August 11-13, 2014
La Jolla, California, USA

I0036242

**Association for
Computing Machinery**

Advancing Computing as a Science & Profession

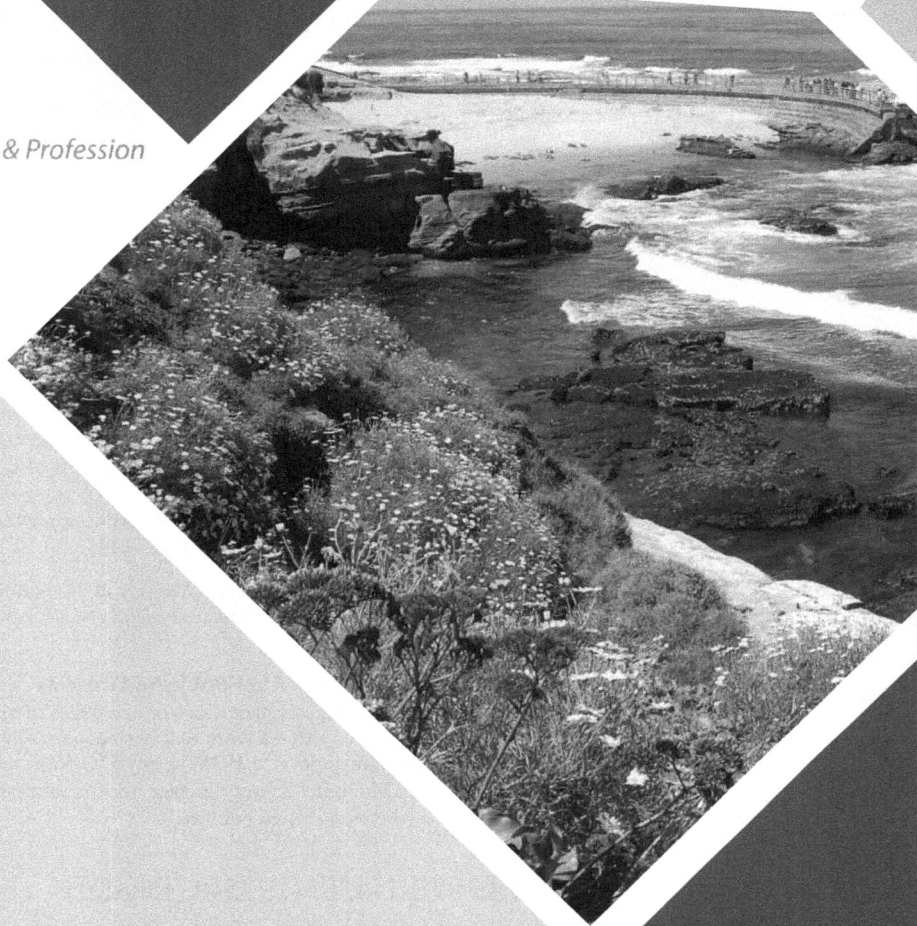

ISLPED'14

Proceedings of the 2014 International Symposium on
Low Power Electronics and Design

Sponsored by:
ACM SIGDA and IEEE

Supported by:
Intel, Synopsys, Qualcomm, IBM, Huawei, Microsoft, SSCS and EDS

**Association for
Computing Machinery**

Advancing Computing as a Science & Profession

The Association for Computing Machinery
2 Penn Plaza, Suite 701
New York, New York 10121-0701

Notice to Past Authors of ACM-Published Articles
ACM intends to create a complete electronic archive of all articles and/or other material previously published by ACM. If you have written a work that has been previously published by ACM in any journal or conference proceedings prior to 1978, or any SIG Newsletter at any time, and you do NOT want this work to appear in the ACM Digital Library, please inform permissions@acm.org, stating the title of the work, the author(s), and where and when published.

ISBN: 978-1-4503-2975-0 (Digital)

ISBN: 978-1-4503-3259-0 (Print)

Additional copies may be ordered prepaid from:

ACM Order Department
PO Box 30777
New York, NY 10087-0777, USA

Phone: 1-800-342-6626 (USA and Canada)
+1-212-626-0500 (Global)
Fax: +1-212-944-1318
E-mail: acmhelp@acm.org
Hours of Operation: 8:30 am – 4:30 pm ET

Printed in the USA

Message from the General Chairs

On behalf of the Organizing Committee, it is our pleasure to welcome you to the 2014 ACM/IEEE International Symposium on Low Power Electronics and Design (ISLPED 2014), which is held in La Jolla, California, on August 11-13, 2014. La Jolla in Spanish means "The Jewel". It is the Jewel of America's finest city, San Diego. La Jolla is located 15 minutes from downtown San Diego. It features shimmering ocean views to timeless landmarks. It is home to renowned institutions, such as the Scripps Institution of Oceanography and the Stephen Birch Aquarium & Museum. This is in addition to the University of California, San Diego. Furthermore, La Jolla is home to many Bio-Tech and software companies. In short, La Jolla is a great place to live in, visit, or do business.

ISLPED (www.islped.org) is the premier forum for presentation of recent advances in all aspects of low-power design and technologies, ranging from process and circuit technologies, simulation and synthesis tools, to system-level design and software optimization. This year we have kept up the tradition of having outstanding contributions from the low-power design community. The Technical Program Chairs, Muhammad Khellah (Intel) and Renu Mehra (Synopsys), have worked hard to put together an excellent Technical Program. Many thanks go to the Technical Program Committee comprising of leading researchers in the area of low-power design, who have generously volunteered their time for the review process to uphold the high quality of the papers. Another ISLPED tradition that has been kept this year is the Low Power Design Contest, chaired by Professors Mingoo Seok and Yiran Chen, and we hope this will inspire more students to showcase the best of their design abilities.

The ISLPED 2014 Organizing Committee has been working tirelessly to bring you a world-class conference experience. Xiangyu Dong and Jack Sampson, as Local Arrangements Co-Chairs, have brought you the first class conference venue, banquet event, sightseeing tours, and all the logistics to make this a truly enjoyable meeting. Industry Liaison, Eren Kursun, has done an outstanding job in raising strong industry support. We thank Yu Wang for serving as Treasurer and Registration Chair, Theo Theocharides as Web Chair, and Deming Chen, Baris Taskin, Jose Ayala as Publicity Chairs. We are also grateful to the Executive Committee, chaired by Massoud Pedram, for their continued guidance in making ISLPED 2014 a great success.

ISLPED 2014 has been fortunate to receive strong support from the industry. In particular, we appreciate the generous financial support from Intel, Synopsys, Qualcomm, IBM, Huawei, and Microsoft for various ISLPED 2014 activities. ISLPED 2014 is sponsored by ACM, ACM-SIGDA, IEEE, and IEEE-CAS, with technical support from the SSCS and EDS. We hope that you will enjoy the excellent ISLPED 2014 program this year, and have a pleasant, enriching and memorable experience at La Jolla.

Yuan Xie
ISLPED'14 General Co-Chair

Tanay Karnik
ISLPED'14 General Co-Chair

Message from the Program Co-Chairs

It is our great pleasure to welcome you to the *2014 ACM/IEEE International Symposium on Low Power Electronics and Design – ISLPED'14,* in the beautiful city of La Jolla, CA, USA. The mission of our symposium is to provide education and technical enrichment for professionals in the area of low power electronics and design and promote advancement of the state-of-the-art in the same area. It provides a forum for technical discussions and a platform for examining new ideas and research topics.

This year, the call for papers attracted 184 submissions from Asia, Africa, Europe, and North & South America. The Technical Program Committee (TPC), consisting of 78 experts from industry and academia, accepted a total of 63 papers divided into 43 for full-length presentations and 20 for poster presentations. The accepted papers cover a variety of low-power topics in technologies, circuits, logic & architecture, CAD Tools & methodologies, systems & platforms, and software and applications. We are very thankful to the authors for contributing to ISLEPD'14. We are also grateful to our TPC members for volunteering their valuable time and effort in reviewing the papers, attending the in-person review meeting, and providing feedback to the authors.

In addition to the above accepted papers, this year's program features:

- Three Keynote Speeches on "Low Power Design Techniques in Mobile Processes" by Dr. Karim Arabi, VP Engineering, Qualcomm Technologies, Inc.; "Accelerator-Rich Architectures — From Single-chip to Datacenters" by Prof. Jason Cong, Chancellor's Professor at the Computer Science Dept., UCLA, and "The New (System) Balance of Power and Opportunities for Optimizations" by Dr. Partha Ranganathan, Principal Engineer, Google.

- Industry Focus Session on the Challenges of Low Power Analog Circuits, Exploiting FD-SOI for Energy Efficient SoCs, and Using Embedded STT-MRAM for Mobile Applications.

- Four Embedded Invited Papers on Emerging Interconnect Technologies, Low Power Processor Design, Leakage Mitigation in Smartphone SoCs, and Powering the Internet of Things.

- Embedded Tutorial by industry DA experts on "Failing to Fail - Achieving Success in Advanced Low Power Design using UPF".

We hope the above talks will complement our main program by providing you with an in-depth understanding of the low-power state-of-the-art as well as gives you valuable insights into future trends. Finally, we hope that you will find the overall program interesting and thought-provoking and that the symposium will provide you with a valuable opportunity to share ideas with other researchers and practitioners from institutions around the world.

Muhammad Khellah
ISLPED'14 Program Co-Chair
Intel, USA

Renu Mehra
ISLPED'14 Program Co-Chair
Synopsys, USA

Table of Contents

Keynote Address

Session Chair: Yuan Xie *(University of California, Santa Barbara)*

Session: Photonics, Spintronics, Approximate Computing and Front-end Throttling

Session Chairs: Hans Jacobson *(IBM)* and Umit Ogras *(Arizona State University)*

Session: Approximate Computing and Quality Driven Power-aware System Design

Session Chairs: Xiangyu Dong *(Qualcomm)* and Vivek Joy *(Intel)*

Session: Emerging Technologies

Session Chairs: Arijit Raychowdhury *(Georgia Institute of Technology)* and
　　　　　　　Patrick Mercier *(University of California, San Diego)*

Session: Energy-efficient Systems using Emerging Non-Volatile Memory Technologies

Session Chairs: Vijay Raghunathan *(Purdue University)* and Zhenyu Sun *(Broadcom)*

Session: Clock and IO Circuit Techniques

Session Chairs: Gordon Gammie *(MediaTek)* and Jie Gu *(Maxlinear)*

Session: Thermal-Aware Design: From Device to System

Session Chairs: Jiang Hu *(Texas A&M University)* and Umit Ogras *(Arizona State University)*

Industry Special Session
Session Chair: Muhammad Khellah *(Intel)*

Embedded Tutorial
Session Chairs: Massimo Poncino *(Politecnico di Torino)* and Renu Mehra *(Synopsys)*

Keynote Address
Session Chair: Tanay Karnik *(Intel)*

Session: GPU Voltage Noise, Uncore Power Modeling, Memory Power Management, and Testing
Session Chairs: John Sampson *(Penn State University)* and Yaojun Zhang *(Qualcomm)*

Session: CAD for Low Power and Reliability
Session Chairs: Zhiru Zhang *(Cornell University)* and Yiran Chen *(University of Pittsburgh)*

Session: Energy Eefficient Digital Circuit Techniques
Session Chairs: Rob Gilmore *(Qualcomm)* and Joyce Kwong *(TI)*

Session: Optimizing Computation and Communication in Mobile Systems
Session Chairs: Sujit Dey *(University of California, San Diego)* and Yiran Chen *(University of Pittsburgh)*

Session: Voltage Reference and Power Converter Circuits
Session Chairs: Swaroop Ghosh *(University of Florida)* and Nilanjan Banerjee *(Qualcomm)*

Session: Variation and Reliability Consideration for Low-Power Systems
Session Chairs: Eli Bozorgzadeh *(University of Calivornia, Irvine)* and Younghyun Kim *(Purdue University)*

Poster Session

Keynote Address
Session Chairs: Muhammad Khellah *(Intel)* and Renu Mehra *(Synopsys)*

Session: Energy Efficient Cache and Memory Design
Session Chairs: Xi Chen *(Qualcomm)* and Zhenyu Sun *(Broadcom)*

Session: Energy Harvesting and Energy-aware System Design
Session Chairs: Naehyuck Chang *(Seoul National University)* and Hyung Gyu Lee *(Daegu University)*

Author Index

2014 International Symposium on Low Power Electronics and Design Organization

General Co-Chairs:	Yuan Xie *(UCSB, USA)*
	Tanay Karnik *(Intel, USA)*
Program Co-Chairs:	Muhammad M. Khellah *(Intel, USA)*
	Renu Mehra *(Synopsys, USA)*
Local Arrangements Co-Chairs:	Xiangyu Dong *(Qualcomm, USA)*
	John (Jack) Sampson *(Penn State University, USA)*
Publicity Co-Chairs:	Deming Chen *(UIUC, USA)*
	Baris Taskin *(Drexel University, USA)*
	Jose Ayala *(UCM, Spain)*
Industry Liaison:	Eren Kursun *(JP Morgan Chase, USA)*
Treasurer:	Yu Wang *(Tsinghua University, China)*
Web Chair:	Theocharis Theocharides *(University of Cyprus, Cyprus)*
Design Contest Co-Chairs:	Mingoo Seok *(Columbia University, USA)*
	Yiran Chen *(University of Pittsburgh, USA)*
Executive Committee:	Massoud Pedram *(University of Southern California, USA)* – **Chair**
	Naehyuck Chang *(Seoul National University, Korea)*
	Pai Chou *(University of California, Irvine)*
	Jason Cong *(University of California Los Angeles, USA)*
	Vivek De *(Intel Corporation, USA)*
	Joerg Henkel *(Karlsruhe Institute of Technology, Germany)*
	Rajiv Joshi *(IBM TJ Watson Research Center, USA)*
	Enrico Macii *(Politecnico di Torino, Italy)*
	Diana Marculescu *(Carnegie Mellon University, USA)*
	Hiroshi Nakamura *(The University of Tokyo, Japan)*
	Vijaykrishnan Narayanan *(Pennsylvania State University, USA)*
	Wolfgang Nebel *(Offis, Germany)*
	Vojin Oklobdzija *(University of Texas at Dallas, USA)*
	Massimo Poncino *(Politecnico di Torino, Italy)*
	Jan M. Rabaey *(University of California Berkeley, USA)*
	Anand Raghunathan *(Purdue University, USA)*
	Kaushik Roy *(Purdue University, USA)*
	Takayasu Sakurai *(The University of Tokyo, Japan)*
	Naresh Shanbhag *(University of Illinois at Urbana-Champaign , USA)*
	Mircea Stan *(University of Virginia, USA)*
	Vivek Tiwari *(Intel Corporation, USA)*

Technical Program Committee:

Track 1.1 – Technologies Subcommittee

Saibal Mukhopadhyay *(Georgia Tech University, USA)* – **Co-Chair**
Arijit Raychowdhury *(Georgia Tech University, USA)* – **Co-Chair**
Jae-Joon Kim *(Pohang University of Science and Technology, Korea)*
Jaydeep Kulkarni *(Intel, USA)*
Azad Naeemi *(Georgia Tech University, USA)*

Track 1.2 - Circuits Subcommittee

Yogesh Ramadass *(TI, USA)* – **Co-Chair**
Srini Sridhara *(TI, USA)* – **Co-Chair**
Mohamed Abu-Rahma *(Apple, USA)*
Kevin Cao *(Arizona State University, USA)*
Vikas Chandra *(ARM, USA)*
Swaroop Ghosh *(University of South Florida, USA)*
Jie Gu *(Northwestern University, USA)*
Roozbeh Jafari *(University of Texax, USA)*
Byunghoo Jung *(Purdue University, USA)*
Amin Khajeh-Djahromi *(Broadcom, USA)*
Tony Kim *(Nanyang Technological University, Singapore)*
Joyce Kwong *(TI, USA)*
Peter Levine *(University of Waterloo, Canada)*
Jae Sun Seo *(Arizona State University, USA)*
Mingoo Seok *(Columbia University, USA)*
Ethan Yi-Chun Shih *(TSMC, Taiwan)*
SengOon Toh *(ARM, USA)*
Carlos Tokunaga *(Intel, USA)*
Lei Wang *(University of Connecticut, USA)*
David Wentzlof *(University of Michigan, USA)*
Matthew Ziegler *(IBM, USA)*

Track 1.3 – Logic and Architecture Subcommittee

Hans Jacobson *(IBM, USA)* – **Co-Chair**
Hai (Helen) Li *(University of Pittsburgh, USA)* – **Co-Chair**
Xi Chen *(Qualcomm, USA)*
David Garrett *(Broadcom, USA)*
Soontae Kim *(Kaist University, S. Korea)*
Nam Sung Kim *(University of Wisconsin, USA)*
Masaaki Kondo *(University of Electro-Communications, Japan)*
Erin Kursun *(IBM, USA)*
Sheng Li *(HP, USA)*
Xiaoyao Liang *(Shanghai Jiao Tong University, China)*
Hiroki Matsutani *(Keio University, Japan)*
Sandeep Navada *(North Carolina State University, USA)*
Dimin Niu *(Samsung, USA)*
John (Jack) Sampson *(Pennsylvania State University, USA)*
Anuradha Srinivasan *(Intel, USA)*
Guangyu Sun *(Peking University, China)*
Sarma Vrudhula *(Arizona State University, USA)*
Thomas Wenisch *(University of Michigan, USA)*
Wei Wu *(Intel, USA)*
Antonia Zhai *(University of Minnesota, USA)*

Track 2.1 – CAD Tools and Methodologies Subcommittee

David Pan *(University of Texas, Austin, USA)* – **Co-Chair**
Deming Chen *(UIUC, USA)* – **Co-Chair**
David Atienza *(EPFL, Switzerland)*
Koushik Chakraborty *(Utah State University, USA)*
Domenik Helms *(OFFIS, Germany)*
Jiang Hu *(Texas A&M University, USA)*
Taemin Kim *(Intel, USA)*
Yongpan Liu *(Tsinghua University, China)*
Enrico Macii *(Polytechnic University of Turin, Italy)*
Mustafa Ozdal *(Intel, USA)*
Ruchir Puri *(IBM, USA)*
Ravishankar Rao *(Synopsys, USA)*

Track 2.2 – Systems and Platforms Subcommittee

Naehyuck Chang *(Seoul National University, Korea)* – **Co-Chair**
Anand Raghunathan *(Purdue University, USA)* – **Co-Chair**
Elaheh Bozorgzadeh *(University of California, Irvine, USA)*
Xiangyu Dong *(Qualcomm, USA)*
Tohru Ishihara *(Kyoto University, Japan)*
Massimo Poncino *(Polytechnic University of Turin, Italy)*
Qinru Qiu *(Syracuse University, USA)*
Li Shang *(University of Colorado, USA)*
Sheldon Tan *(University of California, USA)*
Yu Wang *(Tsinghua University, China)*
Jason Xue *(City University of Hong Kong, Hong Kong)*
Chia-Lin Yang *(National Taiwan University, Taiwan)*
Hao Yu *(Nanyang Technological University, Singapore)*

Track 2.3 – Software and Applications Subcommittee

Vijay Raghunathan *(Purdue University, USA)* – **Co-Chair**
Vivek Tiwari *(Intel, USA)* – **Co-Chair**
Yiran Chen *(University of Pittsburgh, USA)*
Ann Gordon-Ross *(University of Florida, USA)*
Yao Guo *(Peking University, China)*
Barry Pangrle *(Nvidia, USA)*
Zili Shao *(Hong Kong Polytechnic University, Hong Kong)*

Additional reviewers:

Dean Ancajas
Giovanni Ansaloni
Charles Augustine
Raid Ayoub
Ivan Beretta
Srikar Bhagavatula
Andrew Blanksby
Alberto Bocca
Steven Burns
Andrea Calimera
Mu-Tien Chang
Junlin Chen
Ke Chen
Shawn Chen
Yao Chen
Yi-Jung Chen
Ying-Yu (Christine) Chen
Harsha Choday
Shidhartha Das
Ashutosh Dhar
Avijit Dutta
Wael EL-Sharkasy
Zhenman Fang
Jerrica Gao

Jie Guo
Frank Gurkaynak
Hyung Gyu Lee
Yiding Han
Vinay Hanumiah
David Harris
Yuan He
Yun Heo
Anup Holey
Xiaofang Hu
Guoxian Huang
Wenjie Huang
Xin Huang
Amr Hussein
Krishna Jandhyam
Hrishikesh Jayakumar
Yongsoo Joo
Mohammad Karter
Muhammad Khairy
Ashish Khandelwal
Bongchan Kim
Jungsoo Kim
Taeyoung Kim
Younghyun Kim

Additional reviewers (continued):

Minsuk Koo	Mohit Singh
Dileep Kurian	Shana Swarup
Kangwoo Lee	Valerio Tenace
Chen-Hsuan Lin	Cao Thang
Xiaoxiao Liu	Jim Tschanz
Zao Liu	Ridvan Umaz
Mirko Loghi	Sriram Vangal
Jiong Luo	Swagath Venkataramani
Mengjie Mao	Sara Vinco
Sandeep Miryala	Chengke Wang
Sambaran Mitra	Cong Wang
James Myers	Hai Wang
Ragavendra Natarajan	Jue Wang
Kent Nixon	Xue Wang
Jiwoo Pak	Uiqun Wang
Somnath Paul	Zhibo Wang
Arnab Raha	Gustavo Wilke
Ashish Ranjan	Jiang Xu
Phillip Restle	Xiaoqing Xu
Elkim Roa	Jieming Yin
Sanghamitra Roy	Bei Yu
Subhendu Roy	Pengfei Yuan
Martino Ruggiero	Yilin Zhang
Joseph Ryan	Jianfeng Zhao
Mohamed Sabry	Yue Zhao
Alessandro Sassone	Hongbin Zheng
Li Shang	Cheng Zhuo
Donghwa Shin	Wei Zuo

ISLPED 2014 Sponsors & Supporters

Society Sponsors:

Gold Supporters:

Silver Supporters:

Bronze Supporter:

Technical Supporters:

Keynote

Low Power Design Techniques in Mobile Processes

Karim Arabi
Vice President of Engineering,
Qualcomm Technologies, Inc.
San Diego, CA, USA

Abstract

Low power design techniques and efficient wireless solutions have been critical in enabling mobile computing in a ubiquitous and cost-effective manner. While demand for ubiquitous mobile computing continues to rise thanks to an array of new applications, their power budget remains constant due to thermal budget limits and slow improvement in battery technology. Therefore, mobile computing continues to drive innovation in technologies that will enable new use cases and applications in an energy efficient manner. These solutions span from new computing architecture, low power circuits, improved process technology and novel power management techniques. This presentation covers the latest state-of-the-art low power design solutions for mobile devices.

ACM Classification:
B.7.0 Hardware, INTEGRATED CIRCUITS: General -- Advanced; C.1.4 Computer Systems Organization, PROCESSOR ARCHITECTURES, Parallel Architectures -- Distributed architectures; Mobile processors

Author Keywords: AMobile computing; low power design; SoC; CPU; Modem

Bio

Dr. Karim Arabi is Vice President, Engineering at Qualcomm where he is responsible for research and development in ASIC and new product development. Previously, he was VP, Engineering and Technology at Dialog Semiconductor responsible for driving overall technology and new product development. He also held technical positions at PMC Sierra and Cirrus Logic and was co-founder of Opmaxx, an innovative startup in analog design, test and automation. Dr. Arabi obtained his Ph.D. and M.Sc. in Electrical Engineering from Polytechnique Montréal, Canada and his B.Sc. in Electrical Engineering from Tehran Polytechnic. He is interested in technology development for mobile computing and all aspects of mobile SoC design and development including low power design, modem, SoC and CPU architectures, mixed-signal and RFIC design, PMIC design and semiconductor technology. Dr. Arabi has published more than 100 papers and holds several patents covering key SoC design technologies.

ISLPED'14, August 11–13, 2014, La Jolla, CA, USA.
ACM 978-1-4503-2975-0/14/08.
http://dx.doi.org/10.1145/2627369.2631634

EcoLaser: An Adaptive Laser Control for Energy-Efficient On-Chip Photonic Interconnects

Yigit Demir and Nikos Hardavellas

Northwestern University, Department of Electrical Engineering and Computer Science, Evanston, IL, USA

yigit@u.northwestern.edu, nikos@northwestern.edu

ABSTRACT

The high-speed and low-cost modulation of light make photonic interconnects an attractive solution for the communication demands of manycore processors. However, the high optical loss of many nanophotonic components results in high laser power consumption, most of which is wasted during periods of system inactivity. We propose EcoLaser, an adaptive laser control mechanism that saves between 24-77% of the laser power by turning off the laser when not needed. These power savings allow the cores to exploit a higher power budget and achieve speedups of 1.1-2x.

Categories and Subject Descriptions

B.4.3 [**Hardware**]: Interconnections; C.1.2 [**Computer Systems Organization**]: Multiprocessors— *Interconnection architectures*

Keywords

Nanophotonic Interconnection Networks; Adaptive Laser Control

1. INTRODUCTION

Silicon photonics have emerged as a promising solution to meet the growing demand for high-bandwidth, low-latency, and energy-efficient communication in manycore processors. Silicon waveguides can be manufactured alongside CMOS logic on the same die by adding a few new steps in the manufacturing process [5], and they are more efficient for long-distance on-chip communication than electrical signaling [18]. However, the high optical loss of typical silicon waveguides, optical couplers, and on-ring resonators dramatically increase the laser power consumption. While some optical interconnect topologies better balance power and performance [6,18,16] most of these costs are hard to avoid, and the laser power remains a considerable fraction of the total power budget. These costs together with the low efficiency of WDM-compatible lasers (in the range of 5-10% [27]), result in wall-plug laser power that is 10-20x higher than the required laser output power.

The majority of this power is typically wasted when activity is low because photonic interconnects are always on. By comparison, electrical interconnects stay idle until a packet traverses them. It is common for the interconnect to stay idle often for long periods of time, both in scientific computing (compute-intensive execution phases underutilize the interconnect), and in server computing (Google-scale datacenters have a typical utilization of 30% [1]).

ISLPED'14, August 11 - 13 2014, La Jolla, CA, USA

Copyright is held by the owner/author(s). Publication rights licensed to ACM.

ACM 978-1-4503-2975-0/14/08...$15.00.

http://dx.doi.org/10.1145/2627369.2627620

Motivated by these observations, we propose EcoLaser, a collection of static and adaptive laser control mechanisms that react to the demands of the aggregate workload and opportunistically turn the laser off during periods of low activity to save energy, and leave it on during periods of high activity in order to meet the high bandwidth demand. More specifically, our contributions are:

1. We propose laser control as a viable technique to save power and quantify the maximum opportunity.
2. We propose EcoLaser, a collection of static and dynamic laser control mechanisms and policies for SWMR and MWSR crossbars that approximate the maximum possible savings.
3. We evaluate the impact of EcoLaser on the performance and energy of a multicore running a range of synthetic and scientific workloads, under realistic physical constraints, and across a range of optical crossbar sizes.

Our results indicate that EcoLaser saves between 24-77% of the laser power for radix-16 and radix-64 SWMR and MWSR crossbars on real-world workloads. EcoLaser closely tracks (within 2-3% on average) a perfect controller with full knowledge of future interconnect requests. Thus, EcoLaser harvests the vast majority of the energy benefits that can be achieved by controlling the laser source. Moreover, the power savings of EcoLaser leave a higher power budget to the cores, which allows a multicore chip with EcoLaser to outperform a baseline scheme with no control by 1.1-2x.

2. LASER CONTROL SCHEMES

The objective of the laser control is to save laser energy by turning the lasers off whenever the bus (i.e., data channel) is idle. When the laser is off, the messages have to wait for the laser to turn on before transmission. EcoLaser capitalizes on recent advancements in Ge-based lasers [12,14], which enable DWDM-compatible on-chip laser sources that can be turned on within 1 *ns*, during which period the laser consumes the same power as when it is lasing. The laser control schemes we propose aim to maximize energy savings while minimizing the laser turn-on delay overhead.

2.1 Laser Control for SWMR Crossbar

A router in a Single-Reader-Multiple-Writer (SWMR) [11] crossbar (Figure 2) writes to its own dedicated bus, and reads from the other routers' busses. Reservation channels provide exclusion on the data bus [18]. The shaded components in the router microarchitecture in Figure 1 correspond to components added by EcoLaser. The laser controller turns the laser on if there is a message at any of the injection buffers, and it does not turn it off unless (a) there is no message at the injection buffers, and (b) the laser has stayed on for the minimum laser stay-on time *"K"*. The laser controller keeps the switch allocator waiting while the laser turns on. When the laser is ready, the switch allocator moves messages to the modulators.

2.2 Laser Control for MWSR Crossbar

In a Multiple-Writer-Single-Reader [24] (MWSR) crossbar every router reads from its own bus, and writes on the other routers' busses (Figure 2). Because lasers can be built within a waveguide [14],

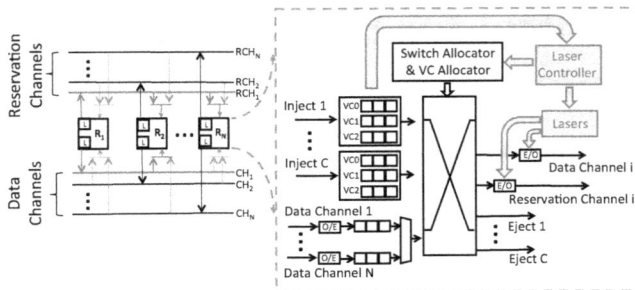

FIGURE 1. SWMR crossbar and router microarchitecture.

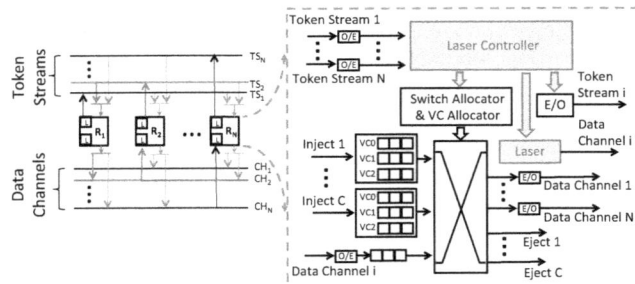

FIGURE 2. MWSR crossbar and router microarchitecture.

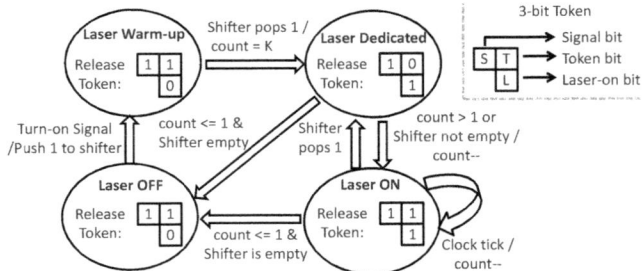

FIGURE 3. 3-bit Token and Laser Controller FSM.

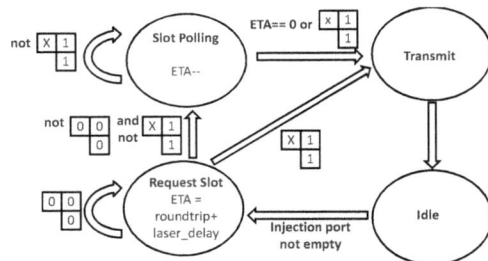

FIGURE 4. Writer Node FSM.

each receiver in EcoLaser holds the lasers for its own bus. This complicates laser control, as the receiver does not know that a sender wants to transmit. Contention in MWSR occurs when two routers try to transmit simultaneously to the same destination. Token-based arbitration [17,24] resolves the contention by using ring-shaped waveguides to move the tokens in the direction of data travel, and one cycle ahead of the data slot. The reader node collects back its returning tokens to control the input buffer utilization [17]. Any writer can exploit this and send a "Laser turn-on request" to the reader with a returning token.

We construct the tokens to perform three tasks: (a) maintain the time share on the bus, (b) indicate if there is light in the data bus hence the writer can write immediately, and (c) bring the laser turn-on requests back to the reader. Note that only the reader can inject tokens in his token stream, and any type of snooping of the token by writers is destructive. In order to meet all these needs, we design 3-bit tokens as shown at the top of Figure 3: the "T" bit provides mutual exclusion on the data bus; the "L" bit indicates if the laser was on when this token was released from the reader node (i.e., the subsequent slot in the data bus has light that can be modulated); the "S" signals the reader to turn on the laser. The photonic links operate at 2x the processor frequency, thus 2 wavelengths suffice (S and T are sent on the same wavelength in a single processor cycle).

Figure 3 shows the **Laser Controller Logic.** When the bus is idle, the data lasers stay at the "Laser OFF" state; they do not consume energy, and the released tokens indicate this with a clear L bit (note that the token-stream laser is always on). Writers send the laser turn-on signal by clearing the S bit of a token. When the laser controller receives the turn-on signal, the data channel lasers move to the "Laser Warm-up" state and the controller pushes a "1" into a 5-bit barrel shifter. During the warm-up the lasers consume full power preparing photons, but cannot emit any light yet. A "1" popping out from the other end of the 5-bit shifter indicates that the lasers are ready (1 ns is 5 cycles at 5 GHz). The lasers start emitting light into the data bus (emit data slots) and move to the "Laser Dedicated" state. The first emitted data slot is dedicated to the writer who requested the laser turn-on; the corresponding token has a

clear T bit, to prevent any other writer from grabbing the slot, thereby guaranteeing freedom from starvation. The lasers move to the "Laser ON" state and remain on for as long as there is a set bit in the shifter. The laser controller keeps track of the duration the laser has stayed on through the counter "$count$". When the laser emits the first (dedicated) slot, the count is assigned the value K. $Count$ decrements on every cycle, and the laser stays on and releases data slots which are available for any writer node to use (tokens indicate this availability with set T and L bits). When $count = 1$ the laser turns off, unless there is another set bit in the shifter, which indicates a new laser turn-on request. If there is, the laser remains on until the set bit pops out from the shifter, at which time the lasers move to the "Laser Dedicated" state like above.

Figure 4 shows the **Writer Node Logic.** When a writer has a message to send, it moves to the "Request Slot" state, and looks for an available data slot. The writer reads the T and L bits of the first token, and if they are both set (i.e., the data slot has light and is available), it modulates the message into the data slot. If T and L are not both set, the writer sends a laser turn-on signal by reading (clearing) the S bit of the token, and expects to receive a dedicated data slot at *Estimated Time of Arrival* (*ETA*) equal to round-trip plus laser-turn-on cycles later. If all token bits are clear, the token has been used to send out a laser turn-on signal already, so the writer stays in the "Request Slot" state and re-tries. After sending a laser turn-on signal, the writer moves to "Slot Polling", in which the writer looks for an available slot (by reading both T and L bits) while waiting for its dedicated slot to arrive. The writer transmits when either an available slot with light arrives, or the writer's dedicated slot arrives. By design the writer sends at most one laser turn-on signal, which avoids wasting laser energy. Also, writers can send a laser turn-on signal using a token that has been through another "Slot Polling" writer, which improves performance.

2.3 Adaptive Laser Control

The static laser control schemes discussed thus far leave the laser on for at least "K" cycles, where "K" is a fixed value. With lower laser stay-on time "K", EcoLaser tends to turn off the laser quicker, which saves more laser energy when the crossbar is not heavily uti-

TABLE 1. Architectural Parameters.

CMP Size	64 cores, 480mm^2
Processing Cores	ULTRASPARC III ISA, up to 5Ghz, OoO, 4-wide dispatch/retirement, 96-entry ROB
L1 Cache	Split I/D, 64KB 2-way, 2-cycle load-to-use, 2 ports, 64-byte blocks, 32 MSHRs, 16-entry victim cache
L2 Cache	Shared, 512 KB per core, 16 way, 64-byte blocks, 14 cycle-hit, 32 MSHRs, 16-entry victim cache
Memory Controllers	One per 4 cores, 1 channel per Memory Controller Round-robin page interleaving
Main Memory	Optically connected memory [2], 10ns access
Networks	SWMR and MWSR crossbars, radix-16 and -64

TABLE 2. Nanophotonic Parameters and Laser Power.

	per Unit	Radix-16 Total	Radix-64 Total
DWDM		64	16
WG Loss	0.3 dB/cm[4]	3 dB	3 dB
Nonlinearity	1 dB	1 dB	1 dB
Modulator Ins.	0.5 dB	0.5 dB	0.5 dB
Ring Through	0.01 dB	10.24 dB	10.24 dB
Filter Drop	1.2 dB	1.2 dB	1.2 dB
Photodetector	0.1 dB	0.1 dB	0.1 dB
Total Loss		**16.04 dB**	**16.04 dB**
Detector		**-20 dBm**	**-20 dBm**
Laser Power	**per Wavelength**	**0.401 mW**	**0.401 mW**
Total Laser Power		**20.1 W**	**78.1 W**

lized. However, under heavier traffic, turning the laser off quickly results in lost opportunities to catch the laser on and send, and increases the number of times the laser has to be turned on anew. The frequent laser turn-on delays decrease performance. On the other hand, when K is high, the laser tends to stay on for longer, which increases performance under heavier traffic, but wastes more laser energy when the utilization is low. Thus, no static scheme is expected to perform best under all traffic conditions.

We propose an adaptive scheme that observes the amount of laser turn-on requests to adjust the laser stay-on time K at run time. Frequent laser turn-on requests hint to lost opportunities to transmit opportunistically, and the adaptive scheme increases K to keep the laser on for longer. A low number of laser turn-on requests hints at potentially wasted laser energy, so the adaptive scheme decreases K to save more laser energy, by turning the laser off more quickly.

To prevent oscillation or overshooting K from its ideal setting, we employ a hysteresis counter which robustly captures the laser turn-on request trends. The hysteresis counter decrements on every cycle on which there is no other counter activity. Upon sensing a laser turn-on signal, the counter increments by adding some value to it. Whenever the counter reaches its upper threshold, K increases by 1; whenever the counter reaches its lower threshold, K decreases by 1. The hysteresis counter controls the value of K in a stable manner, because increasing K results in a reduction of laser turn-on requests, as the likelihood of a writer finding an available data slot with light increases, and vice versa. The threshold settings and the increment and decrement values of the hysteresis counter change its reactive behavior (making it more lazy or aggressive). Through a design space exploration, we identified the settings that provide the highest energy savings for our workloads, and use these settings for the remainder of our study. Other than adapting K at runtime, the rest of the design of the adaptive laser control is the same as the designs described earlier for SWMR and MWSR crossbars.

2.4 The Perfect Laser Control

A perfect laser control scheme has complete knowledge of future interconnect accesses. The perfect scheme saves the maximum laser energy without incurring any performance overhead by turning the laser on ahead of time, so the light reaches the writer at the exact time the writer attempts to transmit. After transmitting, the control deactivates the laser or leaves it on for an upcoming message, if deactivation could cause a delay. Thus, the perfect scheme presents the maximum energy savings for a given laser technology.

3. EXPERIMENTAL METHODOLOGY
3.1 Interconnect Performance and Energy

To evaluate the performance and energy consumption of EcoLaser in isolation from the interference of other system components or application characteristics, we use a cycle-accurate network simulator based on Booksim 2.0 [7], which models radix-16 and radix-64 SWMR and MWSR crossbars servicing random uniform traffic (we use the notation *<type>_XBAR_<radix>* for the crossbars). We model a 480 mm^2 chip with single-cycle routers, 1-cycle E/O and O/E conversions, and a 10 cm waveguide that has a 5-cycle round-trip time. The link latency (1-5 cycles) is calculated based on the traversed waveguide length. The buffers are 20-flits deep, and flits are 300 bits. The maximum core frequency is 5 GHz, and the optical interconnect runs at 10 GHz. We evaluate the load-latency and energy-per-flit of EcoLaser, and compare it against a baseline without laser control (*No-Ctrl*), and against a perfect control scheme (*Perfect*). To demonstrate the merits of the adaptive mechanism, we compare adaptive laser control (*Adaptive*) with two static control mechanisms: *Static-1* and *Static-10*, with 1- and 10-cycle stay-on times respectively. Static-1 is the quickest to turn the laser off; Static-10 saves the most laser energy per packet among all static schemes on average across injection rates.

3.2 Multicore System Performance and Energy

To evaluate the impact of EcoLaser on a realistic multicore, we model a 64-core processor on a full-system cycle-accurate simulator based on Flexus 4.0 [9,25] integrated with Booksim 2.0 [7] and DRAMSim 2.0 [19]. We calculate the power consumption of the electrical interconnect using DSENT [21]. We target a 16 nm technology, and have updated our tool chain accordingly based on ITRS [8]. The simulated system executes a selection of SPLASH-2 and other scientific workloads. We model realistic multicores that use a throttling mechanism (without loss of generality, we use Dynamic Voltage and Frequency Scaling—DVFS) to keep the chip within safe operational temperatures (below 90°C).

We collect runtime statistics from full-system simulations, and use them to calculate the power consumption of the system using McPAT [13], and the power consumption of the optical networks using the analytical power model by Joshi *et al.* [10]. We estimate the temperature of the chip using HotSpot 5.0 [20]. We adjust the leakage power estimate based on the temperature and adjust DVFS based on the stable-state power and temperature estimates.

To put EcoLaser's performance and energy consumption into perspective, we include in our evaluation a 2D-concentrated electrical mesh with express links (*CMesh*). For CMesh we model routers with 8 input and output ports and a 3-cycle routing delay. Routers are connected through 150-bit bi-directional links with 1-cycle local and 3-cycle global delay. To show the range of EcoLaser's impact, we evaluate its application on two optical crossbars that are

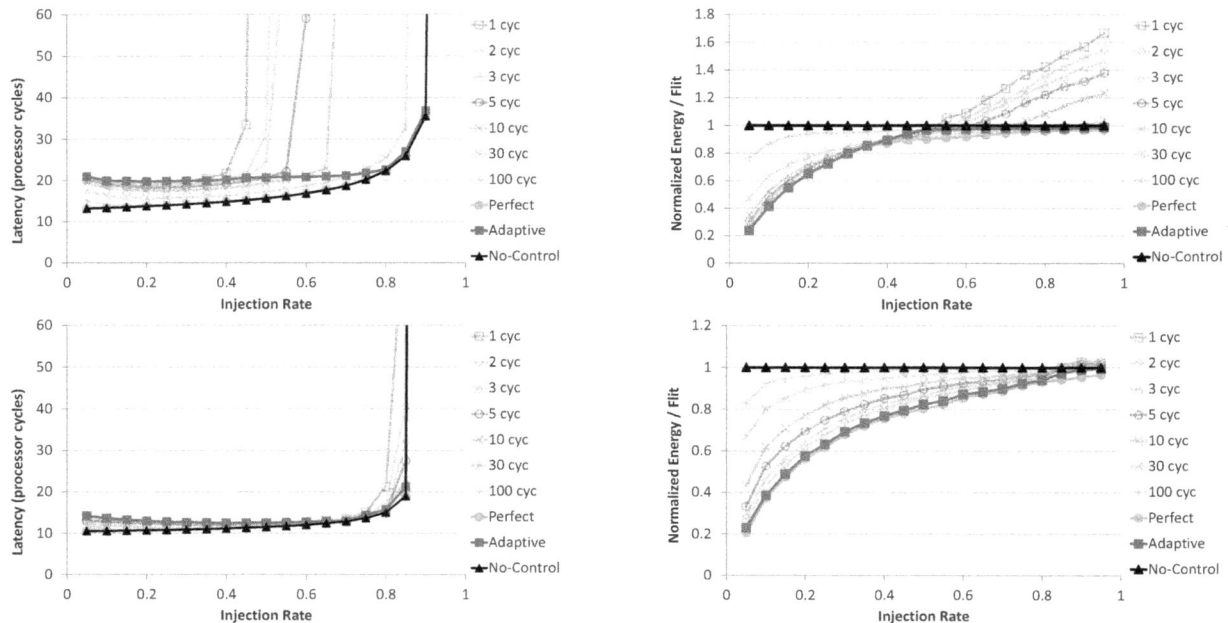

FIGURE 5. Load-Latency (left) and Energy-per-Flit (right) for radix-16 MWSR (top row) and SWMR (bottom row) crossbars.

at the opposite ends of the spectrum, a radix-16 and a radix-64 optical crossbar. The radix-16 crossbar approximates a worst case scenario for EcoLaser. It has low power consumption (similar to the power consumption of CMesh) and its high concentration factor (4) creates heavier traffic. The low power consumption and heavy traffic limit EcoLaser's opportunity. The radix-64 crossbar corresponds to a better case for EcoLaser. It has high laser power consumption and a low concentration (1), which results in light traffic, thus giving ample opportunity to EcoLaser to conserve laser power. For each one of the radix-16 and radix-64 crossbars, we evaluate both SWMR and MWSR designs. The modeling of the optical interconnects is described in Section 3.1. Finally, we contrast Eco-Laser to a power-equivalent optical interconnect design similar to No-Ctrl, but with its interconnect width scaled down to approximate EcoLaser's average energy savings (*Power_Eq*).

3.3 Optical Network Power Consumption

Table 2 shows the assumed optical loss parameters for the modulators, demodulators, drop filters, and detectors, as introduced in [2]. The modulation and demodulation energy is 150 *fJ/bit* at 10 *GHz* [2]. The laser power per wavelength and total laser power are calculated in Table 2 using the analytical models introduced in [10]. Because the number of turned-off rings on a single optical path is high for a radix-64 crossbar, we limit the network to 16 DWDM. The total laser power in Table 2 includes the laser power for both data and reservation channels, plus the laser efficiency of 10%, so it is the wall plug power for the laser. The data bus is 300-bits wide.

To calculate the total ring heating power we extend the method by Nitta *et al.* [15] by additionally accounting for the heating of the photonic die by the operation of the cores. We model the thermal characteristics of a 3D-stacked architecture where the photonic die sits underneath the logic die using the 3D-chip extension of Hot-Spot [20]. When a workload executes, we calculate the ring heating power required to maintain the entire photonic die at the micro-ring trimming temperature during the entire execution. In addition, we account for the individual ring trimming power required to overcome process variations, as described in [10].

Unfortunately, there is little consensus on the optical loss parameters used or projected in literature, as parameters exhibit a variance over 10x across publications. However, the optical components typically drive the design of an optical interconnect (e.g., lower DWDM minimizes off-ring through loss, and low-radix crossbars can be used to implement high-radix ones [18]). In either case, the fraction of laser energy that EcoLaser saves depends on the network utilization, not on the optical loss parameters, and the higher the total optical loss, the higher EcoLaser's impact would be. Thus, we remain conservative in our estimates of optical losses.

4. EXPERIMENTAL RESULTS
4.1 Network Performance

EcoLaser turns off the lasers and saves energy at the cost of higher message latency. At low injection rates, EcoLaser on SWMR has a 4-cycle latency overhead, which is lower than the 5-cycle laser turn-on delay, as some messages catch the laser on (Figure 5). The overhead decreases for higher injection rates as more messages catch the laser on. Similarly, EcoLaser on MWSR exhibits 8 cycles latency overhead, instead of the full 11-cycle laser turn-on delay, as the token design allows senders to transmit immediately when they find the laser on. Static schemes with high laser stay-on time "*K*" (keeping the laser on at least *K* cycles), increase the likelihood of finding the laser on, so they have lower latency overhead and provide higher throughput. However, they don't save much energy at low injection rates, as they may needlessly leave the lasers on. Static schemes with lower *K* turn off the lasers quickly, saving significant laser energy at low injection rates. However, they don't provide enough throughput under heavy utilization, increasing the overall energy consumption. Adaptive outperforms all Static schemes because it adjusts *K* at runtime, thus it achieves high energy savings at low injection rates, and high throughput at high injection rates. Adaptive's performance improvement over Static schemes is higher for MWSR, because it sends turn-on requests through the token stream (which takes longer), while SWMR can turn on or keep the laser on much quicker. Overall, Adaptive's energy consumption is within 2-3% of the Perfect scheme.

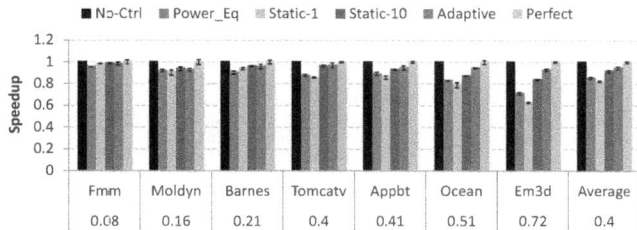

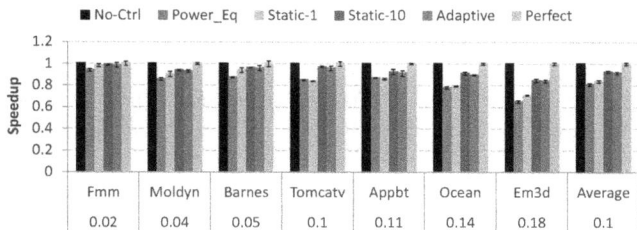

FIGURE 6. Speedup for radix-16 (left) and radix-64 (right) MWSR on a hypothetical multicore without thermal constraints.

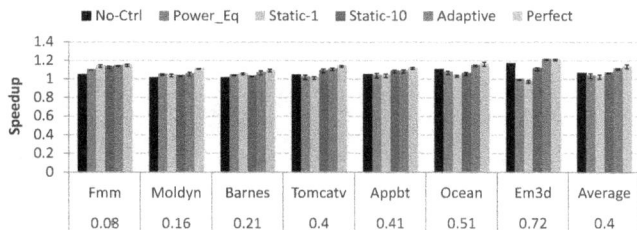

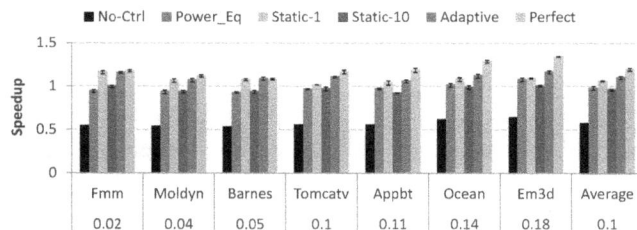

FIGURE 7. Speedup over CMesh for radix-16 (left) and radix-64 (right) MWSR crossbars under realistic thermal constraints.

4.2 The Performance Cost of Laser Control

EcoLaser is expected to degrade performance compared to No-Ctrl, as sometimes transmission is delayed while the laser turns on. In reality, however, EcoLaser recoups the losses and even increases performance by minimizing thermal emergencies and core throttling that DVFS employs to keep a chip within safe operating temperatures. Controlling the laser lowers the power consumption by a significant margin compared to No-Ctrl, which allows for a cooler chip, reduces core throttling, and increases performance. Thus, even though EcoLaser trades off network latency for energy savings, a realistic power-limited system may exhibit higher performance with EcoLaser because the cores will be throttled less often.

We analyze the two effects (increasing the network latency, and reducing core throttling) separately. We analyze the performance cost of EcoLaser by evaluating it on a multicore that is not subject to thermal constraints, thus cores are not throttled and run at maximum frequency (5 GHz). Our workload suite includes both memory-intensive workloads that generate high traffic and are sensitive to interconnect latency (em3d, ocean, appbt, tomcatv), as well as compute-intensive workloads that are less sensitive to message latency (fmm, moldyn, barnes). Figure 6 summarizes our findings. The injection rate of each application appears below its name. Overall, laser control saves more energy on real-world workloads than on synthetic random traffic patterns, because real-world workloads typically have bursty (and sparse) memory access patterns.

In radix-16 MWSR, Static-1 saves the most laser energy (49% on average) at the expense of slowing down the memory intensive workloads. Static-10 achieves high throughput, but it wastes laser energy at compute-intensive workloads (saves 32% on average).

Adaptive combines the benefits of both: it saves 45% of the laser energy on average for radix-16 and 68% for radix-64 MWSR crossbars, at the cost of 4.8% and 7.5% slowdown respectively, while on SWMR it saves 53% and 72% of the laser energy for radix-16 and radix-64 respectively, with only 4% slowdown.

Power_Eq is a scaled-down version of No-Ctrl (150-bit flits for radix-16, and 100-bit flits for radix-64) to approximate Adaptive's laser energy consumption. While it achieves similar energy savings, Power_Eq suffers from high serialization delays and underperforms EcoLaser. Thus, saving laser energy by reducing the width of the interconnect is not a good alternative to laser control.

4.3 EcoLaser on a Realistic Multicore

Under realistic thermal (power) constraints, DVFS in No-Ctrl throttles the cores to keep the chip within a safe temperature. Eco-Laser, however, reduces the laser power and results in a cooler chip, less core throttling, and higher performance. The static schemes typically work well at only one end of the spectrum. Static-1 speeds up workloads with low injection rates, as it saves the most power and reduces throttling, but slows down memory-intensive workloads due to frequent laser turn-on delays (Figure 7-left). Static-10 speeds up workloads with high injection rates, as it increases the likelihood that a sender finds the laser on and transmits without delay, but wastes power when the injection rate is low and leads to more core throttling. Power_Eq achieves low laser power, but at the expense of serialization delays due to its limited width. Overall, the performance and energy-delay product (EDP, Figure 8) of the static schemes is much worse than that of Perfect's. Thus, static laser control or reduced width often lead to slow and energy-inefficient systems.

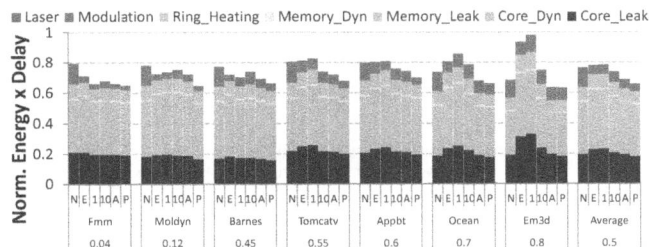

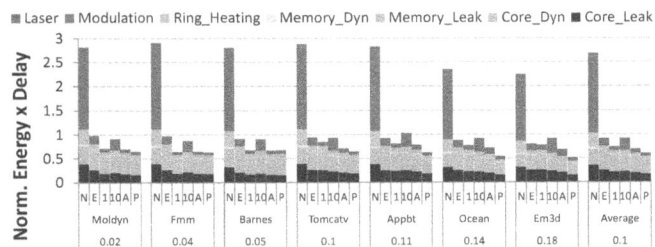

FIGURE 8. Energy x Delay Product in radix-16 and radix-64 MWSR crossbar. The evaluated designs are from left to right: No-Ctrl (N), Power_Eq (E), Static-1 (1), Static-10 (10), Adaptive (A), and Perfect (P).

Adaptive EcoLaser tracks the workload's needs, and provides both low power and high throughput. The impact of EcoLaser is more pronounced on 64-radix crossbars, because their energy savings are a significant fraction of the total chip power, and hence allow the cores to run faster. For example, Perfect runs fmm at 3.25 GHz, Adaptive at 3.2 GHz, and No-Ctrl at only 1.5 GHz. For the same reason, No-Ctrl is 1.7x slower than CMesh even though it has higher bandwidth and lower latency. Compared to No-Ctrl, adaptive EcoLaser on radix-64 MWSR and SWMR crossbars is 2x faster and has 74-77% lower EDP on average (10% faster and 20% lower EDP for radix-16). In all cases, Adaptive's performance and EDP are within 2-6% of Perfect's.

5. RELATED WORK

Corona [24] and many others [23,17,16], implement an MWSR crossbar topology for on-chip communication. Firefly [18] uses partitioned SWMR optical crossbars to connect clusters of electrically-connected mesh networks. Batten *et al.* [2,3] connects a many-core processor to DRAM memory using SWMR crossbars. These works can exploit EcoLaser for laser energy efficiency.

Thonnart *et al.* [22] propose techniques to reduce the static power consumption in electrical interconnects by powering down unused units. Zhou *et al.* [26] identify the constant laser power consumption as an inefficiency, and propose a mechanism to increase average channel utilization, by controlling splitters to tune bandwidth on a binary tree network. Kurian *et al.* [12] propose an optical SWMR crossbar and electrical hybrid network, and mention that a Ge-based laser can be controlled to improve the laser energy efficiency, but don't present nor evaluate a laser control scheme.

6. CONCLUSION

In this paper we propose EcoLaser, a laser-control mechanism that turns the laser off during periods of inactivity to save energy, and meets high bandwidth demands by turning the laser on for as long as necessary. EcoLaser saves between 24-77% of the laser power for radix-16 and radix-64 SWMR and MWSR crossbars on real-world workloads. EcoLaser harvests the vast majority of the energy benefits, as it closely tracks (within 2-3% on average) a perfect controller with full knowledge of future interconnect requests. Moreover, the power savings of EcoLaser allow for providing a higher power budget to the cores, which enables a multicore chip with EcoLaser to achieve speedups of 1.1-2x over a multicore with a traditional optical interconnect that keeps the lasers always on.

7. ACKNOWLEDGEMENTS

This work was partially supported by National Science Foundation award CCF-1218768, and ISEN booster award, and the June and Donald Brewer Chair in EECS at Northwestern University.

8. REFERENCES

[1] L. A. Barroso and U. Holzle. The case for energy-proportional computing. *IEEE Computer*, 40(12):33- 37, 2007.

[2] C. Batten, A. Joshi, J. Orcutt, A. Khilo, B. Moss, C. W. Holzwarth, M. A. Popovic, H. Li, H. I. Smith, J. L. Hoyt, F. X. Kartner, R. J. Ram, V. Stojanovic, and K. Asanovic. Building many-core processor-to-dram networks with monolithic CMOS silicon photonics. *IEEE Micro*, 29(4):8- 21, 2009.

[3] C. Batten, A. Joshi, V. Stojanovic, and K. Asanovic. Designing chip-level nanophotonic interconnection networks. *IEEE Journal on Emerging and Selected Topics in Circuits and Systems*, 2(2), 2012.

[4] J. Cardenas, C. Poitras, J. Robinson, K. Preston, L. Chen, and M. Lipson. Low loss etchless silicon photonic waveguides. *Optics Express*, 17(6):4752- 4757, 2009.

[5] G. Chen, H. Chen, M. Haurylau, N. Nelson, P. M. Fauchet, E. Friedman, and D. Albonesi. Predictions of cmos compatible on-chip optical interconnect. In *7th International Workshop on System-Level Interconnect Prediction (SLIP)*, pp. 13- 20, 2005.

[6] M. J. Cianchetti, J. C. Kerekes, and D. H. Albonesi. Phastlane: a rapid transit optical routing network. In *36th Annual International Symposium on Computer Architecture*, 2009.

[7] W. J. Dally and T. B. *Principles and Practices of Interconnection Networks*. Morgan Kaufmann Publishing Inc., 2004.

[8] European (ESIA), Japan (JEITA), Korean (KSIA), Taiwan (TSIA), and United States (SIA) Semiconductor Industry Associations. The international technology roadmap for semiconductors (ITRS), 2012.

[9] N. Hardavellas, S. Somogyi, T. F. Wenisch, R. E. Wunderlich, S. Chen, J. Kim, B. Falsafi, J. C. Hoe, and A. G. Nowatzyk. SimFlex: a fast, accurate, flexible full-system simulation framework for performance evaluation of server architecture. *SIGMETRICS Performance Evaluation Review, Tools for Comp. Arch. Research*, 2004.

[10] A. Joshi, C. Batten, Y.-J. Kwon, S. Beamer, I. Shamim, K. Asanovic, and V. Stojanovic. Silicon-photonic clos networks for global on-chip communication. In *IEEE International Symposium on Networks-on-Chip (NOCS)*, pp. 124- 133, 2009.

[11] N. Kirman, M. Kirman, R. K. Dokania, J. F. Martinez, A. B. Apsel, M. A. Watkins, and D. H. Albonesi. Leveraging optical technology in future bus-based chip multiprocessors. In *39th IEEE/ACM Annual International Symposium on Microarchitecture*, pp. 492- 503, 2006.

[12] G. Kurian, C. Sun, C.-H. Chen, J. Miller, J. Michel, L. Wei, D. Antoniadis, L.-S. Peh, L. Kimerling, V. Stojanovic, and A. Agarwal. Cross-layer energy and performance evaluation of a nanophotonic manycore processor system using real application workloads. In *26th International Parallel Distributed Processing Symposium*, 2012.

[13] S. Li, J. H. Ahn, R. D. Strong, J. B. Brockman, D. M. Tullsen, and N. P. Jouppi. Mcpat: an integrated power, area, and timing modeling framework for multicore and manycore architectures. In *42nd IEEE/ACM International Symposium on Microarchitecture*, 2009.

[14] J. Liu, X. Sun, R. Camacho-Aguilera, L. C. Kimerling, and J. Michel. Ge-on-Si laser operating at room temperature. *Opt. Lett.*, 35(5), 2010.

[15] C. Nitta, M. Farrens, and V. Akella. Addressing system-level trimming issues in on-chip nanophotonic networks. In *17th IEEE International Symposium on High Performance Computer Architecture*, 2011

[16] Y. Pan, J. Kim, and G. Memik. Flexishare: Channel sharing for an energy-efficient nanophotonic crossbar. In 16th *IEEE International Symposium on High-Performance Computer Architecture*, 2010.

[17] Y. Pan, J. Kim, and G. Memik. Featherweight: low-cost optical arbitration with qos support. In *44th IEEE/ACM International Symposium on Microarchitecture*, pp. 105-116, 2011.

[18] Y. Pan, P. Kumar, J. Kim, G. Memik, Y. Zhang, and A. Choudhary. Firefly: Illuminating future network-on-chip with nanophotonics. In *36th Annual International Symposium on Computer Architecture*, 2009.

[19] P. Rosenfeld, E. Cooper-Balis, and B. Jacob. Dramsim2: A cycle accurate memory system simulator. *Comp. Arch. Letters*, 10(1), 2011.

[20] K. Skadron, M. R. Stan, W. Huang, S. Velusamy, K. Sankaranarayanan, and D. Tarjan. Temperature-aware microarchitecture. In *30th Annual International Symposium on Computer Architecture*, 2003.

[21] C. Sun, C.-H. O. Chen, G. Kurian, L. Wei, J. Miller, A. Agarwal, L.-S. Peh, and V. Stojanovic. Dsent - a tool connecting emerging photonics with electronics for opto-electronic networks-on-chip modeling. In *6th IEEE International Symposium on Networks-on-Chip*, 2012.

[22] Y. Thonnart, E. Beigne, A. Valentian, and P. Vivet. Automatic power regulation based on an asynchronous activity detection and its application to anoc node leakage reduction. In *14th IEEE International Symposium on Asynchronous Circuits and Systems*, pp. 48-57, 2008.

[23] D. Vantrease, N. L. Binkert, R. Schreiber, and M. H. Lipasti. Light speed arbitration and flow control for nanophotonic interconnects. In *42nd Annual International Symposium on Microarchitecture*, 2009.

[24] D. Vantrease, R. Schreiber, M. Monchiero, M. McLaren, N. P. Jouppi, M. Fiorentino, A. Davis, N. Binkert, R. G. Beausoleil, and J. H. Ahn. Corona: System implications of emerging nanophotonic technology. In *35th Annual International Symposium on Computer Architecture*, 2008.

[25] T. F. Wenisch, R. E. Wunderlich, M. Ferdman, A. Ailamaki, B. Falsafi, and J. C. Hoe. SimFlex: statistical sampling of computer system simulation. *IEEE Micro*, 26(4):18- 31, Jul-Aug 2006.

[26] L. Zhou and A. Kodi. Probe: Prediction-based optical bandwidth scaling for energy-efficient NoCs. In *7th IEEE/ACM International Symposium on Networks on Chip (NoCS)*, pages 1- 8, 2013.

[27] A. Zilkie, B. Bijlani, P. Seddighian, D. C. Lee, W. Qian, J. Fong, R. Shafiiha, D. Feng, B. Luff, X. Zheng, J. Cunningham, A. V. Krishnamoorthy, and M. Asghari. High-efficiency hybrid III-V/Si external cavity DBR laser for 3um SOI waveguides. In *9th IEEE International Conference on Group IV Photonics (GFP)*, 2012.

A Model for Array-based Approximate Arithmetic Computing with Application to Multiplier and Squarer Design

Botang Shao
Dept. of Electrical and Computer Engineering
Texas A&M University
College Station, TX
shaobotang@neo.tamu.edu

Peng Li
Dept. of Electrical and Computer Engineering
Texas A&M University
College Station, TX
pli@tamu.edu

ABSTRACT

We propose a general model for array-based approximate arithmetic computing to trade off accuracy for significant reduction in energy consumption, which is realized by identifying input signatures for efficient compensation of approximation errors. Under this model, our approximate 16x16 bits fixed-width Booth multiplier consumes 44.96% and 28.33% less energy and area compared with the most accurate fixed-width Booth multiplier. Furthermore, it reduces average error, max error and mean square by 10.46%, 30.77% and 21.26%, respectively, when compared with the best reported approximate design. Using the same approach, significant energy consumption, area and error reduction is achieved for a squarer unit.

1. INTRODUCTION

As the CMOS technology and VLSI design complexity scales, delivering desired functionalities while managing chip power consumption has become a first-class design challenge. To remedy this grand energy-efficiency challenge, array-based approximate arithmetic computing (AAAC) has been introduced as a promising solution to applications with inherent error resilience including media processing, machine learning and neuromorphic systems. AAAC may allow one to trade off accuracy for significant reduction of energy consumption for such error tolerant applications.

To this end, approximate multipliers and squarers have been a focus of a great deal of past and ongoing work. Two types of approximate multipliers exist: approximate AND-array multipliers, which utilize AND gates for partial product generation and approximate Booth multipliers, which use the modified Booth algorithm to reduce the number of partial products. Constant correction [1] and variable correction [2] schemes are proposed for approximate AND-array multipliers. However, since Booth multipliers are much more efficient than AND-array multipliers, approximate Booth multipliers have been intensively investigated [3]-[8]. In particular, statistical linear regression analysis [3], estimation threshold calculation [4] and self-compensation approach [5] have been utilized to compensate the truncation error. Accuracy is increased by using certain outputs from Booth encoders [6] [7]. To decrease energy consumption, a probabilistic estimation

bias (PEB) scheme [8] is presented. A series of approximate squarers have been proposed [9] [10] [11]. The designs of [9] and [10] compensate truncation error by utilizing constant and variable correction scheme, respectively. A LUT-based squarer [11] employs a hybrid LUT-based structure.

While a diverse set of array-based approximate arithmetic unit designs exist, what is currently lacking is systemic design guidance that allows one to optimally tradeoff between error, area and energy. While the area and energy of a given design can often be easily reasoned or estimated, getting insights on error and thereby providing a basis for optimally trading off between error, area and energy consumption appears to be challenging and not well understood.

To this end, the main contributions of this paper are two-fold. First, we propose a general AAAC model for reasoning about different ways of controlling approximation errors and present optimal error compensation schemes under ideal design scenarios. Our model is general in the sense that it captures the key design structure that is common to a major class of array-based approximate arithmetic units (e.g., multipliers, squarers, dividers, adders/subtractors and logarithmic function units). Our model offers critical insights of optimized error compensation schemes and the corresponding input signature generation logic that is the key to error compensation. Second, as two specific applications, by leveraging the design insights obtained from the proposed model, we present a new approximate Booth multiplier and squarer design that achieve noticeable reduction of error compared with existing designs while maintaining significant benefits in terms of delay, area and energy consumption.

Our approximate 16-bit fixed-width Booth multiplier consumes 44.96% and 28.33% less energy and area compared with the most accurate fixed-width Booth multiplier. Furthermore, it reduces average error, max error and mean square by 10.46%, 30.77% and 21.26%, respectively, when compared with the best reported approximate design. For our 16-bit fixed-width squarer, a 16.28%, 22.00% and 33.25% reduction is achieved on average error, max error and mean square, respectively, when compared with existing designs. Additionally, when operated in the full-width mode, our multiplier and squarer have an even greater improvement of accuracy.

2. AAAC MODEL

Fig. 1 contrasts an Error-Free Computing Unit (EFCU) with n-bit inputs and an m-bit output (left) with its approximate counterpart modeled using the proposed AAAC model (right). The AAAC model consists of three units: Low-Precision Computing Unit (LPCU), Error Compensation Unit (ECU) and Combine Unit (CU).

The LPCU in the AAAC circuit produces a low-precision approximate output, for example, based upon truncation or a fraction of the input bits, with lowered energy, delay and/or area overheads compared with the error-free EFCU. To re-

ISLPED'14, August 11–13, 2014, La Jolla, CA, USA.
Copyright 2014 ACM 978-1-4503-2975-0/14/08 ...$15.00.
http://dx.doi.org/10.1145/2627369.2627617.

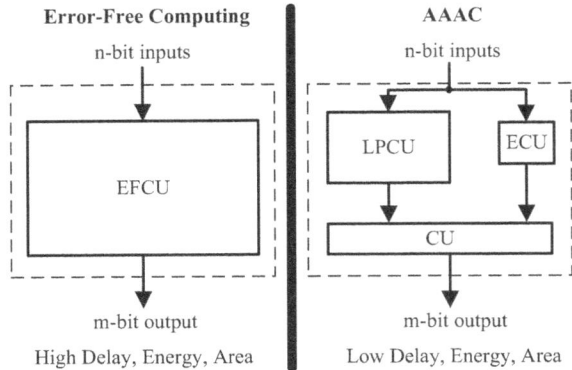

Figure 1: AAAC Model.

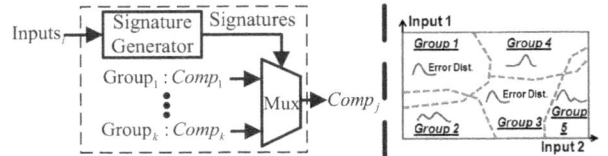

Figure 2: (left) ECU model, (right) Classification of inputs.

duce the error produced by the LPCU, a *low-cost* ECU may be included for error comparison. Finally, the CU combines the error compensation produced by the ECU with the result outputted by the LPCU, generating the final output of the AAAC unit with reduced approximate error.

The *generality* of the AAAC model lies in the fact it reflects the key computing principles behind a wide range of array-based arithmetic units, for example, approximate adders [12], multipliers [1]-[8] and squarers [9]-[11]. For instance, many approximate adders employ carry prediction from low input bits, which can be thought as a particular way of implementing the ECU. Similarly, error compensation is a common scheme in approximate multipliers and squarers.

Clearly, the **key AAAC design problem** is to develop an efficient LPCU and, in particular, an ECU so as to significantly reduce energy, delay and/or area overhead while achieving a low degree of approximation error. While the area and energy of a given design can often be easily reasoned or estimated, the key challenge is to develop insights on error or error distribution so as to optimize the error compensation scheme, which we focus on in the following subsections.

2.1 Error Metrics

We evaluate a given AAAC design with n-bit inputs by defining average error E_{ave}, maximum error E_{max} and mean square error E_{ms}, respectively as

$$E_{ave} = \frac{1}{2^n \cdot N} \sum_{i=1}^{N} |O_{AAAC,i} - O_{EFCU,i}| \quad (1)$$

$$E_{max} = \frac{1}{2^n} \max_i |O_{AAAC,i} - O_{EFCU,i}| \quad (2)$$

$$E_{ms} = \frac{1}{2^{2n} \cdot N} \sum_{i=1}^{N} (O_{AAAC,i} - O_{EFCU,i})^2 \quad (3)$$

where N, $O_{AAAC,i}$ and $O_{EFCU,i}$ denote the number of all possible input combinations, output of the AAAC, and output of EFCU (error-free result), respectively, for each input combination i. Note that the above error metrics are normalized with respect to the range of the output 2^{2n}. As shown in Fig. 1, for each input combination i, the ECU outputs error compensation, denoted by $Comp_i$. Hence the output of the AAAC circuit is: $O_{AAAC,i} = O_{LPCU,i} + Comp_i$, where $O_{LPCU,i}$ is the output of the LPCU. Importantly, the error of the LPCU, *i.e.*, the error of the AAAC before compensation ($E_{BC,i}$) and after compensation ($E_{AC,i}$) is given simply by

$$E_{BC,i} = O_{EFCU,i} - O_{LPCU,i} \quad (4)$$

$$E_{AC,i} = |E_{BC,i} - Comp_i| \quad (5)$$

2.2 Model of Error Compensation Unit (ECU)

Ideally, a specific $Comp_i$ can be computed by the ECU to perfectly zero out the error for each input pattern i. However, this does not serve any purpose for approximate computing as we are re-implementing the error-free operation. We present a practical yet general ECU model, which consists of a *Signature Generator* and a *K-to-1 Mux* as shown in Fig. 2(left). Conceptually, for a given input pattern i, the signature generator produces several signatures that encode certain essential information about the input. Based on the actual values of the extracted input signatures, this input pattern is classified into one of the K predetermined input classes with each having a predetermined error compensation $Comp_j$ ($j = 1,2, ...,$ K). The compensation for this input pattern is produced by using the signature values to select the constant compensation of its corresponding input group via the K-to-1 mux.

It is important to note that the structure of the ECU model may not immediately correspond to the specific logic implementation of the ECU. Nevertheless, it captures the general working principle of error compensation for AAAC.

2.3 Ideal Error Compensation & ECU Design

To shed light on the ECU according to the proposed model, we visualize the classification of the input space based on the chosen signature for the case of two inputs in Fig. 2(right), where the input groups may overlap. In the extreme case, if each input group has only one input pattern, then the optimal compensation for each group/input would be simply the corresponding $E_{BC,i}$ (eqn. 4). However, in practical cases, we need to consider the $E_{BC,i}$ distribution within each group.

Now it is evident that the **key ECU design problem** is to find an optimal signature generation scheme that minimizes one or more error metrics (*i.e.*, E_{ave}, E_{max} and E_{ms}) under a given set of cost constraints (*e.g.*, area, delay and energy). Note that the cost of the ECU often strongly correlates with the number of input groups K. We show several provable results for optimal selection of error compensation constants for a given compensation scheme. We also show an optimal error compensation scheme under an ideal scenario. The proofs are omitted due to space limitation. We first denote the number of input patterns that fall in the jth group by N_{G_j}.

Theorem 1: *The optimal error compensation $Comp_j$ for the jth group that minimizes E_{ave} is the median of $E_{BC,i}$ of the group if N_{G_j} is odd; otherwise it can be any value that falls in the inclusive interval between the two medians of $E_{BC,i}$.*

The above results are illustrated in the example of Fig. 3. Minimizing E_{ave} leads to minimization of the sum of distances from each $E_{BC,i}$ to $Comp_j$.

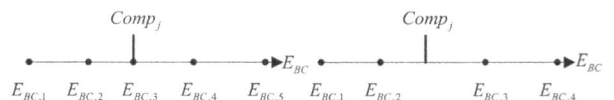

Figure 3: Optimal E_{ave}-minimizing error compensation.

Theorem 2: *The optimal error compensation $Comp_j$ for the jth group that minimizes E_{max} is the mean of $E_{BC,min}$ and $E_{BC,max}$, where $E_{BC,min}$ and $E_{BC,max}$ are the minimum and maximum values of $E_{BC,i}$ in the group, respectively.*

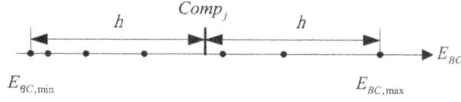

Figure 4: Optimal E_{max}-minimizing error compensation.

This result is illustrated by the example in Fig. 4, in which $h = (E_{BC,max} - E_{BC,min})/2$ is the minimum E_{max} value that can be achieved. Otherwise, either $(Comp_j - E_{BC,min})$ or $(E_{BC,max} - Comp_j)$ will be greater than h.

Theorem 3: *The optimal error compensation $Comp_j$ for the jth group that minimizes E_{ms} is the mean of all $E_{BC,i}$ in this group.*

The above three theorems suggest the following important design guidance. For a given compensation scheme, the compensation $Comp_j$ for each input group can be optimally determined according to the results above to minimize the targeted error metric. Now we turn into the other design problem by presenting the optimal error compensation scheme under an ideal scenario.

Theorem 4: *Assume $E_{BC,i}$ is uniformly and continuously distributed from $\overline{E}_{BC,min}$ to $\overline{E}_{BC,max}$, where $\overline{E}_{BC,min}$ and $\overline{E}_{BC,max}$ are the minimum and maximum values of $E_{BC,i}$, in the entire input range, then the optimal E_{ms}-minimizing error compensation scheme with K input groups partitions the entire $E_{BC,i}$ range into K non-overlapping equal-length intervals with one interval corresponding to a specific input group.*

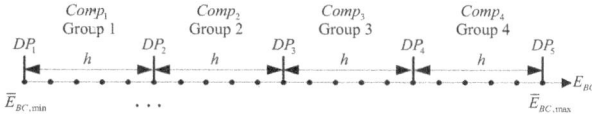

Figure 5: Optimal E_{ms}-minimizing error compensation.

Theorem 4 is illustrated for a 4-group example in Fig. 5. Note that $E_{BC,i}$ is discrete and hence not continuously distributed in reality. This continuous assumption is a good approximation when the error is densely populated between $\overline{E}_{BC,min}$ and $\overline{E}_{BC,max}$.

2.4 Practical ECU Design Guidance

The above theoretical analysis provides optimal design strategies for minimizing a particular error metric. In practice, minimization of one error metric may often lead to near-optimal minimization of other error metrics. We summarize the practical ECU design guidance that is directly resulted from these results:

1) Different input groups shall have no or little overlap on the E_{BC} axis to minimize approximation error;

2) The $E_{BC,i}$ spread of each group shall be largely of equal length;

3) Non-uniformity of $E_{BC,i}$ spread may be reduced by splitting groups with a large spread into smaller sub-groups;

4) For a given compensation/grouping scheme, the optimal compensation values for all groups can be determined to minimize a given error metric according to Theorems 1-3.

3. PROPOSED MULTIPLIER DESIGN

The AAAC model is applied to fixed-width Booth multiplier design and extension to full-width multipliers.

3.1 Fundamentals of Booth Multipliers

Booth multipliers are ideal for high speed applications and the Radix-4 Modified Booth multipliers are most widely applied. The encoding block applies the Radix-4 Booth Algorithm to encode the multiplier B, allowing the selection block

to generate only half number of partial products needed for array multipliers with each product being one of the following: 0, A, 2A, -A, -2A. Then, the compressors in the compression block compress the number of partial products to two. Finally, a $2n$-bit adder is used to generate the final product.

3.2 The Basic Idea

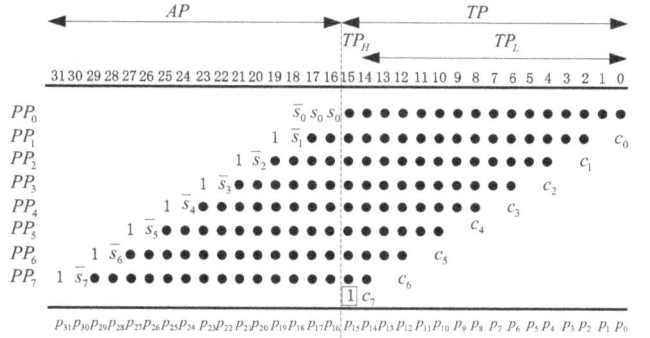

Figure 6: Partial product diagram for fixed-width 16x16 bits Booth multipliers (n=16).

In this paper, we use nxn fixed-width Booth multipliers to refer to approximate Booth multipliers that operate on two n-bit inputs while outputting only an n-bit product [4]. For convenience of discussion, we assume the higher and lower n bits of the multiplicand and multiplier correspond to the integer and fractional parts of the inputs, respectively. In this regard, a fixed-width multiplier outputs, possibly in an approximate manner, the n-bit integer part of the exact product. Fig. 6 shows the full 8-partial product array for a full-precision 16x16 bits Booth multiplier where each dot row (PP_0 to PP_7) is a partial product. The 16 dots (bits) in each PP_i are denoted by $pp_{i,15}pp_{i,14}...pp_{i,0}$ from left to right, c_i is the correction constant required to generate the negative partial product, and s_i is sign of the ith partial product. The vertical dashed line splits the array at the position of the binary (radix) point. A fixed-width multiplier outputs an integer output by approximating the carry-out produced by the fractional part of the array, which is also labeled as the *truncation part (TP)*. On the other hand, the contribution of the bits left of the binary point, *i.e.*, ones in the *accurate part (AP)*, is not approximated.

Direct-Truncated Booth multipliers (DTM) [5], which are an extreme case of fixed-width multipliers, output an n-bit integer product by simply neglecting the bits in the TP part of the array without forming them in the first place, thus potentially producing a large error. As another extreme, Post-Truncated Booth multipliers (PTM) [3] form the complete partial product array, compress all the bits, compute with full precision, add an extra "1" to the $n-1^{th}$ column to exactly round the carry-out to the nth column, and finally output the exact n-bit integer part of the final product (with rounding), as shown in Fig. 6. As such, PTMs are theoretically the *most accurate* fixed-width multipliers.

Our goal in approximate fixed-width multiplier design is to approach the accuracy of a PTM without incurring its high overhead that is commensurate with that of a full-precision multiplier. Under the AAAC model, we associate the accurate part (AP) and the truncation part (TP) of the array in Fig. 6 with the LPCU and ECU, respectively. More specifically, the bits in AP are processed by the LPCU while the effects of the ones in TP are approximated by the ECU in the form of error compensation. The exact product (EFCU output) is $O_{EFCU} = O_{LPCU} + S_{TP}$, where S_{TP} is the partial sum of TP, and O_{LPCU} is the LPCU output corresponding to AP.

To reduce the amount of approximate error, we further divide TP into TP_H (i.e., the $n-1^{th}$ column) and TP_L (Fig. 6) and have [8]

$$S_{TP,H} = \frac{1}{2}SUM_{n-1}, S_{TP,L} = \frac{1}{4}SUM_{n-2} + ... + (\frac{1}{2})^n SUM_0 \tag{6}$$

where $S_{TP,H}$ and $S_{TP,L}$ correspond to the partial sums of TP_H and TP_L, and SUM_i represents the sum of all bits in the ith column, respectively. Now it is clear that $S_{TP} = S_{TP,H} + S_{TP,L}$. The main objective in the design of ECU is to well approximate $S_{TP} \approx O_{ECU}$ such that a fixed-width n-bit output is produced, i.e., $O_{EFCU} = O_{LPCU} + S_{TP} \approx O_{LPCU} + O_{ECU}$. Note again that the ECU of a PTM (most accurate fixed-width multiplier) produces as the output

$$O_{ECU,PTM} = int(S_{TP} + 1) = int(S_{TP,H} + S_{TP,L} + 1) \tag{7}$$

where $int(\cdot)$ returns the integer part of its argument. To approach the PTM, we design our ECU's output to be

$$O_{ECU} = int(S_{TP,H} + \tilde{S}_{TP,L} + 1) \tag{8}$$

where $\tilde{S}_{TP,L}$ is a good approximation to $S_{TP,L}$. In (8), only $\tilde{S}_{TP,L}$ is approximated by the ECU while $S_{TP,H}$ is computed exactly. Regarding to (8), we denote the carry-out from TP_L to TP_H by θ

$$\theta = int(2 \cdot S_{TP,L}) \tag{9}$$

(7) can now be simplified to

$$O_{ECU,PTM} = int(S_{TP,H} + \frac{1}{2}\theta + 1) \tag{10}$$

Going back to (8), it is now clear that the main task of the ECU design is to well approximate θ. Since $S_{TP,H}$ is kept exact in (8), it is also natural to associate both AP and $S_{TP,H}$ with the LPCU, and process them with the LPCU's encoding and selection blocks. In this case, the ECU only produces an approximate θ.

3.3 Design of Error Compensation Unit

According to Section 2.4, the key problem in the ECU design is to classify all input patterns into largely equally sized groups with none or little overlap according to values of $E_{BC,i}$, which is the error before compensation (in this case θ). We first examine the standard Booth encoding that encodes each set of three consecutive bits of multiplier B into five signals and determines the corresponding partial product in terms of multiplicand A in Table 1, where n_i specifies the sign of each partial product, z_i signifies whether the partial product is zero or not, and PP_i is the actual i^{th} partial product generated from the selection block. As in Fig. 6, it is worth noting that Booth encoding is applied across the entire partial product array including the TP part, which is associated with the error. By following the ECU design guidance in Section 2.4, we identify a set of error compensation signatures of low cost from Table 1 to compensate for the error due to TP.

Table 1: Modified Booth encoding.

Inputs			Partial Product	Booth Encoder Outputs				
b_{2i+1}	b_{2i}	b_{2i-1}	PP_i	n_i	t_i	o_i	z_i	c_i
0	0	0	0	0	0	0	1	0
0	0	1	$+A$	0	0	1	0	0
0	1	0	$+A$	0	0	1	0	0
0	1	1	$+2A$	0	1	0	0	0
1	0	0	$-2A$	1	1	0	0	1
1	0	1	$-A$	1	0	1	0	1
1	1	0	$-A$	1	0	1	0	1
1	1	1	$-0(=0)$	1	0	0	1	0

Our key idea is to use *encoded sign* and *magnitude* information of the partial products to classify the input patterns into largely equally sized non-overlapping groups according to the $E_{BC,i}$ value. In the following, we first present a set of error signatures for each partial product, and then compress them for the entire ECU.

3.3.1 Signatures for Each Partial Product Row

The first signature to be chosen is z_i. It is effective since a non-zero value of z_i signifies the zero-valued corresponding partial product PP_i, thereby classifying the inputs into two $E_{BC,i}$ (zero vs. non-zero error) groups independently of the multiplicand A.

Starting from these two input groups, we select our second signature to be n_i, which encodes the sign of PP_i, allowing us to further partition the large non-zero $E_{BC,i}$ input group into two smaller groups of positive vs. negative error.

To further reduce the approximation error, we introduce the third signature to split the large signed error input groups by using the magnitude information of each partial product. For this, we count the number of non-zero bits in multiplicand A: $n_{nza} = \sum_{i=0}^{n-1} a_i$.

3.3.2 Compressed Signatures for ECU

Note that n_i and z_i are defined for each partial product and there are $n/2$ partial products for $n \times n$ bits multiplication. In addition, n_{nza} ranges from 0 to n. Utilizing these signatures for the ECU would create a huge number of input groups and lead to significant area and energy overhead. To simplify the design of the signature generator, we first sum up n_i and z_i to produce CA and CB, respectively, and then introduce a Boolean variable FA that indicates whether n_{nza} is above $n/2$ or not

$$CA = \sum_{i=0}^{\frac{n}{2}-1} z_i, CB = \sum_{i=0}^{\frac{n}{2}-1} n_i, FA = \begin{cases} 0, & \sum_{i=0}^{n-1} a_i < \frac{n}{2} \\ 1, & \sum_{i=0}^{n-1} a_i \geq \frac{n}{2} \end{cases} \tag{11}$$

CA, CB and FA are the final set of compressed signatures we use for the ECU. These signatures can be implemented with low-cost in hardware and possess the desirable properties outlined in Section 2.4 based on the proposed general AAAC model, with carry propagation adders for generating CA, CB and an n-input odd-even sorting network for FA generation.

3.4 The Complete Fixed-Width Multiplier

With the selected signatures and classified input groups, next, we need to determine the actual error compensation for each group, i.e., an approximate to θ in (9). As discussed in Section 2.3, one can follow Theorems 1-3 to choose a fixed compensation for each input group to minimize a targeted error metric. For example, to minimize E_{ms}, the optimal compensation is the average $int(2 \cdot S_{TP,L})$ value for each group. The ECU is designed to run in parallel with the selection block and part of compression block so that it causes little extra delay during runtime.

We take 16x16 bits fixed-width Booth multiplier design as an example to illustrate the signature and compensation generation schemes, and additional possible simplifications. To further simplify the ECU, we consider different ranges and combinations of the signature values in Table 2, where $\wedge$ denotes AND operation. The goal is to identify a smaller set of refined input groups with controlled error spread. $\bar{S}_{TP,L}$ is the average of $S_{TP,L}$ in each input group. To minimize E_{ms}, the optimal integer error compensation $\bar{\theta}$ is set to be the average of (9) in the group.

To further simplify, Case 2 and Case 3 are merged to form Group 1 (G1). Group 2 (G2) consists of Cases 1 and 4. Finally, Case 5 is Group 3 (G3). Each merged group has the same $\bar{\theta}$, and error selection is realized by a simple 3-to-1 mux.

Table 2: Compensation for input groups of 16x16 multiplier.

CA range	Case	Condition	$\overline{S}_{TP,L}$	$\overline{\theta}$
[0,1]	1	$CA = 1 \wedge CB < 3 \wedge FA = 0$	0.9853	1
	2	The rest when CA in [0,1]	1.1259	2
[2,5]	3	$CA = 2 \wedge CB > 3 \wedge FA = 0$	1.0188	2
		$CA = 2 \wedge CB < 3 \wedge FA = 1$		
	4	The rest when CA in [2,5]	0.8580	1
[6,8]	5	CA in [6,8]	0.4001	0

Table 3: Compensation for input groups of 16-bit squarer.

Group	Condition	$\overline{\theta}$	$\overline{S}_{TP,L}$
1	$CA = 0$	0	0.2197
	$\overline{CA} = 1 \wedge CB = 0$		0.4539
2	$CA = 1 \wedge CB = 1$	1	0.6210
	$CA = 2 \wedge CB = 0$		0.8133
3	$CA = 2 \wedge CB = 1$	2	1.0134
	$CA = 3$		1.2902
4	$CA = 4$	3	1.6966
5	$CA = 5$	4	2.1278
6	$CA = 6$	5	2.5838
7	$CA = 7$	6	3.0645

3.5 Proposed Full-Width Booth Multiplier

Approximate full-width multipliers, i. e., ones that approximate accurate $n \times n$ Booth multipliers by outputting a full-width $2n$-bit approximate product, are also useful for many practical applications. The presented fixed-width design can be readily extended to facilitate full-width operation with the difference being that in this case we would like to approximate $S_{TP,L}$ by $\tilde{S}_{TP,L}$ as in (8). Again, to minimize E_{ms}, for instance, the optimal compensation for each input group would be the average of $S_{TP,L}$, denoted by $\overline{S}_{TP,L}$, in that group. For $n=16$, values of $\overline{S}_{TP,L}$ are generated for the same three input groups as proposed fixed-width multiplier (shown in Table 2).

4. PROPOSED SQUARER DESIGN

We demonstrate the application of the AAAC model to approximate fixed-width and full-width squarer designs.

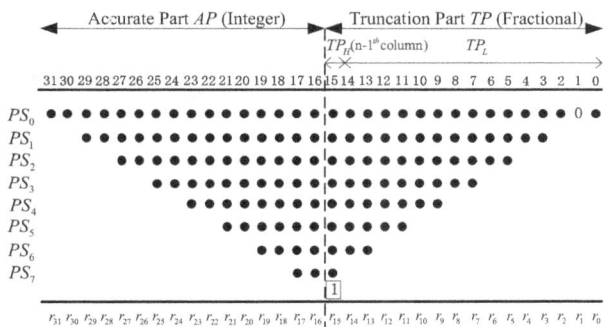

Figure 7: Squaring diagram for 16-bit fixed-width squarers.

Fig. 7 shows the full 8-partial squaring array (PS_0 to PS_7) for a full-precision 16-bit squarer, where the input is denoted by $A(a_{n-1}...a_0)$ [9]. The squarer design process is very similar to the one presented for the proposed multipliers. Again, the **key problem** is to design an ECU to well approximate θ. By following the ECU design guidance in Section 2.4, we consider the signals on the $n - 2^{th}$ column as signatures since they have the highest weight on TP_L and include all input bits which contribute to TP_L. To simplify the design of the signature generator, we sum up the signals on the $n - 2^{th}$ column to produce the first signature CA. To further reduce the approximation error, we introduce one input bit as the second signature (CB) to further split the large input groups formed by CA. Accordingly, input bit a_6 is chosen as the second signature CB for the proposed 16-bit squarer.

The final input groups of the 16-bit squarer classified by CA and CB are shown in Table 3. CA is generated by an odd-even sorting network, which has a low hardware overhead, and CB is selected directly from the input A.

The error compensations $\overline{\theta}$ for the fixed-width squarer are shown in the second last column of Table 3. The values of $\overline{S}_{TP,L}$(error compensation) of different input groups for the full-width squarer are shown in the last column of Table 3.

5. EXPERIMENTAL RESULTS

The proposed 16-bit fixed-width Booth multiplier and squarer are designed in Verilog HDL, synthesized using *Synopsis Design Compiler* with a commercial 90 nm CMOS technology and standard cell library. We also implement four additional fixed-width Booth multipliers: DTM (Direct Truncated Booth Multiplier) [5], PEBM (with probabilistic estimation bias compensation) [8], ZSM (uses sum of $\overline{z}_i$ as signatures) [7] and PTM (Post Truncated Booth Multiplier - most accurate/expensive fixed-width multiplier) [3]. Four additional squarers are implemented: DTS (Direct Truncated Squarer), CCS (with a constant compensation) [9], VCS (the signals on the $n - 2^{th}$ column as the compensation) [10] and PTS (Post Truncated Squarer − most accurate/expensive fixed-width squarer). The Booth multipliers and squarers are implemented using 2:2, 3:2 and 4:2 compressors.

5.1 Comparison of Different Multipliers

Table 4: Comparison of 16x16 bits fixed-width multipliers.

Multiplier	Area (um^2)	Delay (ns)	Energy (pJ)	E_{ms}	EDE ($pJ \cdot ns$)
DTM	2,645	2.61	2.2485	9.8525	57.8202
PTM	5,239	3.72	6.5007	0.0833	2.0144
PEBM	2,937	2.79	2.7272	0.3488	2.6540
ZSM	3,256	2.99	3.3108	0.1961	1.9413
Proposed	3,755	2.99	3.5778	0.1544	1.6517

In Table 4, five fixed-width multipliers are compared for area, delay, energy which is product of delay and power (sum of dynamic power and leakage power) and an energy-delay-mean square error product defined as EDE. The energy consumption and area of the proposed multiplier are slightly larger than PEBM and ZSM, but are much smaller than PTM, with a 44.96% and 28.33% reduction respectively. The proposed design has a significantly reduced EDE, with 14.92% reduction compared with ZSM. This indicates that our design delivers much improved accuracy with a small overhead.

5.2 Accuracy Analysis for Multipliers

5.2.1 Fixed-Width Booth Multipliers

We evaluate the accuracies of the five different designs in terms of E_{ave}, E_{max} and E_{ms}(Section 2.1) as a function of bit width. Fig. 8a shows the error reductions of the proposed fixed-width multipliers over DTM, PEBM and ZSM. Our 16-bit design significantly reduces E_{ave}, E_{max} and E_{ms} by 10.46%, 30.77% and 21.26%, when compared with ZSM.

5.2.2 Full-Width Booth Multipliers

We further compare the accuracies of the five different multipliers in full width in Fig. 8b. The proposed 16x16 full-width Booth multiplier achieves 22.73%, 37.00% and 41.23% reduction on E_{ave}, E_{max} and E_{ms}, respectively, when compared with ZSM and outperforms the most accurate fixed-

(a)

(b)

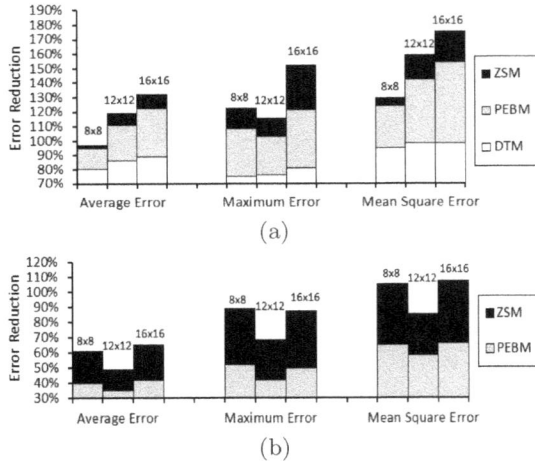

Figure 8: Error reductions of proposed Booth multipliers over DTM, PEBM and ZSM: (a) fixed-width, (b) full-width.

width PTM with an error reduction of 11.20% and 9.12% for E_{ave} and E_{ms}, when $n = 16$.

5.3 Comparison of Different Squarers

According to the results in terms of area, delay, energy which is product of delay and power (sum of dynamic power and leakage power) and $Energy \cdot Delay \cdot E_{ms}(EDE)$ in Table 5, the proposed squarer consumes 42.68% and 30.70% less energy and area than PTS. Despite slightly more energy consumption and area than CCS and VCS, the proposed 16-bit fixed-width squarer reduces EDE significantly, with 23.83% reduction compared with VCS.

Table 5: Comparison of 16-bit fixed-width squarers.

Squarer	Area (um^2)	Delay (ns)	Energy (pJ)	E_{ms}	EDE $(pJ \cdot ns)$
DTS	1,566	2.21	0.7903	4.3389	7.5782
PTS	3,016	2.93	2.0413	0.0831	0.4970
CCS	1,891	2.22	0.9693	0.2842	0.6116
VCS	1,997	2.34	1.0736	0.1612	0.4050
Proposed	2,090	2.45	1.1701	0.1076	0.3085

5.4 Accuracy Analysis for Squarers

5.4.1 Fixed-Width Squarers

Fig. 9a shows the error reductions of the proposed fixed-width squarers over DTS, CCS and VCS. For instance, our 16-bit design has a significant 16.28%, 22.00% and 33.25% reduction in terms of E_{ave}, E_{max} and E_{ms} for 16-bit, when compared with VCS.

5.4.2 Full-Width Squarers

More significant error reduction is achieved when the proposed squarers operate in full width. As shown in Fig. 9b, the proposed 16-bit full-width squarer significantly reduces E_{ave}, E_{max} and E_{ms} by 30.98%, 11.96% and 52.17%, when compared with VCS.

6. CONCLUSIONS AND FUTURE WORK

A general model is presented for array-based approximate arithmetic computing to guide the design of approximate Booth multipliers and squarers. Our proposed 16x16 bits fixed-width Booth multiplier consumes 44.96% and 28.33% less energy and area compared with the most accurate fixed-width Booth multiplier. Additionally, a 10.46%, 30.77% and 21.26%

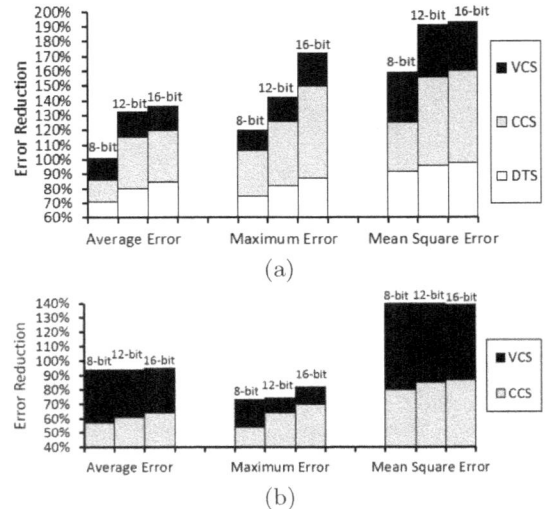

(a)

(b)

Figure 9: Error reductions of proposed squarers over DTS, CCS and VCS: (a) fixed-width, (b) full-width.

reduction is achieved for average error, max error and mean square, respectively, when compared with the best reported approximate design. Using the same approach, our approximate 16-bit fixed-width squarer reduces average error, max error and mean square by at least 16.28%, 22.00% and 33.25%, respectively, when compared with existing designs. Significant error improvements have also been achieved for full-width operation.

Our future work involves applying the approximate designs to practical applications such as hardware based machine learning, in particular, the hardware implementation of Support Vector Machine(SVM). Some initial good results have been got so far. While this effort is still in progress, our results suggest that, for example, our 16-bit approximate multiplier and squarer can lead to 21.18% energy reduction compared with the SVM using full-precision computing while achieving the same training and classifying accuracy.

7. REFERENCES

[1] M. J. Schulte et al. *Truncated Multiplication with Correction Constant.* VLSI Signal Processing, VI, pp. 388-396, 1993.
[2] E. J. King et al. *Data-dependent truncation scheme for parallel multipliers.* Circuits and Systems, 1997.
[3] S. J. Jou et al. *Low-error reduced-width Booth multipliers for DSP applications.* IEEE Trans. Circuits Syst, 2003.
[4] M. A. Song et al. *Adaptive low-error fixed-width Booth multipliers.* IEICE Trans.Fundam, 2007.
[5] H. A. Huang et al. *A self-compensation fixed-width Booth multiplier and its 128-point FFT applications.* Proc. IEEE ISCAS, pp. 3538-3541, 2006.
[6] K. J. Cho et al. *Design of low-error fixed-width modified Booth multiplier.* IEEE Trans .VLSI Syst, 2004.
[7] J. P. Wang et al. *High-accuracy fixed-width modified Booth multipliers for lossy applications.* IEEE Trans.VLSI Syst, 2011.
[8] C. Y. Li et al. *A probabilistic estimation bias circuit for fixed-width Booth multiplier and its DCT applications.* IEEE Trans. Circuits, 2011.
[9] E. G. Walters et al. *Truncated Squarers with Constant and Variable Correction.* Advanced Signal Processing Algorithms, Architectures, and Implementations, August 2004.
[10] E. G. Walters et al. *Efficient function approximation using truncated multipliers and squarers.* IEEE Symposium on Computer Arithmetic, Jun. 2005.
[11] V. P. Hoang et al. *Low-error and efficient fixed-width squarer for digital signal processing applications.* ICCE, 2012.
[12] Y. Kim et al. *An Energy Efficient Approximate Adder with Carry Skip for Error Resilient Neuromorphic VLSI Systems.* ICCAD, 2013.

SPINDLE: SPINtronic Deep Learning Engine for Large-scale Neuromorphic Computing*

Shankar Ganesh Ramasubramanian, Rangharajan Venkatesan, Mrigank Sharad,
Kaushik Roy and Anand Raghunathan
School of Electrical and Computer Engineering, Purdue University
West Lafayette, IN, USA
{sramasub,rvenkate,msharad,kaushik,raghunathan}@purdue.edu

ABSTRACT

Deep Learning Networks (DLNs) are bio-inspired large-scale neural networks that are widely used in emerging vision, analytics, and search applications. The high computation and storage requirements of DLNs have led to the exploration of various avenues for their efficient realization. Concurrently, the ability of emerging post-CMOS devices to efficiently mimic neurons and synapses has led to great interest in their use for neuromorphic computing.

We describe SPINDLE, a programmable processor for deep learning based on spintronic devices. SPINDLE exploits the unique ability of spintronic devices to realize highly dense and energy-efficient neurons and memory, which form the fundamental building blocks of DLNs. SPINDLE consists of a three-tier hierarchy of processing elements to capture the nested parallelism present in DLNs, and a two-level memory hierarchy to facilitate data reuse. It can be programmed to execute DLNs with widely varying topologies for different applications. SPINDLE employs techniques to limit the overheads of spin-to-charge conversion, and utilizes output and weight quantization to enhance the efficiency of spin-neurons. We evaluate SPINDLE using a device-to-architecture modeling framework and a set of widely used DLN applications (handwriting recognition, face detection, and object recognition). Our results indicate that SPINDLE achieves 14.4X reduction in energy consumption and 20.4X reduction in EDP over the CMOS baseline under iso-area conditions.

Categories and Subject Descriptors

C.1.3 [**PROCESSOR ARCHITECTURES**]: Other Architecture Styles (Neural Nets)

Keywords

Spintronics; Emerging Devices; Nanoelectronics; Post-CMOS; Neural Networks; Neuromorphic Computing

1. INTRODUCTION

Neuromorphic algorithms, which mimic the functionality of the human brain, are used for a wide class of applications involving classification, recognition, search, and inference. While the roots of neuromorphic algorithms lie in simple artificial neural networks, contemporary networks have grown to be much larger in scale and complexity. In this work, we focus on deep learning networks (DLNs) [1–3], an important class of large-scale neural networks that have shown state-of-the-art results on a range of problems in text, image, and video analysis. DLNs are currently used in real-world applications such as Google+ image search, Apple Siri voice recognition, house number recognition for Google Maps, etc. [4,5]. In order to achieve high accuracy and robustness to variations in inputs, DLNs utilize several layers with each layer consisting of a large number of neurons and varying interconnectivity patterns. For example, a DLN that recently won the Imagenet visual recognition challenge contains around 650,000 neurons and 60 million synapses, and requires compute power in the order of 2-4 GOPS per classification. The complexity of DLNs, together with the growth in the sizes of data sets that they process, places high computational demands on the platforms that execute them. Several research efforts have been devoted to realizing efficient implementations of DLNs using multi-core processors, graphics processing units, and hardware accelerators [6–8]. All these approaches are limited by one common fundamental bottleneck - in effect, they emulate neuromorphic systems using primitives (instructions, digital arithmetic units, and Boolean gates) that are inherently mismatched with the constructs that they are used to realize (neurons and synapses).

A concurrent trend that has catalyzed the field of neuromorphic computing is the emergence of post-CMOS devices. Although a clear replacement for Silicon and CMOS is yet to be found, many emerging devices have unique characteristics and strengths that are different from CMOS. Among them, spintronics, which uses electron spin rather than charge to represent and process information, has attracted great interest. Spintronic memories promise high density, non-volatility, and near-zero leakage, leading to extensive research, industry prototypes, and early commercial offerings in recent years [9]. Recently, it has been demonstrated that spintronic devices can also be used to directly mimic the computations performed in neurons and synapses while operating at very low voltages [10, 11], leading to greatly reduced area and power over digital and analog CMOS implementations. These advances raise the prospect of realizing large-scale neuromorphic systems such as DLNs in an energy-efficient manner using spintronics. However, several challenges need to be addressed to realize this vision.

First, a direct mapping of a DLN into a network of spintronic neurons and synapses, as envisioned by previous work, leads to a large, inefficient design, especially for DLNs of high complexity (e.g., $\sim 10^6$ neurons and $\sim 10^8$ synapses). Second, for broader utility, it is desirable to have a programmable platform that can implement a wide range of networks of varying complexity and topology, as required by different applications. Third, the low spin diffusion length in most materials mandates the use of charge-based interconnects, imposing overheads for spin$\Longleftrightarrow$charge conversion. Finally, the energy consumed by spin-neurons increases drastically with the precision at which their weights are stored and their outputs are computed. Therefore, careful architectural design is required in order to preserve the intrinsic efficiency of spintronic devices for large-scale neuromorphic computing.

*This work was supported in part by STARnet, a Semiconductor Research Corporation program sponsored by MARCO and DARPA, and in part by the National Science Foundation under grant no. 1320808.

In this work, we propose SPINtronic Deep Learning Engine (SPINDLE), an energy-efficient programmable architecture for Deep Learning Networks (DLNs). We consider various key characteristics of DLNs and spintronic devices in the design of SPINDLE. Notably, DLNs exhibit multiple levels of nested parallelism and are comprised of a few recurring computation patterns. At the lowest level, they contain fine-grained data-parallel computations such as convolution and sub-sampling. These computations are in turn organized into layers, with task parallelism within each layer and producer-consumer parallelism across layers. DLNs exhibit significant data reuse across computations, and exploiting this reuse is critical to reducing off-chip memory accesses, as well as limiting the on-chip storage requirements. Considering these characteristics, we propose a hierarchical three-tiered architecture for SPINDLE, consisting of Spin Neuromorphic Arrays (SNAs), Spin Neuromorphic Cores (SNCs) and SNC Clusters. SPIN-DLE uses a two-level memory hierarchy, consisting of on-chip distributed scratchpad memories that are local to SNCs, and shared off-chip memory. We propose various techniques to enhance the efficiency of SPINDLE, including intra- and inter-layer data reuse, and neuron output and weight quantization. We evaluate SPINDLE using a hierarchical modeling framework, starting with physics-based device simulation, and constructing circuit and architectural macro-models of spin-based neurons and memories. We compare SPINDLE to a well-optimized CMOS baseline using three popular DLN applications - handwriting recognition, face detection, and object recognition. Our analysis shows that SPINDLE achieves 14.4X reduction in energy and 20.4X reduction in energy-delay product under iso-area, establishing the potential of spintronic devices for large-scale neuromorphic computing.

The rest of the paper is organized as follows. Section 2 provides the necessary background on DLNs. Section 3 presents the design of spin-based neurons and memory, which form the building blocks of SPINDLE. Section 4 describes the SPINDLE architecture and the techniques used to improve its energy efficiency. Section 5 details the experimental setup including our device-to-architecture modeling framework. Section 6 presents results comparing SPINDLE with a CMOS baseline. Section 7 provides an overview of prior efforts on hardware for neuromorphic computing, and Section 8 concludes the paper.

2. DEEP LEARNING NETWORKS

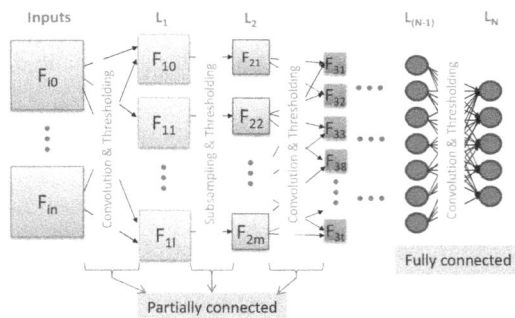

Figure 1: Structure of a DLN

DLNs (Fig. 1) are feed-forward neural networks in which the neurons are organized into well-defined layers. Each layer is composed of multiple features that can be generated in parallel from features of the previous layer using one of two kinds of operations: (i) Convolution-and-Thresholding and (ii) Subsampling-and-Thresholding.
Convolution-and-Thresholding (C-T): A C-T operation takes i features from the input layer ($i \leq N$ where N is the number of features in the input layer), and produces one feature in the output layer. First, a kernel (matrix of weights) is convolved with each input feature (convolution involves

computing dot-product of the kernel with regions of the input feature in a sliding window fashion), and the results are summed up to produce an intermediate output. A bias value is then added and a thresholding operation, also known as an activation function (typically tanh or sigmoid) is applied to produce a feature of the output layer. This process is repeated M times, where M is the number of features in the output layer.
Subsampling-and-Thresholding (S-T): Subsampling takes one input feature and produces one output feature in which each value of an output feature is produced by first computing the average of the neighboring values over a sliding window, adding a bias, and then performing a thresholding operation.

The connectivity between layers falls into two categories: (i) partially connected layers where each feature is connected to a subset of features from the previous layer (ii) fully connected layers where each feature is connected to all features in the previous layer. Note that DLNs contain three levels of parallelism - producer-consumer parallelism across layers, task parallelism within a layer, and fine-grained data parallelism within each C-T or S-T operation. Furthermore there exists significant data reuse across and within these operations.

The computational complexity of a DLN is determined by the number of layers, the number and sizes of network inputs and features in each layer, connectivity between layers, and kernel sizes. For example, CIFAR, an image classification DLN, takes an input of size 3x32x32, and has 685 features spread across 6 layers, requiring 3.77 million multiply-accumulate computations per classification. DLNs are also memory-intensive. For example, CIFAR requires memory accesses amounting to 7.5 MB per input.

3. SPINDLE BUILDING BLOCKS

The fundamental building blocks of SPINDLE are spintronic neurons and memory. In this section, we provide a brief description of their structure and operation.

3.1 Spin-Neurons

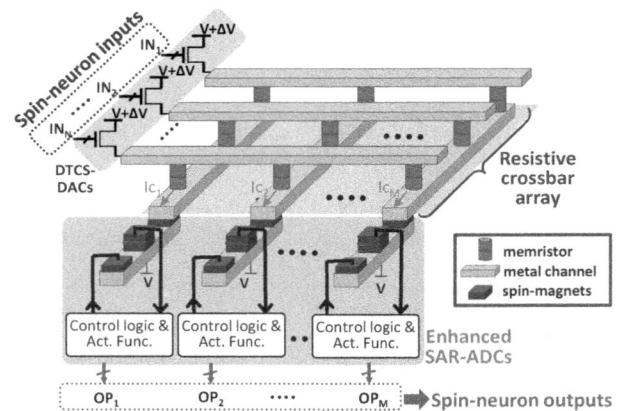

Figure 2: Array of spin-neurons

Fig. 2 shows an array of M spin-neurons that take N inputs each. The spin-neuron array consists of (i) Deep Triode Current Source Digital-to-Analog Converters (DTCS-DACs) that convert the N digital inputs ($IN_1 \ldots IN_N$) into analog currents, (ii) a resistive crossbar array (N x M) that is used to perform weighted summation of the neuron inputs, and (iii) enhanced Successive Approximation Register Analog-to-Digital Converters (SAR-ADCs) that evaluate the activation function and produce the M digital outputs. Although the proposed design utilizes transistors and memristive elements, the spintronic comparator unit in the SAR-ADC is key to the energy-efficiency of the entire neuron since it enables operation at very low voltages (∼10s of mV).

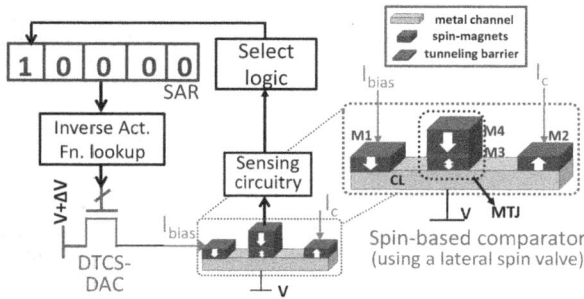

Figure 3: Enhanced spin-based SAR-ADC

The enhanced spin-based SAR-ADC is described in greater detail in Figure 3. The input current (I_C) is received from one of the columns of the resistive crossbar array. The SAR-ADC consists of a successive approximation register (SAR), a lookup table that stores the inverse of the desired neuron activation function, a DTCS-DAC, a spin-based comparator that is based on a lateral spin valve [12], and control logic. The SAR-ADC successively computes the quantized digital neuron output over i cycles where i is the desired precision. In each cycle, it generates a bias current (I_{bias}) using an inverse activation function lookup based on the current SAR value, compares I_{bias} against the input current I_C, and updates one bit of the SAR with the output of the comparator. The spin-based comparator consists of two fixed magnets (M1 and M2) of opposite spin-polarizations and a free magnet (M3) that are all connected to a metallic channel. The free magnet M3 is combined with a fixed magnet (M4) and a tunneling barrier to form a magnetic tunnel junction (MTJ). The comparison is performed by passing I_{bias} and I_C through magnets M1 and M2, respectively, resulting in the injection of spin currents of opposing polarity into the channel (CL). This spin-current injection results in the switching of M3 (the free layer of the MTJ) along a direction given by the greater of I_c or I_{bias}. The output of the comparison is determined by sensing the resistance of the MTJ, much like the read operation in STT-MRAM. Since the magnets and the channels are metallic, the comparator can be operated at very low voltages of the order of 10s of millivolts.

The resistive crossbar array stores weights in the memristors that are located at its cross-points. A memristor storing a k-bit weight needs to support 2^k resistance levels. The memristors can be programmed to different resistance values using current pulses. The number of current pulses required to program the memristor depends on the number of resistance levels. Hence, the programming energy varies exponentially with the precision of weights stored in the memristor.

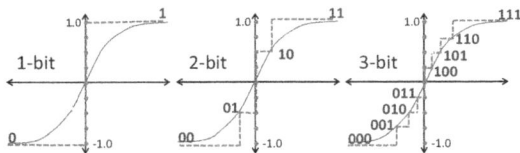

Figure 4: Staircase approximations of tanh()

The enhanced SAR-ADC described in Figure 3 can be used to perform a multi-bit staircase approximation of various activation functions. An example of successive approximation for tanh() is shown in Fig. 4 for different bit-precisions. The 1-bit approximation leads to the step function and as we increase the number of bits the staircase approximation more closely approximates the actual function. However, in order to get a n-bit approximation, we need to repeat the SAR-ADC computation 'n' times with an exponentially increasing bias current. This increases the energy and latency for high precision computations.

The cross-bar based spin-neuron performs a 120-input weighted summation ∼117X and ∼60X more energy efficiently as compared to state-of-the-art digital and analog CMOS (45 nm) implementations, respectively [10, 11]. The energy efficiency of the spin-neuron derives from two primary sources: (i) very low voltages compared to analog and digital CMOS implementations, and (ii) much lower circuit complexity (device count) compared to digital implementations that utilize adders and multipliers. Finally, we believe that the proposed design should be feasible from an integration perspective, since both spintronic and memristive devices have been shown to be compatible with current CMOS fabrication processes.

3.2 Spin Memory

Spintronic memories achieve high density and very low leakage, but require higher write energy compared to CMOS memories. In this work, we utilize a memory bit-cell based on Domain Wall Memory (DWM) [13] that preserves the density and leakage benefits of spintronic memories while significantly reducing the high write energy requirements. The schematic of the utilized bit-cell, which we call 1bitDWM, is shown in Fig. 5. It consists of a ferromagnetic wire, a magnetic tunneling junction (MTJ) and 2 access transistors. The ferromagnetic wire consists of 3 domains – two fixed and one free. When the magnetic orientation of the free domain is parallel (anti-parallel) to the fixed layer of the MTJ, it offers low (high) resistance, representing

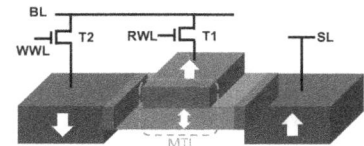

Figure 5: Schematic of spin memory bit-cell [13]

the '0' ('1') state. The read operation is performed by sensing this difference in resistance, similar to conventional STT-MRAM. However, the write operation uses a completely different mechanism based on the phenomenon of domain wall motion. The magnetization of the fixed domains in the left and right ends of the nanowire can be propagated to the free domain by applying a current along the nanowire [13]. The shift-based write mechanism is far more efficient than the MTJ-based writes used in STT-MRAM. The area of the 1bitDWM bit-cell is comparable to a 1T-1R STT-MRAM bit-cell, despite the former using two access transistors, due to the smaller transistor sizes required for 1bitDWM as a result of the lower write current requirement. In summary, 1bitDWM outperforms both SRAM and STT-MRAM [13]; therefore, we use it to design on-chip memories in SPINDLE.

4. SPINDLE ARCHITECTURE

In this section we describe the SPINDLE architecture, which composes spin-neurons and memories to provide a programmable platform for the execution of DLNs.

The SPINDLE architecture, shown in Figure 6, employs a three-level hierarchy to match the nested parallelism present in DLNs. Spin Neuron Arrays (SNAs) constitute the lowest level of the hierarchy, and combine the spin-neurons described in Section 3.2 with peripheral circuitry to realize convolution-and-thresholding or subsampling-and-thresholding operations. SNCs, which represent the second level of the hierarchy, are composed of multiple SNAs, local scratchpad memory, and a dispatch unit. They are typically used to perform a collection of operations that share input features (hence, fostering data re-use from the scratchpad). SNC Clusters form the next level of the hierarchy and consist of multiple SNCs connected by a local bus, and further exploit intra-layer parallelism. SPINDLE is a collection of SNC clusters connected to a Global Control Unit through a common global bus. Inter-layer parallelism is exploited at the top level of the SPINDLE hierarchy.

When the degree of parallelism in the DLN exceeds that supported by SPINDLE, the DLN can be decomposed into partitions that are executed in a serial manner, with intermediate results stored in the memory hierarchy. This allows SPINDLE to execute a wide range of DLNs and makes the architecture scalable and programmable.

The components of SPINDLE are described in greater detail in the following subsections.

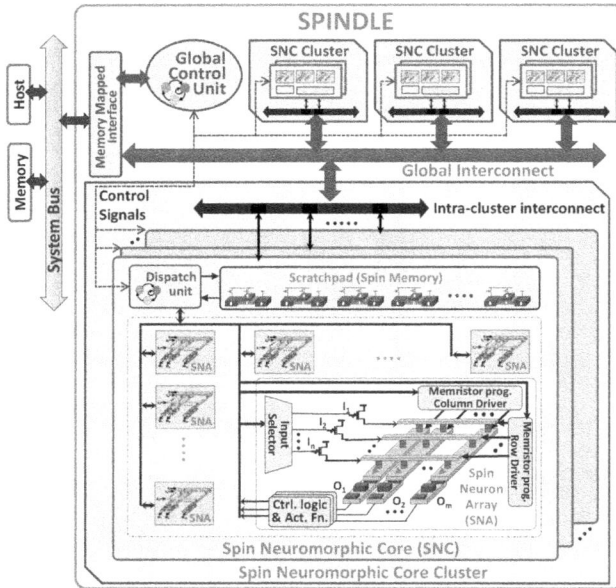

Figure 6: SPINDLE **architecture**

4.1 Spin Neuron Arrays

An SNA performs the smallest unit of computation, namely a convolution or subsampling followed by thresholding. It is fed with the required input features in a streaming manner and produces an output feature. As shown in Figure 6, each SNA consists of a set of spin-neurons (Fig. 2), an input selector unit and a memristor programming circuit.

The dispatch unit within each SNC streams the input features required by all SNAs. The input selector unit in each SNA selects the subset of inputs that SNA uses, and feeds this data to the spin-neurons. The spin-neurons accept the inputs offered by the input selector unit, and perform weighted summations with the kernel (weight matrix) stored in the memristors. Each spin-neuron (column of the crossbar) produces one element of the output feature. The complete output feature is obtained over multiple cycles. The memristor programming circuit consists of row and column drivers. The drivers select a memristor located at a particular row and column (analogous to the decode circuits in RAM), and drive the appropriate current to program the memristor.

A key property of the SNA design is that all the neurons in the array share the same inputs and execute in parallel. This results in substantially lower control overheads, since these overheads are amortized across all spin-neurons. In addition, the computations that produce adjacent elements in an output feature share a large fraction of their inputs, and the crossbar structure is naturally suited for exploiting this fine-grained data reuse. However, each column requires only a subset of the inputs, and the memristor weights for the unused inputs are set to 0. Thus, increasing the data reuse by increasing the number of columns results in a larger fraction of the memristors being programmed to 0, leading to lower energy efficiency. We determine the number of columns in each SNA of SPINDLE by balancing the benefits of data reuse against the overheads of programming zero weights to memristors.

4.2 Spin Neuromorphic Cores

SNCs consist of a group of SNAs, local scratchpad memory, and a dispatch unit. Each SNC executes a set of convolution

or sub-sampling operations from within a layer, while exploiting any available input feature re-use across these operations.

The scratchpad memory forms the highest level of the memory hierarchy and stores the input features used by the SNAs in the SNC as well as the output features that they generate. As described in Section 3.2, we utilize 1bitDWM for designing the scratchpad memory in SPINDLE. The dispatch unit performs three key functions. First, it reads all the input features stored in scratchpad memory and broadcasts them to all SNAs. The input selector in each SNA is programmed to select a subset of input features based on the connectivity of the layer being evaluated. This enables all SNAs in an SNC to perform their respective convolution or subsampling computations in a parallel lock-step fashion. This design choice amortizes control overheads across the SNAs, and enables data reuse across SNAs so that the read traffic to the scratchpad is minimized. Second, the dispatch unit controls the memristor programming circuitry, and supplies weights from the scratchpad memory to each SNA. Finally, the dispatch unit manages communication with the Global Control Unit (GCU).

As described in Section 3.1, the output precision and the number of memristor levels strongly influence the energy expended by SNAs. Therefore, each SNC has suitable tuning knobs to control the output precision by varying the number of successive approximations in the SAR-ADC, and the precision of memristor programming. Fig. 4.2(a) shows the increase in energy required to program a memristor at increasing levels of precision, and Fig. 4.2(b) compares the energy consumption of a spin-neuron to a digital CMOS neuron for various values of output precision. The figures show that it is highly desirable to operate spin-neurons at the lowest possible precision in order to achieve higher energy efficiency.

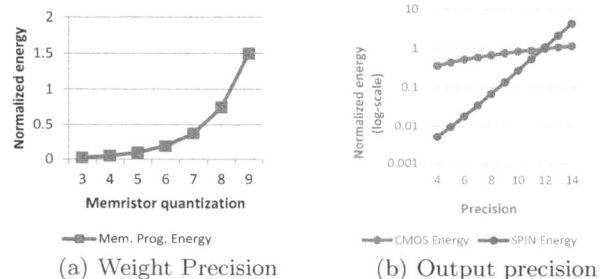

(a) Weight Precision   (b) Output precision

Figure 7: Effect of precision on energy

However, excessively reducing the precision of weights and outputs can lead to a reduction in output quality for the network. Therefore, it is necessary to determine the lowest weight and neuron output precisions that lead to acceptable output quality. For example, Fig. 8 shows the impact of weight and output quantization on the classification accuracy loss for the object detection benchmark (CIFAR). For this benchmark, we choose a weight precision of 7 bits and output precision of 4 bits, since they result in negligible impact on the output accuracy.

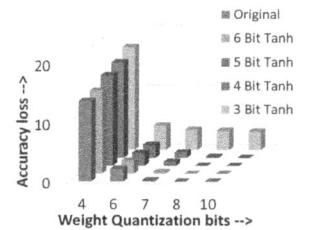

Figure 8: Quantization vs. application accuracy

4.3 SNC Cluster and Global Control Unit

The SNC Cluster consists of a group of SNCs that are connected through a high bandwidth and low-latency local bus. SNC clusters also exploit intra-layer parallelism by generating different features of the same layer in parallel. The hierarchical bus architecture, if combined with a locality-aware

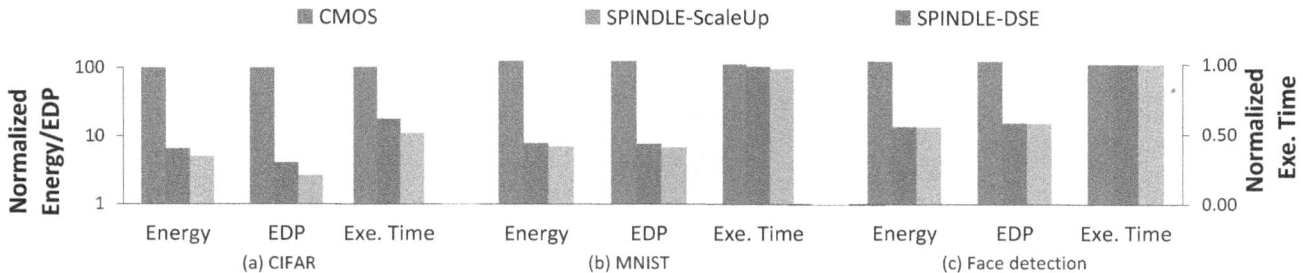

Figure 9: Comparison of benefits for individual benchmarks

mapping of the network to SPINDLE, has a potential to reduce traffic on the high-energy global bus and off-chip memory accesses. The Global Control Unit (GCU) orchestrates the overall execution of the DLN by triggering the execution of parts of the network on each SNC cluster, and the transfer of data between SNC Clusters, and to/from off-chip memory.

5. EXPERIMENTAL METHODOLOGY

In this section, we provide a description of the experimental methodology used to evaluate SPINDLE.

5.1 Modeling Framework

SPINDLE varies from a traditional CMOS architecture in that it is composed of disparate technologies namely spin-neurons, spin memory and CMOS. We model each of these technologies across multiple levels of abstraction using the framework shown in Fig. 10.

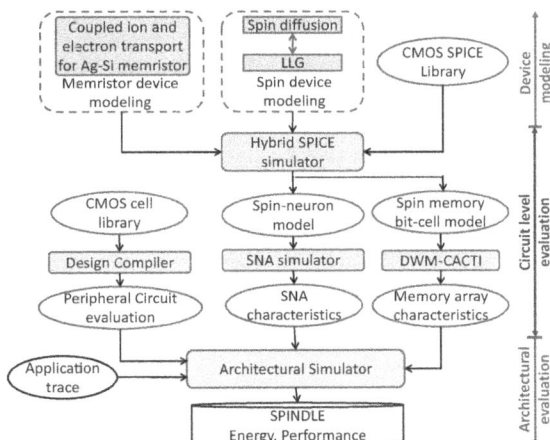

Figure 10: Modeling framework

At the device level, we model spin devices using a physics-based modeling framework [11] that incorporates the effects of variations in order to extract key energy and timing parameters. We model the dynamics of current-induced magnetic switching including the variations caused by thermal noise using Stochastic Landau-Lifshitz-Gilbert equation (LLG), while the transport of spin-current across magnetic devices is modeled using diffusive spin-transport. Parameter variations amounting to 3σ of 15% were considered in critical magnet parameters like saturation magnetization and damping coefficient, and also in the DTCS transistor threshold voltage. We note that the use of hard-axis switching significantly reduces the dependence of switching current on magnet parameters, as a small amount of positive or negative current (greater than thermal noise) can ensure correct switching operation.

At the circuit level, the spintronic devices are abstracted using behaviorally equivalent SPICE models [14]. Similarly, a circuit model for memristors is obtained using the Ag-Si memristor device parameters from [15]. We combine the SPICE models of spin devices, memristors and CMOS tran-

sistors to form a circuit model for spin-neurons. We use this circuit model to characterize SNAs.

In order to model spin memories, we evaluate the bit-cells using SPICE models and use a variant of CACTI [16] called DWM-CACTI [13,17] to evaluate memory array characteristics. We use CACTI [16] to model the CMOS memories in the baseline design. The energy and timing for the control logic in SPINDLE as well as the entire CMOS baseline are obtained by synthesizing RTL implementations using Synopsys Design Compiler to the 45nm NangateOpenCell FreePDK library.

The DLN networks for various benchmarks are built and trained on the Torch framework [18]. We train the application using the training input set and evaluate the application level accuracy using an independent testing input set. We then quantize the weights and activation function to a lower precision and retrain the application until quality bounds (< 1.5% loss in accuracy compared to the original network) are met. The quantized DLNs are executed on the SPINDLE architectural simulator to obtain their execution traces. These traces are analyzed with the appropriate energy and performance models for the components of SPINDLE to compute the application level energy and Energy-Delay-Product (EDP).

5.2 DLN Benchmarks

To evaluate the benefits of SPINDLE, we use 3 representative DLN benchmarks: (i) handwriting recognition on the MNIST database [1], (ii) face detection, and (iii) object classification on the CIFAR-10 dataset [19]. Relevant details of these three benchmarks are given in Table 1.

Table 1: Benchmark characteristics

Benchmark	#Layers	#Features	#MACs (million)	Data Transfers (KB)
MNIST	6	165	0.3	1456
CIFAR	6	685	3.77	7540
Face Detection	4	83	0.14	176

6. EXPERIMENTAL RESULTS

In this section we first present a summary of the results demonstrating the benefits of the SPINDLE architecture compared to the CMOS baseline. We then perform a design space exploration to study the sensitivity of these benefits to various architectural parameters.

6.1 Result Summary

We evaluate the benefits provided by SPINDLE against the CMOS baseline described in Section 5.1 under iso-area conditions. Note that, for the same number of processing elements, SPINDLE achieves considerable area improvements over the CMOS baseline. In order to perform an iso-area comparison, we consider two different designs: (i) SPINDLE-ScaleUp, in which we reinvest the area benefits by increasing the number of SNC Clusters, and (ii) SPINDLE-DSE, in which we perform a design space exploration to determine the best configuration of SPINDLE that uses the same area as the CMOS baseline.

The energy benefits for each of our benchmarks are shown in Fig. 9. Our results show that SPINDLE-ScaleUp can achieve 12.6X lower energy and 15.5X lower EDP compared to the

CMOS baseline. This demonstrates that the SPINDLE architecture largely preserves the intrinsic benefits of spintronic neurons and memory. SPINDLE-DSE further improves the benefits and achieves 14.4X energy and 20.4X EDP improvements, underscoring the value of architectural design space exploration.

6.2 Design Space Exploration

In this section, we study the impact of varying the architectural parameters of SPINDLE on its energy and performance. **Impact of local memory per SNC:** Varying the local memory per SNC results in an initial sharp decrease in overall system energy followed by a gradual increase as shown in Fig. 11. Initially, the increase in local memory enables us to exploit the data reuse inherent in DLNs, resulting in fewer off-chip memory transactions, and leading to significant energy savings. Further, this also reduces the idle time of the SNAs resulting in improved performance. However, once all of the input features fit in the local memory, any further increase only results in costlier reads and writes to local memory, and higher leakage energy without reducing the execution time. This results in the gradual increase in total energy.

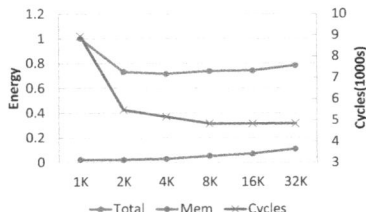

Figure 11: Effect of varying the local memory (MNIST)

Impact of SNAs per SNC: Increasing the number of SNAs per SNC exploits greater inter-feature parallelism resulting in more output features being computed in parallel in each SNC. However, it can also potentially result in memory starvation, leading to longer execution times, since each new SNA may require additional features as inputs. Thus, an increase in the number of SNAs/SNC results in faster execution time up to a point, beyond which the system slows down as shown in Fig. 12.

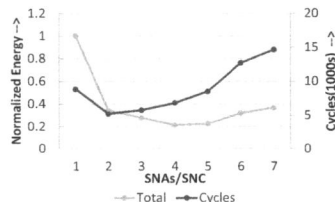

Figure 12: Effect of varying the SNAs/SNC (Face detection)

In summary, our results show that it is possible to achieve order-of-magnitude improvements in energy efficiency for large-scale neuromorphic computing with spintronic devices. The SPINDLE architecture balances efficiency and flexibility, by preserving the intrinsic benefits of spin devices to a large extent, while allowing for programmability across networks of varying sizes and topologies.

7. RELATED WORK

There have been several efforts to realize neuromorphic algorithms using custom accelerators [7,8] and graphics processors [6]. In addition, there have been efforts to more faithfully mimic biological neurons in CMOS circuits to achieve greater computational capability and efficiency [20, 21]. The analog nature of biological neurons has also prompted efforts to realize neuromorphic algorithms using CMOS analog circuits [22]. Despite these efforts, the size and power consumption of CMOS implementations remains a major challenge.

In recent years there have been efforts to use emerging technologies such as PCRAM [23], memristors [24], and spintronics [10] to realize neurons and synapses. Preliminary investigations of these technologies at the device level have shown that they are highly promising for realizing the fundamental building blocks of neuromorphic computing. In particular, PCRAM and memristors enable dense, crossbar memory designs that can store the weights compactly. Spin-based devices can match the basic computation patterns in neuromorphic algorithms while enabling very low-voltage operation [10].

While the above efforts have shown that emerging devices are promising for neuromorphic computing, they are primarily at the device level and form the motivation for our work, which focuses on the design of a large-scale, programmable hardware architecture based on these building blocks.

8. CONCLUSION

Spintronic devices have emerged as a promising technology that can realize the building blocks of neuromorphic computing platforms. To investigate their potential for large-scale neuromorphic systems, we propose SPINDLE, a programmable spintronic processor for deep learning networks. The design of SPINDLE was driven by considering application and device characteristics, and aimed to balance the objectives of energy efficiency and programmability. Our evaluations using a device-to-architecture modeling framework demonstrate over an order-of-magnitude energy benefits over a CMOS baseline.

9. REFERENCES

[1] Y. LeCun et al. Gradient-based learning applied to document recognition. In *Proc. IEEE*, 1998.
[2] G. Hinton et al. A fast learning algorithm for deep belief nets. *Trans. Neural Computation*, 2006.
[3] Y. Bengio. Learning deep architectures for AI. *Foundations and Trends in Machine Learning*, 2009.
[4] George Rosenberg. Improving photo search: A step across the semantic gap http://googleresearch.blogspot.com/2013/06/improving-photo-search-step-across.html. June 2009.
[5] Y. Netzer et al. Reading digits in natural images with unsupervised feature learning. In *NIPS Workshop on Deep Learning and Unsupervised Feature Learning*, 2011.
[6] J. Bergstra. Theano: Deep learning on GPUs with Python. In *Big Learn workshop NIPS, 2011*.
[7] M. Sankaradas et al. A massively parallel coprocessor for convolutional neural networks. In *Proc. ASAP*, 2009.
[8] C. Farabet et al. Hardware accelerated convolutional neural networks for synthetic vision systems. In *Proc. ISCAS*, 2010.
[9] E. Chen et al. Advances and future prospects of spin-transfer torque random access memory. *IEEE Trans. Magnetics*, 46(6):1873–1878, June 2010.
[10] M. Sharad et al. Boolean and non-boolean computation with spin devices. In *Proc. IEDM*, 2012.
[11] M. Sharad et al. Spin neuron for ultra low power computational hardware. In *Proc. DRC*, 2012.
[12] T. Kimura et al. Switching magnetization of a nanoscale ferromagnetic particle using nonlocal spin injection. *Phys. Rev. Lett.*, 2006.
[13] R. Venkatesan et al. DWM-TAPESTRI - An energy efficient all-spin cache using domain wall shift based writes. In *Proc. DATE*, 2013.
[14] G.D. Panagopoulos et al. Physics-Based SPICE-Compatible Compact Model for Simulating Hybrid MTJ/CMOS Circuits. *Trans. TED*, 2013.
[15] L Gao et al. Analog-input analog-weight dot-product operation with Ag/a-Si/Pt memristive devices. In *Proc. VLSI-SoC*, 2012.
[16] CACTI. http://www.hpl.hp.com/research/cacti/.
[17] R. Venkatesan et al. TapeCache: A High Density, Energy Efficient Cache Based on Domain Wall Memory. In *Proc. ISLPED*, 2012.
[18] R. Collobert et al. Torch7: A Matlab-like environment for machine learning. In *BigLearn, NIPS Workshop*, 2011.
[19] Alex Krizhevsky. Learning multiple layers of features from tiny images. Technical report, 2009.
[20] E. Painkras et al. Spinnaker: A multi-core system-on-chip for massively-parallel neural net simulation. In *Proc. CICC*, 2012.
[21] J. Seo et al. A 45nm CMOS neuromorphic chip with a scalable architecture for learning in networks of spiking neurons. In *Proc. CICC*, 2011.
[22] B. Rajendran et al. Specifications of nanoscale devices and circuits for neuromorphic computational systems. *Trans. TED*, 2013.
[23] D. Kuzum et al. Nanoelectronic programmable synapses based on phase change materials for brain-inspired computing. *Nano Letters*, 2012.
[24] S. H. Jo et al. Nanoscale memristor device as synapse in neuromorphic systems. *Nano Letters*, 2010.

Adaptive Front-End Throttling for Superscalar Processors

Wei Zhang, Hang Zhang, and John Lach

ECE Department, University of Virginia, Charlottesville, VA, USA 22904

{wz6pc, hz9xa, jlach}@virginia.edu

ABSTRACT

To achieve high performance, conventional superscalar processors maintain maximum front-end instruction delivery bandwidth, which is often suboptimal when program behavior and priority metrics change. This paper proposes an adaptive front-end throttling technique that dynamically adjusts the front-end instruction delivery bandwidth as program behavior changes to optimize a target metric, being performance, energy, or an arbitrary trade-off between them. Circuit-level synthesis (45nm FreePDK) and simulation show that adaptive front-end throttling incurs negligible overhead but achieves average improvements of 7%, 28%, 28%, and 32% for performance, energy, energy-delay product, and energy-delay-squared product, respectively, over all benchmarks on an 8-way superscalar processor.

Categories and Subject Descriptors

C.1.3 [**Processor Architectures**]: Other Architecture Styles—*adaptable architectures, pipeline processors.*

Keywords

fetch throttling; instruction delivery; low power; energy; adaptive hardware; instruction-level parallelism (ILP)

1. INTRODUCTION

Front-end instruction delivery consumes a significant fraction of energy and has a big impact on the performance of dynamically scheduled superscalar processors. To achieve high performance, the front-ends of conventional superscalar processors deliver instructions at peak rate at all times to expose as much Instruction-Level Parallelism (ILP) as possible. However, this fixed peak-rate instruction delivery scheme is often suboptimal.

Previous work [3, 4, 8, 13] has shown that delivering instructions at peak rate often brings a large number of wrong-path and early-fetched instructions into the pipeline, causing energy waste. In scenarios where high performance is not required (e.g., a user study [12] has shown that the low performance mode of an Intel Pentium CPU with dynamic voltage and frequency scaling already satisfies the users for many applications), instruction delivery could be slowed to save energy without sacrificing user satisfaction. However, conventional peak-rate instruction delivery cannot adapt when the priority metric shifts between high performance and low energy consumption.

ISLPED'14, August 11–13, 2014, La Jolla, CA, USA.

Copyright 2014 ACM 978-1-4503-2975-0/14/08 ...$15.00.

http://dx.doi.org/10.1145/2627369.2627633.

In addition, programs have diverse behaviors. The optimal instruction delivery rate that achieves the lowest energy consumption differs from program to program and from phase to phase in a single program. The conventional fixed-rate instruction delivery cannot adapt to the program behavior changes and often puts the superscalar processor in suboptimal state.

Given the aforementioned problems, it is desirable to have the capability to dynamically adjust the instruction delivery rate of superscalar processors to adapt to changes in priority metrics and program behaviors. This paper proposes an adaptive front-end throttling technique and circuit-level design that dynamically adjusts the front-end width, which controls the instruction delivery bandwidth, using software profiling or a run-time hardware controller to optimize a target metric, being performance, energy, or an arbitrary trade-off between them. In the software profiling approach, programs are analyzed prior to deployment and an optimal front-end width is selected for each program or phase given the target optimization metric. In the run-time approach, a hardware controller samples the program's execution information upon triggering events and automatically adjusts the front-end width to optimize the target metric.

The contributions of this work are as follows:

- Architectural simulations are performed to show that the optimal front-end instruction delivery bandwidth varies as target optimization metric or program behavior changes (Section 2).

- An adaptive front-end throttling technique is proposed that dynamically optimizes a given target metric for superscalar processors using software profiling or a run-time hardware controller (Section 3).

- Circuit-level synthesis (45nm FreePDK) and simulations are performed to accurately evaluate the overhead of adaptive front-end throttling and quantify the resulting energy savings (Section 4).

2. THE NEED FOR FLEXIBILITY

The necessity of a flexible front-end instruction delivery scheme that dynamically adapts to changes in priority metrics and program behaviors is demonstrated in Figure 1, which plots the performance and energy consumption of several SPEC CPU2000 benchmarks executed on an 8-way superscalar processor under different front-end widths. The configurations of the 8-way processor are shown in Table 2.

The optimal front-end width changes as the priority metric changes. When the priority metric is high performance, width 8 is optimal for *gcc*, however, when the priority metric becomes low energy, width 1 is optimal for *gcc*.

The optimal front-end width also changes as the program changes. For example, the lowest energy consumption for *gcc* happens at front-end width 1, while this happens for *bzip* at width 6. Even for a single program, such as *bzip*, the optimal front-end widths in different phases are different.

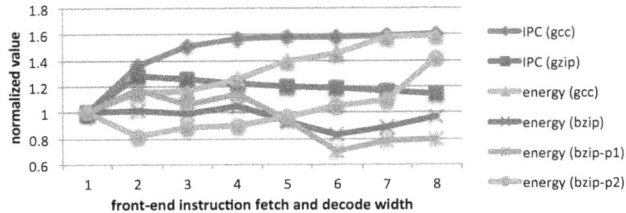

Figure 1: IPC and energy under different front-end widths of an 8-way superscalar processor. Energy is measured for a fixed amount of workload.

For example, the lowest energy consumption for *bzip-p1* and *bzip-p2*, representing two phases of *bzip*, happens at front-end width 6 and 2, respectively.

Surprisingly, the architectural simulations even show that the maximum front-end width does not always yield the best performance, such as *gzip*, the best performance of which happens at front-end width 2 instead of the maximum width 8. The reason behind this phenomenon is twofold. First, larger instruction windows cause more branch mispredictions because of the branch history update latency. This work uses a bimodal branch predictor. Although two-level *gshare* and *gselect* branch predictors with global history register speculatively updated are also tried in this work, they cannot alleviate this problem effectively. Second, larger instruction windows cause more load violations, which could be greatly reduced by using a memory dependence predictor. However, the circuit infrastructure used in this work does not have such a predictor. Both branch mispredictions and load violations have high performance penalty. For *gzip*, when front-end width increases from 1 to 8, branch misprediction rate increases by 3% and load violation rate increases by 7% for a fixed piece of program. While for *gcc*, both rates stabilize as front-end width increases beyond two for a fixed piece of program. This explains why performance degradation at large front-end widths is observed for *gzip*, while not for *gcc*.

In sum, a fixed conventional superscalar processor cannot adapt to priority metric changes or program behavior changes and often works in a suboptimal state, making a flexible front-end instruction delivery scheme that dynamically adapts to these changes highly desirable.

3. ADAPTIVE FRONT-END THROTTLING

Adaptive front-end throttling dynamically searches the optimal front-end width for the target metric by comparing program execution information under all widths and adjusts the front-end to that optimal width. Figure 2 illustrates how the flexible front-end instruction delivery works. The instruction delivery paths, consisting of fetch, decode, rename, and dispatch, are enabled or disabled dynamically by the control registers, which are added to each pipeline stage of the front-end. Corresponding logic in each pipeline stage is modified if necessary to accommodate the flexible instruction processing width. The instruction delivery paths to the branch predictor, branch target buffer, decode units, instruction buffer, rename map tables, dispatch logic, issue queue, and reorder buffer are all selectively enabled or disabled by the control registers. The instruction cache only fetches the required number of instructions dictated by the control register. Unused pipeline resources are clock-gated, but are still powered on.

Special instructions are added to the Instruction Set Architecture to directly access the width control registers, al-

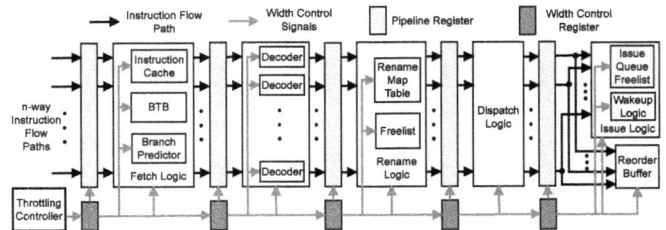

Figure 2: Flexible front-end instruction delivery.

lowing software or compiler based approaches to control front-end throttling. Front-end width changes in a pipeline fashion, starting from the fetch stage and propagating down to the subsequent stages until instructions reach the issue queue and the reorder buffer. Width change can happen in one cycle for a single pipeline stage and does not need to be consecutive. It can jump arbitrarily between any two values ranging from one to the maximum allowable width.

The basic unit that adaptive front-end throttling performs optimization on is an instruction chunk, which consists of a fixed number of instructions. Programs are divided sequentially into equal-sized instruction chunks, and optimization is made chunk-wise. Various control techniques can be proposed to dynamically throttle the front-end width. In this work, software profiling and run-time hardware controller are proposed as two approaches to throttle the front-end.

3.1 Software Profiling

Dynamic program behavior can be analyzed by software profiling, from which the front-end width control information can be extracted and inserted into the programs. To find the optimal width, programs are run once under each front-end width prior to deployment, during which performance and average power consumption of executing each chunk of instructions under that width are collected. Using this information, two types of optimization are applied to the programs. One is optimization by program, which uses a single fixed front-end width throughout the whole program but this width is flexible when choosing it. The target optimization metric for executing the entire program under each front-end width is calculated, and the width that achieves the best result for the target metric is chosen as the optimal front-end width for that program under that metric. For example, on a 4-way superscalar processor, the same program is executed four times under each of the four front-end widths. In each execution, the performance and average power of executing the entire program are collected. Using this information, the target optimization metric under all four different widths are calculated and compared. The width that achieves the best result for the target metric is selected as the optimal width.

The other is optimization by phase, which allows a single program to use different optimal front-end widths for different instruction chunks during execution. Optimization is made chunk-wise, in which the target optimization metric for executing a single chunk of instructions under each front-end width is calculated, and the width that achieves the best result for the target metric is chosen as the optimal front-end width for that chunk of instructions under that given metric. The above optimization process is repeated for each chunk of instructions in the program. For example, on a 4-way superscalar processor, the same program is executed one time under each of the four front-end widths. During each execution, the performance and average power consumption of executing each chunk of instructions in the program are col-

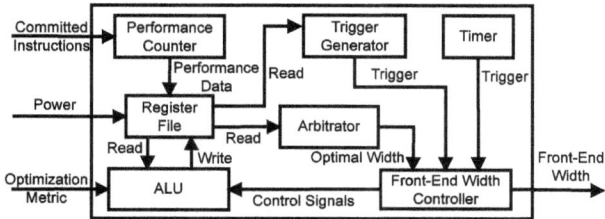

Figure 3: Block diagram of the hardware controller.

lected. For every chunk of instructions in the program, the target optimization metric for that instruction chunk under each width from 1 to 4 is calculated and the width that performs the best is selected as the optimal front-end width for that instruction chunk under that metric.

Width control information can be inserted into the program by compilers via special width control instructions. Alternately, the width control information can be stored in a hardware controller that throttles the front-end width when the width changing point arrives during program execution.

3.2 Run-Time Hardware Controller

Although software profiling is useful for characterizing dynamic program behavior, its efficacy of identifying optimal widths could be degraded when program input changes. To effectively capture dynamic program behavior changes, a dedicated hardware controller is proposed to throttle the front-end width during run-time. The hardware controller samples the program's execution information and uses the sampling results to set the optimal front-end width in the near future. The rationale behind sampling is that programs have such temporal locality that the front-end width that achieves the optimal result for the target metric at present tends to achieve the optimal result in the near future as well. As observed in architectural simulations, this temporal locality can be as long as the time taken to commit hundreds of millions of instructions. The question is when to sample? Software profiling shows that program behavior changes are often accompanied by performance and power changes. The hardware controller uses sudden changes in performance or power as indications of potential program behavior changes, which may necessitate optimal front-end width changes. A number of most recent performance and power data are kept by the hardware controller and their average values are dynamically calculated. When the difference between the new performance or power sample and the average historical performance or power sample, defined as the absolute value of $(newSample - averageSample)/averageSample$, exceeds a threshold, a sudden change in performance or power is identified. The hardware controller monitors the performance and average power of executing each chunk of instructions, and upon detecting a sudden change in either performance or power triggers a sampling process.

The block diagram of the hardware controller is shown in Figure 3. The performance counter counts the number of cycles taken to commit every chunk of instructions. An on-chip digital power meter, such as the one in the Intel Sandy Bridge microprocessor [17], is assumed to have already been built on the processor chip that provides the power information. Performance and power data are written into the register file. The trigger generator triggers a sampling process when detecting a sudden performance or power change. A timer generates periodic trigger signals in case the trigger generator misses certain program behavior changes. The

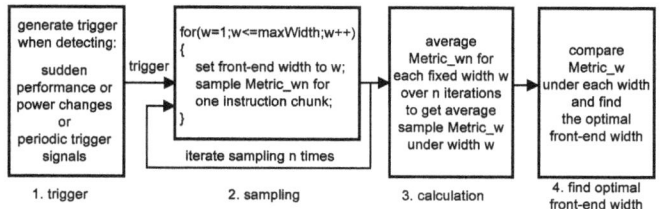

Figure 4: Run-time control flow. $Metric_{wn}$ is the sampling result of the target metric under width w in sampling iteration n. $Metric_w$ is the average sampling result of the target metric under width w. $maxWidth$ is the maximum front-end width.

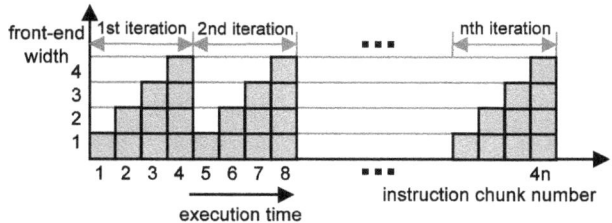

Figure 5: Sampling process on a 4-way processor.

target optimization metric for every single chunk of instructions is calculated in the arithmetic logic unit (ALU), and the results are stored in the register file. The arbitrator compares the sampling results and determines the optimal front-end width. The width controller manages the sampling process and sets the front-end width.

Figure 4 shows the major steps in the control flow using the hardware controller. In step 1, a trigger signal is generated if any of the following events is detected: sudden performance change, sudden power change, and periodic trigger signals. In step 2, upon detecting a trigger signal, the controller initiates a sampling process which consists of n iterations. In each iteration, the controller takes a sample under each front-end width, starting from one and increasing the width until the maximum, by first setting the front-end to that width and then sampling the target metric for executing a single chunk of instructions under that width. Figure 5 shows an example of the sampling process on a 4-way superscalar processor. In each sampling iteration, the controller first sets the front-end width to 1 and takes a sample, then sets the front-end width to 2 and takes a sample, and repeats this until width 4 is sampled. Next, the above sampling iteration is iterated n times. The reason for making n sampling iterations is as follows. The performance and power profile of program execution often fluctuates and Figure 6 shows an example of the performance fluctuations over a few instruction chunks on a 4-way superscalar processor. If a sampling iteration (s1, s2, s3, and s4) happens in locations shown in Figure 6, it would give the result that width 1 yields the best performance, which is not true. The sample under width 1 (s1) just happens to be in the valley. To reduce the influence of program fluctuations, the same sampling iteration is repeated n times to average out the fluctuations. Because of the inherent temporal locality, despite the large fluctuations in some programs the iterated sampling is still very effective as verified by the evaluation results in Section 4. The workload does not have to be very stable in order for the sampling process to work. In step 3, the sampling results under the same front-end width are averaged over n iterations. In step 4, an optimal front-end width is selected by comparing the average sampling results of the target metric

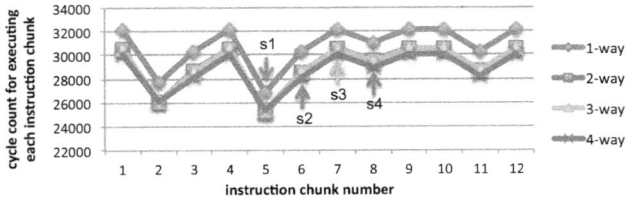

Figure 6: An example of performance fluctuations in *gcc* on a 4-way processor. s1-s4 represent 4 sampling points under front-end width 1 to 4, respectively.

Table 1: Overhead of adaptive front-end throttling on the 8-way superscalar processor.

	Area (μm^2)	Delay (ns)	Power (mW)
Conventional fetch	431267	4.9501	62.2151
Adaptive throttling (Overhead)	444623 (3.1%)	4.9503 ($\approx 0\%$)	63.0909 (1.4%)
Hardware controller (Overhead)	3742 (0.9%)	3.7030 (0%)	0.2720 (0.4%)

under all widths. The width that gives the best result is selected as the optimal width and used to set the front-end.

The run-time controller incurs control overhead, which comes from two sources. One is that the controller needs to try suboptimal front-end widths in the sampling process before settling on the optimal width. To limit this overhead, a minimum interval is enforced to prevent overly frequent sampling. After a sampling process is triggered, a second sampling is not allowed until the minimum interval elapses. Because of the long temporal locality, a properly chosen minimum interval won't miss too many optimal front-end width changes. The other is that the run-time controller may fail to detect some program behavior changes and use suboptimal front-end widths for those program phases. To reduce such misses of program behavior changes, periodic trigger signals are generated by the timer to trigger a sample if no program behavior change is detected for too long.

4. EVALUATION

4.1 Experimental Infrastructure

This work utilizes FabScalar [7] as the experimental platform, which is an open-source infrastructure that automatically generates synthesizable RTL code of diverse superscalar cores. Included in the infrastructure is FabMem, a multi-ported RAM/CAM compiler that can estimate read/write times and energies and area of user-specified RAMs/CAMs and can generate layouts of the desired RAMs/CAMs. For this project, we added a 2-level cache to the FabScalar infrastructure (no cache originally), which consists of an L1 instruction cache, an L1 data cache, and a unified L2 cache.

4.2 Area, Timing and Power Analysis

Circuit-level synthesis and simulation are performed to estimate area, timing and power. RTL synthesis is performed to generate the gate-level netlist and the area and timing report for the design. Next, gate-level simulation is performed on the synthesized netlist to collect the switching activity of the processor when executing the SPEC CPU2000 benchmarks. The switching activity is used to annotate the gate-level netlist, which the power compiler takes to generate the power report. The technology library used is the FreePDK 45nm standard cell library [19]. The power of those unsyn-

Table 2: Configurations of experimental processors.

Core type	4-way	6-way	8-way
Front-end width	4	6	8
Issue width	4	6	8
Functional units (simple,mult./div., branch,ld/st)	1,1,1,1	3,1,1,1	5,1,1,1
Issue queue	32	64	128
Load/Store queue	32	32	64
ROB	128	256	512
Branch predictor, BTB	bimodal, 64K branch history table, 4K BTB		
L1 I-Cache	32K, 64-byte block, 4-way, 1 cycle		
L1 D-Cache	64K, 64-byte block, 4-way, 1 cycle		
Unified L2	2M, 64-byte block, 8-way, 18 cycles		

thesizable RAM/CAM blocks is estimated using FabMem. Because FabMem does not support large-size RAMs/CAMs, the power of caches is estimated using CACTI [1].

4.3 Overhead of Front-End Throttling

Table 1 shows the overhead of adaptive front-end throttling on the 8-way superscalar processor, evaluated by the circuit-level analysis flow. A default switching activity is assumed when estimating the power. The adaptive throttling overhead in the table only represents the overhead of making the front-end instruction delivery flexible and does not include the overhead of the hardware controller, which is evaluated separately. A 64-bit integer ALU already provides enough precision for the arithmetic operations in the hardware controller. Evaluation results show that adaptive front-end throttling has almost no effect on critical-path delay and incurs negligible area and power overhead.

4.4 Evaluation Methodology

To evaluate adaptive front-end throttling, the simulation points, generated by the SimPoint tool [18], of six SPEC CPU2000 benchmarks are executed on the RTL processors. Only integer benchmarks are used because floating point instructions are not supported in FabScalar. SimPoint assigns a weight to each simulation point and the weight sum of the performance of all the simulation points is used to represent the performance of the entire benchmark. Each instruction chunk consists of 10000 instructions and each simulation point is sequentially divided into instruction chunks. The selection of instruction chunk size is flexible, and 10000 is chosen in this evaluation because it is relatively fine-grained but not too small to lose the meaningfulness of averaged program behavior. Optimization is made chunk-wise. The average power of executing each chunk of instructions is estimated using the aforementioned power analysis flow. Energy, ED product, and ED^2 product are calculated for each instruction chunk. Energy consumed by each simulation point is the sum of the energy consumed by all instruction chunks in that simulation point. Energy consumed by each benchmark is estimated as the weight sum of the energy of all the simulation points. In software profiling by phase and run-time hardware controller, it is impossible to optimize the ED or ED^2 of the entire program in run-time. Instead, optimization is made to the ED or ED^2 of each single chunk of instructions, which still optimizes the ED or ED^2 of the overall program. The ED and ED^2 of the overall program are calculated using the performance and energy of the entire program, the estimation of which is described above.

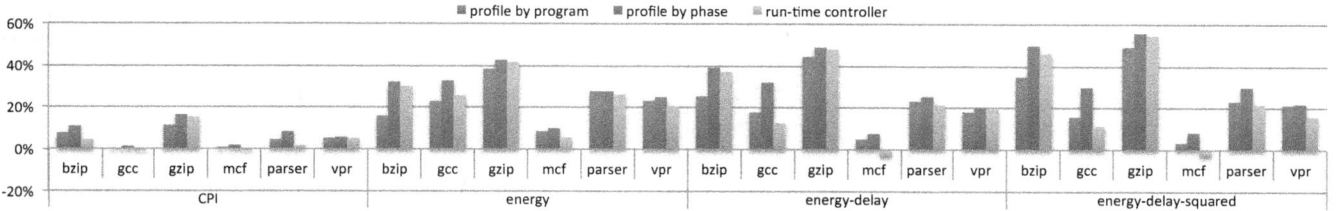

Figure 7: Average improvements of adaptive front-end throttling on the 8-way superscalar processor. CPI, $energy$, ED, and ED^2 are all normalized to the conventional fixed-width 8-way superscalar processor.

Adaptive front-end throttling is applied to three superscalar processors with different superscalar widths (number of pipeline "ways"). Table 2 shows their configurations.

4.5 Evaluating Software Profiling

The results of adaptive front-end throttling using software profiling on the 8-way superscalar processor are shown in Figure 7, in which profiling by program and profiling by phase are evaluated against the conventional fixed-width 8-way superscalar processor. The input to the program is fixed. For each of the four metrics, the adaptive throttling is optimized for that metric. Adaptive throttling is also applied to the 4-way and 6-way superscalar processors. Figure 8 shows the average improvements of the four metrics over all benchmarks on all three processors.

Results show that adaptive throttling using software profiling always does better than conventional fixed-width instruction delivery on all three processors under all four target metrics. Compared with profiling by program, profiling by phase further enhances the average improvements by 2-8% on the 8-way processor. Significant further improvements using profiling by phase are observed for programs with large behavior variations, such as *bzip* and *gcc*. For processors with smaller superscalar widths, 4-way and 6-way, adaptive throttling also achieves significant average improvements over the four metrics, shown in Figure 8.

Performance improvements are mainly due to the fact that instruction delivery pattern influences branch prediction and load speculation, which has been explained in Section 2. However, if a memory dependence predictor is used, performance improvements will become smaller than the numbers presented here. The energy savings mainly come from reducing the number of wrong-path and early-fetched instructions, which waste a significant amount of energy, and from reducing the switching activity of the pipeline by disabling certain instruction delivery paths.

4.6 Evaluating Run-Time Controller

The run-time controller is evaluated by applying the run-time control algorithm to the performance and power data obtained from software profiling. Through trial and error, the threshold for detecting sudden performance or power changes and the number of history performance and power data are chosen as 0.125 and 16, respectively. The sampling iteration number n should be kept small to reduce the overhead of sampling but should also be large enough to average out the program fluctuations. The minimum sampling interval should be much larger than the sampling duration to prevent overly frequent sampling but should not be too large in case program behavior changes are missed. The above two parameters are chosen as 12 and 5 million instructions, respectively. The timer generates a periodic trigger signal every 100 million cycles. Given the above parameters, the

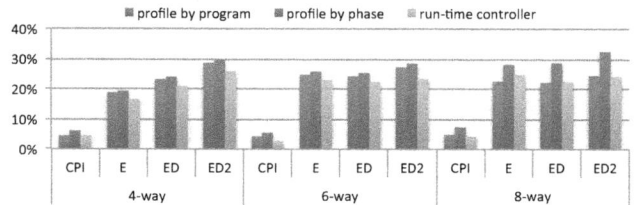

Figure 8: Average improvements of adaptive front-end throttling on 4-way, 6-way, and 8-way superscalar processors.

duration of a complete sampling process on the 4-way superscalar processor is the time taken to execute $4 \times 12 = 48$ instruction chunks, which is very short compared with the time between two adjacent optimal front-end width changes.

The results of adaptive front-end throttling using run-time controller on the 8-way superscalar processor are shown in Figure 7 and the average improvements of the four metrics over all benchmarks on the 4-way, 6-way, and 8-way superscalar processors are shown in Figure 8.

Compared with software profiling by phase with fixed input, which represents the oracle control, the worst-case control overhead of the hardware controller is 7%, 10%, 29%, and 26% for performance, energy, ED product, and ED^2 product, respectively, on the 8-way superscalar processor, and the average control overhead is 3%, 5%, 9%, and 11%, respectively, over all benchmarks on the same processor. The run-time controller causes negative ED and ED^2 results for *mcf*. The reason is that *mcf* has low ILP and the program's performance and power consumption plateau after the front-end width exceeds two, leaving little room for optimization, which is offset by the control overhead of the run-time controller. In this case, the run-time controller can be disabled or better control algorithms can be developed.

Despite the control overhead, the run-time controller still significantly improves all four metrics on the 8-way superscalar processor. The run-time controller also achieves significant improvements over the four metrics on the 4-way and 6-way superscalar processors, shown in Figure 8.

4.7 Further Discussions

Adaptive front-end throttling optimizes each target metric separately. Readers may ask could optimizing energy hurts performance too much, or the opposite happens? Table 3 shows the improvements of CPI, energy (E), ED product, and ED^2 product of different benchmarks on the 8-way superscalar processor when software profiling by program is applied and performance or energy is optimized separately. When the target optimization metric is performance, the results show that energy is improved at the same time for all benchmarks except for *gcc*, for which the maximum front-end width achieves the best performance. When the target optimization metric is energy, performance indeed degrades

Table 3: Improvements of CPI, E, ED, and ED^2 under profile by program on the 8-way processor.

		bzip	gcc	gzip	mcf	parser	vpr
Optimize CPI	CPI	8%	0%	11%	1%	4%	5%
	E	14%	0%	40%	4%	19%	13%
	ED	21%	0%	47%	4%	23%	18%
	ED^2	27%	0%	53%	5%	26%	22%
Optimize energy	CPI	8%	-18%	11%	-4%	-4%	-10%
	E	14%	23%	40%	8%	28%	23%
	ED	21%	8%	47%	5%	25%	15%
	ED^2	27%	-8%	53%	2%	22%	7%

for some benchmarks. However, energy improves more than performance degradation and the ED product is still improved. ED^2 product is also improved for most programs except for *gcc*, which has the worst performance loss.

5. RELATED WORK

A number of techniques have been proposed in the literature to save energy in superscalar processors. Pipeline gating [13] stalls instruction fetch when a low-confidence branch instruction is encountered to reduce wrong-path instructions. Just in time instruction delivery [10] stalls instruction fetch when the number of in-flight instructions exceeds a threshold. Instruction flow based front-end throttling [4] throttles instruction fetch to match the decode rate with the commit rate and reduces early-fetched instructions. Selective throttling [2] focuses on reducing energy dissipated by wrong-path instructions and dynamically chooses the optimal throttling technique applied to each branch depending on the branch prediction confidence level. Fetch halting [14] stops fetching instructions when long-latency critical load misses occur to reduce early-fetched instructions. In [3, 6, 9, 15, 16], the resources of superscalar processors, such as issue queue, reorder buffer, and load/store queue, are dynamically re-sized according to program needs to reduce the energy consumed by these resources.

6. CONCLUSIONS AND FUTURE WORK

This work differs from previous work in a number of ways. First, existing techniques often focus on reducing energy consumption while minimizing performance loss, but adaptive front-end throttling can optimize an arbitrary priority metric. Second, this work is not targeted at improving any existing techniques. Adaptive front-end throttling is orthogonal to, and can even leverage, most existing techniques, providing even greater savings. For example, fetch gating based on branch prediction confidence [2, 13] and dynamic issue queue, reorder buffer, and load/store queue re-sizing [3, 6, 9, 15, 16] can be applied together with adaptive front-end throttling to achieve greater savings. Third, previous work either does not have a direct way to quantify the overhead of the throttling technique and the resulting energy savings, or gets this information relying on architecture-level modeling frameworks, such as Wattch [5] and McPAT [11], which are known to have limited accuracy. In this work, the new architecture is implemented at the register transfer level (RTL), and circuit-level synthesis and simulation are used to accurately analyze the area, delay, and power overhead of the throttling technique and resulting energy savings.

The lack of memory dependence predictor in FabScalar poses a limitation on studying the performance of wide-issue superscalar processors. If a memory dependence predictor was present, adaptive front-end throttling will be less effective in improving performance, but still capable of achieving significant energy savings. In addition, this work focuses on single-thread applications. Applying front-end throttling to multi-thread architectures could be studied in the future. Other future work includes developing more advanced run-time control algorithms with low control overhead and combining adaptive front-end throttling with other existing throttling techniques to achieve even greater savings.

7. ACKNOWLEDGMENTS

This work was supported in part by the National Science Foundation under grants IIS-1065262 and EF-1124931.

8. REFERENCES

[1] HP labs. CACTI. http://www.hpl.hp.com/research/cacti/.
[2] J. L. Aragón, J. González, and A. González. Power-aware control speculation through selective throttling. In *HPCA*, 2003.
[3] R. I. Bahar and S. Manne. Power and energy reduction via pipeline balancing. In *ISCA*, 2001.
[4] A. Baniasadi and A. Moshovos. Instruction flow-based front-end throttling for power-aware high-performance processors. In *ISLPED*, 2001.
[5] D. Brooks, V. Tiwari, and M. Martonosi. Wattch: a framework for architectural-level power analysis and optimizations. In *ISCA*, 2000.
[6] A. Buyuktosunoglu, T. Karkhanis, D. H. Albonesi, and P. Bose. Energy efficient co-adaptive instruction fetch and issue. In *ISCA*, 2003.
[7] N. K. Choudhary, S. V. Wadhavkar, T. A. Shah, H. Mayukh, J. Gandhi, B. H. Dwiel, S. Navada, H. H. Najaf-abadi, and E. Rotenberg. Fabscalar: composing synthesizable rtl designs of arbitrary cores within a canonical superscalar template. In *ISCA*, 2011.
[8] D. Folegnani and A. González. Energy-effective issue logic. In *ISCA*, 2001.
[9] H. Homayoun, A. Sasan, J.-L. Gaudiot, and A. Veidenbaum. Reducing power in all major cam and sram-based processor units via centralized, dynamic resource size management. *IEEE Trans. VLSI*, 2011.
[10] T. Karkhanis, J. E. Smith, and P. Bose. Saving energy with just in time instruction delivery. In *ISLPED*, 2002.
[11] S. Li, J. H. Ahn, R. Strong, J. Brockman, D. Tullsen, and N. Jouppi. McPAT: an integrated power, area, and timing modeling framework for multicore and manycore architectures. In *MICRO*, 2009.
[12] B. Lin, A. Mallik, P. Dinda, G. Memik, and R. Dick. User- and process-driven dynamic voltage and frequency scaling. In *ISPASS*, 2009.
[13] S. Manne, A. Klauser, and D. Grunwald. Pipeline gating: speculation control for energy reduction. In *ISCA*, 1998.
[14] N. Mehta, B. Singer, I. Bahar, M. Leuchten, and R. Weiss. Fetch halting on critical load misses. In *ICCD*, 2004.
[15] P. Petoumenos, G. Psychou, S. Kaxiras, J. M. Cebrian Gonzalez, and J. L. Aragon. MLP-aware instruction queue resizing: The key to power-efficient performance. In *ARCS*, 2010.
[16] D. Ponomarev, G. Kucuk, and K. Ghose. Dynamic resizing of superscalar datapath components for energy efficiency. *IEEE Trans. Comput.*, 2006.
[17] E. Rotem, A. Naveh, D. Rajwan, A. Ananthakrishnan, and E. Weissmann. Power-management architecture of the intel microarchitecture code-named sandy bridge. *Micro*, 2012.
[18] T. Sherwood, E. Perelman, G. Hamerly, and B. Calder. Automatically characterizing large scale program behavior. In *ASPLOS*, 2002.
[19] J. E. Stine, I. Castellanos, M. Wood, J. Henson, F. Love, W. R. Davis, P. D. Franzon, M. Bucher, S. Basavarajaiah, J. Oh, and R. Jenkal. FreePDK: An open-source variation-aware design kit. In *MSE*, 2007.

AxNN: Energy-Efficient Neuromorphic Systems using Approximate Computing *

Swagath Venkataramani, Ashish Ranjan, Kaushik Roy and Anand Raghunathan
School of Electrical and Computer Engineering, Purdue University
{venkata0,aranjan,kaushik,raghunathan}@purdue.edu

ABSTRACT

Neuromorphic algorithms, which are comprised of highly complex, large-scale networks of artificial neurons, are increasingly used for a variety of recognition, classification, search and vision tasks. However, their computational and energy requirements can be quite high, and hence their energy-efficient implementation is of great interest.

We propose a new approach to design energy-efficient hardware implementations of large-scale neural networks (NNs) using *approximate computing*. Our work is motivated by the observations that (i) NNs are used in applications where less-than-perfect results are acceptable, and often inevitable, and (ii) they are highly resilient to inexactness in many (but not all) of their constituent computations. We make two key contributions. First, we propose a method to transform any given NN into an Approximate Neural Network (AxNN). This is performed by (i) adapting the backpropagation technique, which is commonly used to train these networks, to quantify the impact of approximating each neuron to the overall network quality (*e.g.*, classification accuracy), and (ii) selectively approximating those neurons that impact network quality the least. Further, we make the key observation that training is a naturally error-healing process that can be used to mitigate the impact of approximations to neurons. Therefore, we incrementally retrain the network with the approximations in-place, reclaiming a significant portion of the quality ceded by approximations. As a second contribution, we propose a programmable and quality-configurable neuromorphic processing engine (QCNPE), which utilizes arrays of specialized processing elements that execute neuron computations with dynamically configurable accuracies and can be used to execute AxNNs from diverse applications. We evaluated the proposed approach by constructing AXNNs for 6 recognition applications (ranging in complexity from 12-47,818 neurons and 160-3,155,968 connections) and executing them on two different platforms – QCNPE implementation containing 272 processing elements in 45nm technology and a commodity Intel Xeon server. Our results demonstrate 1.14X-1.92X energy benefits for virtually no loss ($< 0.5\%$) in output quality, and even higher improvements (upto 2.3X) when some loss (upto 7.5%) in output quality is acceptable.

Categories and Subject Descriptors

B.7.1 [**INTEGRATED CIRCUITS**]: VLSI (Very large scale integration)

Keywords

Neuromorphic Systems; Large-scale Neural Networks; Approximate Computing; Energy Efficiency

---

*This work was supported in part by the National Science Foundation under grant nos. 1018621 and 1320808.

1. INTRODUCTION

The field of neuromorphic computing has garnered significant interest in the past decade due to a confluence of trends from neuroscience, machine learning, semiconductor technology, and high performance computing. An important development within this field has been the advent of large-scale neural networks (NNs) such as Deep Learning Networks [1–3] (DLNs), Hierarchical Temporal Memory [4] (HTM), *etc.* These biologically inspired algorithms have shown state-of-the-art results on a variety of recognition, classification and inference tasks. Hence, they are deployed in many real world applications such as Google image search [5], Google Now speech recognition [6], and Apple Siri voice recognition [7], among others. However, they are also highly computationally intensive due to their large scale and dense connectivity. For example, SuperVision [2], a DLN that recently won the Imagenet visual recognition challenge, contains 650,000 neurons and 60 million connections, and demands compute performance in the order of 2-4 GOPS per classification. With energy efficiency becoming a primary concern across the computing spectrum from data centers to mobile devices, the energy-efficient realization of large-scale neural networks is of great importance.

In this work, we propose the use of *approximate computing* for energy-efficient implementation of neuromorphic systems. Approximate computing [8–14] is an emerging design paradigm that leverages the intrinsic resilience of applications, *i.e.*, their ability to produce results of acceptable quality even when many of their computations are performed in an approximate manner. This ability to relax the accuracy of computations is translated into significant improvements in energy or performance by utilizing a variety of hardware [9–11,13,14] and software [8,12] techniques.

A key question in approximate computing is which computations to approximate, and by how much. The judicious selection of approximations is critical to maximizing the benefits from approximate computing while ensuring minimal degradation in output quality. For this purpose, it is necessary to determine the impact of approximating various internal computations on the eventual application output quality. In the context of neuromorphic systems, we address this challenge by leveraging backpropagation, an operation that is widely utilized for NN training. We observe that backpropagation provides a measure of the sensitivity of the NN outputs to each neuron in the network; thereby, it can be utilized to identify neurons that are likely to be more resilient to approximations.

The process of training provides a further opportunity to maximize the benefits of approximate computing in NNs. Training is an inherently error-healing process, since it modulates the weights associated with each neuron in the NN such that the error at the network outputs is minimized. Therefore, we suggest that training can also be used to compensate for approximations. Further, this synergy can be exploited in an iterative approximate-and-retrain loop to enhance the benefits of approximate computing.

Based on the above insights, we propose a method to construct ApproXimate Neural Networks (AxNNs) that consists of three key steps. First, it utilizes backpropagation to *characterize* the importance of each neuron in the NN and identify those that impact output quality the least. Next, the AxNN is created by selectively replacing less significant neurons in the network with *approximate* versions that are more energy-efficient. Towards this end, we utilize *precision scal-*

ing, a popular approximate design technique, and modulate the precisions of the inputs and the weights of the neurons to realize versions with different accuracy *vs.* energy trade-offs. Once the approximate NN is formed, we adapt the weights of the neurons in the approximated network by *incrementally retraining* them. Since training is a naturally error-healing process, this allows us to reclaim a significant portion of the quality ceded by approximations. For a given output quality, retraining may create further opportunities to approximate the NN, resulting in increased energy benefits. We develop an automatic design methodology to generate AxNNs by iterating the aforementioned characterize, approximate and retrain steps in a quality-constrained loop.

Another contribution of our work is the design of a quality-configurable Neuromorphic Processing Engine (QC-NPE), which provides a programmable hardware platform for efficiently executing AxNNs with arbitrary topologies, weights, and degrees of approximation. QcNPE features a 2D array of Neural Computation Units (NCUs) and a 1D array of Activation Function Units (AFUs) that together enable the efficient execution of neural networks. We equip the NCUs and AFUs with hardware mechanisms based on precision scaling to effectively translate the reduced precision of neurons into energy benefits at run-time.

In summary, the key contributions of this work are:

- We propose a new avenue for energy efficiency in neuromorphic systems by using approximate computing. We propose the concept of ApproXimate Neural Networks (AxNNs) that leverage backpropagation to maximize the energy benefits from approximate computing, while utilizing the inherent healing nature of the training process to minimize their impact on output quality.

- Embodying the above design principle, we develop a systematic methodology, which can automatically generate AxNNs for any given neural network. The methodology is independent of the NN topology, network parameters and the training dataset.

- We design a programmable and quality-configurable Neuromorphic Processing Engine (QcNPE) that can be used to efficiently execute AxNNs.

- We construct approximate versions of 6 popular large-scale NN applications using the proposed AxNN design methodology and execute them on two different platforms – QcNPE and commodity Intel Xeon server – to demonstrate significant improvements in energy for negligible loss in output quality.

The rest of the paper is organized as follows. Section 2 presents an overview of related efforts. Section 3 provides relevant background on NNs. Section 4 outlines the proposed AxNN design methodology. Section 5 details the architecture of QcNPE. Section 6 describes the experimental methodology and the NN applications used. Section 7 presents the results and Section 8 concludes the paper.

2. RELATED WORK

Our work is at the confluence of two important (and hitherto disconnected) areas of research—efficient realization of neuromorphic systems, and approximate computing. This section presents an overview of research efforts in each of these areas and places our contributions in their context.

Efficient neuromorphic systems: Previous efforts have explored two major directions for the efficient implementation of NNs. The first is accelerator based computing, in which custom architectures that are optimized to the computation and communication patterns of NNs are designed. A spectrum of architectures ranging from application-specific NN designs [15] to programmable neural processors [16,17] have been proposed. Further, NN implementations on other programmable accelerators such as GPUs [18] have also been explored. The second prominent is the use of emerging device technologies such as resistive RAM [19], memristor based crossbar arrays [20], and spintronics [21], to realize neurons and synapses more efficiently.

In this work, we identify a new dimension to optimize neuromorphic systems. We leverage their intrinsic resilience and employ approximate computing to construct NN implementations that are significantly more efficient. Note that the approximate computing techniques presented in this work are *complementary* to the above efforts, *i.e.,* they can be employed together to further enhance efficiency.

Approximate computing: There has been growing interest in the field of approximate computing, leading to efforts at various levels of design abstraction, spanning software, architecture and circuits. At the software level, these techniques improve performance by either skipping computations [8], relaxing dependencies [8], or replacing expensive functions with approximate versions [12]. In hardware, the use of voltage over-scaling and circuit simplification have been explored to gain energy efficiency with some (acceptable) loss in output quality [9, 10, 22]. While these initial efforts targeted application-specific hardware, approximate computing has recently been extended to the domain of programmable processors [13,14]. Finally, with the growing interest in approximate hardware platforms, supporting design automation techniques have also been explored [11].

We extend the state-of-the-art in approximate computing along two key fronts. First, we apply approximate computing to NNs, an important class of applications that demonstrate significant intrinsic resilience. Second, we show how the unique properties of NNs can be exploited to maximize the benefits of approximate computing. The use of backpropagation to systematically identify less significant neurons in NNs leads to a superior energy-quality trade-off. Further, interleaved approximation and training extends the degree to which approximate computing can be utilized in NNs.

3. NEURAL NETS: PRELIMINARIES

Neural networks can be broadly described as systems that functionally abstract the computational behavior of the human brain. The fundamental computation unit of NNs is called a *neuron*, which is densely interconnected with several others to constitute a neural network. Each neuron in the network, as shown in Figure 1(a), computes a weighted sum of all its inputs, followed by a non-linear activation function on the weighted sum to produce the output.

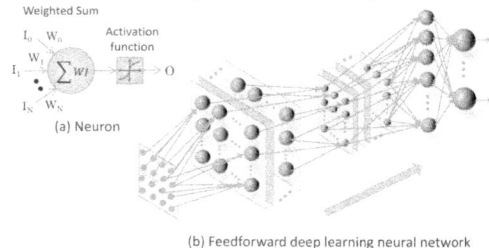

(b) Feedforward deep learning neural network

Figure 1: Neural network preliminaries

While the proposed approach can be applied to various classes of NNs, in our discussions we consider the most prevalent form, *viz. feedforward NNs*, wherein the neurons are connected to form an acyclic network, as illustrated in Figure 1(b). The operation of NNs typically involves 2 phases *viz.* training and testing. In the training phase, the parameters of the NN (weights of each neuron) are identified based on the training dataset. Once the NN is trained, it enters the testing or evaluation phase, in which it is used to perform the desired application. A brief description of the steps involved in testing and training are provided below.

Evaluating NNs—Forward Propagation: Forward propagation, used widely in both testing and training, is the process of evaluating the outputs of the NN. In forward propagation, the inputs are fed to the neurons in the first layer, where they are processed and propagated to the neurons in the next layer. This process is repeated at all the network layers and the NN outputs are eventually computed.

Training NNs—Backpropagation: The training process iterates over a dataset of training instances, pre-labeled with golden outputs for the NN, to identify the values of network

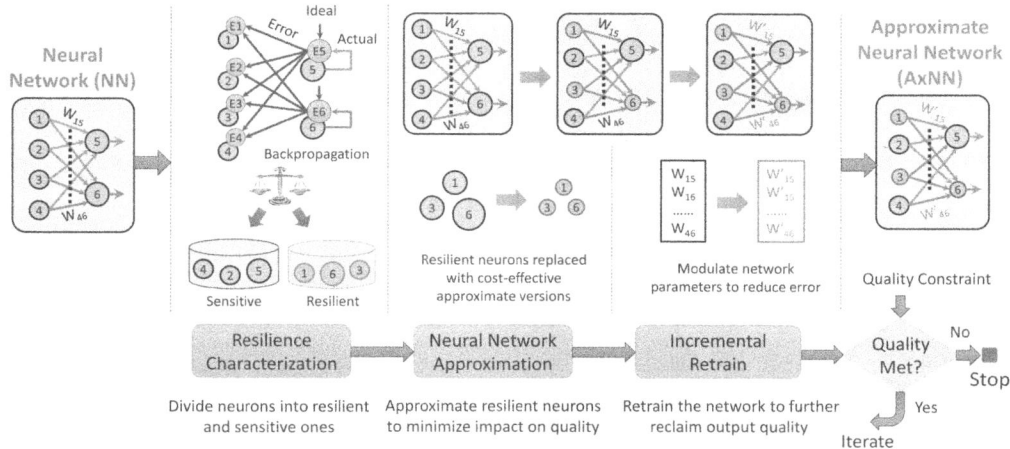

Figure 2: Overview of the Approximate Neural Networks (AxNN) design approach

parameters that maximize the application output quality. The network parameters are typically initialized randomly and are successively refined in each iteration as described below. First, the NN is evaluated for a random training instance using forward propagation, and the error at the network output (with reference to the golden output) is computed. Next, a key step called *backpropagation* is invoked, which redistributes the error at the NN output backward in the network, all the way to its inputs. Thus, backpropagation quantifies the error contributed by each neuron in the network towards the global network error. Knowing the respective error contributions, the network parameters associated with each neuron are modulated such that the error at its output is reduced. Mathematically, the parameter update process is formulated as a gradient descent optimization problem as shown in Equation 1. In this equation, w_{ji} represents the weight of the connection between neuron i and j, E denotes the global error, α denotes the learning rate, and ψ' is the first derivative of the activation function. The Δw_{ji} is computed by propagating the error back in the network through all the connections in the downstream of j to the output.

$$\Delta w_{ji} = -\alpha \frac{\partial E}{\partial w_{ji}} = \sum_{k \in DownStream(j)} \left(\alpha \psi' w_{kj} \frac{\partial E}{\partial w_{kj}} \right) \quad (1)$$

In the proposed methodology to construct AxNNs, we utilize two unique properties: (i) the ability to apportion global errors to local computations by using backpropagation, and (ii) the ability to self-heal local errors in the network during training. A detailed description of the principles behind AxNNs and their design are provided in Section 4.

4. AxNN: APPROACH AND DESIGN METHODOLOGY

Approximate Neural Networks (AxNNs) are neural networks whose constituent computations have been subject to approximations, resulting in improved energy efficiency with acceptable output quality. This section outlines the key ideas behind AxNNs and the proposed design methodology.

4.1 AxNN: Design Approach

An AxNN can be viewed as a transformed version of a trained NN, where the transformation introduces approximations such that the resulting energy is minimized while the output quality meets a specified constraint. As shown in Figure 2, this transformation involves three key steps: (i) Resilience characterization, wherein the neural network is analyzed to identify neurons that impact output quality the least, (ii) Neural network approximation, in which the neurons that were determined to be resilient in the characterization step are approximated, and finally (iii) Incremental retraining wherein the network is retrained with the approximations in-place such that the loss in quality is further

minimized. The following subsections provide an in-depth description of each step in the process.

4.1.1 Neural network resilience characterization

A significant challenge to employing approximate computing in any application is to distinguish computations that the application output is highly sensitive to (and hence cannot be approximated) from resilient ones that may be subject to approximations. In the context of neuromorphic systems, we propose to utilize backpropagation to characterize the resilience of each neuron. Backpropagation apportions the error at the output of the NN to the outputs of individual neurons. Thereby, it provides a measure of the error contributed by each neuron to the outputs of the network. We make the following key observation: neurons that contribute the least to the global error are more resilient *i.e.*, more amenable to approximations. Conversely, neurons contributing the highest error during backpropagation are deemed sensitive.

Based on the above insight, we propose a resilience characterization procedure that involves the following operations. For each instance in the training dataset, the error at the output of the neural network is computed using forward propagation. Next, the errors are propagated back to the outputs of individual neurons and their average error contribution over all inputs in the training set is obtained. The neurons are then sorted based on the magnitude of their average error contribution, and a pre-determined threshold is used to classify them as resilient or sensitive. We note that, unlike the actual training process, the network parameters are not altered during the resilience characterization step.

4.1.2 Approximation of resilient neurons

In the approximation step, the AxNN is formed by replacing *approximate neurons* in place of the resilient neurons identified during resilience characterization. Approximate neurons are inaccurate but cost-effective hardware or software implementations of the original neuron functionality and are the primary source of the energy efficiency in AxNNs. Approximate neurons can be designed using a wide range of approximate computing techniques. In this work, we utilize precision scaling, a popular technique in which the precisions (bit-widths) of the input operands and the neuron weights are modulated based on their degree of resilience. In addition, we also explore the use of piecewise-linear approximations of the activation function. These approximations may lead to improved efficiency on various hardware platforms. However, the proposed QCNPE architecture, described in Section 5, is specifically designed to translate the reduced precision requirements of the approximate neurons into energy improvements.

4.1.3 Incremental retrain of AxNN

Although approximations are themselves introduced in a quality-aware manner, we show how to further minimize their impact by leveraging the training process. As discussed in Section 3, the training process modulates the parameters associated with each neuron such that the global error is minimized. In fully-accurate NNs, the output error originates from untrained or partially trained network parameters. However, in the case of AxNNs, we intentionally supplement this error with a secondary source, *viz.* approximate neurons. Since training by nature has the ability to minimize errors at neuron outputs, we assert that errors introduced by approximations can also potentially benefit from it. Leveraging this insight, we propose to retrain the AxNN parameters with approximations in-place. The retraining process, as shown in Figure 2, suitably adjusts the AxNN parameters, thereby alleviating the impact of approximation-induced errors. Since retraining improves the output quality of the AxNN, it enables new opportunities to perform additional approximations. This synergy between approximation and training can be captured in an iterative approximate-and-retrain loop, as described in the next sub-section.

Retraining the AxNN after approximations increases the overall runtime of the training process. However, we note that the retraining is incremental *i.e.*, it is carried out for very few iterations (2 iterations in our experiments). Typically, the training process in NNs takes several tens to hundreds of iterations and therefore the increase in run-time complexity due to retraining is small. Also, in typical use cases of NN applications, the training process is performed once or very infrequently. On the other hand, the testing or evaluation phase, in which the actual classification is performed using the NN, extends for much longer periods of time. Since AxNNs yield significant energy benefits in the more critical evaluation phase, a small increase in the cost of training is a favorable trade-off. The impact of retraining on the overall energy and quality of AxNNs for different applications is discussed in Section 7.4.

4.2 AxNN Design Methodology

Algorithm 1 describes the pseudocode of the systematic methodology that we propose to automatically construct AxNNs. The inputs are a pre-trained neural network (NN), its corresponding training dataset ($TrData$) and a quality constraint (Q) that dictates the degradation in quality tolerable in the approximate implementation. The quality specifications are application-specific and are typically used during the process of constructing and training the NN itself. The algorithm iteratively builds the AxNN by successively approximating the NN in each iteration (lines 3-15), while ensuring that the quality bounds are satisfied.

Algorithm 1 AxNN: Design methodology

Input: Pre-trained neural network: NN,
  Training dataset: $TrData$, Quality constraint: Q
Output: Approximate neural network: $AxNN$
1: **Begin**
2:   Initialize: $AxNN_{temp} = NN$
3:   **while** $Q_{AxNN} > Q$ **do**
4:     $AxNN = AxNN_{temp}$
5:     $Layer.E_{List} \leftarrow$ Energy estimates of $AxNN$ layers
6:     $Layer_{Emax} \leftarrow$ max ($Layer.E_{List}$)
7:     $Layer_{Emax}.\Delta =$ **backpropagation** ($AxNN, TrData$)
8:     $\Delta_{mean} =$ **mean** ($Layer_{Emax}.\Delta$)
9:     **for** each N: Neuron $\in Layer_{Emax}$ **do**
10:       **if** $Layer_{Emax}.\Delta(N) < \alpha * \Delta_{mean}$ **then**
11:         $AxNN_{temp} =$ Approximate N in $AxNN$
12:       **end if**
13:     **end for**
14:     $AxNN_{temp} =$ train ($AxNN_{temp}$, $TrData$, K epochs)
15:   **end while**
16:   **return** $AxNN$
17: **End**

The following steps are performed in each iteration of Algorithm 1. First, an estimate of energy consumed by each layer of the NN ($Layer.E_{List}$) is computed (line 5). For this purpose, we employ a high-level energy model of the quality-configurable neuromorphic processing engine discussed in Section 5. However, other energy models based on the complexity of neurons and the density of interconnections can also be utilized. We thus identify the most energy-intensive layer ($Layer_{Emax}$) in the network (line 6) and target its constituent neurons for approximations. Next, the resilience of each neuron in $Layer_{Emax}$ is characterized by finding the average error at its output over the entire training set using backpropagation (line 7). We then compute the mean of these errors (Δ_{mean}) and neurons whose error is below a threshold $\alpha * \Delta_{mean}$ are deemed resilient. Each of the resilient neurons previously identified are approximated in steps by gradually reducing their precision of computations (lines 9-13). The approximate neural network ($AxNN$) is thus obtained. Next, the $AxNN$ is incrementally retrained for a small number of iterations (K epochs) to further improve its quality (line 14). After retraining, if the $AxNN$ meets the specified quality constraint, then lines 4-14 are repeated and the network is further approximated. If not, the last valid $AxNN$ is produced as the output.

The above design methodology can be utilized to construct energy-efficient approximate versions of any neural network, subject to the desired quality requirements. Furthermore, any approximation technique may be used, although approximations that result in better energy *vs.* quality tradeoffs are clearly desirable.

5. QUALITY CONFIGURABLE NEURO-MORPHIC PROCESSING ENGINE

In this section, we describe the proposed quality configurable Neuromorphic Processing Engine (QCNPE) that provides a hardware platform to execute AxNNs. The QCNPE is a many-core architecture that exploits the fine-grained data parallelism and data re-use patterns of NNs. A key feature of QCNPE is that it contains specialized processing elements whose accuracies (and energy) are dynamically configurable and hence can be used to efficiently execute neurons with various degrees of approximation.

Figure 3 shows the block diagram of QCNPE. It contains 2 types of processing elements: (i) a 2D array of neural compute units (NCUs), and (ii) a 1D array of activation function units (AFUs). The NCUs contain a 2-level datapath with an accumulator register and compute the weighted sum of a stream of inputs over multiple cycles. The NCUs are connected to their nearest neighbors in the 2D array and receive inputs from the left and top NCUs, which are then propagated to their right and bottom neighbors in the next cycle. The NCUs along the top and left borders of the 2D array receive inputs from two 1D arrays of First-In-First-Out (FIFO) memory elements placed along the borders. Functionally, the NCUs are designed to perform the weighted sum operation associated with each neuron. For this purpose, the inputs are streamed in along the rows and weights along the columns and operated upon within each NCU. Note that the inputs and weights are re-used by all NCUs in a given row and column respectively, which is a typical data flow pattern in NNs, wherein the inputs fan-out to several neurons and the weights are shared amongst neurons/across inputs.

In order to facilitate execution with different accuracies, the NCUs are designed with a *precision control register*, which is initialized at the beginning of the 2D array operation. This is used to modulate the precision of the NCU inputs before they are operated within the NCU. Scaling the precision of input operands naturally results in power savings due to the reduction in switching activity in the NCU. In QCNPE, this is further enhanced by clock gating the LSB bit slices of the NCU accumulator register. In our implementation, the area and power overheads to enable quality configurability amounted to less than 5% of the overall NCU.

The activation function units (AFUs), located on the right border of the 2D array, are designed to perform the non-linear operation on the weighted sum computed in the NCUs. As

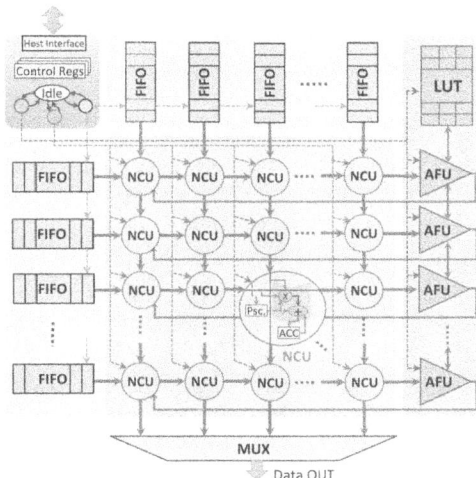

Figure 3: Block diagram of QCNPE

shown in Figure 3, this is carried out in a cyclical fashion, wherein the weighted sums from the NCUs in each row are streamed out and the outputs of the AFUs are stored back to the respective elements.

In summary, the QCNPE architecture provides an energy-efficient hardware platform to execute AxNNs of any given topology, interconnectivity pattern and degrees of approximation in their neurons.

6. EXPERIMENTAL METHODOLOGY

This section describes the experimental methodology and the benchmarks used in our evaluation of AxNNs. The QC-NPE was implemented at the Register-Transfer Level (RTL) in Verilog HDL and mapped to the IBM 45nm technology using Synopsys Design Compiler. Synopsys Power Compiler was used to estimate the energy consumption of the implementation. The key micro-architectural parameters and implementation metrics are shown in Figure 4.

Micro-architectural Parameters	Value	Metric	Value
Array Dimension	16 X 16	Feature Size	45nm
No. of NCU/AFU	256/16	Area	1.7 mm²
FIFO count	32	Power	517.2 mW
FIFO depth	32	Gate Count	390392
		Frequency	1GHz

Figure 4: QCNPE **parameters and metrics**

Neural networks used in 6 popular classification and recognition applications, listed in Figure 5, were used as benchmarks in our experiments. The number of layers, neurons and connections in the networks are also provided in Figure 5. The benchmarks were ported manually to QCNPE and the baseline was well optimized for energy. We utilized classification accuracy, *i.e.*, the fraction of instances correctly classified as the measure of quality for all the benchmarks.

Applications	Dataset	Layers	Neurons	Connections
House Number Recognition	SVHN	8	47818	799616
Object Classification	CIFAR	6	38282	808608
Digit Recognition	MNIST	6	8010	43036
Face Detection	YUV faces	4	13362	25552
Object Recognition MLP	CIFAR	2	1034	3155968
Census Data Analysis	Adult	2	12	160

Figure 5: NN benchmarks

7. RESULTS

In this section, we present the results of experiments that demonstrate the energy efficiency offered by AxNNs.

7.1 Energy benefits of AxNN

Figure 6 shows the energy improvement obtained using AxNNs for various output quality (classification accuracy) constraints. The energy of each AxNN is normalized to a fully-accurate QCNPE implementation in which none of the neurons are approximated. Note that this is already a highly optimized baseline since the QCNPE architecture is highly

customized to the characteristics of NNs. Across all benchmarks, AxNN consistently provides significant energy benefits between 1.14X-1.92X for virtually no loss (< 0.5%) in application output quality. When the quality constraints are relaxed to < 2.5% and < 7.5%, the benefits increase to 1.35X-1.95X and 1.41X-2.3X, respectively. On an average, AxNN achieves 1.43X, 1.58X and 1.75X improvement in application energy for the different quality constraints.

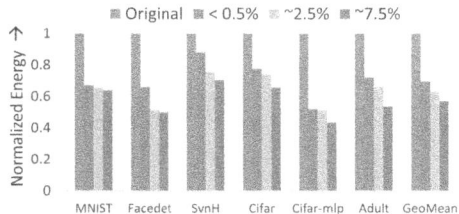

Figure 6: Improvement in energy using AxNN

7.2 Uniform approximation: Comparison

We now illustrate the effectiveness of the proposed resilience characterization methodology for NNs, by comparing it with a naïve approach wherein all the neurons in the NN are approximated uniformly. Figure 7 shows the energy *vs.* accuracy trade-off curves thus obtained for 3 different applications. We observe in all three cases that the energy improvement obtained using AxNNs is substantially better at all quality levels, compared to uniform approximation. Thus, it is critical to identify neurons that are amenable to approximations and directly applying approximate computing techniques without the proposed resilience characterization step would lead to limited benefits.

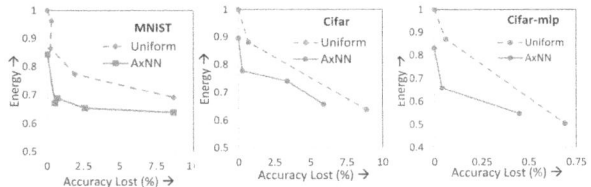

Figure 7: Quality *vs.* energy trade-offs with uniform and AxNN approximations

7.3 Resilience Characterization: Insights

We present insights into the process of identifying resilient neurons in NNs and illustrate them using the digit recognition application (MNIST) [3] as an example. The NN takes a pixel map of a handwritten digit as its input and classifies it amongst digits 0,1 . . . 9. The network contains 6 layers and progressively extracts feature maps from the input image in the first four layers and combines them in layers 5 and 6 to infer the class of the input. Each pixel in each feature map of each layer corresponds to the output of a neuron.

Figure 8 shows the average errors (obtained using back-propagation) at the outputs of all neurons in four selected layers of the digit recognition network. The neurons are color-coded (blue to red) based on the magnitude of their errors and are located on the feature maps corresponding to the pixel they generate. We observe that the resilience of the neurons varies widely (6 orders of magnitude) across all layers and to a substantial extent (4 orders of magnitude) within a given layer. We also find that the fraction of neurons that are resilient decreases sharply as we move closer to the NN outputs. This is attributed to the fact that neurons in the initial layers typically process features local to a certain region of the image, while neurons in the final layers infer global features from the previously extracted local features. Since errors in global inferences are less tolerable, the neurons in the final layers are correspondingly more sensitive. Further, errors in neurons closer to the inputs have a greater chance of being compensated or filtered-out as they propagate through the NN.

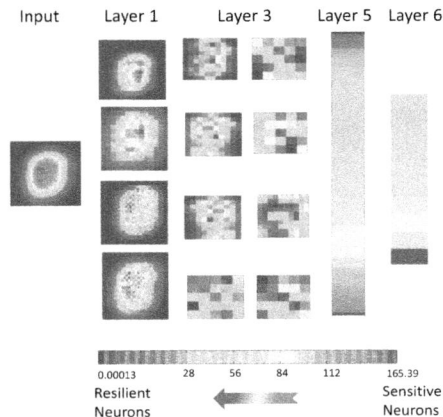

Figure 8: Neuron average error maps in MNIST [3]

We also observe a significant correlation between the resilience of neurons and the region of the image on which they operate. For example, in layer 1 of Figure 8, neurons that process the center of the input image, where information is typically concentrated, are less resilient. The neurons become progressively more resilient when proceeding towards the borders of the image. Thus, the resilience characterization methodology utilized in AxNNs captures the physical intuitions behind the resilience of neurons in NNs.

7.4 Impact of Retraining

To understand the benefits of incrementally retraining the network with the approximations in place, Figure 9 plots the normalized energy-quality trade-off obtained with and without the retraining step in the AxNN methodology for four applications. We observe in all four cases that AxNN with retraining provides a superior trade-off, i.e., lower energy for a given target quality. This is because, retraining recovers a good amount of quality lost due to approximations, thereby allowing additional approximations for the same quality.

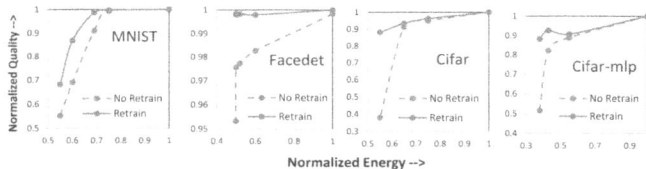

Figure 9: Impact of retraining on energy and quality

Across all our benchmarks, retraining the AxNN increased the run time of the training process on an average by 21.5%. As discussed in Section 4.1.3, we believe that this moderate increase in the training time is quite insignificant relative to the energy benefits provided during the energy-critical testing phase of the application.

7.5 AxNNs on Commodity Platforms

In the previous subsections, the neurons were approximated by scaling the precision of their input operands and the energy benefits were evaluated using the proposed QC-NPE architecture. We now evaluate the benefits of AxNNs on commodity platforms by designing approximate software implementations of NNs. Towards this end, we replace the activation functions of selected neurons in the network, identified by the AxNN methodology, with an approximate but significantly faster piecewise linear function. The original and approximate implementations were executed on a server with an Intel Xeon processor at 2.7 GHz and 132 GB memory. We note that the software baseline implementation was aggressively optimized for performance.

Figure 10 shows the normalized runtime and quality of the software AxNN implementations, with varying fraction of neurons approximated, for three applications. The graphs reveal that, as the fraction of neurons approximated by the AxNN methodology increases, the runtime decreases proportionally. However, the corresponding decrease in the appli-

cation output quality is disproportionately small due to the careful selection of neurons and re-training. On an average, the runtime speedup is 1.35X with $< 0.5\%$ loss in the output quality. These results underscore the generality of the AxNN methodology with respect to both the approximate computing technique employed to create approximate neurons, as well as the hardware platform used for their execution.

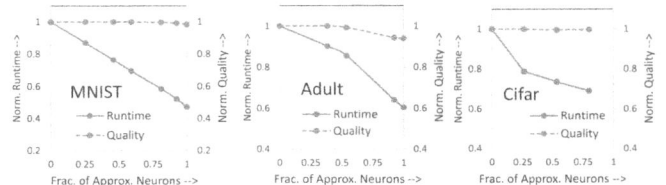

Figure 10: AxNN runtime on commodity platform

8. CONCLUSION

Neuromorphic systems are growing increasingly prevalent and are popularly employed in a wide variety of classification, recognition, search and computer vision applications. In this work, we utilize approximate computing, an emerging design paradigm, to design energy-efficient neuromorphic systems. We propose the concept of Approximate Neural Networks (AxNNs), in which neurons that impact output quality the least are systematically identified and approximated. The AxNN is then retrained with the approximations in place, leading to additional opportunities to further approximate the network. Also, we design a quality configurable neuromorphic processing engine that can be utilized to efficiently execute AxNNs. Our experiments on six NN applications demonstrated significant improvements in energy for negligible loss in the output quality.

9. REFERENCES

[1] K. Kavukcuoglu et. al. Learning convolutional feature hierarchies for visual recognition. In *NIPS*, 2010.
[2] A. Krizhevsky et. al. Imagenet classification with deep convolutional neural networks. In *NIPS, 2012.*
[3] Y. Lecun et. al. Gradient-based learning applied to document recognition. *Proceedings of the IEEE*, 86(11), Nov 1998.
[4] J. Hawkins et. al. Hierarchical temporal memory: Concepts, theory, and terminology. Numenta Inc. Whitepaper, 2006.
[5] George Rosenberg. Improving photo search: A step across the semantic gap. June 2009.
[6] Jeffrey Dean et. al. Large scale distributed deep networks. In *NIPS*, 2012.
[7] Scientists See Promise in Deep-Learning Programs, www.nytimes.com /2012/11/24/science/scientists-see-advances-in-deep-learning-a-part-of-artificial-intelligence.html.
[8] S. Chakradhar and A. Raghunathan. Best-effort computing: Re-thinking parallel software and hardware. In *Proc. DAC '10*.
[9] V. K. Chippa et. al. Scalable effort hardware design: Exploiting algorithmic resilience for energy efficiency. In *Proc. DAC '10*.
[10] R. Hegde et. al. Energy-efficient signal processing via algorithmic noise-tolerance. In *Proc. ISLPED '99*, pages 30–35.
[11] S. Venkataramani et. al. SALSA: systematic logic synthesis of approximate circuits. In *Proc. DAC '12*.
[12] H. Esmaeilzadeh et. al. Neural acceleration for general-purpose approximate programs. In *MICRO, 2012*.
[13] H. Esmaeilzadeh et. al. Architecture support for disciplined approximate programming. In *Proc. ASPLOS 2012*.
[14] S. Venkataramani et al. Quality programmable vector processors for approximate computing. In *Proc. MICRO*, 2013.
[15] C. Farabet et al. Neuflow: A runtime reconfigurable dataflow processor for vision. In *Proc. CVPRW, 2011*.
[16] S. Chakradhar et. al. A dynamically configurable coprocessor for convolutional neural networks. In *Proc. ISCA '10*.
[17] E. Painkras et. al. Spinnaker: A multi-core system-on-chip for massively-parallel neural net simulation. In *Proc. CICC '12*.
[18] J. Ngiam et. al. On optimization methods for deep learning. In *Proc. ICML*, pages 265–272, 2011.
[19] B. Rajendran et. al. Specifications of nanoscale devices and circuits for neuromorphic computational systems. *IEEE Trans. on Electron Devices*, 60(1):246–253, 2013.
[20] Sung Hyun Jo et. al. Nanoscale memristor device as synapse in neuromorphic systems. *Nano Letters '10*.
[21] K. Roy et al. Beyond charge-based computation: Boolean and non-Boolean computing with spin torque devices. In *Proc. ISLPED*, pages 139–142, Sep. 2013.
[22] K. Palem et al. Sustaining moore's law in embedded computing through probabilistic and approximate design: Retrospects and prospects. In *Proc. CASES*, pages 1–10, 2009.

TONE: Adaptive Temperature Optimization for the Next Generation Video Encoders

[1]Daniel Palomino, [2]Muhammad Shafique, [1]Altamiro Susin, [2]Jörg Henkel

[1] Informatics Institute, PPGC, Federal University of Rio Grande do Sul (UFRGS), Brazil
[2] Chair for Embedded Systems (CES), Karlsruhe Institute of Technology (KIT), Germany
dmvpalomino@inf.ufrgs.br, altamiro.susin@ufrgs.br, {muhammad.shafique, henkel}@kit.edu

ABSTRACT

This paper presents an adaptive temperature optimization technique for the next generation video encoders. It exploits both application-specific knowledge (i.e. video encoding configurations) and video content properties in order to efficiently manage the temperature of advanced video coding systems at the software layer. For designing an efficient technique, we perform an extensive offline analysis to understand the impact of different video properties and configurations on the CPU thermal profiles when processing the next generation video encoder. Our temperature optimization technique performs an application-level prediction of the temperature trend followed by an application-level thermal management policy. The policy dynamically manages the temperature by performing an adaptive encoder configuration selection while providing minimum penalties in terms of bit rate and video quality. The experimental results show that our policy meets temperature constraints with negligible encoding performance loss. Moreover, when compared to state-of-the-art techniques, our policy provides a relatively reduced video quality loss while still meeting the temperature constraints.

Categories and Subject Descriptors

C.4 [**Performance of Systems**]: Metrics–*Performance attributes.*

Keywords

Thermal management; HEVC; temperature

1. INTRODUCTION

According to [1], video coding based services will cover 80%-90% of global consumer traffic by 2017. Furthermore, escalating multimedia consumer market demands for more realistic content, ultra-high resolutions (such as 3840x2160) and 3D videos (with 4-8 views) necessitate high compression ratios. The next generation video coding standards such as the emerging High Efficiency Video Coding (HEVC) [2], Google's VP9 [3], and the Audio Video coding Standard (AVS) part 2 [4] have recently been developed to provide high compression ratios for such high-end video contents. Although, these new standards can achieve lower bit rates with high video quality, *the computational complexity of the encoding process can reach ~2.2x* for only the block matching process and inter mode decision when comparing the new HEVC to the state-of-the-art H.264. This increased complexity also corresponds to the escalated power and temperature profiles for the next generation encoders.

This demand for high complexity video processing systems is enabled mainly by the advances in semiconductor technology. Due to the shrinking feature sizes in the nano-era, it is possible to integrate billions of transistors on a single chip. However, this has resulted in high power densities and consequently increased on-chip temperature/thermal hot spots [5]. Besides increasing the cooling costs, thermal hot spots also negatively affect reliability/life time [6][7]. Note, most of the aging effects (such as, electromigration, NBTI, HCI, and TDDB) are aggravated at high temperatures[1]. Therefore, temperature optimizations for embedded video processing systems are necessary to maintain a reliable operation during lifetime, especially for the highly complex next generation video encoding standards.

The temperature optimization works aim at keeping the temperature under safe operational limits or on lowering the overall peak/average chip temperatures. The Dynamic Thermal Management (DTM) policies usually use task migration [8], frequency/voltage scaling [9][10], clock gating [11], or a combination of these as control knobs [12]. These policies usually monitor the temperature or use schemes to predict the workload to perform task migration or/and frequency/voltage scaling at run-time. However, these general purpose state-of-the-art works do not account for application-specific properties and may incur loss in the video quality when applied to video processing systems.

For specifically targeting the video encoding/decoding systems, works such as [13] and [14] use DVFS together with temporal and spatial degradation (by frame drops) as a mechanism to reduce the overall temperature. In these works the key target is to lower the temperature irrespective of the incurred video quality loss, which may be significant in presence of frame drops. Such a video quality loss is not acceptable by the video community as it contradicts the purpose of moving to the next generation video codecs. Additionally, these techniques only target decoding and do not account for encoding, which is more challenging for temperature-aware design due to its >10x times higher complexity compared to decoding [15]. The work [16] offloads the encoder computations for motion estimation to the decoder to balance the encoder/decoder workload, thus reducing the temperature of the encoder. Although this technique can reduce the overall temperature for the encoder, it results in more data to be transmitted between the source (encoder) and receiver (decoder) that leads to increased communication power/energy. The work in [17] selects a video quality degradation mode to compensate for the quality degradation effects of different DTM policies. However, it neither addresses temperature management nor explores the impact of different video properties on the generated temperature. The work [18] uses encoding information to design a predictive DTM technique for MPEG encoding. However, it considers that the power dissipation of encoding all frames is constant which does not happen for HEVC encoding. These state-of-the-art solutions mainly target old standards such as MPEG2 and H.264. Therefore, they may not be efficiently applied to the next generation video encoders due to their novel and highly complex coding tools. Moreover, they do not account for the application-specific characteristics and video properties that may provide a potential for efficient application-level temperature optimization for video coding systems.

ISLPED'14, August 11–13, 2014, La Jolla, CA, USA.
Copyright © 2014 ACM 978-1-4503-2975-0/14/08...$15.00
http://dx.doi.org/10.1145/2627369.2627628

---

[1] As reported in [6], the NBTI leads to the threshold voltage degradation, thus results in either the device slow down or timing errors.

In Summary: There is a need for an application-specific temperature optimization technique for thermal-aware video encoding while keeping the video quality loss to the minimal.

1.1 Our Novel Contributions & Concept Overview

1) TONE – Temperature Optimization for the Next Generation Video Encoders: We propose an adaptive algorithm that optimizes temperature, bit rate and video quality for the next generation video encoders at run time. It employs a temperature prediction that is driven by video content properties. Based on the predicted temperature, TONE employs an application-level thermal management that controls the encoder temperature at run time by selecting an appropriate encoder configuration for a frame, while providing minimum penalties in terms of video quality.

2) Thermal Analysis for the Next Generation Video Encoders: For designing our application-level temperature prediction, we perform an analysis to understand the relationship of video properties (e.g., texture) on the generated thermal profile. Moreover, for designing our application-level thermal management policy we also evaluate the impact of the encoder configuration parameters on the temperature and the resulting encoder efficiency in terms of bit rate and video quality (PSNR).

2. THERMAL ANALYSIS FOR HEVC

In this section, we present the thermal analysis for the next generation HEVC encoder and derive design hints. In our experimental setup we study an Intel Atom 45nm dual-core processor operating at a maximum frequency of 1.8 GHz. *The core temperature is measured using the digital thermal sensor (DTS) provided by Intel's architecture.* In order to obtain thermal maps, we use an IR-camera-based setup as depicted in Figure 1.

Figure 1: Thermal setup used to obtain thermal maps [19].

We have performed an extensive analysis for *various* test videos under diverse encoding configurations (as recommended by the standardization committee). Due to space limitations, in this paper, we provide analysis for only two test sequences *RaceHorses* and *BQMall* (832x480 pixels). For all our thermal evaluations, we use the HEVC test model (HM) software version 11.0 [20].

2.1 Thermal Analysis of Video Content Properties

The efficiency and complexity of advanced video coding tools are usually driven by the properties (e.g., texture, motion) of the input video. For instance, the motion estimation algorithms search for similarities among the sequence content across different frames. In case of videos with irregular, textured, and complex moving objects, it is harder for the motion estimation to find an accurate match. Therefore, video properties such as motion intensity and texture will highly influence the encoding complexity and resulting temperature for a given video and even for different frames in a

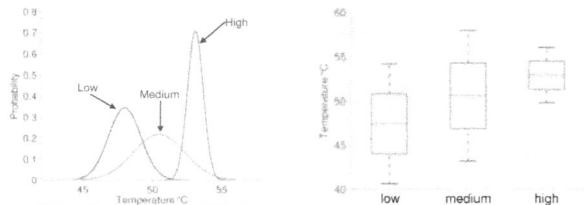

Figure 2: Temperature distribution for different frames.

video. In this work, we classify the frames of a sequence in different complexity classes using the method devised in [21] (i.e. Eqs. 1, 2). In our work, without the loss of generality, we use the texture intensity to classify the frame complexity C_f as *low*, *medium* or *high*; see Eq. (2). The texture is calculated using variance v_f of the luminance samples ρ_i in one frame of dimension $n \times m$ as shown in Eq. (1). Using such a complexity classification, we will be able to observe how these properties influence on temperature behavior.

$$v_f = \frac{1}{n \times m} \sum_{i=0}^{n \times m} (\rho_i - \rho_{avg})^2 \qquad (1)$$

$$C_f = \begin{cases} low & if(v_f \leq Th_{v1}) \\ medium & if(Th_{v1} < v_f \leq Th_{v2}) \\ high & if(v_f > Th_{v2}) \end{cases} \qquad (2)$$

Figure 2 shows the average temperature distribution for different complexity classes when encoding different videos, e.g., *RaceHorses* (*medium-to-high* complexity) and *BQMall* (*medium-to-low* complexity). Figure 2 shows that sequence properties directly influence the temperature behavior of HEVC encoding. The *high* complexity frames will lead to higher temperatures while for the *low* and *medium* complexity frames the temperature distribution is relatively lower. The difference between the *high* and *low* complexity frames can be up to 10 ºC. Another observation (Figure 2) is that high complexity frames have more "concentrated distribution", since the steady temperature is achieved only when these type of frames are encoded. Moreover, the high temperature distribution is mainly from the consecutive *high* complexity frames of videos like *RaceHorses*. The distribution for *medium/low* complexity frames are less concentrated since these types of frames are intercalated between each other. The temperature of encoding these frames is influenced by the "encoding history".

2.2 Thermal Analysis of HEVC Parameters

In the following, we analyze the impact of key parameters employed by all the advanced video encoders on the CPU temperature and encoding quality (in terms of PSNR and bit rate). Examples parameters are: size of coding unit (CU), quantization parameter (QP), number of reference frames (RF), and search area (SA). Independent parameter analysis is performed to understand their impact on temperature. Since each parameter targets a particular functional step during the video encoding, their values are determined independent of each other, thus dependent parameter analysis is not relevant for the contribution of this paper.

Analyzing the Impact of QP on Temperature: The QP controls the bit rate and the resulting video quality. Higher QPs reduce the temperature but incur quality loss. Figure 3 (a) shows the average temperature, bit rate, and PSNR values while Figure 4 (a) shows the temperature over time for four different QPs (22, 27, 32, and 37). It

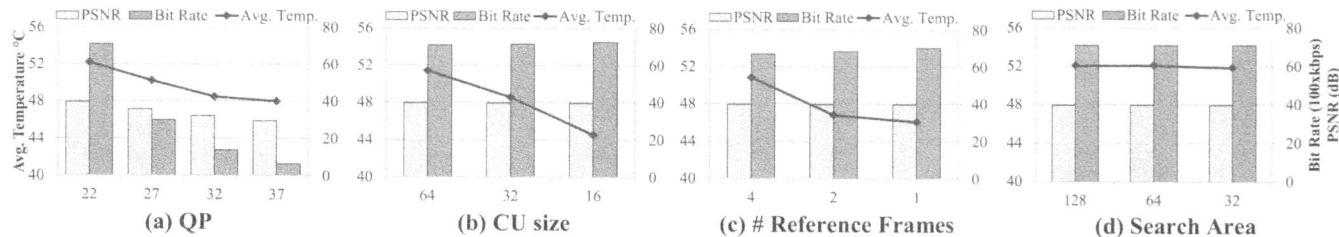

(a) QP	(b) CU size	(c) # Reference Frames	(d) Search Area

Figure 3: Temperature, bit rate and PSNR for different parameters.

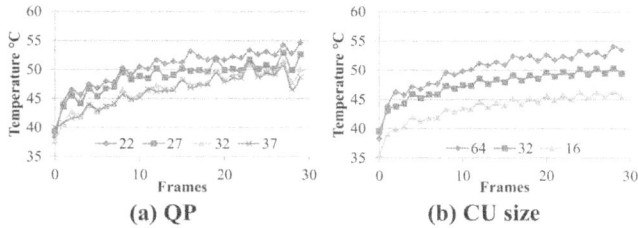

(a) QP   **(b) CU size**

Figure 4: Temperature changing encoder parameters.

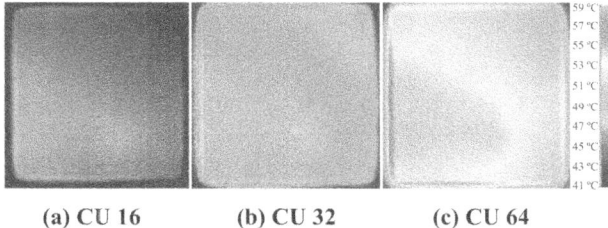

(a) CU 16   **(b) CU 32**   **(c) CU 64**

Figure 5: Thermal maps for different CU sizes.

is noticeable that the *QP selection can provide average temperature reductions of 2 °C between each value*. This provides a hint for designing an application-level temperature optimization algorithm. However, this parameter needs a careful selection to avoid significant quality loss as shown in Figure 3 (a) (white bar).

Analyzing the Impact of CU-size on Temperature: HEVC achieves high compression efficiency using large-sized blocks in a coded tree unit structure with different CU sizes. Unlike earlier standards, the HEVC allows for selecting the maximum CU size between 64x64, 32x32 and 16x16 pixels to capture different object sizes for improved compression efficiency. However, different CU sizes lead to varying thermal profiles. Figure 3 (b) shows the average core temperature, bit rate, and PSNR values while Figure 4 (b) shows the temperature over time for different CU sizes. Bigger CUs lead to high encoding effort per video area, since more options are available for block partitioning resulting in high temperatures. *When using a CU size of 32 instead of 64, the average temperature is decreased by 5 °C and the bit rate increases by 2.17%.* Figure 5 shows example thermal maps at the steady temperature when encoding *RaceHorses* sequence with different CU sizes.

Analyzing the Impact of Number of Reference Frames and Search Area on Temperature: The number of reference frames and the search area control the complexity and quality of motion search (especially for objects with repetitive and high-motion). However, higher values of these parameters also lead to higher temperature. Figure 3 (c) shows the average core temperature, bit rate, and PSNR values for three different selections for the number of reference frames used (1, 2, and 4). When using more reference frames, the temperature of the system is higher. Moreover, *the average temperature decreases by 4 °C when using 2 instead of 4 reference frames at the cost of insignificant quality loss* (less than 0.01 dB). Figure 3 (d) shows the average temperature, bit rate, and PSNR values for three different search areas (128, 64, and 32). Note that for *all three different search areas, there is a slight temperature difference* (less than 0.5 °C). This is due to the type of motion estimator used (i.e., EPZS [20] available in the HM software) as it does not explore the entire search space and adaptively terminates when a good match is found. Therefore, in this case, changing the search area does not impact the resulting temperature significantly. However, for a different type of motion estimator, it may change.

Summary of our Thermal Analysis[2]: Video properties and encoder parameters determine the thermal behavior (average

temperature and temperature variations). Following observations may be exploited by an adaptive temperature optimization algorithm to manage/lower the temperatures at run time.

- High-textured frames require significant workload curtailing to increase the potential of applying temperature optimization.
- Reducing CU size from 64 to 32 reduces the average temperatures by 5 °C.
- Reducing QP by 5 reduces the temperature by 2 °C. However, it has a serious impact on the bit rate and PSNR degradation.
- Reducing the number of reference frames from 4 to 2 lowers the temperature by 4 °C with negligible video quality loss.
- For adaptive motion estimators, changing the search area does not have a significant impact on temperature.

3. TONE: ADAPTIVE TEMPERATURE OPTIMIZATION

TONE is an adaptive thermal management technique for next generation video codecs (like HEVC). It raises the abstraction level of thermal management to the application level such that video quality degradations can be lowered. It performs (1) application-level temperature prediction; and (2) application-level temperature management. Before explaining these two components of our TONE technique, we formulate the application-level temperature optimization problem.

3.1 Optimization Problem

Our temperature optimization for video encoding accounts for three attributes resulted from the encoding process: (1) T as the CPU temperature in °C, (2) Q as the video quality in terms of PSNR and; (3) B as the resulted bit rate. The main **goal** of our optimization algorithm is to minimize QoS degradation in terms of bit rate and PSNR, while keeping the current temperature $T_{current}$ under a specified temperature threshold T_{th} as in Eq. (3).

$$T_{current} < T_{th}, \text{s.t.,} Max\{Q\} \text{ and } Min\{B\} \qquad (3)$$

To achieve this goal, the temperature management at the application-level is performed by appropriate selection of the encoder parameters that determines the workload and affects the resulting temperature. However, efficient parameter selection also requires an application-level temperature prediction.

3.2 Application-Level Temperature Prediction

Eq. (4) shows a simple application-level temperature predictor at the frame granularity. For a given time interval (e.g., between the encoding of two video frames), the predicted temperature T_p (i.e. predicted temperature expected to be obtained after encoding the current frame) can be estimated using: the current temperature $T_{current}$ (temperature at current point in time) and the temperature variation between encoding of current and previous frames.

$$T_p = T_{current} + \Delta T \qquad (4)$$

For obtaining accurate temperature prediction, modeling of the ΔT component in Eq. (4) is the main challenge. As discussed in section 2.1, the temperature behavior of encoding sequences is highly correlated with sequence content properties. These video properties can be leveraged to obtain hints for temperature prediction. However, using the knowledge of only the current frame may not be sufficient because the temperature distribution is also affected by the content of frames previously encoded (as shown in section 2.1). Therefore, it is important to account for the complexity class of the current frame and the previous frame, i.e., the complexity difference between two consecutive frames. Therefore, we model the ΔT parameter as a function of the complexity difference between previous and current frames and their respective temperature distributions. Considering three frame complexity levels (low, medium, and high), we can formulate nine possible temperature variation distributions depending upon the complexity difference between previous and current frames.

---

[2] These temperature results are specific for the studied processor, i.e., Intel Atom. For a high-frequency processor, the temperature variations between different properties and configurations may even be larger.

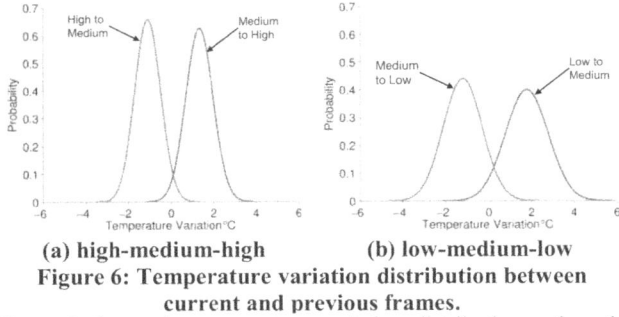

(a) high-medium-high   **(b) low-medium-low**
Figure 6: Temperature variation distribution between current and previous frames.

Figure 6 shows the temperature variation distributions when the complexity between previous and current frames changes (a) from *high-medium-high* and (b) from *low-medium-low* (due to space limitations only these two cases are shown in Figure 6). These temperature variation distributions illustrate that temperature behavior does follow the sequences complexity structure. It means that if current frame complexity is higher than that of the previous, the temperature will increase while if the current frame complexity is lower than that of the previous, the temperature will decrease. *This complexity variation between previous and current frames provides a good hint for temperature prediction.* Since the standard deviation of these temperature variation distributions is not zero, using always the same value for ΔT for a given complexity transition at run time can lead to high prediction errors. *Therefore, our temperature prediction also uses the error history to improve the prediction accuracy.*

Based on the above analysis and discussion, we define our prediction model in Eq. (5). The predicted temperature T_p for the upcoming/current video frame is a summation of current temperature $T_{current}$ and temperature variation ΔT. In Eq. (6) the ΔT parameter is calculate using T_v which is the temperature variation between previous and current frame plus the error history. At run time, the T_v parameter is obtained from the probability distribution functions after computing the complexity difference between the current and previous frame (i.e. one out of nine cases as discussed above). The error history is calculated as the mean value of all errors in a time window w (which is the number of previous frames that will be considered to calculate the error) to compensate for the prediction error. Here, the error e is calculated as the difference between the measured temperature T_m (from the temperature sensors) and the predicted temperature T_p (see eq. (7)).

$$T_p = T_{current} + \Delta T \qquad (5)$$

$$\Delta T = T_v + \sum_{i=0}^{w} e_i / w \qquad (6)$$

$$e = T_m - T_p \qquad (7)$$

Figure 7 shows the accuracy of our application-level temperature prediction for two test sequences *PartyScene* and *Keiba*. For the first three frames the algorithm is not used, since the system is warming up from an idle period, i.e., the temperature increases regardless the complexity level changes between frames. After this warming up period, the prediction starts. It is possible to observe

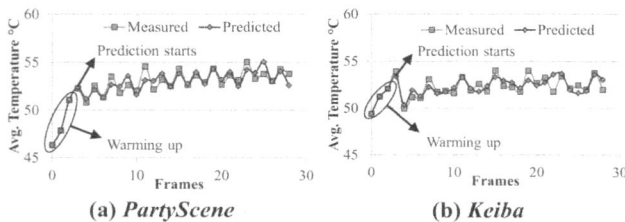

(a) *PartyScene*   **(b) *Keiba***
Figure 7: Evaluating the accuracy of our temperature predictor.

that the predicted temperature (blue line) is indeed close to the measured temperature (red line) for both sequences. In fact the error of our predictor is of only 1.1% on average.

3.3 Application-Level Thermal Management

Based on predicted temperature for the current video frame (T_p), TONE evaluates if T_p may potentially exceed the safe thermal limit and reacts accordingly to keep the temperature below the same limit. As discussed in section 2.2, different sets of encoder parameters will result in different temperature, PSNR and bit rate. Our application-level thermal management controls the encoder temperature at run time by dynamically selecting an appropriate encoder configuration (i.e. set of encoder parameters) for the current video frame, while providing minimum penalties in terms of bit rate and video quality (PSNR) loss. Our technique employs:

(1) *Design-time Pareto analysis of different configurations* for encoding various test video sequences from different complexity class. The outcome is a set of Pareto-optimal configuration point.

(2) *Run-time configuration selection:* depending upon the predicted temperature, an appropriate configuration is selected from the Pareto-optimal points. Since input videos cannot be known at design-time, the temperature, PSNR, and bit rate properties of the Pareto-optimal points for the run-time videos may vary from the design-time analysis. Therefore, our technique dynamically updates the properties of the Pareto-optimal configuration points.

3.3.1 Temperature-aware Configuration Selection

The problem of optimal encoder parameters configuration selection can be solved by Pareto analysis [22] at design time. Algorithm I shows how we extract the optimal Pareto curve for each encoder parameter configuration point for a set of test video sequences. For our experiments, only one Pareto curve is provided as input that is modified at run-time for different videos, thus also avoiding data biasing. For each configuration point c_i we encode a test video sequence v_i in order to extract the resulted temperature t_i, bit rate bit_i and PSNR $psnr_i$. Then, with all the resulted bit rate and PSNR results mapped into temperature points, we can choose the encoder configuration point that provides the desired temperature d_i maximizing the $psnr_i$ and minimizing the bit_i.

Algorithm I Extraction of Pareto optimal curve

Input: Configuration points **C**, Video Sequences **V**;

1: let **T** be all temperature points;
2: **for** each $v \in$ **V** and each $c \in$ **C do:**
3:      encode v_i with configuration c_i and get temperature t_i;
4:      get bit_i and $psnr_i$;
5:      update point t_i in **T** with bit_i and $psnr_i$;
6: let **D** be the desired temperature points;
7: **for** each $v \in$ **V** and each $d \in$ **D do:**
8:      select c_i while maximizing$\{psnr_i\}$ and minimizing$\{bit_i\}$ to satisfy d_i;

Since we use real temperature traces and due to space and time restrictions, we use only a sub-set of the encoder parameters to build our model. Table 1 shows the parameter values we adopt. These parameters are well-studied and recommended by the video standardization committee of HEVC [23]. Considering the analyzed parameters and all combinations, we are interested in the combinations that optimize temperature reduction with our target attributes (bit rate, PSNR) as shown in the Algorithm I.

Table 1. Encoder parameters used to build our model.

Parameters	QP	RF	SA	CU
Values	22, 27, 32, 37	1, 2, 4	128,64,32	64, 32, 16

(a) PSNR   **(b) Bit rate**

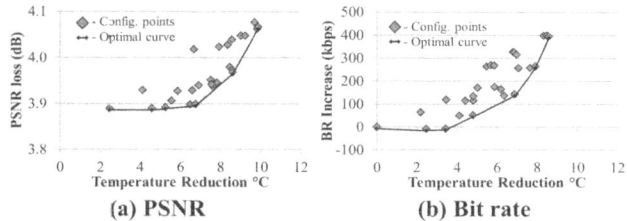

Figure 8: Configuration points for temperature reduction.

Figure 8 shows the configuration points space for all combinations of number of reference frames, search area, and maximum size of coding units with a given QP considering average temperature reduction with PSNR loss and bit rate increase. Due to space limitation, analysis for only *RaceHorses* sequence is shown in Figure 8. Note, for other QPs, the curves are scaled. Figure 8 (a) illustrates that there are many configuration points reducing the average temperature but at the cost of a high PSNR loss. The same happens in Figure 8 (b) where two different configuration points can provide the same temperature reduction but with a different bit rate impact. This way, it is possible to achieve good temperature reduction with low penalties in the encoding results by choosing appropriate encoding parameters.

3.3.2 Run-Time Adaptive Temperature Optimization

Based on the run-time predicted temperature T_p for the current frame, TONE dynamically selects appropriate configuration from the design-time Pareto-optimal points. The configuration selection is illustrated in the Algorithm II. The algorithm starts with initial configuration (line 2) and the current temperature $T_{current}$ is measured from the sensors (line 3). For each frame f, it classifies complexity (line 5) that will be used in the prediction ΔT (line 6, 7). After the temperature prediction, it checks if the temperature exceeds the temperature threshold T_{th} (line 8). In case of temperature violation, the policy reacts by selecting a new set of configuration parameters c based on our Pareto analysis that ensures temperature reduction with minimum losses in bit rate and PSNR (line 9). Finally, we encode the frame f with configuration c (line 10) update the current temperature (line 11), the error list (line 13) and the complexity of previous frame (line 14).

Afterwards, the temperature, PSNR, and bit rate properties of the Pareto-optimal points are updated based on the currently video. It is important to note that, the bit rate and PSNR results are scaled for different videos but the best configuration points are mainly affected by the encoder parameters. The pareto-curves are recalculated only if the parameters used to build the model change.

4. EXPERIMENTAL RESULTS

The input Pareto-curve is obtained from the *RaceHorses* sequence. Therefore, to avoid data biasing, we use three additional sequences (*PartyScene*, *Keiba*, *BasketballDrill*) for evaluating our TONE technique. Our setup is the same as discussed in our thermal analysis in section 2. For thermal management and temperature plots, the temperature is obtained from the thermal sensors. For illustrations, the thermal maps are obtained from the IR-Thermal camera. Figure 9 illustrates the distribution of frames in the evaluated video sequences in terms of complexity (*low*, *medium*, *high*). The *PartyScene*, *RaceHorses* and *Keiba* contain *medium-to-high* while the *BasketballDrill* and *BQMall* sequences have *medium-to-low* complexity frames. We evaluate our TONE technique for three threshold temperatures T_{th}, i.e. 54 ºC, 50 ºC and 46 ºC (as also used by state-of-the-art work [14]) showing how our technique adaptively controls the temperature.

Figure 10-14 show the thermal curves during a part of the encoding process for the *PartyScene*, *RaceHorses*, *Keiba*, *Basketball* and *BQMall* sequences in terms of peak temperature-per-frame being encoded to take various scenarios into account. First, we compared

---

Algorithm II Run Time Adaptive Temperature Optimization

Input: Pareto points **P**, video **V**, Temperature Threshold **T$_{th}$**;

```
1:   error_list = [ ];
2:   c = initial configuration;
3:   T_current = measure_temperature();
4:   for each frame f ∈ V do:
5:       C_current = classify_complexity(f);
6:       ΔT = T_v(C_current, C_previous) + mean(error_list);
7:       T_p = T_current + ΔT;
8:       if T_p > T_th do:
9:           c = pareto_selection(P, T_th); //reaction
10:      encode(f, c);
11:      T_current = measure_temperature();
12:      error = T_current − T_p;
13:      update_error_list(error);
14:      C_previous = C_current;
```

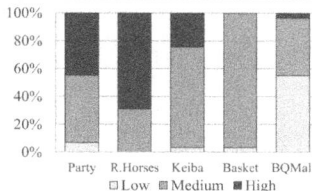

Figure 9: Frames Distribution.   **Figure 10: *PartyScene* profile.**

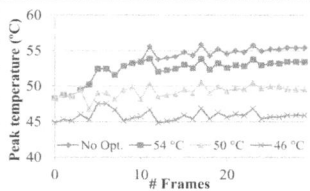

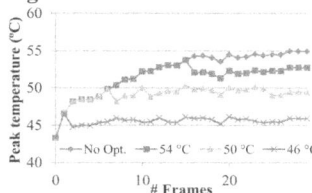

Figure 11: *RaceHorses* profile.   **Figure 12: *Keiba* profile.**

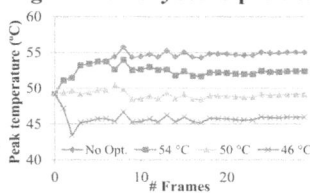

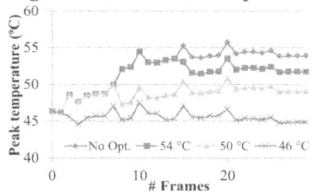

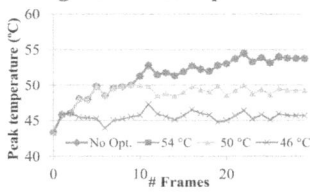

Figure 13: *Basketball* profile.   **Figure 14: *BQMall* profile.**

our TONE technique with three evaluated T_{th} values to the "no thermal optimization" case (i.e., the initial configuration is used in the whole encoding process). Figure 10-14 illustrate that our technique successfully keeps the CPU temperature under the specified T_{th} values by adapting the encoder configurations. As soon as the predicted temperature approaches to T_{th}, our configuration selection dynamically adapts the encoder parameters in such a way that it decreases the current temperature while minimizing the impact on PSNR and bit rate.

Figure 15 compares the thermal maps when using "no thermal optimization" with our optimization set to 54 ºC for encoding the *RaceHorses* sequence. For medium-low complexity sequences like *BasketeballDrill* and *BQMall* it takes more time for increasing the temperature while for medium-high complexity sequences the temperature increases quicker. It means that our optimization algorithm will react earlier in case of the higher complexity videos.

(a) No optimization   **(b) 54 ºC**

Figure 15: Thermal maps of the die for encoding *RaceHorses*.

Figure 16 shows the impact of our TONE technique in terms of (a) PSNR and (b) bit rate in comparison with "no thermal optimization" for the same five sequences. The degradation in PSNR and bit rate increases as the T_{th} decreases. However, as our technique is able to perform appropriate encoder parameter selection, the degradation is low. When T_{th} is set to 54 ℃ the average PSNR loss is of 0.007 dB while the bit rate slightly increases 0.99% on average for all sequences. When T_{th} is set to the lowest value of 46 ℃ the degradation is higher, but not higher than 1.81 dB in terms of PSNR and 0.84% of bit rate increase on average. Furthermore, for *medium-low* complexity sequences like *BQMall* and *BasketeballDrill*, the encoder degradation is lower for both PSNR and bit rate than for *medium-high* sequences like *PartyScene*, *RaceHorses* and *Keiba*. It occurs, since for reducing the temperature of high complexity sequences, the encoder configuration provided by our technique needs to reduce the workload more than for low complexity sequences.

We compare the quality impact of using our TONE with the DTM technique proposed in [13] [14]. These works use frame drop rates varying from 5.7% to 83.3% depending upon the sequence to keep the temperature under a threshold. In our work, the encoder uses the information of the last-encoded frame and skips the encoding process for the dropped frame. This is similar to state-of-the art decoder works that employ frame drop and copy for display.

We establish three frame drop rates, 10%, 20% and 50% to illustrate the negative impact on video quality of using such thermal management technique in comparison to our TONE with the threshold set to 54 ℃. Figure 17 shows the PSNR for five sequences where our technique achieves better quality results than state-of-the-art for all frame drop rates. The frame drop technique significantly degrades the video quality. However, our technique optimizes not only the temperature but also the resulted encoder attributes (PSNR and bit rate) through a temperature-aware configuration selection which is a more sophisticated approach compared to naïvely dropping frames. When the frame drop rate is only 10% the PSNR impact can be of about 12 dB and for 50% the degradation can achieve 20 dB. Such quality degradation is typically intolerable for the users of high-end encoding devices.

Discussion: Our technique is generic and suitable to any hardware platform, since it is applied at the application level using video coding characteristics. Since TONE uses information from the encoder itself, such as parameters and luminance samples, the time overhead of our solution in the whole encoding process is negligible. For instance, the texture intensity calculation for the next frame is performed while the current frame is being encoded.

5. CONCLUSION

We presented an application-level temperature optimization technique for the next generation video encoders. It keeps the temperature within safe operating limits while keeping the video quality degradation to as minimal as possible. Our analysis for different videos and encoder configurations provides design hints for developing an application-level thermal management policy. We developed an application-level temperature predictor, a design-time Pareto-optimal analysis of different encoder configurations, and a run-time policy that dynamically selects an encoder configuration

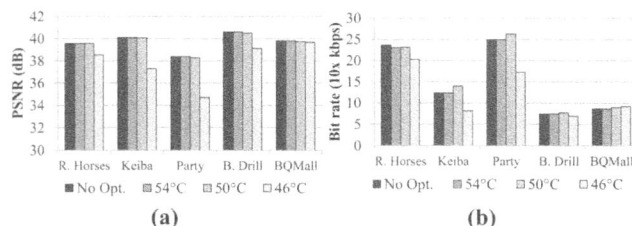

Figure 16: (a) PSNR and (b) Bit rate results.

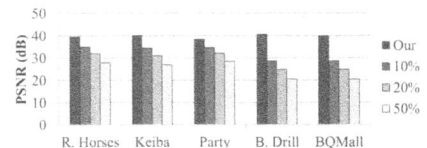

Figure 17: Comparison with works [13] [14].

depending upon the predicted temperature and specific thermal threshold. Managing the thermal behavior of encoders through sophisticated configuration selection enables minimizing the video quality degradation. Our TONE technique raises the abstraction level of thermal management to the application level such that the temperature can be managed proactively based on the content properties while providing a high degree of quality of service.

6. ACKNOWLEDGMENTS
This work is supported in parts by the German Research Foundation (DFG) as part of the priority program "Dependable Embedded Systems" (SPP 1500 - spp1500.itec.kit.edu). We would also like to acknowledge Hussam Amrouch (CES, KIT, Germany) for his help regarding the thermal camera setup.

7. REFERENCES
[1] Cisco, "Cisco Visual Networking Index: Forecast and Methodology, 2012, 2017", May 2013.
[2] ITU-T, "SERIES H: AUDIOVISUAL AND MULTIMEDIA SYSTEMS - Infrastructure of Audiovisual Services - Coding of Moving Video – High Efficiency Video Coding." Apr. 2013.
[3] WebM, "VP9 Video Codec Summary", [Online]. Avialble: http://www.webmproject.org/vp9/. Sep. 2013.
[4] J. Zheng, et al, "Overview of AVS broadcasting standard for high definition video," in IEEE ChinaSIP, pp. 250–254, 2013.
[5] A. K. Coskun, T. Rosing, K. Whisnant, K. Gross, "Static and Dynamic Temperature-Aware Scheduling for Multiprocessor SoCs," IEEE TVLSI, pp. 1127–1140, Sep. 2008.
[6] J. Henkel, L. Bauer, N. Dutt, P. Gupta, S. Nassif, M. Shafique, M. Tahoori, N. Wehn., "Reliable on-chip systems in the nano-era: Lessons learnt and future trends", DAC, 2013.
[7] J. Henkel, T. Ebi, H. Amrouch, H. Khdr, "Thermal management for dependable on-chip systems", ASP-DAC, pp. 113–118, 2013.
[8] I. Yeo, C. C. Liu, E. J. Kim, "Predictive dynamic thermal management for multicore systems", DAC, 2008.
[9] F. Zanini, D.Atienza, G. De Micheli, "A control theory approach for thermal balancing of MPSoC", ASP-DAC, pp. 37–42, 2009.
[10] David Brooks, Margaret Martonosi, "Dynamic thermal management for high-performance microprocessors", HPCA, pp. 171–182, 2001.
[11] M. Powell, M. Gomaa, T. Vijayku, "Heat-and-run: leveraging smt and cmp to manage power density through the operating system", ASPLOS, 2004.
[12] T. Ebi, M. Faruqeu, J. Henkel., "Tape: Thermal-aware agent-based power economy for multi/many-core architectures", ICCAD, pp. 302–309, 2009.
[13] W. Lee, K. Patel, M. Pedram, "Dynamic thermal management for mpeg-2 decoding", ISLPED, pp. 316–321, 2006.
[14] W. Lee, K. Patel, M. Pedram., "GOP-Level Dynamic Thermal Management in MPEG-2 Decoding", TVLSI, vol. 16, no. 6, pp. 662 – 672, 2008.
[15] J. Ostermann, J. Bormans, P. List, D. Marpe, M. Narroschke, F. Pereira, T. Stockhammer, T. Wedi, "Video coding with H.264/AVC: Tools, Performance, and Complexity", IEEE CS Magazine, vol. 4, no. 1, 2004.
[16] D. Forte, A. Srivastava, "Energy and thermal-aware video coding via encoder/decoder workload balancing", ISLPED, pp. 207–212, 2010.
[17] A. Mirtar, S. Dey, A. Raghunathan, "Adaptation of video encoding to address dynamic thermal management effects", IGCC, pp. 1–10, 2012.
[18] Srinivasan, Jayanth, and Sarita V. Adve. "Predictive Dynamic Thermal Management for Multimedia Applications." In Proceedings of the 17th International Conference on Supercomputing (ICSC), 109–20. ACM, 2003.
[19] D. Palomino, M. Shafique, H. Amrouch, A. Susin, J. Henkel, "hevcDTM: Application-Driven Dynamic Thermal Management for High Efficiency Video Coding", in Proceedings of the Design, Automation & Test in Europe (DATE), 2014.
[20] Joint Collaborative Team on Video Coding (JCT-VC), "HM 11.0 Reference Software" [Online]. Available: http://hevc.hhi.fraunhofer.de/
[21] M. Shafique, et al., "Adaptive power management of on-chip video memory for multiview video coding," in Proceedings of the 49th Annual Design Automation Conference, pp. 866–875, 2012.
[22] I. Das, "On characterizing the 'knee' of the Pareto curve based on Normal-Boundary Intersection", Structural and Multidisciplinary Optimization, vol. 18, no. 2-3, pp. 107-115, 1999.
[23] F. Bossen, "Common test conditions and software reference configurations, ITU-T/ISO/IEC Joint Collaborative Team on Video Coding (JCT-VC) document JCTVC-K1100, October 2012." Tech. Rep. 2012.

StoRM: A Stochastic Recognition and Mining Processor *

Vinay K. Chippa, Swagath Venkataramani, Kaushik Roy and Anand Raghunathan
School of Electrical and Computer Engineering, Purdue University
{vchippa,venkata0,kaushik,raghunathan}@purdue.edu

ABSTRACT

Recognition and Mining applications are becoming prevalent across the entire spectrum of computing platforms, and place very high demands on their capabilities. We propose a **Sto**chastic **R**ecognition and **M**ining processor (**StoRM**), which uses Stochastic Computing (SC) to efficiently realize computational kernels from these domains. Stochastic computing facilitates compact, power-efficient realization of arithmetic operations by representing and processing information as pseudo-random bit-streams. However, the overhead of conversion between representations, and the exponential relationship between precision and bit-stream length, are key challenges that limit the efficiency of stochastic designs. The proposed architecture for **StoRM** consists of a 2D array of Stochastic Processing Elements (**StoPEs**) with a streaming memory hierarchy, enabling binary-to-stochastic conversion to be amortized across rows or columns of **StoPEs**. We propose vector processing and segmented stochastic processing in the **StoPEs** to mitigate the unfavorable tradeoff between precision and bit-stream length. We also exploit the compactness of **StoPEs** to increase parallelism, thereby improving performance and energy efficiency. Finally, leveraging the resilience of RM applications to approximations in their computations, we design **StoRM** to support modulation of the stochastic bit-stream length, and utilize this capability to to optimize energy for a desired output quality. **StoRM** achieves 2-3X energy-delay improvements over a conventional design without sacrificing output quality, and upto 10X (20X) improvements when upto 5% (10%) loss in output quality is allowed. Our results also demonstrate that the proposed design techniques greatly enhance the applicability and benefits of stochastic computing.

Categories and Subject Descriptors

B.7.1 [**INTEGRATED CIRCUITS**]: VLSI (Very large scale integration)

Keywords

Stochastic Computing; Recognition and Mining; Approximate Computing; Energy Efficiency

1. INTRODUCTION

Recognition and Mining (RM) refers to an important, emerging class of applications that are used to perform tasks such as classification, search, semantic analysis and inference on real world data. The use of RM applications is being driven by several factors, notably the explosion in various forms of digital data that are stored, analyzed, and interpreted, and the need for mobile and embedded computing systems to interact more naturally with their users and the

environment. Consequently, RM applications are expected to be ubiquitous across the entire computing spectrum, from data centers to mobile and deeply embedded computing systems.

RM applications are highly compute-intensive due to the volumes of data that they process as well as the increasingly complex algorithms that they use. As a result, realizing efficient implementations of RM workloads is a problem that has attracted great interest, with solutions proposed ranging from optimized software on multi-core and many-core processors [1, 2] to specialized hardware accelerators [3, 4] and custom mixed-signal circuits [5].

In this work, we explore stochastic computing [6, 7] as a new direction for the efficient realization of RM applications. Stochastic computing (SC) uses streams of bits to represent data, where the probability of ones in a bit stream denotes its numerical value. A key advantage of SC is that common arithmetic functions can be implemented in an extremely power and area efficient manner in the stochastic domain (for example, a multiplier in the stochastic domain is implemented using a single AND gate and an adder using a MULTIPLEXER). This reduction in complexity, however, comes with a cost – the outputs of stochastic computations are not guaranteed to be accurate due to the intrinsic variations introduced in converting from binary to stochastic representations, correlation between operands, *etc.* [7]. Therefore, SC is only suited to applications where some inaccuracy or approximation in computations is tolerable. While the basic concepts in SC date back to the 1960s [6], SC has witnessed a resurgence of interest in recent years, in part due to the increase in applications that exhibit intrinsic resilience [8]. Stochastic implementations of image processing and error correction coding algorithms, and function approximation using Bernstein polynomials have been demonstrated [9, 10, 11, 12].

We argue that RM applications are a highly suitable target for SC, since (i) they are dominated by arithmetic computations, for which SC promises highly efficient implementations, and (ii) RM applications exhibit significant "intrinsic resilience", and are able to produce outputs of acceptable quality despite inexactness in the underlying computations [8, 13].

We propose **StoRM**, a stochastic processor that executes the compute-intensive kernels of a range of RM applications. Recognizing the abundant parallelism present in RM applications, **StoRM** is organized as a two-dimensional array of Stochastic Processing Elements (**StoPEs**) with a streaming interconnect and memory hierarchy. The architecture of **StoRM** naturally lends itself to amortizing the circuits for binary-to-stochastic conversion across rows and columns of **StoPEs**. We address a key challenge for SC – the length of bit-streams, and hence the number of cycles spent in stochastic computations, increase exponentially with the precision of data. This unfavorable tradeoff significantly impacts the execution time and energy consumption of stochastic designs, and can result in SC being worse than conventional implementations for computations that require even modest precision (*e.g.,* 16 bits).

We present several techniques to address this challenge. First, we propose the use of vector processing, where multiple bits of a stochastic bit-stream are processed in each cycle. Vectorization reduces the execution time of **StoRM** in direct proportion to the vector length while area/power

---

*This work was supported in part by the National Science Foundation under grant no. 1018621.

increase by a significantly smaller factor, leading to a net reduction in energy. Second, we propose segmented stochastic processing, in which a binary number is partitioned into groups or segments of bits, stochastic bit-streams are separately generated to represent these segments, separately processed, and re-combined during conversion back to the binary domain. This technique, which can be viewed as an intermediate choice between the extrema of a conventional binary representation and a fully stochastic representation, limits the exponential increase in bit-streams to the segment length rather than the full bit-width of the numbers being processed. Third, we exploit an interesting attribute of SC – the lengths of stochastic bit-streams presents a natural quality-efficiency tradeoff knob, *i.e.,* they can be dynamically tuned to produce outputs of varying quality, with virtually no additional hardware overheads. We leverage this capability to further improve the efficiency of StoRM by modulating the bit-stream lengths to be the minimum necessary to achieve the specified application output quality.

An implementation of StoRM was designed at the register-transfer level, synthesized to TSMC 65nm technology, and evaluated using representative RM applications. We compare StoRM with an optimized baseline that uses conventional binary processing elements (PEs) under iso-area conditions, where StoRM utilizes a larger degree of parallelism by leveraging the smaller size of StoPEs. StoRM achieves 2-3X improvements in energy-delay product for comparable application quality, and upto 10X (20X) improvements when loss in application output quality of upto 5% (10%) can be tolerated.

In summary, the key contributions of this work are:

- We design and evaluate StoRM, a stochastic processor that uses SC to execute the compute-intensive kernels of RM applications.

- We propose techniques to address the time and energy inefficiency of SC due to the exponential relationship between stochastic bit-stream length and precision.

- We demonstrate that the length of the stochastic bit-stream can be used as an effective mechanism to explore quality *vs.* energy tradeoffs for applications that demonstrate intrinsic resilience.

The rest of the paper is organized as follows. We present related work in the field of SC in Section 2 and discuss the basics of SC in Section 3. Section 4 describes the StoRM processor and presents the proposed techniques used to improve its energy efficiency. We then present our experimental methodology in Section 5, followed by results and conclusions in Sections 6 and 7, respectively.

2. RELATED WORK

In this section, we place our work in the context of previous efforts towards the efficient realization of RM applications, and previous work in the field of stochastic computing.

The prevalence and compute-intensive nature of RM applications has led to efforts to optimize them using parallel software on multi-core and many-core processors [1, 2], specialized hardware accelerators [3, 4, 14] and custom circuits [5]. StoRM is an accelerator for RM applications, but utilizes an entirely different approach (SC), which leads to significant benefits compared to previous efforts.

RM applications exhibit a high degree of intrinsic resilience to inaccuracy in their computations [2, 8]. Approximate computing is a design paradigm that exploits this resilience to realize highly efficient implementations. While approximate computing has been explored at all levels of abstraction from software to circuits, we restrict our attention to hardware techniques since they are closely related to our work. Previous efforts in approximate hardware can be broadly

classified into over-scaling based approximations and functional approximations. Over-scaling based approximation techniques [15, 16] operate hardware under over-scaled voltage conditions, leading to energy efficiency at the cost of timing errors. Functional approximation techniques [17, 18, 19] modify the functionality of hardware or software to reduce complexity, thereby obtaining area and power benefits. Approximate computing techniques have been used to design energy-efficient accelerators [20] and programmable processors [21] for RM workloads. We argue that SC is a promising alternative approach to approximate computing, since the bit-stream length provides a natural quality-energy tradeoff knob. Compared to previous approximate hardware design techniques, which are based on conventional binary implementations, SC provides dynamic quality configurability with minimal hardware overheads, leading to a superior quality-energy tradeoff.

The fundamentals of SC can be traced back to the 1960s [6]. However, due to the accuracy limitations [22], early efforts in SC were restricted to a few applications such as artificial neural networks [23] and hybrid controllers [24]. Recently, there has been a surge in applications that can benefit from SC. The use of SC was explored in Low Density Parity Check (LDPC) decoders [9], and image processing applications such as edge detection and gamma correction [10]. A noteworthy development towards broader applicability of SC was the proposal of a reconfigurable architecture to realize Bernstein polynomials, which in turn can be used to approximate various arithmetic functions [11]. Circuits that judiciously employ correlated stochastic bit streams to implement various image processing applications have been explored [12]. While these efforts have demonstrated promising area and power improvements, they do not address the inherent performance and energy inefficiency of SC due to the exponential relationship between bit-stream length and required precision.

Inspired by the need for efficient realization of RM applications, and their tolerance to approximate computations, we design StoRM, a processor that utilizes SC to efficiently execute RM kernels. We propose vector processing and segmented stochastic processing as techniques to overcome the intrinsic inefficiencies of SC and apply them to improve the energy efficiency of StoRM.

3. BACKGROUND: STOCHASTIC COMPUTING (SC)

In this section, we present the fundamentals of SC, describe the implementation of basic stochastic arithmetic circuits and discuss the overheads and accuracy concerns associated with SC. In SC, numbers are scaled to the range

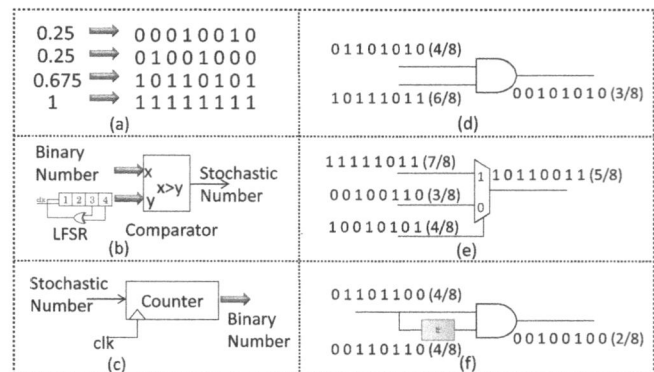

Figure 1: SC basics (a) Stochastic number representation (b) Stochastic number generation (c) Stochastic to binary conversion (d) Multiplication circuit (e) Scaled addition circuit (f) Squaring circuit

[0,1] and represented by bit-streams, such that the probability of ones in a bit stream determines the numerical value of the number that it represents. Examples of stochastic representations of different numbers are shown in Figure 1(a). Stochastic Number Generators (SNGs) consist of a pseudo random number generator, typically implemented using Linear Feedback Shift Registers (LFSR)[1] and a comparator, as shown in Figure 1(b). A counter circuit that counts the number of ones in the bit stream, as shown in Figure 1(c), can be used to convert the stochastic bit-stream back into the binary domain.

The stochastic circuits for three basic arithmetic operations – multiplication, addition and squaring – are shown in Figure 1(d), 1(e) and 1(f) respectively. As shown in Figure 1(d),

A single AND gate can implement the multiplication operation, since the probability of a 1 in the output bit stream is determined by the product of the 1-probabilities in the input bit streams. In the case of addition, in order to constrain the output range to [0,1], scaled addition is implemented using a MUX. A squaring circuit can be realized by an AND gate where one of the inputs is connected directly to the bit-stream and the other input is connected to a delayed version of the bit-stream. The delay element aids in making the two inputs of the AND gate uncorrelated.

The primary benefits of SC are the reduced area and power due to extremely compact implementations of complex arithmetic circuits. However, performance and energy consumption strongly depend on the number of bits in the bit-stream, which grows exponentially with the precision required to represent the input data. For example, a 3-bit binary number can be represented accurately by a bit stream of length 8, whereas an 8 bit binary number needs 255 bits. Therefore, SC becomes highly inefficient in performance and energy as the precision requirements grow. In this paper, we present circuit- and architecture-level techniques in the context of the StoRM processor to overcome this intrinsic limitation of SC.

4. STOCHASTIC RECOGNITION AND MINING PROCESSOR

The design of StoRM was motivated by the observation that the dominant computational kernels in RM applications exhibit a high degree of resilience to approximations [8]. In this section, we present the architecture of StoRM, and describe the design of its stochastic processing elements (StoPEs). Next, we propose two design techniques – vector processing and segmented stochastic processing – to improve the energy efficiency of StoRM. Finally, we discuss the quality configurability and iso-area redesign enabled by the use of SC.

4.1 StoRM: Architecture Overview

Figure 2 presents an architectural overview of StoRM, which consists of a two-dimensional array of stochastic processing elements (StoPEs), stochastic number generators (SNGs), and a two-level memory hierarchy.

The StoPEs are connected in a nearest-neighbor fashion and process streams of data, where input streams are fed to the StoPEs present in the left and top borders of the StoPE array and propagate from left-to-right and top-to-bottom. At the end of a kernel computation, the results available in the counter registers of the StoPEs are scanned out.

The two level memory hierarchy of StoRM consists of first level streaming FIFOs and a second level random access

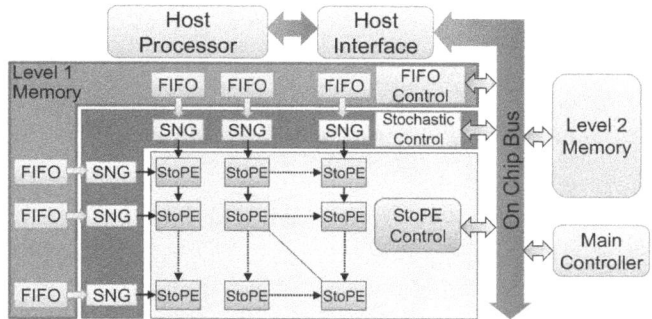

Figure 2: StoRM architecture overview

memory. The FIFOs are located along the top and left borders of the StoPE array, as shown in Figure 2. Data is loaded into the FIFOs from a larger second level random access memory which utilizes a wide interface to provide sufficient bandwidth. Data is stored in binary representation in the memory hierarchy due to increase in volume incurred during conversion to the stochastic domain. Therefore, the SNGs are placed in between the FIFOs and the top and left borders of the StoPE array. It is worth noting that an m × n StoPE array configuration requires only m+n SNGs, as the operands are re-used along the rows and columns of the StoPE array. This significantly amortizes the cost of stochastic bit-stream generation. Since each StoPE internally converts the results back to the binary domain, they can be directly stored back to the level 2 memory.

The steps involved in executing an application kernel on StoRM are explained below. The host processor transfers the data and the program corresponding to the kernel to be executed into the second level memory and program memory inside the main controller, respectively, through an on-chip bus. The main controller then configures the FIFO controller, the SNG controller and the StoPE controller to execute the kernel. The FIFO controller monitors the empty/full status of the FIFOs and orchestrates data transfers from the second level memory to the FIFOs. The SNG controller initializes the seeds for the stochastic bit stream generators and controls the length of the stochastic bit-streams. The StoPE controller initializes the accumulator registers and specifies the kernel operation to be performed by the StoPEs. After these configuration steps, the StoPEs begin to perform computation on the input data, and at the end of computation, the data is scanned out to the level 2 memory and subsequently read by the host processor.

4.2 Stochastic Processing Element (StoPE)

The primary computation element of StoRM is the Stochastic Processing Element (StoPE), which is described in Figure 3. First, let us consider the scalar StoPE, which is shown in Figure 3(a). The StoPE is designed to implement dot product computation and the square of L2-norm computation[2]. The data operands, represented in a stochastic number format, are provided as a sequence of bits at the input. The scalar StoPE processes a single bit in each cycle and provides the kernel output in binary format at the end of computation. The operation of StoPE is explained below.

Let us consider two data vectors of dimensionality n, $\langle a_1, a_2, \cdots a_n \rangle$ and $\langle b_1, b_2, \cdots, b_n \rangle$. The equations representing kernels operating on vectors a and b are shown below:

---

[1]Unlike other applications like cryptographic key generation, SC does not require highly complex random number generators. The key concern is to ensure minimal correlation between bit-streams that are inputs to a stochastic computation. Fortunately, this can be achieved even with low-cost pseudo random number generators such as LFSRs.

[2]In our applications, L2-norm computation is invariably followed by relative computations such as ranking or comparison. Hence, we omit the square-root in the L2-norm as it greatly reduces implementation complexity.

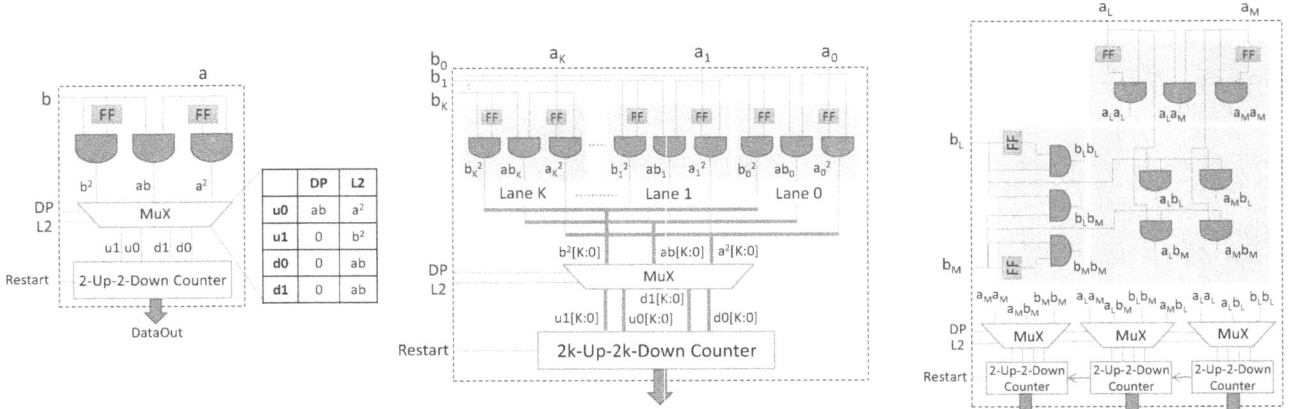

Figure 3: (a) Scalar StoPE. (b) StoPE using vector processing (c) StoPE using segmented stochastic processing.

Dot Product Computation:

$$dot\_product(a, b) = \sum_{i=1}^{n} a_i * b_i \qquad (1)$$

L2-norm distance Computation:

$$L2\_Norm(a, b) = \sqrt{\sum_{i=1}^{n} (a_i - b_i)^2} \qquad (2)$$

which can be re-written as

$$L2\_Norm(a, b) = \sqrt{\sum_{i=1}^{n} a_i{}^2 + b_i{}^2 - 2 * a_i * b_i} \qquad (3)$$

When the vectors are represented in stochastic number format with a stream length of L, $\langle a_{11} \ldots a_{1L}, a_{21} \ldots a_{2L}, \cdots a_{n1} \ldots a_{nL}\rangle$ and $\langle b_{11} \ldots b_{1L}, b_{21} \ldots b_{2L}, \cdots b_{n1} \ldots b_{nL}\rangle$, the kernel computations in the stochastic domain are given by

$$dot\_product(a, b) = \sum_{i=1}^{n} (\sum_{j=1}^{L} a_{ij} \& b_{ij}) \qquad (4)$$

$$L2\_Norm(a, b)$$
$$= \sqrt{\sum_{i=1}^{n} (\sum_{j=2}^{L} a_{ij} \& a_{ij-1} + b_{ij} \& b_{ij-1} - 2 * a_{ij} \& b_{ij})} \qquad (5)$$

The kernels in the stochastic domain require computing the square of each input operand ($a_{ij} \& a_{ij-1}$ and $b_{ij} \& b_{ij-1}$) and their product ($a_i \& b_i$). The StoPE consists of three AND gates and two flip flops to realize this functionality. The second step of the kernel computation viz. accumulation is combined with stochastic to binary conversion; both these functions are realized by a 2-up-2-down counter, as shown in Figure 3(a).

Table 1: Comparison of various StoPE implementations with a baseline binary implementation

	Area (sq um)	Delay (ns)	Power (uW)	Cycle count	Latency (ns)	Energy (fJ)
Binary Scalar	63,714	3.73	0.45	1.00	3.73	1.68
Stochastic	7,552	0.42	0.06	64.00	26.88	1.72
2-way vector	9,288	0.70	0.09	32.00	22.40	2.06
4-way vector	13,145	0.96	0.18	16.00	15.36	2.76
8-way vector	18,068	1.16	0.35	8.00	9.28	3.25
16-way vector	27,564	1.33	0.62	4.00	5.32	3.30
Segmented Stochastic	11,041	0.84	0.11	8.00	6.72	0.77

A comparison of the scalar StoPE with an equivalent binary implementation for a precision requirement of 6 is presented in Table 1, rows 1 and 2. It can be seen that SC results

in a highly compact implementation, resulting in lower area and power consumption. However, the computations in the stochastic domain require multiple cycles, equal to the number of bits in the stochastic bit stream. The length of the bit stream grows exponentially with the precision of the data being represented [6]. As a result, although efficient in area and power, the StoPE consumes more energy than a conventional binary processing element. In order to mitigate this intrinsic limitation (increase in cycle count) of SC, we propose two techniques, vector processing and segmented stochastic processing, which are described in the following subsections.

4.2.1 Vector Processing

The scalar StoPE described above processes a single bit of the stochastic bit-stream in each cycle. We utilize vector processing to realize a space vs. time tradeoff to improve the performance of StoRM. Figure 3(b) shows a vector StoPE where i bits are processed per cycle. As seen from the figure, an i bit vector StoPE requires 3i AND gates and a 2k-up-2k-down counter where the value of k is equal to $\lceil log(i) \rceil$. It can be seen from Table 1 that vector processing improves the performance of StoPEs due to the reduced cycle count, while the increased complexity of the vector StoPE results in higher area and power consumption. The StoPE energy increases with vector length, but much slower than the reduction in processing time, leading to a net benefit in energy-delay product, as shown in Section 6. It has to be noted that, in order to generate multiple stochastic bits in parallel, the SNGs need to updated with multiple random number generators and comparator circuits resulting in additional hardware overheads. A holistic evaluation of vector processing in StoRM considering these overheads is presented in Section 6.

4.2.2 Segmented Stochastic Processing

In SC, all bits in the bit-stream carry equal significance. In contrast, in the case of binary number representation, the significance of bits increases exponentially from LSB to MSB. Considering these representations as two ends of a spectrum, we propose a hybrid representation, referred to as segmented stochastic processing, wherein the binary data is divided into equal segments and a separate stochastic bit-stream is used to represent each of these segments.

Figure 3(c) shows the implementation of a StoPE that employs segmented stochastic processing with 2 segments. a_L and a_M are bit-streams that represent the most significant segment (MSS) and least significant segment (LSS) of a. If the binary data represented by a is 8 bits, the bit-stream length is reduced from 256 to 16 through the use of segmented stochastic processing. Although the segmented StoPE is more complex compared to the original StoPE and hence incurs higher area and power, the disproportionate reduction in cycle count outweighs these overheads and results in energy benefits, as shown in Table 1. It has to be noted that the segmented StoPE element requires two stochastic bit-streams to be generated in parallel, leading to hardware overheads in SNGs. The impact of segmented stochastic processing on the entire StoRM processor is presented in Section 6.

4.3 Quality Configurability through Bit-stream Length Modulation

The functionality of RM applications is defined on a continuous scale of output quality rather than a unique correct output. Thus, for a required output quality, the accuracy of the computations can be modulated to optimize energy consumption. In the case of SC, the accuracy of the computation is determined by the stochastic bit stream length (longer bit streams lead to higher accuracy). Thus, we propose to dynamically modulate the stochastic bit stream length as a means to optimize energy for the desired output quality.

The design of the SNG controller allows bit-stream length modulation with near-zero hardware overheads. This is unlike other popular approximate computing techniques that incur significant hardware overheads (*e.g.*, voltage regulators in the case of voltage overscaling, clock/power gating circuits in the case of precision scaling) in order to effect an energy *vs.* quality tradeoff.

4.4 Iso-area Re-design

RM applications typically operate on large datasets and possess abundant data level parallelism. As described earlier, StoPEs occupy significantly less area compared to their binary counterparts. Thus, for a given area budget, the StoRM processor can accommodate more processing elements, better exploiting the data parallel nature of RM applications. Hence, the StoRM processor can be re-designed by increasing the size of the StoPE array to match the area of its binary equivalent. Increasing the array size allows for more data streams to be processed in parallel and also facilitates better data re-use. This improves the application performance and the overall energy consumption of the StoRM processor.

5. EXPERIMENTAL METHODOLOGY

In this section, we present the experimental methodology and benchmarks used to evaluate the proposed StoRM processor. StoRM was implemented at the register-transfer level (RTL) and was synthesized to TSMC 65nm technology using Synopsys Design Compiler.

Table 2: Applications used for evaluating StoRM

Application	Algorithm	Dataset	Precision
Hand-written Digit Recognition	SVM Classification	MNIST	8
Hand-written Digit Model Generation	SVM Training	MNIST	8
Eye Detection	GLVQ Testing	YUV Faces	6
Optical Character Recognition	K-Nearest Neighbours	OCR Digits	5

We used four popular RM applications, listed in Table 2, and evaluated their energy-quality tradeoffs on the StoRM processor. The application source code was modified to offload selected kernels to StoRM. The precision of the data-set was used to determine the nominal length of the stochastic bit-stream, which was then modulated during execution based on the application's quality requirements.

We performed gate-level simulations of StoRM using Synopsys Power Compiler to obtain its power consumption. Since the gate-level simulation of entire applications takes prohibitively long times, we employed sampling to obtain smaller input traces to use for power simulation. We developed a cycle and bit accurate functional simulator for StoRM to measure the accuracy impact of the proposed techniques on the application output quality. The functional simulator

also outputs the application execution time which, along with the power estimates to determine energy consumption.

6. RESULTS

This section presents the results of various experiments performed to evaluate the energy efficiency of StoRM. To account for the fact that various configurations of StoRM have different performance and energy consumption, we use the energy-delay product as the metric for our comparisons. The delay is computed as the overall application execution time.

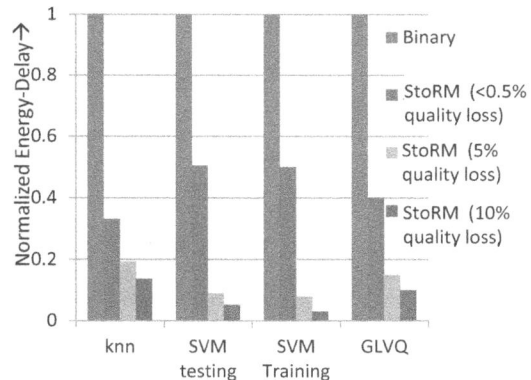

Figure 4: Energy-delay benefits of StoRM for different target quality levels

6.1 Energy-Delay Benefits

Figure 4 shows the normalized energy-delay product of StoRM for various application level quality constraints. The energy-delay is normalized to the binary baseline, which is based on the RM accelerator described in [14] We observe from the figure that StoRM achieves 2X-3X energy-delay benefits for virtually no loss (<0.5%) in the application output quality. When the quality constraints are relaxed, the length of the bit-stream used is reduced accordingly. This results in further improvement in energy-delay, amounting to 2X-10X for moderate loss in output quality (< 5%) and 7X-20X for 10% quality loss.

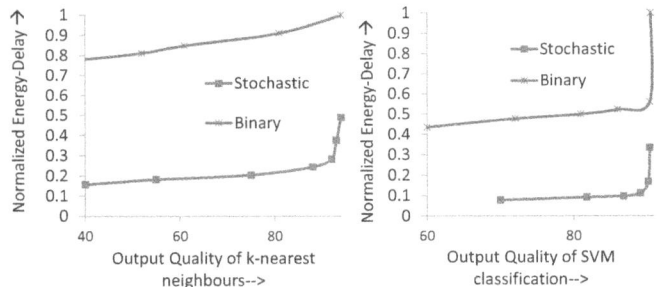

Figure 5: Energy-quality tradeoff for SVM classification and k-nearest neighbors

SC provides a natural knob (bit-stream length) to navigate the energy-quality tradeoff. In binary implementations, this tradeoff is achieved using alternative mechanisms such as precision scaling. We compare the energy-delay *vs.* quality loss obtained through bit-stream length modulation in StoRM with precision scaling for the binary baseline. Figure 5 presents results for 2 representative applications - handwritten digit recognition (SVM classification) and optical character recognition (k-nearest neighbors). It can be inferred from the figure that quality modulation through stochastic bit-stream length modulation comprehensively outperforms binary precision scaling at all target quality levels.

6.2 Impact of Vector Processing

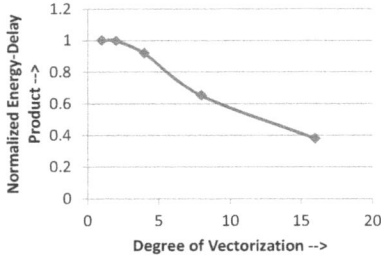

Figure 6: Impact of vectorization on energy-delay benefits

In this subsection, we study the impact of vector processing on the energy efficiency of StoRM. Figure 6 plots the normalized energy-delay product of StoRM for various vector lengths (2-way to 16-way). For this analysis, we used array dimensions of 15x15 and a bit-width of 8 (stochastic bit-stream of length 256). As we increase the degree of vectorization, the execution time decreases linearly, as multiple bits in the stochastic bit stream can be processed in parallel. At the same time, the increased StoPE complexity and the need for additional SNGs result in higher area and power consumption. Overall, the reduction in delay outweighs the increased power consumption, resulting in improved energy-delay.

6.3 Benefits of Increased Parallelism

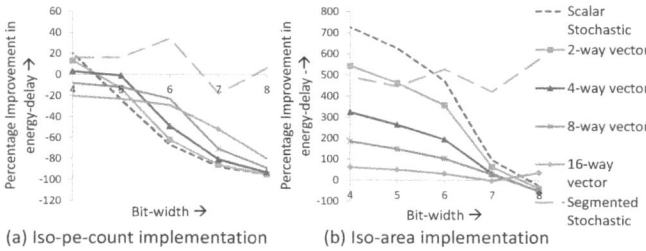

(a) Iso-pe-count implementation   (b) Iso-area implementation

Figure 7: Energy-delay benefits of iso-area re-design

In this subsection, we present results that demonstrate the benefits of re-investing the area savings obtained by SC to increase the array-level parallelism in StoRM. Figure 7(a) shows the energy-delay improvements over the binary baseline *vs.* bit-width, for various versions of StoRM (positive and larger numbers are better). For this experiment, all versions of StoRM and the baseline utilize a 15x15 array. The area and power benefits of StoRM over the binary baseline are outweighed by the exponential increase in bit-stream length. As a result, the energy-delay improvements are negative for most versions of StoRM. The segmented design produces modest improvements for 4-6 bits, and is more efficient for even bit-widths, since they result in segments of equal length.

Exploiting the abundant data parallelism in RM applications, the area and power benefits of SC can be traded off to greatly improve energy efficiency, by increasing the number of StoPEs, *i.e.*, the array-level parallelism in StoRM. Note that increasing the StoPE array size needs to be accompanied with an appropriate increase in the level 1 streaming memory elements and SNGs. Considering all these factors, we performed an iso-area re-design of various versions of StoRM, and the resulting energy-delay products are shown in Figure 7(b). Iso-area re-design significantly improves the energy-delay product of all the stochastic implementations and makes them more efficient than the binary baseline. The scalar and vector implementations still suffer from the exponential increase in cycle counts, resulting in reduced energy-delay benefits for higher bit-widths. However, the segmented stochastic implementation significantly outperforms the binary implementation by 4-5X across the considered bit-width range (4-8 bits). Another point worth noting in Figure 7(b) is that the use of

vector processing negatively impacts energy-delay product. In effect, this suggests that array-level parallelism is more beneficial than vector parallelism within each StoPE. This is due to the differing implications of these techniques on the overheads of SNGs. For a 4X increase in parallelism at the array level, the number of SNGs only increases by a factor of 2 (since SNGs are placed at the array borders). However, for a 4X increase in vector parallelism, in our design, the number of SNGs increases by a factor of 4.

In summary, our results demonstrate that StoRM benefits from the various proposed design techniques (vector processing, segmented stochastic processing, and iso-area redesign), leading to significant improvements in energy efficiency.

7. CONCLUSIONS

Recognition and Mining applications are growing increasingly prevalent and are projected to drive the design of future computing platforms. We proposed a Stochastic Recognition and Mining processor (StoRM), which employs stochastic computing to implement the kernels of RM applications. We proposed different mechanisms such as vector processing, segmented stochastic processing and iso-area re-design to further improve the energy efficiency of StoRM. We identified stochastic bit-stream length modulation as a knob to realize energy-quality tradeoffs in StoRM. Our evaluations suggest that StoRM achieves significant benefits in energy-delay product compared to conventional binary implementations.

8. REFERENCES

[1] C. Chu et. al. Map-reduce for machine learning on multicore. *Proc. NIPS*, 2007.

[2] J. Meng et. al. Best-effort parallel execution framework for recognition and mining applications. In *Proc. IPDPS*, 2009.

[3] A. Majumdar et. al. A massively parallel, energy efficient programmable accelerator for learning and classification. *ACM Trans. Architecture Code Optimization*, 2012.

[4] R. Iyer et. al. CogniServe: Heterogeneous server architecture for large-scale recognition. *IEEE MICRO*, 2011.

[5] S. Lee et. al. A 345mw heterogeneous many-core processor with an intelligent inference engine for robust object recognition. In *Proc. ISSCC*, 2010.

[6] B. R. Gaines. Stochastic computing. In *Proc. SJCC*, 1967.

[7] A. Alaghi et. al. Survey of stochastic computing. *Trans. Embedded Computing Systems*, 2013.

[8] V. K. Chippa et. al. Analysis and characterization of inherent application resilience for approximate computing. In *Proc. DAC*, 2013.

[9] V. C. Gaudet. Iterative decoding using stochastic computation. *Electronics Letters*, 2003.

[10] P. Li et. al. Using stochastic computing to implement digital image processing algorithms. In *Proc. ICCD*, 2011.

[11] W. Qian et. al. An architecture for fault-tolerant computation with stochastic logic. *IEEE Trans. on Computers*, 2011.

[12] A. Alaghi et. al. Stochastic circuits for real-time image-processing applications. In *Proc. DAC*, 2013.

[13] S. T. Chakradhar et. al. Best-effort computing: Re-thinking parallel software and hardware. In *Proc. DAC*, 2010.

[14] V. K. Chippa, H. Jayakumar, D. Mohapatra, K. Roy, and A. Raghunathan. Energy-efficient recognition and mining processor using scalable effort design. In *Proc. CICC*, 2013.

[15] R. Hegde et. al. Energy-efficient signal Processing via algorithmic noise-tolerance. In *Proc. ISLPED*, 1999.

[16] K. Palem et. al. Sustaining moore's law in embedded computing through probabilistic and approximate design: retrospects and prospects. In *Proc. CASES*, 2009.

[17] V. Gupta et. al. IMPACT: Imprecise adders for low-power approximate computing. In *Proc. ISLPED*, 2011.

[18] A. Lingamneni et al. Energy parsimonious circuit design through probabilistic pruning. In *Proc. DATE*, 2011.

[19] S. Venkataramani et. al. SALSA: Systematic logic synthesis of approximate circuits. In *Proc. DAC*, 2012.

[20] V. K. Chippa et. al. Scalable effort hardware design: Exploiting algorithmic resilience for energy efficiency. In *Proc. DAC*, 2010.

[21] S. Venkataramani et. al. Quality programmable vector processors for approximate computing. In *Proc. MICRO*, 2013.

[22] W. J. Poppelbaum et. al. Stochastic computing elements and systems. In *Proc. JCC*, 1967.

[23] B. D. Brown et. al. Stochastic neural computation. I. Computational elements. *IEEE Trans. on Computers*, 2001.

[24] J. M. Quero et. al. Continuous time controllers using digital programmable devices. In *Proc. IECON*, 1999.

Approximate Compressed Sensing: Ultra-Low Power Biosignal Processing via Aggressive Voltage Scaling on a Hybrid Memory Multi-core Processor

Daniele Bortolotti[†], Hossein Mamaghanian[‡], Andrea Bartolini[†], Maryam Ashouei[*]
Jan Stuijt[*], David Atienza[‡], Pierre Vandergheynst[‡] and Luca Benini[†]

[†]DEI - University of Bologna	[‡]ESL, LTS2 - EPFL	[*]Holst Centre/imec
Bologna, Italy	Lausanne, Switzerland	Eindhoven, The Netherlands
{daniele.bortolotti, a.bartolini,	{hossein.mamaghanian, david.atienza,	{maryam.ashouei,
luca.benini}@unibo.it;	pierre.vandergheynst}@epfl.ch;	jan.stuijt}@imec-nl.nl

ABSTRACT

Technology scaling enables the design of low cost biosignal processing chips suited for emerging wireless body-area sensing applications. Energy consumption severely limits such applications and memories are becoming the energy bottleneck to achieve ultra-low-power operation. When aggressive voltage scaling is used, memory operation becomes unreliable due to the lack of sufficient Static Noise Margin. This paper introduces an approximate biosignal Compressed Sensing approach. We propose a digital architecture featuring a hybrid memory (6T-SRAM/SCMEM cells) designed to control perturbations on specific data structures. Combined with a statistically robust reconstruction algorithm, the system tolerates memory errors and achieves significant energy savings with low area overhead.

Categories and Subject Descriptors

C.1.4 [Mobile processors]

Keywords

Compressed Sensing; Approximate Computing; Ultra-Low Power; Hybrid Memory

1. INTRODUCTION

Emerging and future healthcare policies are fueling up an application driven shift toward long term monitoring of biosignals by means of embedded ultra-low power (ULP) devices. Modern human behavior-related diseases, such as cardiovascular pathologies, require accurate and non-stop medical supervision, which is unsustainable for the traditional healthcare system due to increasing costs and medical management needs [1]. Personal health monitoring systems are

able to offer large-scale and cost-effective solutions to this problem.

Wearable health monitoring systems, enabled by Wireless Body Sensor Networks (WBSNs), face opposite requirements such as a continuously tighter power budget and an increasing demand of computation capabilities to pre-process locally the sensors information to reduce the amount of data to be transmitted as well as response time. To ensure minimal energy operation several aspects must be considered, combining optimizations of the signal processing aspects and of the technological layers of the ULP architecture. Recently the Compressed Sensing (CS) paradigm for signal acquisition and compression has proved to be effective in reducing energy consumption in embedded ECG monitors. Enabling a sub-Nyquist sampling rate for sparse signals, authors in [7] show $\approx 37\%$ improved lifetime compared to state-of-the-art compression techniques. Motivated by the inherent parallel nature of medical grade ECG monitoring, where multi-channel signal analysis is often embarrassingly parallel, multi-core architectures demonstrated their efficiency compared to single-core solutions [10, 8]. In [10] is presented a multi-core architecture where individual leads are processed on different cores in parallel. Parallel processing enables more aggressive voltage-frequency scaling than single-core solutions, though at low workload requirements the single-core solution proved to be more efficient. Leakage power, mainly due to data and instruction memories, has a big impact and aggressive voltage scaling cannot be applied due to reliability issues of the memories.

Indeed, the failure probability of the conventional 6 Transistors (6T) SRAM cell increases considerably as the supply voltage is scaled down [11]. The usage of more reliable SRAM bit-cells, such as 8 Transistors (8T) or 10 Transistors (10T) cells, as well as standard cells memories (SCMEM) allows scaling to lower supply voltage, however, such solutions incur in large area penalties.

Approximate computing is an emerging paradigm that exploits intrinsic properties of multimedia and visual applications to tolerate errors to save energy allowing some final QoS degradation. [14] proposes an approximate full adder that reduces design complexity and power (up to 60%) while inducing a negligible QoS loss in JPEG and MPEG compression blocks. [12] uses a custom SRAM design with 6T memory for storing the LSB of each word and an 8T memory to store the MSB, applying such architecture to video decoder applications operating at low voltages. Both solutions are tailored to multimedia accelerators and are built based on the assumption that an error can be tolerated when occurring in the LSBs. As a matter of fact none of the state-of-the-art solution fully exploits the randomly distributed bit-flips errors that are typical in over-scaled SRAMs.

These considerations motivate the idea of the present work: by using a hybrid memory architecture, combining classic 6T-SRAM with SCMEM cells, we are able to offer an architecture that can operate at low voltages with a heterogeneous memory map composed of an error-free portion and an error-prone one. With an accurate data allocation of the CS internal structures between the two different portions, we are able to reduce the size of the SCMEM portion leading to a significantly lower area-overhead and, on the other hand, tolerates error induced by bit-flips in the SRAM by an innovative CS reconstruction algorithm.

The main contributions of this work are the following:

- a novel hybrid memory architecture for ULP multi-core biosignal processors is proposed. The combination of 6T and SCMEM banks enables operating at low-voltage while preserving data-correctness for the most critical data structures.

- the novel Approximate Compress Sensing paradigm is presented. Based on a reconstruction algorithm the proposed Compressed Sensing framework is capable of tolerating random bit-flips errors in the 6T memory.

- the proposed architecture allows to trade-off signal reconstruction quality with voltage supply and this leads to a significant improvement in energy saving. When operating at 0.6V, the hybrid memory architecture proves to be 5x more energy efficient than a purely 6T architecture (@ 0.8V) counterpart with a reduced area overhead ($\approx 13\%$). At 0.7V our architecture saves 60% of power with same reconstruction performance of standard CS for single lead ECG. When compared to SCMEM-only design our architecture has comparable power savings but with almost 10% less area overhead.

The rest of the paper is organized as follows. In Section 2 the hybrid memory multi-core architecture is introduced. Section 3 discusses the CS algorithm, the memory errors in low-voltage operation and the reconstruction algorithm. Next, in Section 4 we describe the experimental setup and the results of the proposed architecture in terms of energy efficiency, reconstruction quality and area overhead. Finally, the conclusions of this work are presented in Section 5.

2. HYBRID MEMORY ARCHITECTURE

We consider for the digital sensor node a baseline architecture similar to several current multi-core architectures targeting biosignal processors [8, 10]. The considered architecture, presented in Figure 1, features 8 Processing Elements (PEs) each one with a private Instruction Memory (IM). The PEs do not have private data caches, therefore avoiding memory coherency overhead, while they all share a L1 multi-banked tightly coupled data memory (TCDM) acting as a shared data scratchpad memory. The TCDM has a

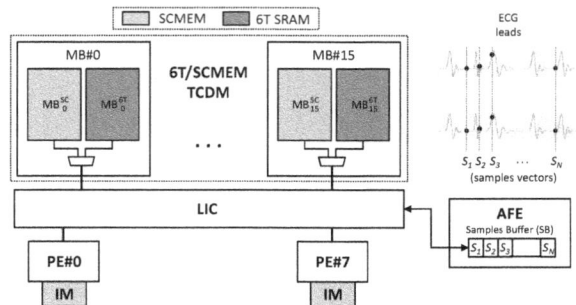

Figure 1: Multi-core architecture with hybrid 6T/SCMEM memory for Compressed Sensing

number of ports equal to the number of banks to have concurrent access to different memory locations. Intra-cluster communication is based on a low-latency high-bandwidth logarithmic interconnect (LIC) able to support single-cycle communication between PEs and memory banks (MBs). In case of multiple conflicting requests, for fair access to memory banks, a round-robin scheduler arbitrates the accesses. To ease the negative impact of banking conflicts we consider a banking factor of 2 (16 banks).

In the considered CS architecture, the input multi-channel signal is sampled by the analog front-end (AFE), with a sampling frequency according to the dynamics of the signal to analyze and the accuracy needed. The AFE is interfaced as a memory mapped buffer (SB in Figure 1) accessible through the LIC and can send interrupts to the PEs when the samples are ready for on the fly compression. Considering the limitations imposed by classic 6T-SRAM memory when operating aggressive voltage scaling and the characteristics of biomedical applications, we consider a hybrid memory architecture. By combining 6T and SCMEM-banks and a careful data allocation in the different memory portions, the system is capable of operating at ultra-low voltage and errors in the 6T portion are handled in the CS reconstruction algorithm. The 6T/SCMEM hybrid architecture is schematized in Figure 1 and it features a single voltage domain for the whole architecture, reducing area overheads and design complexity. The SCMEM portion of the TCDM offers reliable operation down to 400mV, while the 6T portion shows errors below 800mV as will be shown in Section 3.3.

3. ROBUST COMPRESSED SENSING
3.1 Compressed Sensing

Compressed sensing (CS), as an emerging tool has been investigated in many applications from low-power sensing and compression, radar and communication signal processing, high dimensional data analysis. The main idea behind CS is fairly simple and it assumes that given high dimensional data has a sparse representation which could be exploited to highly reduce the dimensionality of data.

Let $\mathbf{x}$ be the real-valued N-dimensional signal vector ($\mathbf{x} \in \mathbb{R}^N$) that is sparse or has a sparse representation in some known dictionary $\mathbf{x} = \mathbf{\Psi}\boldsymbol{\alpha}$. By sparse we mean that $\boldsymbol{\alpha}$ has only few non-zero elements. If we collect a vector of linear measurement $\mathbf{y} \in \mathbb{R}^M$ by $\mathbf{y} = \mathbf{\Phi}\mathbf{x}$, it is possible to recover the original signal $\mathbf{x}$ form measurements vector by solving a convex optimization problem. In the CS context, $\mathbf{\Phi} \in \mathbb{R}^{M \times N}$ is called *sensing matrix* and preferably $M \ll N$, so that the size of the measurement vector is much smaller than the original vector $\mathbf{x}$. To guarantee the recovery, the sensing matrix $\mathbf{\Phi}$ must obey the key *restricted isometry property* (RIP) [17]:

$$(1 - \delta_S) \|\boldsymbol{\alpha}\|_2 \leq \|\mathbf{\Phi}\mathbf{\Psi}\boldsymbol{\alpha}\|_2 \leq (1 + \delta_S) \|\boldsymbol{\alpha}\|_2 \qquad (1)$$

for all S-sparse vectors $\boldsymbol{\alpha}$ and $\|.\|_2$ denotes the 2-norm of the vector. δ_S is the isometry constant of matrix $\mathbf{\Phi}$, which must be not too close to one.

If RIP holds, then an approximate sparse signal reconstruction can be accomplished by solving the following convex optimization problem:

$$\min_{\tilde{\boldsymbol{\alpha}} \in \mathbb{R}^N} \|\tilde{\boldsymbol{\alpha}}\|_1 \qquad \text{s.t.} \qquad \|\mathbf{\Phi}\mathbf{\Psi}\tilde{\boldsymbol{\alpha}} - \mathbf{y}\|_2 \leq \sigma \qquad (2)$$

where σ bounds the amount of noise corrupting the data. Usually in CS context the ℓ_1 norm is used as a sparsity inducing norm and it is proven to reach the sparse solution, while $f(\boldsymbol{\alpha}) = \|\mathbf{\Phi}\mathbf{\Psi}\tilde{\boldsymbol{\alpha}} - \mathbf{y}\|_2$ is named data fidelity or data fitting function which is the least square estimate of the answer to the inverse problem (2).

3.2 Multi-lead ECG and joint Compression

ECG signals are known to be compressible in Discrete Wavelet Domain (DWT). By compressible we mean that even though they are not exactly sparse, it exists an S-sparse approximation which contains most of the information of the signal and the same principles can be applied to some extent [7].

For multi-lead signals we can write the same problem in matrix form. Let $\mathbf{X} \in \mathbb{R}^{N \times L} = [\mathbf{x}_1, \mathbf{x}_2, \ldots, \mathbf{x}_L]$ be the real valued matrix of ECG signals where L is the total number of leads and each column corresponds to a single ECG lead. This matrix could be represented on the DWT domain by $\mathbf{X} = \mathbf{\Psi}\mathbf{A}$, where matrix $\mathbf{A}$ is the sparse coefficients matrix and $\mathbf{\Psi}$ is the DWT matrix. Then the CS recovery problem ((2)) could be solved in multi-lead case too. But in the case of multi-lead ECG compression, where there is a strong correlation between the sparsity structure among the leads, the sparse coefficients model should be refined to take it into account. In such a situation, where non-zero coefficients are naturally partitioned in subsets or groups, the best choice could be using a group-sparsity inducing term [22]. In a recent prior work [21], we proposed to replace the ℓ_1 norm with mixed ℓ_1/ℓ_2 norm. It behaves like an ℓ_1-norm on the vector $(\|\boldsymbol{\alpha}_i\|_2)_{i \in \mathcal{L}}$ in $\mathbb{R}^{|\mathcal{L}|}$, and therefore, induces group sparsity.

3.3 Low Voltage Memory Operation

The classic 6T SRAM is not able to reliably operate at lower supply voltage. One way to address the problem is to have different supply voltages for the memory and the logic sub-blocks [2]. This solution results in the overhead of generating multiple supply voltages and back-end complexity of having separate voltage domains, and the level-shifting overhead between the memory and logic voltage domains. More importantly, the solution does not allow for minimum energy operation due to higher operating voltage of the memory, and therefore not addressing the memory power wall. Another solution is the use of 8T (or even 9T, 10T) cells that were shown operating at lower voltages [3, 4, 5]. While foundries provide 8T SRAM bit cell, the cell is not characterized for low voltage operation. Furthermore, the commercial SRAM generators do not provide characterization points (e.g. timing and power information) for low voltage operation. This prevents proper timing closure at

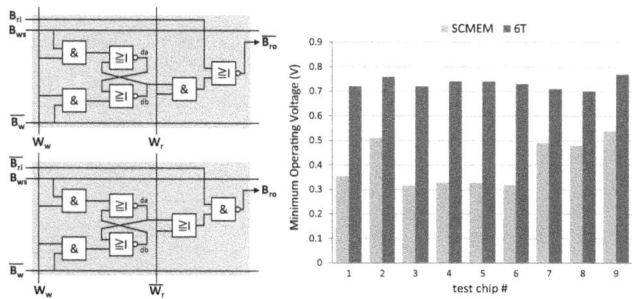

Figure 2: Schematic of SCMEM cell based on AOI/OAI gates (left) and Minimum operating voltage of different chips (right)

low voltage using commercial SRAMs. Custom design of such SRAMs presents a big design effort and can be limited to a few instance sizes. In this work, we use a standard cell-based memory (SCMEM) module. The approach has been proposed in the past [6] and similar to 8T or 10T SRAM, it suffers from an area overhead. We propose to use regular place & route (P&R) in the digital EDA flow for such memory to achieve significant area reduction.

A standard cell-based memory was designed and fabricated in a 40 nm CMOS technology. For comparison reason, also a commercial 6T memory was fabricated on the same chip. The SCMEM uses a cross-coupled pair of AND-OR-INV (AOI) as the storage element (Figure 2, left). The choice of the memory element, combined with the use of regular P&R using the CADENCE Encounter-SoC, results in more than 3x area saving compared to [6] that uses a latch as the storage element. Nine chips were measured and their corresponding minimum operating voltage point is shown in Figure 2 (right) for both the proposed SCMEM and the 6T memory. The results show that for the majority of the chips, the SCMEM operated correctly at voltages below 0.4V and on average it has 400mV lower minimum operating voltage point than the 6T memory. We also measured the minimum retention voltage and both SCMEM and 6T memory have similar retention voltage. The comparison of the memory with state of the art is shown in Table 1.

Error in memory: for the commercial memory, which fails at higher supply voltages, we also measured the errors in memory across the voltage range for nine chips. The errors was characterized by bit-flips randomly placed among all the bits [9]. The measured data was fitted to get the error probability as follows: $P_e = A(V_0 - V_{dd})^k$ where $V_0 = 0.85V$, $k = 6.14$. For the SCMEM, the same fitting equation is accurate when $V_0 = 0.55V$ [9].

3.4 Robust Compressed Sensing

Compressed sensing is known as a robust compression technique in case of noisy measurements vectors corrupted by i.i.d. Gaussian noise. The optimization still works pretty well as long as the amplitude of the noise is small. This is not true if the noise has a very harsh and coarse nature like the bit-flip errors which potentially could be very high in amplitude and not bounded.

Gaussian random distribution are a popular candidate for constructing the sensing matrix $\mathbf{\Phi}$. Such matrix is known to be measurement optimal. The lower bound for the number of measurements is proven to be $M = \Omega(S \log N)$. As far

Table 1: Comparison of different implementations of a 1k x 32b memory (TT corner, 1.1V, 25C)

Feature	Unit	6T commercial 40nm LP	Custom SRAM [3] 40nm LP	SCMEM [6] 65nm LP	SCMEM This work 40nm LP
Dynamic power	pJ	11.9	3.6	-	1.4
(reduced voltage)		-	-	0.93 @ 0.4V*2	0.19 @ 0.4V
Leakage	W	2.15	11*2	-	5.9
(reduced voltage)		-	-	$\geq$ 19.7 @ 0.25V*2	-
Area	mm^2	0.011	0.024*3	$\geq$ 0.186*3	0.058
Min Retention Voltage	V	0.29*1		0.25	0.32*1
Min R/W Voltage	V	0.7*1	-	0.35	0.33*1
Performance (nominal)	MHz	816	454 @ 1.2V	9.5 @ 0.65V	96*1
(reduced voltage)		-	-	0.1-0.2 @ 0.45V	0.4 @ 0.45V*1

*1 measurements results   *2 scaled: $P_{dyn} \propto$ word length   *3 scaled: $A \propto$ total bits $\times (40nm/\lambda_{orig})^2$

as a sparsity S considered, Gaussian matrices are not space optimal and need a huge storage space and nor time optimal since encoding and reconstruction complexity is in the order of O(MN), which makes them not practical for limited resources real-time digital nodes. As an alternative, a sparse binary matrix is used as our sensing matrix $\mathbf{\Phi}$, where each column contains only d non-zero elements equal to 1, $(d \ll M \ll N)$ with required space and time complexity of O(dN) [7]. For such a sensing matrix, the RIP property of (1) is not valid, however, it satisfies a different form of this property, with slightly more required measurements to guarantee the reconstruction [18]. This sensing matrix choice could be very efficient in terms of storage in TCDM, since we only need to store the indexes of non-zero elements that requires O(dN) space instead of O(MN), where $d \ll M$. When storing this matrix in an error-prone memory (6T), it means that the positions of the non-zero elements would change. As a consequence the corrupted sensing matrix $\mathbf{\Phi_c}$ multiplied with the original signal x are represented as $\mathbf{\Phi_c} = (\mathbf{\Phi} + \mathbf{E})$, where $\mathbf{E}$ is the error matrix. $\mathbf{E}$ has only ± 1 entries, $+1$ where an entry is added and -1 where is missed. As long as the number of errors is small and $\mathbf{E}$ is sufficiently sparse, the reconstruction problem (2) can be rewritten with an additional term for minimization and recover the original signal by solving the following optimization problem:

$$\min_{\tilde{\mathbf{A}},\tilde{\mathbf{E}}} \left\| \tilde{\mathbf{A}} \right\|_{1,2} + \lambda \left\| \tilde{\mathbf{E}} \right\|_1 \quad \text{s.t.:} \left\| (\mathbf{\Phi} + \tilde{\mathbf{E}})\mathbf{\Psi}\tilde{\mathbf{A}} - \mathbf{Y} \right\|_2 = 0 \quad (3)$$

where $\|.\|_{1,2}$ denotes the joint ℓ_1/ℓ_2 norm of a matrix. Due to presence of multiplicative noise, the problem (3) in general is not convex and our main goal is to design the recovery algorithm to reach at least the local minimum, and hopefully the global one, if the amount of corrupting noise is limited.

3.5 Reconstruction Algorithm

The formulation of the problem in (2) shows that due to presence of term $\mathbf{EA}$ in constraint, the problem is not convex, but if one of each is given then the problem is very like to the normal Lasso problem and could be treated as a convex optimization problem. If $\mathbf{E}$ is given the problem is the normal Joint CS problem while if $\mathbf{A}$ given then it is similar to the Lasso problem. Similar to the S-TLS problem [24], this suggest to have an iterative decent algorithm yielding successive estimates of the $\mathbf{E}$ and $\mathbf{x}$ with $\mathbf{x}$ and $\mathbf{E}$ fixed respectively. Then the recovery algorithm is two folded and includes two convex optimization problems. First, when $\mathbf{E}$ is considered to be fixed we solve:

$$\tilde{\mathbf{A}}^k = \arg\min_A \left\| (\mathbf{\Phi} + \tilde{\mathbf{E}}^k)\mathbf{\Psi}\mathbf{A} - \mathbf{Y} \right\|_2^2 + \lambda_1 \|\mathbf{A}\|_{1,2} \quad (4)$$

where k is the iteration number and in the next iteration when the estimate of $\mathbf{A}$ is available, we fix $\mathbf{A}$ and try to solve the problem for $\mathbf{E}$:

$$\tilde{\mathbf{E}}^{k+1} = \arg\min_E \left\| \mathbf{E}\mathbf{\Psi}\mathbf{A}^k - (\mathbf{Y} - \mathbf{\Phi}\mathbf{\Psi}\mathbf{A^k}) \right\|_2^2 + \lambda_2 \|\mathbf{E}\|_1 \quad (5)$$

To solve these set of equations we use the proximal gradient methods which are computationally not hard for the type of problems (4) and (5). More specifically, here we are using an accelerated version of the proximal algorithms proposed by [19, 16] which are proven to have faster convergence. Algorithm 1 shows the pseudo code of the proposed algorithm.

Data: $Y, \Phi, \lambda_1, \lambda_2, L_1, L_2$
initialization;
while *not converged* **do**

$\quad G^A = Y^A + \frac{2}{L_1}\left(\Psi(\Phi + \hat{E})^T (Y - (\Phi + \hat{E})\Psi^T Y^A)\right)$;

$\quad \hat{A} = \mathcal{P}_{L12}(G^A, \lambda_1/L_1)$;

$\quad t = \frac{1 + \sqrt{1 + 4*told^2}}{2}$;

$\quad Y^A = \hat{A} + \frac{told-1}{t}(\hat{A} - A\hat{old})$;

$\quad G^E = Y^E + \frac{2}{L_2}\left(Y - (\Phi + Y^E)(\Psi^T \hat{A})\right)(\Psi^T \hat{A})^T (I + \hat{A}\hat{A}^T)^{-1}$;

$\quad \hat{E} = \mathcal{P}_{L1}(G^E, \lambda_2/L_2)$;

$\quad Y^E = \hat{E} + \frac{told-1}{t}(\hat{E} - \hat{E}_{old})$;

$\quad \hat{E}_{old} = \hat{E}, \ \hat{A}_{old} = \hat{A}, \ t_{old} = t$;

end

Algorithm 1: Reconstruction algorithm

The proof is based on the basic convergence of the proximal gradient decent algorithms, the first term of problem (4) and (5) are differentiable and the non differentiable term (ℓ_1 and $\ell_{1,2}$) are separable in the entries of A and E. The convergence to a local minimum is also guaranteed since it always iterates towards a reduced cost for the problem (3). Moreover, simulated tests also demonstrate the convergence of the algorithms and in case of less corrupted data the local optimum is very close to the global optimum.

4. EVALUATION

4.1 Hybrid Memory Partitioning

To implement a multi-lead Compressed Sensing (CS) we have considered a window size of $N = 512$ samples for a fixed Compression Ratio (CR) of 50% and a sampling frequency of 512 Hz. The sensing matrix is constructed off-line and stored at boot time in the error-prone 6T memory portion of the TCDM and shared among all the channels. Since only the indexes of non-zero elements (d) are stored, the required space is equal to $d \cdot N$ (where $d = 16$) and the entries can be represented with a single byte. Considering our multi-core architecture, each processing element works on a separate input data-sets associated to different leads performing on the fly compression. An interrupt generated by the AFE triggers execution on the new sample, thus not requiring to store the input vectors in TCDM. The memory footprint of the CS algorithm consists of 348B for instructions and 16KB for data. The data section comprises the sensing matrix in form of a LUT (8192B), i.e. a vector of random coefficients for the CS projections, and the output buffers for the 16 leads (8KB).

Such CS algorithm analysis was used at design time to choose the appropriate memory cuts and allocate the data. The total TCDM size is assumed to be 18KB (for the data section and 256B of stack per-core), while an instruction memory of 512B (private, per-core) is chosen. The size of the sensing matrix defines the 6T memory portion: 8192B split in 16 banks leading to 512B per-bank. The remaining portion of the TCDM (10KB) is split in 16 SCMEM banks leading to 640B per-bank. Address interleaving performed by the logarithmic interconnect (Section 2) allows a contiguous logical memory map and static allocation in the two portions is easily done by means of linker script sections and compiler variable attributes.

4.2 Area Overhead (iso-size)

To evaluate the area overhead of our solution, in an *iso-size* comparison, we quantified the overhead introduced by the SCMEM memory portion in the hybrid architecture compared to a system where all memory instances are 6T (*6T-only*) and another where all instances are SCMEM (*SCMEM-only*). For the SCMEM memory cuts we considered the numbers presented in Table 1, while for the 6T memory numbers are taken from a low power 40nm technology library. Area figures for the processing elements (PEs) and the logarithmic interconnect are scaled from a 28nm RTL design. Results presented in Table 2 show the evaluation of how of each element impacts on total area.

Table 2: Area comparison (6T/SCMEM, 6T-only, SCMEM-only). Numbers presented in μm^2.

ELEMENT	6T/SCMEM	6T-ONLY	SCMEM-ONLY
PEs	323439	323439	323439
IM	132819	97960	132819
SCM TCDM	332048	-	597686
6T TCDM	195920	431968	-
TOT TCDM	527968	431968	597686
LIC 8x16	88420	88420	88420
TOTAL	1072646	941787	1142364

The extra-circuitry required for the hybrid memory consists of a basic decoder on the address line and a multiplexer on the output line. Memory area is dominated by the memory matrix itself and not by the decoder/muxes making this contribution negligible. The area overhead of the hybrid memory with respect to a 6T-only architecture is $\approx$ 13%. On the other hand, the SCMEM-only architecture incur in a higher area penalty, the overhead on the overall system would be $\approx$ 21%.

4.3 Energy Efficiency

The proposed architecture has been modeled and integrated in a SystemC-based cycle-accurate virtual platform [15] with back-annotated power numbers for the memory subsystem (Table 1) and the rest of the logic (LIC, PEs)

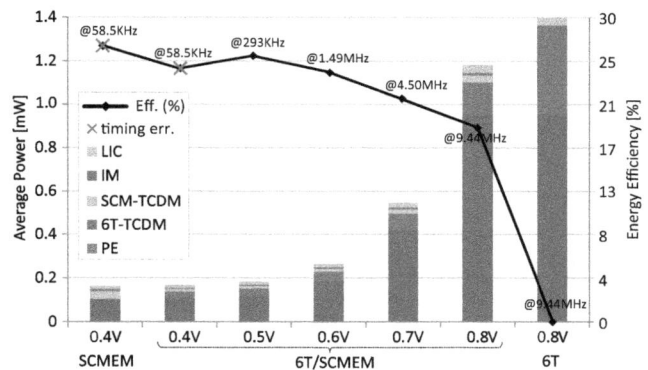

Figure 3: Average power at different operating points for architectures (6T/SCMEM, 6T-only, SCMEM-only) and Energy Efficiency (T=25°C)

extracted from a RTL-equivalent architecture with a customized OpenRISC core for minimum energy. Considering the CS application described in Section 4.1, the virtual platform shows a maximum error in timing accuracy below 6% with respect to RTL simulation. The architecture was configured with 8 cores, an 8x16 logarithmic interconnect and 6T/SCMEM portions as determined in Section 4.1. The CS algorithm, with 16 leads and 8 cores performing compression on 512 samples per window (1 sec), executes in $\approx$ 104 Kcycles.

Figure 4 shows the average power consumption, and its breakdown, during CS execution for the proposed architecture and the 6T-only and SCMEM-only reference designs. In addition the figure shows the energy efficiency (computed in a 512 samples window) at the different design corners for the different cases. The plot clearly shows that the PEs account for the majority of the power consumption and this is mainly due to the small memory size, while the IM and LIC power consumption is negligible. We can notice that the proposed hybrid architecture has a significant power saving (13%) w.r.t. 6T-only at the same voltage (0.8V) and by scaling the voltage supply the proposed architecture gains extra power saving. At 0.6V we save the 81% of power but scaling further ($<$ 0.5V) the system fails to compress the 512 samples within a window. Moreover, when compared to SCMEM-only design our architecture has similar power performance. It results that our hybrid architecture can effectively trade-off the 6T-only and SCMEM-only designs. At 0.6V our architecture has similar power saving and reconstructed quality of the SCMEM-only but with significantly less area overhead.

4.4 Reconstruction Quality

To characterize the error in the 6T memory, 10 trials of separate read/write sequences were performed varying the voltage. Measurements results are shown in Table 3 in the voltage range 400mV-750mV. The probability of er-

Table 3: Probability of bit-flip errors in the 6T memory at different voltages

Voltage [V]	P(bit-flip)	Voltage [V]	P(bit-flip)
0.40	0.0707	0.60	0.0022
0.45	0.0356	0.65	0.0007
0.50	0.0162	0.70	0.0001
0.55	0.0065	0.75	1.3e-5

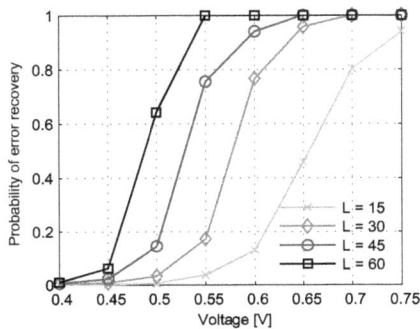

Figure 4: Probability of error recovery in reconstruction for different number of leads and voltages

rors in the whole sensing matrix then can be represented as $P = 1 - (1 - P_b)^{nb}$, where P_b is the probability of the error in each bit (Table 3) and nb represents the number of bits. For very low voltage values the number of errors can be significantly high, situation where the classic CS reconstruction algorithm fails. Figure 4 shows the results of the Reconstruction Algorithm for a simulated data averaged over 100 tests. It is clear that as the number of leads increases, the error recovery improves and more bit-flips in the sensing matrix can be recovered. This feature has major potential benefits for processing biosignals that require a larger number of leads (i.e. EEG).

To validate the performance of the proposed robust compression scheme, we use the PTB Diagnostic ECG Database, available online [20]. The database contains 549 records of 15-lead ECG from 290 subjects. Signals are sampled at 1 KHz with 16-bit resolution. Here we have down-sampled the signals to 512 Hz to be consistent with our system requirements. To quantify the compression performance while assessing the diagnostic quality of the compressed records, we consider the Signal to Noise Ratio (SNR) defined as $SNR = 20 \log_{10} \|\mathbf{x}\|_2 / \|\mathbf{x} - \tilde{\mathbf{x}}\|_2$. Figure 5 shows the average SNR for the Robust CS over different memory voltages. The results are all for 50% compression ration (i.e. $M = N/2$).

To clearly demonstrate the quality of the reconstructed signal, two windows of 1 second for 0.6V and 0.7V are shown in Figure 5 (right). The results show that even for low voltage (0.6V) the algorithm is still able to converge to the solution while the normal CS would fail.

5. CONCLUSIONS

In this work we present a 6T/SCMEM hybrid memory multi-core architecture for biosignal processing. Classic 6T memories face reliability issues when reducing supply volt-

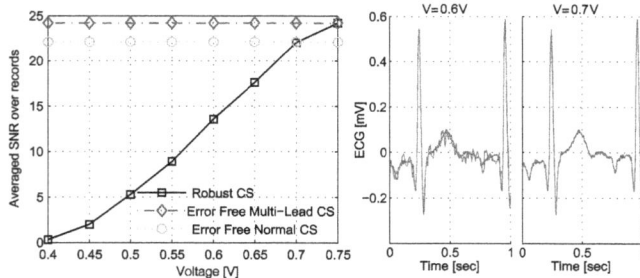

Figure 5: Average SNR for robust CS at different voltages (left). Reconstructed signal quality at 0.6V and 0.7V (right).

age to threshold. By partitioning the compressed sensing data structures in the hybrid memory, combined with a novel reconstruction algorithm, we can tolerate bit-flips in 6T memory trading-off reconstruction quality for energy savings. Our solution offers significant improvements in power ($\approx 60\%$, -2.5dB @ 0.7V) with a low ($\approx 13\%$) area overhead.

Acknowledgments

Work supported by the EU project PHIDIAS (g.a. 318013).

6. REFERENCES

[1] http://www.who.int/mediacentre/factsheets/fs317/en.
[2] Ashouei, M. et al., "A voltage-scalable biomedical signal processor running ECG using 13pJ/cycle at 1MHz and 0.4 V", ISSCC, 2011.
[3] Rooseleer, B. and Wim D., "A 40 nm, 454MHz 114 fJ/bit area-efficient SRAM memory with integrated charge pump", ESSCIRC, 2013.
[4] Sharma, V. et al. "8T SRAM with mimicked negative bit-lines and charge limited sequential sense amplifier for wireless sensor nodes", ESSCIRC, 2011.
[5] Verma, N., and A. P. Chandrakasan, "A 256 kb 65 nm 8T subthreshold SRAM employing sense-amplifier redundancy", Solid-State Circuits, IEEE Journal of 43.1 (2008): 141-149.
[6] Andersson, O. et al., "Dual-VT 4kb sub-VT memories with < 1pW/bit leakage in 65 nm CMOS", ESSCIRC, 2013.
[7] Mamaghanian, H. et al., "Compressed sensing for real-time energy-efficient ECG compression on wireless body sensor nodes", IEEE Transactions Biomedical Engineering, vol. 58, no.9 pp. 2456–2466, 2011.
[8] Dreslinkski, R. G., et al., "An energy efficient parallel architecture using near threshold operation", PACT, 2007.
[9] Gemmeke, T. et al., "Resolving the Memory Bottleneck for Single Supply Near-Threshold Computing", DATE, 2014.
[10] Dogan A.Y. et al., "Multi-core architecture design for ultra-low-power wearable health monitoring systems", DATE, 2012.
[11] Calhoun, B. H. et al., "Analyzing static noise margin for sub-threshold SRAM in 65nm CMOS", ESSCIRC, 2005.
[12] Chang I.J. et al., "A Priority-Based 6T/8T Hybrid SRAM Architecture for Aggressive Voltage Scaling in Video Applications", IEEE transactions on circuits and systems for video technology, vol. 21, no. 2, Feb 2011.
[13] Bortolotti D. et al., "Hybrid memory architecture for voltage scaling in ultra-low power multi-core biomedical processors", DATE, 2014.
[14] Gupta, V. et al., "IMPACT: imprecise adders for low-power approximate computing", ISLPED, 2011.
[15] Bortolotti D. et al., "VirtualSoC: a Full-System SimulationEnvironment for Massively Parallel Heterogeneous System-on-Chip", IPDPWS, 2013.
[16] Beck A. and Teboulle M., "Fast iterative shrinkage-thresholding algorithm with application to wavelet-based image deblurring", ICASSP, 2009.
[17] Candes E. et al., "Stable signal recovery from incomplete and inaccurate measurements", Communications on Pure and Applied Mathematics, 59:pages 1207–1223, 2006.
[18] Chandar V., "A negative result concerning explicit matrices with the restricted isometry property", Tech. report, 2008.
[19] Nesterov, Y. "A method of solving a convex programming problem with convergence rate O(1/k2)", Soviet Mathematics Doklady. Vol. 27. No. 2. 1983.
[20] Goldberger A. L. et al., "Physiobank, physiotoolkit, and physionet components of a new research resource for complex physiologic signals", Circulation,101(23):pp. 215–220, 2000.
[21] Mamaghanian H. et al., "Power-efficient joint compressed sensing of multi-lead ecg signals", ICASSP, 2014.
[22] Kowalski M. et al., "Sparsity and persistence: mixed norms provide simple signal models with dependent coefficients", Signal, Image and Video Processing, 3(3):pages 251–264, 2009.
[23] Lin Z. et al., "The augmented lagrange multiplier method for exact recovery of corrupted low-rank matrices", arXiv preprint arXiv:1009.5055, 2010.
[24] Zhu, H. et al., "Sparsity-cognizant total least-squares for perturbed compressive sampling", Signal Processing, IEEE Transactions on 59, no 5 (2011): pp. 2002–2016.

An On-Chip Autonomous Thermoelectric Energy Management System for Energy-Efficient Active Cooling

Borislav Alexandrov, Khondker Z. Ahmed, and Saibal Mukhopadhyay
Georgia Institute of Technology
Atlanta, GA USA
{balexandrov3, kahmed8}@gatech.edu, {saibal}@ece.gatech.edu

ABSTRACT

This paper presents an on-chip thermoelectric (TE) energy management system for energy-efficient on-demand active cooling of integrated circuits. Embedding a TE module (TEM) within the package has shown potential for on-demand cooling of integrated circuits (ICs); however, the additional cooling energy limits the effectiveness of TE coolers (TEC). The proposed on-chip system monitors the IC temperature and provides cooling during critical thermal events by operating the TEM in the Peltier mode. During normal operation, the TEM is operated in the Seebeck mode to harvest the otherwise wasted heat energy generated by the IC and reduce the net cooling energy. A boost regulator harvests energy in an output capacitor and a programmable current source controls the cooling. The design is implemented in a 130nm CMOS test-chip, and tested with an external thermoelectric device.

Keywords

Thermoelectric Cooling (TEC), Energy Harvesting, Boost Regulator, Programmable current source, Energy Efficiency

1. INTRODUCTION

High power dissipation in integrated circuits, ranging from mobile to high performance processors as well as RF devices, has pushed the limits of today's cooling solutions. Thermal hotspots in particular, have emerged as a major concern for current ICs [1]. The dynamic nature of the power profile, which results in spatiotemporal variation in the on-chip temperature, further exacerbates the cooling challenge. To address the challenge of time-varying hotspots, on-demand active cooling using embedded thermoelectric modules (TEM) has received significant attention [2]. In on-demand active cooling, a finite current is passed through the TEM to provide Peltier cooling and reduce the chip temperature. Active cooling is also a great candidate for mobile devices, where space is a major constraint, and alternative advanced cooling methods are not feasible. The integration of Bi_2Te_3 based thin-film TECs within a microprocessor package has been experimentally demonstrated [3]. The experimental demonstration of embedded TECs has motivated system level studies for TEC based thermal management.

A major concern for TEC based on-demand cooling is the need for additional energy, as processors experience dynamic variations in power dissipation during operation (Fig. 1). The TEC assisted

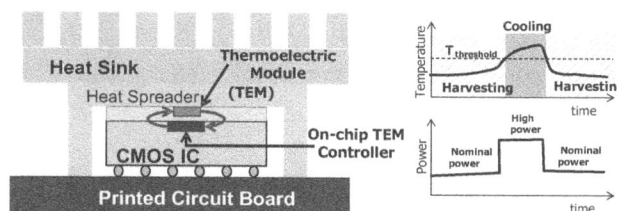

Figure 1. Overview of an embedded TEM and autonomous mode switching in a TEM.

cooling is necessary only during thermally critical high power modes, while the TECs are normally turned off during nominal power modes. The finite heat flux generated during the nominal power modes is wasted as the heat energy is dumped in the environment. It is intriguing to note that this heat flux flows through the TEM and can be harvested to generate electrical energy by operating the TEM in the Seebeck mode (TE generator). The switching of the TEM to the TEG mode allows a part of the otherwise wasted heat energy to be reclaimed and stored. The stored energy can be used to provide cooling during the intermittent high power modes.

This paper explores the implementation of an energy efficient system that uses the same thermoelectric module for cooling a silicon chip's substrate as well as harvesting energy during nominal power modes. This paper, for the first time, presents a fully integrated on-chip system for energy-efficient on-demand active cooling using dynamic mode switching of a single TEM. The proposed system includes a high-efficiency boost regulator encompassing low power design techniques to harvest heat energy and store it in an off-chip capacitor. This capacitor's stored energy is then used to power a constant current source when cooling is required. The current source can deliver the desired current over a wide range of supply voltage. The current source can be programmed digitally to change the cooling current and hence, degree of the achievable cooling. Once the capacitor energy is exhausted, the system automatically switches to powering the cooling from the chip's supply voltage. A comparator and switch matrix control the mode switching of the TEM. A test-chip of the proposed system is designed in 130nm CMOS. The measurement of the test-chip demonstrates the system functionality. The test-chip is tested with a commercial TEM to demonstrate the dynamic mode switching and simultaneous cooling and energy harvesting.

2. RELATED WORK

Much research has been done in the area of using thermoelectrics for chip cooling and energy harvesting. Materials have been investigated recently and thin-film based Bi_2Te_3 super-lattices have been developed to significantly increase the figure of merit of the thermoelectric devices and increase their efficiency. These devices have also been experimentally embedded within a microprocessor package and heat sink solution [2], [3]. This

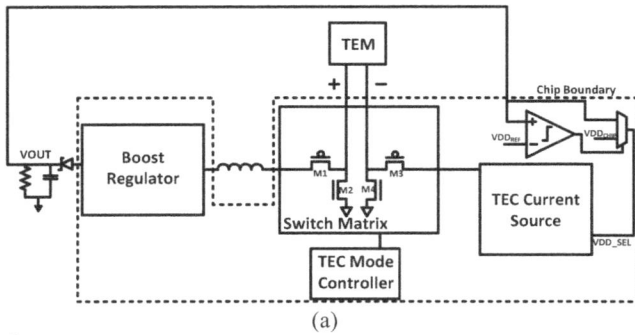

(a)

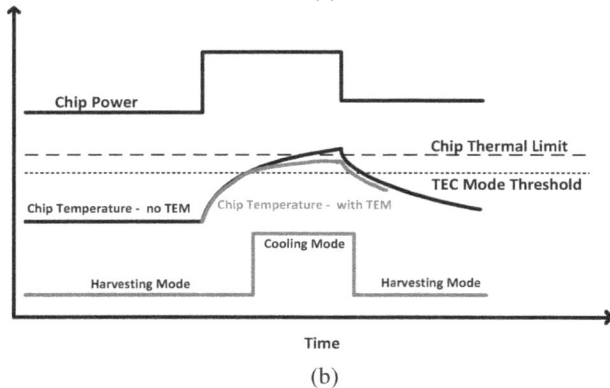

(b)

Figure 2. Overview of the proposed integrated TEM control: (a) schematic of the overall system and (b) system operation.

integration has shown both steady-state as well as transient cooling.

System level analysis has also been explored for efficiently using the TEM within a system. Long et al. have investigated algorithms for optimal placement of TECs in a chip to maximize cooling efficiency when the TEC is active in steady-state [4], [5]. Chaparro et al. have performed system level architectural studies to understand the effect of TEC integration for power overhead and execution time [6]. Alexandrov et al. have explored this further, considering the transient cooling effects in integrated TEC systems and have developed control principles for taking advantage of transient cooling effects [7], [8]. However, the experimental demonstration of an on-chip TEC controller with programmable current source is not reported in the literature.

The concept of using a TEM to harvest wasted heat energy has been proposed and studied in prior work [9]. The dynamic mode switching of a TEM for energy harvesting and cooling has first been discussed by Yang et. al in [10] and the performance benefits and implications have been discussed by Choday et. al in [11]. A high-level control system and board level implementation for dynamic mode switching of TEM is presented by Parthasarathy et. al [12]. However, a board-level controller only shows the feasibility of dynamic mode switching, and does not provide a fully integrated low-power solution. The fully integrated solution is necessary to reduce the system volume. Moreover response time in the order of milliseconds is necessary for chip level embedded cooling, which is difficult to achieve in a board level implementation. This paper is the first to propose a controller for autonomous energy harvesting and cooling that is fully integrated on chip, to meet the volume, performance, and power requirements of chip-scale cooling. Our system demonstrates a boost regulator, a programmable cooling current source, and an autonomous TEM controller, all integrated within the same chip. The system is demonstrated in 130nm CMOS.

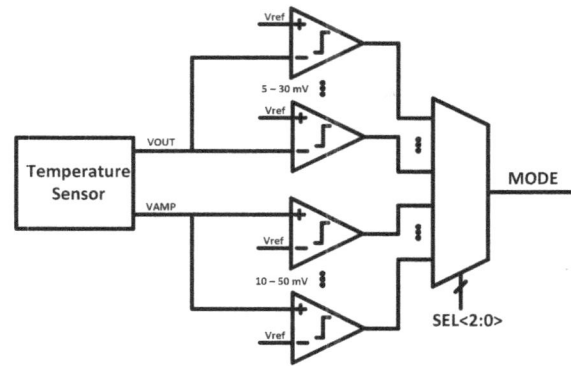

Figure 3. Top level design of the TEC Mode Controller. The MODE signal drives the switch matrix.

3. SYSTEM LEVEL OVERVIEW

Figure 2(a) shows the top level system. The boost regulator boosts the voltage generated by the TEM and dumps charge in an output capacitor. This is called the harvesting mode. Harvesting is active at all times during which the silicon temperature is below a specified user reference, and the TEM operates in the Thermoelectric Generation (TEG) mode. The mode switching is done using a switch matrix, which is responsible for connecting the TEM terminals in the appropriate fashion. When the TEM's negative terminal is grounded and the positive terminal is connected to the inductor, the TEM operates in the harvesting mode by the Seebeck effect. In order to harvest energy, we must connect the positive TEM terminal to the inductor and the negative terminal to ground, so we turn transistors M1 and M4 on, while keeping M2 and M3 off. In the cooling mode, current is forced into the negative terminal of the TEM, making it operate in the Peltier mode and dumping heat from the hot to the cold side of the TEM. Our system does this by turning switches M2 and M3 on and turning M1 and M4 off. The switching logic is implemented in the TEC mode controller and is discussed in the following section.

The system always operates in either the cooling or harvesting mode. During low power events, when the temperature of the silicon is not high, the system will stay in the harvesting mode and dump energy to the output capacitor. This energy is stored in the output capacitor and can be used to power the TEC controller. Once the capacitor gets charged and the voltage reaches the regulation point of the boost regulator, no more energy can be harvested by the TEM. Although this is an issue for long-term operation, a battery charger could be implemented in mobile systems to recharge a battery, while high performance systems can power their local supplies from the output capacitor and run portions of the chip.

Figure 2(b) illustrates the proposed system's behavior in the time domain. When the chip power is low and the chip temperature is low, we operate in harvesting mode. If a high power event occurs in the system, such as a high-power application running, the chip temperature would begin to rise and could go above the thermal limit of the chip and package. With a TEM within the system, once a pre-defined threshold is reached, we can put the system into the cooling mode, reducing the temperature on the chip below the thermal limit and completing the high-power workload. It is important to note that if the chip power is very high or the TEC current is not large enough, we might not be able to avoid the thermal limit with only the use of the TEC, and might require throttling, thread migration, or a more powerful cooling solution.

4. CIRCUIT DESIGN

4.1 TEC Mode Controller

The TEC Mode Controller is responsible for sensing temperature, and making a decision for what mode the system should operate in, TEC or TEG. The goal of the controller is to reduce the temperature of the silicon chip and avoid the thermal limit of the package, while harvesting maximum energy. For the simplicity of design, the controller senses when the temperature crosses an externally adjustable threshold, and turns the TEC on by pushing a constant current through it. If the chip temperature is below the reference we operate in the TEG mode. Figure 3 shows the top level structure of the mode controller. We have a central temperature sensor that generates 2 analog output representations of temperature. The temperature sensor is implemented on chip using a lateral BJT with a constant current being pushed into the BJT, generating a voltage that varies with temperature, VOUT. The output has inverse temperature dependence and only varies by about 2 mV/°C, which is fairly small. We have therefore added another amplification stage on chip in order to boost this to about 4 mV/ °C in order to avoid false triggering of the comparators. This is the VAMP output as shown in figure 3.

A bank of hysteretic comparators, with an externally selectable hysteresis window, is used as the decision engine. We use a 3-bit off-chip select signal for the comparators, with 4 comparators set for each of the temperature outputs. It is important to note that the hysteresis is added to avoid unnecessary mode switching of the comparator when the temperature is hovering near the reference. If the temperature crosses the reference, the comparator trips and the digital signal turns the current source on, pushing current through the TEC off-chip. By changing the hysteresis we effectively change the temperature reduction before the comparator switches again and puts the system in the harvesting mode. The digital outputs of the comparator are then fed to a mux that has externally controlled selection, and the output of the mux is buffered to drive the switch matrix. As stated earlier, M2 and M3 are turned on during TEC mode. Figure 4 shows the design of the current source. We use feedback and sense a portion of the output current, divide it down 100X and compare it to the reference current set to make sure that if the source voltage of the output transistor moves, so does the drain in order to keep the

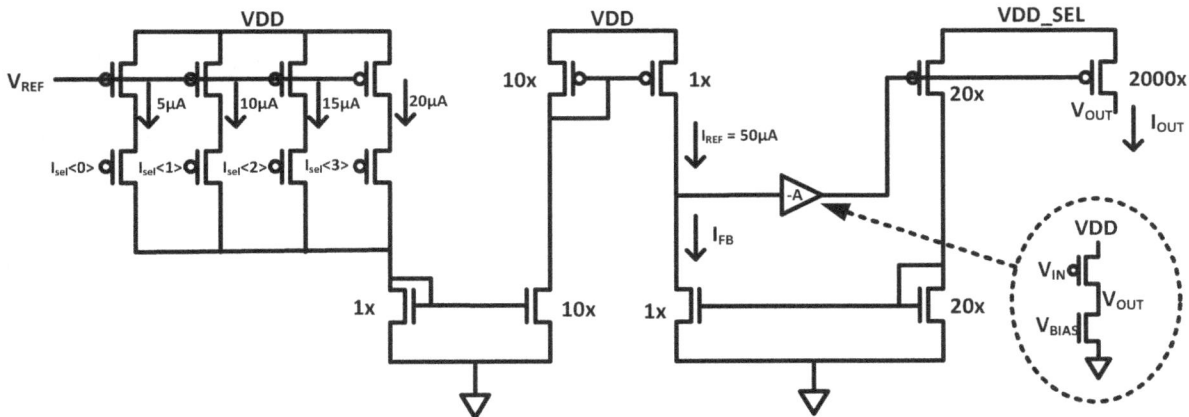

Figure 5. Top Level Diagram of PFM Boost Regulator.

current steady. With the I_{SEL} external signal, we can program the reference current from 0-50µA and hence the output current from 10-100mA. Using this feedback approach, the constant current can be maintained across a 10Ω load from 3.3V all the way down to 1.5V, before the feedback cannot respond further. This represents the discharging voltage in output capacitor. Once the output capacitor is discharged to the point when the current source fails, we switch VDD_SEL using a comparator and analog selector, from the output capacitor to the chip supply voltage. With lower loads, i.e. smaller TEC, we can maintain the current levels down to even lower voltages. This means that we can discharge more stored energy from the output capacitor, achieving higher energy efficiency.

4.2 Boost Regulator

The test chip also includes an integrated Pulsed Frequency Modulation (PFM) boost regulator to boost the low input voltages that the TEM generates in idle power modes to a high voltage for storage to a capacitor. Figure 5 shows the functional block diagram of the boost regulator. The V_{FB} signal monitors the output voltage and uses a hysteretic comparator to compare it with an internally generated reference. The output of the comparator is low when V_{FB} is higher than V_{REF}, meaning that the output is above the regulation point. This means that the oscillator and current limit comparator are both turned off and the output will discharge by the load condition. Once V_{FB} discharges beyond the reference point, the comparator will flip and enable the oscillator

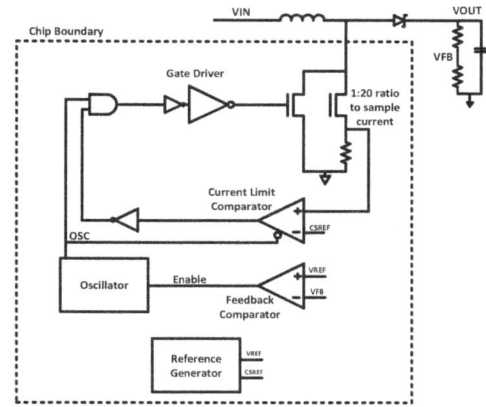

Figure 4. The TEC Current source. Isel<3:0> sets the output current externally, and the feedback ensures constant current even with VDD_SEL reducing (output capacitor being discharged).

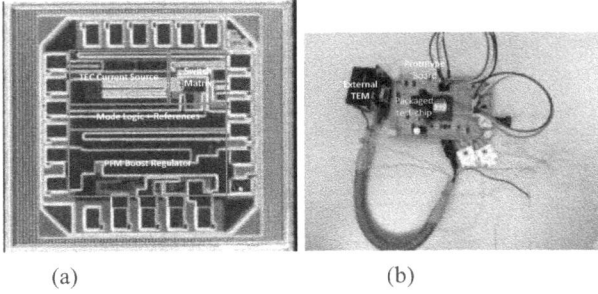

(a)   (b)

Figure 6. (a) Die photo of 1mmX1mm test chip and (b) prototype board and external TEM module used.

and turn the NFET switch on. This will cause the inductor current to build up linearly while the output continues to discharge and the current buildup can be stopped by the current limit comparator or the end of the oscillator pulse, whichever occurs first. When the peak current is reached, the NFET turns off, and the inductor currents discharges to the load, increasing V_{OUT}. Once the inductor current goes to zero the load will start discharging again, causing the process to restart. If the output load is very large, the output voltage might not increase above the hysteresis and the oscillator will not turn off and continue to pulse. Because the oscillator has a very large duty cycle (98% on time), multiple pulses will continue to build up the current and cause the output to slowly charge up and flip the comparator, restarting the process described above. This allows for our booster to service various loads and provide a high conversion ratio.

Table 1. Test chip summary and measurement conditions

Technology	130nm CMOS
Die Size/System Area	1 mm^2/0.49mm^2
Maximum TEC Current	105 mA
Maximum Booster Output	3.3 V
Logic VDD	1.2 V
Total Chip Power Dissipation	5.6 mW
Total VDD Power	0.62 mW
TEC Controller Power	4.98 mW
TEC Current Source Start-up	3.785 ms
TEM	Laird Tech EV56
Maximum TEM Heat Flux	150 W/cm^2
TEM Electrical Resistance	10 Ω
Inductor (External)	100 μH
Output Capacitor	1 mF

5. TEST CHIP IMPLEMENTATION

The proposed design is implemented in a 130nm CMOS process. The chip die photo is shown in figure 6. The chip has a total die area of 1mmX1mm with the boost regulator placed at the bottom of the chip and the cooling mode circuitry and decision making circuits in the top left and middle of the chip. The switch matrix is at the top right of the chip and uses large transistors to reduce the losses across the "on" resistance of the switches. Because a TEM cannot be directly integrated into the packaging solutions of this test chip, we have characterized our system with an external TEM solution. We use the EV56 TEM Evaluation kit from Laird Technologies (formerly Nextreme) [13]. This TEM has an internal resistance of about 10Ω and a heater and heat sink solution. The heater can apply heat fluxes up to 150W/cm^2 to the hot side of the TEM while the fan cools the cold side to generate large ΔT. There are 2 thermocouples to monitor the temperature of both the hot and cold side of the TEM. Although the thermal response of the external system is much slower than an integrated device will be,

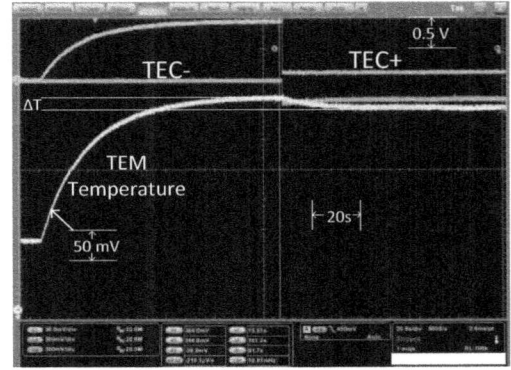

Figure 7. Temperature Characteristics of test chip and external TEM. We observe a ΔT of about 5°C.

the functionality of the energy management solution is presented and with a measured response time less than 4ms for the TEC current, is an ideal candidate for integrated TEM materials. With the ability to function with a 3mmX3mm external TEM, this energy management solution can be integrated under the TEM with about a 10% area overhead on chip. Scaling it down to lower technology nodes can lead to even greater area reductions.

5.1 TEC Mode Controller

The TEC Mode Controller has been fully characterized and tested using the external TEM. We connect the thermocouple leads to an external instrumentation amplifier (AD8495) [14], in order to read the temperature with accuracy of 0.1°C at 5mV/ °C. This ensures an accurate and low noise temperature measurement. We apply a high heat flux to the heater and TEM, 50 W/cm^2 and monitor the temperature at the hot side. We connect the TEM to the test chip and force it in the TEG mode initially using the external voltage (temperature) reference. Figure 7 shows the response of the TEM module. The temperature rises initially as shown by the yellow line in the scope capture. This is the voltage output of the AD8595 amplifier and has an output of 5mV/°C so we see the temperature increases from 25°C to about 75°C. Once the temperature reaches that level, we force the mode controller into the TEC mode using the reference and turn the TEC current source on with a current of 57mA. We observe a reduction of the hot side temperature of the TEM (equivalently the chip temperature in the package integrated TEM). This results in a steady state temperature reduction of about 5°C, a significant reduction. This result illustrates the concept of using the TEC for temperature reduction of the chip, and avoiding the package temperature limit. The blue and green lines show the positive and negative terminals of the TEC respectively.

The current levels of the TEC Current source can be programmed digitally with the external 4-bit I_{SEL} signal as described in section 4.1. The measured test chip can successfully source anywhere from 17-105mA, matching closely with the simulated design. This allows the chip to be programmed depending on the TEC solution that is attached. With larger TECs we require a larger current to achieve a higher ΔT, but smaller form factor TEMs such as ones to be integrated into mobile devices will require a lower current through the TEC for optimal cooling. This allows for our solution to be used with different sizes of TEM materials.

Figure 8 shows the maximum attainable ΔT at the hot side for given TEC currents and heat fluxes. We see that up to 105mA the TEM is able to reduce the temperature of the hot side, meaning that for this TEC we prefer to always run maximum current. It is

54

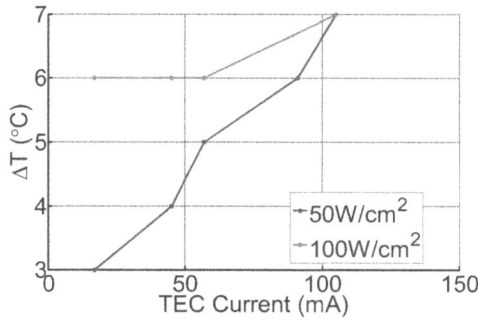

Figure 8. Steady-state temperature reduction for various cooling current levels from the programmable current source.

important to note that with smaller form factor TECs the optimal current can change to a lower value, and our chip can have the current source externally programmed for maximum performance. We also observe that we get a larger ΔT for higher heat fluxes, but it is important to note with $100W/cm^2$ applied, the initial temperature before turning the TEC on was $108°C$, which might is above the thermal limit for many systems. In the $50W/cm^2$ case the initial temperature before the TEC was turned on was $76°C$, making the 7 °C ΔT more effective from a fraction of the initial temperature standpoint.

We also consider the event of the TEC turning on at a pre-defined temperature. Previous work in the literature has investigated this method in order to extend the workload time before a thermal limit [7]. Figure 9 shows the chip and system coupled performance with this method. We turn the TEC on with 57mA at a threshold temperature and observe an immediate cooling effect. We see that the rate of increase in the temperature is decreased and the chip will reach the steady state temperature later. This time allows a chip to complete the workload before having to throttle down.

Lastly it is critical to note the power dissipation of the controller, as well as the time it takes to start-up the current source. Because the controller is based on mostly analog circuits, the major power consumption comes from the biasing networks, and the switching power of the switch matrix transistors. The average power dissipation of the controller, excluding the actual current flowing through the TEC, is 4.98mW. This fairly significant power is due to the feedback network in the current source as noted in section 4.1. Since we need to sample a portion of the output current in order to adjust the voltage, we have to always dissipate a significant biasing current in the current source. We sample 1/100

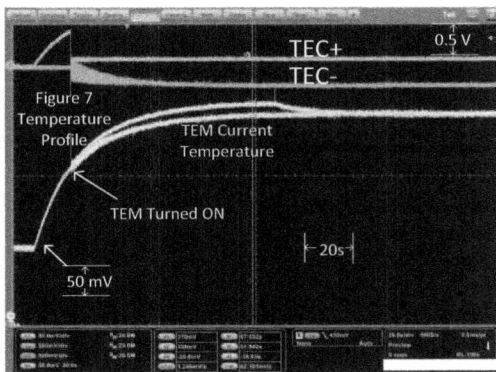

Figure 9. TEC effect on temperature with pre-defined threshold

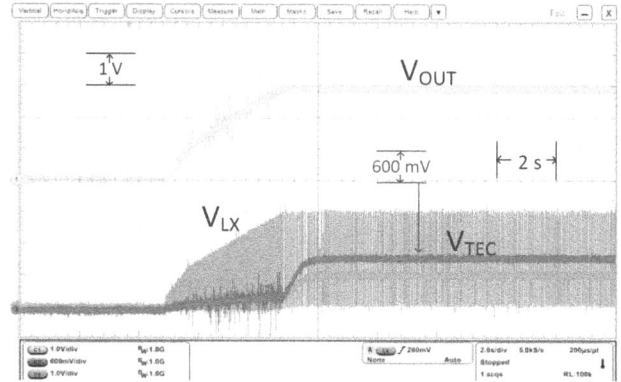

Figure 10. Start-up of PFM boost regulator. The output is regulated at 3V with a 1mF output capacitor

of the output current, as anything smaller than this leads to large errors in current due to process variation. Despite this, the power is a small portion of the total cooling power required by the system, 346 mW with the maximum current programmed. In addition to the power dissipation it is important to consider the start-up time of the current source, once the decision is made. The TEC current source had a measured start-up time of 3.785ms. With the external system that has cooling times on the order of 10's of seconds this is insignificant, and even with an integrated system, where the cooling time scales are on the order of 100s of ms this controller still responds very quickly.

5.2 Boost Regulator (TEG) Mode

The on-chip asynchronous boost regulator has also been characterized for functionality, speed, and efficiency. Figure 10 shows a scope capture showing the functionality of the booster. We use the Nextreme kit again and apply a heat flux to the TEM to generate a voltage across it. We connect the switch matrix in the booster mode which connects the positive TEM terminal to the inductor. As we can see the output voltage (yellow line) begins to rise in a linear fashion as it is heavily loaded (1mF output capacitor) and the oscillator is operating at the highest switching frequency, measured experimentally to be 93.9kHz. The large output capacitor is used in order to be able to store sufficient energy for cooling. The green curve shows the inductor node that connects to the on-chip FET. As we can see there is continuous switching at the node with the voltage steadily rising. The purple curve is showing the positive TEM terminal voltage. As we can see, initially the TEM is loaded by a large inductor current and hence the voltage is effectively reduced due to the load resistance as well as trace and inductor resistances. As the output builds up

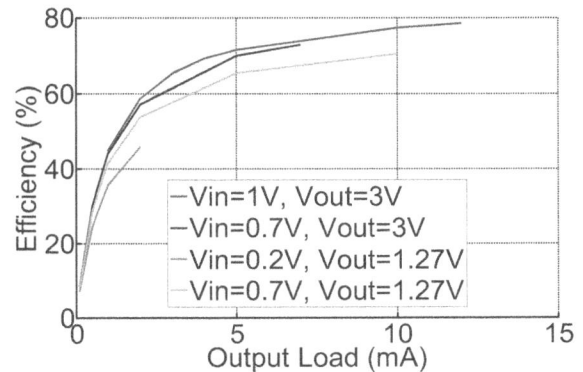

Figure 11. Efficiency characteristics of boost regulator.

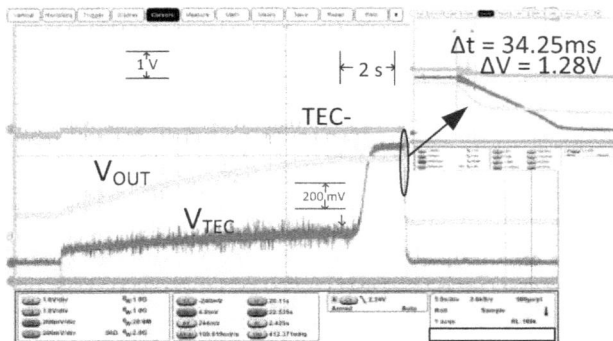

Figure 12. Switching response of full system. The system harvests energy and regulates the output to 3V, before the TEC is turned on the output is used to supply the constant TEC current. This lasts for 34ms when the current source switches to the chip VDD to source the current.

and the current drawn reduces, the voltage begins to steadily rise. Once the regulation point is reached the input voltage settles as the loading decreases, and the switching at the inductor node is also reduced. Since the output voltage is quite high, we are still operating near the maximum switching frequency of the oscillator to keep the output regulated at 3V. We have also characterized the efficiency of the booster considering a DC load. As we can see in figure 11 the maximum efficiency of the booster is near 80% at higher output loads. As the load decreases so does the efficiency.

5.3 Full System Characterization

The full system has also been characterized with the external TEM. Figure 12 shows the scope capture of the integrated system. The yellow line is the output voltage and the purple is the input to the boost regulator. As we can see we turn the system on in the TEG mode and begin harvesting energy into the output. As stated in the previous section, the system takes time to boost up as the input voltage is around 900mV (ΔT of about 30°C) and the output capacitor is 1mF. Once the system has the output regulated, we force the controller into the TEC mode and we force the TEC mode controller's current source to be powered by the output voltage directly. We can see that the output voltage is quickly discharged by the large current that the TEC requires to cool. As we see from the inset scope capture the discharge is linear, meaning that the current source works despite the reduction in output voltage, and sources a constant current, 37mA as programmed in this case. Before the output is fully discharged, a VDD selection comparator flips and the TEC current continues to be sourced from the chip's supply, continuing the cooling operation. The current can be fully sourced from the output capacitor for about 35ms, a time that is quite significant at microprocessor time scales. As the system is fully functional with an external TEM, this low overhead design can be integrated in a chip with an integrated TEM in the package.

6. SUMMARY

We have presented the design of an autonomous system that is able to use a single TEM for cooling as well as harvesting energy. Our system is able to harvest energy and store it in an output capacitor, and when cooling is required draw energy from the output capacitor. This system only takes up $0.49mm^2$ in 130nm CMOS, consumes ~5mW of power (excluding cooling power), and can start-up the cooling operation in ~4ms. The system is suitable for chip-scale on-demand cooling. The small area and moderate power make the design suitable for integration in high-

performance microprocessors. The integration of the proposed system in microprocessor packages with embedded thermoelectric modules can improve the energy-efficiency of on-demand active cooling. The future design needs to reduce the minimum input voltage for the successful start-up of the booster to allow harvesting from even lower chip power. The response time of the booster needs to be improved as well. The future research in this direction needs to consider demonstration of integrated TEM with the test-chip (instead of external TEM), and the co-design of integrated TEM control and processor architecture to better exploit the energy-efficient on-demand cooling.

7. ACKNOWLEDGMENTS

This material is based on work supported by the National Science Foundation (Grant# ECCS-1028569).

8. REFERENCES

[1] A. Watwe, et. al, "Thermal Implications of Non-uniform Die Power Map and CPU Performance," *Proceedings of InterPACK'03*, 2003.

[2] R. Venkatasubramanian et. al, "Thin-Film Thermoelectric Devices With High Room-Temperature Figures of Merit," *Nature*, 2001.

[3] I. Chowdhury et. al, "On-chip cooling by superlattice-based thin-film thermoelectrics," *Nature Nanotechnology*, 2009

[4] J. Long, et. al. "A framework for optimizing thermoelectric active cooling systems," *DAC*, 2010.

[5] J. Long. et. al, "Optimization of an on-chip active cooling system based on thin-film thermoelectric coolers," *DATE* 2010.

[6] P. Chaparro et.al, "Dynamic thermal management using thin-film thermoelectric cooling," *Proceedings of the 14th ACM/IEEE international symposium on Low power electronics and design (ISLPED)*, 2009.

[7] B. Alexandrov, et.al, "Prospects of active cooling with integrated super-lattice based thin-film thermoelectric devices for mitigating hotspot challenges in microprocessors," *ASP-DAC*, 2012.

[8] B. Alexandrov, et. al, "Control Principles and On-chip Circuits for Active Cooling using Integrated Super Lattice Based Thin-Film Thermoelectric Devices", *IEEE TVLSI*, Online:http://ieeexplore.ieee.org/xpls/abs_all.jsp?arnumber= 6595140&tag=1.

[9] S. H. Choday, et. al, "On-chip energy harvesting using thin-film thermoelectric materials," *IEEE SEMI-THERM*, 2013.

[10] Y. Wang, et al. US Patent No. 20120096871, "Dynamic switching Thermoelectric Thermal management systems and methods", 2012.

[11] S. H. Choday, et. al., "Prospects of Thin-Film Thermoelectric Devices for Hot-Spot Cooling and On-Chip Energy Harvesting," Components, *IEEE Transactions on Packaging and Manufacturing Technology (CPMT)*, Dec. 2013.

[12] S. Parthasarathy, et. al, "Enetgy Efficient Active Cooling of Integrated Circuits Using Autonomous Peltier/Seebeck Mode Switching of a Thermoelectric Module," *IEEE SEMI-THERM*, 2014.

[13] Laird Tech EV56 datasheet, http://lairdtech.thomasnet.com/item/thermoelectric-modules-2/etec-series/hv56-72-f2-0203-gg

[14] Analog Devices 8495 datasheet, http://www.analog.com/en/mems-sensors/digital-temperature-sensors/ad8495/products/product.html

Tunnel FET-Based Ultra-Low Power, Low-Noise Amplifier Design for Bio-signal Acquisition

[1]Huichu Liu
[4]Suman Datta
[1,4]Electrical Engineering Dept.,
Pennsylvania State University, PA,
16802, USA
[1]hxl249@psu.edu,
[4]sdatta@engr.psu.edu

[2]Mahsa Shoaran
[5]Alexandre Schmid
[2,5]Swiss Federal Institute of
Technology (EPFL), Lausanne 1015,
Switzerland
{[2]mahsa.shoaran,
[5]alexandre.schmid} @epfl.ch

[3]Xueqing Li
[6]Vijaykrishnan Narayanan
[3,6]Computer Science and Engineering
Dept., Pennsylvania State University,
PA, 16802, USA
{[3]lixueq,[6]vijay} @cse.psu.edu

ABSTRACT

Ultra-low power circuit design techniques have enabled rapid progress in biosignal acquisition. The design of a multi-channel biosignal recording system is a challenging task, considering the low amplitude of neural signals and limited power budget for an implantable system. The front-end low-noise amplifier is a critical component with respect to overall power consumption and noise of such system. In this paper, we present a new design of III-V Heterojunction TFET (HTFET)-based neural amplifier employing a telescopic operational transconductance amplifier (OTA) for multi-channel neural spike recording. Exploiting the unique device characteristics of HTFETs, our simulation shows that the proposed amplifier exhibits a midband gain of 39 dB, a gain bandwidth of 12 Hz-2.1 kHz, and an input-referred noise of 6.27 µVrms, consuming 5 nW of power at a 0.5 V supply voltage. Using the proposed HTFET amplifier, a noise efficiency factor (NEF) of 0.64 is achieved, which is significantly lower than the CMOS-based theoretical limit. Design tradeoffs related to gain, power and noise requirements are investigated, based on a comprehensive electrical noise model of HTFET and compared with the baseline Si FinFET design.

Categories and Subject Descriptors

B.7.1 [**Integrated Circuits**]: Type and Design Styles – *advanced technologies*. B.8.0 [**Performance and Reliability**]: General.

Keywords

Biomedical signal processing, Low-noise amplifier, Neural signal recording, Steep subthreshold slope, Tunnel FETs, Ultra-low power analog design.

1. INTRODUCTION

Technology advancements in micro electromechanical (MEMS) and ultra-low power, low-noise circuit designs have led to rapid progress in biosignal acquisition platforms [1-3]. With the ongoing efforts towards lightweight, miniaturized and power efficient neural recording interfaces, the potential application fields extend to various clinical domains such as diagnosis and treatment of neurological disorders including stroke, Parkinson's disease and epilepsy [4-9]. Fig. 1 illustrates a block diagram of a neural signal

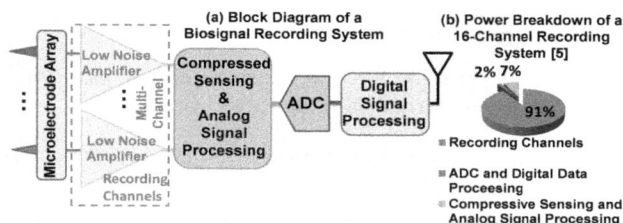

Figure 1. (a) A block diagram of a multi-channel biosignal acquisition system and (b) its power breakdown. [5]

recording system [5]. It is composed of an electrode array for multichannel signal acquisition, an analog front-end for signal conditioning, a data processing unit for reducing the data rate of the following transmitter unit. Biosignals associated with neural activities are classified into different categories, based on their characteristics such as amplitude, bandwidth (*BW*), spatial resolution and invasiveness of the electrodes [3, 6]: electroencephalographic (EEG) (amplitude: 10~20 µV, BW < 100 Hz), electrocorticographic (ECoG) (amplitude < 100 µV, BW: 0.5~200 Hz), local field potential (LFP) (amplitude < 5 mV, BW < 1 Hz), extracellular action potential or neural spikes (amplitude < 500 µV, BW: 100 Hz~7 kHz), etc. Thus, the design objectives of biosignal acquisition systems strongly depend on the application. In general, due to the microvolt range of the neural signals and the stringent heat dissipation limit of implantable devices (< 1 °C temperature increase to avoid tissue damage) [1, 3], the system power consumption should be sufficiently low while minimizing the device area for implantation purpose.

A critical building block in a biosignal acquisition microsystem is the front-end low-noise amplifier. For spike acquisition, an input-referred noise of < 10 µVrms (lower than the background noise) and a power dissipation of < 10 µW/channel are generally required [1-9]. The large dc offsets at the issue-electrode interface should be rejected and the pass band should cover a range from hundreds of hertz to several kilohertz, while providing a high input impedance (~MΩ) to prevent the signal attenuation at the sensor [1, 3, 6]. A gain of 40 dB with sufficient common-mode rejection ratio (*CMRR*) and power-supply rejection ratio (*PSRR*) should also be ensured. The noise efficiency factor (*NEF*) is a widely accepted metric that reveals the design challenge due to the tradeoff between the input-referred thermal noise and the power reduction. Many works have explored the design techniques to reduce the *NEF* [1, 4-10] using CMOS. The subthreshold operation has been introduced for this purpose, to ensure a high transconductance (g_m) at a low bias current (I_{DS}) to reduce the input-referred thermal noise of the amplifier. However, due to the g_m/I_{DS} limit set by the *60 mV/dec* switching in CMOS, further reduction of NEF and power

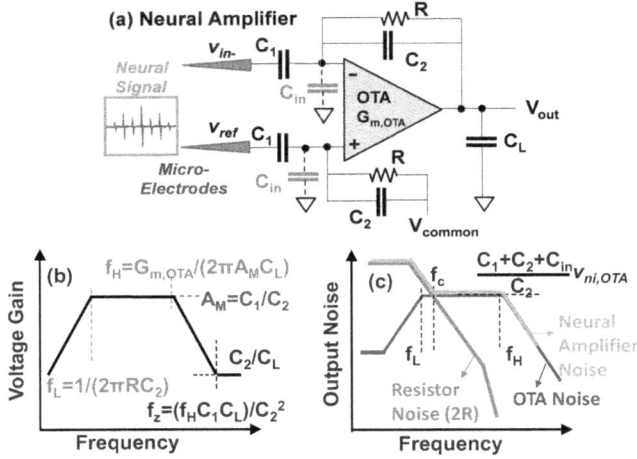

Figure 2. Neural amplifier (a) schematic and (b) gain, (b) output thermal noise characteristics [1, 4].

consumption of the amplifier is inherently difficult in CMOS-based neural recording systems.

The steep subthreshold slope (SS) Tunnel Field Effect Transistor (TFET) has emerged as a prominent candidate for low-voltage applications, taking benefit of the sub-thermal energy switching [11]. Significant progress has been made for the TFET technology such as prototype device demonstration, high-frequency switching and noise characterization, heterogeneous integration and process development [12-15]. Recent work on TFET modeling, circuit designs including variation analysis further explore its energy efficient advantages over CMOS at reduced voltages [16-18]. Authors in [16] first explored the steep SS induced high g_m/I_{DS} to scale the bias current in a SiGe TFET neural amplifier with a degraded gain of 27.7 dB. However, due to the lack of noise models, the power-noise tradeoff was not fully studied. Therefore, it is of great interest to investigate the power-noise tradeoff and explore the design optimizations using TFETs to overcome the technology barriers in neural recording systems.

In this paper, we propose a new design of a III-V Heterojunction TFET (HTFET) neural amplifier for multi-channel neural spike recording based on a shared telescopic OTA through circuit simulations to achieve gain improvement and simultaneous power and noise reduction beyond the CMOS limit. To analyze the design tradeoffs related to power-noise-performance, we apply a comprehensive noise model in [17], and explore the unique device characteristics of HTFETs for neural amplifier design compared to Si FinFETs. The reminder of the paper is as follows. In Section 2, we discuss the fundamental challenges in CMOS-based neural recording system. Section 3 shows the advantages of HTFET and the simulation setup with noise modeling details. Section 4 describes the HTFET telescopic OTA design for performance improvement of the neural amplifier including gain, power and noise. The performance evaluation of the HTFET neural amplifier is shown in Section 5, followed by conclusions.

2. POWER-NOISE CHALLENGES IN CMOS-BASED NEURAL AMPLIFIERS

CMOS-based neural amplifiers have been well studied in literature. The work in [4] proposed a neural amplifier topology based on a capacitive feedback network, which has been widely adopted due to its superior area and power efficiency at a given input-referred noise [10]. Later, the authors in [9] explored the theoretical limit of NEF and achieved a significant power reduction with a modified folded-

cascode OTA. Furthermore, the authors in [7] present a hardware sharing architecture suitable for multi-channel recording. To further reduce the NEF, the design in [8] utilizes a low-noise telescopic cascode topology with source-degeneration resistors. The recent work in [6] explores neural amplifier designs at a low V_{DD} of 1 V, showing good operation compatibility with digital building blocks.

Fig. 2a shows the neural amplifier topology proposed in [4]. It employs the capacitive feedback network (C_1, C_2), pseudo-resistor elements (R) and an OTA with a voltage gain of $G_{m,OTA}$. The voltage gain, A_M, of the neural amplifier is $A_M = C_1/C_2$ (Fig. 2b). The capacitive coupling rejects the dc offset from the electrode-tissue interface. The pseudo-resistor consists of diode-connected MOSFETs with resistance over 10^{12} Ω. The low cutoff frequency is $f_L = 1/(2\pi R C_2)$. The high cutoff frequency is $f_H = G_{m,OTA}/(2\pi A_M C_L)$, where C_L is the load capacitance. $C_2 \ll \sqrt{C_1 C_L}$ must be satisfied to ensure the half-plane-zero f_z higher than the operation bandwidth.

Due to the frequency range of neural signals, the minimization of low frequency flicker and thermal noise is critical. The most effective technique for flicker noise reduction consists of increasing the transistor gate area [4-10]. The thermal noise reduction, however, is constrained by the power requirement, known as power-noise tradeoff. Fig. 2c shows the output thermal noise spectrum of the neural amplifier in [4] and the noise contributions from the OTA and pseudo-resistor (in blue and red, respectively). By ensuring the corner frequency $f_c \ll f_H$, the contribution of the pseudo-resistor thermal noise is minimized. The input-referred thermal noise spectral density $\overline{v_{ni,amp}^2}$ is [1]:

$$\overline{v_{ni,amp}^2} = [(C_1 + C_2 + C_{in})/C_1]^2 \cdot \overline{v_{ni,OTA}^2} \tag{1}$$

where C_{in} is the OTA input capacitance and related to the gate area of the input pair. $\overline{v_{ni,OTA}^2}$ is the OTA input-referred noise. A general expression for $\overline{v_{ni,OTA}^2}$ over a -3dB bandwith of BW is approximated as [1, 7, 9]

$$\overline{v_{ni,OTA}^2} = [\frac{4k_B T}{g_{m,input}}(\frac{1}{\kappa} + \beta \frac{g_{m,load}}{g_{m,input}})] \cdot \frac{\pi}{2} \cdot BW \tag{2}$$

where $g_{m,input}$ and $g_{m,load}$ are the transconductances of the input pair and load transistors in the neural amplifier, respectively. β relates to different OTA topologies and has a value larger than 1. κ is the subthreshold gate coupling factor: $SS = V_t/\kappa \cdot ln10$, where V_t is the thermal voltage ($k_B T/q$) and k_B is Boltzmann constant. According to Eq. (1) and (2), to minimize $\overline{v_{ni,amp}^2}$, we must size the transistors to maximize $g_{m,input}$ and $g_{m,input}/g_{m,load}$. Hence, at a fixed bias current, the input and load transistors are sized to operate in weak inversion (high g_m/I_{DS}) and strong inversion (low g_m/I_{DS}), respectively. However, to reduce the power dissipation, a severely downscaled I_{DS} is required, which in turn reduces $g_{m,input}$ due to the 40 V^{-1} g_m/I_{DS} limit of CMOS. Furthermore, the reduced voltage headroom at low-V_{DD} also degrades the $g_{m,input}/g_{m,load}$. The essence of the power-noise tradeoff is indicated by the NEF [1, 4],

$$NEF \equiv v_{ni,rms}\sqrt{I_{OTA}/(\pi/2 \cdot V_t \cdot 4k_B T \cdot BW)} \tag{3}$$

where I_{OTA} is the total bias current of the OTA, $v_{ni,rms}$ is the rms value of the input-referred noise. Assuming $(C_1+C_2+C_{in})/C_1 \approx 1$, $\beta \cdot g_{m,load}/g_{m,input} \ll 1$, and substituting Eq.(1) and (2) into (3):

$$NEF \approx \sqrt{I_{OTA}/(\kappa \cdot V_t \cdot g_{m,input})} \tag{4}$$

NEF=1 is the theoretical limit in an ideal single-stage bipolar amplifier with only thermal noise considered, while NEF>1 is applied to all CMOS-based circuits. The minimum NEF is calculated as 2.02 (assuming $I_{OTA}=2I_{DS}$ and $\kappa=0.7$ for the input pair)

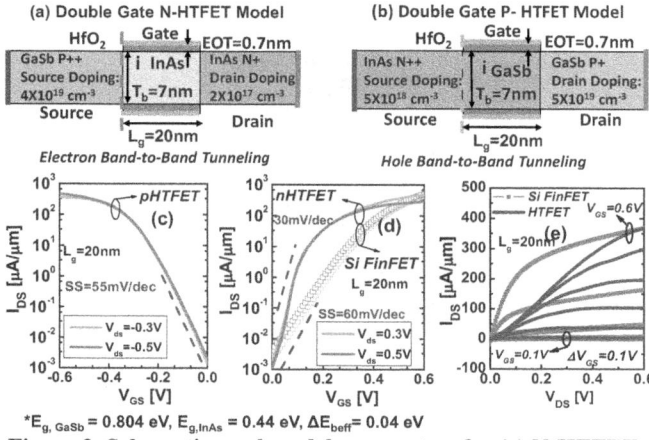

Figure 3. Schematics and model parameters for (a) N-HTFETs (b) P-HTFETs, and device characteristics of (c-d) I_{ds}-V_{gs} and (e) I_{ds}-V_{ds} , comparing with the baseline Si FinFET [17].

for any CMOS neural amplifier using a differential input pair [9], which can be moderately reduced through reference branch-sharing in multi-channel designs [7]. Thus, the power-noise tradeoff in CMOS neural amplifiers inherently limits the design of large-scale multi-channel biosignal acquisition systems.

3. TFETS FOR NEURAL RECORDING APPLICATIONS

3.1 TFET Technology: Advantages of Power-Noise Tradeoff in Neural Amplifier Designs

The fundamental limit of g_m/I_{DS} in CMOS originates from the thermal energy slope of $k_B T$, which results in an over *60 mV/dec SS*. In TFETs, the interband tunneling induced carrier injection mechanism overcomes the thermal energy limit, leading to a *sub-60 mV/dec SS*. Thus, an improvement of g_m/I_{DS} can be achieved in TFETs with SS reduction (Eq. (5)).

$$\frac{g_m}{I_{DS}} = \frac{\partial I_{DS}}{\partial V_{GS}}\frac{1}{I_{DS}} = \frac{\partial \ln I_{DS}}{\partial V_{GS}} = \frac{\ln 10\, \partial \log I_{DS}}{\partial V_{GS}} = \frac{\ln 10}{SS} = \frac{\kappa}{V_t} \quad (5)$$

In this work, we apply the calibrated GaSb-InAs heterojunction TFET (HTFET) models (Fig. 3a-e) reported in [17], which are based on a double-gate device structure with $L_g = 20\ nm$. The device characteristics of g_m/I_{DS} vs. I_{DS} and g_m/I_{DS} vs. V_{GS} are shown in Fig. 4, comparing HTFETs and Si FinFETs. The improved g_m/I_{DS} at low voltage and low I_{DS} provides following advantages in HTFET-based neural amplifier design:

1) Avoiding $G_{m,OTA}$ degradation at low bias current (I_{DS}). A high $G_{m,OTA}$ can ensure a low-noise stable operation of an amplifier. At severely scaled I_{DS}, the high g_m/I_{DS} of HTFETs can significantly improve $g_{m,input}$ compared to Si FinFETs. Hence, a desired $G_{m,OTA}$ can be maintained without increasing the circuit complexity using HTFETs.

2) Reducing $\overline{v_{n,OTA}^2}$ with high $g_{m,input}$ and $g_{m,input}/g_{m,load}$ ratio at low I_{DS}. The steep SS leads to a reduced bias voltage difference to obtain a high $g_{m,input}/g_{m,load}$ ratio. For example, one order magnitude change of g_m/I_{DS} is achieved within a 0.2 V window (Fig. 4a), which reduces the overdrive voltage and hence is suitable for low V_{DD} operation.

**3) Enabling V_{DD} scaling to reduce the power consumption ($V_{DD} \cdot I_{OTA}$) benefitted from the low-V_{DD} operation of HTFETs.

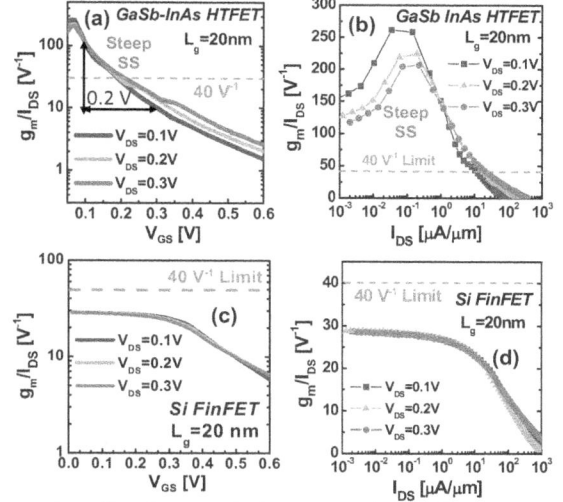

Figure 4. g_m/I_{DS} characteristics comparison of HTFETs (a, b) and Si FinFETs (c, d). The device models are from [17].

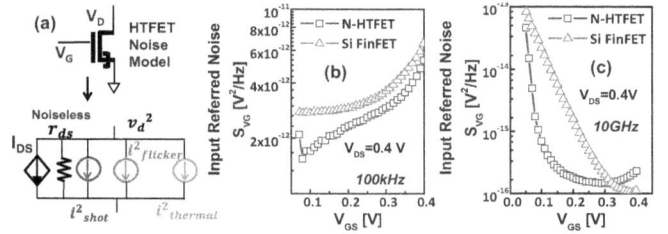

Figure 5. Electrical noise Verilog-A modeling and input-referred noise comparison [17].

4) Reducing the *NEF* by suppressing the thermal energy slope. A steep SS in TFET results in $\kappa > 1$. Substituting (5) into (4), the minimum NEF of a TFET neural amplifier ($NEF_{TFET,min}$) is lower than the CMOS limit ($NEF_{CMOS,min}$):

$$NEF \approx \sqrt{\frac{I_{OTA}}{I_{DS}} \bigg/ \left(\frac{\kappa \cdot V_t \cdot g_{m,input}}{I_{DS}}\right)} = \frac{1}{\kappa}\sqrt{\frac{I_{OTA}}{I_{DS}}} = \frac{SS}{V_t \ln 10}\sqrt{\frac{I_{OTA}}{I_{DS}}} \quad (6)$$

$$NEF_{TFET,min} = NEF_{CMOS,min} \cdot \frac{SS_{TFET,input\ pair}}{SS_{CMOS,input\ pair}} \quad (7)$$

where $SS_{TFET,input\ pair}$ and $SS_{CMOS,input\ pair}$ stand for the SS of the input pair of the TFET OTA and Si FinFET OTA, respectively.

3.2 HTFET Noise Modeling and Circuit Simulation Setup

To design the HTFET neural amplifier, we apply the calibrated Verilog-A device models incorporated with the electrical noise model [17] for HTFETs, and compare the results with the baseline Si FinFET design. The electrical noise model is derived from experimentally validated analytical models, which includes thermal, shot noise and low frequency flicker noise. (The random telegraph noise (RTN) is omitted due to the large transistor gate area in our design.) The modeled noise characteristics comparing HTFETs and Si FinFETs are shown in Fig. 5, where HTFETs exhibit a competitive input-referred noise in the kHz and MHz range compared to Si FinFETs at an operation voltage of 0.3 V. The circuit simulation is performed using Cadence Spectre [19].

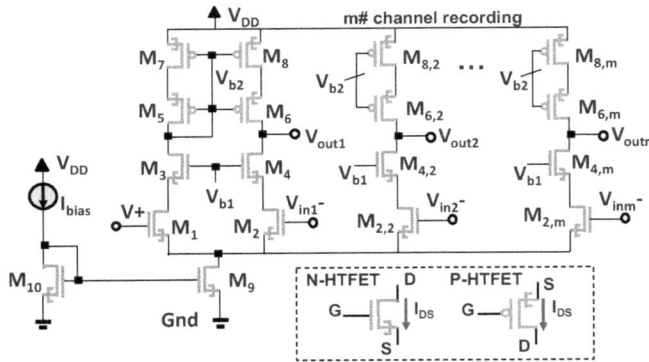

Figure 6. HTFET based telescopic OTA design with sharing architecture for multi-channel recording.

Table 1. Transistor Sizing of the HTFET Telescopic OTA

	W/L [μm/μm]	g_m/I_{ds} [V^{-1}]	V_{ds} [mV]	V_{gs} [mV]
$M_{1,2}$	50/1	**253**	67	50
$M_{3,4}$	1/50	202	150	73
$M_{5,6}$	1/10	40	-92	-92
$M_{7,8}$	0.2/40	**35**	-81	-179
$M_{9,10}$	0.2/10	169	109	82

Table 2. Transistor Sizing of the Si FinFET Telescopic OTA

	W/L [μm/μm]	g_m/I_{ds} [V^{-1}]	V_{ds} [mV]	V_{gs} [mV]
$M_{1,2}$	100/2	**28.7**	220	40
$M_{3,4}$	30/0.2	28.6	79	21
$M_{5,6}$	8/0.2	28.55	-68.4	-68.4
$M_{7,8}$	0.1/80	**9.8**	-423	-492
$M_{9,10}$	2/2	27	209	205

4. HTFET BASED ULTRA-LOW-POWER, LOW-NOISE OTA

4.1 HTFET-Based Telescopic OTA

A modified telescopic OTA topology, inspired from [7] is employed by the HTFET-based OTA (Fig. 6), which utilizes a partial OTA sharing architecture for multi-channel recording. A N-HTFET input pair is used due to its steeper SS (Fig. 3c-d) induced larger g_m/I_{DS}. Cascoded M_3-M_6 are used as gain booster without increasing the input-referred noise-level. Table 1 shows the bias conditions of each transistor in the HTFET OTA. The bias current is 10 nA at V_{DD}=0.5 V, providing a 5 nA bias current for M_1-M_8. As discussed in Section 2, to maximize the $g_{m1,2}$ of the input differential pair $M_{1,2}$, a large W/L ratio is used to achieve high g_m/I_{DS}. Similar to the reported CMOS designs [4-9], a large gate-area (WxL) is used to reduce the flicker noise contribution. For $M_{7,8}$, on the other hand, a minimized W/L is applied to bias the device into strong inversion with small g_m/I_{DS}, which increases the ratio of $g_{m1,2}/g_{m7,8}$ and reduces the thermal noise contribution of $M_{7,8}$. Since the cascoded M_3-M_6 have a negligible contribution to the total input-referred noise, the choice of the sizing for these transistors is based on gain requirement. The balance of the output resistance and intrinsic gain is carefully considered for M_3-M_6. As a result, a high g_m/I_{DS} of 253 V^{-1} is obtained for $M_{1,2}$, while a g_m/I_{DS} of 35 V^{-1} is used for $M_{7,8}$, resulting $g_{m1,2}/g_{m7,8} \approx 7.2$.

For performance comparison, we design a Si FinFET OTA as a baseline with a similar topology and bias current (10 nA). A supply voltage of 1 V is required in Si FinFET OTA due to the overdrive voltage requirement of the stacked devices. Similarly, $M_{1,2}$ operate in subthreshold regime while $M_{7,8}$ are biased in strong inversion regime, using the sizes presented in Table 2. However, due to the limited g_m/I_{DS} and diminished overdrive voltage, $g_{m1,2}$ and the ratio of $g_{m1,2}/g_{m7,8}$ ($\approx$3) are significantly decreased at such low-power level, which is detrimental to noise performance. Performance Analysis

Fig. 7a shows the HTFET OTA gain vs frequency for a single channel compared to the baseline Si FinFET OTA. Benefiting from

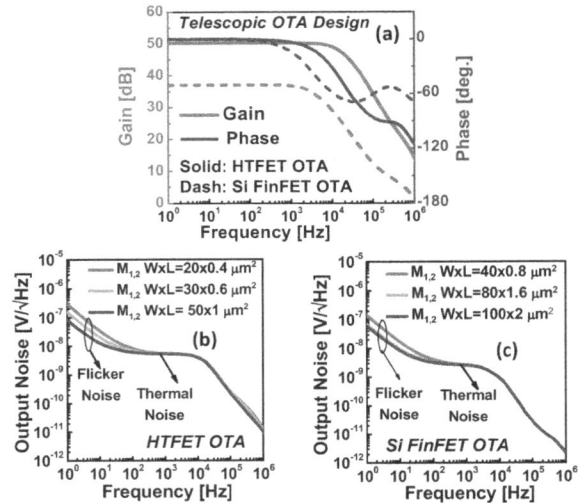

Figure 7. Voltage gain (a) and output noise vs. frequency (b-c) of HTFET and Si FinFET OTAs.

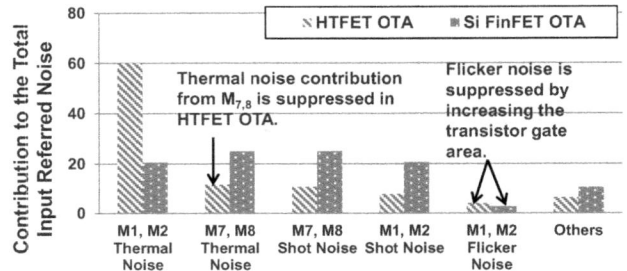

Figure 8. Noise contribution of each transistor to the overall input-referred noise from 10Hz to 1 kHz.

its high g_m/I_{DS} and the cascoding technique, an open-loop gain of 50 dB is achieved in the HTFET OTA at V_{DD}=0.5 V, whereas the Si FinFET OTA shows a degraded gain of 37 dB at V_{DD}=1 V due to extremely limited bias current. The output noise spectrum vs frequency is shown in Fig.7b-c, where the thermal noise dominates the flicker noise which is suppressed owing to the large gate-area of the input pair.

The dominant noise contributor of each transistor and its contribution to the overall input-referred noise is shown in Fig. 8. In the Si FinFET OTA, $M_{7,8}$ contribute to a significant portion of the overall input-referred noise due to the degradation of $g_{m1,2}$ and $g_{m1,2}/g_{m7,8}$. In contrast, an effective suppression of the thermal noise contribution from $M_{7,8}$ is achieved in the HTFET OTA, given its high g_m/I_{DS}. The desired open-loop gain, ultra-low power and competitive noise performance achieved by the HTFET telescopic OTA confirm its advantage for neural amplifier design.

5. THE HTFET NEURAL AMPLIFIER FOR MULTI-CHANNEL BIOSIGNAL RECORDING

5.1 Closed-loop HTFET Neural Amplifier

Using the capacitive feedback topology, we implement the closed-loop HTFET neural amplifier based on the proposed telescopic OTA (Fig. 9). To further eliminate the redundant dc bias circuitry, we use the dc output voltage of the OTA ($V_{out,dc}$) to bias the common voltage (V_{common}) of the input signal through the resistive

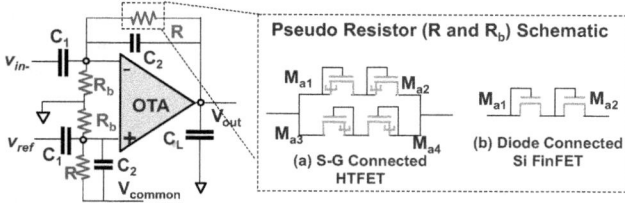

Figure 9. Closed-loop neural amplifier topology and pseudo resistor schematics.

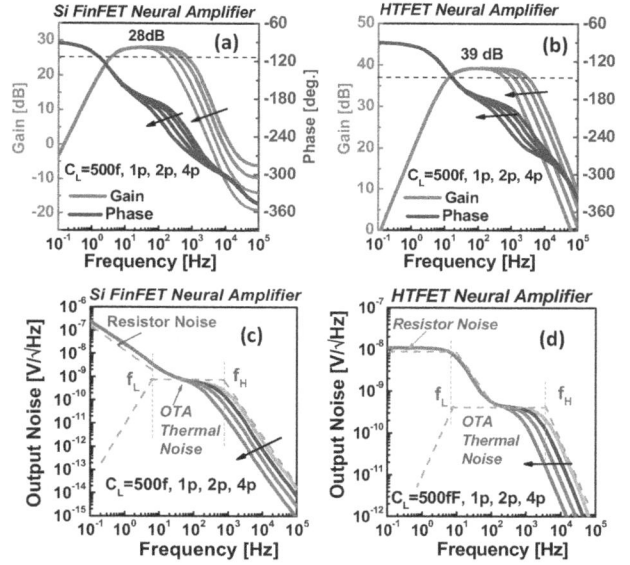

Figure 10. Si FinFET(a, c) and HTFET(b, d) neural amplifier gain vs. frequency and output noise vs. frequency.

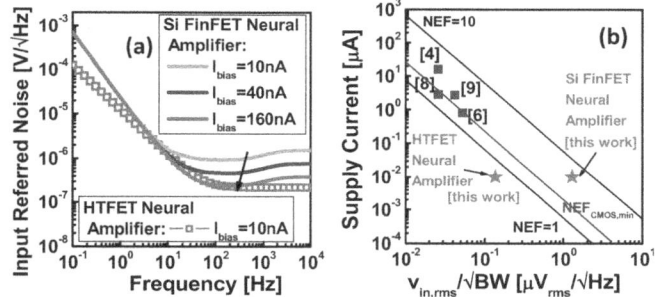

Figure 11. (a) Input referred noise spectrum for HTFET and Si FinFET neural amplifiers and (b) Supply current vs. $v_{in,rms}/\sqrt{\text{bandwidth}}$ for NEF benchmarking.

divider network (R_b) at $V_{common}=V_{out}$. In the OTA simulation, the common dc voltage of the input signal, $V_{in,dc}$, is set to $1/2 V_{out,dc}$. Hence, by setting $R_b=R$, the input signal can be biased at $1/2 V_{out,dc}$. A diode-connected Si FinFET as in [1, 4-10] is used to construct the pseudo-resistor R_b and R for the Si FinFET neural amplifier, where a W/L of 0.2 μm/8 μm is used for M_{a1-2} (Fig. 9b). For the HTFET neural amplifier, shorted source-gate connections [16] can be applied by taking advantage of the asymmetrical source/drain characteristic, while an additional conduction path through M_{a3-4} (Fig. 9a) is required due to the uni-directional characteristics. A W/L of 0.2 μm/6 μm is applied to M_{a1-4} in the HTFET neural amplifier. The values of the capacitors are selected as $C_2 = 500\ fF$, and $C_1/C_2 =100$ to provide a 40 dB mid-band gain. C_L is varied from 500 fF to 2 pF to tune the pass band of the amplifier. For the Si FinFET neural amplifier, $C_2=500\ fF$ and $C_1/C_2 = 50$ are used, due to the degraded open-loop gain.

5.2 Voltage Gain and Noise Performance

The gain and output noise vs. frequency characteristics are shown in Fig. 10, comparing HTFET and Si FinFET neural amplifier designs at different load capacitor conditions (f_H decreases as C_L increases). A midband gain of 39.4 dB is achieved in the HTFET neural amplifier, as compared to 28.1 dB in the Si FinFET neural amplifier. This gain advantage of the HTFET neural amplifier arises from the improved g_m originating from the steep SS induced high g_m/I_{DS}. The output thermal noise spectrum exhibits similar characteristics as in Fig. 2c, for both Si FinFET and HTFET neural amplifiers. For a frequency range below 10 Hz, the noise contribution from the pseudo-resistor dominates the overall output noise, while the thermal noise of the OTA dominates the frequency range between f_L and f_H. As discussed in Section 2, the low cutoff frequency f_L is determined by R and C_2, while C_1/C_2 is constant. Thus, the bandwidth of the designed neural amplifier can be tuned by varying R (R_b) and C_2 to satisfy the operational bandwidth requirement in different application domains.

5.3 Power-Noise Tradeoff

The input-referred noise spectrum for HTFET and Si FinFET neural amplifiers are shown in Fig. 11a. At the same I_{bias} of 10 nA, the HTFET neural amplifier exhibits over 4 times reduction of the input-referred noise within the pass band compared to the Si FinFET neural amplifier. Moreover, reducing the input-referred noise of the Si FinFET neural amplifier can only be achieved by degrading its power performance. When increasing I_{bias} by 4 times (40 nA) and 16 times (160 nA) while increasing all the transistor widths accordingly (4 times at $I_{bias}= 40\ nA$, 16 times at $I_{bias}=160\ nA$), the input-referred noise of the Si FinFET neural amplifier is reduced by 2 times and 4 times, respectively. Such noise reduction is due to the increased $g_{m1,2}$ of the OTA at a fixed g_m/I_{DS} (at a constant NEF). The Si FinFET neural amplifier shows comparable input-referred noise at $I_{bias}=160\ nA$ and $V_{DD}=1\ V$ as the HTFET neural amplifier at $I_{bias}=10\ nA$ and $V_{DD}=0.5\ V$. Hence, an approximate 32 times power reduction over the Si FinFET design is

achieved in the HTFET neural amplifier, considering the design target to obtain the same input-referred noise level.

The performance metrics of the HTFET and Si FinFET neural amplifiers at $C_L=2\ pF$ and $I_{bias}=10\ nA$ are summarized in Table 3 and compared with other designs [8, 16]. A bandwidth of 12 Hz (f_L) to 2.1 kHz (f_H) and power consumption of 5 nW are achieved in the HTFET design with an input-referred noise of 6.27 μVrms integrated over 10 Hz to 1 kHz, which is close to the estimated minimum $v_{ni,rms}$ of 5.26 μV$_{rms}$ achieved by an ideal OTA at $C_L=2\ pF$ and $A_M=40\ dB$ [1]. The Si FinFET neural amplifier, however, shows a bandwidth from 4 Hz to 529 Hz at the same I_{bias} (10 nA), while f_H is degraded due to the limited g_m. The increased $v_{ni,rms}$ at nanowatt power levels imposes inevitable drawbacks on practical applications of the Si FinFET amplifier. Both CMRR and PSRR are improved in the HTFET amplifier compared to the Si FinFET design. A competitive linearity performance of the HTFET and Si FinFET amplifiers, indicated by the total harmonic distortion (THD), is also achieved (compared to Si FinFET, the impact of I_{ds}-V_{gs} non-linearity in HTFET is compensated by the stable operation bias at low-V_{DD}). For a single-channel, the total transistor area of 259.2 μm^2 is achieved in HTFET amplifier compared to 452 μm^2 in Si FinFET amplifier.

Compared to the reported CMOS designs [4, 6, 8, 9], the HTFET neural amplifier exhibits superior power-noise performance (Fig.

Table 3. Performance Comparison with Other Simulation Works

	HTFET Amplifier (this work)	FinFET Amplifier (this work)	Shoaran 2012 [8]	Trivedi 2013 [16]
Technology	20 nm HTFET	20 nm Si FinFET	.18 µm CMOS	90 nm SiGe TFET
Bias Current	10 nA	10 nA	2.84 µA	~3 nA
Supply Voltage	0.5 V	1 V	1.8 V	1 V
Power	5 nW	10 nW	5.11 µW	3.6 nW
Closed-loop Gain	39.4 dB	28.1 dB	39.9 dB	27.7 dB
Bandwidth (f_L-f_H)	12 Hz-2.1 kHz (C_L=2 pF)	4 Hz-529 Hz (C_L=2 pF)	30Hz-2.5kHz (tunable)	0.036 Hz-3.2 kHz (N/A)
Input-Referred Noise	6.27µVrms (10Hz - 1kHz)	29.7µVrms* (10Hz-1kHz)	1.30 µVrms (1Hz-100kHz)	3.1 µVrms** (N/A)
CMRR	56 dB	42 dB	78 dB	64 dB
PSRR	70 dB	58 dB	57 dB	55 dB
THD	0.69% (2 mV$_{p-p}$)	0.67% (2 mV$_{p-p}$)	-	-
NEF	0.64	5.2	1.94	-

*At I_{bias}=160 nA, the integrated input-referred noise of the Si FinFET neural amplifier from 10Hz to 1kHz is 6.99 µVrms with corresponding 16x increase of transistor width. ** Tunnel diode shot noise model with a fano factor of 1 were used for [16] with thermal noise neglected.

11b). A *NEF* of 0.64 (Table 3) is obtained in the HTFET neural amplifier owing to the steep SS, which outperforms the *NEF* of 5.18 in the baseline Si FinFET design. This low *NEF* achieved by the HTFET design also outperforms the optimal *NEF* for both CMOS (*NEF$_{min}$* =2.02) and Bipolar (*NEF$_{min}$*=1) based designs. Moreover, the new HTFET neural amplifier shows significant gain improvement compared to the SiGe TFET design in [16], benefiting from the cascaded transistors and steeper *SS* of III-V HTFETs. The telescopic OTA topology employed by our design is also known to be more power-noise efficient [7, 8] compared to the symmetrical current-mirror OTA topology in [16]. The comparison of the noise performance cannot be applied here because of the different assumption of the Fano factor for shot noise and neglecting of the thermal and flicker noise in [16].

6. CONCLUSIONS

In this paper, we investigate the unique device characteristics of steep slope HTFET for multi-channel biosignal acquisition. By exploring the high g_m/I_{DS} characteristics, we propose a new HTFET neural amplifier design using a shared telescopic OTA topology to enable a nanowatt power-level operation, which also provides a voltage gain improvement and noise reduction compared to the Si FinFET-based design. Using a comprehensive noise model, we analyze the power-noise tradeoff in HTFET neural amplifier designs, which highlights advantages of the steep SS and low-V_{DD} operation for mitigating the aggravated thermal noise limit from the power reduction. At a highly downscaled bias current of 10 nA and supply voltage of 0.5 V, our proposed HTFET neural amplifier design exhibits a midband gain of 40 dB, a -3dB bandwidth from 12 Hz to 2.1 kHz, and an approximate 32 times power reduction over the baseline Si FinFET design to achieve the same input-referred noise level. The performance evaluation further reveals the superior power-noise efficiency of the HTFET-based design, including a *NEF* of 0.64 significant lower than the theoretical *NEF* limits using CMOS or Bipolar technologies. The remarkable performance

improvement and desired power-noise tradeoff confirm the advantages of HTFET technology to overcome the CMOS technology barrier for multi-channel biosignal acquisition system applications.

7. ACKNOWLEDGMENTS
This work is supported in part by the National Science Foundation (NSF) ASSIST ERC 1160483. This work is also supported in part by STARnet, a Semiconductor Research Corporation program sponsored by MARCO and DARPA.

8. REFERENCES

[1] Harrison, R.R. 2008. The Design of integrated circuits to observe brain activity. *IEEE Proceedings.*

[2] Nurmikko et al. 2010. Listening to brain microcircuits for interfacing with external world—progress in wireless implantable microelectronic neuroengineering devices. *IEEE Proceedings.*

[3] Bafar, V. M. and Schmid, A, 2013. *Wireless Cortical Implantable Systems,* Springer New York.

[4] Harrison, R.R. and Charles, C. 2003. A low-power low-noise CMOS amplifier for neural recording applications. *IEEE JSSC.*

[5] Shoaran et al 2014. Compact Low-power Cortical Recording Architecture for Compressive Multichannel Data Acquisition. *IEEE Trans. Biomed. Circuits Syst.*

[6] Zhang et al 2012. Design of Ultra-Low Power Biopotential Amplifiers for Biosignal Acquisition Applications. *IEEE Trans. on Biomed. Circuits and Syst.*

[7] Majidzadeh et al 2011. Energy efficient low-noise neural recording amplifier with enhanced noise efficiency factor. *IEEE Trans. on Biomed. Circuits and Syst.*

[8] Shoaran et al 2012. Design techniques and analysis of high-resolution neural recording systems targeting epilepsy focus localization. In *IEEE EMBC.*

[9] Wattanapanitch, W., Fee, M., Sarpeshkar, R. 2007. An Energy-Efficient Micropower Neural Recording Amplifier. *IEEE Trans. on Biomed. Circuits and Syst.*

[10] Ruiz-Amaya et al 2010. A comparative study of low-noise amplifiers for neural applications. In *ICM'10.*

[11] Seabaugh, A. C. and Zhang, Q. 2010. Low-voltage tunnel transistors for beyond CMOS logic. *IEEE Proceedings.*

[12] Zhou et al. 2012. Novel gate-recessed vertical InAs/GaSb TFETs with record high I_{ON} of 180µA/µm at V_{DS} = 0.5V. In *IEEE IEDM.*

[13] Bijesh et al 2012. Flicker noise characterization and analy-tical modeling of homo and hetero-Junction III-V Tunnel FETs. *In Device Res. Conf. (DRC).*

[14] Bijesh et al. 2013. Demonstration of In$_{0.9}$Ga$_{0.1}$As/GaAs$_{0.18}$Sb$_{0.82}$ near broken-gap tunnel FET with I_{ON}=740µA/µm, G$_M$= 70µS/µm and gigahertz switching performance at V_{DS}=0.5V. In *IEEE IEDM.*

[15] Rooyackers et al 2013. A new complementary heterojunction vertical Tunnel-FET integration scheme. In *IEEE IEDM.*

[16] Trivedi et al 2013. Exploring Tunnel-FET for ultra low power analog applications: A case study on operational transconductance amplifier. In *ACM/EDAC/IEEE DAC.*

[17] Pandey et al 2014. Electrical noise in heterojunction interband tunnel FETs. *IEEE TED.*

[18] Avci et al. 2013. Energy efficiency comparison of nanowire heterojunction TFET and Si MOSFET at L$_g$=13nm, including P-TFET and variation considerations. In *IEEE IEDM.*

[19] Cadence® Virtuoso Spectre Circuit Simulator, 2009.

Performance Modeling for Emerging Interconnect Technologies in CMOS and Beyond-CMOS Circuits

Sou-Chi Chang
Georgia Institute of
Technology
777 Atlantic Dr NW
Atlanta, Georgia 30332-0250
souchi@gatech.edu

Ahmet Ceyhan
Georgia Institute of
Technology
777 Atlantic Dr NW
Atlanta, Georgia, 30332-0250
aceyhan3@gatech.edu

Vachan Kumar
Georgia Institute of
Technology
777 Atlantic Dr NW
Atlanta, Georgia, 30332-0250
vkumar38@gatech.edu

Azad Naeemi
Georgia Institute of
Technology
777 Atlantic Dr NW
Atlanta, Georgia, 30332-0250
azad@gatech.edu

ABSTRACT

In this paper, emerging low-power interconnect options for CMOS and beyond CMOS technologies are reviewed. First, electrical interconnects based on carbon nanotubes and graphene nanoribbons are discussed. It is found that carbon-based electrical interconnects can potentially outperform their conventional Cu counterpart at technology nodes close to or below 10 nm. Next, since using electron spin as a novel state variable has attracted major attention, interconnect options for beyond-COMS spintronic devices will be discussed. We start with metallic interconnects based on the non-local spin-valve and spin-torque-driven switching, and the impact of size effects and dimensional scaling on their potential performance is studied. It is found that the spin signal in the non-local structure decays significantly because of a large degradation in the spin relaxation length as the interconnect width decreases. Next, a spintronic interconnect in the form of a conventional spin-valve configuration is introduced to increase the energy efficiency by eliminating the loss of spins in the non-local structure. Both metallic and semiconducting channels are studied, and the results show that the metallic interconnect is more energy-efficient than the semiconducting one when the interconnect is short (a few hundreds of nanometers) due to a high conductive current path. However, a semiconducting channel is appropriate for an intermediate or long (several microns) interconnect due to a longer spin relaxation time and the possibility of using an electric field to enhance the spin relaxation length. Furthermore, it is shown that for spin interconnects, downscaling the size of the ferromagnets can largely reduce the delay, energy, and energy-delay product at the cost of a shorter retention time.

Categories and Subject Descriptors

B.7.0 [**Hardware**]: INTEGRATED CIRCUITS

Keywords

Interconnects, carbon nanotubes (CNTs), graphene nanoribbons (GNRs), spin injection, spin transport, spin-torques

1. INTRODUCTION

Over the past four decades, the exponentially increasing computing performance in microchips has been realized by the relentless scaling of complementary metal-oxide-semiconductor (CMOS) field-effect transistors (FETs) based on Moore's law [1]. Despite of the improved resistance-capacitance (RC) product in scaled CMOS FETs, the distributed RC product of interconnects has increased with each technology generation [2]. Moreover, for ultra-scaled technology nodes (interconnect width < 20 nm), the RC product is no longer simply determined by the output resistance of the switch and capacitance of the interconnect, since the resistance of the metallic interconnects increases significantly due to dimensional scaling and size effects. Therefore, it is of great interest to explore alternative materials for the use of future nanoscale interconnects for the CMOS technology.

Carbon-based materials such as carbon nanotubes (CNTs) and graphene nanoribbons (GNRs) have become promising candidates for both device and interconnect applications due to their long electron mean free path, high current-carrying capability, and high thermal conductivity. It has been shown that interconnects made of single-wall CNTs and multilayers GNRs can potentially outperform those based on copper/low-κ technology at the 11-nm CMOS technology node and beyond [3][4].

Meanwhile, many beyond CMOS devices are proposed to replace or supplement the conventional Si CMOS technology [5]. However, it is necessary for any emerging logic device to be complemented by a compatible fast and energy-efficient interconnect technology to prevent from the speed or energy penalties imposed by interconnects. Therefore, it is of great interest to look for an energy-efficient interconnect technology for beyond CMOS devices.

Since using spin as a state variable is a promising direction for future logic devices [5], many proposed beyond CMOS devices are based on spintronics. In particular, a device in a non-local spin-valve configuration combined with the spin-transfer-torque switching (see Fig. 1(a)), also known as all spin logic (ASL), provides a complete set of boolean logic functions with an extremely low operating voltage [6] and has become a strong candidate due to its potential to outperform the scaled CMOS technology if certain material targets are achieved [7]. Moreover, in ASL, devices and interconnects are defined according to the operating functions such as INVERT and COPY, since there is no clear boundary in the structure between them. Hence, it is of great importance to look at the impact of dimensional scaling and size effects on interconnects in the ASL configuration. In [8], it was shown that the spin signal decays largely in the metallic channel because the spin relaxation length decreases significantly due to size effects, and this trend implies an increase in the energy needed to pass the spin information in ultra-scaled ASL.

To increase the energy efficiency of spin-transfer-torque interconnects, a conventional spin-valve configuration as shown in Fig. 1(b) is used to eliminate the loss of the spin signal in ASL [9][10]. In [9] and [10], both metallic and semiconducting channels were studied, and it was found that for short interconnects (a few hundreds of nanometers), the metallic channel has a higher energy efficiency than the semiconducting one because of a lower resistive spin signal path; nevertheless, for μm-scale interconnects, a semiconductor is more appropriate as an interconnect material due to longer spin relaxation time. Furthermore, the electric field along the semiconducting channel, enhances the effective spin relaxation length and allows the spin signal to propagate even longer.

This paper aims to provide a comprehensive review on current emerging interconnects for both CMOS and beyond CMOS technologies, and is organized as follows: In Section 2, promising electrical interconnects based on CNTs and GNRs are discussed and compared with those using scaled Cu/low-κ technology. In Section 3, both spin-transfer-torque interconnects in the non-local and conventional spin-valve configurations are discussed. Section 4 concludes the paper.

2. CARBON-BASED ELECTRICAL INTERCONNECTS

At ultra-scaled dimensions, the latency of the Cu/low-κ interconnect technology becomes a significant threat to improving the performance of electronic chips. To address the interconnect problem at the local and intermediate metal levels, a new material solution is required. Carbon-based interconnects have been studied extensively as a potential replacement for the Cu/low-κ technology. Early studies on carbon-based interconnects showed that they are too resistive for high-performance chips due to the limited number of conduction channels [11] and can potentially be used only in ultra low-power circuits [12]. Due to the radical change in the local interconnect behavior at ultra-scaled dimensions;

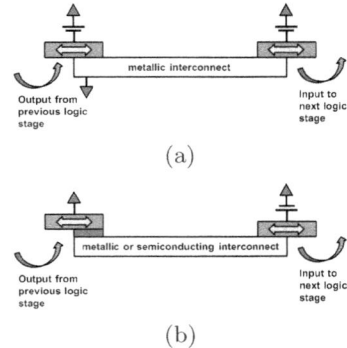

(a)

(b)

Figure 1: (a) spin-transfer-torque interconnects in a non-local spin-valve configuration, also known as all-spin logic. (b) spin-transfer-torque interconnects in a conventional spin-valve configuration for improving energy efficiency.

however, new opportunities arise for carbon-based interconnects. In this section, we investigate the potential for carbon nanotubes (CNTs) and graphene nanoribbons (GNRs).

2.1 Carbon Nanotubes

For many years, researchers have focused on studying CNT bundles to reduce the resistance associated with carbon nanotube interconnects. However, manufacturing horizontal CNT bundles with good ohmic contacts has turned out to be very challenging. On the other hand, there have been promising advances in manufacturing highly dense, perfectly aligned horizontal individual CNTs [13]. Considering these advancements and the significant increase in the resistivity of Cu wires at future technology generations, delay and energy-per-bit of individual or a few parallel SWNT interconnects have been compared to that of Cu/low-κ.

It is assumed that a bed of horizontally aligned tubes is first laid on the substrate before the unwanted tubes are etched away using standard lithography techniques. Per unit length resistances of SWNT interconnects with a certain diameter are constant with technology. As a consequence, the gap between per unit length resistances of Cu and that of SWNT interconnects reduces with technology scaling. It is found that this gap vanishes for a Cu wire with a 7.5nm width and an individual SWNT with a 2nm diameter. The resistances of SWNT interconnect designs can be reduced further by using multiple individual tubes in parallel. Furthermore, per unit length capacitances associated with individual SWNT interconnects are much smaller than Cu interconnects due to their smaller dimensions, which is critical in reducing both the delay and energy-per-bit. CNT bundles have similar capacitances compared to Cu interconnects. Figure 2 illustrates that the intrinsic interconnect energy-delay product (EDP) per unit length cubed associated with SWNT interconnects is significantly better than that of Cu interconnects because of their small capacitance. Furthermore, considering a 5× minimum size inverter at the 7-nm technology node driving 3 similar gates through an interconnect with varied length, Fig. 3 demonstrates that multiple SWNT interconnect options can outperform Cu interconnects in terms of EDP. To achieve this improvement, however, major breakthroughs in fabricating SWNT inter-connects must happen [3].

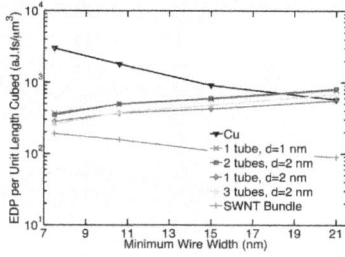

Figure 2: Comparison of the EDP per unit length cubed associated with Cu interconnects, bundles of SWNT and SWNT interconnects considering various number and diameter of tubes in a single layer. The figure is adapted from [3].

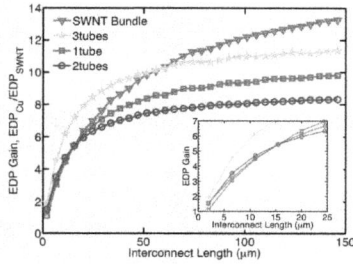

Figure 3: EDP offered by single or a few SWNT interconnect designs with various number of tubes and bundles of SWNTs as a function of interconnect length assuming that drivers and receivers are 5× the minimum size. The figure is adapted from [3].

2.2 Graphene Nanoribbons

Two-dimensional graphene suspended in air has a mean free path of 1.2 μm, which is very high compared to the mean free path of copper (40nm). Additionally, since graphene has a small thickness of 0.35 nm, its capacitance is smaller compared to copper; hence graphene is expected to have a smaller RC delay. However, when graphene is placed on a substrate, the mean free path drops significantly due to the scattering of charge carriers with surface polar phonons, trapped charges at the interface and resonant scatterers [14]. Further, when two-dimensional graphene is patterned into narrow graphene nanoribbons (GNR), the mean free path degrades drastically due to scattering at the rough edges [15]. These non-idealities result in a high resistance and hence a higher RC delay for narrow GNR interconnects. As a result, for high performance applications, technology improvements to obtain smooth edges and good substrates are necessary for GNR interconnects to outperform copper. On the other hand, for low-power applications, GNR interconnects, even with their high resistance, can outperform copper wires. For a simple circuit shown in Fig. 4, the supply voltage is varied to obtain the energy-delay plot for cop-

per and GNR interconnects. For both interconnect lengths shown in Fig. 5, GNR performs better in the low energy (low V_{dd}) region, where the resistance of the driver and interconnect capacitance determine the delay. However, in the high energy (high V_{dd}) region, the intrinsic RC delay of GNR is dominant; hence, copper performs better compared to GNR.

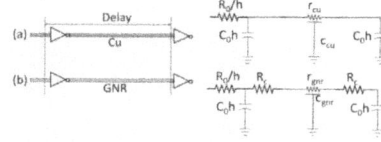

Figure 4: Circuit used for comparison of (a) copper and (b) GNR interconnects. The CMOS inverters are designed using 45 nm low-power technology node. The figure is adapted from [4].

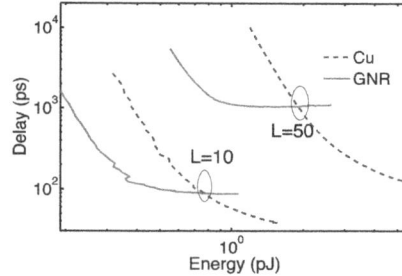

Figure 5: Delay versus energy of 45nm low-power CMOS inverters with copper and GNR interconnects. The inverters are assumed to be minimum sized. The simulations are run for interconnects of length 10 and 50 gate pitches. The figure is adapted from [4].

3. SPIN-TRANSFER-TORQUE INTERCONNECTS

In the past decade, many spin-based devices/interconnects have been proposed to replace or augment FETs in the beyond CMOS era [5]. Applying a large magnetic field used to be the most common way to actively control the magnetic state of a ferromagnet. However, after the discovery of the spin-transfer-torque effect [17], the spin polarization of the nanomagnet can be directly changed by injecting spin-polarized electrons. Recently, a lateral spin valve configuration combined with the spin-transfer-torque switching (ASL) is proposed as a low voltage device for logic computation and interconnection. In this section, we will discuss the scaling effects on ASL interconnects and introduce a new spin-transfer-torque interconnect structure to improve the energy efficiency compared to the ASL one.

3.1 Non-local Spin-valve

As shown in Fig. 1(a), spin-polarized electrons in a non-local structure are injected from the ferromagnet into the interconnect with electrical currents. The ground location near the transmitter is used to maintain the non-reciprocity. These injected electrons diffuse through the metallic channel and transfer their angular momentum to the receiving nanomagnet when they reach the end of the channel. If the spin-torque inserted by injected electrons is large enough, the magnetization of the receiving magnet will align with that of transmitting magnet. A larger spin-torque leads to a faster magnetic response (a shorter delay). However, due to spin-flip scattering in metals, injected electrons lose their spin polarization while traveling through the interconnect, and more spin-polarized electrons are relaxed in a longer interconnect. In Fig. 6, it is shown that the delay and energy increase exponentially with the interconnect length due to the weaker spin-torque inserted onto the receiving nanomagnet. Furthermore, the spin relaxation process becomes more serious in scaled interconnects since the spin-flipping scattering is enhanced by increasing side-wall and grain boundary scattering [16]. Fig. 7 shows that the delay and energy increase significantly as the interconnect width decreases. This trend indicates that the energy needed for the non-local structure increases largely as interconnects are scaled.

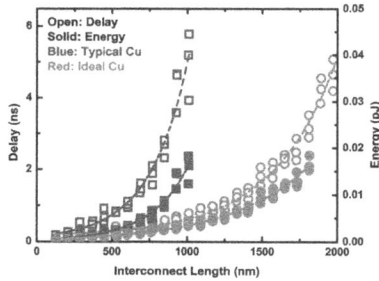

Figure 6: Delay and energy versus the interconnect length. In Fig. 6 and 7, the ideal means that the grain-boundary reflectivity (R) is equal to 0 and the sidewall specularity (p) is equal to 1. The typical means that R is equal to 0.2 and p is equal to 0. The figure is adapted from [8].

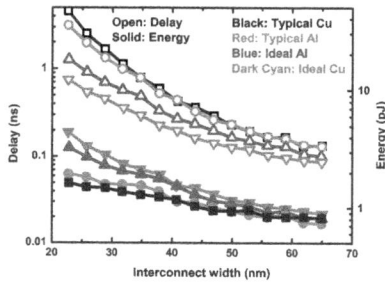

Figure 7: Delay and energy versus the interconnect width. The interconnect length is equal to 400 nm. The figure is adapted from [8].

3.2 Conventional Spin-valve

In the non-local structure, due to the shunt electrical current path, most spin-polarized electrons are directly flowing into the ground, rather than contributing the spin-torque at the end of the channel; therefore, a large energy is needed to correctly pass the spin signal in the non-local spin-torque interconnects. To improve the energy efficiency, a conventional spin-valve is used as a spin interconnect by eliminating the current path responsible for loss of injected spin as shown in Fig. 1(b). Fig. 8 shows the interconnect in a conventional spin-valve configuration is more energy-efficient than that in the non-local structure.

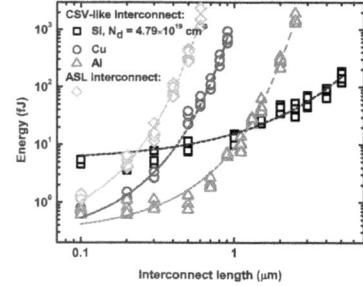

Figure 8: Energy as a function of the interconnect length for CSV-like (conventional spin-valve) and ASL (non-local spin-valve) interconnects under the same magnetic response. Cu, Al, and Si are used for CSV-like interconnects. Cu is used for ASL interconnects. The figure is adapted from [10].

The interconnects based on the conventional spin-valve can be made of metals (e.g. Cu and Al) or semiconductors (e.g. Si). The tunneling oxide in the metallic interconnect is used to maintain the non-reciprocity. For semiconducting interconnects, the tunneling oxide is also necessary to overcome the so-called conductivity mismatch problem even though the non-reciprocity can be achieved by the electric field along the channel.

The performance of this kind of spin interconnects is mainly determined by the spin-polarized tunneling at the transmitter and spin relaxation process in the channel. Large spin tunneling currents with the high spin injection efficiency (the spin current normalized to the electrical current) and slow spin relaxation process are desired for fast and energy-efficient interconnects. In general, it is easier to inject spin into metals than semiconductors due to lack of the Schottky barrier at the interface as shown in Fig. 9. However, the spin-polarized tunneling in semiconductors can be improved by reducing the effect of the Schottky barrier, which can be done by using different ferromagnets and oxides, and increasing doping density of the semiconductor [9].

Due to the strong screening effect, the spin relaxation length in metals is determined by the diffusion coefficient and spin relaxation time, which are material parameters and are difficult to be changed. Thus, similar to the non-local structure, the delay and energy also increase with the interconnect length in the conventional spin-valve configuration as shown in Fig. 10. However, different from the metallic channel, under a weak electric field (in the order of 10^3

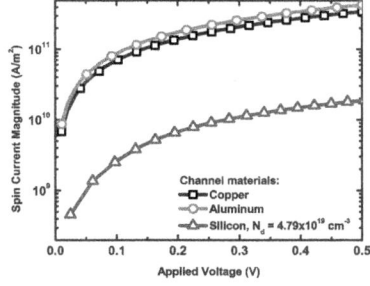

(a)

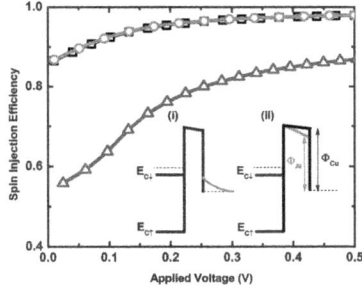

(b)

Figure 9: (a) Spin current and (b) injection efficiency versus the applied voltage for Cu, Al, and Si CSV-like interconnects. The insets in Fig. 9(b) illustrate the effects of the Schottky barrier and metal work function on the energy band diagram. The figures are adapted from [10].

V/cm), how long electrons can preserve their spin polarization is dominated by the spin relaxation time and drift velocity. At a low field, the latter is simply the product of the electron mobility and electric field. This field-assisted spin transport largely increases the effective spin relaxation length in semiconductors.

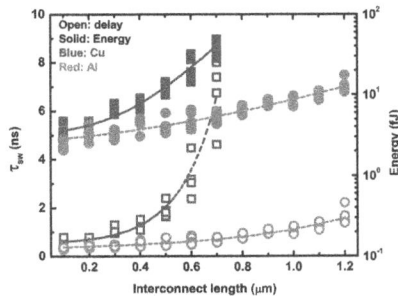

Figure 10: Delay and energy versus the interconnect length for Cu and Al CSV-like interconnects. The figure is adapted from [10].

Silicon, the cornerstone of the modern information technology, has the longest spin relaxation time among the common semiconductors such as Ge and GaAs. The ability of using an electric field to enhance the spin relaxation length allows the delay and energy in μm-scale silicon spin interconnects being independent of the channel length as shown in Fig. 11. Note that increasing the doping density of the channel can reduce the energy dissipation, but makes the delay slightly increase with the interconnect length due to longer spin relaxation time. Further, for short interconnects (several nanometers), since the spin relaxation lengths in metals and silicon are much larger or close to the interconnect length, metals are more suitable due to their low resistance. For intermediate interconnects, it is necessary to use silicon as the channel material to improve the interconnect performance because of its long effective spin relaxation length. As shown in Fig. 8, silicon spin interconnects outperform metallic ones in the channel length equal to several microns.

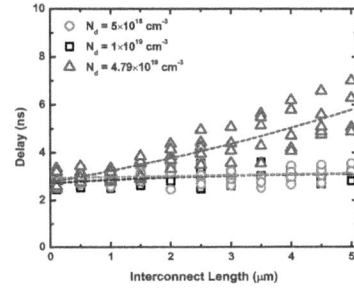

(a)

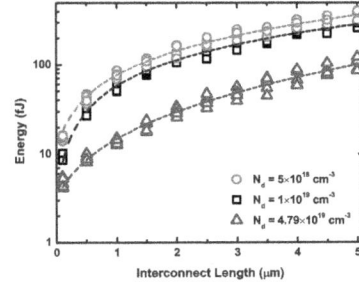

(b)

Figure 11: (a) Delay and (b) energy versus the interconnect length for different doping densities of the silicon channel. The figures are adapted from [9].

The performance of the spin interconnects can be further improved by downsizing the receiving nanomagnet. This is because for a smaller magnet, a weaker spin-torque is needed to change the magnetization of the magnet; that is, a fast magnetic response (a shorter delay) and less energy dissipation can be achieved using a smaller magnet as shown in Fig. 12. Note that a smaller magnet implies a lower energy barrier between the two magnetic states, which degrades the non-volatility property of spin-based devices. Typically, an energy barrier with 40 k_BT can preserve the magnetic state for about 10 yr [18].

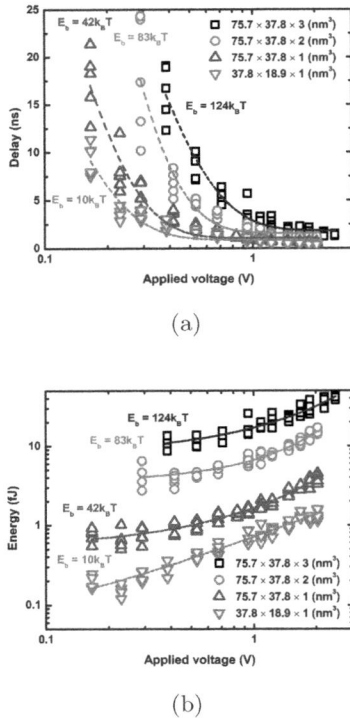

(a)

(b)

Figure 12: (a) Delay and (b) energy versus the applied voltage for different sizes of the receiving nanomagnet. $E_b = 124k_BT$, $83k_BT$, $42k_BT$, and $10k_BT$ can preserve the magnetic state for about 2.25×10^{37} years, 3.52×10^{19} years, 55 years, and 22 μsec, respectively. The interconnect length is 1 μm. The figures are adapted from [9].

4. CONCLUSIONS

In this paper, emerging interconnects for CMOS and beyond CMOS technologies are reviewed. Carbon-based interconnects such as CNTs and GNRs can potentially outperform the copper/low-κ one at the 11-nm CMOS technology node and beyond. Also, interconnects using the spin-valve configuration and spin-transfer-torque effect can potentially provide a low-power interconnect technology for beyond CMOS spin-based devices if proper designs are made.

5. ACKNOWLEDGMENTS

This work was supported by the Interconnect Focus Center, the National Science Foundation (NSF) CAREER Award, and the Intel MSR under Contract 2011-IN- 2198.

6. REFERENCES

[1] G. E. Moore, "Cramming More Components onto Integrated Circuits," *Electronics*, vol. 38, no. 8, pp. 114-117, 1965.

[2] M. T. Bohr, "Interconnect scaling–The real limiter to high performance ULSI," *Proc. Int. Electron Devices Meet.*, pp. 241–244, 1995.

[3] A. Ceyhan and A. Naeemi, "Cu Interconnect Limitations and Opportunities for SWNT Interconnects at the End of the Roadmap," *IEEE. Trans. Electron Devices*, vol. 60, no. 1, pp. 374–382, 2013.

[4] V. Kumar et al., "Performance and Energy-per-Bit Modeling of Multilayer Graphene Nanoribbon Conductors," *IEEE. Trans. Electron Devices*, vol. 59, no. 10, pp. 2753–2760, 2013.

[5] D. E Nikonov and I. A. Young, "Overview of Beyond-CMOS Devices and a Uniform Methodology for Their Benchmarking", *Proceedings of the IEEE*, vol. 101, no. 12, pp. 2498–2533, 2013.

[6] B. Behin-Aein et al., "Proposal for an all-spin logic device with built-in memory," *Nat. Nanotechnol.*, vol. 5, no. 4, pp. 266-270, 2010.

[7] S. Manipatruni et al., "Material targets for scaling all spin logic," arXiv:1212.3362.

[8] R. Mousavi Iraei et al., "Impact of Dimensional Scaling and Size Effects on Beyond CMOS All-Spin Logic Interconnects," *Proc. IEEE IITC/MAM*, to be presented in May, 2014.

[9] S. Chang et al., "Design and Analysis of Silion interconnects for All-spin logic," *IEEE Trans. Magnetics*, accepted, 2014.

[10] S. Chang et al., "Design and Analysis of Copper and Aluminum interconnects for All-spin logic," *IEEE. Trans. Electron Devices*, accepted, 2014.

[11] A. Naeemi and J. D. Meindl, "Design and performance modeling for single-wall carbon nanotubes as local, semi-global and global interconnects in gigascale integrated systems," *IEEE Trans. Electron Devices*, vol. 54, no. 1, pp. 26–37, 2007.

[12] O. Jamal and A. Naeemi, "Ultra-low power single-wall carbon nanotube interconnects for subthreshold circuits," *IEEE Trans. Nanotechnology*, vol. 10, no. 1, pp. 99–101, 2011.

[13] W. Zhou et al., "Synthesis of high-density large-diameter, and aligned single-walled carbon nanotubes by multiple-cycle growth methods," *ACS Nano*, vol. 5, no. 5, pp. 3849–3857, 2011.

[14] Rakheja et al., "Evaluation of the Potential Performance of Graphene Nanoribbons as On-Chip Interconnects," *Proceedings of the IEEE*, vol. 101, no.7, pp. 1740-1765, 2013.

[15] A. H. C. Neto et al., "The electronic properties of graphene," *Reviews of Modern Physics*, vol. 81, no. 1, pp. 109–162, 2009.

[16] S. Rakheja, et al., "Impact of Dimensional Scaling and Size Effects on Spin Transport in Copper and Aluminum Interconnects," *IEEE. Trans. Electron Devices*, vol. 60, no. 11, pp. 3913–3919, 2013.

[17] J. C. Slonczewski, "Current-driven excitation of magnetic multilayers," *J. Magn. Magn. Mater.*, vol. 159, no. 1–2, pp. L1–L7, 1996.

[18] J. Z. Sun, "Spin-current interaction with a monodomain magnetic body: A model study," *Phys. Rev. B*, vol. 62, no. 1, pp. 570–578, 2000.

Making B$^+$-Tree Efficient in PCM-Based Main Memory

Ping Chi, Wang-Chien Lee, Yuan Xie
Department of Computer Science and Engineering, Pennsylvania State University
University Park, Pennsylvania, USA 16802
{pzc139, wlee, yuanxie}@cse.psu.edu

ABSTRACT

Phase change memory (PCM) is a promising technology for building future large-scale and low-power main memory systems. Main memory databases (MMDBs) can benefit from the high density of PCM. However, its long write latency, high write energy, and limited lifetime, bring challenges to database algorithm design for PCM-based memory systems. In this paper, we focus on making B$^+$-tree PCM-friendly by reducing the write accesses to PCM. We propose three different schemes. Experimental results show that they can efficiently improve the performance, reduce the memory energy consumption, and improve the lifetime for PCM memory.

Categories and Subject Descriptors

B.3.2 [**Memory Structures**]: Design Styles—*Primary memory*; H.2.2 [**Database Management**]: Physical Design—*Access methods*

Keywords

B$^+$-Tree, Database, Phase Change Memory

1. INTRODUCTION

Phase change memory (PCM) is an emerging non-volatile random-access memory (NVRAM) with several attractive features [7, 12, 14, 15]. Compared with the modern DRAM technology, PCM offers $2-4\times$ density [14], consumes near-zero idle power, and retains stored data even in a sudden power failure. With the significant density advantage, PCM will be able to store most or all of the data in main memory for many database applications. In addition, PCM can provide traditional main memory databases (MMDBs) [8] with the durability that is not supported by volatile memories. With continuous improvement, the PCM technology is expected to be adopted in large-scale, low-power and non-volatile main memory systems.

Although PCM can bring great benefits to MMDBs, new challenges arise due to its unique characteristics. Different

This work is supported in part by NSF 1218867, 1213052, and 1409798, and Department of Energy under Award Number DE-SC0005026.

from DRAM, the most widely used main memory technology, PCM has asymmetric read/write properties. While the read latency of PCM is comparable to DRAM's, its write latency is about $20\times$ slower than its read latency [7]. In addition, the write operations consume about $5\times$ more energy than the read operations in PCM [7]. Moreover, PCM suffers from the endurance issues. These characteristics, different from the assumptions that have served as the basis in algorithm design of modern database systems, are expected to make the PCM-based MMDBs suboptimal. As writes in PCM are much more expensive than reads, an idea to improve the performance of algorithms running on PCM is to reduce memory writes even at the cost of increasing reads.

In this paper, we focus on enhancing the performance of B$^+$-tree, an efficient index structure widely used in both MMDBs and disk-resident databases, for PCM-based systems. We first design a basic cost model for PCM-based memory systems. Then by analyzing the CPU cost and memory access behavior of the existing PCM-friendly schemes for B$^+$-tree, *i.e.*, the unsorted node schemes proposed by Chen *et al.* [4], we find that: 1) sorting the keys in unsorted nodes before splitting in these schemes involves intensive computations; 2) for small node sizes and small branching factors, these schemes do not effectively reduce the write count; 3) these schemes waste a lot of space in main memory because they do not delete a node until it is empty. To address these issues, we propose three schemes: 1) the *sub-balanced unsorted node* scheme which removes the computational overhead of sorting before splitting in insert operations, 2) the *overflow node* scheme which efficiently reduces the write count in the cases where the existing schemes are ineffective, and 3) the *merging factor* scheme which provides better trade-offs among execution time, PCM wear, memory energy consumption, and space usage in delete operations.

2. BACKGROUND AND RELATED WORK

In this section, we introduce the background and related work of PCM and PCM-based system design.

2.1 Phase Change Memory

PCM is an emerging type of NVRAM, which exploits the unique behavior of chalcogenide glass that enters two different states under different heating temperatures and durations. The two states, termed as amorphous state and crystalline state, have significantly different electrical resistivities. The high-resistance amorphous state represents "0"; and the low-resistance crystalline state represents "1". Furthermore, this material can achieve several distinct intermediary states, thus has the ability to represent multiple bits in a single cell. The multi-level cell technology can further improve the density advantage of PCM [11].

Table 1: Comparisons of different memories [4, 7]

	DRAM	PCM	NAND Flash
Retention	Refresh	10 years	10 years
Density	1×	2-4×	4×
Endurance	$\sim 10^{15}$	10^6-10^8	10^4-10^5
Page size	64 B	64 B	4 KB
Read latency	20-50 ns	$\sim$50 ns	$\sim$25 μs
Write latency	20-50 ns	$\sim$1 μs	$\sim$500 μs
Erase latency	N/A	N/A	$\sim$2 ms /block
Write BW /die	$\sim$1 GB/s	50-100 MB/s	5-40 MB/s
Read energy	0.8 J/GB	1 J/GB	1.5 J/GB
Write energy	1.2 J/GB	6 J/GB	17.5 J/GB
Idle power	$\sim$100 mW/GB	$\sim$1 mW/GB	1-10 mW/GB

Table 1 compares PCM with DRAM and NAND flash. From Table 1, roughly speaking, the properties of PCM lie on the gap between DRAM and NAND flash. Therefore, PCM is considered to be a promising alternative to DRAM as main memory [12, 15] or a promising alternative to NAND flash as storage [3]. Compared with NAND flash, PCM offers several advantages on performance, power saving and lifetime. In this paper, we consider using PCM as main memory.

Compared with volatile DRAM, PCM can provide the following benefits: 1) non-volatility which can maintain data even when power is off; 2) 2−4× as much density as DRAM which implies a larger memory capacity with the same chip area; 3) comparable read latency and energy consumption to that of DRAM; and 4) near zero idle power. Despite of these attractive features, PCM has a couple of challenging issues: 1) the endurance problem that DRAM is free of, which means each cell will be worn out after a limited number of writes; 2) write latency is as $\sim$ 20× long as its read latency and as DRAM's read /write latency; 3) higher write energy consumption. A lot of research work has been done on tackling these challenges of PCM to make it a more feasible and adorable memory/storage replacement. Some improves the lifetime of PCM by using wear leveling strategies [13, 14, 15] and reducing redundant writes [5, 12, 15]; some deals with the long write latency by using a DRAM buffer at architecture level [14] and also by reducing redundant writes at bit level [5, 12, 15]. In this paper, we explore to reduce the write count at algorithm level in order to achieve energy saving and lifetime extension in PCM-based memory systems.

2.2 PCM-based System Design

With the unique characteristics, PCM changes the assumptions regarding the underlying memory systems that have served as the basis for design of various systems, including file systems, operating systems, and database systems. Condit *et al.* proposed a new file system based on the properties of persistent, byte-addressable memory such as PCM [6]. Bailey *et al.* examined the implications of fast, cheap, non-volatile memories such as PCM on OS functions and mechanisms [1].

Chen *et al.* proposed to rethink database algorithm design for PCM, which inspires our work [4]. They present analytic metrics for PCM endurance, energy and latency, and use them to improve two core databases techniques, B$^+$-tree and hash joins, for PCM. Their new design goal for PCM-friendly algorithms is to reduce the number of writes in PCM while keeping good cache performance. To improve B$^+$-tree index, they used unsorted nodes instead of sorted nodes in the tree, saving the writes incurred by sorting a node. The unsorted node schemes are simple and effective. However, we find that they suffer from some issues, which are addressed in the three new schemes proposed in this paper.

Hu proposed a predictive B$^+$-tree, called B^p-tree, for PCM-based database systems [10]. She uses a small DRAM buffer to maintain a small B$^+$-tree for current insertions, and predicts future data distribution based on the summary of previously inserted keys in a histogram. Space is pre-allocated in the memory for near future data so as to reduce the data movements caused by node splits and merges. In this paper, we aim to minimize the hardware overhead and extra design efforts by avoiding the usage of additional DRAM buffer.

3. COST MODEL AND PARAMETERS

In this section, we first present a basic cost model for PCM-based main memory systems. Then we introduce some important parameters in B$^+$-tree algorithm.

3.1 The Basic Cost Model

For each operation on a B$^+$-tree, the execution time T can be divided into three components, the pure CPU time (T_{CPU}, including the access cost to the on-chip L1 cache), the total access time to all the cache levels except L1 (T_{Cache}), and the main memory access time (T_{Mem}):

$$T = T_{CPU} + T_{Cache} + T_{Mem}. \qquad (1)$$

Let I denote the basic instruction count of the algorithm to implement each operation. Let CPI denote the average cycle per instruction of the processor in which memory access latencies in loads and stores are not included, and f denote the frequency of the processor. Then,

$$T_{CPU} = I \times CPI/f. \qquad (2)$$

For a hierarchical memory system with l levels of cache,

$$T_{Cache} = \sum_{i=1}^{l-1} M_i \times L_{i+1}, \qquad (3)$$

in which M_i and L_i denote the miss count and the access latency of the ith level cache separately for $i = 1, 2, \ldots, l$. M_i is determined by a couple of factors, including both the memory access behavior of the algorithm and the characteristics of the ith level cache (*e.g.* capacity, associativity, replacement policies and other cache policies).

To estimate T_{Mem}, we consider two parts, the latency of cache line fetches from the main memory and the impact of cache line write backs to the main memory. The second part can be partially or even completely hidden in conventional DRAM-based main memory systems since the cache line write backs are performed in the background. Let R_{Mem} and W_{Mem} denote the numbers of read and write accesses to the main memory, and Lr_{PCM} and Lw_{PCM} denote the read and write access latencies of PCM. Then

$$T_{Mem} = R_{Mem} \times Lr_{PCM} + \alpha \times W_{Mem} \times Lw_{PCM}, \qquad (4)$$

in which α describes the average impact of the cache line write backs on T_{Mem}, $0 \leq \alpha \leq 1$. For PCM-based main memory, Lw_{PCM} is $\sim 20\times$ as large as Lr_{PCM} (Table 1), so write backs may significantly stall the front-end cache line fetches. Therefore, reducing W_{Mem} might have a large chance to improve performance.

Besides the total execution time T in Eq. (1), the energy consumption of PCM-based main memory, E_{Mem}, is another concern for algorithm design, because PCM suffers from high write energy. We estimate E_{Mem} in three parts: the read dynamic energy, the write dynamic energy, and the background energy. Therefore,

$$E_{Mem} = R_{Mem} \times Er_{PCM} + W_{Mem} \times Ew_{PCM} + E_{background}, \qquad (5)$$

in which Er_{PCM} and Ew_{PCM} denote the average energy consumption of a read access and a write access to PCM. $E_{background}$ is the background energy, which is typically much smaller than the read and write dynamic energy. From Table 1, Ew_{PCM} is $\sim 6\times$ as large as Er_{PCM}. Hence, reducing W_{Mem} is beneficial to energy saving.

As each PCM cell has a limited lifetime, the total wear of PCM should also be considered in algorithm design. Let γ denote the average number of modified bits per modified cache line, then the total wear is

$$Wear_{total} = \gamma \times W_{Mem}. \qquad (6)$$

It can be easily observed that reducing W_{Mem} extends the lifetime of PCM.

3.2 B$^+$-Tree Parameters

B$^+$-tree keeps all data in leaf nodes and uses the information in internal nodes to guide the search. It is easy to maintain and scan while providing fast access time. Thus, it is widely used for metadata indexing in file systems and for table indices in relational database management systems. For different applications, B$^+$-tree may have different key types, *e.g. int* or *string*. Let *key_size* denote the length of a key in unit of bytes. It is determined by the application.

Node size (*node_size*) is an important parameter that affects the performance of B$^+$-tree. Previous work has suggested that the best tree node size is a few cache lines [9]. For modern computers, the cache line size (*cacheline_size*) is usually 32, 64 or 128 bytes.

Let b denote the branching factor (or the order) of a B$^+$-tree, which is the maximum number of children that each internal node can have. For leaves, we assume that a data entry is a tuple of <key, pointer>, in which the pointer points to the external data record. In this case, the leaf node structure is the same with the internal node structure. Therefore, there are at most $b - 1$ keys in either an internal node or a leaf node.

4. ALGORITHMS

In this section, the existing PCM-friendly unsorted node schemes are analyzed before our three schemes are presented.

4.1 Analysis of Unsorted Node Schemes

In the insert and delete operations, keeping the keys of the involved node in order involves a lot of writes. One simple way to reduce the memory write accesses is to leave the node unsorted. Chen et al. proposed three PCM-friendly variants of B$^+$-tree with unsorted node schemes: 1) **unsorted** with all the non-leaf and leaf nodes unsorted, 2) **unsorted leaf** with sorted non-leaf nodes but unsorted leaf nodes, and 3) **unsorted leaf with bitmap** in which each unsorted leaf node uses a bitmap to record valid locations [4]. Since a search incurs a lot of instruction overhead if all the nodes are unsorted, the unsorted leaf scheme captures most of the benefits by reducing the write count and achieves similar search time as the original B$^+$-tree. In our evaluations, we implement the unsorted leaf scheme.

Although the unsorted node schemes reduce the cost of keeping the keys in order in normal insert and delete operations, they make the CPU cost in splits much higher, because it is required to sort the keys before splitting a full unsorted node. The average time complexity for using in-place *Quicksort* is $O(n\log_2 n)$. To reduce the CPU overhead for sorting the keys before a split, the sub-balanced unsorted node scheme is proposed in the next section.

For small branching factors and small node sizes, the unsorted leaf scheme might be inefficient, because keeping keys in order or leaving them unsorted both involve similar write accesses, and splits might incur more write accesses in the unsorted leaf scheme than in the original B$^+$-tree. By exploring different parameters, we find that when $b \leq 10$ and *node_size* ≤ 4, the unsorted leaf scheme cannot efficiently reduce the total write count. Therefore, we introduce the overflow node scheme to cope with such cases of small bs and small *node_sizes*.

In the original B$^+$-tree algorithm, to delete a key from a half-full node, it will either borrow a key from or merge with one of its sibling nodes, which results in a lot of writes. In the unsorted leaf scheme, to reduce the tree reorganization costs, a node will not be deleted unless there is no key in it. However, keeping a lot of near-empty nodes wastes valuable memory space, and even degrade the search performance greatly. We propose the merging factor scheme which provides better trade-off between write count and memory space.

4.2 Sub-balanced Unsorted Node Scheme

As discussed above, the existing unsorted node schemes split a full unsorted node after sorting its keys, and then the two consequent nodes have to be at least half full to keep the tree balanced. However, in our proposed scheme, the new nodes are allowed to be less than half full, *i.e.*, unbalanced, after splitting from a full unsorted node. In this case, we do not need to sort all the keys in a full unsorted node before a split. Instead, we choose a pivot to assign the keys into two nodes – one holds the keys greater than the pivot, and the other holds the rest keys. This enhancement of B$^+$-tree is called *sub-balanced unsorted node scheme*.

The choice of a good pivot is very important to keep the tree balanced and hence efficient. Experiment results show that the middle key value key_{middle} is usually a good choice: $key_{middle} = (key_{max} + key_{min})/2$, so the maximum key ($key_{max}$) and the minimum key ($key_{min}$) in the node should be found first. The time complexity of this scheme for a split is $O(n)$.

4.3 Overflow Node Scheme

When the branching factor and the node size are both small ($b \leq 10$ and *node_size* ≤ 4), we consider reducing the write accesses incurred by splits. In the original B$^+$-tree, a split of a leaf node would involve writes to at least three nodes: 1) the original leaf node which splits, 2) the new leaf node to split to, and 3) the parent node. In our scheme, the updates to the parent node are postponed by splitting the leaf node to an overflow node, and several updates to the parent node are executed in batches later.

In this overflow node scheme, a leaf node can have one or more overflow nodes, and all the nodes are sorted. The overflow nodes have the same structure with ordinary leaf nodes. Here we define two important factors in this scheme.

DEFINITION 1. *The overflow factor of a B$^+$-tree is the maximum number of overflow nodes that each leaf can have.*

DEFINITION 2. *The overflow depth of a leaf node is the number of overflow nodes it attached; the overflow depth of the overflow nodes are the same with the first leaf node.*

For example, if a leaf node has no overflow node, its overflow depth is 0; if a leaf node has one overflow node, the overflow depths of both the leaf node and the overflow node are 1. Only when the overflow depth of a leaf node reaches

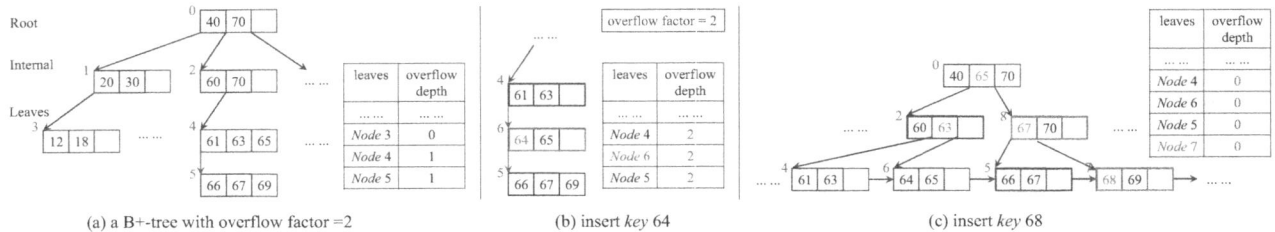

Figure 1: An example of the overflow node scheme. (a) a B$^+$-tree with *overflow factor* = 2; (b) insert a record with *key* 64 to the tree; then *Node* 4 splits to a new overflow node *Node* 6, and its overflow depth becomes 2 reaching the overflow factor; (c) insert a record with *key* 68 to the tree; then *Node* 5 splits to a new node *Node* 7, and *Nodes* 4 − 7 become independent leaves, and a set of keys are inserted to their parent node *Node* 2; then *Node* 2 splits to a new node *Node* 8, and a key is inserted to its parent node *Node* 0.

the overflow factor of the tree, the next split will cause a reorganization of the tree, in which all the overflow nodes of the leaf node become independent leaf nodes and a set of keys are inserted into the parent node all at once.

In the implementation, we maintain the overflow factor of the tree as a global variable, and we modify the structure of leaf nodes to keep the overflow information for each leaf node. We add the overflow depth and an overflow pointer that points to the following overflow node to the original leaf node structure. The overflow depth costs 1 byte, and the overflow pointer is a normal pointer which costs 4 bytes for each leaf node in a 32-bit machine. For *node_size* = 2 cache lines, the space overhead to keep the overflow information in a leaf node is $(1 + 4)/(64 \times 2) \approx 4\%$, assuming the cache line size is 64 bytes. This overhead has little impact on the performance of the algorithm.

4.3.1 Insert

Figure 1 shows an example of the insertion to a B$^+$-tree whose overflow factor is 2. Figure 1(a) is the tree before insertion. It has 6 nodes labeled from 0 to 5, and each node is able to store up to three keys. *Node* 4 is a leaf node, and it has an overflow node, *Node* 5. Figure 1(b) depicts inserting a record with *key* 64 to the tree. *Node* 4 splits to a new overflow node, *Node* 6; and the overflow depth of *Node* 4 becomes 2, reaching the overflow factor of the tree. Figure 1(c) presents the result of the next insertion, inserting *key* 68 to *Node* 5. Firstly, *Node* 5 has to split to a new node *Node* 7. Secondly, because the overflow depth of *Node* 5 has already reached the overflow factor, all the four leaf nodes, *i.e.*, *Nodes* 4 − 7, become independent leaf nodes, and their overflow depths are reset to 0. Thirdly, we need to send all the index information for each independent leaf node to the parent node, so we insert *Node* 2 with a set of three < *key, pointer* > tuples at once. Then *Node* 2 is full and has to split to a new node, *Node* 8, and at last we need to insert a key to its parent node, *Node* 0. From this example, we can see that the overflow node scheme has the ability to postpone the insertions to the parent nodes incurred by splits and to deal with several updates in batches.

4.3.2 Search

It is easy to search a key with our overflow node scheme. Like in the original B$^+$-tree, we can locate the first leaf node, or the 0th overflow node, that may contain the key, and then check if it has overflow nodes. If it has no overflow node, it is the target leaf node, and we can search it and find out the key. Otherwise, the searching key is compared with the last key, also the largest key, of the leaf node. If the key is not greater than the last key, this leaf node is the target leaf node; otherwise, we follow the overflow pointer

to its overflow node, and then check if the overflow node is the target leaf node; and so on. With our overflow node scheme, the path to search a key might be longer, so the overflow node scheme may affect the searching performance.

4.3.3 Delete

The delete operation of the overflow node scheme is similar to the original B$^+$-tree algorithm. To delete a key, we first find it in the target leaf node, and then delete it. If a leaf node (except the root node) is less than half-full, it should borrow a key from or merge with a neighbor node. In the original B$^+$-tree, the neighbor node must be a sibling node. In the overflow node scheme, the neighbor node can also be an overflow node. In our algorithm, an overflow node is preferred since it will not incur writes to the parent node.

4.4 Merging Factor Scheme

In the unsorted node schemes, a node is not deleted unless it is empty. By avoiding tree reorganizations due to deletions, such a delete algorithm reduces writes significantly. However, it may waste too much space and degrade the performance. In the original B$^+$-tree, when a key is deleted from a half full node, it needs to merge with a sibling node if the sibling node has already been half full. However, it may be too early to merge two nodes when they just become less than half full. Therefore, we propose the merging factor scheme, which looses the merging conditions of the original B$^+$-tree. Two important factors in this scheme are defined as follows.

DEFINITION 3. *The filling degree of a node is the ratio of the number of keys in the node to the maximum number of keys that the node can contain.*

DEFINITION 4. *The merging factor of a B$^+$-tree algorithm is the filling degree when two neighbor nodes need to merge with each other if a key is to be deleted from one of them.*

The filling degree is in the range of [0, 1], describing a node's full state, in which "0" means empty and "1" means full. The merging factor is in range of [0, 0.5], whereas the merging factor of the original B$^+$-tree algorithm is 0.5 and the merging factor of the unsorted node schemes is 0.

In our merging factor scheme, the merging factor can be defined less than 0.5, in order to reduce the writes caused by early merges. However, if the merging factor is too small, space may be wasted since many nodes can be near empty.

5. EXPERIMENTAL EVALUATION

In this section, we first introduce our simulation setup, and then present the experimental results.

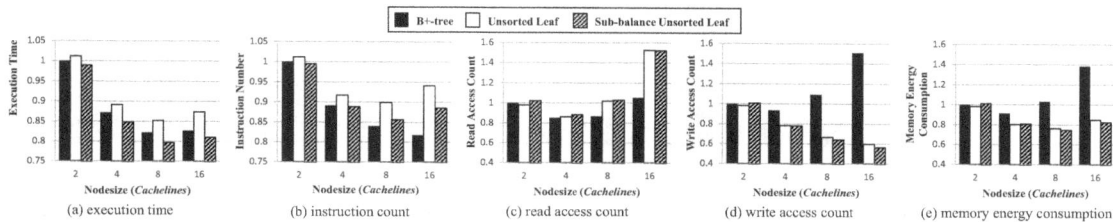

| B+-tree | Unsorted Leaf | Sub-balance Unsorted Leaf |

(a) execution time   (b) instruction count   (c) read access count   (d) write access count   (e) memory energy consumption

Figure 2: Comparison among B⁺-tree, the unsorted leaf scheme, and our sub-balanced unsorted leaf scheme for an insert-only workload (insert one million records with random keys to an empty tree). The results are normalized to those of B⁺-tree with $node\_size = 2$.

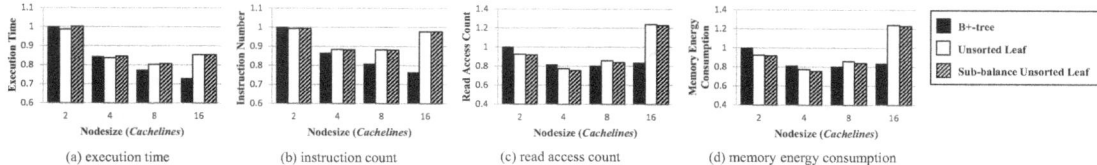

(a) execution time   (b) instruction count   (c) read access count   (d) memory energy consumption

Figure 3: Comparison among B⁺-tree, the unsorted leaf scheme, and our sub-balanced unsorted leaf scheme for a search-only workload (search every record of a tree with one million records in random order). The results are normalized to those of B⁺-tree with $node\_size = 2$.

Table 2: Gem5 Simulation Setup

Processor	1-core, 32-bit alpha, $2GHz$, out of order
Cache	I-L1, $32KB$, 64B line, 4-way, 1-cycle latency
	D-L1, $32KB$, 64B line, 4-way, 1-cycle latency
	L2, 2MB, 64B line, 16-way, 10-cycle latency
Memory	4GB PCM, 2 ranks, 8 banks

5.1 Evaluation Setup

Gem5 [2] is used in our experiments. We modified gem5 to support a PCM model as main memory, and the PCM parameters are set according to Table 1. The processor and memory system configurations are summarized in Table 2.

5.2 Results for The Unsorted Node Schemes

We compare the unsorted leaf scheme and our sub-balanced unsorted leaf scheme with the original B⁺-tree for insert-, search- and delete-only workloads. The key type we use is 16-byte *string*. For the insert- and search-only workloads, we evaluate the node sizes from 2 to 16 cache lines. For the delete-only workload, we test the node size of 4 cache lines.

Figure 2 presents the comparison results for the insert-only workload (insert one million records with random keys to an empty tree). When $node\_size = 2$ ($b = 6$), from Figure 2(d), we find that neither of the two unsorted leaf schemes can reduce the write count. From Figure 2(a) and Figure 2(e), they do not reduce the execution time and memory energy consumption either. That is why we propose the overflow node scheme for small $node\_sizes$ and small bs. As the node size increases, both the two unsorted leaf schemes demonstrate their efficiency in reducing the write count and the total memory energy consumption compared with the original B⁺-tree (Figure 2(d) and Figure 2(e)); meanwhile, the read count increases, as shown in Figure 2(c).

From Figure 2(a), compared with the original B⁺-tree, the execution time of the unsorted leaf scheme is increased by 1.2% to 5.7% among different node sizes. The execution time of our sub-balanced unsorted leaf scheme is decreased to the extent better than that of the original B⁺-tree, by removing the CPU-intensive sorting before splits. As Figure 2(b) shows, its instruction number is decreased compared with the unsorted leaf scheme. It has similar read and write accesses and memory energy consumption to the unsorted leaf scheme (Figure 2(c)-(e)).

Figure 3 demonstrates how the two unsorted leaf schemes affect the search performance compared with B⁺-tree. In

this experiment, we search every record of a tree with one million records in random order. The results show that when $node\_size = 2, 4, 8$ ($b = 6, 13, 25$), the two unsorted leaf schemes incur little performance overhead or memory energy consumption overhead. However, when $node\_size = 16$ ($b = 51$), they have 1.17× execution time and 1.48× total memory energy consumption compared with B⁺-tree. It is because as the branching factor increases, the cost from linear search in the unsorted leaves becomes higher; when the branching factor is large enough, the cost from linear search becomes dominant. These results indicate that, although the unsorted leaf schemes can reduce the write count more efficiently for larger branching factors in insert operations, they may degrade the search performance significantly.

For delete operations, the two unsorted leaf schemes have better performance and lower memory energy consumption than the original B⁺-tree when $node\_size = 4$, as shown in Figure 5. For the delete-only workload, when the merging factor ($mgf = 0.5$, the unsorted leaf scheme can reduce 4.0% write accesses, and save 6.8% execution time and 2.7% memory energy compared with B⁺-tree; the sub-balanced unsorted leaf scheme can reduce 5.1% write accesses, and save 5.0% execution time and 4.3% memory energy.

5.3 Results for The Overflow Node Scheme

We evaluate the overflow node scheme for the cases of small node sizes and branching factors. Figure 4 presents the results of the overflow node scheme with overflow factors (ovf) from 1 to 4 when $node\_size = 2$ and $b = 6$. For the insert-only workload (insert one million records with random keys to an empty tree), as Figure 4(a) shows, the overflow node scheme reduces the write count by 5.8% to 11.8% and saves memory energy by 3.3% to 6.3% as the overflow factor increases from 1 to 4, without hurting the performance. However, for the search-only workload (search every record of a tree with one million records in random order), the overflow node scheme incurs 0.5% to 5.3% performance overhead and increases the total memory energy consumption by 0.9% to 10.9% with the overflow factor from 1 to 4, as shown in Figure 4(b). Therefore, $ovf = 1$ and $ovf = 2$ are two good choices when considering the performance and memory energy of both the insert and search operations.

For delete operations, Figure 5 shows the results of the overflow node scheme with $node\_size = 4$ and $ovf = 2$. Compared with the original B⁺-tree, it reduces execution

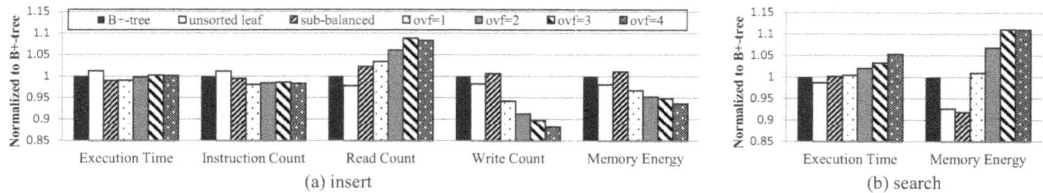

Figure 4: Comparison results of the overflow node schemes for (a) insert-only and (b) search-only workloads when $node\_size = 2$ and $b = 6$ (normalized to the B$^+$-tree results).

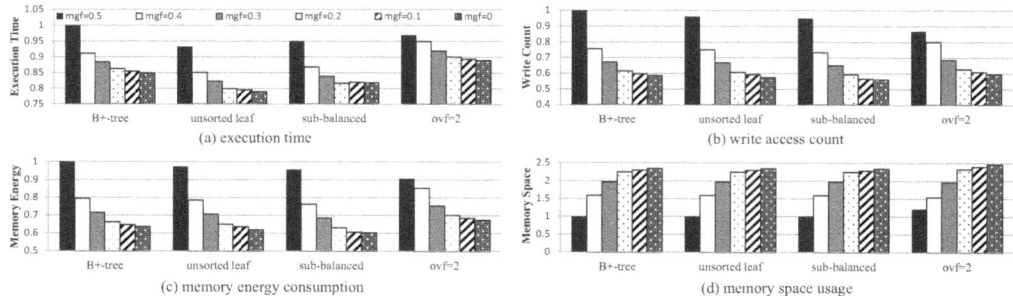

Figure 5: The results of the merging factor scheme for a delete-only workload (randomly delete half the records from a tree holding one million records) with $node\_size = 4$ (normalized to the B$^+$-tree results).

time by 3.0% ($mgf = 0.5$). It also decreases write accesses by 13.1% and saves memory energy by 9.3%. However, these benefits come at the cost of 21.2% more memory space. The reason is that the write accesses due to merge and borrow are reduced; and the leaves can be sparser since a leaf node can borrow keys and merge with an overflow node.

5.4 Results for The Merging Factor Scheme

The merging factor scheme is implemented with the merging factor varied from 0 to 0.5. We use $key\_size = 16$ and $node\_size = 4$ in the experiment. The original B$^+$-tree, the unsorted leaf node scheme, the sub-balanced unsorted leaf node scheme, and the overflow node scheme with $ovf = 2$ are evaluated, for a delete-only workload (randomly delete half the records from a tree holding one million records with random keys). The results are shown in Figure 5. As shown, with the decrease of the merging factor from 0.5 to 0, the write accesses of all the four schemes are decreased greatly (up to $\sim 40\%$) and so are their execution time (up to $\sim 20\%$) and memory energy consumption (up to $\sim 40\%$). However, the space usage is increased dramatically (up to $\sim 2.5\times$). For MMDB applications, space efficiency is also important for algorithm design, although PCM can provide $2 - 4\times$ the capacity of DRAM with the same area. With the merging factor scheme, a proper merging factor can be chosen to make better trade-offs among execution time, total wear, memory energy and space usage.

6. CONCLUSION

As PCM is becoming a promising technology for building large-scale and low-power main memory systems, it may benefit MMDB systems with its high density and other nice features. This paper focuses on the ubiquitous B$^+$-tree and aims to make it efficient in PCM-based memory systems. A new algorithm design goal is to reduce the number of PCM writes that have long latency, high energy consumption, and endurance problems. In this paper, we propose three schemes to address the problems suffered in the existing unsorted node schemes. Experimental results show that the schemes proposed in this paper can provide more algorithm options and better trade-offs among performance improvement, PCM lifetime extension, memory energy saving, and space usage reduction under different workloads.

7. REFERENCES

[1] K. Bailey et al. Operating system implications of fast, cheap, non-volatile memory. In *HotOS*, 2011.

[2] N. Binkert et al. The gem5 simulator. *SIGARCH Comput. Archit. News*, 39(2):1–7, 2011.

[3] A. M. Caulfield et al. Moneta: a high-performance storage array architecture for next-generation, non-volatile memories. In *MICRO*, 2010.

[4] S. Chen et al. Rethinking database algorithms for phase change memory. In *CIDR*, 2011.

[5] S. Cho et al. Flip-n-write: a simple deterministic technique to improve pram write performance, energy and endurance. In *MICRO*, 2009.

[6] J. Condit et al. Better i/o through byte-addressable, persistent memory. In *SOSP*, 2009.

[7] E. Doller. Phase change memory and its impacts on memory hierarchy. *http://www.pdl.cmu.edu/SDI/2009/slides/Numonyx.pdf*, 2009.

[8] H. Garcia-Molina et al. Main memory database systems: An overview. *IEEE Trans. Knowledge and Data Engineering*, 4(6):509–516, 1992.

[9] R. A. Hankins et al. Effect of node size on the performance of cache-conscious b$^+$-tree. In *SIGMETRICS*, 2003.

[10] W. Hu. Redesign of database algorithms for next generation non-volatile memory technology. Master's thesis, National University of Singapore, 2013.

[11] L. Jiang et al. Fpb: fine-grained power budgeting to improve write throughput of multi-level cell phase change memory. In *MICRO*, 2012.

[12] B. C. Lee et al. Architecting phase change memory as a scalable dram alternative. In *ISCA*, 2009.

[13] M. K. Qureshi et al. Enhancing lifetime and security of pcm-based main memory with start-gap wear leveling. In *MICRO*, 2009.

[14] M. K. Qureshi et al. Scalable high performance main memory system using phase-change memory technology. In *ISCA*, 2009.

[15] P. Zhou et al. A durable and energy efficient main memory using phase change memory technology. In *ISCA*, 2009.

Sleep-Aware Variable Partitioning for Energy-Efficient Hybrid PRAM and DRAM Main Memory

Chenchen Fu*   Mengying Zhao*   Chun Jason Xue*   Alex Orailoglu†

*Department of Computer Science, City University of Hong Kong, Hong Kong
†Department of Computer Science and Engineering, University of California, San Diego, USA

ABSTRACT

Energy consumption of memories is always a significant issue for computing systems. Recently, hybrid PRAM and DRAM memory architectures have been proposed. It combines the advantages of DRAM and PRAM, such as low leakage power in PRAM and short write latency in DRAM. However, the leakage power in DRAM is still considerable in hybrid memories. The leakage power can only be reduced by turning DRAM into sleep state. In this paper, a novel proximity concept is proposed to guide the variable partitioning to maximize the possibility of turning DRAM into sleep mode. A novel Sleep-Aware Variable Partition Algorithm (SAVPA) is then proposed with the objective of maximizing the sleep time of DRAM while satisfying the performance and endurance constraints. The experiment results show that SAVPA reduces the energy consumption by 11.25% in average (up to 15.84%) compared to the state-of-art work with simple sleep technique.

1. INTRODUCTION

Energy consumption is always a major concern in the design of memory architecture in computing systems. Dynamic Random Access Memory (DRAM) is commonly used for main memory, but it is facing the challenges such as high leakage power and poor scalability. Recently, non-volatile memories (NVMs) have been emerged as a promising candidate for memory architectures, because of their non-volatility, near-zero leakage power and high density [14]. They have been studied and applied in many areas, such as Flash, main memory, Cache, Scratch-pad Memory, etc. [5,7,8]. Phase change Random Access Memory (PRAM), as a non-volatile memory, is a promising alternative of DRAM to serve as the main memory. However, the disadvantages of PRAM exist with its strengths. The write latency in PRAM is longer and the lifetime of PRAM is limited. In order to exploit the advantages of both PRAM and DRAM, hybrid main memories have been proposed [3,9,11]. An example DRAM and PRAM hybrid memory chip is produced by Samsung [1]. In this paper, we propose a technique to improve energy efficiency of the hybrid memory through a sleep-aware variable partition algorithm.

Hardware and operating system supports for the hybrid

DRAM and PRAM memory are proposed in [3]. Liu et al. [9] propose variable partition algorithms to achieve satisfied trade-offs among energy saving, performance and the number of PRAM writes by putting write intensive variables into DRAM bank. However, the leakage power of DRAM is not considered in [9]. Park et al. [11] reduce the energy consumption of the hybrid memory by minimizing the refreshes in DRAM. They develop a run-time adaptive method of DRAM decay by dynamically writing dirty data to PRAM, and apply a long time out to dirty data to guarantee the acceptable PRAM writes. While [11] focuses on reducing the dynamic DRAM energy, this paper discusses about reducing the leakage power of DRAM. Leakage power is a significant part in the energy consumption of DRAM, and cannot be reduced unless DRAM is turned into sleep mode. In this paper, we discuss how to obtain a proper variable partition to maximize the sleep time of DRAM in hybrid memory to improve energy saving.

There are several previous work considering turning DRAM into sleep state for dual DRAM banks. Wang and Hu [12] introduce a method to partition variables and generate an instruction schedule to reduce the energy consumption by maximizing consecutive, long idle time. In [10], variable partitioning and decisions of when to put DRAM into different operation modes are discussed for energy saving. These work cannot be directly applied in the hybrid memories. For hybrid DRAM and PRAM memory, different memory access latencies and limited number of write operations in PRAM need to be considered to guarantee the performance and the endurance.

In this paper, we define a new concept proximity to explore the sleep potential of DRAM, and propose a novel Sleep-Aware Variable Partition Algorithm (SAVPA) that maximizes the sleep time for hybrid memory, with the guiding of proximity. Experiment results show that the proposed variable partition approach can effectively reduce the energy consumption while meeting the given performance and endurance constraints.

The main contributions of this paper are:

- Constructs graph models to represent the relations between memory operations and between variables.

- Proposes a new concept proximity to evaluate the sleep potential of a partition, and formulates the relationships between proximity and the other metrics, such as parallelism and write ratio, defined in this paper.

- Proposes a novel sleep-aware variable partition algorithm that reduces the energy consumption compared to the state-of-art work.

The rest of this paper is organized as follows: The architecture features and motivating example are given in Section 2. In Section 3, problem formulation and definitions are presented. Section 4 proposes the Sleep-Aware Variable Partition Algorithm. Experiment results and analysis are given in Section 5. Finally, Section 6 concludes this paper.

2. PRELIMINARIES AND MOTIVATION

2.1 Architecture Features

To quantitatively evaluate and compare the performance and energy characters of DRAM and PRAM, in this section, we compare the read/write latency, read/write dynamic energy, and the leakage power of DRAM and PRAM. CACTI [13] and NVSim [4] are employed to derive the parameters of DRAM and PRAM respectively. Results are shown in the following table.

Table 1: Parameters per read/write access for 50nm, 64 MB PRAM and DRAM (*RS for Reset and S for Set*).

	DRAM	PRAM	Ratio	
read latency	12.92ns	21.72ns	$t_{rd} = 3$	$t_{rp} = 5$
write latency	12.92ns	49.64ns(RS) 159.64ns(S)	$t_{wd} = 3$	$t_{wp} = 24$
leakage power	1.12W	0.09W	$e_{ld} = 2$	$e_{lp} = 0$
read energy	0.35nJ	0.74nJ	$e_{rd} = 6$	$e_{rp} = 1$
write energy	0.35nJ	5.30nJ	$e_{wd} = 6$	$e_{wp} = 5$
Evaluation setup	Device Roadmap = LOP, Temperature = 340°C Write Type = conservation, Word Width = 64bit			

From this table, we observe that the leakage power is significant compared to dynamic read/write energy in DRAM. The actual read/write energy is calculated by adding the dynamic energy with leakage power multiplied by the read/write latency. The leakage energy during a read/write access in DRAM is $12.92ns \times 1.12W = 14.47nJ$, which is much larger than dynamic read/write energy $0.35nJ$. The parameter comparison ratios of different access latencies and energy in DRAM and PRAM are abstracted according to the real values. The read access latency is set to 3 cycles in DRAM ($t_{rd} = 3$), and the write latency in PRAM is set according to the average value of SET and RESET operations ($t_{wp} = 24$). The read/write energy in DRAM is set to 6 ($e_{rd} = 6$). Accordingly, in the standby mode, the leakage energy is 2 per cycle, while in PRAM, the leakage power is negligible for 1 cycle. For simplicity, the parameter comparison ratios are used in the motivating example and the experiments instead of the real values.

2.2 Motivating Example

In this section, a motivating example is presented to illustrate that different variable partitions lead to different sleep time in DRAM, and longer DRAM sleep time significantly reduces the energy consumption. The target architecture under study has one DRAM bank and one PRAM bank with two Function Units (FUs). An input DSP application is presented as a Date Flow Graph (DFG) in Figure 1(a). The formal definition of DFG is given in Section 3.

The latency and energy parameters of read/write access to DRAM and PRAM use the ratios as listed in Table 1. Assume that each computing operation takes 1 cycle, and the transition cost between sleep mode and active mode is 1 cycle.

Figure 1 shows the partition and schedule results obtained by different variable partition algorithms. In Figure 1(b), variables a, d, c are partitioned into DRAM and b, e are in PRAM. Most of the time PRAM is idle while DRAM being accessed frequently, which means that the leakage power is on almost all the time. The advantages of the hybrid memory are not fully utilized, as PRAM consumes much less energy than DRAM but seldom used. In Figure 1(c), a, b, c are in DRAM and d, e are in PRAM. DRAM can sleep for 18 cycles to reduce the leakage power at the cost of one

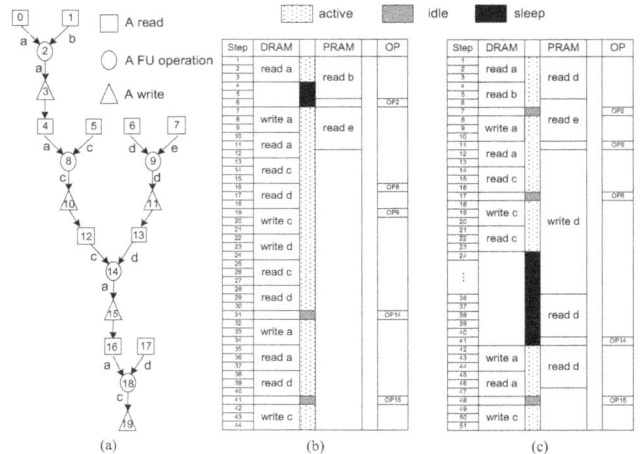

Figure 1: The motivating example. (a) DFG; (b) A solution using algorithm in [9]: DRAM: a, d, c; PRAM: b, e. Valid sleep time = 3. Energy consumption = 88. (c) A solution using the proposed algorithm: DRAM: a, b, c; PRAM: d, e. Valid sleep time = 18. Energy consumption = 79.

extra write in PRAM. The total energy consumption can be reduced from 88 to 79 by assuming both solutions can turn DRAM to sleep as long as the idle period is no less than 2 cycles. The partition in Figure 1(b) is obtained by the algorithm in [9], which does not consider the sleep potential of DRAM. The proposed algorithm in this paper, which outputs the partition in Figure 1(c), targets the critical problem of maximizing the DRAM sleep time through variable partitioning with considering the features of the hybrid memory. This motivating example reveals that further energy reduction can be achieved by appropriately partitioning the variables and turning off the DRAM accordingly.

Note that the schedule length is increased by 7 cycles. If the schedule length deadline comes after step 51, and the algorithm in [9] can turn DRAM to sleep from step 45 to 51, the energy consumed by applying algorithm in [9] is 89 by adding an extra sleep mode transition cost. It implies that under this case, the proposed algorithm effectively reduces energy consumption without leading overhead on performance. In Section 3, we will show that flexible solutions can be derived by using the performance and the endurance constraints as inputs.

3. PROBLEM FORMULATION AND DEFINITIONS

In this section, several definitions used in the variable partition algorithm are presented. The main idea of the proposed variable partition algorithm lies in two aspects. In one hand, to take full advantages of the asymmetric features of DRAM and PRAM, variables that can be accessed in parallel need to be assigned to different banks, with considering write intensive variables should be put in DRAM because of the long write latency and the endurance in PRAM. On the other hand, variables in DRAM are expected to be gathered in terms of access timing as clusters so that DRAM can have a chance to sleep. Two metrics, pertaining to *parallelism* and *proximity*, are accordingly proposed to guide the variable partition. Before introducing these two metrics, we first introduce Data Flow Graph (DFG), Interference Graph (IG), Access Set, Write Ratio and Mobility Window in the following.

Data Flow Graph (DFG): $G_{DFG}(V_d, E_d, X)$, is a directed graph, where V_d is a set of memory and computing operations, $E_d \in V_d \times V_d$ is the edge set that represents the

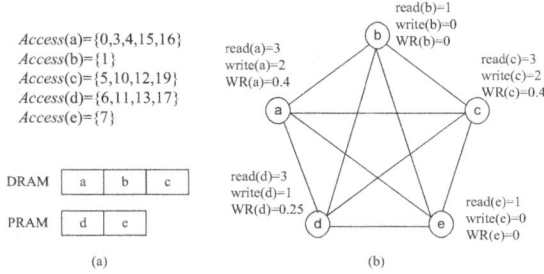

Figure 2: (a) The variable partition and Access Set of the motivating example; (b) IG of the motivating example.

precedence relations between the operation nodes in V_d, and X is the weight set that represents the variables accessed by the memory operations. A DFG example is presented in Figure 1(a).

In order to obtain the access information of a certain variable, the definition of Access Set is introduced as following.

Access Set: Given DFG $G_{DFG}(V_d, E_d, X)$, an Access Set is a set of memory operations that access a particular variable. Access Set for each variable based on the motivating example is listed in Figure 2(a).

Interference Graph (IG) is a widely used graph model in variable partitioning [6]. The definition of IG, especially the weight, varies with different target problem. In this paper, the definition of IG is given as follows.

Interference Graph (IG): IG is an undirected weighted graph $G_{IG}(V_i, E_i, W)$, where $v_i \in V_i$ represents the variable, and $E_i \in V_i \times V_i$ represents the edges that connect variables. In addition, two attributes are associated with each node v_i: $write(v_i)$ and $read(v_i)$, represent the number of write and read operations of each variable respectively. The function W maps from E to two real values including parallelism and proximity, which will be introduced in the following. IG of the motivating example is given in Figure 2(b).

Write Ratio: Given IG $G_{IG}(V_i, E_i, W)$, $write(v_i)$ and $read(v_i)$ attributes of all the nodes $v_i \in V_i$, Write Ratio is defined as $WR(v_i) = write(v_i)/(write(v_i) + read(v_i))$. Considering the number of writes affecting the lifetime of PRAM, Write Ratio is defined to protect the endurance of PRAM. Since a write access takes more time in PRAM than in DRAM, for the sake of both performance and endurance, variables with high Write Ratio are more likely to be partitioned into DRAM.

Mobility Window [15]: For $v_d \in V_d$ in a given DFG $G_{DFG}(V_d, E_d, X)$, $MW(v_d)$ is a set of steps on which a mem-

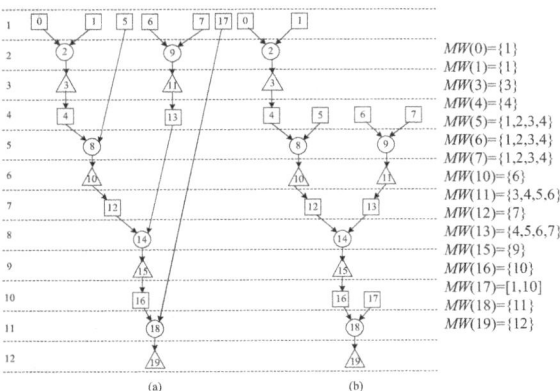

Figure 3: Mobility Window of each memory operation based on the motivating example: (a) Operations are scheduled by ASAP; (b) Operations are scheduled by ALAP.

ory operation v_d can be scheduled. Note that v_d can be scheduled by any scheduling schemes. Mark the step that v_d is scheduled by As Soon As Possible (ASAP) and As Late As Possible (ALAP) as s_{v_d} and e_{v_d} respectively. The Mobility Window of v_d is $MW(v_d) = \{s_{v_d}, ..., e_{v_d}\} = [s_{v_d}, e_{v_d}]$. Figure 3 shows the possible schedule steps and the Mobility Window of each variable.

Based on these defined notations, we introduce two vital concepts for guiding sleep-aware variable partitioning, parallelism and proximity.

Parallelism is used to estimate the possibility of two memory accesses happening at the same step. Different from the previous work [15] [12], in this paper, parallelism is first defined between each pair of memory operations. As a variable may involve multiple operations, we then define parallelism between each pair of variables.

DEFINITION 1. *Parallelism between memory operations $p_a(x, y)$: Given DFG $G_{DFG}(V_d, E_d, X)$ and Mobility Window of each memory operation, the parallelism between two memory operations x and y is*

$$p_a(x, y) = \frac{|MW(x) \bigcap MW(y)|}{|MW(x) \bigcup MW(y)|}$$

DEFINITION 2. *Parallelism between variables $p_a(u, v)$: Given IG $G_{IG}(V_i, E_i, W)$ and Access Set of each variable, the parallelism between every two variables u and v is*

$$p_a(u, v) = \sum_{\forall x \in Access(u)} \sum_{\forall y \in Access(v)} p_a(x, y)$$

Proximity is used to estimate the distance between variables in the scheduling. Two variables with smaller proximity, which means that the memory operations that access them are relatively close in the scheduling, are better to be put into the same memory bank. In this way, memory operations of different variables in a memory bank are gathered as clusters. Each cluster are within a few scheduling steps. DRAM is then more likely to obtain idle period, and be turned into sleep state to reduce leakage energy. In the following, first we define the proximity between memory operations, and then the proximity between variables is presented accordingly. Finally, the proximity of a variable based on a given partition is developed.

DEFINITION 3. *Proximity between memory operations $p_r(x, y)$: Given DFG $G_{DFG}(V_d, E_d, X)$ and the Mobility Window of each memory operation, the proximity is defined in two different ways depending on whether there is a path between two operations x and y or not in the DFG.*

Case 1: There is a path from x to y.

Assume there is a path from x to y in the given DFG. $MV(x) = [s_x, e_x]$, $MV(y) = [s_y, e_y]$. It is possible to schedule x at each step of $MV(x)$. Without loss of generality, assume that x is scheduled at step $s_x + i$, denoted as $S(x, i) \in |MW(x)|$, where $0 \leqslant i \leqslant |MW(x)| - 1$. The mobility range of y, denoted as $P(y, i) \subseteq MW(y)$, might be affected by $S(x, i)$, and squeezed to a subset of $MV(y)$. The problem can be discussed in two subcases.

Subcase(1): If x is in the longest path to y,

$$p_r(x, y) = \frac{s_y + e_y}{2} - \frac{3s_x + e_x}{4}$$

Under this case, the mobility range of y, $P(y, i)$ is determined by $S(x, i)$, and $|MV(x)| \leqslant |MV(y)|$. The proof is straightforward and is omitted due to the space. When x is scheduled at $S(x, i)$, $P(y, i)$ is squeezed to $[s_y + i, e_y]$. Let $mean(P(y, i))$ represent the arithmetic mean of all the values in $P(y, i)$. The average distance between x and y is

$$Dist(x, y, i) = mean(P(y, i)) - S(x, i) \qquad (1)$$

77

Table 2: Details of calculating $S(x,i)$ and $P(y,i)$ for two subcases: (a) Subcase(1); (b) Subcase(2).

$S(x,i)$	$P(y,i)$	$S(x,i)$	$P(y,i)$
s_x	$[s_y, e_y]$	s_x	$[s_y, e_y]$
s_x+1	$[s_y+1, e_y]$	s_x+1	$[s_y, e_y]$
$\vdots$	$\vdots$	$\vdots$	$\vdots$
s_x+i	$[s_y+i, e_y]$	s_y-d	$[s_y, e_y]$
s_x+i+1	$[s_y+i+1, e_y]$	s_y-d+1	$[s_y+1, e_y]$
$\vdots$	$\vdots$	$\vdots$	$\vdots$
e_x	$[s_y+e_x-s_x, e_y]$	e_x	$[e_x+d, e_y]$
(a)		(b)	

The proximity of x and y is obtained:

$$p_r(x,y) = \frac{\sum_{i=0}^{|MW(x)|-1} Dist(x,y,i)}{|MW(x)|} \quad (2)$$

Subcase(2): If x is not in the longest path to y,

$$p_r(x,y) = \frac{s_y - s_x + e_y - e_x}{2} + \frac{(e_x - s_y + d + 1)(e_x - s_y + d)}{4(e_x - s_x + 1)}$$

where d represents the minimal distance from x to y. This situation implies that the mobility of y is also constrained by another incoming path. Note that d, which is the minimal distance, cannot be smaller than $s_y - e_x$, therefore $s_y - d \leqslant e_x$. Similarly, it can also be noted that $e_x + d \leqslant e_y$. When $S(x,i)$ is set between $[s_x, s_y - d]$, the mobility range of y, $P(y,i) = MW(y)$, will not be affected or squeezed. This is because that until now $P(y,i)$ is fixed by the longest path to y. When $S(x,i) \in [s_y - d + 1, e_x]$, $P(y,i)$ is squeezed from $[s_y+1, e_y]$, to $[e_x+d, e_y]$. The rest calculations are similar by using Equation (1) and (2).

The detailed $S(x,i)$ and $P(y,i)$ for each subcase are listed in Table 2.

Case 2: There is no path between x and y.

$$p_r(x,y) = \left| \frac{s_x + e_x}{2} - \frac{s_y + e_y}{2} \right| \times (p_a(x,y) + 1)$$

The first part of the proximity is the absolute value of the distance of two memory operations' average scheduling steps. Then it is multiplied by the parallelism correction which is defined as $p_a(x,y) + 1$, to get the final proximity. This is because if $p_a(x,y)$ is a very big number, which means potentially variable u and v can run in parallel, then putting u and v in the same memory bank may sacrifice too much of the schedule length. As a result, the proximity should be large to guarantee that these two variables are more likely to be partitioned into different memory banks.

DEFINITION 4. *Proximity between variables* $p_r(u,v)$: *Given the proximity between memory operations and Access Set, proximity between variables* $p_r(u,v)$ *can be calculated as follows. For each memory access* $x \in Access(u)$, *find one operation* $y \in Access(v)$ *that* $p_r(x,y)$ *is the minimal among all memory operations related to variable* v. *All the memory operations in* $Access(u)$ *are calculated in the same way.* $p_r(u,v)$ *is the average value of* $\min\{p_r(x,y)\}$ *for all* $x \in Access(u)$.

$$p_r(u,v) = \frac{\sum_{\forall x \in Access(u)} \min\{p_r(x,y)\}, \forall y \in Access(v)}{|Access(u)|}$$

Note that $p_r(u,v)$ *may not be equal to* $p_r(v,u)$.

The reason that we only care about the minimal memory operation distance of two variables is that the minimal operation distance determines whether the memory accesses to two variables are close or not in a schedule. For example, if each minimal operation pair of a variable pair always has a small proximity, it means that the accesses to two variables are always close. As a result, it is clear that these two variables should be put into the same bank. According to the definition of proximity between variables, the proximity of one variable is given as follows.

DEFINITION 5. *Proximity of variable* $p_r(u)$: *For a hybrid DRAM and PRAM memory, variables are partitioned into two groups. Given a partition* $\{B_1, B_2\}$, *considering variable* $u \in B_1$, *for any variable* $i \in B_1$, *the proximity* $p_r(u,i)$ *is obtained. Denote* $p_r(u, B_1)$ *as the average value of* $p_r(u,i)$ *for each* $i \in B_1$. *Similarly, for any variable* $j \in B_2$, *we get the average value of proximity denoted as* $p_r(u, B_2)$. *We define*

$$p_r(u) = p_r(u, B_1) - p_r(u, B_2)$$

In next section, we will use the above definitions of parallelism and proximity to guide the sleep-aware variable partition.

4. SLEEP-AWARE VARIABLE PARTITION

In this section, a novel Sleep-Aware Variable Partition Algorithm (SAVPA) is proposed to compute a variable partition that maximizes the sleep time of DRAM to save energy while satisfying the performance and endurance constraints. The input of the algorithm is a PRAM bank and a DRAM bank with an application presented as DFG, as well as the performance constraint Δ, and the endurance constraint η (which limits the number of writes in PRAM). In SAVPA, variables are first partitioned into two banks by only considering the parallelism. Then variable pairs are picked out of each bank and exchanged between two banks according to the weight value defined in Equation (3). The exchange is evaluated based on whether the new partition can meet the conditions of performance, endurance and sleep time maximization constraints. For each variable i chosen from DRAM and variable j from PRAM, the weight of each pair is defined as follows:

$$w(i,j) = w_1 \times (WR(j) - WR(i)) + w_2 \times (p_r'(i) + p_r'(j)) \quad (3)$$

where w_1, w_2 are the coefficients that represent the tradeoff between proximity and write ratio (which also affects the performance since write access in PRAM has longer latency). For each variable $u \in V_i$, let $p_r'(u) = p_r(u)/\max\{|p_r(v)|\}$ for $\forall v \in V_i$, since the proximity $p_r(u)$ should be normalized between $[-1, 1]$ to match with $WR(u)$.

In SAVPA, first of all, Mobility Window for each operation, the Access Set and Write Ratio of each variable, and the parallelism between each pair of variables are calculated. IG is constructed to be used for variable partitioning. Maximum-Cut is a well known NP-Complete problem. In the initial variable partition, SAVPA uses balanced maximum cut (Line 3) with parallelism sum for the sake of efficiency instead of maximum cut. It is acceptable because the parallelism balanced cut is not a crucial step since variables will be exchanged many times considering energy, performance and endurance. Next, SAVPA schedules the operations. Note that switching DRAM between active mode and sleep mode requires extra overhead in energy. Denote the overhead as a critical threshold ξ. The valid sleep time is the sum of each sleep period which is larger than 2ξ.

However, obtaining an optimal schedule that maximizes the valid sleep time with limited number of FUs is difficult. Considering that the definition of proximity helps enlarge the consecutive idle time, a priority-based scheduling scheme is applied in SAVPA: an available operation with longer critical path has higher priority than others, where critical path

Sleep-Aware Variable Partition Algorithm(SAVPA)

Input: DFG, a DRAM bank and a PRAM bank, Δ, η
1: Calculate the $MW(x)$, $Access(u)$, $WR(u)$, and $p_a(u,v)$ for all memory operations x and variables u, v;
2: Construct IG;
3: Balance cut variables with maximum parallelism into two groups;
4: Partition the group with smaller sum of Write Ratios into PRAM;
5: Schedule the operations, and set L_{crt}, S_{crt} and W_{crt} according to the current partition;
6: **while** Binary search dose not stop **do**
7:     Find the best value of w_1/w_2 for energy saving.
8:     **while** there exists new variable pairs not be scanned **do**
9:         Obtain $w(i,j)$ for each pair of variables i and j;
10:        Ignore the scanned variables pairs, exchange variable i and j with max $w(i,j)$, and obtain L_{new}, S_{new} and W_{new};
11:        **if** $W_{new} \leqslant \max\{W_{crt}, \eta\}$ **then**
12:           **if** $L_{new} = L_{crt}$ & $S_{new} > S_{crt}$ **then**
13:              Keep the exchange, and update L_{crt}, S_{crt}, W_{crt};
14:           **else if** $L_{crt} < L_{new} < \Delta$ & $\frac{S_{diff}}{L_{diff}} \geqslant \theta_1$ **then**
15:              Keep the exchange, and update L_{crt}, S_{crt}, W_{crt};
16:           **else if** $L_{crt} \leqslant \Delta$ & $\frac{S_{diff}}{L_{diff}} \leqslant \theta_2$ or $L_{crt} > \Delta$ **then**
17:              Keep the exchange, and update L_{crt}, S_{crt}, W_{crt};
18:           **else**
19:              Undo the exchange;
20:           **end if**
21:        **else**
22:           Undo the exchange;
23:        **end if**
24:     **end while**
25: **end while**
Output: Variable Partition P

means the longest execution time from this operation to the end of the application.

Before the variable exchanging process, a binary search is conducted within $[0.1, 10]$ for w_1/w_2 in Equation (3). The binary search outputs a minimal energy consumption. For efficiency, the search area is limited to the set of $\{0.1, 0.2, ..., 0.9, 1, 2, ..., 10\}$, as experiments show that a smaller spacing leads to negligible variation of the result. In each iteration of the binary search, for each w_1/w_2 value, we try two neighbor values of the same distance on its left and right side. As long as two schedule results are different, binary search chooses the better direction (with the smaller energy consumption) or stops if both ways are worse. Let L_{crt} be the current schedule length, S_{crt} be the current sleep time and W_{crt} be the number of writes in PRAM.

In each iteration of the exchange process, pick a variable i from DRAM bank and a variable j from PRAM bank that $w(i,j)$ as defined in Equation (3) is the maximal among all (i,j) pairs. Exchange these two variables with each other. The schedule length, DRAM sleep time and the number of writes in PRAM are recalculated according to the new partition, denoted as L_{new}, S_{new} and W_{new} respectively (Line 10). There are several conditions to decide whether the exchange should be kept or not. If W_{new} is either smaller than W_{crt} or threshold η, three subcases are checked: (1) Keep the exchange if schedule length is the same but the valid sleep time is longer; (2) If the new schedule length is longer but dose not exceed the threshold Δ, keep the exchange if $\frac{S_{diff}}{L_{diff}} > \theta_1$. Here, $S_{diff} = S_{new} - S_{crt}$, $L_{diff} = L_{new} - L_{crt}$; (3) If the new schedule length is shorter, keep the exchange if $\frac{S_{diff}}{L_{diff}} < \theta_2$ or $L_{crt} > \Delta$. The value of the threshold parameters θ_1 and θ_2 will be discussed in Section 5. The goal of all the conditions is to guarantee that the sleep potential of DRAM is improved while the performance and endurance constraints are satisfied. After a successful exchange, update $L_{crt} = L_{new}$, $S_{crt} = S_{new}$ and $W_{crt} = W_{new}$. To guarantee the loop finishes, the scanned variable pairs in this iteration, no matter exchanged or not,

will not be chosen again in the following iterations. At the end of the algorithm, a variable partition with maximizing the DRAM sleep time within the constraints of performance and endurance is obtained.

5. EXPERIMENT RESULTS

5.1 Algorithms Evaluation

In this section, the proposed algorithm, SAVPA is evaluated and compared with the state-of-art variable partition algorithm, VPHDP, proposed in [9]. VPHDP achieves satisfied tradeoffs among performance, energy and endurance by putting variables with high write ratios into DRAM. Without considering significant leakage power of DRAM, VPHDP does not try to turn DRAM into sleep state. In this paper, we compare SAVPA with the original VPHDP and a modified VPHDP approach with simple sleep transition scheme.

Benchmarks are selected from DSPstone [16] and mediabench [2], including Finite Impulse Response filter (*FIR*), 2-Dimensional Finite Impulse Response filter (*FIR2D*), 4-stage lattice filter (*4lattice*), 8-stage lattice filter (*8lattice*), volterra filter (*volterra*), MPEG filter (*MPEG*) and Auto Regression Filter (*ARF*). For each benchmark, we use GCC for compilation, obtain its variable access dependency and construct the DFG. PRAM and DRAM are configured using the ratio data from Table 1. The critical sleep length of DRAM, ξ, which is determined by the transition cost between active mode and sleep mode, is set to 2 cycles.

In the experiment, we set θ_1 to 0.9 and θ_2 to 1.1. When the algorithm tries to determine whether a new schedule is better than the original one, $\frac{S_{diff}}{L_{diff}} = 1$ is an obvious metric. It implies that increased (decreased) schedule length works in the sleep mode. The new schedule is at least as good as the original one. The initial partition, which only considers the parallelism, has a partition for better performance than energy. SAVPA encourages a schedule to achieve better energy consumption. As a result, when a new schedule is longer, the metric θ_1 is relaxed a bit, while θ_2 is tighten a little for a shorter schedule. The schedule length is constrained by Δ to guarantee the feasibility of the application, while the endurance of PRAM is protected by the input parameter η. In the following evaluation, we set Δ to $1.2\times$ the schedule length developed by VPHDP, and η to 5 extra writes plus the write number given by VPHDP as inputs.

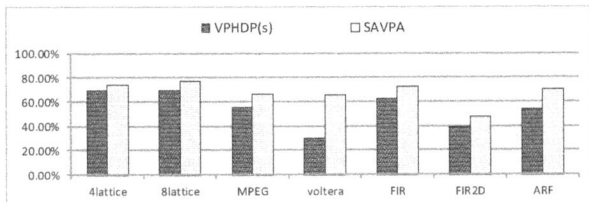

Figure 4: Percentages of sleep time over schedule length on VPHDP(s) and SAVPA.

Sleep time is calculated by counting the valid idle cycles in the algorithm. The valid sleep time over the total schedule length is given in Figure 4. Note that the original VPHDP has no sleep mode transition mechanism. For a more realistic comparison, we assume that VPHDP can also turn DRAM into sleep mode when there is no memory access, denoted as VPHDP(s). The ratio of sleep time over schedule length is improved by 13.21%. The ratio comparison implies that SAVPA can turn DRAM into sleep state for a longer period than VPHDP(s), by which, the leakage power can be reduced.

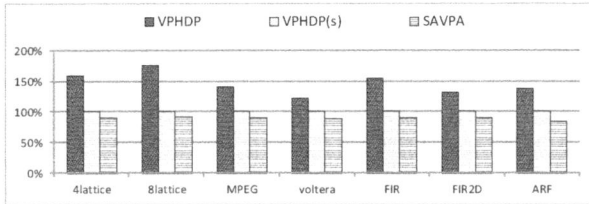

Figure 5: Comparison of the energy consumption of VPHDP, VPHDP(s) and SAVPA.

The energy comparison is shown in Figure 5. The results of the original VPHDP and SAVPA are normalized to VPHDP(s). For the original VPHDP, SAVPA reduces the energy consumption by 38.14% in average. Over the sleep version of VPHDP, SAVPA improves the energy saving by 11.25% in average (up to 15.84%).

The schedule length and the number of writes in PRAM are always in control according to the input performance and endurance constraints. The application feasibility and reasonable number of writes in PRAM make SAVPA a good energy-efficient and practical variable partition algorithm.

5.2 Parameter Variation Analysis

In this section, two sets of experiments are presented to show how the critical sleep length ξ and schedule constraint parameter Δ affect the improvement of energy savings respectively.

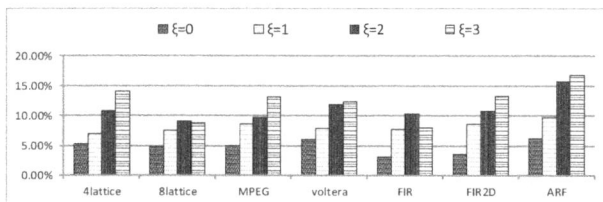

Figure 6: Energy saving improvement of SAVPA over VPHDP(s) on different critical sleep cycles ξ.

The energy saving improvement with different critical sleep cycles are shown in Figure 6. When there is no transition cost between active and sleep mode, the energy saving improvement of SAVPA compared with VPHDP(s) is the smallest. The improvement increases with the critical sleep length being larger. It implies that there are short idle cycles in VPHDP(s). Sometimes they are not long enough to be the valid sleep length. On the contrary, SAVPA has higher potential to obtain consecutive and valid sleep time. Note that the improvement ratio decreases for *8lattice* and *FIR*, when $\xi = 3$. This is because even though SAVPA maximizes the consecutive sleep time, it is difficult to let DRAM sleep if the transition cost is large, especially for compact applications.

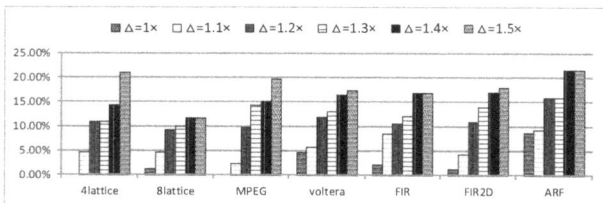

Figure 7: Energy saving improvement of SAVPA over VPHDP(s) on different performance constraints Δ.

Next, we show that with different performance constraints for an application, how is the improvement of energy savings of SAVPA compared with VPHDP(s). From Figure 7, it can be noted that even the performance constraint is the same as the schedule length of VPHDP, SAVPA consumes the same or less energy compared to VPHDP(s). Furthermore, when the performance constraint is relaxed to $1.5\times$ the schedule length of VPHDP, the improvement of energy savings can become as much as 21.51%.

6. CONCLUSIONS

In this paper, we propose a novel variable partition algorithm to maximize DRAM sleep time to reduce the high leakage power of DRAM for hybrid PRAM and DRAM memoriese. Important metrics, such as parallelism and proximity are defined to help construct a better partition for energy consumption, while the performance and endurance constraints are set as inputs to guarantee the schedulability and the lifetime of PRAM. Experiment results show that the proposed algorithm effectively improves the energy saving by 11.25% in average (up to 15.84%) compared to the state-of-art work.

7. ACKNOWLEDGMENTS

This work is partially supported by a grant from the Research Grants Council of the Hong Kong Special Administrative Region, China [Project No. CityU 117913].

8. REFERENCES

[1] Samsung Mobile Memory: http://www.samsung.com/global/business/semiconductor/product/mobile-dram/resource.

[2] MediaBench: http://euler.slu.edu/~fritts/mediabench/.

[3] G. Dhiman, R. Ayoub, and T. Rosing. Pdram: A hybrid pram and dram main memory system. In *Proceedings of the 46th Annual Design Automation Conference*, DAC. ACM, 2009.

[4] X. Dong, C. Xu, Y. Xie, and N. Jouppi. Nvsim: A circuit-level performance, energy, and area model for emerging nonvolatile memory. *IEEE Transactions on Computer-Aided Design of Integrated Circuits and Systems*, 31(7):994–1007, July 2012.

[5] J. Hu, C. Xue, Q. Zhuge, W.-C. Tseng, and E.-M. Sha. Towards energy efficient hybrid on-chip scratch pad memory with non-volatile memory. In *Design, Automation Test in Europe Conference Exhibition (DATE)*, 2011.

[6] R. Leupers and D. Kotte. Variable partitioning for dual memory bank dsps. In *IEEE International Conference of the Acoustics, Speech, and Signal Processing.*, ICASSP, 2001.

[7] D. Liu, T. Wang, Y. Wang, Z. Qin, and Z. Shao. Pcm-ftl: A write-activity-aware nand flash memory management scheme for pcm-based embedded systems. In *Real-Time Systems Symposium (RTSS)*, 2011.

[8] D. Liu, T. Wang, Y. Wang, Z. Shao, Q. Zhuge, and E. Sha. Curling-pcm: Application-specific wear leveling for phase change memory based embedded systems. In *Design Automation Conference (ASP-DAC)*, 2013.

[9] T. Liu, Y. Zhao, C. Xue, and M. Li. Power-aware variable partitioning for dsps with hybrid pram and dram main memory. In *DAC*, 2011.

[10] C. Lyuh and T. Kim. Memory access scheduling and binding considering energy minimization in multi-bank memory systems. In *Design Automation Conference*, 2004.

[11] H. Park, S. Yoo, and S. Lee. Power management of hybrid dram/pram-based main memory. In *DAC*, 2011.

[12] Z. Wang and X. S. Hu. Energy-aware variable partitioning and instruction scheduling for multibank memory architectures. *ACM Trans. Des. Autom. Electron. Syst.*, 10(2):369–388, April 2005.

[13] S. J. E. Wilton and N. Jouppi. Cacti: an enhanced cache access and cycle time model. *IEEE Journal of Solid-State Circuits*, 31(5):677–688, May 1996.

[14] C. J. Xue, Y. Zhang, Y. Chen, G. Sun, J. J. Yang, and H. Li. Emerging non-volatile memories: Opportunities and challenges. CODES+ISSS. ACM, 2011.

[15] Q. Zhuge, E.-M. Sha, B. Xiao, and C. Chantrapornchai. Efficient variable partitioning and scheduling for dsp processors with multiple memory modules. *IEEE Transactions on Signal Processing*, 52(4):1090–1099, April 2004.

[16] V. Zivojnovic, J. Martinez, C. Schager, and H. Meyr. Dspstone: a dsp-oriented benchmarking methodology. In *Proceedings of the International Conference on Signal Processing Applications and Technology*, 1994.

DR. Swap: Energy-Efficient Paging for Smartphones

Kan Zhong   Xiao Zhu   Tianzheng Wang[†]   Dan Zhang
Xianlu Luo   Duo Liu[*]   Weichen Liu   Edwin H.-M. Sha

College of Computer Science, Chongqing University, liuduo@cqu.edu.cn
Key Lab. of Dependable Service Computing in Cyber Physical Society (Chongqing Univ.), Ministry of Education
[†]Department of Computer Science, University of Toronto, tzwang@cs.toronto.edu

ABSTRACT

Smartphones are becoming increasingly energy-hungry to support feature-rich applications, posing a lot of pressure on battery lifetime and making energy consumption a non-negligible issue. In particular, DRAM is among the most demanding components in energy consumption. In this paper, we propose DR. Swap, an energy-efficient paging design to reduce energy consumption in smartphones. We adopt emerging energy-efficient non-volatile memory (NVM) and use it as the swap area. Utilizing NVM's byte-addressability, we propose direct read which guarantees zero-copy for read-only pages in the swap area. Experimental results based on the Google Nexus 5 smartphone show that our technique can effectively reduce energy consumption.

Categories and Subject Descriptors

D.4.2 [**Operating Systems**]: Storage Management—*Main memory, storage hierarchies*

Keywords

Swapping; paging; energy; non-volatile memory; smartphone

1. INTRODUCTION

Thanks to the advances in mobile microprocessors and operating systems, smartphones nowadays integrate more functionality than they ever had, such as the ability to install third-party applications, multi-tasking and gaming. These functionalities, on the one hand bring great user experiences; on the other hand they accelerate the depletion of the limited energy that could be carried by a smartphone in the form of batteries with a capacity of around 1000–2000mAh. Such resource-constrained nature of smartphones in turn affects user experience. For example, in most smartphone OSes, applications are not terminated (thus resources not released) when they are switched to backend to allow faster switch-back. Various daemons also keep running all the time to pull

---

[*]Duo Liu is the corresponding author.

ISLPED'14, August 11–13, 2014, La Jolla, CA, USA.
Copyright 2014 ACM 978-1-4503-2975-0/14/08 ...$15.00.
http://dx.doi.org/10.1145/2627369.2627647.

Table 1: Comparing PCM, DRAM and NAND flash [5, 21].

Attributes	DRAM	PCM	NAND
Non-volatility	No	Yes	Yes
Idle power	~100mW/GB	~1mW/GB	~10mW/GB
Bandwidth	~GB/s	50-100MB/s	5-40MB/s
Write latency	20-50ns	~1us	~500us
Erase cycles	∞	$10^6 - 10^7$	$10^4 - 10^5$

useful information for the user (e.g., notifications for new instant messages). As a result, a lot of energy is consumed by the DRAM-based main memory to maintain these run-time data, leading to high energy consumption.

What makes the situation worse is the trend of adopting large main memories to support feature-rich applications. For example, Google Nexus 5 has as much as 2GB main memory.[1] Larger main memory improves system performance, but inevitably leads to higher energy consumption [4, 18]. It is reported that smartphone's main memory can consume more than 30% of the overall energy [4]. Reducing the energy consumption of main memory becomes critical in smartphones. Most existing work [8, 13] suggests turning off inactive DRAM banks or reducing memory usage. However, these approaches may degrade performance as they essentially reduce usable system memory.

We argue that smartphones should re-adopt swapping with the help of emerging byte-addressable, non-volatile memory (NVM). Swapping is an effective way of extending memory using storage spaces [17]. It has long been a standard feature in modern OSes, but smartphones seldom use it because of the sub-optimal storage (NAND flash) performance. Though flash memory has much better energy consumption parameters than DRAM, it could not be used as the swap area while maintaining acceptable performance. Compared to flash, byte-addressable NVMs such as phase change memory (PCM) [26] and memristor [23] offer not only faster (near-DRAM) performance, but also lower energy consumption. As shown in Table 1, PCM exhibits much better energy parameters when compared to both DRAM and NAND flash. It also exhibits much shorter write latency when compared to NAND flash [27]. A plethora amount of work have been proposed to further achieve near-DRAM performance and better endurance for PCM [2, 7, 9, 12, 16, 19, 28]. Other NVMs such as STT-RAM [6] could promise even faster performance and better endurance than DRAM [10]. Thus, we do not specifically consider endurance or latency issues

---

[1]http://www.google.com/nexus/5

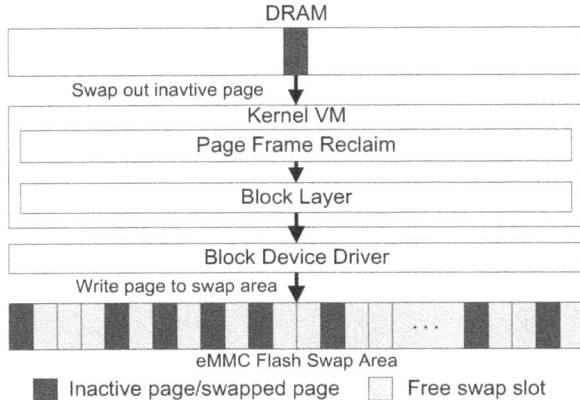

Figure 1: Traditional NAND flash backed swapping.

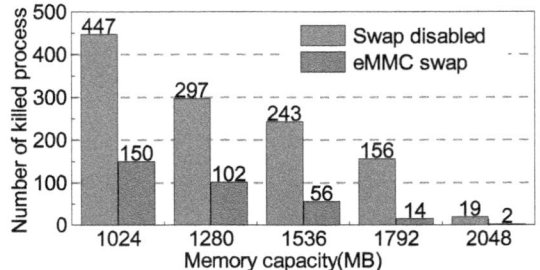

Figure 2: The number of processes killed with and without a swap area under different DRAM sizes.

and focus on energy consumption in this paper. Unlike flash, these NVMs are byte-addressable and can be placed on the memory bus, available to `load` and `store` instructions. Such combination of high performance and low energy consumption makes NVM an ideal candidate for swapping.

In this paper, we propose an in-memory paging architecture called *DR. Swap*, to re-adopt swapping in smartphones by replacing part of the DRAM with NVM, and using NVM as a swap area. With less DRAM, we reduce energy consumption, while the NVM based swap area extends memory capacity to still allow feature-rich applications to run. In addition, utilizing the NVM's byte-addressability, we allow direct read (DR) for read requests directly from the swap area, guaranteeing zero-copy for read-only pages. With DR, read requests are satisfied by mapping the virtual address to the physical page in the NVM-based swap area, instead of by copying the memory page from the swap area to user space. DR is made possible because of the byte-addressability of NVM. In DR. Swap, the NVM-based swap area is attached to the memory bus, eliminating I/O and the whole storage stack overhead. With the traditional swap approach which has to go through the whole storage stack to access a page, we avoid unnecessary memory copying to DRAM, thus reducing energy consumption.

In summary, we make the following contributions:

- We explore the feasibility of re-adopting swapping for better energy consumption behaviors in smartphones;

- Based on byte-addressable NVMs, we propose an in-memory paging architecture to reduce energy consumption while maintaining high performance;

- We propose direct read (DR) to further avoid unnecessary memory copying induced by read-only requests, thus reducing energy consumption.

In Section 2 we first give related backgrounds. Section 3 details the design of DR. Swap. Evaluation results are shown in Section 4. We summarize related work and conclude in Sections 5 and 6, respectively.

2. BACKGROUND

We give background on swapping and energy-related issues in smartphones. We use Google Android as an example as it is the most widely adopted smartphone OS. Note that this work can also be extended to support other platforms.

2.1 Swapping and Paging in Smartphones

Swapping is an effective way to extend memory space by borrowing space backed by storage devices (e.g., NAND flash) in modern OSes [17]. With paging, swapping becomes more flexible as processes could be swapped in and out in units of non-contiguous pages. However, usually swapping is not enabled by smartphones due to the sub-optimal storage (NAND flash) performance [11]. As shown in Figure 1, a traditional swap area is backed by storage, such as flash memory. The swap area is divided into *slots*, each of which is precisely the size of a page. As shown in Figure 1, when memory is under pressure, the kernel will start to swap inactive pages out to the I/O device via the block layer to make room for incoming memory allocations.

To avoid poor performance, mainstream mobile OSes such Android disables swapping and implements a low memory killer (LMK) to reclaim memory by terminating certain processes when the system is under pressure. Despite the poor performance, we find that a swap area can significantly reduce the number of killed processes and improve user experience should we have high performance storage. We plot the number of killed processes by LMK (y-axis) with varying memory capacity (x-axis) in Figure 2. With a flash backed swap area, the number of killed processes could be significantly reduced (e.g., from 447 to 150 with 1G memory). Figure 3 highlights the amount of block I/O induced by a flash backed swap. Swapping greatly increases I/O operations. Recent research has shown that storage plays a significant role in application performance [11]. In particular, when pages are swapped out from main memory to the on-board eMMC flash, a significant portion of bandwidth is occupied, leading to sub-optimal overall performance. Moreover, the erase count of eMMC flash is limited to 10^5 [3]; frequently writing to the swap area further reduces the lifetime of NAND flash.

2.2 Energy Consumption in Smartphones

Due to size, weight and heat dissipation constraints, smartphones nowadays usually can only be equipped with batteries of very limited capacity (e.g., 1000–2000mAh). This implies that energy becomes a first-class citizen in smartphones. In particular, the energy consumed by DRAM is non-negligible [1]. DRAM could account for as much as 34.5% of the overall energy consumption of a smartphone [20]. What makes the situation worse is the trend of adopting large main memories to support feature-rich applications. For example, the Google Nexus 5 smartphone has as much as 2 GB memory. In most smartphone OSes, applications are not fully closed (thus resources not released) when they

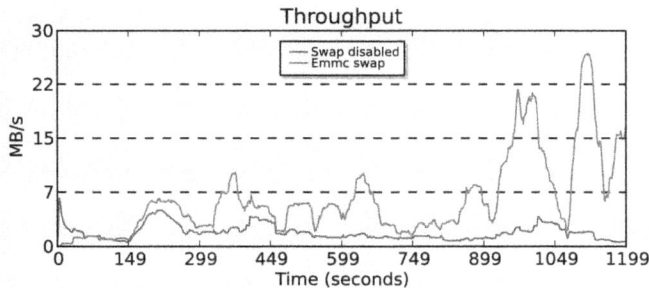

Figure 3: Comparison I/O between eMMC swap and native Android OS with swap disabled.

are switched to backend to allow faster switch-back. Various daemons also keep running all the time to pull useful information for the user (e.g., notifications for new instant messages). As a result, excessive energy is consumed by the DRAM-based main memory to maintain these run-time data, leading to high energy consumption.

3. ENERGY-EFFICIENT PAGING

We first give details on DR. Swap, which consists of our energy-efficient in-memory paging (IMP) architecture and the direct read optimization. In the end, we discuss IMP's energy efficiency.

3.1 In-Memory Paging Architecture

Utilizing NVM's energy-efficiency and byte-addressability, DR. Swap consists of an in-memory paging architecture and the direct read (DR) optimization. Our in-memory paging architecture attaches NVM to the memory bus, side by side with DRAM to make it directly accessible by the `load` and `store` instructions. Different from hybrid memory approaches which treat NVM as part of main memory, we dedicate the NVM region as the swap area, which is usually backed by some I/O device (e.g., NAND flash) in existing systems. Compared to hybrid memories, swapping effectively re-uses the infrastructure that is already existed in mobile OSes and much less intrusive to implement. With IMP, swapping requests become pure memory copying, instead of I/O requests, thus eliminating the need to go through all the storage stack to access data in the swap area, and allowing better utilization of NVM's high performance.

Since we attach NVM to the memory bus, the OS sees an NVM area that shares part of the physical address space with DRAM. We focus on the software side in this paper, but expect the memory controller to provide information on which part of the whole address space belongs to NVM (e.g., through the E820 table in the x86 architecture). The OS can then manage the NVM area by reading such information at boot time. We still use DRAM as main memory and eMMC flash as secondary storage for system and user data. On top of the OS kernel, all system libraries and user space applications work as usual.

Figure 4 shows the details of adopting IMP in existing OSes. When the system is under pressure (i.e., no enough memory for satisfying allocation requests), the memory management subsystem will try to reclaim page frames from running applications and swap them out to the swap area. We replace the traditional swap subsystem with our NVM-based swap subsystem, which accesses NVM directly without going

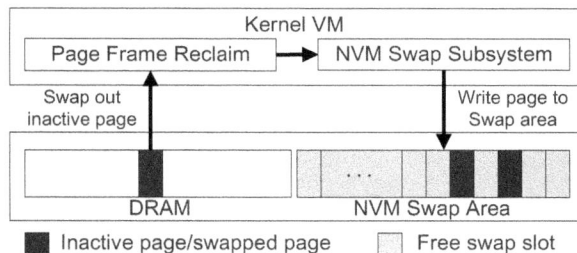

Figure 4: In-memory paging architecture. We replace the traditional storage-based swap area with memory-attached NVM. The memory management subsystem interacts with memory, instead of I/O devices (e.g., flash) to swap in/out pages.

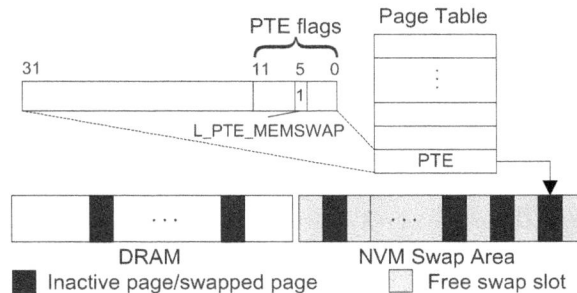

Figure 5: Overview of direct read. DR directly maps the NVM page to the user space from the swap area, saving extra memory copying for page reads.

through the storage stack. Victim pages selected by the kernel's page frame reclaim routine are directly written to the swap area through simple `memcpy` calls. Compared to NAND flash, though NVM could have similar read/write power, it exhibits lower idle power and much faster read/write speed than NAND flash. Compare to the traditional I/O based swap architecture shown in Figure 1, IMP achieves both high performance and energy efficiency.

3.2 Direct Read

In a traditional paging system based on I/O devices (e.g., NAND flash), victim memory pages will be copied first to the swap area and then copied back to main memory (i.e., DRAM) when the page is requested again from the user space. The kernel handles such requests through the page fault handler, which reads the I/O device to fetch the requested page, set up new page table mappings and return to the user application. The whole operation will involve at least one I/O device read, one DRAM page write and one page table entry (PTE) write. It fits nicely with its target architecture. In the IMP architecture, the whole operation now will involve one memory read, one memory write and one PTE write. However, this approach incurs unnecessary memory copying, especially for page reads, since the requested memory page already resides in memory – the NVM – though in a different region.

To remove unnecessary memory operations between NVM and DRAM, as shown in Figure 5, DR directly sets up the PTE mappings from the user space virtual address to the physical address of the NVM page in the swap area, instead of first reading and then copying the page from NVM to

DRAM. In this way, we remove the need of both reading and writing of NVM and DRAM, respectively. Compared to the traditional approach, we save the energy for reading and writing a whole page. The only overhead left is for the PTE write, which only involves writing a 32-bit entry.

DR naturally utilizes the fast read performance of most NVM technologies. We do not allow "direct write" for write requests, due to the asymmetric nature of most NVM's latency (e.g., PCM has much faster reads than writes), wear leveling concerns, and the complication brought by intrusive changes to support writes.

3.3 Energy Model

We analyze the energy efficiency of different paging architectures with the following model. Table 2 lists the power consumption mnemonics and values of read, write, idle and refresh operations for DRAM, NVM, and NAND flash. Energy parameters used in our model are shown in Table 3. We compare the energy consumed by DR. Swap, NAND flash backed swap and `ramdisk` (DRAM-backed) swap. By comparing the energy consumption of DR. Swap with `ramdisk` swap, we show how much energy is saved by our IMP architecture and the DR optimization.

Note that idle power is not included in our model for simplicity. The idle power of different memory technologies have obvious larger-than relationships, and will only add a constant to each pair of comparison result. Thus, the omission will not affect the accuracy of our model when comparing different architectures.

DR. Swap. Swapping pages out involves copying them from DRAM to NVM and then setting up PTEs to indicate that these pages are not present in memory (see details in Section 2). Thus, the energy consumed by W swap-outs is:

$$E_{WN} = W \times S \times (P_{RD} + P_{WN}) + W \times P \times (P_{RD} + P_{WD}) \quad (1)$$

For each page read, no memory copy is required with DR. The only overheads are one NVM read for the processor to access the page in NVM, the PTE write to setup new memory mapping and one DRAM read to read the mapping by the MMU. The energy consumed by R swap-ins is:

$$E_{RN} = R \times S \times P_{RN} + R \times P \times (P_{WD} + P_{RD}) \quad (2)$$

NAND flash backed swap. Swap-out is similar to DR. Swap, except that accessing NAND flash is slower:

$$E_{WF} = W \times S \times (P_{RD} + P_{WF}) + W \times P \times (P_{RD} + P_{WD}) \quad (3)$$

Direct read cannot be applied in this case, thus the energy consumed by R swap-ins is:

$$E_{RF} = R \times S \times (P_{RF} + P_{WD}) + R \times P \times (P_{WD} + P_{RD}) \quad (4)$$

DRAM backed swap. The only difference with NAND flash backed swap is the latency values. For swap-outs:

$$E_{WD} = W \times S \times (P_{RD} + P_{WD}) + W \times P \times (P_{RD} + P_{WD}) \quad (5)$$

Swap-in is similar, with DRAM's latency:

$$E_{RD} = R \times S \times (P_{RD} + P_{WD}) + R \times P \times (P_{WD} + P_{RD}) \quad (6)$$

Comparison. Based on Equations (2) and (4), the difference on swap-ins with DR. Swap and NAND flash is:

$$D = R \times S \times (P_{RF} + P_{WD} - P_{RN}) \quad (7)$$

Similarly, we can derive the difference between DR. Swap and DRAM swap by replacing P_{RF} in Equation (7) with

Table 2: Power consumption mnemonics and values for DRAM, NVM and NAND flash in our energy model. Values are shown in the corresponding parentheses.

	Read (nJ/Byte)	Write (nJ/Byte)	Idle (mW/GB)	Refresh (mW/GB)
DRAM	P_{RD} (0.8)	P_{WD} (0.8)	P_{ID} (100)	P_{FD} (1.35)
NVM	P_{RN} (0.8)	P_{WN} (8)	P_{IN} (1)	P_{FN} (0)
eMMC	P_{RF} (1)	P_{WF} (1.3)	P_{IF} (10)	P_{FF} (0)

Table 3: Energy model parameters.

Parameter	Explanation
R	Number of swap-ins
W	Number of swap-outs
S	Page size, default 4KB
P	PTE length, default 4 bytes

P_{RD}. As we expect that P_{RN} is smaller than both P_{RF} and P_{RD}. When taking idle power and refresh power(for DRAM) into consideration, we conclude that DR. Swap is capable of reducing energy consumption when compared to existing swap architectures. In Section 4 we verify these projections by running various smartphone applications.

4. EVALUATION

We implement and evaluate DR. Swap based on Google Nexus 5 with Android 4.4 (Linux kernel version 3.4). The Nexus 5 smartphone features a Qualcomm Snapdragon 8974 processor clocked at 2.3GHz, 2GB DRAM and 16GB eMMC NAND flash. We focus on energy issues in this paper, though it is obvious that a fast NVM-based swap area will definitely improve performance. We left performance evaluation as future work. The rest of this section first gives our experimental setup. We then present and discuss the results.

4.1 Experimental Setup

We use the Android Debug Bridge (ADB) provided by the Android SDK to communicate with the Nexus 5 smartphone which is connected to a desktop PC. To understand the effect of eMMC flash backed swap, we use blktrace to collect block layer I/O activities. Before each test, we reboot the phone and set aside for few minutes to ensure the device is roughly in the same state (e.g. number of background process). For all the experiments, we connect the phone to a charger and make sure the phone is working in its full performance capability.

We use PCM as the NVM in our experiments. Note that we do not specifically emulate the latency values of PCM, though it is slower than DRAM. As we mentioned in Section 1, a lot of work on improving the endurance and performance of PCM has been proposed. In our future work, we will study how to improve the endurance for NVM backed swap area. Moreover, our system does not rely on any specific type of NVM and can be easily adopted by different NVM-based systems. In our work, we do not focus on which NVM can be served as the swap area, and instead, we focus on the how to design and implement the NVM backed swap area. The energy consumption values for DRAM, PCM, and eMMC flash is shown in Table 2. Table 4 lists the applications we used in the experiments. We classify them into seven categories, including browser, social network, multimedia, office,

Table 4: Workload applications.

Category	Application
Internet	Android Browser, Firefox Browser for Android, Google Chrome, Opera
Social networking	Facebook, Google+, Pinterest, QQ, Sina Weibo, Skype, Twitter, WhatsApp
Multimedia	Google Play Music, MX Player, TTpod Player, Youtube
Office	Evernote, Gmail, Google Drive, Google Maps, Office Mobile
Gaming	Angry Brid, Asphalt 8 , Temple Run 2
Shopping	Amazon, Ebay, Fancy, Google Play, TaoBao
News	BBC News, Engadget, Flipboard, Google Newsstand, NBC News, NetEase News, Netflix, TED, Zaker

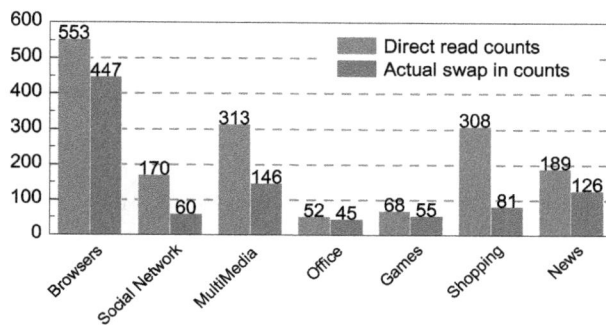

Figure 6: The number of direct reads in 30 minutes.

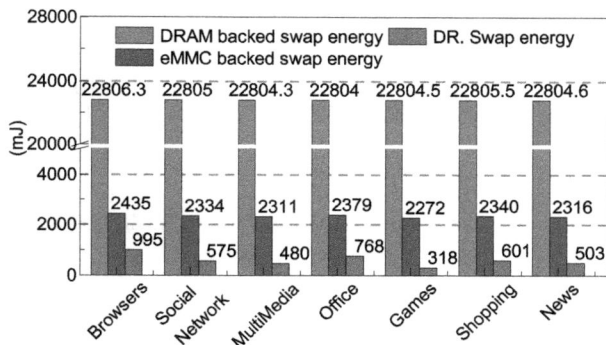

Figure 7: Comparing energy consumption between DR. Swap, eMMC swap and DRAM swap.

games, shopping and news. Those categories have covered the applications we daily used and the application we choice are worldwide popularity. Therefore we use those applications to evaluate our work. By running these applications, we collect data for the following metrics:

Memory copy reduction. To evaluate the effectiveness of direct read, we run all the applications in each category for 15 minutes shown in Table 4 and count the number of reduced memory copy. Accessing a non-present page in DRAM could cause a page fault, we modified the page fault handler to support read a swapped out page in NVM swap area directly. A read counter is used to counts the number of reduced memory copy and a write counter is used to counts the actually swap-ins.

Energy consumption. To evaluate the energy consumption of DR.Swap, we run all the applications in each category to compare the energy consumption under different swap implementations including DRAM backed, eMMC flash backed and DR.Swap. The energy consumption by each swap implementations is computed using the model proposed in section 3 according to the swap-ins and swap-ous.

4.2 Results

Figure 6 compares the number of direct reads and the "real" swap-ins. With an eMMC flash backed swap architecture, the total number of swap-ins can be count as the sum of DR. Swap's direct reads and DR. Swap's "real" swap-ins. With DR. Swap, we reduce the number of required memory copy by around 50% for browsers, office and gaming applications. Moreover, for other applications such as shopping, DR. Swap reduces more than 70% "real" swap-ins.

Figure 7 shows that DR. Swap consumes much less energy when compared to eMMC flash backed swap and DRAM backed swap architectures. The paging architecture we proposed is energy efficient. The energy consumption is computed under the energy model proposed in Section 3. The total energy consists of three parts: swap-in/swap-out energy, idle energy and refresh energy. For eMMC flash swap and DR. Swap, the refresh energy is zero as neither PCM nor eMMC flash requires constant voltage to maintain its data. Because of the limited swap-ins and swap-outs during the 15 minutes, the energy is dominated by the idle energy and refresh energy. Therefore, our results in Figure 7 could hardly show the difference among different categories of ap-

plications when using DRAM backed swap. However, we observe uniformly much lower energy consumption for DR. Swap compared to eMMC flash backed swap. Though eMMC flash backed swap also reduces a considerable amount of energy consumption, it greatly degrades performance due to the sub-optimal I/O design. Therefore, we conclude that an in-memory paging architecture with the help of emerging byte-addressable NVM is the ultimate solution for effective and efficient swapping for smartphones.

5. RELATED WORK

Reducing energy consumption in smartphones has been a focus in the research community. Wang et al. [24] uses profile-based battery traces to estimate the power consumption of mobile applications. To better understand energy consumption in smartphones, Perrucci et al. [18] measured and compared the energy consumed by different components in mobile devices. Shen et al. [22] proposed an energy-efficient caching and prefetching by considering the characteristics of mobile systems such as data update and user request patterns. Lee et al. [14] focused on the optimization of the power delivery network(PDN) in smartphones.

Due to its low standby power, high density and byte addressability, PCM is considered as a promising DRAM alternative [12, 21]. To improve PCM's performance and lifetime, various techniques and systems have been proposed [2, 7, 9, 12, 16, 19, 25, 28]. Hybrid approaches are also used, such as hybrid cache [15] and using mobile RAM and NVM together [4]. Though we do not target at any specific NVM products, we expect them to be energy-efficient, fast, and cheap as predicted. Our system could be easily ported to work with different future NVM technologies.

6. CONCLUSIONS

Reducing energy consumed by DRAM is critical for saving battery lifetime in smartphones. Emerging NVM's energy-efficiency and byte-addressability make it attractive for swapping in smartphones. In this paper, we have proposed *DR.Swap*, an energy-efficient in-memory paging (IMP) architecture to reduce energy consumption in smartphones. We re-adopt swapping in smartphones by replacing part of the DRAM with NVM, and using it as a swap area. We also propose direct read which guarantees zero-copy for read-only pages in the swap area. Experimental results based on Google Nexus 5 show that on average DR. Swap can reduce more than 60–80% energy consumption when compared to flash and DRAM based swap architectures, respectively.

ACKNOWLEDGEMENTS

This work is partially supported by the National Natural Science Foundation of China (61309004), National 863 Program (2013AA013202), Research Fund for the Doctoral Program of Higher Education of China (20130191120030), Chongqing cstc2012ggC40005 and cstc2013jcyjA40025, Fundamental Research Funds for the Central Universities (CDJZR14185501).

REFERENCES

[1] A. Carroll and G. Heiser. An analysis of power consumption in a smartphone. *USENIX ATC*, 2010.

[2] S. Cho and H. Lee. Flip-N-Write: A simple deterministic technique to improve PRAM write performance, energy and endurance. *MICRO*, pages 347–357, 2009.

[3] J. Cooke. Flash memory technology direction. *Micron Applications Engineering Document*, 2007.

[4] R. Duan, M. Bi, and C. Gniady. Exploring memory energy optimizations in smartphones. *IGCC*, pages 1–8, 2011.

[5] S. Eilert, M. Leinwander, and G. Crisenza. Phase change memory: A new memory enables new memory usage models. *IMW*, pages 1–2, 2009.

[6] M. Hosomi, H. Yamagishi, T. Yamamoto, K. Bessho, Y. Higo, K. Yamane, H. Yamada, M. Shoji, H. Hachino, C. Fukumoto, H. Nagao, and H. Kano. A novel nonvolatile memory with spin torque transfer magnetization switching: spin-ram. *IEDM*, pages 459–462, 2005.

[7] J. Hu, C. J. Xue, Q. Zhuge, W.-C. Tseng, and E. H.-M. Sha. Write activity reduction on non-volatile main memories for embedded chip multiprocessors. *ACM TECS*, pages 77:1–77:27, 2013.

[8] H. Huang, P. Pillai, and K. G. Shin. Design and implementation of power-aware virtual memory. *ATEC*, 2003.

[9] L. Jiang, B. Zhao, Y. Zhang, J. Yang, and B. Childers. Improving write operations in MLC phase change memory. *HPCA*, pages 1–10, 2012.

[10] A. Jog, A. Mishra, C. Xu, Y. Xie, V. Narayanan, R. Iyer, and C. Das. Cache revive: Architecting volatile STT-RAM caches for enhanced performance in CMPs. *DAC*, pages 243–252, 2012.

[11] H. Kim, N. Agrawal, and C. Ungureanu. Revisiting storage for smartphones. *FAST*, 2012.

[12] B. C. Lee, E. Ipek, O. Mutlu, and D. Burger. Architecting phase change memory as a scalable DRAM alternative. *ISCA*, pages 2–13, 2009.

[13] M. Lee, E. Seo, J. Lee, and J.-S. Kim. PABC: Power-aware buffer cache management for low power consumption. *IEEE TC*, 56(4):488–501, 2007.

[14] W. Lee, Y. Wang, D. Shin, N. Chang, and M. Pedram. Optimizing the power delivery network in a smartphone platform. *IEEE TCAD*, pages 36–49, 2014.

[15] J. Li, L. Shi, C. Xue, C. Yang, and Y. Xu. Exploiting set-level write non-uniformity for energy-efficient nvm-based hybrid cache. *ESTIMedia*, pages 19–28, 2011.

[16] D. Liu, T. Wang, Y. Wang, Z. Qin, and Z. Shao. PCM-FTL: A write-activity-aware NAND flash memory management scheme for PCM-based embedded systems. *RTSS*, pages 357–366, 2011.

[17] J. Park, H. Han, and S. Cho. Extending main memory with flash – the optimized SWAP approach. *NVMW*, 2014.

[18] G. P. Perrucci, F. H. P. Fitzek, and J. Widmer. Survey on energy consumption entities on the smartphone platform. *VTC*, pages 1–6, 2011.

[19] M. K. Qureshi, J. Karidis, M. Franceschini, V. Srinivasan, L. Lastras, and B. Abali. Enhancing lifetime and security of PCM-based main memory with Start-gap wear leveling. *MICRO*, pages 14–23, 2009.

[20] A. Rice and S. Hay. Decomposing power measurements for mobile devices. *PerCom*, pages 70–78, 2010.

[21] Z. Shao, Y. Liu, Y. Chen, and T. Li. Utilizing PCM for energy optimization in embedded systems. *ISVLSI*, pages 398–403, 2012.

[22] H. Shen, M. Kumar, S. K. Das, and Z. Wang. Energy-efficient data caching and prefetching for mobile devices based on utility. *Mob. Netw. Appl. 2005*, 10(4):475–486.

[23] D. B. Strukov, G. S. Snider, D. R. Stewart, and R. S. Williams. The missing memristor found. *Nature*, 2008.

[24] C. Wang, F. Yan, Y. Guo, and X. Chen. Power estimation for mobile applications with profile-driven battery traces. *ISLPED*, pages 120–125, 2013.

[25] J. Wang, X. Dong, Y. Xie, and N. Jouppi. i2WAP: Improving non-volatile cache lifetime by reducing inter- and intra-set write variations. *HPCA*, pages 234–245, 2013.

[26] H. S. P. Wong, S. Raoux, S. Kim, J. Liang, J. P. Reifenberg, B. Rajendran, M. Asheghi, and K. E. Goodson. Phase change memory. *Proceedings of the IEEE*, 98(12):2201–2227, 2010.

[27] C. Xue, G. Sun, Y. Zhang, J. J. Yang, Y. Chen, and H. Li. Emerging non-volatile memories: Opportunities and challenges. *CODES+ISSS*, pages 325–334, 2011.

[28] P. Zhou, B. Zhao, J. Yang, and Y. Zhang. A durable and energy efficient main memory using phase change memory technology. *ISCA*, pages 14–23, 2009.

Quasi-Resonant Clocking: A Run-time Control Approach for True Voltage-Frequency-Scalability

Visvesh Sathe
Department of Electrical Engineering
University of Washington, Seattle
sathe@uw.edu

ABSTRACT

Resonant clocking has emerged as a promising approach for achieving energy-efficiency in high-performance digital systems. However, the limited frequency range of efficient resonant clocking operation restricts its applicability in widely-used Dynamic Voltage and Frequency Scaling (DVFS) systems. Existing frequency-scalable resonant clocking implementations are either not voltage-scalable, or provide only modest frequency range extension. This paper presents a *true* voltage and frequency-scalable quasi-resonant clock architecture. Simulations on a 64-bit pipelined multiply-accumulate unit in 65nm CMOS demonstrate continuous frequency scalability over 2–200MHz. Efficient operation during dynamic voltage frequency-scaling is demonstrated over 0.8V–1.3V, resulting in a 54% energy-per cycle reduction over conventional distributions.

1. INTRODUCTION

Clock energy dissipation continues to play a significant role in determining the energy-efficiency of a wide range of digital systems, from high performance microprocessors [8–10, 13] to ultra-low power digital circuits employing aggressive pipelining [7]. Following several prototype demonstrations [1–3, 6, 14–16, 18], resonant clocking has emerged as a promising technique to reduce the substantial power dissipated in commercial processor clock distributions [5, 10, 13].

A reliance on mesh-like structures to provide a common point in global clock distributions for low skew and high race-immunity is pervasive among high-volume, high-performance microprocessors [9–11, 17]. With its significant load capacitance, this clock mesh structure accounts for a sizable fraction of average power dissipation of the processor [12, 17].

The main concept behind resonant clocking is to employ inductance to achieve efficient LC resonance, enabling efficient oscillation of the capacitive global clock distribution. A simplified resonant global clock distribution with a single equivalent driver driving a large distributed clock network (modeled as a lumped RC element) is shown in Figure 1a. Although practical integrated implementations typically involve an array of distributed inductors, a single inductor is shown for simplicity.

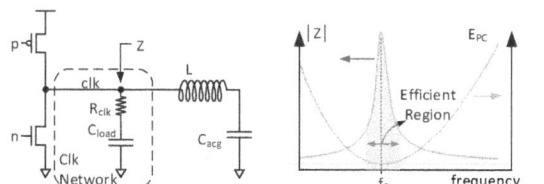

(a) Simplified Schematic using lumped clock capacitance and a single inductor

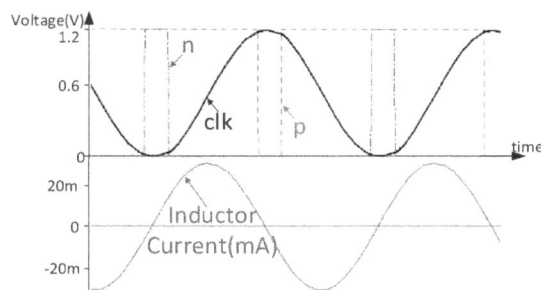

(b) Clock voltage and inductor current waveforms

Figure 1: Basic resonant clock architecture

Figure 1b shows the observed voltage at clk and current flow I_L through the inductor. At frequencies close to the natural frequency f_0 the impedance of the resulting tank circuit increases, consuming lower lower power dissipation while sustaining the desired oscillation amplitude.

With resonant clocking, the per-cycle energy dissipation (E_{PC}) incurred in driving oscillations on a load capacitance C_{load} with peak-to-peak amplitude V_{dd} at frequency f_0 can be expressed as [13]:

$$E_{PC} = \frac{\pi}{4Q} C_{load} V_{dd}^2, \qquad (1)$$

where Q is the system quality factor. Improving Q through low-loss inductors and clock networks reduces clock power dissipation in comparison to conventional clocking. At near-resonance frequencies, E_{PC} remains low as shown in Figure 1a, whereas it increases considerably away from f_0. Furthermore, as reported in [1], operating at frequencies sufficiently below f_0 warps the clock, compromising functionality. For this reason, current resonant clock implementations [10, 12] employ mode switches to disconnect the inductors, using conventional clocking at frequencies further away from f_0. Careful selection of f_0 is required to optimize the system for either Thermal Design Power (TDP) limited peak performance (higher f_0), or average battery life (lower f_0).

Dynamic Voltage and Frequency Scaling (DVFS) is a widely-used runtime technique for energy-efficiency in digital systems [5,

8,9]. Depending on workload, performance and battery-life considerations, the system is tuned at runtime to operate over a wide range of voltage-frequency settings. In such systems, resonant clocking is only effective for a fraction of the operating time of the system, when the frequency is close to f_0. A wide-voltage-frequency range resonant clock architecture which will afford resonant-clocking efficiencies across the entire operating voltage-frequency range is therefore highly desirable.

More recently, an intermittent resonant clocking technique that generates a "blip" waveform, has been proposed [4]. Another approach involves using multiple parallel inductors, each connected by a series switch, to tune f_0 [10]. These methods are however, either limited in achievable frequency range, or are not voltage scalable due to reliability concerns driven by design and clock generator topology.

This paper proposes quasi-resonant clocking (QRC), a novel resonant clock architecture which demonstrates *true* voltage-frequency scalability while meeting several key requirements:

1. No adverse reliability impact: All circuit nodes remain within the supply voltage rails.
2. On-the-fly frequency and voltage scalability.
3. Energy-efficient operation over a wide, *continuous* tuning range from 0 to f_0.
4. Readily controllable clk duty-cycle.

The key observation enabling the proposed architecture is that resonant clock operation can (with the correct circuit topology) be periodically "suspended" for an arbitrary duration of time while the clock is held at V_{dd} or V_{ss}, allowing for true frequency scalability. Runtime-control plays a central role in enabling this scalability. The efficacy of QRC is demonstrated with post-layout simulations of the clock distribution network of a 64-bit pipelined Multiply-Accumulate(MAC) design.

The rest of this paper is organized as follows. Section 2 provides an overview of the related work in the field. Section 3 presents the QRC architecture, including the clock generator topology and the control module which ensures robust DVFS support. Simulation results of the extracted 64-bit MAC unit clock network are discussed in Section 4, including voltage-frequency scaling, duty-cycle control, and energy dissipation.

2. RELATED WORK

Figure 2a illustrates a recently proposed solution involving the use of separate shunt inductors in parallel with a mode switch to make discrete f_0 adjustments [10]. Selecting the appropriate inductor combination enables the system to operate at the most efficient resonant configuration, extending the effective bandwidth.

While well-suited to its specific application and fabrication technology, the approach has limited frequency range, insufficient for wide-tuning range DVFS systems. Furthermore, placing extra inductors under already challenging placement constraints is not feasible in most commercial process technologies.

Another approach, illustrated in Figure 2b involves an intermittent resonant clock generator which creates a frequency-tunable "blip" [4] to enable frequency-scaling. This system has a number of limitations, however. By construction, the clock voltage transitions significantly outside the CMOS voltage rail. In addition to added power dissipation, the near-$2V_{dd}$ swing of the clock is a reliability concern due to oxide-stress in connected MOS devices, limiting the feasibility to near-threshold voltage systems. Finally, the system does not allow for duty-cycle control, a key post-silicon test-optimization.

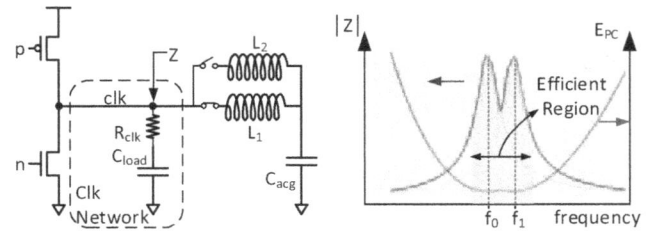

(a) Resonant clocking with bandwidth extension using multiple inductors [10]

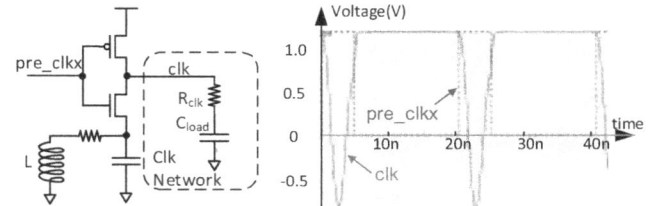

(b) Intermittent clocking generating blip waveform [4]

Figure 2: Existing frequency-scalable resonant clock implementations

3. PROPOSED ARCHITECTURE

The central idea behind the proposed system stems from the observation in Figure 1b that as the clock reaches V_{dd} or V_{ss}, the current flow through the inductor, I_L equals 0. If L is disconnected from the network at this time, clk could be held to the appropriate supply rail indefinitely. Resonant clocking operation can be subsequently resumed by reconnecting the inductor to the clock distribution.

By relying on efficient LC resonance for clock transition, and conventional drive to retain clock-state at either V_{dd} or V_{ss}, QRC achieves robust and efficient wide-ranging frequency scalability, extending resonant clocking benefits across the entire frequency range of DVFS systems.

Figure 3 shows a simplified quasi-resonant clock implementation and timing diagram. The implementation discussed in this paper involves the use of an off-chip inductor. The resulting package parasitics shown in the figure are therefore included in all simulations. A conduction switch M_c, is added to the resonant clock architecture to disconnect the inductor from the clock network. A run-time control unit provides timing for n, p and t by evaluating the potential across conduction switch to determine current flow.

Consider the steady-state operation of the QRC system. The voltage across C_{acg} ($C_{acg} >> C_{load}$) is nearly steady at $Vdd/2$ throughout (for a 50% duty-cycle clock). At the start of the clock cycle, $V(ref\_clk) = 0$, $V(clk) = 0$. As ref_clk transitions to V_{dd}, t is asserted and connects the inductor to the resonant system, resulting in an RL current build-up in the inductor. After a duration τ_{iBuild}, n transitions to 0, turning off the hitherto conducting M_n. This begins the LC driven transition of clk toward V_{dd}. After a delay of $\tau_{riseEdge}$, clk arrives at its peak voltage, the control module senses the clk peak and de-asserts t, disconnecting the inductor from the network, and drives p to 0, turning on M_p and bringing clk to the V_{dd} rail. At the end of this sequence, clk has transitioned to V_{dd}, the inductor remains disconnected from the grid, enabling M_p to hold clk to V_{dd} indefinitely until the next transition of clk toward 0. The sequence of events orchestrating the falling clk edge is conceptually similar to the rising edge sequence and is illustrated in Figure 3b. The detection of the time instant of clk maxima or

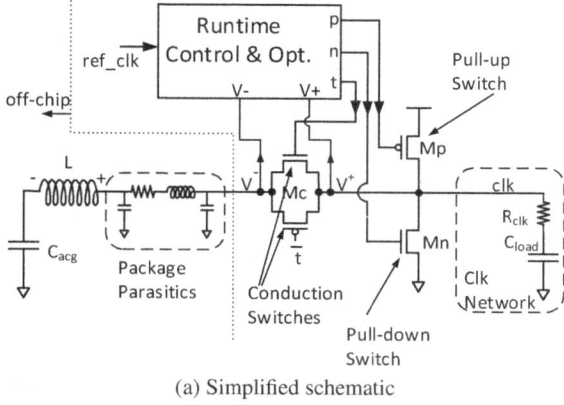

(a) Simplified schematic

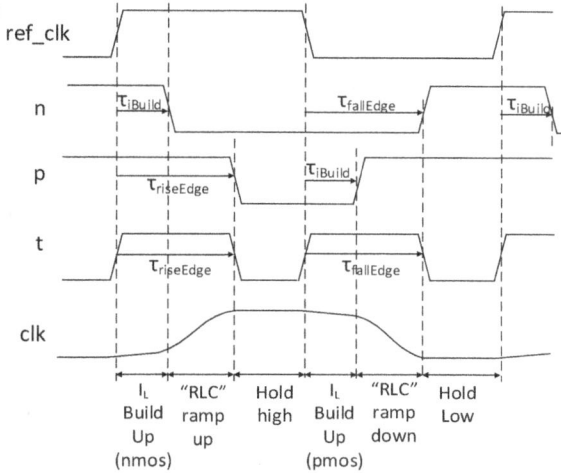

(b) Timing diagram of the quasi-resonant clock system

Figure 3: Proposed QRC architecture

minima coinciding with $I_L = 0$, is performed by comparing the potential difference across M_c.

Quasi-resonant clocking simulation waveforms are shown in Figure 4. The clock transitions between alternate resonant transition phases and conventional hold phases. It is noteworthy that even with perfect timing, I_L does not remain 0 after M_c is off (during the *conv.phase*). The parasitic capacitance in the package trace at V^-, which is at one of the supply rail voltages at the time of disconnection, experiences an under-damped LC oscillation. Ensuring that this oscillation remains contained within the supply rails and does not adversely affect reliability requires accurate timing control of t.

The *continuous* range of frequencies that can be obtained by QRC is $0 < f \leq f_{max}$, where:

$$f_{max} \approx \frac{1}{\sqrt{LC_{load}}}, \qquad (2)$$

Considerations that govern the slew rates of QRC waveforms are identical to those of regular resonant clocks. These slew rates will be lower than conventional clocks [1,4,10,12,16]. Degraded slews impact efficiency and performance due to increased crowbar current and process-dependent clock skew respectively. These challenges can be effectively addressed using a variety of circuit and architectural approaches [7,12,16], and are outside the scope of this work.

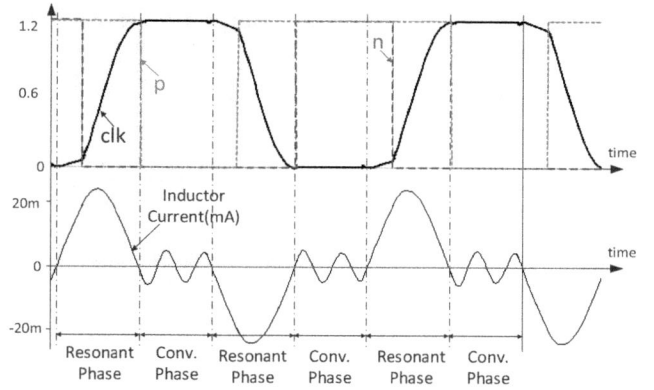

Figure 4: Quasi-resonant clocking simulation waveforms

3.1 Dual-Delay-Locked Loop

Timing requirements for n, p and t relative to ref_clk pose a number of design challenges. It is crucial that t be de-asserted at the exact time that $I_L = 0$, regardless of current-sense delay, or pre-driver latency. Furthermore, the timing for n and p differ for rising and falling transitions of clk. Notice from Figure 3b that while the timing of n (p) during the clk rise (fall) is driven by current build-up requirements, it is the clock transition duration (determined mainly by L and C_{load}) which governs timing during the fall (rise) of clk. Achieving a zero-delay signal-path between the current-sensing mechanism, and t, and enabling context-specific timing requirements for the n and p signals was best achieved by devising a Dual-Delay-Locked-Loop (Dual-DLL).

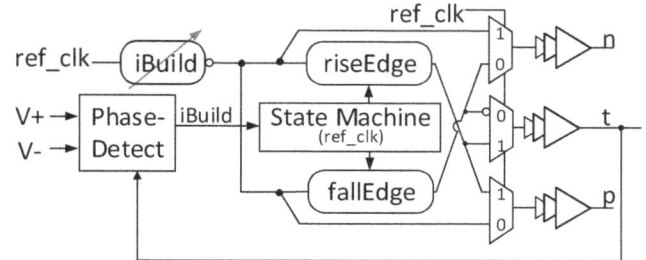

Figure 5: Proposed Dual-DLL for context-specific timing control

Figure 5 shows the Dual DLL module which performs runtime control and optimization of the M_c, M_n and M_p switches. The $iBuild$ delay chain determines the current-buildup duration in the inductor before launching a clock transition. The $riseEdge$ and $fallEdge$ delay chains control the time duration from the de-assertion of M_n (M_p) and the assertion of M_p (M_n). As depicted in Figure 3b, this duration corresponds to the RLC transient driving the clock to V_{dd} (V_{ss}).

The phase detector senses I_L polarity using V^+ and V^-, and provides the dual-DLL with an $iSink$ signal, indicating whether the inductor is sourcing current to, or sinking current from clk. This feedback allows the DLL to adjust $riseEdge$ ($fallEdge$) delays, enabling de-assertion of t when $I_L = 0$ independent of pre-driver latency. Consequently, it is crucial that the phase detector sampling edge and the asserting/de-asserting edge of M_c be driven by the same physical signal.

Given the "double-pumped" nature of the phase-detector, with two evaluations per-cycle (peak and valley detection), $riseEdge$ ($fallEdge$) delay adjustments are made during the falling (rising) edge of the ref_clk to ensure glitch-less n, p and t signals.

Multiplexers at the end of the control path provide the necessary "context-switching" for n, p and t between rising and falling clk edges. The $iBuild$ module is currently not controlled at run-time in the current implementation, resulting in an opportunity loss for further energy optimization.

During an initial power-up or reset sequence, the dual-DLL will not be in lock, resulting in mis-timed inductor disconnection and beyond supply-rail V^- oscillations. To address this issue, the control module "warms-up" to the final state by starting with only a sub-bank of M_c switches, interleaving delay-locking with the additional MC banks until lock is achieved with all M_c banks on. Subsequently, the control module goes into a low-bandwidth (low-power) thermal-tracking mode, and reverts to high-frequency re-lock only during a voltage or frequency change event.

3.2 Phase-detector

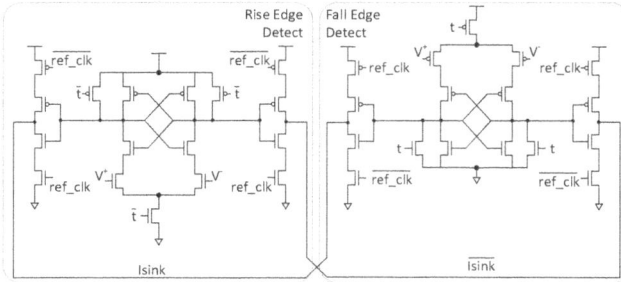

Figure 6: Phase detector used in Dual-DLL implementation

The phase-detector used in the control module is shown in Figure 6. The voltages V^+ and V^-, are both close to either V_{dd} and V_{ss} when sampled to determine I_L direction. Resolving differences at such extreme common-mode voltages with a single latch would be ineffective. Consequently, a dual-sense-amp latch structure was developed. Phase detection is always triggered by a de-assertion of t. Toward the end of a clk rise (fall) transition, if $V^+ > V^-$ at the sampling instant, then the inductor is sinking current and t needs to be de-asserted sooner (later).

The voltages of V^+ and V^- remain close to V_{dd} or V_{ss} and are sampled by the Dual-DLL control before the evaluating phase of the phase-detector resets, enabling the omission of keepers and the traditionally-employed connection device between the differential and cross-coupled inverter pairs.

To address metastability, the phase detector output is double-latched by both rising and falling edge flops, and used by the appropriate Dual-DLL control logic sections to affect $fallEdge$ and $riseEdge$ respectively.

4. EXPERIMENTAL RESULTS

To validate the operation and efficiency of the QRC architecture, a pipelined 64-bit Multiply-ACcumulate (MAC) unit was implemented using commercial Synthesis, Auto Place and Route (SAPR) tools in an industrial 65nm CMOS process. All simulations include post-layout parasitics from the MAC design, back-annotated parasitics for the drivers, conduction switches.

4.1 Setup

Three separate MAC variants were implemented to accurately quantify the benefits of the proposed clock architecture.

4.1.1 Quasi-resonant clock (res_clk)

An industrial place-and-route tool was augmented with a parameterizable resonant clock tree and mesh generator to build the quasi-resonant distribution. The remainder of the design was implemented using a conventional place-and-route flow. Package trace RLC parasitics leading from the conduction switch to the off-chip inductor were included in all simulations, as was power dissipation of the control module, the pre-driver leading up the final resonant clock driver. Following the completion of the MAC design, the clock distribution network was extracted and used for analysis of power. Simulation measurements of the quasi-resonant distribution indicate a clock skew of 6.1ps when V_{dd}=1.2V. Consistent with expectations, the skew remains unchanged at 0.8V.

The QRC controller was implemented using a conventional SAPR flow and its power dissipation is included in the total power dissipation reported.

4.1.2 Conventionally-driven resonant clock distribution (res_conv_clk)

This variant of the design uses the resonant clock tree network but employs *conventional* drive to achieve the same clock skew and slew targets (The inductor, decap and conduction switch are omitted). This variant serves only as a baseline to evaluate the efficiency of res_clk over CV^2 dissipation while driving the same load. Consequently, the significant electromigration (SigEM) challenges at M_n and M_p, resulting from the removal of the inductor are ignored.

4.1.3 Conventional clock tree (conv_clk)

To enable a fair assessment of the efficiencies of quasi-resonant clocking efficiency, a conventional clock distribution was implemented using the SAPR flow with a relaxed skew target of 70ps, and a slew target similar to that of the resonant clock distribution. As in the res_conv_clk implementation, SigEM challenges in this implementation are ignored.

The clock tree synthesis tool did not take advantage of the entire slew budget. The consequent sharper edges in the conventional design would result in lower post-silicon variation-driven skew. Monte-Carlo simulations were therefore performed to quantify the variation-driven clock skew benefit of the conventional clock over res_clk. A 3σ skew-credit was then provided, resulting in a relaxed skew target of 70ps.

4.2 Frequency-only Scaling

Figure 7 demonstrates the capability of the QRC system to perform on-the-fly frequency-scaling. Clock waveforms corresponding to frequency points a, b and c on the frequency-time plot are overlaid. For larger time-periods, the controller need make no adjustments to the delay-chains as frequency scales, and remains locked since the current build-up and transition times are independent of clock frequency – Directly scaling ref_clk achieves the desired scaling result. At lower cycle-times, the under-damped response at V^- following the de-assertion of t has a minor timing impact on clk node maximum and minimum, requiring some delay-chain setting adjustment.

4.3 Voltage-Frequency Scaling

Unlike QRC frequency-scaling, which is relatively straightforward, voltage-scaling is more challenging since voltage-scaling varies delay-chain latencies that need to be maintained. To demonstrate DVFS support, the ref_clk was sourced from a ring-oscillator in the same voltage domain to provide the necessary accompanying change in frequency.

DVFS simulation results of the clock are shown in Figure 8. The initial voltage of 1.3V was scaled down to 0.8V continuously with an accompanying frequency reduction. The runtime control mod-

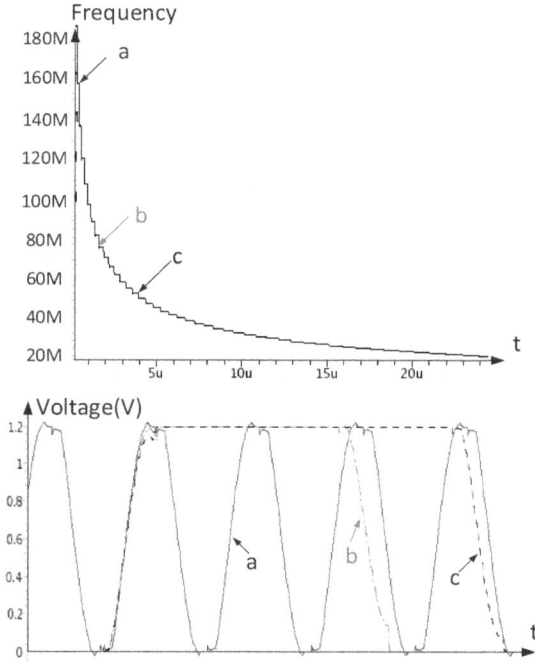

Figure 7: On-the-fly wide-range frequency scaling resonant clocking: clk simulation waveforms

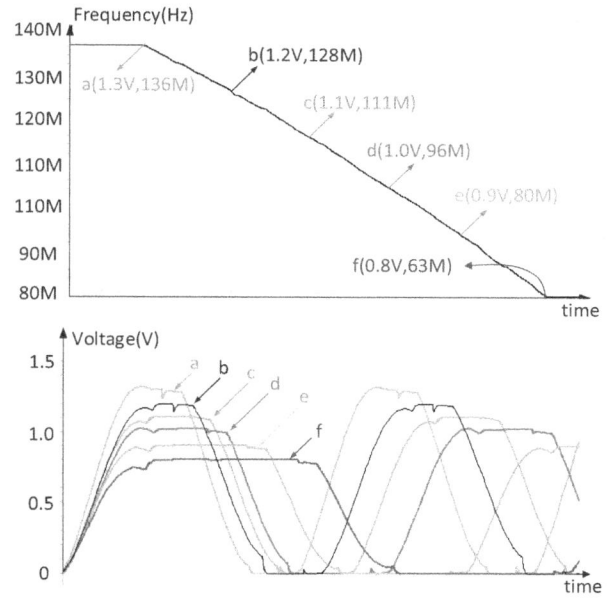

Figure 8: On-the-fly wide-range voltage-frequency scaling resonant clocking: clk simulation waveforms

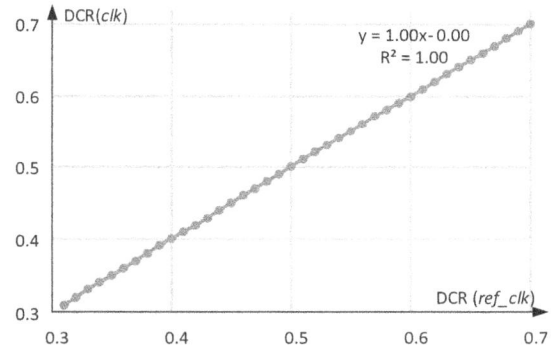

Figure 9: QRC simulation demonstrating ref_clk DCR vs clk DCR

ule bandwidth is sufficient to maintain lock. Clock waveforms corresponding to various voltage-frequency combinations are overlaid and demonstrate correct QRC operation.

4.4 Duty-cycle Control

Duty-cycle control is an important requirement in most clock designs. Dynamic-logic, level-sensitive latches, or other phase-paths require clock duty-cycle control for robust operation. Duty-cycle tuning is also a common post-silicon yield and performance optimization. To the best of the author's knowledge, QRC is the only wide-frequency range resonant clock architecture capable of programmable duty-cycle support. Figure 9 shows the duty-cycle ratio (DCR) of clk as ref_clk DCR varies, demonstrating a wide duty-cycle tuning range.

4.5 Decoupled Efficiency-Frequency behavior

To illustrate the key difference between existing resonant designs and the proposed QRC architecture, constant-voltage frequency scaling in the 2MHz–200MHz range is conducted while monitoring the active E_{PC}.

Figure 10 illustrates the *active* (no leakage) E_{PC} of the quasi-resonant clock and a baseline corresponding to the E_{PC} incurred in driving the same capacitance conventionally (res_conv_clk). QRC energy-efficiency remains nearly constant over 2 decades of frequency-scaling, resulting in approximately 60% savings compared to res_conv_clk . This is in stark contrast to the narrow frequency range of efficient resonant clock operation in current designs [1, 10, 12], even at a constant voltage. QRC always operates "at resonance" from an energy dissipation perspective, regardless of the operating frequency.

One interesting observation from Figure 10 is the fluctuation in E_{PC} of the quasi-resonant distribution at high frequencies. This is caused by the voltage oscillations at node V^- (infer from Figure 4) after the inductor is disconnected. Depending on the fractional re-

lationship between load capacitance and parasitic capacitance on V^-, I_L can either be constructive or destructive at the onset of resonant transition. This interference gradually diminishes at lower frequencies as the V^- oscillations die out and $I_L = 0$ at the onset of the next resonant transition.

4.6 Energy Efficiency

The energy efficiency of the three design variants, res_clk, res_conv_clk and $conv\_clk$ were evaluated. Starting with a 1.3V supply at 200MHz, supply voltage and frequency were scaled following a DVFS profile down to V_{min} at 0.8V. All measurements are made at $25\,^{\circ}$C

Figure 11 shows total E_{PC} dissipation of the three variants across the voltage-frequency scaling range. In this experiment, res_clk efficiency relative to res_conv_clk and $conv\_clk$ vary with frequency because voltage scaling increases the resistance of the M_n, M_p and M_c devices (Figure 3a). Maintaining efficient operation at a lower voltage requires drive strength modulation of drivers [13] or voltage-boosting techniques [4] which have not been implemented in the current work. Nevertheless, throughout the entire voltage range, res_clk dissipates at least 54% lower energy per cycle then

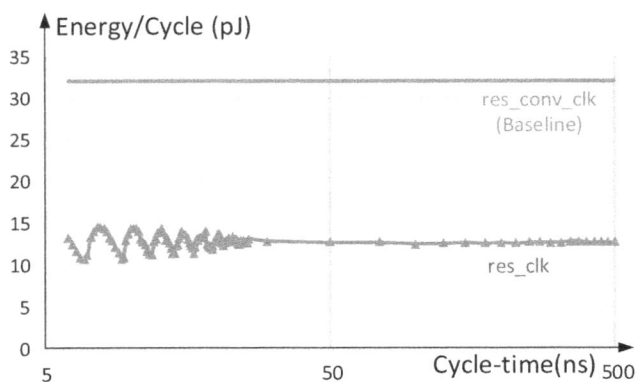

Figure 10: E_{PC} vs. cycle-time

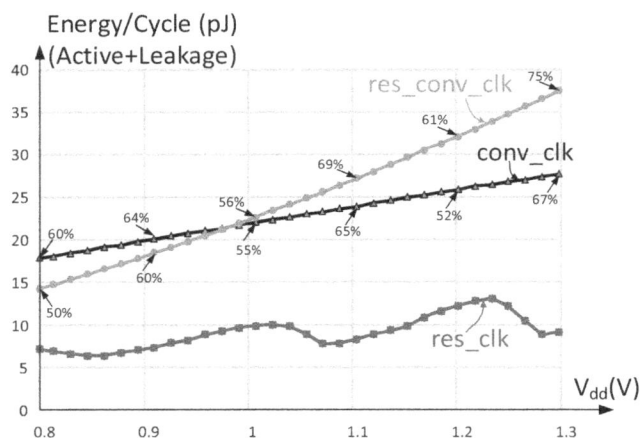

Figure 11: E_{PC} vs. V_{dd}. QRC savings annotated.

either res_conv_clk or $conv\_clk$. E_{PC} fluctuation for res_clk is expected as explained in section 4.5. The resonant clock distribution has a higher total clock load compared to a conventional clock tree due to the wider metal wires and the use of a clock grid. Consequently at higher voltages, $conv\_res\_clk$ dissipates more power than $conv\_clk$. As voltage scales however, energy dissipation in $conv\_clk$ reduces less rapidly due to the increased leakage in the clock buffers, resulting in comparable E_{PC} at 1.0V.

5. CONCLUSION

Quasi-resonant clocking (QRC) is presented in this paper. The proposed solution for the first time, enables true voltage-frequency scalability, allowing resonant clocking efficiencies to be effectively harnessed along with Dynamic Voltage and Frequency Scaling (DVFS) techniques. QRC enables a continuous operating frequency range of $0^+ - f_0$. Simulations of a pipelined 64-bit Multiply-Accumulate clock distribution in a commercial 65nm CMOS process are presented to demonstrate on-the-fly voltage-frequency scaling from 0.8V–1.3V. Energy savings of 50%-75% over a conventional clock distribution are demonstrated. QRC simulations over a frequency range of 2MHz-200MHz are also presented.

6. ACKNOWLEDGEMENTS

The author thanks Sanjay Pant and Radha Poovendran for helpful discussions.

7. REFERENCES

[1] S. Chan et al. A Resonant Global Clock Distribution for the Cell Broadband Engine Processor. *Journal of Solid State Circuits*, 44(1):64–72, Jan. 2009.

[2] S. Chan, P. Restle, and K. Shepard. A 4.6GHz resonant global clock distribution network. In *International Solid State Circuits Conference*, Feb. 2004.

[3] A. J. Drake et al. Resonant Clocking using Distributed Parasitic Capacitance. *Journal of Solid State Circuits*, 39:1520–1528, Sep. 2004.

[4] H. Fuketa, M. Nomura, M. Takamiya, and T. Sakurai. Intermittent resonant clocking enabling power reduction at any clock frequency for 0.37v 980kHz near-threshold logic circuits. In *International Solid State Circuits Conference*, pages 437–437, Feb. 2013.

[5] K. Gillespie et al. Steamroller: An x86-64 Core Implemented in 28nm bulk CMOS. In *International Solid State Circuits Conference*, Feb. 2014.

[6] M. Hansson, B. Mesgarzadeh, and A. Alvandpour. 1.56GHz On-Chip Resonant Clocking in 130nm CMOS. In *Custom Integrated Circuits Conference*, pages 241–244, Sep. 2006.

[7] D. Jeon et al. A Super-Pipelined Energy Efficient Subthreshold 240MS/s FFT Core in 65nm CMOS. *IEEE Journal of Solid-State Circuits*, 47(1):23–34, Jan. 2012.

[8] N. Kurd et al. Next generation intel core micro-architecture (nehalem) clocking. *IEEE Journal of Solid-State Circuits*, 44(4):1121–1129, Apr. 2009.

[9] H. McIntyre et al. Design of the Two-Core x86-64 AMD Bulldozer Module in 32nm SOI CMOS. *IEEE Journal of Solid-State Circuits*, 47(1):164–176, Jan. 2012.

[10] P. Restle et al. Wide-Frequency-Range Resonant Clock with On-the-Fly Mode Changing for the POWER8 Microprocessor. In *International Solid State Circuits Conference*, pages 100–101, Feb. 2014.

[11] P. J. Restle et al. A Clock Distribution Network for Microprocessors. *Journal of Solid State Circuits*, 36:792–799, May. 2001.

[12] V. Sathe et al. Resonant-clock Design for a Power-efficient, High-volume x86-64 Microprocessor. In *International Solid State Circuits Conference*, pages 68–69, Feb. 2012.

[13] V. Sathe et al. Resonant-Clock Design for a Power-Efficient, High-Volume x86-64 Microprocessor. *IEEE Journal of Solid-State Circuits*, 48(1):140–149, Jan. 2013.

[14] V. S. Sathe, J. Y. Chueh, and M. C. Papaefthymiou. Energy-Efficient GHz-Class Charge Recovery Logic. *Journal of Solid State Circuits*, 42(1):38–47, Jan. 2007.

[15] V. S. Sathe, J. C. Kao, and M. C. Papaefthymiou. RF2: A 1GHz FIR Filter with Distributed Resonant Clock Generator. In *IEEE Symposium on VLSI Circuits*, pages 44–45, Jun. 2007.

[16] V. S. Sathe, J. C. Kao, and M. C. Papaefthymiou. Resonant-Clock Latch-Based Design. *Journal of Solid State Circuits*, 43(4):864–873, Apr. 2008.

[17] G. Shamanna, N. Kurd, J. Douglas, and M. Morrise. Scalable, sub-1w, sub-10ps Clock Skew, Global Clock Distribution Architecture for Intel Core i7/i5/i3 Microprocessors. In *VLSI Circuits (VLSIC), 2010 IEEE Symposium on*, pages 83–84, June 2010.

[18] J. Wood, T. Edwards, and S. Lipa. Rotary Traveling-wave Oscillator Arrays: a New Clock Technology. *Journal of Solid State Circuits*, 36:1654–1665, Nov. 2001.

An Energy-efficient 2.5D Through-silicon Interposer I/O with Self-adaptive Adjustment of Output-voltage Swing

Dongjun Xu[1,2], Sai Manoj P. D.[1], Hantao Huang[1], Ningmei Yu[2] and Hao Yu[1]
[1]School of Electrical and Electronic Engineering, Nanyang Technological University, Singapore 639798
[2] Dept. of Electronic Engineering, Xi'an University of Technology, Xi'an, China 710048
Email: haoyu@ntu.edu.sg.

ABSTRACT

A self-adaptive output swing adjustment is introduced for the design of energy-efficient 2.5D through-silicon interposer (TSI) I/Os. Instead of transmitting signal with large voltage swing, Q-learning based self-adaptive adjustment is deployed to adjust I/O output-voltage swing under constraints of both power budget and bit error rate (BER). Experimental results show that the adaptive 2.5D TSI I/Os designed in $65nm$ CMOS can achieve an average of $13mW$ I/O power, $4GHz$ bandwidth and $3.25pJ/bit$ energy efficiency for one channel under 10^{-6} BER, which has 21.42% reduction of power and 14.47% energy efficiency improvement.

Categories and Subject Descriptors: B.4.2 [Input/Output Devices]:Channels and controllers

Keywords: output-voltage swing tuning; TSI I/O; 2.5D integration; I/O Channel controller; Q-learning.

1. INTRODUCTION

There is an emerging need to process large amount of data with high bandwidth and low power consumption I/Os for an energy-efficient cloud-server, which is mainly based on the integration of many-core processors with shared memory [1]. A 3D integration by stacking several layers of dies vertically using through-silicon via (TSV) [2, 3, 4] has better scalability of integration but worse thermal density for heat dissipation [5, 6]. A 2.5D integration by through-silicon interposer (TSI) in common substrate has gained recent interest for memory-logic integration in cloud-server design due to better thermal dissipation capability [7, 8]. Compared to the 3D integration by TSV, TSI based 2.5D also enables the integration of transmission line (T-line) based I/O design to achieve high bandwidth and low power [9]. It has no area overhead because the interposer based T-line can be deployed underneath the substrate. Hence it has become an interest to design energy-efficient I/Os using TSI based T-line for the integration of many-core microprocessors with shared memory.

Previous work of wire-line communication by PCB trace of backplane [10] has large latency and poor signal-to-noise ratio of the transmission channel. Moreover, all previous works [11, 12] assume uniform output-voltage swing that consumes large I/O communication power. To meet a low communication power budget, output-voltage swing at transmitter can be reduced. However, the reduction in output-voltage swing increases bit error rate (BER) at receiver [13, 14]. Therefore it has become a trade-off to balance the BER and energy efficiency during the

I/O communication by TSI. In this paper, we have proposed an adaptive 2.5D I/O design that can automatically adjust output-voltage swing with balanced consideration of energy efficiency and BER. An error correcting code (ECC) is developed for checking BER. One Q-learning based management is applied to adjust the level of output-voltage swing at transmitter (associated with cores) such that one can achieve a reduced power under specified BER requirement.

The adaptive I/Os are integrated with the TSI based transmission line (T-line) implemented in $65nm$ CMOS process. Experimental results show that the adaptive 2.5D TSI I/Os designed in $65nm$ CMOS can achieve an average of $13mW$ I/O power, $4GHz$ bandwidth and $3.25pJ/bit$ energy efficiency for one channel under 10^{-6} BER, which has 21.42% reduction of power and 14.47% improvement of energy efficiency. The remainder of this paper is organized as follows. Firstly, we describe the memory-logic integration architecture by 2.5D TSI integration with an adaptive I/O design; and the according problem of adaptive control in Section 2. Section 3 presents the circuit blocks of 2.5D TSI based receiver/transmitter, error-correcting code and adaptive tuning. In Section 4, the adaptive output-voltage swing tuning by the Q-learning algorithm is presented. The experimental results are shown in Section 5 with conclusion in Section 6.

2. 2.5D TSI I/O COMMUNICATION

In this section, we will present memory-logic integration architecture by TSI I/O followed by problem formulation of the adaptive I/O design for power versus BER.

2.1 Memory-logic Integration by 2.5D TSI I/O

The traditional interconnection between processors and memories is by printed circuit board (PCB) with backplane [10] containing sockets into which other boards can be plugged in (See Fig. 1(a)(i)). However, long trace ($\geq 25cm$) and non-ideal vias are needed at PCB scale, hence there is a severe loss on the backplane, which requires current-starved circuits to reach the high data rate and equalizers to compensate the channel loss [10]. For the 2.5D TSI technology [7], the processors and memories dies are integrated on one common substrate by silicon interposer underneath (See Fig. 1(a)(ii)). Unlike traditional backplane based interconnects, 2.5D TSIs are much shorter with a few mm in length and are deployed underneath the substrate with less routing overhead. The channel loss vs. frequency is shown in Fig. 1(b) for PCB backplane I/O and 2.5D TSI I/O, respectively. When comparing the loss at $5GHz$ clock frequency, the PCB backplane with long ($25cm$) trace has nearly $24dB$ channel loss; and the TSI with small trace ($10\mu m$ width, $3mm$ length) has only $1dB$ loss. Hence, the 2.5D TSI based integration has much less loss with better performance for the memory-logic-integration. When compared to the 3D through-silicon-via based integration, the 2.5D TSI based integration further shows much better thermal dissipation capability [7, 8].

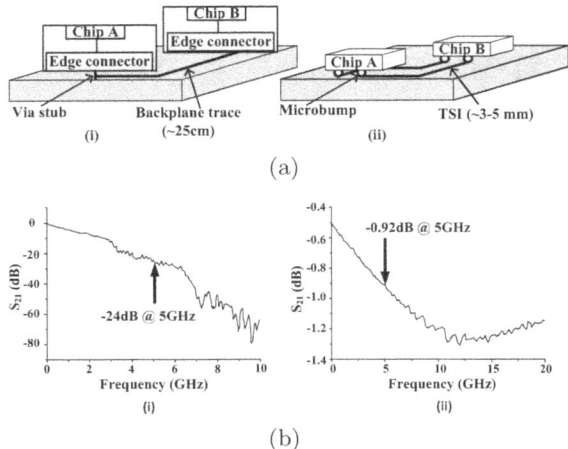

Figure 1: (a) Interconnect by: (i) Backplane trace (ii) TSI T-line; (b) Channel loss for: (i) Backplane trace; (ii) TSI T-line

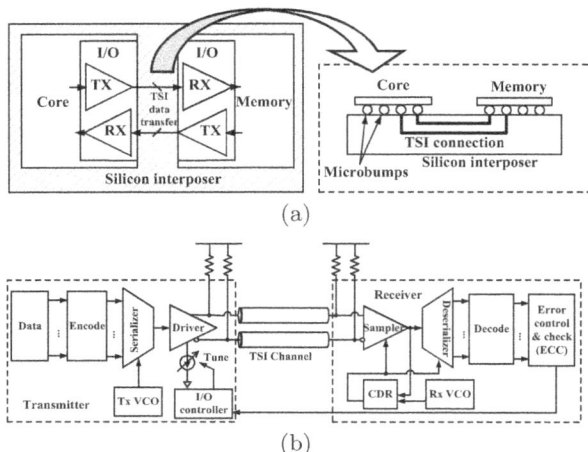

Figure 2: (a) Core-memory integration by 2.5D TSI I/O interconnect and its cross sectional view; (b) Adaptive tuning I/O based on error checking and correction

To achieve high bandwidth and energy efficiency, we will study 2.5D TSI I/O in this paper for the integration of multi-core microprocessors and memories. In order to improve the energy efficiency, we propose a self-adaptive design with tuning of the output-voltage swing by checking the BER and power. Compared to the previous designs [11] with fixed full output-voltage swing, the proposed design can save I/O communication power and improve energy efficiency.

Architecture for memory-logic integration by the 2.5D adaptive TSI I/O is shown in Fig. 2(a). Each of the memory and core will have transmitter as well as receiver to enable a full duplex communication. The data is encoded by adding the redundant parity check bits as input to the transmitter. Serializer converts the parallel data into serial data for transmission through the TSI channel. At the receiver end, the encoded data is decoded and BER is calculated by ECC block. One I/O controller tunes the output-voltage swing adaptively by varying the driver tail current at the transmitter. The transmitter adjusts its output-voltage swing adaptively based on the feedback of the BER and I/O communication power. Thus, the output-voltage swing can be tuned adaptively to save the power along with considering the BER constraint. Detailed description of each of the transmitter, receiver, coding and the adaptive tuning of output-voltage swing is presented in Section 3. In the following, we further show how to formulate an adaptive control problem of the proposed I/O.

2.2 Problem Formulation

Note that a large output-voltage swing may be not required when certain amount of error in the data can be accepted for the trade-off of power saving. This is particularly true for some applications involving data such as imaging, audio and video. Therefore, one can reduce the output-voltage swing at transmitter though some error can happen when detected at receiver. By employing the error-correcting code (ECC) block at the receiver side, one can determine the BER and check if there exists margin. Based on this phenomenon one can design a controller at transmitter to balance the trade-off between the I/O communication power and BER by tuning the voltage levels of the output-voltage swing, which can be formulated as:

Problem: Tune the output-voltage swing at the transmitter to achieve low power at the cost of BER based on the logic-memory communication characteristics.

$$Opt. < P_i, \ BER_i >$$
$$S.T.(i) \ P_i \ \leq \ P_B \qquad (1)$$
$$(ii) \ BER_i \ \leq \ BER_T$$

where P_i and BER_i denotes the I/O communication power and BER under the i-th output-voltage swing level V_{s_i}. Note that the BER and power are both functions of the output-voltage swing. P_B and BER_T represents the targeted I/O communication power and BER of one TSI I/O under the normal operation. With the increase in the output-voltage swing, the I/O communication power increases and BER goes down and vice-versa. Output-voltage swing level V_{s_i} needs to be adaptively tuned for optimizing the I/O communication power and BER simultaneously.

In this paper, a self-adaptive tuning of the output-voltage swing at transmitter is performed based on one Q-learning algorithm with feedback of the BER and power as inputs, presented in Section 4. In the next section, we first discuss the detailed circuit blocks of 2.5D adaptive TSI I/Os.

3. 2.5D TSI I/O CIRCUIT DESIGN

In this section, we discuss in detail about each component of the overall 2.5D TSI I/O link such as transmitter (Tx) and receiver (Rx) presented in Fig. 2(b). To operate high bandwidth by single channel of 2.5D TSI I/O, we employ 8:1 serializer in the Tx and 1:8 de-serializer at the Rx. Each of the Tx and Rx has a voltage-controlled-oscillator (VCO) to generate the required clock signal ($2GHz$). Both the Tx and Rx are terminated for the 2.5D TSI based T-line with matched 50Ω resistor. At the Rx, the serial bit stream is sampled and de-serialized; and is re-synchronized by the recovery clock from the clock data recovery (CDR) block.

3.1 Receiver and Transmitter

In details, the Tx employs a 8:1 serializer to convert 8-bit parallel data into serial data as shown in Fig. 3(a). Four digital D flip-flops are implemented as a shift-register chain for each of the odd (D_1, D_3, D_5, D_7) and even (D_0, D_2, D_4, D_6) bits of data. This is followed by a 2:1 MUX to combine them altogether. A current-mode logic (CML) output driver is used to drive the TSI T-line from the Tx to the Rx on the common substrate. The CML output stage is powered by the fixed supply ($1.2V$). The I/O communication power P depends on the output-voltage swing and the tail current of the driver. I/O Communication power and BER are considered as state of the system, and can be tuned by the output-voltage swing, which will be considered as the corresponding action. For example, one can generate control bits to tune the tail current of the CML driver and thus the output-voltage swing, as shown in Fig. 3(b).

What is more, compared to the traditional serial I/Os based on the backplane PCB trace [15, 16], the 2.5D TSI I/Os do not need the complex equalizer circuits at the receiver due to the small signal loss in the TSI T-line channel. A sampler at the front-end receiver is employed to convert the current-mode signals into digital levels. After the data decision, this data is processed in the digital domain, which saves more power compared to analog demultiplexer. A delay-locked loop (DLL) based clock-data recovery

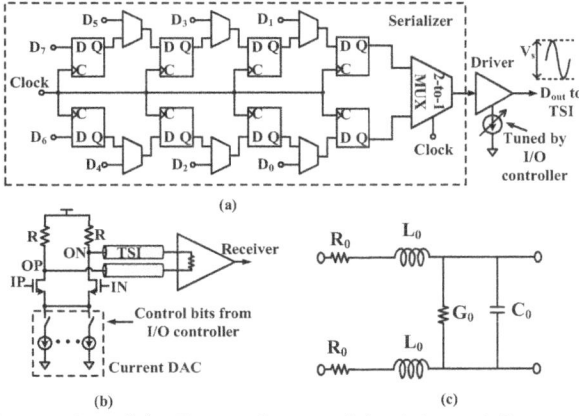

Figure 3: (a) Transmitter with 8:1 serializer; (b) Adaptive tuning of driver tail current; (c) TSI realized by a T-line

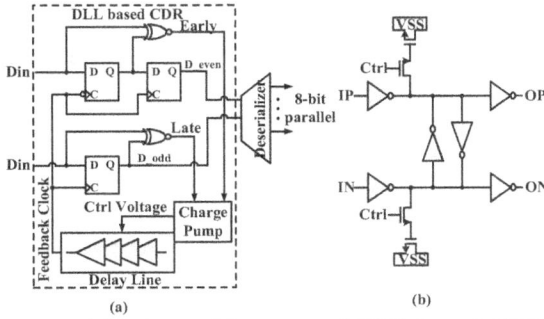

Figure 4: (a) The architecture of DLL based CDR; (b) The voltage controlled delay cell in the DLL

(CDR) at receiver is implemented to de-skew the sampling clocks, as shown in Fig. 4(a).

In this CDR design, a half-rate clock architecture is employed to decrease digital circuit working frequency and save power consumption. Two exclusive-or (XOR) gates in Fig. 4(a) form a phase detector to judge the sampling clock position compared to input data. It compares the input data edge with rising edge sampled signal to obtain the "early" pulse and the "late" pulse. And then a charge-pump block converts these pulses into variable voltage to control the DLL delay line, which can tune the delay phase of clocks and also provide feedback to the sampler. The schematic of voltage-controlled delay cell (in Fig. 4(a)) is illustrated in Fig. 4(b), which are based on inverter chain for reducing the constant current consumption. This implementation of DLL in the CDR circuit makes inherently stable and avoids jitter accumulation.

3.2 Error Correcting Code

To determine the historical BER for future control, data is encoded using the hamming code and transmitted along with the parity check bit. As shown in Fig. 5, 32-bit parallel data $(D-32)$ is initially stored in the output FIFO of the transmitter. For the data bits, 7 parity bits are generated by the parity generator and an additional MSB of parity check vector is set as 0. Parity generator uses the code generator matrix C to generate parity bit vector p, where the parity generator consists of set of AND and XOR gates. As such, the total encoded data to be transmitted will be 40-bit for every 32-bit of data. One MUX is implemented for serial transmission.

At the receiver, the first 32-bit of data is stored in the input FIFO $(D-32$ bits$)$ and 7-bit of the last 8-bit (parity) is utilized for error checking and correction. The checking result vector (R) is generated from the parity code p. By summing the result vector, one can detect if any bit is wrong and a left-shifter is used to correct 1-bit error. The current implementation of ECC has capability to correct 1-bit error but detect multiple bit

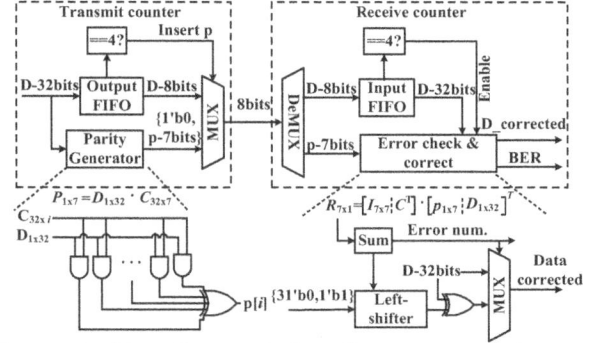

Figure 5: Encoding and decoding at transmitter and receiver

errors. It can be used to obtain the historical BER at the receiver and is further feedbacked to the transmitter. BER for a certain time interval is calculated by the total number of errors found to the total number of bits transmitted.

3.3 Adaptive Tuning

Based on the calculated BER from the ECC, a feedback signal is sent back to the I/O controller at the transmitter. This signal is considered as one of the component for control that forms a look-up-table (LUT). The I/O controller generates the corresponding control bits. The control bits can control the DAC current at the tail of CML buffer driving the TSI T-line. Thus, the output-voltage swing is tuned by varying the tail current of CML buffer. As shown in Fig. 3(c), the CML driver with variable current source is set by the DAC current and load resistor. The DAC tail current source is composed of a group of current sources in parallel with switches controlled by the control bits generated from the I/O controller. Generally, the load resistor is set 50Ω for the TSI T-line impedance matching. In this paper, tail current source is varied from $2mA$ to $5mA$.

4. Q-LEARNING BASED ADAPTIVE TUNING

In this section, we will discuss about the Q-learning theory and its application to have a self-adaptive tuning of the output-voltage swing for the 2.5D TSI I/Os.

4.1 Q-learning Theory

The Q-learning theory [17] is generally practised to find an optimal action-selection policy from the set of states S. The Q-learning algorithm evaluates *state* and *action* pairs form the previous inputs. To solve (1), we formulate the Q-learning algorithm that takes the I/O communication power P_i and BER BER_i as the state vector; and uses the output-voltage swing level V_{s_i} as the action by

$$S = <P_i, BER_i>.$$

In order to obtain the state and action pairs and form a look-up-table (LUT), the input samples are trained. A sample LUT will be as follows:

Action (Voltage swing)	State	
	Power	BER
V_{s_1}	P_1	BER_1
⋮	⋮	⋮

The input samples are collected at a time periods of control cycle, in scale of ns. Duration of control cycle is based on the speed of I/O controller circuit. The next state variable needs to be predicted with an action for the next input sample. This can be done by calculating a reward function to achieve an optimally estimated value based on the existing state s_k by

$$R_w = f(\mathbf{S}_{k+1}) - f(S_k). \tag{2}$$

Here **S** denotes the predicted state and k indicates the number of control cycle. The reward R_w denotes the direction of state transition. The optimal estimation is chosen among the set of states to satisfy the required criteria by taking the corresponding action selected from the formed LUT. The optimal estimation E of the states S can be calculated as follows:

$$E = min\{f(S_{k+1-i})\}, i = 0, ..., M. \tag{3}$$

Here M denotes the number of samples to make the optimal estimation. Based on the optimal estimation E, the action to be taken for next state is calculated as

$$f(S_{k+1}) = f(S_k)(1 - \alpha) + \alpha(R + \gamma E) \tag{4}$$

where $f(s_{k+1})$ is the determined action for the next control cycle $k + 1$; α denotes learning rate and γ denotes discount factor. In the following, we show the system power and BER models with predictions.

4.2 System Power Model

The first component of the state vector is the I/O communication power. The system power model refers to the I/O communication power of driver and the TSI T-line power, both depending on the output-voltage swing V_{s_i}. For the CML based driver with TSI T-line [18] the I/O communication power is given by

$$P_i = V_{s_i} \cdot (I_t + \frac{\eta * V_{dd} * s}{(R_D + Z_{diff})} * f). \tag{5}$$

Here I_t is driver tail current; s is duration of signal pulse; η is activity factor; R_D is the resistance of driver; and Z_{diff} is the characteristic impedance of the TSI T-line.

The tail current I_t at the current control cycle can be obtained from measurement and is predicted for the next control cycle by auto-regression (AR)

$$\mathbf{I}_t(k + 1) = \sum_{i=0}^{M-1} w_i I_t(k - i) + \xi. \tag{6}$$

Here $\mathbf{I}_t(k + 1)$ denotes the predicted tail current at $k + 1$-th control cycle; w_i represents the auto-regression coefficient; ξ is the prediction error and M represents the order of the AR prediction. Based on the predicted tail current, the I/O communication power for next control cycle is calculated as $\mathbf{P}_i(k + 1)$.

4.3 System BER Model

The second component of the state vector is the BER, the feedback from the receiver. The BER is affected by the output-voltage swing, external noise, channel noise etc. [19]. In a wireline communication system [20], the BER has a relationship with the output-voltage swing as follows

$$BER_i = \frac{1}{2} erfc(\frac{V_{s_i}}{\sqrt{2}\sigma_v}). \tag{7}$$

Here the $erfc$ is complementary error function and σ_v is the standard deviation of the noise.

The BER can be obtained as the feedback from ECC at the receiver. During the training process, σ_v is calculated from (7) for the given output-voltage swing at the current control cycle. By knowing σ_v, the BER for the next control cycle can be can be predicted accordingly.

4.4 Q-learning Control Flow

The self-adaptive tuning of the output-voltage swing at the CML buffer is performed based on the Q-learning discussed in Section 4.1. The I/O communication power P_i and BER BER_i are considered as the state vectors with output-voltage swing level V_{s_i} as the corresponding action.

The proposed self-adaptive output-voltage swing tuning is presented in Algorithm 1. LUT is formed with output-voltage

---

Algorithm 1: Q-learning based adaptive tuning of output-voltage swing

Input: Communication power trace P_i, BER feedback from receiver and look-up-table (LUT)
Output: Adaptive tuning of output-voltage swing V_s
1: Predict tail current: $I_t(k + 1) = \sum_{i=0}^{M-1} w_i I_t(k - i) + \xi$
2: Calculate corresponding communication power and BER
3: Reward: $R_w = a_1 \Delta V_s(\mathbf{P}_i) + a_2 \Delta V_s(\mathbf{BER}_i)$
4: Optimal value estimate: $E = min\{(V_{s_i}(t - j + 1))\}$, $j = 0, ..., M$
5: $V_{s_i}(t + 1) \leftarrow V_{s_i}(t)(1 - \alpha) + \alpha(R_w + \gamma E)$
6: By adjusting tail current using control bits, tune corresponding V_{s_i}

---

swing as action based on the I/O communication power and BER in (5) and (7) as state vectors. The tail current of the CML buffer is predicted, as given in (6), Line 1 of Algorithm 1. Based on the predicted tail current, the I/O communication power for the control cycle is calculated using (5). Similarly, BER is predicted using the feedbacked σ_v.

Based on the present and predicted power and BER values, reward R_w is calculated similarly to (2). Since we have two factors, we consider the weighted sum, as given in Line 3 of Algorithm 1. Here a_1 and a_2 denote the weighted coefficients for normalized rewards of the communication power $\Delta V_{s_i}(\mathbf{P}_i)$ and normalized BER $\Delta V_{s_i}(\mathbf{BER}_i)$. After calculating the reward, the optimally estimated value for the output-voltage swing is calculated, as in Line 4 of Algorithm 1. Finally, the output-voltage swing is selected (4), given in Line 5 of Algorithm 1. The LUT can be implemented online with the corresponding control bits calculated and feedbacked to CML buffer to tune the DAC current of the CML buffer. This is how the adaptive tuning is performed. Note that LUT can be implemented in the hardware with multiple AND/OR partial matching logic circuit instead of read only memory (ROM). This LUT based implementation has higher speed and lower power compared to the ROM. As a summary, the whole flow of adaptive tuning by the Q-learning algorithm is shown in Fig. 6.

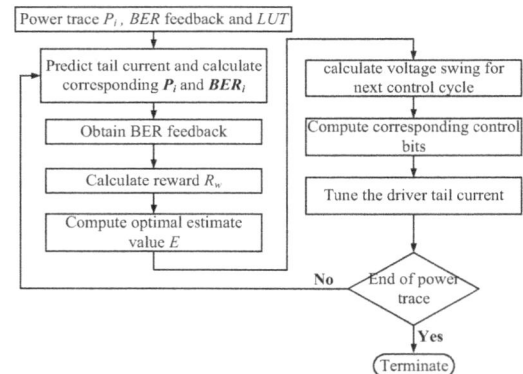

Figure 6: Flowchart showing Q-learning based self-adaptive voltage swing tuning

5. SIMULATION RESULTS

The 2.5D adaptive TSI I/O verification is performed in Cadence Virtuoso (Ultrasim-Verilog) and Matlab. An 8-core MIPS microprocessor with 8-bank of SRAM memory is designed with GF $65nm$ CMOS. The 2.5D TSI T-line is of length $3mm$ and $10\mu m$ width, driven by the CML buffer. The power traces are measured from Cadence Virtuoso and control cycle is set as $1ns$, larger than switching time of I/O controller. The look-up-table (LUT) is designed with ECC coding for adaptively tuning the output-voltage swing. The controller is based on the Q-learning of the I/O communication power and BER at receiver respectively. The multiple setup parameters are from:

$(100mV, 4.98E-2mW, 5.05E-2), (150mV, 1.75E-1mW, 1.10E-3), (200mV, 2.55E-1mW, 1.12E-4)$ and $(300mV, 3.48E-1mW, 8.40E-6)$. This LUT is almost robust, since this depends on characteristics of the circuit rather than the application. The other geometry settings are presented in Table 1. Area overhead and power overhead of the adaptive tuning is nearly same as that of the I/O controller, presented in Table 1. The circuit is designed in Cadence with the according technology PDK. The overall I/O performance can provide $76mV - 190mV$ peak-to-peak signal swing with $4Gb/s$ bandwidth, and the power consumption is only $13mW$. The adaptive self-tuning of output-voltage swing may come with a little area overhead of $0.03mm^2$ for additional control circuits and a latency of $100 - 200ps$.

Simulation results are presented in following manner. Firstly, we show the adaptive tuning of the output-voltage swing with the resulting eye-diagrams. Secondly, we present the Q-learning results based on the I/O communication power and the BER. Finally, we compare the saving in I/O communication power as well as energy efficiency under different benchmarks of workloads.

Table 1: System settings for memory-logic integration with TSI I/O

Item	Description	Value	Size
Microprocessor	Technology node	$65nm$	
	Frequency	$500MHz$	$0.3mm^2$
	Dissipation power	$15mW$	
I/O controller	Output-voltage swing	$0.1V, 0.15V, 0.2V, 0.3V$	
	Driving current	$2mA, 3mA, 4mA, 5mA$	$0.03mm^2$
	Number of levels	4	
	Switching time	$0.4ns$	
TSI	Length	$3mm$	
	Inductance	$300pH$	$3mm^2$
	Resistance	5Ω	
	Capacitance	$60fF$	
Memory	SRAM	16 KB	$0.2mm^2$
	Power dissipation	$6mW$	

5.1   2.5D I/O Eye-diagram

The characteristics of eye-diagrams with the driver currents are presented in Fig. 7 by introducing 10% clock cycle-to-cycle jitter (noise) at the TSI I/O channel. Note that different driving currents can make different eye openings under the noise in channel. A larger eye opening is associated with a higher current driving ability (or a larger output-voltage swing), which can reach $190mV$ peak-to-peak signal swing with $300mV$ output-voltage swing and $95ps$ timing margin. Compared to the lowest level at $76mV$ signal swing with $100mV$ output-voltage swing and $77ps$ timing margin, one can obtain nearly twice the eye amplitude (signal swing) and the according reduction in BER at the cost of triple the output-voltage swing. Thus, one can leverage the trade-off between the power reduction and the necessary BER.

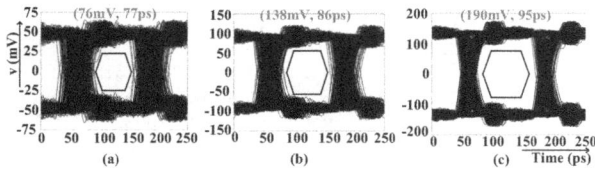

Figure 7: Eye diagram of output data with different driver current (or output-voltage swing) levels: (a) $2mA$; (b) $3mA$; (c) $4mA$

We further study the eye diagram under the control of adaptive tuning. Fig. 8 shows the current consumption under the tuned output-voltage swings. The sources of error are introduced in three stages: enlarging the clock jitter to 20%; increasing Rx sampler offset to 10%; and importing 10% power supply noise. As discussed previously, with the increase in noise, the tail current at the CML buffer is varied when tuning the output-voltage swing. For example, for stage 1, which has only clock jitter, the current is increased to $5mA$; With the increase in noise i.e., for stage 3, the current is increased adaptively. The difference in eye diagram with tuning the output-voltage swing and without tuning the output-voltage swing is shown in Fig. 8.

One can observe that for stage 3, without tuning the tail current, the eye opening is $96mV$, but the eye opening increases to $112mV$ by adaptively changing the current. Similar improvement in eye openings is shown for other stages as well.

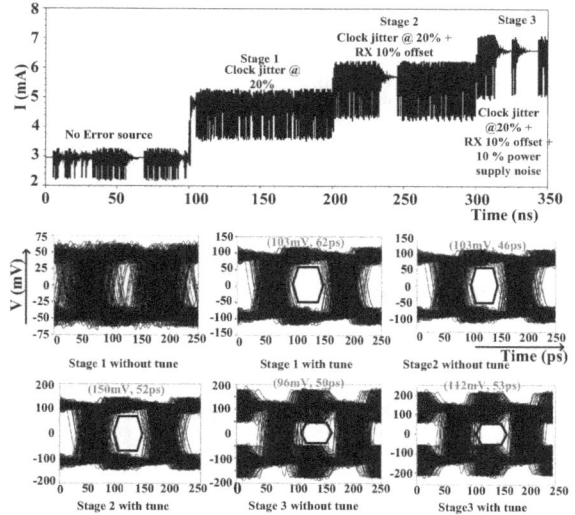

Figure 8: The adaptive current (or power) adjustment by the adaptive output-voltage swing tuning

5.2   BER versus Power Curve

We further discuss the trade-off curve of the I/O communication power and BER under the change of output-voltage swing. Fig. 9 shows the change in BER (black rectangle) and the I/O communication power (blue circle). With the increase in output-voltage swing, BER decreases at the cost of I/O communication power. For example, at an output-voltage swing of $350mV$, I/O communication power is $0.56mW$ with a BER of $4.14E-6$; whereas at an output-voltage swing of $400mV$, BER goes down to $4.54E-8$ at the cost of increased communication power to $1.14mW$. Since different applications can tolerate different amount of errors, I/O communication power thereby can be traded off for BER.

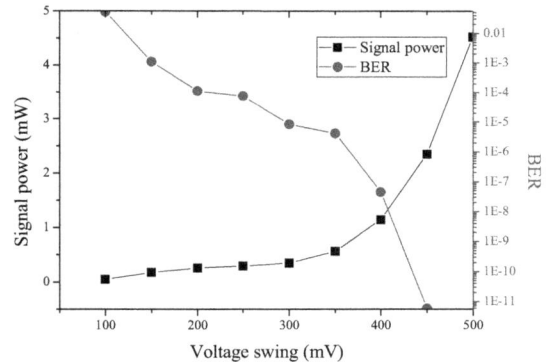

Figure 9: Various I/O communication power and BER under different output-voltage swing levels

5.3   Adaptive I/O Control by Q-learning

To obtain an optimal trade-off between the I/O communication power and BER, we further discuss the self-adaptive tuning of the output-voltage swing based on the Q-learning Algorithm 1. The learning rate α and discount factor γ are set as 0.3 and 0.7 respectively. Auto-regression (AR) of order 8 is used for load current (or I/O communication power) prediction. Fig. 10(a) shows the I/O communication power trace and the corresponding predicted one using AR for the *bzip2* benchmark. The error between the predicted and actual values are less than 0.3%. Fig. 10(b) further shows the I/O communication power by tuning the output-voltage swing. There is 19.08% saving on average for the I/O communication power by the one with the adaptive tuning when compared to the one without the adaptive tuning.

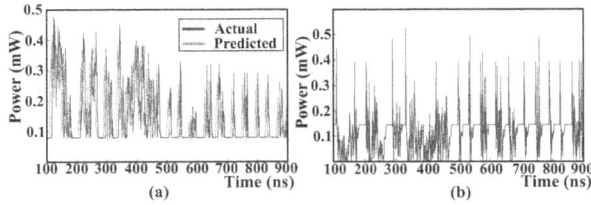

Figure 10: (a) Power trace for *bzip2* benchmark: actual and predicted; (b) Power with adaptive tuning

5.4 Performance Comparison with Benchmarking

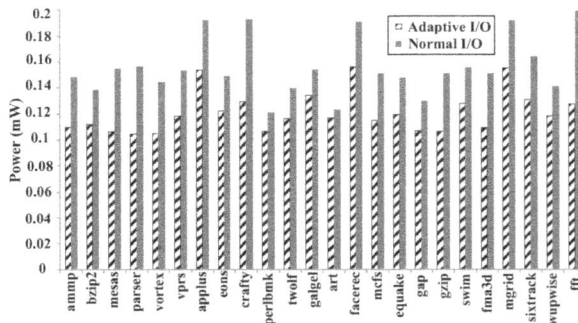

Figure 11: I/O communication power saving by self-adaptive tuning under different benchmarks

The communication power saving by the self-adaptive tuning using Q-learning algorithm is illustrated in Fig. 11. Various benchmarks such as *SPEC* [21] and *fft* are used to evaluate the communication power savings. For example in Fig. 11 for the *fft* benchmark, the I/O communication power with and without the self-adaptive tuning are $0.127mW$ and $0.199mW$ respectively. The power consumption is $19mW$ with energy efficiency of $4.75pJ/bit$ for the I/O without the self-adaptive tuning. On an average, 21.42% power saving and 14.47% energy-efficiency improvement can be achieved by the self-adaptive tuning.

6. CONCLUSION

In this paper, we have investigated the low-power 2.5D TSI I/O with adaptive adjustment of output-voltage swing. Based on the predicted I/O communication BER and power, the Q-learning based self-adaptive control is developed to control the output-voltage swing of 2.5 TSI I/Os for energy efficiency upon the workload characteristics. Experimental results have shown that the adaptive 2.5D TSI I/Os designed in $65nm$ CMOS can achieve an average of $13mW$ I/O power, $4GHz$ bandwidth and $3.25pJ/bit$ energy efficiency for one channel under 10^{-6} BER, which has 21.42% reduction of power and 14.47% improvement of energy efficiency.

7. ACKNOWLEDGMENTS

This project is sponsored by Singapore MOE TIER-2 fund MOE2010-T2-2-037 (ARC 5/11).

8. REFERENCES

[1] R. Kumar, V. Zyuban, and D. M. Tullsen, "Interconnections in multi-core architectures: Understanding mechanisms, overheads and scaling," in *IEEE Int. Symp. on Computer Arch.*, 2005.

[2] Y. Xie and et.al., "Design space exploration for 3D architectures," *ACM JETC*, vol. 2, no. 2, pp. 65–103, Apr 2006.

[3] M. Motoyoshi, "Through-silicon via (TSV)," *IEEE proceedings*, vol. 97, no. 1, pp. 43–48, 2009.

[4] M. P. D. Sai and et.al., "Reliable 3-D clock-tree synthesis considering nonlinear capacitive TSV model with electrical–thermal–mechanical coupling," *IEEE Trans. on Computer-Aided Design of Integrated Circuits and Systems*, vol. 32, no. 11, pp. 1734–1747, Nov 2013.

[5] H. Yu and et.al., "Thermal via allocation for 3-D ICs considering temporally and spatially variant thermal power," *IEEE Trans. Very Large Scale Integr. Syst.*, vol. 16, no. 12, pp. 1609–1619, Dec 2008.

[6] H. Yu, J. Ho, and L. He, "Allocating power ground vias in 3D ICs for simultaneous power and thermal integrity," *ACM Trans. on Design Automation of Electronic Systems (TODAES)*, vol. 14, no. 3, p. 41, 2009.

[7] J. R. Cubillo and et.al., "Interconnect design and analysis for through silicon interposers (TSIs)," in *IEEE 3DIC*, 2012.

[8] S.-S. Wu and et.al., "A thermal resilient integration of many-core microprocessors and main memory by 2.5D TSI I/Os," in *ACM/IEEE DATE Conf.*, 2014.

[9] T. Ishii and et.al., "A 6.5-mW 5-Gbps on-chip differential transmission line interconnect with a low-latency asymmetric Tx in a 180nm CMOS technology," in *IEEE ASSCC*, 2006.

[10] J. F. Bulzacchelli and et.al., "A 10-Gb/s 5-tap DFE/4-tap FFE transceiver in 90-nm CMOS technology," *IEEE J. of Solid-State Circuits*, vol. 41, no. 12, pp. 2885–2900, 2006.

[11] J. Tschanz and N. Shanbhag, "A low-power, reconfigurable adaptive equalizer architecture," in *Asilomar Conf. on Signals, Systems, and Computers*, 1999.

[12] J.-S. Seo and et.al., "High-bandwidth and low-energy on-chip signaling with adaptive pre-emphasis in 90nm CMOS," in *IEEE Int. Solid-State Circuits Conf.*, 2010.

[13] I. Foster, A. Roy, and V. Sander, "A quality of service architecture that combines resource reservation and application adaptation," in *IEEE Int. Workshop on Quality of Service*, 2000.

[14] M. Boniface and et.al., "Platform-as-a-service architecture for real-time quality of service management in clouds," in *IEEE Int. Conf. on Internet and Web Applications and Services (ICIW)*, 2010.

[15] S. Gondi and B. Razavi, "Equalization and clock and data recovery techniques for 10-Gb/s CMOS serial-link receivers," *IEEE J. of Solid-State Circuits*, vol. 42, no. 9, pp. 1999–2011, 2007.

[16] M. Pozzoni and et.al., "A multi-standard 1.5 to 10Gb/s latch-based 3-tap DFE receiver with a SSC tolerant CDR for serial backplane communication," *IEEE J. of Solid-State Circuits*, vol. 44, no. 4, pp. 1306–1315, 2009.

[17] E. E-Dar and Y. Mansour, "Learning rates for Q-learning," *J. of Machine Learning*, vol. 5, pp. 1–25, 2003.

[18] I. Ndip and et.al., "High-frequency modeling of TSVs for 3-D chip integration and silicon interposers considering skin-effect, dielectric quasi-TEM and slow-wave modes," *IEEE Tran. on Components, Packaging and Manufacturing Technology*, vol. 1, no. 10, pp. 1627–1641, 2011.

[19] S. K. Das, S. K. Sen, and R. Jayaram, "Call admission and control for quality-of-service provisioning in cellular networks," in *IEEE Int. Conf. on Universal Personal Communications Record*, 1997.

[20] R. A. Shafik and et.al., "On the extended relationships among EVM, BER and SNR as performance metrics," in *IEEE Int. Conf. on Electrical and Computer Engineering*, 2006.

[21] "SPEC 2000 CPU benchmark suits," http://www.spec.org/cpu/.

Reconfigurable Regenerator-based Interconnect Design for Ultra-Dynamic-Voltage-Scaling Systems

Seongjong Kim, Mingoo Seok
Columbia University, New York, NY, USA, sk3667@columbia.edu

Abstract. Ultra-dynamic-voltage-scaling (UDVS) is a compelling technique to use nominal supply voltage (V_{DD}) for providing peak performance while achieving high energy efficiency by opportunistically using near/sub-threshold V_{DD}s under average and low workload. One of the challenges in developing UDVS systems is that circuit fabrics optimized for a specific V_{DD} can exhibit largely sub-optimal performance and energy efficiency at other V_{DD}s. One critical example is the repeater-based interconnect design where the optimal interval of repeater insertion varies with V_{DD}. In this paper, we propose a reconfigurable interconnect design based on an optimized regenerator to improve performance and energy efficiency across a wide range of V_{DD}s.

Keywords. Ultra-dynamic-voltage-scaling, UDVS, ultra-low-voltage, ULV, interconnect, repeater, regenerator

1. Introduction

In VLSI systems, ultra-dynamic-voltage-scaling (UDVS) has been proposed to further extend the range of the conventional dynamic-voltage-scaling [1]. UDVS can provide peak performance by operating at nominal supply voltage (V_{DD}) while it can also achieve extremely high energy efficiency by scaling V_{DD} down to near or below device threshold voltage (V_{th}) under average and low workload. UDVS can be applicable to a wide range of computing applications including data centers, personal computing, mobile electronics, and embedded computing systems, for further improving performance and energy-efficiency limits.

For developing UDVS systems, one of critical challenges is to mitigate the inflexibility in various circuit fabrics. Circuit fabrics such as pipeline structures, clock networks, and on-chip memory bitcells are often optimized for only a single V_{DD} [2,3]. Those circuit fabrics, however, can exhibit highly sub-optimal performance, energy-efficiency, variability, and robustness when operating at the different V_{DD}s. Conventionally, designers have made compromised decisions for favoring the operation at a specific V_{DD} [3,4,11-14].

One of the critical examples of such inflexibility is the design of long (> mm) interconnects on a chip. In the conventional techniques, repeaters are inserted throughout wires at a certain interval, called an optimal interval of repeater insertion or $L_{optimal}$, for optimizing total delay [5-8]. This $L_{optimal}$ is, however, a strong function of V_{DD}. In high V_{DD} regime, $L_{optimal}$ becomes smaller as the delay improvements from shorter wire segments are larger than the penalties incurred by inserting more repeaters. Contrarily in near and sub-threshold regime, $L_{optimal}$ tends to be longer since the intrinsic delay of repeaters exponentially grows. The delay overhead of an additional repeater can therefore outweigh the delay improvement enabled by the short interconnect segments [3]. Our simulations show that $L_{optimal}$ can vary by 6× across the range of V_{DD}s from 1.0V to 0.35V. This widely varying $L_{optimal}$ makes an interconnect design optimized for a specific

V_{DD} to exhibit significantly lower performance and energy efficiency when operating at the V_{DD}s that they are not optimized for.

Reconfigurable circuits and architecture can be a promising direction to mitigate the challenges of the inflexibility of circuit fabrics in UDVS systems. Unfortunately, for the repeater-based interconnect-designs, it is not trivial to dynamically reconfigure the number of repeaters with minimal invasiveness since repeaters are inserted *in series with* wires and the wire segments are physically disconnected by the repeaters (Fig. 1(a)). One naïve solution for the reconfiguration ability is to implement multiple interconnect lanes with different insertion intervals, and the UDVS system dynamically selects the optimal lane based on the V_{DD} currently used. This approach, however, can cause large area overhead as the number of lanes quickly increase with the number of V_{DD} options in UDVS systems.

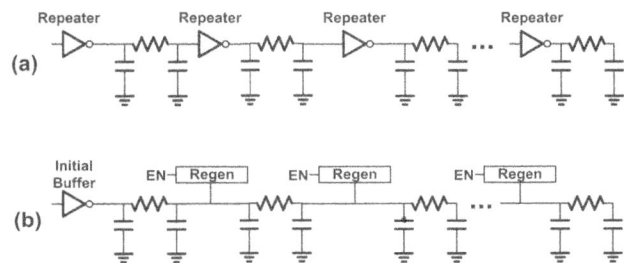

Fig. 1. Interconnect designs using (a) the conventional repeaters and (b) the proposed reconfigurable regenerators

In this paper, we instead focus on an alternative interconnect design technique based on regenerators for their use in UDVS systems. Regenerators have been proposed to enable bi-directional signaling with often better performance and energy-efficiency over repeater-based interconnect designs for primarily nominal super-threshold V_{DD} operation [9,10]. They can sense the signal transitions appeared in wires, and when sensing, they can rapidly source current to quickly complete the transitions.

A regenerator is particularly different from a repeater in the sense that it has a single signal port to serve both input and output, which is connected to a wire *in parallel*, without physically dividing wires (see Fig. 1(b)). This parallel connection can facilitate to dynamically reconfigure the number of regenerators that contribute signal transitions for different V_{DD} options in UDVS systems. If a regenerator is disabled it simply becomes a dangling capacitance with minimal energy and delay impacts. Such reconfigurability is hard to achieve in the repeater-based interconnect design.

In this paper, we, therefore, investigate a reconfigurable and regenerator-based interconnect design technique. We first optimize the existing regenerator circuits to enable dynamic reconfiguration and also to improve functional robustness at V_{DD}s from nominal to near and sub-threshold regime. We then design and analyze the interconnects based on the regenerators which can dynamically reconfigure the number of active regenerators for different V_{DD} operations. We compare the proposed design to the three conventional repeater-based interconnect ones each of which is optimized for the operations at V_{DD}s = 0.35V, 0.7V, and 1.0V, respectively. In the case study of driving 10-mm long and 0.1μm wide wires in an industrial 65nm CMOS technology, SPICE simulations show that the proposed design achieves 2.1-3× improvement in delay and 1.4-6.3× improvement in energy efficiency across V_{DD}=0.35-1V, as compared to the three conventional repeater-based interconnect designs. The similar amount of gains are observed for non-minimum width wires.

2. Challenges of Repeater-Based Interconnect Design for UDVS Systems

In this section, we analyze the challenges of the conventional repeater-based interconnect design in the context of UDVS systems. Inverters are used as a repeater element throughout this paper since they are considered to provide the best performance and energy-efficiency [7].

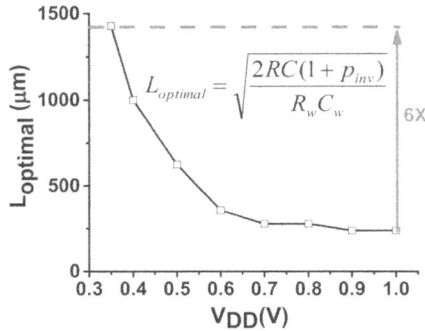

Fig. 2. Simulation shows a 6× variation in $L_{optimal}$ over V_{DD}=1-0.35V. (R/C: the on-resistance and gate capacitance of unit-size inverters; R_w/C_w: the resistance and capacitance of unit-length wires; p_{inv}: the ratio of diffusion and gate capacitance of unit-size inverters.)

2.1. Optimal Interval of Repeater Insertion

One of the critical challenges in the repeater-based interconnect design for UDVS systems is that $L_{optimal}$ is a strong function of V_{DD}. Fig. 2 shows (i) the analytical solution of $L_{optimal}$ [7] and (ii) the simulated $L_{optimal}$ across V_{DD}s in an industrial 65nm CMOS. When V_{DD} is scaled down to near and sub-threshold regimes, $L_{optimal}$ rapidly increases since the on-resistance of the repeaters (R) exponentially increases while the capacitances of repeaters (C and p_{inv}) remains relatively constant and also the resistance and capacitance of wires

remain constant (R_w and C_w). It is shown that $L_{optimal}$ varies by up to 6× from nominal V_{DD} (1.0V in this technology) to sub-threshold (0.35V) V_{DD}. In nominal V_{DD}, $L_{optimal}$ is smaller since delay improvements from shorter wire segments are greater than the delay added by extra repeaters. In ULV regime, however, the $L_{optimal}$ becomes larger since the delay of repeaters exponentially grows and thus favoring less number of repeater insertion.

2.2. Repeater-based Interconnect Design

The large difference in $L_{optimal}$ across V_{DD}s can make repeater-based interconnect designs highly sub-optimal if *operation V_{DD}* deviates from *optimization V_{DD}*. To confirm this, we design three interconnects which are optimized at three V_{DD}s, 1V (Design I), 0.7V (Design II), and 0.35V (Design III), respectively. In each design, $L_{optimal}$ is first found by sweeping the number of repeater insertion. At this point we do not need fully optimized repeater sizing since $L_{optimal}$ at a given V_{DD} is not a strong function of repeater sizing (see the equation in Fig. 2). Next, using the $L_{optimal}$ just found, we search the size of repeaters for achieving the best delay performance. The optimized designs are summarized in Table 1. In this experiment, we consider the third layer wire whose length is 10mm and width is minimum-sized (i.e., 0.1μm). The wire is modeled with the distributed RC π-model with 1000 segments (i.e., each segment is 10μm long).

Design	Optimization V_{DD} (V)	Device Width of a Repeater (μm)	# of Repeaters
I	1.0	24	42
II	0.7	33	36
III	0.35	170	7

Table. 1. Implementation details of the Design I, II, and III.

The delay, slew, and energy consumption of the Design I, II, and III are simulated across V_{DD}=0.35-1.0V. As shown in Fig. 3, the Design I which is optimized at 1.0V achieves the best performance at V_{DD}=1.0V. At V_{DD} = 0.35V, however, it exhibits 3× worse delay than the Design III since the excessive number of repeaters in the Design I significantly increase delay. Contrarily, the Design III optimized at 0.35V achieves the shortest delay among the three designs at V_{DD}=0.35V while exhibiting 2.8× longer delay at V_{DD}=1.0V than the Design I. The Design II achieves a balanced delay performance across V_{DD}s, yet still exhibiting 2.1× longer delay at 0.35V than the Design III and 1.1× longer delay at 1.0V than the Design I.

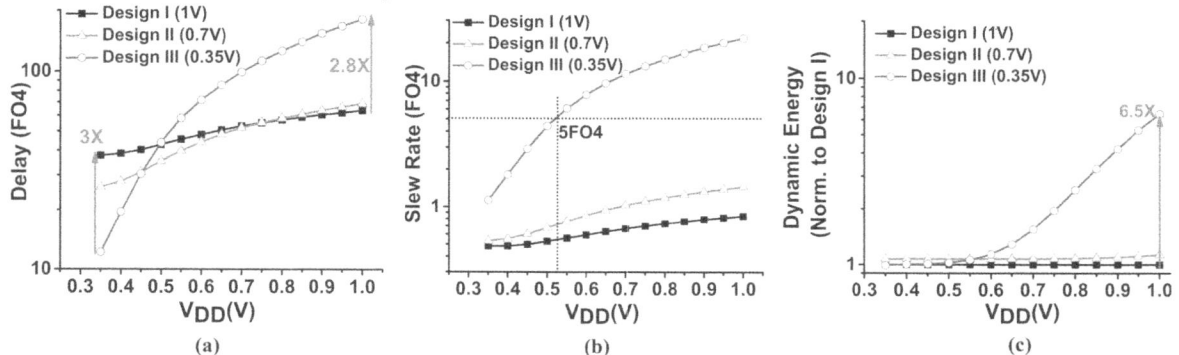

Fig. 3. Any single repeater-based interconnect design cannot simultaneously achieve optimal delay, slew and energy-consumption across a wide range of V_{DD}s. (a) At 0.35V, the Design III outperforms the Design I and II. At 1V, however, the Design I exhibits 2.8× shorter delay than the Design III. (b) All the designs achieve acceptable slew rates at the V_{DD}s that they are optimized for. The Design III exhibits large slew at 1V. (c) The three designs consumes similar amounts of energy since the total widths of inserted repeaters are similar. Only the Design III shows a large energy consumption at V_{DD}=0.6-1V due to the short circuit current induced by large slew.

The slew rates of all three designs are less than two fan-out-of-4 (FO4) delay at the V_{DD}s that those designs are optimized for. When operation V_{DD} deviates from optimization V_{DD}, however, some of the designs, particularly the Design III, exhibit significantly degraded slew and energy consumption. As shown in Fig 3(b), the Design III exhibits the slew of more than 5 FO4 delays at $V_{DD} > 0.5V$ due to the less than ideal number of repeater insertions. This large slew also degrades energy efficiency due to the increased short-circuit current As shown in Fig 3(c), the Design III consumes 6.5× more energy than the Design I and II at 1V.

3. Optimized Regenerator Circuit Design

In this section, we introduce several conventional regenerator circuits and their challenges in the context of UDVS operation. We then propose our optimized regenerator circuits based on the self-timed regenerators (STR, [10]).

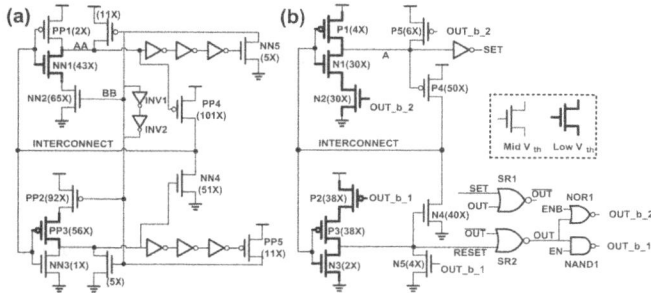

Fig. 4. (a) The STR with original sizing [10] and (b) the optimized regenerator design.

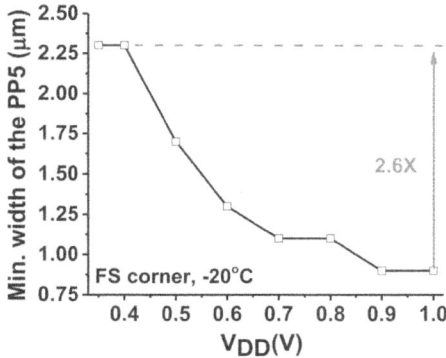

Fig.5. The required size of the writing devices (NN5 and PP5) rapidly increases under the worst-case process and temperature corner.

3.1. Self-Timed Regenerator (STR)

Several regenerator designs have been proposed primarily targeting at nominal V_{DD} operation [9,10]. In [9], the Booster was proposed as an alternative solution for driving long on-chip wires. The Booster has several advantages over repeaters. It can achieve shorter delays and can also allow bi-directional signaling with a single wire. The delay is less sensitive to the variations of regenerator placement. The more number of regenerators than the optimal number can still achieve near-optimal delay since the propagation delays of the extra Boosters are not added to the overall interconnect delay.

In [10], another regenerator design called STR was proposed to further improve performance and energy efficiency

over the Booster (see Fig. 4(a)). The detail operations of the STR are as follows. When it detects transitions in the wire (i.e., the node INTERCONNECT), it turns on PP4 or NN4, supplying current to accelerate the transitions. The transition-high detection (NN1, NN2, PP1) and transition-low detection circuits (PP2, PP3, NN3) are highly skewed using both transistor sizing and multi-V_{th} transistors for fast signal transition detections. Specifically in [10], the three devices, PP2, PP3, and NN3, are sized to have the effective ratio of PMOS to NMOS of ~46×. Also, the devices, NN1, NN2, and PP1, are set to have the ratio of ~16.3×. The main current-supplying devices (PP4 and NN4) are switched off after a certain amount of time which is defined by the inverter chains. This self-timed operation can avoid the situation that the node INTERCONNECT is actively held by the previous state, thereby improving delay. The cross-coupled inverters (the INV1 and INV2 in Fig. 4(a)) are added to hold the states at the node BB, which is critical for maintaining the correct inputs for the devices, NN2 and PP2.

3.2. Robustness Challenges in the STR design

Since the original STR design targets at only nominal and super-threshold V_{DD} operation, its robustness can be compromised in UDVS systems when near and sub-threshold V_{DD} is used.

The first robustness challenge of the conventional STR design comes from the cross-coupled inverters (INV1 and INV2) and the inverter-chain based feedback path (NN5 and PP5 in Fig. 4(a)). The writing devices, NN5 and PP5, need to be sized up so that they can overwrite the state (i.e., the node BB) of the cross-coupled inverters even under the worst-case process, temperature, and voltage (PVT) variation. In UDVS systems, this demands very large NN5 and PP5 since the variations at near and sub-threshold regime significantly grow. This apparently increases the overhead of area and energy to design the STR to operate reliably across a wide range of V_{DD}s. As shown in Fig. 5, the process and temperature corner simulations show that 2.6× larger writing devices are needed at 0.35V than at 1V. Random process variations and other dynamic variations can demand even larger device size, significantly increasing area and energy consumption.

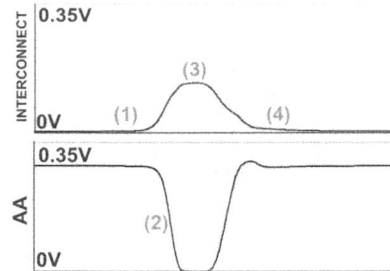

Fig.6. Leakage through PP4 and strongly-skewed devices, NN1 and NN2 (Fig. 4[a]), can induce false transition detections at low V_{DD}s. An example operation at 0.35V is shown.

Another robustness challenge is the false transition detection induced by (i) the leakage of the current-supplying devices (PP4 and NN4) and (ii) the use of highly skewed circuits in the transition detection circuitry (i.e., devices PP1, NN1, NN2, PP2, PP3, and NN3). At the steady-state and when the node INTERCONNECT is low, the PP4 and NN4 are turned off, and therefore the node INTERCONNECT becomes floating. If some process, temperature, and voltage (PVT) variations make the PP4 to leak more than the NN4, the potential of the node INTERCONNECT can start to increase (Fig. 6(1)). Since the transition detection circuits are highly skewed, the increase can be easily interpreted as a signal transition, and thereby causing false transition detection (Fig. 6(2)). This flips the node INTERCONNECT to the wrong high state (Fig. 6(3)). The STR can still return to the correct state (Fig. 6(4)) since the initial buffer (see Fig. 1) drives the node INTERCONNECT to the correct state. The glitch induced by false transition detections, however, can increase delay, consume more energy, and even propagate wrong states to the receiving registers.

The use of highly skewed and multiple-V_{th} circuits can significantly increase the probability of such false transitions in UDVS systems. While the optimal skew can be set based on noise margin at $V_{DD}=1V$, the skew can largely increase at near and sub-threshold regime since the on and off-current of low-V_{th} devices are orders of magnitude larger than mid-V_{th} devices in those V_{DD} domains. This can create the excessive skew in detection circuits, resulting in much higher rate of false transition detection.

3.3. Robustness and Reconfiguration

In order to improve robustness in the context of UDVS systems, we optimize the STR regenerators. First of all, we avoid the use of multi-V_{th} devices in the detection circuitry. In addition, a smaller amount of skew is introduced. The effective ratio of PMOS to NMOS sizes is ~9.5× in P2,P3, and N3. The effective ratio of NMOS to PMOS sizes is ~3.75× in N1,N2, and P1. This significantly improves the robustness. While the original STR design exhibits the false detection rate of 9%, the proposed design has that of 0% when 1-k Monte-Carlo simulations with all the process variations is ran with 1µs leaking period. The delay penalty from the reduced skew is only about 3%. In addition, in order to avoid over-sizing in the writing devices NN5 and PP5, the proposed regenerator employs a SR-latch (SR1, SR2 in Fig. 4(b)). Since the SR-latch is free from the contention problem, it can be designed with nearly minimum sized devices. The use of SR-latch can reduce area by about 12% at the same delay.

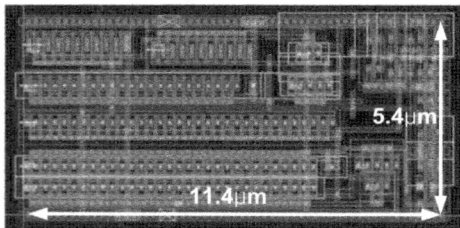

Fig. 7. Layout of the proposed regenerator design. The height is set as multiples of the height of standard cells in this technology.

Dynamically enabling and disabling regenerators is critical to avoid unnecessary switching activities when $L_{optimal}$ is large at low V_{DD} regime. Therefore, in addition to the above optimizations for higher robustness, we also add two gates, NAND1 and NOR1 which can enable and disable the regenerator controlled by the external signals EN and ENB. When EN is high (ENB is low), the regenerator are enabled. When EN is low, the regenerator is disabled by forcing the node

OUT_b_1 to be high (and OUT_b_2 to be low). This disables the transition detectors. Only some of the gate capacitances in the transition detection circuitry (i.e., N1, P1, N3, P3) and the diffusion capacitance of the main driving devices (i.e., P4 and N4) are exposed to the wire. The additional gates for dynamic reconfiguration causes 5% area overhead.

The proposed regenerator is sized and drawn for our experiment with a 10mm interconnect (Fig. 7). The total area is 61.56µm^2 in a 65nm CMOS. Note that, the main driving devices (N4 and P4) use medium V_{th} transistors for fair comparison with the repeater-based interconnect design that also use medium V_{th} devices.

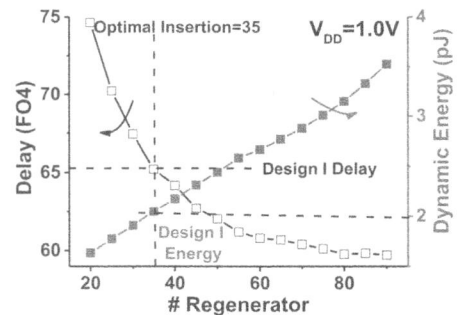

Fig. 8. The optimal number of regenerator is found to be 35 at 1V with 1mm, minimum-width wires.

4. Reconfigurable Regenerator-Based Interconnect Design for UDVS Systems

In this section, we propose a reconfigurable regenerator-based interconnect design technique for UDVS systems (Fig. 1). Applied for driving 10mm-long, minimum-width wires, the proposed design significantly outperforms the conventional repeater-based design across a wide range of V_{DD}s.

4.1. Design Process of the Proposed Interconnects

In order to design the reconfigurable and regenerator-based interconnect for UDVS systems, we introduce the two-step design process.

Step I: We sweep the size of the initial buffer, the size of the regenerator, and the number of regenerators to find the combination that achieve the same delay of the repeater based design at 1.0V (66 FO4 delays). As shown in Fig. 8, the optimal number of the regenerators is found to be 35. It is possible to further improve delay performance at lower energy efficiency since the performance benefit of adding regenerators outweighs the capacitance penalty beyond the optimal insertion count. The interconnect design with 90 regenerators, for example, can achieve 10% shorter delay but consume 72% more energy per switching.

Step II: Similarly to the conventional repeater based interconnect design, the proposed design also has the optimal numbers of regenerators to be enabled at different V_{DD}s. Enabling all regenerators can achieve shorter delay but it can also incur a considerable amount of energy-efficiency penalty.

We find the optimal number of regenerators enabled for each V_{DD}, which can be used to dynamically enable and disable regenerators during runtime. The target performance is the best performance among three repeater based designs (Design I-III)

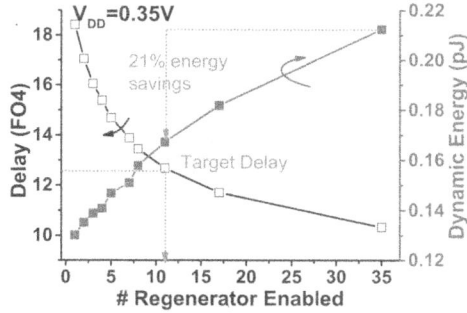

Fig. 9. At lower VDDs, some of the regenerators can be disabled while still meeting the target performance. At 0.35V, for example, only 11 out of 35 regenerators are enabled, achieving 21% reduction in energy consumption compared to when all enabled.

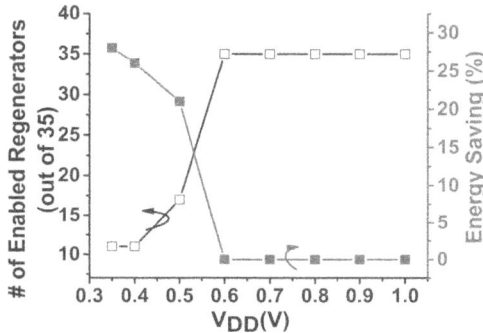

Fig. 10. The optimal numbers of enabled regenerators to achieve the target performance across V_{DD}s are found. The proposed reconfigurable interconnect design reduces energy consumption by up to 28% by disabling a subset of regenerators.

at each V_{DD}s. As shown in Fig. 9, at 0.35V, only 11 out of 35 regenerators need to be enabled to achieve the same performance of the design III (12.2 FO4 delays). The remaining 24 regenerators can be disabled, reducing energy consumption of regenerators by 21% compared to when all regenerators are enabled. At V_{DD}s=0.35-0.5V, it is sufficient to enable a subset of regenerators (11 to 17 out of 35) for achieving the target performance (Fig. 10). At V_{DD}=0.6-1.0V, all of the 35 regenerators need to be enabled. As shown in Fig.10, the reconfiguration can reduce energy consumption by up to 28% as

compared to the repeater based design with targeting performance.

4.2. Comparisons

The proposed interconnect design are compared to the three conventional repeater based designs, Design I, II, and III, each of which is optimized for the best performance at 1V, 0.7, and 0.35V, respectively. The total active area for the proposed and the conventional designs are shown in Fig. 11 (d). Although, all four designs have the similar total device width, the proposed regenerator-based interconnect design have 29-45% active area overhead due to the more complex topology of the regenerator. The performance, slew, and energy efficiency of the four interconnect designs are compared across V_{DD} ranging from 0.35 to 1.0V.

As shown in Figs. 11(a) and (b), the proposed interconnect design achieves 3× improvement in performance and 28% improvement in energy efficiency at VDD=0.35V as compared to the Design I. The Design I exhibits a large amount of performance degradation in low VDDs due to the excessive number of repeaters. At VDD=1V, where the Design I is optimized for, the proposed interconnect design still achieves a comparable performance with less than 3% degradation and energy efficiency. As the Design II is optimized at the intermediate VDD of 0.7V, it exhibits more balanced performance and energy efficiency across VDDs than the Design I and III. As shown in Fig. 11(a), the Design II, however, has 2.1× longer delay and 49% more energy consumption than the proposed interconnect design at 0.35V. In addition, the Design II is slower by 5% than the proposed design at 1V operation as the number of added repeaters is not optimal. As shown in Fig. 11(b), the proposed interconnect design also has comparable delay with < 3% degradation and 28% lower energy consumption at the VDD=0.35V than the Design III. The proposed design also achieves 2.8× shorter delay and 6.3× higher energy efficiency at VDD = 1V than the Design III. Note that the Design III exhibits largely compromised performance at higher VDDs since the number of inserted repeaters is far smaller than the optimal values.

As regenerators rely on the detection of interconnect transition, the slew of the proposed interconnect design is found to be worse than that of the conventional repeater based designs (see Fig. 11(c)). However, the slew of the proposed interconnect is still less than 6 FO4 delays which can be considered to be acceptable [15, 16]. Another overhead of the proposed interconnect design is higher static power consumption. The Design I, II, and III have the similar static power consumption due to the similar total device width. The regenerator have 3× higher static power consumption due to more leakage path and the usage of low V_{th} devices. Static power reduction techniques

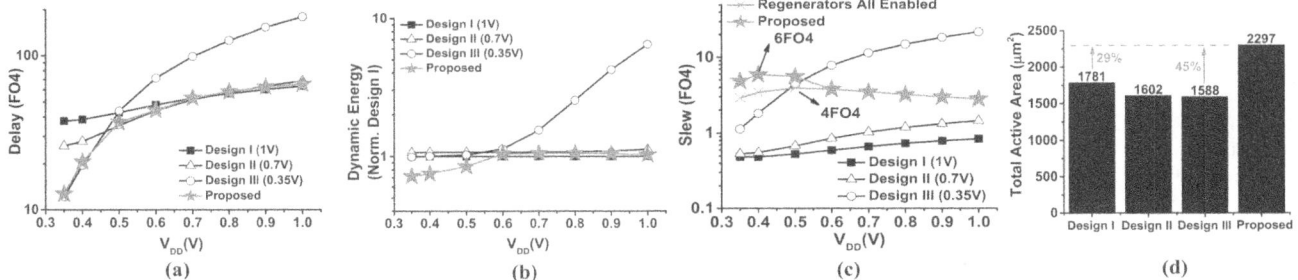

Fig. 11. The simulation results of (a) delay, (b) energy consumption, (c) slew, and (d) area of the proposed reconfigurable interconnect design and the three conventional repeater-based interconnect designs.

(e.g., power gating switches) can be used to mitigate this overhead.

4.3. Non-Minimum Width Wire

So far the minimum width wire has been used throughout the paper. In this section, we reiterate the experiments for confirming the effectiveness of the proposed interconnect design technique across non-minimum-width wires. We use five different wire widths from 0.1 (minimum) to 0.5 μm. The lengths of wires are 10 mm. The optimal size and the optimal number of repeaters and regenerators are re-searched. As shown in Fig. 12, the simulation results shows that the proposed interconnect design technique achieves the similar amount of improvement both in delay and energy consumption across different wire widths, confirming the proposed technique is effective for wider wires.

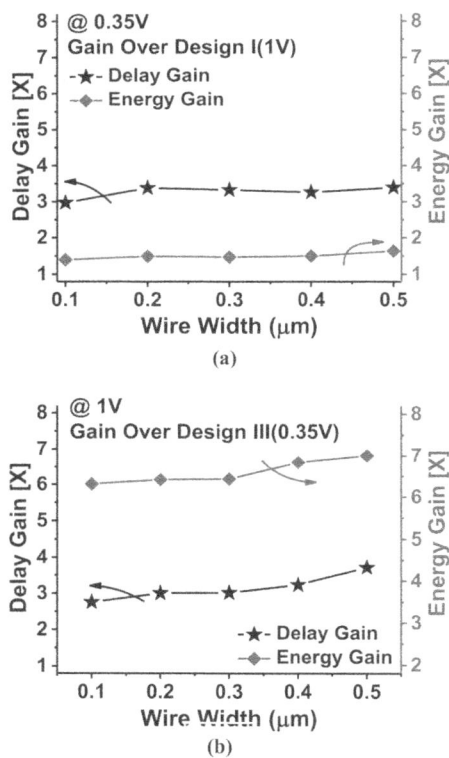

Fig. 12. The proposed design demonstrates the similar amounts of delay and energy improvement over the wires of different widths. The proposed design is compared to (a) the Design I(1V) at 0.35V, and (b) the Design III(0.35V) at 1V.

5. Conclusion

In this paper, we propose a reconfigurable interconnect design technique based on regenerators for UDVS systems. The proposed interconnect design outperforms all the three repeater-based interconnect designs in performance by 2.1×-3× and in energy efficiency by 1.4×-6.3×. Even compared to the best case among the three repeater based design across V_{DDS}, the proposed interconnect design achieves near-best performance with <3% degradation at 28% higher energy efficiency.

Acknowledgement

This work was supported by DARPA PERFECT.

References

[1] B. H. Calhoun, et al., "Ultra-Dynamic Voltage Scaling (UDVS) Using Sub-Threshold Operation and Local Voltage Dithering," *Journal of Solid-State Circuits*, Vol. 41, No. 1, pp. 238-245, 2006.

[2] M. Seok, et al., "Pipeline Strategy for Improving Optimal Energy Efficiency in Ultra-Low Voltage Design," *Design Automation Conference*, pp. 990-995, 2011.

[3] M. Seok, et al., "Robust Clock Network Design Methodology for Ultra-Low Voltage Operations," *Journal on Emerging and Special Topics on Circuits and Systems*, pp. 12-130, 2011.

[4] B. Zhai, et al., "A Variation-Tolerant Sub-200mV 6-T Subthreshold SRAM," *Journal of Solid-State Circuits*, Vol. 43, No. 10, pp. 2338 – 2348, 2008.

[5] H. B. Bakoglu, et al., "Optimal Interconnection Circuits for VLSI," *Trans. Electron Devices*, Vol. ED-32, pp. 903-909, 1985.

[6] V. Adler, et al., "Repeater Design to Reduce Delay and Power in Resistive Interconnect," *Trans. Circuits Syst. II*, Vol. 45, pp. 607-616, 1998.

[7] N. H. E. Weste and D. Harris, *CMOS VLSI Design A Circuits and Systems Perspective*, Reading, MA: Addison-Wesley, 2005.

[8] R. Ho, et al., "The Future of Wires," *Proceedings of IEEE*, Vol. 89, No. 4, pp.490-504, 2001.

[9] A. Nalamalpu, et al., "Boosters for Driving Long Onchip Interconnects – Design Issues, Interconnect Synthesis, and Comparison with Repeaters," *Transaction on Computer-Aided Design of Integrated Circuits and Systems*, Vol. 21, No. 1, pp. 50-62, 2002.

[10] J.-S. Seo, et al., "Self-Timed Regenerators for High-Speed and Low-Power Interconnect," *International Symposium on Quality Electronic Design*, pp. 621-626, 2007.

[11] R. Krambeck, et al., "High Speed Compact Circuits with CMOS," *Journal of Solid-State Circuits*, Vol. SC-17, No. 3, pp. 614-619, 1982.

[12] F. Klass, et al., "A New Family of Semidynamic and dynamic Flip-Flops with Embedded Logic For High Performance Processors," *Journal of Solid-State Circuits*, Vol. 34, No. 5, pp. 712-716, 1999.

[13] S. Hanson, et al., "Performance and Variability Optimization Strategies in a Sub-200mV, 3.5pJ/inst, 11nW Subthreshold Processor," *Symposium on VLSI Circuits*, pp. 152-153, 2007.

[14] B. H. Calhoun, et al., "Modeling and Sizing for Minimum Energy Operation in Subthreshold Circuits," *Journal of Solid-State Circuits*, Vol. 40, No. 9, pp. 1778-1786, 2005.

[15] Y. Peng., "Low-Power Repeater Insertion With Both Delay and Slew Rate Constraints," *Design Automation Conference*, pp. 302-307, 2006.

[16] A. B. Kahng., "Interconnect Tuning Strategies for High-Performance ICs," Design, Automation and Test in Europe, pp. 471-478, 1998.

Dynamic Thermal Management for FinFET-Based Circuits Exploiting the Temperature Effect Inversion Phenomenon

Woojoo Lee, Yanzhi Wang, Tiansong Cui, Shahin Nazarian and Massoud Pedram
University of Southern California, CA, USA
{woojoole, yanzhiwa, tcui, snazaria, pedram}@usc.edu

ABSTRACT

Due to limits on the availability of the energy source in many mobile user platforms (ranging from handheld devices to portable electronics to deeply embedded devices) and concerns about how much heat can effectively be removed from chips, minimizing the power consumption has become a primary driver for system-on-chip designers. Because of their superb characteristics, FinFETs have emerged as a promising replacement for planar CMOS devices in sub-20nm CMOS technology nodes. However, based on extensive simulations, we have observed that the delay vs. temperature characteristics of FinFET-based circuits are fundamentally different from that of the conventional bulk CMOS circuits, i.e., the delay of a FinFET circuit decreases with increasing temperature even in the super-threshold supply voltage regime. Unfortunately, the leakage power dissipation of the FinFET-based circuits increases exponentially with the temperature. These two trends give rise to a tradeoff between delay and leakage power as a function of the chip temperature, and hence, lead to the definition of an optimum chip temperature operating point (i.e., one that balances concerns about the circuit speed and power efficiency.) This paper presents the results of our investigations into the aforesaid *temperature effect inversion* (TEI) and proposes a novel dynamic thermal management (DTM) algorithm, which exploits this phenomenon to minimize the energy consumption of FinFET-based circuits without any appreciable performance penalty. Experimental results demonstrate 40% energy saving (with no performance penalty) can be achieved by the proposed TEI-aware DTM approach compared to the best-in-class DTMs that are unaware of this phenomenon.

Categories and Subject Descriptors

B. m [**Hardware**]: MISCELLANEOUS

Keywords

Low-power designs; FinFET; Thermal management

1. INTRODUCTION

With the dramatic downscaling of layout geometries, the traditional bulk CMOS technology has hit critical roadblocks, namely increasing leakage current and power consumption induced by the short-channel effects (SCEs) and the increasing variability levels. To overcome such drawbacks, FinFET devices, a special kind of quasi-planar double gate (DG) devices, have been proposed as an alternative for the bulk CMOS as technology scales down below the 20nm technology node [1, 2]. This is due to more effective channel

control, higher ON/OFF current ratios, and superior voltage scalability features of FinFET devices.

DVFS (Dynamic Voltage and Frequency Scaling) is a well-known technique for minimizing power in VLSI designs by reducing the supply voltage and clock frequency to the minimum values that are needed to meet a given performance level. Indeed, a number of recent studies of ultra-voltage scaled designs (i.e., circuits that operate at near/sub-threshold supply voltage levels) have proven the value of voltage scaling to very low supply voltage levels esp. when the performance targets are loose [3, 4]. The wide-range voltage scalability of FinFET devices enables them to outperform bulk CMOS devices in ultra-low power designs [5].

Meanwhile, as power density has continued to increase with the technology scaling, the accompanying high rate of heat generation has become a growing concern. The leakage current of a circuit increases exponentially with the increasing temperature [6] and this positive feedback mechanism between leakage power and temperature can result in a thermal runaway situation. Dynamic thermal management (DTM) has been proposed as an effective technique to control the over-heating of the circuit by maintaining the circuit temperature below a critical temperature threshold, while affecting circuit performance as little as possible. Several DTM response mechanisms (control knobs) e.g., fetch-toggling, dynamic thread migration, frequency throttling and DVFS, have been introduced [7, 8, 9]. A few of researchers have focused on developing resource management, task assignment, and scheduling policies to achieve the highest performance [6, 10] or the minimum energy consumption [11] under the condition that the target system hardware remains temperature-safe.

The previous DTM works have tackled the question of how to limit the peak temperature on circuit substrates comprised of planar CMOS devices running in the super-threshold voltage regime to save power or maximize performance. To the best of our knowledge no previous work has studied the question of optimal DTM policy design for FinFET-based VLSI circuits that can operate in any of the super, near or sub-threshold regimes. This is an important point because the delay versus temperature behavior of FinFET devices and circuits is different from that of the conventional bulk CMOS devices operating in the super-threshold regime.

For commercial bulk CMOS standard cell library operating at super-threshold V_{dd} supply voltages, the worst-case (longest) path delay occurs at the highest temperature. However, in the near/sub-threshold regime [12, 13] or in high-vt devices [14], it has been reported that the delay of these circuits decreases with increasing temperature. On the other hand, for various circuits designed using the PTM-MG FinFET libraries under 20nm bulk CMOS technology [15], a first observation from our SPICE simulations is that the circuits run faster at higher temperatures in all supply voltage regimes (including the super-threshold one.) This will be called as the *Temperature Effect Inversion* (TEI) phenomenon. A second observation is that, in the near/sub threshold regimes, the delay decrease for a fixed amount of die temperature increase is larger in FinFET-based designs compared to planar CMOS based designs.

This paper starts from exploring the delay vs. temperature behavior of FinFET-based designs, which forces the worst-case delay of these circuits to occur at low temperatures (e.g., -25°C). Our objective is to minimize the circuit energy consumption without any performance penalty. Given a DVFS schedule derived from the worst-case (at, say, -25°C) delay at various voltage levels, the motivation is to scale down the voltage level when the circuit temperature is high enough such that the delay from the lower voltage level is no larger than the worst-case delay from the original higher voltage level. This method can achieve significant energy reduction without performance penalty due to the following three reasons: (i) lowering down the voltage level will quadratically reduce the dynamic energy of the circuit and also reduce the leakage energy/power, (ii) lowering down the voltage level may slow down the rising speed of temperature, or may even reduce the temperature in presence of a heatsink (e.g., the ambient environment for mobile devices), and will exponentially reduce the leakage power, and (iii) the operating frequency determined by the worst-case delay of the higher original voltage can be maintained after the voltage scaling.

Based on in-depth studies of the influence of the TEI on the energy consumption of the FinFET circuits and the key idea described above, we present a novel DVFS-based thermal management method to minimize energy consumption with no performance loss. In this proposed DTM, we effectively find the optimal temperature point to maximize energy efficiency of the circuits, and introduce new voltage scaling policies to make the circuits operate at the optimal point.

Along with a detailed description of our experimental work, we validate the proposed thermal management algorithm on the four different FinFET circuits designed based on various PTM-MG technology libraries. We perform SPICE simulations on each circuit with various voltage levels in the full (possible) operating temperature range. Experimental results demonstrate some 40% energy saving (with no performance penalty) can be achieved by the proposed TEI-aware DTM approach compared to the best-in-class DTMs that are unaware of this phenomenon.

2. TEMPERATURE EFFECT INVERSION (TEI) PHENOMENON IN FinFETs

For VLSI circuits, the delay of a logic gate is directly affected by the driving current (I_{on}). As I_{on} increases, the logic gate switches faster, and vice versa. For a conventional MOSFET operating at superthreshold V_{dd} (e.g., 0.9 V), it is well known that the rising temperature will result in a reduced I_{on} and eventually aggravate the speed of circuit. That is why the worst-case timing corner for the commercial MOSFET standard cell library at superthreshold V_{dd} occurs at the highest temperature (e.g., 125°C).

It has been reported that fabricated FinFETs operating at superthreshold V_{dd} show the opposite behavior of MOSFET, i.e., I_{on} increases as the die temperature rises [16]. Some FinFET-based circuits based on 32nm PTM have shown the similar result when operating at superthreshold V_{dd} [17]. Reference [18] analyzed this opposite temperature influence on I_{on}, illustrating that this effect results from the bandgap narrowing and carrier mobility changes, which are induced by *tensile stress effect* of the insulator in the FinFET structure. As technology scales down (e.g., beyond 30nm), the tensile stress from the insulator layer to the fin body (cf. Figure 2) affects the device characteristics more significantly. In other

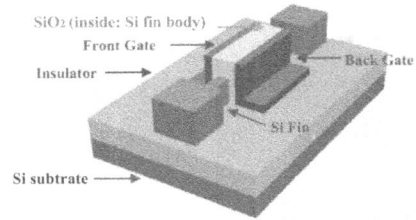

Figure 2: Three-dimensional structure of the bulk FinFET

words, because the thinner fin body has larger stress, the stress-induced bandgap narrowing results in a more significant decrease of the threshold voltage V_{th}. And, with increasing of the temperature, the tensile stress becomes larger, which decreases V_{th} as well as induces a slight change of the carrier mobility μ for FinFETs.

Finally, the changes of V_{th} and μ can directly affect I_{on} of Fin-FET in the super-threshold operation regime. Generally, $I_{on}(T)$ as a function of the temperature T can be expressed as:

$$I_{on}(T) = \begin{cases} \mu(T)e^{\frac{V_{gs}-V_{th}(T)}{S(T)}} & : \text{if } V_{gs} < V_{th} \\ \mu(T)(V_{gs}-V_{th}(T))^{\beta} & : \text{otherwise,} \end{cases} \quad (1)$$

where V_{gs} is the gate-source voltage, S is the subthreshold swing, β is the velocity saturation effect factor. S, μ, and V_{th} are the temperature dependent parameters. Due to the tensile stress with rising T, decreasing V_{th} along with a slight change of μ result in an increasing I_{on}, thereby decreasing the delay of logic gate.

Meanwhile, conventional MOSFETs operating in the sub/near-threshold regime or high-vt devices have shown the similar phenomenon (indeed, more significant than what was observed in Fin-FETs with super-threshold V_{dd}) that the circuit delay decreases with the increasing temperature [12, 13, 14]. As temperature increases, μ and V_{th} of MOSFETs decrease while S increases. From (1), I_{on} in the sub-threshold regime is exponentially and dominantly dependent on V_{th} and S, which is different from the case that I_{on} is a nearly linear function of V_{th} and μ in the super-threshold regime. As a consequence, different from the super-threshold regime where the slightly stronger effect of μ than that of V_{th} causes decreasing I_{on} with increasing T, the changes of V_{th} and S considerably increases I_{on} in the sub/near-threshold regime, and thus the gate can run much faster.

I_{on} of FinFETs operating in the sub/near-threshold regime also has the same exponential dependency on V_{th} and S. Combined with the tensile stress effect, FinFETs in the sub/near-threshold regime exhibit a significant delay reduction as the temperature goes high. We conclude that temperature increase makes FinFETs run faster at all the supply voltage levels. As stated earlier, we call this phenomenon temperature effect inversion (TEI) in FinFETs.

Figure 1 shows simulated results from four FinFET technologies: 20nm, 16nm, 14nm and 10nm. We can observe that all the technologies beyond 20nm clearly show the TEI phenomenon. The delay results of each technology is normalized by the delay at the nominal V_{dd} (in the super-threshold) at 125°C, which is shown as the dashed line in the figure. We can see that the delay at 125°C is not the worst case any more, but in fact the best case. Rather, the

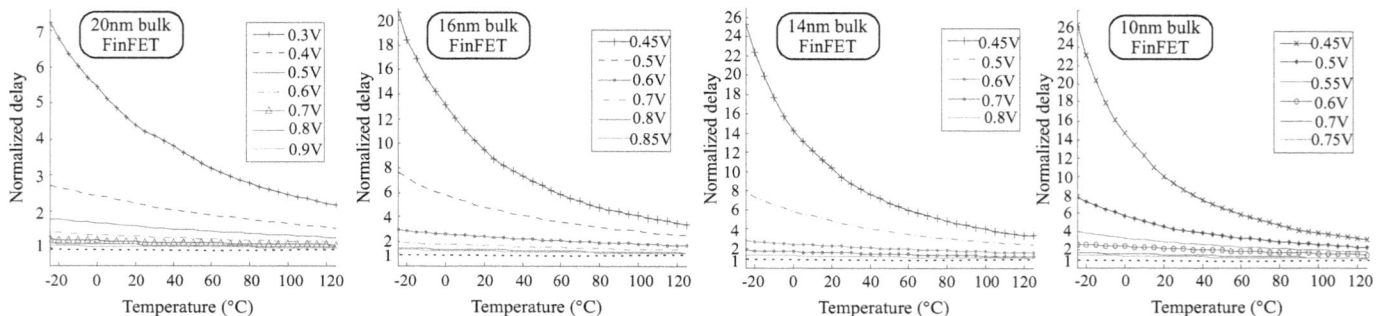

Figure 1: Delay at different temperatures and supply voltage levels, from FinFET-based FO4 inverter chain simulations.

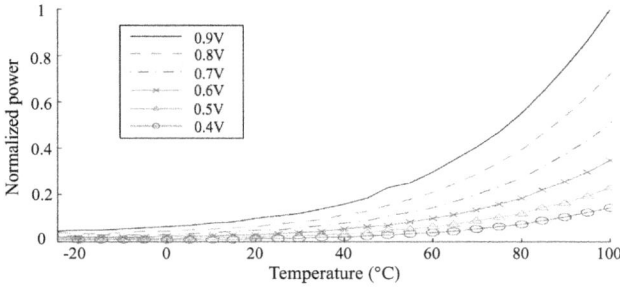

Figure 3: Leakage power at different temperatures and supply voltage levels, based on the 20nm FinFET technology.

worst case delay for each V_{dd} level occurs at the lowest temperature (e.g., -25°C).

3. POWER AND THERMAL MODELS

The power consumption of VLSI circuits has two components: a dynamic part and static (leakage) part. The dynamic power $P_{dynamic}$ is given by $P_{dynamic} = \alpha C V_{dd}^2 f$, where α is the activity factor, C is the switching capacitance, and f is the clock frequency. It is known that the static power P_{static} has a dependence on the die temperature T_{die} and V_{dd}, which can be expressed as:

$$P_{static}(T_{die}, V_{dd}) = V_{dd}\left(c_1 T_{die}^2 e^{\left(\frac{c_2 V_{dd} + c_3}{T_{die}}\right)} + c_4 e^{(c_5 V_{dd} + c_6)}\right), \quad (2)$$

where the first term is the sub threshold leakage, and the second term after the plus symbol is the gate leakage; c_1 to c_6 are technology dependent parameters [11]. Figure 3 shows the changes of P_{static} as a function of the elevated T_{die} at different V_{dd}'s, resulted from the simulations based on the 20nm bulk FinFETs.

We use the conventional RC-circuit thermal model, which is shown in Figure 4 (a) [19]. In the figure, $P_{circuit}$ denotes the heat generated by the circuit, which is the sum of $P_{dynamic}$ and P_{static}; P_{amb} is the heat dissipated to the ambience; T_{amb} is the ambient temperature; and C_{die} and $R_{die-amb}$ are the thermal capacitance of the circuit die and the thermal resistance from the die to the ambiance, respectively. Because we target the whole mobile device, modeling the on-chip thermal variations within the device [20] is less critical. Thus we do not account for thermal variations in this paper. Additionally, we do not include a separate heat sink, because in our target device there is none. Notice that, if we target a large scale chip that equips heatsinks or coolers, the spatial thermal variations should be taken into consideration, which may require to develop the more sophisticated thermal models and accompanying control logics (e.g., the feedback controller) to be robust to the modeling errors. However, they are beyond the scope of this paper.

Applying Kirchhoff equations to the RC-circuit thermal model in Figure 4 (a), we have:

$$C_{die}\frac{dT_{die}}{dt} = P_{circuit} - \frac{T_{die} - T_{amb}}{R_{die-amb}}. \quad (3)$$

Figure 4 (b) shows a conceptual relationship between $P_{circuit}$ and P_{amb}, where the two $P_{circuit}$ levels are resulted from the high V_{dd} and low V_{dd}. When $P_{circuit} = P_{amb}$, i.e., $dT_{die}/dt = 0$ in (3), T_{die} is stable. We call this point the equilibrium temperature T_{eq}. T_{eq}^{high} and T_{eq}^{low} in the figure denote the equilibrium temperatures for the high V_{dd} case and low V_{dd} case, respectively.

Due to the strong dependence of P_{static} on T_{die} and V_{dd} from (2), the amount of differences between the two $P_{circuit}$ levels from the high V_{dd} and low V_{dd}, which is indicated by the arrows in Figure 4 (b), increases super-linearly with increasing T_{die} and V_{dd}. Similarly, the differences between the two T_{eq}'s also follow the super-linear trend for the given $R_{die-amb}$, a fixed design parameter. Hence, for some high V_{dd} levels, it is possible that the corresponding T_{eq}'s exceed the die temperature limit (e.g., 90°C), or such T_{eq}'s do not

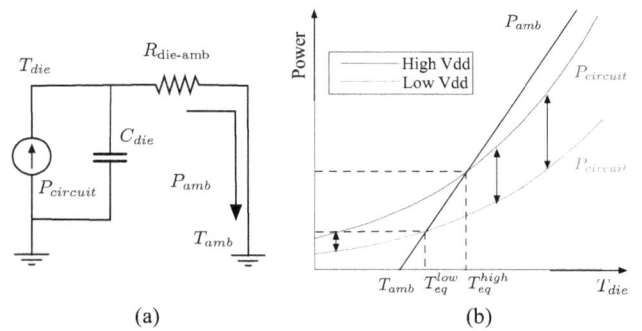

| (a) | (b) |

Figure 4: (a) RC-circuit thermal model, and (b) the effect of the temperature and power variation

Table 1: Simulation results of T_{eq} and the time to reach T_{eq} or 90°C from 20nm FinFET test circuits

$V_{dd}(V)$	0.50	0.55	0.60	0.65	0.70	0.75	0.80
T_{eq}(°C)	31.8	34.2	38.2	44.5	N/A	N/A	N/A
$Time(sec)$	1310	1465	1873	2375	3231	1600	1039

exist at all. While $R_{die-amb}$ directly affects T_{eq}, another design parameter, C_{die}, influences how fast the die temperature reaches either T_{eq}, if it exists, or the die temperature limit, otherwise. Especially, the time to reach the die temperature limit is an important design factor, because it determines how long a circuit can operate under the high voltage level. Table 1 shows the T_{eq} levels and the times from 0°C to T_{eq} or the die temperature limit, 90°C, from the 20nm bulk FinFET test circuits. From the measurement on ARM Cortex-A8, $R_{die-amb}$, C_{die} and T_{amb} are set to be 35.8 K/W, 9.0 J/K and 25°C, respectively [19]. The power from the test circuit is scaled so that the circuit with $V_{dd} = 0.7$V has the same trend of temperature increase that ARM Cortex-A8 shows with the measured $R_{die-amb}$, C_{die} and T_{amb}. The details will be explained at Section 5.

The previous work on DTM has mainly focused on cases where T_{eq} does not exist, and focused on how to avoid exceeding the die temperature limit with inevitable performance penalties: for example, lowering the clock frequency or both frequency and voltage levels to reduce $P_{circuit}$, thereby to cool down T_{die}. Different from the previous work, we present a novel DTM algorithm in the following section, which exploits the TEI phenomenon to improve energy efficiency of the circuit while neither exceeding the die temperature limit nor losing any performance.

4. TEI-AWARE DTM

4.1 Influence of TEI on energy consumption

Due to the TEI phenomenon, the worst-case delays occur at the low temperature in FinFET circuits. Therefore, for a given target clock frequency, the corresponding voltage level of the circuit should be set according to the worst-cased circuit delay, which occurs at the lowest die temperatures. This is needed to guarantee correct circuit operation in the full range of the operating temperature. We call this voltage level the *base voltage level*, V_{base}, associated with a target clock frequency, f_{target}.

Consider a FinFET-based circuit running at f_{target}. As time goes by, the die temperature T_{die} rises. Because of the TEI phenomenon, the FinFET-based circuit is getting faster with rising temperature, which allows us to drop the supply voltage level below V_{base} while maintaining f_{target}. Of course, we have to wait for T_{die} to reach a predetermined level (which we will call the *threshold temperature*, T_{th}) before we can drop the supply voltage level. This is because we have a finite number of discrete supply voltage levels, so the move from a higher initial voltage level to the next lower voltage level can only happen when the delay decrease due to the temperature rise is some minimum amount so that correct circuit operation at lower voltage level can be ensured. Note that if T_{th} exists, then this can significantly reduce the power consumption of the circuit due to the

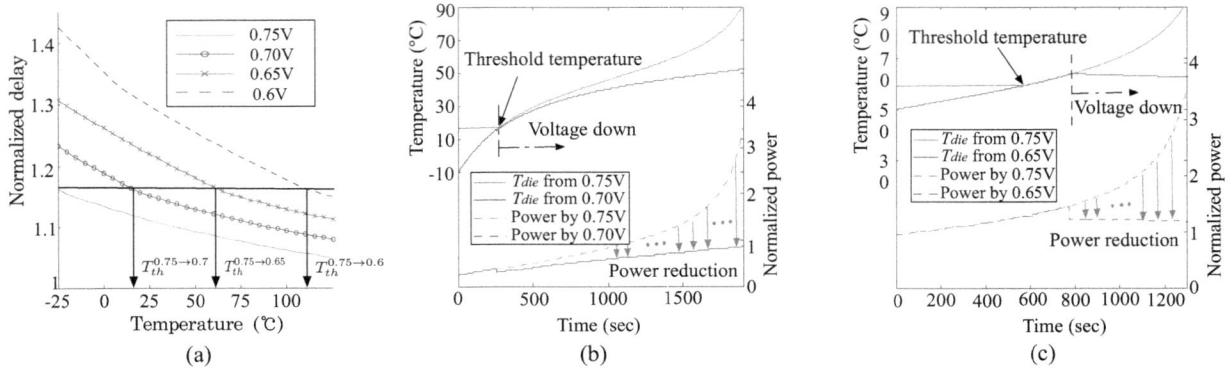

Figure 5: (a) Threshold temperatures (T_{th}'s) at different voltage levels, and two different cases after lowering down the voltage level at T_{th}: (b) T_{die} increases, and (c) T_{die} decreases, based on the 20nm FinFET based FO4 inverter chain simulation.

quadratic dependence of $P_{dynamic}$ and the exponential dependence of P_{static} on the supply voltage level. Furthermore, differently from the conventional DTM methods, our approach does not scale down the clock frequency, so there will be no performance loss. Finally, note that because power dissipation is going down, the temperature rise in the substrate will be curbed.

Figure 5 (a) shows an example of T_{th} levels from multiple different voltage levels, based on the delay values with 20nm FinFET technology. Note that, for the figure and the remaining part of this paper, we assume the lowest temperature of test circuits is -25°C, and the die temperature limit is 90°C. We also assume that a fine-grained (0.05V) input voltage control can be supported, similar to existing voltage controllers that power Intel CORE2 E6850 processor and ARM CORTEX-A8 with 0.05V difference in adjacent voltage levels. Then, in the figure, the operating frequency is set by the worst-case delay from the base voltage level, 0.75V, at -25°C. We use notation $T_{th}^{base\ voltage \to target\ voltage}$ in the figure to denote T_{th} in each case. While $T_{th}^{0.75 \to 0.6}$ exceeds the die temperature limit, the other threshold temperatures can be exploited in DTM.

Lowering down the voltage levels right after the increased temperature reaching T_{th} leads to two possible cases: (Case I) T_{die} keeps increasing, or (Case II) T_{die} begins decreasing. Case I is because the equilibrium temperature T_{eq} of the lowered voltage level is higher than T_{th}, or such T_{eq} does not exist. Case II is because T_{eq} of the lowered voltage level lies below T_{th}. For Case I, it is intuitive that the immediate voltage change at T_{th} will not degrade the performance of the circuit, but give us the opportunity to save energy. This is illustrated on Figure 5 (b). Because 0.7V voltage level does not have T_{eq} (from Table 1), lowering down the voltage from 0.75V to 0.7V at $T_{th}^{0.75 \to 0.7}$ =18°C allows the circuit to operate with the scheduled frequency but consume significantly less energy. On the other hand, the immediate voltage change at T_{th} for Case II will result in timing violation because the temperature will begin to decrease. Therefore, we have to wait for a certain amount of time, until T_{die} exceeds T_{th} by a certain amount. Then, we can lower down the voltage level to reduce the power consumption, and keep the lowered voltage level until the decreasing temperature reaches T_{th}. This is illustrated in Figure 5 (c). Because $T_{th}^{0.75 \to 0.65}$ equals 61°C, and T_{eq} corresponding to the 0.6V voltage level is 44.5°C (from Table 1), T_{die} decreases after the voltage change.

Different from Figure 5 (b) and (c), each of which considers simply two available voltage levels, there can be more than two available voltages levels in reality that can meet the scheduled frequency condition in the whole temperature range. The availability of the multiple voltage levels requires more detailed analysis and more elaborate DTM policy. The following subsections will discuss all the possible cases in a DVFS schedule to complete a given task. The proposed optimal DTM policy can be generalized to arbitrary DVFS schedules.

4.2 Energy optimization

With the given deadline specification of a task, the required (min-imum) operating frequency f_{target} and corresponding base voltage level V_{base} can be determined in order to finish task execution by deadline. Conventional DTMs of the circuit try not to exceed the temperature limit T_{limit} by forcing to lower down the frequency or stop execution with performance penalties. Our proposed DTM method targets to minimize the energy consumption for a given task, or a given set of tasks, without violating the operating frequency of the initial schedule, and thereby without any performance loss. Simultaneously, our DTM slows down the speed of temperature increase, or makes the die temperature stable at a certain point below T_{limit}, thereby avoiding the performance loss from such situations when the conventional DTMs inevitably lower the frequency or stop execution.

Among all the possible voltage levels, if one voltage level V_i has a threshold temperature such that $T_{th}^{V_{base} \to V_i} < T_{limit}$, then V_i may be exploited instead of V_{base} in a certain temperature range. For the remainder of paper, we use a simple notation $T_{th}^{V_i}$ to denote $T_{th}^{V_{base} \to V_i}$. Then, we can separate the operating temperature regions by each available T_{th}. More specifically, the ith region is $R_i \triangleq [T_{th}^{V_i}, T_{th}^{V_{i+1}})$ for $1 \leq i \leq N$, where N is the number of the candidate voltage levels of the target frequency f_{target}. We have $V_1 = V_{base} > V_2 > ... > V_N$.

Figure 6 (a) and (b) show an example that has three candidate voltage levels, $V_{High} = V_{base}$, V_{Mid} and V_{Low}, and thus the temperature regions are divided into three regions. The red curves in both figures show the minimum energy consumption at each temperature, according to the lowest voltage level that makes the circuit work with f_{target} at that temperature point. As can be seen from the figure, the minimum energy point in each region locates at the temperature point where the voltage level is changed, i.e., the threshold temperature level. Furthermore, from extensive simulations based on various FinFET libraries, we find that the energy consumption at $T_{th}^{V_{i+1}}$ is always higher than that at $T_{th}^{V_i}$. This is because the leakage power increases fast as the temperature rises. Therefore, we start the optimization process from a premise:

▶ The minimum energy point in R_i is always at $T_{th}^{V_i}$, and the corresponding energy consumption is smaller than that at $T_{th}^{V_{i+1}}$.

The equilibrium temperature level $T_{eq}^{V_i}$ depends on the ambient temperature, and hence, it is an uncontrollable factor. The potential inequality between $T_{eq}^{V_i}$ and $T_{th}^{V_i}$ will not let the circuit operate with stable temperature $T_{th}^{V_i}$. Suppose that the initial die temperature is T_{init}, which is in region R_i. Then the movement of die temperature T_{die} follows the following two rules:

▶ If $T_{init} < T_{eq}^{V_i}$, T_{die} will increase, until $T_{die} = \min\{T_{eq}^{V_i}, T_{th}^{V_{i+1}}\}$.

▶ If $T_{init} > T_{eq}^{V_i}$, T_{die} will decrease, until $T_{die} = \max\{T_{eq}^{V_i}, T_{th}^{V_i}\}$.

We use Figure 6 (a) as an example of the above rules. Suppose that T_{init} is in R_{Mid}, the temperature will eventually be stable at

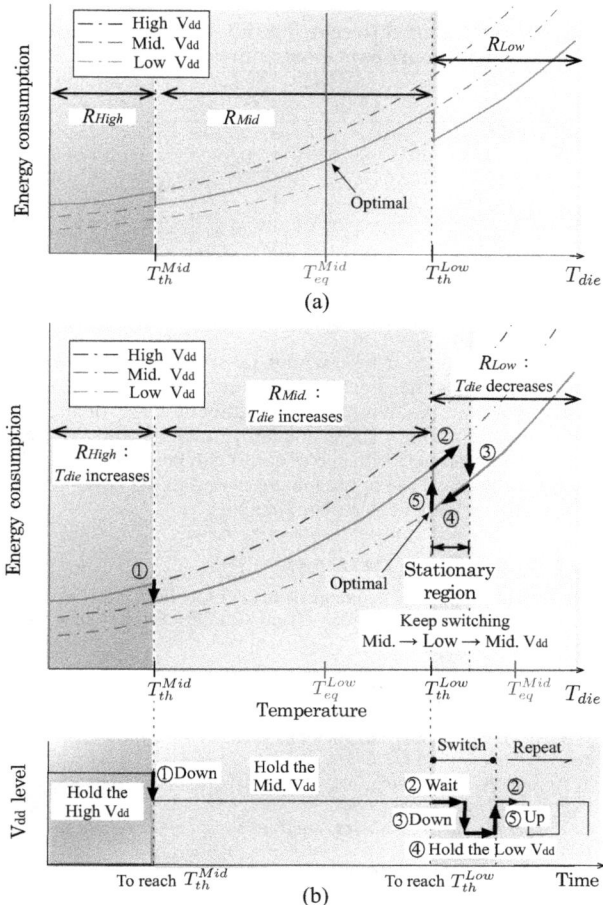

Figure 6: Case studies for (a) Policy I, and (b) Policy II.

T_{eq}^{Mid} which is also in R_{Mid}. Then, T_{eq}^{Mid} is the optimal temperature point where the circuit can achieve the maximum energy saving for the given task. Similarly, suppose that T_{init} is in R_{Low}, and T_{eq}^{Mid} is still in R_{Mid}. Then T_{eq}^{Mid} is still the optimal point. That is because T_{eq}^{Low} is lower than T_{eq}^{Mid}, T_{die} with initial voltage V_{Low} decreases from T_{init} to T_{th}^{Low}. Then the voltage level switches to V_{Mid} in order to maintain the speed of the circuit. Finally, T_{die} will be stable at T_{eq}^{Mid}. The opposite case that T_{init} is in R_{High} results in the same outcomes, because T_{eq}^{High} is higher than T_{eq}^{Mid} and this fact makes T_{die} move to T_{eq}^{Mid}. Therefore, we propose a policy as:

▶ Policy I: Check if there exists a k such that $T_{eq}^{V_k} \in R_k$ for $1 \leq k \leq N$: we have proved that at most one such k exists. If k exists, the optimal voltage level is V_k and the optimal and stable temperature is $T_{eq}^{V_k}$. Whatever region T_{init} starts in, we need to use the corresponding voltage level of the region, i.e., the lowest voltage in the region that meets the frequency condition, and then keep changing the voltage level whenever T_{die} reaches a region boundary. Eventually die temperature will arrive at $T_{eq}^{V_k}$.

Now we discuss the case when no such k exists. In this case, T_{die} keeps increasing in all the regions until the region i with $T_{eq}^{V_i}$ lower than $T_{th}^{V_i}$. In this case T_{die} should decrease in R_i. Then, the minimum energy consumption of the circuit is at $T_{th}^{V_i}$, because (i) using high voltage level than V_i only makes T_{die} increase, thus consuming more energy, (ii) T_{die} can not further decrease than $T_{th}^{V_i}$. This case is illustrated in Figure 6 (b). In the figure, T_{eq}^{Mid} locates higher than

T_{th}^{Mid}, and T_{eq}^{High} should be higher than T_{eq}^{Mid}. Hence, T_{die} always increases in both R_{High} and R_{Mid}. But, because T_{eq}^{Low} lies below the region R_{Low} (in R_{Mid} in the figure), T_{die} will decrease in R_{Low} if V_{Low} is applied. Finally, the optimal temperature is T_{th}^{Low}.

Although we know the optimal temperature point in Figure 6 (b), it is impossible to maintain operating at this point during circuit operation. Therefore, we propose to use V_{Mid} for a certain amount of time to warm up. This process is indicated by ②. Then continue to perform: ③ lower down the voltage to V_{Low}, and ④ maintain voltage V_{Low} until T_{die} decreases to T_{th}^{Low} where we need to ⑤ increase the voltage to V_{Mid}. Repeating these process makes the circuit operate near the optimal temperature without timing violation. We call this region the *stationary region* because when T_{die} enters this region, it continues staying in that region by doing proper voltage switchings. The blue-colored region in Figure 6 (b) shows an example of the stationary region.

Meanwhile, the amount of time for the warm-up process affects how far the circuit operates from the optimal point. The shorter the time is, the higher energy efficiency is achieved. The minimum constraint of such warm-up time is determined by the voltage switching time (i.e., the voltage transition latency of DC-DC converters) that the voltage controller can provide. However, this responsiveness issue of the voltage controller is beyond the scope of this paper.

Based on the previous discussion, we propose the second policy of our DTM:

▶ Policy II. if Policy I cannot be applied, check whether there exists k such that $T_{eq}^{V_k} < T_{th}^{V_k}$. Find the smallest k value if such k exists, and then the optimal temperature point should be $T_{th}^{V_{\min(k)}}$. Whatever the region T_{init} starts in, use the corresponding lowest voltage level of the region. Keep changing the voltage level whenever T_{die} reaches a region boundary until T_{die} enters the stationary region. In the stationary region, we keep performing ②→③→④→⑤.

At the end, we point out that if there exists no k such that $T_{eq}^{V_k} < T_{th}^{V_{k+1}}$, T_{die} will eventually exceed T_{limit} and the task will fail to finish in time. Of course, conventional DTMs that use only the base voltage level of the task will make T_{die} reach T_{limit} even earlier. Compared to conventional DTMs, the proposed DTM could save a considerable amount of energy before T_{die} reaches T_{limit}, because the proposed DTM always selects the lowest (possible) voltage level in each region. Furthermore, using lower voltage levels slows down the temperature rise so that the circuit can operate with at a high frequency for longer time, while the circuit controlled by conventional DTMs would have to reduce the frequency earlier than the proposed DTM.

5. EXPERIMENTAL WORK

We validated our proposed DTM with various FinFET-based circuits, namely, 50 FO4 inverter chain, 16-bit carry-select adder, 16-bit multiplier, and 16-bit comparator based on 10nm, 14nm, 16nm, and 20nm PTM-MG bulk FinFET libraries. All the circuits are designed in the shorted gate mode. We performed Hspice simulation to obtain the delays and power consumptions of each circuit for different V_{dd} setups and different temperatures. The delays were obtained from the worst case inputs of the circuits. Notice that we did not attempt to consider interconnect delays in our simulations. That is because the characteristics of interconnects used for deeply scaled FinFET-based circuit fabrics is unknown (i.e., although the R and C parasitic values of the interconnect go up with temperature, the current strength of the driver also improves, which can reduce the wire delay.) We determined the minimum and maximum temperature that the circuits operate as -25°C and 90°C, respectively. Based on the worst delay at -25°C for each V_{dd}, we found the available voltage levels, which are lower than the base V_{dd} but have

Table 2: Simulation results from the four kinds of FinFET-based circuits based on the four different FinFET technology libraries. The number of * indicates different reasons why 0.1V below V_{base} can not be used: details are explained at the end of Section 5.

Tech.	Gain from V_{base}= 0.75V and V_i, the lower voltage level(s)				Tech.	Gain from V_{base}= 0.55V and V_i, the lower voltage level(s)			
	Inverter chain	Adder	Multiplier	Comparator		Inverter chain	Adder	Multiplier	Comparator
20nm	32.44% 0.7V and 0.65V	22.60% 0.7V and 0.65V	22.51% 0.7V **	20.14% 0.7V *	20nm	38.19% 0.5V and 0.45V	40.82% 0.5V and 0.45V	33.85% 0.5V **	42.20% 0.5V and 0.45V
16nm	22.17% 0.7V and 0.65V	32.56% 0.7V and 0.65V	8% 0.7V *	35.22% 0.7V and 0.65V	16nm	28.51% 0.5V ***	19.95% 0.5V ***	20.91% 0.5V ***	17.99% 0.5V ***
14nm	28.62% 0.7V and 0.65V	17.01% 0.7V ***	22.95% 0.7V ***	30.06% 0.7V and 0.65V	14nm	19.25% 0.5V ***	18.93% 0.5V ***	19.51% 0.5V ***	18.46% 0.5V ***
10nm	16.49% 0.7V and 0.65V	13.65% 0.7V ***	8.96% 0.7V ***	15.60% 0.7V *	10nm	14.82% 0.5V ***	15.81% 0.5V ***	16.33% 0.5V ***	15.48% 0.5V ***

smaller delays than the worst delay of the base V_{dd} in some higher temperature regions.

For the power and thermal modeling, we used data from ARM Cortex-A8, which resulted that $R_{die\text{-}amb}$= 35.8 K/W, and C_{die}=9.0 J/K, and the chip increased from 25°C to 36°C in 500 sec. The detailed explanation of the measurement can be referred from [19]. Finally, we scaled the obtained power data of the test circuits in order to make the data compatible to using the measured $R_{die\text{-}amb}$ and C_{die}. In this scaling work, we found the scaling factor s, such that multiplying s to the power data from the 20nm based inverter chain makes the temperature increase of the circuit (working with 0.7V) follow the same trend of ARM Cortex-A8. Then the derived s was multiplied to other circuits. Based on the scaled power and the ambient temperature set to 25°C, we finally derived the equilibrium temperature for each circuit and each voltage level.

We defined $Gain = \frac{Saved\ energy\ w/\ the\ proposed\ DTM \cdot 100(\%)}{Energy\ consumption\ w/\ the\ conventional\ DTM}$. We also determined the simulation conditions as follows: (i) the base V_{dd} in the simulation is assumed to be the minimum voltage level, that the circuit controlled by the conventional DTM can finish a given task with the base V_{dd} before the temperature exceeds 90°C or its T_{eq}, and (ii) the circuit starts the operation at the ambient temperature (25°C). Note that the resulted gains under these conditions are almost the minimum gain that the proposed DTM can achieve, because (i) there can be the case that the proposed DTM makes the circuit finish a given task in time, while the conventional DTM does not, (ii) if the circuits starts with the higher temperature, then $Gain$ may significantly increase than that can be derived from starting at the ambient temperature.

Table 2 shows the simulation results that includes $Gain$ and the possible voltage levels in the given operation conditions. We set the base V_{dd} to 0.75V and 0.55V. Some cases in the table show that the test circuits can lower down the voltage level by 0.1V, i.e., two levels down, while the others can not. The other cases are because (i) the voltage level that 0.1V below V_{base} could not satisfy $T_{th}^{V_i} < T_{limit}$ (indicated by * in the table) (ii) the setup for conventional DTM made the temperature increase too fast to reach T_{limit}, thereby the simulation was done earlier, otherwise our DTM could exploit the 1V low level voltage (indicated by **), or (iii) the circuit with 0.05V low level voltage has the equilibrium temperature with the given thermal conditions, which is below T_{th} of the 0.1V low level voltage (indicated by ***). The reason (ii) and (iii) prove the potential of our DTM that can enhance the more energy savings than those in the table. Finally, the proposed DTM has been demonstrated to significantly improve the energy efficiency of the FinFET-based circuits.

6. CONCLUSION

This paper started by presenting a key observation of TEI phenomenon that the delay of a FinFET gate decreases with increasing die temperature both in the near and super-threshold voltage regimes, which is different from that exhibited by planar CMOS devices operating at the super-threshold V_{dd}. Next it introduced the TEI-aware DTM algorithm to minimize the energy consumption of FinFET-based circuits without any appreciable performance penalty. More precisely, instead of choosing the smallest possi-

ble voltage to complete a task within its specified deadline, the proposed DTM algorithm dynamically adjusts the supply voltage of the chip so as to maintain the chip temperature at or near its optimum operation point. Experimental results showed 40% energy saving (with no performance penalty) can be achieved by the proposed TEI-aware DTM approach compared to the best-in-class DTMs that are unaware of this phenomenon.

7. ACKNOWLEDGEMENTS

This research is supported by grants from the PERFECT program of the Defense Advanced Research Projects Agency and the Semiconductor Research Corporation.

8. REFERENCES

[1] E. J. N. et al., "Turning silicon on its edge," IEEE Circuits and Devices Magazine, 2004.

[2] T. Sairam, W. Zhao, and Y. Cao, "Optimizing FinFET technology for high-speed and low-power design," GLSVLSI, 2007.

[3] B. Zhai et al., "Energy efficient subthreshold processor design," IEEE T. on VLSI, 2009.

[4] R. Dreslinski et al., "Near-threshold computing: reclaiming moores law through energy efficient integrated circuits," IEEE, 2010.

[5] F. Crupi et al., "Understanding the basic advantages of bulk FinFETs for sub- and near-threshold logic circuits from device measurements," IEEE.T on CAS II, 2012.

[6] W.Liao et al., "Temperature and supply voltage aware performance and power modeling at micro architecture level," IEEE T. on CAD, 2005.

[7] D. Brooks and M. Martonosi, "Dynamic thermal management for high performance microprocessors," HPCA, 2001.

[8] R. Jayaseelan and T. Mitra, "Temperature aware task sequencing and voltage scaling," ICCAD, 2008.

[9] H. Jung, P. Rong, and M. Pedram, "Stochastic modeling of a thermally-managed multi-core system," DAC, 2008.

[10] R. Jayaseelan and T. Mitra, "Dynamic thermal management via architectural adaptation," DAC, 2009.

[11] D. Shin et al., "Energy-optimal dynamic thermal management: Computation and cooling power co-optimization," IEEE T. on Industrial Informatics, 2010.

[12] Y. Pu et al., "Misleading energy and performance claims in sub/near threshold digital systems," ICCAD, 2010.

[13] M. Ashouei et al., "Novel wide voltage range level shifter for near-threshold designs," ICECS, 2010.

[14] A. Calimera et al., "Reducing leakage power by accounting for temperature inversion dependence in dual-vt synthesized circuits," ISLPED, 2008.

[15] "PTM," available at http://ptm.asu.edu.

[16] X. Huang et al., "Sub-50 nm P-Channel FinFET," IEEE T. on Electron Devices, 2001.

[17] S. Soleimani, A. AfzaliKusha, and B. Forouzandeh, "Temperature dependence of propagation delay characteristic in finfet circuits," ICM, 2008.

[18] S. Kim et al., "Temperature dependence of substrate and drain-currents in bulk FinFETs," IEEE T. on Electron Devices, 2007.

[19] Q. Xie et al., "Dynamic thermal management in mobile devices considering the thermal coupling between battery and application processor," ICCAD, 2013.

[20] A. Bansal et al., "Compact thermal models for estimation of temperature-dependent power/performance in FinFET technology," ASPDAC, 2006.

Buffered Clock Tree Synthesis Considering Self-Heating Effects[*]

Chung-Wei Lin[1], Tzu-Hsuan Hsu[2], Xin-Wei Shih[2], and Yao-Wen Chang[2,3]
[1]Department of Electrical Engineering and Computer Sciences, UC Berkeley, Berkeley, CA 94720
[2]Graduate Institute of Electronics Engineering, National Taiwan University, Taipei 106, Taiwan
[3]Research Center for Information Technology Innovation, Academia Sinica, Taipei 115, Taiwan
cwlin@eecs.berkeley.edu, {thhsu,raistlin}@eda.ee.ntu.edu.tw, ywchang@ntu.edu.tw

ABSTRACT

A clock tree typically consumes substantial dynamic power, and thus the considerable heat generated by itself can cause serious clock-skew variations. In this paper, we propose a self-heating-aware buffered clock tree synthesis flow. A mixed integer linear programming (MILP) formulation is proposed to simultaneously model heat spreading, place buffers, and determine a temperature-aware clock tree topology. The formulation is then transformed into a succession of low-complexity feasibility problems to further reduce the runtime. In addition, a fast superposition approach is proposed to incrementally update thermal profiles to reduce simulation time. Experimental results show that our synthesis flow can achieve averagely 50.57% worst-case clock skew reduction, compared with the original symmetrical clock tree.

Categories and Subject Descriptors

B.7.2 [**Integrated Circuits**]: Design Aids; J.6 [**Computer-Aided Engineering**]: Computer-Aided Design

Keywords

Clock tree synthesis; clock skew; thermal; self-heating

1. INTRODUCTION

To synchronize sequential elements in a chip, a clock tree is used to distribute clock signals with buffers and interconnects. The synchronization degree is evaluated by *clock skew*, which is the difference between the maximum and the minimum delays of clock signal paths. Temperature variation is a critical issue [6] for such synchronization because temperature would affect the signal delays. Temperature gradients of high performance chips could be up to 80° [11]. Such significant gradients may result in very different temperature environments for clock signal paths. Consequently, the actual clock-skew variations could be serious if the temperature gradients are not considered.

Most previous temperature-aware clock-tree synthesis techniques simplify the problem by neglecting the heat generated

[*]This work was partially supported by Genesys Logic, IBM, MediaTek, TSMC, and NSC of Taiwan under Grant No's. NSC 103-2918-I-002-012, NSC 102-2221-E-002-235-MY3, NSC 102-2923-E-002-006-MY3, NSC 101-2221-E-002-191-MY3, and NSC 100-2221-E-002-088-MY3.

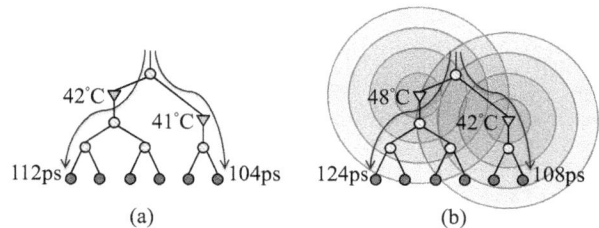

Figure 1: (a) Without considering heat generated by a clock tree itself, the analysis of sink latencies is not accurate. (b) Heat generated by a clock tree itself would change temperature environments and have significant impact on sink latencies.

from a clock tree itself. That is, only the background heat generated from other placed circuit elements is considered when optimizing the clock skew. However, in high performance chip designs, a clock tree, one of the main power sources, also generates considerable heat. As reported in [14, 18], a clock tree could consume about 40% overall dynamic power. Due to such high consumption which is usually distributed non-uniformly, the difference of temperatures in different regions can be large enough to affect clock skew. Figure 1 gives an example. In Figure 1(a), the clock skew is 8 ps as the heat generated by the clock tree is neglected. In contrast, such heat leads to an actual clock skew of 16 ps as shown in Figure 1(b). This problem is difficult because the heat generated from a clock tree cannot be modeled as the background heat during clock tree construction, and it is too late to consider the heat after the clock tree is fixed. Therefore, it is desirable to develop new self-heating-aware techniques for the practical clock-tree synthesis problem that considers temperature.

For self-heating-aware clock-tree synthesis, we need an efficient, yet sufficiently accurate estimation of the impact of temperature on signal path delays. On one hand, the estimation can be realized by constructing a timing model and then calculating the model. However, the model construction and calculation have an intrinsic difficulty due to the interaction between the carrier mobility and the threshold voltage of devices (e.g., clock buffers) [13, 17]. On the other hand, although we can apply SPICE simulation to improve the accuracy, the simulation might not be feasible for self-heating-aware clock-tree synthesis due to its high complexity. It is thus desirable to develop a new efficient and effective mechanism to facilitate the delay estimation for the self-heating-aware clock-tree synthesis.

1.1 Previous Work

To minimize delay difference of interconnects, many previous works [9, 10, 12] develop thermal-aware routing methods to prevent interconnects from passing through hotspot regions. These methods [9, 10] often can achieve good results

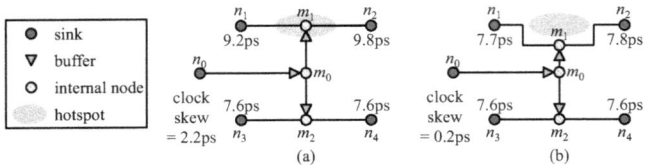

Figure 2: Post-processing example for clock-skew reduction. (a) The path $< n_0, m_0, m_1, n_2 >$ runs through a hotspot region and incurs a larger delay compared to other paths. (b) The modified clock tree relocates the tree node m_1 to a lower location to avoid passing through a hotspot region. As a result, the clock skew is reduced.

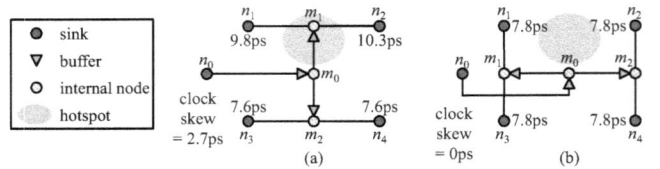

Figure 3: An example of insufficient post-processing. (a) Simply relocating internal tree nodes to nearby locations cannot avoid from passing through hotspot regions. (b) However, changing the clock tree topology could result in a smaller clock skew.

without considering buffer insertion. If buffers are considered [12], they often generate considerable heat, change temperature environments, and incur mutual temperature influence with other buffers. Therefore, it is desirable to develop an effective technique to consider the self-heating effects of buffers and place buffers into suitable locations to minimize the temperature difference of buffers.

On the other hand, to cope with temperature effects, existing temperature-aware techniques optimize a pre-constructed clock tree for given thermal profiles by postprocessing, where a profile is a value table that represents temperature of each uniformly divided grid on the chip. The thermal profiles can be obtained by performing a thermal simulation based on power distribution after placement. TACO [8] works on two thermal profiles, a uniform and the worst-case thermal profiles. To consider the time-variant issue, PECO is proposed to handle multiple thermal profiles [21]. Both TACO and PECO adopt postprocessing techniques to reduce worst-case clock skew. Figure 2 illustrates how postprocessing could reduce clock skew. These postprocessing techniques reduce clock skew by relocating nodes of a pre-constructed clock tree. Such postprocessing can be effective in some cases, but they could fail in other cases. As shown in Figure 3, the hotspot region is larger than that in Figure 2. For this case, simply relocating internal tree nodes to nearby locations cannot prevent the clock tree from running through a hotspot region.

1.2 Our Contributions

This paper considers temperature effects *during* clock tree synthesis for skew minimization, unlike the previous works that resort to *postprocessing*. We evaluate various clock tree topologies and select one with the smallest worst-case skew under different thermal profiles. For example, if we change the tree topology of Figure 3(a) to that in Figure 3(b), the resulting clock skew can be reduced because the new clock tree topology makes each path from the clock source to sinks run through similar temperature environments. Refinement with only postprocessing may not resolve the problem shown in Figure 3(a) due to its limited solution space.

In this paper, we consider self-heating effects of buffers. We propose a mixed integer linear programming (MILP) formulation to simultaneously model heat spreading, place buffers, and determine a temperature-aware clock tree topology. To guide optimization with temperature information, we propose a fast superposition approach based on the alternating-direction-implicit-based (ADI-based) thermal simulation [20, 19]. By adopting this approach, background thermal profiles could be obtained before clock tree construction and updated incrementally to avoid time-consuming thermal simulations during clock tree construction. To further reduce the runtime, the original MILP formulation is transformed into successive low-complexity feasibility problems. Experimental results show that our method can reduce runtime by 17.29X and meanwhile maintain same solution quality. Compared

with the original symmetrical clock tree, our synthesis flow can achieve averagely 50.57% worst-case clock skew reduction.

The remainder of this paper is organized as follows. Section 2 presents some preliminaries and then formulates the addressed problem. Section 3 presents our clock tree synthesis flow. Section 4 reports experimental results. Section 5 concludes this paper.

2. PRELIMINARIES

2.1 Temperature Superposition

To analyze temperature distributions, we first divide a chip into an array of uniform grids. With power settings, the initial temperature of each grid point can be estimated. Then, a thermal simulation is performed to compute the temperature of each grid point. The basic idea of thermal simulations is to solve the heat conduction equations for each grid point. An efficient transient thermal simulation algorithm based on the ADI method is proposed in [19, 20]. With a finite difference method of partial differential heat conduction equations, the ADI-based 3D thermal simulator discretizes the space domain and the time domain to obtain

$$T_{i,j,k}^{n+1} - T_{i,j,k}^n = \frac{\Delta t}{\rho C_p} g + r_x \frac{\delta_x^2}{2}(T_{i,j,k}^{n+1} + T_{i,j,k}^n) +$$
$$r_y \frac{\delta_y^2}{2}(T_{i,j,k}^{n+1} + T_{i,j,k}^n) + r_z \frac{\delta_z^2}{2}(T_{i,j,k}^{n+1} + T_{i,j,k}^n), \quad (1)$$

where (i, j, k) represents the coordinate of a grid point in the corresponding (x, y, z) directions, $T_{i,j,k}^n$ denotes the temperature of the grid point (i, j, k) at the time step n, Δt is the time increment, ρ is the material density, C_p is the specific heat, and g is the heat energy generation rate. The term $r_x/r_y/r_z$ controls the simulation steps of the time and space domains in the $x/y/z$ direction. The term $\delta_x^2 T_{i,j,k}^n$ is defined as $T_{i-1,j,k}^n - 2T_{i,j,k}^n + T_{i+1,j,k}^n$ and represents the spatial temperature relation at the time step n in the x direction ($\delta_y^2 T_{i,j,k}^n$ and $\delta_z^2 T_{i,j,k}^n$ are defined similarly). The ADI method transforms a three-dimensional problem into successive three one-dimensional problems. By expanding Equation (1) in the x direction, we can obtain

$$(1 + r_x)T_{i,j,k}^{n+1} - \frac{r_x}{2}(T_{i-1,j,k}^{n+1} + T_{i+1,j,k}^{n+1}) = \alpha, \quad (2)$$

where α is a constant value. Based on the above observation, computing temperatures at the time step $n + 1$ by the ADI-based method can be seen as solving a linear system. Then, we adopt the superposition technique to compute background temperatures and clock tree temperatures separately and sum them up to get final temperatures, as shown in Figure 4.

2.2 Symmetrical Clock Tree

The symmetrical clock tree is a state-of-the-art work presented in [15] to better handle the challenges for modern large-scale clock-tree synthesis, compared with the classical DME method [5, 7] and industrial practice with iterative timing

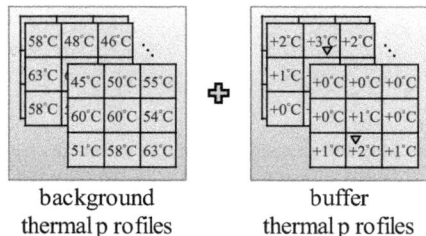

Figure 4: By adopting the superposition approach, thermal profiles can be obtained by adding background thermal profiles and a set of buffer thermal profiles together.

simulations, by avoiding insufficiently accurate timing model, time-consuming simulation, and considerable capacitance usage. The concept of the symmetrical clock tree is making paths from the clock source to sinks as similar as possible. In other words, configurations such as the number of branches, the length of interconnects, and the type of buffers are kept identical in the same level of a clock tree. Once paths are similar, and so are latencies on sinks. Consequently, clock skew can be minimized this way.

2.3 Problem Formulation

To overcome the above disadvantages of post temperature-aware optimization methods, we propose to simultaneously determine a clock tree topology and place buffers at the locations with similar temperature configurations. Furthermore, heat generated by a clock tree itself and the mutual temperature influence of clock buffers are also considered. In addition, a fast superposition approach based on the ADI thermal simulation is proposed to rapidly compute and update thermal profiles. We define the self-heating-aware buffered clock tree synthesis problem as follows:

- **Self-Heating-Aware Buffered Clock Tree Synthesis Problem (SHAB-CTS):** Given clock sinks, thermal profiles, a slew-rate constraint, and a library of buffers, construct a buffered clock tree to distribute clock signals to all sinks such that the worst-case clock skew under different thermal profiles is minimized subject to no slew-rate violation.

3. ALGORITHM

We adopt the symmetrical clock tree [15] as the basic clock tree topology because it does not rely on any timing models or time-consuming simulation during clock tree synthesis. However, the symmetry properties mentioned in Section 2.2 are not sufficient while considering temperature effects. To follow the concept of the symmetrical clock tree, buffers in the same level need to be placed at locations with similar temperature environments, and thus the difference of buffer propagation delays can be minimized. In the original symmetrical clock tree construction flow, however, buffers are inserted after detailed routing, and thus the solution space of buffer locations are often limited. To overcome the disadvantages, we simultaneously determine clock tree topologies and place buffers.

3.1 Objectives

Our objective is to minimize the worst-case clock skew under different thermal profiles. Since our method adopts the symmetrical clock tree structure and aligns received temperatures of buffers in each tree level. The key problem of minimizing the worst-case clock skew is transformed into minimizing the maximum difference of temperatures received by buffers in each tree level.

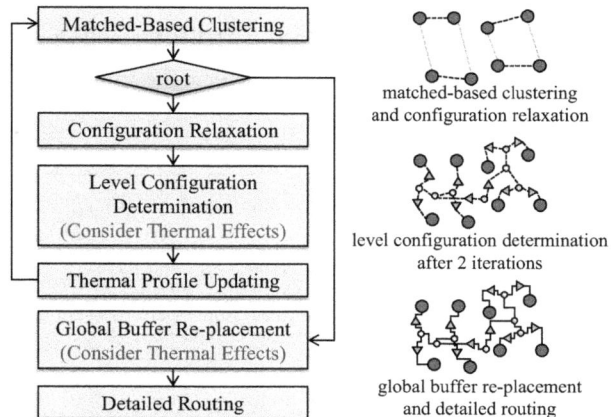

Figure 5: A self-heating-aware buffered clock tree synthesis flow.

3.2 Overall Flow

Figure 5 shows our proposed self-heating-aware clock tree synthesis flow. First, the Minimum-Bottleneck Maximum Matching (MBMM) algorithm [16] is applied to cluster sinks into connection sets and to obtain an initial matching. With the MBMM algorithm, total wirelength can be minimized in a certain tree level. Considering temperature effects, a matching with the minimum bottleneck interconnect is then relaxed to obtain more clustering combinations and enlarge the solution space for temperature alignment problems. To choose a proper configuration which satisfies the temperature alignment requirement and to consider the mutual temperature influence of buffers, an MILP-based algorithm is applied to simultaneously determine clustering configurations and place buffers into locations with similar temperature environments. After a clustering configuration (matching) is determined, we apply the superposition approach mentioned in Section 2.1 to incrementally update temperatures in all thermal profiles. The above process is iteratively performed from sinks (tree leaves) to the clock source (tree root) to obtain a clock tree topology. However, determining clock tree structures level-by-level may unbalance a thermal profile, i.e., heat generated by later placed buffers may affect already placed buffers. Therefore, under the same clock tree topology, we re-place all buffers simultaneously to get a better solution. As a clock tree topology is determined and buffers are placed, interconnects can then be routed to connect sinks, buffers, internal nodes, and the clock source.

3.3 Clustering and Relaxation

To balance the trade-off between wirelength minimization and temperature alignment, a matching obtained by the MBMM algorithm with the minimum bottleneck interconnect is relaxed to provide more potential configurations for temperature alignment. To relax a matching, some unmatched, yet potentially matched edges are put back into the resulting matching. Since long wirelength is undesirable, an upper bound on wirelength is provided to select potentially matched edges. Our method is to restrict the number of buffers; in other words, we set the upper bound wirelength as the longest wirelength which can be driven by the buffer number used in the minimum bottleneck interconnect.

3.4 Level Configuration Determination

After obtaining a set of potential edges (clustering configurations) from the previous stage, we simultaneously place buffers and select a proper clustering configuration for each level (from sinks to the clock source) by an MILP-based method.

See Table 1 for the notations used in the MILP formulation. Note that $\mathcal{E}$ is the set of potential edges obtained in Section 3.3

Table 1: Notations used in the MILP formulation.

SETS AND ELEMENTS	
$\mathcal{P}$	set of thermal profiles
$\mathcal{G}$	set of uniform grids
$\mathcal{N}$	set of nodes (sinks or subtrees)
$\mathcal{E}$	set of potential edges
$\mathcal{B}$	set of potential buffers
p_q	thermal profile q
$g_{k,m}$	the grid in column k and row m
n_i	node i
$e_{i,j}$	edge between nodes n_i and n_j
$b_{i,j}$	buffer between nodes n_i and n_j
CONSTANTS	
$C_{i,j,r}$	constants of linear equations enclosing the embedding region of buffer $b_{i,j}$ ($1 \leq r \leq 4$)
L	length of one side of a grid
$T_{q,i,j}$	background temperature of buffer $b_{i,j}$ under thermal profile p_q
$T'_{i,j,k,m,i',j',k',m'}$	temperature increment of buffer $b_{i,j}$ if buffers $b_{i,j}$ and $b_{i',j'}$ are placed into grid $g_{k,m}$ and $g_{k',m'}$ respectively
VARIABLES	
$(x_{i,j}, y_{i,j})$	coordinates of buffer $b_{i,j}$
$s_{i,j}$	0-1 variable that denotes if edge $e_{i,j}$ is selected (i.e., buffer $b_{i,j}$ is selected)
$l_{i,j,k,m}$	0-1 variable that denotes if buffer $b_{i,j}$ is placed into grid $g_{k,m}$
$t_{q,i,j}$	received temperature of buffer $b_{i,j}$ under thermal profile p_q

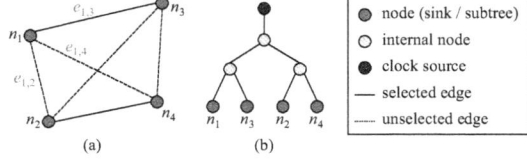

Figure 6: An example configuration (edge) selection.

(not all pairwise edges between nodes), and $\mathcal{B}$ is the set of buffers on edges in $\mathcal{E}$. The objective function is given by

$$\text{minimize} \quad \max_{p_q \in \mathcal{P}} \left(\max_{b_{i,j} \in \mathcal{B}} (t_{q,i,j}) - \min_{b_{i,j} \in \mathcal{B}} (t_{q,i,j}) \right), \quad (3)$$

where $\left(\max_{b_{i,j} \in \mathcal{B}} (t_{q,i,j}) - \min_{b_{i,j} \in \mathcal{B}} (t_{q,i,j})\right)$ is the maximum received-temperature difference of thermal profile p_q. We have explained the objective function in Section 3.1. We can also consider capacitance and wirelength by using a weighted summation in the objective function. The constraints of the MILP formulation will be explained in the following subsections.

3.4.1 Configuration Selection

$$\forall n_i \in \mathcal{N}, \quad \sum_{n_j \in neighbor(n_i)} s_{i,j} = 1. \quad (4)$$

Clustering configuration is determined through edge selection. We use node notation to represent sinks (subtrees) and assume that the number of nodes is even. If the number of nodes is not even, we add one *pseudo sink* [15]. Since each node should be exactly connected with another node, there is only one edge to be selected for a specific node, which is derived from Equation (4). If an edge $e_{i,j}$ is selected ($s_{i,j} = 1$), it means that buffer $b_{i,j}$ is selected, and buffer $b_{i,j}$ will receive and contribute some temperature increments in Equation (8). Note that $e_{i,j} = e_{j,i}$ because the edges here are undirected. For the example shown in Figure 6(a), node n_1 should be exactly clustered with another node; thus, equation $s_{1,2} + s_{1,3} + s_{1,4} = 1$ must hold. After solving an MILP problem, assuming that $s_{1,3} = 1$ and $s_{1,2} = s_{1,4} = 0$, we have the resulting clustering configuration shown in Figure 6(b), where nodes n_1 and n_3 are clustered together.

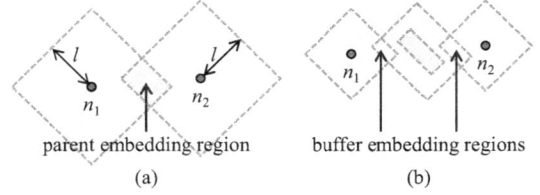

Figure 7: (a) Parent embedding region. (b) Buffer embedding regions.

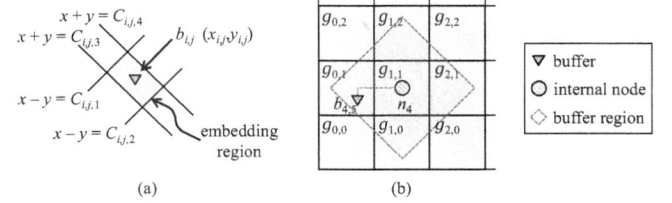

Figure 8: (a) Embedding region of $b_{i,j}$. (b) An example of buffer location determination. $l_{4,5,0,1} = 1$ since $b_{4,5}$ is placed into $g_{0,1}$.

3.4.2 Embedding Region Constraints

$$\forall b_{i,j} \in \mathcal{B}, \quad C_{i,j,1} \leq x_{i,j} - y_{i,j} \leq C_{i,j,2}; \quad (5)$$

$$\forall b_{i,j} \in \mathcal{B}, \quad C_{i,j,3} \leq x_{i,j} + y_{i,j} \leq C_{i,j,4}. \quad (6)$$

To allocate potential locations for internal tree nodes and buffers, embedding regions are represented by the tilted rectangular region (TRR) [5, 7]. In our clock tree synthesis, we lengthen shorter interconnects through snaking to be equal to the bottleneck wirelength in a specific tree level. Nodes which are clustered together should be routed to a parent node with the same wirelength. Therefore, we construct a parent embedding region to allocate potential locations for a parent node. As shown in Figure 7(a), we first extend child nodes (n_1 and n_2) with the Manhattan distance l which is the bottleneck wirelength. Then, the parent embedding region is obtained by performing an intersection operation. Each location in the parent region can be reached by child nodes with the distance l. Another issue is that according to the driving strength of a buffer, the distance between a parent node and child nodes should be limited to keep the slew rate in an acceptable range. As a result, we construct buffer embedding regions to allocate proper locations for buffers. Figure 7(b) shows how we build up buffer embedding regions. To start with, we extend child nodes with a suitable distance which can be driven by a buffer. Next, similar process is applied to the parent embedding region. Finally, buffer embedding regions are obtained through performing intersection operations. Since an embedding region is a tilted rectangular region as shown in Figure 8(a), it can be defined by four values $C_{i,j,1}, C_{i,j,2}, C_{i,j,3}, C_{i,j,4}$ in Equations (5) and (6), which enclose the region.

3.4.3 Buffer Location Determination

$$\forall b_{i,j} \in \mathcal{B}, g_{k,m} \in \mathcal{G}, \quad l_{i,j,k,m} = 1 \iff$$
$$Lk \leq x_{i,j} \leq L(k+1) \wedge Lm \leq y_{i,j} \leq L(m+1). \quad (7)$$

To minimize the received-temperature difference of buffers, locations of buffers should be evaluated and temperatures of those locations should be computed. If buffer $b_{i,j}$ is placed into grid $g_{k,m}$, $l_{i,j,k,m}$ is equal to 1. Otherwise, it is equal to 0. For the example shown in Figure 8(b), buffer $b_{4,5}$ is placed into grid $g_{0,1}$; therefore, $l_{4,5,0,1}$ is equal to 1. On the other hand, $l_{4,5,1,1}$ is equal to 0 because buffer $b_{4,5}$ is not in grid $g_{1,1}$. Note that Equation (7) can be transformed into equivalent linear constraints.

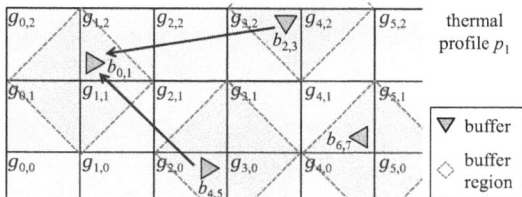

Figure 9: An illustration of heat spreading.

3.4.4 Heat Spreading

$$\forall p_q \in \mathcal{P}, b_{i,j} \in \mathcal{B}, \qquad t_{q,i,j} = T_{q,i,j} + \sum_{b_{i',j'} \in \mathcal{B}, g_{k,m}, g_{k',m'} \in \mathcal{G}}$$

$$\left(T'_{i,j,k,m,i',j',k',m'} \cdot l_{i,j,k,m} \cdot l_{i',j',k',m'} \cdot s_{i,j} \cdot s_{i',j'} \right). \qquad (8)$$

In our formulation, the key is to formulate received temperatures of buffers. As mentioned in Section 1.1, heat generated by a clock tree itself and the mutual temperature influence of buffers are considered. We regard buffers as heat sources and formulate equations to describe heat spreading of buffers. The received temperature of buffer $b_{i,j}$ under thermal profile p_q is denoted as $t_{q,i,j}$ and can be formulated by Equation (8); it is composed of the background temperature and the buffer temperature. The background temperature is generated by already placed circuit elements and varies under different operation modes. Therefore, we use $T_{q,i,j}$ to denote the background temperature of buffer $b_{i,j}$ under thermal profile p_q, where $T_{q,i,j}$ only needs to be simulated once before clock tree construction as mentioned in Section 2.1. On the other hand, other placed buffers would have impact on the temperature of buffer $b_{i,j}$. The activated temperature increment is expressed as the summation term. If buffers $b_{i,j}$ and $b_{i',j'}$ are selected and placed into grid $g_{k,m}$ and $g_{k',m'}$ respectively, the term $(l_{i,j,k,m} \cdot l_{i',j',k',m'} \cdot s_{i,j} \cdot s_{i',j'})$ will be 1, and the temperature increment will be activated; otherwise, it will not be activated. Note that the multiplication of binary variables can be transformed into equivalent linear constraints. An example of heat spreading is shown in Figure 9. The temperature of $b_{0,1}$ is affected by $b_{2,3}$ and $b_{4,5}$, which can be expressed as $t_{1,0,1} = T_{1,0,1} + T'_{0,1,1,2,2,3,3,2} + T'_{0,1,1,2,4,5,2,0}$. On the other hand, $b_{6,7}$ is far away from $b_{0,1}$; therefore, it has no impact on $b_{0,1}$.

3.5 Global Buffer Re-Placement

As mentioned in Section 3.2, placing buffers in the current level would change temperature distributions and affect buffers placed in the previous levels. Therefore, after constructing a clock tree topology level-by-level, we perform global optimization to simultaneously adjust all buffer locations under the same clock tree topology. Formulations of global buffer re-placement is same as what we did in level configuration determination. Since we do not preform edge selection in this stage, the MILP formulation is simpler; as a result, we can re-place all buffers into suitable locations in a short time. Another issue is that we need to align temperatures in different tree levels at the same time. Nevertheless, it is hard to achieve multiple objectives in all tree levels. Therefore, we transform the multiple objective optimization problem into a single objective optimization problem by combining all objectives into a single one and associating each objective with a weight to indicate its importance. Note that the received-temperature difference of buffers in higher levels is more sensitive to clock skew. The reason is that if buffers in higher levels (close to the source) receive different temperatures and thus have different propagation delays, the slew rate for each downstream path can vary significantly, and it is hard to remedy slew-rate differences in lower levels. Based on this observation, we assign larger weights to higher levels.

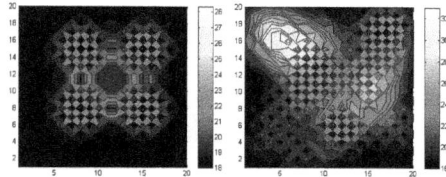

Figure 10: Examples of thermal profiles used for *ispd'09-f11*.

3.6 Speed-Up Methods

The objective of level configuration determination is to minimize the maximum received-temperature difference under different thermal profiles. Since we have multiple thermal profiles, finding the maximum and minimum temperatures for all thermal profiles may introduce a large number of variables and constraints and significantly complicate our MILP formulation. Therefore, we transform a minimization problem into successive low-complexity feasibility problems. The main idea is that we iteratively reduce received-temperature differences of each thermal profile. To begin with, an upper-bound and a lower-bound temperatures are set for each thermal profile. That is, buffers cannot be placed into a location with temperature higher than the upper-bound temperature or lower than the lower-bound temperature. Then, we formulate a feasibility problem to find a proper configuration which satisfies temperature settings. If a feasible solution is found, we can try to minimize received-temperature differences (increase the lower-bound temperature or decrease the upper-bound temperature). As a result, we re-formulate a feasibility problem with a new temperature setting and try to find a new feasible solution. The above process is iteratively performed until we cannot find a feasible solution when the received-temperature differences cannot be further reduced.

4. EXPERIMENTAL RESULTS

The proposed self-heating-aware clock tree synthesis was implemented in the C++ programming language. All the experimental data were measured on a Linux workstation with an Intel Xeon 2.5GHz CPU and 40GB memory. The CPLEX 12.3 [1] library was used to solve our MILP problems. The benchmark circuits are from the 2009 and 2010 ISPD clock network synthesis contests [2]. We followed the parameter settings of the 45nm process technology [4] and used ngspice [3] to evaluate the quality of resulting clock trees. We focus on handling temperature effects between buffers and do not consider blockages; therefore, only those benchmark circuits with no blockages were used to evaluate our results.

Since the original ISPD benchmark circuits do not have thermal profiles, we generated several thermal profiles for each benchmark. First, we divided a chip into a uniform grid and assigned power consumption to each grid point based on sink information. For example, the benchmark circuit, *ispd'09-f11*, was divided into a 20×20 uniform grid. In this stage, we randomly inserted some power sources to represent already placed circuit elements and simulated real applications. Then, we performed the ADI-based thermal simulation with power setting and obtained background thermal profiles. For each thermal profile, we used different power settings to simulate different operation modes. In the following experiments, we used ten thermal profiles including one uniform thermal profile and nine non-uniform ones for each benchmark. See Figure 10 for two thermal profiles used for *ispd'09-f11*.

The following two experiments were performed: (1) we evaluate three different synthesis flows to explore the effects of temperature on clock skews, and (2) we verify the effectiveness of our speed-up method for the MILP computation.

Table 2: Comparison between Symm-CTS, Post-CTS, SHAB-CTS*, and SHAB-CTS. All of the algorithms adopt the symmetrical clock tree concept. We report the worst-case clock skew (skew) in *ps*, capacitance (cap) in *fF*, and runtime (time) in *s*. The results are first normalized and then averaged for the comparison.

Benchmark	#Sinks	Symm-CTS (no self-heating-aware)			Post-CTS (post optimization)			SHAB-CTS* (self-heating-aware)			SHAB-CTS (SHAB-CTS* w/o speed-up)		
		skew	cap	time	skew	cap	time	skew	cap	time	skew	cap	time
ispd'09-f11	121	16.521	73,733	0.05	13.332	78,251	168.3	8.127	78,804	126.2	8.102	81,209	1,348.9
ispd'09-f12	117	19.242	65,172	0.06	16.387	68,542	84.2	9.733	68,854	24.6	9.828	69,856	514.6
ispd'09-f21	117	18.686	77,576	0.06	12.615	78,692	49.3	9.681	77,934	47.2	9.579	79,215	957.8
ispd'09-f22	91	17.026	43,819	0.04	13.598	47,174	28.6	9.983	45,562	25.6	9.953	48,143	441.5
ispd'10-f07	1,915	28.086	152,342	30.5	19.468	152,816	303.9	13.214	152,673	251.9	N/A	N/A	> 12 hrs
ispd'10-f08	1,134	33.710	115,974	12.1	25.625	117,137	298.4	14.238	116,155	283.2	N/A	N/A	> 12 hrs
comparison		2.023	0.973	0.028	1.544	1.007	1.530	1.000	1.000	1.000	0.998	1.030	17.286

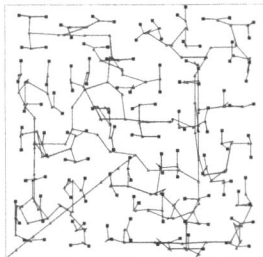

Figure 11: The resulting clock tree for the benchmark circuit *ispd'09-f11*.

Table 2 shows our comparative studies with three different clock tree synthesis flows, where "Symm-CTS" denotes the original symmetrical tree construction [16] without considering temperature effects, "Post-CTS" denotes a flow which performs post temperature-aware optimization to improve the worst-case clock skew, and "SHAB-CTS*" denotes our complete flow which simultaneously determines a clock tree topology and buffer placement to minimize the received-temperature differences of buffers. As shown in the table, SHAB-CTS* achieves averagely 50.57% worst-case clock skew reduction, compared with Symm-CTS, with only 2.7% capacitance overhead which results from longer wirelength. Compared with Post-CTS, SHAB-CTS* also achieves averagely 35.22% worst-case clock skew reduction. In particular, the capacitance and runtime of SHAB-CTS* are even smaller than those of Post-CTS. The reason is that although Post-CTS only places buffers and does not consider clustering configurations, it may be hard to find proper locations for buffers. In other words, with a poor clustering configuration, it might take longer wirelength and longer time to minimize received-temperature differences of buffers.

Table 2 also gives the results on the second experiment, where "SHAB-CTS" denotes our original self-heating-aware buffered clock tree synthesis (without the speed-up method). Adopting the speed-up method can reduce the runtime by more than 17.29X. Without the speed-up method, we cannot obtain solutions for the benchmark circuits, *ispd'10-f07* and *ispd'10-f08*, within 12 hours. In particular, the resulting worst-case clock skew of SHAB-CTS* is almost the same as SHAB-CTS, implying that our speed-up method can substantially reduce the runtime while maintaining high solution quality. The resulting clock tree for the benchmark circuit *ispd'09-f11* is shown in Figure 11.

5. CONCLUSIONS

We have presented a self-heating-aware buffered clock tree synthesis flow to minimize the worst-case clock skew under time-variant thermal profiles. Our flow extends the symmetrical clock tree by placing buffers in the same tree level at similar temperature environments by using an MILP formulation. To reduce the runtime, we transform the formulation into successive low-complexity feasibility problems. The ex-

perimental results have shown that our method can achieve a 17.29X speedup while maintaining good solution quality. Compared with the original symmetrical clock tree, our flow achieves averagely 50.57% worst-case clock skew reduction.

6. REFERENCES

[1] *IBM ILOG CPLEX Optimizer.* http://www-01.ibm.com/software/integration/optimization/cplex-optimizer/.

[2] *ISPD Clock Network Synthesis Contest.* http://www.ispd.cc/contests/.

[3] *ngspice.* http://ngspice.sourceforge.net/.

[4] *Predictive Technology Model.* http://engineering.asu.edu/.

[5] K. D. Boese and A. B. Kahng. Zero-skew clock routing trees with minimum wirelength. In *IEEE ASIC*, pages 17–21, Sept. 1992.

[6] S. Bota, J. Rossello, C. de Benito, A. Keshavarzi, and J. Segura. Impact of thermal gradients on clock skew and testing. *IEEE Design & Test of Computers*, 23(5):414–424, May 2006.

[7] T.-H. Chao, Y.-C. H. Hsu, and J.-M. Ho. Zero skew clock net routing. In *ACM/IEEE DAC*, pages 518–523, June 1992.

[8] M. Cho, S. Ahmedtt, and D. Pan. TACO: temperature aware clock-tree optimization. In *IEEE/ACM ICCAD*, pages 582–587, Nov. 2005.

[9] C. Liu, R.-X. Chen, J. Tan, S. Fan, J. Fan, and K. Makki. Thermal aware clock synthesis considering stochastic variation and correlations. In *IEEE ISCAS*, pages 1204–1207, May 2008.

[10] C. Liu, J. Su, and Y. Shi. Temperature-aware clock tree synthesis considering spatiotemporal hot spot correlations. In *IEEE ICCD*, pages 107–113, Oct. 2008.

[11] F. J. Mesa-Martinez, E. K. Ardestani, and J. Renau. Characterizing processor thermal behavior. In *ACM ASPLOS on Architectural Support for Programming Languages and Operating Systems*, pages 193–204, Mar. 2010.

[12] J. Minz, X. Zhao, and S. K. Lim. Buffered clock tree synthesis for 3d ics under thermal variations. In *IEEE/ACM ASP-DAC*, pages 504–509, Mar. 2008.

[13] C. Park, J. John, K. Klein, J. Teplik, J. Caravella, J. Whitfield, K. Papworth, and S. Cheng. Reversal of temperature dependence of integrated circuits operating at very low voltages. In *IEEE Int. Electron Devices Meeting*, pages 71–74, Dec. 1995.

[14] R. S. Shelar and M. Patyra. Impact of local interconnects on timing and power in a high performance microprocessor. In *ACM ISPD*, pages 145–152, Mar. 2010.

[15] X.-W. Shih and Y.-W. Chang. Fast timing-model independent buffered clock-tree synthesis. In *ACM/IEEE DAC*, pages 80–85, June 2010.

[16] X.-W. Shih, H.-C. Lee, K.-H. Ho, and Y.-W. Chang. High variation-tolerant obstacle-avoiding clock mesh synthesis with symmetrical driving trees. In *IEEE/ACM ICCAD*, pages 452–457, Nov. 2010.

[17] S. Sze and K. Ng. *Physics of Semiconductor Devices*. Wiley, 2007.

[18] V. Tiwari, D. Singh, S. Rajgopal, G. Mehta, R. Patel, and F. Baez. Reducing power in high-performance microprocessors. In *ACM/IEEE DAC*, pages 732–737, June 1998.

[19] T.-Y. Wang and C. C.-P. Chen. 3-D Thermal-ADI: a linear-time chip level transient thermal simulator. *IEEE TCAD*, 21(12):1434–1445, Dec. 2002.

[20] T.-Y. Wang and C. C.-P. Chen. Thermal-ADI—a linear-time chip-level dynamic thermal-simulation algorithm based on alternating-direction-implicit (ADI) method. *IEEE TVLSI*, 11(4):691–700, Aug. 2003.

[21] H. Yu, Y. Hu, C. Liu, and L. He. Minimal skew clock embedding considering time variant temperature gradient. In *ACM ISPD*, pages 173–180, Mar. 2007.

Therminator: A Thermal Simulator for Smartphones Producing Accurate Chip and Skin Temperature Maps

Qing Xie, Mohammad Javad Dousti, and Massoud Pedram

University of Southern California, Los Angeles, CA, USA

{xqing, dousti, pedram}@usc.edu

ABSTRACT

Maintaining safe chip and device skin temperatures in small form-factor mobile devices (such as smartphones and tablets) while continuing to add new functionalities and provide higher performance has emerged as a key challenge. This paper presents *Therminator*, an early stage, fast, full-device thermal analyzer, which generates accurate steady-state temperature maps of the entire smartphone starting from the Application Processor and other key device components, extending to the skin of the device itself. The thermal analysis is sensitive to detailed device specifications (including its material composition and 3-D layout) as well as different use cases (each case specifying the set of active device components and their activity levels). Therminator considers all major components within the device, builds a corresponding compact thermal model for each component and the whole device, and produces their steady-state temperature maps. Temperature results obtained by using Therminator have been validated against a commercial computational fluid dynamics-based tool, i.e., Autodesk Simulation CFD, and thermocouple measurements on a Qualcomm Mobile Developer Platform. A case study on a Samsung Galaxy S4 using Therminator is provided to relate the device performance to the skin temperature and investigate the thermal path design.

Categories and Subject Descriptors

C. 5. 3 [**Computer System Implementation**]: Microcomputers – *Portable devices (e.g., laptops, personal digital assistants)*

Keywords

Smartphones, embedded systems, thermal management, thermal modeling, temperature maps simulator, skin temperature, CFD

1. INTRODUCTION

The popularity of mobile devices, such as smartphones and tablets, has surpassed that of personal computers, thanks to their portability and ease-of-use. (In the remainder of this paper we will use smartphones as the popular and archetypical mobile device.) Additional enablers for the rapid increase in the number of smartphones have been their improving functionality and ever-increasing performance capabilities. This has in turn happened due to introduction of high performance (heterogeneous, multi-core) processors inside smartphones. Unfortunately, high performance processors cause two adverse effects: 1) They tend to experience higher average and peak die temperatures. 2) They tend to result in higher device *skin (surface) temperatures*. High die temperature increases the leakage power consumption [1], speeds up aging processes [2], and may eventually cause permanent defects. High skin temperatures can cause first or even second degree burns on

device users, with obvious and immediate adverse user reactions. Hence, thermal design (i.e., designing the heat flow path and a cooling method) and thermal management (i.e., employing thermal response mechanisms to avoid hot spots and high die temperatures) are crucial for a mobile device to improve its performance and energy efficiency while maintaining safe temperatures.

Proper thermal design effectively removes heat away from a VLSI circuit die. In smartphones, *application processors* (APs) incorporate CPU, GPU, *digital signal processor* (DSP), sometimes a baseband radio unit, and so on. The AP is a major heat generator in the smartphone [3]. Due to the cost, form factor, noise, and safety issues, smartphones rely on passive cooling methods that dissipate the heat generated by the AP through thermal conduction to the device skin. Thermal pads are usually attached on top of the AP chip package to ease the heat removal [3][4]. Thermal management techniques, such as frequency throttling and voltage/frequency scaling, are also exploited to avoid high die temperatures. For example, one can observe that the CPU and GPU performance (and consequently their power consumption) are throttled in Samsung Exynos 5250 so as to prevent the AP's junction temperature from exceeding an upper threshold [5].

As noted above, thermal design and management of smartphones are also concerned a *skin temperature constraint*. This constraint refers to the fact that the temperature at the device skin must not exceed a certain upper threshold. According to [6][7], most people experience a sensation of heat pain when they touch an object hotter than 45°C. Ideally speaking, distributing the heat uniformly onto the device skin results in the most effective heat dissipation. However, in practice, majority of the heat flows in vertical direction from the AP die, and thus hot spots are formed on the device skin above the AP location [8]. It is reported that the hottest spot on iPad 3 can reach as high as 47°C while playing graphic intensive games [9]. Usually, a skin temperature thermal governor is implemented to maintain the skin temperature at a desired *setpoint* by using a control feedback.

To address this design challenge, it is necessary to model the temperature map (temperature at different locations) for the smartphone in an accurate and efficient manner. Knowing the detailed temperature map on the device skin at the design time is helpful in the device implementation. For example, using materials with high thermal conductivity in the thermal path enhances heat removal from the AP and in turn causes high skin temperature, whereas using low thermal conductivity materials cannot remove the heat from the AP fast enough and hence the die temperature goes up. Moreover, knowing how the temperature of a particular component depends on use cases helps to derive the optimal thermal management policy for that component. For instance, setting CPU frequency throttling levels is affected by how skin temperature depends on the CPU frequency.

Analyzing temperature maps at the early stage of the design flow can significantly reduce the device time. Even though *computational fluid dynamics* (CFD) tools generate accurate temperature maps, they are expensive and not compatible with other performance/power simulators. *Compact thermal modeling* (CTM) method has been proposed for thermal analysis with reasonable accuracy and low computational complexity [10][11]. This method builds an RC thermal network based on the well-known duality between the thermal and the electrical phenomena, and solves for temperatures in the network in a similar way to finding voltage values in an electrical circuit.

In this work, we present *Therminator*, a CTM-based component-level thermal simulator targeting small form-factor mobile devices (such as smartphones and tablets). Major contributions of this work are the following:

1) Therminator is the first thermal simulator targeting at smartphones. It produces temperature maps for all components, including the AP, battery, display, and other key device components, as well as the skin of the device, with high accuracy and fast runtime. Therminator results have been validated against thermocouple measurements on a Qualcomm Mobile Developer Platform (MDP) [12] and simulation results generated by Autodesk Simulation CFD [13].

2) Therminator is very versatile in handling different device specifications and component usage information, which allows a user to explore impacts of different thermal designs and thermal management policies. New devices can be simply described through an input specification file (in XML format).

3) Therminator supports parallel processing, allowing users to employ GPU to reduce the runtime by more than two orders of magnitude for high-resolution temperature maps.

4) A detailed case study has been conducted for Samsung Galaxy S4 by using Therminator. The temperature results relate the device performance to the device skin temperature, as well as the impact of the thermal path design.

Therminator is available for download at http://atrak.usc.edu/downloads.

The rest of paper is organized as follows. Section 2 reviews related work. Section 3 introduces Therminator. The modeling methodology and implemented features are elaborated in Sections 4 and 5. We validate Therminator results in Section 6 and provide a case study in Section 7. Section 8 concludes the paper.

2. RELATED WORK

HotSpot [11] is a successful early-stage CTM methodology targeting thermal analysis of the silicon die and its packaging which are cooled with a heat sink and possibly a fan. It generates accurate temperature maps quickly. *Temptor* [14] is a tool based on HotSpot which allows the temperature prediction using performance counters instead of components' power trace. Meng *et al.* [15] improved HotSpot by adding the 3-D chip simulation support. *Teculator* [16] instruments HotSpot to support thermoelectric coolers. *3D-ICE* [17] is another thermal simulator targeting 3-D ICs equipped with liquid cooling. However, neither HotSpot nor 3D-ICE can be modified or extended to analyze small form-factor devices as they target a single IC package along with its cooling equipment. In fact, modeling smartphone is much more complicated due to: 1) multiple heat generators, including battery, display, and a number of IC chips; 2) complex 3-D layout where each component may be in vertical and horizontal contact with several other components; and 3) necessity of considering the internal air in the device. Comparing to those tools, Therminator focuses on component-level thermal modeling, in which the architecture-level details inside a single chip package are ignored.

Several researches have been conducted in studying the thermal design for smartphones and tablets [3][4][18]. Luo *et al.* established a simple thermal resistance network to analyze the whole mobile phone system [18]. However, the thermal resistance network built in [18] is oversimplified as each component is modeled as one block with a single uniform temperature value. Gurrum *et al.* modeled the smartphone in CFD tools and analyzed the thermal effect of using materials with different thermal conductivities through CFD simulation [3]. Rajmond and Fodor [4] used CFD tools to show that attaching thermal pad on top of the AP

significantly reduces the AP temperature. To the best of our knowledge, Therminator is the first tool targeting smartphones that automatically builds a compact thermal model from the device specifications, and solves for temperature maps of all components accurately with a fast runtime.

3. THERMINATOR OVERVIEW

Figure 1 depicts the overview of Therminator. Therminator takes two input files provided by users. The `specs.xml` file describes the smartphone design, including components of interest and their geometric dimensions (length, width, and thickness) and relative positions. Therminator has a built-in library storing properties of common materials (i.e., thermal conductivity, density, and specific heat) that are used to manufacture smartphones. In addition, users can override these properties or specify new materials through the `specs.xml` file. The `power.trace` file provides the usage information (power consumption) of those components that consume power and generate heat, e.g., ICs, battery, and display. The `power.trace` can be obtained through real measurements or other power estimation tools/methods such as [19][20]. `power.trace` is a separate file so that one can easily interface a performance-power simulator with Therminator.

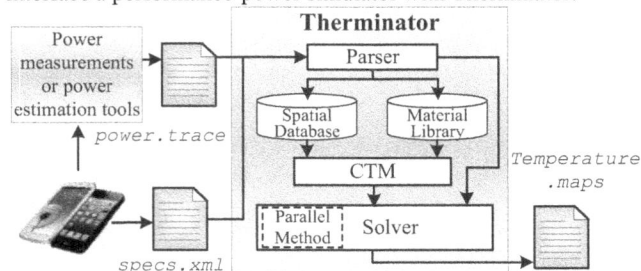

Figure 1. Overview of Therminator.

Therminator has three main modules. A *parser module* parses input files, updates the *material library*, and makes a set of components specified by the input file. Parser performs multiple sanity checks after it finishes parsing to detect inappropriately specified components, e.g., the positions of two components are set such that they overlap in space. A *CTM module* takes the valid components set from the parser, divides them into fine-grained sub-components, and stores them into a spatial database. Next, the CTM module detects physical contacts among sub-components and builds a compact thermal model. Finally, the compact thermal model is given to a *Solver module*. The solver uses the thermal model along with the power trace coming from the parser to compute temperature maps of all components. The Solver applies a *parallel method* using GPUs to solve for temperature results more quickly when GPU hardware is available.

4. COMPACT THERMAL MODELING

There is a well-known duality between the thermal and electrical phenomena [21]. The compact thermal modeling methods build an equivalent RC circuit based on the original thermal system. In this paper, we focus on generating the steady-state temperature maps for components inside a smartphone because the objective of thermal design and management is to ensure that the device can run continuously without exceeding a given temperature threshold. Therefore, the device is modeled by using a thermal resistance network only.

To build a compact thermal model, Therminator divides specified components into *sub-components* with smaller dimensions and checks for physical contacts among sub-components. Finer granularity of sub-component division helps to produce more accurate temperature maps at the cost of increased runtime and memory usage. Each sub-component is modeled as a node in the thermal resistance network and has a single temperature value. A thermal resistance is calculated for every contacted sub-component pairs, based on their material properties, dimensions, and relative positions.

Figure 2 shows a small part of thermal resistance network for the Qualcomm MSM8660 Mobile Developer Platform (MDP) [12]. The components in Figure 2, from top to bottom, include screen protector, display module, PCB and IC chips, battery, and rear case. Terminator breaks various components into non-equal number of sub-components according to their importance and requirements of solution quality. For two adjacent sub-components i and j, the thermal resistance is calculated by serially connecting two thermal resistors from their centers to the shared surface,

$$r(j,i) = r(i,j) = r_i + r_j = \frac{1}{A}\left(\frac{t_i}{k_i} + \frac{t_j}{k_j}\right) \qquad (1)$$

where A is the common area between these two contacted sub-components, k_i and k_j are the thermal conductivity, and t_i and t_j are the perpendicular distances from the center of sub-components to the shared surface, respectively. Note that adjacencies between sub-components are detected in a 3D space and thereby, we account for orthotropism in the material thermal conductivity.

At the boundary of the device, heat diffuses to the ambient environment (air). Thus, the boundary thermal resistance between the i-th sub-component and the ambient air is calculated as,

$$r(i, amb) = r_i + r_{amb} = \frac{1}{A}\left(\frac{t_i}{k_i} + \frac{1}{h_{air}}\right) \qquad (2)$$

where h_{air} is the air heat transfer coefficient. In the natural convection condition, h_{air} has the value of $5\sim25\ W/(m^2K)$ [22].

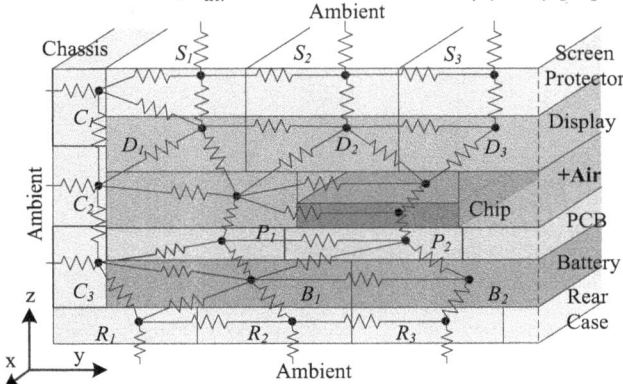

Figure 2. A cross-section view of the thermal resistance network in a simple smartphone model.

Note that empty spaces, shown as orange areas in Figure 2, are left in the design specifications. Ignoring these empty spaces, i.e., not calculating the thermal resistance between them and adjacent components will completely disable the heat flow through them and subsequently result in temperatures over-estimation. Thus, to avoid this issue, Terminator does *VoidFill* – i.e., it automatically identifies these empty spaces and fills them with air, as shown in Figure 2. Note that it is not practical to model the internal air using compact modeling of fluids in our problem, due to the lack of specific air circulation channels in smartphones. Therefore, in the steady-state, the air flow is ignored and the air is modeled like other sub-components. We apply a correction factor to the thermal conductivity of the air to account for this simplification.

Having built the resistance network, we obtain heat flow equations for all sub-components in a matrix format as follows,

$$G\vec{T} = \vec{P} \qquad (3)$$

where $\vec{T}$ is the vector of all sub-component temperatures, G is the conductance matrix derived from the thermal resistance network, and $\vec{P}$ is the heat generation vector, which includes the heat generation of sub-components and heat diffusion from the device to the ambient environment. Terminator adopts the *LUP decomposition* method to decompose G into a lower and upper

triangular matrices, and then applies *forward and backward substitution* to solve for $\vec{T}$. Advanced matrix solver libraries enabling GPU-acceleration are also included to reduce the runtime for fine-grained temperature maps.

5. THERMINATOR IMPLEMENTATION

Therminator is implemented using C++ and compiled by GCC 4.7. The parser adopts *PugiXML* [23], an open source, light-weight, and fast C++ XML processing library. The built-in material library is a class called `Materials` which holds default material properties and its data are updated by the parser. All components and sub-components are instances of `Component` and `Subcomponent` classes, respectively. A `Device` class keeps track of sub-components objects using a spatial database. Another class called `Model` takes the `device` object and builds the thermal model based on Equations (1) and (2). Several geometric utility methods are implemented in order to perform basic spatial queries on sub-components, e.g., checking the physical contact between every two sub-components, determining if they have overlap in space, and calculating their common area. Moreover, the `Model` class calls another parser to read the `power.trace` file which contains the power consumption of each component.

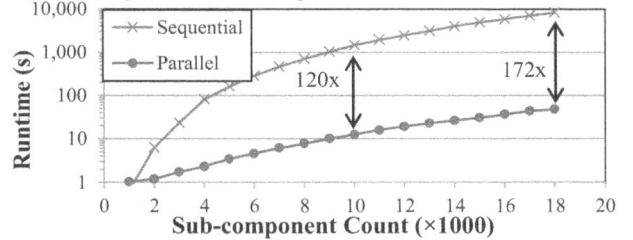

Figure 3. Comparison of runtime of sequential and parallel methods for different sub-component counts.

Matrix solving techniques, namely, the LUP decomposition method followed by the forward and backward substitution method, are implemented using the sequential method (which utilizes the CPU) and the parallel method (which utilizes the GPU), respectively. For the parallel method, Therminator adopts *CULA Dense* [24], which is a set of GPU-accelerated linear algebra libraries utilizing the *NVIDIA CUDA* parallel computing platform. One can observe that the parallel method speeds up Therminator by more than two orders of magnitude against the sequential method, as shown in Figure 3. Runtime results of both methods are measured on a server with 4×Intel Xeon E7-8837 CPUs, 64GB of memory, and an NVIDIA Quadro K5000 GPU.

6. THERMINATOR EVALUATION

6.1 Validation of the Therminator Results

We use a Qualcomm MSM8660 MDP [12] as the target system to validate Therminator results. The MSM8660 MDP has a dual-core 1.5GHz CPU, Adreno 220 GPU, 1GB LPDDR2 RAM, 3.61-inch touch screen, and a 1,300mAh Li-ion battery. A smartphone consists of a large number of small components with irregular geometric shapes and complicated material compositions. In this work, we try our best to identify the major components in the MSM8660 MDP and obtain the thermal properties of these components. Figure 4(a) shows a teardown of the MSM8660 MDP. We create a model for MSM8660 MDP device by identifying major components that have thermal impact to the entire device and measure their dimensions and relative positions. Components identified include rear case, chassis, battery, PCB, display, screen protector, and some ICs, such as AP, DRAM, eMMC, GPS and WiFi. The detailed material properties and dimensions for components are not shown due to the limited paper space. We draw the MSM8660 MDP model in Autodesk software, as shown in Figure 4(b), and perform CFD thermal analysis. We treat CFD results as golden results and compare Therminator results with

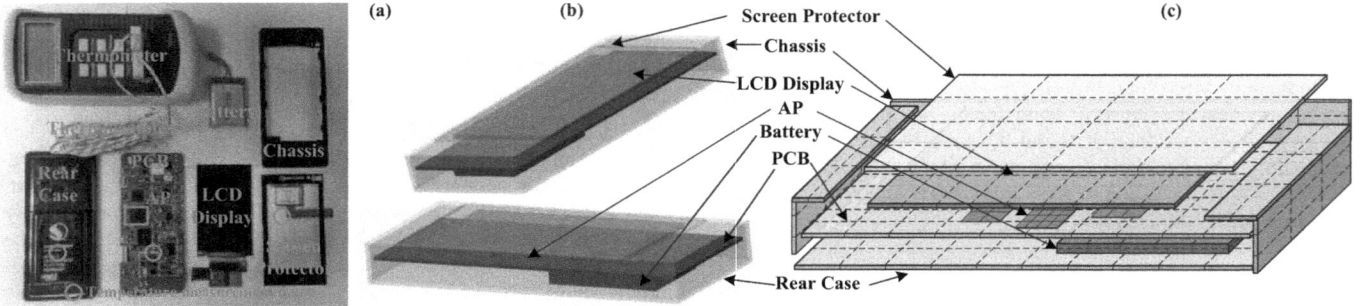

Figure 4. (a) Teardown of MSM8660 MDP device and temperature measurement kits (circle marks are temperature measurement points. Note for the PCB, thermocouple is attached onto the other side), **(b)** CFD drawing, and **(c)** Therminator 3-D visualization.

Table 1. Temperatures obtained from the thermocouple measurement (TCM), Autodesk Simulation CFD, and Therminator. Note the AP junction temperature is read from temperature register (Reg) instead of measurement. The ambient temperature is 23.0°C.

Use Case	$T_{screen\ hot\ spot}$ (°C)			$T_{rear\ case\ hot\ spot}$ (°C)			$T_{PCB\ (near\ battery)}$ (°C)			$T_{AP\ junction}$ (°C)		
	TCM	CFD	Therminator	TCM	CFD	Therminator	TCM	CFD	Therminator	Reg	CFD	Therminator
StabilityTest	38.1	38.4	38.5	38.4	39.1	38.7	44.9	44.5	44.4	60	58.6	59.3
Candy Crush	37.2	37.8	37.7	38.4	39.2	38.9	46.2	44.6	44.8	59	59.0	59.5
YouTube	35.8	37.0	36.7	34.6	34.4	34.2	39.3	38.4	38.3	43	45.2	45.4
Camcorder	31.7	32.2	32.1	33.3	32.6	32.4	36.9	36.2	36.2	42	42.7	43.3
Video playback	30.2	30.8	30.7	30.5	30.8	30.7	33.3	33.4	33.4	39	39.4	40.0

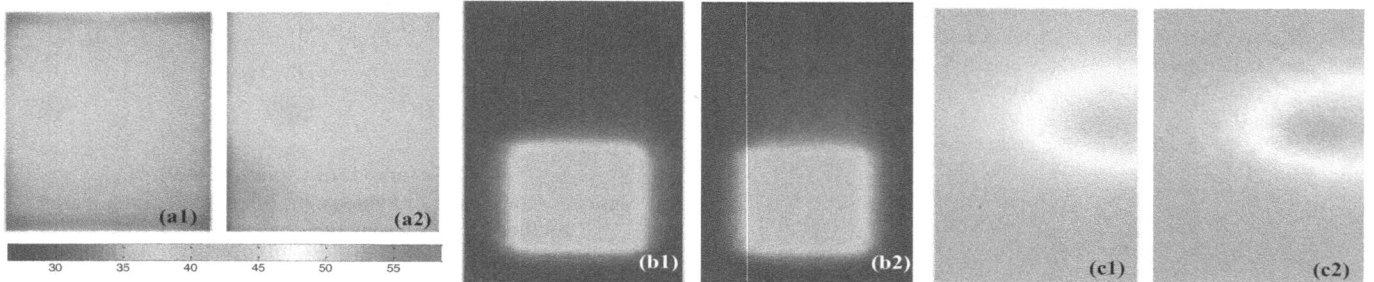

Figure 5. Temperature maps produced by Autodesk Simulation CFD (a1, b1, c1) and by Therminator (a2, b2, c2) for the screen protector (a), rear case (b), and PCB (c) for the StabilityTest use case.

them. Thus, a similar MDP device model, including the aforesaid components, their dimensions, relative positions and material properties, is specified in the *specs.xml* file for Therminator. Figure 4(c) visualizes the 3-D layout model that Therminator creates from the input file. Note that Therminator applies different granularity to different components.

We run a few representative use cases that utilize different components and consume various amounts of power. Use cases tested in this work are *StabilityTest* (an app that heavily stresses CPU and GPU [25]), casual gaming (*Candy Crush*), *YouTube* video streaming, camcorder (video recording), and a local video playback. We adopt *Trepn Profiler* [26] to record the per component power consumption breakdown of this device, and provide as inputs for both CFD simulation software and Therminator. Note that we assign the total power consumption of some small components (interconnects, sensors, etc.) to the PCB uniformly because we have no access to the schematic diagram of the MSM8660 MDP to precisely locate them.

We use thermocouples to measure temperatures at three locations in MSM8660 MDP, shown as red circles in Figure 4(a). We measure 1) hot spot on the screen right above the AP; 2) hot spot on the rear case below the battery (because there is a big air gap between PCB and rear case, the hot spot on the rear case is located below the battery); and 3) the PCB (the opposite side of the board shown in Figure 4(a).) The ambient temperature is measured as 23.0°C during the experiments. We access *Sysfs* of the MDP device through the *Android Debug Bridge* interface and obtain the AP junction temperature by reading the temperature register in `/sys/class/thermal/thermal_zone2` directory. Note that the temperature register only has the accuracy of ±1°C.

Table 1 compares temperature of aforementioned regions obtained through thermocouple measurements, CFD simulations, and Therminator. We first compare thermocouple measurement results and CFD simulation results. One can see that CFD simulation produces accurate results for all tested use cases and all regions. The maximum and average temperature error are 2.4°C and 0.7°C (11.0% and 4.7%), respectively. The error mainly comes from simplifications in modeling the real device and inaccuracies in determining component material properties. Note that the largest error (2.4°C) comes from the AP junction temperature in YouTube use case. A potential reason might be the inaccuracy of the temperature register (i.e., ±1°C).

Next, CFD results are used as golden results and we compare Therminator results with them. We divide specified components into 7,336 sub-components in total in Therminator. Table 1 shows that for all use cases and temperature points, the maximum and average errors of Therminator are only 0.7°C and 0.25°C (3.65% and 1.42%), respectively, compared to CFD results. Figure 5 shows more detailed comparisons of temperature maps, produced by CFD simulation and Therminator, of front screen, rear case, and PCB. One can see that Therminator is able to accurately capture not only the temperature of a particular hot spot, but also temperature maps of the entire smartphone device. Therefore, Therminator matches very well with the commercial CFD tool, given the same input models.

6.2 Convergence of the Therminator Results

Therminator can generate more detailed temperature maps at higher resolution with longer runtime. We study the convergence of temperature versus total the number of sub-components created by

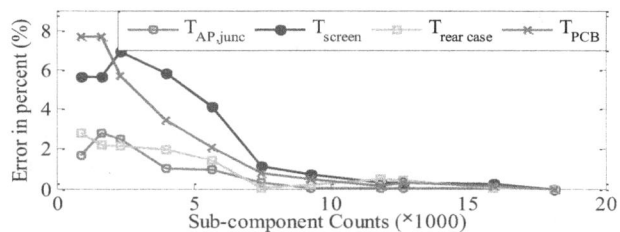

Figure 6. Therminator results convergence and runtime versus sub-component counts for the StabilityTest use case.

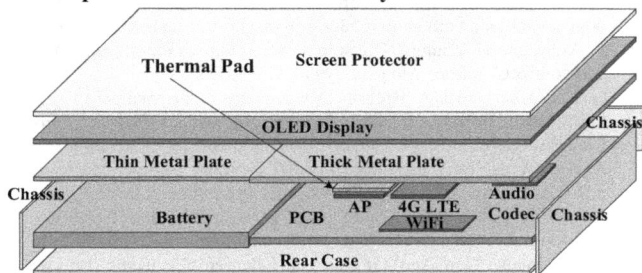

Figure 7. 3-D layout for Samsung Galaxy S4. Sub-components are not shown.

Therminator for MSM8660 MDP in Figure 6. We calculate *convergence errors* at different resolutions by comparing temperature results obtained at a particular resolution to those obtained at the highest resolution that we have tested (18,109 sub-components in total). One can see that the convergence errors of all four temperature points drop below 1% when the total sub-components number is above 7,000. According to results reported in Section 6.1, the difference of Therminator results compared to CFD results is only 1.42% for 7,500 sub-components. The runtime of Therminator at that resolution is less than seven seconds.

7. CASE STUDY

Therminator is versatile in handling different form-factor devices as long as input files are provided properly. In this section, we provide a case study targeted at Samsung Galaxy S4. Samsung Galaxy S4 is a flagship commercial smartphone released in 2013. Unlike the MSM8660 MDP device, Samsung Galaxy S4 does not provide power consumption due to some commercial reasons. Thus, the power consumption for major components, i.e., AP (CPU and GPU) and display, are estimated by measuring the total power consumption of Galaxy S4 at the battery output terminals and scaling them to the power breakdown ratio as reported in [27]. A simplified model of Galaxy S4 is also created, as shown in Figure 7. An AP floorplan describing locations of CPU and GPU is specified in the specs.xml file for better estimation accuracy.

We notice that in Galaxy S4, the thermal governor throttles the CPU, GPU, and memory operating frequency such that the skin temperature will not exceed 45°C, i.e., the skin thermal governor has the temperature setpoint of 45°C. The critical temperature of AP junction is usually quite high, say 85°C, and thereby the frequency throttling we have observed is triggered by the skin thermal governor. We validate Therminator results for the maximum skin temperature located on the front screen (denoted as T_{skin}) and the AP junction temperature ($T_{AP,junc}$) against the thermocouple measurement results. The measurements results and Therminator results in the same condition of power consumption are underlined in Table 2. One can see that the temperature error produced by Therminator is within 0.5°C (2%).

To simulate the effect of frequency throttling utilized by the thermal governor, we scale the total power consumption to produce different steady-state skin temperatures. Table 2 reports the corresponding T_{skin} and $T_{AP,junc}$ values for different AP power consumption values. To better study the effect of skin temperature

Table 2. Skin temperature and AP junction temperature obtained by thermocouple measurement (TCM) and Therminator at different AP power consumption levels.

Method	Temperature (°C)		Power (W)		
	$T_{AP,junc}$	T_{skin}	P_{AP}*	$P_{AP,leak}$	$P_{AP,dyn}$
TCM	62.5	44.8	2.20	0.15	2.05
Therminator	68.0	47.7	2.64	0.18	2.46
	66.5	47.1	2.53	0.17	2.36
	65.1	46.5	2.42	0.16	2.26
	63.7	45.9	2.31	0.15	2.16
	62.3	45.3	2.20	0.15	2.05
	60.9	44.7	2.09	0.15	1.94
	59.4	44.1	1.98	0.13	1.85
	58.0	43.5	1.87	0.13	1.74
	56.1	42.9	1.76	0.12	1.64
	55.2	42.4	1.65	0.12	1.53
	53.8	41.8	1.54	0.11	1.43
	52.3	41.2	1.43	0.11	1.32
	50.9	40.6	1.32	0.11	1.21
	49.5	40.0	1.21	0.10	1.11
	48.1	39.4	1.10	0.10	1.00

* P_{AP} includes power consumption of both CPU and GPU.

on the device performance, we obtain the dynamic power consumption by subtracting the leakage power consumption, estimated by using McPAT [28], from the total AP power consumption values. Note that we use average AP temperature to estimate leakage power consumption values. Each row in Table 2 indicates a dynamic power consumption level when that specific skin temperature is met. In other words, when the skin thermal governor sets the target T_{skin} as the values listed in the third column of Table 2, the approximated AP's dynamic power consumption allotment are shown in the fifth column.

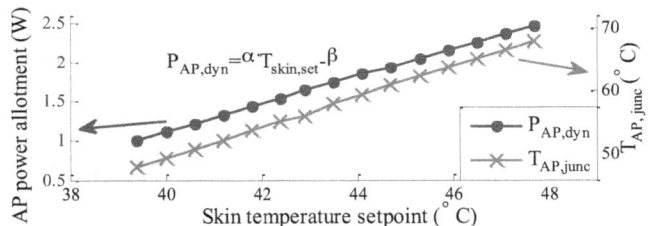

Figure 8. AP power consumption and junction temperature versus various skin temperature setpoints.

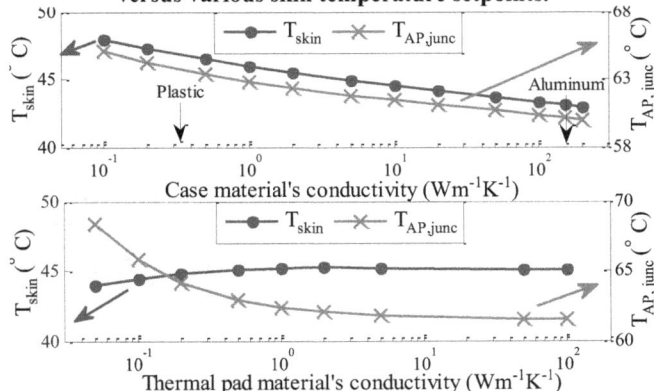

Figure 9. Skin and AP junction temperature versus rear case material (a) and thermal pad material (b) for $P_{AP} = 2.2W$.

Figure 8 plots the AP's dynamic power consumption allotment, denoted by $P_{AP,alt}$, versus the skin temperature setpoint, denoted by $T_{skin,set}$, as the latter is a typical variable in various thermal management policies. The blue dots indicates that $P_{AP,alt}$ (which is proportional to the device operating frequency and therefore, the device performance) has a linear relationship with the setpoint value of skin temperature. From the data presented in Figure 8, we capture this relationship as,

$$P_{AP,alt} = \alpha \cdot T_{skin,set} - \beta \qquad (4)$$

where $\alpha = 0.18$ W/K and $\beta = 5.92$ W. Since the device performance highly depends on $T_{skin,set}$, allowing high skin temperature results in significant performance improvement. For instance, increasing $T_{skin,set}$ from 45°C to 48°C results in 15.5% increase of $P_{AP,alt}$, i.e., an increase from 1.93W to 2.23W. On the other hand, decreasing $T_{skin,set}$ from 45°C to 42°C results a decrease from 1.93W to 1.63W. In addition, one can also observe from Figure 8 that the AP's junction temperature also linearly depends on the skin temperature setpoint (red crosses).

Clearly, modifying the thermal path design for a device affects its peak performance level. We study the thermal impact of thermal properties of the device exterior case by exploring its thermal conductivity from very low value (insulation material) to a high value (conductive material). Figure 9 (a) shows that both of T_{skin} and $T_{AP,junc}$ decrease when using higher thermal conductivity materials for the exterior case of the device. More precisely, adopting aluminum as the device case results in 2~3°C lower T_{skin} and $T_{AP,junc}$, comparing with using pure plastic as the device case. This temperature reduction is helpful in improving the device performance. In practice, device manufacturers may also account for other factors such as the manufacturing cost.

We also investigate the impact of the material composition of the thermal pad, which is attached on top of the AP, and report the results in Figure 9 (b). A clear trade-off can be observed between T_{skin} and $T_{AP,junc}$ at various types of materials. This observation complies with results reported by a group of researchers at Texas Instrument [3]. The optimal thermal path design should touch the AP junction temperature constraint and skin temperature constraint at the same time. According to our study, from the thermal path design perspective, adopting a thermal pad with lower thermal conductivity on top of the AP achieves better performance. This is because T_{skin} is usually more critical in smartphones and a low thermal conductivity material hinders the heat flow to the device skin. However, in practice, some other factors (such as accelerated aging of AP and high leakage power at high temperatures) may prevent the usage of low thermal conductivity material.

8. CONCLUSION

We presented Therminator, a component-level compact-thermal-modeling-based thermal simulator targeting small form-factor devices in this work. Therminator is an early-stage, full-device thermal analyzer that produces accurate steady-state temperature maps of all components (ICs, boards, screens, cases, etc.) in a smartphone, from the application processor to the skin of device, with a fast runtime. Therminator provides great flexibility in handling different user-specified design specifications and use cases. We validated temperature results produced by Therminator against real temperature measurements using thermocouples and simulations using a commercial computational-fluid-dynamics tool on the Qualcomm MSM8660 MDP device. We also provided a case study on Samsung Galaxy S4 by using Therminator, showing that the device performance is linearly related to the device skin temperature. In addition, the impact of the thermal path design on the skin and AP junction temperature was also studied.

ACKNOWLEDGEMENT

This research is supported by grants from the PERFECT program of the Defense Advanced Research Projects Agency and the Software and Hardware Foundations of the National Science Foundation.

REFERENCES

[1] M. Pedram and S. Nazarian, "Thermal Modeling, Analysis, and Management in VLSI Circuits: Principles and Methods," *Proc. IEEE*, vol. 94, no. 8, pp. 1487–1501, 2006.

[2] J. Srinivasan *et al.*, "The case for lifetime reliability-aware microprocessors," in *ISCA*, 2004.

[3] S. P. Gurrum *et al.*, "Generic thermal analysis for phone and tablet systems," in *ECTC*, 2012, pp. 1488–1492.

[4] J. Rajmond and A. Fodor, "Thermal management of embedded devices," in *ISSE*, 2013, pp. 30–34.

[5] A. L. Shimpi, "The ARM vs x86 Wars Have Begun: In-Depth Power Analysis of Atom, Krait & Cortex A15." [Online]. Available: http://www.anandtech.com/show/6536/arm-vs-x86-the-real-showdown.

[6] E. Arens and H. Zhang, "The skin's role in human thermoregulation and comfort," *Indoor Environ. Qual.*, Oct. 2006.

[7] G. L. Wasner and J. A. Brock, "Determinants of thermal pain thresholds in normal subjects," *Clin. Neurophysiol. Off. J. Int. Fed. Clin. Neurophysiol.*, vol. 119, no. 10, pp. 2389–2395, Oct. 2008.

[8] A. Ku, "Asus Transformer Pad TF300T Review: Tegra 3, More Affordable - An Affordable Transformer Prime Derivative?," *Tom's Hardware*. [Online]. Available: http://www.tomshardware.com/reviews/transformer-pad-tf300t-tegra-3-benchmark-review,3179.html.

[9] J. A. Kaplan, "New Apple iPad hits 116 degrees, Consumer Reports says," *FoxNews.com*. [Online]. Available: http://www.foxnews.com/tech/2012/03/20/ipads-not-overheating-apple-says/.

[10] M.-N. Sabry, "Compact thermal models for electronic systems," *IEEE Trans. Compon. Packag. Technol.*, vol. 26, no. 1, pp. 179–185, 2003.

[11] K. Skadron et al., "Temperature-aware Microarchitecture: Modeling and Implementation," *ACM TACO*, no. 1, pp. 94–125, Mar. 2004.

[12] "Snapdragon MDP Mobile Development Platform - Legacy Devices," *Qualcomm Developer Network*. [Online]. Available: https://developer.qualcomm.com/mobile-development/development-devices-boards/mobile-development-devices/snapdragon-mdp-legacy-devices.

[13] "Simulation Software | Mechanical, CFD, Plastics | Autodesk." [Online]. Available: http://www.autodesk.com/products/autodesk-simulation-family/overview.

[14] Y. Han *et al.*, "Temptor: A Lightweight Runtime Temperature Monitoring Tool Using Performance Counters," in *TACS*, 2006.

[15] J. Meng *et al.*, "Optimizing Energy Efficiency of 3-D Multicore Systems with Stacked DRAM Under Power and Thermal Constraints," in *DAC*, 2012.

[16] M. J. Dousti and M. Pedram, "Platform-dependent, leakage-aware control of the driving current of embedded thermoelectric coolers," in *ISLPED*, 2013.

[17] A. Sridhar *et al.*, "3D-ICE: Fast Compact Transient Thermal Modeling for 3D ICs with Inter-tier Liquid Cooling," in *ICCAD*, 2010.

[18] Z. Luo *et al.*, "System thermal analysis for mobile phone," *Appl. Therm. Eng.*, vol. 28, no. 14–15, pp. 1889–1895, Oct. 2008.

[19] L. Zhang *et al.*, "Accurate online power estimation and automatic battery behavior based power model generation for smartphones," in *CODES+ISSS*, 2010.

[20] A. Pathak *et al.*, "Where is the Energy Spent Inside My App?: Fine Grained Energy Accounting on Smartphones with Eprof," in *EuroSys*, 2012.

[21] F. Kreith, *The CRC handbook of thermal engineering*. CRC Press, 2000.

[22] Y. A. Çengel, *Heat and mass transfer: a practical approach*. Boston: McGraw-Hill, 2007.

[23] "pugixml," *pugixml*. [Online]. Available: http://pugixml.org/.

[24] "CULA." [Online]. Available: http://www.culatools.com.

[25] "StabilityTest." [Online]. Available: https://play.google.com/store/apps/details?id=com.into.stability&hl=en.

[26] "Trepn Profiler," *Qualcomm Developer Network*. [Online]. Available: https://developer.qualcomm.com/mobile-development/performance-tools/trepn-profiler.

[27] X. Chen *et al.*, "How is Energy Consumed in Smartphone Display Applications?," in *HotMobile*, 2013, pp. 3:1–3:6.

[28] S. Li et al., "McPAT: An integrated power, area, and timing modeling framework for multicore and manycore architectures," in *MICRO*, 2009, pp. 469–480.

Challenges in Low-Power Analog Circuit Design for sub-28nm CMOS Technologies

Amr Fahim
Semtech Corporation
5141 California Ave, Suite #150
Irvine, CA 92617
+1 949 269-4492
afahim@semtech.com

ABSTRACT

In this paper, we discuss some of the most pressing challenges in low-power analog circuit design for sub-28nm technologies. A design methodology suitable for deep submicron low-power analog design is first described. Using the proposed figure of merit, several technologies as they scale down towards 28nm are compared. This is followed by a discussion of some of the issues that are unique to 28nm CMOS technologies and beyond. The effect of FinFETs devices in analog circuit design is also explored.

Categories and Subject Descriptors

B.7 [INTEGRATED CIRCUITS]: Miscellaneous;

Keywords

Low power analog circuit design, FinFET, 28nm CMOS technology, leakage current, device mismtach

1. INTRODUCTION

The aggressive scaling of CMOS technologies has presented both opportunities and challenges to analog circuit designers. Scaling down to 28nm CMOS technologies has forced many analog circuit designers to revisit classical analog circuit design methodologies. Some of these challenges are similar to what digital circuit designers face, such as leakage current, but their effects on the performance of analog circuit design is quite different. Other effects such as device matching and worsened device linearity have presented new challenges. The importance of physical implementation, such as well proximity and STI effects [4] cannot be ignored and must be included during the initial circuit design phase.

In order to support aggressively scaled gate oxide thicknesses, the power supply of deep submicron devices must also be scaled. Although this power supply scaling has been one of the main tools of decreasing the power consumption of digital circuits, it causes several issues in analog circuit design. Its main effect is loss of dynamic range. As will be shown later, in order to compensate for the loss of dynamic range, more current must be

burned in order to lower the analog circuit's noise floor. This means that voltage scaling, in the context of analog circuit design, usually entails higher power consumption.

The other effect of scaled gate oxide thickness is the increase of gate leakage. Gate current leakage is caused by quantum tunneling effect where electrons can escape the gate and show up in the diffusion channel. Despite technological solutions to solve gate leakage, it has been shown to worsen dramatically as technology scales down to the 28nm node and beyond. As will be shown later, the effect of gate leakage in analog circuit design is twofold. Firstly, the low-frequency input impedance can no longer be considered high-impedance, and now consists of an effective gate conductance that is dependent on the gate voltage. Secondly, the matching of two current sources is no longer a monotonic function of device area.

This paper is organized as follows. In Section 2, the traditional g_m/I_{ds} analog circuit design methodology [1] is revisited by including dynamic range and circuit bandwidth. A new figure-of-merit (FOM) is developed and is used to compare different technology nodes. In Section 3, a discussion of some of the circuit design challenges in 28nm CMOS technologies and beyond are given. In Section 4, some circuit design techniques that can be used to remedy some of the challenges in sub-28nm CMOS technologies are discussed. Finally, conclusions are drawn in Section 5.

2. DESIGN METHODOLOGY

In [1]-[3], a design methodology suitable for low-power operation is proposed called g_m/I_{ds} design methodology. The main metric used in this design methodology is the ratio of transconductance, g_m, to the current consumed by a certain device, I_{ds}. In essence, it is a measure of the current efficiency of a device for analog design. Fig. 1 shows a sample of g_m/I_{ds} versus the gate overdrive voltage, V_{ov}. An amplifier circuit design is usually specified by the desired gain-bandwidth product, ω_T, and capacitive load, C_L. This constrains the transconductance to be given as

$$g_m = \omega_T C_L . \tag{1}$$

Using square law equations for CMOS devices, it can be shown that g_m/I_{ds} quantity is independent of gate width, W. This means that for a given device length, a characteristic width can be chosen and simulated to obtain a constant, $(g_m/I_{ds})^*$. This ratio can then be used as a scaling ratio to scale the device width, W, to obtain a desired g_m to satisfy (1).

ISLPED'14, August 11–13, 2014, La Jolla, CA, USA.
Copyright 2014 ACM 978-1-4503-2975-0/14/08 …$15.00.
http://dx.doi.org/10.1145/2627369.2631639

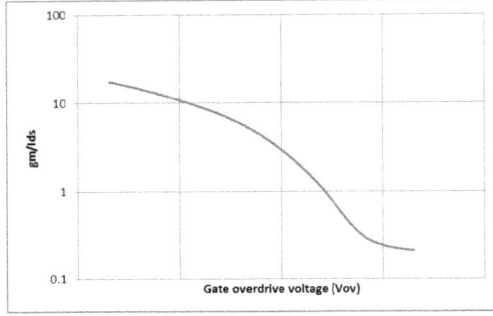

Fig. 1. g_m/I_{ds} versus gate overdrive voltage V_{ov}

Although g_m/I_{ds} is a good figure of merit for characterizing a device's current efficiency in obtaining a certain transconductance, there are other practical metrics that an analog circuit designer must consider. Other metrics include gain-bandwidth product (GBW), and dynamic range (DR). The lower boundary of dynamic range is set by the circuit's noise floor; whereas the upper boundary of the dynamic range is set by the linearity. A common expression used for dynamic range [5] in communication systems is given as:

$$ DR = \frac{2}{3}\left(IIP3 - MDS\right) \qquad (2) $$

where IIP3 is the input referred third intercept point and MDS is the minimum detectable signal. The IIP3 and MDS are expressed in decibels. In this study, the minimum detectable signal is simply substituted by the integrated noise floor over the amplifier's bandwidth. When considering a common source amplifier with no load, the GBW is simply given as g_m/C_{gs} or the unity current gain frequency, f_T, of the device. Hence a figure-of-merit encompassing both DR and GBW of an amplifier can be given as

$$ FOM = 10\log\left(f_T\right) + \frac{2}{3}\left(IIP3 - 10\log\left(\int v_n^2 df\right)\right) \qquad (3) $$

where the noise is integrated over the amplifier's bandwidth.

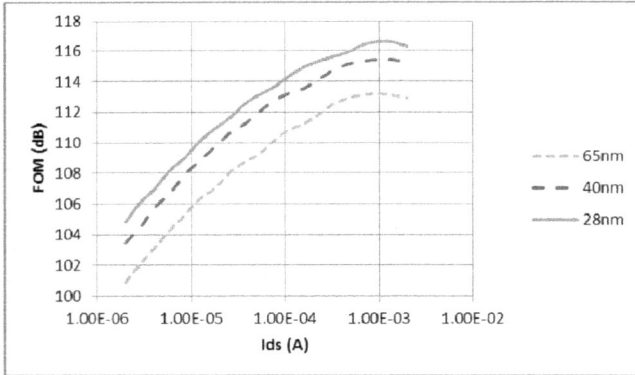

Fig. 2. FOM versus current evaluated for various technologies

This FOM, however, does not include any measure of current efficiency, which is important for low-power design. Using the g_m/I_{ds} metric, the FOM can be modified as:

$$ FOM2 = 10\log\left(\frac{g_m}{I_{ds}}\right) + 10\log\left(f_T\right) + \frac{2}{3}\left(IIP3 - 10\log\left(\int v_n^2 df\right)\right) \qquad (4) $$

The FOM and FOM2 are evaluated for 65nm, 40nm and 28nm CMOS technologies as shown in Fig. 2 and 3 below, respectively.

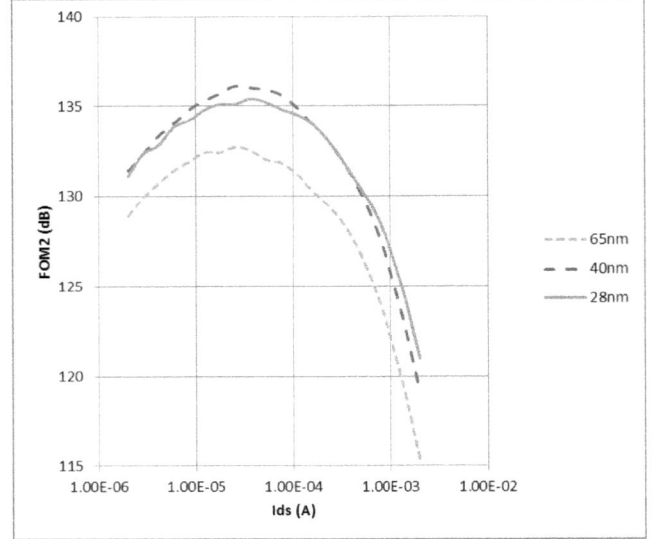

Fig. 3. FOM2 versus current evaluated for various technologies

As Fig. 2 shows, to achieve the maximum possible dynamic range and gain-bandwidth product, a fair amount of current must be burned per transistor. As technology is scaled, the FOM improves, mainly due to higher device f_T. The improvement, however, scales slower than f_T, due to worse linearity and noise as devices are scaled. This explains the smaller margin between 40nm and 28nm CMOS technologies. One interesting result is that this optimal current setting seems to be independent of technology.

Fig 3 shows FOM2 versus current for 65nm, 45nm and 28nm CMOS technologies. As stated earlier, FOM2 is a weighted version of FOM, where current efficiency is taken into account, which is important for low-power design. As FOM2 reveals, a different optimal point for biasing the transistor is achieved. The graph shows two interesting results. Firstly, although better speeds are achievable with scaled technologies, from a low-power perspective, there seems to be a diminishing advantage that 28nm CMOS has over 40nm CMOS. Secondly, the optimal point seems to be independent of technology.

Using the figure-of-merits of (3) and (4), one can obtain a set of curves that can help the designer optimally bias an amplifier design. As long as transistor width, W, is chosen to be large enough to avoid small width effects, both figure of merits can be shown to be largely independent of transistor width. These curves can then be used in the same manner as in the g_m/I_{ds} design methodology.

3. CHALLENGES IN SUB-28NM CMOS

The previous section gave a quantitative method of evaluating different technologies for low-power analog circuit design. This methodology results in a set of curves which can then be used as design references to choose an optimal operating point. In this section, the design challenges that arise from aggressively scaled technologies are given. These design challenges change some of the basic conclusions that are reached from classical analog circuit design.

The first of these issues is gate leakage. As stated earlier, gate leakage is caused by quantum tunneling effect of electrons on the gate terminal appearing in the transistor's inversion layer due to the thin gate oxide thickness. The tunneling effect is a strong function of the gate overdrive voltage, V_{ov}. The gate leakage causes an effective conductance, g_{tunnel}, which is in parallel with the input capacitance of the transistor, C_{in}. This means that the low frequency input impedance of the transistor is lowered by g_{tunnel}. The cut-off frequency where this occurs is important and is given as

$$f_{gate} = \frac{g_{tunnel}}{2\pi C_{in}} \qquad (5)$$

The interpretation of f_{gate} is important in analog circuit design. Equation (5) reveals the minimum frequency where sample and hold circuits can be used, below which a voltage cannot be held reliably. This has a profound impact on the usability of circuit design in data converters as well as phase-locked loops (PLLs).

Fig. 4 below shows the f_{gate} as a function of technology. As the trend shows, the gate leakage current grows exponentially with technology down to the 28nm technology node and cannot be ignored in analog circuit design.

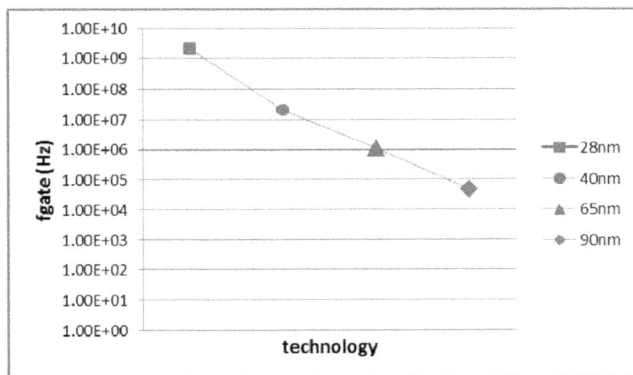

Fig. 4. f_{gate} as a function of technology.

Another impact of gate leakage is limited current gain. It can be shown that the gate current due to gate tunneling is given as [6]:

$$i_{GS} \approx C_{ox} \cdot W \cdot L \cdot f_{gate} \qquad (6)$$

Using the square law expression for FET current, it can be shown that the current gain of a FET is now limited to

$$\frac{i_{DS}}{i_{GS}} \approx \frac{1}{L^2} \cdot \frac{\mu(v_{GS} - V_T)^2}{2 \cdot f_{gate}} \qquad (7)$$

Another adverse effect of gate leakage is on the current matching between current sources. Since gate leakage is a quantum effect with random characteristic, it causes a random spread on the FET output current, I_{DS}. Classical matching equations for FET current sources is given as

$$\left(\frac{\Delta I}{I}\right)^2 = \left(\frac{A_{VT}}{\sqrt{WL}} \cdot \frac{g_m}{I}\right)^2 \qquad (8)$$

Where A_{VT} is a technology related coefficient related to the V_T mismatch between 2 nearby devices. Equation (8) assumes that the total mismatch is dominated by V_T mismatches. As the equation shows, current matching is improved by simply increasing the area. The only practical upper bounds on area are die cost and parasitic capacitance due to the large FET area. In sub-28nm technologies, gate tunneling must be taken into account. This means that (8) must be rewritten as [7]:

$$\left(\frac{\Delta I}{I}\right)^2 = \left(\frac{A_{VT}}{\sqrt{WL}} \cdot \frac{g_m}{I}\right)^2 + \left(\frac{X_{IGS}}{\sqrt{WL}} \cdot \frac{i_G}{I}\right)^2 \qquad (9)$$

where X_{IGS} is a constant related to the tunneling effect. Closer observation of (9) yields the following analysis. The first term on the right hand side of the equation is the classical matching and is improved by increasing the area. The second term on the right hand side is the new term taking into account gate tunneling effect. As (7) shows, i_G/I is proportional to L^2. This means that this second term in (9) actually increases with area. This indicates that there is an optimum point beyond which matching cannot be improved. As stated earlier, gate leakage is only important in analog circuit design for frequencies below f_{gate}. For fast switching devices, this mismatch component would be less of an issue.

The last important effect of gate leakage in analog circuit design is the effect of noise. Gate leakage shows up as a gate shot noise component given as:

$$i_{g,n}^2 = 2qI_{GS} \qquad (10)$$

where I_{GS} is given by (6). Although not a major component of noise, it is still important to take into account when designing ultra-low-noise sensors or low noise amplifiers (LNAs) for wireless applications.

Many other analog circuit design challenges arise in deep submicron technologies due to the physical implementation of these devices. Some of these effects include V_T shifts resulting from proximity of the gate to the well edge and mobility shifts resulting from the shallow-trench effect (STI). [4].

4. SUB-28NM CMOS CIRCUIT DESIGN

The previous section outlines some of the more important challenges in sub-28nm CMOS circuit design. Indeed, most of these issues area related to the gate tunneling effect. There are a variety of techniques, however, that designers use for deep submicron technologies.

One of these techniques is to stack devices in order to be able to use higher supply voltages. This has the advantage of recovering the dynamic range and being able to operate at lower current levels. This technique, however, is being limited by the shrinking maximum V_{GB}, gate-to-bulk voltage, that the technology can handle.

Another technique that has found widespread acceptance is the use of digitally assisted analog circuit design [8]-[11]. In such techniques, digital calibration loops make up for analog circuit non-idealities. For example, wireless transmitters use digital predistortion to improve the linearity of the transmitter. This is accomplished by having a priori knowledge of the nonlinear transfer function of the transmitter, then predistorting the input to the transmitter with an equivalent inverse transfer function to counteract the nonlinearity of the transmitter.

Digitally assisted analog circuit design has also found its way in high-speed and high-resolution data converters. Instead of sizing up devices to achieve a certain bit resolution, a calibration loop can be inserted to determine the distortion in the data converter, then applying a digital correction value to each code word of the data converter to recover the linearity. This has the advantage of avoiding overly large areas for data converters, which would otherwise be necessary to achieve a certain static linearity. Lower area has the two advantages of less gate leakage effects as well as higher speed of operation.

One interesting development in sub-28nm CMOS technologies is the widespread use of FinFET technologies. In FinFET technologies, a transistor is rotated and a gate is applied to three sides of the transistor. This achieves a tighter control on the gate leakage. It also has the effect of having better output resistance than a bulk CMOS technology for equivalent gate length. For example, a single-stage amplifier designed in 28nm CMOS achieved a DC gain of 42dB; whereas in 16-nm FinFET achieved nearly 70dB.

5. CONCLUSIONS

In this paper, the classical g_m/I_{ds} design methodology was reviewed. Using this design methodology as a starting point, two figure-of-merits describing analog circuit performance (dynamic range and bandwidth) were described. The second figure-of-merit, FOM2, took transistor current efficiency into account. Some of the design challenges in deep sub-micron analog CMOS design have been outlined. Most of these challenges listed are due undesirable effects due to quantum gate tunneling. Some design techniques were reviewed that are commonly used in sub-28nm CMOS analog circuit design.

6. REFERENCES

[1] P. Jespers, "Sizing low-voltage, low-power CMOS analog circuits," *Faible Tension Faible Consommation*, pp. 58-8, 2011.

[2] P. Jespers, "Sizing low-voltage CMOS analog circuits," *ISCAS*, pp. 752-755, 2007.

[3] W. Sansen, "Analog design procedures for channel lengths down to 20nm," *20th Int'l Conf. on Electronics, Circuits and Systems (ICECS)*, pp. 337-340, 2013.

[4] L. Lewyn, et. al., "Analog Circuit Design in Nanoscale CMOS Technologies," *Proc. Of the IEEE*, vo. 97, no. 10, Oct. 2009, pp. 1687-1713.

[5] A. Jerng, C. Sodini, "A Wideband SD Digital-RF Modulator for High Data Rate Transmitters," *IEEE J. of Solid-State Circuits*, vol. 42, no. 8, pp. 1710-1722, Aug 2007.

[6] Annema, et. al., "Analog Circuits in Ulta-Deep-Submicron CMOS," *IEEE J. of Solid-State Circuits*, vol. 40, no. 1, pp. 132-143, Jan 2005.

[7] A. Marshall, "Noise and mismatch in sub 28nm silicon processes," *IEEE Int'l SOC Conference (SOCC)*, pp. 88-93, 2012.

[8] M. Li, et. al, "Signal Processing Challenges for Emerging Digital Intensive and Digitally Assisted Transceivers with Deeply Scaled Technology (Invited)," *IEEE Workshop on Signal Processing Systems*, pp. 324-329, 2013.

[9] T. Cao, et. al., "A 9-bit 50MS/s Asynchronous SAR ADC in 28nm CMOS," *NORCHIP*, pp. 1-6, 2012.

[10] J. Xiao, et. al., "A 13-bit 9GS/s RF DAC-Based Broadband Transmitter in 28nm CMOS," *IEEE VLSI Circuits*, pp. 262-263, 2013.

[11] B. Verbruggen, et. al., "A 2.1mW 11b 410 MS/s Dynamic Pipelined SAR ADC with Background Calibration in 28nm Digital CMOS," *IEEE VLSI Circuits*, pp. 268-269, 2013.

Process and Design Solutions for Exploiting FD-SOI Technology Towards Energy Efficient SOCs

Philippe Flatresse
STMicroelectronics
850, rue Jean Monnet
38926 Crolles Cedex
+33 (0) 476925106
philippe.flatresse@st.com

ABSTRACT

Planar UTBB FD-SOI technology is an opportunity for energy efficient SOCs in deeply scaled technologies. Thanks to its excellent responsiveness to power management design techniques, this technology brings a significant improvement in terms of performance and power savings. The unique features offered by this technology at process and design levels enable a differentiation in terms of flexibility, cost and energy efficiency with respect to any process available on the market.

Keywords

UTBB FD-SOI; multi-V_T; energy efficiency; low voltage; ultra wide voltage range; process compensation; body biasing, SOC.

1. INTRODUCTION

With the increasing demand of processing power to be delivered by the System On Chips, it is now key to improve their energy efficiency, not only for thermal or battery life duration purpose but also for environmental considerations such as green supercomputers, wireless base stations and micro servers [1-2]. The conventional CMOS on Bulk silicon has become highly inefficient to meet SOC speed and power requirements. Despite of all possible process and design techniques that have been applied in the last decade, the conventional bulk technology has reached its limits today. That is the reason why the industry has decided to move to fully depleted technologies as a way to continue the technology roadmap. Thin-body structures such as finFETs and fully-depleted SOI devices (FDSOI) offer much better control over the charge in the channel and therefore much better off characteristics of the device [3].

Using fully depleted devices, and in particular FD-SOI, enable designing energy efficient SOCs running at very high frequency over an ultra-wide voltage range while minimizing power dissipation [4]. In this context, STMicroelectronics is implementing planar fully depleted silicon technology.

The work presented in this paper has contributed to the development of the first design platform in FDSOI planar technology on Ultra-Thin Body and Box (UTBB) for the 28nm and below technology nodes [9], [11]. This paper is organized as follows: Section II introduces the main features of the UTBB FDSOI CMOS technology. Section III discusses the process-design co-optimization solutions deployed to improve the performance and energy-efficiency. Section IV presents several silicon demonstrations showing the capabilities of the technology for energy efficiency applications.

2. UTBB FD-SOI Technology

2.1 Device Architecture

28nm Ultra-thin body and box FD-SOI technology is a planar HKMG CMOS technology fabricated in a very thin layer of silicon sitting over a buried oxide (BOX). The thin active silicon film (7nm) ensures that all electrical paths between source and drain of the transistor are confined close to the gate, leading to a significant improvement of the sub-threshold slope and DIBL. The Box thickness of 25nm guarantees a good trade-off between Drain/Source-to-Substrate parasitic capacitance and body factor. A cross-section of UTBB FD-SOI transistor is shown in Fig. 1. This technology has no channel doping nor pocket implant making the process much simpler with respect to bulk technology.

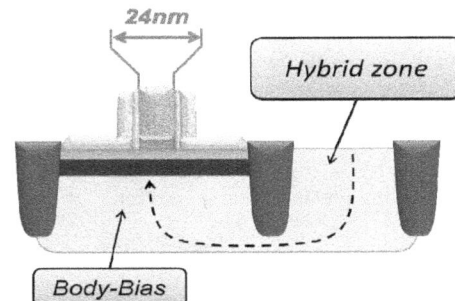

Fig. 1:   UTBB FD-SOI transistor cross-section

ISLPED'14, August 11–13, 2014, La Jolla, CA, USA.
Copyright © 2014 ACM 978-1-4503-2975-0/14/08...$15.00.
http://dx.doi.org/10.1145/2627369.2631640

3. Threshold Voltage adjustment

To adjust the the threshold voltage and keep control of the short channel effect, a back plane, either n-type or p-type, is implemented underneath the Box. The back-plane doping type is chosen as function of the type of transistor implemented: it is identical to the gate type for regular-V_T (RVT) devices and opposite to the gate type for low-V_T (LVT) devices. Thanks to the thin BOX, a hybrid scheme co-integrating both Bulk and FD-SOI devices on the same die is allowed. This also permits to realize Well taps that are used to apply a bias voltage on the back-plane. The BOX dielectric electrically isolates the well from the source and drain of the transistors, which expands the range of possible well bias voltages (VB) and therefore improves the range of possible VT adjustments, through a high body factor of 85mV/V. This gives an added degree of freedom to chip designers, by providing them with a back-gate common to a group of transistors, which can be used for finely tuning the V_T of transistors, even dynamically. The threshold voltage of transistors can be strongly varied by applying a bias voltage on this back-interface. Thanks to the absence of drain- and source-to-body junctions, the UTBB FD-SOI technology enables an extended body-bias range from -3V (RBB) up to +3V (FBB) [10].

Since NMOS and PMOS transistors are isolated by junction, the body bias range is asymmetrical between RVT and LVT transistors as shown in Fig.2. This asymmetry comes from the p-Well/n-Well diode, which must never be in forward mode e.g., by making the p-Well bias significantly higher than the n-Well bias. So, the circuit designer must ensure that the p-Well/n-Well diode is always maintained in reverse mode when applying body biasing. In a conventional well approach (RVT) where NMOS and PMOS sit on p-Well and n-Well like in bulk technology, a huge reverse back-biasing till -3V and an intermediate forward back-biasing up to [VDD/2 + 300mV] can be applied. The range is defined by the breakdown voltage and the threshold voltage of the p-Well/n-Well diode. To take advantage of the very wide forward back-biasing range offered by the technology and go beyond [VDD/2 + 300mV], a unique body bias design technique called flip well (FW) has been proposed [4]. The solution implements an n-Well under the BOX of NMOS transistors and a p-Well under the BOX of PMOS transistors – wells are flipped compared to the configuration used in conventional bulk CMOS. This presents the advantage of enabling a very wide forward back-biasing range up to 3V, since in this configuration increasing FBB (i.e. increasing back-plane voltage under NMOS and decreasing it under PMOS) goes in the direction of further reverse-biasing the junction between wells. Flip well approach is specific to UTBB FD-SOI because the wells have no impact on the electrical characteristics of the transistors and thanks to the buried oxide that ensures a total dielectric isolation of the device.

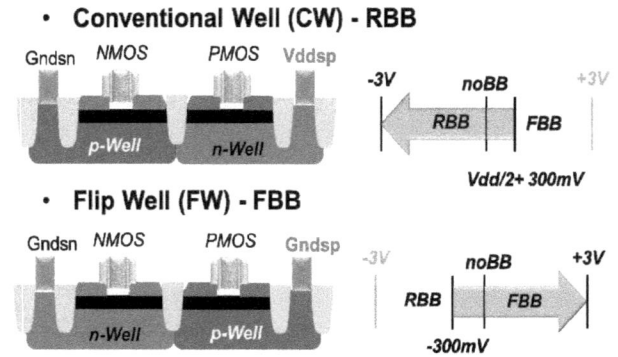

Fig. 2: Well architecture of RVT & LVT transistors in UTBB FD-SOI technology.

Furthermore, UTTB FD-SOI exhibits an improved DIBL and thus scalability with respect to bulk. At transistor level, this means for a given leakage target, the minimum channel length can be further scaled down over its bulk counterpart, leading to much higher speed. At 28nm node, the minimum channel of the UTBB transistor is 24nm while in bulk it cannot be scaled below 28nm. It is one of the key differentiator of UTBB FD-SOI offering circuit designers a wider range of static power optimization thanks to poly biasing The poly biasing technique consists in modulating the gate length of the transistor in order to optimize the static power consumption of a digital block. In UTBB FD-SOI, the range goes from 24nm up to 40nm giving to FD-SOI much more flexibility in power optimization wrt bulk for which the range is 10nm only going from 30nm to 40nm.

Combining body biasing and poly biasing techniques, it offers to designers more flexibility in terms of frequency / leakage power optimization as shown in figure 3.

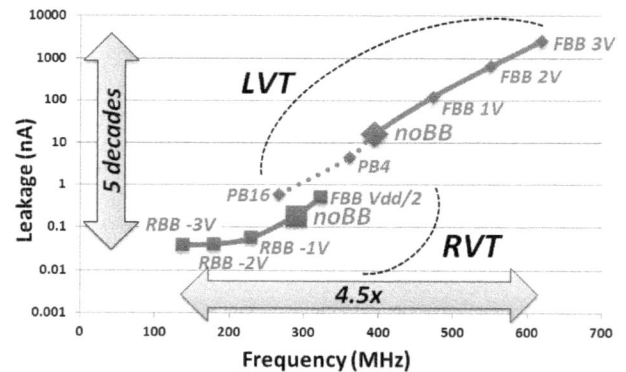

Fig. 3: Leakage vs. Frequency trends of LVT and RVT at VDD=1V for several back-bias voltages and poly bias conditions. Ring oscillator silicon measurement results.

Fig. 4 (right) demonstrates an efficient frequency boost for various supplies when applying FBB. At 3V FBB, LVT transistors exhibit attractive speed gains from 34% at 1.3V up to 5.5x at 0.5V. On the opposite, at low voltage when performance is not required, RVT transistors enable a drastic cut of the leakage by a factor of 50 at -3V RBB (Fig. 4 left).

128

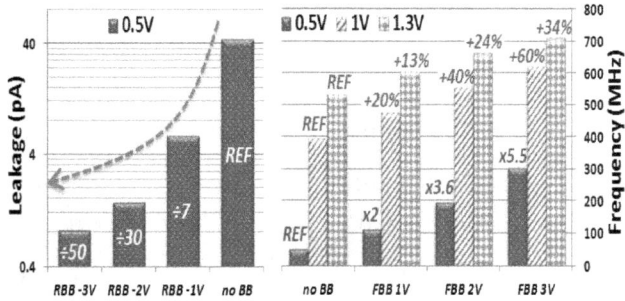

Fig. 4: Ultra wide BB range enables RVT leakage reduction (left) and LVT performance boost (right)

3.1 Generation and distribution of body voltages

Generation and distribution of body voltages one of the key aspect when developing a SOC in FDSOI. Body Bias voltages are distributed classically to the standard Nwell and Pwell taps through the Power and Ground grid (Fig.4), as is done in Bulk implementations [6], [7]. Nwell and Pwell ties are spaced like they were in Bulk implementations. However they can be spaced further apart since there are no static body currents in FD-SOI (and therefore no risk of latchup). For the same reason IR drop in the Body Bias grid is no longer a concern.

Integrating the body bias generator inside the SoC is essential allowing direct and fast control of the body bias voltage. The body bias generator is built in a symmetrical way: one half (gnds grid in Fig.5) is supplied in the positive domain at 1.8V (the SoC IO supply) and the other half (vdds grid in Fig.4) is supplied in the negative domain at -1.8V which is generated locally. Two DACs allow independent programming of the buffered outputs. The embedded charge pump has to provide static current consumed by all blocks in the negative domain, while fast transitioning currents are sunk by the external tank capacitor. The body bias generator uses the standard thick oxide FD-SOI transistors, in their Regular-Vt and Low-Vt flavors.

Output buffers must be able to provide large currents during body voltages transitions to feed the body network capacitance. Static power is constrained by the charge pump current drive capability. Therefore an AB-class structure is chosen. The same amplifier is used for both positive and negative outputs. Hence, care must be taken with the wells and substrate diodes: Low-Vt Nmos transistors have their Nwells tied to the high-side supply to avoid turning on the Nwell-Psub diodes.

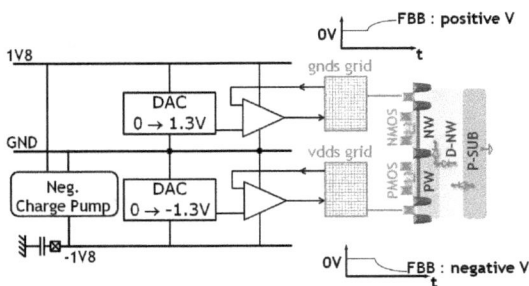

Fig. 5: On-die Body Bias generator structure & connection

4. Silicon demonstration

In this section, silicon results from two demonstrators are presented showing the capabilities of UTBB FD-SOI technology for very high energy efficiency applications.

The first example presents 802.11n Low-Density Parity-Check (LDPC) decoder, the first 28nm UltraThin Body and BOX Fully Depleted SOI (UTBB FDSOI) VLSI circuit designed to demonstrate the performance gains of this circuit versus 28nm LP High-K Metal Gate CMOS bulk technology [4]. Fig 6 shows the optimal (Vdd, Vbb) couple to achieve the lowest Energy-Delay-Product (EDP) for both bulk and FD-SOI technologies. This metric enables designers to select the best tradeoff in delay and energy for a given operating point. The measurements show a reduction of the minimum bulk EDP (1V, 0.3V) by 34% when moving to FD-SOI (0.8V, 0V). An extra 24% EDP reduction can be achieved by simply optimizing the (Vdd,Vbb) couple from (0.8V, 0V) to (0.7V, 1V). This result highlights the compelling energy efficiency capability offered by UTBB FD-SOI technology.

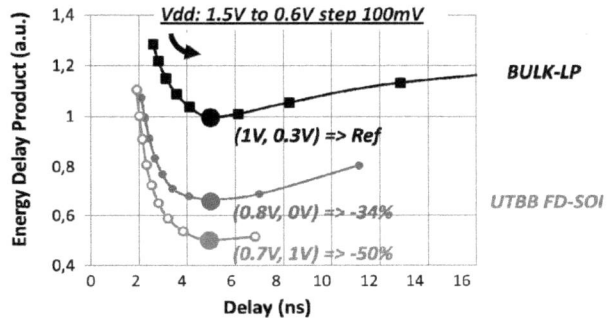

Fig.6: Switching energy vs. delay showing an optimal (Vdd;Vbb) couple

In Fig.7, a dual-core ARM CortexTM-A9 (A9) is presented [8]. The design exploits the flexibility provided by FD-SOI technology, especially the wide Dynamic Voltage and Frequency Scaling (DVFS) range, from 0.52V to 1.37V, and Forward Body Bias (FBB) techniques up to 1.3V. The system integrates all the advanced IPs for energy efficiency as well as the body bias generator and a fast dynamic body bias management solution. The measured dual core CPU maximum operation frequency is 3GHz (for 1.37V) and it can be operated down to 300MHz (for 0.52V) in full continuous DVFS. The obtained relative performance, with respect to an equivalent planar 28nm bulk CMOS chip, shows an improvement of +237% at 0.6V, or +544% at 0.61V with 1.3V FBB. The relative (28FDSOI versus 28LP) energy efficiency of the CPU system as a function of the frequency and FBB voltage shows a minimum of 33% power reduction at high frequency w/o FBB and a maximum of 48% w. FBB at low frequency.

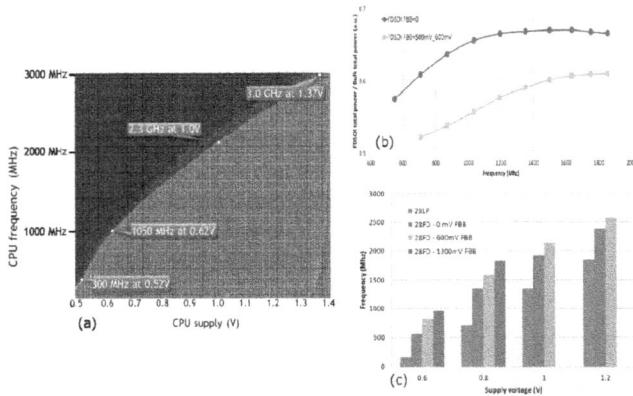

Fig. 6. Measured performance of the dual core A9 CPU in 28FDSOI and comparison with measured data from an equivalent chip in 28nm planar bulk CMOS (28LP)

(a) Schmoo plot of the CPU system maximum frequency versus the external supply voltage: from 300 MHz @0.52V to 3 GHz @1.37V in full continuous DVFS.

(b) The relative (28FDSOI versus 28LP) energy efficiency of the CPU system as a function of the frequency and FBB voltage.

(c) CPU maximum frequency versus V and FBB voltage in 28LP and 28FDSOI.

5. Conclusion

UTBB FD-SOI is becoming a must for SOC applications targeting very high energy efficiency without major changes in the design infrastructure. This technology provides designers a new lever for energy efficiency optimization, performance boosting, ultra-low-voltage functionality and leakage reduction. In the future, FD-SOI will remain the most compelling solution thanks to its ability to extend the life of 2D planar process and design architectures to offer best in class energy efficient solutions.

6. Acknowledgement

The author would like to thank the ST Technology Development and Design teams, CEA-LETI and BWRC for their valuable contributions and support.

7. References

[1]   Y. Shin et al, "28nm high- metal-gate heterogeneous quad-core CPUs for high-performance and energy-efficient mobile application processor", 2013 IEEE International Solid-State Circuits Conference Digest of Technical Papers (ISSCC), Page(s): 154 –155

[2]   Jakubczak, S. ; Katabi, D., "SoftCast: Clean-slate scalable wireless video", 2010 48th Annual Allerton Conference on Communication, Control, and Computing (Allerton), Page(s): 530 – 533

[3]   B. Nikolić, M. Blagojević, O. Thomas, P. Flatresse, A. Vladimirescu „Circuit Design in Nanoscale FDSOI Technologie", 2014 MIEL Conference

[4]   Flatresse, P. ; Giraud, B. ; Noel, J. ; Pelloux-Prayer, B. ; Giner, F. ; Arora, D. ; Arnaud, F. ; Planes, N. ; Le Coz, J. ; Thomas, O. ; Engels, S. ; Cesana, G. ; Wilson, R. ; Urard, P., "Ultra-wide body-bias range LDPC decoder in 28nm UTBB FD-SOI technology", 2013 IEEE International Solid-State Circuits Conference Digest of Technical Papers (ISSCC), Page(s): 424 – 425.

[5]   Arnaud, F. ; Planes, N. ; Weber, O. ; Barral, V. ; Haendler, S. ; Flatresse, P. ; Nyer, F., "Switching energy efficiency optimization for advanced CPU thanks to UTBB technology", 2012 IEEE International Electron Devices Meeting (IEDM), Page(s): 3.2.1 - 3.2.4

[6]   Pique, G.V. ; Meijer, M., "A 350nA voltage regulator for 90nm CMOS digital circuits with Reverse-Body-Bias", 2011 Proceedings of the ESSCIRC (ESSCIRC), Page(s): 379 – 382

[7]   Meijer, M. ; de Gyvez, J.P. ; Kup, B. ; van Uden, B. ; Bastiaansen, P. ; Lammers, M. ; Vertregt, M., "A forward body bias generator for digital CMOS circuits with supply voltage scaling", Proceedings of 2010 IEEE International Symposium on Circuits and Systems (ISCAS), Page(s): 2482 – 2485

[8]   Jacquet, D. ; Cesana, G. ; Flatresse, P. ; Arnaud, F. ; Menut, P. ; Hasbani, F. ; Di Gilio, T. ; Lecocq, C. ; Roy, T. ; Chhabra, A. ; Grover, C. ; Minez, O. ; Uginet, J. ; Durieu, G. ; Nyer, F. ; Adobati, C. ; Wilson, R. ; Casalotto, D., "2.6GHz ultra-wide voltage range energy efficient dual A9 in 28nm UTBB FD-SOI", 2013 Symposium on VLSI Technology (VLSIT), Page(s): C44 - C45

[9]   Philippe Magarshack, Philippe Flatresse, Giorgio Cesana: UTBB FD-SOI: a process/design symbiosis for breakthrough energy-efficiency. DATE 2013, Page(s): 952-957, 2013.

[10] Noel, J.-P. ; Thomas, O. ; Jaud, M. ; Weber, O. ; Poiroux, T. ; Fenouillet-Beranger, C. ; Rivallin, P. ; Scheiblin, P. ; Andrieu, F. ; Vinet, M. ; Rozeau, O. ; Boeuf, F. ; Faynot, O. ; Amara, A., "Multi- UTBB FD-SOI Device Architectures for Low-Power CMOS Circuit", IEEE Transactions on Electron Devices, Volume: 58 , Issue: 8, 2011, Page(s): 2473 – 2482Tavel, P. 2007. *Modeling and Simulation Design*. AK Peters Ltd., Natick, MA.

[11] Planes, N.et al, "28nm FD-SOI technology platform for high-speed low-voltage digital applications", 2012 Symposium on VLSI Technology (VLSIT), Page(s): 133 – 134.

Unified Embedded Non-Volatile Memory for Emerging Mobile Markets

Kangho Lee
Corporate R&D, Qualcomm
Technologies Incorporated
5775 Morehouse Drive
San Diego, CA 92121USA
+1-858-845-3023
kanghol@qti.qualcomm.com

Jimmy J. Kan
Corporate R&D, Qualcomm
Technologies Incorporated
5775 Morehouse Drive
San Diego, CA 92121 USA
+1-858-845-5319
jkan@qti.qualcomm.com

Seung H. Kang
Corporate R&D, Qualcomm
Technologies Incorporated
5775 Morehouse Drive
San Diego, CA 92121 USA
+1-858-651-8689
seungk@qti.qualcomm.com

ABSTRACT

Emerging mobile markets such as wearable electronics and Internet of Things necessitate innovations in embedded non-volatile memory (eNVM) for energy-efficient mobile computing and connectivity. In this paper, we briefly review how conventional eNVM has served current markets and investigate emerging eNVM in light of new mobile applications on the horizon. We propose spin-transfer-torque MRAM as a unified eNVM solution that can realize an eNVM-only memory configuration and enable emerging mobile products with high energy efficiency at low cost.

Categories and Subject Descriptors

B.0 [**Hardware**]: GENERAL

General Terms

Design

Keywords

Non-volatile memory; STT-MRAM; eFlash; RRAM; FRAM; connectivity; Internet of Things

1. INTRODUCTION

CMOS technology scaling driven by Moore's law has continually propelled growth in IT infrastructure and a prospering mobile industry. In the past 10 years, we have witnessed drastic improvements in the performance of mobile chipsets. Multi-core application processors (AP) with clock speed over 2 GHz are already available in the market. A Level-3 cache is being introduced to the state-of-the-art mobile chipsets. The prevalence of 4G LTE has also increased the performance and complexity of baseband chip designs in order to process more data from multiple channels in parallel. Along with these innovations in design, the logic technology has been moving toward the 10 nm transistor node.

Meanwhile, emerging mobile markets are gathering attention, driven by Internet of Things (IoT), wearable electronics, and context-aware computing. New products are already being introduced into various consumer markets, bringing the paradigm shifts in mobile computing and connectivity into our everyday lives. These new product domains include home automation, wireless healthcare, wireless automobiles, security, energy monitoring, and wearable gadgets. In comparison to the high performance AP, mobile chips for these products have drastically different requirements. Many of these mobile products are designed to be always-on or indefinitely in a standby state, making low power consumption a key figure of merit. As a result, performance may be traded off in favor of low cost and battery life.

For connectivity and wearable devices to be integrated into our lives seamlessly, it is desirable for smartphones to remain constantly 'on', acting as a control tower and connected to multiple wireless devices in the background. For such applications, smartphones may need a dedicated co-processor to perform this function while the power-hungry AP rests in sleep mode. This co-processor should be able to support low-power wireless connectivity and post-processing of collected data from connected devices. This would enable always-on features in a smartphone without compromising battery life. Some recent smartphones have already implemented a low power co-processor to control integrated motion sensors and process data independent of the primary AP.

Considering the new challenges and requirements for the next era of mobile computing and connectivity, it is unclear how performance gains obtained from CMOS technology scaling can provide direct benefits for emerging mobile products. Instead, technology innovations might need to focus on further reducing cost and power consumption. In this paper, we explore the role of embedded non-volatile memory (eNVM) as a key enabler of emerging mobile products and propose spin-transfer-torque MRAM (STT-MRAM) as a unified eNVM solution.

2. OVERVIEW OF EMBEDDED NVM TECHNOLOGY

As software complexity increases in modern systems, there have been increasing demands for eNVM in microcontrollers (MCU) and digital signal processors (DSP). Embedded Flash (eFlash) has been the dominant eNVM, primarily driven by automotive and smartcard applications. The eFlash adoption rate in MCU has steadily increased and is projected to reach 88% in 2017 [1].

While eFlash has served a wide range of MCU, the current MCU markets are too diversified for a single eFlash architecture to satisfy a variety of technology requirements. For example, automotive applications require reliable high-temperature operations with sub-ppm defect controls. In contrast, smart cards demand low-power consumption, low cost and security. Some medical applications place primary emphasis on ultra-low power operations. Various eNVM architectures have been used to meet these diversified requirements in memory capacity and critical parameters. eNVM suppliers in recent years have typically only supported a few eFlash platforms, depending on specific combinations of requirements such as cell size, endurance, read/write speed, power consumption, operating temperature, etc

In general, there are three types of eFlash bitcells [2-4]: 1T-NOR, split gate (also called 1.5T-NOR), and 2T-NOR. All of these have a NOR configuration. 1T-NOR is similar to that of standalone flash and has the smallest cell size, which makes it suitable for applications that require relatively large memory capacity. However, 1T-NOR does not provide good scalability, hence performance is often traded off with reliability. To address this challenge, eFlash technology has evolved to split gate and 2T-NOR designs, enhancing performance, power efficiency, and reliability at the sacrifice of cell size. In addition to eFlash, one-time or multi-time programmable (OTP, MTP) memory has also been drawing significant attention. OTP and MTP memory densities are generally very low, only about a few Kbytes or less. Yet it provides indispensable functions in various SOC applications such as after-package trimming and calibration, chip ID, security keys, etc. Electrically programmable fuses (eFuse), which utilize electromigration of poly Si have also been widely used. For a more scalable OTP solution, anti-fuse OTP (based on gate oxide breakdown of a logic transistor) has become a common choice recently [5].

One general challenge for any eNVM technology is the requirement of compatibility with baseline logic platforms. Historically, eFlash lagged behind logic technologies by a few generations and this gap has become wider [4]. Currently, most advanced eFlash under development is at the 40-nm node while logic platforms are moving toward 10 nm. eFlash is expected to face significant scalability challenges at deeply-scaled technology nodes. First, shrinking tunnel oxide thickness is becoming more difficult due to data retention constraints. This would limit the potential for cell size reduction and voltage scaling. Second, integration of conventional eFlash device structures into advanced CMOS technology at 28 nm or beyond is challenging due to increased complexity in front-end-of-line (FEOL) processes.

While the current eNVM technology landscape is complicated due to diversified technology requirements and scalability challenges, emerging eNVM markets for mobile applications demand more cost-effective and energy-efficient eNVM solutions at advanced technology nodes. By far, ferroelectric RAM (FRAM), resistive RAM (RRAM), and magnetoresistive RAM (MRAM) have been productized. FRAM and RRAM were adopted in low-power MCU products [6-7], though only at legacy nodes (130 and 180 nm, respectively). Field-switching MRAM technology has also been used in embedded applications, however addressing only niche markets. The specification of embedded field-switching MRAM has not been disclosed. However, since the first standalone MRAM product was shipped in 2006, the reliability and endurance qualities of MRAM have well been recognized [8]. Although these products may not represent the

true potential of each eNVM technology, they clearly show on-going innovations in emerging eNVM.

The eNVM mentioned above use a simple 1T-1R (MRAM, RRAM) or a 1T-1C (FRAM) bitcell architecture, which is basically one transistor serially connected to one resistive or capacitive memory element. Unlike eFlash that requires separate front-end processes to form double-gate structures, emerging eNVM cells are inserted into a back-end-of-line (BEOL) logic platform. This is an advantage because they can be developed independent of front-end processes, a feature that positions emerging eNVM attractively at advanced technology nodes.

In general, endurance, power consumption, and write speed are dramatically improved by replacing eFlash with emerging eNVM. For instance, FRAM and RRAM were employed in ultra-low power MCU, replacing eFlash and EEPROM. In contrast to eFlash that requires charge pumps to generate high internal write voltages (~10V), system core and IO voltages may be directly used for read and write operations. In addition, the write speed was improved by two orders of magnitude. A 2× reduction in total system power consumption has been demonstrated with these ultra-low power MCU.

However, scalability of emerging eNVM needs to be evaluated carefully. For example, it is questionable whether FRAM can be scaled down below 90 nm due to fundamental limitations in the scalability of ferroelectric materials [9]. Similarly, the only RRAM product demonstrated so far is at 180 nm node in small density (64 Kbytes), indicating that it is still challenging to achieve solid functionality and reliability in smaller features. Field-switching MRAM is not scalable below 65 nm because switching fields tend to increase with decreasing cell size. Since the switching fields are generated by flowing current through local interconnect metal lines, shrinking MRAM memory elements increases active power consumption. The 2nd generation MRAM, spin-transfer-torque MRAM (STT-MRAM), employs current-induced magnetization switching without involving magnetic fields. This operating mechanism fundamentally provides more room to scale the technology down beyond 65 nm. At the moment, STT-MRAM and RRAM are regarded as the only scalable emerging eNVM.

3. EMBEDDED NVM REQUIREMENTS FOR EMERGING MOBILE MARKETS

There are at least four product categories in emerging mobile markets where emerging eNVM can play a role as a key enabler or differentiator:

1. Low-power wireless connectivity chips for IoT

2. Low-power AP for wearable devices (e.g. smart watch)

3. Co-processor chips to control integrated sensors in a smartphone with the main AP in the sleep mode

4. Companion DSP chips for context-aware features of a smartphone (e.g. voice activation)

In this section, we discuss generic memory configurations for emerging mobile products and examine how implementing emerging eNVM will improve cost and power consumption at the system level.

3.1 Memory Configurations

Duty cycle is one of the key parameters that needs to be considered to optimize a memory configuration for minimum total power consumption in emerging mobile products. The inset in Fig. 1 illustrates a simplified current consumption profile over time. The total standby current may include various sources such as analog and SOC components in the system. For the sake of discussion, we assume that the standby current is dominated by memory leakage current. Figure 1 shows the percentage of standby power in total power consumption as a function of the duty cycle. As the duty cycle increases, the impact of standby power on total power consumption quickly diminishes particularly when the active to standby current ratio is high.

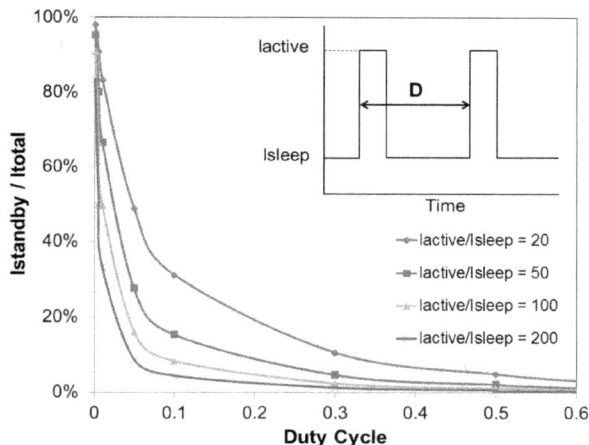

Figure 1. The percentage of standby power in total power consumption as a function of the duty cycle. The inset illustrates a simplified current consumption profile over

In general, there are three possible memory configurations: 1) SRAM-only 2) SRAM and eNVM and 3) eNVM-only. For the SRAM-only configuration, software code is stored in external Flash. Since static leakage power from SRAM has sharply increased at advanced technology nodes, this configuration is not desirable for applications with a low duty cycle. In contrast, emerging eNVM can replace both SRAM and Flash (either embedded or external), enabling the eNVM-only memory configuration. This simplifies the overall system design and eliminates SRAM cell leakage power and unnecessary IO transactions. However, the active current of emerging eNVM, particularly write current, is typically larger than that of SRAM. Hence, for a duty cycle above 5% or so, this would increase the total power consumption. Between these two options, one can use SRAM for dynamic operations and eFlash or emerging eNVM for code storage.

Table 1 compares memory attributes of SRAM, eFlash, RRAM and STT-MRAM. Note that the macro size information is only an estimation based on a 40 nm logic technology node. Due to smaller bitcell sizes, RRAM and STT-MRAM can reduce the memory block size by a factor of 2~3, which leads to cost reduction or increased memory capacity. When memory elements are well-optimized to guarantee sufficient write margins, the minimum bitcell size of emerging eNVM is determined by logic design rules, not the physical dimension of memory elements. Due to this fact, the minimum bitcell size for any of the aforementioned emerging eNVM would be comparable. At 40 nm, the bitcell size is expected to be at least 2~3× smaller than SRAM and at least 10~20% smaller

than eFlash. The demand to add more software features and improve signal processing algorithms has created a requirement for larger memory capacity. With smaller bitcells and die sizes, emerging eNVM could serve this need optimally at low cost. In addition to the bitcell size reduction, when a charge pump is not needed for high voltage generation, the array efficiency can also be improved, reducing die sizes further.

Compared to eFlash, emerging eNVM is much more energy-efficient. eFlash requires a charge pump to generate high voltages (> 10V) for write operations. This is a significant overhead for a battery-powered system. Furthermore, eFlash does not allow truly random access and the write cycle time is very slow (~1 ms). For emerging eNVM, only system core and IO voltages are used for read and write (R/W) operations. The write cycle time is typically 100 ns or less and for STT-MRAM, sub-10 ns write operations have even been demonstrated at a chip level [10].

Table 1. Comparison of SRAM, eFlash, RRAM and STT-MRAM

	SRAM	eFlash	RRAM	STT-MRAM
Macro size (normalized to SRAM)	1	0.4 ~ 0.6	0.3 ~ 0.5	0.3 ~ 0.5
Standby power	High	Low	Low	Low
Active power	Low	High	Medium	Medium
Charge pump	No	Yes	Yes	No
Read speed	1 ns	10~30 ns	10 ns	4~20 ns
Write speed	1 ns	0.1 ~1 ms	0.1 ~1 us	4~100 ns
Endurance	10^{15}	10^4	10^5	10^{12}~10^{15}
Retention	Volatile	10 years	10 years	10 years

While it is straightforward to swap eFlash with RRAM or STT-MRAM in emerging mobile products, replacing SRAM requires sufficiently high R/W speed and nearly unlimited endurance. Since STT-MRAM is superior to RRAM in terms of write speed and endurance (Table 1), it has been considered as a promising candidate to replace working memories (SRAM and eDRAM) in embedded applications and even standalone DRAM. As STT-MRAM has continually advanced over the last few years, write speed and active power consumption have significantly improved, mitigating the energy gap between SRAM and STT-MRAM. Further development may eventually allow STT-MRAM to replace high-density SRAM, bringing overall system-level benefits owing to non-volatility and increased memory capacity. Since the write energy per bit of STT-MRAM is minimized around 5~10 ns, the STT-MRAM-only memory configuration may eventually be adopted for emerging mobile products whose effective write cycle falls below 100~200 MHz. Furthermore, system architecture simulations have shown that STT-MRAM can be competitive over SRAM for L3-cache [11].

3.2 Connectivity Products

Connectivity products generally include a low-power MCU, a low-power wireless module (e.g. Bluetooth Low Energy, Zigbee, etc.), NOR Flash for code storage, and possibly one or more sensors. For this type of MCU, the system clock frequency is typically very low (~20 MHz) and low-density (e.g. 1~2 Mbits)

SRAM is usually used for working memory. The clock frequency is often optimized to minimize dynamic power consumption while only assuring adequate computing power for low-power wireless connectivity and data processing.

Battery-powered connectivity products usually have small form factors, limiting the battery capacity to 200 mAh or less. Connectivity products tend to have a low duty cycle. This means that the total power consumption can be minimized by adopting an eNVM-only configuration, eliminating static power consumption as much as possible. In fact, many low-power MCU products are still using legacy logic technology platforms (90 nm or older) partly because static leakage current tends to increase at more advanced technology nodes, in addition to the fact that eFlash lags behind the logic by 3 ~ 4 generations.

To be more accurate, power consumption from power-mode transitions and various peripheral components also need to be evaluated. Retention flip-flops have been used in low-power MCU to eliminate IO transactions between power-mode transitions and to minimize wake-up time. For this application, high-speed non-volatile retention flip-flops based on emerging eNVM have also been demonstrated [12, 13]. Various peripheral components such as analog sensors, ADC, voltage reference generator, digital interfaces also need to be considered. When peripheral power consumption is considerable during the standby mode, the impact of emerging eNVM adoption on total power consumption diminishes.

While low memory capacity and low operating frequency make connectivity products attractive candidates for early adoption of emerging eNVM, sufficient endurance is required for an eNVM-only memory configuration. For this reason, STT-MRAM has a higher chance to enable an eNVM-only memory configuration than RRAM.

3.3 Wearable Devices

Many wearable devices related to healthcare or wellness applications (pedometers, sleep trackers, etc) belong to the category of connectivity products. This means that an eNVM-only memory configuration is desirable for overall system performance and cost reduction as discussed in the previous sections. However, there is another class of wearable products that require higher performance and larger memory capacity. The best example in this category would be "smart watches" which have gathering attention from the mobile community. Table 2 compares five smart-watch products currently available on the market.

Figure 2 shows two memory configurations for smart-watch products. In low-performance smart watches (Fig. 2(a)), 120~180 MHz low-power MCU with 128~256 Kbyte SRAM and 512 ~ 1024 Kbyte eFlash have been used. External NOR Flash with or without PSRAM has been used for code storage. A dedicated small-size SRAM can be incorporated as a backup memory to retain data between power-mode transitions. Some SRAM blocks may be core-coupled to maximize computation efficiency for DSP operations.

While emerging eNVM can easily replace eFlash in Fig. 2(a), this may not significantly impact overall system cost, power, and performance. With its fast R/W speed and good endurance, embedded STT-MRAM can replace SRAM as well as eFlash (although core-coupled SRAM may remain in the system). STT-

MRAM can make power-mode transitions and data retention much more efficient. Non-volatile retention flip-flops based on magnetic tunnel junctions (MTJ) can also be incorporated to further improve the wake-up time. External Flash may eventually be replaced by low-cost standalone STT-MRAM when available. For further cost and power optimization, standalone STT-MRAM can be embedded into the MCU provided that the memory capacity is not too large.

Table 2. Comparison of smart watch product specifications

Product	Pebble Watch [14]	Qualcomm Toq [15]	Samsung GearFit[14]	Samsung Gear 2 [14]
Battery Life	7 days	5 days	3~4 days	2~3 days
Battery Capacity	130 mAh	240 mAh	210 mAh	300 mAh
Wireless	BT, BLE	BT	BLE	BLE
CPU	120MHz ARM Cortex M3	120MHz ARM Cortex M3	180 MHz ARM Cortex M4	1GHz Dual-Core + 84MHz Cortex M4
SRAM in MCU	128 KB	128 KB	256 KB	64 KB
eFlash in MCU	512 KB	1 MB	2 MB	128 KB
Main Memory	N/A	16MB pSRAM	8MB pSRAM	512MB DRAM
Storage	4MB NOR	2GB NAND	16MB NOR	4GB NAND

Figure 2(b) shows the memory configuration for high-end smart watches. 2~4 Gbyte NAND flash is used to store various software applications, photos, videos, etc. DRAM or PSRAM are used for main memory. A low-performance co-processor may be used to support always-on features. The role of emerging eNVM in high-end smart watches can vary widely depending on product requirements and system specifications. Initial introduction of emerging eNVM into high-end smart watches may be limited to the co-processor. When the main memory capacity is relatively small (e.g. 16~32 Mbyte PSRAM), high-speed STT-MRAM may be embedded into AP or MCU with significant advantages in power consumption and form factor. If the memory capacity requirement is high, DRAM would be the only available choice

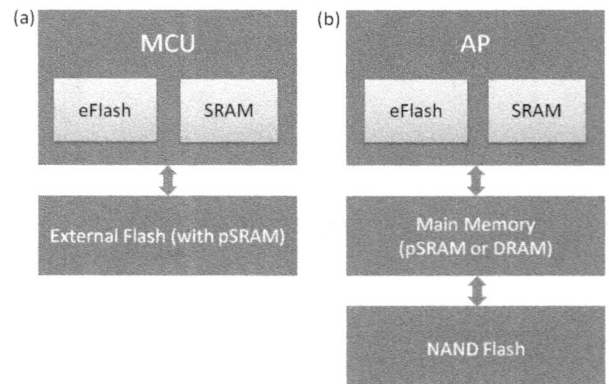

Figure 2. Conventional memory configurations for wearable devices

until standalone STT-MRAM becomes competitive against DRAM in terms of density and cost.

3.4 Smartphone Co-processor and Companion Chip

Co-processor or companion chips, typically 20~150 MHz MCU, have been incorporated in smartphones to support always-on features (e.g. voice activation, motion sensor control, etc.) with a primary AP completely in sleep mode. The standby current of a modern smartphone is less than 10 mA. Since the effective current consumption of co-processor and companion chips are added to the standby current, these products tend to have a stringent power consumption requirement. However, they need to have sufficient computing power to collect and process sensor data without waking the primary AP due to false alarms. This often requires adding more features and improving signal processing algorithms, which leads to increasing demands for higher memory capacity.

The duty cycle of co-processor or companion chips may not be low in comparison to connectivity products. This means that active current consumption accounts for a significant portion of the total power consumption. If eFlash is present in these products, emerging eNVM can replace it and provide all the system-level benefits explained above. However, an essential question for emerging eNVM adoption in this category of products is whether it can lower active power consumption at a low or intermediate operating frequency and allow larger memory capacity at comparable or lower cost.

At 40 nm or beyond, the active current of SRAM is typically 15 μA/MHz or less (symmetric R/W currents at ×32 or ×64). For STT-MRAM with switching current density of 2 MA/cm^2 at 50 MHz and MTJ size of 50 nm, the switching current of an average memory cell is ~40 μA, which is equivalent to 25 μA/MHz at ×32. While the write energy per bit of STT-MRAM can further be optimized by materials and process engineering and may become comparable to that of SRAM at future technology nodes, read current of STT-MRAM also tends to be larger than that of SRAM because both memory and reference cells need to be accessed during comparative read operations. Read current consumption is dependent on reference cell schemes so that read power consumption can be traded off with read speed. Hence, for a given MIPS required to perform a specific computation, it would be challenging for low-density STT-MRAM to compete with SRAM in terms of active power consumption. However, it is worth noting again that the bitcell size of STT-MRAM is ~3× smaller than that of SRAM. Increased memory capacities can be utilized to adopt memory-intensive computing, resulting in significant MIPS reduction. Such co-optimization of software and hardware may decrease the total power consumption while adding additional software features and improving signal processing algorithms.

4. STT-MRAM AS UNIFIED EMBEDDED NVM

While eNVM is expected to play an important role in innovating emerging mobile products, it is not trivial to drive eNVM technology toward this end because of diversified market segments and the presence of numerous eNVM technologies. A system engineer needs to consider various memory components to optimize overall system performance, cost and power consumption. For example, conventional low-power MCU have eFlash for code storage, SRAM for data memory, e-fuse OTP for chip ID and security keys, and SRAM-based retention flip-flop for efficient power-mode transitions.

If a single technology platform can serve all these various needs in emerging mobile products, it would greatly simplify system architecture. Furthermore, this platform could support an eNVM-only memory configuration because many applications in emerging mobile markets have low duty cycles. This means that fast R/W speed and good endurance are important to enable a unified eNVM solution for emerging mobile products. Note that emerging mobile products typically operate over a range of 0°C to 70°C or 85°C. Mitigating technology attributes required for high-temperature reliability can provide more room to tune emerging eNVM toward low cost and power saving.

Here, we propose embedded STT-MRAM as a unified eNVM solution for replacing eFlash, OTP, retention flip-flop, and even SRAM when needed. In particular, for battery-powered emerging mobile products with low duty cycles, the STT-MRAM-only memory configuration would be a highly efficient way of maximizing battery life and reducing cost, providing greater system-level benefits than replacing eFlash alone. While STT-MRAM has all the technology potential to become such a single eNVM platform, careful engineering of materials, devices and bitcells can provide useful knobs to further tune the technology to serve various memory configurations and memory components in emerging mobile products. In general, MTJ device properties can be tuned to trade off between write power and stand-by data retention in order to achieve minimum total power consumption for a given cost requirement. The same MTJ device used in a memory block can also be used to implement OTP by intentionally applying larger voltage across a MTJ device and breaking down the insulating barrier. This has been successfully demonstrated using one of our 45 nm STT-MRAM test chips, showing clear advantages of MTJ-based OTP over e-fuse OTP solution (at 45 nm 70% reduction in cell size and > 90% reduction in write power). In addition, a high-speed MTJ-based retention flip-flop has been demonstrated [16] and successfully implemented in a low-power MCU [13].

Since Sony first reported a chip-level demonstration of STT-MRAM in 2005 [17], there have been numerous chip-level demonstrations for STT-MRAM. Referring to two recent demonstrations with comprehensive chip-level testing data, Everspin presented fully functional standalone 64 Mb DDR3 STT-MRAM using in-plane MTJ technology [18]. Here, 20 ns R/W operations with low bit error rates were demonstrated. TDK recently demonstrated fully functional 8 Mb perpendicular STT-MRAM, showing remarkable high-temperature data retention at 150 °C and sub-5ns write operations [10]. Both demonstrations were built on 90 nm CMOS technology.

Many technology hurdles for enabling STT-MRAM have been cleared through relentless engineering endeavors in the MRAM community. More details about the current status of embedded STT-MRAM technology has recently been discussed elsewhere [19]. A significant hurdle for enabling STT-MRAM now lies with development of MTJ etching processes to ensure sufficiently good MTJ device uniformity and high yield at a target MTJ size. Fortunately, the MTJ device pitch for embedded applications tends to be quite relaxed (~150nm at 28nm). This relaxes the constraints for optimizing MTJ etching processes compared with commodity DRAM-like STT-MRAM arrays that require an extremely tight pitch (~40nm) due to stringent bitcell size constraints (6 F^2).

5. CONCLUSION

Realizing the advantages provided by emerging eNVM in cost and battery life would likely propel the introduction and adoption of next-generation mobile products. To ensure mainstream industry adoption, emerging eNVM must provide competitive advantages over conventional eNVM in energy, speed, density, endurance, logic compatibility, and cost. Overall, STT-MRAM is regarded as the most promising and capable eNVM for providing a unified eNVM solution for emerging mobile products. In particular, when a mobile system has a low duty cycle, the values of embedded STT-MRAM can be maximized by replacing eFlash, OTP, retention flip-flop, and SRAM simultaneously, delivering the eNVM-only memory configuration. As STT-MRAM technology continues to improve in areas of performance and energy efficiency, it will play a key role in enabling innovative non-volatile memory subsystems in emerging mobile products.

6. ACKNOWLEDGMENTS

We thank Taehyun Kim, Sungryul Kim, and Jung-Pill Kim for valuable technical discussions.

7. REFERENCES

[1] A. Niebel. 2013. Semiconductors and Memory Shaping Up for Growth in 2013. (January 2013). Retrieved July 1, 2014 from http://www.kilopass.com/semiconductors-and-memory-shaping-up-for-growth-in-2013

[2] H. Hidaka, "Evolution of Embedded Flash Memory Technology for MCU", Proc. ICICDT, (May 2011), 1-4.

[3] R. Strenz, "Embedded Flash Technologies and their Applications: Status & Outlook", Proc. IEDM, (Dec. 2011), 9.4.1-9.4.4.

[4] K. Baker, "Embedded Nonvolatile Memories: A Key Enabler for Distributed Intelligence", Proc. IMW, (May 2012), 1-4.

[5] E. Hsiao. 2013. Using Non-volatile Memory IP in System on Chip Designs. (June 2013). Retrieved June, 20 2014 from http://www.eetimes.com

[6] MSP430FRxx series product spec. Retrieved June, 20 2014 from http://www.ti.com

[7] AM1(MN101) series product spec, Retrieved June, 20 2014 from http://www.semicon.panasonic.co.jp

[8] MR series product spec, Retrieved June, 20 2014 from http://www.everspin.com

[9] C. Bohac. 2013. Comparing FRAM and MRAM. Application Note 02130. Everspin Technologies, Inc., Chandler, AZ.

[10] G. Jan, L. Thomas, S. Le, Y.-J. Lee, H. Liu, J. Zhu, R.-Y. Tong, K. Pi, Y.-J. Wang, D. Shen, R. He, J. Haq, J. Teng, V. Lam, K. Huang, T. Zhong, T. Torng, and P.-K. Wang, "Demonstration of fully functional 8Mb perpendicular STT-MRAM chips with sub-5ns writing for non-volatile embedded memories," Symp. VLSI, (June 2014)

[11] H. Noguchi, K. Ikegami, N. Shimomura, T. Tetsufumi, J. Ito, and S. Fujita, "Highly Reliable and Low-Power Nonvolatile Cache Memory with Advanced Perpendicular STT-MRAM for High-Performance CPU", Symp. VLSI, (June 2014).

[12] S. C. Bartling, S. Khanna, M. P. Clinton, S. R. Summerfelt, J. A. Rodriguez, H. P. McAdams, "An 8MHz 75uA/MHz Zero-Leakage Non-Volatile Logic-Based Cortex-M0 MCU SoC Exhibiting 100% Digital State Retention at VDD=0V with <400ns Wakeup and Sleep Transitions", Proc. ISSCC, (Feb. 2013), 432-434.

[13] N. Sakimura, Y. Tsuji, R. Nebashi1, H. Honjo, A. Morioka, K. Ishihara, K. Kinoshita, S. Fukami, S. Miura, N. Kasai, T. Endoh, H. Ohno, T. Hanyu, and T. Sugibayashi, "A 90nm 20MHz Fully Nonvolatile Microcontroller for Standby-Power-Critical Applications", Proc. ISSCC, (Feb. 2014), 184-185.

[14] iFixit. 2013. Teardown. (March 2013). Retrieved March 5, 2014 from http://www.ifixit.com

[15] Tech Insights. 2013. Qualcomm Toq Smartwatch Sample Report. (Dec 2013). Retrieved March 5, 2014 from http://www.techinsights.com

[16] N. Sakimura, T. Sugibayashi, R. Nebashi, and N. Kasai, "Nonvolatile Magnetic Flip-Flop for Standby-Power-Free SOCs", JSSCC, (Aug. 2009), 2244-2250.

[17] M. Hosomi, H. Yamagishi, T. Yamamoto, K. Bessho, Y. Higo, K. Yamane, H. Yamada, M. Shoji, H. Hachino, C. Fukumoto, H. Nagao, and H. Kano, "A Novel Nonvolatile Memory with Spin Torque Transfer Magnetization Switching: Spin-RAM," Proc. IEDM, (Dec. 2005), 459-462.

[18] J. M. Slaughter, N. D. Rizzo, J. Janesky, R. Whig, F. B. Mancoff, D. Houssameddine, J. J. Sun, S. Aggarwal, K. Nagel, S. Deshpande, S. M. Alam, T. Andre and P. LoPresti, "High Density ST-MRAM Technology", Proc. IEDM, (Dec. 2012), 29.3.1-29.3.4.

[19] S. H. Kang, "Embedded STT-MRAM for Energy-efficient and Cost-effective Mobile Systems", Symp. VLSI, (June 2014).

Failing to Fail - Achieving Success in Advanced Low Power Design using UPF

Rick Koster
Mentor Graphics
13355 Noel Road, Suite #500
Dallas, TX 75240
+1-972-391-2419
rick_koster@mentor.com

Sushma Honnavara Prasad
Broadcom Corporation
2431 Mission College Blvd
Santa Clara, CA 95124
+1-408-505-5823
sushma@broadcom.com

Shreedhar Ramachandra
Synopsys
700 E Middlefield Rd
Mountain View, CA 94086
+1-650-584-5598
shreedr@synopsys.com

ABSTRACT

Low power designs demand aggressive power management, which adds complexity and creates both verification and implementation challenges. IEEE Standard 1801 Unified Power Format (UPF) enables early capture of power intent, early verification of power management, and automated implementation of power intent in low power systems. This tutorial presents a high-level overview of UPF concepts, commands, applications, and flows, for both IP blocks and systems. Attendees will become familiar with basic power management concepts, how UPF captures power architecture, UPF commands, a methodology for modeling IP power intent and reusing that at a system level, and how to leverage UPF to verify power management.

Categories and Subject Descriptors

D.3.3 [**Programming Languages**]: Language Constructs and Features

B.7.0 [**Hardware**]: Integrated Circuits - General

Keywords

Low power design and verification, UPF

1. INTRODUCTION

Power density on a system on chip (SoC) is increasing with every new process node due to shrinking geometries and an increase in design frequencies. Form-factor limited chips are becoming thermally constrained, calling for aggressive power reduction techniques. Every new generation of SoCs is adding more and more features, and demanding more performance that needs to be met under aggressive schedules to remain competitive in the ever changing consumer/technology market. These collectively result in aggressive power management schemes that tend to make the design and verification process complex. Enabling early capture of power intent is therefore critical for complex low power SoCs. UPF is a standard that is used to define power intent of a design, describe the power management and enable early modeling of the power intent. This tutorial gives a high level overview of the concepts, command and applications of UPF, and how these can be applied at an IP level and reused at a system level for both implementation as well as verification.

ISLPED'14, August 11–13, 2014, La Jolla, CA, USA.
ACM 978-1-4503-2975-0/14/08.
http://dx.doi.org/10.1145/2627369.2631637

2. UPF

UPF is an evolving standard; it started as Accellera UPF1.0 and eventually became IEEE1801-2009 aka UPF2.0, and the latest version of the standard is IEEE1801-2013. UPF is a standard format for defining power management of a design. It is an extension of Tool Command Language (TCL). It is defined separately from the HDL, thus making the HDL power-agnostic. It enables early verification of power intent, drives verification and implementation from RTL to Layout.

Using UPF, one can describe the power distribution architecture, which is composed of power-domains, supply rails and the power control signals. Power state tables and operating voltages are captured in the UPF. Special power management cells like isolation, level shifters, power switches and retention registers are also described using UPF commands. Power intent is different from functional intent in that functional intent specifies design architecture, logic functionality and IP usage.

2.1 Power Domains

A power domain is a collection of instances that are treated as a group for power management purposes. The instances of a power domain typically, but do not always, share a primary supply.

2.2 Power Supply Network

Power supply network describes the logical connectivity of the power supplies, or power rails in the design. This may include connectivity through power switches. The major components of the power supply network are: supply ports, supply nets, supply sets and power switches. Supply sets are a group of related supply nets that contain functions to represent the supply nets, which can be defined later and constitute an electrically complete model. Some supply sets are created implicitly upon creation of a power domain; these are also called predefined supply sets.

2.3 Strategies

Strategies are rules that specifies where and how to apply isolation, level-shifting, state retention, and buffering in the implementation of power intent.

2.3.1 Isolation Strategies

Isolation is a technique used to provide defined behavior of a logic signal when its driving logic is not active. An Isolation cell is used to pass normal logic value during normal operation and clamps its output to some specified logic value when a control signal is asserted.

Two power domains interact if one contains logic that is the driver of a net and the other contains logic that is a receiver of the same net. If the driving logic is powered down, the input to the receiving logic may float between 1 or 0. This can cause significant current to flow through the receiving logic, which can damage the circuit. To avoid this problem, isolation cells are inserted at the boundary of a power domain to ensure that receiving logic always sees an unambiguous 1 or 0 value.

2.3.2 Level Shifting Strategies

Two interacting power domains may also be operating with different voltage ranges. In this case, a logic 1 value might be represented in the driving domain using a voltage that would not be seen as an unambiguous 1 in the receiving domain. Level-shifters are inserted at a domain boundary to translate from a lower to a higher voltage range, and sometimes from a higher to a lower voltage range as well. The translation ensures the logic value sent by the driving logic in one domain is correctly received by the receiving logic in the other domain.

3. IP POWER INTENT MODELING

IPs are a piece of functionality optimized for power, area and performance. Soft IPs are handed off as synthesizable HDL (technology agnostic), while hard IPs are handed off as LEF/GDS (technology specific). Soft IPs are typically handed off with their full design UPF, while Hard IPs can be delivered as either UPF power models or Liberty models.

IP power intent goes through a process of incremental refinement from constraints to final delivery. The first step involves creation of IP level constraints, which in turn the following actions:

- Identify "atomic" power domains in the design
- Identify state elements to be retained
- Identify isolation clamp values on ports
- Specify legal power states and sequencing

In the next step, the constraints are configured along with the RTL. In this step, we do the following:

- Uniquify power domains based on RTL configuration
- Merge power domains
- Create the required power-management ports
- Create isolation strategies to fulfill isolation needs
- Create retention strategies to fulfill retention needs
- Update power states and power transitions

The final step involves implementing the configured power intent. This is composed of the following:

- Create supply ports and nets
- Update supply set functions
- Update power states with supply values
- Create power switches
- Map strategies to technology specific library cells

4. POWER AWARE VERIFICATION

Traditionally verification of non-Power-Managed design involves verifying the functionality of the design statically or dynamically using vectors which do not involve voltage transitions. Power Aware verification means verifying Power Managed (or Low Power) designs which involves verifying the complex Power management schemes of the Power Controller and make sure that the design can successfully operate in all the Power states it is designed for. During the process of verification, various kinds of bugs are detected which can be categorized into Structural, Control Sequence and Architectural issues.

4.1 Static Verification

Static Verification is used at both RTL and implemented netlist level to catch structural Low Power bugs in the design.

Static verification relies on the possible power states of the design. The objective of static verification is to validate that the design can function properly in all the possible Power states.

Examples of structural bugs are

a) Missing Isolation on a path that connects a shutdown domain to a ON domain.

b) Missing Level Shifter between two Power Domains operating at different voltages.

c) Power Control signals for a block that is ON is driven from a shutdown block.

d) Incorrect supplies to Always ON buffers, ISO cells

e) Incorrect PG connectivity

4.2 Power Aware Simulation

Power Aware Simulation is used to catch Control sequence and Architectural Low Power bugs in the design. Power Aware simulation on top of functional simulation does the following.

a) Simulation of the Supply Network described in the UPF.

b) Shutdown Corruption: When a Power Domain is shutdown, the gates and registers that are a part of the domain propagate 'X' values during simulation.

c) Virtual Isolation Insertion: Virtual Isolation is simulated in RTL as described in UPF using Isolation Strategies.

d) Retention Simulation: Retention flops are simulated in RTL based on retention strategies in UPF by instantiating shadow latch if required.

Examples of Control Sequence and Architectural bugs are

a) Delayed Isolation Control enable or early Isolation Control disable

b) Save Restore signal sequencing

c) Corrupt on Activity Simulation: When a Power Domain is in the Corrupt on Activity state, the inputs to the domain need to be stable since the domain cannot handle switching. Any input change in this state is illegal.

d) Illegal Transitions of the Power states

5. REFERENCE

[1] IEEE Standard for Design and Verification of Low-Power Integrated Circuits (IEEE 1801™-2013), IEEE, New York, NY

Keynote

Accelerator-Rich Architectures — From Single-chip to Datacenters

Jason Cong

University of California, Los Angeles
Los Angeles, CA 90024
cong@cs.ucla.edu

Abstract

In order to drastically improve energy efficiency, we believe that future processor architectures will make extensive use of accelerators from single-chip implementation to datacenter-level integration, as custom-designed accelerators often provide 10-1000X performance/energy efficiency over the general-purpose processors [1]. Such an accelerator-rich architecture presents a fundamental departure from the classical von Neumann architecture, which emphasizes efficient sharing of the executions of different instructions on a common pipeline, providing an elegant solution when the computing resource is scarce. In contrast, the accelerator-rich architecture features heterogeneity and customizaiton for energy efficiency, which is better suited for energy-constrained design where the silicon resource is abundant.

There are several concerns with the extensive usage of accelerators: (1) low utilization, (2) narrow workload coverage, (3) high design cost, and (4) unfamiliar programming interfaces. In this talk, I shall discuss recent progresses and ongoing work to address these concerns. Due to tight power and thermal budgets, only a fraction of computing elements on-chip can be active in future technologies (so called dark silicon [2]). This means low utilization (but much higher energy efficiency) will be an inherent characteristic of future chips. To address the problem of narrow workload coverage, we look to the use of composable accelerators and programmable fabrics to virtualize and accelerate larger blocks of computation [3]. The design cost can properly managed by leveraing the recent advances in high-level synthesis coupled with efficient parameterized architecture template generation. The programming interface is a critical issue for successful adaption of accelerator-rich architectures. It needs to support extensive use of accelerators from single-chip to datacenter scales [4]. We have made significant progress in compilation and runtime support to enable programmers to make use the existing programming interfaces (e.g. C/C++ for computation tasks and MapReduce or Hadoop for large-scale distributed computation in dataceners) for efficient use of accelerators at all scales.

ACM Classification:

C.1.3 [PROCESSOR ARCHITECTURES]:

Other Architecture Styles—Heterogeneous (hybrid) systems

Author Keywords: Energy-efficient computing, accelerators.

ISLPED'14, August 11–13, 2014, La Jolla, CA, USA.
ACM 978-1-4503-2975-0/14/08.
http://dx.doi.org/10.1145/2627369.2631636

Speaker Bio

Jason Cong received his B.S. degree in computer science from Peking University in 1985, his M.S. and Ph. D. degrees in computer science from the University of Illinois at Urbana-Champaign in 1987 and 1990, respectively. Currently, he is a Chancellor's Professor at the UCLA Computer Science Department and the director of Center for Domain-Specific Computing (CDSC). He served as the department chair from 2005 to 2008. Dr. Cong's research interests include synthesis of VLSI circuits and systems, energy-efficient computer architectures, reconfigurable systems, nanotechnology and systems, and highly scalable algorithms. He has over 400 publications in these areas, including 10 best paper awards, and the 2011 ACM/IEEE A. Richard Newton Technical Impact Award in Electric Design Automation. He was elected to an IEEE Fellow in 2000 and ACM Fellow in 2008. He is the recipient of the 2010 IEEE Circuits and System Society Technical Achievement Award "For seminal contributions to electronic design automation, especially in FPGA synthesis, VLSI interconnect optimization, and physical design automation."

Dr. Cong has graduated 31 PhD students. Nine of them are now faculty members in major research universities, including Cornell, Fudan, Georgia Tech., Peking Univ., Purdue, SUNY Binghamton, UCLA, UIUC, and UT Austin. Dr. Cong has successfully co-founded three companies with his students, including Aplus Design Technologies for FPGA physical synthesis and architecture evaluation (acquired by Magma in 2003, now part of Synopsys), AutoESL Design Technologies for high-level synthesis (acquired by Xilinx in 2011), and Neptune Design Automation for ultra-fast FPGA physical design (acquired by Xilinx in 2013). Dr. Cong is also a distinguished visiting professor at Peking University.

References

[1] J. Cong et al. "Customizable Domain-Specific Computing", IEEE Design Test of Computers, 28(2):6–15, 2011.

[2] H. Esmaeilzadeh et al. "Dark Silicon and the End of Multicore Scaling", ISCA '11, pages 365–376.

[3] J. Cong et al. "Accelerator-Rich Architectures: Opportunities and Progresses", DAC'14.

[4] A. Putman et al. "A Reconfigurable Fabric for Accelerating Large-Scale Datacenter Services", ISCA'14.

GPUVolt: Modeling and Characterizing Voltage Noise in GPU Architectures

Jingwen Leng[1], Yazhou Zu[1], Minsoo Rhu[1], Meeta S. Gupta[2], Vijay Janapa Reddi[1]

[1] The University of Texas at Austin, [2] IBM T.J. Watson

ABSTRACT

Voltage noise is a major obstacle in improving processor energy efficiency because it necessitates large operating voltage guardbands that increase overall power consumption and limit peak performance. Identifying the leading root causes of voltage noise is essential to minimize the unnecessary guardband and maximize the overall energy efficiency. We provide the first-ever modeling and characterization of voltage noise in GPUs based on a new simulation infrastructure called *GPUVolt*. Using it, we identify the key intracore microarchitectural components (e.g., the register file and special functional units) that significantly impact the GPU's voltage noise. We also demonstrate that intercore-aligned microarchitectural activity detrimentally impacts the chipwide worst-case voltage droops. On the basis of these findings, we propose a combined register-file and execution-unit throttling mechanism that smooths GPU voltage noise and reduces the guardband requirement by as much as 29%.

Categories and Subject Descriptors

C.4 [**Performance of Systems**]: Modeling techniques, Reliability, availability, and serviceability

Keywords

di/dt, inductive noise, GPU architecture, GPU reliability

1. INTRODUCTION

Voltage guardbands [1–3] have been a long-standing and established mechanism to ensure robust execution. By raising the voltage regulator's output from its nominal operating voltage (e.g., 20% in IBM POWER6 [4]), the processor can meet its frequency target under the worst-case operating conditions such as process, temperature and voltage variations, and aging. However, an over-provisioned guardband consumes additional power and limits peak performance [5].

Prior measurement results show that throttling the processor's frequency and voltage according to its runtime activity can reduce power consumption by 24% on average without violating program correctness [3], simply because worst-case conditions occur rarely in the real world [6]. On the basis of such insightful characterization, several throttling mechanisms have been proposed that intelligently mitigate

ISLPED'14, August 11–13, 2014, La Jolla, CA, USA
Copyright 2014 ACM 978-1-4503-2975-0/14/08$15.00.
http://dx.doi.org/10.1145/2627369.2627605.

the worst-case voltage guardband requirement [1–3, 6–8]. A majority of these studies concluded that current resonance and surge (e.g., the $L\frac{di}{dt}$ effect caused by quick increases in microarchitectural activities after pipeline stalls) are the major causes of voltage noise in CPUs [6, 8].

No such prior work exists for GPUs, even though measurements of GPU's voltage guardband in prior work indicate that they can be as large as the CPUs' [9]. A fundamental reason is the lack of infrastructure support along with critical insights. Thus, the goals of this paper are to provide a platform to support new work and to demonstrate critical insights that uniquely pertain to the GPU. Architectural differences between CPUs and GPUs motivate us to conduct such a study. For instance, a GPU has a much larger register file, supports thousands of threads, and has a large number of cores. Such differences alter the *root causes* of voltage noise in a GPU architecture versus a CPU architecture.

We provide the first detailed modeling of GPU voltage noise, and a quantitative characterization of voltage droops' leading causes. First, we propose *GPUVolt*, a new GPU-specific voltage simulation framework that models the GPU on-die voltage noise behavior accurately. It is based on prior work [10], and has 0.9 correlation with hardware measurements. GPUVolt is integrated with GPGPU-Sim [11] and GPUWattch [12], which are robustly validated GPU performance and power simulators, respectively. GPUVolt adds a new dimension that allows researchers to perform different types of trade-off studies between the GPU's performance, power, and reliability (i.e., the voltage guardband).

Second, we perform an in-depth analysis of voltage droops for both single-core and chip-wide GPU-specific microarchitectural activities. We demonstrate that the root causes of large voltage droops in the GPU architecture are global synchronous activity across multiple cores at the second-order droop frequency, and core-level register file activity at the first-order droop frequency. The global synchronous activity is caused by activity occurring in specific microarchitectural units, such as special functions and floating-point units.

Third, we propose a throttling mechanism to reduce the GPU's worst-case voltage guardband. Our mechanism, which throttles the register-file and functional units, reduces the guardband by up to 29%. The key contribution, however, is the identification of voltage noise root causes and the ability to throttle them effectively with minimal performance loss.

The paper is organized as follows: Sec. 2 describes the GPUVolt modeling methodology. Sec. 3 focuses on the in-depth characterization of GPU voltage noise root causes, both at the individual core level and chip-wide activity. Sec. 4 demonstrates a use case of GPUVolt, discussing the register-file and functional-unit throttling mechanism that targets GPU-specific voltage droops root causes. Sec. 5 discusses the related work. We conclude the paper in Sec. 6.

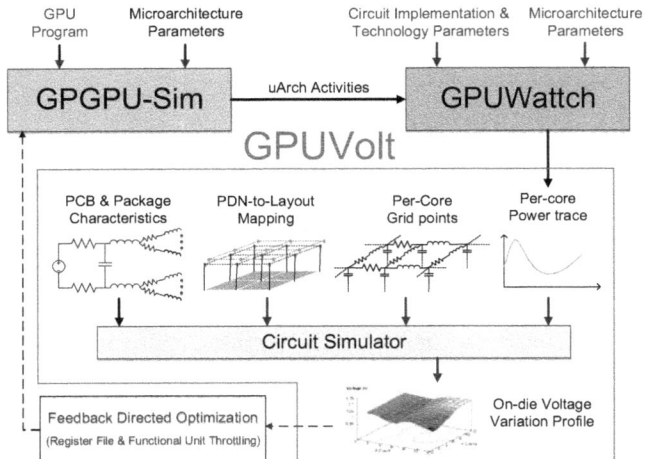

Fig. 1: An integrated and configurable voltage-noise simulation framework for the GPU many-core architecture.

2. GPU VOLTAGE-NOISE MODELING

In this section, we describe the voltage noise modeling methodology of GPUVolt. We start by providing an overview of the necessary co-simulation infrastructure, with which GPUVolt is tightly integrated to create a robust and flexible voltage noise simulation framework. Next, we provide the description of the voltage noise modeling methodology, with the details of important components. Finally, we validate GPUVolt against hardware measurements, showing that it has a strong 0.9 correlation across a range of applications.

2.1 Simulation Framework Overview

GPUVolt simulates the voltage noise behavior by calculating the time domain response of the power (voltage) delivery model under current input profiles of each core (Fig. 1). We use GPUWattch [12], a cycle-level GPU power simulator, to approximate the current variation profile of each GPU core under a certain supply voltage level. GPUWattch takes the microarchitectural activity statistics from GPGPU-Sim [11], a cycle-level performance simulator, and calculates the power consumption of each microarchitectural component.

We assume the widely established GTX 480 architecture for our study. We tested and evaluated the accuracy of both GPGPU-Sim and GPUWattch for this architecture. Both tools simulate the architecture with high accuracy. GPGPU-Sim has a strong 97% correlation with the hardware, whereas GPUWattch has a modest 10% modeling error.

We omit a table listing all the simulated architecture details because of space constraints, and also because we do not modify the architecture's default configuration. But, briefly, the GTX 480 architecture consists of many cores that are called streaming multiprocessors (SMs) in NVIDIA terms. The GTX 480 has 15 such SMs. Each SM contains a 64 KB L1 cache/scratchpad, and all SMs share a large 768 KB L2 cache that is backed by six high-bandwidth memory channels. In addition, each SM has a large 131 KB register file and a set of SIMD pipelines to support the execution of a large number of logically independent scalar threads.

2.2 Modeling Methodology

GPUVolt's power delivery model consists of three parts (Fig. 3a): the printed circuit board (PCB), the package, and the on-die power delivery network (PDN). We abstract the PCB and package circuit characteristics into a lumped model for simplicity; whereas for the most important component, on-die PDN, we use a distributed model that can capture the on-die voltage fluctuations accurately across the chip. A distributed model can reflect both intra-SM voltage noise as well as inter-SM voltage noise interference [10].

Accurately modeling the GTX 480's PDN characteristics is challenging because there is no public information on its actual PDN design. Therefore, we derive our initial model from the original Pentium 4 model developed by Gupta et al. [10]. However, we scale its PDN parameters in accordance to the GPU's peak thermal design power (TDP), because designers must design the PDN to match the target processor architecture's peak current draw [1, 2]. The GTX 480 has a high TDP of over 200 W, whereas the Pentium 4 model has a TDP of only 60-70 W [10]. Because high-performance processor package impedance is no longer scaling linearly [2], we only scale GPUVolt's grid parameters by 2× (compared to the 4× TDP ratio between two processors). The parameters and their values are shown in Fig. 3a. Other scaling values (e.g., 1.5× and 3×) are also possible, which simply result in different PDN characteristics. Thus, they are in fact valid configurations in GPUVolt (Sec. 2.3).

We lay out the SMs, L2 caches, network on chip (NoC), and memory controllers into the PDN grid based on publicly available die photos of GTX 480 (Fig. 3b); the die photos show an aspect ratio of each SM not being 1, so we use 2×3 grid points to model each SM (Fig. 3c) and 4×6 grid points to model the L2 cache, NoC, and memory controllers.

We do not model the intra-SM floorplan in detail, for two main reasons. First, the goal of GPUVolt is to focus on inter-SM voltage variations and to study such variations' impact on other SMs in the many-core GPU architecture with a shared-PDN; the intra-SM variations are relatively small, and therefore adding more detail does not necessarily provide additional insights at the chip level. Second, there is no publicly available intra-SM floorplan information for any of the contemporary GPU architectures. However, it is entirely feasible to extend GPUVolt with intra-SM floorplan details. We leave this as future work.

Fig. 2 justifies our grid point allocation scheme (i.e., 2×3 grid points for each SM and 4×6 grid points for the rest). It captures the trade-off between simulation accuracy and simulation speed as the number of total on-chip PDN grid points varies. We inspect the *peak intra-die voltage variation* under maximum SM current variation, which reflects the highest

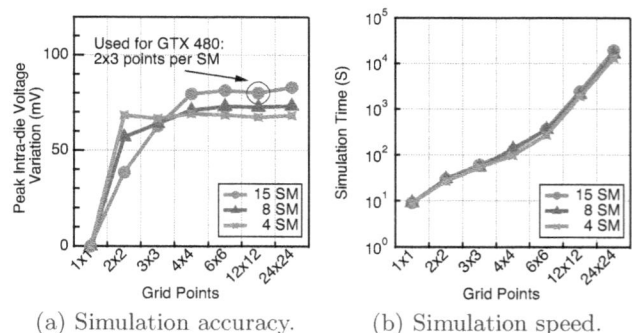

(a) Simulation accuracy.   (b) Simulation speed.

Fig. 2: GPUVolt's simulation accuracy versus speed trade-off (without GPGPU-Sim and GPUWattch overheads).

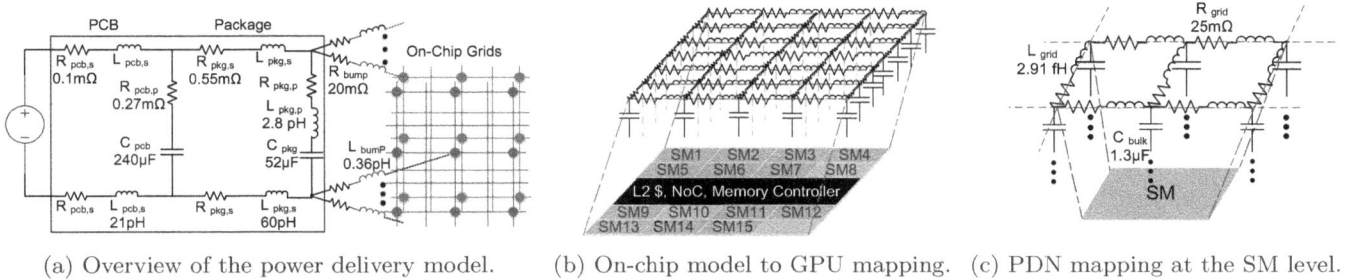

(a) Overview of the power delivery model.   (b) On-chip model to GPU mapping.   (c) PDN mapping at the SM level.

Fig. 3: Simulated voltage model in GPUVolt. (a) Global view of the power delivery model, including PCB, package, and on-chip PDN. (b) Mapping between the on-chip model and the GPU layout. (c) The on-chip PDN model for each SM.

voltage minus the lowest voltage on the die at the same cycle. In effect, it lets us quantify the impact of voltage noise on one core in response to another core's activity, which may be adjacent or located elsewhere on the chip. If we assume a lumped model with a single grid point, the intra-die voltage variation in Fig. 2a is nonobservable, which can lead to incorrect conclusions. However, the model begins to capture peak intra-die voltage variation as the grid size increases. With a total of 12×12 (144) grid points, we can achieve a reasonable balance between simulation accuracy and simulation time. The peak intra-die variation starts saturating as the grid size exceeds our choice while the simulation time continues to increase (Fig. 2b).

Fig. 2 also shows how the intra-die variation magnitude varies with the number of GPU SMs. We show this primarily to emphasize configurability of our modeling methodology. GPUVolt can readily support a varying number of SMs, depending on the assumption of the target architecture.

2.3 Model Validation

We validate GPUVolt by first showing the impedance versus frequency profile of our PDN, which establishes consistency with prior modeling work. Fig. 4 shows the impedance profile, extracted using GPUVolt's modeled PDN. As expected, the impedance profile shows two peak values due to the RLC effects of the PDN. Among the two peak values, the higher peak corresponds to voltage droops that occur at the order of tens of cycles, which is commonly referred to as the *first-order droop* (around 100 MHz). The lower peak impedance corresponds to voltage droops that occur at the order of hundreds of cycles, known as *second-order droop* (around 1 MHz). Our results are in line with previous studies [10, 13] and validate GPUVolt's PDN modeling methodology. We include other scaling factor results to demonstrate the ability to correctly model cheaper (i.e., high impedance) or costlier (i.e., low impedance) PDNs.

To further validate the PDN, we compare it against measurement results. Ideally, one would measure and compare the hardware's impedance-frequency profile with that of the simulator. Unfortunately, we do not have access to the required hardware V_{sense} pins [14]. Therefore, we perform a best-effort validation of GPUVolt by comparing the simulated worst-case voltage droops against the *critical voltage* measured on real hardware, using a variety of GPU applications. We measure an application's critical voltage by progressively reducing the GTX 480's supply voltage until the application crashes (i.e., produces a segmentation fault or wrong output compared to the reference run at nominal volt-

age). We decrement the processor's supply voltage from its default value (1.063 V, 700 MHz) in 10 mV steps, checking the program's correctness after each step. The first voltage at which the application produces an incorrect result is recorded as its critical voltage.

For robust validation, we use applications from a diverse set of benchmark suites, with a large range of worst-case voltage droops. The application set includes five large programs from the CUDA SDK: BlackScholes (BLS), convolutionSeparable (CVLS), convolutionTexture (CVLS), dct8×8 (DCT), and binomialOptions (BO); seven from Rodinia [15]: BACKP, KMN, SSSP, NNC, CFD, MGST, and NDL; and the DMR program from LoneStarGPU [16]. The worst-case droop ranges from 5% to 12%. Because of measurement limitations, we can only validate the whole program's worst-case droop, although kernel-level droops can be analyzed (Sec. 3).

Fig. 5 shows the correlation between the measured critical voltage and simulated worst-case voltage droop. GPUVolt faithfully captures the expected critical voltage behavior. As explained previously, programs with a high measured critical voltage would show a large simulated voltage droop, and vice versa. The Pearson's correlation between the two parameters is 0.9 assuming the default 2× scaling factor for the GTX 480 architecture for the 13 applications minus the four outliers. Thus, we conclude the GPUVolt's modeling methodology achieves reasonable modeling accuracy.

3. GPU VOLTAGE-NOISE ANALYSIS

We use GPUVolt to characterize GPU voltage noise at the kernel, SM component, and global inter-SM interference level. Our analysis reveals that large voltage droops occur rarely in the GPU, and as such the GPU voltage guardband

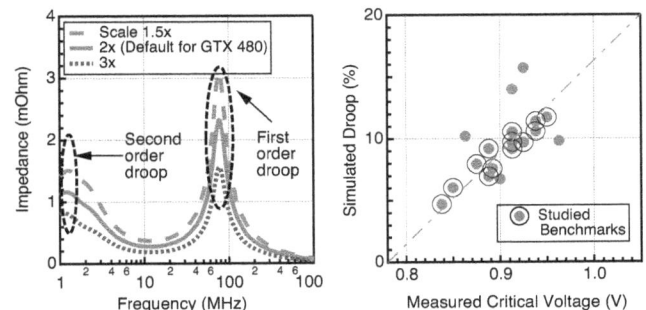

Fig. 4: Our PDN model's impedance-frequency profile. Fig. 5: Simulated droop versus measured critical voltage.

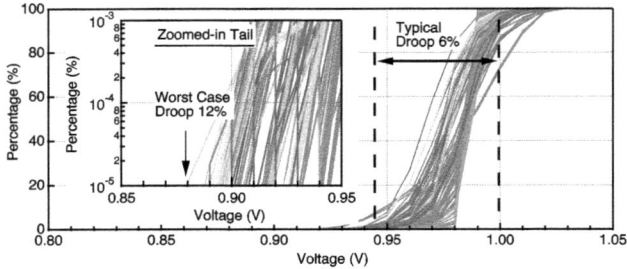

Fig. 6: Cumulative distribution of voltage droops: each line represents the CDF of a kernel. The typical droop is about 6%. The inset plot zooms into the tail portion.

is overprovisioned. Although this insight has been observed in CPUs, we are the first to report such analysis on GPUs.

The differences between the typical- and worst-case droop motivate us to understand the GPU's voltage-noise root causes. It is important to understand the root causes in order to mitigate them successfully. We focus mainly on characterizing the worst-case voltage droop of the architecture components and their power consumption levels, because the first step is to uncover the key microarchitectural components that are responsible for the large voltage droops.

We show that key microarchitecture components, such as the large register file and SIMD functional units, are the main contributors of voltage droops in the GPU architecture. Furthermore, we show that functional units' activity at the intra-SM level when in synchronization with other SMs' functional units' activity can lead to global current surge, causing large chip-wide voltage droops.

3.1 Kernel-Level Voltage Droop

To understand the typical voltage noise profile on GPUs, we gathered the voltage traces of all the programs mentioned in Sec. 2.3. Fig. 6 shows a cumulative distribution profile of the voltage droops for the different GPU programs. Each GPU program consists of one or more kernels, where a kernel is defined as a single unit of execution. Different kernels in the same program may have different droop behaviors. Thus, we plot each distinct program kernel execution as a line in Fig. 6. We analyze the data from over 200 kernels executed across all the programs.

We observe that the vast majority of the voltage samples (over 99.9% of the time) are greater than 0.94 V. We refer to these droops as the typical voltage droops, which are half the magnitude of the worst-case droop (i.e., 0.88 V) indicated by the zoomed-in tail portion. The large voltage droops rarely occur, with a cumulative frequency that is less than 0.02%.

It is also important to note that both typical- and worst-case voltage droop behaviors are strongly program or kernel dependent. On one hand, the lines in Fig. 6 are not overlapping, which indicates that the typical droop behavior varies across the programs and their kernels. On the other hand, as the inset plot shows, the worst-case droop of some kernels is as small as 5% (i.e, 0.95 V), whereas the worst-case droop of other kernels is as large as 12% (i.e, 0.88 V).

Understanding the differences between the typical- and worst-case droop requires us to understand how runtime program behavior impacts component current variation, as well as the intra- and inter-SM voltage droop. To draw general and broad conclusions, from here on in this section we only focus on aggregate kernel behavior across all the programs.

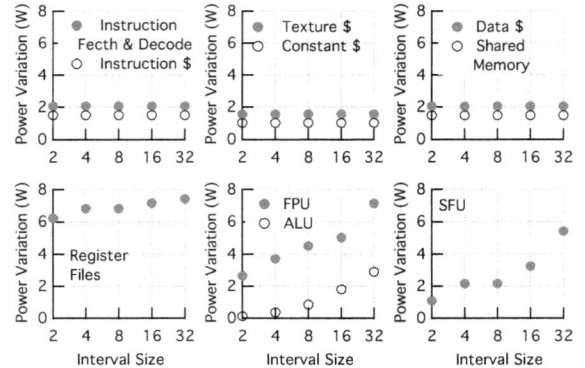

Fig. 7: The power variation for all the major GPU components over several different interval sizes, ranging from 2 cycles to 32 cycles (only consider power increase).

3.2 Component Current Variation

We want to identify the voltage noise root causes in GPU architectures. The first step is to characterize each component's contribution to the total $L\frac{di}{dt}$ effect. We approximate each microarchitectural component's per-cycle current draw using the per-cycle power consumption results from GPUWattch [12]. A large power variation in a short time period would lead to a large voltage droop.

We quantify the power varying "speed" of each component by recording its peak power variation within a timing interval. Using various interval lengths of size N, we capture the peak current draw characteristics of the different components accurately. We sweep N over 2, 4, 8, 16, and 32 cycles, enough to cover the first-order droop impedance (Fig. 4). We find that power variation plateaus for all components with a time scope larger than 32 cycles; therefore, we do not increase N beyond 32. The microarchitecture components include front-end (i.e., fetch and decode); various on-chip caches (i.e., texture, constant, and data); shared memory; register file; and integer, floating-point, and special-function units (ALU/FPU/SFU). The list is comprehensive and includes all the major components.

Fig. 7 shows the characterization results. We make three important observations. First, power variation of the front-end and various caches is stable and low across different interval sizes. For example, power variation of the instruction cache is constantly 2 watts with different interval sizes in the x-axis. We expect this because instruction cache access only takes one cycle. Other caches (data/constant/texture) and shared memory have a similar power variation profile, with slightly different magnitudes.

Second, the register-file has the most rapid power variation among all components. Its behavior is closely tied to the unique characteristics of the GPU architecture. Modern GPUs require a large register file to hold the architectural states of thousands of threads in each SM core. In our simulated GTX 480 architecture, the register file size is 131 KB, which is much larger than the 16/48 KB L1 cache sizes. Consequently, the register file access rate and power consumption are much higher compared to the RF in CPUs [12, 17].

Third, the functional units (ALU/FPU/SFU) also have large power variation, because they are all SIMDized and consume lots of power. However, compared to the RF, these components exhibit large variation at the interval size of 32 cycles, which is due to their multicycle execution latencies.

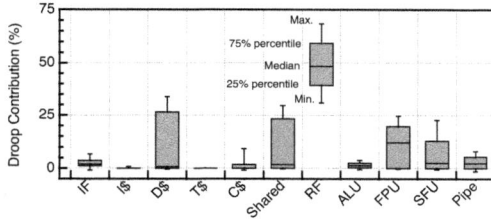

Fig. 8: Component contribution to any voltage droop that is greater than 3% at the intra-SM level.

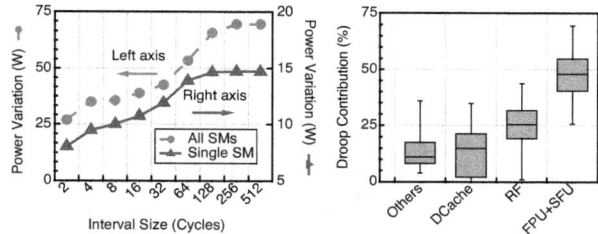

Fig. 9: SM power variation at different interval sizes.

Fig. 10: Component impact on chip-wide voltage droops.

3.3 Intra-SM Voltage Droop

We must quantify each component's contribution to an SM's voltage-noise profile over its execution duration. This is because even though a component may experience high power variation, it does not necessarily imply that it will be the leading contributor of large voltage droops in the GPU. Its impact may vary depending on its utilization frequency.

We leverage the linear property of our voltage model to quantify each component's contribution to a single SM's voltage noise. The linear property of GPUVolt's RLC circuit model implies that the temporal response of the PDN's on-chip voltage noise is the sum of the individual parts over time. Therefore, we can establish each component's contribution to the SM's total voltage noise by feeding the individual component's current profile separately into GPUVolt.

Fig. 8 shows the contribution of the major components to voltage droops in a single SM. We perform the quantitative analysis of each component's contribution to the magnitude of voltage droops that are larger than 3% of the nominal supply voltage. We pick this value because the maximum droop at the intra-SM level is about 5%. Therefore, a 3% threshold filters out the typical droop behavior, letting us isolate and focus on the large droops in the intra-SM level.

Fig. 8, shown as a box plot, captures the maximum, 75%, and 25% quartiles, and the minimum contribution of each component for the cycle-by-cycle voltage samples gathered during a run. Even at the intra-SM level, the register file remains the single most dominant source of voltage droops, with a maximum of 70% and median of 50% contribution to the droops. Other components, such as FPU, SFU, shared memory, and data cache, also contribute to large droops, but their influence is smaller as compared to the register file.

3.4 Chip-Wide Voltage Droop

We expand our analysis to chip-wide voltage droops to understand how intra-SM component activity, combined with activity from all SMs, can lead to large voltage droops with magnitudes larger than 8%. We find that aligned activity and second-order droop effects are the dominant root causes.

Chip-wide droops are caused by aligned component activity across different SMs because GPUVolt assumes a *shared* PDN (i.e., all SMs are connected to the same power grid); prior work demonstrates that a shared PDN is more robust to voltage noise than a split power grid where cores are connected to separate power grids [4]. An unfortunate side effect of a shared PDN is that one SM's aggregate component activity can impact another SM's voltage; such behavior has been studied in CPUs [6, 8], but its characterization and root-cause analysis have not been unveiled in GPUs.

Unlike in the intra-SM scenario, where rapid power variation occurs at the first-order droop frequency, the aligned chip-wide power variation occurs at the second-order droop frequency. Fig. 9 shows the total peak power variation for a single SM and all the 15 SMs. We study interval ranges between 2 and 512 cycles. This range captures both the first- and second-order droop frequencies. The single SM's power variation begins to saturate at the 64-cycle interval with a peak of 14 watts, which corresponds to a single SM's maximum instantaneous power consumption. In contrast, the total power variation for all SMs reaches a peak between the 256- or 512-cycle interval, which matches with the second-order droop frequency. The peak value is about 70 watts, which indicates that there are at least six SMs whose activities are in strong alignment to cause large droops.

To understand global component activity impact on chip-wide voltage droops, we carry out a characterization study as in Sec. 3.3. We feed GPUVolt with components' currents from all SMs to expose each component's droop contribution to all droops that are larger than 8% of the nominal supply voltage. Fig. 10 presents our results, and it shows that the global aligned activities are from the execution units across SMs. The execution units (mainly FPU and SFU) contribute most to the chip-wide droops (maximum 75% and median 50%). Compared to the single or intra-SM case, the register file only accounts for 25% to 45% of the total chip-wide droops.

Our insights emphasize that it is important to understand both intra-SM and chip-wide activity in a combined fashion to comprehensively identify voltage noise root causes in GPU architectures.

4. GPU VOLTAGE-NOISE MITIGATION

We conduct a proof-of-concept study to demonstrate that it is possible to mitigate the GPU's worst-case guardband on the basis of our intra-SM and chip-wide inter-SM voltage droop characterization. Our goal is *not* to comprehensively evaluate a wide variety of mechanisms and demonstrate which is best; rather, it is to demonstrate that our root-cause analysis is sound and that throttling the key components (i.e., execution units and the register file) will reduce the worst-case voltage droop.

We evaluate a solution similar to "Pipeline Damping" [7], which limits the key components' activity increase over an interval of consecutive cycles. In our work, we set the interval size such that it matches the components' droop-impact characteristics. For example, the power variation of the register file (RF) causes large voltage droop at the first-order droop frequency. Similarly, the execution units (Exe.) cause large voltage droops at the second-order droop frequency. Consequently, we set 8 and 800 cycles as the throttling interval size for the RF and Exe., respectively.

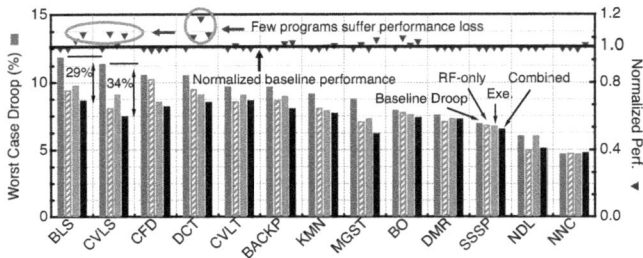

Fig. 11: Worst-case voltage droop reduction caused by throttling components identified to cause the most voltage droop.

Fig. 11 shows the throttling results in terms of the worst-case droop with and without our throttling evaluation. The key insight is that we have to perform a combination of RF and execution unit throttling because the root cause of a large voltage droop can be due to either component. Combined throttling can effectively mitigate the worst-case droop, because the worst-case voltage droop in a program may be caused by only one or both components. In BLS, the droop reduces from 12% to 8.5%, with a 29% improvement. However, RF-only throttling barely reduces the droop to 10.25% in CFD from its maximum droop of 10.6%. The geometric-average performance overhead of throttling both components is 4.1% for the evaluated programs.

5. RELATED WORK

Gupta et al. were the first to use a distributed PDN model to model on-die voltage noise [10]. GPUVolt is a natural but GPU-specific extension of the prior work. GPUVolt is configurable and useful to study GPU voltage-noise characteristics with different SMs (e.g., Fig. 2a), package characteristics (e.g., Fig. 4), microarchitecture configurations (Fig. 1), etc.

At the single-core (SM) level, prior work concluded that rapid current increases and resonant current behavior caused by microarchitectural activities–e.g., pipeline flushing and cache misses–are the root causes of voltage droops [1,2,7]. In contrast, our GPU component-level characterization shows that the GPU's throughput-architecture design causes new sources of $L\frac{di}{dt}$ problems, such as its large register file.

Multicore CPU voltage noise studies focused on thread interference and how to mitigate the effect at the global level by scheduling threads [6,8]. We took a different approach by studying the contribution of various components and their combined effect on voltage noise across the different SMs. We find that synchronized global activity of the SMs' execution units and register files can lead to large chip-wide voltage droops. On the basis of such insights, we perform a case study of voltage smoothing by throttling these units.

6. CONCLUSION

GPUVolt is an integrated voltage noise simulation framework specifically targeted at GPU architectures. We validated it against hardware measurements, and it shows a 0.9 correlation for a range of programs. Using GPUVolt, we demonstrate that the current surge of register file at the first-order droop frequency and aligned execution unit (i.e., ALU/FPU/SFU) activity at the second-order droop frequency are the main sources of voltage noise in GPU architectures. Controlling their utilization can reduce the worst-case voltage droop magnitude by as much as 29% with a marginal impact on the performance.

Acknowledgments

This work is supported by the National Science Foundation grants CCF-1218474, in addition to the support provided by Defense Advanced Research Projects Agency, Microsystems Technology Office, under contract no. HR0011-13-C-0022. The views expressed are those of the authors and do not reflect the official policy or position of the NSF, the Department of Defense, or the U.S. Government. This document is: Approved for Public Release, Distribution Unlimited.

7. REFERENCES

[1] E. Grochowski et al., "Microarchitectural simulation and control of di/dt-induced power supply voltage variation," in Proc. of HPCA, 2002.

[2] R. Joseph et al., "Control techniques to eliminate voltage emergencies in high performance processors," in Proc. of HPCA, 2003.

[3] C. R. Lefurgy et al., "Active management of timing guardband to save energy in power7," in Proc. of MICRO, 2011.

[4] N. James et al., "Comparison of Split-Versus Connected-Core Supplies in the POWER6 Microprocessor," in Proc. of ISSCC, 2007.

[5] D. Ernst et al., "Razor: a low-power pipeline based on circuit-level timing speculation," in Proc. of MICRO, 2003.

[6] V. Reddi et al., "Voltage Smoothing: Characterizing and Mitigating Voltage Noise in Production Processors via Software-Guided Thread Scheduling," in Proc. of MICRO, 2010.

[7] M. D. Powell et al., "Pipeline damping: a microarchitectural technique to reduce inductive noise in supply voltage," in Proc. of ISCA, 2003.

[8] T. Miller et al., "VRSync: characterizing and eliminating synchronization induced voltage emergencies in manycore processors," in ISCA, 2012.

[9] J. Leng et al., "Energy efficiency benefits of reducing the voltage guardband on the Kepler GPU architecture," in Proc. of SELSE, 2014.

[10] M. Gupta et al., "Understanding Voltage Variations in Chip Multiprocessors Using a Distributed Power-delivery Network," in DATE, 2007.

[11] A. Bakhoda et al., "Analyzing CUDA Workloads Using a Detailed GPU Simulator," in Proc. of ISPASS, 2009.

[12] J. Leng et al., "GPUWattch: Enabling Energy Optimizations in GPGPUs," in Proc. of ISCA, 2013.

[13] K. Aygun et al., "Power Delivery for High-Performance Microprocessors," in Intel Technology Journal, Nov. 2005.

[14] M. Laurent et al., "Impact of power-supply noise on timing in high-frequency microprocessors," IEEE Tran. on Advanced Packaging, 2004.

[15] S. Che et al., "Rodinia: A benchmark suite for heterogeneous computing," in Proc. of IISWC, 2009.

[16] M. Burtscher, R. Nasre, and K. Pingali, "A Quantitative Study of Irregular Programs on GPUs," in Proc. of IISWC, 2012.

[17] M. Gebhart et al., "Energy-efficient mechanisms for managing thread context in throughput processors," in Proc. of ISCA, 2011.

Empirically Derived Abstractions in Uncore Power Modeling for a Server-Class Processor Chip

Hans Jacobson, Arun Joseph*, Dharmesh Parikh*, Pradip Bose, Alper Buyuktosunoglu

IBM T. J. Watson Research, *IBM Systems & Technology Group

hansj@us.ibm.com, arujosep@in.ibm.com, dhparikh@in.ibm.com, pbose@us.ibm.com, alperb@us.ibm.com

ABSTRACT

Early-stage power modeling is an essential aspect of the process of defining efficient, yet high-performance microarchitectures. Pre-silicon power modeling has been an active area of research and development for well over a decade, although primarily focused on the processor cores. In this paper, we examine the challenge of developing practical abstractions in uncore power modeling in an industrial setting. We report a systematic methodology of abstractions in modeling with a focus on key uncore elements of the POWER8™ processor chip from IBM. The results show that the active power of these uncore elements can be modeled with acceptable levels of precision, by: (a) using just a few activity markers: e.g. reads, writes, retries and snoops; and (b) using a small set of systematically crafted microbenchmark stress test cases to measure the activity frequencies on a detailed, cycle- and latch-accurate RTL reference model.

Categories and Subject Descriptors

C.4 [**Performance of Systems**]: Modeling techniques, measurement techniques, design studies

General Terms

Performance, Design.

Keywords

Energy-efficient design, power modeling, levels of abstraction, speed-accuracy trade-offs, power proxy

1. INTRODUCTION

The onset of the so-called power wall [1] at the beginning of the new millennium necessitated a deep look at the ways of assessing the inherent energy-efficiency of processor microarchitectures at the earliest stages of definition. Early processor power modeling innovations (e.g. Wattch [2], SimplePower [3], the Cai-Lim model [4], TEMPEST [5], PowerTimer [6]) were largely focused on the processor core – and these methods helped motivate the need for and then quantify the benefits of core-level power reduction and management strategies: e.g. progressively finer-grain modes of clock-gating [6], defining the optimal choice of microarchitectural parameters like pipeline depth or super scalar width [7, 8], various forms of adaptive (or dynamic) power management [9] and even unit-level power gating within a core [10]. As designs evolved into the multi- and many-core era (as a consequence of the power wall), the attention has shifted to the so-called "uncore" elements of a processor chip. Multi-core, multi-threaded application workloads are complex and detailed. Hence, cycle-accurate simulation of target processor chips has become progressively more difficult for early-stage performance and power modeling teams in industry. As such, abstractions in modeling are needed in order to characterize the relative power-performance trade-offs in an acceptably accurate manner before key design decisions are "frozen" into register-transfer-level (RTL) specifications of the design.

In this paper, we provide a modern perspective of the pre-silicon power modeling challenge. We take a deep look at the "uncore" elements of the chip microarchitecture and examine the feasibility of a drastic abstraction in power modeling. In particular, we focus on the memory controller and key on-chip bus interconnect components of the IBM POWER8™ processor. Our results indicate that uncore elements of such a modern multi-core processor can be modeled in terms of just a few activity event frequencies: reads, writes, retries and snoops, without appreciable loss of accuracy. Based on this result, and noting similar abstraction methods for processor cores [11, 12, 13], we envision the use of full-chip, empirically derived abstractions in power modeling and discuss a few use-case scenarios in section 4.

2. DETAILED PRE-SILICON POWER MODELING REFERENCE

Before discussing levels of abstraction in pre-silicon power modeling, we review the fundamentals of how a very detailed and accurate power modeling reference can be established. Abstractions of varying degrees can then be defined with respect to the detailed reference. Such a reference model focused on the processor core was discussed in [11]. Here, we generalize that view by extending the scope to the uncore elements of the chip, and thereby covering the full multi-core chip.

Figure 1 depicts a simplified overview of the flow in the detailed reference chip power analysis tool chain used at IBM. This very accurate contributor based power modeling framework forms the reference point in our power abstraction work. The ability to create process, voltage and temperature (PVT) independent standard cell power contributor abstracts and the ability to create PVT-independent gate level power abstracts for IP blocks, and its use for enabling efficient multi-corner hierarchical chip power analysis was discussed by Dhanwada et al [18, 16]. The accuracy of the detailed reference chip power analysis tool chain was validated against POWER7+ microprocessor hardware power measurements for a range of unique hardware parts, voltage and temperature conditions [16, 19]. The guiding principles of the methodology are as follows:

ISLPED'14, August 11-13, 2014, La Jolla, CA, USA.
Copyright 2014 ACM 978-1-4503-2975-0/14/08...$15.00.
http://dx.doi.org/10.1145/2627369.2627619

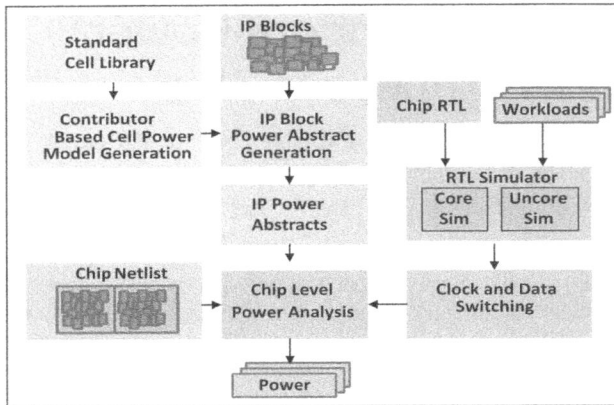

Figure 1. Reference power modeling methodology

1. PVT-independent power abstracts are derived for the standard cell library and IP library to enable rapid hierarchical chip power analysis for multiple sets of process, voltage and temperature corner conditions and RTL workload switching.

2. Core and uncore simulation models are built from chip RTL specifications. Multiple workloads are simulated and switching information is collected for latch clocking, latch and primary input data switching, and array accesses. The switching data is collected at a per-latch and per-net basis to improve accuracy. Due to simulation speed limitations of large designs modeled at the detailed RTL level, application workloads need to be abstracted into representative loop kernels. In this work, we generate a set of such small kernels that are representative of the different activities seen in the uncore part of the chip.

3. For performance analysis purposes high level event activities are extracted during RTL simulation. We select a subset of these performance events to form the independent variables of the regression analysis that generates the abstract power models.

4. The RTL switching data, the standard cell power abstracts, the IP block power abstracts, and chip netlist are input to a chip level power modeling and analysis tool [16], and power is computed for each workload for a range of different corners.

5. Leakage power is calculated by the reference power tool chain by other means [16, 18], driven by estimates of total gate width, supply voltage, threshold voltage, and "sort point" information available through separate technology-specific analysis toolsets.

The workload-specific power and event counts produced by the reference model, as outlined above, form the data points we use in generating an uncore abstract power model.

3. UNCORE POWER MODELING

In this section, we focus on selected uncore elements of the IBM POWER8[TM] [14] state-of-the-art multi-core server processor to explain how detailed power modeling for these elements are pursued in an industrial setting. We then propose abstractions in event selections, similar in spirit to what has been proposed before for the processor core [11] and present experimental results to demonstrate the accuracy achievable. As seen from the power breakdown pie chart for POWER7[TM] (see Figure 4 in [12]), the uncore elements within each chiplet (namely: the L2, L3 caches) constitute 20% of the power for a thermal design point workload. The uncore elements within a chip further include large macros that

are shared by all the chiplets: e.g. multiple memory controller units, several PowerBus related on-chip communication elements, and a variety of high bandwidth I/O links. In the rest of this section, we'll focus on the macros involved on the path taken by memory requests starting at the L3 out to the chip memory I/O links. The major macros involved on this path are the PowerBus Ramp (PBIEX) which acts as an interface between the L3 and PowerBus, the PowerBus Unit (PBEH) which routes read and write requests and associated data to the correct memory controller unit (MCU) which buffers and frames the data of the memory requests and transmits and receives the requests on the I/O links. In each case, we propose and experiment with a drastic modeling abstraction by considering only four activity markers, namely: *reads, writes, retry* and *snoop* events. We show that for such uncore macros, this simple abstraction is sufficient in terms of achieving an average power modeling accuracy of 1.4-2.4%.

Figure 2 shows the POWER8[TM] chip photomicrograph with superimposed demarcations to indicate regions occupied by cores, L2/L3 caches, chip interconnect, memory controllers, etc. This chip has 12 cores with 8-way simultaneous multi-threading (SMT) per core. The total on-chip L2+L3 cache capacity is 102 MB. The chip was fabricated using a 22nm CMOS SOI technology, and has a die size of 649 mm^2, with 4.2 billion transistors [14]. Each core is an aggressive, wide-issue super scalar design, with 16 execution pipelines for massive data crunching. The uncore supports a massive 7.6 Tb/s off-chip bandwidth including memory and SMP links, PCIe links, an off-chip coherent accelerator interface, as well as on-chip bus-attached data accelerators, etc.

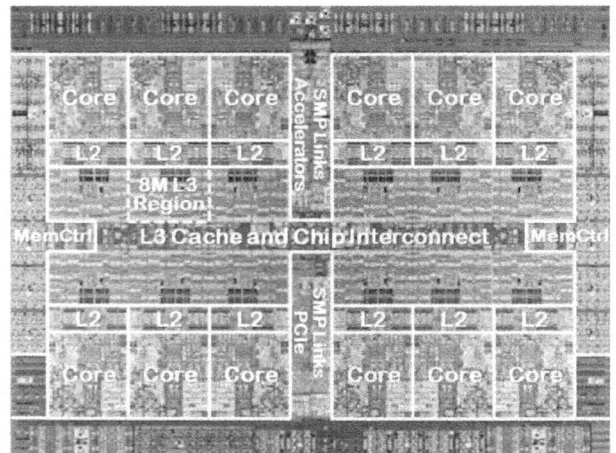

Figure 2. 12-core, 96-thread POWER8 microprocessor

Figure 3 provides a detailed block-diagram view of the chip, with clearly defined "uncore" elements (in blue). The processor "uncore" (in IBM terminology usually referred to as "nest") comprises of a 512KB private L2 per core, an 8 MB L3 instance per core – which adds up to 96 MB of L3 eDRAM cache for the chip. The so-called "memory stack" is separated into four on-chip memory controllers (MCU) each partitioned into two sub-controllers for a total of 8 memory I/O links and an off-chip Centaur L4 buffer chip per link. The on-chip interconnect, called PowerBus (PB) provides coherent communication support across the cache-memory subsystem. In this paper, we focus on the MCU, and key components within the PB namely, PBIEX and PBEH. The interface between the cores and the PowerBus is called the PBIEX (combination of PBI and PBEX depicted in Figure 3) and the actual

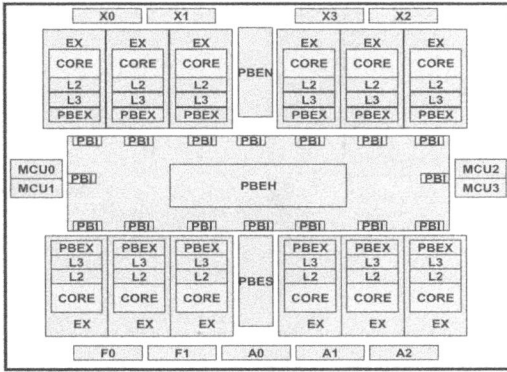

Figure 3. Block diagram view of the POWER8 chip

command and data transport layer is called the PBEH. Cache regions are known to be amenable to accurate power modeling in terms of activity abstractions and hence are not considered in the uncore modeling of this paper. We instead focus on the interconnect and I/O control interfaces which have not been examined in detail in prior power modeling abstraction studies.

3.1 Reference power for uncore macros

The detailed reference power model of Figure 1 can be abstracted along several dimensions: (a) the RTL simulator could be an early-stage microarchitecture-level pipeline timing model; (b) the application workload could be a suite of representative loop kernels; (c) the switching statistics could be reduced to a smaller subset; (d) the circuit-level detailed analysis could be approximated by area or gate count based analytical equations. In this paper, we focus our abstraction experiments to (b) and (c) above. That is, we retain the reference power tool chain in its detailed, accurate form, working with an RT-level cycle simulator that produces activity statistics as well as data switching factors (see Figure 4). The POWER8^{TM} design was supported by an extensive power modeling framework, centered on the reference power tool chain of Figure 1. In this framework clock and data switching factors are derived from chip level RTL simulation and applied to circuit level extracted C-effective values for each component of the chip to calculate the dynamic switching power to a high level of accuracy. Simulations of such large and detailed models are necessarily limited to a small number of simulated clock cycles due to simulation speed limitations. Power analysis of larger benchmarks therefore necessitates abstracted power models. Such abstraction can be performed by applying linear regression techniques to data points obtained from RTL simulations. The RTL simulations must thus provide power along with event counts for the set of high level events that are to be used in the context of the abstract model.

To obtain the data points needed to perform the regression analysis, a chip level POWER8^{TM} simulation model was built from the design RTL. An overview of the methodology used is shown in Figure 4. In this model the L2, L3, and the rest of the uncore and the Centaur buffer chips are represented by actual RTL while the 12 cores are represented by drivers that generate a programmable stream of L1-cache misses. We program the drivers to implement a set of read-only, write-only, and mixed read/write (similar to the application kernel called daxpy) streams.

The chip model is run for approximately 20,000 simulated clock cycles for each stream and clock and data switching is extracted

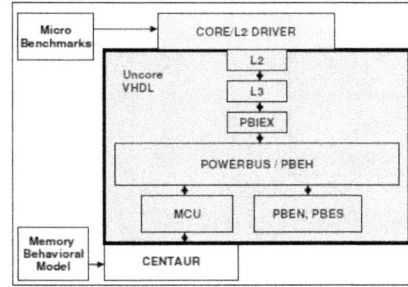

Figure 4. Uncore simulation environment

along with event counts for the high level events. We wish to apply a drastic abstraction in the number of high level event activities applied in the regression to make the abstract power model easily applicable in a variety of environments. In our case the monitored high level events are therefore only reads, writes, retries and snoops. The switching data is fed into a power tool that applies the per-net switching factors to the corresponding C-effectives for each macro in the chip design. The power values output by the tool along with the event counts are fed into a linear regression tool and the best fit is determined.

Since the RT-level simulator is very slow, there is a need to limit power analysis to small representative kernels. Table 1 describes the micro-benchmark characteristics that were used for modeling the uncore power. Each micro-benchmark has a certain number of cores performing reads, writes or a mixture thereof. The amount of address and data-switching is also varied to capture its impact on power. Each column in the table is one workload with varying number of cores, memory controllers (MCU), reads (RD), writes (WR) and data switching (DSW). This mix of benchmarks should sufficiently cover the behavior of the targeted uncore components even when some cores are power gated or MCUs are turned off.

Table 1. Characteristics of workloads used

Workload	W1	W2	W3	W4	W5	W6	W7	W8	W9	W10	W11	W12	W13	W14	W15	W16	W17
Cores	1	1	2	2	4	4	8	8	8	10	12	12	12	12	12	12	12
MCU	8	8	2	8	8	8	8	8	8	8	8	8	8	8	8	8	8
RD	Y	Y	Y	Y	Y	Y	N	Y	Y	N	Y	Y	Y	Y	Y	N	Y
WR	N	N	Y	Y	Y	N	Y	Y	N	Y	Y	N	N	N	N	Y	Y
DSW	Y	N	Y	Y	Y	Y	Y	Y	N	N	Y	Y	N	N	N	Y	Y

3.2 Modeled uncore units

3.2.1 Power Bus Ramp

The Power Bus Ramp (PBIEX) is the interface between a chiplet and the Power Bus Unit. The PBIEX buffers memory requests initiated by the L3 upon a cache miss or flush event until the Power Bus is available. As each chiplet can vary its voltage and frequency dynamically, the PBIEX also acts as an asynchronous interface and voltage translator between each chiplet and the rest of the uncore. Since the main responsibility of the PBIEX is to send and receive memory requests to the power bus unit PBEH, the activity of a PBIEX instance is foremost determined by the read and writes bandwidth to and from its associated chiplet. However, the PBIEX must also handle coherence requests on the Power Bus. The PBIEX activity is thus further determined by snooping activity resulting from reads and writes originating from other chiplets.

As illustrated by Figure 5, it is evident that a good regression fit can be obtained even when drastically cutting the number of independent variables down to as little as three (reads, writes, snoops) for which the worst case model error is 5.9% and average

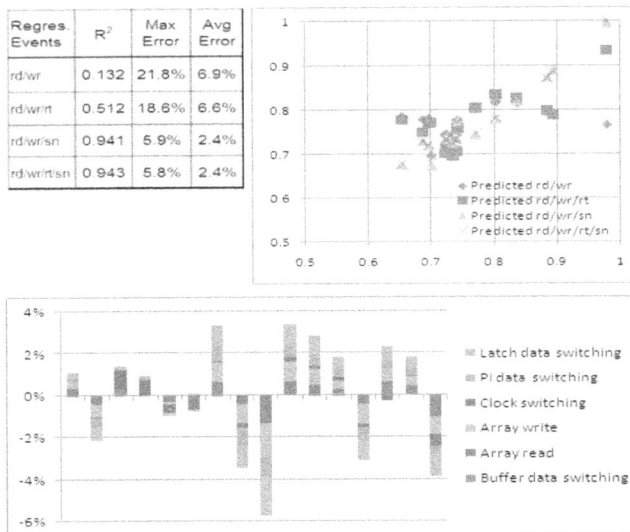

Regres. Events	R^2	Max Error	Avg Error
rd/wr	0.132	21.8%	6.9%
rd/wr/rt	0.512	18.6%	6.6%
rd/wr/sn	0.941	5.9%	2.4%
rd/wr/rt/sn	0.943	5.8%	2.4%

Figure 5. PBIEX regression statistics and predicted vs. actual power scatter plot for four different combinations of events (rd=reads, wr=writes, rt=retries, sn=snoops) and bar graph showing error sources for predicted power for each workload

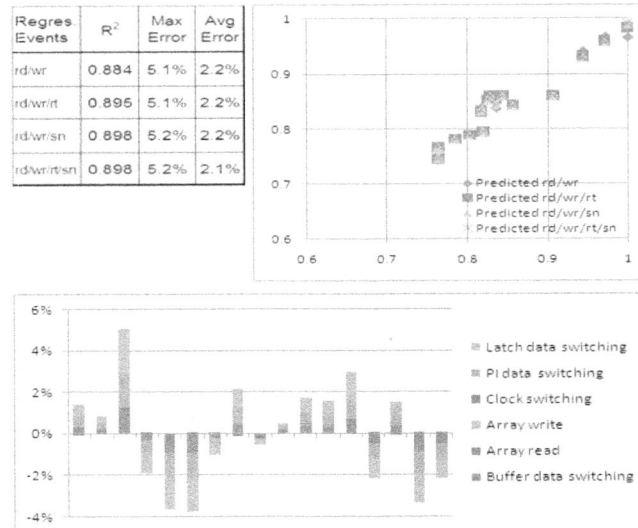

Regres. Events	R^2	Max Error	Avg Error
rd/wr	0.884	5.1%	2.2%
rd/wr/rt	0.895	5.1%	2.2%
rd/wr/sn	0.898	5.2%	2.2%
rd/wr/rt/sn	0.898	5.2%	2.1%

Figure 6. PBEH regression statistics and predicted vs. actual power scatter plot for four different combinations of events (rd=reads, wr=writes, rt=retries, sn=snoops) and bar graph showing error sources for predicted power for each workload

error is only 2.4%. The PBIEX is heavily dependent on the snoop event to get a good regression fit. This is evident by the well-centered green triangle and cross points of the scatter plot in Figure 5 as compared to the rather scattered blue diamonds and red box points of the two regressions that do not contain the snoop event. As part of the analysis we also explored the power sensitivity to data switching as this impacts the accuracy of the abstract model. A read stream with minimum address and data switching was therefore compared to a read stream with maximum address and data switching. The difference in power for the PBIEX unit was only 2.2%. This validates that the PBIEX model can be built with acceptable accuracy even when events expressing the address and data patterns are not obtainable.

To figure out where the errors of the regression model come from we take advantage of the unique features of the detailed uncore power modeling framework which allows us to break down the sources of errors by performing separate regressions on each available power type of the unit such as clock, buffer, data switching and array read and write power. The bar graph in Figure 5 shows the breakdown of the sources of errors of the PBIEX regression model for each of the workloads. It is interesting to note that for the PBIEX there is virtually no cancellation effect (positive errors cancelling out negative errors) to mitigate the prediction errors. It can furthermore be noted that the clock switching power is very accurately captured by the model with very small errors. As expected, since none of the events used to form the regression model capture address- or data-bit switching, the errors of the model are dominated by data switching dependent on latch outputs and primary input (PI) nets of unit macros as well as array reads and writes that include data switching internal to the arrays.

3.2.2 Power Bus Unit

The Power Bus Unit (PBEH) is the routing fabric between each chiplet and the memory and network controllers. The PBEH performs coherency checks on each memory request received from the chiplets. Each L3 cache miss results in the PBEH broadcasting a request to each chiplet to check whether some other L3 contains

the requested cache line. If not, the request is forwarded to the correct memory controller. Since the main responsibility of the PBEH is to communicate coherence requests and responses between chiplets as well as memory requests to and from the MCU, the activity of the PBEH is foremost determined by the read and writes bandwidth of the chip as well as coherence requests and responses on the Power Bus.

As illustrated in Figure 6, the PBEH is only dependent on the read and write events to get a good regression fit. The worst case error, when using only these two events, is 5.1% and the average error is 2.2%. The difference between read streams with minimum and maximum address and data switching in the PBEH unit was 8.6%. This sensitivity to address and data switching was not unexpected for a unit that consists mainly of long and wide buses. While the effect of address and data switching is notable for this unit it is certainly not excessive and is within an acceptable range for a high level abstract model. As a mitigating factor, the centering of the regression model also ensures that the max error does not exceed 5.1% (of the workloads tested). The bar graph in Figure 6 breaks down the error sources of the PBEH regression model. Similar to the PBIEX there is no cancellation effect to mitigate the errors for PBEH. The errors of the PBEH model are dominated by data switching dependent on latch outputs, primary inputs, and buffers as expected from a bus dominated unit. Error from clock switching is very low for this unit as it has predictable utilization behavior.

3.2.3 Memory Controller Unit

The memory Controller Unit (MCU) is the interface between the PBEH and the high speed serial I/O links going to and from memory. Each request is assembled into a transmission frame and sent over the link. The MCU buffers each request until the read data or write acknowledge is returned from memory. Since the main responsibility of the MCU is to handle requests to and from memory, the activity of the MCU is foremost determined by the read and write bandwidth of the PBEH. However, the MCU must also reject a request if it cannot handle more requests due to full buffers. Such rejections result in requests being tried again and this

Regres. Events	R^2	Max Error	Avg Error
rd/wr	0.943	6.1%	1.9%
rd/wr/rt	0.962	6.0%	1.5%
rd/wr/sn	0.964	5.9%	1.4%
rd/wr/rt/sn	0.966	5.9%	1.4%

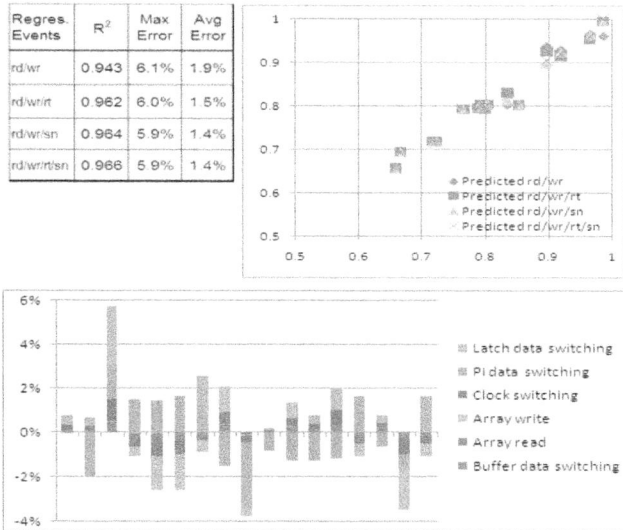

Figure 7. MCU regression statistics and predicted vs. actual power scatter plot for four different combinations of events (rd=reads, wr=writes, rt=retries, sn=snoops) and bar graph showing error sources for predicted power for each workload

can amount to a number of retries being performed in situations of very high bandwidth utilization.

The activity of the MCU is therefore also dependent on the number of such retries. As illustrated in Figure 7 the MCU is mainly dependent on the read and write events to get a good regression fit although adding retries and snoops can improve the fit a bit further. The worst case error when using all four events is 5.9% and the average error is 1.4%. The difference between read streams with minimum and maximum address and data switching in the MCU unit was 7% which we deem as acceptable. The bar graph in Figure 7 shows that there are clear error cancellation effects that help mitigate the prediction errors for the MCU. The errors of the MCU model are dominated by data switching dependent on latch outputs and primary inputs. Errors from clock switching and array power are low for this unit as its utilization behavior can be accurately captured by the regression events. Buffer power errors are also low as the unit does not contain a significant amount of buffers.

3.3 Regression model conclusions

The breakdown of error contributors to the uncore unit regression models indicate that the utilization of the units, captured by the clock switching power, is modeled very accurately even with the very few (four) event markers used. The error breakdown analysis clearly points out that any work to refine the models further should be focused on providing events that capture the degree of bit switching on addresses and data that move through the uncore units. However, in light of what has been learned from the < 9% power difference observed for the minimum vs. maximum address and data switching workloads and the < 6% maximum errors of the regression models, we argue that the models are sufficiently accurate for the abstract level at which they are intended to be used.

4. ILLUSTRATIVE USE OF ABSTRACT POWER MODELS

One of the key uses of abstract, analytically formulated power models of the type discussed in this paper is the ability to assist in making correct decisions in the choice of early-stage microarchitectural parameters e.g. the sizes of various queues, caches and other buffers, or even higher level decisions: e.g. number of cores, superscalar width, pipeline depth, number of memory controllers and various other bandwidth or latency parameters. An abstract modeling toolset for the core-uncore combination for a given chip is of great assistance in making early-stage choices for a follow-on chip in the same family. For microarchitectural scaling of this type, prior work [11] has described such capabilities with regard to core power models.

Another use of such power model abstractions is in the definition of so-called digital power proxies [20]. These are activity counter based hardware power "sensors" that may be used in energy accounting for billing purposes, or for chip-wide power management. In the latter instance, per-core or per-chiplet power estimates are needed in order to "shift" power between cores to maximize chip throughput performance without violating chip peak power limits. Without an uncore power proxy, the dynamic power management policy has to conservatively estimate a constant, high power level for the uncore which would reduce the opportunity for maximizing performance/watt at the chip level. Based on the power analysis work in Section 3 of this paper along with additional I/O models we have calculated that adding an uncore power proxy to a POWER8[TM] chip, would improve the accuracy of chip power estimation by 15% compared to a baseline where only core, L2 and L3 level power proxies [20] are present with the rest of the uncore elements lumped into a constant worst-case power value. For scenarios where the uncore is largely idle this could translate to an opportunity to boost the frequency by at least 5% for a given chip power cap assuming chip-wide DVFS. With *per-core* DVFS control and the ability to shift power across core domains, the boost in performance could be much higher.

Yet another use of an acceptably accurate abstract uncore power model is in the task of predicting the trends of several important metrics: power density, bandwidth-limited growth in the number of cores or maximum inductive noise, etc. with the evolution of technology nodes. Realistic, application-driven power estimation is key to predicting trends with relative accuracy. Let us consider the challenge of quantifying the maximum voltage noise trend in future multi-core processors. Voltage noise (ΔV) adds non-determinism to the supply voltage (V) that powers on-chip circuits in a microprocessor. For a given operating clock frequency level, f (which corresponds to a worst-case path delay within any given pipeline stage of the processor), there is a minimum supply voltage level $V_{min}(f)$ below which the processor would fail because of circuit timing violation. Let us assume that the worst-case power consumption of the chip is P and that the fraction of power in the cores is C regardless of technology node. Assume further that the cores can be power-gated off when not in use, while the uncore elements always burn a constant, worst-case power. Let us assume that with technology scaling, the supply voltage scales down by a factor of S in each step of such scaling, causing a factor S increase in supply current at fixed P which leads to (max-$\Delta V/V$) increasing by a factor of S^2 for each technology step. Figure 8 shows the worst-case progression of (max-$\Delta V/V$) as a function of technology nodes, under the assumptions stated above, and specifically for the case C=0.5, and for values of S = 0.85, 0.90 and 0.95. Note that we have not shown the case for the Dennard-regime scaling factor S = 0.7, since voltages are not likely to scale per Dennard-prescribed rate any more. From Figure 8, we see that for the reasonably

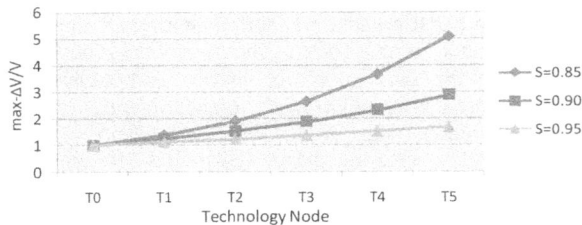

Figure 8. Progression of (max-ΔV/V) with technology node, relative to current node (T0).

realistic assumption of S = 0.85, the (max-ΔV)/V is expected to increase by a factor of 5 within the next five technology nodes; and, even with a more conservative S=0.9, the factor of increase is 3. The above analysis is conservative, assuming worst-case (maximum) power for cores and uncore – leading to a maximum (fixed) chip power of P. With core and uncore abstract (analytical) power models, one can capture the worst-case (peak) and best-case (minimum) chip power much more accurately – and project the trend forward accordingly. With workload-driven analytical power models one can show that the 5X and 3X conservative bounds in Figure 8 can be trimmed down to more realistic 3.5X and 2X bounds (respectively) for realistic core centric workloads.

5. SUMMARY AND CONCLUSIONS

With the escalating core count trend and its inherent increase in uncore complexity and focus on dynamic power management of uncore components, accurate modeling of uncore power and identification of power reduction opportunities in the uncore elements is a critical aspect of future power-efficient micro-processor design. In this paper, we present a practical methodology for use in an industrial setting for deriving abstract analytical power models for selected key uncore elements within a state-of-the-art server-class processor chip. We show that even with very few power event markers and a small set of stressmarks, it is possible to develop accurate regression-based analytical power models for the uncore elements of a modern chip with average power prediction errors as low as 1.4%-2.4%. We further quantify the accuracy impact such abstract power models have in providing improved power proxies for power shifting and in predicting worst-case bounds on chip level inductive noise in future technologies.

Acknowledgements

This work is sponsored, in part, by Defense Advanced Research Projects Agency, Microsystems Technology Office (MTO), under contract no. HR0011-13-C-0022. The views expressed are those of the authors and do not reflect the official policy or position of the Department of Defense or the U.S. Government. This document is: Approved for Public Release, Distribution Unlimited.

6. REFERENCES

[1] Brooks, D., et al. 2000. Power-Aware Microarchitecture: Design and Modeling Challenges for Next-Generation Microprocessors. IEEE Micro 20(6): 26-44 (2000).

[2] Brooks, D., Timari, V., Martonosi, M. 2000. Wattch: a framework for architectural level power analysis and optimization. In Proc. of Int'l. Symp. on Computer Architecture (ISCA), June 2000.

[3] Vijaykrishnan, N., et al. 2000. Energy-driven integrated hardware-software optimization using SimplePower, In Proc. of 27th ISCA, pp. 95-106, June 2000.

[4] Cai, G. and Lim, C.H. 1999. Architectural level power/performance optimization and dynamic power estimation. In Proc. of Cool Chips Tutorial collocated with MICRO, Nov. 1999.

[5] Dhodapkar, A., Lim, C.H. and Cai, G. 2000. Tempest: a thermal enabled multi-model power/performance estimator. In Proc. of Power-Aware Computer System (PACS) Workshop, Nov. 2000.

[6] Brooks, D., et al. 2003. New methodology for early-stage microarchitecture-level power-performance analysis of microprocessors. IBM Journal of R&D, 47 (Sep. 2003), pp. 653-670.

[7] Zyuban, V., et al. 2004. Integrated analysis of power and performance for pipelined microprocessors. IEEE Trans. Computers 53(8): 1004-1016 (2004)

[8] Palacharla, S., Jouppi, N., Smith, J. E. 2007. Complexity-effective superscalar processors. In Proc. of 24th. Int'l. Symp. on Computer Architecture (ISCA) June 2007.

[9] Albonesi, A. et al. 2003. Dynamically Tuning Processor Resources with Adaptive Processing. IEEE Computer 36(12): 49-58 (2003).

[10] Hu, Z., Buyuktosunoglu, A., Srinivasan, V., Zyuban, V., Jacobson, H. M., Bose, P. 2004. Microarchitectural techniques for power gating of execution units. In Proc. Int'l. Symp. on Low Power Electronics and Design (ISLPED), 2004, pp. 32-37.

[11] Jacobson, H., Buyuktosunoglu, A., Bose, P., Acar, E., Eickemeyer, R. 2011. Abstraction and Microarchitecture Scaling in Early-Stage Power Modeling. In Proc. Int'l. Symp. on High Performance Computer Architecture (HPCA), 2011, pp. 396-405.

[12] Zyuban, V. et al. 2011. Power Optimization methodology for the IBM POWER7 microprocessor. IBM Journal of R&D, vol. 55, no. 3, May/June 2011.

[13] Powell, M.D., et al. 2009. CAMP: A technique to estimate per-structure power at run-time using a few simple parameters. In Proc. 15th Int'l. Symp. on High-Performance Computer Architecture (HPCA-2009).

[14] Fluhr, E.J., et al. 2014. POWER8: A server-class processor in 22nm SOI with 7.6 Tb/s off-chip bandwidth. In Proc. Int'l Solid State Circuits Conference (ISSCC), Feb. 2014.

[15] Lefurgy, C. et al. 2011. Active management of timing guardband to save energy in POWER7. In Proc. Int'l. Symp. on Microarchitecture (MICRO-44), December 2011.

[16] Dhanwada, N., et al. 2013. Efficient PVT independent abstraction of large IP blocks for hierarchical power analysis, In Proc. Int'l Conference on Computer-Aided Design (ICCAD), pp.458-465, 18-21 Nov. 2013.

[17] Taylor, S. 2012. POWER7+™: IBM's next generation POWER microprocessor, Hot Chips 24, 2012.

[18] Dhanwada, N., et al. 2012. Leakage Power Contributor Modeling, Design & Test of Computers, IEEE , vol.29, no.2, pp.71-78, April 2012.

[19] Zyuban, V., et al. 2013. IBM POWER7+ design for higher frequency at fixed power, IBM Journal of Research and Development, vol.57, no.6, pp.1:1,1:18, Nov.-Dec. 2013.

[20] Floyd, M. et al. 2011. Introducing the adaptive energy management features of the POWER7 chip, IEEE Micro, vol. 31, no. 2, March/April 2011.

Content-Driven Memory Pressure Balancing and Video Memory Power Management for Parallel High Efficiency Video Coding

Felipe Sampaio[1], Muhammad Shafique[2], Bruno Zatt[3], Sergio Bampi[1], Jörg Henkel[2]

[1]Informatics Institute, PPGC, Federal University of Rio Grande do Sul (UFRGS), Brazil
[2]Chair for Embedded Systems (CES), Karlsruhe Institute of Technology (KIT), Germany
[3]GACI, PPGC, CDTec, Federal University of Pelotas (UFPel), Brazil
{felipe.sampaio, bampi}@inf.ufrgs.br, bzatt@inf.ufpel.edu.br, {muhammad.shafique, henkel}@kit.edu

ABSTRACT

We present a novel content-driven memory pressure balancing and video memory power management scheme for parallel High Efficiency Video Coding (HEVC). The key is to leverage the application-specific knowledge to balance the (instant) access pressure on Scratchpad-based Video Memories (SVMs) for parallelized video processing. Our scheme accurately predicts the memory requirements of each processing core based on monitored memory usage and leverages this knowledge to perform a categorization of different video regions. Afterwards, it employs an adaptive policy for memory pressure balancing by rescheduling encoding of different video blocks based on their categories. This balancing also facilitates our scheme to perform efficient power-gating of unused parts of SVMs. Experimental results show that our scheme reduces the variations in the memory pressure by 37%-83% when compared to the traditional raster scan processing for 4- and 16-core parallelized HEVC encoder. Our content-driven power management saves 56% (on average) of SVM leakage energy.

Categories and Subject Descriptors

C.3 [**Special-Purpose and Application-Based Systems**]: Real-time and embedded systems; B.3.2 [**Design Styles**]: Cache memories

Keywords

On-chip memory; memory pressure reduction; application-specific optimization; HEVC; adaptivity; power management; low-power.

1. INTRODUCTION AND RELATED WORK

Parallelization of video processing applications under stringent energy budget is a significant challenge for the next-generation embedded manycore multimedia systems. Moreover, the memory hierarchy consumes a significant portion of the chip footprint and power/energy in such systems. Meeting these constraints becomes quite intricate when considering the escalating complexity of emerging video coding standards, like HEVC [1].

The *High Efficiency Video Coding* (HEVC) standard [1] aims at providing 2x higher compression efficiency compared to that of the state-of-the-art H.264/AVC standard. To achieve this, HEVC introduces novel data structures and coding tools that increase the computational effort by 40% and memory requirements by >2x compared to H.264/AVC (see Figure 1a). To alleviate this increased computation, HEVC provides parallelization support in form of *Video Tiles* that are independently processed on different cores. However, this further complicates the memory design in an embedded multimedia system through the following means: (1) More on-chip video memories are required to feed the processing

ISLPED'14, August 11 - 13 2014, La Jolla, CA, USA
Copyright 2014 ACM 978-1-4503-2975-0/14/08…$15.00.
http://dx.doi.org/10.1145/2627369.2627615

cores that incur an increase in the leakage and dynamic energy. (2) External memory pressure is increased since multiple cores try to access the data at the same time, thus also leading to an increase in the off-chip energy. Moreover, the number of scenarios with unbalanced memory pressure may increase due to the run-time variation of the video content (as shown in Figure 1b) that lead to high instant power dissipation and may surpass the maximum available memory bandwidth. Therefore, *it is crucial to balance the memory pressure while performing efficient power management of video memories in parallel HEVC encoding*.

Recently, the use of scratchpad memories has proliferated in the manycore systems (like in IBM Cell [10]) as power-efficient on-chip memories to complement or replace large-sized shared caches [8]. The scratchpad memories avoid energy overhead of tags and write replacement management to provide >30% energy reduction compared to a full cache design [8]. Power efficient management of these scratchpad memories is of key importance. External memory pressure and on-chip scratchpad memory management for high-performance manycore systems have been explored in [12][13]. However, these works do not account for the application-specific properties, thus may not be efficiently employed for on-chip video memories. From the application-driven perspective, several works proposed dedicated power management schemes for video encoding regarding both off-/on-chip video memories [2]-[4]. However, these works lack support for *parallel* HEVC video encoding and corresponding memory constraints. Therefore, these techniques may perform inefficient under scenarios with (1) unbalanced memory pressure during parallel HEVC encoding (as we motivate in Section 1.2); and (2) simultaneously accessed multiple on-chip memories.

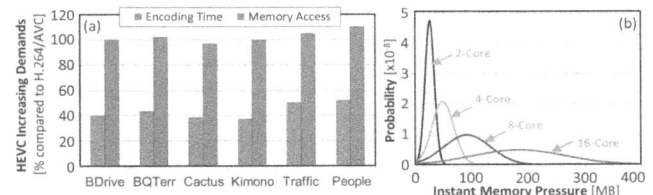

Figure 1. (a) HEVC increasing demands compared to H.264/AVC (b) memory pressure Probability Density Function for *BasketballDrive*.

Summarizing, *the challenge is to obtain balanced pressure for off- and on-chip memories based on multiple Scratchpad-based Video Memories (SVMs) used by different Video Tiles in parallel HEVC encoding and to provide efficient SVM power management by exploiting this knowledge .*

Before proceeding further, we first provide preliminaries of HEVC.

1.1 HEVC Preliminaries

The HEVC introduces the *Coding-Tree Unit* (CTU, e.g., a 64x64 block) as a basic encoding entity within a video frame. The CTU is divided using a recursive splitting into blocks of NxN or 2Nx2N sizes (e.g., 32x32, 16x16 and so on) [1]. An example partitioning is shown in Figure 2b. The Motion Estimation is performed for all possible blocks. For each block it searches for the most similar block within a *search window* in one or more reference frames (i.e. already encoded and reconstructed frames).

The search window is defined as the maximum range of motion search in both horizontal and vertical directions. This motion search process for multiple blocks may consume up to 90% of the total HEVC encoding energy [2]. Besides CTUs, HEVC supports rectangular *Video Tiles* (each containing multiple CTU) that can be processed in parallel without any data dependency [7]. Figure 2a presents an example of a 2x2 Video Tiles configuration (4-Tile scenario) for a video frame with 8x4 CTUs.

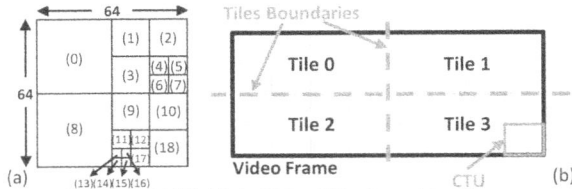

**Figure 2. (a) Multiple Video Tiles in a video frame;
(b) An example CTU partitioning.**

1.2 Motivational Case Studies

We have performed an experimental analysis (see experimental setup in Section 4) for (1) memory pressure and access imbalance when processing multiple Video Tiles concurrently; (2) memory pressure and access correlations; and (3) Intra-Video Tile access behavior. These analyses provide a foundation for our novel contributions.

1) Memory Pressure Analysis: We define memory pressure as the memory access requirement caused by a CTU processing during a specific time. When considering multiple processing cores, the memory pressure may be (1) core-specific, or (2) accumulated (sum of all core-specific pressures). Typically, the motion estimation is performed in the traditional raster scan order (i.e., from top-left to bottom-right corner in row-by-row order). However, this may lead to unbalanced external memory pressure, as depicted in the 4-Tile example of Figure 3a. The maximum and minimum memory pressure peaks can be seen in Figure 3b. There are significant memory access variations compared to the average access case (that typically does not happen). This unbalanced memory pressure leads to high power peak dissipations and high instant memory bandwidth requirements, which may surpass the maximum availability constraints. Moreover, such unbalancing also leads to inefficient memory power management due to (1) fluctuations in the sleep durations, (2) frequent P_{ON}-P_{OFF} switching, and (3) memory usage prediction errors due to sudden access variations. Therefore, *the key is to leverage application specific-properties to adapt and re-schedule the CTU processing in order to achieve the best possible memory pressure balancing.*

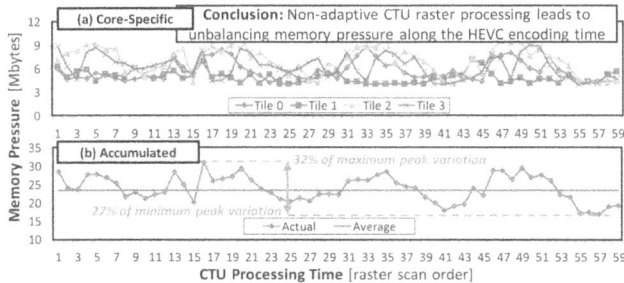

Figure 3. Memory pressure for (a) each processing core; and (b) accumulated and average cases for *BasketballDrive*.

2) Spatial/Temporal Neighboring Analysis: If it is possible to accurately predict the memory requirements for a given CTU, it can be exploited by a power manager to balance the memory pressure in a very efficient way. In case of high frame rates (30-60 fps), significant temporal correlation exists, i.e. the neighboring frames have similar memory access behavior, as depicted in Figure 4. Additionally, high video frame resolutions (e.g., FullHD=1920x1080 to 4K=3840x2160) increase the spatial correlations between

neighboring CTUs within the same frame. Furthermore, we can note that the memory pressure for each CTU also depends upon their corresponding video content characteristic (like texture and motion content). Therefore, *the key is to leverage the knowledge from the monitored memory pressure of spatially- and temporally-neighboring CTUs to obtain a high quality prediction of the actual memory pressure for a given CTU.*

3) Intra-Video Tile Memory Analysis: While balancing the memory pressure is important from the external memory perspective, it is also crucial to take care of the core-private on-chip SVMs. In this case, long sleep durations (and consequently more leakage energy savings) can be achieved by consecutively encoding CTUs with similar video content properties (like texture and motion), thus similar memory pressure. Figure 5 shows Video Tiles with *less* memory requirements (like Video Tile 1) and *more* memory demands (like Video Tile 2). In this case, longer sleep durations and higher energy savings can be obtained for the SVM of core processing the Video Tile 1. Furthermore, re-scheduled CTU processing orders for a well-balanced memory pressure tends to group similar properties CTUs to be consecutively encoded, providing even higher sleep durations (as we will demonstrate in Section 3). Hence, the *key challenge here is how to leverage the CTU re-schedule for memory pressure balancing and increased sleep durations for efficient SVM power management.*

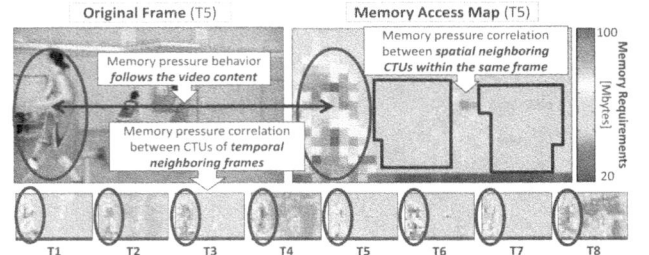

Figure 4. Video content and neighborhood correlation analysis for *BasketballDrive* test sequence.

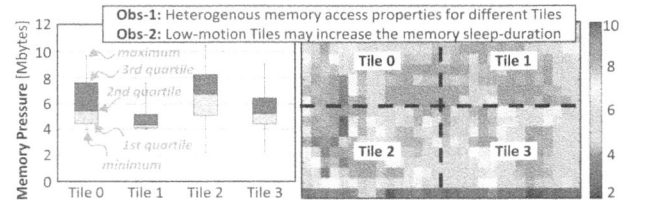

Figure 5. Intra-Tile memory pressure analysis for *BasketballDrive*.

The goal of our work is *to leverage application-specific properties for memory pressure balancing and SVM's leakage energy reduction targeting parallelized HEVC encoding.*

1.3 Our Novel Contributions

We propose content-driven memory pressure balancing along with SVM power management for HEVC parallelized on manycore processors. The key is to leverage the memory access correlation *within* and *across* different Video Tiles (i.e. Intra- and Inter- Video Tile correlation). Our scheme employs:

- **A Memory Pressure Prediction Algorithm (Section 2.1)** that leverages the monitored memory pressure of Video Tiles in the previously encoded CTUs in order to accurately predict the memory requirements for Video Tiles in the current frame.

- **Run-Time Statistics-Based CTU Memory Classification (Section 2.2)** that dynamically adapts the parameters involved in our memory power management scheme according to the predicted memory pressure statistics.

- **CTU Re-Scheduling for Memory Pressure Balancing (Section 2.3)** our scheme groups the CTUs of a *Video Tile* into variable-size groups (called CTU-groups). The size of the CTU-groups depends on the Video Tile-specific motion activity properties. Depending upon the predicted memory pressure, we schedule the CTU-groups to closely meet the target pressure.

- **Content-Driven Power Management of SVMs (Section 3):** since the CTU-groups may also exhibit similar properties blocks, our scheme analyzes the predicted memory usage of different CTU to increase the potential of the sleep-duration of different SVM regions and thereby increasing the leakage energy savings.

To the best of authors' knowledge, this is the first work towards *managing the memory pressure in parallel video processing* that exploits the video content properties and memory access correlation.

1.4 Overview of Our Memory System

Figure 6 depicts the overall system with our content-driven memory power management. To support HEVC encoding parallelized using *n* Video Tiles, our system has (1) a multicore processor with *n* cores and (2) a memory infrastructure containing *n* SVMs, such that every core has its private on-chip SVM for search window storage used during the motion estimation process. The SVMs are connected to the external memory by data/address bus interfaces. Our content-driven memory pressure balancing scheme is composed of the following three modules: (a) memory pressure prediction, (b) run-time statistics-based CTU memory classification, and (c) CTU re-scheduling for memory pressure balancing. Furthermore, our memory management system also employs a content-driven power management of SVMs. It leverages the run-time statistical analysis performed by (a) and (b). A memory monitoring unit feeds the statistics about the current memory requirements to our system.

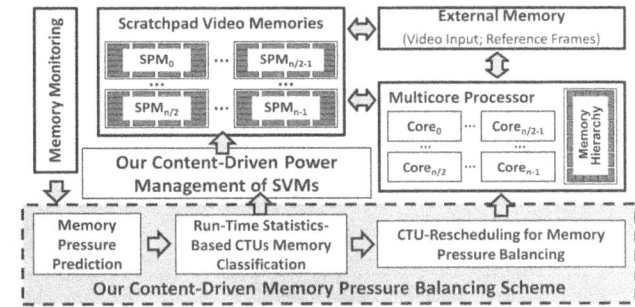

Figure 6. n-Tile HEVC encoding system with our application-specific memory power management scheme.

Although traditional scratchpad memories require programmer driven control, recent works have demonstrated run-time management of these memories where data allocation is managed by a virtual manager, like [8][9]. In our case, instead of explicitly passing the control to the programmer, we have an application-specific hardware management of these SVMs (which is much simpler compared to the management circuitry of cache memories).

2. CONTENT-DRIVEN MEMORY PRESSURE BALANCING SCHEME

2.1 Memory Pressure Prediction

As demonstrated in Section 1.2, highly correlated memory pressure may exist (1) among spatial neighboring CTUs (within the same frame); and (2) among CTUs of temporal neighboring frames. Therefore, based on the actual memory usage of previously processed CTUs (*ActualMem*), our prediction algorithm estimates the memory requirements of the CTUs in the current frame[1]. Figure 7 depicts an example of used CTU predictors in the current and reference frames. Four spatial predictors from the current frame and nine temporal predictors from each reference frame are selected as input to a

weighted prediction. Eq. (1)-(2) presents the spatial and temporal predictors selected for a given CTU: $Pred_{Temp}$ and $Pred_{Spatial}$, respectively. The letters *A-M* correspond to the spatial and temporal predictors depicted in Figure 7. As statistical parameters for the prediction, we apply different weighting factors[2] according to the spatial location of the predictor related to the current CTU position. Possible cases of CTU position are: center (α_C), horizontal/vertical (α_A), and diagonal (α_D). Eq. (3)-(5) present the weighted prediction formula for predicting the memory pressure considering a given CTU. The weighting factors were statistically generated based on the memory access correlations of real video test sequences. First, the predicted memory pressure considering only the temporal references is estimated: $PredMem_{Temp}$ in Eq. (3). Then, the spatial predictors are used to calculate the $PredMem_{Spatial}$, as in Eq. (4). Finally, both spatial and temporal predictions are used to derive the predicted memory pressure for the given CTU: $PredMem$ in Eq. (5).

$$Pred_{Temp}(F_{Ref}) := WP(ActualMem(F_{Ref}[A...I]), [\alpha_C, \alpha_A, \alpha_D]) \quad (1)$$

$$Pred_{Spatial} := WP(ActualMem(F_{Curr}[J...M]), [\alpha_A, \alpha_D]) \quad (2)$$

$$PredMem_{Temp} = \sum_{\forall F_{Ref}} \left\{ \left[\sum_{P_T \in Pred_{Temp}(F_{Ref})} (P_T) \right] * \frac{1}{D[F_{Ref}]} \right\} \quad (3)$$

$$PredMem_{Spatial} = \sum_{P_S \in Pred_{Spatial}} (P_S) \quad (4)$$

$$PredMem(CTU) = WP(PredMem_{Temp}, PredMem_{Spatial}, [\alpha_S, \alpha_T]) \quad (5)$$

When some predictors are unavailable (e.g., in case of CTUs at the frame boundaries) the weighted prediction is performed only with the available predictors.

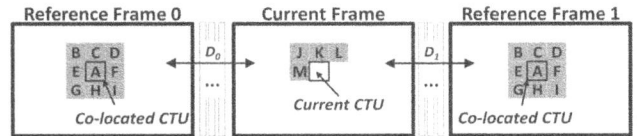

Figure 7. Example: spatial and temporal predictors selecting.

The predicted memory requirements of the CTUs need to be analyzed to classify each video frame, Video Tile and CTU-groups to characterize their memory access behavior.

2.2 Run-Time Statistics-Based CTU Memory Classification

As motivated in Section 1.2, in order to avoid the memory pressure imbalance problem of traditional raster scan order processing, our scheme re-schedules the order of CTU evaluations for motion estimation. To achieve this, our scheme partitions the CTUs of a Video Tile into so-called *CTU-groups*, which are rectangular regions of CTUs such that, all CTUs of a given CTU-group are processed consequently; see an example in Figure 8. The goal is to assign CTUs with similar memory requirements/pressure into one group while balancing the overall memory pressure of Video Tiles.

Figure 8. Example: CTU-groups division for re-scheduling.

The memory access distribution follows specific properties (i.e., motion and texture) of each video sequence. Hence, we use the video

---

[1] A current frame refers to the frame being encoded at that moment.

[2] Statistically defined parameters using the experimental methodology described in Section 4: α_C=0.5, α_A=0.3, α_D=0.2, α_S=0.5 and α_T=0.5.

properties to decide the number of CTU-groups. Our scheme adapts the number of CTU-groups at frame level according to the predicted memory access distribution of Video Tiles. At first, a base number of groups is defined, N_B in Eq. (6). It is based on the Probability Density Function (PDF) of the predicted memory pressures at frame level (μ_F is the average, σ_F is the standard deviation) and the average number of CTUs per Video Tile ($N_{CTUPerTile}$). Later on, we define the actual number of groups for each Video Tile (N_G in Eq. (7)) by comparing the predicted memory access distribution of a given Video Tile (μ_T, σ_T) with that of the with the overall frame. Video Tiles with spread memory pressure distributions are divided into more CTU-groups to enable fine-grained management (first clause of Eq. (7)). The goal is to have a fine-grain management because we may have very diverse memory behaviors within a Video Tile. In contrast, Video Tiles with concentrated memory pressure distribution (second clause of Eq. (7)) lead to few (but large-sized) CTU-groups as their texture and motion properties tend to be correlated inside such a Video Tile. The decision of having smaller CTU-groups must be carefully taken because the SVM data reuse among adjacent CTUs is not available between each CTU-group processing, causing efficiency loss in the SVM data management. Due to the CTU order inside one CTU-group (see Figure 8), the SVMs are more efficient for large-groups.

$$N_B = \lceil (\sigma_F/\mu_F)\, N_{CTUPerTile} \rceil \qquad (6)$$
where: $\{\mu_F, \sigma_F\} = PDF(PredMem(CTU)|\forall\, CTU \in Frame\, F)$

$$N_G(T) = \begin{cases} (\sigma_T > \sigma_F),[N_B + [(\sigma_T/\mu_T)-(\sigma_F/\mu_F)]N_{CTUPerTile}] \\ (\sigma_T \le \sigma_F),[N_B - [(\sigma_F/\mu_F)-(\sigma_T/\mu_T)]N_{CTUPerTile}] \end{cases} \qquad (7)$$

Where: $\{\mu_T, \sigma_T\} = PDF(PredMem(CTU)|\forall\, CTU \in Video\, Tile\, T)$

The predicted memory pressure distribution is used to classify the Video Tile in terms of motion property. By comparing the average behavior of each Video Tile-specific distribution to the overall frame distribution, Eq. (8) defines three categories: *H-type* (high motion), *M-type* (medium motion), and *L-type* (low motion). Moreover, each CTU-group also has its own PDF (given in Eq. (9)) that will be used for the re-scheduling decision during the memory pressure balancing.

$$C_{Tile}(T) = \begin{cases} (\mu_T \ge \mu_F + 0.5\sigma_F),(H)\ High \\ (\mu_F + 0.5\sigma_F > \mu_T > \mu_F - 0.5\sigma_F),(M)\ Medium \\ (\mu_F + 0.5\sigma_F > \mu_T),(L)\ Low \end{cases} \qquad (8)$$

$$\{\mu_G, \sigma_G\} = PDF(PredMem(CTU)|\forall\, CTU \in CTUgroup\, G) \qquad (9)$$

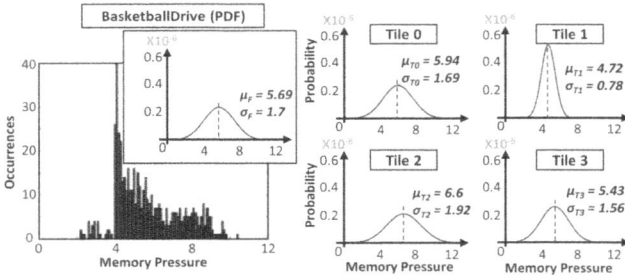

Figure 9. Memory pressure statistics for each Video Tile of the *BasketballDrive* test sequence (PDFs and histogram).

An Example: Figure 9 presents the run-time statistics of the predicted memory pressure of a frame in the HD1080 *BasketballDrive* video encoded with 4-Tiles. The N_{Base} value, which is only dependent on the overall frame statistics, is calculated using Eq. (6), i.e. $N_{Base}=6$. Using Eq. (7), the number of CTU-groups at is calculated: $N_G(0)=6$, $N_G(1)=2$, $N_G(2)=8$, $N_G(3)=4$. Using Eq. (8), the motion classification of Video Tiles are: $C_{Tile}(0)=M$-*type*, $C_{Tile}(1)=L$-*type*, $C_{Tile}(2)=H$-*type*, and $C_{Tile}(3)=M$-*type*.

The above analysis and predicted memory pressure statistics are used by our CTU re-scheduling algorithm for memory pressure balancing and by the corresponding power management policy.

2.3 CTU Re-Scheduling for Memory Pressure Balancing

The goal of our CTU re-scheduling is to balance the accumulated memory pressure at the Video Tiles level, reducing the mean squared deviance (MSD) related to the average memory pressure (ideal case). Different number of CTU-groups leads to variable-sized groups, containing more or less CTUs within each Video Tile. Our scheme also classifies the Video Tiles according to the motion properties in three classifications $C_{Tile}=\{H$-type, M-type, L-type\}$ using the Eq. (8). Different Video Tile types will contributes in different ways for the accumulated balancing: *H-type* Video Tiles start by occupying the most part of the memory bandwidth, *M-type* Video Tiles contribute by median memory occupation, and the *L-type* Video Tiles aim to alleviate the memory pressure. The main task of our scheme is to schedule the CTU-groups processing.

Figure 10 depicts our CTU-groups scheduling functionality that is called at two points: (1) at the initial frame processing, when the decision about CTU-groups scheduling has not already taken, and (2) at the end of one CTU-group processing, when a new group must be scheduled. The call for this routine is performed at Video Tile-level, when the algorithm analyzes the current scenario to take the best decision. So, as input parameters we have the *ID* of the Video Tile $Tile_{ID}$ and the list of CTU-groups ($L_{CTU\text{-}Groups}$) that are inside the target Video Tile (*line 1*). For the first frame of the video, there are no temporal references for memory predictors, so the traditional raster scan order is performed (*lines 2-3*). If it is not the first frame, all memory predictions and run-time memory-related classifications are performed at the beginning of the frame processing. In case of the first CTU-group scheduling, the algorithm takes the motion Video Tile classification C_{Tile} into account to decide the CTU-group that will be next coded ($G_{ToBeCoded}$) (*lines 6-9*). Otherwise, our adaptive scheme analyzes the gap (*gapAccumPress*) between the current memory pressure (*currMemPress*) and an approximate average case prediction (*averageAccumPress* in *line 11*). So, the algorithm selects the CTU-group which has the predicted memory pressure and that has the best fit to the predicted gap (*lines 11-14*). After this decision, the CTU-group is removed from the non-coded groups list and the CTUs according are encoded according to the CTU-groups internal processing order depicted in Figure 8 (*line 17*).

1.	**scheduleCTUGroup(*Video Tile:* Tile$_{ID}$, *List of CTU-groups:* L$_{CTU\text{-}Groups}$)**
2.	**If** *first frame* **Then**
3.	G$_{ToBeCoded}$:= L$_{Groups}$.*first()*; //CTU-group equals to Video Tile
4.	**Else** //not the first frame
5.	**If** *frame start* **Then** //run-time statistical knowledge of Video Tiles
6.	Tile$_{class}$:= C$_{Tile}$(Tile$_{ID}$); //Eq. (8) – statistical classification
7.	**Case**(Tile$_{Class}$: L-type): G$_{ToBeCoded}$:= L$_{CTU\text{-}Groups}$.*min()*;
8.	**Case**(Tile$_{Class}$: M-type): G$_{ToBeCoded}$:= L$_{CTU\text{-}Groups}$.*median()*;
9.	**Case**(Tile$_{Class}$: H-type): G$_{ToBeCoded}$:= L$_{CTU\text{-}Groups}$.*max()*;
10.	**Else**
11.	averageAccumPress:= $\sum_{T=0}^{N_{Tiles}}(\mu_T)$; //sum of av. pressures
12.	currAccumPress := *getCurrentMemoryPressure()*; //monitoring
13.	gapAccumPress := averageAccumPress – currAccumPress;
14.	G$_{ToBeCoded}$:= (G | μ_G has the best fit to gapAccPress);
15.	**End If;**
16.	**End If;**
17.	L$_{CTU\text{-}Groups}$.*remove*(G$_{ToBeCoded}$); *encode*(G$_{ToBeCoded}$);

Figure 10. CTUs re-scheduling algorithm.

Besides memory pressure balancing, we also develop an on-chip power management that controls the low-power states of different blocks of the SVMs while increasing their sleep durations.

3. CONTENT-DRIVEN POWER MANAGEMENT

Our power management policy monitors each core's private SVM usage to capture the current video motion property and power-gate less-likely used sectors to save on-chip leakage energy.

Memory Power Model: We consider a memory technology with three power states: P_{ON}, P_{DR} *(Data Retentive)* and P_{OFF}, where:

$V_{ON}=V_{dd}$, $V_{DR}=0.3*V_{dd}$ and $V_{OFF}=0$, and the wake-up energies (WE) for power states transitions[3] are $WE_{T0}=1/2*C_{Circuit}*V_{dd}^2$, and $WE_{T1}=0.65*WE_{T0}$. V_{dd} is the memory supply voltage, and $C_{Circuit}$ is the total capacitance of the memory [5]. Our SVMs are divided into N_{Secs} memory sectors that are power gated by the same sleep transistor. One memory sector supports a 16x16 search window block ($S_{Sector}=16*16*8bits=2048bits$). This sectors organization *allows fine-grain memory management* during the encoding, since variable blocks sizes are processed and very accurate memory power states assignment is required. The SVMs are sized to *store one complete search window in a private way for each core*. Hence, we have $N_{SVM}=N_{Tiles}=N_{Cores}$ number of SVMs and each SVM has $S_{SVM}=(SW_H+64)*(SW_V+64)*8$ Kbits, where SW_V and SW_H are the search window vertical and horizontal dimensions.

Run-Time SVM Usage Analysis: Our evaluations in Figure 11 illustrate that we can *increase the potential of long sleep durations once the memory pressure is balanced*. For example, Figure 11a presents the SVM usage for the core 1 when encoding the *BasketballDrive* sequence. The SVM usage (SVM_{Usage}) calculated as the percentage of accessed SVM memory positions (measured by our memory monitoring unit) during one ME operation ($AccSVM$), see Eq. (10). As shown in Figure 11(b), the SVM usage for the entire CTU can be determined as the Probability Density Function of the SW_{Usage} values of all blocks within the CTU, see Eq. (11).

$$SVM_{Usage}(CU_{ID}) = AccSVM(CU_{ID})/S_{SVM} \qquad (10)$$

$$SVM_{UsagePDF}(CTU) = \{\sigma_{SVM}, \mu_{SVM}\} = \\ PDF(SPM_{Usage}(Block_{Node})|\forall\ Block_{Node} \in CTU) \qquad (11)$$

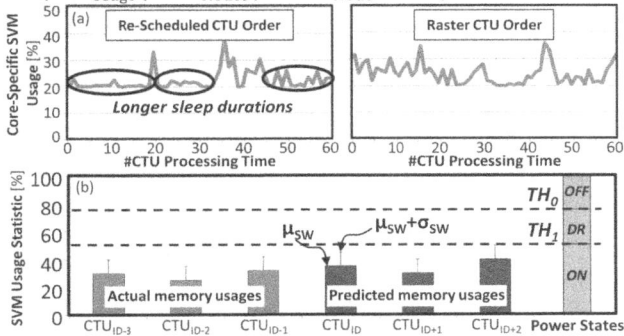

Figure 11. (a) Increased memory pressure correlation; (b) power states determination based on the SVM usage PDFs.

Our Power Management Scheme: At the beginning of a CTU encoding, the algorithm predicts the number of the memory sectors that can be put into different power state (i.e., N_{ON}, N_{DR} and N_{OFF}). As basis for this prediction, we analyze (1) the actual search window usage for previously processed CTUs (e.g., CTU_{ID-3}, CTU_{ID-2}, and CTU_{ID-1}); (2) the predicted usage for the current CTU_{ID} and the next CTU_{ID+1} and CTU_{ID+2}. The goal is to have the knowledge of the past, present and predicted future memory requirements to increase the on-chip leakage energy savings while minimizing the overhead for memory sectors waking-up. Figure 11(b) presents an example of SVM usage PDFs and the corresponding power states assignment.

Figure 12 presents our power management policy. The actual SVM usage PDFs of the past CTUs ($List_{ActualSVMusagePDF}$) and the next predicted SVM usage PDFs ($List_{PredSVMUsagePDF}$) are used to determine the power states of the SVM sectors (*lines 3-5*). As in Figure 11, we define two thresholds (TH_0 and TH_1) based on the average and standard deviation of all cited PDFs (*lines 6-7*). Afterwards, the SVM sectors corresponding to each power states are derived (*lines 8-9*). The physical assignment of the power states to the SVM cells is performed at the beginning of every block processing within a CTU (*lines 10-13*). In the case data

---
[3] Power states transitions: *T0* ($P_{OFF}\rightarrow P_{ON}$), and *T1* ($P_{DR}\rightarrow P_{ON}$).

retransmission is required (SVM cells wake-up from the P_{OFF} state), the control unit inserts stalls in the execution pipeline. Still, this penalty implies a negligible energy/performance overhead since in our experiments the worst-case scenario is observed <0.2% times.

1. **managePowerSVM** (*VideoTile:* Tile$_{ID}$, *CTU:* CTU$_{ID}$)
2. PowerMap$_{SVM}$:= Φ; N$_{ON}$:= 0; N$_{DR}$:= 0; N$_{OFF}$:= 0;
3. List$_{ActualSVMUsagePDF}$:= (SVM$_{UsagePDF}$ (ActualMem(CTU$_{ID}$) | ID $\in$ {-3..-1}));
4. List$_{PredSVMUsagePDF}$:= (SVM$_{UsagePDF}$ (PredMem(CTU$_{ID}$) | ID $\in$ {0..2}));
5. List$_{PDF}$.*append*(List$_{ActualSVMUsagePDF}$, List$_{PredSVMUsagePDF}$);
6. TH$_0$:= $max(\mu_{SVM}+3.\sigma_{SVM}$ | $(\mu_{SVM},\sigma_{SVM}) \in$ {List$_{PDF}$}); //TH's definition
7. TH$_1$:= $max(\mu_{SVM}+1.\sigma_{SVM}$ | $(\mu_{SVM},\sigma_{SVM}) \in$ { List$_{PDF}$});
8. N$_{OFF}$:= (1–TH$_0$)*N$_{Sec}$; N$_{DR}$:= (TH$_0$–TH$_1$)*N$_{Sec}$; N$_{ON}$:= TH$_1$ *N$_{Sec}$;
9. PowerMap$_{SVM}$.*assignPowerStates*(N$_{ON}$, N$_{DR}$, N$_{OFF}$);
10. **For** *all* Block $\in$ CTU$_{ID}$
11.   SVM[Tile$_{ID}$].*powerGate*(PowerMap$_{SVM}$); //apply power gating
12.   *encode*(Block);
13. **End For;**

Figure 12. On-chip power management of SVMs.

4. RESULTS AND DISCUSSIONS
4.1 Experimental Methodology
The experiments are performed using the HEVC software (HM 11.0) using the common test conditions adopted by the video coding community [6]. Four HD1080p (1920x1080) test video sequences with different properties were adopted: *BasketballDrive (BDrive)*, *BQTerrace (BQTerr)*, *Cactus* and *Kimono*. We consider 4-/16-Tile scenarios, 128x128 search window size (typical dimension for HD1080p [7]), GOP=8, FRExt, CABAC, and TZ Search algorithm for motion estimation. We use 4 and 16 threads (i. e., Video Tiles), each executing on a dedicated/specific processing core. Therefore, we use 4-, and 16-core x86 processor in our setup. Table 1 presents the on-chip SVM parameters as per the model defined in Section 3.

Table 1. On-Chip SVMs Sizing Parameters

SVM Sizing Parameter	Value
Number of SVMs	4, 8, 16 (one SVM per core)
SVM Sector Size	2048 bits = 256 B
SVM Size	(128+64) * (128+64) * 1B = 36 KB
Memory Size (4-Core)	114 KB
Memory Size (16-Core)	576 KB

We developed a custom simulator that takes the HM 11.0 memory traces for each thread (independent Video Tile) as input and estimates the accumulated memory pressure and the on-chip leakage energy. Our simulator contains memory models for the external memory and for the on-chip SVMs. For the external memory, we used a Low-Power DDR2 DRAM (LPDDR2) memory model (from Micron technical specification [14][15]) to derive the memory pressure. For the on-chip memory leakage energy estimation, we extracted the electrical parameters (for the 65nm SRAM technology node) using the CACTI 6.5 tool [11], as well as the multiple power states model described in Section 3.

MSD metric: Let the $Mem_{[0...m]}$ be the discretized memory pressure measurements along the time. The mean squared deviance (MSD) calculates the squared different between each memory pressure measured point and the Mem average value (μ_{Mem}), as in Eq. (12).

$$MSD(Mem_{[0...m]}) = \frac{1}{|Mem|}\sum_{i=0}^{m}(\mu_{Mem} - Mem_i)^2 \qquad (12)$$

4.2 Memory Pressure Balancing Results
Figure 13 presents a temporal evaluation of the memory pressure comparing (1) the traditional CTU raster processing order; (2) our application-specific memory pressure balancing scheme using CTU-rescheduling; and (3) the optimal corner case where the memory pressure is continuously equals to the average pressure. The case (3) is a theoretical approximation used to evaluate the gaps of our and the traditional schemes related to the best possible balancing case. Figure 13 shows that our scheme balances the pressure for each processing core. Compared to the traditional raster order, the

maximum-minimum peak variations are reduced from 27%-32% to 9%-13%, respectively. Our scheme achieves this balancing by effectively predicting the memory requirements, capturing the Video Tile-specific properties, and managing the processing order.

Figure 14 presents our results regarding the memory pressure balance. As already discussed, more Video Tiles potentially leads to more unbalanced accumulated memory pressure, since more concurrent memory accesses are performed during each time slot. In this scenario, there is a high probability of having very different motion properties being processed by different cores at the same time. So, the balancing gap when more Video Tiles are used is higher. Our scheme successfully exploits this potential, as shown in Figure 14. The MSD efficiency reduction ranges from, on average, 37% to 83%, for 4 to 16 Video Tiles. Therefore, our application-specific memory power management is efficiently scalable when working with an increased number of Video Tiles.

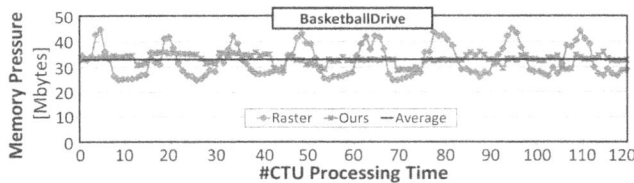

Figure 13. Accumulated memory pressure results of our scheme.

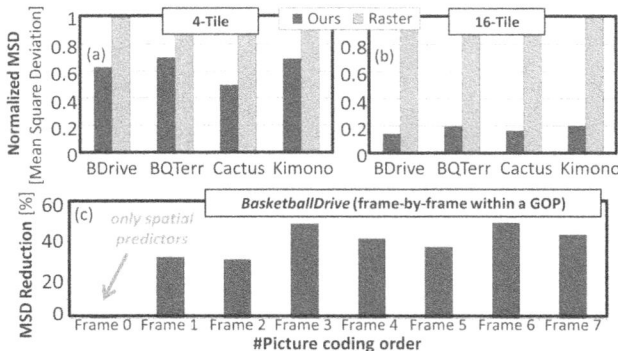

Figure 14. (a)(b) Memory pressure balancing analysis compared to the original raster scan order and (c) frame-by-frame analysis.

Figure 14c depicts a frame-by-frame MSD reduction analysis. During the first frame processing, as only spatial references can be used as input for our memory pressure predictor, our scheme achieves results close to the original raster order. However, by acquiring the temporal knowledge, our scheme fits the CTU-Groups accordingly to capture the motion properties and achieves increased memory pressure balancing for the other remaining frames. Thus, we can increase the accumulated memory pressure balancing by up to 49% in the case of 4-Tile *BasketballDrive* scenario (Figure 14c).

4.3 On-Chip Leakage Energy Savings

Figure 15a depicts the on-chip leakage energy savings of our content-driven SVM power management policy for different video sequences. On average, our scheme saves 56% of on-chip energy by power gating the unused and less-likely used memory sectors. The wake-up energies overhead is already included into the results of Figure 15. Our energy reductions are high in case of the low-motion Video Tiles by achieving longer sleep durations due to consecutive processing of CTU with similar texture and motion. This behavior is demonstrated in Figure 15b where the total energy savings are decomposed for each core-private SVM. The low-motion Video Tiles provide the highest savings while the medium- and high-motion Video Tiles required more energy due to higher memory usage as a result of an extensive search. When considering SVMs, the energy/performance overhead of waking up the memory cells are negligible, since one block of the search window is continuously

accessed during one ME operation over a given block of the CTU. Thus, the energy/performance penalty is completely amortized, not leading to significant overhead for the overall memory system.

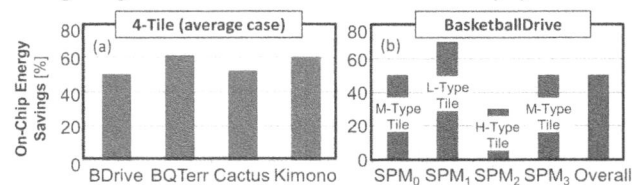

Figure 15. On-chip static energy reduction due to our content-driven power management of SVMs.

5. CONCLUSIONS

This work presented a content-driven memory pressure balancing scheme with an integrated power management policy. Our scheme is composed of: (1) a prediction unit that estimates the memory pressure due to the monitoring of past CTUs encoding; (2) a run-time statistics-based CTU memory classification that adapts the involved parameters of our schemes to the current video content; (3) a memory pressure balancing strategy that adaptively changes the CTU processing order to reduce the accumulated memory pressure variations; and (4) a power management policy that analyzes the actual and predicted memory usage for the CTUs to accordingly power-gate unused (or less-likely used) video memory sectors. Our experimental results demonstrated that our scheme can reduce the memory pressure peak variation by 37%-83% compared to the state-of-the-art raster processing order, for 4-/16-core processors. The SVM leakage energy is reduced by 56%. This work illustrates that the reducing memory pressure and on-chip SVM leakage energy are crucial for parallel HEVC on real-world embedded systems.

6. AKNOLEDGEMENTS

This work was partly supported by DFG as part of Transregional. Collaborative Research Centre "Invasive Computing" (SFB/TR 89); and partly by DAAD/CAPES as part of PROBRAL project VideoArch[3D].

7. REFERENCES

[1] JCT-VC, "High Efficiency Video Coding (HEVC) text specification draft 10 (for FDIS & Consent)", Doc.: JCTVC-L1003_v9, 2013.

[2] B. Zatt, M. Shafique, F. Sampaio, L. Agostini, S. Bampi, J. Henkel, "Run-time adaptive energy-aware motion and disparity estimation in multiview video coding", IEEE DAC, pp. 1026-1031, 2011.

[3] M. Shafique, B. Zatt, S. Bampi, J. Henkel, "Adaptive Power Management of On-Chip Video Mem. for Multiview Video Coding", DAC, pp. 866-875, 2012.

[4] F. Sampaio, B. Zatt, M. Shafique, J. Henkel, S. Bampi, "Energy-Efficient Memory Hierarchy for Motion and Disparity Estimation in Multiview Video Coding", IEEE DATE, pp. 665-670, 2013.

[5] H. Singh et al., "Enhanced leakage reduction techniques using intermediate strength power gating", IEEE Transactions on Very Large Scale Integration, vol. 15, no. 11, pp. 1215-1224, 2007.

[6] F. Bossen, "Common test conditions and software reference configurations", ITU-T/ISO/IEC JCTVC-K1100, 2012.

[7] K. Misra et al., "An overview of tiles in HEVC," JSTSP, no.99, 2013.

[8] D. Cho et al., "Adaptive Scratch Pad Memory Management for Dynamic Behavior of Multimedia Applications," TCAD, v.28, n.4, pp.554-567, 2009.

[9] I. Issenin, et al. "Data-Reuse-Driven Energy-Aware Cosynthesis of Scratch Pad Memory and Hierarchical Bus-Based Communication Architecture for Multiprocessor Streaming Applications". TCAD, v. , n. , pp. 1439-1452, 2008.

[10] IBM, "The Cell Project", Last Accessed: Sep. 2013, <researcher.watson.ibm.com/researcher/view_project.php?id=2649>.

[11] S. Thoziyoor, N. Muralimanohar, J.-H. Ahn, and N. P. Jouppi, "CACTI 5.1 technical report," HP Labs, Tech. Rep. HPL-2008-20, 2008.

[12] M. Jeong, et al. "A QoS-aware memory controller for dynamically balancing GPU and CPU bandwidth use in an MPSoC," DAC, pp. 850–855., 2012.

[13] L. L. Pilla, et al. "A hierarchical approach for load balancing on parallel multi-core systems," In: ICPP'12, pp. 118–127, 2012.

[14] Micron. "4Gb: x16, x32 Mob. LPDDR2 SDRAM S4", 168p, 2013.

[15] Micron. "TN-46-03 – Calculating DDR Mem. System Power"., 26p, 2005.

Software Canaries: Software-based Path Delay Fault Testing for Variation-aware Energy-efficient Design

John Sartori† and Rakesh Kumar‡
†University of Minnesota, ‡University of Illinois at Urbana-Champaign

ABSTRACT

Software-based path delay fault testing (SPDFT) has been used to identify faulty chips that cannot meet timing constraints due to gross delay defects. In this paper, we propose using SPDFT for a new purpose – aggressively selecting the operating point of a variation-affected design. In order to use SPDFT for this purpose, test routines must provide high coverage of potentially-critical paths and must have low dynamic performance overhead. We describe how to apply SPDFT for selecting an energy-efficient operating point for a variation-affected processor and demonstrate that our test routines achieve ample coverage and low overhead.

1. INTRODUCTION

Traditionally, processors have been designed and operated at worst case operating points determined by static critical path delays. This ensures timing safety under all circumstances, including worst case process, voltage, and temperature (PVT) variations, but also entails a significant energy overhead, since worst case conditions are rare [5] and provisioning for the worst case means operating at a much higher voltage and/or lower frequency than required on average. In response to the energy overheads of conventional worst case design, designers have sought more aggressive design styles that permit better-than-worst-case (BTWC) operation [8, 5, 1, 6, 7, 22, 28, 29, 2, 16, 12]. For example, the BTWC design technique that has found the most success in commercial processors is canary circuits [20, 7, 28]. A canary circuit is a protection circuit that attempts to mimic the static critical path delay of a design and is built to fail first in the event of an impending timing violation due to an aggressive voltage or frequency setting caused by variations or by design. Thus, failure of a canary circuit indicates the limit of safe operation (e.g., minimum voltage or maximum frequency) for the static critical path in a processor.

Whereas previous BTWC design techniques have been based on hardware mechanisms that measure slack in timing margins, we propose that testing for available timing slack can be performed with software-based techniques (that may not even require hardware changes to the processor). Software-based path delay fault testing (SPDFT) is a technique that tests for gross delay defects on the paths in a design to identify faulty chips that cannot meet timing constraints. We propose to leverage SPDFT as a software-based approach to BTWC operation by generating software routines that test for timing slack on the potentially-critical paths of a design and adapt the operating point to exploit available slack for improved energy efficiency.

This paper makes the following contributions.

• We demonstrate the use of SPDFT to select a variation-aware energy-efficient operating point for a design. To this

ISLPED'14, August 11–13, 2014, La Jolla, CA, USA.
Copyright 2014 ACM 978-1-4503-2975-0/14/08 ...$15.00.
http://dx.doi.org/10.1145/2627369.2627646.

end, we propose a methodology for generating SPDFT routines based on microarchitectural analysis. Since the distribution of potentially-critical paths for an individual chip also depends on variations, our test generation methodology accounts for the potential impact of variations on the slack distribution. We also present microarchitectural and system support for using SPDFT to select an energy-efficient operating point.

• Using SPDFT to select an energy-efficient BTWC operating point requires software-based test routines that provide high coverage of potentially-critical paths and that incur low dynamic performance overhead. We show that it is possible to generate test sequences for a processor that achieve ample coverage (e.g., 96.4%) while maintaining low performance overhead (e.g., < 1%). We also present usage models for our test routines, including when they are used in conjunction with hardware canary circuits to ensure 100% coverage of potentially-critical paths.

• We show that using SPDFT to select a BTWC operating point can result in same or better energy efficiency as hardware-based BTWC design techniques like canary circuits. Average energy savings are 12% compared to a hardware canary circuit-based design and 27% compared to a conventionally guard-banded worst case design.

2. RELATED WORK

The closest related work is on software-based testing for path delay faults that render a processor defective [4, 26, 11]. To the best of our knowledge, this is the first work to use SPDFT to improve energy efficiency by selecting a BTWC operating point in a variation-affected design. Also, because we perform SPDFT periodically during runtime, the test routines must have significantly lower overhead than typical delay fault testing routines.

We use SPDFT to test for timing slack on the potentially-critical paths in a processor. Fine-grained hardware-based BTWC mechanisms (e.g., timing speculation [5, 1]) can test for timing slack on the critical paths of a processor but have considerable static and dynamic overhead when all potentially-critical paths are targeted (e.g., 25% [15] to 87% [9]), especially in the context of microprocessors where a large fraction of timing paths are potentially-critical [23, 14]. Note that it is possible to use timing speculation and SPDFT synergistically to maximize system efficiency (see Section 3.6).

Another related body of work is on built-in self test (BIST) [21, 25, 30] and software-based self-test (SBST) [24, 4, 11]. A BIST routine uses on-chip hardware to check for defects in logic by exercising the logic and checking the test results. On the other hand, SBST, like SPDFT, uses a processor's instruction set to perform at-speed defect testing. BIST and SBST focus on testing for permanent defects that render a chip faulty. In contrast, we focus on using SPDFT to improve the energy efficiency of a processor through exploitation of timing slack in the presence of static and dynamic variations.

3. EXPLOITING TIMING SLACK IN SOFTWARE

In this section, we describe a framework for deriving instruction sequences that test for path delay faults on the potentially-critical paths in a given microarchitecture. We follow with a description of system support required to use SPDFT to dynamically select an energy-efficient operating point for a design affected by static and dynamic variations.

3.1 Deriving Instruction Sequences to Test Potentially-Critical Paths

SPDFT routines are instruction sequences that test for timing slack on the paths in a processor and produce outputs that are checked against the known correct outputs for the instruction sequences. A valid test sequence must set up and propagate a transition on a path from start to end. We design instruction sequences in such a way that if there is insufficient timing slack at the present operating point, SPDFT will generate an incorrect output or an exception, signaling that the voltage of the processor must be increased. If correct outputs are produced, the present operating voltage is safe, and there may be additional timing slack that allows the voltage of the processor to be reduced. For our objective of using SPDFT to select a BTWC operating point, we focus testing on the set of potentially-critical paths (i.e., the paths that might become critical as the processor is affected by variations). We distinguish between *potentially-critical paths* in a design and *the critical path* in a design because as chips are affected by variations it is possible for different chips to have different critical paths or for the critical paths of a chip to change over time due to aging. If variations (e.g., local and global PVT variations) can cause the delay of a path to change by up to X%, then any path with delay that is within X% of the critical path delay is a potentially-critical path. **By testing the potentially-critical paths in a design for timing safety, SPDFT can ensure timing safety for the entire design**, even the non-architectural state, since the absence of errors on all potentially-critical paths indicates that all shorter paths are also free of errors. Stated another way, if any shorter path fails, one of the potentially-critical paths (tested exhaustively by our test routines) must have failed as well, resulting in an observable failure during testing.

Some approaches exist for generating SPDFT routines for a processor [24, 4, 11], and approaches in previous work target exhaustive path coverage. Since our objective is energy efficiency, not identification of faulty chips, we target test routines that provide ample coverage of potentially-critical paths and have low performance overhead. Our approach for deriving SPDFT routines for a given processor design involves (1) identifying the set of potentially-critical paths (i.e., all paths that may become critical due to variations) and (2) formulating instruction sequences that test those paths with high coverage. Providing coverage for all potentially-critical paths, rather than only a few static critical paths, enables adaptation to *local* as well as global variations. For example, within-die process variations caused by factors such as sub-wavelength lithographic inaccuracies can cause the critical paths on different dies to be different. By providing coverage for all potentially-critical paths, we ensure that **even if local variations change the expected delay distribution of a design, SPDFT can track available timing slack accurately**.

To identify potentially-critical paths, we perform static timing analysis (STA) to identify which paths may become critical as a result of variations. The potentially-critical paths identified by STA are the paths with delays that are within X% of the critical path delay, where X% corresponds to the delay guardband for sources of trackable variations (see Section 4).

Since the number of potentially-critical paths in modern processor designs can be large [23, 14], using conventional instruction-based path delay test generation procedures that generate instruction pairs to test specific paths for delay defects may result in very long test sequences [24, 4, 11]. Instead, we use microarchitectural analysis of potentially-critical paths to design SPDFT routines. Our approach for test routine generation consists of using microarchitectural analysis to formulate *generator templates* that characterize instruction patterns that test for path delay faults on the critical paths in a design, and expanding the generator templates to create an instruction sequence that exhibits high coverage for a particular microarchitecture.

```
(A)                    (B)                       (C)
sw R_K,X               bne R_K,$0,FAIL           ori R_K,$0,-1
lw R_K,X               bne R_K,$0,FAIL           addi R_{K+1},R_K,1
Expansion:             Expansion:                Expansion:
insert sw R_{i-1},X    append bne R_K,$0,FAIL    append addi R_{i+2},R_{i+1},±1
after sw R_i,X                                   after addi R_{i+1},R_i,∓1
```

Figure 1: Generator templates are instruction patterns that excite transitions on critical paths in a logic stage and are expanded to provide adequate coverage of potentially-critical paths.

We find that this approach satisfies our goals of ample coverage and low overhead (see Section 5). Generalized automation of test routine generation is a subject of ongoing work.

3.2 Derivation of Generator Templates

In this section, we describe the derivation of instruction sequences that create transitions on critical paths in a generic superscalar processor [3]. The FabScalar processor is an open-source, typical out-of-order pipeline that supports a range of configurations, from a wide superscalar design to a narrow scalar design. Thus, our work demonstrates the viability of using SPDFT to select a BTWC operating point for a range of simple to complex cores. Detailed evaluation of applying SPDFT to set processor operating point in the context of other microarchitectures is a subject of ongoing work.

For ease of exposition, we first explain how we use microarchitectural analysis to derive a SPDFT generator template for the load-store unit, as several other pipeline stages in the FabScalar processor demonstrate similar criticality behavior.

Load-Store: The load-store unit (LSU) performs memory disambiguation. This involves checking for dependences between loads and stores. Load disambiguation begins with a search through the store queue address CAM to determine if the load depends on any in-flight stores, followed by generation of a mask vector that indicates all preceding in-flight stores in program order. If there are matching entries from the CAM search, they are filtered by the mask vector, and the latest resulting entry accesses the store queue data RAM and forwards its data to the load. If forwarding is not required, the memory request is forwarded to the memory subsystem. Paths that perform load disambiguation involving store-to-load forwarding are critical paths in the LSU, and longer paths are exercised when the in-flight dynamic dependence chain is longer. Thus, a generator template for the LSU, shown in Figure 1(A), consists of dependent instructions that necessitate store-to-load forwarding. We observe that increasing the length of the dependence chain increases critical path coverage. Thus, the generator template is expanded by adding dependent stores to the chain until the resulting instruction sequence exhibits adequate coverage of potentially-critical paths, as described in Figure 2.

Fetch: Next PC generation logic and priority selection between multiple branch targets constitute the most critical paths in the fetch stage. Branches in the fetch group check the branch target buffer, branch predictions are generated by the branch prediction buffer, and the next PC is selected based on the predicted branch outcome of the highest priority branch. The critical paths are exercised when all the instructions in the fetch group are branches. A generator template for the fetch stage (Figure 1(B)) consists of back-to-back branches. Branch conditions are written such that the branch outcomes are never mispredicted. We observe that expanding the template by appending additional branches (up to the length of the fetch group) increases coverage of potentially-critical paths.

Decode: For the RISC ISA implemented by FabScalar, decode logic has a regular structure. There are several possible instruction sequences that exercise critical paths in the decode stage, including the generator template for the Register-Read, Execute, and Writeback stages (described below, Figure 1(C)). We observe that expanding the generator template (as described in Figure 2) increases coverage of potentially-critical paths.

```
// Identify potentially-critical paths
Use STA to identify potentially-critical paths P_PC
  with delay within X% of the static critical path delay
// Expand generator templates
foreach(generator template GT)
    do
        Expand length of GT by one unit in test routine
        Test coverage C_PC of P_PC
    while(C_PC increases)
// Select test with highest P_PC coverage and lowest overhead
Select canary with maximum C_PC that has minimum length
```

Figure 2: Pseudocode for test routine generation.

Rename: A large number of critical paths in the rename stage are exercised when a true dependence chain exists between the entire group of instructions for which register renaming is being performed. When the instructions enter the rename stage, new tags are popped from the freelist for the destination registers of the instructions. Comparators indicate that one or more of the source operand(s) of the dependent instructions are the destinations of the other instruction, so instead of reading the source tags from the rename map table, the tags popped from the freelist must be selected for the dependent instructions' sources. Finally, the rename map table is also updated with the renamed register mappings. A generator template for the rename stage (Figure 1(C)) consists of back-to-back instructions that form a chain of true dependences. We observe that expanding the chain length up to N for an N-wide processor by adding dependent operations increases coverage of potentially-critical paths.

Dispatch: The dispatch stage is the gateway between the processor frontend and backend. It checks for free slots in the re-order buffer, issue queue, and load-store queue, and dispatches instructions to free slots. Like decode, dispatch has a regular structure. The generator template used for decode also works well for dispatch.

Issue: The wakeup / select loop contributes the most critical paths in the issue stage. This critical loop is exercised when there is a true dependence chain between successive instructions, such that a source operand for each dependent instruction is the result of the preceding instruction. A newly awoken instruction passes through selection logic, is read from the payload RAM, and broadcasts its destination tag, which hits in the wakeup CAM, closing the loop as the dependent instruction becomes ready. As with rename, the generator template for issue consists of back-to-back dependent instructions that can be expanded into a dependence chain. Thus, we observe that the same generator template can generate test routines that provide good coverage for both stages.

RegisterRead, Execute, Writeback: The critical paths in the register read, execute, and writeback stages are also excited by back-to-back dependent instructions. In this case, one or more source operands for each dependent instruction is obtained from the bypass network from writeback rather than from the physical register file. Critical paths in these stages consist of reading the physical register file, navigating the MUX logic joined to the bypass network, executing the instructions, and writing back the results to the writeback latches and bypass network. Again, a generator template containing back-to-back dependent instructions (Figure 1(C)) works well for these stages. For the arithmetic operations in the chain, we ensure (using gate-level simulation) that the operands selected will excite the static critical paths in the ALU.

3.3 SPDFT Test Generation

Based on the above analysis, we can generate test routines that target the potentially-critical paths in all stages in the pipeline using the three generator templates in Figure 1. The generator templates are expanded into (A) a chain of dependent memory operations that necessitate store-to-load forwarding, (B) a cluster of back-to-back branches, and (C) a chain of dependent arithmetic operations and concatenated to create a SPDFT routine for a particular processor.

```
ori  $2,$0,-1
addi $3,$2,1
addi $4,$3,-1
addi $2,$4,1
sw   $4,20($30)
sw   $3,20($30)
sw   $2,20($30)
lw   $4,20($30)
bne  $4,$0,FAIL
bne  $4,$0,FAIL
bne  $4,$0,FAIL
bne  $4,$0,FAIL
PASS: [test passed]
FAIL: [test failed]
```

Figure 3: SPDFT routine that provides good coverage for a 4-wide superscalar processor.

```
Read test routine pointer
Begin checkpoint and set watchdog
Remove safety margin
do
    Execute test routine at pointer
    if(!FAIL)
        Decrease voltage by one step
while(!FAIL)
if(recovery or timeout)
    Revert checkpoint
Increase voltage by one step
Add safety margin
Reset watchdog
Return to normal execution
```

Figure 4: Pseudocode describing testing procedure.

Figure 2 describes the process of test generation. The test generation procedure begins by using STA to produce a path timing distribution. Potentially critical paths are identified (using STA) as the subset of paths with delays that are within X% of the critical path delay, where X% corresponds to the delay guardband for sources of trackable variations. Each of the generator templates (described in Section 3.1) is expanded in turn within the test routine while recording the resulting routine's coverage of potentially-critical paths. For each generator template, the length of the instruction chain is iteratively increased by one step until the marginal increase in coverage is negligible (coverage is maximized). Among test routines that provide maximum coverage, we select the one that incurs the least overhead (i.e., the shortest instruction sequence). Figure 3 shows an example of a generated test routine that provides good coverage of potentially-critical paths for a 4-wide superscalar processor.

Compared to the traditional instruction sequences used in SPDFT, which use instruction pairs that target PDFs on individual paths, the test sequences we generate may be more efficient because they focus specifically on potentially-critical paths and target large groups of potentially-critical paths rather than individual paths. We show in Section 5 that our SPFDT routines provide high coverage (96.4%) of potentially-critical paths in our test design (FabScalar [3]), comparable to other approaches for software-based path delay fault testing [24, 4, 11]. We also propose that potentially-critical paths not covered by SPDFT can be covered using hardware canary circuits.

3.4 Microarchitectural and System Support for Selecting an Energy-efficient BTWC Operating Point Based on SPDFT

Using SPDFT to select a BTWC operating point involves using SPDFT routines to monitor availability of timing slack and adapting a processor's voltage to exploit available timing slack that exists due to guardbanding for static and dynamic variations. Since some sources of variations (e.g., temperature, aging) change dynamically, SPDFT routines should be executed periodically. The minimum interval between successive tests that guarantees timing safety can be determined based on the maximum rate of change of trackable variations. During normal operation between testing intervals, a safety margin is added to the operating voltage to protect against potential increase in delay over a single interval due to trackable variations. For example, if trackable variations can change delay at a maximum rate of 1ns per 1ms of execution time, and the length of a testing interval is $1\mu s$, then a guardband must be applied during normal operation to protect against a potential 1ps increase in delay during the interval between tests. Our results account for this overhead, as well as all other power and performance overheads introduced by our SPDFT execution framework (see Section 4). We set the interval length and safety margin such that **performance degradation from periodic testing is less than 1%**. At each testing interval, the safety margin that protects against delay drift is removed and testing is performed to determine the minimum safe operating voltage for the processor. If testing passes, there may be additional timing slack available, and the processor may lower the supply voltage and perform testing again to check for safety at a lower voltage. When testing fails (either at the original voltage or a lower voltage), the voltage is increased by one increment plus all required margins, and program execution resumes. Proper selection of testing interval (Section 3.6) and intelligent testing patterns [19] can be used to limit the number of voltage points evaluated before arriving at the new optimal voltage. Performance overhead of testing can potentially also be reduced by scheduling testing when the processor is idle [25].

To protect the processor during testing, which may result in errors, we use a checkpointing and recovery mechanism established in prior work [25]. During testing, updates to registers are buffered in a checkpoint memory and updates to memory are buffered in the cache (marked as volatile). If a failed test necessitates recovery, updated registers are reverted, volatile cache lines are marked as invalid, the pipeline is flushed, and execution resumes from the checkpointed state after increasing the voltage to include required guardbands. We account for the overhead introduced by recovery in our evaluations (see Section 4). There are many possible frameworks that support checkpointing and recovery [25, 10], and processors that support speculative execution (like the FabScalar architecture we evaluate) already provide most of the necessary mechanisms. We use the same fault-tolerant checkpointing and recovery mechanism as Bulletproof [25], which prevents any erroneous writes made during testing from being committed to architectural state. We conservatively assume an area overhead of 1.6% for implementing BulletProof, as quoted in [25]. However, since we only require the checkpointing and recovery mechanisms of BulletProof (not the defect testing hardware), overhead in our implementation should be less.

In addition to checkpointing and recovery mechanisms, we include additional support to ensure that the processor can recover from segmentation faults and hangs that might occur due to timing violations during testing. Control errors caused by incorrect branching may cause the processor to jump to an incorrect location or to hang. We use a watchdog timer to protect against control errors and hangs. Before testing, the watchdog timer is set, and the last action of the test routine is to reset the watchdog timer. If a control fault causes the processor to hang or jump to an incorrect location, the watchdog timer expires, and recovery is initiated. Incorrect R/W or O accesses can result in segmentation faults. However, since any segmentation fault during testing can be attributed to a timing error, we suppress normal handling of R/W/O segmentation faults and instead treat them as error detections, which initiate recovery. Context switches and external interrupts are delayed during testing, as SPDFT routines are only a few instructions long. The testing routine is stored in memory as an interrupt service routine that executes at a periodic rate. Since the exact test routine is small, deterministic, and executes at a known rate, it can easily be prefetched just before testing. Figure 4 shows pseudocode for the SPDFT execution framework.

3.5 The Impact of PVT Variations

Our SPDFT execution framework allows a processor to select an energy-efficient operating point in face of process, voltage, temperature (PVT), and aging-induced variations. Figure 5 estimates potential power savings for a FabScalar [3] processor implemented with 65nm technology if SPDFT can enable operating point adaptation to all sources of PVT variations. Results are nearly identical for an OpenSPARC [27] processor implemented in the same technology. Power savings are measured by synthesizing, placing, and routing the processor design at a worst case corner and evaluating the processor at the minimum safe voltage required to meet timing over the range of worst, typical, and best case corners. The figure shows that

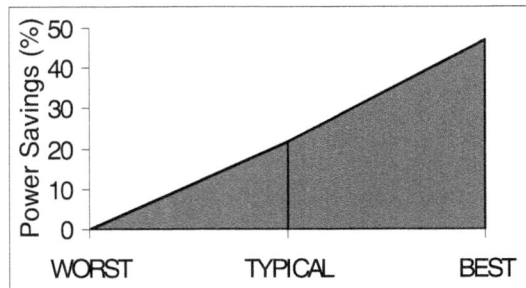

Figure 5: SPDFT can allow a processor that experiences BTWC variations to reduce power through supply voltage reduction. Additional power savings enabled by adapting to PVT variations can be up to 22% under typical case conditions and up to 47% in the best case if SPDTF allows adaptation to all sources of PVT variations.

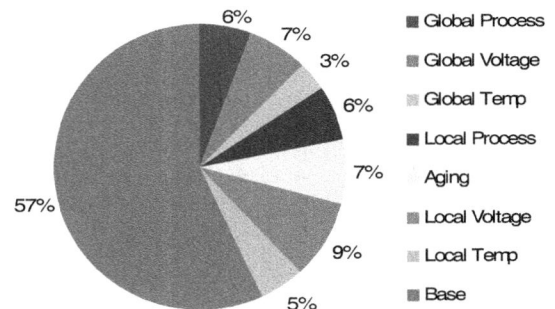

Figure 6: This figure breaks down the power consumption associated with worst case guardbands for various types of variations. If any source of variations can be tracked by SPDFT, the power associated with that guardband can be reduced under BTWC conditions.

the power savings available from typical case and best case operation could be up to 22% and 47%, respectively. These savings represent benefits from idealized BTWC operation under typical case and best case conditions.

In reality, only a subset of these benefits may be possible from SPDFT, since test routines cannot track delay fluctuations caused by all sources of variations. For example, fast-changing variations, e.g., most global and local voltage variations, cannot be tracked by SPDFT due to the latency of processor adaptation through voltage or frequency scaling and the interval between successive tests, which is long relative to the rate of change of fast-changing variations. Figure 6 breaks down the power consumption associated with worst case guardbands for various sources of variations. Note that actual design guardbands would be mostly in terms of operating frequency. However, since we use voltage scaling to target BTWC operating points in this paper, Figure 6 quantifies how much power could potentially be reduced by translating each design guardband into a voltage reduction. The size of a segment corresponding to a particular type of variations shows how much power can potentially be reduced under best case conditions (fast corner) if a hardware or software testing can track delay changes caused by that source of variations. For sources of variation that can be tracked, design margins can be partially reduced, depending on the actual amount of variations observed during operation. In Section 5, we evaluate the potential energy savings enabled by SPDFT both with and without the additional benefits enabled by adapting to a subset of PVT variations.

3.6 Other Implementation Considerations

Critical Path Coverage: SPDFT can allow adaptation to local variations only if the canary routines test all the potentially-critical paths that may become critical due to local variations [5]. Otherwise, guardbands must be used to protect against local variations. In cases where SPDFT provides high but incomplete coverage of potentially-critical paths, it may be beneficial to use hardware canaries synergistically with SPDFT, such that hardware canaries (e.g., Razor II [5]) provide protection for any potentially-critical paths not covered by SPDFT. Such an organization allows elimination of guardbands for slow-changing local variations while keeping the hardware overhead introduced by canary circuits low (since most paths are protected by SPDFT). In Section 5, we evaluate the critical path coverage of SPDFT, as well as the potential benefits of a SPDFT + hardware canary hybrid design.

Testing Interval Size and Number of Voltage Levels: The interval between successive tests is determined by the maximum rate of change of trackable variations, to balance the performance overhead of testing (higher for a shorter interval) and the cost of providing a safety margin to protect against the maximum drift of critical path delay due to dynamically changing trackable variations in a single time interval (higher for a longer interval). Note that if the interval size is selected properly (to bound the maximum change in delay variation during an interval), SPDFT routines should not need to be run for more than a maximum of three voltages per interval (in the case when voltage step granularity is finest and the optimal voltage is lower than the present operating voltage). In Section 5, we perform analysis of SPDFT execution for different testing intervals and numbers of voltage levels in order to determine appropriate values for design parameters.

4. METHODOLOGY

To quantify the potential benefits of SPDFT, we use a detailed methodology to measure power, performance, timing, and activity. Designs are implemented with the TSMC 65GP library (65nm), using Synopsys Design Compiler for synthesis and Cadence SoC Encounter for layout. To evaluate the power and performance of designs at different voltages and design corners, Cadence Library Characterizer was used to generate libraries at each voltage (V_{dd}) between $1.0V$ and $0.5V$ at $0.01V$ intervals for worst, typical, and best case corners. Designs are implemented at 500 MHz. Power, area, and timing analyses are performed in Synopsys PrimeTime. Gate-level simulation is performed with Cadence NC-Verilog to gather activity information for the design, which is subsequently used for dynamic power estimation and test coverage measurement. Evaluation of potential energy savings is performed by implementing the processor at the worst case corner (conventional design) and evaluating the design at a BTWC corner (e.g., typical, best).

To measure the coverage achieved by our test routines, we use PrimeTime STA to determine the set of paths that can become critical when affected by worst case variations (P_{PC}). We use Cadence NC-Verilog to execute our SPDFT routines on the synthesized, placed, and routed netlist for the processor and produce a VCD file which is used to trace toggled paths from destination to source to determine the paths that are tested by the test routines (P_{SPDFT}). Coverage is computed as the cardinality of the set intersection between P_{SPDFT} and P_{PC} divided by the cardinality of P_{PC}.

We perform evaluations for a collection of benchmarks from the SPEC and EEMBC benchmark suites. Benchmarks are executed on a synthesized, placed, and routed processor. SPEC benchmarks are fast-forwarded to their Simpoints [13], while EEMBC embedded benchmarks are run in their entirety.

4.1 Energy Impact of Dynamic Adaptation

To calculate the expected power of the processor, we use parameters from the technology library to characterize the distribution of variations from best to worst, where the range from best to worst covers six standard deviations (6σ). We take the number of discrete voltage levels as an input and use Prime-Time to measure the power of the placed and routed processor at each voltage level. We then use the cumulative distribution function ($\Phi(x) = \frac{1}{2}[1 + erf(\frac{x-\mu}{\sqrt{2}\sigma})]$), along with the delay vs.

voltage relationship of the processor to calculate the probability that the variations are in the range corresponding to each discrete voltage level (erf is the error function). Let us denote the power at the voltage level corresponding to a certain deviation of variations as $Power(x)$. We then calculate the expected value of power as $E[Power] = \sum_{i=1}^{N} \Phi(x)|_{x=x_{i-1}}^{x_i} \cdot Power(x_i)$.

We measure performance (IPC) for each benchmark by executing benchmarks on our processor RTL using NC-Verilog and derate the performance based on the overheads imposed by the dynamic execution framework. First, we calculate the maximum number of voltage level changes per interval using the maximum rate of change of trackable variations, the interval length, and the number of voltage levels. We calculate the maximum expected overhead of switching between voltage levels based on the maximum number of level switches per interval and the cost of switching voltage levels. The cost of switching voltage levels depends on the size of the voltage step, which in turn depends on the number of voltage levels. We perform evaluations for two different voltage regulators – an on-chip voltage regulator that can scale the voltage at a rate of 1 V / 100 ns [18, 17] and an off-chip voltage regulator that is 1000 times slower (1 V / 100 μs) [18]. We calculate the performance overhead for each execution of the test routines as the product of the maximum number of times testing is applied per interval and the number of cycles required to execute the test routines. The maximum number of tests per interval is one more than the maximum number of level switches. Recovery, when required, incurs performance and power overheads for performing the recovery as well as performance lost due to flushing the pipeline. To obtain the derated performance of a benchmark for SPDFT-based execution, we derate the IPC observed during execution of the benchmark based on the total number of overhead cycles devoted to executing SPDFT routines, context switching, switching voltage levels, and recovery. We calculate energy as power divided by performance (W/IPC).

5. RESULTS

Using SPDFT as described in Section 3 can result in improved energy efficiency for a variation-affected design. In practice, available energy savings depends on the extent of variations observed as well as the ability of SPDFT routines to track delay changes due to those variations. Tracking of local variations is enabled only if test routines provide coverage for all potentially-critical paths. Coverage analysis (described in Section 4) reveals that our SPDFT routines provide coverage for *96.4% of potentially-critical paths*. For the remaining 3.6% of the potentially-critical timing paths, we have the option of using Razor II [5] as a canary circuit to provide coverage. Razor II is modeled following the methodology described in [15]. (Note that Razor II [5] is different than Razor-based timing speculation [8] and can be used as a canary circuit.) Due to the high coverage of our SPDFT routines, adding canary circuits for unprotected potentially-critical paths only adds 0.2% power overhead. When Razor II is used as a canary circuit without SPDFT, the overhead introduced by canary circuits is 7.5%.

As discussed in Section 3.5, SPDFT routines cannot track changes in timing slack due to all types of variations. Local and global voltage variations (such as Ldi/dt) can change very quickly, and likely do not allow enough response time for SPDFT routines to adapt the processor's voltage. SPDFT for fast-changing variations is a subject of ongoing work.

Since SPDFT cannot track all sources of variations (e.g., fast-changing voltage variations), SPDFT-based designs still use worst case guardbands for untrackable variations. Table 1 quantifies the power savings afforded by SPDFT-based designs that adapt to various sources of trackable variations and use worst case guardbands for untrackable variations (denoted in the first column). Results are shown for typical and best case corners. The first row corresponds to a SPDFT-based design

Table 1: Power savings (%) for adapting to trackable variations.

Worst-Case Guardbands	TYPICAL	BEST
Full Voltage, Local Temp and Aging	19.5	25.4
Full Voltage	27.4	38.1

that does not provide coverage for all potentially-critical paths. Note that such a design cannot adapt to voltage, local temperature, or aging variations because the coverage of potentially-critical paths is less than 100%. The design can, however, adapt to slow-changing and static global variations. The second row of the table quantifies power savings for a synergistic SPDFT + hardware canary-based design where adaptation to slow-changing local aging and temperature variations is possible because the paths uncovered by SPDFT are covered using Razor II as a canary circuit. The results show that using SPDFT to select a BTWC operating point may significantly improve energy efficiency, with or without the synergistic use of hardware canary circuits. Benefits are significantly higher when a synergistic SPDFT + hardware canary-based approach is used to provide coverage for all potentially-critical paths.

The next set of results quantifies the energy savings enabled by SPDFT for a real execution framework that allows dynamic adaptation to variations (details in Section 4.1). These results consider all performance and power overheads for voltage scaling, test routine execution, and error recovery. We quantify energy savings with respect to both conventional and canary circuit-based baselines. We explore the design space by varying the testing interval size and number of voltage levels.

Figure 7 shows energy savings over conventional and canary circuit-based designs averaged over our benchmark suite. SPDFT achieves energy savings of up to 28% over conventional design and 12% over canary circuit-based design. Energy savings enabled by our dynamic adaptation framework are 96% of the ideal energy savings that could be achieved without any power or performance overheads. Performance overhead introduced by periodic testing and adaptation is low, ranging from around 1% to 3% for different testing interval lengths.

From the results, we observe that testing interval size does not affect energy savings much, though savings are greater for a shorter interval because the cost of providing a larger safety margin to protect against delay drift due to dynamically changing variations during a longer interval outweighs the cost of additional testing incurred with a shorter interval. Energy savings are 5% closer to ideal when 4 voltage levels are used instead of 2. There is a small (2%) boost in energy savings from increasing the number of voltage levels from 4 to 8, however, we use 4 voltage levels for the remaining evaluations, since several conventional voltage scaling designs have up to 4 voltage levels.

The results in Figure 7 assume an on-chip voltage regulator that can scale the voltage at a rate of 1 V / 100 ns [18, 17], as described in Section 4.1. We also performed evaluations for an off-chip voltage regulator that is 1000 times slower (1 V / 100 μs) [18] than the on-chip regulator. In this case, energy savings are 24% over conventional design, 10% over canary circuit-based design, and 83% of the ideal energy savings that assume no overheads.

6. CONCLUSION

In this paper, we propose using SPDFT to select an energy-efficient operating point for a variation-affected design. We describe a procedure for generating software-based PDF tests with low performance overhead that provide ample coverage of potentially-critical paths in a processor. We also describe microarchitectural and system support for SPDFT-based execution and show the potential for energy reduction from using SPDFT to select an operating point in a variation-affected design. Average energy reduction at a typical case corner is 12% compared to a hardware canary circuit-based design and 27% compared to a conventionally guardbanded worst case design.

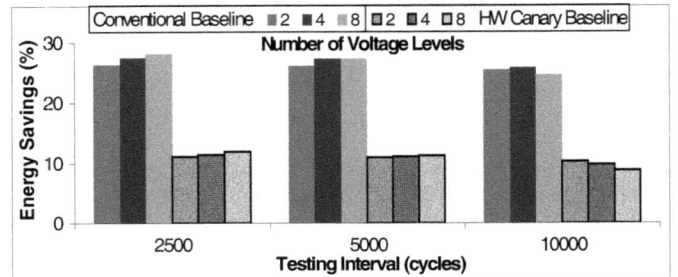

Figure 7: SPDFT in the context of a dynamic adaptation framework achieve up to 28% energy savings over a conventional worst case design and 12% energy savings over a canary circuit-based design. To make results more conservative, we do not account any overhead for canary circuits in the baseline design. Benefits are averaged over all benchmarks in our suite.

7. REFERENCES

[1] K. Bowman, J. Tschanz, C. Wilkerson, S. Lu, T. Karnik, V. De, and S. Borkar. Circuit techniques for dynamic variation tolerance. In DAC, pages 4–7, 2009.

[2] T. Burd, S. Member, T. Pering, A. Stratakos, and R. Brodersen. A dynamic voltage scaled microprocessor system. IEEE Journal of Solid-State Circuits, 11(35):1571–1580, 2000.

[3] N. Choudhary, S. Wadhavkar, T. Shah, H. Mayukh, J. Gandhi, B. Dwiel, S. Navada, H. Najaf-abadi, and E. Rotenberg. Fabscalar: Composing synthesizable rtl designs of arbitrary cores within a canonical superscalar template. In ISCA, 2011.

[4] K. Christou, M. K. Michael, P. Bernardi, M. Grosso, E. Sanchez, and M. Sonza Reorda. A novel sbst generation technique for path-delay faults in microprocessors exploiting gate- and rt-level descriptions. In VTS, pages 389–394, 2008.

[5] S. Das, C. Tokunaga, S. Pant, W. Ma, S. Kalaiselvan, K. Lai, D. Bull, and D. Blaauw. Razor II: In situ error detection and correction for PVT and SER tolerance. Proc. ISSCC, pages 400–622, 2008.

[6] S. Dhar, D. Maksimovic, and B. Kranzen. Closed-loop adaptive voltage scaling controller for standard-cell ASICs. ISLPED, 2002.

[7] A. Drake, R. Senger, H. Deogun, G. Carpenter, S. Ghiasi, T. Nguyen, N. James, M. Floyd, and V. Pokala. A distributed critical-path timing monitor for a 65nm high-performance microprocessor. In ISSCC, pages 398–399, 2007.

[8] D. Ernst, Nam Sung Kim, Shidhartha Das, Sanjay Pant, Rajeev Rao, Toan Pham, Conrad Ziesler, David Blaauw, Todd Austin, Krisztian Flautner, and Trevor Mudge. Razor: A low-power pipeline based on circuit-level timing speculation. In MICRO, pages 7–18, 2003.

[9] M. Fojtik, D. Fick, Y. Kim, N. Pinckney, D. Harris, D. Blaauw, and D. Sylvester. Bubble razor: An architecture-independent approach to timing-error detection and correction. In ISSCC, pages 488–490, 2012.

[10] M.S. Gupta, K.K. Rangan, M.D. Smith, Gu-Yeon Wei, and D. Brooks. Decor: A delayed commit and rollback mechanism for handling inductive noise in processors. In HPCA, pages 381–392, 2008.

[11] Sankar Gurumurthy, Ramtilak Vemu, Jacob A. Abraham, and Daniel G. Saab. Automatic generation of instructions to robustly test delay defects in processors. In ETS, pages 173–178, 2007.

[12] V. Gutnik and A. Chandrakasan. An efficient controller for variable supply-voltage low power processing. IEEE Proc. Symposium on VLSI Circuits, pages 158–159, 1996.

[13] Greg Hamerly, Erez Perelman, J. Lau, and Brad Calder. Simpoint 3.0: Faster and more flexible program analysis. In JILP, 2005.

[14] Andrew Kahng, Seokhyeong Kang, Rakesh Kumar, and John Sartori. Designing processors from the ground up to allow voltage/reliability tradeoffs. In IEEE HPCA, pages 119–129, 2010.

[15] Andrew B. Kahng, Seokhyeong Kang, Rakesh Kumar, and John Sartori. Recovery-driven design: Exploiting error resilience in design of energy-efficient processors. IEEE Trans. on CAD of Integrated Circuits and Systems, 31(3):404–417, 2012.

[16] T. Kehl. Hardware self-tuning and circuit performance monitoring. ICCD, pages 188–192, 1993.

[17] Wonyoung Kim, D.M. Brooks, and Gu-Yeon Wei. A fully-integrated 3-level dc/dc converter for nanosecond-scale dvs with fast shunt regulation. In ISSCC, pages 268 –270, 2011.

[18] Wonyoung Kim, M.S. Gupta, Gu-Yeon Wei, and D. Brooks. System level analysis of fast, per-core dvfs using on-chip switching regulators. In HPCA, pages 123 –134, 2008.

[19] S. Lee, S. Das, T. Pham, T. Austin, D. Blaauw, and T. Mudge. Reducing pipeline energy demands with local dvs and dynamic retiming. In ISLPED, pages 319–324, 2004.

[20] Charles R. Lefurgy, Alan J. Drake, Michael S. Floyd, Malcolm S. Allen-Ware, Bishop Brock, Jose A. Tierno, and John B. Carter. Active management of timing guardband to save energy in power7. In MICRO, pages 1–11, 2011.

[21] Edward McCluskey. Built-in self-test techniques. IEEE Des. Test, 2(2):21–28, March 1985.

[22] M. Najibi, M. Salehi, A. Afzali Kusha, M. Pedram, S. M. Fakhraie, and H. Pedram. Dynamic voltage and frequency management based on variable update intervals for frequency setting. In ICCAD, pages 755–760, 2006.

[23] Janak Patel. Cmos process variations: A critical operation point hypothesis, 2008.

[24] M. Psarakis, D. Gizopoulos, E. Sanchez, and M.S. Reorda. Microprocessor software-based self-testing. Design Test of Computers, IEEE, 27(3):4–19, 2010.

[25] Smitha Shyam, Kypros Constantinides, Sujay Phadke, Valeria Bertacco, and Todd Austin. Ultra low-cost defect protection for microprocessor pipelines. In ASPLOS, pages 73–82, 2006.

[26] Virendra Singh, Michiko Inoue, Kewal K. Saluja, and Hideo Fujiwara. Instruction-based self-testing of delay faults in pipelined processors. IEEE TVLSI, 14(11):1203–1215, November 2006.

[27] Sun. Sun OpenSPARC Project, 2010.

[28] James Tschanz, Keith Bowman, Chris Wilkerson, Shih-Lien Lu, and Tanay Karnik. Resilient circuits: enabling energy-efficient performance and reliability. In ICCAD, pages 71–73, 2009.

[29] A.K. Uht. Going beyond worst-case specs with teatime. IEEE Micro Top Picks, pages 51–56, 2004.

[30] Bardia Zandian, Waleed Dweik, Suk Hun Kang, Thomas Punihaole, and Murali Annavaram. Wearmon: Reliability monitoring using adaptive critical path testing. In DSN, pages 151–160, 2010.

Algorithms for Power-Efficient QoS in Application Specific NoCs

Hao He
Department of ECE
Texas A&M University
haohe2012fall@tamu.edu

Gongming Yang
Department of ECE
Texas A&M University
edward_yang@tamu.edu

Jiang Hu
Department of ECE
Texas A&M University
jianghu@ece.tamu.edu

ABSTRACT

Quality-of-Service (QoS) is a fundamental part of Networks-on-Chip (NoC) design. In application specific NoCs, guaranteed QoS is often obtained by static bandwidth reservation at design-time. The bandwidth allocation inevitably affects power-efficiency, which is crucial yet largely neglected in prior NoC QoS methods. In this work, we develop two algorithmic techniques that concurrently address power-efficiency and QoS. One is path-based integer linear programming (ILP) and the other is a negotiation-based heuristic. Both techniques support multiple user-cases. Simulation results show that our techniques significantly outperform an iterative greedy heuristic and are order of magnitude faster than conventional edge-based ILP.

Keywords

Networks-on-Chip, Quality-of-Service, power-efficiency

1. INTRODUCTION

As chip complexity continues to grow, more resources, including clock cycle time and energy, are spent on moving data around than on computing operations. On-chip communication therefore plays a pivotal role on determining the overall chip performance and power. To cope with the increasingly large demand for communication bandwidth, people recently exploit ideas from computer network technology and establish the new field of Networks-on-Chip (NoC). Unlike computation units, whose performance is mostly decided by their speed, NoC performance also relies on how its bandwidth is allocated among different communication requests. An imbalanced allocation may create bottleneck threads and thereby degrade the overall application execution. This problem is the main subject of Quality-of-Service (QoS), which is often categorized into best efforts (BE) and *guaranteed service* (GS). Guaranteed service is obviously more desirable, but more difficult to achieve than best efforts. A main focus of our work is NoC bandwidth allocation for guaranteed service in MultiProcessor System-on-Chip (MPSoC) designs. The bandwidth use inevitably involves power – a grand challenge faced by the semiconductor industry. In this regard, our work also emphasizes power-efficiency and addresses it in conjunction with QoS.

An MPSoC often has multiple operation user-cases. For example, a smart phone processor may perform text editing, voice recognition or video streaming at different times. Each user-case entails a specific traffic pattern on NoC. This application specific nature, as opposed to the largely random traffic in chip multiprocessors, allows guaranteed service to be obtained by reserving resources at design-time [1–6]. The resources include both physical ones - links along a packet routing path, and temporal ones - time slots at each link, i.e., the resource allocation is based on Time Division Multiplexing (TDM). Many works [1–6] take this approach, but pay almost no attention on the power issue. Perhaps the only work that seems to touch both power-efficiency and NoC QoS is [7]. It mainly solves task mapping/scheduling assuming fixed routing and fixed link/buffer capacity. As such, the role of NoC in [7] is more of background than design space.

We propose design-time algorithms of simultaneous packet routing, time slot assignment and link/buffer capacity optimization for guaranteed service. Distinguished from the previous works [1–6], we minimize the total of dynamic energy, which depends on packet routing, and static energy, which is decided by link capacity and buffer size. NoC capacity optimization is studied in [8], but without handling QoS. We first introduce a new Integer Linear Programming (ILP) formulation, which has substantially lower computation cost than conventional ILP formulation [5]. We also develop a heuristic inspired by layout routing algorithm [9, 10]. Both techniques support multiple user-cases and reserve bandwidth for best efforts packets. Like in [4,5], the solutions are deadlock free by construction. Our ILP technique also permits multi-route and in-order delivery [4]. Since flit-level static scheduling and routing has been shown feasible in Æthereal network [4] and FPGA [5], we focus on algorithmic techniques instead of hardware implementation. To the best of our knowledge, this is the first algorithmic work on power-efficient QoS for application specific NoCs. For comparison, we extend two previous works with related but different goals. One is the NoC capacity optimization algorithm [8], which is an iterative greedy heuristic, and the other is bandwidth allocation algorithm for only QoS [5], which is conventional edge-based ILP approach. Experimental results show that our techniques significantly outperform iterative greedy heuristic and are dramatically faster than edge-based ILP.

2. PREVIOUS RELATED WORKS

An early work on TDM-based NoC QoS is [1] where packet routing and time slot assignment are performed separately. In [2,3], routing paths are searched exhaustively and the search is coupled with a naïve time slot assignment scheme. The work of [4] conducts simultaneous routing and time slot assignment using a network flow approach. An edge-based Integer Linear Programming (ILP) method for the bandwidth allocation is described in [5]. Boolean satisfiability and wire routing-based techniques are reported in [6]. These works [1–6] are mostly focused on NoC QoS alone without optimizing power-efficiency.

Power and performance are simultaneously considered in task mapping/routing [11], NoC topology synthesis [12] and voltage/task scheduling [13]. However, latency constraints are enforced for overall tasks and there is no performance guarantee for individual packets in these works. In video applications, such approaches may result in significant delays for some image frames and consequent viedo quality degradation. A NoC capacity optimization algorithm is proposed in [8]. It is similar as minimizing the static power of NoC, but does not address QoS. The work of [7] attempts to minimize energy subject to deadline constraint. However, its main emphasis is on task mapping/scheduling and NoC mostly serves as the context. It also assumes fixed link/buffer capacity and neglects static energy.

3. PROBLEM FORMULATION

The problem inputs include a set of user-cases on a fixed NoC topology. In a user-case, each GS packet has a range of available time and a latency constraint. Additionally, there is the minimum bandwidth required for overall BE packets. In a router, BE buffers and GS buffers are separated. Otherwise, BE flits may block GS flits for an arbitrarily long time. Time on each link/buffer is divided into slots that can be assigned to different flits, i.e., TDM.

For each GS packet/flit, the decisions are to find routing path in terms of links/buffers, and time slots along the path[1]. Additionally, a lumped sum of BE bandwidth is reserved, and link/buffer capacities are also decided like in [8]. The objective is to minimize an average energy dissipation among all user-cases, including dynamic and static energy.

Ideally, a flit is routed along the shortest physical path in the network without waiting in a buffer. If there is resource contention between different flits, the decisions face three options: (1) increasing link capacity, (2) waiting in a buffer and (3) routing detour. Options (1) and (2) increase static energy while option (3) causes more dynamic energy. Hence, there is a tradeoff among these options and it is likely a link/buffer has zero capacity in a solution, i.e., a link/buffer is removed. The problem formulation is given as follows.

PEQoS (Power-Efficient QoS): *Given an NoC topology, a set of traffic user-cases, find routing paths and time slot assignment for each GS flit, and decide link and GS buffer capacity such that a weighted average of energy dissipation among all user-cases is minimized, every GS packet satisfies its latency constraint and sufficient link bandwidth remains for BE packets.*

The weighting factors for user-cases are design parameters. For example, they can be the estimated probabili-

ties of individual user-cases. Customers can also decide how much link bandwidth should be kept for BE packets, which are routed in a distributed manner. In contrast, GS packets employ source routing. Since the TDM switchings are determined at design time, deadlock can be easily avoided for GS packets like in [4,5]. As GS buffers are separated from BE buffers, there will be no deadlock between GS and BE packets. Our techniques can be applied to various NoC topologies, from regular mesh to customized topology. We also allow flits of the same packet to take different routes while the in-order delivery constraint is satisfied.

4. GRAPH MODEL

The physical and temporal resources of an NoC can be described in a unified graph model, where solving PEQoS is equivalent to finding a path for every flit. We first define physical graph $G(V, E_L, E_B)$, which does not contain temporal information. It has a set of nodes V, each of which represents a router, and two sets of edges, E_L for links and E_B indicating buffers. An example is shown in Figure 1(a), where dashed edges are for E_B.

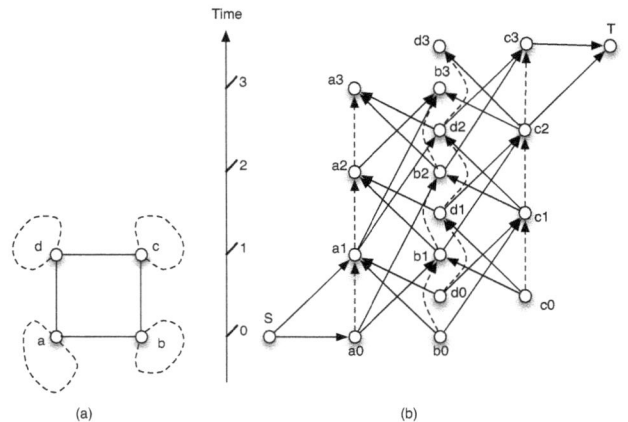

Figure 1: (a) Physical graph; (b) Resource graph.

In a resource graph, temporal resource is embraced by duplicating physical nodes along the time axis and connecting nodes at different time planes with edges. This is illustrated in Figure 1(b), where two adjacent time planes are separated by one clock cycle. If the latency of a link is m clock cycles, the corresponding edge spans $m + 1$ time planes. In order to limit the graph size, we assume that the traffic patterns are repeated in periodic time windows. This assumption is reasonable if the window size is sufficiently large [4,6]. In a resource graph $\mathcal{G}(\mathcal{V}, \mathcal{E}_L, \mathcal{E}_B)$, a node $v \in V$ is duplicated into $v^0, v^1, ..., v^\Psi \in \mathcal{V}$ at time plane $0, 1, ..., \Psi$, where Ψ is the window size. Any time τ corresponds to $k\Psi + \tau$, where k is an integer. An edge elapsing through two adjacent windows wraps around in the graph [4,6]. For example, an edge starting from $v_i^\Psi \in \mathcal{V}$ may end at $v_j^1 \in \mathcal{V}$. The time range for a packet ready to inject can be modeled by a super source node like S In Figure 1(b). The deadline for a flit can be enforced by super target node. In Figure 1(b), the super target node T requires that the corresponding flit must arrive physical node c by time 3. Edges $\mathcal{E}_L$ and $\mathcal{E}_B$ correspond to links and buffers, respectively.

[1] The flit level static scheduling and routing is demonstrated to be feasible in Æthereal network [4] and FPGA [5].

5. PROPOSED TECHNIQUES

PEQoS is a combinatorial optimization problem, which can often be solved by greedy heuristic or Integer Linear Programming (ILP). For complex problems, however, greedy heuristic is easily trapped into low-quality solutions while ILP is computationally too expensive. We approach the PEQoS problem from two directions: (1) starting from ILP and reducing its computation cost, and (2) starting from greedy heuristic and improving solution quality.

5.1 Path-Based Integer Linear Programming

Integer Linear Programming has been applied to solve NoC QoS before [5]. In their approaches, the binary decision variables are defined to indicate if *edges* in the resource graph are selected to transport flits. Such formulation guarantees that optimal solution is in the search space. However, such approach does not scale well with problem size and can be applied at only very small cases in practice.

We propose a path-based ILP formulation, where a decision variable tells if to select a *path* in the resource graph for a flit. This approach requires that a set of candidate paths are generated for each flit in advance. Since it is not practical to include all possible paths in this set, there is no guarantee for optimality. However, by carefully generating the candidates, one can attain near optimal solutions with much better scalability than the edge-based ILP method.

We describe the path-based ILP formulation followed by an introduction to the candidate paths generation. An MPSoC design has a set of $\mathcal{M}$ user-cases. In each user-case $\mu \in \mathcal{M}$, there is a set of packet requests per time window and each packet is composed by one or multiple flits. To simplify the description without loss of generality, we specify the requests in flits, i.e., a set of flit requests Φ_μ for each user-case μ per time window. A set of candidate paths $P_i = \{p_{i,1}, p_{i,2}, ...\}$ on $\mathcal{G}$ are found for flit ϕ_i, and each of the paths has a variable $x_{i,j} \in \{0,1\}$ indicating if path $p_{i,j}$ is selected. Each link $l \in E_L$ has a variable capacity y_l telling how many flits it can simultaneously transport. Similarly, each buffer $b \in E_B$ has capacity z_b, which is the number of flits it can accommodate. Dynamic energy for a time window in user-case μ is represented by Δ_μ. The static energies per time window for unit link and buffer capacity are denoted by ϵ_l and ϵ_b, respectively. We use $\phi_i \prec \phi_j$ to indicate that ϕ_i is injected into the network earlier than ϕ_j and they belong to the same packet. The ILP formulation is as follows.

$$\text{Min} \quad \sum_{\mu \in \mathcal{M}} \omega_\mu \Delta_\mu + \sum_{l \in E_L} \epsilon_l y_l + \sum_{b \in E_B} \epsilon_b z_b \quad (1)$$

$$\text{s.t.} \quad \Delta_\mu = \sum_{\phi_i \in \Phi_\mu} \sum_{p_{i,j} \in P_i} \delta_{i,j} x_{i,j} \quad (2)$$

$$\sum_{p_{i,j} \in P_i} x_{i,j} = 1, \quad \forall \phi_i \in \Phi_\mu, \quad \forall \mu \in \mathcal{M} \quad (3)$$

$$\sum_{e_l \in p_{i,j}} x_{i,j} \leq y_l \leq U_l, \quad \forall e_l \in \mathcal{E}_L, \quad \forall \mu \in \mathcal{M} \quad (4)$$

$$\sum_{e_b \in p_{i,j}} x_{i,j} \leq z_b \leq U_b, \quad \forall e_b \in \mathcal{E}_B, \quad \forall \mu \in \mathcal{M} \quad (5)$$

$$\sum_{p_{i,j} \in P_i} |p_{i,j}| x_{i,j} \leq \sum_{p_{k,q} \in P_k} |p_{k,q}| x_{k,q}, \forall \phi_i \prec \phi_k \quad (6)$$

$$\Psi y_l - \sum_{e_l \in \mathcal{E}_l, \in p_{i,j}} x_{i,j} \geq \beta_l, \quad \forall l \in E_L \quad (7)$$

$$x_{i,j} \in \{0,1\}, \quad \forall x_{i,j} \quad (8)$$

$$y_l, z_b \in Z^*, \quad \forall y_l, z_b \quad (9)$$

The objective (1) is to minimize total energy consumption per time window. The first term is in (1) is a weighted average of dynamic energy among all user-cases. The weighting factors ω_μ are user specified parameters, and can be obtained

by system level characterization. The dynamic energy of each user-case is defined by constraint (2). The dynamic energy of propagating flit ϕ_i through path $p_{i,j}$ is represented by $\delta_{i,j}$. The second (third) term in (1) is for the static energy of all links (buffers). Constraint (3) enforces that one and only one path is selected for each flit. Constraints (4) and (5) ensure that each link/buffer capacity does not exceed certain bound U_l/U_b. In (6), $|p_{i,j}|$ means the path length in term of clock cycles for path $p_{i,j}$. Then, this is the constraint for in-order delivery. The last significant constraint (7) is to make sure at least β_l bandwidth is left for BE flits at link l per time window.

Now we discuss the candidate paths generation. The candidate paths should all satisfy latency constraints and consist of short paths so as to increase the chance of low dynamic energy solutions. To this end, we first generate all the paths that has minimum number of hops, which can be found by Breadth First Search. In addition, the candidate paths for a flit need to be diversified so that contention with other flits can be easily avoided. Thus, we also generate candidate paths by the same method as [6]. For each flit, our method iteratively performs the shortest path algorithm on the resource graph and the result is added to the candidate path set. At the end of each iteration, the cost of each edge along this path is increased by a fixed amount so that later iterations attempt to circumvent these edges and thereby improve path diversity.

After the candidate path generation, the ILP formulation is fed to a ILP solver which tries to optimize it and may use different algorithms such as Branch and Bound and Cutting Plane Method.

5.2 Negotiation-Based Heuristic

Besides seeking the shortest paths on the resource graph, a key point is to increase link/buffer sharing among different flits so that static energy (or equivalently link/buffer capacity) is reduced.

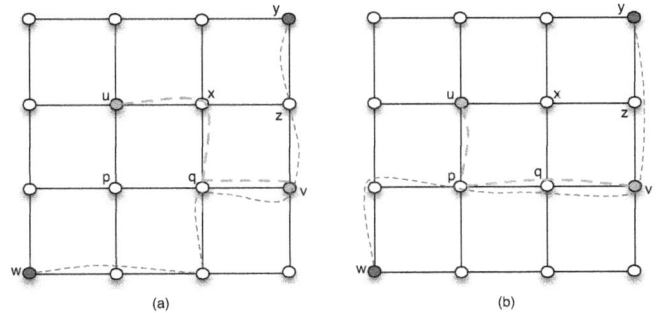

Figure 2: Greedily rerouting one flit at a time may get stuck at (a) while a better solution is (b).

A related work [8] is an iterative greedy heuristic for minimizing only link capacities. It iteratively routes a flow along the minimal cost path in the network. If a link capacity has already been used in previous iterations, its cost is regarded as zero to encourage reuse. By employing the resource graph described in Section 4, this heuristic can be easily extended to solve PEQoS. However, it sometimes misses good solutions due to its greedy nature. In Figure 2(a), flit-1 ($u \leadsto v$)

is first routed like the thick (red) dashed trace. When flit-2 ($w \rightsquigarrow y$) is routed next, the thin (blue) dashed path is found in order to share the use of link (q, v). Assume that both flits are injected into the network at the same time, flit-1 would traverse link (q, v) earlier than flit-2. Hence, there is no temporal contention between them. If we simply extend [8], when flit-1 is rerouted in later iterations, it would take the same route as before in order to share link (q, v) with flit-2. Likewise, rerouting flit-2 would not alter its route. In other words, the solution gets stuck at Figure 2(a) even though a better solution (b), where two links are shared, exists.

We introduce a new heuristic composed by three phases: (1) initial GS routing, (2) GS rerouting, and (3) BE bandwidth allocation. In the initial routing, all packets are sorted in non-decreasing order of flexibility in terms of the number of shortest paths. Then, all packets are routed one by one using Dijkstra's shortest path algorithm. The latency of a link $(u, v) \in E_L$ is denoted by $\lambda(u, v)$. In a resource graph $\mathcal{G}$, an edge from node u at time plane τ to node v at time plane $\tau + \lambda(u, v)$ is represented by $(u, v)^{\tau, \tau+\lambda(u,v)}$. The edge cost is defined by

$$w((u, v)^{t, t+\lambda(u,v)}) = \delta_u + \delta_{(u,v)} + \hat{\epsilon}_{(u,v)} \qquad (10)$$

where δ_u and $\delta_{(u,v)}$ are the dynamic energy to send a flit through the switch at u and link (u, v), respectively. The term $\hat{\epsilon}_{(u,v)}$ is the static energy cost, which is 0 if the number of flits through (u, v) during time $(\tau, \tau + \lambda(u, v))$ is less than the maximum number of flits through (u, v) during any other time. The cost for buffer edges can be defined similarly.

In the GS rerouting phase, some flits are selected to be rerouted in order for increasing link/buffer sharing. Our approach is inspired by the negotiation technique in layout routing [9,10], where an edge cost is unremittingly increased as long as the edge has capacity violation. Compared to a cost that is oblivious to how long a violation exists, the increasing cost is more effective on driving wires away from congested regions. A naïve application of this idea to our case is to continuously decrease an edge cost such that flits can be attracted to the same link/buffer. However, a simple exercise on Figure 2 tells that such application only results in detour instead of solution (b). Moreover, continuously decreasing edge cost may end up with negative edge cost, which disallows the use of the Dijkstra's algorithm.

Our idea is to identify those troublesome edges, which prevent link/buffer sharing, and increase their cost using negotiation like in [9,10]. We define a link as *non-preferred* if it has at least one flit passing through, the minimum bounding box of a passing through flit is contained within the minimum bounding box of any other flit, and the link direction is against a shortest path of any flit whose minimum bounding box encloses this link. In Figure 2(a), link (x, q) is non-preferred as flit-1 passes through it, the minimum bounding box of flit-1 is contained within the minimum bounding box of flit-2, and a shortest path of flit-2 can be found to go through (q, x). At each rerouting iteration, all flits passing through any non-preferred links are ripped up, the cost of every non-preferred link is increased and then the ripped flits are rerouted like in the initial phase. The negotiation is implemented by using a history factor $h(u, v)$ for each link $(u, v) \in E_L$. Then, the edge cost is redefined to

$$w((u, v)^{t, t+\lambda(u,v)}) = (\delta_u + \delta_{(u,v)}) \cdot (1 + \log h(u, v)) + \hat{\epsilon}_{(u,v)} \qquad (11)$$

At the very beginning, $h(u, v) = 1$ and is increased by 1 at each iteration when (u, v) is non-preferred.

In Figure 2(a), link (x, q) is non-preferred and hence the history factor of its corresponding edge in $\mathcal{E}_L$ is increased. Then, rerouting flit-1 would take path $u \rightarrow p \rightarrow q \rightarrow v$ as the thick (red) dashed trace in Figure 2(b). Next, flit-2 would take the thin (blue) dashed route in Figure 2(b) as (p, q) and (q, v) have already been used by flit-1 and do not cost additional static energy for flit-2.

The adoption of negotiation in our case is more subtle than it seems to be. In layout routing, moving a wire away from congested region is almost always desirable. For solving PEQoS, deflecting one flit away from a non-preferred link does not always help as other flits passing through the same link may have less link sharing. Quite often, one wants to deflect many or all flits away from a non-preferred link so that the chance of sharing in other links is increased. This is why the history factor in our heuristic never decreases, unlike that in layout routing [9,10]. Since rerouting a flit may or may not increase link sharing, the total energy does not always decrease over iterations. However, our heuristic does dig out more opportunities of capacity sharing as illustrated by the example in Figure 2.

Input : Resource graph $\mathcal{G}$, GS flits Φ and their initial routing on $\mathcal{G}$, iteration count k
Output: Rerouting of Φ on $\mathcal{G}$

1 **while** $(--k > 0)$ **do**
2     $\Phi_R \leftarrow \emptyset$;
3   **for** *each non-preferred link* $\hat{l}$ **do**
4   Increase history factor for edges corresponding to $\hat{l}$;
5   **for** $\phi \in \Phi$ **do**
6   **if** $\hat{l} \in path(\phi)$ **then**
7   Rip up ϕ from $\mathcal{G}$; $\Phi_R \leftarrow \Phi_R \cup \{\phi\}$;
8   **end**
9   **end**
10   **end**
11   Sort Φ_R in non-decreasing order of flexibility;
12   **for** $\phi \in \Phi_R$ **do**
13   Route ϕ on $\mathcal{G}$ using Dijkstra's algorithm;
14   **end**
15   Save the min-cost solution;
16 **end**
17 Apply the min-cost solution;

Algorithm 1: GS flits rerouting.

An algorithm sketch for the GS rerouting phase is provided in Algorithm 1. The GS routing described so far, including phase 1 and 2, is for only one user-case. For multiple user-cases, we first sort them according to an estimated bandwidth demand. Assuming that every GS flit is routed with the minimum-hop path, then the total dynamic energy of a user-case provides a credible estimate of the bandwidth demand by this user-case. All user-cases are processed one after another in a non-decreasing order of bandwidth demand. If a link/buffer capacity is used in earlier cases, the corresponding static energy is treated as zero for later cases.

Finally, we check unallocated bandwidth of each link, and add the minimum capacity needed to satisfy the demand by BE packets.

Table 1: Main results for TGFF cases.

Testcases	#cases	Total $|\mathcal{V}|$	$|\mathcal{M}|$	Iterative Greedy		Path-Based ILP		Negotiation	
				Energy	Runtime (s)	Energy	Runtime (s)	Energy	Runtime (s)
Group 1	9	1250-1500	1,5	459	161	324	288	355	377
Group 2	14	2000-2250	3,10	299	224	222	1022	262	502
Group 3	12	2400-2500	3,5	375	320	273	2047	321	721
Group 4	14	3000-3200	5,8,15	235	233	177	1642	217	547
Group 5	10	4800	10, 15	146	188	116	2961	142	433
Group 6	10	5000	8, 10	220	192	151	5239	206	465
Group 7	5	6400	8	266	529	208	3817	268	1132
Group 8	9	7200-7500	12, 15	178	329	141	5439	176	763
Normalized total	83			1	1	0.75	10.3	0.92	2.3

6. EXPERIMENT

In the experiment, we attempt to evaluate the effectiveness of our techniques by comparing with extensions of two related but different works. One is the *iterative greedy* method for NoC capacity optimization [8] and the other is the conventional *edge-based ILP*, which is recently used [5] in NoC QoS without considering power dissipation.

The comparisons are conducted on two types of testcases. One is random benchmarks generated by TGFF [14], which has been employed in many other NoC works such as [7,11]. The other is a more realistic benchmark developed for multimedia SoC in the NaNoC project (http://www.nanoc-project.eu). The energy dissipation, including both dynamic and static energy, is estimated by ORION3.0 [15] based on 65nm technology. All methods are implemented and simulated with C/C++ and ILP is solved by LP-Solve (http://lpsolve.sourceforge.net/). The experiment is performed on AMD Opteron processor with 2.2GHz frequency and Linux operating system.

The first experiment is on 83 TGFF cases and the results are summarized in Table 1. To save space, the results are presented in 8 groups and the second column tells the number of cases in each group. The third column lists the total number of nodes $|\mathcal{V}|$ for the resource graphs of all user-cases in one testcase. Please note $|\mathcal{V}| = |V| \cdot \Psi \cdot |\mathcal{M}|$, where $|V|$ is the number of physical nodes and takes value of 10, 16 or 25 for each case. The number of user-cases $|\mathcal{M}|$ is in the fourth column. Please note that the runtime also depends on the number of flits in addition to $|\mathcal{V}|$. Each packet contains 1-3 flits and the latency across each link can be 1 or 2 clock cycles. The energy and computation runtime results are shown in the right six columns. As the energy is a weighted average among all user-cases, it does not necessarily grow with the total $|\mathcal{V}|$. The last line indicates that our path-based ILP can reduce energy dissipation by 25% compared to extension of [8]. Our negotiation-based heuristic also brings 8% energy savings. Among these cases, $10\% - 60\%$ bandwidth is allocated to GS packets and the others are to be used by BE packets. Please note that the greedy heuristic terminates when it gets stuck at a local optima, hence further iterations would not improve its results.

In the second experiment, we compare our path-based ILP with optimal edge-based ILP solutions. Since the edge-based ILP is very slow, this part of experiment is carried out only on small cases. The results are displayed in Table 2. One can see that our technique is only 1% worse than the optimal but over 2000X faster than the edge-based ILP. In a small example, our path-based ILP entails about 1K vari-

Table 2: Optimality test on small TGFF cases.

	Total $|\mathcal{V}|$	Edge-ILP (Optimal)		Path-Based ILP	
		Energy	Runtime	Energy	Runtime
Case 1	216	3.18	466	3.23	<1
Case 2	220	1.81	249	1.81	<1
Case 3	240	1.59	18	1.59	<1
Case 4	250	2.67	3009	2.71	<1
Case 5	288	2.80	279	2.84	<1
Case 6	288	3.13	1179	3.17	<1
Case 7	300	2.29	5769	2.34	<1
Case 8	312	2.93	6934	2.93	<1
Case 9	405	2.14	2807	2.14	<1
Norm. Ave.		1	2301	1.01	1

ables while the edge-based ILP requires 54K variables. This explains why the path-based ILP is much faster.

The third experiment is on a set of relatively large TGFF cases. Although our path-based ILP often reaches near optimal solutions and is much faster than the edge-based ILP, its runtime is not ideal for large cases. On the other hand, our negotiation-based heuristic demonstrates its value on large cases. This is shown in Table 3 where the negotiation-based heuristic obtains 14% energy reduction compared to the iterative greedy heuristic. The runtime is increased but still at a manageable level.

Table 3: Results on large TGFF cases.

	Total $|\mathcal{V}|$	Iterative Greedy		Negotiation	
		Energy	Runtime	Energy	Runtime
Case 1	9000	844	3347	718	7239
Case 2	9900	1694	9126	1358	17461
Case 3	10010	1336	6018	1178	12712
Case 4	10080	1541	7556	1289	14744
Case 5	10200	1275	5680	1135	12337
Case 6	10200	1331	6990	1117	13725
Case 7	10260	1458	7487	1217	14961
Case 8	10400	1216	6095	1088	13215
Case 9	10500	798	3292	697	7097
Case 10	10500	1269	6173	1090	12253
Case 11	10500	1050	5618	966	11090
Norm. Ave.		1	1	0.86	2.03

The multimedia SoC case (http://www.nanoc-project.eu) has 25 cores and 8 user-cases. The NoC topology of 10 router nodes and traffic patterns are given. We vary the latency constraints and window size to obtain 9 variants of this case. The energy comparison among different techniques for these cases are depicted in Figure 3. Compared to the iterative greedy heuristic, our path-based ILP and negotiation-based algorithm achieve energy reduction of 15% and 9%, respectively. The runtime of our path-based ILP is actually less than the greedy heuristic in these cases.

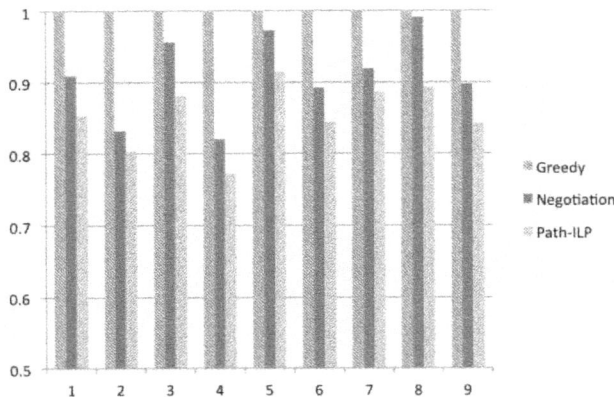

Figure 3: Normalized energy comparison for multi-media SoC cases.

In the last part of the experiment, we examine the energy-latency tradeoff that can be obtained by our technique. For three TGFF cases, we vary the latency constraints and observe the impact on energy consumption. Figure 4 exhibits the results from our path-based ILP. Its horizontal axis indicates normalized packet latency and the vertical axis is normalized energy dissipation. The curves show a few small kinks because the problem is non-convex and our technique cannot guarantee the optimality. The overall trend of these curves does provide tradeoff between energy and latency.

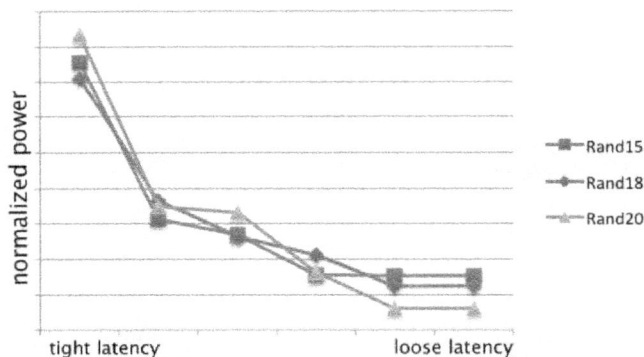

Figure 4: Energy-latency tradeoff of 3 different cases.

7. CONCLUSIONS

In this work, we propose new algorithms for TDM-based NoC QoS with consideration of power-efficiency. To the best of our knowledge, this is the first dedicated work that simultaneously achieves QoS and optimizes power for application-specific NoCs. Our path-based ILP approach provides solutions that cost about 25% less energy dissipation than an iterative greedy heuristic and are near to the optimal solutions, and is order of magnitude faster than the optimal method. Our negotiation-based heuristic is even faster and still outperforms the iterative greedy heuristic, especially for large cases.

8. REFERENCES

[1] A. Hansson, K. Goossens, and A. Rădulescu. A unified approach to constrained mapping and routing on network-on-chip architectures. In *Proceedings of the IEEE/ACM/IFIP International Conference on Hardware/Software Codesign and System Synthesis*, pages 75–80, 2005.

[2] S. Stuijk, T. Basten, M. C. W. Geilen, A. H. Ghamarian, and B. D. Theelen. Resource-efficient routing and scheduling of time-constrained network-on-chip communication. *Elsevier Journal of Systems Architecture*, 54(3-4):411–426, March 2008.

[3] Z. Lu and A. Jantsch. TDM virtual-circuit configuration for network-on-chip. *IEEE Transactions on VLSI Systems*, 16(8):1021–1034, August 2008.

[4] R. Stefan and K. Goossens. A TDM slot allocation flow based on multipath routing in NoCs. *Elsevier Journal on Microprocessors and Microsystems*, 35(2):130–138, March 2011.

[5] M. Schoeberl, F. Brandner, J. Sparsø, and E. Kasapaki. A statically scheduled time-division-multiplexed network-on-chip for real-time systems. In *Proceedings of the IEEE/ACM International Symposium on Networks-on-Chip*, pages 152–160, 2012.

[6] G. Yang, H. He, and J. Hu. Resource allocation algorithms for guaranteed service in application-specific NoCs. In *Proceedings of the IEEE International Conference on Computer Design*, pages 483–486, 2013.

[7] J. Hu and R. Marculescu. Energy-aware communication and task scheduling for network-on-chip architectures under real-time constraints. In *Proceedings of Design, Automation and Test in Europe Conference*, pages 234–239, 2004.

[8] I. Walter, E. Kantor, I. Cidon, and S. Kutten. Capacity optimized NoC for multi-mode SoC. In *Proceedings of the ACM/IEEE Design Automation Conference*, pages 942–947, 2011.

[9] L. McMurchie and C. Ebeling. PathFinder: a negotiation-based performance-driven router for FPGAs. In *Proceedings of ACM International Symposium on Field-Programmable Gate Arrays*, pages 111–117, 1995.

[10] J. A. Roy and I. L. Markov. High-performance routing at the nanometer scale. *IEEE Transactions on Computer-Aided Design*, 27(6):1066–1077, June 2008.

[11] J. Hu and R. Marculescu. Energy- and performance-aware mapping for regular NoC architectures. *IEEE Transactions on Computer-Aided Design*, 24(4):551–562, April 2005.

[12] Y. Hu, Y. Zhu, H. Chen, R. Graham, and C.-K. Cheng. Communication latency aware low power NoC synthesis. In *Proceedings of the ACM/IEEE Design Automation Conference*, pages 574–579, 2006.

[13] Y. Liu, Y. Yang, and J. Hu. Clustering-based simultaneous task and voltage scheduling for NOC systems. In *Proceedings of the IEEE/ACM International Conference on Computer-Aided Design*, pages 277–283, 2010.

[14] D. Rhodes, R. Dick, and K. Vallerio. Task graph for free. http://ziyang.eecs.umich.edu/ dickrp/tgff/.

[15] J. Fong, S. Nath, A. B. Kahng, and B. Lin. ORION3.0: a power-performance simulator for interconnection networks. http://vlsicad.ucsd.edu/ORION3/.

Design and CAD Methodologies for Low Power Gate-level Monolithic 3D ICs

Shreepad Panth[†], Kambiz Samadi[§], Yang Du[§], and Sung Kyu Lim[†]
[†]School of ECE, Georgia Institute of Technology, Atlanta, GA
[§]Qualcomm Research, San Diego, CA
{spanth,limsk}@ece.gatech.edu

ABSTRACT

In a gate-level monolithic 3D IC (M3D), all the transistors in a single logic gate occupy the same tier, and gates in different tiers are connected using nano-scale monolithic inter-tier vias. This design style has the benefit of the superior power-performance quality offered by flat implementations (unlike block-level M3D), and zero total silicon area overhead compared to 2D (unlike transistor-level M3D). In this paper we develop, for the first time, a complete RTL-to-GDSII design flow for gate-level M3D. Our tool flow is based on commercial tools built for 2D ICs and enhanced with our 3D-specific methodologies. We use this flow along with a 28nm PDK to build layouts for the OpenSPARC T2 core. Our simulations show that at the same performance, gate-level M3D offers 16% total power reduction with 0% area overhead compared to commercial quality 2D IC designs.

Categories and Subject Descriptors

B.7.2 [**Integrated Circuits**]: Design Aids—*Placement and routing*

Keywords

Monolithic 3D; Timing Closure

1. INTRODUCTION

Monolithic 3D ICs (M3D) are an emerging technology that offers orders of magnitude higher integration density than other 3D integration technologies such as through-silicon-via (TSV), silicon interposer, etc, thanks to its nano-scale monolithic inter-tier vias (MIVs) [1]. There are three design styles possible for monolithic 3D ICs: transistor-level, gate-level, and block-level. In transistor-level monolithic 3D ICs [2, 5], the PMOS and NMOS within each standard cell is split into different tiers, and MIVs are used for intra-cell as well as inter-cell connections. This is the finest-grained integration style, and has the advantage that the PMOS and NMOS fabrication process can be optimized separately. However, it requires redesign and re-characterization of the standard cells themselves, which takes significant effort. Also, the standard cell foot-

This work is supported by Qualcomm Research.

Permission to make digital or hard copies of all or part of this work for personal or classroom use is granted without fee provided that copies are not made or distributed for profit or commercial advantage and that copies bear this notice and the full citation on the first page. Copyrights for components of this work owned by others than ACM must be honored. Abstracting with credit is permitted. To copy otherwise, or republish, to post on servers or to redistribute to lists, requires prior specific permission and/or a fee. Request permissions from permissions@acm.org.
ISLPED'14, August 11–13, 2014, La Jolla, CA, USA
Copyright 2014 ACM 978-1-4503-2975-0/14/08 ...$15.00.
http://dx.doi.org/10.1145/2627369.2627642.

print does not reduce by 50% in 3D due to the mismatch in the PMOS and NMOS sizes. This leads to an increase in total silicon area and cost.

The next design style is gate-level monolithic 3D ICs, where existing standard cells and memory can simply be reused. Gates are placed onto multiple tiers, and MIVs are used to connect them together. The authors of [2] provided a rudimentary design flow that is not capable of handling any hard macros such as memory, and therefore cannot be applied to real designs. The last design style is block-level monolithic 3D ICs, where functional blocks are floorplanned onto different tiers [7]. This style has the benefit of IP reuse, but does not fully take advantage of the fine-grained nature of MIVs. Since the blocks are implemented in 2D, the power benefit of this style is limited.

This paper focuses on gate-level monolithic 3D ICs because they offer the reuse of existing standard cells and memory, zero total silicon area overhead (unlike transistor-level), and a sufficiently high integration density to obtain significant power benefits (unlike block-level). In addition, we focus only on the two-tier case, as it requires only one silicon attachment step. This paper proposes, for the first time, a CAD methodology that is capable of taking gate-level monolithic 3D IC designs all the way though place, route, clock-tree-synthesis, and timing optimization. We use the OpenSPARC T2 [6] core as a case study, and demonstrate that monolithic 3D ICs offer *significant* power benefits compared to *commercial-quality* 2D IC designs.

We demonstrate that using multiple MIVs per signal net can help reduce the total wirelength by 10.03%, giving us a 4.53% net power reduction, which in turn translates into 2.66% total power savings. Next, we present a CTS methodology, that when compared with existing techniques, reduces the clock wirelength and buffer count by 21.91% and 21.56% respectively. This leads to a clock power reduction of 29.82%. When compared to a 2D clock tree, our CTS method enables monolithic 3D to have 23.20% less clock power. All these techniques enable us to achieve 15.57% total power reduction when compared to commercial-grade 2D ICs. Finally, we demonstrate that the power benefit of M3D carries over even when using dual-V_t libraries, and the total power savings rises to 16.08%.

2. DIE STACKING TECHNOLOGIES

We show the various design styles for monolithic 3D ICs in Figure 1(a). As seen from this figure, transistor-level integration is the most fine-grained technique. However, since MIVs are required with each cell, there is an increase in the total cell area (as seen in the INV cell). In addition, each cell will need to be redesigned from scratch. In gate-level monolithic 3D ICs, we observe that there is no area overhead for each cell. We also observe that since

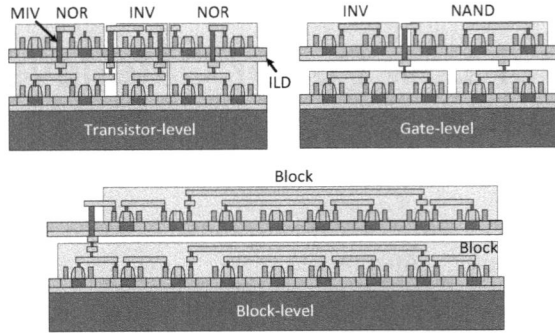

(a) Monolithic 3D ICs

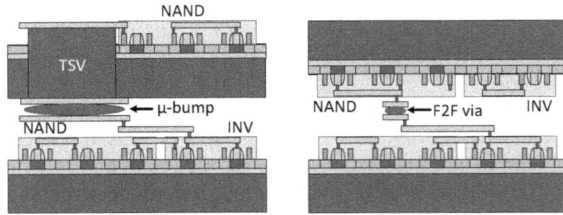

(b) Gate-level TSV-based 3D IC   (c) Gate-level face-to-face 3D IC

Figure 1: Various design styles available for different die stacking technologies.

MIVs can be placed anywhere in between cells, a sufficiently high integration density can be obtained, which will lead to significant power savings. Lastly, we observe that in block-level integration, since each block is the same in 2D and 3D, the potential power benefit is limited.

Out of the three styles considered, gate-level offers the greatest balance between integration density and reuse of existing libraries. Therefore, we focus on gate-level integration in this paper. For gate-level designs, we also show diagrams for TSV-based 3D ICs in Figure 1(b) and face-to-face 3D ICs in Figure 1(c). We clearly see that in TSV-based 3D ICs, the via size is so large that the power benefit is limited. However, face-to-face 3D ICs offer only slightly larger via sizes than monolithic 3D, and can also be considered fine-grained. Therefore, we also include results for gate-level face-to-face 3D ICs in this paper.

3. CAD METHODOLOGY

This section presents our sign-off CAD methodology for monolithic 3D ICs. This methodology is based on the fact that the z-dimension is negligible in monolithic 3D ICs (only a few μm), which enables us to utilize commercial 2D IC tools to perform place and route for M3D.

3.1 Overall Methodology

Consider a true 3D analytical placer that solves equations in the x,y, and z dimensions. Since we consider only the rectilinear half-perimeter wirelength (HPWL), each axis is independent of the other, and is therefore solved independently. Now, since the z dimension is so small (and discrete), all z solutions for a given x and y solution will have more or less the same HPWL. This implies that a 2D placer can be used to first find the x and y solutions, and the z location can be determined as a post-process. Note that this entire process is contingent on the 2D placer being able to place all the gates in a monolithic 3D IC footprint, which is half the footprint area of a 2D IC. This requires several techniques to utilize the

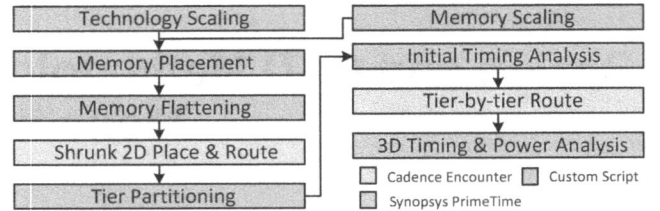

Figure 2: The overall CAD methodology flow used in this paper.

commercial 2D IC tool. In addition, memory complicates the issue, as they are pre-placed in *both* tiers, and this somehow needs to be fed into the commercial tool.

The overall design flow is shown in Figure 2. First, in order to utilize the 2D tool to handle all the standard cells in a reduced footprint, several technology files are scaled, and this process will be described in detail in Subsection 3.2. Next, memory handling requires several steps such as memory scaling, memory placement and memory flattening, which will be described in detail in Subsection 3.3. Once this is done, the commercial 2D engine (Cadence Encounter) can be run on this "shrunk 2D" design (described in Subsection 3.4). This result is then split into multiple tiers to obtain a DRC-clean sign-off design as described in Subsection 3.5, and finally timing and power analysis is performed as described in Subsection 3.6.

3.2 Scaling Technology Files

The goal of this step is twofold. We need to utilize the commercial 2D tool into placing all the gates in half the footprint area, and we also need to make sure that the wire RC information that the tool sees accurately reflects what will be present in the final 3D design. Note that this subsection assumes a gate-only design, and handling memory will be introduced in Subsection 3.3.

Placing all the gates into half the area can be achieved by shrinking the area of each standard cell by 50%. We scale the width, height and the location of all the pins within the cell by $1/\sqrt{2}$ (0.707). In addition, the chip width and height are scaled by 0.707 to reduce the 2D footprint area by half. This will also be the footprint of each tier in the final M3D design. Note that since the x and y axis equations in an analytical placer are linear, scaling all the dimensions by 0.707 will simply make the cell locations 0.707 of what they used to be in the 2D placement solution. This leads to a theoretical HPWL improvement of 29.3%.

Next, in order to make the routing in the shrunk 2D accurately represent the routing in monolithic 3D, we shrink both the metal width and pitch of each metal layer by 0.707. Since the chip width and height are also shrunk by the same amount, the total routing track length does not change between 2D and shrunk 2D. The total track length will also be the same once we go to 3D; hence, this method gives a good estimate of wire length. Note that we *do not* change the wire RC per unit length, even though the wire width is smaller. Therefore, the extracted RC values from the tool does not reflect the geometry of shrunk 2D, but that of a M3D wire of equivalent length using the original metal geometries.

3.3 Handling Memory Macros

While standard cells can be handled by shrinking their footprint, this is not the case for memory. This is because standard cells can be moved by the placer, while memory is pre-placed. Since no standard cell can be placed in the location where a memory is pre-placed, simply shrinking the memory is not an option. We utilize the fact that a pre-placed memory can be thought of as a combina-

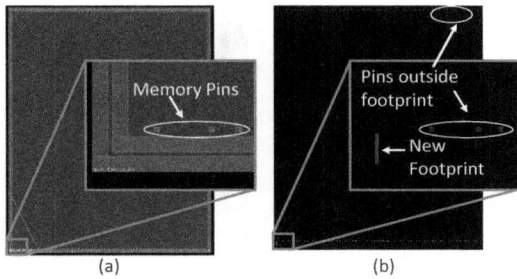

Figure 3: Isolating the memory pins by shrinking the memory footprint. (a) Initial memory footprint, and (b) Memory footprint reduced to size of filler cell.

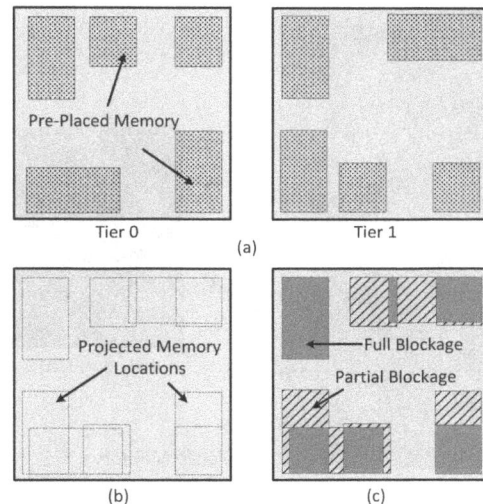

Figure 4: Handling pre-placed memory from a placement blockage perspective. (a) Initial pre-placed locations, (b) Projection of both tiers onto the same plane, and (c) Final placement blockages for shrunk 2D P&R.

tion of its pins, which serve as anchors for standard cell placement, and a placement blockage over its footprint, which prevents cells from being placed over it. We now describe how we utilize the 2D tool to handle memory pins and placement blockages independently.

In order to isolate the memory pin portion, we shrink down the footprint of the memory to the minimum size possible (that of a filler cell). However, we do not scale the relative locations of its pins. This is shown in Figure 3. This will lead to memory pins that are placed outside the memory footprint. These pins will be in the same location they would have been if the memory was its original size. Therefore, from a memory pin perspective, the pre-placed memory in both tiers can simply be shrunk down as described, and fixed in the shrunk 2D footprint.

Handling the placement blockage portion of the memory is more complicated. Consider the pre-placed memories in both tiers as shown in Figure 4(a). First, we project both these tiers onto the same plane as shown in Figure 4(b). Those regions that have two memories overlapping cannot contain cells in any tier, and hence will become full placement blockages in the shrunk 2D footprint. Those regions that have only one memory can contain cells in the tier where the memory is not placed. In the shrunk 2D design, we will need to reduce the maximum placement density of these regions to reflect this fact. This can be achieved by using partial placement blockages. This is shown in Figure 4(c). For example, if the target density of the final 3D design is 70%, then we set the maximum placement density of the partial placement blockages to be 35%. Therefore, this region will have only half the cells of regions not containing memory, representing the fact that those regions only have free space in one tier.

3.4 Shrunk 2D Place and Route

We feed the shrunk technology and standard cell libraries along with the memory related pins and blockages into Cadence Encounter. This commercial 2D IC tool is then used to run through *all* the design stages such as placement, post-placement optimization, CTS, routing, and post-route optimization. Unlike conventional 3D flows, this approach avoids the problem of tier-by-tier timing optimization. The advantage of this is that the tool can see the entire 3D path, and will insert the minimum buffers required to meet timing.

3.5 Obtaining a 3D Design

There are several steps involved in going from a shrunk 2D design to a monolithic 3D IC design. First, we need to split the logic into two tiers. Next, we need to ensure that an adequate clock tree is built. We also need to ensure that signal MIVs are inserted into whitespace locations. Finally, we need to perform tier-by-tier rout-

ing with real design rules (unlike shrunk 2D), so that the design is DRC clean.

3.5.1 Splitting the Logic

We need to split the shrunk 2D design into two tiers ensuring minimum perturbation to the solution. First, the cells are expanded back to their original areas. This will cause overlaps in the placement solution. Next, the memories are moved to their respective tiers. Standard cells placed over partial placement blockages are moved to the tier not containing memory. What remains are cells in those regions without memory in either tier. To partition this, we first create placement bins in a regular fashion. We wish to partition the design such that half the cells in each bin are in tier 0 and the other half in tier 1. This is done by modifying the traditional Fiduccia-Mattheyses [3] (FM) min-cut partitioner. The only difference during partitioning is that we check for area balance within each placement bin instead of area balance in the whole chip. A screenshot of this entire process of obtaining a 3D design using shrunk 2D is shown in Figure 5.

3.5.2 3D Clock Tree Synthesis

Once the logic is split into two tiers, we need to create a 3D clock tree. The conventional approach for 3D ICs (using commercial tools) is to create one separate clock tree per tier, and tie them together using a single MIV. However, the OpenSPARC T2 core has several clock gates built into the RTL. So, to use the conventional approach, we fix all the clock gating cells onto tier 0 (as shown in Figure 6(a)), and construct one clock tree per tier for each gating group. We term this technique as source-level CTS, as MIVs are inserted close to the clock source. This approach does not use the clock tree from shrunk 2D at all, so if we are using this approach, we do not construct a clock tree in shrunk 2D, and instead set a fixed clock uncertainty value during optimization.

In this paper, we propose a new CTS methodology that will help reduce the clock power. Since MIVs are very small, we can safely assume that we can insert as many as required. We propose to utilize the existing CTS result of shrunk 2D. This clock tree contains several levels of logic as shown in Figure 6(b). During the logic splitting process, we fix the entire clock backbone (clock buffers

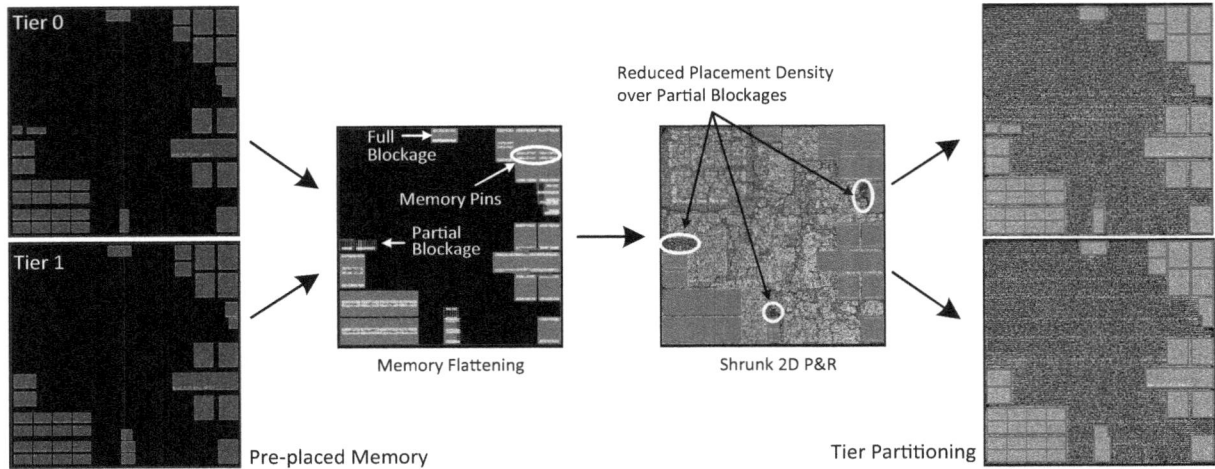

Figure 5: Pre-placed memory is flattened to get a shrunk 2D footprint, on which 2D P&R is performed. This is then partitioned to get a monolithic 3D solution.

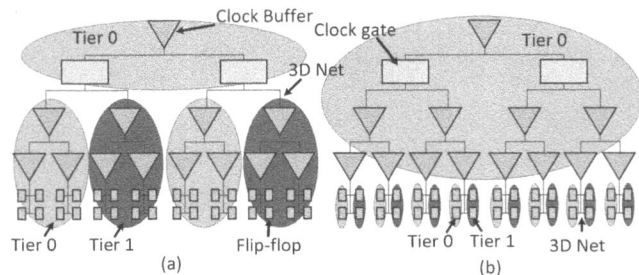

Figure 6: Two different types of 3D CTS possible (a) One clock tree per tier for each gating group (source-level), and (b) The entire backbone is fixed onto tier 0 (leaf-level).

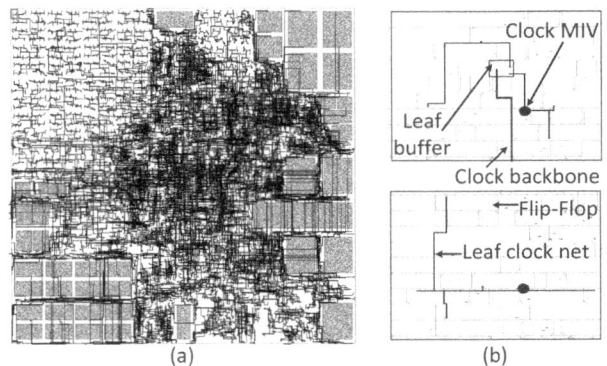

Figure 7: Our proposed CTS methodology (a) The clock backbone in tier 0, and (b) Zoom-in shot of leaf-level flip-flops in both tiers connected to a leaf clock buffer in tier 0.

and clock gates) onto tier 0. Only the leaf-level flip-flops are free to be partitioned to maintain area balance. Therefore, MIVs will be inserted following all leaf clock buffers that drive flip-flops in both tiers. We determine these clock MIV locations using an approach similar to what will be described in Subsection 3.5.3, and then once the tiers are split, we re-route the leaf-level clock nets. This approach is termed leaf-level CTS, and an example of this approach for the OpenSPARC T2 core is shown in Figure 7.

3.5.3 Signal MIV Insertion

We utilize a 2D router that is capable of routing to pins on multiple metal layers to perform MIV insertion for us. First, all the metal layers in the technology LEF are duplicated to yield a new 3D LEF with twice the number of metal layers. Next, for each cell in the LEF file, we define two flavors – one for each tier. The only difference between the two flavors is that their pins are mapped onto different metal layers depending on tier. Next, each cell in the 3D space is mapped to its appropriate flavour, and forced onto the same placement layer. Note that this will lead to cell overlap in the placement layer, but there will be no overlap in the routing layers. We also place routing blockages in the via layer between the two tiers, to prevent MIVs being placed over cells. This entire structure is then fed into Cadence Encounter. Once routed, we trace the routing topology to extract the MIV locations, and generate separate verilog/DEF files for each tier.

Note that for certain nets, the router is bound to insert multiple MIVs. Since existing 3D tool flows use tier-by-tier optimization,

timing constraints need to be derived for each tier. In each tier, MIVs are defined as I/O ports, and the timing constraints are captured as input/output delays. However, if a single net contains multiple MIVs, then it becomes very difficult to capture multiple input/output delays on a single net, as such conditions do not arise in 2D ICs (which current tools are designed for). Therefore, multiple MIV insertion is converted to single MIV insertion by picking the best MIV (in terms of HPWL) from those inserted, and re-routing the net. This could potentially increase the wirelength, but is unavoidable for conventional 3D flows. In our flow, since the optimization is performed in the shrunk 2D design and not tier-by-tier, we can use multiple MIV insertion, which will reduce wirelength and give us a power benefit. Routing topologies for single and multiple MIV insertion for a given net are shown in Figure 8.

Note that the approach proposed here is not limited to monolithic 3D ICs, and can also be applied to other fine-grained 3D integration technologies such as face-to-face (F2F) integration. This can be achieved by simply changing the order of the metal layers in the generated 3D technology LEF file, and not adding a routing blockage over cells, thereby allowing F2F vias to be placed over cells. This is because F2F vias occupy the top metal layer only, and do not require placement space. Sample MIV and F2F vias after insertion are shown in Figure 9.

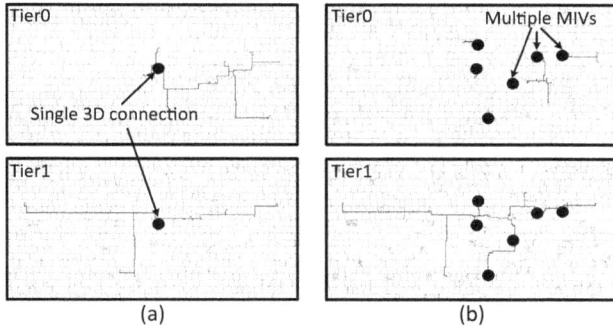

Figure 8: Two types of MIV insertion for a 3D net (a) Single, (b) Multiple

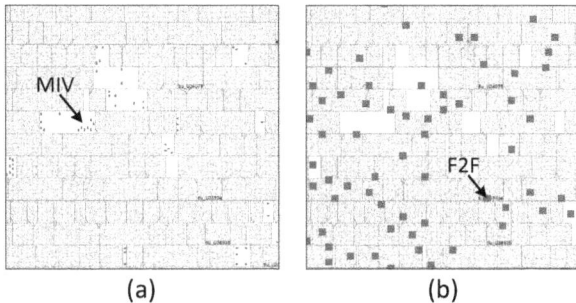

Figure 9: (a) Monolithic 3D integration, and (b) Face-to-face 3D integration. MIVs are limited to whitespace, while F2F vias are not.

3.6 Timing and Power Analysis

Once the MIV/F2F locations are determined, each tier is first trial routed and estimates of parasitics for each tier are dumped. The netlist for each tier, along with its parasitics is then fed into Synopsys PrimeTime. In addition, a top-level netlist and parasitic file is created that contains the MIV/F2F connectivity and parasitics. With all this information, an initial timing analysis is performed to derive timing constraints for each tier. With these timing constraints, we go back to each tier, and run timing-driven routing. The real sign-off parasitics for each tier are then fed back into PrimeTime to get the final timing and statistical power simulation numbers.

4. POWER BENEFIT STUDY

We choose the OpenSPARC T2 core as a case study, implement it in a 28nm technology library and explore the power benefit that monolithic 3D ICs offer when compared to a commercial quality sign-off 2D design. All the numbers presented in this section are for timing closed designs, with a frequency of $1Ghz$. This is the maximum frequency that we could design the 2D version using a high-effort timing-driven flow in Cadence Encounter. The footprint area of the monolithic 3D IC design is exactly half that of the 2D design, and therefore, all 3D designs presented here have zero total silicon area overhead when compared to 2D.

The MIV diameter is assumed to be $100nm$, and its resistance and capacitance are assumed to be 2Ω and $0.1fF$ respectively. We also provide comparisons with face-to-face integration and the F2F via diameter, resistance and capacitance are assumed to be $500nm$, 0.5Ω and $0.2fF$ respectively. All required scripts are implemented in C/C++, Python and Tcl.

Table 1: Comparison of single vs. multiple MIV/F2F insertion. Power values are reported in mW, and wirelength in meter.

	Monolithic 3D			Face-to-face		
	Single	Multiple	Diff(%)	Single	Multiple	Diff(%)
Total WL	15.61	14.29	-8.43	15.44	13.89	-10.05
#MIV/F2F	106k	235k	+120.44	106k	202k	+89.72
Total Pwr	**534.10**	**522.10**	**-2.25**	**538.30**	**524.00**	**-2.66**
Cell Pwr	126.90	126.10	-0.63	127.30	126.40	-0.71
Net Pwr	293.90	282.70	-3.81	297.80	284.30	-4.53
Lkg Pwr	113.30	113.30	0.00	113.30	113.30	0.00

Table 2: Comparison of two different types of 3D CTS. Power values are reported in mW, and wirelength in meter.

	Monolithic 3D			Face-to-face		
	Source-level	Leaf-level	Diff (%)	Source-level	Leaf-level	Diff (%)
#MIV/F2F	871	11,376	+1.2k	871	11,376	+1.2k
Skew (ps)	197.42	103.00	-47.83	172.90	117.07	-32.29
Clock Pwr	**68.40**	**48.00**	**-29.82**	**69.00**	**48.50**	**-29.71**
Tier0 WL	0.55	0.62	+11.89	0.53	0.62	+16.61
Tier1 WL	0.48	0.19	-60.50	0.48	0.17	-64.85
Total WL	1.03	0.80	-21.67	1.01	0.79	-21.91
#Tier0 Buf	14,610	21,687	+48.44	14,958	21,687	+44.99
#Tier1 Buf	12,444	0	-100	12,691	0	-100
#Total Buf	27,054	21,687	-19.84	27,649	21,687	-21.56

4.1 Single vs. Multiple MIV Insertion

We first discuss the power benefit offered by using multiple MIVs (or F2F vias) for each 3D net. A summary of results for both single and multiple MIV insertion is tabulated in Table 1. From this table, we observe that using multiple vias offers 8.4% and 10.04% wirelength reduction for M3D and F2F respectively. We also note that the number of 3D vias double. This means that each net is, on average, using approximately two MIV/F2F vias. This wirelength reduction does not reduce leakage power, but it does reduce some cell power. The biggest reduction is in net power, which reduces by 3.81% and 4.53% for M3D and F2F, which translates to 2.25% and 2.66% total power reduction, respectively.

4.2 CTS: Source-level vs. Leaf-level

In this section, we discuss the power benefit that our proposed CTS methodology (leaf-level) offers over existing 3D techniques (source-level). A summary of results is tabulated in Table 2. From this table, we first observe that leaf-level CTS offers huge reductions in clock skew, as well as a 29.82% reduction in the clock tree power. There are 871 clock-gating related cells in the design, which is why source-level CTS uses that number of MIV/F2F vias. We observe that leaf-level uses far more 3D vias, which helps reduce the clock power.

These power reduction numbers can be explained on the basis of per-tier wirelength and buffer count. We observe that leaf-level uses far more buffers and has a longer WL on tier 0, which is the tier with the clock-backbone. On the other hand, the number of buffers is zero in tier 1 and the WL is much smaller. In comparison, source-level has a more balanced clock WL and buffer count between the tiers, but this comes at the cost of an increase in the total clock WL and buffer count.

4.3 Overall Comparisons: 2D vs. 3D

Using the techniques that give us the best power reduction (i.e. multiple MIV insertion and leaf-level CTS), we now make a comparison of M3D and F2F with a 2D IC designed using Cadence Encounter. A summary of results is tabulated in Table 3. From this

Table 3: Overall comparisons between 2D and different 3D implementation styles

	Encounter 2D	Shrunk 2D		Monolithic 3D		Face-to-face	
Total WL(m)	17.96	13.10	(-27.05%)	14.29	(-20.40%)	13.89	(-22.65%)
# MIV/F2F	-	-		235,394		235,394	
# Buffers	164,917	128,098	(-22.33%)	128,098	(-22.33%)	128,098	(-22.33%)
#Total Gates	458,824	421,959	(-8.03%)	421,959	(-8.03%)	421,959	(-8.03%)
Total Power (mW)	**618.40**	**514.40**	**(-16.82%)**	**522.10**	**(-15.57%)**	**524.00**	**(-15.27%)**
Cell Power (mW)	135.60	126.80	(-6.49%)	126.10	(-7.01%)	126.40	(-6.78%)
Net Power (mW)	356.30	274.30	(-23.01%)	282.70	(-20.66%)	284.30	(-20.21%)
Leakage Power (mW)	126.50	113.30	(-10.43%)	113.30	(-10.43%)	113.30	(-10.43%)
Memory Power (mW)	49.00	45.10	(-7.96%)	45.10	(-7.96%)	45.00	(-8.16%)
Combinational Power (mW)	385.10	300.00	(-22.10%)	305.30	(-20.72%)	306.80	(-20.33%)
Clock Tree Power (mW)	62.50	46.90	(-24.96%)	48.00	(-23.20%)	48.50	(-22.40%)
FF Clock Pin Power (mW)	9.70	9.90	(+2.06%)	9.60	(-1.03%)	9.70	(0.00%)
Register Power (mW)	112.10	112.50	(+0.36%)	114.00	(+1.69%)	114.00	(+1.69%)

table, we first observe that shrunk 2D reduces the wirelength by 27.05% compared to 2D. This is very close to the 29.3% HPWL bound predicted in Section 3. The improvement number goes down for both M3D and F2F, which is to be expected. In addition, M3D has slightly higher WL compared to F2F because the MIVs are limited to whitespace, while F2F vias are not. Next, we observe that the 3D implementations reduce the buffer count by 22.3%, which translates to a 8.03% reduction in total gate count. Since MIV and F2F designs are obtained by simply splitting the shrunk 2D design, all three have the same gate counts. The reduced wirelength and gate count lead to a total power reduction of 15.57% and 15.27% for M3D and F2F respectively. We observe that F2F has a higher power consumption than M3D even though it has lower WL, which is due to increased parasitics of F2F vias. Also, both M3D and F2F power numbers are quite close to the shrunk 2D numbers, which shows that the shrunk 2D design is a very good estimate of M3D and other fine-grained 3D technologies.

We first divide the total power into cell, net, and leakage power. From the table, we observe that the cell power reduces at a number roughly equal to the total gate count reduction. The net power reduces roughly proportional to wirelength, and finally, the leakage reduction is slightly larger than cell count reduction due to smaller buffer sizes. We can also split up the total power by lumping the internal, net and leakage power of certain classes of gates/memory together. This is also tabulated in Table 3. We observe that the flip-flop clock pin power and register power are virtually unchanged in 3D. The biggest savings in power come from combinational logic (20.72% savings), and from the clock tree (23.20% savings). We also observe some memory power savings due to reduction in the output net length that the memory drives.

4.4 Impact of Dual-Vt Gates

All the results discussed so far have used only the regular V_t standard cell library for both 2D and 3D designs. However, it is known that converting cells on non-critical paths to a high V_t flavor can help reduce leakage power. In this section, we evaluate dual V_t designs (DVT), and investigate whether the power benefit of M3D carries over from the single V_t designs (SVT).

For both 2D and 3D (shrunk 2D), we initially use Encounter to perform leakage optimization during the P&R flow. We also perform leakage optimizations in PrimeTime using a script similar to [4], and tabulate the results in Table 4. From this table, we observe that M3D designs reduce the total power of 2D designs by 16.08%. This is a slightly better improvement number than the SVT case alone. This is due to the fact that there are more paths that become non-critical in 3D. We also observe that the F2F improvement numbers are better than the SVT case. Therefore, the 3D power benefit not only carries over to dual-V_t designs, it actually improves.

Table 4: Dual-Vt comparisons between 2D and different 3D implementation styles. Power is in mW.

	Enc. 2D	Monolithic 3D		Face-to-face	
Total WL(m)	17.94	14.29	(-20.33%)	13.89	(-22.59%)
#MIV/F2F	-	235,394		202,593	
Total Pwr	**572.10**	**480.10**	**(-16.08%)**	**482.20**	**(-15.71%)**
Cell Pwr	131.80	123.00	(-6.68%)	123.30	(-6.45%)
Net Pwr	356.60	282.70	(-20.72%)	284.30	(-20.27%)
Leak. Pwr	83.60	74.40	(-11.00%)	74.60	(-10.77%)
Mem. Pwr	48.80	45.10	(-7.58%)	45.00	(-7.79%)
Comb. Pwr	361.60	283.00	(-21.74%)	284.30	(-21.38%)
Clk Tree Pwr	62.50	48.00	(-23.20%)	48.50	(-22.40%)
FF Clk Pin Pwr	9.10	9.20	(+1.10%)	9.20	(+1.10%)
Reg. Pwr	90.00	94.90	(+5.44%)	94.80	(+5.33%)

5. CONCLUSION

In this work, for the first time, we have demonstrated a CAD methodology that is capable of taking gate-level monolithic 3D IC designs all the way though place, route, CTS, and timing optimization. We have used the OpenSPARC T2 core as a case study, and demonstrated that monolithic 3D ICs offer significant power benefits when compared to commercial-quality 2D ICs. We have demonstrated several low-power techniques such as multiple MIV insertion and a leaf-level CTS methodology. All these techniques enable us to achieve 15.57% total power reduction when compared to commercial-grade 2D ICs. In addition, we demonstrate that the power benefit of M3D carries over even when using dual-V_t libraries, and we can achieve a total power reduction of 16.08%.

6. REFERENCES

[1] P. Batude et al. Advances in 3D CMOS Sequential Integration. In *Proc. IEEE Int. Electron Devices Meeting*, 2009.

[2] S. Bobba et al. CELONCEL: Effective design technique for 3-D monolithic integration targeting high performance integrated circuits. In *Proc. Asia and South Pacific Design Automation Conf.*, 2011.

[3] C. M. Fiduccia and R. M. Mattheyses. A linear-time heuristic for improving network partitions. In *Proc. ACM Design Automation Conf.*, 1982.

[4] P. Gupta, A. Kahng, P. Sharma, and D. Sylvester. Gate-length biasing for runtime-leakage control. *IEEE Trans. on Computer-Aided Design of Integrated Circuits and Systems*, 2006.

[5] Y.-J. Lee, D. Limbrick, and S. K. Lim. Power Benefit Study for Ultra-High Density Transistor-Level Monolithic 3D ICs. In *Proc. ACM Design Automation Conf.*, 2013.

[6] Oracle. OpenSPARC T2.

[7] S. Panth, K. Samadi, Y. Du, and S. K. Lim. High-Density Integration of Functional Modules Using Monolithic 3D-IC Technology. In *Proc. Asia and South Pacific Design Automation Conf.*, 2013.

Efficient NBTI Modeling Technique Considering Recovery Effects

Reef Eilers, Malte Metzdorf,
Domenik Helms
OFFIS Institute for Computer Science
Escherweg 2, 26121 Oldenburg, Germany
{reef.eilers, domenik.helms}@offis.de

Wolfgang Nebel
University of Oldenburg
26129 Oldenburg, Germany
nebel@informatik.uni-oldenburg.de

ABSTRACT

The aging effect "Negative Bias Temperature Instability",
which is highly dependent on device history, has a direct
impact on the design of integrated circuits. In order to
make realistic predictions available in the design process,
simulation durations of existing history aware models must
be significantly reduced. Therefore, a performance-oriented,
yet accurate abstraction of the switching trap NBTI model
is presented within this paper. Evaluation results for various
stress scenarios demonstrate very precise NBTI simulations
and a major improvement to another performance-oriented
model abstraction. Simulation durations facilitate realistic
aging predictions of larger components in a reasonable period of time.

Categories and Subject Descriptors

B.8.2 [**Hardware**]: Performance and Reliability—*Performance Analysis and Design Aids*

Keywords

NBTI; Reliability; Aging; CET map; Mission scenarios

1. INTRODUCTION

With the pace of Moore's law, industry is driving technology dimensions further towards the atomic regime. With
this scaling, the technology picked up more and more physical artifacts, influencing the usage of such devices. The
advent of various flavors of static currents such as gate tunneling in 65nm and gate induced drain leakage in 45nm [9],
also introduced an increasing susceptibility to process variations as well as an electro-thermal coupling. Currently, it
seems, as if aging effects could become one of the main challenges for this decade. Similar to the static currents, there
is not just a new physical phenomenon - there is rather a
vast selection of aging mechanisms.

We can separate these aging effects into different classes:
At first, there are degradation effects, slowly varying relevant process parameters over time. At high temperatures,

ISLPED'14, August 11–13, 2014, La Jolla, CA, USA.
ACM 978-1-4503-2975-0/14/08.
http://dx.doi.org/10.1145/2627369.2627618.

degradation is dominated by negative bias temperature instability (NBTI), where chemical traps in the gate oxide
can capture and emit charges, thus increasing the devices
threshold voltage [4]. At lower temperatures hot carrier
degradation (HCD) dominates, where fast (hot) carriers can
get trapped in the oxide thus again influencing the threshold voltage of the device [10]. From an abstract view, all
degradation effects result in a change of power demand and
path timing. As soon as the available slack within one path
is exceeded, degradation will also lead to a timing failure.

Permanent failures are thus the second class of aging.
Electro-migration specifies a force, introduced by the high
current density, that can dislocate interconnect material at
elevated temperatures, resulting in a total connection-loss.
Time dependent dielectricity breakdown (TDDB) may occur
in oxides, having collected a vast number of trapped oxide
charges, forming a conductive path through the oxide and
thus to a permanent device failure [3]. Finally, there are radiation induced permanent failures like single event latchup
(SEL) and others, each of which finally leads to a thermal
destruction of a device as a result of ionizing radiation.

Research and industry are currently trying to develop
tools and methodologies, helping to cope with aging at all
design levels from system design, where parameter adaption
and redundancy may be employed, down to devices, where
direct reduction of the effects are the main focus. Our contribution to this challenge, as presented in this work, is a
simple, yet accurate abstraction of the state of the art description of NBTI [7], reducing the per transistor description
form over a thousand parameters to just three without losing details such as healing behavior or the behavior against
time varying stress as induced by system idle phases or techniques as power gating. The resulting abstraction is more
than three orders of magnitude faster, enabling either the
simulation of the total lifetime of a device or the simulation
of a huge system of such devices in a reasonable time scale.

Before we introduce the implementation details of our
model in Sections III and IV, we present the recent state of
the art in NBTI modeling. Afterwards, Section V presents
direct comparisons between our model and the standard
model using industrial characterization data directly from
the author of [7]. Section VI finally concludes our work.

2. RELATED WORK

Early in the last decade, a first NBTI model, called reac-
tion-diffusion (RD) model was proposed [2]. It explained
NBTI with a good agreement to the measurement data available. [2] proposed that NBTI is caused by passivation hydro-

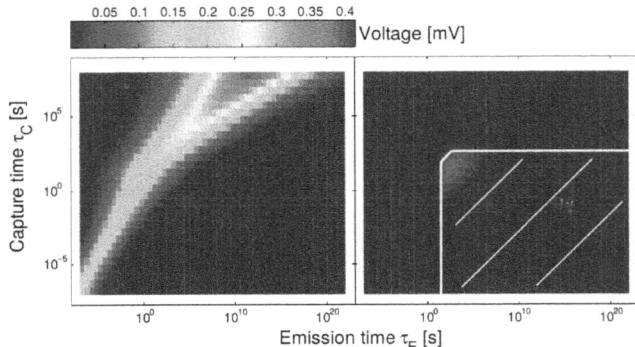

Figure 1: Left: Characteristic distribution histogram of the trap density over emission and capture time per trap. The color indicates total V_{th} shift induced by all traps within one (τ_C, τ_E) bin. Right: Distribution histogram for a partially charged transistor state. Occupied and unoccupied traps of a device are always separated by a monotone function. Accurately abstracting this shape is the core idea of the proposed model.

gen atoms from the gate-oxide interface, which were freed under stress by hole trapping (reaction) and then drifting through the oxide (diffusion) with a potential annealing over a short annealing distance. Much later, it was shown, that RD can neither explain the ultra-short time behavior of NBTI, nor the long time for recent devices, giving favor to the switching trap (ST) model as proposed by [4].

The recent ST based NBTI model proposes huge numbers (thousands) of traps inside each device's oxide, each of which is formed between two adjacent SiO2 molecules. Each uncharged trap may capture an electron and the charged trap may re-emit it back with potential barriers and thus related transition times in the order of milliseconds. Additionally, for a charged trap, the local crystalline structure of the oxide can swap, driving the trap over a potential barrier large enough to also explain the macroscopic transition times (seconds to month) observed in measurements. Depending on the exact configuration of the molecules, the potential barriers between the states may significantly vary leading to characteristic capture τ_C and emission times τ_E per trap. Figure 1 (left) shows such a distribution as a two dimensional histogram. As can be seen, capture and emission times are weakly correlated: While capture and emission times spread over several orders of magnitude, usually capture and emission time are in the same order of magnitude; e.g. traps with a long capture time also tend to have long emission times. During ST simulations occupation probabilities of the existing traps are calculated based on given stress scenarios.

Besides the abstraction, we propose, there have been several other approaches. [6] proposed a first abstraction of the NBTI conditions, lumping all transient NBTI defects into two components. Even though the model itself is too simplistic, the authors propose a useful gate-netlist reduction technique, eliminating nodes, which are irrelevant for the circuits timing correctness. In [5], an abstract model for system level NBTI and HCD description is presented. It models NBTI with an extended RD model, called the composite model. It introduces good prediction of a full system's timing behavior under degradation. However, the composite

model as other closed-form solutions of the NBTI degradation only handles constant stress over the entire system life time and does not feature varying stress conditions within the device's history. Additionally, as it still bases on the RD model, it cannot be characterized with recent (ST based) technology data.

There are already industrial tools for aging simulation available such as RelExpert [1], which can accurately predict aging of a circuit under static conditions by simulating the fresh transistor netlist, compute per device stress conditions and apply a per device aging model. With the degraded netlist, the simulation at SPICE level is repeated to get power and timing figures of the system after stress. However, the accuracy of such methods depends on the employed aging model, which is today also bound to static stress conditions.

Best to our knowledge, all existing NBTI models are either too slow for a full chip and/or full life-time simulation, or they cannot handle varying stress conditions as typically occurring in most systems, or they are not accurately following silicon measurements.

3. ABSTRACTED DEFECT OCCUPATION

The initial model assumption, as already proposed by [7], is that the discrete traps, which can either be fully charged or fully uncharged can be replaced by a continuous statistical process, which can also be described using RC circuits. This step is necessary when compacting the explicit traps into a trap distribution map as presented in Figure 1. Thus we assume to having a two dimensional histogram $\Delta V_{th}(\tau_C, \tau_E)$ and the occupation state over time of all these traps can be described by a defect occupation $P(\tau_C, \tau_E, t)$ with

$$1 - P(\tau_C, \tau_E, t + \Delta t) = (1 - P(\tau_C, \tau_E, t)) \cdot e^{-\frac{\Delta t}{\tau_C}} \quad (1)$$

if the system is stressed for a time Δt and

$$P(\tau_C, \tau_E, t + \Delta t) = P(\tau_C, \tau_E, t) \cdot e^{-\frac{\Delta t}{\tau_E}} \quad (2)$$

if the stress is removed for a time Δt. The transient threshold damage due to NBTI over time be computed as

$$\Delta V_{th\ tran}(t + \Delta t) = \int d\tau_C \int d\tau_E P(\tau_C, \tau_E, t + \Delta t)$$
$$\cdot \Delta V_{th}(\tau_C, \tau_E) \quad (3)$$

Examples for P functions under different stress loads are visualized in Figure 2. As can be seen, occupied and unoccupied traps are separated by a monotone function, since trap charging and discharging always starts at low values of τ_C and τ_E, respectively. For a wide range of stress scenarios this monotone function is typically almost rectangularly shaped. Figure 1 (right) also depicts this function and illustrates the connection between defect occupation and distribution histogram for a partially charged transistor state. The permanent threshold shift is modeled similar to Equation 1 and 3 with the only difference that the histogram $\Delta V_{th\ perm}(\tau_C)$ and the defect occupation are only one-dimensional.

First step in order to develop a history aware and efficient NBTI model is an abstraction of the switching trap transistor state using only a few parameters. In this way, the device history can be tracked by observing the alteration of the abstraction parameters. Obviously, permanent $\Delta V_{th\ perm}$ and transient threshold shift $\Delta V_{th\ trans}$ are used

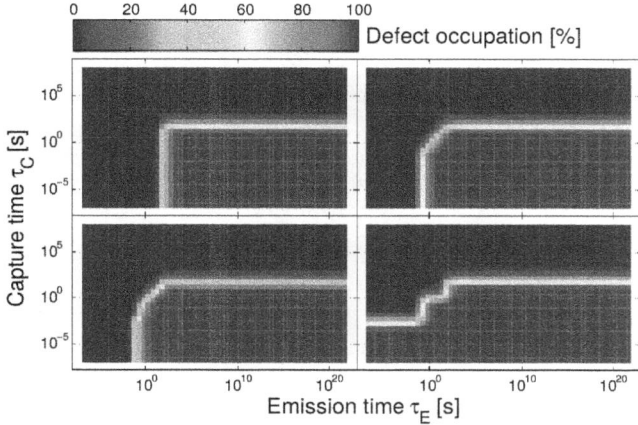

Figure 2: Defect occupation (P function) for stress scenarios of 30s stress - 30s relax (top left), 10Hz - 50% duty cycle (top right), binary Markov graph with $P_{01}=1\frac{\%}{ms}$, $P_{10}=2\frac{\%}{ms}$ (bottom left) and a worst case scenario with a very generic minutes stress - minutes relax - seconds stress - seconds relax - milliseconds stress sequence (bottom right).

as the first abstraction parameters. A third parameter H is used to characterize the slope within the defect occupation due to peridioc stress (compare Figure 2 (top right and bottom left)). Since the gradient is an intrinsic feature of the ST model [8], H only describes the logarithmic temporal length (emission time) of the interval stated by Equation 4. Since this parameter characterizes the short-time healing ability of the system, it is called "healability" within this paper.

$$\frac{\int d\tau_C P(\tau_C, \tau_E)}{\int d\tau_C P(\tau_C, \tau_{E\ Max})} \in [0.01, 0.99] \quad (4)$$

A conversion between the original defect occupation of the ST model and the abstract representation is mandatory for our approach. The calculation of the abstraction parameters based on the defect occupation is a straight forward process using Equations 3 and 4. However, the generation of a defect occupation based on the abstraction parameters is a complex operation with various degrees of freedom. Therefore, this conversion is the key point of our approach and will be evaluated extensively in Section V.

The generation process of the defect occupation as indicated in Figure 3 (top) is based on the monotone function described above. The one-dimensional occupation of permanent defects is reconstructed by increasing a virtual capture time (rf. Equation 1) until $\Delta V_{th\ perm}$ has reached the intended value. The two-dimensional occupation of transient defects that occur under typical stress conditions can't be reconstructed based on a single parameter. However, the virtual capture time of the permanent component is a perfect estimate of the height of the defect occupation at $\tau_{E\ Max}$, since the maximal emission time is too high to be reached under normal operation conditions. At first, the virtual capture time is used for the complete range of emission time values and a slope characterized by H is added in the short time regime. Afterwards, a virtual emission time (rf. Equation 2) is increased, while the slope is always restored, until $\Delta V_{th\ trans}$ has reached the intended value. In this way, the parameter $\Delta V_{th\ trans}$ also determines the position of the slope on the emission time scale. The result of

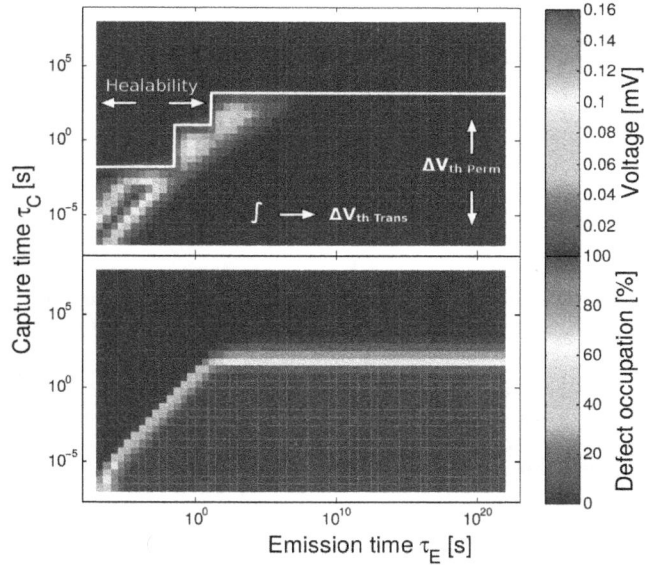

Figure 3: Top: Distribution histogram for the worst case scenario. $\Delta V_{th\ perm}$ is a measure for the height of the defect occupation at $\tau_{E\ Max}$ and H characterizes the temporal length with reduced (but nonzero) defect occupation. Bottom: Recreated defect occupation for the worst case example in Figure 2 based on $\Delta V_{th\ perm}$, $\Delta V_{th\ trans}$ and healability H.

Stress scenario	Integrated difference between occupation and recreation[%]
30s stress, 30s relax	$4 \cdot 10^{-7}$
10Hz, 50%	0.35
P_{01}=1%, P_{10}=2%	0.4
Worst case	2.92

Table 1: Failure of recreated defect occupation for the examples in Figure 2.

the generation process is always a rectangular shaped defect occupation, which may have an additional slope (rf. Figure 3 (bottom)).

Failure values of the recreated defect occupations for the examples in Figure 2 are shown in Table 1. A clear deviation only occurs for the short time regime of the worst case scenario (compare Figure 2 (bottom right) and Figure 3 (bottom)). Naturally, such generic defect occupations can't be characterized precisely using only three parameters. However, as long as different defect occupations that are characterized by the same parameter values produce nearly the same results in a consecutive ST simulation, this characterization is sufficient for our phase space approach.

4. PHASE SPACE APPROACH

Instead of a NBTI simulation that is based on the transformation of the complete defect occupation, the phase space approach tracks the transformation of the three parameter abstraction (rf. Section III). However, the ST model can't be easily modified to rely directly on the abstraction parameters. Consequently, the new approach uses a precomputed phase space to perform a NBTI simulation by following a (interpolated) phase space trajectory. The phase space is

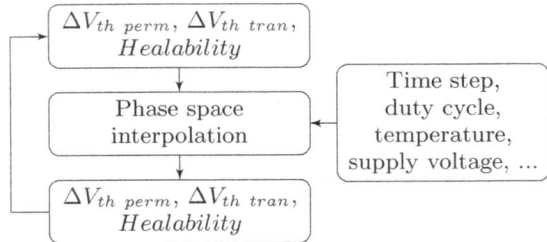

Figure 4: Flow chart of the phase space based simulation method. Various additional input arguments (e.g. temperature) may be used in a future version.

defined by the abstraction parameters $\Delta V_{th\ perm}$, $\Delta V_{th\ tran}$ and "healability" H. A flow chart of the general simulation method is shown in Figure 4. During a phase space based simulation the abstraction parameters and additional input arguments (e.g. stress scenario) are used to interpolate a step on a phase space trajectory. The resulting values of $\Delta V_{th\ perm}$, $\Delta V_{th\ tran}$ and H can be used for the next time step, which may have different values of the additional input arguments. In this way, the simulation simply follows the phase space trajectory as long as the additional input arguments don't change.

In order to construct the phase space (rf. Figure 5), the defect occupation is generated with the method described in Section III and the actual transformation of the abstraction parameters during a time step is directly calculated with the ST model. The phase space construction can be processed in parallel and has to be done only once for each transistor technology and geometry. Step size of the three abstraction parameters defines the interpolation failure of the phase space simulations as well as the construction duration. Since $\Delta V_{th\ perm}$, $\Delta V_{th\ tran}$ and H are restricted to certain ranges, the phase space incorporates all system states and a trajectory can't leave the area of precomputed values. It is possible to simulate NBTI induced aging with the same time resolution as with the ST model. Every time step on a phase space trajectory will induce a small interpolation failure and a failure due to the three parameter abstraction. However, the phase space approach facilitates the usage of longer simulation time steps, if there is a reasonable abstraction of the stress (e.g. signal probability) and the stress scenario changes only on macroscopic time steps (e.g. power gating or ambient temperatures). These longer time steps vastly reduce the simulation duration.

5. EVALUATION

5.1 Model setup

As the main reference to assess all other model's accuracy, we use the model of [7], with all model parameters based on direct silicon measurement at $440\,\mathrm{K}$ temperature and $2.2\,\mathrm{V}$ supply voltage (accelerated aging conditions), directly from the author of [7] (rf. Figure 1 (left)). We will refer to it as full switching trap model (FST). Under different generic and realistic stress conditions, we used the FST model with a time resolution of $1\,\mathrm{ms}$ per step, lumping together the cycle based activity statistics into milliseconds of 100% busy or 100% idle. Going from cycle base to milliseconds was mandatory for the evaluation - its drawbacks will be discussed later.

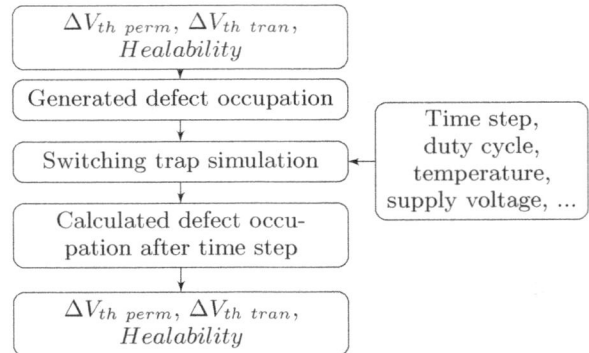

Figure 5: Flow chart of the phase space construction. Various additional input arguments (e.g. temperature) may be used in a future version.

Defect number	Capture time τ_C [s]	Emission time τ_E [s]	Maximal induced ΔV_{th} [mV]
#1	6.49	4.99	42.16
#2	$5.11 \cdot 10^6$	$8.45 \cdot 10^9$	48.47
#3	$1.37 \cdot 10^3$	∞	10.43
#4	$1.19 \cdot 10^7$	∞	81.53

Table 2: Parameters chosen for the lumped switching trap model [6], representing transient and permanent NBTI.

Additionally, we re-implemented the model, used in [6], being closest to our own approach. We will refer to this model as the lumped switching trap model (LST). Even though it is not fully disclosed in [6], we tried to optimize their free model parameters for our evaluation by using the same silicon data. To improve fairness of comparison, we also increased the number of defects from 2 to 4 by introducing two additional permanent defects. In order to define the defect properties of LST, we devided the capture time scale of transient and permanent defects within the silicon data in two regions. While the induced ΔV_{th} of each lumped defect is simply a summation of all defects within the region, the new time constants are calculated using a weighted mean of all corresponding time constants (rf. Equation 5). The particular regions are chosen in order to attain optimal evaluation results in the scenario 1 day, 10Hz and 50% duty cycle (rf. Figure 6). Table 2 summarizes the parameters of the 4 defects.

$$\tau_C = 10^{\frac{\sum log(\tau_C)\Delta V_{th}(\tau_C,\tau_E)}{\sum \Delta V_{th}(\tau_C,\tau_E)}} \tag{5}$$

We call our model as described in Sections III and IV the phase space based model (PSB). Taking the FST as a reference, we pre-compute the phase space for a time step of $60\,\mathrm{s}$. For the sake of comparison of the abstraction itself, we use a very fine mesh to avoid additional interpolation errors.

5.2 Stress scenarios

We defined 24 stress scenarios to evaluate different aspects of our PSB model. A continuous stress scenario gives the upper bound of reachable threshold shift. 30s stress, 30s relax is an example for a perfectly rectangular defect occupation (rf. Figure 2 (top left)) that doesn't need the "healability" abstraction parameter; worst case generically constructs the worst defect occupation we could reach by setting the system under a very generic minutes stress - minutes relax - seconds stress - seconds relax - milliseconds stress sequence. Nine scenarios represent typical frequency - duty cycle stress to make this work comparable with other publications. All these stress scenarios were applied for a simulation time of 1 hour, 1 day and 1 week. Therefore, the PSB simulations comprise of 60, 1440 and 10080 conversions between defect occupation of FST and the abstract representation, respectively. Evaluation results of these scenarios are shown in Figure 6.

Additional evelution results with a simulation time of 1 day are shown in Figure 7. There are 5 binary Markov graph scenarios, showing non periodic, yet strictly characteristic signals with parameterized up- P_{01} and down-switching P_{10} probability. In order to demonstrate short-time effects within these scenarios, a relaxation time of 0.1 s was added in additional examples. The corresponding frequency - duty cycle scenarios were also implemented as a reference. Quasi-period f_q and signal probability P_1 can be computed as

$$P_1 = P_1 * P_{11} + P_0 * P_{01} = P_{01}/(P_{01} + P_{10}) \quad (6)$$

$$f_q = (P_0 * P_{01} + P_1 * P_{10})\frac{1}{\Delta t} = \frac{2P_{01}P_{10}}{P_{01} + P_{10}}\frac{1}{\Delta t} \quad (7)$$

Finally, there are three tri-state Markov graphs, generating stress scenarios, which are typical for devices with long idle times (e.g. from power gating). These systems remain for a macroscopic time (several minutes, as specified by P_{PG}) either in idle ($P_1 = 0$) or in active with given P_{01} and P_{10} values. For each scenario, two examples with a on- and off-state in the last macroscopic time step are implemented. These realistic scenarios are currently not supported by any other model, but the three models, evaluated here.

5.3 Result discussion

At first we have to notice, that PSB partially over- and underestimates the correct threshold in the scenarios of Figure 6 with a worst case error smaller than 4%. Neither the variation of simulation time, signal frequency nor duty cycle has a distinct impact on the accuracy of the simulation results. It is also worth mentioning, that the error for the permanent part of the threshold damage is never larger than 0.05 mV. This can be explained by the modeling methodology: In the FST, permanent damage is represented by an occupation of traps with different capture times. Since there's no emission, the occupation distribution is directly determined by Equation 1 using a transistor lifetime that is reduced by all relaxation times. This behavior is directly modeled with the phase space based approach. For much longer simulation times, we may therefore see a slightly larger modeling error of the transient part, but the permanent part will still be almost perfectly modeled. Accuracy of the scenario with almost rectangularly shaped defect occupation (30s stress, 30s relax) coincides with other periodic stress scenarios, showing that the slope within the defect occupation of peridioc stress examples is well abstracted by the healability.

Parameters of our implementation of LST were characterized to have minimal deviation for the scenario 1 day, 10Hz and 50% duty cycle. However, clear deviations up to -64% and +139% occur in other scenarios. LST shows the tendency to underestimate the threshold shift in scenarios with 10% duty cycle or long duration times and to overestimate ΔV_{th} for 90% duty cycle or short simulation times. Since

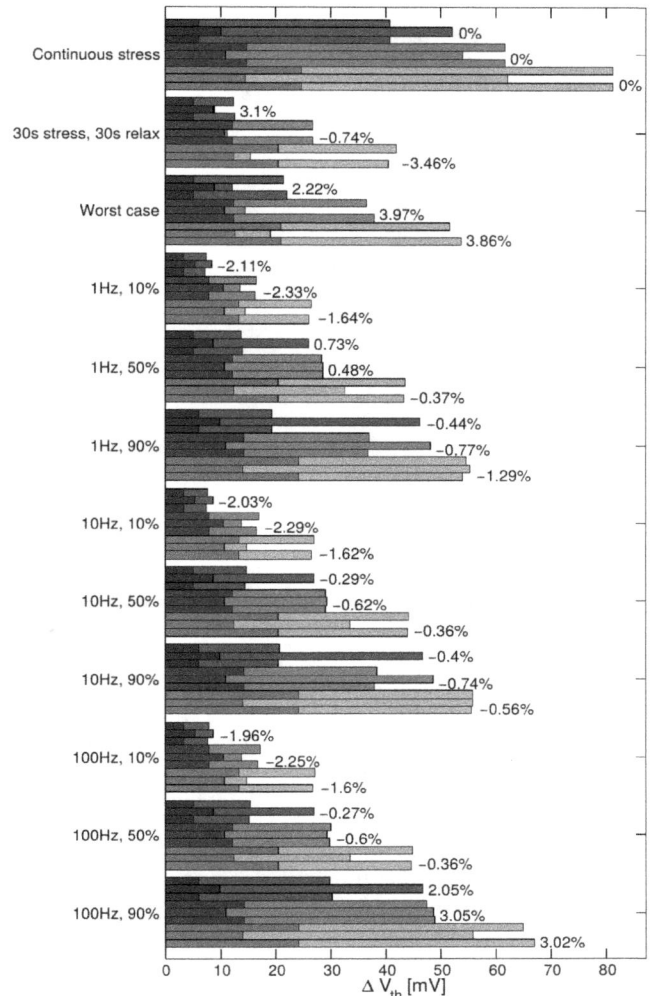

Figure 6: Permanent (dark color) and transient threshold shift (light color) for different stress scenarios. Each scenario was applied with a simulation time of 1 hour (blue), 1 day (red) and 1 week (green). First, second and third bar in each group represent full switching trap model (FST), lumped switching trap model (LST) and phase space based model (PSB), respectively. Numerical data stands for percentual difference between FST and PSB.

there is only a minor influence of the signal frequency on LST and almost no impact on PSB, it may be suggested that these results are also valid for real components, surely having much higher switching frequencies.

Much longer on and off times are possible in the binary Markov graph scenarios in comparison to quasi frequency signals. However, differences in threshold voltages are only simulated for scenarios with quasi duty cycle of 67% and 83% (rf. Figure 7). An additional relaxation time of 0.1 s is needed in these Markov graph scenarios to align ΔV_{th} with the quasi frequency scenarios. This relaxation time corresponds to an off-time that is 4 or 10 times larger than the nominal value of the quasi frequency signal, respectively. Hence, this difference cannot be modeled with static NBTI models, such as [1] or [5], leading to an underestimation of the NBTI effect. Although LST operates close to the char-

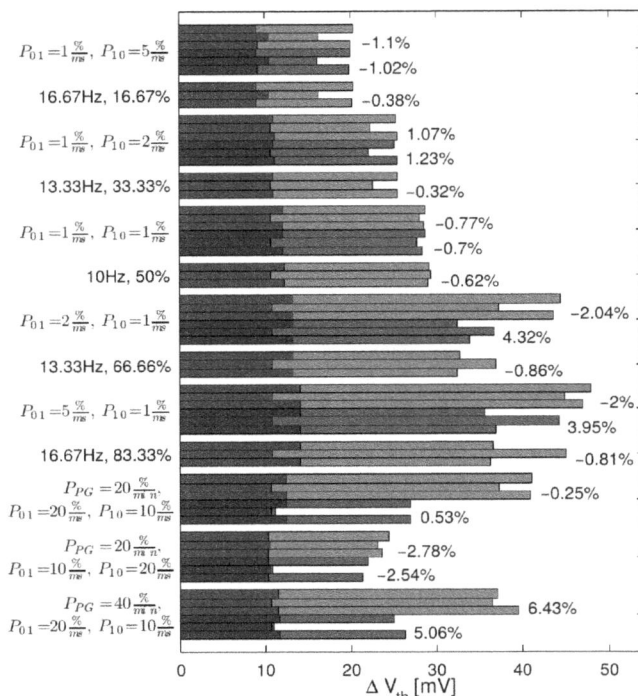

Figure 7: Permanent (dark color) and transient threshold shift (light color) for different stress scenarios with a simulation time of 1 day. Blue bars represent additional examples with a relaxation time at the end of the stress signal. First, second and third bar in each group represent FST, LST and PSB, respectively. Numerical data stands for percentual difference between FST and PSB.

6. CONCLUSION

Several abstract NBTI models are already known, some of which show a good accordance to silicon data, when assessed for periodic signals with arbitrary duty cycles. Assuming long and non-periodic off times, e.g. induced by components that are idle or actively waiting or even power gated, the NBTI model has to incorporate the complete device history. In these scenarios only the original switching trap model and our new model can accurately regard the transient healing effects for a wide range of signal probabilities and simulation times. Our model shows a moderate error in the transient part and a negligible error in the permanent part of NBTI and speeds up the simulation by more than three orders of magnitude. The model we presented is focusing on the device description only and could be easily integrated into sophisticated simulation environments, such as RelExpert [1], the academic path pruning [6] or any other ageism flow.

Our follow-up research will focus on a support for varying temperature and voltage stress. Finally, we intend to include an accurate model into a fast simulation environment enabling long time all system assessment of the NBTI and the effect of optimization techniques such as power gating.

7. ACKNOWLEDGMENT

This work presents results achieved within the European ICT FP7 project MoRV (619234) and within a subcontract from Infineon in the European Catrene project RELY (CA 403). We would like to thank Infineon for their friendly cooperation.

8. REFERENCES

[1] Cadence white paper. *Reliability Simulation in Integrated Circuit Design*, 2003.

[2] S. Chakravarthy et al. A Comprehensive Framework For Predictive Modeling of Negative Bias Temperature Instability. *Proc. of IEEE Intl. Reliability Physics Symp.*, 2004.

[3] M. Choudhury et al. Analytical model for TDDB-based performance degradation in combinational logic. *Design, Automation & Test in Europe conf.*, 2010.

[4] T. Grasser et al. A Two-Stage Model for Negative Bias Temperature Instability. *Proc. of IEEE Intl. Reliability Physics Symp.*, 2009.

[5] V. Huard et al. A Predictive Bottom-up Hierarchical Approach to Digital System Reliability. *Proc. of IEEE Intl. Reliability Physics Symp.*, 2012.

[6] D. Lorenz et al. Aging analysis at gate and macro cell level. *Intl. conf. on CAD*, 2010.

[7] H. Reisinger et al. The statistical analysis of individual defects constituting NBTI and its implications for modeling DC- and AC-stress. *Proc. of IEEE Intl. Reliability Physics Symp.*, 2010.

[8] H. Reisinger et al. Understanding and Modeling AC BTI. *Proc. of IEEE Intl. Reliability Physics Symp.*, 2011.

[9] K. Roy et al. Leakage Current Mechanisms and Leakage Reduction Techniques in Deep-Submicrometer CMOS Circuits. *Proc. of the IEEE*, 91(2), Feb. 2003.

[10] S. Tyaginov et al. Physics-Based Hot-Carrier Degradation Models. *Electrochemical Society Transactions*, 35(4), 2011.

acterization example, simulation results of PSB are slightly more precise within these scenarios. The aforementioned difference between Markov graph and quasi frequency scenarios can also only be simulated by FST and PSB. While the effect of the additional relaxation time is only slightly underestimated by PSB, LST simulates almost no transformation in threshold voltage.

Both abstract models are able to simulate components with long off times, as induced by idle, active waiting, or power gating. This is a great advantage in comparison to static NBTI models ([1] or [5]). Examples having an off-state in the last macroscopic time step show that LST clearly overestimates the relaxation within such a large time step.

We implemented all three models in an interpreter language for a 64 core 2.3GHz AMD Opteron with 512GB memory. In the very accurate FST model could compute 1 hour device lifetime in about half an hour. Thus it would need prohibitive 5 years to simulate a 10 year transistor lifetime. Both alternative models, the LST and our PSB were over 3 orders of magnitude faster, simulating 1 hour device life in about one second. Thus a 10 year simulation would become feasible, needing less than 2 days computation time. The PSB model needs to do one phase space characterization run in advance which has to be repeated for each transistor technology and geometry. Such a characterization needs some hours of computation time (36 hours for our very fine characterization for evaluation purposes).

Bridging High Performance and Low Power in Processor Design

Ruchir Puri, Mihir Choudhury, Haifeng Qian, Matthew Ziegler
IBM Thomas J Watson Research Center, Yorktown Hts, NY 10598

ABSTRACT

The design complexity of modern high performance processors calls for innovative design techniques and methodologies for achieving time-to-market goals. New design techniques are also needed to curtail power increases that inherently arise from ever increasing performance targets. This paper describes new processor design and optimization approaches that bridge the gap between high performance and low power. These techniques are flexible as they rely on automated synthesis-centric optimizations to enable power reduction without sacrificing performance. These methodology innovations contributed to the industry leading performance of the POWER8 processor.

Keywords

Design methodology; High performance design; Low power design; Synthesis; Processors; Servers; Design space exploration

1. INTRODUCTION

The design complexity of high performance processors continues to increase as the goals of higher throughput and functionality needed for large scale data centers pushes transistor counts into the multi-billions. But, as the complexity and performance of high-end chips rises, power consumption emerge as a first order design limitation. Power is now a focal point for high-end servers targeting maximum performance. In addition, the industry looks to boost productivity by increasingly relying on synthesis for even high performance designs that have conventionally employed more custom methodologies. Time-to-market pressures and the desire for cost savings via smaller design teams further fuel the shift towards synthesis-centric methodologies.

This paper describes new design techniques and methodologies for bridging the gap between high performance and low power and overcoming the productivity challenges while designing the IBM POWER8^{TM} processor [11]. Leveraging synthesis and automation to a higher degree addressed the complexity and productivity goals. To meet performance levels conventionally attained by custom design an enhanced synthesis flow called Structured Synthesis provided the abil-

ity to employ custom design techniques within the synthesis flow. Scaling to larger synthesized blocks further improved productivity as well as provided area and power improvements through a flow we call Large Block Synthesis (LBS). We refer to the overall flow that merges custom capabilities and allows scaling macro size as Large Block Structured Synthesis (LBSS) [2].

High-end servers have conventionally relied on transistor-level custom design techniques for achieving high performance, e.g., the POWER6 processor which achieves frequencies over 5GHz [25]. At a lower frequency envelope, ASIC design has conventionally achieved design efficiency over high performance processors by more heavily relying on synthesis. While this gap between custom and ASIC design efficiency has been noted in prior publications [7][36], it has not been until recently that synthesis has made major inroads in the realm of high performance servers running in the 4-5GHz range.

One representative metric that conveys the evolution of synthesis in IBM's server design flow is the percentage of synthesized macros in the processor core, as Fig. 1 illustrates. The core is typically the portion of the chip that limits performance from a frequency perspective and where custom design is more conventionally utilized. During the POWER6 and POWER7 time frame, improving custom design productivity was a major focus. These innovations allowed reducing the cost associated in custom design tasks in key areas, such as, automated leaf cell generation, placement, and routing [12][25]. This focus on custom design productivity was quite appropriate at the time, seeing that custom design represented 50% of the core macros and the majority of the most challenging macros. Following significant custom design productivity improvements, productivity efforts began focusing more heavily on synthesis, eventually evolving into the POWER8 LBSS methodology.

As Fig. 1 shows, a significant increase in synthesized macros between the POWER7 and POWER7+ chips. POWER7+ provided an ideal situation to push for higher use of synthesis. Underlying improvements in IBM's PDSrtl synthesis tool [27] combined with the higher logic stability of POWER7+, with respect to POWER7, lowered the risk of shifting towards synthesis. The Structured Synthesis methodology was a key catalyst for the transition to higher use of synthesis for core macros. Structured Synthesis provided techniques to span any remaining gap for timing closure. For example, if a macro could not close timing using the standard synthesis flow, the designer could intervene and apply custom techniques to only the critical portions of the macro.

Building on the success of POWER7+, the trend of higher synthesis use continued in the POWER8 core. The adoption of Large Block Synthesis (LBS), which improved synthesis turn-around-time, in combination with Structured Synthesis techniques led not only to a greater use of synthesis, but also to larger macros. Entire core units on the chip were

ISLPED'14, August 11–13, 2014, La Jolla, CA, USA.
Copyright 2014 ACM 978-1-4503-2975-0/14/08 ...$15.00
http://dx.doi.org/10.1145/2627369.2631642.

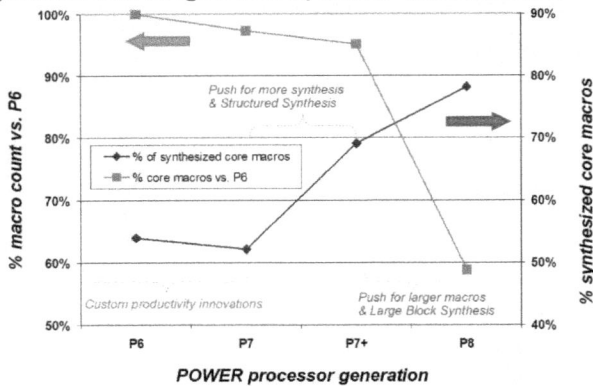

Figure 1: POWER processors have leveraged synthesis heavily in recent generations, driven by both Structured Synthesis and Large Block Synthesis methodologies.

synthesized as single large block macros and the number of core macros in POWER8 was reduced by 50% compared to POWER6, as Fig. 1 shows.

1.1 Structured synthesis

Structured Synthesis aims to merge the productivity of a synthesis flow with the fine grained designer intervention of a custom design flow. Conceptually, it strives to allow custom design to be applied to only the portion of the macro that is critical, while allowing the remainder of the macro to be synthesized. Prior to enabling custom techniques within synthesis, the entire macro would have had to be designed custom to allow even a small customized portion. Allocating significant custom design effort late in a design cycle creates schedule risk. Structured Synthesis alleviates this risk by allowing custom techniques to be applied incrementally to only the most critical portions of a design. Thus more challenging macros can be synthesized without the risk of having to revert to complete custom designs late in the schedule, should timing closure difficulty arise.

Figure 2: Preplacement and embedded custom IP blocks are used in this example to close timing, achieve 8% power, and 16% area savings.

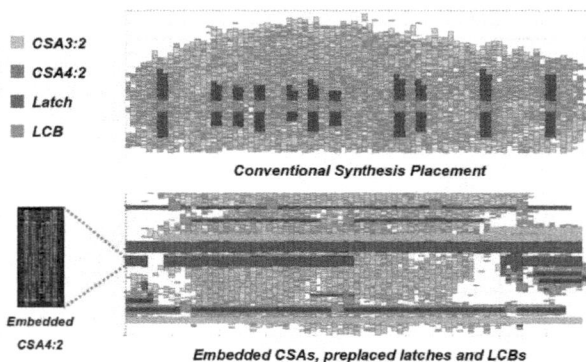

Structured Synthesis is based on a portfolio of custom techniques that can be applied within the server synthesis flow, as needed. The general philosophy is to attempt to close macro timing using the standard synthesis flow and then incrementally apply Structured Synthesis techniques, as needed, which attempts to minimize design effort. Once a macro achieves timing closure, additional customization can be applied to further optimize the macro from a power or area perspective, if the return-on-investment (ROI) for

additional design effort appears favorable. Although the design effort for specific application of a custom solution can vary greatly, the general approach is to look to lower-effort techniques first. The choice of using a technique depends on the macro specific problem to be solved as well as the expected ROI in implementing the technique.

Figure 3: Designer supplied latch placement and automated structured latch placement provide various degrees of control and automation.

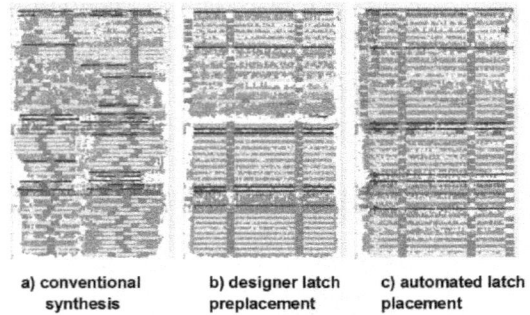

| a) conventional synthesis | b) designer latch preplacement | c) automated latch placement |

Improvements over conventional synthesis

design version	timing	wire length	area
b) designer latch preplacement	28%	30%	5%
c) automated latch placement	16%	27%	2%

Fig. 2 depicts a design example showing conventional synthesis, i.e., synthesis without Structured Synthesis techniques, in comparison to a structured implementation. In this example latches and LCBs (local clock blocks) are preplaced. In addition, two types of custom components are embedded preplaced. Whereas the conventional synthesis result does not meet the timing requirements, for this example the Structured Synthesis techniques close timing as well as provide an 8% power reduction and 16% reduction in area.

The Datapath Synthesis placement algorithm was added to the PDSrtl synthesis program to build upon designer supplied preplacement [32]. Using preplaced cells and macro pins as anchors, this new placement algorithm infers structure in the macro and attempts to align datapath portions of the macro to the anchors, while non-datapath portions of the macro revert to convention placement algorithms more appropriate for "random logic". In addition, an automated latch and LCB placement algorithm was added to PDSrtl to emulate the style of preplacements designers supply [3]. Fig. 3 shows an example of a macro containing many latches and the a) conventional synthesis placement, b) designer supplied preplacement, c) the new datapath latch placement algorithm. From this example we see automated latch placement resembles the placements from an experienced custom designer. Although the automated latch placement algorithm does not fully attain the level of improvements as the designer directed preplacements, the design effort of the automated approach was far less and in many cases provides an attractive ROI.

1.2 Large block synthesis

While Structured Synthesis provides a continuum of techniques to attain near-custom quality from synthesis, scaling to larger macro sizes allows another level of synthesis gains. The core benefit of scaling to larger macro sizes is a lower reliance on macro boundary conditions, such as timing assertions and physical constraints, e.g., macro size, aspect ratio, and pin positions. The maintenance and accuracy of these boundary conditions are persistent challenges for physical design. Moving to larger macro sizes removes the need for boundary conditions between the previously small macros within the larger macro and allows the synthesis tool to fully optimize paths across the small macros as native internal paths. On the other hand, larger macros present challenges in terms of design complexity, tool runtime, and design efficiency via partitioning work among designers.

To address these challenges, the PDSrtl synthesis tool was optimized for issues that arise in larger macros as well to generally improve runtime for large macros. Routing congestion is one issue often facing larger macros. For these macros, the synthesis tool must find solutions for the routing complexities conventionally handled by experienced human unit integrators. These challenges were addressed in POWER8 by enhancing the PDSrtl tool with options for automated congestion aware placement and wire assignment, e.g., [16].

In addition, new design techniques for controlling portions of the large block design were developed during POWER8, providing designer guided facilities for improving congestion, timing, and power. The Soft Hierarchy flow allows designers to cluster subsets of logic gates within a large block macro [4], thereby allowing the synthesis tools to increase focus on localized critical portions of the design. This requires low design effort in that it only requires specifying the sub-macro hierarchy to physically group and optionally a bounding box for the sub-macro placement. The Hierarchical LBS flow (hLBS) allows designers to embed pre-synthesized sub-macros in a large macro. A key aspect of the hLBS flow is that only the synthesis step is needed for the sub-macro as the sub-macro boundary dissolves during the top-level synthesis process, allowing synthesis to operate on paths crossing the sub-macro boundary. In addition, hLBS allows division of labor among designers and allows each sub-macro to be synthesis with unique synthesis options. Further custom design precision can be attained by designing a flattened embedded IP block using either synthesis or custom design techniques. In this case the sub-macro is designed using standard cells and routed; however the sub-macro is flattened prior to top-level signoff. Finally, embedded hard IP allows full customization, such as using non-standard cell gates, but requires highest degree of design effort, i.e., full signoff of the sub-macro.

Figure 4: The IFU (Instruction Fetch Unit) is a unit scale LBSS macro that employed a number of structured techniques for design closure.

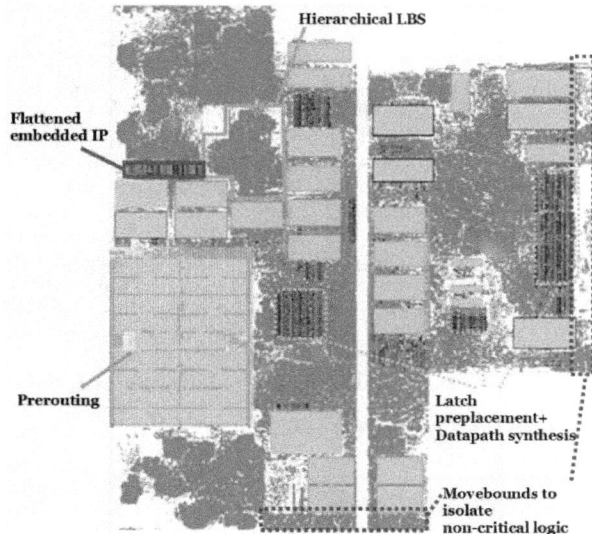

Finally, the runtime of tools was improved by adopting a gate-level signoff (GLSO) methodology for macros designated as large blocks. Prior POWER processors mostly em-

ployed a transistor-level signoff (TLSO) methodology requiring flat transistor-level extraction. The GLSO tools provide a 3-10x speedup over TLSO for verifying the timing, power, electrical integrity, compliance to electromigration reliability rules, and manufacturing design rules using a gate-level extracted netlist [11]. Prior to POWER8, many of the GLSO tools were not yet adequate for analyzing many of the custom design styles that enabled processor operation in the frequency range of 4-5 GHz. However, an extensive GLSO correlation effort to TLSO and SPICE level simulation led to an accurate and efficient signoff flow for high frequency designs. Note that the TLSO methodology was still extensively used by the POWER8 team for custom macros, dynamic logic, arrays, register files, clock distribution and analog design components.

The IFU, shown in Fig. 4, is responsible for fetching, decoding and dispatching instructions to the sequencing unit, expanding complex instructions into sequences of primitive instructions, predicting and executing the program control flow instructions such as branches and tracking the addresses of all in-flight instructions. The IFU design includes 37 instances of SRAM and register files arrays, 580K standard cells and 640K nets. Area savings was a motivating factor in moving to a single LBSS design for POWER8. Overall, it is estimated that the LBSS implementation of the IFU saved 15% in area versus a conventional server implementation.

Preplacement of the arrays was among the first techniques employed in the IFU to provide an underlying structure to the unit. Both movebounds, that confine logic to designer specified regions, and preplacement of latches and LCBs provided additional structure and were effective in guiding the synthesis tools to give better timing and reduce wiring congestion. Approximately 12K out of over 50K total latches were preplaced. The Datapath Synthesis placement algorithm, described in section 3.2, was used to effectively place the regularly structured portions of logic, building upon the preplaced latches as anchors. Fig. 4 depicts the dataflow regions as vertical colored lines. The hLBS flow was used to tackle a timing critical, physically irregular, control oriented sub-macro within the IFU, allowing high synthesis effort to focus on a specific portion of the unit. Likewise, a critical set of muxes were designed as a custom sub-cell and embedded in the unit, employing the flattened embedded IP process.

In terms of routing, applying layer and width assignments, i.e. wirecodes, to specific nets during synthesis proved effective for timing critical nets. Furthermore, the nets requiring a precise routing topology, such as the IFU cache output bus, were prerouted to ensure a regular topology across the bits of the bus.

2. HIGH-PERFORMANCE DESIGN

With technology scaling, transistor performance improvements and power reductions have saturated and it is becoming increasingly difficult to improve chip performance, primarily limited by the total power budget. In this era of nanometer scaling, delivering higher performance to applications would require chip architects and EDA developers to step up innovations across micro-architechture, logic, and physical design to enable designs to maximize energy efficiency for target application.

Datapath logic constitutes a significant portion of a general purpose microprocessor and frequently occurs on the timing-critical paths in high-performance designs. Arithmetic components, such as adders, multipliers, shifters are the basic building blocks in datapath logic and hence, to a great extent dictate the performance of the entire chip. Binary addition is one of the most fundamental and widely used in microprocessors because other complex arithmetic operations can be built upon adders.

Figure 5: (a) Prefix graph for the carry propagate logic with evenly distributed fanout. (b) Performance-power trade-off for a 64-bit adder.

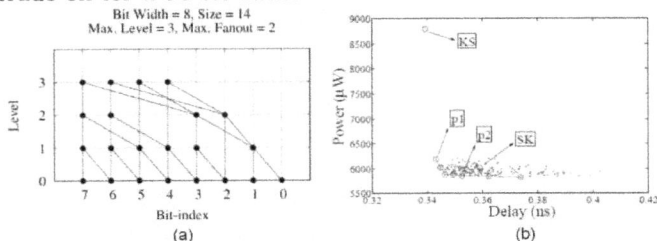

High-performance datapth logic today typically uses regular adders such as Kogge-Stone, Ladner-Fisher and Han-Carlson, because besides having minimum logic levels, these adders provide an evenly distributed fanout and netlist connectivity that minimizes wire delay and congestion during physical design. A recent work [21] demonstrated an automated solution to generating adder structures with desirable logic and physical design characteristics. Regular adders such as Kogge-Stone (KS) and Sklansky (SK) are not able to achieve pareto-optimal energy-efficiency of adders designed using [21] shown as points p1 and p2 in Fig. 5. Although the adders generated using [21] did not have a regualar logic structure (like Kogge-Stone or Sklansky adders), the adder was 25% smaller than regular high-performance adders and had fanout evenly distributed across adder gates (see Fig. 5(a)). Together these properties resulted in better performance due to reduced wire delay, congestion and better gate sizing opportunities during physical design. As shown with points p1 and p2 in Fig. 5(b), the highest performance adders generated with [21] consumed 40% less power than regular adders.

Recent progress in multi-level logic synthesis has been driven towards achieving optimal area-delay decompositions. For instance, [18] proposes pre-computing optimal decompositions for functions with up to four or five input variables. These pre-computed structures are then selectively used four or five input logic cuts occurring in larger designs. The advantage of this technique is that it is very fast and several iterations can be applied on large designs to achieve significant area and delay reduction. In contrast to the rewriting approach, that uses smaller functions as building blocks for larger functions, bidecomposition is a logic optimization technique that breaks down a large function recursively into smaller functions. Bidecomposition techniques are useful because they can discover decompositions that would be missed by local restructuring techniques like rewriting, rewiring, and algebraic factoring technuques. The biggest hurdle in bidecomposition techniques is the computational complexity of computing the variable partition in each recursive step. Recent work on bidecomposition algorithms have used structural properties of BDDs [34] and pairwise variable cofactoring [5] to scale this approach to functions with a large number of variables.

Even with state-of-the-art synthesis algorithms, there is no silver bullet to finding optimal multi-level logic structures. Most synthesis algorithms are sensitive to the input netlist format and the order in which gates and nets are processed by the algorithm. Many algorithms are tailored for specific classes of logic such as arithmetic logic, XOR-intensive logic, AND-OR logic, etc. Improving multi-level decomposition for large designs requires tedious application of several synthesis algorithms on different parts of the design and cut enumeration techniques [9] might be the only option for uncovering sub-optimalities within large designs.

In future technology generations, with diminishing improvements coming from transistor performance, higher performance will be delivered by leveraging higher device density to build even more complex designs with heterogeneous parallelism that targets specific applications. This would require logic and physical design tools to handle new levels of complexity. To meet these challenges, we believe that logic design (including logic restructuring, optimization, and technology mapping) and physical design (placement, gate sizing, buffer optimization, and routing) will have to be tightly integrated and co-optimized. To achieve better integration requires better timing models during synthesis, faster and more deterministic placement algorithms, and metrics for measuring and predicting design complexity.

3. POWER OPTIMIZATION TECHNIQUES

This section discusses various power reduction techniques that work on different dimensions of circuit design: gate sizing, threshold voltage assignment, voltage islands, and logic optimizations. The focus of the discussion is how each of these well-established optimizations can be re-targeted for the purpose of power minimization in high-performance microprocessors.

3.1 Physical design techniques

The most widely studied optimization techniques are gate sizing and threshold voltage assignment, as well as simultaneous optimization of the two [6][10][13][17][19][20][22][23][24][30], for both performance and power optimization. Established methodologies can be roughly divided into two categories. The first is sensitivity-based discrete heuristics represented by TILOS [10][22]. The second is continuous nonlinear optimization, followed by snapping gates to the technology-imposed cell choices [6]; it is known to give better results for the sole gate sizing problem, but loses when incorporating the more discrete threshold voltage decisions.

Another important aspect of simultaneous gate sizing and threshold voltage assignment, which often does not get enough attention in literature, is the critical role of accurate work load analysis and circuit activity analysis [8]. For example, given two identical gates in the netlist, one is a control signal that rarely switches while the second is a data signal that changes value during 30% of the clock cycles, we would use a larger cell with higher threshold voltage for the first gate and use a smaller cell with lower threshold voltage for the second gate. At application level, such trade-off situation varies widely due to intended work load of the chip; at circuit level, it varies widely from gate to gate, e.g., output of an XOR tree switches more than output of an AND tree.

For recent chips [11], we use the algorithm from [1][20], driven by accurate activity analysis all the way from work load level to gate level. The algorithm of [20] belongs to the first category of sensitivity-based discrete heuristics, and iteratively solves the optimization as a weighted maximum independent set problem. It is well suited to perform simultaneous gate sizing and threshold voltage assignment, exploiting per-gate trade-off based on detailed switching activity information. It is used twice during the design flow, once before routing and once after routing. Table 1 shows the pre-routing optimization results on a set of macros with varying activity profiles, and the optimization is conservative to account for routing uncertainty. Table 2 shows the post-routing optimization results, which translates the slack left by the pre-routing call to further power savings. For both tables, the timing performance is neutral before and after the optimization.

3.2 Dual Vdd

Utilizing voltage islands is an effective and widely used way of reducing power consumption of a chip. In particular, having voltage islands enables power gating, where an idle circuit block can consume zero power, as well as dynamic voltage scaling, which exploits performance-power tradeoff

Table 1: Pre-routing Gate Sizing and Threshold Voltage Assignment

	Before (mW)	After (mW)	Reduction
Leakage Power	87.70	83.63	4.65%
Dynamic Power	270.75	247.23	8.68%
Total Power	358.45	330.86	7.70%

Table 2: Post-routing Gate Sizing and Threshold Voltage Assignment

	Before (mW)	After (mW)	Reduction
Leakage Power	61.56	53.76	12.66%
Dynamic Power	187.55	175.31	6.53%
Total Power	249.11	229.07	8.04%

on the fly [26]. However, existing multiple-voltage designs typically form voltage islands at a coarse level of granularity, where an island size is at least thousands of gates. There are a few works on fine-grained multiple-voltage methods [19][24], but without hardware implementation and targeted at low-frequency designs.

We implemented a fine-grained dual-Vdd design flow targeted at high-performance microprocessors, which can run at as high as 5GHz. The flow allows island sizes as low as a single cell, with typical sizes being dozens of cells. Part of the flow is detailed in [33]. It is comprised of two major optimization steps, – topological clustering and physical island generation, – as well as specialized dual-Vdd power grid routing and other supporting dual-vdd design utilities.

The first optimization step is topological clustering. The input is a single-Vdd design that is optimized at the higher supply voltage. The output is a dual-Vdd design, as illustrated in Figure 6. Note that a high-Vdd gate is allowed to drive low-Vdd gates, yet a low-Vdd gate must go through a level shifter in order to drive a high-Vdd gate. The objective of the optimization is to minimize power consumption while maintaining the same timing performance as the initial single-Vdd design. In other words, instead of trading off between two dimensions of gate size and threshold voltage as discussed in the previous section, this optimization trades off among three dimensions, with a new dimension being the Vdd of a gate. The algorithm employed is a generalization of the ECVS method [29][28] in combination of [20].

The second optimization forms placement islands such that dual-Vdd power grids are feasible and that each gate is reachable by the appropriate voltage grid, while maintaining the timing performance and power savings from the first optimization. Our dual-Vdd power grid design uses segmented power rails in lower metal layers and interleaved power rails in upper metal layers; the feasibility of such a design translates to a placement constraint that is the minimum length of a voltage island, as well as special placement rules for level shifters. Details can be found in [33]. The output is illustrated in Figure 7.

3.3 Logic restructuring

Another big lever for power minimization is via logic changes. At RTL level, for example, encoding a finite-state machine differently could have substantial power implications. At combinatorial logic level, different implementations of the same logic function could result in designs with widely varying power consumption. This section focuses on the latter

Figure 6: Dual-Vdd Topological Clustering

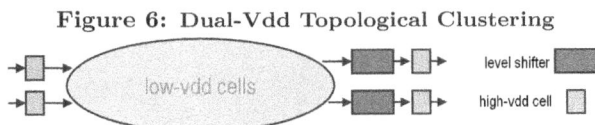

Figure 7: Dual-Vdd Placement Islands. Dark green gates are low-Vdd gates, light blue ones are high-Vdd gates, purple gates are level shifters, cyan gates are local clock buffers, placement islands are outlined by red rectangles [33].

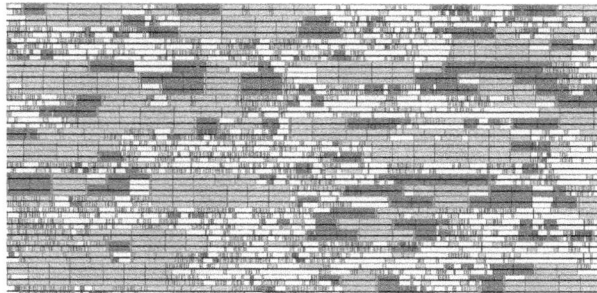

case: assume a given RTL description with fixed latches and try to find a low power combinatorial implementation.

Many existing logic optimization techniques in literature can be readily adapted for power minimization. Specifically, any technique that works on timing-area tradeoff can be retargeted by replacing the area metric with a power metric, driven by accurate power analysis as discussed earlier. The algorithm of [14][15], which implicitly enumerates all mapping solutions of a logic section, has been extensively used for timing optimization in high-performance microprocessors [11]. By replacing the area metric with leakage power, dynamic power, or sum of the two, the algorithm of [15] switches its goal to enumerate for the best power solution with a timing constraint. Note that leakage power reduction is achieved by mapping logic to complex gates with more stack effect.

Another group of logic optimization techniques, namely rewiring [31][35], is more targeted and suitable for dynamic power reduction. These methods work by identifying a signal to be removed, and looking for either a replacement signal or a set of additional signals that make the target signal redundant.

4. CONCLUSION

The design complexity of modern high performance processors calls for innovative design techniques and methodologies for achieving time-to-market goals. This paper described new processor design and optimization approaches that bridge the gap between high performance and low power which were critical for the industry leading power-performance tradeoff of the POWER8 processor.

5. REFERENCES

[1] E. Acar and H. Qian. Simultaneous power and timing optimization in integrated circuits by performing discrete actions on circuit components. *U.S. Patent 7689942*, 2010.

[2] M. Cho et al. Converged large block and structured synthesis for high performance microprocessor designs. *U.S. Patent 8271920*, 2012.

[3] M. Cho et al. Latchplanner: Latch placement algorithm for datapath-oriented high-performance vlsi designs. In *International Conference on Computer-Aided Design Digest of Technical Papers*, 2013.

[4] M. Cho et al. Soft hierarchy-based physical synthesis for large-scale high-performance circuits. *U.S. Patent 8516412*, 2013.

[5] M. Choudhury and K. Mohanram. Bi-decomposition of large boolean functions using blocking edge graphs.

In *Proceedings of the International Conference on Computer-Aided Design*, ICCAD '10, pages 586–591, Piscataway, NJ, USA, 2010. IEEE Press.

[6] A. R. Conn et al. Gradient-based optimization of custom circuits using a static-timing formulation. In *Proceedings of Design Automation Conference*, pages 452–459, 1993.

[7] W. J. Daily and A. Chang. The role of custom design in asic chips. In *Proceedings of the Design Automation Conference*, 2000.

[8] N. Dhanwada et al. Efficient pvt independent abstraction of large ip blocks for hierarchical power analysis. In *International Conference on Computer-Aided Design Digest of Technical Papers*, pages 458–465, 2013.

[9] M. Elbayoumi, M. Choudhury, V. Kravets, A. Sullivan, M. Hsiao, and M. Elnainay. Tacue: A timing-aware cuts enumeration algorithm for parallel synthesis. In *Proceedings of the 51st Annual Design Automation Conference on Design Automation Conference*, DAC '14, pages 189:1–189:6, New York, NY, USA, 2014. ACM.

[10] J. P. Fishburn and A. E. Dunlop. Tilos: A posynomial programming approach to transistor sizing. In *International Conference on Computer-Aided Design Digest of Technical Papers*, pages 326–328, 1985.

[11] E. J. Fluhr et al. Power8: A 12-core server-class processor in 22nm soi with 7.6tb/s off-chip bandwidth. In *IEEE International Solid-State Circuits Conference Digest of Technical Papers*, pages 96–97, 2014.

[12] J. Friedrich et al. Design methodology for the ibm power7 microprocessor. *IBM Journal of Research and Development*, 55(3):9:1–9:14, 2011.

[13] M. Ketkar and S. S. Sapatnekar. Standby power optimization via transistor sizing and dual threshold voltage assignment. In *International Conference on Computer-Aided Design Digest of Technical Papers*, pages 375–378, 2002.

[14] V. N. Kravets and P. Kudva. Implicit enumeration of structural changes in circuit optimization. In *Proceedings of the Design Automation Conference*, pages 438–441, 2004.

[15] V. N. Kravets and K. A. Sakallah. Resynthesis of multi-level circuits under tight constraints using symbolic optimization. In *International Conference on Computer-Aided Design Digest of Technical Papers*, pages 687–693, 2002.

[16] W.-H. Liu et al. Routing congestion estimation with real design constraints. In *Proceedings of the Design Automation Conference*, 2013.

[17] Y. Liu and J. Hu. A new algorithm for simultaneous gate sizing and threshold voltage assignment. *IEEE Transactions on Computer-Aided Design of Integrated Circuits and Systems*, 29(2):223–234, Feb 2010.

[18] A. Mishchenko, S. Chatterjee, and R. Brayton. DAG-aware AIG rewriting a fresh look at combinational logic synthesis. In *Proceedings of the 43rd Annual Design Automation Conference*, DAC '06, pages 532–535, New York, NY, USA, 2006. ACM.

[19] P. Pant, V. K. De, and A. Chatterjee. Simultaneous power supply, threshold voltage, and transistor size optimization for low-power operation of cmos circuits. *IEEE Transactions on Very Large Scale Integration Systems*, 6(4):538–545, December 1998.

[20] H. Qian and E. Acar. Timing-aware power minimization via extended timing graph methods. *ASP Journal of Low Power Electronics*, 3(3):318–326, 2007.

[21] S. Roy, M. Choudhury, R. Puri, and D. Z. Pan. Towards optimal performance-area trade-off in adders by synthesis of parallel prefix structures. In *Proceedings of the 50th Annual Design Automation Conference*, DAC '13, pages 48:1–48:8, New York, NY, USA, 2013. ACM.

[22] J. M. Shyu, A. Sangiovanni-Vincentelli, J. P. Fishburn, and A. Dunlop. Optimization-based transistor sizin. *IEEE Journal of Solid State Circuits*, 23(2):400–409, April 1988.

[23] S. Sirichotiyakul, T. Edwards, C. Oh, R. Panda, and D. Blaauw. Duet: An accurate leakage estimation and optimization tool for dual-vt circuits. *IEEE Transactions on Very Large Scale Integration Systems*, 10(2):79–90, April 2002.

[24] A. Srivastava, D. Sylvester, and D. Blaauw. Power minimization using simultaneous gate sizing, dual-vdd and dual-vth assignment. In *Proceedings of Design Automation Conference*, pages 783–786, 2004.

[25] B. Stolt et al. Design and implementation of the power6 microprocessor. *IEEE Journal of Solid State Circuits*, 43(1), 2008.

[26] Z. Toprak-Deniz et al. Distributed system of digitally controlled microregulators enabling per-core dvfs for the power8 microprocessor. In *IEEE International Solid-State Circuits Conference Digest of Technical Papers*, pages 98–99, 2014.

[27] L. Trevillyan et al. An integrated environment for technology closure of deep-submicron ic designs. *IEEE Design and Test of Computers*, 21(1):14–22, 2004.

[28] K. Usami et al. Automated low-power technique exploiting multiple supply voltages applied to a media processor. *IEEE Journal of Solid State Circuits*, 33(3):463–472, 1998.

[29] K. Usami and M. Horowitz. Clustered voltage scaling technique for low-power design. In *Proceedings of the international symposium on Low power design*, pages 3–8, 1995.

[30] Q. Wang and S. B. K. Vrudhula. Static power optimization of deep submicron cmos circuits for dual vt technology. In *International Conference on Computer-Aided Design Digest of Technical Papers*, pages 490–496, 1998.

[31] X. Wei, W. Tang, Y. Wu, C. Sze, and C. Alpert. Wrip: logic restructuring techniques for wirelength-driven incremental placement. In *Proceedings of the Great Lakes Symposium on VLSI*, pages 327–332, 2012.

[32] H. Xiang et al. Network flow based datapath bit slicing. In *ACM International Symposium on Physical Design*, 2013.

[33] H. Xiang, H. Qian, C. Zhou, Y. Lin, F. Yee, A. Sullivan, and P. Lu. Distributed system of digitally controlled microregulators enabling per-core dvfs for the power8 microprocessor. In *Proceedings of Design Automation Conference*, 2014.

[34] C. Yang and M. Ciesielski. Bds: a bdd-based logic optimization system. *Computer-Aided Design of Integrated Circuits and Systems, IEEE Transactions on*, 21(7):866–876, Jul 2002.

[35] X. Yang, T. Lam, and Y. Wu. Ecr: a low complexity generalized error cancellation rewiring scheme. In *Proceedings of the Design Automation Conference*, pages 511–516, 2010.

[36] V. Zyuban et al. Design methodology for semi custom processor cores. In *Proceedings of the Great Lakes Symposium on VLSI*, 2004.

CASA: Correlation-Aware Speculative Adders

Gai Liu, Ye Tao, Mingxing Tan, and Zhiru Zhang

Computer Systems Laboratory, Electrical and Computer Engineering
Cornell University, Ithaca, NY
gl387@cornell.edu, yt434@cornell.edu, mingxing.tan@cornell.edu, zhiruz@cornell.edu

ABSTRACT

Speculative adders divide addition into subgroups and execute them in parallel for higher execution speed and energy efficiency, but at the risk of generating incorrect results. In this paper, we propose a lightweight correlation-aware speculative addition (CASA) method, which exploits the correlation between input data and carry-in values observed in real-life benchmarks to improve the accuracy of speculative adders. Experimental results show that applying the CASA method leads to a significant reduction in error rate with only marginal overhead in timing, area, and power consumption.

Categories and Subject Descriptors

B.2 [**Arithmetic and Logic Structures**]: General

Keywords

Speculative Adders, Low Error Rates, Low Power

1. INTRODUCTION

Opportunistic computing [3] is an emerging design paradigm to improve the performance and energy efficiency of digital computer systems. By allowing inaccurate or occasionally incorrect results to occur, designers are offered a choice to more easily trade the quality of solution for cost. The central idea of opportunistic computing is to speed up the common-case execution while allowing errors to happen in rare occasions. In applications such as signal processing [8, 7] where inexact results are tolerable, opportunistic computing techniques can improve both speed and energy efficiency. On the other hand, when exact results are desired, appropriate error detection and recovery mechanisms are necessary to correct the errors.

Being one of the essential building blocks of the digital circuits, adders have been recently re-examined and "retooled" in the context of opportunistic computing. The main idea is to exploit the fact that the typical length of the carry propagation is usually much shorter than the full width of the adder. Therefore, an opportunistic adder built with short carry chains can potentially operate at a much faster speed with reasonably accurate results. Broadly speaking, opportunistic adders can be categorized into two classes, namely, approximate adders and speculative adders. Approximate adders [4, 17, 12] are more concerned with minimizing the error amplitude to ensure the accuracy of the output value. Speculative adders [11, 13, 10, 14, 16, 15, 2, 9], on the other

hand, primarily aim to improve the speed of the addition by making speculations about the carry-in values. When a misspeculation results in an incorrect output, the error recovery circuit will be triggered to correct the result. Since the error recovery logic usually incurs considerable overhead in latency and energy consumption, a speculative adder is expected to operate with a low error rate (i.e., the number of errors divided by the total number of additions).

In this work, we focus on speculative adders considering that they are applicable to a wider range of problems. Clearly, minimizing the error rate without significant timing/area/power degradation is one of the key challenges for designing an effective speculative adder. Although a variety of techniques [10, 16, 15, 2] have been proposed to address this issue, the existing speculative adders are mostly tested against uniformly distributed random vectors, which often do not reflect the actual data patterns from the real-life benchmarks. In fact, according to our experiments on MiBench [5], two representative speculative adders exhibit high error rates (above 30%) for multiple benchmarks, suggesting that random test vectors are insufficient for evaluating the effectiveness of existing and new speculation techniques.

In this paper, we address the problem of reducing error rate of speculative adders in the context of real-life applications. Our method intelligently exploits the correlation between the most significant bit of the input operands and the carry-in values to improve the "correctness" of speculative adders. Our major contributions are as follows:

1. We present a systematic study using real-life benchmarks to evaluate the effectiveness of state-of-the-art speculative adders. We show that significant room exists for reducing the error rates of existing techniques.

2. We propose the correlation-aware speculative addition (CASA), which is a generic lightweight extension to existing speculative adders. We show that CASA achieves a significant reduction in error rate with small overhead in timing and area. Compared with a fast parallel prefix adder, CASA can also achieve substantial power reduction with comparable speed.

The rest of the paper is structured as follows: Section 2 reviews the related work on speculative adder designs; Section 3 provides background and preliminaries of the operating principles of the speculative addition; Section 4 presents the quantitative study of two existing speculative adders and motivates our own method; Section 5 presents our correlation-aware speculative addition approach; Section 6 reports the experimental results followed by conclusions in Section 7.

2. RELATED WORK

One of the early attempts to build a speculative adder is described in [11] where a long addition is divided into smaller groups of length K, with each group responsible for generating the result only for the most significant bit in that group adder. Since each group adder only handles a window size of K bits, an error would occur when the actual length of the carry propagation exceeds K. Variable latency speculative adder (VLSA) [13] employs a similar scheme formed by K-bit group adders and further proposes resource sharing techniques to significantly reduce the overall circuit area. Error detection and recovery circuits are also introduced in this work.

In the error-tolerant adder (ETA) [16, 15], a different design is proposed where the original adder is divided into several non-overlapping groups and each group also has a separate carry generation logic. The carry-in value for a group adder depends on the result of the carry generation from the preceding group adder. A different method of carry-in prediction is used in the speculative carry select adder (SCSA) [2], which pre-computes both cases with and without the carry-in. The carry-out value from the preceding group will be used to determine the actual outcome. Although this method can achieve higher speed and accuracy, pre-computations are quite expensive in terms of both area and energy. Accuracy configurable adder (ACA) [10] only uses the result of upper half part of each addition so as to improve accuracy. They also propose a pipelined accuracy-reconfigurable scheme where results are incrementally corrected in different pipeline stages. Since error amplitude of ACA can be limited within certain range by the incremental correction scheme, ACA can also be viewed as a hybrid adder combining the feature of approximate and speculative adders. In [14], a reconfigurable prediction scheme is proposed where carry-in value of current window is predicted by previous K windows, where K is a configurable parameter. This serves as an improvement for ACA achieving accuracy-configurability during compute stage.

3. PRELIMINARIES

In this section, we review the basics of the speculative adders in terms of how they achieve speed improvement with short carry chains and detect errors. In particular, we will examine VLSA and ACA, which are two representative speculative adder designs, in more detail.

3.1 Group Adders

The rationales of the existing speculative adder designs are similar. The key insight is that the typical length of the carry propagation is much shorter than the worst-case scenario. Hence, dividing a long addition into smaller groups and executing them in parallel would lead to smaller delay and potentially lower power consumption.

Existing speculative adders can be roughly categorized into two classes based on how addition groups are defined and how the final sum is composed from the result of each group adder. In the first class [11, 13], each group adder only contributes one bit to the final sum, i.e., only the most significant bit (msb) of each group adder will be used. VLSA is a good representative design for this class of speculative adders. In the second class [10, 14, 16, 15, 2], the addition is divided into multiple windows with each window responsible for generating a range of bits for the final sum. The existing window-based speculative adders are logically similar, but usually exhibit different trade-offs among delay, area and power consumption. In this paper, we focus on ACA [10] in the subsequent discussion since it is a good representative of the window-based speculative adders and has a low area overhead.

Figure 1 illustrates the circuit structures of group adders in VLSA and ACA. In VLSA, only the msb of each group addition will be used in the final result. VLSA can achieve relatively high accuracy because each bit in the final sum is calculated from one dedicated group adder. However, the circuit cost is also relatively high for VLSA because of the large number of group adders needed. In contrast, window-based speculative adders such as ACA organize group additions in a manner of overlapping windows. Area overhead is reduced in this case since less amount of redundant computation is conducted.

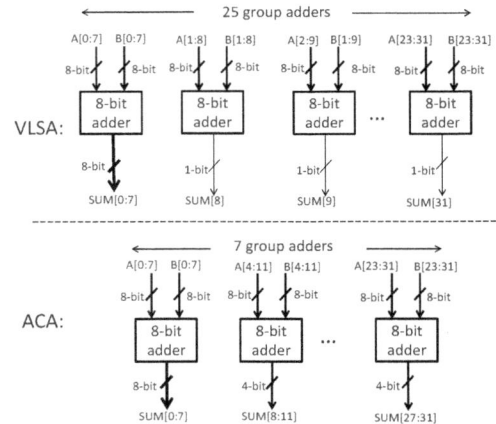

Figure 1: Group adders of VLSA and ACA.

The key design technique to ensure high accuracy is that only certain part (usually left-most bits) of the group sum goes into the final result. In this scenario, even if there exists a carry propagation from the previous group, the result of current group addition may not necessarily be wrong. This is because there is a high probability that carry will be generated or killed inside the lower bits in the group adder, so that carry-in from the previous group will have no impact on the correctness of the current group addition.

3.2 Error Condition

Speculative adders truncate the original addition into group additions of length K, and assume that the carry-in values will not propagate across more than K bit positions. Hence it is not too difficult to derive the error condition of a speculative adder as follows:

$$ErrorFlag = \sum_{i=0}^{n-k-1} p_i p_{i+1} \cdots p_{i+k} g_{i+k+1} \qquad (1)$$

The definitions g_i and p_i signals in the above equation are described below. We also define the kill signal (k_i) to facilitate the later discussions.

- Generate g_i: $g_i = 1$ if both operands are 1 at position i;
- Kill k_i: $k_i = 1$ if both operands are 0 at position i;
- Propagate p_i: $p_i = 1$ if two operands differ at position i.

It is worth noting that having a long sequence of propagate signals p's does not necessarily result in an error. In fact, only when this sequence is trailed by a g signal (instead of k), the actual carry propagation would occur, resulting in an error.

4. QUANTITATIVE STUDY OF REPRESENTATIVE SPECULATIVE ADDERS

In this section, we present a quantitative study using real-life benchmarks to evaluate the effectiveness of VLSA and ACA.

4.1 Error Rate Evaluation

We have set up a comprehensive evaluation flow based on the GEM5 [1] architectural simulator to assess the effectiveness of existing speculative adders against real-life benchmarks. Specifically, we have modified the arithmetic logic units in a MIPS32 processor and tested benchmarks from the MiBench [5] suite. Results of two representative speculative adders, i.e., VLSI and ACA, are compared against the correct results to obtain error instructions and derive the error rates.

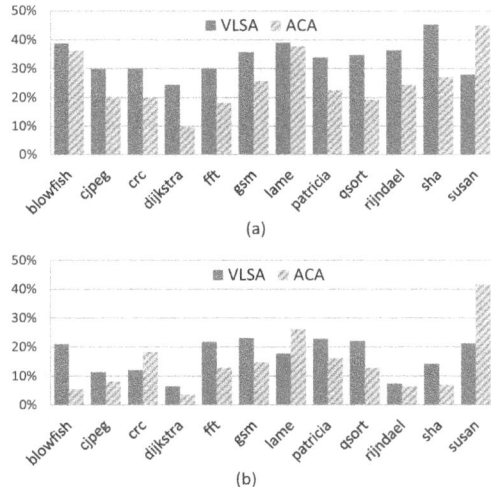

Figure 2: Error rates for VLSA and ACA. (a) K=4; (b) K=8.

The error rates of VLSA and ACA on 12 MiBench benchmarks are shown in Figure 2. Among these benchmarks, the error rates vary widely from below 10% to above 40%. This suggests that the common practice of using uniformly distributed random test vectors is insufficient for evaluating the effectiveness of existing speculative addition techniques. Furthermore, this study shows that significant room exists for reducing the error rates of state-of-the-art speculative adders.

4.2 Diagnosis of Erroneous Additions

In this section, we examine the data patterns in MiBench benchmarks that frequently trigger errors in speculative adders. We compile the benchmark code of MiBench, analyze the assembly, and keep track of the operands of the addition instances during execution.

We identify the most frequently executed and error-prone instructions and examine the characteristic patterns of their source operands. Figure 3 shows several instances of such

Figure 3: Example of long carry propagation chain causing errors.

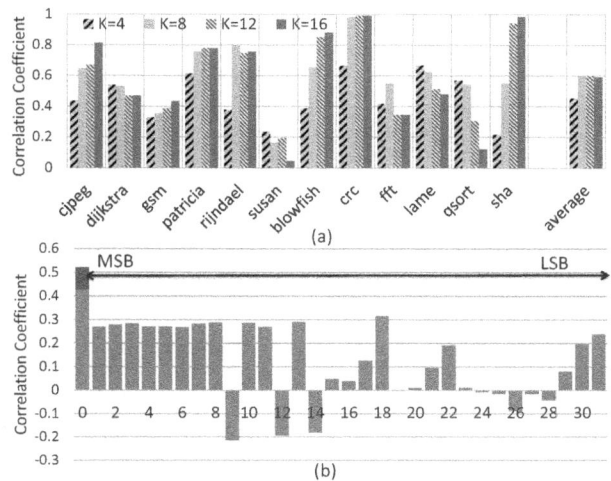

Figure 4: (a) Correlation coefficient for different benchmarks. (b) Correlation coefficient for each of the 32 bits for benchmark *fft*.

additions that are executed many times and prone to errors. It can be observed that the carry propagation chains in the above examples are usually long. Any speculative adder that fails to anticipate such long carry propagation will result in an error. In fact, we observe that in most cases these long carry propagation chains arise from sign bit extensions. In other words, long sequence of propagate signals usually happen when adding numbers of different signs. These long carry chains are the major source of errors.

Given this observation, we hypothesize that there exists a correlation between the difference of the most significant bits (i.e. $XOR(msb)$) and the length of the carry propagation chain. We will further justify the correlation in the following section, and show that this correlation-based speculation technique can be used as a lightweight extension to speculative adders, achieving significant reduction in error rate.

4.3 Correlation Analysis

As previously mentioned, we hypothesize that there exists correlation between the length of the carry propagation and the $XOR(msb)$ value. In this section, we will examine this hypothesis based on the well-known Pearson's correlation coefficient for additions from MiBench. To facilitate our test, we define the following two random variables:

- Random variable X: $X = 1$ $if XOR(msb) = 1$; $x = 0$ if $XOR(msb) = 0$.

- Random variable Y: $Y = 1$ if there exists a sequence of propagate signal ending with generate g (i.e. $ppp \ldots g$) whose length is equal to or greater than the group size.

The Pearson's correlation coefficient between X and Y can be defined as:

$$\rho_{X,Y} = \frac{\text{cov}(X,Y)}{\sigma_X \sigma_Y} \quad (2)$$

where cov is the covariance and σ_X and σ_Y are the standard deviation of X and Y respectively. Intuitively, large $\rho_{X,Y}$ indicates strong correlation between X and Y, while small $\rho_{X,Y}$ indicates weak correlation between X and Y.

To investigate the Pearson's correlation coefficient of X and Y, we have sampled 12 benchmarks from MiBench. Figure 4 shows the Pearson's correlation coefficient of X and

Y in these designs. Results show that the correlation coefficient are greater than 0.5 in a majority part of benchmarks, which largely confirms our hypothesis. [1]

5. CASA DESIGN

In this section, we present the design of our correlation-aware speculative addition (CASA) and the corresponding error rate evaluation. CASA is a lightweight carry prediction scheme that can serve as an extension to most existing speculative adders. Here we use ACA adder [10] as our baseline design, while extensions to other speculative adders can be fulfilled in a similar manner.

5.1 Implementation of CASA

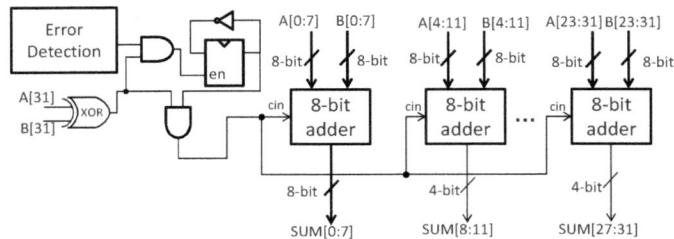

Figure 5: Circuit implementation of CASA.

Figure 5 shows the structural diagram of the CASA extension based on ACA. The first modification to the original ACA adder is an XOR gate connecting the msb of two operands to the carry-in of group adders. When $XOR(msb) = 0$, the carry-in to the group adders will be all zeros, which is the same in the original ACA. As long as the length of carry propagation chain does not exceed K, CASA will always generate the correct result. On the other hand, when $XOR(msb) = 1$, the carry-in to the group adders will be set to one to account for the potential long carry propagation that are frequently encountered when the most significant bits differ. In this case, CASA will achieve higher accuracy compared to the baseline design because it often correctly predicts the carry-in signal generated from previous group adders.

In order to improve the error rate for applications with relatively small correlation coefficient, we also propose a dynamic 1-bit prediction scheme to further reduce error rate for certain benchmarks. The high-level idea of this 1-bit prediction scheme is similar to a simple 1-bit branch predictor. Instead of always predicting carry-in equals one when $XOR(msb) = 1$, we make CASA adaptive by keeping some history information and update the prediction value every time an error occurs. In our case, if the prediction is wrong for the current instruction leading to an error, the prediction outcome will be reversed. This way, the carry prediction unit can dynamically adapt to the characteristics of the input vector, thus further reducing the error rate.

Prediction is realized by one flip-flop enabled by the error detection circuit. We only apply dynamic prediction when $XOR(msb) = 1$ by introducing an AND gate connecting the XOR gate and the output of the flip-flop. Also, to ensure that the state of prediction is only updated when $XOR(msb) = 1$, we implement an enable signal driven by

---

[1] It is worth noting that [6] also observed that long carry propagation chains are more likely to occur when adding small numbers with opposite signs in DCT/IDCT algorithms. Based on this observation, approximate adders with reduced bitwidths are used to improve the area and timing of the design.

the result of an AND gate that takes as inputs the error flag and output of XOR gate. Then each group adder will conduct addition based on the predicted carry-in and two operands, and the final result will be selected from the group adders accordingly.

Our CASA implementation is lightweight and flexible. CASA only requires one extra XOR gate and one additional flip-flop to conduct correlation-based speculation and dynamic prediction. Although we are extending ACA in this case, CASA can be applied to other speculative adders such as VLSA.

5.2 Error Rate Analysis of CASA under Uniformly Distributed Random Inputs

Although CASA is motivated by observations from real-life input vectors, we can also show that CASA does not significantly degrade the performance under uniformly distributed random input vectors. First of all, we note that for uniformly distributed random inputs, dynamic 1-bit prediction is unbiased and have no impact on the overall error rate. This is confirmed by our Monte Carlo simulation. For simplicity, we restrict our analytical evaluation to CASA with correlation speculation and take VLSA as our baseline design.

Let us first define function $G_n(x)$ as the total number of n-bit long sequences in which the longest run of $pppp\ldots g$ does not exceed x. $G_n(x)$ can be calculated using the following recursive relation:

$$G_n(x) = \sum_{i=1}^{x} 2^i \times G_{n-i}(x) + \sum_{i=x+1}^{n} 2^{i-1} \times G_{n-i}(x) + 2^n \quad (3)$$

with the boundary condition:

$$G_n(x) = 4^n, n \leq x \quad (4)$$

where the first summation corresponds to run of p that is shorter than x and is terminated by g or k; the second summation corresponds to run of p longer than or equal to x but is terminated by k; and the third term corresponds to a run of p whose length is exactly n. Now using $G_n(x)$, error rate of CASA for $XOR(msb) = 0$ and $XOR(msb) = 1$ can be separately calculated as:

$$ErrorRate^{xor=0} = \frac{4^{n-1} - G_n^{xor=0}(x)}{4^{n-1}} \quad (5)$$

$$ErrorRate^{xor=1} = \frac{4^{n-1} - G_n^{xor=1}(x)}{4^{n-1}} \quad (6)$$

where

$$G_n^{xor=0}(x) = G_{n-1}(x) \quad (7)$$

$$G_n^{xor=1}(x) = G_{n-1}(x) - \sum_{i=x+1}^{n-1} 2^i \times 4^{n-i-1} \quad (8)$$

The additional sum in Equation 8 accounts for the fact that when $XOR(msb) = 1$, the msb itself contributes to possible propagate chains starting from msb. The overall error rate for CASA is the expectation of Equation 5 and Equation 6:

$$ErrorRate = \frac{1}{2} \times (ErrorRate^{xor=0} + ErrorRate^{xor=1}) \quad (9)$$

As a reference, the error rate for VLSA can be calculated as:

$$ErrorRate = \frac{4^n - G_n(x)}{4^n} \quad (10)$$

Based on above derivations, we provide theoretical error rates for VLSA and CASA under uniformly distributed random input vectors.

Table 1: Theoretical error rate for VLSA and CASA with uniformly distributed random input vectors.

K	4	6	8	10	12
VLSA	37.44%	9.87%	2.33%	0.54%	0.12%
CASA	39.50%	10.29%	2.43%	0.56%	0.13%

From Table 1, we observe that CASA achieves similar accuracy compared to baseline design, confirming the feasibility of CASA even for uniformly distributed random vectors.

5.3 Error Detection for CASA

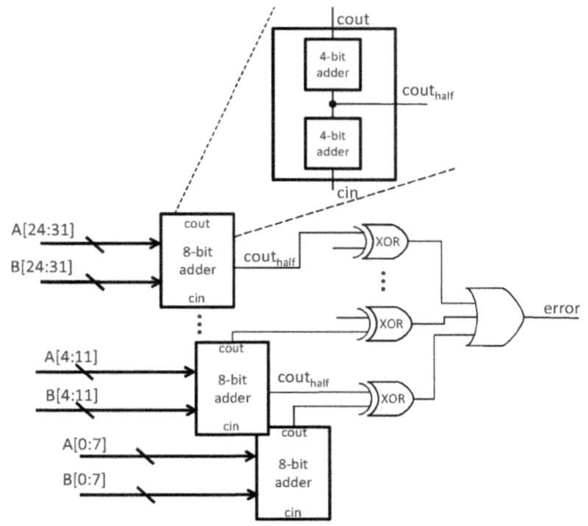

Figure 6: Error detection circuit for CASA. ($cout_{half}$ represents carry-out signal generated by the lower 4 bits in the group adder.)

Our error detection logic is similar to the ACA adder [10] but with slight modification to account for the different carry-in values predicted by the XOR gate. A naive way of implementing error detection circuit is to search in the original input operands for every sequence of $ppp\ldots g$ or $ppp\ldots k$ for $XOR(msb) = 0$ and $XOR(msb) = 1$, respectively. Then the error detection circuit will flag an error if the length of such sequences is longer than the available look-ahead bits in the group adder. Here we introduce a logically equivalent but much simpler version of error detection circuit: For each group addition, error detection circuit compares the carry-out value from the previous window with the carry-out value generated by the lower-half of the current group adder, as shown in Figure 6. If the error detection circuit finds a mismatch between these two values in any of the group adders, it means that the upper-half of the group adder fails to capture the correct carry-in value. Thus the final result will be wrong and error detection circuit will flag an error. Otherwise, if no mismatch is found, the result is guaranteed to be correct.

6. EXPERIMENTAL RESULTS

In this section, we first present error rate reduction of CASA applying to both VLSA and ACA. Then we report the timing, area, and power results of our CASA design.

6.1 CASA Error Rate Evaluation

We evaluate the error rate reduction of using the proposed CASA method on VLSA and ACA, under two different group sizes with $K = 4$ and $K = 8$. Table 2 shows that CASA can significantly reduce the average error rate of VLSA from 16.7% to 3.5% when $K = 8$. For ACA, CASA

reduces the average error rate from 14.4% to 2.1%. When $K = 4$, the error rate reductions are also substantial.

Figure 7 shows the breakdown of the error rate reductions by CASA due to prediction and correlation. It is important to note that dynamic prediction alone does not provide sufficient error rate reductions without correlation-based speculation. For example, the error rate for fft only decreases from 12.7% to 11.9% if we employ a naive dynamic prediction scheme where carry-in prediction is always updated regardless of the result of $XOR(MSB)$. In contrast, the final error rate is down to 3.7% with CASA. For $patrica$, the error rate even increases from 16.1% to 17.8% after applying naive dynamic prediction. With CASA, the error rate is as small as 2.0%. From our experiments, coordinated prediction and carry-in speculation leads to most significant error rate reduction.

6.2 Circuit Implementation

We have implemented CASA in behavioral *Verilog* and synthesized the circuit using Synopsys Design Compiler with a Synopsys 90nm technology library. Table 3 compares the timing, area, and power results of parallel prefix adder, ACA, and CASA. Comparing to the original ACA, CASA can lead to significant error rate reduction with only marginal hardware overhead.[2] We also compare CASA with a fast parallel prefix adder provided by the Synopsys DesignWare library. According to Table 3, CASA is able to achieve 25.6% power savings without any compromises in speed.

Table 3: Implementation results for 32-bit ACA and CASA, K=8.

	prefix adder	ACA	CASA
delay (ns)	0.594	0.559	0.560
area (μm^2)	4238	3063	3300
power (mW)	1.29	0.93	0.96
CASA vs. ACA			
timing overhead			0.2%
area overhead			7.7%
power overhead			3.2%
CASA vs. prefix adder			
power savings			25.6%

7. CONCLUSIONS

In this paper, we conduct quantitative study of existing speculative adders with realistic benchmarks and propose a lightweight extension called CASA to significantly reduce the error rate. Our approach is based on the correlation between the MSB of input operands and the carry-in values for the group adders. To validate our observation, we provide detailed correlation analysis based on the input vectors extracted from real-life benchmarks. We further perform circuit implementation of CASA and detailed performance and power analysis to validate the feasibility of our method.

ACKNOWLEDGMENTS

This work was supported in part by NSF Award CCF-1337240 and a research gift from Xilinx, Inc.

---

[2]Note that we can potentially use a CASA adder with a smaller group size to meet the same accuracy requirement, leading to even higher speed and better energy efficiency than the baseline speculative adders.

Table 2: Error rate reduction after applying CASA.

	VLSA vs. CASA				ACA vs. CASA			
	K=4		K=8		K=4		K=8	
	VLSA	CASA	VLSA	CASA	ACA	CASA	ACA	CASA
blowfish	38.7%	23.4%	20.9%	1.3%	36.1%	5.1%	5.4%	0.1%
cjpeg	29.8%	14.5%	11.4%	3.6%	20.2%	6.4%	7.9%	2.5%
crc	30.1%	14.8%	12.0%	0.1%	20.2%	0.0%	18.2%	0.1%
dijkstra	24.3%	6.7%	6.3%	2.4%	9.6%	3.5%	3.6%	1.8%
fft	30.0%	7.2%	21.7%	2.5%	18.0%	5.2%	12.7%	3.7%
gsm	35.7%	27.2%	23.1%	18.5%	25.6%	17.4%	14.6%	9.0%
lame	39.0%	10.6%	17.6%	1.2%	37.8%	2.7%	26.2%	0.4%
patricia	33.9%	12.4%	22.8%	3.4%	22.4%	4.7%	16.1%	2.0%
qsort	34.7%	7.5%	22.0%	3.9%	19.1%	5.4%	12.7%	3.6%
rijndael	36.4%	13.7%	7.3%	0.9%	24.3%	3.4%	6.4%	0.2%
sha	45.3%	24.6%	14.1%	1.7%	27.0%	6.6%	6.9%	0.9%
susan	27.9%	13.0%	21.2%	2.4%	45.0%	8.3%	41.6%	0.6%
average	33.8%	14.6%	16.7%	3.5%	25.4%	5.7%	14.4%	2.1%

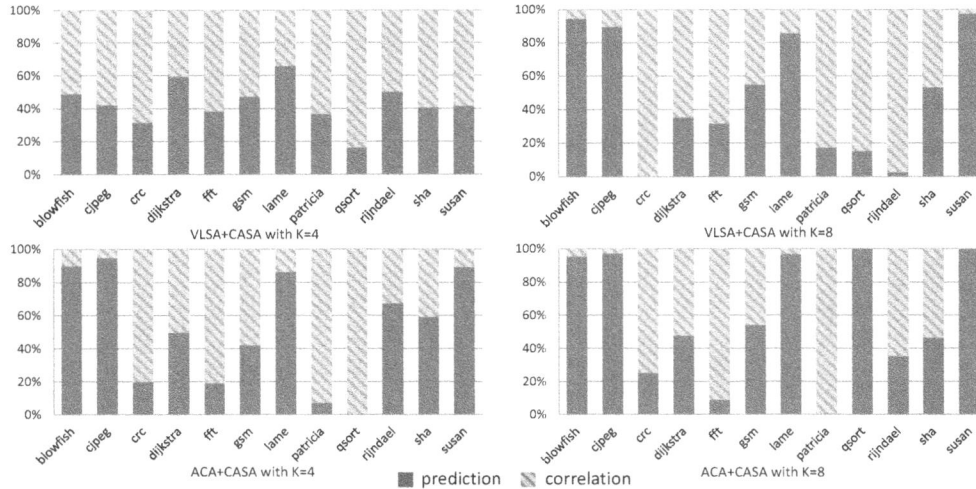

Figure 7: Breakdown of error rate improvements for CASA due to dynamic prediction and correlation-based speculation.

REFERENCES

[1] N. Binkert, B. Beckmann, G. Black, S. K. Reinhardt, A. Saidi, A. Basu, J. Hestness, D. R. Hower, T. Krishna, S. Sardashti, et al. The gem5 simulator. *ACM SIGARCH Computer Architecture News*, 39(2):1–7, 2011.

[2] K. Du, P. Varman, and K. Mohanram. High performance reliable variable latency carry select addition. In *Proceedings of the conference on Design, automation and test in Europe*, pages 1257–1262, 2012.

[3] P. Gupta, Y. Agarwal, L. Dolecek, N. Dutt, R. K. Gupta, R. Kumar, S. Mitra, A. Nicolau, T. S. Rosing, M. B. Srivastava, et al. Underdesigned and opportunistic computing in presence of hardware variability. *Computer-Aided Design of Integrated Circuits and Systems, IEEE Transactions on*, 32(1):8–23, 2013.

[4] V. Gupta, D. Mohapatra, A. Raghunathan, and K. Roy. Low-power digital signal processing using approximate adders. *Computer-Aided Design of Integrated Circuits and Systems, IEEE Transactions on*, 32(1):124–137, 2013.

[5] M. R. Guthaus, J. S. Ringenberg, D. Ernst, T. M. Austin, T. Mudge, and R. B. Brown. Mibench: A free, commercially representative embedded benchmark suite. In *Workload Characterization, 2001. WWC-4. 2001 IEEE International Workshop on*, pages 3–14, 2001.

[6] K. He, A. Gerstlauer, and M. Orshansky. Circuit-level timing-error acceptance for design of energy-efficient dct/idct-based systems. *Circuits and Systems for Video Technology, IEEE Transactions on*, 23(6):961–974, 2013.

[7] R. Hegde and N. R. Shanbhag. Energy-efficient signal processing via algorithmic noise-tolerance. In *Proceedings of the 1999 international symposium on Low power electronics and design*, pages 30–35, 1999.

[8] R. Hegde and N. R. Shanbhag. Soft digital signal processing. *Very Large Scale Integration (VLSI) Systems, IEEE Transactions on*, 9(6):813–823, 2001.

[9] J. Huang, J. Lach, and G. Robins. A methodology for energy-quality tradeoff using imprecise hardware. In *Proceedings of the 49th Annual Design Automation Conference*, pages 504–509, 2012.

[10] A. B. Kahng and S. Kang. Accuracy-configurable adder for approximate arithmetic designs. In *Proceedings of the 49th Annual Design Automation Conference*, pages 820–825, 2012.

[11] S.-L. Lu. Speeding up processing with approximation circuits. *Computer*, 37(3):67–73, 2004.

[12] J. Miao, K. He, A. Gerstlauer, and M. Orshansky. Modeling and synthesis of quality-energy optimal approximate adders. In *Proceedings of the International Conference on Computer-Aided Design*, pages 728–735, 2012.

[13] A. K. Verma, P. Brisk, and P. Ienne. Variable latency speculative addition: a new paradigm for arithmetic circuit design. In *Proceedings of the conference on Design, automation and test in Europe*, pages 1250–1255, 2008.

[14] R. Ye, T. Wang, F. Yuan, R. Kumar, and Q. Xu. On reconfiguration-oriented approximate adder design and its application. In *Proceedings of International Conference on Computer-Aided Design*, 2013.

[15] N. Zhu, W. L. Goh, G. Wang, and K. S. Yeo. Enhanced low-power high-speed adder for error-tolerant application. In *Proceedings of the 7th International SoC Design Conference*, pages 323–327, 2010.

[16] N. Zhu, W. L. Goh, and K. S. Yeo. An enhanced low-power high-speed adder for error-tolerant application. In *Proceedings of the 12th International Symposium on Integrated Circuits*, pages 69–72, 2009.

[17] N. Zhu, W. L. Goh, W. Zhang, K. S. Yeo, and Z. H. Kong. Design of low-power high-speed truncation-error-tolerant adder and its application in digital signal processing. *Very Large Scale Integration (VLSI) Systems, IEEE Transactions on*, 18(8):1225–1229, 2010.

Synergistic Circuit and System Design for Energy-Efficient and Robust Domain Wall Caches

Seyedhamidreza Motaman, Anirudh Iyengar and Swaroop Ghosh
Computer Science and Engineering, University of South Florida.
motaman@mail.usf.edu, anirudh@mail.usf.edu, sghosh@cse.usf.edu

ABSTRACT

Non-volatile memories are gaining significant attention for embedded cache application due to their low standby power and excellent retention. Domain wall memory (DWM) is one possible candidate due to its ability to store multiple bits per cell in order to break the density barrier. Additionally, it provides low standby power, fast access time, good endurance and retention. However, it suffers from poor write latency, shift latency, shift power and write power. DWM is sequential in nature and latency of read/write operations depends on the offset of the bit from the read/write head. This paper investigates the circuit design challenges such as bitcell layout, head positioning, utilization factor of the nanowire, shift power, shift latency and provides solutions to deal with these issues. A synergistic system is proposed by combining circuit techniques such as merged read/write heads (for compact layout), flipped-bitcell and shift gating (for shift power optimization), wordline (WL) strapping (for access latency), shift circuit design with micro-architectural techniques such as segmented cache to realize energy-efficient and robust DWM cache. Simulations show 3-33% better performance and 1.25X-14.4X better power over a wide range of PARSEC benchmarks.

Categories and Subject Descriptors

B.3.2 [Memory Structures]: Design Styles --- *Cache memories*

General Terms

Algorithms, Design, Performance, Theory

Keywords

Design Domain wall memory, shift power, cache segregation, synergistic systems

1. INTRODUCTION

Modern processors dominated by multi-core and graphics engines demand greater memory bandwidth that can only be sustained by larger on-die cache. The large cache requires a dense and an energy-efficient memory technology to substitute the current embedded memory solutions like SRAMs and embedded DRAMs (eDRAM) [1]. Emerging high density embedded memories such as Spin-Torque Transfer RAM (STTRAM) [2] are 4-10X denser than the standard SRAM. However, future processors would need 50-100X denser memories with extremely low standby power. Resistive RAM (RRAM) [3] is a promising candidate due to its

ISLPED'14, August 11–13, 2014, La Jolla, CA, USA.
Copyright 2014 ACM 978-1-4503-2975-0/14/08...$15.00.
http://dx.doi.org/10.1145/2627369.2627643

better MLC capability but it suffers from long write-cycle time and limited write endurance. Domain wall memory (DWM) is a strong alternative for a low-power and high density on-chip memory. The fundamental advantage of DWM is its ability to store multiple bits per cell in order to break the density barrier [4, 5, 6]. Due to its non-volatility, it offers low standby power, fast access time, good endurance and retention [3]. Due to these properties, DWM has a great potential to be used as an on-chip random access cache. DWM based array has been proposed for cache application in [7, 8] and a 256 bit in-plane DWM array has been experimentally demonstrated by IBM [5].

Circuit level challenges in DWM such as joule heating, process variations, shift logic design have been addressed in [9, 10], however the layout details have not been presented. A cross-layer design technique using DWM is described in [11]. Although the micro-architectural implementation has been presented, the detailed circuit issues have not been discussed. In [7], a multiple port DWM optimized for read operations considering the asymmetry in the read/write characteristics has been proposed. It also provides a new cache organization and head management policies that mitigate the performance penalty arising from serial access of bits. An all-spin cache design that utilizes DWM at all level of cache hierarchy is described in [8]. A shift-based write and separate WLs for read/write access is employed at the circuit level. Pre-shifting is used at the architectural level to hide the latency of shift operations. Although the layout is described in detail, the impact of shift-based write and multiple WLs in density, and design challenges due to multiple heads have not been addressed.

We investigate circuit design challenges in DWM and provide solutions to address them. We extract circuit level knobs (e.g., shift current dependency on shift latency) to enable micro-architectural optimization for a synergistic design paradigm. In particular, we make following contributions in this paper:

- We study circuit design challenges such as compact bitcell layout, subarray metal planning, head positioning, multiple heads selection, utilization factor (UF) of the nanowire (NW), shift power and shift latency. We also propose solutions such as NW grouping, shift gating, wordline strapping and low-overhead decoding to address the above issues.

- We provide a merged read-write head design which creates space to accommodate multiple heads for faster read/write access and improved UF.

- We propose a methodology to estimate and optimize the UF of the NW while maintaining fast access latency.

- We exploit the inter-dependency of shift current and shift latency for cache segregation. The faster ways implement higher shift current to improve latency whereas slower ways implement lower shift current to save power. This creates synergy between circuit and micro-architecture.

- A novel cache replacement policy is proposed which stores most recently used block in fast ways and least recently used (LRU) in slow ways.

The rest of the paper is organized as follows. In Section 2, we describe the basics of DWM. The bit-cell design including merged read/write head, access transistor sizing and a methodology to estimate the UF are discussed in Section 3. The bitcell layout and circuit level details are covered in Section 4. The energy-efficient subarray and the proposed segmented cache design and organization is introduced in Section 5. The power and energy results are also described in this section. Conclusions are drawn in Section 6.

2. BASICS OF DWM

As described before the DWM provides better density compared to contemporary memory technologies such as STTRAM, RRAM etc. This is due to storage of multiple bits per bitcell that share the read/write access transistors. Magnetic NW is the crucial component that holds the bits. In essence, the NW is analogous to a shift register. DWM is serial in nature and the desired bit needs to be brought under the read/write Magnetic Tunnel Junctions (MTJ) (Fig. 1). Therefore shifting is an added overhead on the read/write latency. Multiple read/write heads (i.e., MTJ and access transistor) can be used to reduce the shift overhead at the cost of lower memory bit density. Few points that can be observed in this context are: (a) read and write operation is linked with shifting of bits; (b) buffering of bits is required to ensure that the useful bits are preserved in the NW. Therefore, only a fraction of bits from the NW can be used for computation defined as 'utilization factor' (UF). The overhead bits are shown in Fig. 1; (c) the shift latency depend on the offset from read/write heads. Therefore multiple heads are desirable to reduce the access latency; and, (d) bitcell footprint depends on both the NW dimensions as well as on the number and size of read/write heads.

3. BITCELL DESIGN

In the previous section, we presented the basics of DWM as well as factors limiting the bitcell footprint and memory density. In this section we propose merged read and write heads for improving density and latency. We also describe the sizing methodology for the heads and utilization factor.

3.1 Merged Read-Write Head Design

Merged read-write head uses the same MTJ and access transistor for memory operations. The access transistor is sized to meet the write current requirement while ensuring lower read disturb. Fig. 2 illustrates a single NW with the proposed merged heads (two heads are shown in this example) and corresponding read-write circuitry. The bitlines (BL and BLB) are shared over all heads across the local columns, thus reducing the routing density per cell. However appropriate changes in column circuitry are necessary to differentiate between read and write operation. Separate column selects are generated for read and write ('ysel_r' and 'ysel_w') signals to connect the bitlines to sense-amp or write driver. Following paragraphs summarize the read and write operations with the proposed design:

Read: The BLB is switched to ground and the BL is connected to the read circuitry (comprising of a two-stage sensing circuitry).

Write: The BL and BLB are connected to the two ends of the write driver. In the case where a '0' needs to be written the current from the write driver is made to flow from top to bottom and vice versa in the case of writing a '1'.

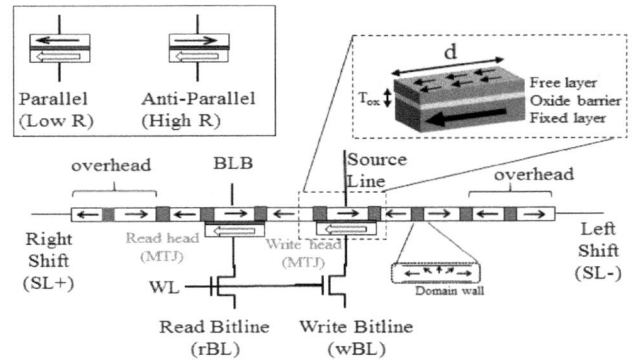

Fig. 1 Schematic of a conventional Domain Wall Memory. The read/write MTJ and overhead bits are shown.

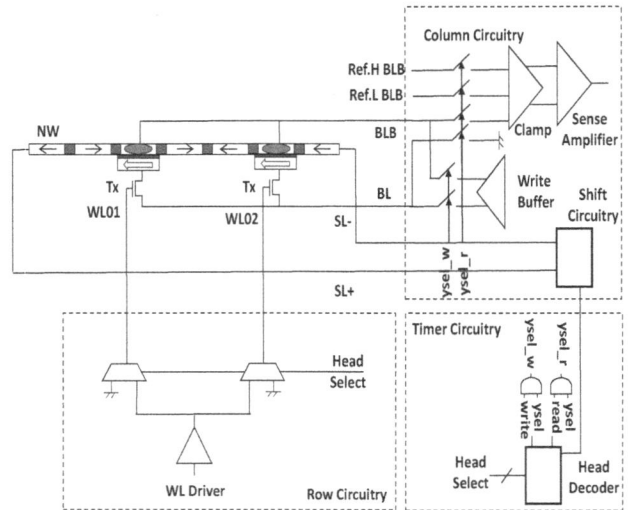

Fig 2. Proposed merged head design. The shared read/write circuit, head selection and shift select is also shown.

Head and shift selection: The selection of the head is performed dynamically using a head decoder in the timer. The decoder accepts last few bits of the address and determines the segment of the NW that needs to be accessed. The corresponding merged head closest to the accessed bit is selected. Note that the WL driver is shared between heads since only one head is active at a time. The inactive heads are driven to ground to prevent activation of multiple heads and avoid contention on the bitlines. Furthermore head select signals can be shared among all WL drivers in the subarray because the selected heads in unselected WL will be driven to ground by the corresponding WL driver. The sharing of head select reduce interconnect overhead in tight pitch WL driver. Since the position of the bits in the NW is known ahead of time, the head decoding is also used to provide

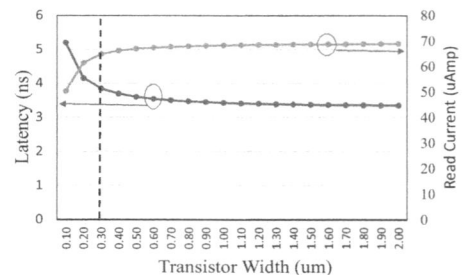

Fig.3 Read current vs write latency and access transistor size.

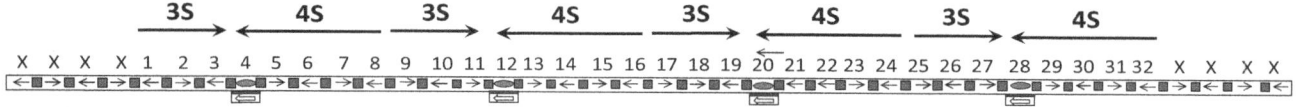

Fig. 4 NW used in our simulation with 4 heads placed at bit number 3, 7, 11, 15 of the usable bits. Buffer bits are shown by 'X'.

information about number of shifts required to access the desired bit. Head and shift circuit delay overhead could be hidden by parallelly performing WL pre-decoding.

3.2 Access Transistor Sizing

For finding the appropriate R/W head size which optimizes area and latency we have considered both read disturb and write latency. Read disturb can be controlled by reducing the read current. Write latency can be addressed either by increasing write current or increasing access transistor size. However, increasing access transistor size may result in more read current resulting in read-disturb. Access transistor size has a weak dependency on the read current flowing in the data leg. Fig. 3 demonstrates the relation between access transistor sizes, write latencies and read currents. Due to area overhead of access transistor we pick the size (0.31um in this case) that satisfies good write latency (3.9ns) and reasonable read current. The read latency is determined by finding the time needed to develop 100mV sense margin for store-0 and store-1.

3.3 Positioning of Merged Head and UF

As described before, a certain number of bits per NW are dedicated for buffering the functional bits during shift. The number of heads and their positioning in the NW determine the amount of buffer space required for preserving the functional bits. For better bitcell density it is desirable to achieve higher UF which in turn depends on the number of heads, their positioning and the physical dimension of the NW. The positioning of the heads also determines the shift latency. Fig. 4 shows the NW used in our design with appropriate number of heads to maximize UF

(32 useful bits out of 40 bits) and minimize latency (worst case is 4 shifts). It comprises of 32 usable bits and 8 buffer bits. The physical dimension of the NW and number of bits/NW are determined during bitcell layout optimization process described in Section 4.

4. BITCELL LAYOUT

In the previous sections we described the NW and head design (e.g., merged head, number/position of heads in the NW, UF, access transistor sizing). In this section, we propose the DWM bitell layout considering the access transistor size, metal pitch, number/position of heads, shift power/latency etc.

4.1 Sharing Diffusion, Bitlines and Shift Lines

The proposed DWM is nT-1NW structure where n is the number of heads. The access transistor size found in Section 3 corresponds to 7F in Intel 22nm technology [13] whereas the width of the NW is F (the pitch is 2F). This brings the need of sharing the diffusion width to accommodate 4 NWs. There are several advantages of sharing multiple NW that belong to the same column: (a) the bitlines (BL and BLB) can be shared in 8F pitch. Therefore the bitline widths can be increased (3.5F) and, (b) the shift lines (SL+ and SL-) can be shared with larger widths (3.5F), to reduce resistance. Plus, (c) the grouping of NWs provides a knob to segregate shift operation in the column for reducing shift power (discussed in Section 5).

By sharing 4 access transistors (for 4 NWs), the width of one NW group is 11F (10F for the diffusion and 1F for NW-NW spacing). The number of bits in the NW when its length is matched with the group width is 9. This is with the assumption that the width of

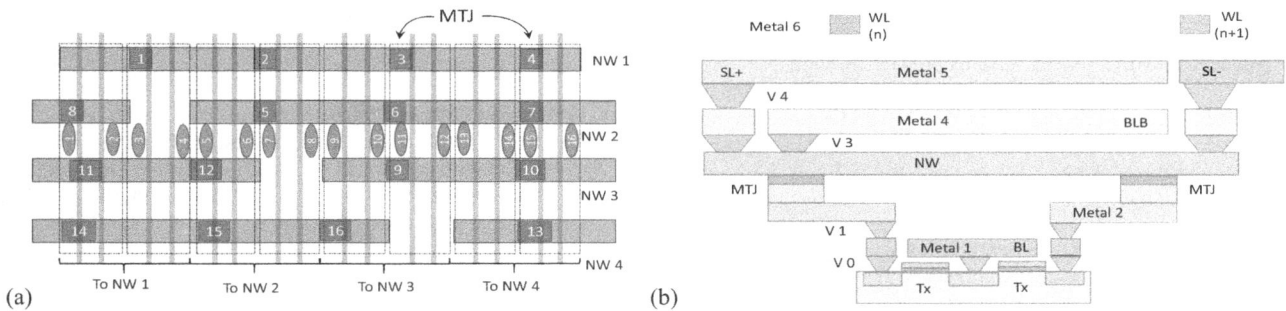

Fig. 5 (a) Bitcell layout (4-bit, $2.56F^2$/bit). MTJs and diffusion contacts are numbered, (b) Cross section of the bitcell.

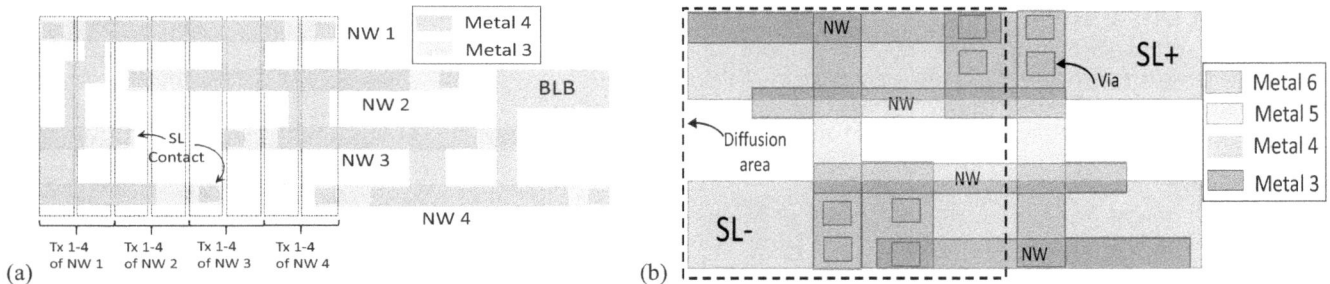

Fig. 6 (a) Metal plan of BLB. The SL stubs are also shown, (b) metal plan of shift lines.

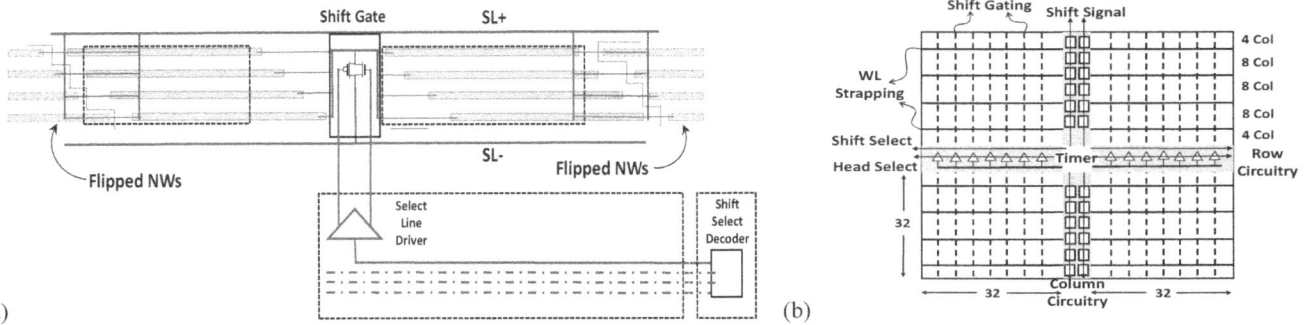

Fig. 7 (a) Shift gating circuitry and, (b) proposed subarray with shift select, gating select and head selects. WL strap is also shown.

each domain is 1F and the space allocated for landing the shift line contact on the NW is 1F. Since one head per NW is associated with longer shift latency it is prudent to increase the number of heads which in turn increases the NW group width and NW length. In this work we have used 4 heads per NW to optimize the shift latency, number of bits/NW, UF and architectural simplicity. The NW group width with this choice of heads is 41F. Therefore a NW of length 40F that is capable of holding 40 bits (where number of useful bits=32) is used. The effective bitcell footprint for this bitcell layout is $2.56F^2$ per bit and the UF is 0.8. It is important to mention that the NWs in the NW group cannot be aligned w.r.t each other because it aligns the M4 stubs in the SL+/SL- at the end of NWs and would block the routing of BLB (Fig. 6(b)). To create space for local routing of BLB, the NWs are staggered (Fig. 6(a)).

Fig. 5(a) shows the proposed DWM layout. The access transistors (Txs) share the bitline (BL), and the other two ends of Txs are connected to the MTJs. There are a total of 16 MTJs on the 4 NWs that connects to the respective diffusion contacts as illustrated by numbers in Fig. 5(a). Each NW is controlled by single WL that is muxed and shared among 4 Txs (Fig. 2). Fig. 5 (b) provides the cross-sectional view of the DWM layout where Tx is connected to the MTJ that is built in the via space between M2 and M3. The NW rests on top of the MTJs in M3 layer. Note that M3 layer is completely occupied by NW in the bitcell area. BL is connected to the source terminal of Tx through M1 and BLB (directly above MTJ and NW) is routed in M4. The left and right shift lines (SL+ and SL-) are routed in M6 and connect to the ends of the NW through M5 and V4. M5 serves two purposes namely, shorting the SL+ and SL- for the NWs in the NW group and routing the VDD/VSS tracks. The WLs are run orthogonally in M7 for periodic connection to the poly WL for better slew rate. The details of WL strap (Fig. 7(b)) cell are omitted for brevity. The sizing of the bitcell is based on the Tx size, NW size and the pitch of BL, BLB, SL+/SL-1 and WL. Therefore, it is necessary to take metal pitch of each layer into account [13].

4.2 DWM Integration

In the following paragraphs we list the requirements from the process integration standpoint for successful integration of DWM in the logic process for embedded cache application:

- WL: The WL is routed in poly in the orthogonal direction. M7 also runs orthogonally and carries WL signal. M7 is connected to poly in strap area.
- BL: This is shared between two Txs and routed in M1 in horizontal direction.
- Connection to the MTJ: The other ends of Txs are connected to the MTJs that are located at appropriate places in the NW. M2 is used for local connection to the MTJ and runs horizontally.

- MTJ: The MTJ lies in the via space between M2 and M3.
- NW: The NW is built in M3 region and also runs horizontally.
- BLB: The NW above the MTJ is connected to the BLB through V3. BLB uses M4 and runs horizontally. The routing of M4 for BLB connection to all NWs in the group is shown in Fig. 6(a).
- SL+/SL-: Fig. 6(b) shows the routing of SL+ & SL- in M6 that runs horizontally. The SLs connect to the ends of the NW. The jogging of SLs to connect every NW is done in M5.

From above discussion it is obvious that M1, M2, M3, M4 and M6 must be routed horizontally whereas poly and M7 should be routed orthogonally and should have same pitch to enable strapping. This contradicts the logic design rules where subsequent metals are routed orthogonally. Furthermore, M1 to M7 is fully occupied in the bitcell area and cannot be used for routing other signals. Global data (in and out) should be routed in higher metal layers (M8). The pre-decoded signals and control signals can run in row and column area where the design rules are relaxed.

5. CACHE DESIGN AND SEGMENTATION

In the previous section we explained the bitcell layout and process requirements. This section is focused on subarray details and cache segregation for synergistic circuit and micro-architecture design where the relationship between shift current and DW velocity is exploited.

5.1 Sub-Array Design

Fig. 7(b) shows the proposed sub-array design. There are a total of 64 WLs (32 in each sector), 512 local columns that are muxed to provide 64 bits of data. The column area holds read/write and shift circuitries. Timer contains a decoder to provide the number and direction of shift. WL decoder consists of WL driver and head selection muxes. The select signals are provided by decoder in the timer. It can be noted that shift operation consumes more power as the NWs of entire column share the SL+/SL-. In order to mitigate the shift power we group 8 NWs (i.e., two NW groups) and add a

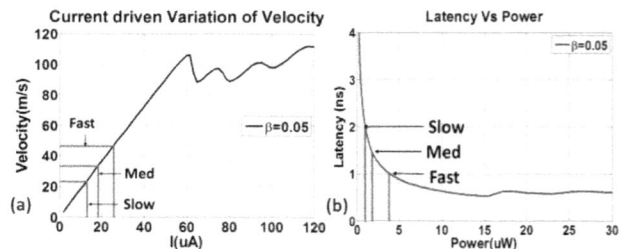

Fig. 8 (a) DW velocity vs input current using 1D model. (b) Shift latency vs power. Power for fast, med and slow shift are

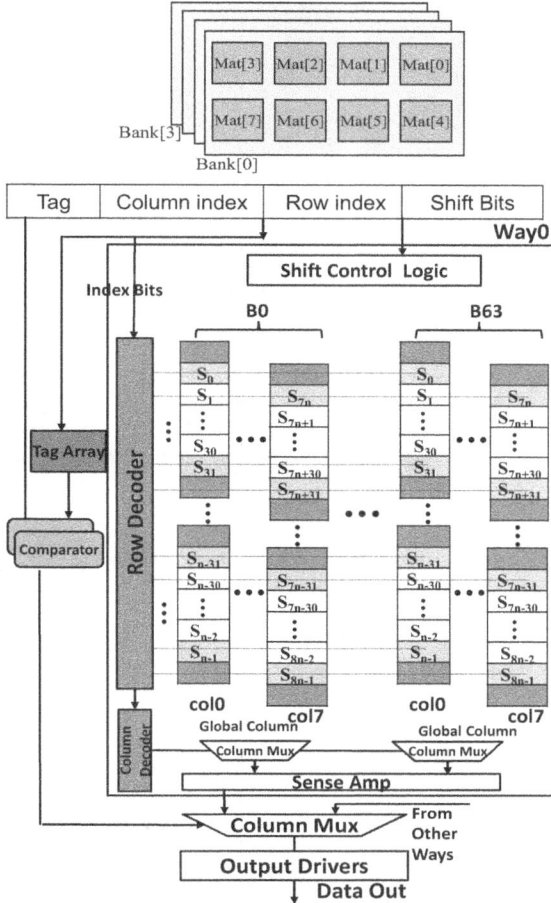

Fig. 9 Cache and sub-array organization.

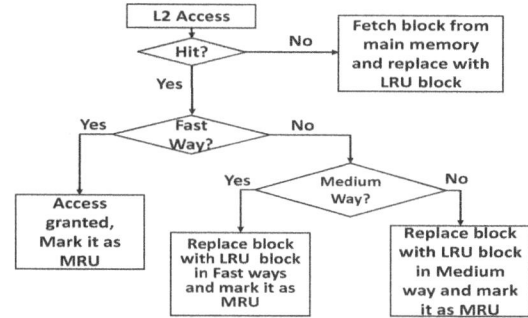

Fig. 10 Proposed cache replacement policy.

transmission gate in between that is controlled by shift gating signal. The shift gate is accommodated in Silicon by flipping the NW group so that SL+ and SL- can be shared between NW groups eliminating NW-NW spacing. The shift gate is full CMOS and will require a nwell. Therefore two extra poly space is incorporated to insert the gating mux. The gating signal is generated in WL decoder by using the pre-decoded addresses to determine the selected NW groups. The details are described in Fig. 7(a). A 4X shift power reduction is gained by the proposed gating. The DW motion depends on shift current. Higher current increases the DW velocity but also increases the power consumed. Fig. 8(a) shows the DW velocity vs shift current by using the 1D NW model described in [12, 14]. The corresponding DW shift latency with shift power is plotted in Fig. 8(b). We leverage this property to segregating our cache for a trade-off between the shift power and latency. The fast, medium and slow caches are shifted with high, medium and low currents respectively. In the proposed design we take the shift latency for the fast, medium and slow cache to be 1ns, 1.5ns & 2ns respectively. The shift circuit of the fast, medium and slow cache is sized accordingly to enable variable shift latency.

5.2 Cache Organization

The L2 cache is divided into following sections (Fig. 9): (a) Sub-array, (b) Mat that consists of a group of sub-arrays which share a common pre-decoder. Each mat contains multiple ways. A group of mats provides output cache-line (e.g., 8 mats provide 64 bits each totaling 512 bits) and, (c) Bank that operates independently. Each way in L2 is implemented in a different subarray in mat for parallelism. The column mux selects the desired BL and senseamp

senses bit-cell states in either data or tag array. For n-way set-associative cache we use n-comparators to compare the tag bits in Tag Array against input address to detect the set containing the desired data. Next the tag hit signal is routed to the respective mat and the desired cache-line is routed to the I/O ports. Logical to physical mapping of a mat inside a bank is shown in Fig. 11.

The L1 cache comprises of traditional SRAMs, whereas the segmented L2 cache contains the DWM. Fig. 10 shows different steps in proposed cache replacement policy. If an access to L2 cache is considered as a hit, we check whether this access is to fast way or not. If so, the access is granted and the way is marked as most recently used (MRU). For the medium way access the block is moved to fast way and marked as MRU after granting the access. LRU block from the fast way is replaced. The block replacement policy in fast way can be explained as follows: During cache access both the tag and data array is accessed simultaneously. The data is temporarily buffered in each mat. In case of hit the content of buffer is routed to I/O ports (Fig. 12). The latency from edge of mat to the CPU is longest and the block can be replaced during this interval by embedding swap-enable (SWE) in each way. A hit signal to a slow and medium way will trigger the SWE. For example, if the desired data is present in way5 and way0 is LRU way in fast ways, the accessed set from way0 is copied to way5 and the corresponding set of way5 (from buffer) will be placed into way0 (Fig. 12). Hence, the latency due to block swapping could be hidden.

5.3 Simulation Setup and Result

We evaluate and compare 32MB L2 cache for four different cases namely, SRAM, STTRAM, base DWM (with one head and medium shift latency), and RPL-DWM (Proposed DWM with novel replacement policy). We performed our evaluation on a 4-core Alpha processor in Gem5 [16] (Table 1). Gem5 is modified accordingly to implement cache segmentation and replacement policy. The simulations are performed over a wide range of Parsec Benchmarks [17]. The cache latency and energy is achieved using CACTI [15] and Hspice model of DWM (Table 2). Base DWM has same parameters as RPL-DWM except 1 head, $4F^2$ footprint and medium shift latency.

Fig. 13 demonstrates the performance result represented by the normalized instruction per cycle (IPC). It can be observed that RPL-DWM architecture shows ~33% improvement over Base-DWM. This is due to significant reduction of number of shift operations. We also achieve ~3% (~12%) improvement over SRAM (STTRAM). Even though DWM requires shift operations the small footprint of the bitcell and less routing latency helps in improving the performance. For power simulation we used McPAT [18] multi-core power simulator with modified CACTI which is integrated in Gem5 simulator. Fig. 14 shows that the total energy of the RPL-DWM is ~14.4X less than SRAM due to small leakage

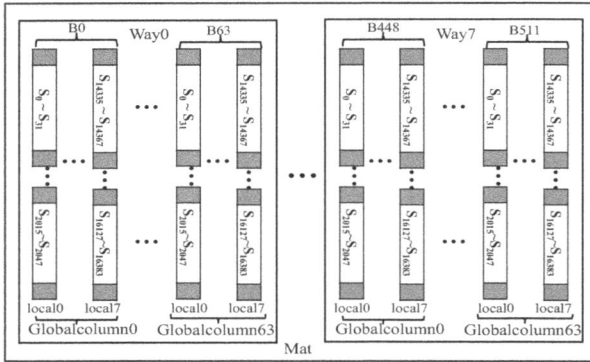

Fig. 11 Logical to physical mapping of a Mat.

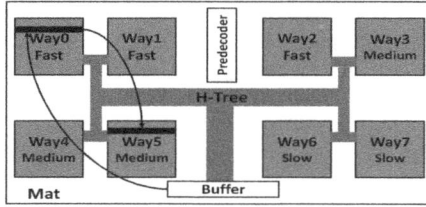

Fig. 12 Proposed cache replacement in a Mat.

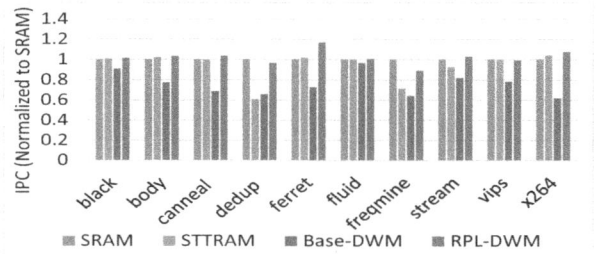

Fig. 13 Performance comparison across different memory technologies.

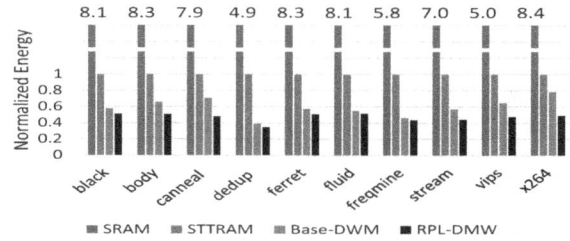

Fig. 14. Comparison of energy consumption of L2 cache across different memory technologies.

Table1: Processor Configuration

Processor	Alpha,O3,4 cores, 2GHz, 8-way issue
SRAM L1-Cache	Private, Icache=16KB, Dcache=16KB, 64B Cache-line, Write back, 2 cycle read/write latency.
LLC Cache	Shared, 32MB, 4 banks, 8 ways, 64B cache-line, writeback, R/W latency based on memory tech.
Main Memory	4GB, DDR3, 200-cycle latency.

power. Furthermore, it achieves 1.25X less energy compare to Base-DWM due to reduction in number of shift operations.

6. CONCLUSION

We presented a synergistic circuit and system design for DWM caches. Our design comprehends several important factors such as bitcell layout for maximizing effective footprint, process requirements to allow seamless integration of DWM, optimization of heads, utilization factor, shift-power and latency. We proposed cache segmentation by controlling the shift current and exploited it at the system level for power and performance optimization.

ACKNOWLEDGEMENT

This paper is based on work supported by Semiconductor Research Corporation (#2442.001).

REFERENCES

[1] PW Diodato, "Embedded DRAM: more than just a memory", IEEE Communications Magazine, 2000.

[2] M. Hosomi, et al. "A novel nonvolatile memory with spin torque transfer magnetization switching: Spin-RAM." IEDM, 2005.

[3] M. H. Kryder et al., "After hard drives what comes next," TMag, 2009.

[4] S. Ghosh, "Path to a TeraByte of on-chip memory for petabit per second bandwidth with< 5watts of power." In Proceedings of the 50th Annual Design Automation Conference, p. 145. ACM, 2013.

[5] A. J. Annunziata et al., "Racetrack memory cell array with integrated magnetic tunnel junction readout, IEDM 2011.

[6] S. Parkin, et al. "Magnetic domain-wall racetrack memory." Science, 2008.

[7] R. Venkatesan et al., "TapeCache: a high density, energy efficient cache based on domain wall memory," ISLPED, 2012.

[8] Venkatesan, et.al "DWM-TAPESTRI-an energy efficient all-spin cache using domain wall shift based writes." EDA Consortium, 2013.

[9] S. Ghosh, "Design methodologies for high density domain wall memory." NANOARCH, 2013.

[10] A. Iyengar, et.al. "Modeling and Analysis of Domain Wall Dynamics for Robust and Low-Power Embedded Memory." DAC, 2014.

[11] Z. Sun, et al. "Cross-layer racetrack memory design for ultra high density and low power consumption." ACM, 2013.

[12] M. Hayashi, "Current driven dynamics of magnetic domain walls in permalloy nanowires." PhD diss., Stanford University, 2006.

[13] www.chipworks.com, for information regarding the 22nm SoC.

[14] S. Fukami, et.al, "Micromagnetic analysis of current driven domain wall motion in nanostrips with perpendicular magnetic anisotropy." JAP, 2008.

[15] CACTI. http://www.hpl.hp.com/research/cacti/.

[16] Gem5, http://www.gem5.org.

[17] Parsec, http://parsec.cs.princeton.edu/index.htm.

[18] McPAT, http://www.hpl.hp.com/research/mcpat.

Table 2: Design parameters for different cache configurations (22nm technology).

Cache parameters	Cell Size	Total Area	Read Latency	Write Latency	Read Energy	Write Energy	Shift Power/Block (Fast/medium/Slow)	Shift Latency (Fast/medium/Slow)	Write Pulse	Leakage Power (W)
SRAM	146 F²	57.03 mm²	8.1 ns	5ns	1.1nJ	0.8nJ	-------	-------	------	36.7
STTRAM	40 F²	21.3 mm²	5.5ns	7.1ns	0.9nJ	1.4nJ	------	-------	3.9 ns	4.5
Base-DWM	4 F²	7.2 mm²	2.9ns	4.9ns	0.63nJ	0.74nJ	16mW/8mW/4mW	1ns/1.5ns/2ns	3.9 ns	2.4
RPL-DWM	2.5 F²	5.2 mm²	2.81ns	4.63ns	0.6nJ	0.7nJ	16mW/8mW/4mW	1ns/1.5ns/2ns	3.9 ns	2.31

Timing Errors in LDPC Decoding Computations with Overscaled Supply Voltage

Behnam Sedighi[*]
University of Notre Dame
Notre Dame, IN 46556, USA
bsedighi@nd.edu

N. Prasanth
Anthapadmanabhan
Bell Labs, Alcatel-Lucent
Murray Hill, NJ 07974,USA
prasanth.anthap@alcatel-
lucent.com

Dusan Suvakovic
Bell Labs, Alcatel-Lucent
Murray Hill, NJ 07974,USA
dusan.suvakovic@alcatel-
lucent.com

ABSTRACT

Decoders for Low Density Parity Check (LDPC) codes, used commonly in communication networks, possess inherent tolerance to random internal computation errors. Consequently, it is possible to apply voltage over-scaling (VOS) in their implementation to save energy. In this paper, the impact of VOS on timing errors is characterized for a typical min-sum LDPC decoder architecture using circuit simulations. Failure modes are analyzed for arithmetic circuits performing variable and check node computations. It is shown that a rather unconventional register placement in the variable node unit is beneficial for voltage scaling, and that the check node unit may be designed such that only the least significant bits are more likely to experience errors. Insights into timing error characteristics obtained through this analysis can be used to estimate the limits of voltage scaling and associated energy saving in practical LDPC decoder designs.

Categories and Subject Descriptors

B.8.1 [**Performance and Reliability**]: Reliability, Testing, and Fault-Tolerance; B.7.1 [**Integrated Circuits**]: Types and Design Styles—*advanced technologies, algorithms implemented in hardware*

Keywords

Voltage over-scaling; Error-resilience; Computation errors; Arithmetic and signal processing circuits; Noisy decoder

1. INTRODUCTION

Voltage scaling is an effective power-saving method [1, 2]. However, digital circuits are more prone to the fabrication process variations and variations in operating conditions [2]

---

[*]This work was completed when B. Sedighi was with CEET, University of Melbourne, Melbourne, VIC 3010, Australia.

ISLPED'14, August 11–13, 2014, La Jolla, CA, USA.
Copyright 2014 ACM 978-1-4503-2975-0/14/08 ...$15.00.
http://dx.doi.org/10.1145/2627369.2627638.

when operated at low voltages. The mainstream industry approach to this problem is to design for the worst-case condition and to use sufficiently large design margins to avoid logic faults. However, despite the reliability and ease of design, such over-designed circuits are not optimal from the power dissipation and throughput perspective. An alternate approach, when the application can tolerate some errors, is to employ error-resilient design [4, 5, 6, 7], where the circuit is designed with small margins and the supply voltage is scaled below the critical level thus allowing for some errors resulting from timing violations to occur. This method requires overhead circuitry for detection and correction of the errors, or for monitoring the circuit performance and adjusting the operating conditions appropriately. Error-resilient designs require a full analysis of the impact of the timing errors [1] which is the subject of this paper.

A low-density parity-check (LDPC) decoder (cf. Sec. 2) is a complex and power hungry circuit implementing an iterative algorithm. In [8], it is shown that LDPC decoders show error-tolerance by analyzing the error-correction performance of the decoder under a given rate of random errors. Previous works have proposed error-resilient designs of LDPC decoders using different error mitigation circuitry such as replication (e.g., triple modular redundancy) [13], algorithmic noise tolerance (e.g., using a reduced precision replica) [9, 10], RAZOR flip-flop [11], and convergence damping [14]. A theoretical analysis based on density evolution of an error-prone LDPC decoder along with an error mitigation mechanism is provided in [20]. However, the aforementioned studies focus mainly on the system design, and a thorough understanding of the characteristics of internal timing errors in LDPC decoder computations has so far been lacking. The error generation probability and error magnitudes need to be understood in a low-voltage decoder in order to efficiently design the error mitigation circuits.

This paper focuses on the timing errors in voltage-overscaled LDPC decoders. We show that both the smart placement of the pipelining registers (D-flip-flops) and proper gate-level implementation of a functional block play an important role in the error generation and resiliency in the decoder. Examples of data-dependent timing error with respect to voltage over-scaling (VOS) are presented for different parts of an LDPC decoder. The impact of the error-aware design and process variations on the total power saving are also discussed. Thus, the results in this paper complement the previous works allowing an improved error-resilient design that accounts for the internal error model.

The paper is organized as follows. A brief introduction to LDPC decoding is provided in Sec. 2. Our method of analysis is explained in Sec. 3. Sec. 4 describes a simple and intuitive error model which is useful in understanding the simulation results presented in Sec. 5. Finally, some guidelines and conclusions are provided in Sec. 6 and Sec. 7.

2. LDPC MIN-SUM DECODING

A common method for decoding LDPC codes is using the min-sum algorithm [16] due to it's reduced complexity. A small correction term is typically used with min-sum to obtain an improved decoder performance and the particular instance considered in this paper employs a scaling (or attenuation) factor denoted by S below. The decoder of an LDPC code of length N and dimension K consists of N variable node units (VNUs) and $N-K$ check node units (CNUs) which are interconnected in the form of a bipartite graph, exchanging messages in an iterative manner until the decoding converges. Each message represents a log-likelihood ratio (LLR), i.e., the logarithm of the ratio of the probabilities of a particular bit being 1 vs. being 0. The operations within a VNU of degree L and CNU of degree M are given by the following equations.

$$\text{VNU: } \beta_i = \alpha_{\text{channel}} + \sum_{j \in [L] \setminus i} \alpha_j, \quad \forall i \in [L], \quad (1)$$

$$\text{CNU: } \alpha_j = \prod_{i \in [M] \setminus j} \text{sign}(\beta_i) \cdot S \cdot \min_{i \in [M] \setminus j} |\beta_i|, \quad \forall j \in [M] \quad (2)$$

where α_j (resp. β_i) denotes the input messages to the VNU (resp. CNU), which corresponds to the output messages from the CNU (resp. VNU), α_{channel} is the LLR calculated based on the observed value over the channel, and the shorthand $[n] := \{1, \ldots, n\}$ is used for convenience.

3. METHOD

As a representative candidate for our study, we consider a VNU with degree 3 and a CNU with degree 6. The messages α_j and β_i are assumed to be in sign-magnitude (SM) format with a word-length of 4 bits. The hardware architecture of the VNU is shown in Fig. 1(a) [15]. The SM inputs are first converted to 2's complement (2sC) format and then added together. After calculating the sum, three subtractions are performed to find three 6-bit 2sC outputs OUT_i. Finally, the OUT_i are saturated to 4 bits and converted back to SM format. The saturation operation checks if the 6-bit number is higher than +7 or lower than -7, in which case it is saturated to either +7 or -7, respectively. The CNU shown in Fig. 1(b) has two parts: (i) magnitude calculation which mainly consists of finding the minimum among the input magnitudes; (ii) sign calculation which may be accomplished using XOR gates. The minimum computation in (2) essentially reduces to finding the first and second minimums (Min_1 and Min_2), and also a scaling factor of $S = 0.75$ is used here. It is quite clear, and simulations have confirmed as well, that the sign calculation has a significantly smaller propagation delay and essentially does not experience timing errors in the range of VOS considered here. At least one set of pipelining registers is needed in the VNU/CNU loop. For the moment, we assume one set of registers at the outputs of VNUs and another set at the outputs of CNUs. The impact of the location of the VNU registers (see Fig. 1(a)) is discussed later.

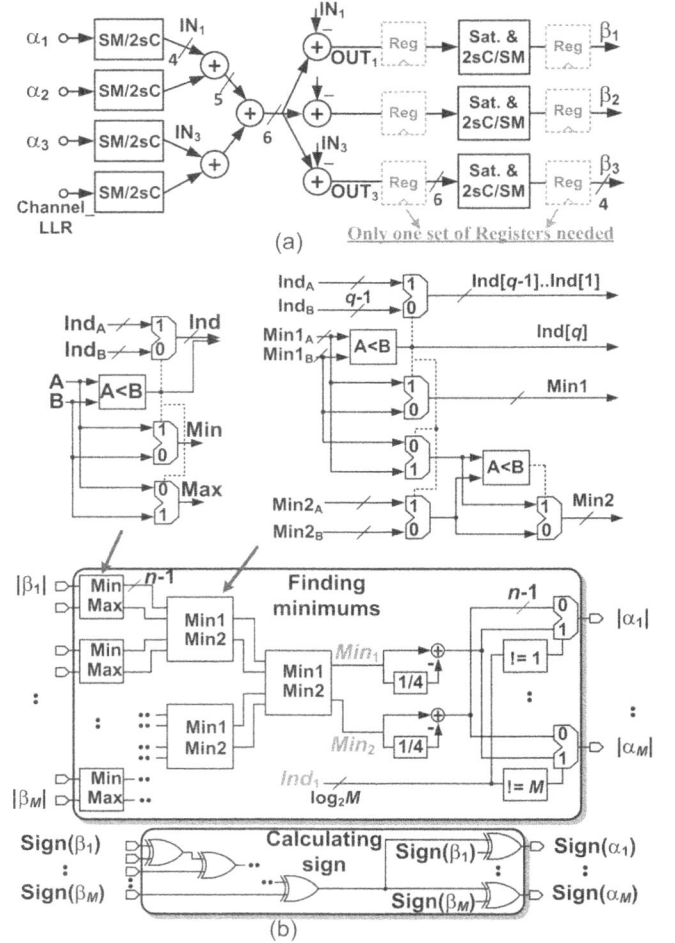

Figure 1: (a) Variable node unit. (b) Check node unit.

In order to study the effects of VOS, the VNU and CNU are each first implemented in Verilog and then synthesized in 90 nm CMOS using Design Compiler. The resulting gate-level netlist is transferred into SPICE netlist. The transistor-level simulation in presence of VOS is carried out in SPICE using BSIM3 model for MOSFETs. The simulation results are finally processed in MATLAB to analyze the errors.

The relationship of the propagation delay and dynamic power dissipation against supply voltage (V_{DD}) in the 90 nm technology used here is expressed as [17]

$$T_D = k_1 V_{DD}/(V_{DD} - V_{TH})^{1.6} \quad \text{and} \quad E = k_2 V_{DD}^2 \quad (3)$$

where k_1 and k_2 are constants that depend on the circuit. V_{TH} is the threshold voltage and is about 0.3 V in this technology. The exponent 1.6 was found by curve fitting on the simulation results. Fig. 2 shows the close match between equation (3) and the simulation results. Note that equation (3) is provided only to give insight, while the simulation results shown later make direct use of the transistor models.

4. SIMPLE ERROR MODEL

In order to provide some insight into the computation errors produced in the circuits, a simple and intuitive error

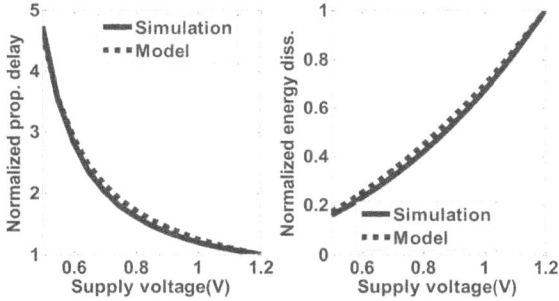

Figure 2: Delay and energy dissipation as a function of supply voltage in 90 nm CMOS (for a ring oscillator consisting of NAND gates).

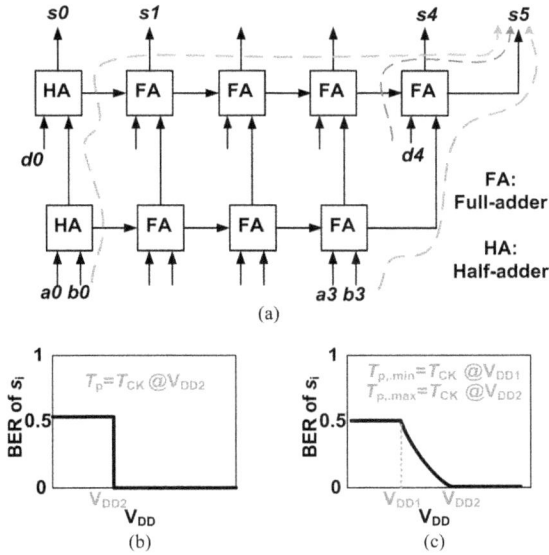

(a)

(b)

(c)

Figure 3: (a) Cascaded adders with dashed lines showing the propagation paths. (b) Simple error model. (c) Error model considering different propagation paths.

model is described here. Fig. 3(a) shows a circuit with cascaded additions where two 4-b numbers $A = a_3 \ldots a_0$ and $B = b_3 \ldots b_0$ are added and the result is then added to a 5-b number $D = d_4 \ldots d_0$. This is illustrative of the operations inside a VNU. Furthermore, similar observations would also apply to the CNU if the comparison operations involved in finding the minimum magnitude are performed using subtractions. It is worth pointing out that the objective here is not to provide an optimal circuit, but rather to analyze a simple and tractable circuit to later aid understanding of the simulation results presented in Sec. 5. Nevertheless, the simulations in Sec. 5 indeed use the optimal circuits synthesized by Design Compiler.

The inputs and outputs are registered with a given clock period T_{CK} which dictates the time available for the signal to propagate. For every output bit s_i in Fig. 3(a), there are several propagation paths from the inputs. The maximum

propagation delay T_{s_i} for each bit s_i is given by

$$T_{s_0} = 2T_A, \quad T_{s_1} = 3T_A, \quad \ldots \quad T_{s_5} = 7T_A, \quad (4)$$

where we assume the same delay T_A for both a half-adder (HA) cell and a full-adder (FA) cell for simplicity. If V_{DD} is large enough, then $T_{s_i} < T_{CK}$ for all output bits and there will be no errors. However, as V_{DD} is reduced, the circuit becomes slower and below a certain voltage denoted by V_{DD2}, we will have $T_{s_i} > T_{CK}$. To obtain a simple error model, shown in Fig. 3(b), we assume the bit-error rate (BER) is 50% below V_{DD2}.

The above simplification considers only the worst-case path; however, there are indeed several propagation paths from the inputs to every output bit. For example, in Fig. 3(a), a transition in s_5 may be caused by a change in a_0 or d_4, with the latter having a significantly lower delay. Consequently, not all the transitions of s_5 will result in a timing violation when $7T_A > T_{CK}$. Thus, the BER transition as V_{DD} is reduced may not be as sharp as shown in Fig. 3(b). In principle, one can compute the probability of an output change caused by a signal propagating along a certain path [1, 18, 19, 20]. For the purpose of our discussion, an approximation suffices and so we omit this detailed computation. For a given output bit, let $T_{p,\min}$ and $T_{p,\max}$ denote the minimum and maximum propagation delays along two different paths. For example, for the output bit s_5, we have $T_{p,\min} = T_A$ and $T_{p,\max} = 7T_A$. The error rate is taken as 50% if $T_{p,\min} > T_{CK}$, whereas the error rate is zero if $T_{p,\max} < T_{CK}$. The BER is then linearly interpolated for the delay values between $T_{p,\min}$ and $T_{p,\max}$. The delay is then related to the voltage supply using (3) to obtain an error model as shown in Fig. 3(c). This simple model is useful in interpreting the simulation results in the next section.

5. SIMULATION RESULTS

The circuits are simulated with uniformly random inputs in every clock period. The outputs are observed 1.8 ns after the inputs change, corresponding to a clock frequency of 500 MHz and 0.2 ns for the setup/hold times for DFFs. The output bits are compared to $V_{DD}/2$ to decide for logic 0 or 1. We study the bit-wise error probability as well as the probability mass function (pmf) on the error magnitude as this captures the dependence across bits. Due to the long duration taken by SPICE simulations, we capture errors with probability up to about 10^{-4}, with the justification that errors with even smaller probability will not be a dominant influence on decoder performance. In fact, high-level decoder simulations in [8, 11] show that internal error probabilities around 0.1% result in negligible SNR penalties provided that proper error mitigation schemes (e.g. protecting the sign of the messages) are employed.

5.1 VNU with registers before saturation

Due to the cascaded additions/subtractions involved in computing OUT_i in Fig. 1(a), we expect that the LSBs have a relatively lower delay and therefore less prone to errors. Indeed, Fig. 4(a) confirms that LSBs have a lower BER and also shows a fast roll-off. The error magnitude pmf at $V_{DD} = 0.6$ V is shown in 4(b). As only bits 3–5 experience any errors at this V_{DD}, the error magnitude is a multiple of 8.

Next, we compare and interpret the results using the simple error model in Sec. 4. Using SPICE simulation, the propagation delay of a FA cell T_A is found as 260 ps at

(a)

(b)

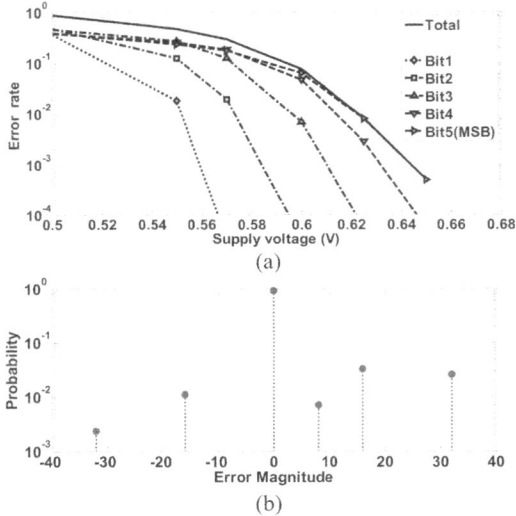

Figure 4: VNU with registers placed *before* saturation. (a) Probability of bit errors. (b) Probability mass function of error magnitude at V_{DD}=0.6 V.

Table 1: Maximum propagation delay in VNU for **OUT**$_i$ at $V_{DD} = 0.6$ V

Bit0	Bit1	Bit2	Bit3	Bit4	Bit5
$4T_A$	$5T_A$	$6T_A$	$7T_A$	$8T_A$	$9T_A$
1.04 ns	1.3 ns	1.56 ns	**1.82 ns**	**2.08 ns**	**2.34 ns**

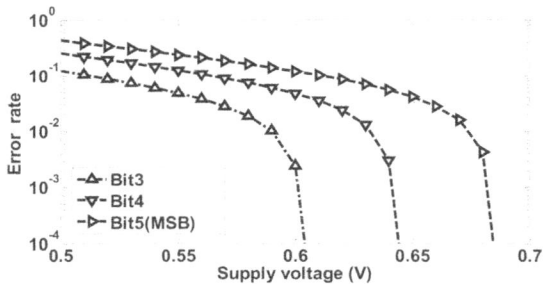

Figure 5: Error rate estimate using the simple model for the VNU with registers placed *before* saturation.

$V_{DD} = 0.6$ V in this technology. The maximum propagation delay for each bit of **OUT**$_i$ is calculated in Table 1. For bits 0–2, the worst-case delay is less than 1.8 ns, and hence no error is observed, which is in agreement with the SPICE simulation result in Fig. 4. At $V_{DD} = 0.7$ V, we find $T_A = 180$ ps. Therefore, even the delay for the MSB of $9T_A$ is only 1.62 ns. So, none of the output bits are expected to face errors at $V_{DD} = 0.7$ V, which is again consistent with Fig. 4. Fig. 5 illustrates the complete result of the simple error modeling for bits 3–5 and it captures the general behavior of the VNU before saturation.

5.2 VNU with registers after saturation

On the other hand, placing the registers after the saturation operation yields contrasting results. Interestingly,

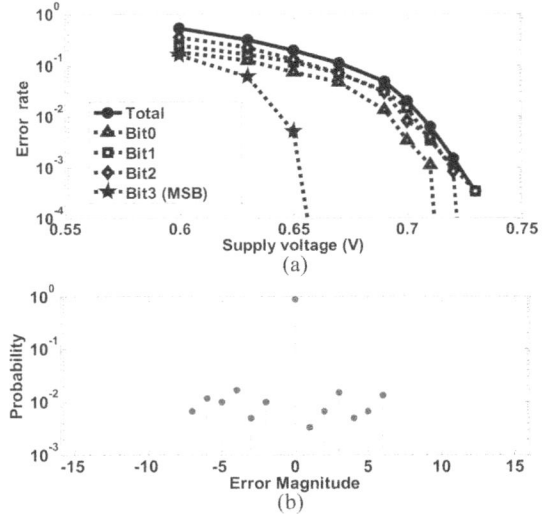

(a)

(b)

Figure 6: VNU with registers placed *after* saturation. (a) Probability of bit errors. (b) Probability mass function of error magnitude at V_{DD}=0.67 V.

Fig. 6(a) shows that the MSB of β_i has the lowest error rate whereas all the remaining bits have almost similar error rates. The pmf of the error magnitude in Fig. 6(b) reaffirms that the errors are almost equally likely in all the bits except for the MSB. The reason for this contrast is as follows. As observed earlier, the MSBs of the **OUT**$_i$ have larger delay. However, the saturation operation can be performed only when the MSBs of **OUT**$_i$ are determined. Once this is done, the saturation operation itself is relatively simple and has a small delay. Therefore, the overall delay from α_i to β_i in Fig. 1(a) is dominated by the delay to **OUT**$_i$. Moreover, the MSB (i.e. sign) of β_i is simply the MSB of **OUT**$_i$ resulting in no delay for the MSB in the saturation block.

5.3 CNU

Recall from Fig. 1(b) that the calculation of $\text{sign}(\alpha_i)$ involves XOR operations only and does not contribute to the timing errors. Considering the calculation of the magnitude $|\alpha_i|$, we again study whether the timing errors are more likely to occur in the MSBs or LSBs. The simulation results given in Fig. 7 show in fact that the LSBs have higher bit-error rate. This is explained as follows.

The main operations in the magnitude calculation are the comparisons (COMPs) which in turn dictates the error performance of the CNU. Each input experiences a propagation delay of $(1 + \lceil \log_2 M \rceil)$ COMPs. There are two possible ways of implementing a COMP operation: (i) using bit-wise comparisons proceeding from the MSB to LSB, (ii) using a subtraction. We use the first approach here for reasons that will be clear soon. Indeed, in this case, a COMP has the lowest delay if MSBs of its two input words are different. If the MSBs are the same, then MSB-1 bits determine the results, and so on. As a result, the most likely case for a timing violation occurs when only LSBs of the two inputs are different. Therefore, we expect the LSBs of the outputs to have the largest error rate. Furthermore, this also implies that the errors occur when the inputs have close values

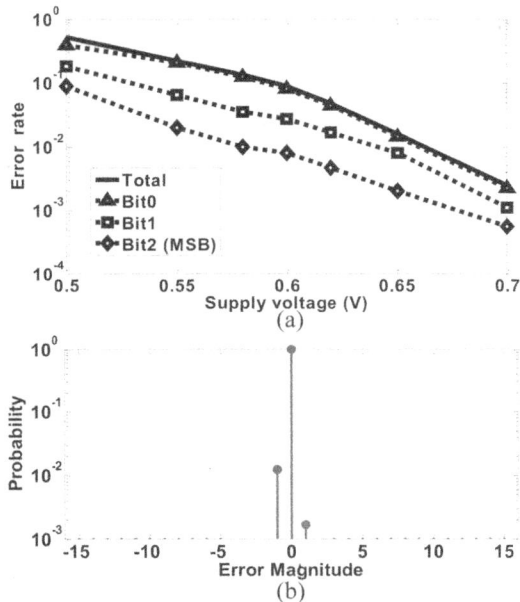

Figure 7: CNU. (a) Probability of bit errors. (b) Probability mass function of error at $V_{DD}=0.65\,\mathrm{V}$.

meaning that the error magnitudes are small as shown in Fig. 7(b). Compared to the VNU, observe also in Fig. 7(a) that the error rate increase is gradual as the supply voltage is reduced. This indicates the presence of several propagation paths with varying delays from the inputs to the output. On the contrary, with the second COMP implementation using a subtraction, the signal propagates from LSB to MSB and so, the MSBs are more likely to have errors. Hence, the first implementation using bit-wise comparisons is in fact better in the presence of timing errors.

6. DISCUSSION

Fig. 4 and Fig. 6 illustrate that in the VNU, the MSBs face a longer propagation until the point OUT$_i$ before saturation, but in fact the LSBs constrain the delay beyond this point. Thus, placing the registers after saturation (β_i) does not allow for the best possible voltage scaling. Indeed, comparing the error rates at supply voltage around 0.65 V, we see that an incorrect MSB at OUT$_i$ already ripples to corrupt all bits of β_i. Therefore, an efficient error-resilient design requires that the pipelining registers be placed before the saturation and 2sC-SM operations in the VNU. An undesired by-product of this is that the number of DFFs in the VNU increases. However, the benefits of better voltage scaling should outweigh the power consumed by the small number of additional registers in most application scenarios. Moreover, the number of interconnects between VNUs and CNUs can remain the same by physically placing the saturation and 2sC-SM conversion block within the VNUs. In the CNU, we know from Fig. 7 that LSBs constrain the delay. Thus, combining the LSB-constrained and relatively simple saturation/2sC-SM block in the VNU into the pipeline with the CNU still results in shorter paths for MSBs, with errors more likely in LSBs similar to Fig. 7.

With the above architecture, the MSB (sign bit) has the highest error rate in the VNUs. Since an error in the sign bit significantly deteriorates the performance of the LDPC decoder [8], additional error detection and correction circuitry are necessary preventing the error from propagating to the CNUs. On the other hand, in the CNUs, since errors are more likely in the LSBs and the error rate changes gradually with supply voltage, we may do away without a specific error mitigation mechanism.

A toolbox of such error mitigation mechanisms is already available from schemes previously proposed in the literature. Such techniques include simple replication (e.g., triple modular redundancy) [13], algorithmic noise tolerance (e.g., using a reduced precision replica) [9, 10], RAZOR flip-flop [11, 5], and convergence damping [14]. The error models provided in this paper are useful in customizing the error mitigation by highlighting the areas where such mitigation is necessary, and by comparing the performance of different schemes. Additionally, by incorporating these error models in BER vs. SNR simulations (together with the error-mitigation mechanism), it is possible to determine the computation error rates that can be tolerated, and thus the amount of tolerable VOS, for a given acceptable SNR penalty (e.g., 0.1–0.2 dB) in achieving a specified BER.

Let V_{DD} denote the supply voltage in the conventional error-free design and ΔV_{DD} denote the amount of supply voltage reduction, giving the new supply voltage of the system as $V'_{DD} = V_{DD} - \Delta V_{DD}$. For example, in the 90 nm CMOS technology that we consider, V_{DD} is determined from

$$\frac{0.9k_{1,\min}V_{DD}}{(0.9V_{DD} - V_{TH,\max})^{1.6}} = T_{\text{target}} \qquad (5)$$

where T_{target} is the desired delay. The coefficient 0.9 is introduced as the minimum supply voltage is often 10% lower that the typical value. $k_{1,\min}$ and $V_{TH,\max}$ are the worst case values and a function of process variations.

The total dynamic energy dissipation E for a decoding operation in the conventional design is given by

$$E = N_{\text{iter}}E_{\text{iter}} = N_{\text{iter}}\left(NE_{\text{VNU}} + (N-K)E_{\text{CNU}}\right),$$

where N_{iter} is the number of decoding iterations and $E_{\text{iter}} := N_{\text{iter}}(NE_{\text{VNU}} + (N-K)E_{\text{CNU}})$ is the energy dissipation per iteration in a decoder with N VNUs and $N-K$ CNUs. The new total dynamic energy dissipation E' with VOS is calculated as

$$E' = N'_{\text{iter}}\left(\left(V'_{DD}/V_{DD}\right)^2 E_{\text{iter}} + E_{\text{iter,oh}}\right),$$

where $E_{\text{iter,oh}}$ is the energy dissipation overhead (per iteration) of the error mitigation scheme and N'_{iter} is the new number of decoding iterations. Consequently, with $N'_{\text{iter}} = \rho_{\text{iter}}N_{\text{iter}}$ and $E_{\text{iter,oh}} = \rho_{\text{oh}}E_{\text{iter}}$, we obtain

$$E' = \rho_{\text{iter}}\left(\left(V'_{DD}/V_{DD}\right)^2 + \rho_{\text{oh}}\right)E. \qquad (6)$$

The exact value of the power saving depends on several factors including the LDPC code that is chosen, clock frequency, process technology, the error mitigation scheme and its overhead. The effectiveness of the new design depends on the supply voltage in the original error-free design V_{DD} and the amount of the supply voltage reduction ΔV_{DD}, which is the sum of two components $\Delta V_{DD,\text{pv}}$ and $\Delta V_{DD,\text{data}}$. $\Delta V_{DD,\text{pv}}$ comes from allowing some of the VNUs and CNUs to have a small error-rate in presence of transistor variations.

Addressing process variation through statistical analysis is well understood by designers and the only difference here is the more relaxed requirement on the probability of timing errors. $\Delta V_{DD,\text{data}}$ is obtained by permitting the input-data dependent errors. For complicated circuits, when the number of gates in the signal propagation paths is large, $\Delta V_{DD,\text{pv}}$ will be smaller since the local process variations will be averaged out. On the other hand, such circuits are likely to have a large number of signal propagation paths and hence a larger $\Delta V_{DD,\text{data}}$.

Assuming computation error rates of 10^{-3} are tolerable [8, 11], we estimate $V'_{DD} = 0.65$ V using Figs. 4 and 7. Using (6), this leads to an estimated power savings of 50.8%, i.e., about $2\times$ assuming $V_{DD} = 1.2$ V, the number of iterations increases by 25% (i.e., $\rho_{\text{iter}} = 1.25$) and the error mitigation overhead is 10% of E_{iter} (i.e., $\rho_{\text{oh}} = 0.1$). It should be added that using a different CMOS process other than 90 nm will change the exact relationship between delay and V_{DD}, but it will not change the observed trends and provided guidelines which are more general. Furthermore, since the analysis in this paper is by nature circuit-dependent, it is beyond the scope of the paper to address all possible LDPC decoding algorithms and decoder architectures. Nevertheless, the similarity in the decoder structure can be exploited to draw similar guidelines, and the analysis methodology developed here can also be similarly applied to other circuits.

7. CONCLUSIONS

The timing error behavior under voltage over-scaling of the main computation circuits, namely the variable node unit and the check node unit, of a min-sum LDPC decoder have been studied. The results complement the previous works, enabling an improved error-resilient design that accounts for the internal error model.

It has been shown that, in the VNU, a rather unconventional placement of the pipelining registers before the saturation operation and 2sC-SM conversion results in more efficient voltage scaling than their natural placement. However, such an architecture results in the the MSB (sign bit) having the highest error rate. Therefore, it is necessary to include an additional circuitry that detects/corrects the error preventing it from propagating further to the CNUs. In the CNUs, comparison (COMP) operations mainly dictate the error performance. With an appropriate implementation of the COMP operations, we show that timing errors are more likely in the LSBs and the error rate increases gradually as supply voltage is reduced. Hence, we may do away without a specific error mitigation mechanism in CNUs. As a future step, the computation error models studied here can be incorporated in a high-level decoder simulation to obtain a more accurate picture of the BER performance and convergence behavior under different error mitigation mechanisms.

8. REFERENCES

[1] Y. Liu, T. Zhang, and K. K. Parhi. Computation error analysis in digital signal processing systems with overscaled supply voltage. *IEEE Trans. Very Large Scale Integ. Syst.*, 18(4):517–526, Apr. 2010.

[2] M. E. Sinangil et al. Design of low-voltage digital building blocks and ADCs for energy-efficient systems. *IEEE Trans Circuits Syst.-II*, 59(9):533 537, Sep. 2012.

[3] Y.-H. Lee et al. A near-optimum dynamic voltage scaling in 65-nm energy-efficient power management with frequency-based control for SoC system. *IEEE J. Solid-State Cir.*, 47(11):2563–2575, Nov. 2012.

[4] G. Karakonstantis, N. Banerjee, and K. Roy. Process-variation resilient and voltage-scalable DCT architecture for robust low-power computing. *IEEE Trans. Very Large Scale Integ. Syst.*, 18(10):1461–1470, Oct. 2010.

[5] S. Das et al. A self-tuning DVS processor using delay-error detection and correction. *IEEE J. Solid-State Cir.*, 41(4):792–804, Apr. 2006.

[6] N. R. Shanbhag, R. A. Abdallah, R. Kumar, and D. L. Jones. Stochastic computation. *ACM/IEEE Design Automation Conf. (DAC)*, 859–864, Jun. 2010.

[7] R. A. Abdallah and N. R. Shanbhag. Minimum-energy operation via error resiliency. *IEEE Embedded Syst. Lett.*, 2(4):115–118, Dec. 2010.

[8] V. C. Gaudet. Low-power LDPC decoding by exploiting the fault-tolerance of the Sum-Product algorithm. *Contemporary Mathematics*, 523:165-172, 2010.

[9] J. Cho, N. R. Shanbhag, and W. Sung. Low-power implementation of a high-throughput LDPC decoder for IEEE 802.11n standard. *IEEE Workshop on Signal Processing Systems (SiPS)*, 40–45, Oct. 2009.

[10] E. P. Kim and N. R. Shanbhag. Energy-efficient LDPC decoders based on error-resiliency. *IEEE Workshop on Signal Processing Systems (SiPS)*, 149–154, Oct. 2012.

[11] M. Alles, T. Brack, and N. Wehn. A Reliability-Aware LDPC Code Decoding Algorithm. *IEEE Vehicular Technology Conference-Spring*, 1544–1548, Apr. 2007.

[12] A. M. A. Hussien et al. A class of low power error compensation iterative decoders. *IEEE GLOBECOM*, 1–6, Dec. 2011.

[13] M. May, M. Alles, and N. Wehn. A case study in reliability-aware design:a resilient LDPC code decoder. *Proc. Design Automation Test Europe*, 456–461, 2008.

[14] H. Cho, L. Leem, and S. Mitra. ERSA: Error Resilient System Architecture for Probabilistic Applications. *IEEE Trans. Comput.-Aided Design Integr. Circuits Syst.*, 31(4):546–558, Apr. 2012.

[15] A. J. Blanksby and C. J. Howland. A 690-mW 1-Gb/s 1024-b, rate-1/2 low-density parity-check code decoder. *IEEE J. Solid-State Circuits*, 37(3):404–412, Mar. 2002.

[16] J. Chen and M. Fossorier. Near optimum universal belief propagation based decoding of low-density parity check codes. *IEEE Trans. Commun.*, 50(3):406-414, Mar. 2002.

[17] L. Yan, J. Luo, and N. K. Jha. Joint dynamic voltage scaling and adaptive body biasing for heterogeneous distributed real-time embedded Systems. *IEEE Trans. Comput.-Aided Design Integr. Circuits Syst.*, 24(7):1030–1041, Jul. 2005.

[18] T. Rejimon, K. Lingasubramanian, and S. Bhanja. Probabilistic error modeling for nano-domain logic circuits. *IEEE Trans. Very Large Scale Integ. Syst.*, 17(1):55–65, Jan. 2009.

[19] J. Huang, J. Lach, and G. Robins. Analytic error modeling for imprecise arithmetic circuits. *Silicon Errors in Logic - System Effects (SELSE)*, 2011.

[20] C-H Huang, Y. Li, and L. Dolecek. Gallager B LDPC Decoder with Transient and Permanent Errors. *IEEE Trans. Commun.*, 62(1):15–28, Jan. 2014.

A Case for Leveraging 802.11p for Direct Phone-to-Phone Communications

Pilsoon Choi[1], Jason Gao[1], Nadesh Ramanathan[2], Mengda Mao[2], Shipeng Xu[2],
Chirn-Chye Boon[2], Suhaib A. Fahmy[2], Li-Shiuan Peh[1]
[1]Massachusetts Institute of Technology, USA
[2]Nanyang Technological University, Singapore
pilsoon@mit.edu

ABSTRACT

WiFi cannot effectively handle the demands of device-to-device communication between phones, due to insufficient range and poor reliability. We make the case for using IEEE 802.11p DSRC instead, which has been adopted for vehicle-to-vehicle communications, providing lower latency and longer range. We demonstrate a prototype motivated by a novel fabrication process that deposits both III-V and CMOS devices on the same die. In our system prototype, the designed RF front-end is interfaced with a baseband processor on an FPGA, connected to Android phones. It consumes 0.02uJ/bit across 100m assuming free space. Application-level power control dramatically reduces power consumption by 47-56%.

1. INTRODUCTION

Direct device-to-device (D2D) communication between smartphones has been available for years via WiFi's ad-hoc mode, but as operating system modifications are required to set this up, D2D has not been widespread until recently, with the adoption of the WiFi Direct standard. Video sharing, file sharing, as well as multiplayer games have started to leverage WiFi Direct. Clearly, there are peer-to-peer applications that benefit from the faster response times of D2D communications; these applications gather user input and sensor data from nearby phones, perform computations in-situ, and output results and user interface updates with higher responsiveness. However, existing D2D communication only works for short-range, low mobility scenarios. WiFi is challenged in long-range or high-mobility scenarios [1]. WiFi Direct facilitates easier setup of device-to-device networks, but one device must serve as an access point (the group owner) and all other devices must communicate through it, thus not supporting highly mobile networks with rapidly changing topologies. This largely limits WiFi Direct applications to close-range, static deployments between a few phones. LTE Direct can be regarded as a promising new D2D technology, but as it leverages LTE infrastructure, it requires modifications to the LTE base stations which may hinder adoption.

Vehicle-to-vehicle (V2V) communication is, in essence, a form of D2D communication, and has been burgeoning with the adoption of the IEEE 802.11p DSRC standard around the world [2, 3]. Nu-

ISLPED'14, August 11 - 13, 2014, La Jolla, CA, USA.
Copyright 2014 ACM 978-1-4503-2975-0/14/08 ...$15.00.
http://dx.doi.org/10.1145/2627369.2627644 .

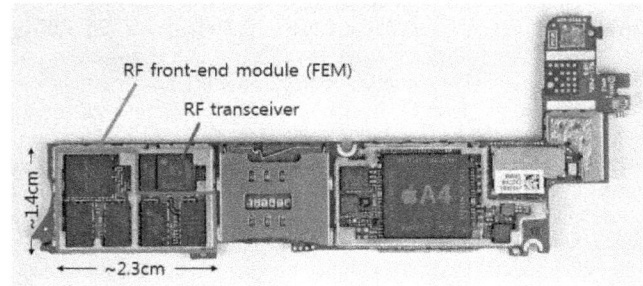

Figure 1: RF front-end modules (FEMs) on the Apple iPhone 4.

merous V2V applications in the transportation domain have been proposed or deployed, such as mobile multimedia, safety, road pricing, and others [4]. These applications leverage the high mobility, long range and fast response times of 802.11p for next-generation transportation applications. 802.11p's increased transmit power enables longer range communications, but the high power consumption of 802.11p radios has, until now, precluded their integration into non-vehicular mobile devices[1].

In this paper, we demonstrate the feasibility of realizing 802.11p on phones by bringing together materials, devices, circuits, and systems researchers. We see this development opening up D2D communications to a much larger class of applications, with mobile devices on pedestrians, passengers, and drivers now interconnected at low latency and high bandwidth, enabling highly interactive mobile applications.

Among several building blocks for a communications system, the RF front-end is one of the most critical, with III-V semiconductor devices (e.g. GaN, GaAs, InGaP) showing much better power density and efficiency than CMOS. Figure 1 (photo from [5]) shows multiple RF front-end modules (FEMs) for a variety of standards in an Apple iPhone 4; together, these occupy a large portion of real estate. In addition, each FEM includes multiple semiconductor dies within it, further increasing area footprint, power, as well as cost.

In our work, we leverage a unique process, the LEES (Low Energy Electronics Systems) process, where both CMOS and III-V semiconductor devices can be fabricated on a *single* die. This allows the use of the most suitable III-V devices grown on top of a conventional CMOS device, interfaced via metal layers. Such single-die integration offers the superior performance required by 802.11p specifications at the small form factor and within the tight

---

[1]The recently-released Qualcomm Snapdragon Automotive Solutions support DSRC for short-range vehicular safety detection, but not 802.11p and its extended range with high transmit power.

power budget of a smartphone implementation. In Section 2, we will show how the process can shrink the 802.11p front-end module and how the FEM can plug into the existing communications subsystem circuitry on a phone.

LEES devices and the relevant semiconductor processes are now being developed in conjunction with a commercial CMOS foundry, targeting to release the first prototype devices and circuits at the end of 2014. In parallel, device modeling and p-cell layout for the LEES devices are also in progress to develop a PDK, which will be the first integrated CMOS and III-V design kit for circuit designers to create innovative circuits using a conventional design flow. To demonstrate chip functionality before the LEES process is ready, we first design and fabricate a reference front-end circuit for our system prototype using standard commercial 0.18um CMOS and 0.25um GaN technologies on separate dies. This front-end incorporates a novel circuit design to realize the high transmit power (28.8dBm, 4× or 19× that of WiFi) required by 802.11p, at low power.

We demonstrate compatibility with existing phones by emulating an 802.11p baseband on FPGA (using a modified 802.11a baseband) and interfacing the FPGA with the fabricated 802.11p transmitter. Our system prototype is a transmitter chain consisting of the designed front-end circuits in standard CMOS and GaN technologies, a baseband processor in an FPGA board interfaced to an Android smartphone through USB, all 802.11p compliant. Application-level adaptive control of the radio's transmit power through a gain control interface means the Android application can tune the radio's transmit power (and thus its power dissipation) to match actual desired D2D communication distance. This joint hardware-software power optimization enables substantial further power reduction, allowing the prototype to meet the aggressive smartphone power budget.

2. BACKGROUND

2.1 LEES Process and Design Flow

By enabling monolithic integration of III-V materials with CMOS, the new process presents new challenges to integrated circuit design that are fundamentally different. It thus prompted the setting up of a materials-circuit-system team to explore new application drivers that can best leverage the monolithic, vertically integrated process.

The LEES process is based on conventional front-end silicon CMOS processing by a commercial foundry, followed by III-V integration and processing in a research lab, before returning the processed wafer back to the commercial foundry for back-end silicon CMOS processing. Figure 2 illustrates an example structure of III-V monolithically integrated with CMOS/Si devices. In this paper, we focus on GaN HEMTs as these are particularly suitable for the high-power RF circuits necessary for 802.11p.

As the LEES process is based on a commercial CMOS foundry, CMOS circuit design can leverage the existing CMOS PDK provided by the foundry. The III-V portion of the die, however, will require a new PDK which includes III-V device models, layout p-cells, and interconnect models between III-V and CMOS devices. The PDK has been developed with a physics-based compact model of III-V devices [6] (i.e. GaN HEMT first) coupled with device layout, sizing and spacing rules defined by device and process researchers, enabling CMOS+III-V circuit simulation using conventional CAD tools and layout for both the CMOS and GaN portions of the die. This integrated CAD flow enables joint CMOS+III-V circuit design and eases migration of the LEES process to commercialization.

2.2 Phone Communications Circuits

A typical smartphone incorporates several two-way communications radios, including WiFi (IEEE 802.11a/b/g/n/ac), Bluetooth,

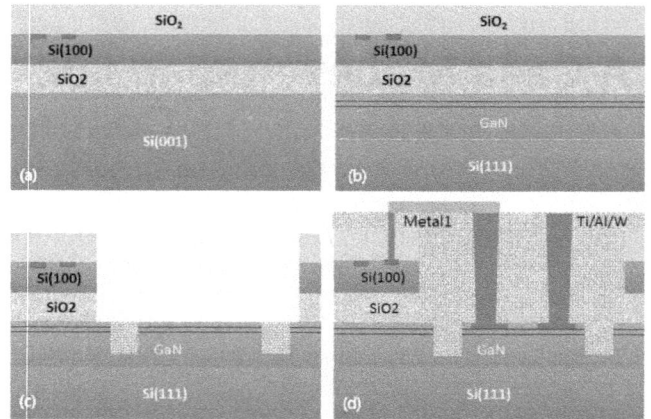

Figure 2: LEES process integration of III-V (GaN) and CMOS: (a) A silicon-on-insulator (SOI) wafer with fabricated Si devices; (b) Si CMOS/GaN-on-Si wafer realized by two-step bonding technology; (c) GaN window open and device isolation; (d) Schematic cross-section view of the monolithically integrated GaN HEMT devices with final metal interconnection of fabricated HEMTs and Si CMOS devices.

and the cellular radios. The cellular radios in mobile phones available today do not support direct device-to-device (D2D) communications, and only communicate with the cellular base stations that coordinate access to the medium. WiFi Direct is a recent standard that allows D2D communications between mobile phones, and thus enables networks with star topologies, but not mesh or full peer-to-peer topologies. Ad-hoc WiFi is a pre-existing standard that allows for direct D2D communication without needing to appoint one of the devices as a centralized controller or access point, but is not widely supported among the major mobile operating systems, and thus requires kernel modifications.

Each radio typically contains a PHY (physical layer) and MAC (medium access control) implemented in hardware, with upper MAC and higher networking layers implemented in software at the device driver, operating system and application level. Most of the building blocks of the communications subsystem within a phone are increasingly being integrated with current standard CMOS processes, except for the RF power amplifier. While there is significant ongoing circuit research targeting CMOS power amplifiers to enable higher level of integration of the entire communications subsystem, the intrinsic low power density and efficiency of current CMOS devices presents a tough challenge [7]. As shown in Figure 1, a power amplifier for each communication standard is still a separate chip fabricated using III-V technology which enables higher output power and efficiency, but worsens system form factor.

2.3 802.11p Compatibility with 802.11a

IEEE 802.11p DSRC is an emerging standard originally proposed for vehicle-to-vehicle (V2V) and vehicle-to-infra structure (V2I) communication, enabling truly distributed mesh D2D networking like ad-hoc WiFi. Table 1 compares the 802.11p specification with 802.11a. 802.11p adopts the same OFDM modulation as 802.11a, but its time domain parameters are double those of 802.11a to mitigate highly mobile and severe fading vehicular environments. Thus, when we implement the digital baseband processor for 802.11p, we can use 802.11a hardware as is, but run it at half the clock frequency.

However, with the increased transmit power and robustness necessary for longer range V2V communications, the high power con-

	802.11p (DSRC)	802.11a (WiFi)
User mobility	Vehicular (outdoor)	Personal (indoor)
Operating frequencies	5.85-5.925GHz	5.15-5.825GHz
Channel bandwidth	10MHz	20MHz
Max. output power	760mW	40/200mW
Data rate	3-27Mbps	6-54Mbps
Modulation	BPSK-64QAM	BPSK-64QAM
OFDM symbol duration	8us	4us
Guard time	1.6us	0.8us
Preamble duration	32us	16us
Subcarrier spacing	156kHz	312kHz

Table 1: 802.11p vs. 802.11a specifications.

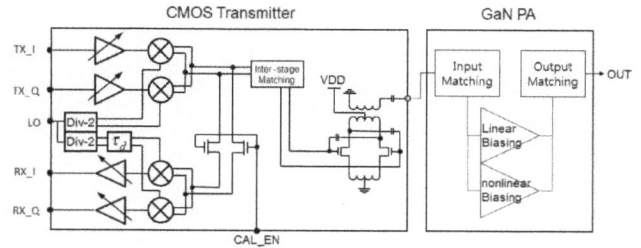

Figure 3: Proposed interfacing of the 802.11p LEES single-die solution with existing phones' WiFi chipset.

sumption of 802.11p radios has precluded their use in mobile phones until now. The LEES process can resolve this issue through its novel CMOS/III-V integration technology that can optimize high power density III-V devices' performance for specific applications and integrate them with CMOS on a single die. This new device and process technology, combined with a novel circuit design, along with adaptive gain control by the application software, make it possible to implement a low-power and small form-factor 802.11p-based D2D solution in a smartphone. Figure 3 depicts how the 802.11p system can be implemented with the existing WiFi chipset and application processor on a phone using LEES technology, such that only a 802.11p RF front-end chip needs to be added.

3. SYSTEM PROTOTYPE DESIGN

Our system prototype is a transmitter chain from phone to FPGA to the RF front-end, enabling 802.11p compliant signal transmission with application level gain control for power saving. A USB-Ethernet adapter is used to communicate between the Android phone and the FPGA. To interface the baseband processor on FPGA to our custom RF front-end, commercial DAC evaluation boards are used to feed analog I/Q signals into the RF transmitter. As mentioned in Section 2.2, all these digital and ADC/DAC components can be shared with existing WiFi communications circuitry, and a single RF front-end can readily support both 802.11a and 802.11p by slightly extending its maximum carrier frequency range from 5.875GHz to 5.925GHz. Thus, to demonstrate the feasibility of 802.11p implementation and its compatibility with existing WiFi solutions, we first design and fabricate a CMOS transmitter and GaN PA using commercial foundries, then leverage existing 802.11a IP to implement 802.11p baseband on an FPGA, before interfacing the FPGA to the Android kernel.

3.1 RF Front-End

Figure 4 shows the circuit schematics of the CMOS+GaN RF front-end consisting of a CMOS transmitter and a GaN PA. A simple CMOS receiver circuitry is also designed for calibration to enhance

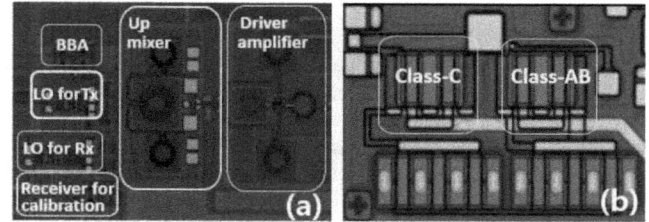

Figure 4: CMOS+GaN RF front-end block diagram

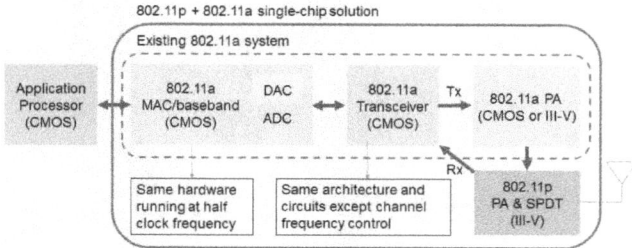

Figure 5: Fabricated die microphotographs: (a) CMOS transmitter circuit (b) GaN PA circuit.

the RF performance. A CMOS driver amplifier is designed using cross-coupled neutralization capacitors to improve linearity, along with the center-tapped on-chip inductor for source degeneration. A center-tapped on-chip transformer is used to remove an external balun. The CMOS circuits are fabricated in 0.18um CMOS technology and occupy $1.4mm^2$ including a whole transmitter chain and a receiver for I/Q mismatch calibration excluding the pad area, as shown in Figure 5(a).

A GaN PA is designed and fabricated using a commercial 0.25um GaN-on-SiC process [8]. Since GaN HEMTs are depletion mode devices with a negative pinch-off voltage, the PA requires external negative biases. To satisfy the EVM requirement at 28.8dBm maximum output power, we propose a new in-phase power combining technique utilizing both Class AB and C biasing devices, achieving both linearity and efficiency across output power levels, while eliminating complex design issues in traditional power amplifiers. Figure 5(b) shows the fabricated GaN circuit occupying $1.28mm^2$ die area.

3.2 FPGA Subsystem

FPGAs provide an ideal platform for prototyping complex radio baseband implementations in real-time, offering high performance, low power, and portability, in comparison with other software radio platforms [9]. The FPGA platform performs two vital functions in our setup: baseband processing and providing the interface between the application software on the Android phone and the analog/RF circuitry via the DAC. The FPGA system is implemented on a Xilinx XC5VLX110T FPGA on the XUPV5 development board. We have implemented the complete transmitter chain as described in Figure 6. Packets are transmitted from the Android handset, via the RRR Abstraction layer and Ethernet physical interface, into the 802.11p Airblue baseband on the FPGA. The resultant baseband output is passed through a digital low pass filter and scaled before delivery to the DAC circuitry.

The Airblue baseband [10] was originally designed for the 802.11a standard. Since the two standards are largely similar, we run the entire baseband design at half the clock frequency (10MHz) to achieve compatibility with the 802.11p standard. It is worth noting that for

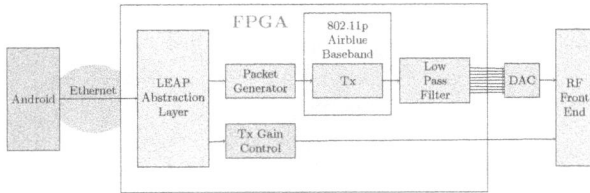

Figure 6: FPGA system diagram.

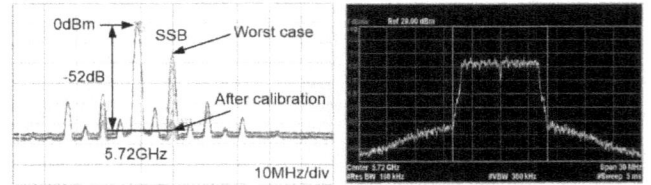

Figure 7: RF performance: (a) SSB rejection of CMOS transmitter, (b) GaN PA output spectrum.

actual 802.11p deployment, more stringent output spectrum shaping is required than for 802.11a [11]. The Android handset can access two functions in the FPGA hardware: the packet generator and the gain control module. The packet generator is responsible for configuring parameters, buffering, and synchronizing, the baseband transmission. The gain control module allows the Android handset to directly control power settings on the RF front-end. The FPGA receives and decodes power control commands from handset, applying the appropriate settings at the front-end via a parallel pin interface. This enables power saving capability to be applied from the Android application software. We add a digital low pass filter to reduce the noise caused by the sampling effect within the 40MHz spectrum range.

The Asim Architect's Workbench (AWB) [12] is the development environment for hybrid hardware-software design. FPGA support is provided in AWB via the Logic-based Environment for Application Programming (LEAP) framework [13] that provides the Remote Request-Response (RRR) framework, an abstracted communication layer.

3.3 Phone-FPGA Interface

The Android smartphone is interfaced to the FPGA through a USB-Ethernet adapter connected via Ethernet to the FPGA and via USB On-the-Go (OTG) to the Android device.

In order to have the Android device recognize and enumerate the USB-Ethernet adapter, we recompiled the Linux kernel for the device to include the USB-Ethernet drivers for the particular ASIX AX88178 and SMSC 7500 chipsets in the adapters. We then loaded this kernel onto the phones, replacing the default kernel. This allowed the Android device to become a USB host and recognize the USB slave Ethernet adapters attached to it via the USB OTG cable.

4. EVALUATION

4.1 Circuit Measurements

For the CMOS transmitter, after the calibration process, -52dB single-sideband (SSB) rejection is achieved as depicted in Figure 7(a). With the same calibration settings and using the IEEE 802.11p baseband I/Q signals, -36.5dB EVM is achieved at the output. The GaN PA achieves -30.5dB EVM and 22% drain efficiency across one-decade output power ranges with its maximum output power of 28.8dBm. This circuit characteristic is suitable for system level power saving across all output power levels at high efficiency, unlike a conventional PA whose efficiency exponentially decreases as output power drops. Figure 7(b) shows the output power spectrum using the 802.11p 64-QAM signals.

4.2 System Prototype Evaluation

Figure 8 shows the experimental setup of the system prototype, illustrating that a smartphone, an FPGA board and commercial DAC evaluation boards are interfaced to the designed CMOS and GaN

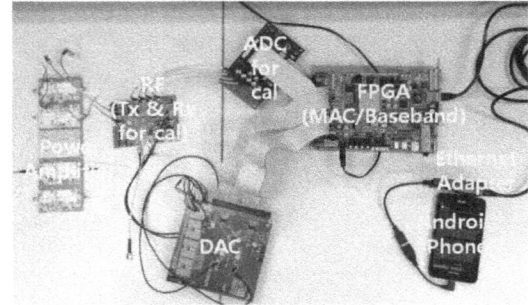

Figure 8: Snapshot of the system prototype.

PCB boards. An 802.11p compliant digital baseband implemented in the FPGA along with the TI dual 12-bit DAC, DAC2902, sampling at 40MHz, feeds the analog I/Q baseband signals into the CMOS transmitter. An Android application on the smartphone controls packet generation/transmission and RF gain.

Since the transmit mode dominates power consumption, we design and implement an entire transmitter chain to validate the LEES feasibility as well as potential power reduction through application-level adaptive power control (ALAPC). In addition, the DC power of the PA is more than 90% of the whole transmitter power with a complex modulation scheme like OFDM in 802.11p, since it requires back-off due to its high PAPR signals and the power efficiency is dramatically reduced as output power decreases from the saturation point. Thus, power management of the PA is crucial to fit the 802.11p front-end within a smartphone's stringent power budget.

In the following subsections, we demonstrate that ALAPC, combined with our GaN PA's improved power efficiency across all output power levels, can achieve dramatic power reductions. We cannot yet deploy our prototype system due to its complex system configuration, FPGA and DAC boards, and multiple power supplies for the transmitter and PA boards. However, we can use traces from prior deployments of two mobile apps which originally used off-the-shelf D2D communications, to estimate the potential system power savings that can be achieved if we replace those COTS D2D radios with our proposed single-die 802.11p radios integrated within phones.

4.2.1 RoadRunner Evaluation

RoadRunner [14] is an in-vehicle Android app for road congestion control, and speaks turn-by-turn navigation instructions to the driver, like existing navigation systems, while enforcing road-space rationing by allocating tokens among vehicles in the background. Tokens permit a vehicle to drive on a specific road segment, and are distributed to vehicles from a server over the cellular network (LTE), or exchanged directly between vehicles over 802.11p DSRC.

Original deployment. The original deployment took place in Cambridge, MA, USA, consisting of 10 vehicles driving among

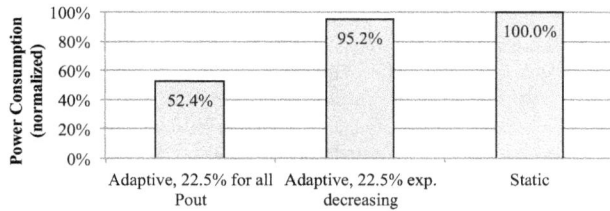

Figure 9: Average power consumption of RoadRunner V2V exchanges with and without adaptive power control.

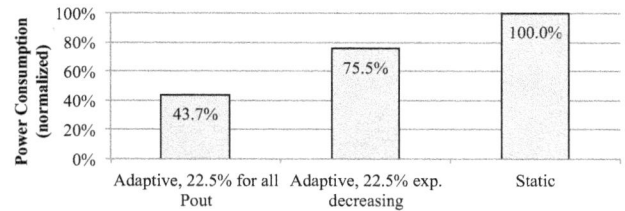

Figure 10: Average power consumption of SignalGuru broadcasts with and without adaptive power control.

multiple possible congestion-controlled routes. Three different scenarios were evaluated: RoadRunner using only the cellular network as a baseline; additionally using ad-hoc WiFi for V2V communications; and additionally using 802.11p DSRC for V2V communications. With 802.11p, each smartphone was tethered via USB to an off-the-shelf 802.11p DSRC radio [15]. Using 802.11p enabled network response time improvements of up to 80% versus the cellular network, and cellular network usage reductions of up to 84%. Ad-hoc WiFi's performance did not suffice: with ad-hoc WiFi, only 5 V2V communications sessions occurred at an average distance of 29.2 meters, resulting in only 6.8% of requests being offloaded to V2V from the cellular network, while with 802.11p, 47 V2V sessions occurred at an average distance of 175.7 meters, offloading 43% of requests. This original deployment thus motivates the use of 802.11p as a mobile D2D communication standard for phones, while the cumbersome setup tethering a COTS 802.11p radio to a phone motivates a single-die 802.11p chip.

Adaptive power control. We obtained the RoadRunner traces and assume that with our adaptive power control, each V2V communications session (a token exchange) would be transmitted at the minimum power required to reach the other vehicle. We compare this to the original deployment traces as a baseline, in which every V2V token exchange is conducted at full radio power. The traces include vehicle location, communications on all radio interfaces, and distances at which V2V token exchanges occurred during the deployment. For each V2V exchange, we look up the minimum power level to transmit a packet across that distance from our experimental measurements of the GaN PA, using 64-QAM coding. We normalize the sum of these estimates to a situation with no adaptive power control, shown in Figure 9.

With ALAPC and our new PA design (22.5% efficient for all power levels), the V2V exchanges use 47% less power (from 3.37 W down to 1.77 W), indicating that many V2V communications sessions did not need the full transmit power in the original deployment to reach the other vehicle. With ALAPC, but without our new PA design (so efficiency is exponentially decreasing), V2V token exchanges use 4.8% less power than the baseline (from 3.37 W down to 3.21 W), underscoring the importance of the improved PA efficiency of our circuits in realizing gains from ALAPC.

4.2.2 SignalGuru Evaluation

SignalGuru [16] is a vehicular traffic light detection iPhone app that shares data among multiple phones to collaboratively learn traffic signal transition patterns and provide GLOSA (Green Light Optimal Speed Advisory) to drivers. Each vehicle contains a windshield-mounted iPhone that observes traffic signal transitions via the phone's camera and broadcasts the observations over ad-hoc WiFi every 2 seconds.

Original deployment. The original SignalGuru deployment also occurred in Cambridge, MA, USA, along three consecutive inter-

sections on Massachusetts Avenue. 5 vehicles followed a route for 3 hours, generating GPS location traces. To surmount the limited range of ad-hoc WiFi, a phone stationed near an intersection acted as a relay.

Adaptive power control. We obtained the SignalGuru traces, and in the simulation of our proposed 802.11p radio's performance, whenever a vehicle broadcasts a packet (every 2 seconds), we calculate the power level required to reach the nearest vehicle to it, from 19.8 to 28.8 dBm. We compare this to baseline static power control, in which every broadcast is transmitted at the maximum power level of 28.8 dBm.

With ALAPC and our new PA design (22.5% efficient for all power levels), SignalGuru broadcasts use 56.3% less power (from 3.37 W down to 1.47 W), shown in Figure 10. With ALAPC, but without our new PA design (efficiency exponentially decreasing), SignalGuru broadcasts use 24.5% less power than the baseline (from 3.37 W down to 2.54 W), highlighting again that the improved power efficiency of our single-die circuits is important to substantially lowering overall system power consumption.

4.2.3 Power Reduction Summary

To put our power reductions of 1.6 W (RoadRunner) and 1.9 W (SignalGuru) in context, we measured the dynamic range of a Samsung Galaxy S4 smartphone's power consumption to be between 1 W (screen on, idle) and 11 W (running a CPU-intensive benchmark) using a Monsoon Power Monitor [17]. This indicates a significant power reduction in the overall platform power budget can be realized with our new power amplifier.

4.3 Simulations on the new PDK

To predict the circuit functionality and layout area of the combined CMOS + GaN design using LEES process technology, the LEES PDK is used for the simulation and layout of our prototype circuits. Since the PDK includes an unmodified commercial CMOS PDK, we validate only the III-V portion. At one GaN device's three terminals, we achieve the same waveforms at 5.9GHz, which means RF parasitics as well as intrinsic AC/DC parameters are successfully reflected in the model. We also model large-signal nonlinearity using the physics-based compact model to match the PA's nonlinear characteristics at high output power, which is essential for predicting accurate performance of a III-V (or III-V + CMOS) PA with CMOS power control circuitry on a single die.

Figure 12 depicts a draft layout for the designed CMOS transmitter combined with a GaN PA using the p-cells in the PDK. Compared with the sum of two separate die areas at $1.4 + 1.28 = 2.68mm^2$, the combined CMOS + GaN layout using our PDK totals $1.98mm^2$, demonstrating the proposed process integration can further shrink the form factor (as pads are no longer needed). Along with the smaller single die area, the technology can integrate all FEMs and

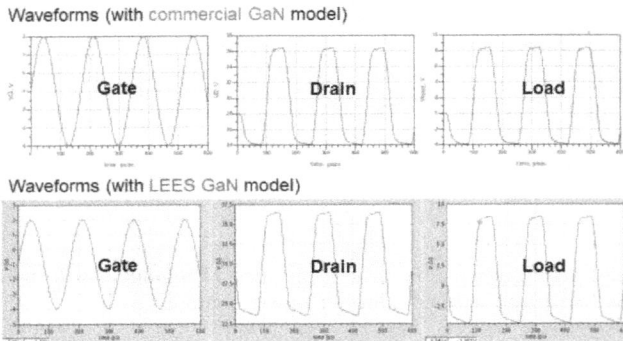

Figure 11: Simulation comparison between a commercial and LEES GaN models.

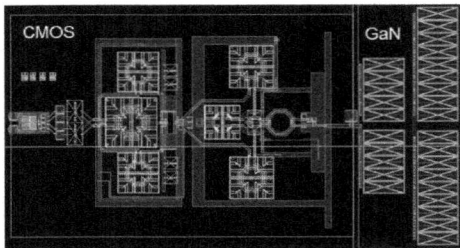

Figure 12: Layout for the designed CMOS transmitter and GaN PA using the integrated PDK.

related components currently in a smartphone into a single die (or package) in the near future.

5. CONCLUSIONS

This work is the result of collaboration between materials and device researchers, circuits designers and mobile systems and software architects. Motivated by the novel GaN-CMOS monolithic process, we leveraged the GaN HEMT devices to realize the high-power power amplifier necessary for 802.11p specifications, and coupled that with a CMOS transmitter. The RF front-end circuits were tailored for adaptive power control, targeting good power efficiency across a wide range of transmit power. An 802.11p baseband processor was emulated on an FPGA (using an existing 802.11a baseband) to connect an Android phone to the RF front-end, creating a full system prototype to demonstrate the feasibility of incorporating the RF front-end into a phone. Our results show that the GaN-CMOS process can realize an 802.11p front-end within the stringent power and area budgets of a smartphone.

6. ACKNOWLEDGEMENTS

We thank Zhihong Liu for detailed discussions on the LEES process, Zhaomin Zhu for the development of the LEES PDK, in SMART, Ujwal Radhakrishna for the compact modeling of the GaN HEMTs, and Kermin Fleming for helping with porting of the AirBlue baseband, at MIT. This research was supported by the Singapore National Research Foundation through the Singapore-MIT Alliance for Research and Technology (SMART)'s Low Energy Electronic Systems (LEES) and Future Urban Mobility (FM) research programmes, and by the United States Department of Defense NDSEG fellowship.

7. REFERENCES

[1] A. Balasubramanian, R. Mahajan, A. Venkataramani, B. N. Levine, and J. Zahorjan, "Interactive Wifi connectivity for moving vehicles," in *Proc. ACM SIGCOMM, 2008.*

[2] "The connected vehicle test bed," www.its.dot.gov/factsheets/connected_vehicle_testbed_factsheet.htm, US Department of Transportation, 2013.

[3] "CAR 2 CAR Communication Consortium," car-to-car.org.

[4] P. Papadimitratos, A. La Fortelle, K. Evenssen, R. Brignolo, and S. Cosenza, "Vehicular communication systems: Enabling technologies, applications, and future outlook on intelligent transportation," *IEEE Communications Magazine*, vol. 47, no. 11, pp. 84–95, 2009.

[5] "iFixit iPhone 4 teardown," ifixit.com/Teardown/iPhone+4/3130, iFixit, 2010.

[6] U. Radhakrishna, L. Wei, D.-S. Lee, T. Palacios, and D. Antoniadis, "Physics-based GaN HEMT transport and charge model: Experimental verification and performance projection," in *Proc. IEEE IEDM, 2012.*

[7] G. Liu, P. Haldi, T. K. Liu, and A. M. Niknejad, "Fully integrated CMOS power amplifier with efficiency enhancement at power back-off," *IEEE Journal of Solid-State Circuit*, vol. 3, no. 43, pp. 433–435, March 2008.

[8] P. Choi, C. Boon, M. Mao, and H. Liu, "28.8 dBm, high efficiency, linear GaN power amplifier with in-phase power combining for IEEE 802.11p applications," *IEEE Microwave and Wireless Components Letters*, vol. 23, no. 8, pp. 433–435, August 2013.

[9] J. Lotze, S. A. Fahmy, J. Noguera, B. Ozgul, L. Doyle, and R. Esser, "Development framework for implementing FPGA-based cognitive network nodes," in *IEEE Global Communications Conference – GLOBECOM*, 2009.

[10] M. C. Ng, K. E. Fleming, M. Vutukuru, S. Gross, and H. Balakrishnan, "Airblue: A system for cross-layer wireless protocol development," in *Proc. ACM/IEEE Symposium on Architectures for Networking and Communications Systems*, 2010.

[11] T. H. Pham, I. V. McLoughlin, and S. A. Fahmy, "Shaping spectral leakage for IEEE 802.11p vehicular communications," in *Proc. of the IEEE Vehicular Technology Conference – Spring*, 2014.

[12] J. Emer, P. Ahuja, E. Borch, A. Klauser, C.-K. Luk, S. Manne, S. Mukherjee, H. Patil, S. Wallace, N. Binkert, R. Espasa, and T. Juan, "Asim: a performance model framework," *Computer*, vol. 35, no. 2, pp. 68–76, 2002.

[13] A. Parashar, M. Adler, K. Fleming, M. Pellauer, and J. Emer, "LEAP: A virtual platform architecture for FPGAs," in *Proc. of Workshop on the Intersections of Computer Architecture and Reconfigurable Logic*, 2010.

[14] J. Gao and L. Peh, "RoadRunner: Infrastructure-less vehicular congestion control," in *ITS World Congress*, in press 2014.

[15] "MK2 WAVE-DSRC Radio," cohdawireless.com/product/mk2.html.

[16] E. Koukoumidis, L.-S. Peh, and M. R. Martonosi, "SignalGuru: leveraging mobile phones for collaborative traffic signal schedule advisory," in *Proc. ACM MobiSys*, 2011.

[17] Monsoon Solutions, "Monsoon Power Monitor," http://msoon.com/LabEquipment/PowerMonitor/.

Leakage Mitigation Techniques in Smartphone SoCs

John Redmond
Broadcom
16340 W Bernardo Dr
San Diego
949-926-7989
jcredmon@broadcom.com

ABSTRACT

This paper outlines leakage mitigation in smart phone SoCs. Leakage power will be investigated across the disparate smart phone use-cases. Leakage mitigation techniques will be covered at architecture, design, and run-time.

1. INTRODUCTION

The rapid increase in compute power and convergence of point portable devices into the smartphone coupled with the increasing leakage in deep submicron silicon processes has led to leakage power becoming a first class challenge.

The smartphone SoC architecture has integrated dedicated hardware accelerators and high performance processor cores. In order to realize the performance gains, silicon process has shifted from low leakage(LP) silicon processes to higher leakage processes.

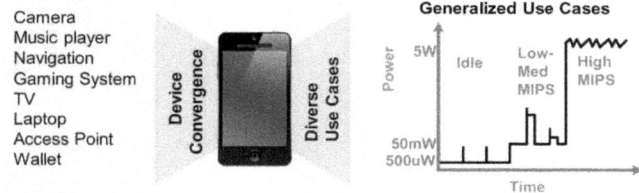

Figure 1. Device convergence leads to diverse use-cases

User expectation for standby and talk times has remained unchanged and battery technology hasn't kept pace with the performance increases. In order to meet the power envelopes, advanced techniques are required to keep leakage under control.

This paper is organized around three general classes of use-cases: 1) idle, 2) low-medium MIPS use-cases, and 3) high MIPS use-cases. Each of these general classes has unique power requirements that will be addressed.

2. IDLE MODE

Idle mode is when phone is paging for calls, texts, emails, and other updates. There are two phases, deep-sleep and paging.

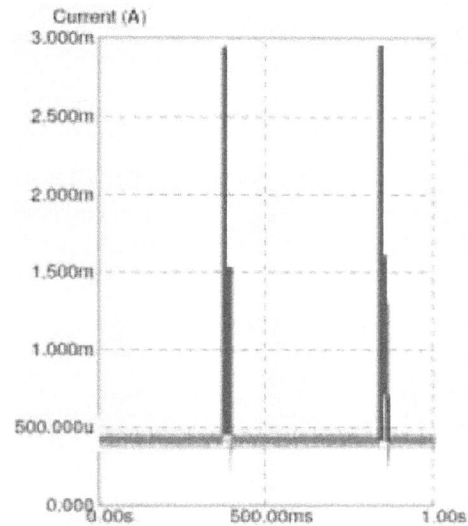

Figure 2. Idle mode

Leakage power dominates overall power in idle mode. Due to the very low power requirement in this mode, leakage needs to be addressed at an architectural level. In idle mode, reduction of leakage is the first priority.

Aggressive power gating is critical to reduce leakage in this mode. Leading edge cellular SoCs have greater than 30 different independent power islands to minimize leakage. Correctly implementing and verifying complex power architecture can only be done with a power intent flow. We use IEEE1801 power intent standard to accomplish this.

Additional techniques are to reduce VDD to minimum voltage determined by bit-cell retention voltage and reducing the amount of state that needs to be retained.

3. LOW – MEDIUM MIPS USE CASES

Low and medium MIPS use-cases include voice call, audio playback and video playback. User expect higher fidelity with each new generation of smartphones while maintaining similar or increased use times.

Active power, consisting of dynamic and leakage power, minimization is the key to meet the power requirements in these modes.

Techniques such as multi-Vt cells and gate length biasing provide design time leakage reduction. These techniques may lead to higher dynamic power, so careful trade off between leakage and dynamic power is required to achieve optimized power.

Leakage power varies across process, voltage, and temperature. Designing at the typical environmental conditions is critical to reduce power for the aggregate of devices. Additionally, a design needs to be robust for correct operation at the corner process and temperatures.

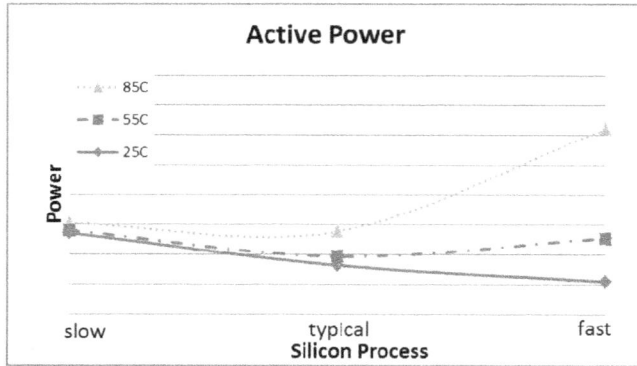

Figure 3. Active Power across temperature and silicon process

Other design techniques to reduce active leakage include guard band reduction and keeping memories at retention voltage when not in use.

4. HIGH MIPS USE CASES

In order for cores to meet multi-GHz frequency requirements, extensive use of low Vth cells are required. High frequencies lead to high dynamic power and low Vth cells lead to high leakage power. This power increases leads to temperature increase which can lead to thermal run away.

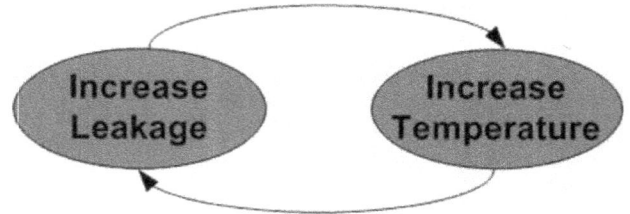

Figure 4. Thermal runaway

Runtime power and thermal management is the key to prevent thermal run away. Real-time leakage monitoring is required as input to these algorithms to provide optimal performance.

5. CONCLUSION

Leakage mitigation techniques for smartphone SoCs across diverse use-cases in order to meet power requirements have been presented. Techniques are implemented at the architectural, design, and run-time phases.

2.3 ppm/·C 40 nW MOSFET-Only Voltage Reference

Oscar E. Mattia
Microelectronics Graduate
Program
Federal University of Rio
Grande do Sul
Porto Alegre, Brazil
oemneto@inf.ufrgs.br

Hamilton Klimach
Electrical Engineering
Department
Federal University of Rio
Grande do Sul
Porto Alegre, Brazil
hklimach@ufrgs.br

Sergio Bampi
Informatics Institute
Federal University of Rio
Grande do Sul
Porto Alegre, Brazil
bampi@inf.ufrgs.br

ABSTRACT

A MOSFET-only sub-bandgap voltage reference at less than 50 nW and with very low temperature coefficient is introduced. It consists of a threshold voltage extractor circuit and a proportional to absolute temperature voltage generator, using no resistors. The behavior of the circuit is analytically described, a design methodology is proposed and simulation results for a $0.13\mu m$ CMOS process are presented. It allows a reference voltage below the bandgap, 625 mV in this design example, achieving a temperature coefficient of 2.3 ppm/°C for the -40 to 125 °C temperature range. The circuit consumes 40 nW at 27 °C and under 1.2 V supply, being the implemented silicon area 0.0099 mm^2.

Categories and Subject Descriptors

B.7 [**INTEGRATED CIRCUITS**]: Miscellaneous

Keywords

Voltage Reference; Nano-Power; Resistorless Reference; CMOS Analog Design

1. INTRODUCTION

Voltage references are fundamental circuit blocks ubiquitously used in analog, mixed-signal, RF and digital systems, including memories. Mobile and energy harvesting applications require ultra low power designs, which should be extended to all circuits, including the analog ones. Resistorless analog blocks have the advantage of implementation in standard digital processes. Basically, voltage references can be divided into three fundamental functions: the generation of two voltages (or currents), one proportional and the other complementary to absolute temperature (PTAT and CTAT, respectively) and biasing. The biasing function is sometimes implemented together with the PTAT generator, reducing area and complexity, as done in the traditional bandgap reference (BGR), introduced by Widlar in 1971 [19].

ISLPED'14, August 11–13, 2014, La Jolla, CA, USA.
Copyright 2014 ACM 978-1-4503-2975-0/14/08 ...$15.00.
http://dx.doi.org/10.1145/2627369.2627621.

In BGR circuits the CTAT voltage is implemented with a p-n junction, which presents a slightly non-linear behavior over temperature [15]. This non-linearity is the main contributor to the curvature over temperature usually seen in these implementations, impacting directly the thermal coefficient of the reference. Through the years many curvature compensation techniques were proposed [7], [14] and [10]. Still, even in modern CMOS approaches they consume high power [8]. References that do not implement curvature compensation usually do not achieve low temperature coefficients [9] or operate under a limited temperature range [6]. Switched capacitors can also be used to reduce fabrication variability [4], but the curvature effect is still present.

The MOSFET threshold voltage, in turn, presents an alternative way to implement a CTAT voltage. It has been used in recent voltage references to achieve low power consumption and low power supply voltages [3], [17], [5], [12] and [20]. The temperature range of these references varies widely, but nano-watt power consumption, resistorless circuits and sub-1 V power supplies are common to almost all.

In this paper we propose a novel voltage reference based on the sum of two almost linear temperature dependent terms. A threshold voltage extractor, based on the self-biased current source topology presented in [1], provides the CTAT voltage. The PTAT voltage is generated by two PMOS unbalanced differential pairs operating in weak inversion. The sum of these two linear terms results in a significant reduction of the thermal coefficient over a wide temperature range, while power consumption is kept low by the use of transistors operating under weak and moderate inversion.

The text is organized as follows: section 2 presents the threshold voltage extractor and the PTAT voltage generator circuits. A design methodology is proposed in section 3, followed by simulation results of the implemented reference in $0.13\mu m$ CMOS - section 4 - including Monte Carlo variability analysis. To conclude, we compare our results against typical results of recently published works.

2. CIRCUIT DESCRIPTION

The transistors used in the proposed circuit operate both under weak and moderate inversion levels, meaning that circuit analysis requires a model that describes all operation regions using one equation, as done in the ACM MOSFET model [2].

2.1 ACM MOSFET Model

In the ACM model, the drain current I_D of a long-channel MOSFET is expressed as

$$I_D = I_F - I_R = SI_{SQ}(i_f - i_r) \quad (1)$$

Where I_F and I_R are the forward and reverse currents, $S = W/L$ is the aspect ratio, W being the width and L the length of the transistor. i_f and i_r are the forward and reverse inversion coefficients, related to the source and drain inversion charge densities, while I_{SQ} is the sheet normalization transistor current, defined as

$$I_{SQ} = \frac{1}{2}n\mu C'_{ox}\phi_t^2 \quad (2)$$

Where n is the subthreshold slope factor, μ is the channel effective mobility (both slightly dependent on the gate voltage V_G), C'_{ox} is the gate capacitance per unit area, and ϕ_t is the thermal voltage. The relationship between current and voltage is given by

$$\frac{V_P - V_{S(D)}}{\phi_t} = F(i_{f(r)}) = \sqrt{1 + i_{f(r)}} - 2 + \ln(\sqrt{1 + i_{f(r)}} - 1) \quad (3)$$

Where V_S and V_D are the source and drain voltages (all terminal voltages are referenced to the transistor bulk), and V_P is the pinch-off voltage, approximated by (4).

$$V_P \simeq \frac{V_G - V_{T0}}{n} \quad (4)$$

Where V_{T0} the threshold voltage for zero bulk bias. The first term (the square root one) in the right side of (3) is related to the drift component of the drain current, being predominant under strong inversion. The last term (the logarithmic one) is related to the diffusion component, being predominant under weak inversion operation. In forward saturation $I_F \gg I_R$ and consequently $I_D \simeq I_F = SI_{SQ}i_f$.

2.2 V_{T0} Extractor

The proposed V_{T0} extractor circuit, shown in Fig. 1, is a variation of a self-biased current source presented in [1]. In the work of [1], both M1 and M2 were operating in weak inversion. Here, we take a different approach on the same circuit to extract the threshold voltage of transistors M1 and M2.

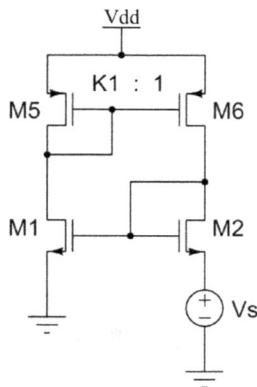

Figure 1: Threshold voltage extractor schematic.

From (3) and (4), one can see that a saturated nMOS-FET with grounded source and operating under a constant

inversion level equal to 3 ($i_f = 3$) will have a gate voltage V_G equal to the threshold voltage V_{T0}. It happens because under these conditions, the right side of (3) becomes zero.

In the circuit shown in Fig. 1, M1 is made to operate under such condition, being in the moderate inversion region. Also in Fig. 1, M2 is designed with the same geometry of M1, kept saturated too and sharing the same gate voltage, but with a source voltage different from zero. Using (3) and (4) for M2, knowing that $V_{G2} = V_{G1} = V_{T0}$, leads to (5).

$$-V_{S2} = \phi_t F(i_{f2}) \quad (5)$$

So, one can conclude that if the resulting M1 current I_{D1}, that was chosen to keep M1 operating with $i_{f1} = 3$, is also used to control the drain current of M2 (through the M5-M6 current mirror), M2 also operates under a constant inversion level, making $F(i_{f2})$ constant. Thus, if a voltage proportional to ϕ_t is attached to the source terminal of M2, with the right proportionality factor $F(i_{f2})$ adjusted (using the current mirror aspect relation K1), the equality of (5) can be satisfied. A non-zero equilibrium point is then reached in this circuit, that keeps $V_{G1} = V_{G2} = V_{T0}$ for any temperature. Since M2 operates with higher source voltage than M1, its inversion level has to be lower, or $F(i_{f2}) < 0$. This means that in our circuit M2 operates in the weak inversion region, and its PTAT source voltage can be generated by the self-cascode topology, presented in the next section.

The temperature dependence of the threshold voltage V_{T0} can be approximated by the linear equation (6).

$$V_{T0}(T) = V_{T0(nom)} + K_T(T - T_{nom}) \quad (6)$$

Where T is the absolute temperature, $V_{T0(nom)}$ is the threshold voltage at the nominal temperature T_{nom} and K_T is the thermal coefficient of the threshold voltage.

2.3 Self Cascode PTAT Generator

A well-known circuit used to generate a PTAT voltage independent of process parameters is the self-cascode MOSFET, introduced by Vittoz in 1977 [18] and shown in Fig. 2.

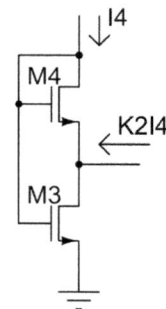

Figure 2: Self-Cascode PTAT generator schematic.

Transistor M3 has higher drain current than M4 but smaller aspect ratio, leading to different inversion levels on each transistor. While M4 must be in saturation, M3 can be in saturation or in triode. The difference between their gate-source voltages appear across the drain-source terminals of M3. As done in [11], (3) and (4) demonstrate that this voltage is proportional to the thermal voltage. It is given by

$$V_{SC} = V_{DS3} = \phi_t[F(i_{f3}) - F(i_{if4})] \quad (7)$$

Usually both transistors operate in weak inversion, but (7) shows that as long as the inversion levels of both transistors are kept constant over temperature, they generate an ideal PTAT voltage under any inversion level [11]. This can be achieved by biasing them with current $I_4 = K_3 I_{SQ}$, where K_3 is constant with process and temperature. (7) then becomes

$$V_{SC} = \phi_t \left[F\left(\frac{K_3}{S_3}(K_2 + 1) \right) - F\left(\frac{K_3}{S_4} \right) \right] \quad (8)$$

From (8) it is clear that the PTAT voltage generated by the self-cascode MOSFET depends only on geometrical factors, and not on fabrication process parameters.

2.4 Unbalanced Differential Pair PTAT Generator

Another common PTAT generator structure is the unbalanced differential pair, introduced by Tsividis in 1978 [16], that operates in weak inversion. This circuit is shown in Fig. 3, where K_4 and K_5 are the aspect ratio relations of M8-M9 and M11-M10, respectively.

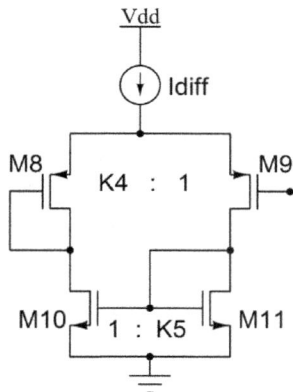

Figure 3: Differential Pair PTAT generator schematic.

In this circuit, M8 and M9 share the same source connection, and the PTAT voltage develops across the two gates. This is an interesting alternative that doesn't load the previous circuit, since it is connected to a gate terminal. By using the ACM model, it is possible to extend the operation of this circuit to all inversion levels, as was done for the self-cascode structure. Assuming that all transistors are in saturation and using (3) and (4), the PTAT voltage generated by the differential pair V_{DIFF} is given by (9).

$$V_{DIFF} = V_{G9} - V_{G8} = n\phi_t[F(i_{f9}) - F(i_{f8})] \quad (9)$$

Eq. (9) is very similar to (7), only differing by the multiplying factor n. Since the M8-M9 pair is biased by the M10-M11 mirror, one can conclude that $i_{f9}/i_{f8} = K_4 K_5$. Thus also this circuit generates a PTAT voltage independent of the inversion region, as long as the inversion levels i_{f8} and i_{f9} themselves are kept constant. Again, this is achieved by biasing the differential pair with a current $I_{DIFF} = K_6 I_{SQ}$, that can be obtained by mirroring the current I_{D1} of the

V_{T0} extractor of Fig. 1. Eq. (9) then becomes

$$V_{DIFF} = n\phi_t \left[F\left(\frac{K_4 K_5 K_6}{(1 + K_4)S_8} \right) - F\left(\frac{K_6}{(1 + K_4)S_8} \right) \right] \quad (10)$$

This voltage is less ideal than that generated by the self-cascode (8), because the subthreshold slope n varies slightly with process and temperature.

2.5 Voltage Reference Circuit

The complete circuit of the proposed voltage reference can be seen in Fig. 4. Transistors M1-M7 form the threshold voltage extractor, being transistors M3-M4 the self-cascode PTAT generator. The unbalanced differential pairs are made of transistors M8-M17, and are sized exactly the same to produce a total PTAT voltage that is twice that of a single cell. Since we choose $i_{f1} = 3$, $I_{D1} = 3S_1 I_{SQ}$, and this current is mirrored to bias the rest of the circuit through pMOS transistors M5-M7, M12 and M17.

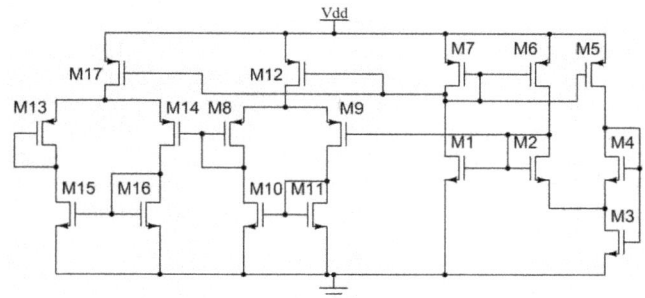

Figure 4: Proposed voltage reference schematic.

The reference voltage V_{REF}, at the gate of M13, is the sum of a CTAT term given by (6) and twice the PTAT term given by (9), hence:

$$V_{REF} = V_{G1} + 2V_{DIFF} = V_{T0} + 2n\phi_t[F(i_{f9}) - F(i_{if8})] \quad (11)$$

3. DESIGN METHODOLOGY

The design procedure starts by setting the forward inversion level of M1 $i_{f1} = 3$. A small aspect ratio for M1 and M2 is necessary to achieve low power operation. Through current mirror gain K_1 the inversion level of M2 can be defined. A high value of K1 favors low power consumption, but it also forces the source voltage of M2, generated by the self-cascode pair M3-M4, to be higher. According to (8), this can be done by increasing the ratio S_4/S_3, or by bringing M3 and M4 into moderate or strong inversion. If too high a PTAT voltage is generated, it can put transistor M2 in triode, since its drain voltage is decreasing and its source voltage is increasing with temperature. A good compromise can be reached between power consumption and aspect ratio gain by setting M5 = M6, making $I_{D3} = 2I_{D4}$.

Once the threshold voltage extractor is designed, differentiating (11) with respect to temperature, and equating it to zero provides the necessary inversion level of M8-M9 and M13-M14, together with aspect ratio and current gains K_4 and K_5 to make the output V_{REF} temperature independent. Since M8-M17 are all operating in weak inversion, to keep the power consumption low, the value of the current mirror gain K_6 doesn't affect heavily the PTAT voltage generated. It is designed to guarantee that all transistors are kept in saturation over the whole operating temperature range. The same is true for the nMOS current mirrors M10-M11 and M15-M16 aspect ratios. The resulting voltages and their derivatives, simulated in Matlab, can be seen in Fig. 5.

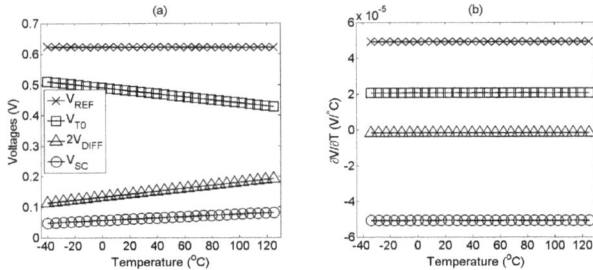

Figure 5: Analytical model. (a) Voltages versus temperature; (b) first derivative over temperature.

The MOSFET parameters used for this demonstration come from a standard I/O transistor from the $0.13\mu m$ process design kit library. V_{T0} was extracted through simulation using the gm/id methodology described in [13], being $V_{T0(nom)} = 476$ mV, $T_{nom} = 27\,°C$ and $K_T = -500\,\mu V/°C$. The constant design factors used are $K_1 = 6$, $K_2 = 2$, $K_3 = 1$, $K_4 = 2$, $K_5 = 4$ and $K_6 = 1.5$, while the aspect ratios are $S_1 = 1/30$, $S_3 = 2/50$, $S_4 = 6.6/50$ and $S_8 = 1$.

4. SIMULATION RESULTS

The results presented here are for SPICE post-layout simulations, and accurately match the analytical design of section 3. The implementation takes into consideration good matching layout practices such as common-centroid structures and dummies. The occupied silicon area is 0.0099 mm^2, as shown in Fig. 6, while the final MOSFET sizes are presented in Table 1.

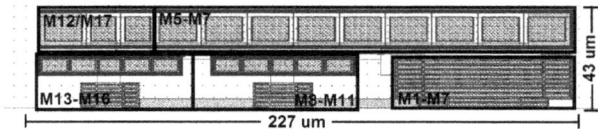

Figure 6: Layout of the proposed voltage reference in $0.13\mu m$ CMOS.

Table 1: Implemented MOSFET sizing.

	M1	M2	M3	M4	M5	M6	M7	M8	M9
W (μm)	1	1	2*1	6*1.1	10	10	6*10	2*5	5
L (μm)	30	30	50	50	15	15	15	10	8.4

	M10	M11	M12	M13	M14	M15	M16	M17
W (μm)	1	4*1	10	2*5	5	1	4*1	10
L (μm)	10	10	10	10	8.4	10	10	10

The voltage extractor circuit employs positive feedback, and the stability of the equilibrium point $V_{G1} = V_{T0}$ must be guaranteed. Opening the loop on the gate of M1, and by varying V_{G1} while observing the resulting V_{G2}, the operating

point can be found and the loop gain can be calculated. This is shown in Fig. 7.

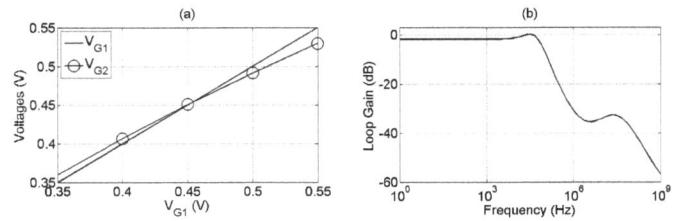

Figure 7: (a) DC operating point; (b) Loop gain versus frequency around DC operating point.

There is only one crossing point of both lines, which happens for $V_{G1} = V_{T0}$ - Fig. 7(a). Fig. 7 (b) shows the loop gain at the crossing point, being less than 0 dB and thus providing a stable operating point.

Fig. 8(a) presents V_{T0} over temperature estimated by the gm/id method [13] (labeled ACM), and simulated in the V_{T0} extractor circuit of Fig. 4 (labeled VTEX). The error defined as $Error(\%) = 100(V_{TEX} - V_{ACM})/V_{ACM}$ is presented in Fig. 8(b). The circuit tracks the ideal threshold with an error inferior to 1.5% under the whole operating temperature range.

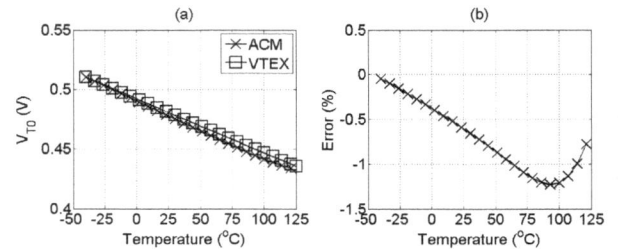

Figure 8: (a) Proposed circuit and gm/id extracted threshold voltage. (b) Error.

This CTAT voltage can then be added to the PTAT voltage generated by the unbalanced differential pairs, resulting in a reference voltage of 625 mV, as shown in Fig.9a. The effective temperature coefficient, as given by (12), is 2.3 ppm/°C for the temperature range of -40 to 125 °C, operating at $V_{DD} = 1.2$ V.

$$TC_{EFF} = \frac{V_{REF_{max}} - V_{REF_{min}}}{(T_{max} - T_{min})V_{REF(27°C)}} \quad (12)$$

In Fig.9b the behavior of each voltage over temperature is presented. It shows the extracted threshold voltage V_{T0}, the unbalanced differential pairs PTAT voltage $2V_{DIFF}$ and the temperature independent V_{REF}. It also presents the PTAT voltage V_{SC}, generated by the self-cascode structure M3-M4 used in the threshold voltage extractor circuit. Fig.9c presents the currents in each branch over the -40 to 125 °C temperature range. The current consumption at 27 °C for the whole circuit is 33 nA, reaching a maximum of 44 nA at 125 °C. This results in power consumptions of 39.6 nW and 52.8 nW respectively, for a 1.2 V supply.

Startup behavior of the circuit was simulated, having a settling time of less than 3 ms, which is acceptable for this proof of concept. We expect that leakage currents are enough

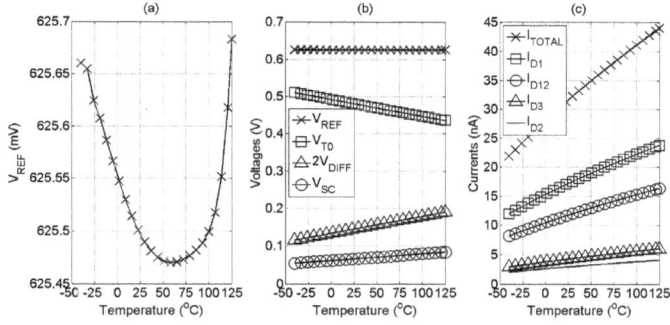

Figure 9: (a) V_{REF}; (b) V_{T0}, V_{DIFF} and V_{PTAT} voltages; (c) Currents over temperature.

to start the circuit, but in real applications a startup circuit could be necessary for faster settling.

Even though the nominal supply voltage of the process used is 1.2 V, the proposed implementation starts operating around 0.9 V with acceptable TC, as shown in Fig. 10b. The circuit was designed to reach a minimum TC at 1.2 V. Shown in Fig. 10(c), the line sensitivity of V_{REF} is 35.2 mV/V, while the current consumption sensitivity is 21.88 nA/V, both from 0.9 V to 1.2 V supply. The power supply rejection ratio (PSRR) measured at 100 Hz and $V_{DD} = 1.2$ V is around -30 dB - Fig. 10a.

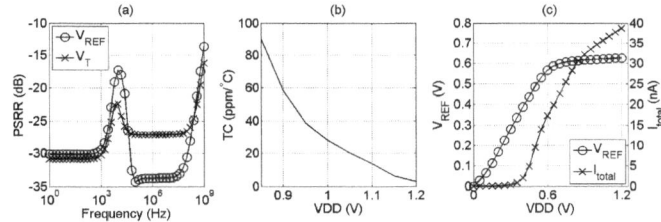

Figure 10: (a) PSRR; (b) TC_{EFF}; (c) V_{REF} and I_{TOTAL} line sensitivities.

Table 2 presents a comparison of recently published low-power, resistorless voltage references in different CMOS technologies. Since most of these works report experimental data, we have selected the best case for each reference in order to compare them with our simulation results. The greatest advantage of our circuit topology is the low temperature coefficient over the widest temperature range, consuming low power while occupying a small silicon area. A clear drawback of our reference resides in its high supply sensitivity and consequently low PSRR. These could be increased by adding cascode current sources, for example, at the penalty of increasing the minimum supply voltage.

As noted before by other authors [9], reports of variability results in such voltage references are still somewhat poor, specially regarding experimental results from a significant number of samples, and from different fabrication batches, which would reveal the average process variability dependencies. To analyze the fabrication variability of the circuit, Monte Carlo (MC) simulation was done separately for local mismatch effects and average process variations, with 1000 runs each. For average process MC all the transistors have their parameters changed equally in each run. For local

mismatch MC, the parameters of each transistor are varied individually in each run. Both effects are taken into account in a full variability analysis.

Fig. 11(a) shows the spread of the reference voltage, with a $\sigma/\mu = 3.63\%$ for mean process variation, while local mismatch, shown in Fig.11(c), yields $\sigma/\mu = 1.32\%$. Since both are relevant, Fig. 11(e) also shows simulation results for the two types of variability combined, yielding $\sigma/\mu = 4\%$. Another relevant parameter that is affected by fabrication spread is the thermal coefficient, which suffers more from local mismatch - Fig. 11(d), than from mean process variations - Fig. 11(b). This is expected since the thermal voltage dependence constant K_T and the PTAT voltage derivative are fairly insensitive to such mean variations. When both local mismatch and average process are considered, the TC reaches a maximum value of 76 ppm/°C - Fig. 11(f).

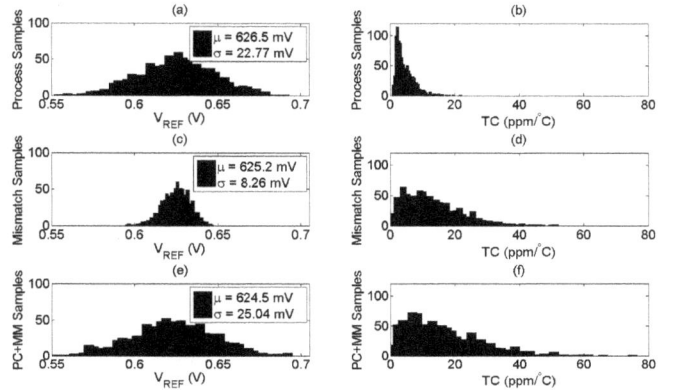

Figure 11: V_{REF} and TC_{EFF} Monte Carlo results. Average process variation on (a) and (b); Local mismatch on (c) and (d); Both on (e) and (f).

The circuit has been sent to fabrication in a 0.13μm CMOS process through the MOSIS educational program. Similar results were obtained from simulations using other MOSFETs from the same 0.13μm technology, and re-designed on a 0.18μm process as well.

5. CONCLUSIONS

A novel resistorless ultra-low-power voltage reference circuit was presented. It is composed by a threshold voltage extractor circuit and a PTAT generator working in weak inversion. Post-layout simulations for a 0.13μm CMOS technology demonstrate a reference voltage of 625 mV with a power consumption of 40 nW under 1.2 V supply at 27 °C. The main advantage is the low temperature coefficient of 2.3 ppm/°C from -40 to 125 °C, with an implemented silicon area of 0.0099 mm^2. Monte Carlo simulations show that the spread of the reference voltage is $\sigma/\mu = 4\%$ for both process mean variation and local mismatch, while the maximum temperature coefficient is 75 ppm/°C. The design presented is a proof of concept, optimized for thermal stability. Other metrics such as silicon area, power consumption and line sensitivity can be improved, according to the ultra-low-power application requirements.

Table 2: Comparison of recent resistorless CMOS Voltage References

(+) experimental; (*) simulation	[3]+	[17]+	[8]+	[5]+	[12]+	[9]+	[20]*	[6]*	**This Work***	Unit
Technology	0.35	0.35	0.5	0.18	0.18	0.18	0.18	0.18	**0.13**	μm
CTAT Voltage	V_{T0}	V_{T0}	V_{EB}	V_{T0}	V_{T0}	V_{EB}	V_{T0}	V_{EB}	V_{T0}	–
Temperature Range	0 – 80	-20 – 80	-40 – 120	0 – 125	-20 – 80	-40 – 120	-20 – 80	0 – 125	**-40-125**	°C
Temperature Coefficient	10	7	11.8	142	176.4	114	19.4	7	**2.3**	ppm/°C
Power @ $V_{DD_{nom}}$, 27°C	36	300	$6.48 \cdot 10^5$	3.15	0.011	52.5	180	5.7	**39.6**	nW
V_{REF}	670	745	1.23	263.5	328	548	633	479	**625**	mV
V_{DD}	0.9 – 4	1.4 – 3	3.6	0.45 – 2	0.5 – 3.6	0.7 – 1.8	0.85 – 2.5	0.85 - 1.8	**0.9 – 1.2**	V
Line Sensitivity	2700	20	-	4400	440	-	0.024	2112	**35200**	ppm/V
PSRR @ 100 Hz	-47	-45	-31.8	-45	-49	-56	-76	-48	**-30**	dB
Silicon Area	0.045	0.055	0.1	0.043	0.0014	0.0246	–	0.0014	**0.0099**	mm²

6. ACKNOWLEDGMENTS

The authors gratefully acknowledge the support of CI-BRASIL, MOSIS Educational Program and CNPq.

7. REFERENCES

[1] E. Camacho-Galeano, C. Galup-Montoro, and M. Schneider. A 2-nw 1.1-v self-biased current reference in cmos technology. *Circuits and Systems II: Express Briefs, IEEE Transactions on*, 52(2):61–65, Feb 2005.

[2] A. Cunha, M. Schneider, and C. Galup-Montoro. An mos transistor model for analog circuit design. *Solid-State Circuits, IEEE Journal of*, 33(10):1510–1519, 1998.

[3] G. De Vita and G. Iannaccone. A sub-1-v, 10 ppm/c, nanopower voltage reference generator. *Solid-State Circuits, IEEE Journal of*, 42(7):1536–1542, 2007.

[4] H. Klimach, M. Monteiro, A. Costa, and S. Bampi. Resistorless switched-capacitor bandgap voltage reference with low sensitivity to process variations. *Electronics Letters*, 49(23):1448–1449, 2013.

[5] L. Magnelli, F. Crupi, P. Corsonello, C. Pace, and G. Iannaccone. A 2.6 nw, 0.45 v temperature-compensated subthreshold cmos voltage reference. *Solid-State Circuits, IEEE Journal of*, 46(2):465–474, 2011.

[6] O. E. Mattia, H. Klimach, and S. Bampi. 0.9 v, 5 nw, 9 ppm/'c resistorless sub-bandgap voltage reference in 0.18um cmos. In *Circuits and Systems (LASCAS), 2014 IEEE Fifth Latin American Symposium on*, 2014.

[7] G. Meijer, P. C. Schmale, and K. Van Zalinge. A new curvature-corrected bandgap reference. *Solid-State Circuits, IEEE Journal of*, 17(6):1139–1143, 1982.

[8] X. Ming, Y.-Q. Ma, Z. kun Zhou, and B. Zhang. A high-precision compensated cmos bandgap voltage reference without resistors. *Circuits and Systems II: Express Briefs, IEEE Transactions on*, 57(10):767–771, 2010.

[9] Y. Osaki, T. Hirose, N. Kuroki, and M. Numa. 1.2-v supply, 100-nw, 1.09-v bandgap and 0.7-v supply, 52.5-nw, 0.55-v subbandgap reference circuits for nanowatt cmos lsis. *Solid-State Circuits, IEEE Journal of*, 48(6):1530–1538, 2013.

[10] G. Rincon-Mora and P. Allen. A 1.1-v current-mode and piecewise-linear curvature-corrected bandgap reference. *Solid-State Circuits, IEEE Journal of*, 33(10):1551–1554, 1998.

[11] C. Rossi, C. Galup-Montoro, and M. C. Schneider. Ptat voltage generator based on an mos voltage divider. In *NSTI Nanotech*, volume 3, pages 625–628, 2007.

[12] M. Seok, G. Kim, D. Blaauw, and D. Sylvester. A portable 2-transistor picowatt temperature-compensated voltage reference operating at 0.5 v. *Solid-State Circuits, IEEE Journal of*, 47(10):2534–2545, 2012.

[13] O. F. Siebel, M. C. Schneider, and C. Galup-Montoro. {MOSFET} threshold voltage: Definition, extraction, and some applications. *Microelectronics Journal*, 43(5):329 – 336, 2012. Special Section {NANOTECH} 2011.

[14] B.-S. Song and P. Gray. A precision curvature-compensated cmos bandgap reference. *Solid-State Circuits, IEEE Journal of*, 18(6):634–643, 1983.

[15] Y. Tsividis. Accurate analysis of temperature effects in i/sub c/v/sub be/ characteristics with application to bandgap reference sources. *Solid-State Circuits, IEEE Journal of*, 15(6):1076–1084, 1980.

[16] Y. Tsividis and R. Ulmer. A cmos voltage reference. *Solid-State Circuits, IEEE Journal of*, 13(6):774–778, 1978.

[17] K. Ueno, T. Hirose, T. Asai, and Y. Amemiya. A 300 nw, 15 ppm/c, 20 ppm/v cmos voltage reference circuit consisting of subthreshold mosfets. *Solid-State Circuits, IEEE Journal of*, 44(7):2047–2054, 2009.

[18] E. Vittoz and J. Fellrath. Cmos analog integrated circuits based on weak inversion operations. *Solid-State Circuits, IEEE Journal of*, 12(3):224–231, 1977.

[19] R. Widlar. New developments in ic voltage regulators. *Solid-State Circuits, IEEE Journal of*, 6(1):2–7, 1971.

[20] Y. Zeng, Y. Huang, Y. Luo, and H.-Z. Tan. An ultra-low-power {CMOS} voltage reference generator based on body bias technique. *Microelectronics Journal*, 44(12):1145 – 1153, 2013.

A Bipolar ±40 mV Self-Starting Boost Converter with Transformer Reuse for Thermoelectric Energy Harvesting

Nachiket V. Desai
Massachusetts Institute of Technology
77 Massachusetts Avenue
Cambridge, Massachusetts 02139
ndesai@mit.edu

Yogesh K. Ramadass
Texas Instruments
12500 TI Boulevard
Dallas, Texas 75243
yogesh.ramadass@ti.com

Anantha P. Chandrakasan
Massachusetts Institute of Technology
77 Massachusetts Avenue
Cambridge, Massachusetts 02139
anantha@mtl.mit.edu

ABSTRACT

This paper presents a converter for boosting the low-voltage output of thermoelectric energy harvesters to power standard CMOS circuits. The converter can start up from a fully de-energized state off a bipolar ±40 mV input and can harvest net positive energy from voltages as low as ±30 mV in steady state. A single transformer is multiplexed between an oscillator that is used during startup and a flyback converter that is used during steady-state operation. During steady-state operation, the converter is automatically shut off if the input power is found to be too low. Simulation results on the converter designed in a 0.35 μm CMOS process demonstrate a peak steady-state conversion efficiency of 68% at an output voltage of 5.5 V and input voltage range between 30 mV and 500 mV in magnitude.

Categories and Subject Descriptors

B.7.1 [**Integrated Circuits**]: Types and Design Styles

General Terms

Design, Performance

Keywords

energy harvesting, thermoelectric generators, flyback converters, Meissner oscillator, bipolar input, flux-commutation

1. INTRODUCTION

Advances in low-power biomedical and industrial sensor design [9, 3, 13] have made energy harvesting an attractive alternative to batteries for powering wearable or otherwise hard-to-reach sensors. Such constraints on the location of these sensors also preclude the use of solar or vibration energy harvesters as a source of energy. Thermal energy har-

vesting is a likely candidate owing to the presence of reasonable thermal gradients in industrial settings, or between the human body and the environment. Thermoelectric generators (TEGs) that are capable of powering wristwatches and sub-mW radios have been explored and demonstrated [8, 11].

Bulk-mode TEGs typically generate 20-30 mV at open-circuit for every 1 K of temperature difference across them and are typically modeled as a Thevenin source with output impedance as low as 2 Ω [10]. Harvesting energy using these devices usually implies working off an output voltage as low as 30 mV in the worst case, when the temperature difference across the device is around 2 K and the converter loads the TEG to 70% of its open-circuit voltage. Boost converters are typically used to convert these voltages to levels where CMOS circuits can be powered. Starting up these converters proves to be a significant challenge since most switches have threshold voltages far exceeding the output of the TEG. This problem has been addressed by incorporating a battery [5] to operate the switches during startup or a motion-activated mechanical switch [10]: approaches that can significantly increase the cost and complexity of integration. A low-voltage negative resistance oscillator along with a charge multiplier using native MOSFETs is used for startup in [12].

In addition to the low magnitude, the polarity of the induced voltage depends on the direction of heat flow, which could vary across different applications or within the same application (such as HVAC systems). Two separate transformer-based oscillators are used in [1] for both low-voltage startup and steady-state operation, one each for each polarity. A transformer-based oscillator for startup and a transformer-based boost converter are used in [6], leading to higher efficiency but with the capability to support a single polarity. This paper presents a circuit topology that uses a single transformer for starting up and operating in steady state from a bipolar supply. The transformer-based Meissner oscillator is modified to ensure the conditions for oscillation are maintained irrespective of supply polarity, and the flyback converter uses flux commutation inside the core for steady-state operation.

2. MEISSNER OSCILLATOR

The harvester uses a transformer-based oscillator for starting up from a state of zero energy in the system. Once enough energy has been built up to power the clock gener-

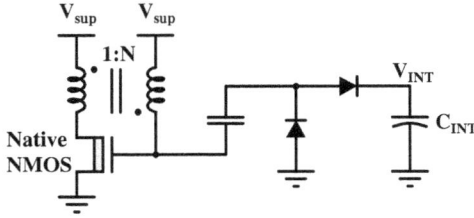

Figure 1: Schematic of Meissner oscillator

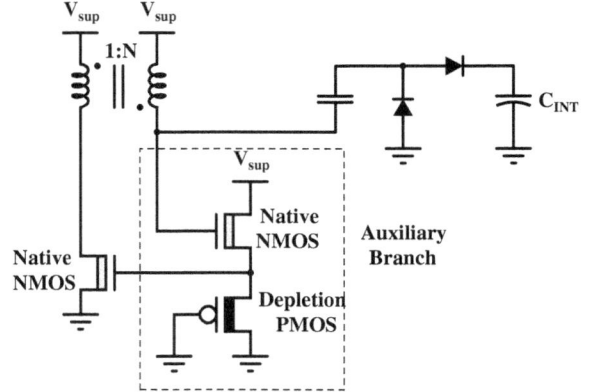

Figure 2: Schematic of modified Meissner oscillator for bipolar operation

ators and gate drives, the flyback converter is activated for steady-state operation. An intermediate crude flyback stage is also used to speed up the startup process. The operation of the transformer-based Meissner oscillator and its derivative capable of operating from bipolar supply voltages are described in detail below.

2.1 Unipolar Operation

A schematic of the Meissner oscillator is shown in figure 1. This oscillator is similar to the one presented in [4]. Since oscillations in the zero energy state need to start up from the low (≈ 30 mV) supply, a native NMOS device with zero threshold voltage is used to obtain reasonable g_m without sacrificing voltage gain due to the low output impedance of depletion mode devices. Connecting the secondary to the supply instead of ground also serves to increase the g_m and thus the loop gain during startup. A transformer with large (N = 20, 50, 100) turns ratio is used to satisfy the loop gain condition. The phase condition is satisfied by the specific connection of the terminals of the transformer. Neglecting leakage inductances, the loop gain of the oscillator is

$$L_{pos}(s) = (-g_m s L_1) \cdot (-N) \cdot \frac{1}{s^2 L_2 C_g + s R_2 C_g + 1} \quad (1)$$

where C_g is the total capacitance from the gate of the native MOS transistor to ac ground, which includes the gate-source capacitance of the transistor and the winding capacitance of the transformer secondary coil. L_1 and L_2 are the inductances measured looking into the primary and secondary of the transformer respectively and R_2 is the winding loss referred to the secondary side of the transformer. The first term in equation (1) is the gain of the common-source amplifier formed by the transistor and the primary side of the transformer, the second term captures the transformer turns' ratio and the way the terminals of the transformer are connected, and the third term corresponds to the loading of the transformer secondary by the gate capacitance C_g.

From equation (1), the circuit oscillates at $f = \left(2\pi\sqrt{L_2 C_g}\right)^{-1}$. The secondary terminal is coupled to a diode rectifier through a DC-blocking capacitor. The diode rectifier charges a low capacitance node V_{INT}, since the oscillator cannot supply a large load current while satisfying conditions for oscillation.

2.2 Bipolar Operation

The expression for loop gain in equation (1) is valid when the supply voltage is positive. For negative supply voltage the loop gain changes to

$$L_{neg}(s) = \frac{g_m s L_1}{1 + g_m s L_1} \cdot (-N) \cdot \frac{1}{s^2 L_2 C_{gs} + s R_2 C_{gs} + 1} \quad (2)$$

The change in the first term of equation (2) compared to equation (1) results in a reduction in magnitude and inver-

sion of phase of the loop gain, which makes the circuit incapable of oscillation when the supply voltage is negative. An intuitive explanation for this is that the native NMOS acts as a source follower instead of a common source amplifier when the supply voltage is negative. The phase shift encountered upon traversing the loop at the frequency where the loop gain is real is then π radians, which causes the oscillation conditions to not be met.

In figure 2, we introduce a circuit that can oscillate with a supply voltage of either polarity. This is done by introducing an auxiliary amplifier/source follower branch to complement the action of the native NMOS. This branch acts as a source follower when the supply voltage is positive and has no effect on the phase of the loop function at resonance. For negative supply voltages, the auxiliary branch acts as a common source amplifier and inverts the phase of the loop gain to satisfy the oscillation criteria. Instead of using a resistive load on the auxiliary branch, an appropriately-sized depletion mode PMOS is used so that the branch can be turned off after the startup phase is completed.

With the auxiliary branch, the loop transfer functions change to

$$L_{pos,aux}(s) = L_{pos}(s) \cdot \frac{g_{m,aux} r_{o,aux}}{1 + g_{m,aux} r_{o,aux}} \quad (3)$$

$$L_{neg,aux}(s) = L_{neg}(s) \cdot (-g_{m,aux} r_{o,aux}) \quad (4)$$

where $L_{pos}(s)$ and $L_{neg}(s)$ are as defined in equations (1) and (2), $g_{m,aux}$ is the transconductance of the native MOS transistor in the auxiliary branch and $r_{o,aux}$ is the small-signal output resistance of the auxiliary branch. The current through the auxiliary branch is scaled down from that through the transformer primary branch to ensure the $g_m r_o$ product remains the same in magnitude at the resonant frequency. This ensures that the magnitude of the startup voltage remains the same irrespective of the polarity of the supply.

3. FLYBACK CONVERTER

In order to use the same transformer that was used in section 2 as the magnetic energy storage element for a boost converter, the standard inductor-based topology has been modified to a topology resembling the flyback converter. An unoptimized version of this modified topology is shown in

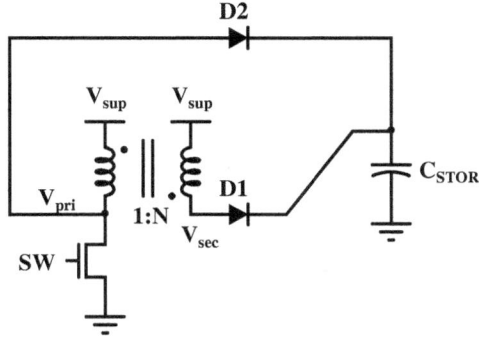

Figure 3: Schematic of unoptimized flyback converter

Table 1: Energy harvesting transformer parasitics

Turns Ratio	Primary Winding Capacitance (C_p)	Secondary Winding Capacitance (C_s)
1:20	4.05 nF	6 pF
1:50	26.7 nF	4.8 pF
1:100	84.4 nF	2.8 pF

figure 3. A switch connected to the primary side of the transformer stores energy in the transformer core in one phase of the driver clock cycle. The stored energy is transferred to the output in the complementary phase by the secondary. Diodes D1 and D2 conduct when the supply is negative and positive respectively.

The converter operates in DCM using PFM control. The low-power control circuits used for the main flyback converter that monitor the output OV, UV etc. operate at 2 kHz [7]. Based on the output resistance of the TEG being used for an application, the on-time of the switch can be set to achieve near-MPPT condition.

3.1 Transformer Flux Commutation

The transformers used for the targeted application [2] have large turns ratios and thus large primary winding capacitances, as shown in table 1. Due to this large parasitic capacitance on the primary, the node V_{pri} in figure 3 cannot rise a diode drop above V_{STOR} for diode D2 to turn on when the supply is positive. Instead, when the switch turns off under a positive supply the flux in the transformer core *commutates* as a result of the resonance between the primary winding inductance and its associated parasitic capacitance. Diode D1, being connected to the secondary, can easily conduct once the flux in the core changes directions. This is shown in figure 4. This also prevents the large voltage generated by the transformer on the V_{sec} node in the case where D2 conducts in figure 3. Since diode D2 in figure 3 is not used for either polarity of the converter input V_{sup}, it can be dropped from the circuit.

In order to allow for the transformer flux to commutate when V_{sup} is positive, the flyback converter switch needs to be turned off for sufficient time. Based on the secondary winding inductance values in [2] and the capacitance values in table 1, the worst case oscillation period is 2.8 μs for the

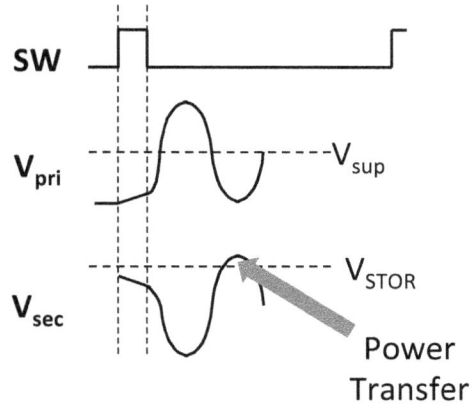

Figure 4: Waveforms for flux commutation in transformer core for positive supply voltage

1:100 transformer. To accommodate this minimum off-time, the switching period of the flyback converter is chosen to be 16 μs and the maximum possible on-time is 12 μs. Since the flux commutation requires less than a full oscillation period of the secondary winding inductance and capacitance, this allows sufficient time for flux commutation for every on-time setting.

3.2 Intermediate Crude Flyback Converter

If the bipolar Meissner oscillator of section 2 were used to charge the large (≈ 5 μF) output capacitor C_{STOR}, it would either cease to oscillate or slow down the startup process considerably because of its limited current-driving capability. Instead, the oscillator is made to charge up a relatively small capacitor C_{INT}, which is isolated from C_{STOR}, to around 600 mV. The energy stored in C_{INT} is used to operate a ring oscillator that drives a small, low-V_{th} switch that drives the flyback converter and charges the output capacitor C_{STOR}. The low-V_{th} crude-stage switch and normal V_{th} main switch in figure 5 can be connected in parallel since flux-commutation ensures that the drain of the switches doesn't rise enough to damage the former. The main low-side switch that operates during steady-state is switched at the output voltage, which can be as high as 5.5 V, and achieves higher efficiency.

4. CONVERTER STARTUP AND STATE TRANSITIONS

4.1 Transformer Multiplexing

The secondary coil of the transformer in the flyback converter of figure 5 is connected to the output through a diode and a pass gate. The pass gate allows the path to C_{STOR} to be turned off when the bipolar Meissner oscillator is operating. The complete schematic of the oscillator is shown in figure 5. The diode rectifier branch going to C_{INT} goes through a depletion mode PMOS device which is only turned off when the flyback converter is operating.

On the primary side, the native NMOS transistor from the bipolar Meissner oscillator is connected in series to a depletion mode PMOS switch that turns off the branch when the flyback converter commences operation, as shown in figure 5.

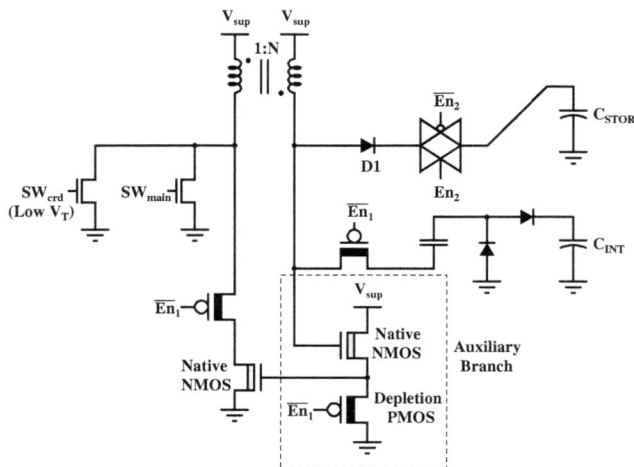

Figure 5: Complete schematic of converter with bipolar Meissner oscillator on the bottom and dual flyback stages on the top

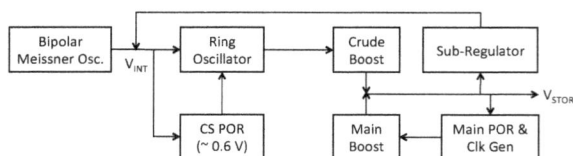

Figure 6: Block diagram of complete thermoelectric energy harvesting system

This branch is connected in parallel to the two switches from the flyback converter on the primary side of the transformer.

4.2 Startup State Transitions

A complete block diagram of the converter is shown in figure 6, while the states transitioned by the converter before reaching steady state are shown in figure 7. During cold-start, the bipolar Meissner oscillator charges C_{INT}. Once V_{INT} crosses the cold start Power-On Reset (POR) threshold, the flyback converter is operated in the crude-boost mode to charge C_{STOR} till V_{INT} falls below a hysteretic threshold (between 630 mV and 540 mV at 25°C and nominal corner). The bipolar Meissner oscillator then takes over again to charge C_{INT} back to the POR level. The POR trigger-on threshold varies from 630 mV at 25°C and nominal process corner to 500 mV at 100°C and fast corner. During this period C_{STOR} holds most of its stored charge since the main sensing and control circuits driven by V_{STOR} have not yet been activated.

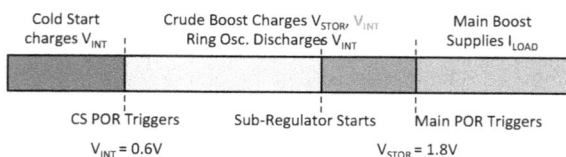

Figure 7: State transition diagram of converter during startup

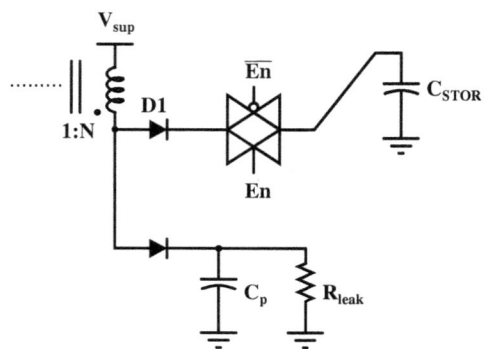

Figure 8: Schematic of circuit used to store maximum value of voltage on anode of diode D1. The circuit on the primary side of the transformer is the same as in figure 5.

Once V_{STOR} exceeds the POR trigger-on level by the threshold voltage of a low-V_{th} switch, energy can be directly transferred from C_{STOR} to C_{INT} using a sub-regulator, considerably speeding up the startup. Once C_{STOR} is charged to 1.8 V, the main-POR goes high, the main oscillator and control circuits [7] (operating at 2 kHz) are activated, and the main primary side switch is used. Upon reaching steady-state operation the startup circuits are disabled using depletion-mode PMOS gating switches to reduce loss in the converter.

5. AUTOMATIC SHUTDOWN

The thermoelectric energy harvester's output can drop to arbitrarily low power levels depending on the operating conditions. Below a threshold, the net energy stored in the magnetic core of the transformer when the low-side of the flyback converter is on becomes insufficient to charge the parasitics on the high-side and turn on D1 in figure 5 while the switching losses stay the same irrespective of the TEG voltage. In this scenario, the net energy harvested is negative and it is beneficial to shut down the converter till more favorable conditions arise.

To detect this condition, the maximum value of the voltage at the anode of diode D1 is stored on a capacitor C_p with a large shunt resistor R_{leak} to leak the stored charge with a large time constant, as shown in figure 8. When the input is large enough to turn D1 on and supply net positive energy, the voltage stored on the capacitor C_p is a few hundred mV above V_{STOR}. This voltage is compared against V_{STOR} using a clocked strong-ARM comparator with 1:2 sized input transistors. This provides enough input offset across PVT variation to prevent a small difference (< 100 mV) between the voltages across C_p and C_{STOR} from making the comparator signal that the TEG voltage is large enough to supply net positive energy. The output of the comparator is checked at the 2 kHz system clock frequency. When the converter shuts off in the absence of adequate power to harvest, only the control circuits that run on the 2 kHz system clock with 330 nA quiescent current are left on. The converter is turned on for 16 cycles every two seconds to check if net positive energy can be harvested.

6. SIMULATION RESULTS

The converter was designed and simulated in a 0.35 μm high-voltage CMOS process. TEGs were modeled as a volt-

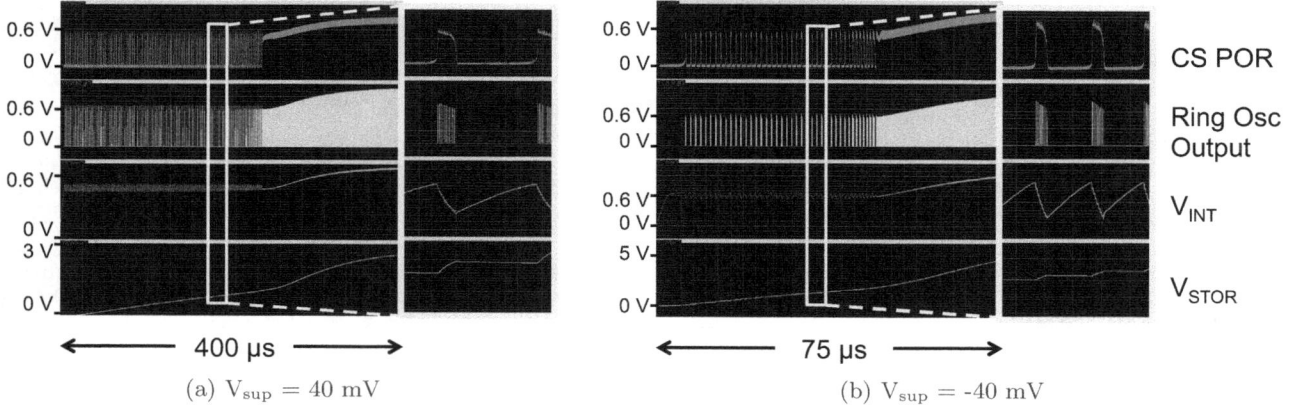

(a) $V_{sup} = 40$ mV

(b) $V_{sup} = -40$ mV

Figure 9: Simulated transient waveforms for startup with 1:100 transformer and bipolar harvester output voltages

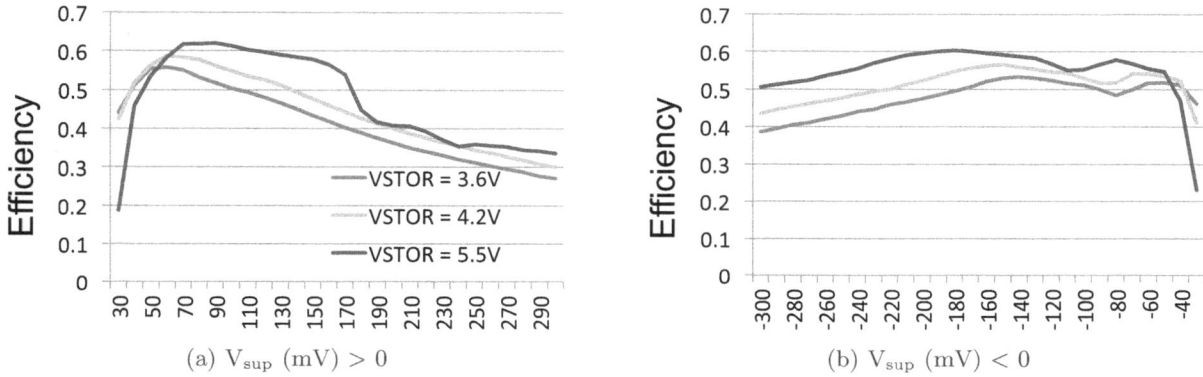

(a) V_{sup} (mV) > 0

(b) V_{sup} (mV) < 0

Figure 10: Flyback converter efficiency plots for different input voltages for N=100 transformer and a TEG with 5 Ω output resistance, at 70% input regulation and with different V_{STOR} values

age source in series with a source resistance varying from 1 Ω to 5 Ω, based on which the on-time of the low-side switch in the flyback converter would be set to achieve near-MPPT condition. The transformer was modeled using measured values for the primary and secondary coil inductance, parasitic series resisistance and shunt capacitance, and the intercoil coupling coefficient.

Simulated waveforms for the converter startup at nominal process corner and 27°C are shown in figure 9 for N=100 and input voltages of ±40 mV. The V_{STOR} node drives the main control circuits which are power-gated off until the main POR triggers. In this simulation, the crude flyback converter is allowed to operate beyond the main POR trigger threshold (1.8 V) on V_{STOR} to demonstrate its reliability in charging the node. As described in section 4.2, the converter initially switches back and forth between the bipolar Meissner oscillator (ring oscillator, CS POR OFF) mode and the crude flyback (ring oscillator, CS POR ON) mode. The zoomed portion of the waveform shows the value of V_{STOR} rising in small increments for each cycle the ring oscillator is on. Once the sub-regulator turns on, the voltage V_{STOR} rises rapidly due to the positive feedback effect of V_{INT} rising increasing the amount of charge transferred in each cycle.

The self-start voltage rises to ±100 mV at 100°C and fast process corner.

In figure 9, the V_{STOR} node is charged up much faster in the case where the input voltage is negative than when the input in positive. This is because the POR voltage on V_{INT} where the bipolar Meissner oscillator turns off is set to be attainable by the oscillator across corners. This gate-drive level for the small switch on the primary side of the crude flyback converter is close to its V_{th}. The additional bias on this switch along with the lower threshold voltage when the input is negative increases the stored flux substantially, which strengthens the forward turn-on of the diode D1 in figure 6 and increases the amount of energy flowing to V_{STOR} in each iteration of the charge-discharge cycle of V_{INT}.

Simulated efficiency plots for the flyback converter with a 1:100 transformer and input voltage varying between ±30 mV and ±100 mV are shown in figure 10 with the output voltage clamped at voltage levels typical for power management IC inputs. For positive input voltages (section 5), the conversion efficiency drops sharply around 30 mV input because the initial flux in the transformer core is insufficient to charge the parasitic capacitance on the secondary side of the transformer to a diode drop above V_{STOR} and turn on the high-side diode. The efficiency decreases for larger

Table 2: Comparison with state-of-the-art thermoelectric energy harvesters

	Im et al.[6]	LTC3109[1]	**This work**
Input polarity	Unipolar	Bipolar	Bipolar
Xformer count	1	2	1
1:N	1:60	1:100	1:100 - 1:20
$V_{startup}$	40 mV	±30 mV	±40 mV
η_{peak}	61%	36%	68% [a]
P_{OUT}	2.7 mW [b]	600 μW [c]	470 μW [c]
V_{out}	2 V	2.35 - 5 V	1.8 - 5.5 V

[a] Efficiency at V_{sup} = 200 mV and V_{STOR} = 5.5 V with a 1:50 transformer

[b] At V_{sup} = 300 mV and V_{out} = 2 V

[c] At V_{sup} = 100 mV and V_{out} = 3.3 V with 1:100 transformer

positive input voltages because most of the energy transfer occurs through voltage transformation when the primary-side switch is on instead of flux commutation after the switch turns off. As positive V_{sup} increases, the open circuit voltage at the transformer secondary increases when the primary-side switch is on. Since the output is clamped at a fixed voltage, this decreases the efficiency of power transfer by increasing dissipation in the transformer. Depending on the input voltage range for the chosen application, a transformer with smaller turns ratio may be chosen to achieve maximum efficiency at the desired value of V_{sup}.

The efficiency for negative input voltages (section 5) stays fairly steady around the 60% mark. The conversion efficiency for negative inputs also falls sharply around 30 mV in magnitude for reasons similar to the case where the input is a small positive value. Since the high-side diode is reverse biased when the low-side switch of the flyback converter is on irrespective of the input voltage, the efficiency does not drop as sharply as it does for positive input voltage. Instead the losses at larger input voltage magnitudes arise from increased on-resistance of the low-side switch due to body-biasing of the transistor. A comparison with the state-of-the-art is presented in table 2.

7. CONCLUSIONS

A system for converting the low-voltage output of thermoelectric energy harvesters to higher voltages usable by CMOS circuits has been presented. The converter achieves bipolar input voltage-operation with the use of a single transformer. The transformer is multiplexed to allow for both ±40 mV input cold-startup using a bipolar Meissner oscillator and steady state operation at ±30 mV using a flux-commutating flyback topology. The flyback converter achieves 60% steady-state conversion efficiency for bipolar input voltages as low as 80 mV in magnitude with a 1:100 transformer and 68% at 200 mV with a 1:50 transformer. To the best of the authors' knowledge, this is the first system capable of low-voltage cold-startup and high-efficiency steady-state conversion from bipolar input voltages using a single multiplexed transformer.

8. REFERENCES

[1] LTC3109 - Auto-Polarity, Ultralow Voltage Step-Up Converter and Power Manager - Linear Technology.

[2] WE-EHPI Energy Harvesting Coupled Inductor - Product Catalog Passive Components - Würth Electronik.

[3] J. L. Bohorquez, M. Yip, A. P. Chandrakasan, and J. L. Dawson. A biomedical sensor interface with a sinc filter and interference cancellation. *IEEE J. Solid-State Circuits*, 46(4):746–756, Apr. 2011.

[4] J. Damaschke. Design of a low-input-voltage converter for thermoelectric generator. *IEEE Trans. Ind. Appl.*, 33(5):1203–1207, Sept. 1997.

[5] I. Doms, P. Merken, R. Mertens, and C. Van Hoof. Integrated capacitive power-management circuit for thermal harvesters with output power 10 to 1000μW. In *IEEE Int. Solid-State Circuits Conf. (ISSCC) Dig. Tech. Papers*, pages 300–301, Feb. 2009.

[6] J.-P. Im, S.-W. Wang, S.-T. Ryu, and G.-H. Cho. A 40 mV transformer-reuse self-startup boost converter with MPPT control for thermoelectric energy harvesting. *IEEE J. Solid-State Circuits*, 47(12):3055–3067, Dec. 2012.

[7] K. Kadirvel, Y. K. Ramadass, U. Lyles, J. Carpenter, V. Ivanov, V. McNeil, A. P. Chandrakasan, and B. Lum-Shue-Chan. A 330nA energy-harvesting charger with battery management for solar and thermoelectric energy harvesting. In *IEEE Int. Solid-State Circuits Conf. (ISSCC) Dig. Tech. Papers*, pages 106–108, Feb. 2012.

[8] M. Kishi, H. Nemoto, T. Hamao, M. Yamamoto, S. Sudou, M. Mandai, and S. Yamamoto. Micro thermoelectric modules and their application to wristwatches as an energy source. In *Proc. Intl. Conf. on Thermoelectrics*, pages 301–307, 1999.

[9] R. Min, M. Bhardwaj, E. Shih, A. Sinha, A. Wang, and A. Chandrakasan. Low-power wireless sensor networks. In *Intl. Conf. on VLSI Design*, pages 205–210, 2001.

[10] Y. K. Ramadass and A. P. Chandrakasan. A battery-less thermoelectric energy harvesting interface circuit with 35 mV startup voltage. *IEEE J. Solid-State Circuits*, 46(1):333–341, Jan. 2011.

[11] P. Spies, M. Pollak, and G. Rohmer. Energy harvesting for mobile communication devices. In *Intl. Telecomm. Energy Conf.*, pages 481–488, 2007.

[12] H.-Y. Tang, P.-S. Weng, P.-C. Ku, and L.-H. Lu. A fully electrical startup batteryless boost converter with 50mV input voltage for thermoelectric energy harvesting. In *Dig. Symp. VLSI Circuits*, pages 196–197, June 2012.

[13] M. Yip, J. L. Bohorquez, and A. P. Chandrakasan. A 0.6V 2.9μW mixed-signal front-end for ECG monitoring. In *Dig. Symp. VLSI Circuits*, pages 66–67, June 2012.

Impact of Process Variation in Inductive Integrated Voltage Regulator on Delay and Power of Digital Circuits

Monodeep Kar*, Sergio Carlo*, Harish Krishnamurthy‡, Saibal Mukhopadhyay*

*School of ECE, Georgia Institute of Technology, Atlanta, GA‡ Intel Corporation, Hillsboro, OR

∗{monodeepkar, sergio.carlo}@gatech.edu,saibal@ece.gatech.edu,‡ harish.k.krishnamurthy@intel.com

ABSTRACT

This paper analyzes the effect of variations in the parameters of an Integrated Voltage Regulator (IVR) and its impact on the power/performance of a system of IVR driven digital logic circuit. The coupled analysis of IVR and digital logic considering variations in the integrated passives, power train FETs and controller transistors shows, compared to an off-chip VR, variations in IVR induce much larger shifts in the operating frequency of the logic and total system power. Variations in the output filter passives cause most prominent variations in the system power and performance, particularly pronounced at low voltage operation of the core. We also show that the mean performance of the system can be traded-off to reduce the variability by modifying IVR parameters, such as controller zeroes or output capacitors.

Categories and Subject Descriptors

B.0. [**Hardware General**]: Integrated Voltage Regulator

Keywords

Integrated Voltage Regulator; Process Variation;

1. INTRODUCTION

The integration of switched inductor based voltage regulator with the digital processors on the same die eliminates the parasitic impedances due to pins, package, and board traces (Fig. 1). The reduced impedance of the power traces and use of lower inductance and capacitance (higher frequency) in the integrated voltage regulators (IVR) improve the dynamic response and reduce the power supply noise. Due to the above mentioned advantages, the high-frequency IVRs are emerging as a key approach to power delivery in microprocessors [1-7]. The 4th generation Intel Haswell Processor uses fully integrated voltage regulators as demonstrated in [7]. IVRs working above 100MHz with fast transient response have been presented [4-7].

The IVRs need to cope with the higher variability that exists in state-of-the-art digital processes. The transistors in the power stage and in the controller (conventional digital devices) experience process variations. The on-chip or on-package inductors and capacitors and their electrical series resistances (ESR) also experience variations. The variability in the IVR ultimately manifests as shifts in (i) the transient characteristics and the steady-state ripple of the output voltage and (ii) power loss. In the system of an IVR followed by a core, the variability in the IVR couples with the process variations in the digital cores [8]. The net effect is a higher variability in the core's performance and the system (core + IVR) power, the two *observable* parameters of the system.

ISLPED'14, August 11–13, 2014, La Jolla, CA, USA
Copyright 2014 ACM 978-1-450-2975-0/14/08...$15.00.
http://dx.doi.org/10.1145/2627369.2627637

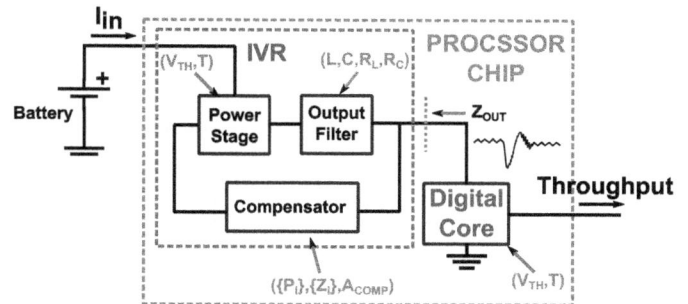

Figure 1. A system of IVR and digital core and different sources of variations affecting the system, indicated in red color

This paper models and analyzes the effect of process variations on an IVR. We consider the digitally controlled voltage mode inductive buck converter to illustrate our analysis. We analyze the effect of variations in inductor, capacitor, the power transistors, and the delay of the digital control loop, on the IVR parameters by performing Monte-Carlo simulations. We perform sensitivity based analysis to identify the relative magnitude of the process control tolerance of different design parameters to achieve a robust IVR design. Further, the IVR's variation analysis is coupled with voltage-dependent delay and power characteristics of a generic digital logic, to characterize the effect of process variation in IVR on core performance and system power.

Our analysis identifies the critical parameters that significantly increase IVR's variability. The variations in the output filter passives, specifically the inductor dominate the variability in the power loss, output voltage ripple, and *load* transient response (overshoot and settling time) of the IVR. The variation in the delay of the controller dominates spread in the voltage transients during transition of *power state* (i.e. change of output voltage during voltage scaling). The coupled analysis of core and IVR shows that due to the elimination of the board/package level power delivery network, the variation in the IVR has a much stronger influence on the variations in power/performance of the digital circuits. The effect of IVR's variation on the system is amplified at specific operating conditions of the core, namely, at low-voltage/low-frequency. The analysis shows the need for improving process tolerance as well as exploring design techniques to improve robustness of the system under IVR variations, potentially by trading off nominal design specifications for reduced spread.

2. MOTIVATION AND RELATED WORK

To understand the motivation behind the proposed work, consider the overall power delivery system of a processor with off-chip and on-chip VRs (Fig. 2). The power supply impedance looking from the core into the converter determines the supply noise that the core will experience due to transitions in its operating voltage or power. As the supply noise is used to determine the voltage margin of the core for a target frequency, any variation in the generated noise will essentially translate into a variation in the core performance as illustrated in Fig. 3.

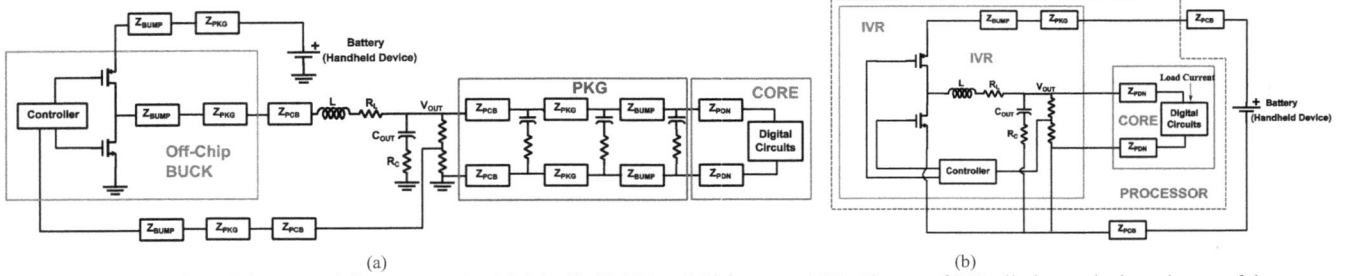

Figure 2: The overview of the power delivery network with (a) off-chip VR and (b) integrated VR. The use of IVR eliminates the impedances of the power traces in the board and package as well as the decoupling capacitors.

With off-chip VRs, the power supply impedance looking from the core into the converter is a series combination of closed loop impedance of the VR ($Z_{OVR,CL}$), the impedance of the power traces in the package and PCB including the decoupling capacitances used to control high-frequency droops (Z_{PKG}), and impedance of the on-chip power delivery network (Z_{PDN}, which is much smaller than Z_{PKG}) (Fig. 2a). The larger passive elements used in off-chip VRs limit their bandwidths. Consequently, the impedance profile at high frequency is determined solely by the Z_{PKG} and the changes in the characteristics of the VR due to process variations are less critical. The output of IVR on the other hand is directly connected to the digital core only through the on-chip PDN (Fig. 2b). As the IVRs are distributed spatially across the chip in multiple phases the on-chip PDN impedance drops significantly making the supply impedance observed by the core to be largely dominated by $Z_{IVR,CL}$. Hence, process variation in IVR has a much more pronounced effect on the core performance (see Section 4.F) than the variations in the off-chip VRs. This shows the need for characterization of the effects of variation in IVR.

The impact of process variation on off-chip inductive VRs has been studied and post-fabrication tuning of off-chip VRs has been explored to tolerate shifts in L/C passives by directly sensing parameters like phase margin and cross-over frequency [9-10]. While these studies show the need for variation analysis in IVR, they do not study the impact of IVR variation on the performance of the core. Compared to an off-chip VR, direct sensing of parameters, and hence, tuning, is more challenging for IVR. Therefore, the IVR should be treated as a part of the digital core itself and the variations in the core performance and total power (core power + IVR losses) should be studied considering the IVR variations. On the other hand, architecture level co-analysis of digital core and VRs (inductive or linear) has been explored. For example, Kim et al. analyzed the effect of VR transient performance on the performance of the core and the system wide energy efficiency with DVFS [11]. However the coupled analysis of IVR and core has so far only focused on the nominal process corners, assuming no variability in the IVR. The variation analysis of IVR and its impact on the delay/power spread of a digital system is a unique contribution of this paper.

3. MODELLING OF INDUCTIVE IVR
A. Components of an IVR

The IVR consists of a power stage driven by a set of non-overlapped clocks (Fig. 4). IVRs typically use high density magnetic thin film based inductors ([1]) or package integrated air-core or magnetic core inductors with much smaller inductance (less than 50nH) than what is used for off-chip VRs. The parasitic resistance (R_L) of the inductors (~100mΩ-500mΩ [1]) typically tends to be higher than off-chip inductors. To maintain dynamic response and power quality with small passive elements, IVRs are driven with high switching frequency (F_{SW}) typically more than 100 MHz. The output capacitor (C_{OUT}) is implemented either using on-chip deep-trench (DT) capacitor or MOS capacitors. The on-chip or on-package capacitors used in IVRs have very low ESR which shifts the zero created by the C_{OUT} and its ESR at high frequency, typically more than F_{SW} [5]. Also the on-chip capacitors have low parasitic inductances (ESL) with high self-resonant frequency. For external VRs that use electrolytic capacitors having low frequency ESR zero, a type II compensator is used in the controller. The IVRs generally use a type III compensator with two zeroes and two/three poles. The IVRs can also have an extra transient management loop ([5-7]) to provide a non-linear gain depending on the magnitude of the transient overshoot/undershoot and achieve fast response. Although the transient management varies between IVR designs, the basic control law remains similar in all the IVRs. Hence, for the sake of simplicity and generalization, *we will consider a standard type III control scheme for the IVR in this paper.*

B. Modeling Of IVR Output Parameters

In this section we will present the modelling of a standard inductive IVR. A discrete time control is an attractive choice due to implementation using all digital transistors and robustness in the controller parameters against variation [2]. A standard discrete time PWM controller consists of an ADC sampled at F_{SW} that

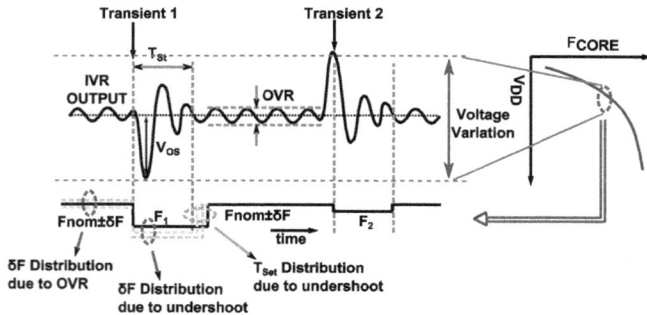

Figure 3: Impact of IVR variations on its output voltage fluctuations and the corresponding variations in core frequency. The transient variations and Output Voltage Ripple (OVR) reduce maximum operating frequency (F_{MAX}) and increase the settling time (lower throughput).

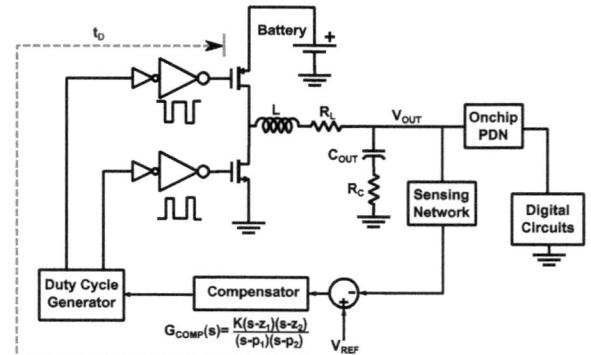

Figure 4. Architecture of a PWM buck converter showing the transfer function of the controller.

Table I Models of IVR Parameters

Power Efficiency $\eta = \frac{P_{CORE}}{P_{IN}} = \frac{P_{CORE}}{P_{CORE}+P_{LOSS}} = \frac{P_{CORE}}{P_{CORE}+P_{COND}+P_{RPL}+P_{SW}}$ P_{CORE}: Core Power P_{SW}: power consumed by the power FET drivers P_{COND}: conduction loss due to $R_{DS,ON}$ of the FETs and parasitic R_L of the inductor P_{RPL}: Loss due ESR of the output capacitor $$P_{COND} = \left(I_{LOAD}^2 + \frac{I_{RPL}^2}{3}\right)\left(DR_{DS,P} + (1-D)R_{DS,N} + R_L\right) + \frac{I_{RPL}^2}{3}R_C; \quad I_{RPL} = \frac{(V_{in}-V_{ref})D}{2LF_{SW}}; \quad P_{SW} = C_G V_{in}^2 F_{SW}$$	(1)
Output Voltage Ripple $OVR = \frac{V_{in}(1-D)}{16LCF_{sw}^2} + 2I_{RPL}R_C; \quad I_{RPL} = \frac{(V_{in}-V_{ref})D}{2LF_{SW}}$ Vin: Input Voltage D: Duty Cycle L: Inductor C: Capacitor F_{sw}: Switching Frequency R_C: ESR of Capacitor	(2)
Loop Gain $L(z) = G_{vd}(z) * G_C(z)$ Power Stage Gain $G_{vd}(z) = \frac{\hat{v}_{out}}{\hat{d}} = \frac{C(1-\Phi z^{-1})^{-1}\gamma}{z}$ $\Phi = e^{AT_s}$ $\gamma = e^{A(T_s-t_d)}BV_{in}T_s$ A, B, C: Matrices in the state space equation of the power stage; T_S: switching period t_D: loop time delay $t_D = t_{ADC} + t_{Compensator} + t_{DPWM}$ Compensator Transfer Function $G_C(z) = K\frac{(z-z_1)(z-z_1)}{z(z-1)}$ z_1, z_2: zeroes	(3)
Output Impedance: Open Loop: $Z_{o,OL}(s) = R_L\frac{\left(1+\frac{s}{w_L}\right)\left(1+\frac{s}{w_C}\right)}{1+\frac{s}{Qw_o}+\frac{s^2}{w_o^2}}$ Closed Loop: $Z_{o,CL}(s) = \frac{Z_{o,OL}(s)||R_{LOAD}}{1+L(s)}$ $w_L = \frac{R}{L}$ $w_C = \frac{1}{RC}$ $Q = \frac{\sqrt{L/C}}{R_L+R_C}$	(4)
Load transient response: $V_{OUT}(t) = D * V_{In} - L^{-1}\left(\frac{\Delta I}{s}Z_{o,CL}(s)\right)$ L^{-1}: Inverse Laplace Transform ΔI=Height of the load Step	(5)
Line transient response: $V_{OUT}(t) = L^{-1}\left(\frac{\Delta V}{s}\frac{G_{vd}(z)G_C(z)}{1+G_{vd}(z)G_C(z)}\right) = L^{-1}\left(\frac{\Delta V}{s}\frac{L(z)}{1+L(z)}\right)$ Δv=Height of the reference Step	(6)

digitizes the error between scaled output and a reference voltage. The digitized error signal (e[n]) is processed by the compensator which receives digital inputs K, z_1 and z_2 and generates a duty cycle command d[n]. The digital PWM engine converts the truncated digital data d[n] to a pair of non-overlapped clock signal with the desired duty cycle.

The models of the output parameters of an IVR are presented in Table I in terms of the design components. The steady state characteristics of IVR include its power loss and output voltage ripple. The power loss of the IVR consists of conduction loss, ripple loss and switching loss (detailed equations are given in Table I). The power efficiency (η) is defined as the ratio of total power transferred to the core (P_{CORE}) to the input power to the system (P_{IN}). The output voltage ripple (OVR) at the IVR output is the sum of inductor current (I_{RPL}) integrated by the output capacitor and the resistive drop across the capacitor ESR. The digital compensator is assumed to have two zeroes (compensating for the filter double pole of the power stage) and two poles (acts as an integrator and makes the steady state error zero). The closed loop output impedance is the impedance looking from the core into the converter after the voltage mode feedback is applied. We have used a bilinear transformation to convert the loop gain from z to Laplace domain while calculating $Z_{O,CL}$. The loop gain and the output impedance manifest their effects in the transient response of the IVR output. Given an ideal load current step of height ΔI the voltage droop (V_{DROOP}) and the settling time ($T_{S,LOAD}$) of the output node are defined as the load transient parameters. Similarly when the processor makes a power state transition which typically involves a step transition in reference voltage (Δv) (neglecting change in output current), the response of the converter is called as power state transient response and the equivalent response parameters are called overshoot value (OV_{REF}) and the settling time ($T_{S,REF}$). The variation in the power stage and output filter (due to passive elements) and the compensator (due to controller delay) affects the transient response of the IVR.

C. Impact of IVR Variations on Digital Core

Variations in the IVR eventually manifest as variations in the supply voltage (as shown in Fig. 3) and hence, maximum frequency (F_{MAX}) of the digital circuit. The OVR of the IVR is included in the steady state supply voltage margin of the cores. During sharp load transients the V_{DROOP} limits the maximum operating frequency of the processor for a time duration of $T_{S,LOAD}$ which affects the average throughput of the load. During power state transients the processor is generally stalled till the output settles and variation in $T_{S,REF}$ adds to the variation in that time margin. The OV_{REF} variation contributes to the variation in the upper limit of the voltage margin that can pose reliability issues due to overstressing the digital transistors.

The input power of the system can be expressed as:

$$P_{In} = P_{Core} + P_{Loss} = P_{Core} + P_{SW} + P_{COND} + P_{RPL} \tag{7}$$

It can be observed that IVR variations contribute to system power variation in two ways. First, the conduction and ripple losses (marked in red) of the IVR directly add to the variation in the total power (the switching loss remains almost constant). Second, supply voltage variations due to variation in the output ripple and transient response of the IVR, result in the variations in the core power. Hence variations in P_{CORE} and P_{LOSS} are not independent and together contribute to the variability of P_{IN}. This paper assumes variations only in the IVR to specifically illustrate the variation in the system parameters contributed only by the IVR and mask the variability of the core. The variability is expected to increase in presence of process variation in core.

4. VARIATION ANALYSIS AND RESULTS

A. Sources of Variations

The IVR is affected by variations in the inductor, capacitors, the ESR values, and threshold voltage variation in the power train and the controller transistors. We assume each variable to be independent Normal distribution. External ferrite power inductors are shown to have ±18% ($3\sigma/\mu$) worst case tolerance [12]. The maximum variation of the on-chip inductors depends on the fabrication process. The with-in-die variation of the trench capacitors for a 45nm PDSOI process is ±6% ($3\sigma/\mu$) [13]. However the variation is expected to increase for die-to-die variation. For our analysis, we assume a ±18% ($3\sigma/\mu$) variation for

Table II Design Parameters of IVR and Off-chip VR

Parameter	L	C	R_L	R_C	F_{SW}
IVR	20nH	50nF	200mΩ	50mΩ	130MHz
Off-Chip VR	2.2μH	15μF	50 mΩ	200 mΩ	2MHz

all the parameters. The threshold voltages of PFET and NFET in the power train are modeled as independent random variables. As the control system is implemented completely in digital domain, the pole and zero locations do not vary, unlike an analog compensator. To simplify the analysis, we assume the total delay of the controller path has a normal distribution and the mean (μ_{t_D}) and standard deviation (σ_{t_D}) are estimated considering the gates in the critical path. If an analog or hysteretic controller is used for the IVR compensation, both the gain of the compensator as well as the locations of the poles and zeroes will vary also. In such cases the sensitivity of the pole zero locations can be studied to observe the impact on the IVR output parameters and the core performance.

B. Design of a System of an IVR Driven Core

We have designed an illustrative IVR to demonstrate the impact of component variations on the output parameters of the IVR. The IVR in context uses a single phase and discrete time control although the analysis is applicable for any standard IVR using type III compensation. To illustrate the comparison between variability of the designed IVR and an off-chip VR, we also design an off-chip buck converter as demonstrated in [14] with the design parameters shown in the Table II. A type II analog compensator is used to compensate the off-chip buck. The package impedance (Z_{PKG}) is assumed to be a bump of 1nH inductance followed by a 10nF on-chip decoupling capacitor [15]. We assume that the IVR designed above is driving a core designed in 130nm technology having a total of 1 million logic gates and a critical path depth of 30 gates. The maximum frequency of the core is calculated from the model presented in [8]. The core power and hence the corresponding load current are calculated using the maximum frequency at a given supply, the activity factor and other relevant technology parameters. To evaluate the role of IVR variations, we assume that the core model does not contain any variations.

We have performed Monte-Carlo simulations considering variations in one parameter at a time as well as all parameters at the same time and at two core power corners: High Power Mode, Vdd 1.2V and activity factor of 0.3 (I_{CORE}: 0.96A) and Low Power Mode, Vdd 0.6V and activity factor of 0.1 (I_{CORE}: 2mA). To simulate the effect of variations on the load transient, a 500mA (both HP and LP mode) of transient step with no change in the

output voltage is considered. For analyzing the power state transient, a reference voltage step of 1V without any change in load current is considered. In state-of-the-art SoCs load current steps occur as fast as 500mA/100pS and power state transients can occur at 0.5V/100nS [5]. As we have considered ideal step with zero rise time during simulation of transient waveforms, the values estimated in our analysis are pessimistic.

C. Variation Results of IVR

Variation in Power Loss: The distribution of P_{LOSS} is shown in Fig. 5a. The standard deviation of P_{LOSS} is lower at low output power as the switching loss, which does not suffer from variations, dominates the total loss. At higher output power the conduction loss due to the power FET resistances and ESR_L dominates, and hence, the overall loss variations increases.

Variation in Output Voltage Ripple (OVR): Fig. 5b shows the distribution of the OVR. The standard deviation of OVR is independent of the load current drawn and depends only on the output voltage. However the dependence of OVR on output voltage is not a strong function of the Vout value. Hence the variability is less sensitive to change in operating conditions.

Variation in Transient Responses: Fig. 6a and 6b show the distribution of undershoot (V_{DROOP}) and the settling time ($T_{S,LOAD}$) considering the *load transients* and 6c and 6d show the distribution of overshoot voltage (OV_{REF}) and settling time ($T_{S,REF}$) for *power state transient*. The $T_{S,LOAD}$ distribution has discrete peaks at 540nS and 630nS. The transient voltage during load transient rings with a frequency close to the resonant frequency of the output filter (the closed loop Z_{OUT} peaks). Hence the intersection points of the transient response with the settling time error band occur in clusters separated by one half of a ringing cycle. As a result we see discrete peaks in the distribution, separated by 90nS (F_{Filter}: 5.7MHz). The distributions of OV_{REF} and $T_{S,REF}$ both have a typically long tail. This is due to the skewed distribution of the crossover frequency as IVRs with higher crossover frequency exhibit improved response time.

D. Sensitivity Analysis of IVR Outputs

The sensitivities of IVR outputs at low power (LP) and high power (HP) mode to the design components are summarized in Table III.

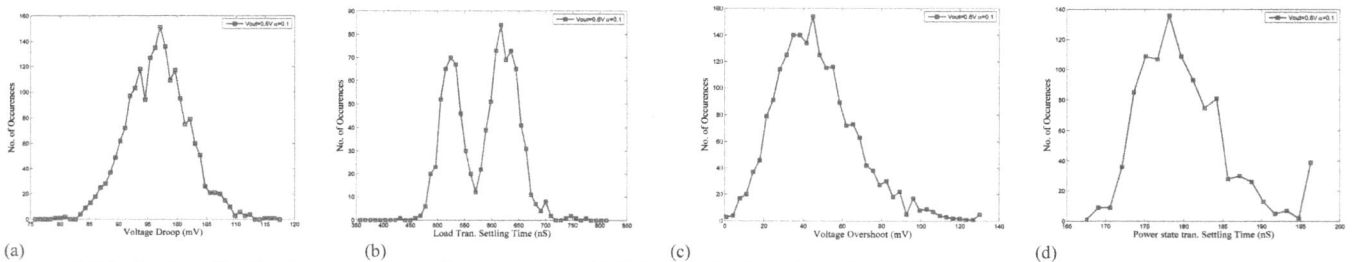

Figure 6. Distribution of load and power state transient parameters :(a) Voltage undershoot during load transient (b) Settling time during load transient (c) Voltage overshoot during power state transient (d) Settling time during power state transient. The distributions of parameters for power state transitions show skewed distributions. (No. of Monte Carlo Runs = 500)

Table III The sensitivity table for different IVR output parameters (3σ/μ=18% for all components)												
3σ/μ(%)	P_{LOSS}		OVR		V_{DROOP}		$T_{S.LOAD}$		OS_{REF}		$T_{S,REF}$	
Power Mode	HP	LP	HP	LP	HP	LP	HP	LP	HP	LP	HP	LP
L	2.37	0.51	18.08	18.24	9.93	11.22	1.56	28.83	20.97	27.6	7.56	11.7
R_L	9.63	0.18	0	0	0.03	0.03	0.6	17.82	10.95	30.99	1.74	2.04
C	1.62	0.01	9.27	12.63	8.49	9.90	1.14	7.77	21.54	81.87	6.30	13.05
R_C	1.5	0.04	8.58	5.64	3.18	3.78	0.24	8.55	0.24	69.87	0.40	0.57
$V_{th,PWR}$	3.42	0.03	0	0	*	*	*	*	*	*	*	*
$t_{D,CTRL}$	0	0	0	0	4.29	5.07	0.12	0.09	1.68	72.81	0.36	0.63
All Varying	10.92	0.54	21.24	22.53	13.74	16.23	6.9	28.02	28.74	123.45	15.84	30.57

* Negligible Variations   Most significant source   2nd most significant source   HP= Vdd:1.2V α:0.3   LP= Vdd:0.6V α:0.1

Table IV: The sensitivity table for total power and performance of system (3σ/μ=18% for all components)

3σ/μ	P_{In}		$F_{CORE,OVR}$		$F_{CORE,TRAN}$	
Vdd	1.2V	0.6V	1.2V	0.6V	1.2V	0.6V
α	0.3	0.1	0.3	0.1	0.3	0.1
Mean	1.31W	0.073W	943MHz	144MHz	806MHz	103MHz
L	1.53	0.12	1.5	2.28	2.4	6.39
R_L	2.07	0.15	0	0	0.01	0.03
C	1.17	0.36	0.81	1.5	2.04	5.7
R_C	1.05	0.12	0.75	0.72	0.78	2.13
$V_{th,PWR}$	0.72	0.03	0	0	0	0
$t_{D,CTRL}$	0	0	0	0	1.02	2.88
All	**3.39**	**0.48**	**1.92**	**2.85**	**3.36**	**9.39**

Most significant source   2nd most significant source

We present the 3σ/μ values of the output parameters for 18% (3σ/μ) variation the components.

- The *power loss* at low load current is most sensitive to capacitor ESR variation (R_C), as the major source of power loss is ripple loss (note, switching loss does not suffer from variation). At higher load, the sensitivity to variations in the Vth of the power FET and ESR of L (R_L) are higher as conduction loss is the dominant component.

- The *OVR* variation is sensitive to L (results in variation in the ripple current) and C, ESR of C (R_C) (voltage change due to ripple current) variation. The variability is not very sensitive to the operating condition of the core.

- The *load transient response* is sensitive to the location of filter poles and loop gain. Hence L and C are the dominant sources for both V_{DROOP} and $T_{S,LOAD}$. The V_{DROOP} variation is also sensitive to $t_{D,CTRL}$ as V_{DROOP} is dependent on the phase margin of the loop (see Table I). The $T_{S,LOAD}$ variation is determined by the impedance of the closed loop response and the overall loop gain, and hence sensitive to ESR of L (R_L) and $t_{D,CTRL}$. The variability increases particularly at LP mode as the phase margin of the loop drops at low load current along with impedance peaking in the $Z_{O,CL}$.

- For the *power state transient response*, we observe very high sensitivity of OV_{REF} on C and $t_{D,CTRL}$ as the phase margin of the loop drops at low load and increases the sensitivity of overshoot. The $T_{S,REF}$ variation is again sensitive to the filter pole locations and hence L and C variation is dominant.

E. System Level Variation Analysis

In this section we translate the variation in the output parameters of the IVR to variability in the total power (P_{IN}) and performance (F_{CORE}) of the core (Table IV). The variation in F_{CORE} (the max. frequency) due to OVR is dominated mostly by L and C variations and is higher at lower power corner as the output voltage is lower at that point. The variation in OVR results in 1.92% and 2.85% variability in F_{CORE} at HP and LP condition respectively. The variability of F_{CORE} due to V_{DROOP} increases significantly also at lower power corner. We observe that 18% variation in the different components of IVR introduce about 9.39% variation in the F_{CORE} at LP condition. Apart from the filter passives the controller loop delay can introduce additional (~2.9%) performance variation. The inductor still remains the dominant source of variation (6.4%). At higher power, similar variation in all the components leads to smaller (~only 3.36%) variation in the performance. However the variation in the throughput will be significantly more than F_{CORE} variation when impact of the settling time variation is added to it.

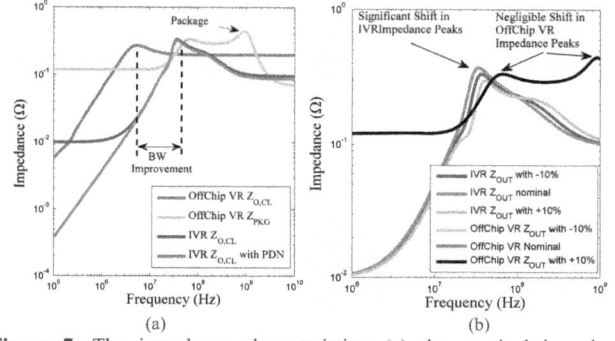

Figure 7: The impedance characteristics: (a) the nominal impedance values, and (b) variation in the impedance observed by the core due to variation in the VR parameters (impedance response of the off-chip VRs are overlapped on top of each other due to negligible effect of variation

TABLE V Comparison of the nominal value and variability of the output parameters and impact on the core performance for off-chip VR and IVR under variation

Mean Value	V_{DROOP} (mV)	$T_{S,LOAD}$ (nS)	OV_{REF} (mV)	$T_{S,SET}$ (nS)	F_{CORE} (MHz)
Off-Chip VR	171.3	3056.2	231.2	4347.7	49.2
IVR	96.4	584.3	46.1	181.8	103.7

3σ/μ (%)	V_{DROOP}	$T_{S,LOAD}$	OV_{REF}	$T_{S,SET}$	F_{CORE}
Off-Chip VR	0.78	14.07	26.01	29.55	2.46
IVR	16.17	29.13	135.21	30.57	9.24

We observe that at the higher power corner the ESR_L is the most dominant source of variation in the total power (2.07% variability). However, it is important to note that variability in the total power is much smaller than the variation in the power loss. The σ/μ of the total power can be related to the σ/μ of the converter power loss as (assuming no variation in core power):

$$\left(\frac{\sigma}{\mu}\right)_{Pin} = \frac{\sigma_{Pin}}{\mu_{PLoss} + \mu_{PCore}} \simeq \frac{\sigma_{PLOSS}}{\mu_{PLoss}} * (1 - \eta_{eff}) = \left(\frac{\sigma}{\mu}\right)_{PLOSS} (1 - \eta_{eff}) \quad (8)$$

Evidently the higher efficiency (η_{eff}) at higher power reduces the overall variability of the system power. Although, we consider the variation in the core power due to variation in the OVR, the effect was observed to be small at high power case (i.e. equation (8) remains mostly valid). At lower power corner, however, the variation in P_{CORE} becomes important for the total power variation. The most dominant source of variability becomes C as it introduces OVR variation (F_{CORE} variation) thereby modulating the power loss. The reduced η_{eff} at low load also makes the variation in power loss more observable at the input.

F. Comparative Analysis: IVR vs Off-chip VR

We have observed that in the case of IVR, the overall supply impedance is determined mainly by the IVR output impedance (Fig. 7a). Hence, shifts in the IVR components directly impact the total supply impedance observed by the core (Fig. 7b, ±10% variation in the components). However, for the off-chip case the total impedance is largely independent of the VR variations. Table V compares the impact of the IVR and off-chip-VR on the transient voltage variations experienced by the core and associated F_{CORE}. As expected, the mean values of the transient parameters improve for IVR, compared to the off-chip VR, due to higher bandwidth of the control loop and elimination of the package impedance. However, variability in the transient parameters (σ/μ ratio) is much higher for the IVR. This is because the effects of variations in the VR components are desensitized by the loop gain and impedance profile is dominated by Z_{PKG} for off-chip VRs. Therefore, the variation in the F_{CORE}, for example due to V_{DROOP}

TABLE VI Design examples on trade-off between variability and nominal design value for different output capacitor

Capacitor Value (nF)	V_{DROOP}		OV_{REF}		F_{CORE}	
	μ (mV)	$3\sigma/\mu$ (%)	μ (mV)	$3\sigma/\mu$ (%)	μ (MHz)	$3\sigma/\mu$
45	102	14.5	71.24	131	99.7	10.8
50	96.6	16.2	43.00	162	103.6	9.03
55	93.6	16.5	24.32	216	106.6	8.4

TABLE VII Design examples on trade-off between variability and nominal design value for different controller zero locations

Controller Zeros	$\mu T_{S,LOAD}$ (nS)	σ/μ $T_{S,LOAD}$ (%)	$\mu T_{S,REF}$ (nS)	σ/μ $T_{S,REF}$ (%)
0.89±0.09i	533	23.28	310.3	1.04
0.89±0.17i	578	29.49	181.8	24.36
0.89±0.22i	684	36.81	163.7	75.78

variations at Vdd=0.6V and α=0.1, is increasing with IVR (~9.3%) from off-chip VR (~2.4%).

5. DISCUSSIONS

We have discussed the sensitivities of the output parameters of IVR and the system on different sources of variations for the illustrative design presented in section 4.B. However, the sensitivities of the output parameters of an IVR depend on design. The variation-aware pre-silicon and/or post-silicon tuning can be useful to minimize variation in IVR parameters and core performance. To motivate future work in this direction, we present illustrative examples in design time and post-silicon tuning. First, consider the impact of choice of the capacitance (Table VI, design-time). As μV_{DROOP} and μOV_{REF} are sensitive to the output capacitor; the variability of overshoot voltage is sensitive to the capacitor value and variability of F_{CORE} can be reduced from 10.5% to 8.4% by choosing suitable capacitor value by reducing the mean value in V_{DROOP}. Second, consider the example of tuning of the controller zero in a digital controller (Table VII, post-silicon). As $\mu T_{S,LOAD}$ increases its variability increases; but with the changing zero location an increase in $\mu T_{S,REF}$ results in lower σ/μ ratio. If power state transitions are less frequent for a core, a higher $T_{S,REF}$ can be tolerated (first zero). However, if power state transients are frequent then the third zero location can help reduce mean value of $T_{S,REF}$, but that will lead to higher variability in $T_{S,REF}$ and hence, more unpredictability in the system performance. The preceding discussion shows the need for variation-aware design time and run-time tuning of IVRs for robust system design.

6. CONCLUSIONS

This paper analyses the effect of parametric variations on a system of high-frequency inductive integrated voltage regulator (IVR) followed by a digital core. We observe that, an IVR achieves better transient performance compared to an off-chip VR, but the performance of a core can suffer significantly due to variability in the IVR. The IVR variability and its impact on the core performance are pronounced at the low voltage/low power conditions and will be enhanced when the variation of the settling time and the process variation in the core are added to the calculation of effective throughput. The process and design techniques need to be investigated to improve the robustness of the system against process variation in IVR. From a process perspective, the variation in the inductor value should be minimized to reduce variation in power loss and transient response. In parallel, design techniques should be adopted to minimize the delay spread of the controller. Pre silicon design choices and post silicon tuning options can be adapted to optimally trade-off the mean system performance and the variability. At the system level, the core's operating condition, for example, voltage or frequency, can be co-designed considering IVR's variation to increase the system's robustness. The future work needs to focus on methodologies like variation-aware design optimization of the IVR to improve variation tolerance of the system (core + IVR).

7. ACKNOWLEDGEMENTS

This material is based on work supported in part by Semiconductor Research Corporation (SRC) through Texas Analog Center of Excellence at the University of Texas at Dallas (Task ID: 1836.110) and National Science Foundation (CNS-1218745)

REFERENCES

[1] Gardner, D.S. et. al., "Integrated on-chip inductors using magnetic material (invited)," Journal of Applied Physics, Apr 2008

[2] A. V. Peterchev, et. al, "Architecture and IC implementation of a digital VRM controller," IEEE TPEL, Jan 2003

[3] J. Wibben, et. al, "A High Efficiency DC-DC Converter Using 2nH On-Chip Inductors," IEEE VLSI Circuits, June 2007

[4] P. Hazucha, et. al, "A 233-MHz 80%-87% efficient four-phase DC-DC converter utilizing air-core inductors on package," IEEE JSSC, April 2005

[5] N. Sturcken, et. al, "A Switched-Inductor Integrated Voltage Regulator With Nonlinear Feedback and Network-on-Chip Load in 45 nm SOI," IEEE JSSC, Aug. 2012

[6] N. Sturcken, et. al, "A 2.5D Integrated Voltage Regulator Using Coupled-Magnetic-Core Inductors on Silicon Interposer," IEEE ISSCC, Feb. 2012

[7] N. Kurd, et. al, "Haswell, a Family of IA 22nm Processors" IEEE ISSCC, Feb. 2014

[8] R. Rao, et. al, "Parametric yield estimation considering leakage variability," ACM DAC, July 2004

[9] J. Morroni, et.al. "Adaptive tuning of digitally controlled switched mode power supplies based on desired phase margin," IEEE PESC June 2008

[10] J. Morroni, et. al, "An Online Stability Margin Monitor for Digitally Controlled Switched-Mode Power Supplies," IEEE TPEL, November 2009.

[11] W. Kim, et. al, "System level analysis of fast, per-core DVFS using on-chip switching regulators," IEEE HPCA Feb. 2008

[12] http://www.coilcraft.com/do3316h.cfm#table

[13] Agarwal, K. et. al. "In-situ measurement of variability in 45-nm SOI embedded DRAM arrays," IEEE VLSIC, June 2010.

[14] http://www.ti.com/lit/ds/symlink/tps62290.pdf

[15] S. Carlo, et. al, "On the potential of 3D integration of inductive DC-DC converter for high-performance power delivery," DAC, June 2013

[16] A. Papoulis, Probability, Random Variables and Stochastic Processes, McGraw-Hill Education, Oct 25, 2001.

Aging Mitigation of Power Supply-Connected Batteries

Jaemin Kim[1] , Alma Pröbstl[2] , Samarjit Chakraborty[2] , and Naehyuck Chang[1]
[1]Seoul National University, Seoul, Korea
[2]Technische Universität München, München, Germany
[1]{jmkim,naehyuck}@elpl.snu.ac.kr, [2]{alma.proebstl,samarjit}@tum.de

ABSTRACT

Battery-operated portable electronics, from smartphones to notebook computers, are generally sold with a dedicated power supply. The power supply operates the device and also charges the built-in battery. Most users are concerned about the battery aging while the device is operated by the built-in battery. This is the first paper to our knowledge that discovers, analyzes and mitigates the built-in battery aging when the device is operated with the provided power supply. We focus on the fact that in an effort to reduce size and weight, the capacity of the power supply is optimized for the average power demand rather than the maximum power demand. Such a *reduced-capacity* power supply brings advantages in terms of size, weight and cost but it accelerates the battery aging because the aging progresses even when the device is operated by the power supply, which is different from the expectation of most users. We quantitatively analyze such battery aging with various operating scenarios based on standard benchmark programs. We show that the battery experiences significant aging, i.e., the battery lifetime can be reduced to 23% of its shelf lifetime. Finally, we propose a cost-effective supercapacior hybrid to mitigate such battery aging when the device is operated using the power supply. The simulation results show that 10, 1 and 0.1 mF supercapacitors can reduce the battery aging by 68.6%, 55.1% and 4.6%, respectively.

1. INTRODUCTION

Battery-operated portable electronics range from small form factor smartphones to high performance laptop computers. Manufacturers claim that their devices are functional for hours to days without recharging but users are often frustrated by depleted batteries in the middle of operation. Therefore, many users carry a power supply and use it to operate and recharge their device where possible.

It is a trend by manufacturers to reduce the size and weight of portable devices such as notebooks. Also the chargers shipped by the manufacturers are reduced in size. This development is of course welcomed by the consumers. The general expectation of a user is that a smaller power supply does not affect the build-in battery of the notebook. However, we show in this paper that if a *reduced-capacity* power supply is used, the battery is exposed to aging. The reason is that in case of a high power demand, the

charger cannot meet this demand and the additional power is drawn from the battery. This leads to increased aging of the battery. Even for a shortfall between charger power and accumulated component power of only 4W, the aging is significant and the battery lifetime might be reduced to 23% of the shelf lifetime when the battery is connected to an insufficiently dimensioned power supply under normal usage conditions. Shelf life is the time it takes until the capacitance of a stored and unused battery has faded to 80% of its initial capacity. A solution to this problem, which is still small and light, but eases the burden on the battery, is to add a supercapacitor as a charge buffer.

This is the first paper to our knowledge that points out battery aging when the battery is still connected to the power supply. We first select devices that are designed with a *reduced-capacity* power supply, we estimate the maximum potential power consumption of a device by the specification and compare it with the power supply specification. The second step is to measure the built-in battery current while we run various benchmarking programs. We create various representative usage scenarios. We convert the battery charging/discharging profiles to the battery aging using an existing battery aging model, which is based on the state of charge (SOC) swing and average SOC. Finally, we apply a supercapacitor charge buffer between the charger and the device that mitigates the battery aging while the device is operated by the power supply. In our design space exploration, we explore the impact of the supercapacitor capacity on the battery aging mitigation. The experimental results show that 10, 1 and 0.1 mF supercapacitors can reduce the battery aging by 68.6%, 55.1% and 4.6%, respectively.

The implications of our case study go beyond the aging with the manufacturer provided power supply. Our solution can also be applied to further reduce the charger size for business notebooks, which usually are exposed to lower workloads but their battery will be protected from aging by buffering charge with a supercapacitor.

2. PROPOSED BATTERY AGING MITIGATION METHOD

For solving the problem of battery aging mitigation with a reduced-capacity power supply, we first identify the battery charging and discharging current while the notebook computer is operated with the power supply. We set up the usage scenario and select suitable workloads. Then we run the workloads and measure the battery current while the notebook is plugged into the power supply.

The second step is to identify battery aging, i.e., state of health (SOH) degradation, using the battery current profile. The SOH describes the condition of the battery related to its specification. Here, battery condition refers to the state of the battery capacity degradation. The capacity degradation leads to a reduced life time of the battery. The ratio of remaining lifetime to expected lifetime of an unused battery is used as a measure of SOH. We convert the time series of the battery current profiles to statistical data because the existing SOH degradation model only considers periodic charging and discharging sequences. This means that the average battery SOC and the SOC swing do not vary over time. The SOC is the ratio of available charge in the battery to the maximum available charge of a recharged battery. We estimate the battery aging from the statistical data and the SOH degradation model.

Next, we consider a supercapacitor as charge buffer and determine its capacitance. We perform a design space exploration and explore the battery aging mitigation rate versus the supercapacitor capacitance.

The remainder of this paper is organized as follows. We give an overview of related work in Section 3. Next, we describe our experimental setup in Section 4. We first show that there is a discharge current on the battery when under heavy workload, define representative user profiles and calculate the battery aging for these profiles in Section 5. We explore the design space in order to find a suitable supercapacitor capacitance which reduces battery degradation and discuss its cost in Section 6. The paper concludes with Section 7, where we discuss the implications of our work.

3. RELATED WORK

Battery aging has been studied for batteries in different setups. Even if the battery is not used, it is exposed to calendar aging. The calendar aging depends on the storage conditions of the battery such as the SOC of the stored battery and the environmental temperature [1]. Considering a battery which is in use, the dependency of battery aging on different discharge C-rates has been studied in [2]. Instead of the C-rate, the discharge can be represented by average SOC and SOC swing, as done in [3], where additionally temperature effects are considered. Other settings study the effect of capacity fading with data measured from electric vehicles [4]. For predicting battery degradation, empirical data is fitted to a model [3][5].

After having measured the battery current while the notebook is connected to the power supply, we apply the current profile to the aging model in [3] and derive the degradation of battery life. For the sake of completeness, we will repeat the model. The aging model relates the SOH degradation to SOC swing, average SOC and battery temperature. The time series profile we measure from the benchmarking test has mixed cycles of charge and discharge with arbitrary SOC. Therefore, we convert the profile to derive the mean SOC ($\overline{SOC}$), and a normalized deviation from average SOC (σ_{SOC}), where T_m is the duration of the m-th time interval of the battery being charged and discharged and T is the total duration of all intervals:

$$\overline{SOC} = \frac{\int_{T_m} SOC(t)dt}{T},$$

$$\sigma_{SOC} = 2\sqrt{\frac{3\int_{T_m}(SOC(t) - \overline{SOC})^2 dt}{\int_{T_m} dt}}.$$

The effective number of throughput cycles N deals with microcycles:

$$N = \frac{\int_{T_m}|i(t)|dt}{2Q_{nom}},$$

where Q_{nom} is the nominal charge capacity of the battery.

The increment of the life parameter in a cycle accounting for SOC swing and throughput, L_1 is given by

$$L_1 = K_{co}Ne^{\left((\sigma_{SOC}-1)\frac{T_{ref}+273}{K_{ex}(T_B+273)}\right)} + 0.2\frac{T_{cycle}}{T_{life}},$$

where T_{cycle} is time in seconds of a cycle, T_{life} is the total expected shelf life in seconds to 80% capacity at 25°C and 50% SOC, T_{ref} is the reference battery temperature, which is 25°C. K_{co} is a constant coefficient of throughput, K_{ex} is a constant exponent for depth of discharge (DOD), and T_B is the battery temperature, which we set to a constant value of 30°C. The DOD is an alternative measure of the battery SOC, where a DOD of 1 denotes an empty battery and 0 a full battery.

The increment of the life parameter accounting for average SOC and decrease in Li-ion concentration, L_2, is given by

$$L_2 = L_1 e^{\left(4K_{soc}(\overline{SOC}-0.5)\right)}(1-L),$$

where K_{soc} is a constant coefficient for average SOC.

The increase of aging for T_m while using the battery is given by

$$L_{active}(T_m) = L_2 e^{\left(K_t(T_B-T_{ref})\frac{T_{ref}+273}{T_B+273}\right)},$$

where K_t is a doubling of decay rate for each 10°C rise in temperature [3].

In [6], the aging model is extended to consider idle times of the battery. During idle times, the battery is not used and no increased aging due to average SOC and SOC swing is taking place. Therefore, only calendar aging needs to be taken into account. In case of battery idle times, the life parameter is calculated by the following equation:

$$L_{1idle} = 0.2\frac{T_{idle}}{T_{life}},$$

where T_{idle} is the total amount of idle time and T_{life} is the shelf life, which is assumed to be 15 years. The amount of aging for T_m while idle is given by

$$L_{idle}(T_m) = L_{1idle}e^{\left(K_t(T_B-T_{ref})\frac{T_{ref}+273}{T_B+273}\right)}.$$

Depending on the battery usage (active or idle), the life parameter L is incremented by either L_{active} or L_{idle}. Note that due to the dependence of L_2 on the previous value of L, the chronological order of the sequence is important.

$$L = \begin{cases} L + L_{active}, & \text{in the active case,} \\ L + L_{idle}, & \text{if battery idle.} \end{cases}$$

The life parameter L can take on values in the range of [0,1], where 0 means a new battery and 1 a battery with no capacity left.

The model in [3] is developed for an electric vehicle battery while we are considering a notebook battery. We assume that aging mechanisms are the same because both cell chemistries are Li-ion. Unfortunately, it is hard to access concrete life data for parameter fitting of the target battery. Instead, we use the same parameters as presented in [3], which are derived for the A123 ANR26650M1A Li-ion battery cell such that $K_{co} = 3.66 \times 10^{-5}$ for DOD 0.35 to 0.95, $K_{ex} = 0.717$, $K_{soc} = 0.916$ and $K_t = 0.0693$. Battery temperature T_B is assumed to be 30°C, the reference temperature T_{ref} is set to 25°C. In conclusion, electric vehicles are different to batteries of laptop computers, but they are both Li-ion batteries and therefore, the results we report still help us to draw meaningful conclusions for laptop batteries.

As a solution to battery aging for power supply connected batteries, we suggest a hybrid energy storage consisting of a battery and a supercapacitor. Electric double layer capacitors, more commonly known as supercapacitors, have a superior cycle efficiency defined as the ratio of the energy output to energy input, which reaches almost 100%. Moreover, supercapacitors have a high charge-discharge cycle frequency and no aging effects [7]. However, supercapacitors also have some disadvantages such as a relatively small capacity and higher cost compared to Li-ion batteries. Therefore, a

Table 1: Maximum power consumption of Lenovo T530-2359-A44, Apple MacBook Pro 2013 components [8][9][10][11][12].

Model	T530-2359-A44		MacBook Pro 2013	
Component	Specification	Power	Specification	Power
CPU	i7-3610QM	45 W	i7-3840QM	45 W
LCD	15.4"	6 W	15.4"	6.2 W
VGA	NVS5400M	35 W	GT650M	45 W
HDD	7200rpm	5.5 W	7200rpm	5.5 W
RAM	DDR3 8G	2.5 W	DDR3 8G	2.5 W
Total		94 W		104 W
Adaptor		90 W		85 W

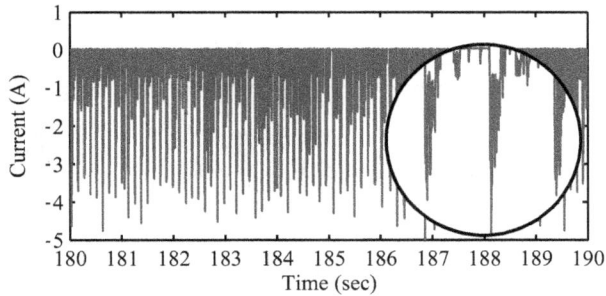

Figure 1: Current profile of gaming workload with almost fully charged battery. Negative current indicates discharging of the battery.

supercapacitor suits well as a charge buffer to mitigate load current fluctuations. This idea is not new, hybrid energy storage systems consisting of supercapacitors and Li-Ion batteries have been used before to compensate the disadvantages of Li-Ion batteries [7].

4. EXPERIMENTAL SETUP

In the following, we show the existence of a discharge current when the notebook is connected to a power outlet. Then, we define user profiles using benchmark programs which will later be used to calculate the battery aging for these profiles.

Table 1 compares the maximum specified power consumption of two notebook computers with the power made available by their provided power supplies. In case of the Lenovo notebook, the specified power demand exceeds the power provided by the charger by 4 W, in case of the Apple notebook, the gap is even bigger and comes to 19 W.

Let us consider the case that the power consumption exceeds the power supplied by the charger. We use a Lenovo T530-2359-A44 notebook with a 90 W power supply and run a heavy gaming workload for a short period of time while the notebook is connected to the power supply. Figure 1 shows that the battery is exposed to a discharge current. This is the a 10 second excerpt of the current that results in the SOC discharge profile in Figure 2. As can be seen in Figure 2, the battery discharges because the power supply is not capable of providing the peak power demand. The SOC decreases to compensate the power shortage. However, this is only the case for a high SOC. If the battery has a lower SOC, e.g., 25%, we still have discharge currents but the power supply meets the average power consumption as can be seen in Figure 3. This will be of importance when building the usage profiles. Note that if we remove the battery and run the same benchmarking programs, the power manager of the operating system reduces the CPU frequency and limits the performance of the notebook.

We determine the available capacity of the battery, which is then used as the 100% SOC limit in the profiles by discharging until 20%, which is the cut-off SOC of the battery internal safety circuit, and then recharge the battery by the external power supply while

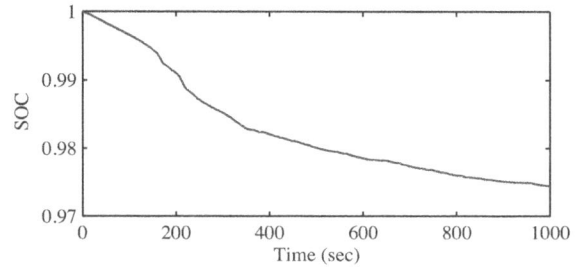

Figure 2: Overall discharge profile of gaming workload.

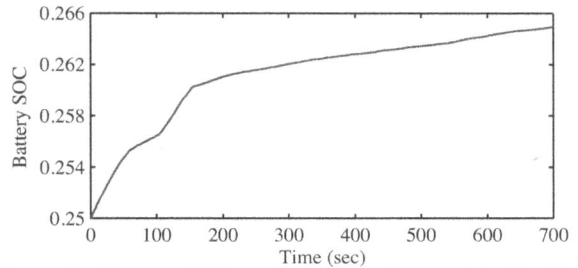

Figure 3: Battery SOC profile of gaming workload with 25% charged battery.

the notebook computer is turned off. Figures 4 and 5 show the battery charging profile. Note that we set the 20% cut-off SOC to 0% SOC in our graphics.

We measure the SOC profile for two categories of workloads. We run Futuremark's gaming benchmarks 3DMark06, 3DMark08, as well as the online 3D based urban planning simulation video game SimCity(2013) from EA Games as real gaming workloads and Futuremark's PCMark Home, Creative, and Work test as office workloads [13][14]. There is no remarkable difference in affecting the battery SOC between workloads within a category. Consequently, we decide to consider only two workload characteristics, the real game SimCity as a high gaming workload and PCMark Work as an office work workload. We run the tests in a loop and schedule the workloads and idle times for user types defined by us.

5. AGING RESULTS

The battery current is recorded for the two different workloads and exemplary daily usage profiles are designed, which then are used for calculating the battery degradation of a new battery within 24 hours under the assumption that the user will expose the same behavior seven days a week every day of a year. Instead of running the game or benchmark for a whole day, the data is looped and concatenated such as to simulate the notebook usage during one day. The four profiles are shown in Table 2 and Figure 6 shows the SOC of the four different use cases.

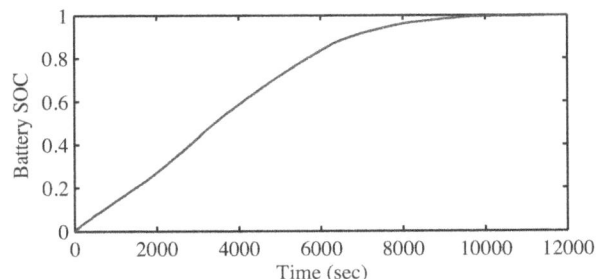

Figure 4: Battery SOC profile while charging.

Table 2: Usage profiles: 24 slots for the 24 hours of the day. Game workload is marked by "g", office workload, generated by the office Work benchmark, is marked by "w". Trailing idle hours ensure the full recharge at the end of a daily profile.

Hour	0	1	2	3	4	5	6	7	8	9	10	11	12	13	14	15	16	17	18	19	20	21	22	23
User 1	-	-	-	-	-	-	-	g	-	g	-	g	g	g	-	g	-	-	g	g	g	-	-	-
User 2	-	-	-	-	-	-	-	-	-	-	g	g	g	g	g	-	g	g	g	g	g	-	-	-
User 3	-	-	-	-	-	-	w	-	w	-	w	w	w	-	w	-	-	w	w	g	g	-	-	-
User 4	-	-	-	-	-	-	-	-	-	-	g	w	g	g	-	w	w	w	g	g	-	-	-	-

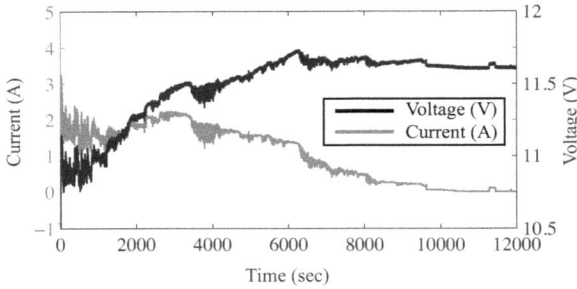

Figure 5: Battery current and voltage profile while charging.

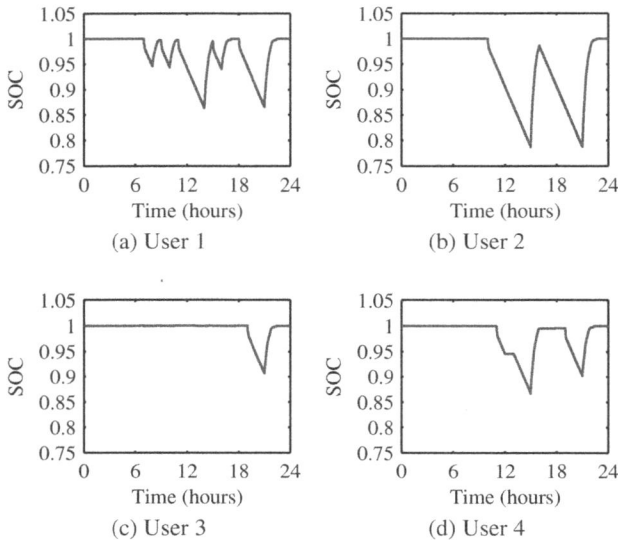

Figure 6: Usage profiles.

Table 3: Battery degradation per day and total lifetime reduction in terms of years for the four usage profiles and calendar aging if the battery is not in use. A life time of 100% denotes the full 15 years of shelf life, while, e.g., 17.95% means that the battery capacity is reduced to 80% of its initial value after 2.69 years.

Profile	Degradation per day in %	Life time in %
User 1	2.25×10^{-4}	17.95
User 2	1.75×10^{-4}	22.96
User 3	1.85×10^{-4}	21.66
User 4	1.79×10^{-4}	22.43
Idle (30°C)	0.51×10^{-4}	71.12
Idle (25°C)	0.37×10^{-4}	100

Table 4: Comparison of weight and dimensions of chargers with different power [15].

Charger	Weight (g)	Dimension (mm) WxDxH
90 W	0.36	$50 \times 126 \times 30$
135 W	0.83	$80 \times 165 \times 35$

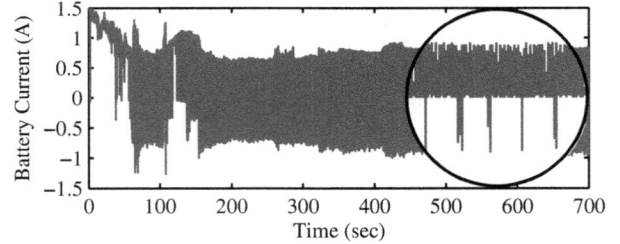

Figure 7: Battery current profile of high workload while battery SOC is approximately at 25%. The profile is centered around zero, hence, the battery is charged as well as discharged.

When applying the aging model to the profiles, the degradation can be calculated. We assume a new battery and calculate the degradation after one day. Using this value we can derive the lifetime reduction in case a user profile is applied to the notebook every day. As can be seen in Table 3, the lifetime reduction varies between 17.95% and 22.96%. Assuming a shelf life of 15 years, this means that the battery capacity will be reduced to 80% of its initial capacity after approximately 3 years and needs to be replaced. The results suggest that the battery ages due to higher peak power demand that cannot be fully met by the power supply. The results indicate that even a shortfall of 4W between charger power and the accumulated maximum power demand of the notebook components leads to significant battery aging.

6. AGING MITIGATION USING A CAPACITOR

The easiest way to prevent the battery from aging in the considered scenario would be to use a bigger power supply. However, users value small size and light weight of chargers. Table 4 compares the weight and dimensions of two chargers. It can be seen that a reduction of the charger power by one third results in a reduction of weight by more than half of its original weight.

We now want to identify the current that an inserted supercapacitor charge buffer would be exposed to. We assume that when the notebook is plugged in to an outlet the battery SOC is or will soon be close to 100%. The charging protocol of the battery then is in CV (constant voltage) mode and the charging current is not at its maximum. In order to find a more realistic current that may charge a supercapacitor buffer, we perform the same gaming workload test at a lower SOC of approximately 25%. The battery is charged and discharged (Figure 7), while the accumulated battery SOC increases slightly (Figure 3). In other words, the external power supply satisfies the average power requirements even if the external power supply fails to feed enough power to the notebook computer.

We select the User 2 profile, which has the deepest depth of discharge, for the design space exploration and we take into account

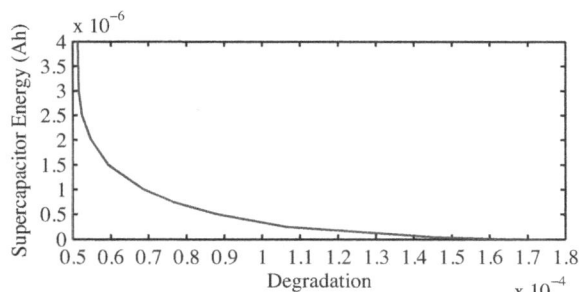

Figure 8: Minimum energy storage amount related to SOH degradation per day.

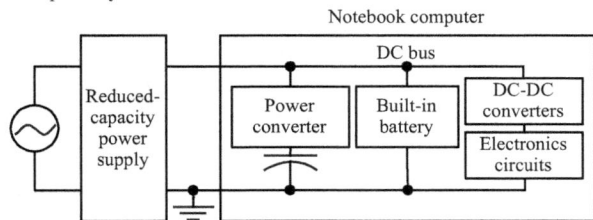

Figure 9: Suggested supercapacitor-battery hybrid system.

the CC-CV charging protocol of Li-ion batteries for a more realistic approach. Figure 8 shows the relationship between the daily SOH degradation and the minimum amount of energy to be stored in the supercapacitor.

We introduce a built-in battery aging mitigation setup based on a supercapacitor-battery hybrid architecture. We use the architecture shown in Figure 9 considering the fact that the terminal voltage almost linearly varies by its SOC. The large swing of the supercapacitor terminal voltage also results in significant variation in the power converter efficiency, which is connected between the supercapacitor and the DC bus. The charger efficiency is affected by input voltage, output voltage and input current [16].

We assume that users who usually put the notebook on the desk generally also connect external power supply with the notebook in order to not to discharge the battery during night, therefore, we also assume that there is no cold starting situation of the supercapacitor. We set the lower bound of the supercapacitor voltage level to 10 V and the upper bound of the supercapacitor voltage level to 15 V to explore the design space. The charger efficiency model and its parameters come from [17]. Figure 10 shows the relationship between SOH degradation and capacitance of the supercapacitor considering the charger efficiency.

These results are verified by replacing the laptop battery by a 120mF supercapacitor which has a voltage rating of 15V and running a gaming benchmark (3DMark06[13]). For verification, we

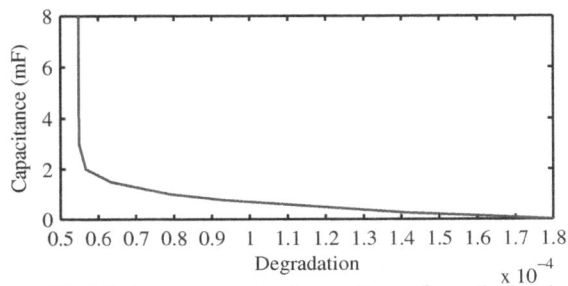

Figure 10: Minimum amount of capacitance for reducing battery SOH degradation.

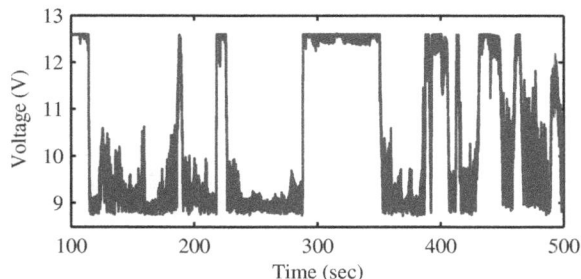

Figure 11: Voltage profile of a supercapcitor that replaces a battery when running a gaming benchmark.

Table 5: Comparison of 3DMark06 benchmark scores when running the notebook with a battery, replacing the battery by a supercapacitor or removing the battery. Note that 3DMark06 utilizes both CPU and GPU severely [13].

	No charger	135 W charger	90 W charger
With battery	8361	9615	9634
No battery	-	9613	7709
Supercapacitor	-	-	9588

do not use any additional charging circuit. The size of the supercapacitor is chosen approximately 10 times higher than our calculated minimum size in order to be able to buffer all the energy required and also to tolerate some losses. We compare the benchmark results for different combinations of chargers, with / without battery and supercapacitor. The results in Table 5 show that replacement of the battery by a supercapacitor of this size leads to no reduction of the benchmark results considering small measurement inaccuracies in the benchmark results. One can also see that in case an outlet is available, the power supply should be used to improve battery life and performance. Battery aging will be reduced because deep battery discharge at high currents is still worse than little currents to meet the peak demand. And the notebook performance is better in terms of benchmark results.

We now have determined the approximate capacitor size. If we add some capacitance to compensate losses, we can say that the capacitance has to be at least 5mF to 10mF to prevent additional power from being drawn from the battery. This range lies in the transition from Electrolytic capacitors to supercapacitors. As can be seen in Table 6, the main difference between these two types are in terms of their price and dimensions. Electrolytic capacitors are cheaper, but supercapacitors have a smaller size. The decision has to be made by the manufacturer. If size matters more, then a supercapacitor should be selected. If cost is the most important factor, a normal capacitor is the preferable choice. Any of these options is much cheaper than buying a new battery.

A lifetime of 55% in our case study corresponds to 8.25 years. Figure 12 shows the cost of the desired lifetime for the different options - Electrolytic capcacitor, supercapacitor and a new battery. For the supercapacitor, only the minimum cost is given according to Table 6 as the cost does not progress linearly. The supercapacitor cost ranges between $2.13 and $10.225. The drop of costs for electrolytic capacitors after 55% of the lifetime is assumed to be due to higher demand of this specific capacitance. It can be seen that the cost per battery replacement of $139.99 exceeds the other options significantly. In this usage scenario, the battery needs to be replaced approximately every three years. Although the supercapacitor is more expensive than the Electrolytic capacitor, it might be prefered due to its small dimensions which are given in Table 6.

In summary, we found that the use of a supercapacitor buffer, whose stored energy is used to satisfy power peaks, is a much

Table 6: Price and dimension of electrolytic capacitors, supercapacitors [18] and a replacement battery [15]. Multiple 10mF, 20mF, 30mF supercapacitor should be used due to their voltage ratings.

Capacitance	Price ($)	Dim. (mm), W×D×H	Type
$0.27mF$	0.131	$8.0 \times 8.0 \times 12.0$	Electrolytic
$0.47mF$	0.173	$8.0 \times 8.0 \times 10.2$	Electrolytic
$1mF$	0.655	$12.5 \times 12.5 \times 13.5$	Electrolytic
$2mF$	0.959	$16.0 \times 16.0 \times 16.5$	Electrolytic
$5mF$	0.873	$18.0 \times 18.0 \times 16.5$	Electrolytic
$8mF$	1.011	$22.0 \times 22.0 \times 27.0$	Electrolytic
$18mF$	1.359	$22.0 \times 22.0 \times 42.0$	Electrolytic
$33mF$	1.950	$25.0 \times 25.0 \times 52.0$	Electrolytic
$6.8mF$	10.225	$20.0 \times 15.0 \times 5.8$	Supercap
$10mF \times 3$	0.710×3	$(11.0 \times 11.0 \times 5.0) \times 3$	Supercap
$20mF \times 5$	1.615×5	$(3.8 \times 3.8 \times 1.1) \times 5$	Supercap
$30mF \times 5$	0.506×5	$(3.8 \times 3.8 \times 1.1) \times 5$	Supercap
$47mF \times 3$	2.487×3	$(13.5 \times 13.5 \times 9.5) \times 3$	Supercap
new battery	139.99	-	Battery

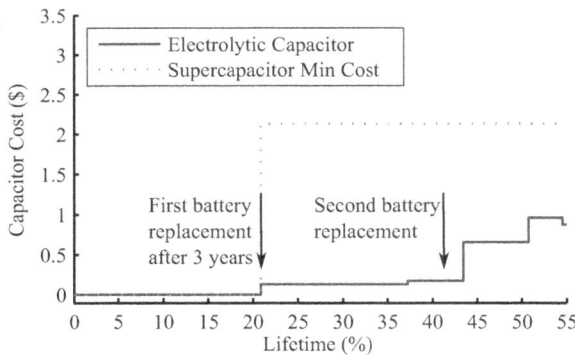

Figure 12: Relation of capacitor cost and lifetime degradation. Two arrows point out the times of battery replacements in case no capacitor is applied. A new battery costs $139.99. This is much higher than both capacitor types, electrolytic and supercapacitor, and therefore not indicated on the y-axis but marked by arrows.

more cost-efficient solution than drawing the power from the battery which therefore ages faster and needs to be replaced after a short time.

7. CONCLUDING REMARKS

In our case study, we see that a mere $4W$ difference between charger power and accumulated power demand of notebook components can lead to significant battery aging, i.e., a lifetime reduction to only 22.96% of the calendar life. In addition, we showed that our solution of mitigating the aging by the use of a capacitor is more cost efficient than replacing the aged battery by a new battery.

As an implication of our study, we suggest that in future the charger size and power could be further reduced by the manufacturers which would be beneficial for the users. We showed that the problem of discharging the battery while the notebook is connected to the power supply only occurs for high workloads, i.e., the benchmark that represented office use did not affect the battery. This benchmark represents the situation of business notebooks whose owners will surely welcome smaller charger. Therefore, there should be room for further reducing the charger size, and using a supercapacitor as buffer for peak demands. The shortfall between provided and demanded power could be designed even higher compared to what we studied in this paper and would lead to even more aging acceleration. Again, one can apply our solution

which helps to mitigate the aging at a negligible cost. The savings should be explored by further experiments.

In summary, this paper discovered that the battery ages even when the notebook is powered by a reduced-capacity power supply, where the power supply capacity is smaller than the maximum power demand. Despite numerous advantages of such reduced-capacity power supplies in terms of cost, weight, form factor, etc., this method incurs significant battery aging even when the notebook is powered by the power supply. We analyze the battery aging issue with the reduce-capacity power supply by measurements and simulations. We quantify the battery aging under practical usage scenarios consisting of representative benchmarking programs. Finally, we propose to use a supercapacitor buffer to mitigate the battery aging. Experimental results show that a supercapacitor of only $2mF$ capacitance increases the lifetime by approximately three times compared to the lifetime without using a capacitor.

Acknowledgement

This work is supported by the Center for Integrated Smart Sensors funded by the Ministry of Science, ICT & Future Planning as Global Frontier Project (No.201373718) and the Bavarian Ministry of Economic Affairs and Media, Energy and Technology as part of the EEBatt project.

8. REFERENCES

[1] M. Kassem, J. Bernard, R. Revel, S. Pélissier, F. Duclaud, and C. Delacourt, "Calendar aging of a graphite/LiFePO4 cell," *JPS*, vol. 208, pp. 296 – 305, 2012.

[2] J. Wanga, P. Liua, J. Hicks-Garnera, E. Shermana, S. Soukiaziana, M. Verbruggeb, H. Tatariab, and P. F. James Musserc, "Cycle-life model for graphite-LiFePO4 cells," *JPS*, vol. 196, pp. 3942 – 3948, 2011.

[3] A. Millner, "Modeling Lithium ion battery degradation in electric vehicles," in *IEEE CITRES*, 2010.

[4] S. B. Peterson, J. Apt, and J. Whitacre, "Lithium-ion battery cell degradation resulting from realistic vehicle and vehicle-to-grid utilization," *JPS*, vol. 195, pp. 2385 – 2392, 2010.

[5] L. Lam and P. Bauer, "Practical capacity fading model for Li-ion battery cells in electric vehicles," *IEEE TPE*, vol. 28, no. 12, 2013.

[6] S. Karagiannopoulos, M. González, M. Hildmann, and G. Andersson, "Battery modeling within plug-in vehicle fleet simulations in smart-grids," Master's thesis, ETH Zürich, 2012.

[7] D. Shin, Y. Kim, Y. Wang, N. Chang, and M. Pedram, "Constant-current regulator-based battery-supercapacitor hybrid architecture for high-rate pulsed load applications," *JPS*, vol. 205, pp. 516–524, 2012.

[8] Intel, Product information, http://ark.intel.com/products.

[9] Beyondinfinite, LP154WX4-TLC3 datasheet, http://beyondinfinite.com/lcd/Library/LG-Philips/LP154WX4-TLC3.pdf.

[10] HGST, Travelstar-Z7K500 datasheet, http://www.hgst.com/hard-drives/mobile-drives/7mm-thin-and-light-drives/travelstar-z7k500, 2013.

[11] Kingston, KVR16N11-8 datasheet, http://www.kingston.com/dataSheets/KVR16N11_8.pdf, 2013.

[12] Wikipedia, http://en.wikipedia.org/wiki/Comparison_of_Nvidia_graphics_processing_units.

[13] Futuremark benchmarks, http://www.futuremark.com, 2014.

[14] Simcity, http://www.simcity.com, 2014.

[15] Lenovo, http://shop.lenovo.com, 2014.

[16] Y. Kim, N. Chang, Y. Wang, and M. Pedram, "Maximum power transfer tracking for a photovoltaic-supercapacitor energy system," in *IEEE/ACM ISLPED*, 2010.

[17] Y. Choi, N. Chang, and T. Kim, "DC-DC converter-aware power management for low-power embedded systems," *IEEE TCAD*, vol. 26, 2007.

[18] Digikey Corporation, http://www.digikey.com, 2014.

Variation Tolerant Design of a Vector Processor for Recognition, Mining and Synthesis*

Vivek Kozhikkottu,
Swagath Venkataramani,
Anand Raghunathan
School of ECE, Purdue University
{vkozhikk,venkata0,raghunathan}@purdue.edu

Sujit Dey
School of ECE, UC San Diego
dey@ece.ucsd.edu

ABSTRACT

Variations have emerged as one of the most significant challenges facing the design of integrated circuits in nanoscale technologies. As a consequence, variation tolerant design has become essential at all levels of design abstraction.

In this work, we investigate the design of a variation tolerant vector processor for applications from the emerging domains of recognition, mining and synthesis (RMS). We demonstrate how leveraging domain-specific application and architectural characteristics can lead to new and highly effective variation tolerance mechanisms. A predominant fraction of the processing elements in the target processor perform vector reduction operations, which leads to two key properties that we exploit for variation tolerance. First, the circuit delay of a processing element can be bounded a few cycles in advance based on its micro-architectural state. Second, vector reduction operations may be decomposed by performing operations on smaller vectors and combining the partial results. These properties allow us to create a joint hardware-software variation tolerance mechanism, wherein the hardware is enhanced with the ability to predict timing errors during the execution of vector instructions and effectively preempt their occurrence, while software is tasked with restoring the correct outputs. We enhance the proposed scheme with a dynamic voltage control mechanism that further improves energy efficiency by exploiting variations in data characteristics seen across different applications. Our experiments on six RMS applications demonstrate that the proposed variation tolerant design technique achieves an average of 32% energy improvement over a traditional guardband based design.

Categories and Subject Descriptors

B.7.1 [**INTEGRATED CIRCUITS**]: VLSI (Very large scale integration)

Keywords

Vector Processors; Variations; Variation Aware Design; Variation Tolerance; HW/SW co-design

1. INTRODUCTION

In recent years, variations in the manufacturing process has emerged as one of the biggest challenges confronting designers of integrated circuits. Traditionally, process variations have been addressed by employing conservative voltage (or

*This work was supported in part by the National Science Foundation under Grant Nos. 0916117 and 1018621.

frequency) guardbands to ensure that the required timing constraints are met even under variations. However, with the continued scaling of transistors into the deep nanometer regime and the corresponding increase in the magnitude of variations, guardband based worst case design has become highly expensive. For example, variation measurements on a many-core processor at the 45nm technology node demonstrated a 30% spread in the frequencies of cores [1].

Realizing the significant penalties associated with conservative design, various research efforts have proposed variation-tolerant design methodologies at different levels of design abstraction, spanning circuits to systems. As variations are inherently a bottom up phenomenon, initial research efforts focussed on the lower levels of design abstraction, leading to techniques such as statistical timing analysis [2], variation-aware gate sizing [3], *etc.* However, the incessant increase in the magnitude of variations has prompted designers to address them earlier in the design process, at the architecture and system levels. This has resulted in variation-tolerant design techniques for micro-processors [4,5], multi-cores [6,7], graphics processing units [8], SIMD processors [9,10] and heterogeneous system-on-chips [11].

In this work, we investigate the variation tolerant design of an important class of architectures *viz.* vector processors, which enable efficient execution of workloads with fine-grained data parallelism and regular data accesses. These patterns are abundant in a wide range of existing and emerging application domains such as multimedia, graphics, recognition, mining, synthesis, and vision. We focus on QUORA [12], a vector processor designed for recognition, mining and synthesis, which consists of processing elements that primarily perform vector reduction operations on input vectors or streams.

We identify two key properties specific to the target vector processor architecture that enable the design of new and highly effective variation tolerance mechanisms. The first property exploits the *delay predictability* of Vector Processing Elements (VPEs) that perform vector reduction operations. Vector reductions are typically carried out over multiple cycles; in each cycle, individual data elements of the input vector(s) are operated upon and partial results are reduced or accumulated. We make the key observation that, while executing vector reduction operations, the worst case delay of a VPE in the next few cycles is a strong function of its current micro-architectural state. This allows us to *predict*, based on the values of selected registers in the VPE, whether timing errors due to variations are imminent during the course of the current instruction. The ability to predict timing violations in advance, without significant circuit-level enhancements [13,14] to detect them, is key to the proposed variation tolerant design approach.

Another intrinsic feature of vector reductions is the property of *decomposability*, which enables them to be broken up into smaller vector reductions, whose partial results can subsequently be combined to obtain the final reduction output. We utilize the dynamic decomposition of vector reduction operations as a strategy to *preempt* timing errors that may occur due to variations. This is possible because decomposing a vector reduction into operations on smaller vector streams effectively limits the circuit delays in the VPE on which it executes. Finally, the intermediate results produced as a result of the decomposition process are composed together to *restore* the correct output at the end of a reduction operation.

Based on the above insights, we propose a joint hardware-software variation tolerance scheme wherein we equip the hardware with logic required to predict and preempt the occurrence of timing errors during instruction execution and instrument the software with recovery routines that restore the correct output at the end of each vector reduction. While this approach enables us to eliminate conservative design guard-bands employed for process variations, it does not exploit the wide variation in data characteristics seen across different applications. We exploit this opportunity by augmenting the design with a voltage control mechanism that monitors the number of preemption operations performed by the vector processor and appropriately regulates the supply voltage so as to minimize the overall application energy.

In summary, the key contributions of this work are as follows:

- We propose the first approach to design variation tolerant vector processors that leverages the unique properties of vector reduction to predict and preempt the occurrence of timing errors under variations, and subsequently restore the correct output at the end of execution.
- Embodying the above predict-preempt-restore design approach, we develop a low-overhead hardware-software variation tolerance mechanism for a recently proposed vector processor for RMS applications.
- We further improve the energy efficiency of the proposed scheme by embedding it in a dynamic voltage control loop that reacts to variations in the data characteristics by appropriately modulating the supply voltage of the vector processor.
- We demonstrate the utility of the proposed variation tolerance mechanisms on six RMS applications and achieve significant (average of 32%) energy benefits.

The rest of this paper is organized as follows. Section 2 provides an overview of previous work in variation tolerant design. Section 3 gives an architectural overview of the vector processor considered in this work. Sections 4 and 5 detail our proposed variation tolerant design approach. Section 6 describes our experimental methodology and the results obtained are subsequently presented in Section 7. Finally, Section 8 concludes the paper.

2. RELATED WORK

In this section, we discuss previous efforts that have addressed variations at different levels of design abstraction.

At the circuit level, Razor [13] proposed the use of shadow latches to detect timing errors caused due to variations, and techniques such as clock-gating and counter-flow pipelining to recover from them. Subsequently, tunable replica circuits (TRC) and embedded error-detection circuits (EDS) were proposed [14] to help detect and recover from process, voltage and temperature variations. While effective, these techniques incur considerable area and power overheads and require significant modifications to the architecture and design flow. Further, these techniques cannot address the impact of within-die variations [11]. These shortcomings are further amplified in the context of vector processors, since: (i) unlike general purpose processors, they do not possess the necessary control logic that facilitates low-overhead implementations of error recovery such as counter-flow pipelining and (ii) they contain a large number of processing cores operating in lock-step and are hence more susceptible to within-die variations. Variation-tolerant designs have been proposed for micro-processors [4,5], multi-cores [6,7], Graphic Processing Units (GPUs) [8], SIMD processors [9, 10] and accelerator-rich SoCs [11]. For micro-processors, globally asynchronous locally synchronous design [5] and fine grained body-biasing [4]

have been proposed as mechanisms to combat the impact of variations. In the context of multi-core platforms, traditional dynamic voltage and frequency scaling (DVFS) was extended to incorporate the impact of variations on the frequency and leakage power of individual cores [6]. Disproportionate shared resource (*e.g.*, cache) allocation was proposed to redress the impact of variations in multi-core platforms on the performance of multi-threaded programs [7]. For GPUs, shutting down slower cores and allowing each streaming multi-processor (SMP) to run at its maximum frequency have been proposed as variation tolerance strategies [8]. In the context of SIMD processors a combination of localized error recovery and lane weaving was used to mitigate the impact of variations [9]. Similarly, memoization [10] was shown to be effective in reducing the timing error recovery penalty under variations for SIMD architectures. The concept of "recovery islands" was proposed to enable scaling the recovery based design paradigm to large SoCs and to handle within-die variations [11].

This work proposes new variation-tolerance schemes for the important domain of vector processors. The proposed schemes leverage the unique characteristics of the target applications and architecture, leading to highly effective and low-overhead variation tolerance.

3. BACKGROUND

Over the years, vector processor architectures and programming models have been explored extensively [15,16] and have been successfully deployed in various commercial applications. In this work, we demonstrate the proposed variation-tolerant design approach using QUORA, a recently developed vector processor [12] that is designed to efficiently execute applications from the Recognition, Mining and Synthesis (RMS) domains. RMS applications are commonly characterized by 2 levels of reduction operations. In the first level, matrix-matrix and matrix-vector reduction operations are performed on the input data to generate significant amounts of intermediate data. These intermediate data are further subject to a second level of reduction to result in a small number of outputs.

To realize RMS applications efficiently, the QUORA architecture, shown in Figure 1, utilizes a 3 tiered hierarchy of processing elements, *viz.* 2D-array vector processing elements (2d-VPEs), 1D-array vector processing elements (1d-VPEs) and a scalar processing element (scPE). These PEs vary significantly in their complexity and programmability. QUORA also contains 2 sets of streaming memory (SM) elements that feed data to the PEs.

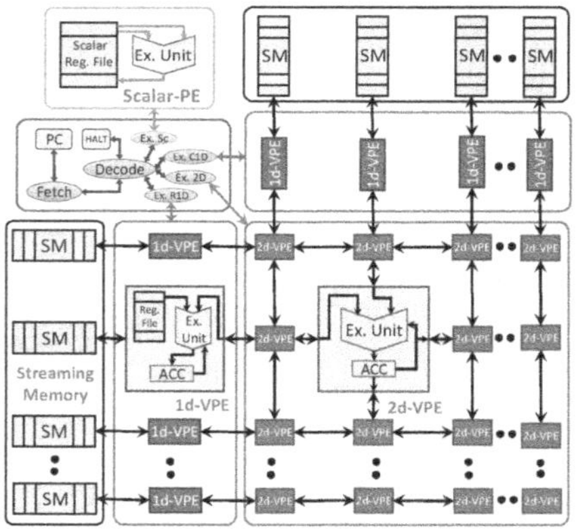

Figure 1: QUORA architectural overview

The 2d-VPEs are arranged as a 2D systolic array with each 2d-VPE receiving inputs from the left and top neighbours, which are subsequently propagated to the right and bottom neighbours respectively in the next cycle. The 2d-VPEs along the top and left borders of the 2D array receive inputs from SM elements located in the corresponding row/-column. The 2d-VPEs are optimized to carry out vector-vector reduction operations such as Dot product, Euclidean distance, Sum of absolute differences *etc.* The 2d-VPEs contain one accumulator register that stores the output of the vector reduction operation.

QUORA also contains two sets of 1d-VPEs arranged along the left and top borders of the 2d-PE array, as shown in Figure 1. The 1d-VPEs receive their inputs from the accumulators of the 2d-VPEs and operate together in an SIMD fashion. The 1d-VPE elements are designed to carry out complex reduction operations such as finding min/max, and evaluate kernel functions like tanh, exponential, *etc.* Hence, their execution units are more sophisticated compared to the 2d-VPEs. The processor also contains a scalar processing element, which is similar to a conventional scalar microprocessor. It is typically used to execute computations for loop control, address calculation, pointer arithmetic, *etc.*

A detailed energy analysis of the QUORA processor synthesized to the IBM 45 nm technology reveals that the energy consumption of the applications is dominated by the 2D array VPE's (upto 88%). We hence focus our variation tolerance efforts on the 2D array and guardband the other cores. It is also noteworthy that we utilize this architecture only as an illustration and the design approach is applicable to any vector processor that performs vector reduction operations.

4. VARIATION TOLERANT VECTOR PROCESSOR DESIGN

The proposed approach for tackling the impact of variations involves deterministically predicting whether timing errors can occur during execution and subsequently preempting such errors and recovering from their impact. Towards this end, we first describe in detail how the unique properties of QUORA enable us to design low-overhead prediction, preemption and recovery schemes. We then present a joint hardware-software variation tolerance mechanism that applies this design approach.

4.1 Preliminaries and Design Approach

As described in Section 3, the vast majority of the processing elements in QUORA perform reduction operations on input data vectors to evaluate a scalar output. Examples of vector reduction operations include multiply-and-accumulate, Euclidean distance, sum-of-absolute-differences, *etc.* These operations can be decomposed into scalar computations on individual vector elements, whose outputs are then accumulated together. A typical implementation of a vector processing element (VPE) thus consists of several scalar execution units followed by an accumulator as

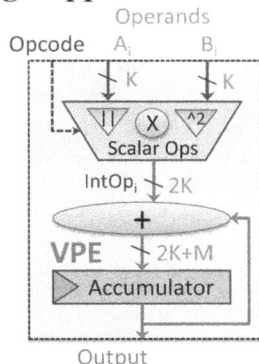

Figure 2: VPE micro-architecture

shown in Figure 2. The VPE executes a vector reduction operation over multiple cycles, wherein in each cycle, individual data elements of the input vectors (A_i, B_i) are sequentially fed into the VPE and the corresponding intermediate output ($IntOp_i$) from the scalar execution unit is used to update the accumulator register. Note that the bit-width of the accumulator ($2K + M$) has to be significantly wider than both the data operands (K). Therefore, the adder that performs the accumulation is responsible for a large portion of the circuit delay within each VPE.

The vector reduction computation pattern and the corresponding micro-architectural characteristics of the VPE can be leveraged to design low overhead variation tolerance mechanisms, as explained below.

First, the worst case delay of the VPE is a strong function of its intrinsic micro-architectural state, i.e., the magnitude of the value held in its accumulator register. This is attributed to the fact that the accumulator register is used in

every VPE execution cycle and has a wider bit-width compared to other input operands. In order to illustrate the above property, we analyze the delay characteristics of a synthesized 2D-VPE unit of the QUORA processor with input operands and accumulator registers of size 8 and 32 bits respectively.

Figure 3 plots the normalized worst case delay of the VPE as a function of the value in the accumulator register. The figure shows that the worst case delay of the circuit monotonically increases with the accumulator value. For small accumulator values, less than the magnitude of the intermediate scalar output (2^{16}), the worst-case delay of the circuit is

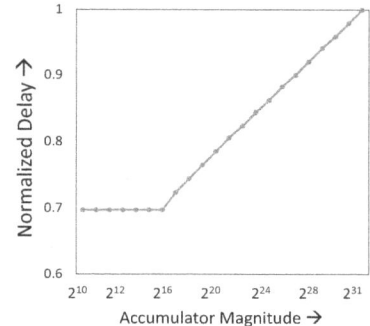

Figure 3: Normalized VPE delay *vs.* accumulator state

strongly influenced by the input operands and therefore does not vary with accumulator magnitude. However as the accumulator magnitude increases, the worst-case delay of the circuit is determined primarily by the accumulator state. In this case, the spread in worst-case delay amounts to 30% of the maximum delay of the VPE. This unique property allows us to bound the delay of the VPE based on its intrinsic software state.

The second key property of the VPE is that *in each execution cycle, the magnitude of its intrinsic micro-architectural state (and hence the VPE circuit delay) can at most increase by the maximum possible value of the intermediate scalar output ($IntOp_i$).* Thus, based on the current value of the accumulator register, this property enables us to obtain a delay bound for the VPE not just for the current execution cycle but also for a given number of successive execution cycles. Since process variations impact the delay of the circuit, these properties allow us to deterministically predict whether a given VPE can perform correct computations (without timing violations) for a given number of future execution cycles. This ability to predict timing errors under variations is unique to vector reduction operations and forms a key component of the proposed variation tolerance scheme.

Finally, we note that *vector reductions operations can be decomposed into reduction operations of smaller length, whose outputs can then be accumulated together to compute the final reduction output.* Therefore, under variations, when the accumulator value (and by extension the delay of the VPE) exceeds a safe threshold, we save the current value of the accumulator and reset the accumulator register to zero. Resetting the accumulator considerably reduces the delay of the VPE and enables the VPE to resume the vector reduction computation without suffering from timing violations. Finally, at the end of the reduction operation, we can recompute the correct reduction output by composing the current value in the accumulator with the previously saved partial reduction outputs. Note that the safe threshold value is unique to each VPE and depends on how it has been impacted by variations.

In summary, the delay dependence of a VPE on its accumulator state can be utilized to design an efficient timing error prediction mechanism. This prediction mechanism is paired with a preemptive reset and restore mechanism which leverages the decomposability of vector reductions.

4.2 Hardware Software Co-design for Variation Tolerance

In this section, we demonstrate the proposed approach by designing joint hardware-software variation tolerance framework for the QUORA processor.

In the proposed framework, outlined in Figure 4, the hardware is responsible for deterministically predicting when tim-

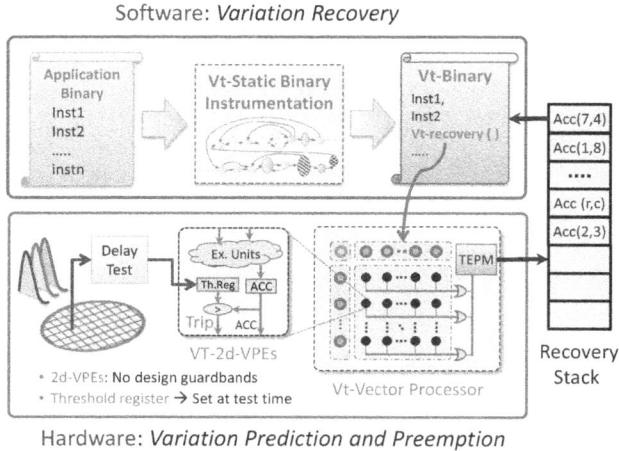

Software: *Variation Recovery*

Hardware: *Variation Prediction and Preemption*

Figure 4: Hardware-software variation tolerance framework overview

ing violations occur in the VPEs and performing the required steps to preempt their occurrence. All the VPEs in the 2D-array are instrumented with a programmable *threshold register*, which holds the maximum accumulator value until which the VPE can perform computations without timing violations under variations. The threshold register for each VPE is set through post-manufacturing delay test and hence considers its individual variation-profile. The VPE is also augmented with additional logic that can detect if its accumulator register exceeds the value set in the threshold register. If so, a *Timing Error Preemption Module* (TEPM) saves the current accumulator value on to a *recovery stack* and resets the accumulator to zero. The VPE then resumes normal execution. If further threshold violations occur, the accumulator is again saved to the stack and reset to zero for each violation.

While the hardware is equipped to carry out variation prediction and preemption, the software is tasked to ensure that the correct output is computed at the end of each vector reduction operation by composing the accumulator states saved in the recovery stack. As shown in Figure 4, a static binary instrumentation tool is utilized to instrument the application with appropriate *recovery routines* that parse the recovery stack and perform the operations required to compute the correct output at the end of the vector reduction. The following sections describe the hardware and software variation tolerance mechanisms in more detail.

4.2.1 Hardware: Variation Prediction and Preemption

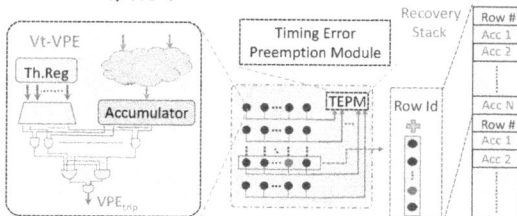

Figure 5: Variation tolerant hardware: Prediction and preemption of timing errors

As described previously, each VPE in the 2D array is equipped to detect if variations can lead to timing errors during execution and further preempt their occurrence by storing and resetting their software state. Figure 5 shows the block diagram of the proposed variation-tolerant VPE (VT-VPE), augmented with a threshold register and timing error prediction logic. The timing error prediction logic ensures that the accumulator value is within the value specified in the threshold register. If not, it asserts the VPE_{trip} signal. In our implementation, we restrict the value stored in the threshold register to powers of 2. This quantization of the

threshold greatly simplifies the complexity of the error prediction logic and the associated power and area overheads. For instance, when the threshold register is set to 2^K, the timing error prediction logic only needs to check if the accumulator bits above bit position K are all zeros (accumulator $< 2^K$) or all ones (accumulator $> -2^K$), in-order to ensure that the magnitude of the accumulator is within the desired range.

The VPE_{trip} signals from all VPEs are then routed to the timing error preemption module (TEPM) that is global to the entire vector processor. The TEPM is responsible for identifying the VPE asserted its VPE_{trip}, storing the VPE's accumulator state onto the recovery stack and resetting the VPE. The TEPM in our implementation performs the above operations at the granularity of rows of the 2D array *i.e.*, even if the VPE_{trip} signal of one of the VPEs is asserted, the software state of all the VPEs in its row are preempted. This design choice is driven primarily by three factors: (i) The overheads of saving a single VPE's accumulator and that of the entire row are essentially the same, since the interconnect structure of the 2D array dictates that the accumulators need to be scanned out sequentially, (ii) Since all the VPEs in a row have one operand in common, their accumulator values tend to be similar in practice, and (iii) Due to the spatial correlation exhibited by within-die variations, the threshold registers for multiple VPEs in a row are often similar.

The TEPM checks every cycle whether any of the VPE_{trip} signals have been asserted. If so, it initiates the preemption process and first stalls the entire 2D array of VPEs. It then proceeds to shift out the contents of all VPE accumulator registers and writes them out, along with a unique row identifier, to the top of the recovery stack (Figure 5). Subsequently, all the VPEs in the row are reset and normal execution is resumed. In the above scheme, routing and collating the VPE_{trip} signals from all VPEs within a single execution cycle can prove to be challenging for large dimensions of the 2D array. Therefore, we suitably lower the magnitude of the threshold register to provide sufficient look-ahead such that all the VPE signals can be safely collated inside the timing error preemption module. We evaluated the QUORA processor augmented with the proposed prediction and preemption modules and found the area and power overheads to be less than 4%.

Thus, the vector processor is equipped with hardware mechanisms to efficiently identify and preempt the occurrence of timing errors under variations.

4.2.2 Software: Variation Recovery

The key responsibility of software is to ensure that the outputs of vector instructions are computed correctly, even when they are preempted to avoid timing errors. This requires composing the intermediate accumulator states stored in the recovery stack with the corresponding VPE's accumulator register. The instruction set of QUORA allows us to carry out these computations as a sequence of native instructions. A static binary instrumentation tool is used to transform the application assembly code by inserting variation recovery routines that guarantee overall program correctness. The instrumentation ensures that all possible execution paths between instructions that modify the accumulator registers to those that consume it have at least one call to a recovery routine.

The variation recovery routine utilizes the 1d-VPEs to perform the operations required to restore the correct outputs. On each invocation, the recovery routine first checks whether the recovery stack is empty and if so it returns immediately. If not, the intermediate values stored in the recovery stack and the corresponding accumulator values (based on the row-id stored along with the intermediate values) are gathered in the 1d-PE array and are accumulated before being stored back to their respective locations in the 2D array. The above process is repeated until the recovery stack is empty. In our implementation, the recovery routine takes 47 cycles per unique row entry in the recovery stack.

In summary, the proposed predict-preempt-restore design approach, and the hardware-software framework that embodies it, provide a new alternative to design variation-tolerant vector processors.

5. EXPLOITING DATA CHARACTERISTICS

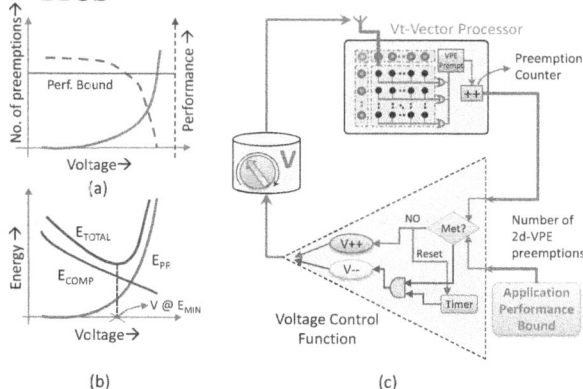

Figure 6: Dynamic voltage control mechanism and corresponding tradeoffs

While the design framework discussed in the previous section enables us to greatly reduce the conservative guardbands associated with process variations, we can further improve energy efficiency by considering the variations present in application data characteristics. For instance, the length of input vectors over which reduction operations are performed, as well as the sparsity of data (*i.e*, number of non-zero elements in input vectors) vary widely across applications. As a consequence, the maximum value of VPE accumulators (and by extension their maximum delay) can change drastically from one application to another.

We augment the proposed variation-tolerant vector processor design with an adaptive voltage control mechanism, as shown in Figure 6, which can dynamically exploit data characteristics to improve energy efficiency. Scaling the supply voltage allows us to lower the energy required to perform the vector computations (E_{COMP}). However decreasing the supply voltage increases the VPE delay and therefore necessitates decreasing each VPE's threshold. This can lead to an increase in the number of preemptions and thereby increase the number of cycles and energy spent in the preemption and recovery operations (E_{PR}). The voltage controller therefore tries to achieve an optimal tradeoff between these two conflicting factors by operating as close to the optimal energy point that minimizes $E_{TOTAL} = E_{COMP} + E_{PR}$.

The voltage controller takes as it inputs the number of preemptions and a bound on the performance loss and tries to minimize the overall energy. The controller is invoked every million cycles, or if the number of preemptions exceeds a given threshold. On every invocation, if the number of preemptions exceeds the computed threshold (based on the performance bound) it increments the supply voltage. Similarly, if the number of preemptions is below the threshold, we decrement the voltage. However, to avoid frequent voltage transitions, we wait for 20 million cycles after a voltage increment to decrement the voltage any further.

The dynamic voltage control scheme described above enables the HW-SW variation tolerance framework to adapt to the application's data characteristics and further improve energy efficiency.

6. EXPERIMENTAL METHODOLOGY

In this section, we describe our experimental methodology for energy and performance estimation, explain our variation modeling framework and finally provide an overview of the application benchmarks used in our experiments.

Energy and Performance Estimation: For our experiments, we developed a cycle accurate simulator for the QUORA processor described in Section 3. We synthesized the RTL imple-

Technology node = 45 nm;
Nominal Core Frequency: 250Mhz
V_{th}: 150mV; V_{dd}: 1V; T: 300K; ϕ: 0.5;
α: 1.3; V_{th}'s σ/μ: 0.09

Table 1: Technology Parameters

mentation of QUORA to the IBM 45nm technology library using Synopsys Design Compiler and utilized Synopsys Power Compiler to estimate power consumption. For estimating application energy, we first perform gate level power analysis to obtain the energy consumed by each instruction in the instruction set. We applied this instruction-level energy model to the statistics (dynamic instruction counts) reported by the instruction set simulator to obtain the total application energy.

Variation Modelling: For modelling the impact of process variations, we utilized VARIUS [17] along with a chip floorplan to obtain the frequency distributions for each processing element in our vector processor, in accordance with the technology parameters shown in Table 1. For each of our experiments we generated 100 distinct chip instances, each of which has a unique delay distribution, and we report energy benefits averaged across these 100 chip instances.

Applications	Algorithm	Dataset
Document Recognition (SVM)	Support Vector Machines	MNIST
Digit Classification (CNN)	Neural Networks	MNIST
Eye Detection (GLVQ)	Generalized Learning Vector Quantization	YUV faces
Character Recognition (k-NN)	K-nearest Neighbors	OCR digits
Image Segmentation (Img-Seg)	K-means Clustering	Berkeley dataset
Optical Character Clustering (OCR)	K-means Clustering	OCR digits

Figure 7: Application Benchmarks

Application Benchmarks: We evaluate the proposed variation tolerant vector processor using a suite of data-parallel applications from the domains of recognition, mining and synthesis. Figure 7 lists the six applications, the underlying algorithm and the dataset on which the application was run. We ported these applications to the QUORA ISA and instrumented the application assembly with the required variation recovery routines.

7. RESULTS

In this section, we present the results of various experiments that demonstrate the ability of our joint hardware-software variation tolerance framework to eliminate guardbands and achieve significant improvements in overall energy efficiency.

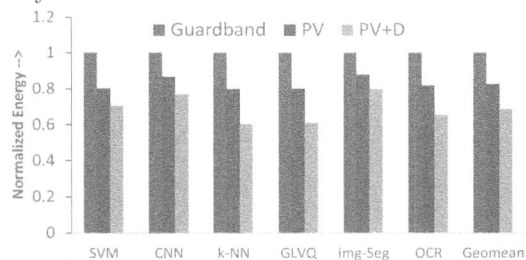

Figure 8: Energy consumption under variations

Figure 8 plots the normalized energy consumption for all of our applications for three different designs: (i) *Guardband*: Traditional guardband based design wherein the voltage is set conservatively such that no timing errors occur even under variations, (ii) *PV*: The proposed variation-tolerant design without the dynamic voltage control mechanism, and (iii) *PV+D*: The proposed design with the dynamic voltage control scheme that enables it to adapt to each application's data characteristics and further improve energy benefits. For the *PV* and *PV+D* designs the application performance loss was bounded to be less than 1%. We note that the energy savings reported are an average obtained over 100 chip instances, each with a distinct frequency profile. The figure shows that the *PV* design on an average reduces the overall energy consumption between 12-20% (geometric mean:

18%), compared to the guardbanded design. Further, leveraging the variations in the application data characteristics, the *PV+D* design obtains an additional 9-20% energy benefits, resulting in an average of 32% energy savings over the guardbanded baseline.

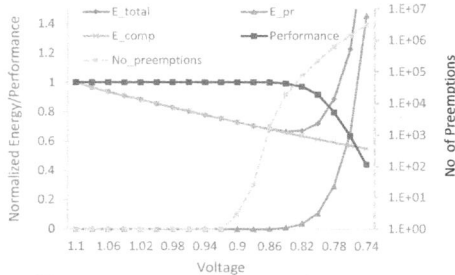

Figure 9: Energy consumption for the SVM application at different supply voltages

Figure 9 plots the normalized energy consumption E_total of the SVM application as well as its constituent components, *viz.* (i) E_comp: energy spent in performing useful computations, and (ii) E_pr: energy spent in performing the necessary preemption and restore operations, while varying the supply voltage. It also plots the normalized performance of the application as well the number of preemption operations that occurred as a function of the supply voltage. As we can see from the figure, scaling the voltage past the guardbands (associated with die-to-die and within-die variations) allows us to reduce the energy spent in performing useful computations (E_comp). However scaling the voltage beyond a point (0.92 V in the figure) exponentially increases the number of preemptions as well as the energy spent in performing the required preempt and restore operations (E_pr). As a result of these conflicting factors, the overall application energy (E_total) is minimum at 0.84 V. In a similar manner, due to the performance overheads associated with preempt and restore operations, application performance also starts degrading with increased voltage scaling. For any given application, the proposed dynamic voltage control scheme tries to operate at the supply voltage that minimizes the overall application energy, while simultaneously ensuring that the performance constraints are satisfied.

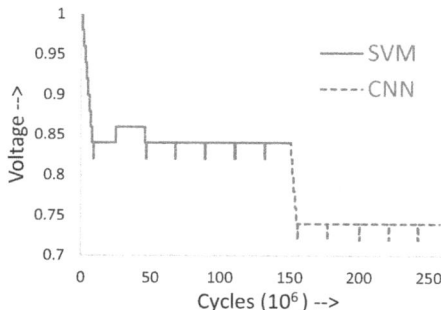

Figure 10: Voltage *vs.* time during the execution of SVM and CNN applications

Figure 10 plots the voltage selected by the dynamic voltage control mechanism over a period of 250 million execution cycles, while the vector processor consecutively executes two different applications, namely SVM and CNN. The figure shows that the voltage controller initially adapts to the data characteristics of the SVM application and operates around its optimal operating voltage (0.84 V). However, in the case of the CNN application, the maximum value reached by the accumulator register is much smaller compared to SVM, due to smaller vector lengths over which the reduction operations are performed (SVM: 784 *vs.* CNN: 25). Hence, as the vector processor starts executing the CNN application, the supply voltage is further lowered by the voltage control mechanism, resulting in improved energy benefits.

Finally, in Figure 11 we plot the overall energy savings obtained for all six of our application benchmarks as a function of the magnitude of underlying variations. The figure shows that with increasing variations, the overall energy savings obtained by our variation tolerance framework increases across all application benchmarks.

In summary, our experimental results clearly demonstrate the effectiveness of our

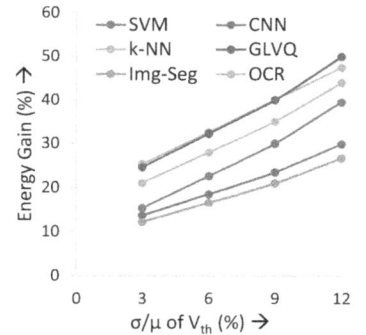

Figure 11: Overall energy benefits with increasing magnitude of variations

joint hardware-software variation tolerance framework in improving energy efficiency under variations. We also illustrate the additional energy benefits that can be obtained by dynamically adapting the supply voltage in response to application data characteristics. Finally, our results show improvements in energy savings with increasing magnitude of variations, which are a likely consequence of further technology scaling.

8. CONCLUSION

In this work, we presented a predict, preempt and restore based variation-tolerant design scheme for vector processors, that leverages the unique domain specific properties of vector reduction operations to create a highly efficient variation tolerance mechanism. We implemented this scheme in a joint hardware-software framework, wherein the hardware performs prediction and preemption and the software handles restore operations. We evaluated the proposed scheme on six applications from the domains of recognition, mining and synthesis and demonstrated significant improvements in overall application energy.

9. REFERENCES

[1] S. Dighe et al. Within-die variation-aware dynamic voltage frequency scaling with optimal core allocation and thread hopping for the 80-core teraflops processor. *Trans. ISSC*, 46(1), 2011.
[2] D. Blaauw et al. Statistical timing analysis: From basic principles to state of the art. *Trans. TCAD*, 27(4):589–607, 2008.
[3] A. Kahng et al. Designing a processor from the ground up to allow voltage/reliability tradeoffs. In *Proc. HPCA*, pages 1 –11, 2010.
[4] S. Sarangi et al. EVAL: Utilizing processors with variation induced timing errors. In *Proc. MICRO*, pages 423–434, 2008.
[5] D. Marculescu et al. Variability and energy awareness: a microarchitecture-level perspective. In *Proc. DAC*, 2005.
[6] S. Herbert et al. Variation-aware dynamic voltage/frequency scaling. In *Proc. HPCA*, pages 301–312, 2009.
[7] V. Kozhikkottu et al. Variation aware cache partitioning for multithreaded programs. In *Proc. DAC*, 2014.
[8] J. Lee et al. Analyzing throughput of gpgpus exploiting within-die core-to-core frequency variation. In *Proc. ISPASS*, April 2011.
[9] R. Pawlowski et al. A 530mv 10-lane SIMD processor with variation resiliency in 45nm soi. In *Proc. ISSCC*, pages 492–494, Feb 2012.
[10] A. Rahimi et al. Spatial memoization: Concurrent instruction reuse to correct timing errors in SIMD architectures. *Trans. TCAS*, 60(12):847–851, Dec 2013.
[11] V. Kozhikkottu et al. Recovery-based design for variation tolerant SoCs. Proc. DAC '12, New York, NY, USA, 2012. ACM.
[12] S. Venkataramani et al. Quality programmable vector processors for approximate computing. In *Proc. MICRO*, pages 1–12, 2013.
[13] D. Ernst et al. Razor: a low-power pipeline based on circuit-level timing speculation. In *Proc. MICRO*, pages 7–18, 2003.
[14] K. Bowman et al. Circuit techniques for dynamic variation tolerance. In *Proc. DAC*, pages 4–7, 2009.
[15] Y. Lee et al. Exploring the tradeoffs between programmability and efficiency in data-parallel accelerators. In *Proc. ISCA*, 2011.
[16] C. Kozyrakis et al. Overcoming the limitations of conventional vector processors. In *Proc. ISCA*, pages 399–409, June 2003.
[17] S.R. Sarangi et al. VARIUS: A Model of Process Variation and Resulting Timing Errors for Microarchitects. *Semiconductor Manufacturing, IEEE Trans.*, 21(1):3 –13, 2008.

Thermal-aware Layout Planning for Heterogeneous Datacenters

Reza Azimi
School of Engineering
Brown University
Providence, RI 02912
reza_azimi@brown.edu

Xin Zhan
School of Engineering
Brown University
Providence, RI 02912
xin_zhan@brown.edu

Sherief Reda
School of Engineering
Brown University
Providence, RI 02912
sherief_reda@brown.edu

ABSTRACT

Cooling power represents a significant portion of total power consumption in datacenters. Heterogeneous datacenters deploy clusters of servers with different hardware configurations, each offering its own performance and power characteristics. We observe that heterogeneous datacenters offer a unique opportunity to reduce cooling power through appropriate planning. In this paper we formulate the problem of rack layout for planning of heterogeneous datacenters, where the goal is to identify the best locations of the server racks with different hardware capabilities to improve the supply temperatures of the CRAC units and the total cooling power. We provide optimal solutions that take into account the impact of varying utilizations of datacenters and job scheduling methods. Using state-of-the-art thermal modeling tools, we prove that our methods lead to datacenter layouts with significant improvements in cooling power reduction, between $15.5\% - 38.5\%$ based on the datacenter utilizations and an average of 28.3% without any negative side effects.

Categories and Subject Descriptors

H.3.4 [**Systems and Software**]: Performance evaluation (efficiency and effectiveness)

Keywords

Energy efficiency, heterogeneous datacenters, cooling power

1. INTRODUCTION

Cooling power is a major source of energy consumption in datacenters. Recent studies show that cooling power can contribute 42% of the total energy consumption of datacenters [3]. Cooling power of the Computer Room Air Conditioners (CRACs) is used to extract the heat produced from the servers and to supply cold air back to the facility through the perforated tiles. The supply temperatures of the cold air from the CRAC units should be set as high as possible to reduce cooling power while not violating the red temperature specifications of the servers.

The planning of homogeneous datacenters is relatively simple as servers are all identical in their configurations; thus, there is no inherent advantage from changing the locations of the racks as the servers will have the same power consumption behavior irrespective of their locations. In homogeneous datacenters, it is the allocation of workloads to the servers that only determines the spatial power distribution inside the datacenter, which consequently determines the thermal characteristics and the cooling power.

Modern datacenters are heterogeneous in nature. They deploy clusters of heterogeneous server platforms where the hardware configuration of the servers can be completely different. Heterogeneous servers can use different processor types, number of cores, and DRAM capacities. The heterogeneous makeup helps datacenters cater to workloads with different characteristics (e.g., transactional, batch, numerically intensive, etc) by matching workloads with the right platforms to better achieve the datacenter's target metrics (e.g., performance and energy consumption). Another reason for heterogeneity arises from multiple replacement, upgrades and the deployment of more cost-efficient systems that become available over time [3].

We observe that heterogeneous datacenters provide an interesting opportunity to plan their facilities in a way to reduce cooling power. Heterogeneous servers have different power specifications, and thus, the spatial positions at installment will lead to inherent thermal characteristics in the datacenter. Thus, we can reduce cooling power by carefully laying out the racks of heterogeneous servers during the planning phase of datacenters. We believe the contributions of this paper are as follows.

- We formulate the problem of rack layout for planning of heterogeneous datacenters, where the goal is to identify the best locations of the racks of servers with different hardware capabilities to improve the supply temperatures of the CRAC units and the total cooling power.

- Given the nature of modern datacenters with varying utilization that is a function of time and sophisticated job schedulers, we reformulate the rack layout problem in a probabilistic manner to identify layouts that are likely to provide the best cooling subject to various operating conditions.

- We propose a number of of heuristics and an optimal solution methodology based on integer linear programming (ILP) and evaluate them for realistic datacenter configurations. Since the planning of datacenters occur only once, the ILP runtime is practically feasible.

- Using a state-of-the-art Computational Fluid Dynamics (CFD) thermal modeling tool for datacenters, we demonstrate the effectiveness of our approach in reducing total cooling power between $15.5\% - 38.5\%$ based on the datacenter utilizations with an average of 23.3%. This improvement is realized by planning the datacenter using the rack locations identified from our algorithm and without any side effects.

The organization of this paper is as follows. In Section 2 we provide the basic background information for thermal modeling of data centers. In Section 3 we formulate the layout planning problems for heterogeneous datacenters to reduce cooling power and propose methods to solve it. Our experimental setup and results are provided in Section 4, where we demonstrate significant improvements in cooling power. Finally, Section 5 provides the main conclusions for this work and future research directions.

2. BACKGROUND

In this section we provide the necessary background to understand our work and its context with respect to related work. We discuss techniques (a) to model the cooling power of datacenters, and (b) to improve the thermal characteristics and cooling power.

a. Modeling Cooling Power. CRAC units consume cooling power to remove the heat generated by the computing servers. The cooling power p_{cool} of a CRAC is a function of the inlet heat flowing into the CRAC, its supply temperature t_{sup}, and its coefficient of performance CoP, such that

$$p_{cool} = \frac{\text{inlet heat from racks}}{CoP(t_{sup})}, \qquad (1)$$

where the $CoP(\cdot)$ gives the efficiency of the CRAC unit as a function of its supply temperature [8]. The exact function of the CoP is determined empirically by the CRAC manufacturer [8]. Achieving the minimum sufficient cooling power is equivalent to finding the maximum t_{sup} that guarantees that the inlet temperatures of all the servers are below the manufacturer's redline temperature t_{red}.

The inlet temperatures t_i^{in} of rack r_i is impacted by the CRAC supply temperature and the heat recirculation from all the racks in the datacenter. Given a floor plan of the datacenter, the heat recirculation matrix $\mathbf{D}$ can be derived using CFD simulations [13]. Each element $\mathbf{D}(i,j)$ of the heat circulation matrix defines the contribution of the power consumption of rack j to the temperature increment of rack i. For a datacenter that consist of n racks, let $\mathbf{t}^{out} = [t_1^{out}, t_2^{out}, \cdots, t_n^{out}]$ denotes the vector of the outlet temperatures of the racks, while $\mathbf{t}^{in} = [t_1^{in}, t_2^{in}, \cdots, t_n^{in}]$ denotes the vector of inlet temperatures. If $\mathbf{p} = [p_1, p_2, \cdots, p_n]$ denotes the vector of power consumption of racks in datacenter, we can compute the inlet temperatures as [13]:

$$\mathbf{t}^{in} = \mathbf{t}^{sup} + \mathbf{D}\mathbf{p} \qquad (2)$$

where $\mathbf{t}^{sup}$ is a vector of length n that denotes the supply temperatures of the racks in the datacenter, where each element is equal to t_{sup} of the CRAC units.

b. Reducing Cooling Power. Previous works in reducing cooling power focused on thermal-aware job scheduling, where the main goal is to schedule jobs in a way to minimize the heat recirculation effect [12, 9, 1, 8, 2, 10]. Moore *et al.* [8] introduced the concept of Heat Recirculation Factor (HRF), and proposed to distribute the computational power budget to servers with respect to each server's HRF. Shamalizade *et al.* minimized the thermal heat recirculation of homogeneous datacenters considering servers allocation constraints [10]. In [5], authors proposed techniques for High Performance Computing (HPC) cloud datacenters where they allocate the virtual machines to physical machines using linear programming.

Their goal is to minimize the computation power considering the recommended maximum operating temperature of servers.

Tang and Gupta proposed to minimize the heat recirculation by using a genetic algorithm based job scheduler [12] and afterwards, they extended their job scheduling techniques for heterogeneous and Internet datacenters [9, 1]. For heterogeneous datacenters, Al-Qawasmeh *et al.* [2] considered linear programming techniques to select the p-states and allocated jobs of servers to minimize the power consumption under performance constraints and also to maximize performance under power constraint.

None of the previous works leverage the inherent differences in the specifications of heterogeneous servers to provide layouts during the datacenter planning phase to reduce cooling power during operation. We believe that our work is the first to formulate and address this issue.

3. PROPOSED LAYOUT METHODOLOGY

In our datacenter organization we assume the existence of multiple racks of heterogeneous servers, where each rack holds a number of servers of the same configuration. The assumption that a rack holds servers of the same type is not restricting, and it is natural given typical datacenter purchases and upgrade cycles.

Rack Layout Problem formulation: Given n heterogeneous server racks each consuming power p_i, the objective is to find the optimal layout that maps the n racks to n locations in the datacenter such that the sufficient cooling power of the datacenter's m CRAC units is minimized.

While the proposed problem formulation bears resemblance to the thermal-ware job scheduling problem, there is an important distinction between the two. The rack layout problem determines the inherent thermal characteristics of the datacenter, and a bad rack layout can handicap a thermal job scheduler from achieving its target. By solving the rack layout problem, we enable the design of data centers with inherently less cooling requirements, which can be leveraged for further improvements using thermal-aware job scheduling algorithms.

Given a datacenter with a heat recirculation matrix $\mathbf{D}$ that represents the heat recirculation relations among the locations in this datacenter, a greedy algorithm that can solve the proposed rack layout problem is given in Algorithm 1:

---

for *each rack location i of the n locations* **do**
    Compute $h_i = \sum_{j=1}^{n} \mathbf{D}(i,j)$;
end
Sort h_i in ascend order;
Sort the racks based on p_i in descending order;
Allocate the racks to locations based on their sorting order;

Algorithm 1: Greedy layout planning algorithm.

This algorithm allocates servers racks based on their power consumption rank to the locations based on their heat recirculation rank in the reverse order so the server with the highest power consumption gets in the position where it has the least recirculation effect on other servers and so on for other servers and locations.

Another solution to solve the proposed rack layout problem is through local search techniques as given in Algorithm 2. The local search method changes the allocations at random and will save the one with the lowest heat recirculation effect.

The greedy and local search methods are only heuristics and cannot guarantee finding optimal layouts. Thus we investigate an integer linear programming based algorithm to find the optimal so-

for *each rack r_i of the n racks* **do**
| allocate r_i to a free location picked at random
end
Assemble the **p** vector based on allocated rack locations;
let $t_{curr} = $ max of **Dp**;
let $t_{min} = t_{curr}$;
while *the maximum iteration is not reached* **do**
| **for** *each rack r_i* **do**
| | swap the location of r_i with a random rack;
| | recompute t_{curr};
| | **if** $t_{curr} \leq t_{min}$ **then**
| | | let $t_{min} = t_{curr}$;
| | **end**
| | **else**
| | | swap racks back to their original locations;
| | **end**
| **end**
end

Algorithm 2: Local search-based layout planning algorithm.

lution for the rack layout problem. We use the greedy and local search for comparison in the experimental results section 4.

3.1 Thermal-aware Layout Optimization

To maximize the $\mathbf{t}^{sup}$ while ensuring the resulted $\mathbf{t}^{in}$ will not exceed the red line temperature t_{red}, we can instead minimize the maximum element in **Dp**. Let **X** be an $n \times n$ permutation matrix, where $x_{ij} \in \{0, 1\}$ is equal to 1 if and only if rack r_j is placed to location i. The rack layout problem can be formulated as follows.

$$\text{minimize} \quad ||\mathbf{DXp}||_\infty$$
$$\text{subject to} \quad \forall i : \sum_j^n x_{ij} = 1 \quad (1),$$
$$\forall j : \sum_i^n x_{ij} = 1 \quad (2),$$
$$x_{ij} \in \{0, 1\},$$

where the infinity norm $||\mathbf{DXp}||_\infty$ gives the maximum element in the vector $\mathbf{DXp}$. Constraint (1) guarantees each location is assigned at most one rack, while constraint (2) guarantees that each rack r_j is assigned to a location. To solve this optimization problem, we can transform the problem into an integer linear program by adding a slack variable s, where:

$$s = ||\mathbf{DXp}||_\infty \quad (3)$$

Then we can establish relationship between s and the temperature increment of each rack location i:

$$\forall i : t_i \leq s, \quad (4)$$

where $t_i = \sum_{k=1}^n \mathbf{D}_{ik}(\sum_{j=1}^n x_{kj} p_j)$. Thus, the formulation can be rewritten as:

$$\text{minimize} \quad s$$
$$\text{subject to} \quad \forall i : \sum_{k=1}^n \mathbf{D}_{ik}(\sum_{j=1}^n x_{kj} p_j) \leq s$$
$$\forall i : \sum_{j=1}^n x_{ij} = 1,$$
$$\forall j : \sum_{i=1}^n x_{ij} = 1,$$
$$x_{ij} \in \{0, 1\}.$$

The integer linear program accurately describes the optimization objectives and constraints and by solving it we can guarantee the

optimal rack layout during the datacenter planning phase for minimizing the cooling power later during operation.

3.2 Probabilistic Layout Planning

In the previous subsection, we assumed that the power distribution vector **p** is constant over time. However, in reality, the power consumption of each rack, $\mathbf{p}(\lambda)$, varies as a function the datacenter job arrival rate λ and the decisions of the job scheduler. In this case, the optimal rack layout will change with varying server utilization distributions. However, once located, the rack layout cannot be changed dynamically. Thus, it is important to find the optimal layout that minimizes the cooling power on the average over the distribution of utilization cases.

Integrating an accurate server power model that captures the impact of utilization will lead to a better layout that saves cooling power over a larger range of datacenter operation. In this work, we consider two power models:

1. **Servers with idle power consumption.** In datacenters where the number of service requests fluctuates frequently over a large range, the under-utilized servers should remain active in idle mode to enable immediate response. However, when idle, servers still consume $40\% - 50\%$ of their peak power [3]. Let p_{idle} denote the power consumption of a rack in idle mode and p_{dyn} denote the extra power when the rack is fully utilized, then the power p_i of each rack r_i can be modeled as:

$$p_i(\lambda) = p_{idle} + u_i(\lambda) p_{dyn}, \quad (5)$$

where $0 \leq u_i(\lambda) \leq 1$ is the utilization of rack i for a job arrival rate λ to the datacenter. Since our datacenters are heterogeneous, the racks could have different p_{idle} and p_{dyn} depending on their servers configurations.

2. **Servers with power nap states.** To eliminate the idle power, especially when there is no hard requirement for request response time, some datacenters put under-utilized servers to power nap states to eliminate their idle power consumption. In this case, the power of rack i is given by

$$p_i(\lambda) = \begin{cases} p_{idle} + u_i(\lambda) p_{dyn}, & u_i(\lambda) > 0 \\ 0, & u_i(\lambda) = 0 \end{cases} \quad (6)$$

It is important to stress that the utilizations of the racks, which determine their power consumption and consequently the vector **p**, is a function of both the job arrival rate λ and the policy of the job scheduler of the datacenter. For each arrival rate λ, the corresponding utilization u_i for each server rack i can be estimated using a discrete-event simulation with the datacenter's job scheduler.

To solve the rack layout problem with the consideration of utilization dynamics, we propose a probabilistic formulation for the rack layout problem. For a job arrival rate λ with probability density function $\text{pdf}(\lambda)$, the objective of the optimal rack layout can be formulated as:

$$\mathbf{X}_{OPT} = \operatorname*{argmin}_{\mathbf{X}} \int_0^\infty ||\mathbf{DXp}(\lambda)||_\infty \times \text{pdf}(\lambda) d\lambda \quad (7)$$

In reality datacenters are provisioned to operate under a maximum job arrival rate $\lambda_{\max}$. Thus we can approximate the integration in Equation (7) with a summation over the discrete integer

Figure 1: the CFD simulation results and configuration of our experimental datacenter.

values for λ. Using a slack variable s_λ for every possible λ, the integer linear program can be formulated as:

$$\text{minimize} \quad \sum_{\lambda=0}^{\lambda_{\max}} s_\lambda \times \text{pdf}(\lambda)$$

$$\text{subject to} \quad \forall i, \lambda : \sum_{k=1}^{n} \mathbf{D}_{ik}(\sum_{j=1}^{n} x_{kj} p_j(\lambda)) \leq s_\lambda$$

$$\forall i : \sum_{j=1}^{n} x_{ij} = 1,$$

$$\forall j : \sum_{i=1}^{n} x_{ij} = 1,$$

$$x_{ij} \in \{0, 1\}.$$

4. EXPERIMENTAL RESULTS

We setup our datacenter space to accommodate 80 U42 racks for a total of 3200 servers organized in the form of 8 aisles with 10 racks per aisle. We used the CFD modeling tool 6SigmaRoom Lite [4] to simulate the thermal and airflow characteristics of the datacenter. The tool is used to generate the heat circulation matrix. Our datacenter configuration and an example of the simulation result are illustrated in Figure 1. We consider a baseline of four classes of different servers to emulate the architectural heterogeneity in realistic datacenters. The configurations for servers of the four classes are given in Table 1. We collect execution traces of SPEC CPU2006 benchmarks [11] on each of the four types of servers using the pfmon tool, while simultaneously measuring the power consumption trace using an Agilent 34410A digital multimeter. We consider 20 racks for every server type. The datacenter has 8 CRAC units located at the sides as illustrated in Figure 1. We use the HP CRAC model given in Moore et al. with a $CoP(t_{sup}) = 0.0068t_{sup}^2 + 0.0008t_{sup} + 0.458$ [8]. We assume maximum inlet temperature is 25°C. To simulate the dynamic behavior of the datacenter under different loading scenarios, we implement a discrete event queuing simulator [7], which uses the execution and power traces and the heat recirculation matrix to esti-

Table 1: Server configurations.

server	CPU	num CPUs	num cores	freq (GHz)	DRAM (GB)
A	Intel Core i7 920	1	4	2.67	4
B	Intel Core i5 3450S	1	4	2.80	8
C	Intel Xeon E5530	2	8	2.27	12
D	AMD Phenom II X4	1	4	3.40	16

Table 2: Supply tempereture and cooling power for the first experiment

Method	t_{sup} (°C)	cooling power (kW)
ILP	22.1	117
Local Search	20.6	133
Greedy	21.4	124
Heterogeneous oblivious	16.6	191

mate the power and thermal characteristics as a function of time. The job arrival rates are drawn from a random exponential distribution with parameter λ, which controls the mean job arrival rate (jobs/second). The simulator uses a greedy job scheduler to assign jobs to servers, where it assigns an incoming job in the queue to the most energy-efficient free server i.e., the server with highest throughput per Watt [8].

Exp 1. Layout Planning with no Utilization Knowledge. In this experiment, we demonstrate our rack layout method under the scenario that the utilization is not a priori known. Thus, we assume that all servers are running at their highest power consumption which corresponds to maximum utilization. Because we assume full utilization, this planning experiment does not make value of the queueing simulations, and it corresponds to a case where the datacenter is designed based on the plate specifications of the servers regardless of the workloads. We solve the rack layout problem by our proposed ILP algorithm, local search and greedy approaches. The estimated CRAC units supply temperature requirement and minimum cooling power computed from each algorithm are given in Table 2. We also compare against the case of heterogeneous oblivious planning, where the racks are placed randomly independent of their specifications.

Our results show that the optimal locations identified by our ILP algorithm can achieve 38.5% savings in cooling power from 191 kW to 117 kW. The results also show that the use of the ILP-based method is justified compared to easier and faster alternatives such as greedy and local search, as the ILP method saves 11.8% of cooling power over local search and 5.6% over greedy. The runtime of the ILP took 60 seconds on server configuration A, which is quite reasonable given the large size of our experimental datacenter and given that the ILP needs to be solved only once during the planning phase of the datacenter.

The datacenter layouts using ILP and greedy method are given in Figure 2. The slight difference between these two layouts il-

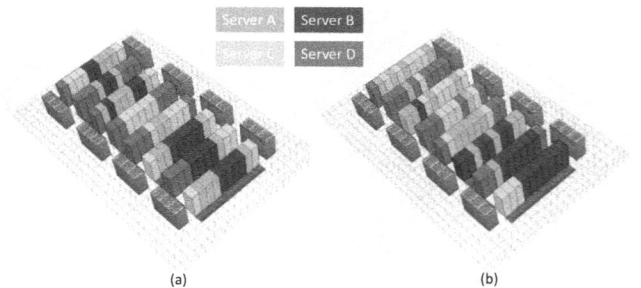

Figure 2: The layout planning of the experimental datacenter. (a) using greedy on the left and (b) using ILP on the right.

lustrates that placing the high power servers in locations with low heat recirculation effect is not enough. While both techniques have similar general trends in their layouts, ILP is able to find a global optimal solution while the greedy heuristics reaches a local optimal.

Exp 2. Layout Planning with known Utilization. When the utilization is known, our proposed method can find the optimal layout planning for a given utilization. We repeat the queuing simulation five times with five different mean job arrival rates from low mean arrival rate ($\lambda = 8$) to high arrival rate ($\lambda = 24$), which cover all service conditions from undersubscribed to oversubscribed operation. The average server utilizations of the four different server types for different job arrival rates are given in Figure 3. Note that for a given λ, the servers show different utilizations, which arise from the role of the job scheduler, which prefers to schedule jobs on the most energy-efficient servers first. Thus, at low job arrival rates, the most energy-efficient servers (e.g., servers of configuration D) will be mostly utilized but other servers will be relatively idle, while all servers tend to become more utilized as the mean job arrival rate increases.

To determine the optimal server rack layout, we consider two power management policies: (a) one where non-utilized servers consume a base amount of idle power depending on their specifications, and (b) one where non-utilized servers are put into near-zero power-saving state (e.g., power nap states [6]).

a. **Servers with idle power consumption.** When service requests transition rapidly, free servers must stay at idle state so that they can respond to new requests immediately. Given the non energy-proportional characteristics of servers [3], an idle server still consumes $40\% - 50\%$ of its peak power consumption. We evaluate the minimum cooling power achieved by our proposed algorithm and demonstrate its power saving performance. In Figure 4, the layouts produced by the ILP reduce the cooling power by $25.5\% - 36.9\%$ compared to heterogeneous-oblivious planning, whereas local search and greedy methods reduce the cooling power requirements by $21.1\% - 33.2\%$.

b. **Servers with power nap states.** In some datacenters where the service request rate is relatively stable, power management techniques could turn the free servers into near-zero power napping states to improve the energy-efficiency. In this case, the optimal layouts identified by our ILP method

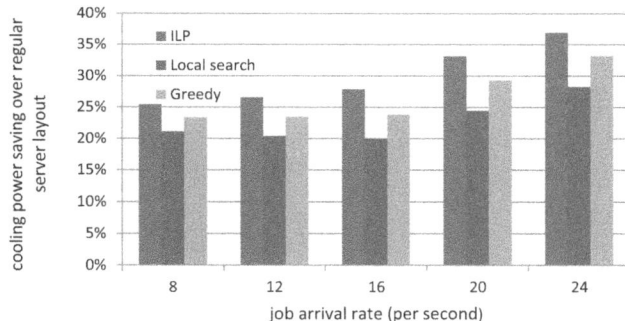

Figure 4: Reductions in cooling power over heterogeneous-oblivious planning when non-utilized servers consume idle power.

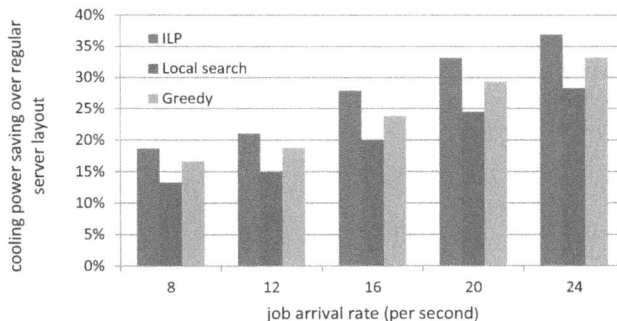

Figure 5: Reductions in cooling power over heterogeneous-oblivious planning when non-utilized servers switch to nap states.

algorithm reduce the cooling power by $18.6\% - 36.9\%$ depending on the utilization rate as given in Figure 5, where local search and greedy algorithm give only $13.2\% - 33.2\%$ of improvements over heterogeneous oblivious rack layout. Our job scheduler prioritizes energy-efficient servers with low power consumption; thus, at low job arrival rates, the low-power servers have higher utilization while the high-power servers are under utilized and switch to nap mode, which leads to a relatively uniform power consumption by the racks. Thus, the optimization searching space and the reductions in cooling power are limited for small λ.

In both cases, ILP improves the cooling power reduction a maximum of 12.1% over local search and 5.6% compare to greedy method.

Exp 3. Layout Planning with Variable Utilization. In a real datacenter, the mean job arrival rate and utilization are not static but they rather change over time reflecting user trends. Thus, for this experiment we used real datacenter utilization traces to drive the distribution of job arrival rate for our datacenter simulator. Figure 6 shows the probability density function (pdf) of our institution's datacenter utilization (i.e., Brown University) over a year and the pdf of a Google datacenter during 24 hours over a week [14]. We mapped these distributions to the corresponding job arrival rate for our datacenter configuration. Using the probability of each job arrival rate and utilization distribution of each job arrival rate, we use our probabilistic ILP formulation to identify the optimal layout planning.

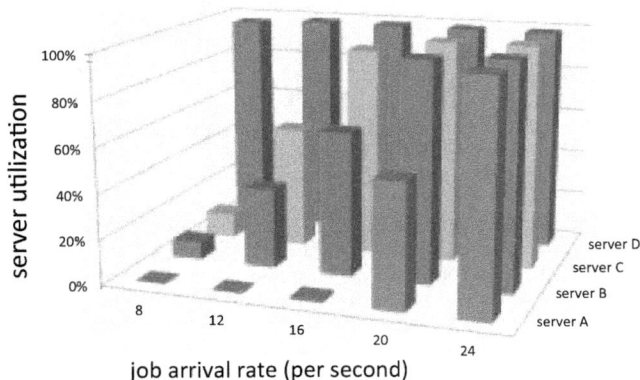

Figure 3: The average utilization of each server type.

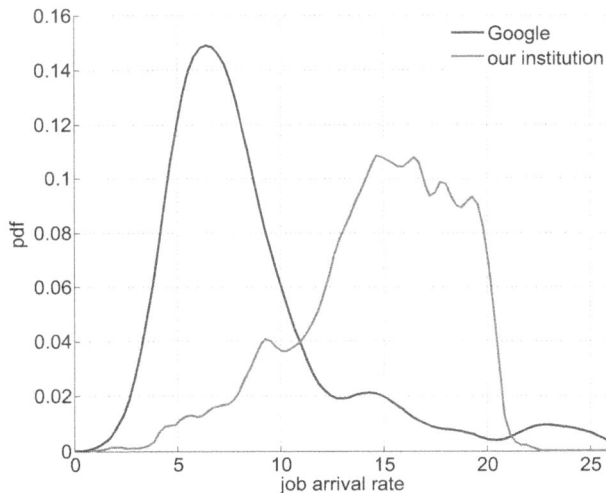

Figure 6: Probability density functions (pdfs) for job arrival rate distribution for two datacenters: one at our institution and one at Google.

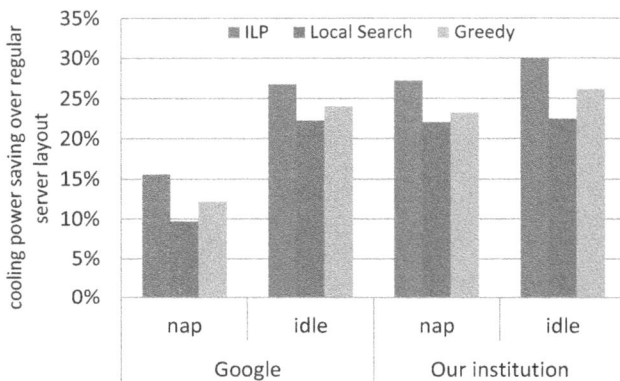

Figure 7: Cooling power reductions achieved by layout from our methods compared to heterogeneous-oblivious planning.

Figure 7 gives the result for our datacenter using the PDFs from Google and our institution for the two power management cases: (a) free servers remain idle and (b) free servers are switched to nap modes off. Result shows that our methods are able to consistently deliver layouts that lead to reduced cooling power for various utilization trends. The magnitude for improvement is higher for our institution's datacenter because it has a higher mean job arrival rate.

5. CONCLUSION AND FUTURE WORK

In this paper we have formulated the problem of rack layout for heterogeneous datacenters, where the goal is to identify the locations of the server racks during the planning phase of the datacenter to reduce cooling power. Whereas homogeneous racks offer no incentive to lay them out in a particular way, heterogeneous racks offer different power specifications that can be exploited to produce layouts with improved thermal characteristics and cooling. We also

investigated the impact of varying datacenter utilization and the impact of the job scheduler on cooling power and reformulated the rack layout problem to identify the locations that are likely to reduce cooling power under different operating conditions. We devised optimal solution methods to the rack layout problem using integer linear programming. For the experimental results, we devised a realistic model for datacenters using state-of-the-art CFD modeling tools and demonstrated that our methods lead to significant improvements in the thermal characteristics and cooling power.

Planned future work and improvements include analyzing the impact of layout planning on thermal aware job scheduling and exploring potential additional savings.

6. ACKNOWLEDGMENTS

This work is partially supported by the NSF grants 0952866 and 1305148.

7. REFERENCES

[1] Z. Abbasi, G. Varsamopoulos, and S. K. S. Gupta. Thermal aware server provisioning and workload distribution for internet data centers. In *Proceedings of the 19th ACM International Symposium on High Performance Distributed Computing*, pages 130–141, 2010.

[2] A. Al-Qawasmeh, S. Pasricha, A. Maciejewski, and H. Siegel. Power and thermal-aware workload allocation in heterogeneous data centers. *Computers, IEEE Transactions on*, PP(99):1–1, 2013.

[3] L. A. Barroso and U. Holzle. *The Datacenter as a Computer*. Morgan and Claypool Publishers, 2009.

[4] FutureFacilities. 6sigmaroom lite. http://www.futurefacilities.com/.

[5] E. K. Lee, H. Viswanathan, and D. Pompili. Vmap: Proactive thermal-aware virtual machine allocation in hpc cloud datacenters. In *High Performance Computing (HiPC), 2012 19th International Conference on*, pages 1–10, 2012.

[6] D. Meisner, B. Gold, and T. Wenisch. PowerNap: Eliminating Server Idle Power. In *International Conference on Architectural Support for Programming Languages and Operating Systems*, pages 205–216, 2009.

[7] D. Meisner, J. Wu, and T. Wenisch. Bighouse: A simulation infrastructure for data center systems. In *IEEE International Symposium on Performance Analysis of Systems and Software*, pages 35–45, 2012.

[8] J. Moore, J. Chase, P. Ranganathan, and R. Sharma. Making Scheduling "Cool": Temperature-Aware Workload Placement in Data Centers. In *Proceedings of USENIX Annual Technical Conference*, pages 61–75, 2005.

[9] T. Mukherjee, A. Banerjee, G. Varsamopoulos, S. K. Gupta, and S. Rungta. Spatio-temporal thermal-aware job scheduling to minimize energy consumption in virtualized heterogeneous data centers. *Computer Networks*, 53(17):2888–2904, 2009.

[10] H. Shamalizadeh, L. Almeida, S. Wan, P. Amaral, S. Fu, and S. Prabh. Optimized thermal-aware workload distribution considering allocation constraints in data centers. In *Proceedings of the 2013 IEEE International Conference on Green Computing and Communications*, pages 208–214, 2013.

[11] C. D. Spradling. SPEC 2006 Benchmark Tools. *SIGARCH Computer Architecture News,*, 35(1):13–134, 2007.

[12] Q. Tang and S. Gupta. Thermal-Aware Task Scheduling for Data Centers through Minimizing Heat Recirculation. *Cluster Computing*, pages 129–138, 2008.

[13] Q. Tang, T. Mukherjee, S. Gupta, and P. Cayton. Sensor-based Fast Thermal Evaluation Model for Energy Efficient High-Performance Datacenters. In *Intelligent Sensing and Information Processing*, pages 203–208, 2006.

[14] J. Wilkes. More Google cluster data. Google research blog, Nov. 2011.

QPR.js: A Runtime Framework for QoS-Aware Power Optimization for Parallel JavaScript Programs

Wonjun Lee[†‡]   Channoh Kim[‡]   Houp Song[†]   Jae W. Lee[‡]

[†]Samsung Electronics
Suwon, Korea
{wonjun44.lee, hu.song}@samsung.com

[‡]Sungkyunkwan University
Suwon, Korea
{wonjun.lee, channoh, jaewlee}@skku.edu

ABSTRACT

JavaScript has become a general-purpose programming environment that enables complex, media-rich web applications. An increasing number of JavaScript programs are parallelized to run efficiently on today's multicore CPUs, which are capable of dynamic core scaling (DCS) and voltage/frequency scaling (DVFS). However, significant power savings are still left on the table since an operating point (in terms of the number of active cores and CPU voltage/frequency) is selected by monitoring CPU utilization or OS events, without considering the user's performance goal. To address this, we propose QPR.js, a **Q**oS-aware **p**ower-optimizing **r**untime system for **J**avaScript. Using the QPR.js API, the application developer can specify a QoS goal and provide a fitness function to quantify the current level of QoS. During execution the QPR.js runtime system uses this information to autonomously find an optimal operating point minimizing power consumption while satisfying the QoS goal. Our evaluation with five parallel JavaScript programs demonstrates an average of 35.2% power savings over the Linux Ondemand governor without degrading user experience.

Categories and Subject Descriptors

D.1.3 [**Programming Techniques**]: Concurrent Programming—*Power Optimal Programming*; D.3.2 [**Programming Languages**]: Language Classifications—*JavaScript*

Keywords

Power Optimization; DVFS; JavaScript; multi-core

1. INTRODUCTION

As more applications go online, there are strong demands for power-efficient performance of JavaScript. Many modern web browsers support HTML5, which enables sophisticated media-rich applications on the web, such as media players, 3D graphics and games. These applications are compute-

intensive and consume a large amount of power, which is a serious concern, especially on mobile devices.

On the hardware front multicore CPUs have become commonplace in all scales of computing platforms to offer abundant execution resources. To efficiently utilize these resources, multiple JavaScript parallelization frameworks have emerged, such as WebCL [3] and Web Workers [2]. Besides, modern multicore CPUs expose to software some knobs to improve power efficiency such as dynamic voltage/frequency/-core scaling (DVFCS) [9]. In a DVFCS-capable CPU, the number of active cores and their voltage/frequency settings constitute the CPU's operating point.

To maximize power efficiency of parallel JavaScript programs, it is required to find an optimal operating point for a given workload and performance goal. However, most of the popular DVFCS algorithms, such as Linux CPUFreq Governor [1] and Windows DVFS [5], only use *system* metrics, such as CPU utilization and event counts visible to OS, and do not take into *user* metrics (i.e., performance perceived by the user). This often leads to overly conservative voltage/frequency/core settings, to significantly increase the system's power and temperature with only marginal improvement, or even degradation, of user experience.

There are proposals to take user metrics into account to control DVFCS to expose additional opportunities for power savings. However, they either take a human-in-the-loop approach, requiring human intervention to quantify user satisfaction [6,7], or infer it from UI events (e.g., touches), which may erroneously interpret the user's intention and degrade use experience [8,10,11].

This paper proposes QPR.js, an API and runtime system that enables quality-of-service (QoS) aware DVFCS for parallel JavaScript programs. Using the QPR.js API, the user can specify a QoS goal and a fitness function that quantifies the current level of QoS. The QPR.js runtime system finds an optimal operating point that minimizes power consumption subject to satisfying the QoS goal (e.g., minimum frame rate). QPR.js is implemented on Intel's Sandy Bridge quad-core system running Linux and evaluated using 5 WebCL-based parallel JavaScript programs. Compared with the default Ondemand governor for DVFCS control, QPR.js reduces power consumption by 35.2% on average while satisfying the QoS goal specified by the user.

2. QOS-POWER TRADE-OFFS

There is a class of applications that require not only correctness but also performance to be useful. Many multimedia applications on the web fall in this category, such as me-

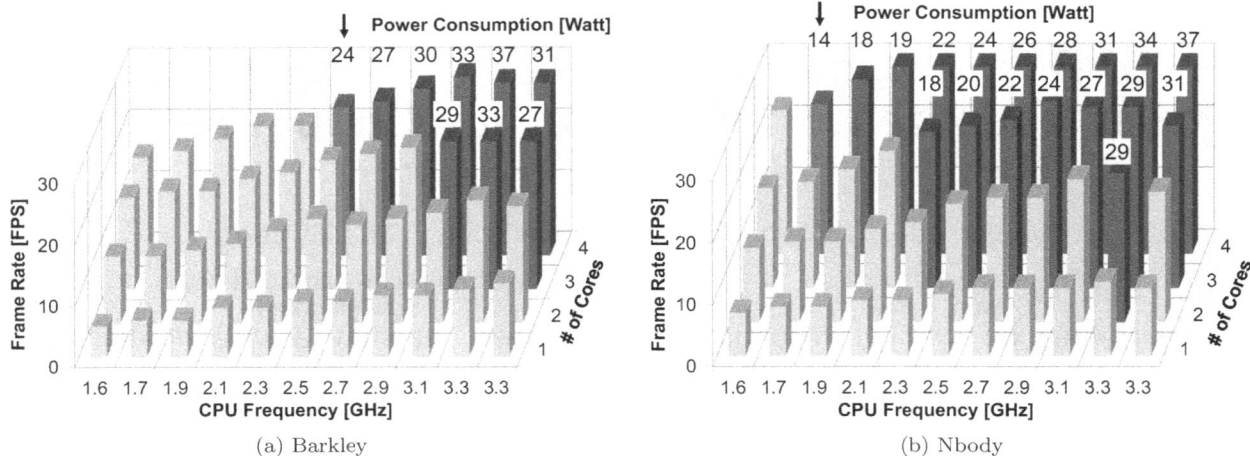

Figure 1: Trade-off between frame rate and power; the number above a bar shows power consumption at the operating point.

dia players and 3D games. For example, a video player has a minimum performance (QoS) constraint in terms of frames per second (FPS) to guarantee user satisfaction. Once this constraint is met, the improvement of user satisfaction by further increasing the FPS is only marginal. For this class of applications it is possible to achieve additional power savings by exploiting QoS-power trade-offs.

Figure 1 illustrates this QoS-power trade-off controlled by varying the operating point via DVFCS for two parallel JavaScript applications: Barkley and Nbody. The graphs show the achieved FPS for all operating points on a quad-core desktop machine. Assuming the QoS constraint to be 24 FPS, those operating points that satisfy this constraint are colored in blue; the red bar (indicated by an arrow) shows the optimal operating point, which has minimum power consumption while satisfying the constraint. The operating points that fail to satisfy the constraint are shown in gray.

We can infer two points from the results: (1) The optimal operating point is determined by the QoS constraint. This motivates *QoS-aware* DVFCS control to reduce power consumption. (2) Even for the same QoS constraint (say, 24 FPS), the optimal operating point differs by applications. In the previous example, Barkley runs optimally with 4 cores at 2.5 GHz, and Nbody with 4 cores at 1.7 GHz. However, conventional DVFCS governors, which control the voltage/frequency/core scaling daemon, do not take into account either QoS constraints or application characteristics, hence leaving potential power savings on the table. Therefore, it is highly desirable to have a runtime support for communicating the application's QoS constraint and its current level of QoS to the DVFCS governor.

3. QPR.js RUNTIME SYSTEM

3.1 Overall Structure

Figure 2 illustrates the block diagram of the QPR.js runtime system. The main component is the *optimizer* module in JavaScript, which builds on lower-level hooks for DVCFS control and power monitoring. Our prototype system is based on WebKit-WebCL [4] running on Intel's OpenCL driver (Version 1.2). We use parallel JavaScript applications based on WebCL for performance evaluation in Section 4.

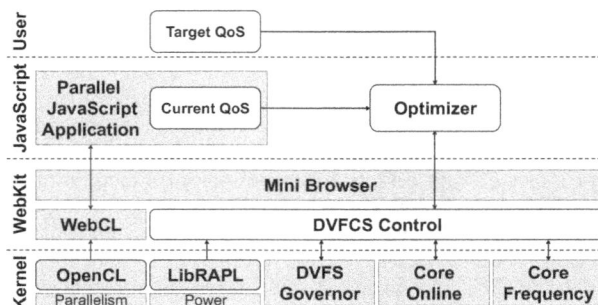

Figure 2: Overall structure of QPR.js runtime

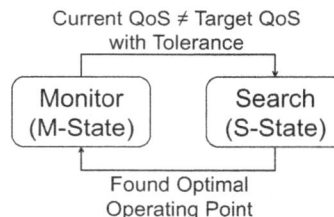

Figure 3: Optimizer two-state FSM

To control DVCFS we add a JavaScript binding to the kernel-level DVFS and Hotplug governors to QPR.js using Web Interface Description Language (WebIDL). The DVCFS control module monitors and changes the governor policy, the number of active cores, and voltage/frequency settings by reading and writing to DVFCS node files.

To monitor instantaneous power we exploit energy counters provided by modern multicore CPUs. For our prototype we provide a JavaScript binding to read the Running Average Power Limit (RAPL) values in Model-Specific Registers (MSR) through LibRAPL on Intel's Sandy Bridge CPU. By reading RAPL values we can easily measure the power consumption of each hardware component, such as CPU, GPU, package, and caches.

The optimizer exposes an API for the programmer to specify a QoS goal and a fitness function to calculate the current level of QoS. By combining this information with the capabilities of power monitoring and DVFCS control, the optimizer searches for an optimal operating point while a parallel JavaScript application is running.

3.2 Optimizer Algorithm

Figure 3 illustrates the two-state finite state machine (FSM) implemented by the optimizer. Initially, the system starts with the monitoring state (M-State). In M-State the optimizer monitors the current QoS level (provided by the user-provided fitness function) and compare it with the target QoS level. If the difference is greater than the threshold, the optimizer enters the search state (S-State). To improve the stability of the algorithm, the current QoS takes a running average of the last ten samples.

In S-State the optimizer sets the initial operating point by turning on all cores and scaling up to the maximum frequency. The search algorithm first scales down the frequency step by step until the operating point yields the current QoS ($QoS_{current}$) equal to or lower than the target QoS (QoS_{target}). Then the algorithm turns off one core and repeat the process except that it does not go below the frequency limit ($limit_{freq}$) found with one more core turned on. If the search is finished, optimizer sets the optimal core and frequency. Once search is finished and an optimal operating point is found, the system enters M-State again.

Algorithm 1 presents the pseudo code of this algorithm. Note that this algorithm is invoked periodically, and that the search state ($freq, core$) is preserved across invocations. Since it is time consuming to search all operating points, we employ heuristics to reduce the size of search space using $limit_{freq}$; the main idea is that an operating point with fewer cores and the same frequency cannot perform better than the current operating point. Also, we stop searching with one fewer cores if there are relatively few frequencies that satisfy the QoS constraint with the current core count. By default this threshold is set to a half of the number of frequency steps on the platform.

4. EVALUATION

Table 1 summarizes the experimental setup. Five rendering JavaScript programs are selected since it is easy to define the QoS goal for them: `Barkley`, `Nbody`, `PathIntegrals`, `VideoCube`, and `XY` [4]. Note that, QPR.js is flexible enough to accommodate applications from other domains as well. We set 24 FPS (minimum FPS for TV) to be the target QoS level and adjust the iteration count of an inner loop, if necessary, for all applications to achieve at least 30 FPS at the maximum operating point.

Name	Descriptions
Core	Intel i5-2500 CPU (4 ea)
Frequency	1.6GHz-3.3GHz (11 steps)
Memory	8GB
GPU	Nvidia Geforce GT 530
OS	Ubuntu 12.04 64bits
Platform	WebKit-WebCL EFL Port [4]
Power	RAPL (Intel Sandy Bridge)
Parallel JavaScript	WebCL (Intel OpenCL v1.2 CPU)

Table 1: System specifications

Figure 4 compares the power consumption of QPR.js-enabled parallel programs against QoS-oblivious Linux DVFS

Algorithm 1 Search Algorithm

Input: $QoS_{current}, QoS_{target}$
Output: $core_{opt}, freq_{opt}$
Initialize: $core \leftarrow core_{max}, freq \leftarrow freq_{max}$
1: **if** $QoS_{current} = QoS_{target}$ **then**
2:    **if** $freq > sizeof(freqsteps)/2$ **then**
3:       $core_{opt} \leftarrow core, freq_{opt} \leftarrow freq$
4:       **return**
5:    **else if** $core = core_{min}$ **then**
6:       $core_{opt} \leftarrow core, freq_{opt} \leftarrow freq$
7:       **return**
8:    **else**
9:       $limit_{freq} \leftarrow freq + 1$
10:       **decrease** $core, freq \leftarrow freq_{max}$
11:    **end if**
12: **else if** $QoS_{current} < QoS_{target}$ **then**
13:    **if** $freq = freq_{max}$ **then**
14:       $core_{opt} \leftarrow core, freq_{opt} \leftarrow freq$
15:       **return**
16:    **else**
17:       **decrease** $core, freq \leftarrow freq_{max}$
18:    **end if**
19: **else**
20:    **if** $freq \neq freq_{min}$ **and** $freq > limit_{freq}$ **then**
21:       **decrease** $freq$
22:    **else if** $freq > sizeof(freq)/2$ **then**
23:       $core_{opt} \leftarrow core, freq_{opt} \leftarrow freq$
24:       **return**
25:    **else**
26:       **decrease** $core, freq \leftarrow freq_{max}$
27:    **end if**
28: **end if**

---

governors. Compared to the default Ondemand governor, QPR.js achieves 35.2% of power savings while satisfying the QoS goal. Note that, both Performance and Ondemand governors run at the maximum operating point most of time to yield low power efficiency. The power consumption of the Powersave governor is minimal, but at the cost of violating the QoS constraint.

Figure 5 illustrates the runtime behavior of the two applications: `Barkley` and `Nbody`. `Barkley` is an example with stable optimal operating point, where the optimal operating point does not fluctuate once entered. `PathIntegrals`, `VideoCube`, and `XY` all follow this pattern. However, the optimal operating point of `Nbody` is not stable, making the optimizer continuously switch between M-State and S-State. Nevertheless, the overall power consumption is still signif-

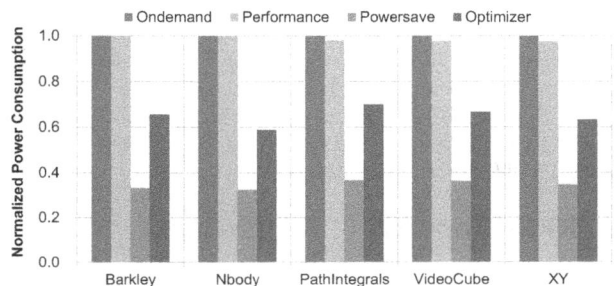

Figure 4: Power comparison against Linux DVFS governors

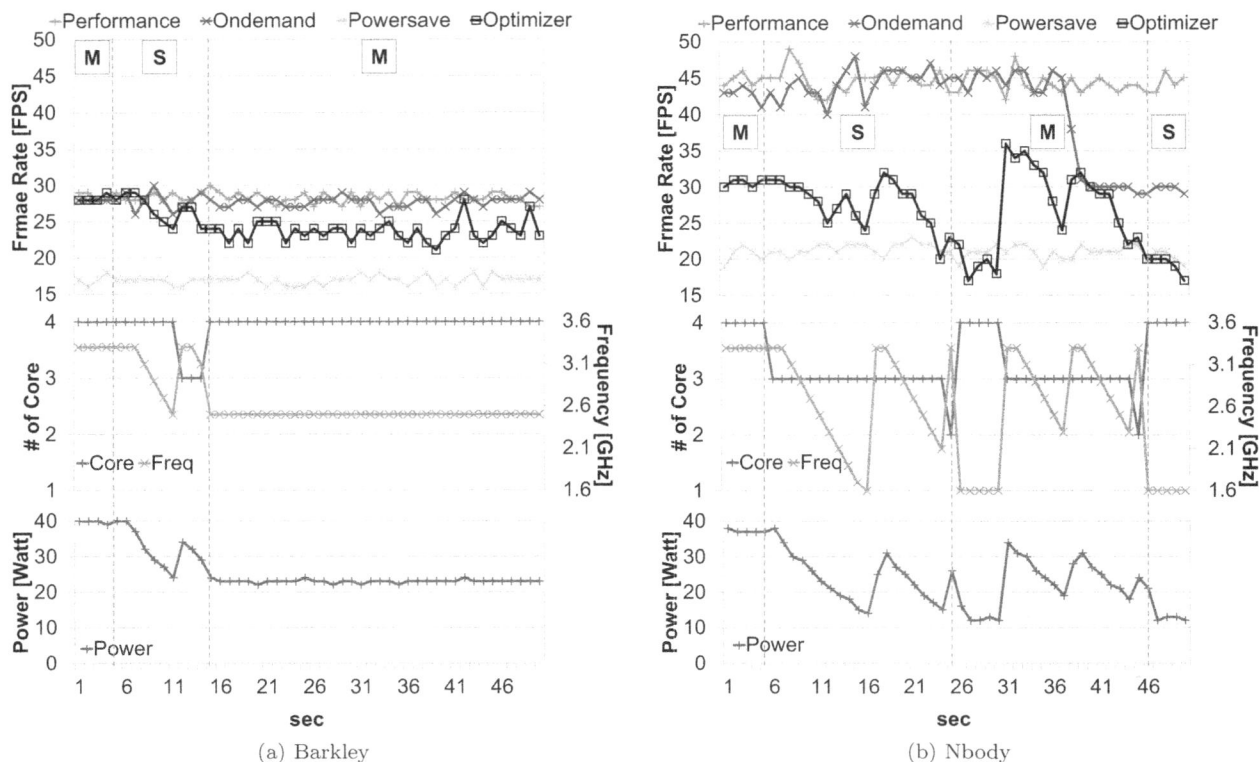

(a) Barkley

(b) Nbody

Figure 5: Runtime behavior of QPR.js-enabled parallel execution

icantly lower than the QoS-oblivious DVFS governors as shown in Figure 4.

5. CONCLUSION

The demands for power-efficient JavaScript performance are higher than ever with widespread adoption of web applications. As web applications become more complex and compute-intensive, the demands will continue to grow. In this paper we present QPR.js, the first JavaScript API that enables QoS-aware power reduction while satisfying user-specified QoS constraints. Our evaluation with five WebCL-based parallel JavaScript applications shows promising results; QPR.js achieves an average of 35.2% power savings compared to the default Ondemand Linux governor. This benefit is realized with relative simple modifications to the original program. We plan to extend this work to accommodate applications with more complex QoS constraints and improve the efficiency of the optimizer algorithm.

6. ACKNOWLEDGMENTS

This work was supported in part by the Korean Evaluation Institute of Industrial Technology funded by the Ministry of Science, ICT & Future Planning (KEIT-10047038) and the IT R&D program of MKE/KEIT [KI001810041244, Smart TV 2.0 Software Platform].

7. REFERENCES

[1] CPU frequency and voltage scaling code in Linux(TM) kernel. https://www.kernel.org/doc/Documentation/cpu-freq/governors.txt.

[2] Web Worker. http://dev.w3.org/html5/workers/.

[3] WebCL. http://www.khronos.org/webcl/.

[4] WebCL for WebKit. https://github.com/SRA-SiliconValley/webkit-webcl.

[5] Windows Power Management and ACPI - Architecture and Driver support.

[6] B. Lin, A. Mallik, P. Dinda, G. Memik, and R. Dick. User-and process-driven dynamic voltage and frequency scaling. In *Performance Analysis of Systems and Software, 2009. ISPASS 2009. IEEE International Symposium on*, pages 11–22. IEEE, 2009.

[7] A. Mallik, B. Lin, G. Memik, P. Dinda, and R. P. Dick. User-driven frequency scaling. *Computer Architecture Letters*, 5(2):16–16, 2006.

[8] A. Shye, Y. Pan, B. Scholbrock, J. S. Miller, G. Memik, P. A. Dinda, and R. P. Dick. Power to the people: Leveraging human physiological traits to control microprocessor frequency. In *Proceedings of the 41st Annual IEEE/ACM International Symposium on Microarchitecture*, MICRO 41, pages 188–199, Washington, DC, USA, 2008. IEEE Computer Society.

[9] H. Wang, V. Sathish, R. Singh, M. J. Schulte, and N. S. Kim. Workload and power budget partitioning for single-chip heterogeneous processors. In *Proceedings of the 21st International Conference on Parallel Architectures and Compilation Techniques*, PACT '12, pages 401–410, New York, NY, USA, 2012. ACM.

[10] S. Woo, W. Seo, C. Kim, and J. Huh. User input based power reduction technique for smartphone. In *Proceedings of the Korean Institute of Information Scientists and Engineers*, 2013.

[11] L. Yan, L. Zhong, and N. K. Jha. User-perceived latency driven voltage scaling for interactive applications. In *Proceedings of the 42Nd Annual Design Automation Conference*, DAC '05, pages 624–627, New York, NY, USA, 2005. ACM.

Ultra-Low Voltage Mixed TFET-MOSFET 8T SRAM Cell

Yin-Nien Chen, Ming-Long Fan, *Student Member, IEEE*, Vita Pi-Ho Hu, *Member, IEEE*,
Pin Su, *Member, IEEE*, Ching-Te Chuang, *Fellow, IEEE*
Dept. of Electronics Engineering and Institute of Electronics, National Chiao-Tung University, Hsinchu, Taiwan
E-mail: snoopyfairy@gmail.com chingte.chuang@gmail.com

Abstract

In this work, we propose a mixed TFET-MOSFET 8T SRAM cell comprising MOSFET cross-coupled inverters, dedicated TFET read stack and TFET write access transistors. Exploiting both the merits of TFET and MOSFET devices, the proposed SRAM cell provides significant improvement in SRAM stability, V_{min} and performance. The proposed cell is evaluated and compared with the conventional MOSFET 8T cell and pure TFET 8T cell using mixed-mode TCAD simulations. The results indicate that the proposed mixed TFET-MOSFET cell topology is viable for ultra-low voltage operation.

Keywords

Tunnel FET, TFET SRAMs, ultra-low voltage, ultra-low power.

1. Introduction

Voltage scaling is an efficient way to reduce the power consumption. The conventional 6T SRAM cell achieves large storage capacity. However, it suffers from read disturb, half-select disturb, and the conflicting read/write requirements. Consequently, the stability of 6T SRAM cell degrades significantly as V_{DD} scales down, limiting the achievable V_{min} for overall system.

Tunnel FET (TFET) device, with the band-to-band tunneling as the major current transport mechanism, enables steeper than 60mV/dec subthreshold swing and is a promising device to replace MOSFET device for ultra-low voltage/power operation [1]-[5]. However, the asymmetric source/drain design and transport mechanism result in uni-directional current conduction [6], which severely impacts the pass-gate based circuits and SRAMs [6]-[9].

In this work, we propose a mixed TFET-MOSFET 8T SRAM cell which exploits both the advantages of TFET and MOSFET devices for ultra-low voltage operation. The merits of the proposed cell versus the conventional MOSFET 8T SRAM cell and the pure TFET 8T SRAM cell in stability and performance are comprehensively assessed.

2. Device Design, TCAD Methodology and Switching characteristics

2.1 Device Design and TCAD Methodology

In this work, we consider the PNPN type TFET [3] for its capability to achieve sub-threshold swing below 60mV/dec at room temperature. The device structures of the TFET and conventional MOSFET are shown in Fig. 1.

Double-gate (DG) structures are used, and the detailed parameters used in this work are listed in Table 1. Fig. 2 shows the Ids-Vgs characteristics of the TFET (PNPN/NPNP), LV_T and HV_T MOSFET (N/PMOS) at Vds = 0.6V. The TFET and MOSFET devices/circuits are analyzed using atomistic TCAD mixed-mode

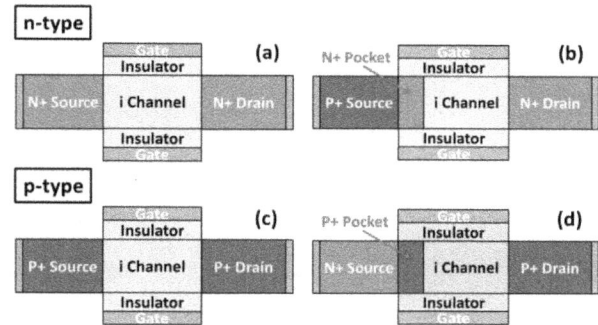

Fig. 1. Structures of (a) n-type MOSFET, (b) n-type PNPN TFET, (c) p-type MOSFET and (d) p-type NPNP TFET.

Table 1. Parameters for n-type MOSFET and n-type TFET devices

Parameters		n-MOSFET	n-TFET
Leff	(nm)	25	25
Tox	(nm)	0.6	0.6
T_{si}	(nm)	6	6
$WF_{HVT/LVT}$	(eV)	4.69/4.58	4.42
N_s	(cm^{-3})	n-2x10^{20}	p-2x10^{20}
N_d	(cm^{-3})	n-2x10^{20}	n-2x10^{20}
N_{pocket}	(cm^{-3})	-	n-1.2x10^{20}

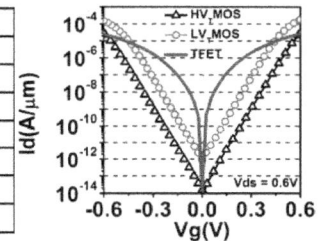

Fig. 2. Ids-Vgs characteristics at Vds = 0.6V of n-/p-type DG LV_T and HV_T MOSFETs and DG PNPN/NPNP TFETs.

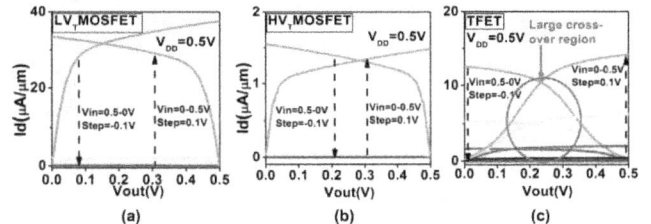

Fig. 3. Device switching characteristics of (a) DG LV_T MOSFET, (b) DG HV_T MOSFET and (c) DG TFET in an inverter.

simulations. The nonlocal band-to-band tunneling model which is applicable to arbitrary tunneling barrier with non-uniform electric field is used for TFET simulations [16]. The tunneling paths are dynamically determined according to the gradient of the band energy. The I_{on}/I_{off} ratio and S.S. of PNPN TFET device are calibrated with [3] and the OFF state current is set with available Si TFET experimental data. The DG MOSFET devices with two different V_T value designs are considered to investigate the impact of different MOSFET V_T designs on the SRAM stability and performance. The HV_T MOSFET device is designed with the same OFF state current as the TFET device for low power operation baseline, while the LV_T MOSFET device is designed with higher leakage current around pA/μm. The TFET device can be seen to have superior current drive and subthreshold slope at very low gate bias, followed by a broad soft transition region before its current saturates. While at high gate bias region, the current drive of TFET device is less effective than the LV_T MOSFET.

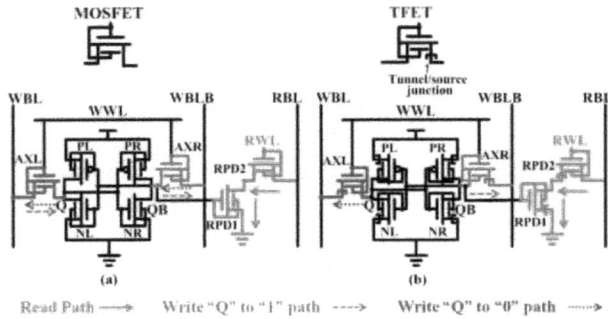

Fig. 4. Cell structures and corresponding read/write paths for: (a) conventional MOSFET 8T SRAM cell and (b) TFET 8T SRAM cell.

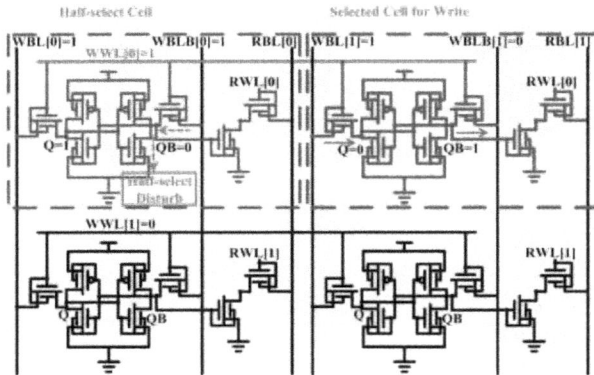

Fig. 5. Schematic of 8T SRAM cell array showing the selected cell for Write and half-select disturb current path through the half-selected cell for MOSFET 8T SRAM.

2.2 Device and Circuit Switching/Output Characteristics

Figs. 3 show the switching Id-Vds characteristics of LV_T, HV_T MOSFET and TFET devices in an inverter. The delayed saturation in TFET device results in large cross-over region/current between the n-type and p-type devices in TFET inverter which degrades the sharpness of voltage transfer characteristic (VTC) of the TFET inverter and the stability in TFET SRAM cell.

3. Ultra-Low Voltage SRAM Cell Designs
3.1 Conventional MOSFET/TFET 8T SRAM Cell

The conventional 6T SRAM cell faces many challenges with increasing variations in deep sub-100nm technologies [10], especially at low supply voltages. Alternative SRAM cells such as 8T cell and 10T cell have been proposed for robust low voltage operations [11]-[15]. In this work, the conventional 8T SRAM cell [11] is used as the basic cell structure due to its technical viability with uni-directional TFET devices. Fig. 4 shows the schematics of MOSFET/TFET 8T SRAM cell structures and the corresponding read/write current paths. The bracket in the symbol of TFET device indicates the tunnel junction in the TFET device.

For MOSFET 8T SRAM cell, the read disturb is eliminated through the dedicated read stack which decouples the cell storage nodes from read current while the bi-directional write access transistors provide the "push-pull" action to enhance write-ability during write operation. However, MOSFET 8T SRAM cell suffers from write half-select disturb (Fig. 5) where the half-select cells on the selected row (WWL[0] = V_{DD}) perform "dummy" read, thus experiencing cell disturb similar to the read disturb in the conventional 6T cell. The MOSFET 8T SRAM cell is thus not suitable for bit-interleaving architecture.

For TFET 8T SRAM cell, the read stability is improved by the dedicated read stack as in the MOSFET 8T cell. Moreover, the

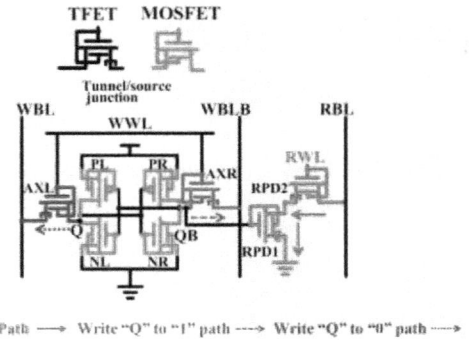

Fig. 6. Cell structure and corresponding read/write paths of proposed mixed TFET-MOSFET 8T SRAM cell where MOSFET devices are used in the cross-coupled inverter pair.

superior current drive and subthreshold slope of TFET at low voltage significantly enhance the read performance over the MOSFET 8T cell at low voltage. Furthermore, the uni-directional write access transistors eliminate write half-select disturb, thus facilitating bit-interleaving architecture for enhanced soft error immunity with error correction code (ECC) [17]. However, there are two drawbacks for the TFET 8T cell. First, the large cross-over region in TFET device degrades the hold/read static noise margin (HSNM/RSNM) and write static noise margin (WSNM). Secondly, the lack of "push-pull" action during write operation due to uni-directional write access transistors degrades the write-ability.

3.2 Mixed TFET-MOSFET 8T SRAM Cell

Based on the previous discussion of the pros and cons of MOSFET and TFET 8T SRAM cells and realizing that mixing TFET and MOSFET devices is manufacturly possible since the process of TFET device is compatible with CMOS process [5], Fig. 6 shows the proposed mixed TFET-MOSFET 8T SRAM cell and corresponding read/write paths. The cell features MOSFET cross-coupled inverters for improved HSNM and RSNM, dedicated TFET read stack for enhanced read stability and read performance and TFET write access transistors to facilitate bit-interleaving architecture. Furthermore, with MOSFET cross-coupled inverters, the write-ability of the proposed mixed TFET-MOSFET 8T cell is significantly enhanced over the MOSFET 8T cell and TFET 8T cell due to the disparity of the current drive between the write access TFET device and the holding (pull-up) PMOSFET at low voltage. By properly designing the TFET and MOSFET devices hence the voltage range of the disparity current in between, the effective voltage range for improved Write-ability of the mixed TFET-MOSFET will be broader. The impact of the V_T design of the MOSFET device on the SRAM stability and performance of the mixed TFET-MOSFET 8T cell will be addressed in section IV.

4. Stability and Performance

In this section, the stability and performance of the MOSFET, TFET and mixed TFET-MOSFET 8T SRAM cell are comparatively assessed.

4.1 Stability

Fig. 7 shows the respective hold, read, write and half-select SNM of the LV_T and HV_T MOSFET 8T cell, TFET 8T cell and mixed TFET-MOSFET 8T cell comprising of LV_T and HV_T MOSFET cross-coupled inverters, respectively, for V_{DD} ranging from 0.2V to 0.5V.

4.1.1 Hold/Read SNM

For 8T cell configuration, the read SNM (RSNM) equals hold SNM (HSNM). As shown in Fig. 7(a) and 7(b), both the LV_T and HV_T MOSFET 8T cell and mixed TFET-MOSFET 8T cell comprising of LV_T and HV_T MOSFET cross-coupled inverters exhibit

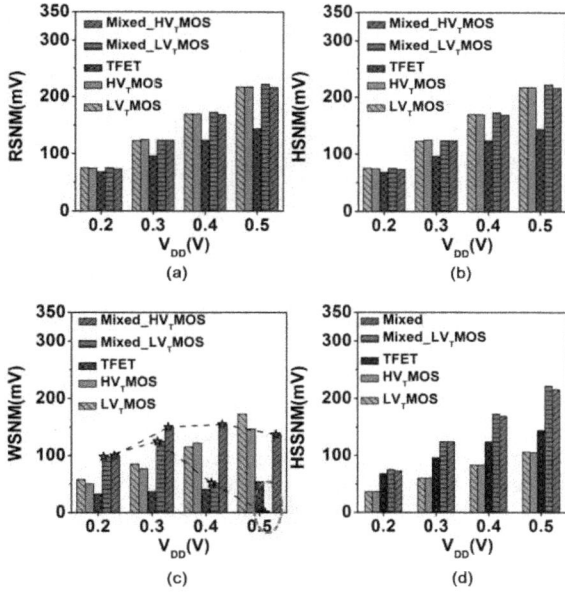

Fig. 7. Stability of LV_T and HV_T MOSFET 8T SRAM cell, TFET SRAM cell and Mixed TFET-MOSFET 8T SRAM cell comprising LV_T and HV_T MOSFET cross-coupled inverter, respectively, across $V_{DD} = 0.2V$-$0.5V$: (a) Hold static noise margin (HSNM), (b) Read static noise margin (RSNM), (c) Write static noise margin (WSNM) and (d) Half-select static noise margin (HSSNM).

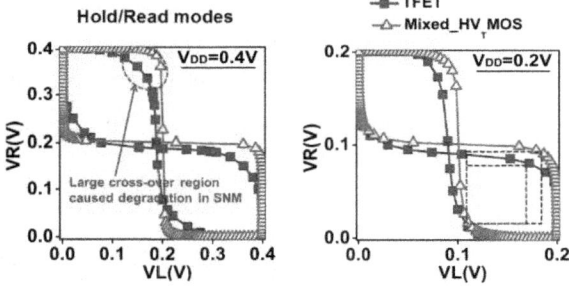

Fig. 8. Butterfly curves of TFET and mixed TFET-MOSFET 8T SRAM cell comprising HV_T MOSFET cross-coupled inverter in hold/read modes at $V_{DD} = 0.4V$ and $V_{DD} = 0.2V$.

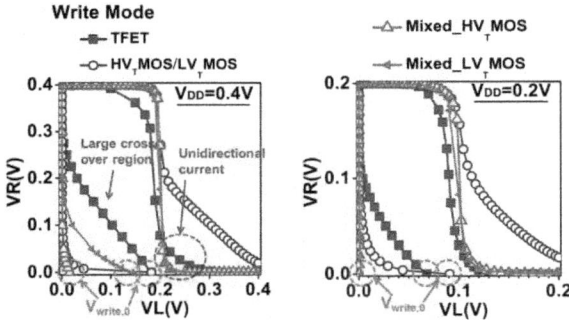

Fig. 9. Butterfly curves of LV_T and HV_T MOSFET 8T SRAM cell, TFET 8T SRAM cell and mixed TFET-MOSFET 8T SRAM cell comprising LV_T and HV_T cross-coupled inverters, respectively, in write mode at $V_{DD} = 0.4V$ and $V_{DD} = 0.2V$.

comparable HSNM and RSNM. The TFET 8T cell shows inferior HSNM and RSNM, especially for $V_{DD} \geq 0.3V$, due to the large cross-over region in TFET devices which degrades the sharpness of cell inverter VTC as can be observed in the transition region of the butterfly curves shown in Fig. 8. The actual amount of degradation

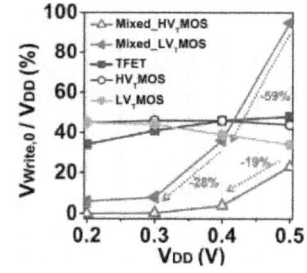

Fig. 10. Weighting of $V_{Write,0}$ versus V_{DD} of LV_T, HV_T MOSFET 8T SRAM cell, TFET 8T SRAM cell and mixed TFET-MOSFET 8T SRAM cell comprising LV_T and HV_T MOSFET cross-coupled inverter.

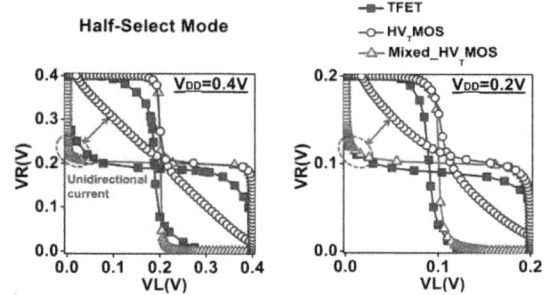

Fig. 11. Butterfly curves of HV_T MOSFET 8T SRAM cell, TFET SRAM cell and Mixed TFET-MOSFET 8T SRAM cell comprising HV_T MOSFET cross-coupled inverter, respectively, in half-selected mode at $V_{DD} = 0.4V$ and $V_{DD} = 0.2V$.

depends on the output conductance of the TFET devices and MOSFET devices in weak inversion conditions. As V_{DD} scales down to 0.2V, the HSNM/RSNM degradation of the TFET 8T cell becomes less as the cross-over region in TFET devices is reduced.

4.1.2   Write SNM

Fig. 7(c) shows the write SNM (WSNM) of the SRAM cell topologies versus V_{DD}. The TFET 8T cell shows significant degradation in WSNM across V_{DD} ranging from 0.2V to 0.5V compared to other SRAM topologies. It is because the uni-directional conduction of TFET write-access transistor deprives the push-pull action during write operation, and can be observed in the write butterfly curves of TFET and mixed TFET-MOSFET 8T cells in Fig. 9(a). Meanwhile, the large cross-over region in TFET devices causes large $V_{Write,0}$ (determined by the current balance between the write access transistor and the holding transistor) as shown in Fig. 9(a), thus further degrading the write-ability. As V_{DD} scales down to 0.2V, the WSNM of TFET 8T cell becomes comparable to that of MOSFET 8T cells as shown in Fig. 9(b) since the cross-over transition region is reduced. Among these SRAM cell topologies, the proposed mixed TFET-MOSFET 8T cell comprising HV_T MOSFET cross-coupled inverter exhibits superior WSNM. While the proposed cell still lacks push-pull action during write operation, the $V_{Write,0}$ is significantly reduced, especially at low voltages, due to the steep swing of the TFET device and hence the disparity of current drive between the write access TFET and the holding PMOSFET, thus providing significant improvement in write-ability among all these SRAM topologies. However, for the proposed mixed TFET-MOSFET 8T cell comprising LV_T MOSFET devices, it demonstrates worse Write-ability and the WSNM diminishes at $V_{DD} = 0.5V$. It is due to decrease of the drive current disparity between the write access TFET devices and holding PMOSFET with the use of LV_T MOSFET. Also, at $V_{DD} = 0.5V$, the current drive of the LV_T MOSFET device overwhelming that of the TFET device results in write failure.

It should be noted that the proposed mixed TFET-MOSFET SRAM topology is suitable for other MOSFET and TFET structures.

However, the TFET device without such sharp subthreshold swing as PNPN TFET device, and MOSFET device with lower threshold voltage, may results in worse write-ability and narrower write operation range. Hence the device designs between the MOSFET and TFET device should be carefully designed to have larger write operation range.

It should also be noticed that the WSNM of the mixed TFET-MOSFET 8T cells shows an unique reflective trend as indicated by the two dashed line shown in Fig. 7(c), while the WSNM of MOSFET/TFET 8T cells exhibit monotonic trend with scaled V_{DD}. This is because as V_{DD} scales down from 0.5V to 0.4V/0.3V for mixed TFET-MOSFET 8T cell comprising HV_T/LV_T MOSFET devices, the decrement of $V_{Write,0}$ of the proposed cell is larger than the reduced margin caused by decreased supply voltage and can be seen with the weighting of the $V_{Write,0}$ versus V_{DD} in Fig. 10.

4.1.3 Half-Select SNM

Fig. 7(d) shows the half-select SNM (HSSNM) of the SRAM cell topologies versus V_{DD}. It is observed that TFET and mixed TFET-MOSFET 8T cells with uni-directional TFET write access transistors show larger HSSNM than the MOSFET 8T cells. At $V_{DD} = 0.5V$, the enhancement of HSSNM of mixed TFET-MOSFET 8T cells are about 106% and 50% compared with the MOSFET 8T cells and TFET 8T cell, respectively. The large improvement results from the fact that with uni-directional TFET write access transistors, the "dummy" read current of the half-selected cells cannot flow through the cell storage nodes, hence the half-selected disturb is significantly reduced. This can be clearly observed in the butterfly curves shown in Fig. 11 indicated by the spanning arrows. For the proposed mixed TFET-MOSFET 8T cells with the MOSFET cross-coupled inverters, the HSSNM improves further due to sharper VTC (reduction of the cross-over region) compared with the TFET cross-coupled inverters as shown in Fig. 11.

The stabilities of the SRAM cell topologies are summarized in Table 2. It is clear that the proposed mixed TFET-MOSFET 8T cell comprising HV_T MOSFET cross-coupled inverters provides merits for ultra-low voltage operation.

Table 2. Comparison of stability among the 8T SRAM topologies.

Type	Mixed HV_T MOS	Mixed LV_T MOS	HV_T MOS	LV_T MOS	TFET
Hold SNM	O	O	O	O	Δ
Read Disturb Free	O	O	O	O	O
Write-ability	O	Δ*	Δ	Δ	X
Half-Select Disturb Free (Bit-interleave)	O	O	X	X	O

4.2 Performance

The performance of SRAM arrays with 16 cells per bit-line are assessed considering the worst case bit-line data pattern and bit-line loading. As shown in Fig. 13(a), TFET 8T cell and mixed TFET-MOSFET 8T cells significantly outperform the HV_T MOSFET 8T cell in "cell" read access time (defined as the time from when selected read word-line (RWL) reaches half-V_{DD} to when the read bit-line (RBL) is pulled down to half-V_{DD}), providing 1.6x and 4000x improvement at $V_{DD} = 0.5V$ and 0.2V, respectively. While for V_{DD} larger than 0.4V, the LV_T MOSFET 8T cell demonstrates better read performance among the SRAM cells. Fig. 13(b) shows the "cell" time-to-write (defined as the time from the 50% activation of the write word-line (WWL) to the time when the voltage of the cell high-going storage node reaches 90% V_{DD}). HV_T MOSFET 8T cell exhibits severely degraded cell time-to-write at low supply voltage due to the low current drive of MOSFET devices. For mixed TFET-MOSFET 8T

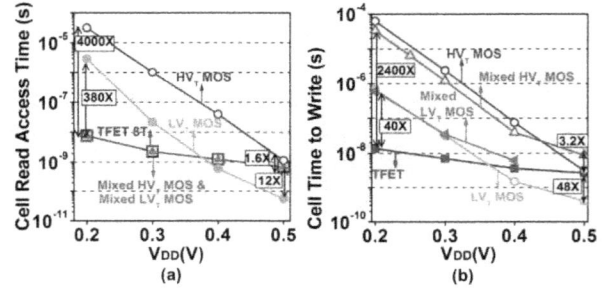

Fig. 13. Performance comparison of the LV_T and HV_T MOSFET 8T SRAM cell, TFET 8T SRAM cell and mixed TFET-MOSFET 8T SRAM cell comprising LV_T and HV_T cross-coupled inverters, respectively, for (a) cell read access time and (b) cell time-to-write.

cell comprising HV_T and LV_T cross-coupled inverter, owing to lack of push-pull action and the low current drive of pull-up PMOSFET, shows substantial longer time-to-write than the TFET 8T cell. While the LV_T MOSFET 8T cell provides better time-to-write for V_{DD} larger than 0.4V due to the higher current drive.

5. Conclusions

We propose a mixed TFET-MOSFET 8T SRAM cell comprising MOSFET cross-coupled inverters, dedicated TFET read stack and TFET write access transistors. The use of MOSFET cross-coupled inverters improves hold static noise margin (SNM) over the pure TFET cell. The TFET read stack improves the "cell read access time" by 1.6x and 4000x at $V_{DD} = 0.5V$ and 0.2V, respectively, compared with the HV_T MOSFET 8T cell due to the superior current drive and subthreshold slope of TFET at low voltage. The uni-directional TFET write access transistors eliminate the write half-select disturb. The disparity in current drive between TFET write access transistor and HV_T MOSFET holding (pull-up) transistor improves WSNM. The proposed cell improves the cell stability, read performance, and eliminate half-select disturb to facilitate bit-interleaving architecture for enhanced soft error immunity with error correction code (ECC). The performance of the MOSFET, TFET, and proposed mixed TFET-MOSFET 8T cells are comparatively assessed. With superior stability and read performance, the proposed mixed cell comprising HV_T MOSFET cross-coupled inverters, provides merits for ultra-low voltage operation.

Acknowledgment

This work was supported in part by the Ministry of Science and Technology in Taiwan under Contracts MOST 101-2221-E-009 -150-MY2 and MOST 103-2917-I-009-181. The authors are grateful to National Center for High-Performance Computing in Taiwan for computational facilities and software.

References

[1] J. Appenzeller et al., *Phys. Rev. Lett.*, Nov. 2004.
[2] S. H. Kim et al., *VLSI Tech.*, 2009.
[3] V. Nagavarapu et al., *IEEE Trans. Electron Devices*, Apr. 2008.
[4] A. C. Seabaugh et al., Proc. IEEE, Dec. 2010.
[5] F. Mayer, et al., *IEDM. Tech. Dig.* 2008.
[6] J. Singh et al., *Proc. ASP-DAC*, 2010.
[7] D. Kim et al., *Symp. Low Power Electronics and Design*, 2009.
[8] X. Yang et al., *Proc. Design Automation and Test in Europe*, 2011.
[9] V. Saripalli et al., *Symp. Nanoscale Architectures*, 2011.
[10] C.-T. Chuang et al., in *IEEE Int. Workshop on Memory Technology, Design and Testing*, 2007
[11] L. Chang et al., in *Symp. VLSI Technology Dig.*, 2005
[12] R. Joshi et al., in *IEEE Symp. VLSI Circuits Dig.*, 2007
[13] M.-H. Chang et al., in *Proc. Int. Symp. Low Power Electronics and Design (ISLPED)*, 2011
[14] I. J. Chang et al., *IEEE J. Solid-State Circuits*, Feb. 2009.
[15] T.-H. Kim et al., *IEEE J. Solid-State Circuits*, Feb, 2008.
[16] *Sentaurus User's Manual*, 2011.
[17] L. Chang et al., *IEEE J. Solid-State Circuits*, Apr. 2008.

a-SAD: Power Efficient SAD Calculator for Real time H.264 Video Encoder Using MSB-Approximation Technique

Le Dinh Trang Dang
IEEE Student member
Electronics and Radio Engineering
Kyunghee University,Yong-in, Korea
Trangdld@khu.ac.kr

Ik Joon Chang
IEEE member
Electronics and Radio Engineering
Kyunghee University,
Yong-in, Korea
ichang@khu.ac.kr

Jinsang Kim
IEEE senior member
Electronics and Radio Engineering
Kyunghee University,Yong-in, Korea
jskim27@khu.ac.kr

ABSTRACT

We propose a power efficient SAD calculator, namely a-SAD. We use MSB-approximation where some highest-order MSB's are approximated to single MSB. Our theoretical analysis shows that this technique simultaneously improves performance and power of SAD circuit. We obtain optimal number of approximated MSB's from video experiments, which is the largest number not to affect video compression rate. In our simulations, our a-SAD circuit delivers higher performance compared to previous SAD circuits. We compare power dissipation under *iso-performance* scenario, where our a-SAD circuit shows 27% power saving compared to a previous design.

Categories and Subject Descriptors

B.5.1 [**Register-Transfer-Level Implementation**]: Design – *Data-path design.*

Keywords

Approximate Computing, Motion Estimation, MSB-Approximation, SAD Circuit Design

1. INTRODUCTION

Motion estimation (ME) is one of most critical parts in video encoder since this requires very large computational complexity. To conduct ME, we need to find the best matching *macro block* (MB) within a given *searching window range* (SWR), namely block matching. Here, *Sum of absolute difference* (SAD) has been most widely used as a metric to determine the best matching MB [1]. Previous studies show that block matching operations occupy a substantial portion of total ME computation (mostly 50~90%) [2]. We need to note that for single block matching, SAD calculation should be repeated for all MB's within a given SWR. These imply that performance and power of SAD calculation highly affect those of video encoding hardware.

We aim to design power efficient SAD calculator for H.264 video encoder. To achieve real time H.264 video encoding, high throughput is required [2, 3]. Hence, we need to develop power reduction techniques while providing high performance. Due to the high throughput requirement, previous researches regarding

SAD calculator design have mostly focused on performance improvement. For instance, J. Vanne et al. proposed compression array units to enhance performance of SAD circuit [4]. Although they do not consider low power techniques, their performance improvement may be translated to power saving by applying supply power scaling. H. Kaul et al. improved energy efficiency of SAD calculator by using wide dynamic voltage scaling [5]. However, the voltage scaling degrades performance. They compensated this problem by some performance techniques such as speculative difference computation and 4:2 compression units [5]. They commonly used compression units such as *carry-save adders* (CSA's). These compression units preclude long carry-propagation delay, providing high performance.

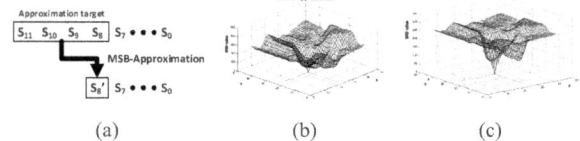

Figure 1. (a) MSB-Approximation diagram, (b) Original SADs in a SWR. (c) Approximated SADs in a SWR

In this work, we propose *approximate SAD* (a-SAD) calculator to simultaneously improve performance and power by employing our MSB-approximation technique. We note that in block matching, the best matching MB shows minimum SAD within a given SWR. To find a MB having minimum SAD, previous works [2, 4-7] fully estimated SAD's corresponding to all MB's within the given SWR. However, some MB's have much larger SAD than the best matching MB. For these MB's, accurate SAD estimation may not be necessary.

We affirmatively take into consideration such a fact for our design. Unlike previous works, our design is based on *ripple-carry adders* (RCA's). RCA suffers from long carry-propagation delay from *least significant bits* (LSB's) to *most significant bits* (MSB's), which may degrade performance of SAD circuit. However, this problem can be compensated by our MSB-approximation technique, illustrated in Fig. 1. Here, we select some MSB's as our approximation target (S_{11}, S_{10}, S_9, S_8 in Fig. 1 (a)), sequentially chosen from the highest-order bit. The selected MSB's are approximated to single MSB (S_8' in Fig. 1 (a)), which is enabled as far as target MSB's are not fully '0'. Then, we mask the selected MSB's to the single MSB, as shown in Fig. 1 (a). In such a scheme, SAD's are bounded by a certain value and hence, original SAD's of Fig. 1 (b) are approximated to those of Fig. 1 (c). In spite of these approximations, we can still find the best matching MB having minimum SAD under the condition that the minimum SAD is smaller compared to the boundary value. From extensive video experiments, we are able to decide optimal number of target MSB's to mostly satisfy the above condition.

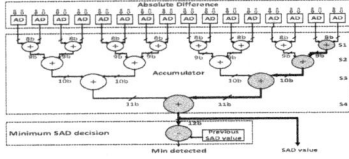

Figure 2. General SAD module for 16 pairs input pixels

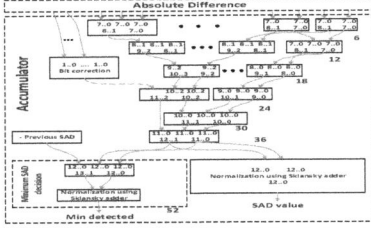

Figure 3. CSA-based SAD for 16 pairs input pixels

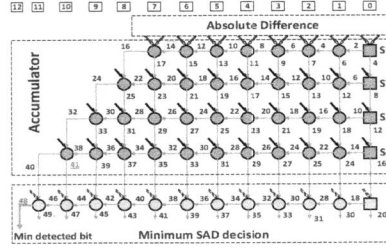

(a)

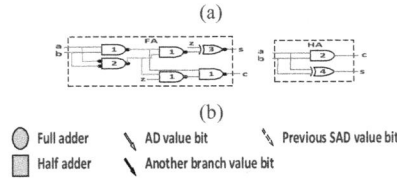

(b)

○ Full adder   ⬧ AD value bit   ⬧ Previous SAD value bit
□ Half adder   ⬧ Another branch value bit

Figure 4. (a) RCA-based SAD for 16 pairs input pixels, (b) full adder (FA), half adder (HA)

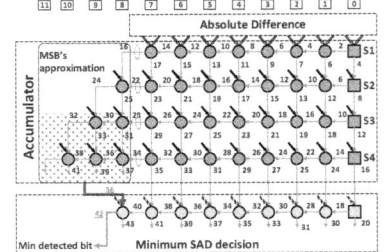

(a)

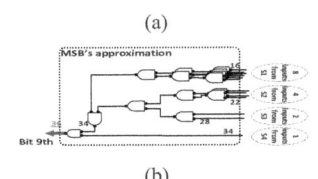

(b)

Figure 5. (a) RCA-based SAD apply MSB-approximation technique, (b) 4-MSB's approximation circuit

In original RCA-based design, MSB's are computed by some full adders. In our design, we replace these full adders with our MSB-approximation circuit. This circuit reduces long carry-propagation delay of RCA and number of logic gates. Hence, the a-SAD circuit simultaneously improves performance and power compared to original one. We verify this by simulating performance and power in Synopsis Design Compiler and Primetime. We also simulate performance and power of previous SAD calculators. Then, we compare these simulation results to those of our a-SAD circuit. Here, our a-SAD circuit shows highest performance and lowest power dissipation.

The remainder of this paper is organized as follows. Section 2 discusses the related works along with their pros and cons. In Section 3, we analyze properties of RCA-based SAD design, and present the a-SAD circuit. Simulation results are provided in Section 4. Section 5 concludes our study.

2. PREVIOUS SAD CALCULATORS

We further discuss previous SAD calculators of [4, 5]. Before this, we briefly introduce SAD and its structure in VLSI implementation. The definition of SAD is given as follows:

$$SAD = \sum_{i=0}^{M \times N - 1} \left| C_i - R_i \right| \qquad (1)$$

, where C_i and R_i are 8-bit luma or chroma value of pixels in current and reference MB's, respectively. $M \times N$ is the size of a single MB, which is varied dependently on defined video compression standard. In H.264 video standard, 4×4 MB is employed considering tradeoff between performance and complexity of the system [6]. To design an SAD calculator having high throughput, we can employ the fully-folded architecture of Fig. 2. Here, an SAD calculator is divided into three parts: AD, accumulation and minimum SAD decision. In the AD part, AD estimators of sixteen pair pixels are paralleled, whose outputs are fed to the accumulation. Then, the accumulation produces SAD between current and reference MB's. In the minimum SAD decision part, the output of the accumulation is compared to previous minimum SAD of the current SWR.

Researchers have developed many techniques to improve performance or power of SAD calculator under the architecture of Fig. 2. In [4], J. Vanne et al. improved performance of

accumulation part by using compression array units based on *carry-save adder* (CSA). Fig. 3 shows their accumulation design. This design requires a final addition to convert compressed values to normal values, which is simultaneously conducted with minimum SAD decision. This effectively reduces delay of the accumulation part. By using theoretical analysis, they showed that their design delivers smaller delay compared to other SAD designs. H. Kaul et al. presented four-way speculative computation of AD's to make better performance. They merged S1-level additions of Fig. 2 with AD's by employing this technique, resulting in performance advantage translated to 30% energy savings under same throughput. They presented a 4:2 compression unit for accumulation part and optimized this unit in gate/circuit-levels. They achieved optimal energy efficiency by applying wide dynamic voltage scaling (230mV ~ 1.4V). Such an approach incurs considerable performance penalties, which are compensated by the above techniques.

We implemented these two designs at RTL-level using standard-library cells of Samsung 130nm CMOS technology and simulated their performance and power dissipation under nominal voltage condition (1.2V). Here, we suitably modified the architecture of H. Kaul's design to that of Fig. 2 for fair comparison. We do not take into account some circuit-level techniques of Kaul's design since these techniques cannot be implemented at RTL-level. Our simulation results show that under nominal voltage condition, J. Vanne's design delivers higher performance and better power efficiency compared to the other one. This is due to long critical-path delay and large power dissipation of 4:2 compression units. Hence, J. Vanne's design is used as our comparison target in this work.

3. PROPOSED a-SAD CIRCUIT DESIGN

In this section, we propose MSB-approximation technique to simultaneously improve performance and power of the accumulation part. This technique is easily implemented in RCA-based accumulation, which will be discussed in section 3.3. Hence, we design accumulation part of our a-SAD calculator by employing RCA's.

3.1 RCA-based Accumulation

Figure 4 (a) shows RCA-based accumulation design, where S1, S2, S3 and S4 describe S1, S2, S3 and S4 levels of Fig. 2, respectively. Here, we consider that minimum SAD decision is also implemented by RCA. RCA consists of full adder (FA) and half adder (HA), which are implemented as Fig. 4 (b) at gate-level. In Fig. 4 (b), the numbers written inside gate symbols express delay times of each logic gate obtained from our theoretical analysis. Based on these delay times, we are able to theoretically compute delay times of the RCA-based accumulation design of Fig. 4 (a). Our computation results are stuck to each module. In these theoretical analyses, we make four assumptions as follows. Firstly, all logic gates are combinations of only three basic gates, which are 2-input NAND/NOR gates and inverter. Secondly, all basic gates have unit time delay. Thirdly, all outputs of AD part are simultaneously fed to accumulation part. This feeding time is regarded as the initial time of our analysis. Lastly, we do not consider effects of fan-out, fan-in and interconnection for simplicity. Under these assumptions, the critical-path delay of 'accumulation + minimum SAD decision' is estimated to 48 timing units.

In the same way as the above estimation, we calculate the critical-path delay of 'accumulation + minimum SAD decision' for J. Vanne's design of Fig. 3. We suppose that the normalization adder of Fig. 3 is implemented by using a *Sklansky Adder* (SKA), which is the fastest *carry-look-ahead adder* (CLA) under our assumptions (We do not consider the effect of fan-out, as mentioned above). Nonetheless, the critical-path delay is 52 timing units, which is slightly larger than that of Fig. 4 (a). Such counter-intuitive observation is due to the fact that in Fig. 4 (a), carry–propagations of S1, S2, S3 and S4 levels are concurrently conducted, alleviating long carry-propagation delay problem of RCA's.

On the other hand, in the design of Fig. 4 (a) this addition cannot be paralleled with accumulation, incurring extra delay in AD part. Hence, when we estimate the critical path delay of total SAD circuit (= 'AD + accumulation + minimum SAD decision'), the design of Fig. 4 (a) probably shows comparable delay to J. Vanne's one.

Using theoretical analysis, we also compare power dissipation of accumulation module for the designs of Fig. 3 and Fig. 4 (a). Since it is difficult to directly estimate power dissipation, we compare the number of full-adders used in each design as an indirect method. Under the assumption that switching probabilities of all full-adders are same, the number of full-adders obviously has high correlation to power dissipation. The accumulation of Fig. 4 (a) consists of 131 full-adders while 156 full-adders are employed in that of Fig. 3. This implies that the first one dissipates lower power compared to the latter one.

These theoretical analyses lead to the motivation of our work. If MSB-approximation technique significantly reduces carry-propagation delay of RCA-based accumulation, our a-SAD calculator may obtain higher performance than J. Vanne's one. If the circuit for MSB-approximation requires smaller number of logic gates than RCA's to compute approximation target MSB's, then our a-SAD calculator will show lower power dissipation compared to the above two designs.

3.2 Determining Optimal Number of Approximation Target MSB's

In RCA-based accumulation, MSB signals are summation of corresponding input signals and carry-in signals. Then, we can implement the proposed MSB-approximation circuit by OR-gating the input and the carry-in signals. In such a scheme, the output of the MSB-approximation circuit is disabled only when all input and carry-in signals are disabled. Since we do not fully estimate output MSB's, such a scheme reduces carry-propagation delay and the number of logic gates at the same time. As we increase the number of approximation target MSB's, the reductions are expected to be larger. However, it is obvious that this lowers boundary value of approximate SAD. When minimum SAD of a SWR is larger than the boundary value, we fail to find the minimum SAD as aforementioned. This degrades video compression rate due to the following reason. After finding the best matching MB within the SWR, *motion compression* (MC) process is conducted. Here, residual data is generated by subtracting the found reference MB from the current MB. This residual data is transformed to DCT coefficients [3]. If we find wrong reference MB in block matching, the residual data becomes relatively larger. This increase the number of high frequency DCT coefficients, degrading compression rate.

These imply that optimal number of approximation target MSB's is the largest one not to affect video compression rate. We conducted video experiments to find the optimal number by using JM reference software [8] with H.264/AVC baseline profile. We customize SAD computation function of JM reference software to survey the influence of MSB-approximation upon video compression rate. We made our experiments for five test video sequences having 640x460 resolutions, which are Akko&Kayo (30fps), Race1 (30fps), Rena (30fps), Ballroom (25fps), and Exit (25fps) (we only show 3 of them). We conducted same experiments for various searching algorithms of Full Search (FS), Fast Full Search (FFS), and UMHexagon Search (UHS). Table 1 shows total bit-rates of compressed video sequences. Under 4×4 MB, SAD value has 12-bit information. Here, up to the approximation of 4-MSB's compressed bit-rates are hardly affected (less than 2% variation). Hence, we decide optimal number of approximation target MSB's as four. We do not show PSNR value of video output since our MSB-approximation does not affect the video output quality.

3.3 Performance and Power Analysis of Our a-SAD Calculator

Based on the discussion of section 3.2, we design our a-SAD calculator. Fig. 5 (a) shows the a-SAD calculator, where we approximate four highest-order MSB's of original SAD to single

MSB. The approximate MSB is enabled as far as original MSB's are not fully disabled. In RCA-based accumulation, such a scheme can be easily implemented by OR-gating carry-in signals as shown in Fig. 5 (b). In the proposed a-SAD calculator, we properly modify minimum SAD decision part, as shown in Fig. 5 (a). We theoretically estimate the critical-path delay of 'accumulation + minimum SAD decision', which is 42 timing units. Compared to original design of Fig. 4 (a), our a-SAD circuit shows 12.5% smaller delay in our theoretical analyses.

In our a-SAD circuit, we replace six full adders of accumulation with MSB-approximation circuit and remove three full adders of minimum SAD decision. As shown in Fig. 4 (b), single full adder consists of 12 basic logic gates (2-input NAND: 8 and inverter: 4). Hence, nine full adders have 108 basic logic gates while our MSB-approximation circuit is made of 42 basic logic gates (2-input NAND: 14 and inverter: 28). This implies that our a-SAD circuit shows significantly lower power dissipation compared to original one of Fig. 4 (a).

Table 1. Compressed video: total bitrate (Kb/s)

Search ALG	Video	Normal	Approximation		
			3 MSBs	4 MSBs	5 MSBs
FS	Race1	2055	2057	**2098**	2636
	Akko&Kayo	1155	1156	**1180**	1359
	Rena_	727	727	**727**	732
FFS	Race1	2090	2091	**2120**	2207
	Akko&Kayo	1161	1161	**1162**	1177
	Rena	728	728	**730**	731
UHS	Race1	3883	3883	**3890**	3895
	Akko&Kayo	1885	1894	**1900**	1901
	Rena	748	748	**750**	750

Table 2. Performance and power simulation after optimization synthesis

Design	Critical path delay (ns)	At clock period = 5.4ns	
		Power (mW)	Area (um²)
RCA_based SAD	4.546684	4.6388	14971
J. Vanne's SAD	4.899782	5.7086	17034
4-MSB a-SAD	4.004959	4.1796	14737

4. SIMULATION RESULTS

We verify the proposed design by logic simulations. We synthesize three SAD designs (J. Vanne's design of Fig. 3, the design of Fig. 4 (a), our a-SAD circuit) by using standard cell libraries of 130nm Samsung 130nm CMOS. Then, delays and powers of these designs are simulated by Synopsys Primetime and Design Compiler. Unlike our theoretical analysis, we estimate delay and power of full SAD circuit including AD part and consider the effects of fain-in, fan-out and interconnection. Hence, we can obtain more accurate performance and power comparisons.

It should be noted that Design Compiler conduct delay optimization based on given timing constraints. To compare performances of several designs, we gradually reduced the timing constraint and performed logic synthesis. Then, at a certain timing constraint, timing violation was observed after the logic synthesis. Such work informs of minimum clock period of each design where timing violation does not occur. We simulated the critical-path delay of each design at their minimum clock period, whose results are shown in the second column of Table 2. Here, the SAD design of Fig. 4 (a) shows higher performance to J. Vanne's one. Our a-SAD circuit reduces the critical-path delay of the SAD design of Fig. 4 (a) (12.1% improvement). Compared to J. Vanne's design (our comparison target as mentioned in section 2), our a-SAD shows 18% higher performance.

In power comparisons, we assume that all designs have same clock period for fairness. We selected 5.4ns clock period where timing violation is not observed for all designs. Under this timing constraint, we synthesize the above three designs. Then, Design Compiler automatically inserts buffers to meet the given timing constraint. Under such an *iso-performance* condition, our a-SAD

circuit shows the lowest power dissipation among three designs. The third column of Table 2 shows power simulation data. This shows that MSB-approximation of our a-SAD circuit results in 10% power reduction compared to original one of Fig. 4 (a). Compared to J. Vanne's design, our a-SAD circuit shows 27% smaller power under this *iso-performance* condition.

We also compare areas of the above three designs. The automatic buffer insertion of Design Compiler considerably affects circuit area. This implies that for fair area comparison, we have to perform logic synthesis under *iso-performance* condition. We employ the same timing constraint as power comparison, which is 5.4ns. The fourth column of Table 2 shows the estimation results, where our proposed design delivers smallest area. This proves that our design improves area efficiency also.

5. CONCLUTION

We present a power efficient SAD calculator, named as *approximate SAD* (a-SAD) calculator. In the accumulation design based on ripple-carry adders, we can easily implement the MSB-approximation circuit by OR-gating some carry-in signals and input signals. From extensive video simulations, we conclude that optimal number of approximation target MSB's are four. The MSB-approximation technique reduces carry-propagation delay and number of logic gates, thereby improving performance and power at the same time. This implies that the proposed design delivers good power efficiency. In Samsung CMOS 130nm technology, we compared performance and power of our a-SAD circuit to those of previous SAD designs. Here, our a-SAD circuit shows highest performance and best power efficiency.

6. ACKNOWLEDGMENTS

This research was supported by the Basic Science Research Program through the National Research Foundation of Korea (NRF) funded by the Ministry of Science, ICT and Future Planning (Grant 2012R1A2A2A01011 and NRF-2013R1A1A1005832).

7. REFERENCES

[1] Fore June. *An introduction to Video compression in C/C++*. CSIPP, 2010, ch.9, sec.9.4, pp. 132

[2] T.-C. Chen, S.-Y. Chien, Y.-W. Huang, C.-H. Tsai, C.-Y. Chen, T.-W. Chen and L.-G. Chen. *Analysis and architecture design of an HDTV720p 30 frames/s H.264/AVC encoder*. IEEE Trans. Circ. Syst. Video Tech. vol.16, issue 6, pp.673-688, June.2006

[3] Iain E. Richardson *The H.264 Advanced Video Compression Standard*. 2nd edition, A John Wiley and Sons 2010.

[4] Vanne, J., Aho, E., Hamalainen, T.D. and Kuusilinna, K. *A High-Performance Sum of Absolute Difference Implementation for Motion Estimation*. IEEE Trans. Circ. Syst. Video Tech. vol. 16, issue 7, July.2006

[5] Kaul, H., Anders, M.A., Mathew, S.K., Hsu, S.K., Agarwal, A., Krishnamurthy, R.K. and Borkar, S. *A 320 mV 56µW 411 GOPS/Watt Ultra-Low Voltage Motion Estimation Accelerator in 65 nm CMOS*. IEEE, Journal of Solid-state Cirt. Vol. 44, no. 1, January

[6] Swee Y.Y. and John V. McCanny. *A VLSI Architecture for Variable Block Size Video Motion Estimation*. IEEE Trans. Circ. Syst. – II express briefs, vol. 51, no. 7, Juny 2004

[7] Seong S. Lee, Jeong-M. Kim and Soo-Ik Chae, *New Motion Estimation Algorithm Using Adaptively Quantized Low Bit-Resolution Image and Its VLSI Architecture for MPEG2 Video Encoding*. IEEE Trans. Circ. Syst. Video Tech. vol. 8, issue 6, Oct 1998

[8] JM ver.18.6 http://iphome.hhi.de/suehring/tml/

Design Exploration of Racetrack Lower-level Caches

Zhenyu Sun
Broadcom Corporation, San Diego, CA, USA
zhenyus@broadcom.com

Xiuyuan Bi, Alex K. Jones and Hai Li
University of Pittsburgh, Pittsburgh, PA, USA
{xib5, akjones, hal66}@pitt.edu

ABSTRACT

The recent successful integration of magnetic racetrack memory forecasts a new computing era with unprecedentedly high-density on-chip storage. However, racetrack memory accesses require frequent magnetic domain shifting, introducing overheads in access latency and energy consumption. In this paper, we evaluate and compare several different physical layout strategies and array organizations. From this evaluation, a workload-oriented racetrack LLC architecture is proposed that combines different array types, each of which is tailored to a specific data access pattern. Further, a resizable cache access strategy is applied to reduce shifting overheads at runtime. Our simulation results show that compared with the leading racetrack-based cache, the proposed racetrack LLC can improve system performance by 13.2% reduce LLC energy consumption by 30.4%.

Keywords

Racetrack Memory; Cache Memory

1. INTRODUCTION

The wide adoption of *chip multiprocessors* (CMPs) has generated an explosive demand for on-chip memory resources. Unfortunately, as technology scaling continues, the reliance on conventional SRAM technology for on-chip caches raises several concerns including the large memory cell size, the high leakage power consumption, and the low resilience to soft errors. A very recent emerging nonvolatile memory technology, the *racetrack* memory [1], has been projected to overcome the density barrier and high leakage power of existing memory solutions. Demonstrations in single devices and array structures have been presented by IBM [2], NEC [3, 4], and CNRS [5], supporting its feasibility and potential.

In contrast to conventional array-based memories, including SRAM and *spin-transfer torque random access memory* (STT-RAM), racetrack memory realizes random data accesses by introducing a *racetrack shift* to ensure correct data access in a read or write operation. Racetrack shifts enable the sharing of an access port by multiple memory bits so the array density is determined only by the physical dimension of magnetic domains within the racetrack, which could be as small as $2F^2$. However, the extra delay and energy

overheads due to shifting during read and write operations can degrade the overall system performance and efficiency. Therefore, *minimizing racetrack shifts is the key concern in racetrack-based cache design.*

In this work, a **design exploration study** of racetrack *last-level caches* (LLCs) at the physical design level is performed. We find that the access port organization of racetracks significantly impacts the number of shifts per access. An access port supporting read and write operations (RW-port) must be large enough to provide sufficient writing current. Due to the large area of RW-port, it must be shared by many magnetic domains to overlay the transistor with the racetrack efficiently, inducing a high average shift overhead. In contrast, a read-only port (R-port) can be implemented with a smaller transistor, allowing more R-port access points along a racetrack, reducing the shift overhead for each read access. We present multiple possible layout strategies with different combination of these ports and evaluate the impact of various access port organizations of racetrack LLCs.

At architecture level, we proposed of a **mixed array organization** cache design comprised of both hybrid-port and uniform-port arrays, each of which are optimized to handle different common access patterns efficiently. The hybrid-port array with many R-ports and few RW-ports is efficient for regular and read-intensive cache accesses, such as instruction requests. The uniform-port array with homogeneous but fewer overall RW-ports is more suitable for heavily written data and/or potentially highly random data accesses. On top of the mixed array organization, a **resizable racetrack LLC** is presented, which adjusts the number of accessible ways in a set-associative cache organization based on the application access requirements on-the-fly to further minimize shifting when cache pressure is low. Efficiently adjusting the effective racetrack size in the racetrack LLC can eliminate 57.9% of the required racetrack shifts, thereby significantly improving the system performance and energy efficiency.

2. BASICS OF RACETRACK MEMORY

Figure 1 shows the basic structure of a planar racetrack nanowire within which many *magnetic domains* are stored and separated by ultra narrow *domain walls* [6]. Each domain has its own magnetization direction, representing one-

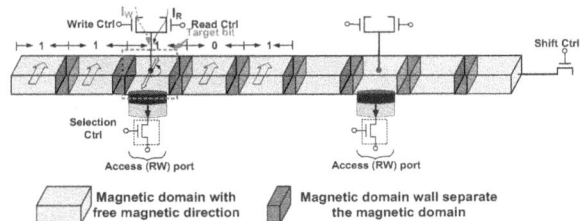

Figure 1: A racetrack nanowire and associated read/write access ports.

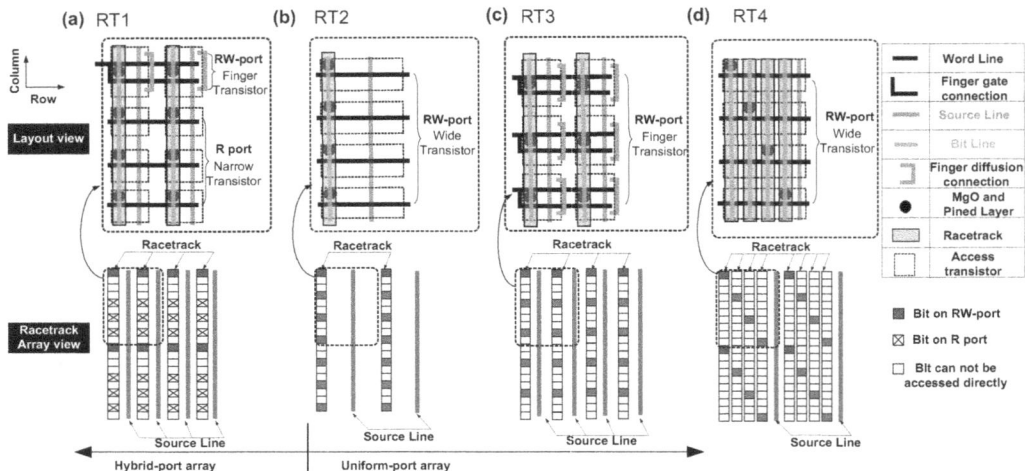

Figure 2: Four example racetrack array organizations: (a) hybrid-port array; (b-d) uniform-port arrays.

bit of binary data. Data is accessed through a shared *access port*. Each access port contains an access transistor connected to fixed magnetic layers similar to the construction of a magnetic tunnel junction (MTJ) used to construct STT-RAM [7]. Because the number of port is much smaller than the number of magnetic domain, accessing a particular magnetic domain (i.e., bit) requires two steps: *Step 1—shift & align* the target magnetic domain to an access port; *Step 2— read or write* by applying an appropriate voltage/current, which is intrinsically as same as STT-RAM.

3. RACETRACK ARRAY DESIGN

Unlike STT-RAM in which all the access transistors are identical, the access port for racetrack memory can be designed to conduct only read operations (***R-port***) or reads and writes (***RW-port***) [8]. The fundamental circuit implementation difference is the transistor size. An R-port requires a smaller transistor due to the relatively small current required for data detection. The RW-port is considerably bigger to provide sufficient current and enough torque to switch the magnetization direction of magnetic domains during write operations.

3.1 Hybrid and Uniform Arrays

The hybrid-port array in Figure 2(a) contains both R-ports and RW-ports. To fit into the width-wise footprint of the small R-port transistors, a wide RW-port transistor is broken into two or more parallel-connected segments, or *fingers*. In the array view, the dark square indicates the magnetic domain aligned with the RW-port, that can be directly read and written. A square with cross corresponds to a domain aligned with a R-port in similar fashion. Accessing a magnetic domain in a blank square (or writing to a cross location), first requires shifts to align the domain with an R/RW-port prior to access. Thus, the shift cost of a data bit is determined by both its physical location and access type. Typically, writes to hybrid arrays incur more shifts than reads due to the heterogeneous availability of the access ports.

A uniform-port array containing only RW-ports can be implemented in different RW-port layouts and racetrack connections. Figure 2(b) is the first-generation array design [8]. Due to the mismatch between the large RW-port transistors and narrow racetrack nanowires, a large portion of the area due to the footprint of access transistors is wasted. Fig-

ure 2(c) utilizes the RW-port design in (a), which breaks a wide access transistor into a few fingers. As such, the RW-port size is reduced along the row direction but extended in the column direction. This design avoids wasted area but increases the distance between adjacent access ports. Figure 2(d) adopts the wide 1-finger layout of RW-ports. Multiple racetracks are placed above a column of transistors and share a source line. The design fully utilizes the unused area and achieves an improved density. However, the distance between adjacent access ports further increases.

3.2 Array Design Impact on Caches

We consider these racetrack array organizations (RT1~RT4) (Figure 2) in the context of a 4MB LLC under 32nm technology and compare them with caches constructed of conventional SRAM ($125F^2$) and the latest STT-RAM technology [10]. Tables 1&2 summarize the related cache latency and energy parameters obtained from a modified version of NVsim [11]. The domain wall shifting energy is calculated based on micro-magnetic simulations [9].

From the result we can see hybrid-port RT1 achieved best read performance and energy after taking shift cost into account, thanks to sufficient amount or R-ports which help reduce the shifts. On the other hand, uniform-port RT4 provides best domain-level R/W performance and energy consumption (not including shifts). The reason is that high density leads to small area of the array, so a great amount of the latency and energy on the peripheral circuit can be saved. However, RT4 also introduces the most shift overheads among all arrays, therefore proper optimization should be applied to fully take advantage of this design.

4. RACETRACK LLC OPTIMIZATION

Section 3 demonstrates a tradeoff between racetrack array layout density with the resulting cache performance and en-

Table 1: Comparison of Cache Access Latencies

	SRAM	STT-RAM	RT1	RT2	RT3	RT4
Rd Lat.[1]	9+1	7+1	4+1	5+1	4+1	2+1
Wr Lat.[1]	9+1	7+10	4+10	5+10	4+10	2+10
Shift [2]			Rd: 3; Wr: 8	3	4	8

[1] *Latency in clock cycles = peripheral + cell latency*
[2] *One shift means a racetrack moves the distance of a magnetic domain. Each shift takes 0.5ns [9], that is, one clock cycle in this work.*

Table 2: Energy Consumption Parameters

	SRAM	STT-RAM	RT1	RT2	RT3	RT4
Read Energy (nJ)	0.42	0.34	0.16	0.22	0.16	0.074
Write Energy (nJ)	0.35	1.52	0.97	1.07	0.97	0.57
Shift Energy (nJ/shift)	–	–	0.62	0.62	0.62	0.62
Leakage Power (mW)	4100	120	65	83	70	46

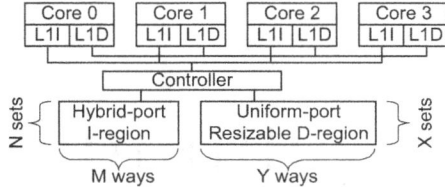

Figure 3: The mixed array organization.

ergy overheads from additional shifting during access. Based on these observations, we propose a two-step cache architecture optimization to mitigate shifting:*mixed-array cache* and *dynamic resizable RT cache*.

4.1 Mixed Array Organization

At the application level, we observe that different types of cache blocks within the application demonstrate very different read and write access characteristics. Instruction blocks are dominated by read access as blocks of instructions are often reused many times such as in loops. In contrast, the read and write frequencies of data blocks are more balanced. Additionally, from Section 3 the results indicate that hybrid-port arrays are well suited to frequently read data while uniform-port arrays are often better when write accesses are more frequent.

The *mixed array* cache leverages these observed access properties and provides both hybrid-port arrays optimized for heavily read blocks such as instruction blocks and uniform-port arrays that are well suited for data blocks. Figure 3 illustrates mixed array concept as applied in a LLC that segregates instruction and data caches. The instruction region (*I-region*) is constructed with hybrid-port arrays while the uniform-port arrays (*D-region*) are used for data blocks with diverse and random access patterns.

4.2 Dynamic Resizable Racetrack Cache

The usage frequency of cache blocks in LLC is often heavily biased. Some applications may only utilize a few ways in an set associative cache. In this case, reducing the number of active ways would not have a dramatic negative impact on the performance.

Based on this phenomenal, a *dynamic resizable racetrack LLC design* is designed which can adjust the cache capacity based on application needs at runtime, to improve data proximity to access points, therefore reduce the amount of shifts. First of all, a physical to logical mapping shows in Figure 4 is applied. Within a cache set, the data bits for each racetrack nanowire are separated into different associative ways. The resizability of the racetrack LLC is achieved by changing the associativity, *i.e.*, the number of ways in a cache set, using a *way mask*. For example, when reducing the associativity from 32 to 8 for the design in Figure 4, the maximum shift distance decreases from two to zero. Conse-

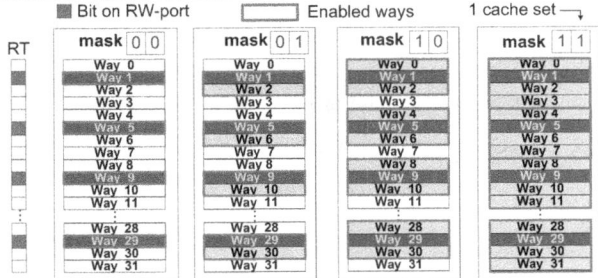

Figure 4: Resizable implementation for a 32-way racetrack cache.

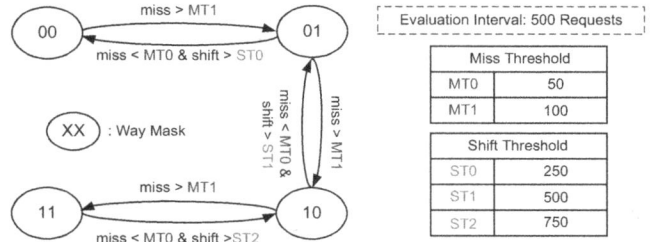

Figure 5: The resizing policy.

quently, the latency and energy costs of a cache hit become much lower. Benefiting from the unique structure of racetrack memory, the associativity of each set can be controlled independently without interfering other sets. Please note for I-region in the mixed array design, the amount of shifts is already quite low for most access, *i.e.*, read access, which leaves very limited optimization space. Therefore, the proposed resizing scheme is only applied to the D-region.

The resizing policy: Figure 5 shows the policy which is used to control the resize procedure. Each state represents a size configuration and determines the way mask. The resizing condition is checked periodically at the end of a fixed monitoring interval (500 requests). Basically, when the miss rate increases beyond a threshold, the policy will enlarge the cache capacity.

5. EVALUATION AND COMPARISON

5.1 Experimental Setup

MacSim [12] with our own custom racetrack cache module was used for real-time micro-architecture estimation. The latency and energy parameters of the 4MB LLC in SRAM, STT-RAM, and racetrack technologies have been summarized in Table 1 & 2. The processor configuration and memory hierarchy parameters can be found in Table 3. And Table 4 provides detailed parameters for the mixed array (combining RT1 and RT4, see Section 3), resizable racetrack LLC design. The SPEC CPU2006 benchmark suite [13] provided the evaluation workloads.

5.2 Mixed Array Organization

Figure 6 shows the performance and energy consumption of the racetrack LLC after adopting the mixed array organization normalized to RT4. On average, splitting the I-region and D-region achieves 6.6% improvement in IPC over the uniform RT4 design [Figure 6 (a)]. The major benefit comes from the reduced shift operations: on average 12.7% of racetrack shifts (black line) are removed in the mixed

Table 3: The CPU Configuration

CPU	2GHz, 2 Cores, out-of-order, 2-way issue
L1 Cache (SRAM)	32K I/D, 32B cache line, write-back, 2-cycle R/W, private
L2 Cache	4MB, 32B cache line, write-back, shared
Main Memory	1GB, 400 cycle

Table 4: Optimized Racetrack LLC Configuration

Baseline Racetrack LLC	I-region	D-region
Capacity & Design	0.5 MB, RT1	3.5 MB, RT4
Latency[1]	R: 5/ W:14	R: 3/ W:12
Shift of Read[2]	3	8
Shift of Write[2]	8	8
Dynamic energy	0.084 nJ/read; 0.62 nJ/write	
Leakage power	48 mW	
Shift Latency	0.5 ns/shift [9]	
Shift energy	0.62 nJ/shift	

[1] *Latency = peripheral + cell latency (in cycles)*
[2] *Shift is represented by the number of magnetic domains.*

265

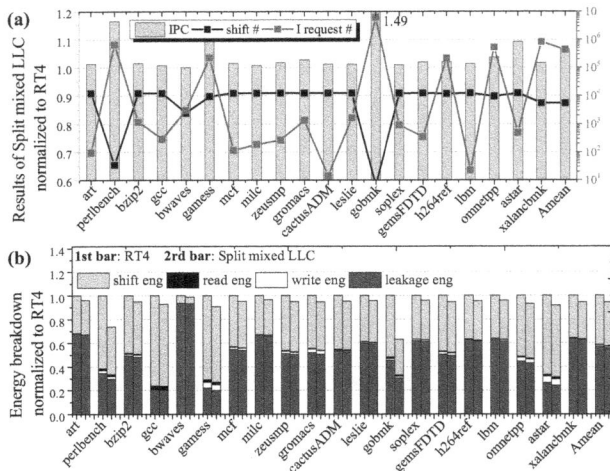

Figure 6: Mixed Array LLC Efficiency. (a): IPC and number of shifts normalized to RT4; Number of instruction requests. (b) Energy breakdown.

array design. As expected, the workloads with more instruction requests (blue line), such as `perlbench` and `gobmk`, achieve the highest performance improvements due to heavy access density to RT1 arrays, which have higher port density and result in considerable shift reduction (black line) over RT4 arrays of the baseline. The improved performance and reduction of domain shifts result in a 6.7% energy reduction.

5.3 Resizable Racetrack Cache

The effectiveness of resizable racetrack (r_rt) approach is examined by comparing with the latest *history based way reorder* (HBWR) scheme which monitors the racetrack position and dynamically controls its movement [9]. Compared to the baseline RT4, (r_rt) obtains a 57.9% reduction in racetrack shifts, resulting in an average system performance improvement of 13.2% with a 30.4% savings in LLC energy, as shown in Figure 7. Compared to HBWR, which tends to migrate access-intensive data blocks to access ports, r_rt is more efficient in shift reduction and removes 31.3% of racetrack shifts. Consequently, r_rt obtains 3.0% performance improvement and 15.9% energy savings over HBWR. Although the motivation of HBWR is also reducing the amount of shifts, our proposed design achieved better performance and energy because: (1) HWBR does not take advantage of the strongly biased read/write ratio of instruction block and (2) the maximum number of shift in HWBR is not reduced.

6. CONCLUSION

In this paper, we explore several possible array organizations of racetrack LLC. Based on these explorations, a statically (design time) partitioned, mixed array organization is proposed which integrates both hybrid-port arrays and uniform-port arrays to reduce racetrack shifts. In addition, a resizable cache scheme is applied to dynamically adjust associativity selections to further reduce shifts. The simulation results show that the proposed design can achieve 13.2% performance improvement and 30.4% energy saving over the baseline design.

7. ACKNOWLEDGEMENT

This work was supported in part by NSF grants of CNS-1311706 and CNS-1342566. Any opinions, findings and con-

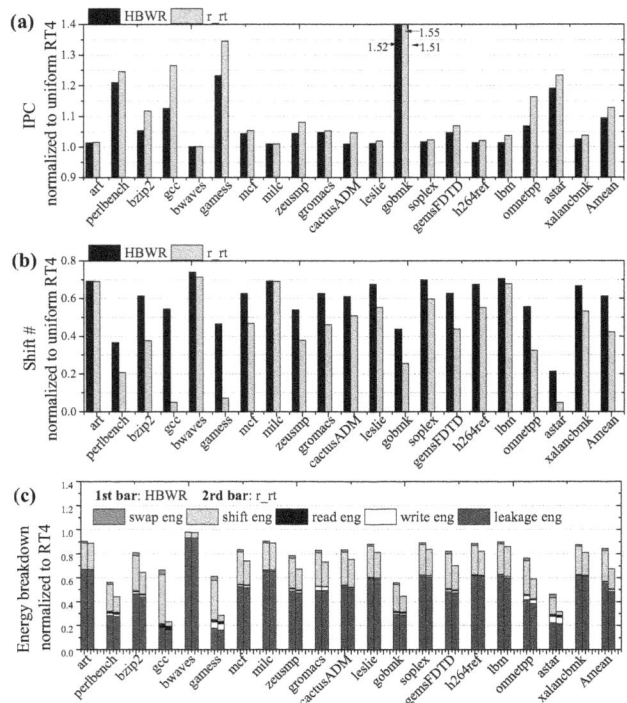

Figure 7: Efficiency of the resizable cache.

clusions or recommendations expressed in this material are those of the authors and do not necessarily reflect the views of NSF or their contractors.

8. REFERENCES

[1] S. Parkin, "Racetrack Memory: A Storage Class Memory Based on Current Controlled Magnetic Domain Wall Motion," *DRC-67*, pp. 3–6, 2009.

[2] Annunziata *et al.*, "Racetrack Memory Cell Array with Integrated Magnetic Tunnel Junction Readout," *IEDM-58*, pp. 24–3, 2011.

[3] S. Fukami *et al.*, "Low-Current Perpendicular Domain Wall Motion Cell for Scalable High-Speed MRAM," *VLSIT-29*, pp. 230–231, 2009.

[4] R. Nebashi *et al.*, "A Content Addressable Memory using Magnetic Domain Wall Motion Cells," *VLSIC-25*, pp. 300–301, 2011.

[5] J. Sampaio *et al.*, "Coupling and Induced Depinning of Magnetic Domain Walls in Adjacent Spin Valve Nanotracks," *Journal of Applied Physics (JAP)*, vol. 113, p. 133901, 2013.

[6] Y. Zhang *et al.*, "Perpendicular-Magnetic-Anisotropy CoFeB Racetrack Memory," *Journal of Applied Physics (JAP)*, vol. 111, no. 9, pp. 093 925–093 925, 2012.

[7] M. Hosomi *et al.*, "A novel nonvolatile memory with spin torque transfer magnetization switching: Spin-RAM," *IEDM*, pp. 459–462, 2005.

[8] R. Venkatesan *et al.*, "TapeCache: a High Density, Energy Efficient Cache based on Domain Wall Memory," *ISLPED-12*, pp. 185–190, 2012.

[9] Z. Sun, W. Wu, and H. Li, "Cross-Layer Racetrack Memory Design for Ultra High Density and Low Power Consumption," *DAC-50*, pp. 1–6, 2013.

[10] Z. Sun *et al.*, "Multi Retention Level STT-RAM Cache Designs with a Dynamic Refresh Scheme," *MICRO-44*, pp. 329–338, 2011.

[11] X. Dong *et al.*, "NVSim: A Circuit-Level Performance, Energy, and Area Model for Emerging Nonvolatile Memory," *TCAD*, vol. 31, no. 7, pp. 994–1007, 2012.

[12] MacSim, *http://code.google.com/p/macsim/*.

[13] SPEC2006, *http://www.spec.org/cpu2006/*.

A Compact Macromodel for the Charge Phase of a Battery with Typical Charging Protocol *

Donghwa Shin
Yeungnam University
donghwashin@yu.ac.kr

Alessandro Sassone, Alberto Bocca,
Alberto Macii, Enrico Macii, and

Massimo Poncino †
Politecnico di Torino
{alessandro.sassone, alberto.bocca,
alberto.macii, enrico.macii,
massimo.poncino}@polito.it

ABSTRACT

Availability of a simulation model of a battery is one of the most important requisites in the system-level design of battery-powered systems. The vast majority of the models describe the *discharge* behavior of the battery; so far, the estimation of charging time has been in fact only marginally studied because the charging phase is regarded as a relatively controlled process compared to discharge.
In this paper, we present a compact macro-model for the estimation of charging time under the most widely used charge protocol, i.e., Constant Current-Constant Voltage (CC-CV). This model is derived under the consideration of the context of the existing models including the well-known Peukert's law and equivalent electric circuits. The estimation result with the proposed model based on the manufacturer's data of commercial Li-ion batteries shows fair accuracy, especially when compared to estimates on parameters extracted from discharge characteristics.

Categories and Subject Descriptors

I.6.5 [**Simulation and Modeling**]: Model Development.

Keywords

Battery charging, Battery Modeling, Peukert's law, Datasheet, Constant Current - Constant Voltage (CC-CV).

1. INTRODUCTION

Battery modeling plays a fundamental role in the design of battery-powered systems in many applications domains (e.g., automotive, aerospace, smart grids). The availability of mathematical models

---

*This work was supported by the EC co-funded SMAC (SMArt systems Co-design) project Grant Agreement FP7-ICT-288827, Basic Science Research Program through the National Research Foundation of Korea(NRF) funded by the Ministry of Education (grant number: 2012R1A6A3A03038938). This work was also supported by the 2014 Yeungnam university research grant.

†Corresponding author

of the battery characteristics has the primary purpose of estimating *battery performance* (e.g., lifetime, state of charge, output voltage) and secondly that of helping *battery design* by evaluating how the design of a battery impacts its performance. However, still in many contexts, designers usually rely on simple macromodels such as the Peukert's law [1], as a quick estimator for the sizing of the battery sub-system or for preliminary what-if analyses.

The Peukert's law expresses a non-linear relationship between the discharge current and the delivered capacity; for this reason, the majority of the battery models that rely on this law are usually focused on the *discharge* behavior of a battery.

Estimation of the battery charging behavior through specific model has been considered generally less interesting than discharging; this is because battery charge, unlike discharge, is usually a quite controlled process, and the current/voltage charge profiles normally follows well-defined standard "protocols" like the popular Constant Current-Constant Voltage (CC-CV) scheme [2].

Nevertheless, for specific tasks like the design of a charger circuit or the sizing of a power source used to charge a battery a light model that allows to accurately estimate charging time under different conditions would be a very desirable design aid.

In this paper we propose a compact macromodel for the estimation of charging time under the most widely used CC-CV protocol. The proposed model is derived taking into account the existing models including the Peukert's law and equivalent electrical circuits. We refer to the most widely adopted charge protocol for lead-acid and Li-Ion batteries, i.e., the CC-CV protocol. We achieve this by keeping the empirical nature of Peukert's equation, and by relying only on manufacturers' data, as done recently by several modeling frameworks ([3, 4]).

2. BACKGROUND

2.1 Battery Models and Peukert's Equation

In literature, there are many different approaches to model the fundamental battery properties. models. Among the various models, a popular battery "model" is a simple empirical equation that has been widely used in the past in order to estimate the lifetime or the residual capacity of a battery discharged at a constant current, known as Peukert's law [1], which is generally expressed as:

$$t = C_p / I^k \tag{1}$$

where C_p is the Peukert's Capacity, I the constant discharge current; and t is the time to totally discharge the battery; k is the Peukert's number or coefficient, a dimensionless quantity having values > 1 when considering the discharge case. Typical values of k de-

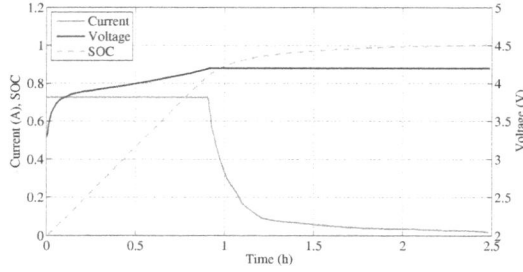

Figure 1: CC-CV Charging Profile of the Sony US18650 Li-Ion Battery [8].

pend on the battery chemistry and the manufacturing process and typically range from 1.1 to 1.3. A generalization of the Peukert's coefficient was presented in [5]. The Peukert's capacity C_p corresponds to a battery discharged at $I = 1A$. The capacity measured by other current rate can be transformed to C_p by the following relation $C_p = C(\frac{C}{R})^{k-1}$ where C is the rated capacity at that discharge rate (in ampere-hours) and R is the rated discharge time (i.e., the time to discharge the battery, in hours).

2.2 Battery Charging Protocols

Charging protocols have been widely analyzed in the literature (e.g., [6]). Regardless of all drawbacks, the CC-CV protocol is considered as the standard charging protocol for Li-ion batteries because of its simplicity, ease of implementation while meeting important safety requirements including over-voltage and over-current protection. The protocol consists of two phases. The battery is initially charged at a constant current (typically in the range 0.7C-0.8C*) until its voltage rises to a pre-determined limit that depends on the type of Li-ion battery. At this point, the voltage remains constant while the battery current drops until a pre-determined lower limit. In practice, the end-of-charge time is defined depending on the specific battery, and can occur when reaching (i) a minimum current, (ii) a maximum voltage level, or (iii) a total charge time. During the CC phase the state of charge (SOC) grows linearly as the integral of the current, as shown in Figure 1 which depicts a typical CC-CV profile.

3. MACROMODEL OF THE BATTERY CHARGING PHASE

The main characteristic of our model consists of expressing the total charge time t_{charge} as the sum of two distinct contributions, one for each of the two phases (CC and CV), i.e., $t_{charge} = t_{cc} + t_{cv}$. For the calculation of a constant-current charging time, t_{cc}, we use the principle of Peukert's law but applied to the charge phase (Section 3.1), whilst the calculation of a constant-voltage charging time t_{cv} relies on two assumptions that will be justified in Section 3.2 and 3.3:

1. *The current profile during the CV phase is roughly independent of the current value used in the CC phase;*

2. *The charge accrued during the CC phase for a given current value up to meeting CV phase is approximately the same as the charge that would be accrued by the current profile corresponding to a CV charging before reaching the same voltage.*

3.1 Calculation of t_{cc}

In Peukert's law, the discharge time (1) represents the time to reach the pre-determined cut-off voltage using a given discharge

---

* C denotes the C-rate, i.e., a current discharge rate normalized with respect to the capacity value. For instance, a 1C current for a 1200 mAh battery corresponds to 1200mA.

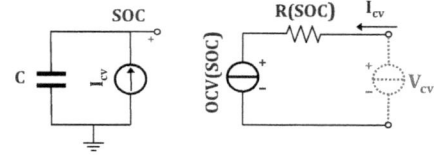

Figure 2: Schematic of Circuit Equivalent Model of a Battery

current. Let us now simply apply this scenario to the charge phase, in which the battery is charged with a constant current until the battery reaches the required voltage V_{cv} after which the CV phase starts.

Conceptually, these two processes are equivalent: both of them identify a time at which a certain cut-off voltage is reached with a given current. Therefore, the time duration of CC phase, t_{cc}, can be modeled in the same manner using Peukert's law, i.e.:

$$t_{cc} = C_p / I_{cc}^{k_{cc}}, \qquad (2)$$

where I_{cc}, C_p, and k_{cc} denote the constant charging current, the Peukert's capacity of the battery, and the Peukert's coefficient, respectively. Notice that k_{cc} will be in general different from the one describing the discharge process and has to be characterized using different data.

3.2 Relation between CV Current Profile and CC Current

In order to relate the current profile during CV with the CC current used before the CV phase, we need to express the battery charge current in terms of the intrinsic parameters of the battery, in particular, the internal resistance (R), the open-circuit voltage (OCV) and the capacity, which are usually used to consider in the battery model for the system-level design [7]. This can be done by analyzing a simple circuit equivalent model of the battery behavior, described in Figure 2. C denotes the nominal capacity, while internal resistance and OCV are modeled as a function of the SOC. The dashed section on the right represents the constant charging voltage V_{cv}. Based on simple circuit analysis, the charging current I_{cv} during the CV phase at a certain SOC can be defined as:

$$I_{cv} = (V_{cv} - OCV(SOC))/R(SOC), \qquad (3)$$

The charging current is determined by SOC, which in turn is the result of the integral of the current I_{cv} where R and OCV are in general complex non-linear functions.

The behavior of I_{cv} over time is thus governed by (3), and, in turn, the I_{cv} always follows the same curve even with the different starting SOC values. Therefore, in the CC-CV charging protocol, regardless of the value of I_{cc}, as soon as the battery voltage reaches the target voltage V_{cv}, the battery current profile follows a curve determined only by the SOC and the battery internal parameters.

Figure 3 shows the abstract shape of current and SOC profile of CC-CV charging, with two different CC current I_{cc1} and I_{cc2} ($< I_{cc1}$) when the current during CV phase follows the same shape. A manufacturer's data also reports this aspect of CV charging current [8]. In the figure, I_{eoc} denotes the end-of-charge current, i.e., the current value used to define the end of the charge phase.

3.3 Equivalence of Total Charge before CV

The fact that the CC current curves typically merge on the CV current curve regardless of I_{cc}, as discussed in Section 3.2, suggests that the charge cumulated by CC charging and CV charging, from the respective time origin to the time when the CC and CV curves intersect, should be roughly equivalent. An intuitive explanation of this claim derives from the observation that, from the electrical

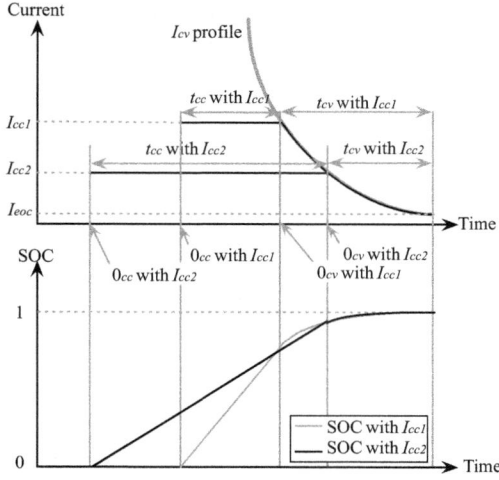

Figure 3: Conceptual Shape of Current and SOC Profiles of CC-CV Charging with Different I_{cc}s.

circuit equivalent (3) there is unique I_{cv} value at a certain SOC. For a given I_{cc}, at the time point in which $I_{cc} = I_{cv}(t)$ the battery SOC should be the same. In some sense, CC current profile can be regarded as a folded and prolonged CV current profile due to the safety and efficiency reason.

This is pictorially represented in Figure 4. The two slanted regions in the figure represent the total cumulated charges. The right slanted region is the total charge (integral of current) accumulated during CC time under I_{cc}, while the left slanted region is the total charge with I_{cv} between 0 and t^*, defined as the time point at which $I_{cv} \equiv I_{cc}$. Notice that in order to plot two different curves with different starting points there are two conceptual time origins, i.e., 0_{cc} (where CC curve starts), and 0_{cv} (where CV curve starts).

We now derive analytically an expression for t_{cv} based on this assumption. Let t^* be the time point in which the CC and CV curve intersect, i.e., such that $I_{cv}(t^*) = I_{cc}$. The total charge with a constant current over time is given by $I_{cv} \cdot t_{cc}$. Now, since $I_{cc} = I_{cv}(t^*)$, and t_{cc} is determined by (2), the total CC charge is:

$$I_{cc}t_{cc} = I_{cc} \cdot \frac{C_p}{I_{cc}^{k_{cc}}} = I_{cv}(t^*) \cdot \frac{C_p}{I_{cv}(t^*)^{k_{cc}}}, \qquad (4)$$

This should be same as the total charge during a full CV charging before I_{cv} reaches I_{cc} at t^*, which is given by the integral of the CV current between $0 (= 0_{cv})$ and t^* over time. From (4) we get:

$$\int_0^{t^*} I_{cv}(t)dt = C_p \cdot I_{cv}(t^*)^{1-k_{cc}} \qquad (5)$$

Taking the derivative d/dt^* of both terms we obtain:

$$\frac{dI_{cv}(t^*)}{dt^*} = \frac{I_{cv}(t^*)^{1+k_{cc}}}{C_p \cdot (k_{cc} - 1)}. \qquad (6)$$

Solving (6) yields the following equation:

$$I_{cv}(t^*) = (\alpha_{cv}t^* + \beta_{cv})^{\gamma_{cv}} \qquad (7)$$

where

$$\alpha_{cv} = -\frac{k_{cc}}{C_p(1-k_{cc})}; \quad \beta_{cv} = I_{cv}(0)^{-k_{cc}}; \quad \gamma_{cv} = -\frac{1}{k_{cc}} \qquad (8)$$

$I_{cv}(0)$ denotes the current value that we will get at time 0 when applying V_{cv} to the completely discharged battery (SOC=0), and can

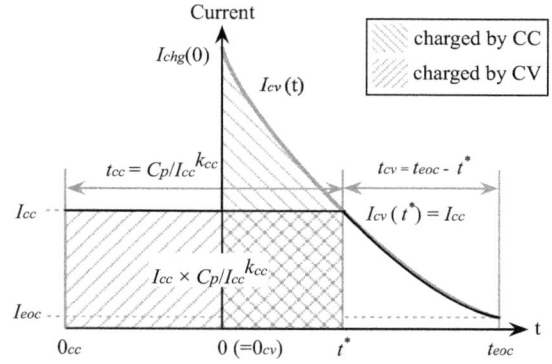

Figure 4: Total Charge During CC and CV Phases.

be calculated by knowing V_{cv} and the battery parameters ($R(SOC = 0)$, and $OCV(SOC = 0)$), as $I_{cv}(0) = \frac{V_{cv} - OCV(SOC=0)}{R(SOC=0)}$. The analytical expression of I_{cv} of (7) allows calculating the value of t^* as:

$$(\alpha_{cv}t^* + \beta_{cv})^{\gamma_{cv}} = I_{cc} \Rightarrow t^* = (I_{cc}^{1/\gamma_{cv}} - \beta_{cv})/\alpha_{cv} \qquad (9)$$

The CV time t_{cv} can be obtained as $t_{eoc} - t^*$, where t_{eoc} is the end-of-charge time, defined as the time point at which $I_{cv}(t_{eoc}) = I_{eoc}$. The latter is a known value given by the charge specifications of the battery. Therefore, t_{eoc} has an expression similar to that of t^*, with I_{eoc} in place of I_{cc}. Therefore, t_{cv} is given by:

$$t_{cv} = t_{eoc} - t^* = (I_{eoc}^{1/\gamma_{cv}} - I_{cc}^{1/\gamma_{cv}})/\alpha_{cv} \qquad (10)$$

This model for t_{cv} also correctly models the two limit conditions in which t_{cv} reduces to 0. One condition is when $I_{cc} = I_{eoc}$; the second one is when $k_{cc} = 1$. In other terms, if we initially charge the battery with a constant current corresponding to I_{eoc}, or if the stored charge in the battery is exactly proportional to the charging current (i.e., ideal battery), then there is no CV phase.

3.4 Overall Macromodel of Charge Time

Putting together the results of the two previous sections the total (CC-CV) charging time is given by:

$$t_{charge}(I_{cc}, k_{cc}) = \frac{C_p}{I_{cc}^{k_{cc}}} - C_p \frac{(1-k_{cc})}{k_{cc}} \cdot \left[\frac{1}{I_{eoc}^{k_{cc}}} - \frac{1}{I_{cc}^{k_{cc}}}\right]. \qquad (11)$$

Notice that both α_{cv} and γ_{cv} has now been expressed in terms of k_{cc}. (11) can be rewritten as:

$$t_{charge} = C_p/(k_{cc}I_{cc}^{k_{cc}}) + \sigma \qquad (12)$$

where $\sigma = \frac{C_p(1-k_{cc})}{k_{cc}} \cdot \frac{1}{I_{eoc}^{k_{cc}}}$. This rewritten general expression approximates the CC-CV charging time with a given I_{cc} depending on only three parameters, i.e., k_{cc}, C_p, and σ (which in turn depends on k_{cc}, C_p, and I_{eoc}). σ reflects the terminating condition of the charging, which can be variable according to the types of the batteries.

4. EXPERIMENTS

4.1 Parameters Extraction

We validate the proposed macromodel and assess its accuracy by comparing the estimated results with the manufacturer's data of two Li-ion rechargeable batteries: US18650 by Sony [8] (1.6Ah nominal) and MP174565 by Saft [9] (4.8Ah nominal). Datasheet of

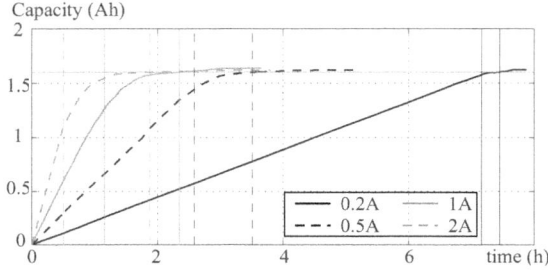

Figure 5: Charged capacity profiles of Sony 18650 Li-ion battery with different constant charging current.

each target battery provides multiple charging profiles with different charging currents suitable for the purpose of model parameter extraction and validation.

We obtain the CC and CV charging time as follows. After digitizing the plots, we set the switching point between the CC and CV phases when the slope of the current profile is higher than 10% (in fact, at CC it is 0%). Next, we determine the end of the charging time by detecting when the SOC value meets 100%. The datasheet of the Sony US18650 battery provides 1A charging profile, therefore, we use it to derive the Peukert's capacity C_p. The datasheet of the Saft MP174565 provides 0.96A charging profile; so, in this case, we rescale C_p. Then, we derive k_{cc} for each given constant current from the CC phase of the corresponding charging profile. Figure 5 shows the digitization result of the target battery from Sony. For the Sony US18650, the obtained k_{cc} values range from 1.1299 to 1.2044 (1.1628 on average), whereas for the Saft MP174565 battery they range between 1.1685 and 1.2036 (1.1860 on average). Table 1 summarizes the parameters estimation result, for each target battery, after taking into account the datasheet information only.

4.2 Charging Time Estimation

The estimated CC and CV times are computed considering: (i) the k_{cc} obtained with a certain current-rate in CC and (ii) an averaged k_{cc}. For the Sony US18650 battery, when using the k_{cc} extracted from 0.5A CC-CV charging profile, the estimation error of CC time is up to 4.0% and, on average, 1.9%, while the estimation error of CV time is up to 11.6% and 3.5% on average. The total charge time error t_{charge} is up to 7.6%, and 1.4% on average. When using the averaged k_{cc} value, the maximum estimation error of CC and CV times are up to 5.45% and 8.63%, respectively, and the total charge time estimation error is up to 5.53%, and 1.44% on average. Table 1 summarizes both the time values extracted from the datasheets and the estimations.

Table 1: Extracted parameters and charging time estimation.

I_{cc} (A)	k_{cc}	C_p	Extracted (h)			k_{cc} @ 0.5A (h)			average k_{cc} (h)		
			t_{cc}	t_{cv}	t_{charge}	t_{cc}	t_{cv}	t_{charge}	t_{cc}	t_{cv}	t_{charge}
0.2	1.13		7.16	0.29	7.45	7.45	0.29	7.74	7.55	0.31	7.87
0.5	1.15		2.59	0.93	3.51	2.59	0.93	3.53	2.60	1.01	3.61
1	-*	1.16*	1.16	1.19	2.35	1.16	1.13	2.29	1.16	1.21	2.37
2	1.20		0.50	1.38	1.88	0.52	1.21	1.74	0.52	1.30	1.82

Sony US 18650 Li-ion battery (header spans top)

I_{cc} (A)	k_{cc}	C_p	Extracted (h)			k_{cc} @ 2.4A (h)			average k_{cc} (h)		
			t_{cc}	t_{cv}	t_{charge}	t_{cc}	t_{cv}	t_{charge}	t_{cc}	t_{cv}	t_{charge}
0.96	-*	4.30*	4.47	1.02	5.50	4.50	1.08	5.58	4.51	1.20	5.71
2.4	1.17		1.53	1.65	3.19	1.54	1.50	3.05	1.52	1.67	3.19
4.8	1.20		0.65	1.85	2.49	0.69	1.63	2.32	0.67	1.80	2.47

SAFT MP174565 Li-ion battery (header spans lower portion)

---

* The extracted t_{cc} values with 1A and 0.96A are used to derive C_p for the target batteries. In these cases, k_{cc} cannot be determined (C_p is equal to $t_{cc} \cdot I_{cc}$). It is an intrinsic characteristics of Peukert's equation.

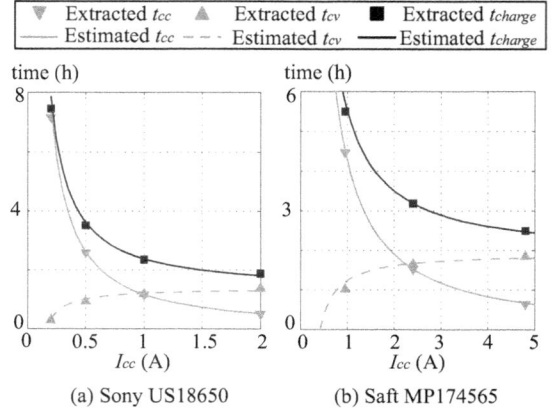

(a) Sony US18650   (b) Saft MP174565

Figure 6: Extracted and estimated t_{cc}, t_{cv}, t_{charge} with average k_{cc} for each target battery.

The same experiment is done for the Saft MP174565 battery. When we use the k_{cc} extracted from 0.5C (i.e., 2.4A) CC-CV charging profile then the total charging time estimation error is up to 7.1% and 3.2% on average, while using the averaged k_{cc}, the total charging time estimation error is up to 3.9% and 1.1% on average. Figure 6 shows the extracted and estimated CC, CV, and total charging time with the averaged k_{cc}. Overall, values for the coefficient k_{cc} are similar to the original Peukert's number for the discharging phase (i.e., from 1.1 to 1.3) and, similarly, also the charging time estimation error.

5. CONCLUSIONS

In this paper, we have proposed a compact model for the CC-CV charging time, similar to Peukert's equation, based on the theoretical and empirical observations while maintaining the consistency with existing models The proposed model is validated by comparing the estimation results with the manufacturer's data of commercial Li-ion batteries. The experimental results show that the exponential coefficient for the proposed model lies between 1.1 to 1.3, which is similar to the original Peukert's coefficient for the discharging time estimation. The error of the charging time estimation is also similar to that of the original Peukert's law, and its value is up to 5.5% and 1.4% on average.

6. REFERENCES

[1] W. Peukert. Über die Abhängigkeit der Kapazität von der Entladestromstärke bei Bleiakkumulatoren. *Elektrotechnische Zeitschrift*, 20, 1897.

[2] H.A.-H. Hussein, I. Batarseh. A Review of Charging Algorithms for Nickel and Lithium Battery Chargers. *IEEE Transactions on Vehicular Technology*, 60(3):830-838, March 2011.

[3] M. Petricca et al. An Automated Framework for Generating Variable-Accuracy Battery Models from Datasheet Information. *Proc. of ISLPED 2013*, pages 365-370. IEEE, 4-6 Sept. 2013.

[4] A. Sassone et al. Modeling of the Charging Behavior of Li-Ion Batteries based on Manufacturer's Data. *Proc. of GLSVLSI'14*. ACM, 21- 23 May 2014.

[5] N. Omar, P. Van den Bossche, T. Coosemans and J. Van Mierlo. Peukert Revisited—Critical Appraisal and Need for Modification for Lithium-Ion Batteries. *Energies*, 6(11):5625-5641, 2013.

[6] W. Shen, T.T. Vo, A. Kapoor. Charging algorithms of lithium-ion batteries: An overview. *Proc. of ICIEA 2012*, pages 1567-1572. IEEE, 18-20 July 2012.

[7] D. Shin, K. Kim, N. Chang, W. Lee, Y. Wang, Q. Xie, and M. Pedram, Online estimation of the remaining energy capacity in mobile systems considering system-wide power consumption and battery characteristics. *Proc. of ASP-DAC.* 22-25 Jan. 2013

[8] Sony Corporation. *Lithium Ion Rechargeable Batteries Technical Handbook*.

[9] Saft Specialty Battery Group. *Rechargeable lithium-ion battery MP 174565 Integration*.

Energy Efficient Task Scheduling on a Multi-core Platform using Real-time Energy Measurements

Digvijay Singh and William J. Kaiser

Electrical Engineering, University of California, Los Angeles

digvijay@ucla.edu, kaiser@ee.ucla.edu

ABSTRACT

This paper presents a large advance in energy-efficient operating system multiprocessor task scheduling with experimentally proven benefits for standard Linux multi-core computing platforms. This Energy Aware Scheduler (EAS) introduces micro-Operations executed Per Joule (OPJ) as a metric representing run-time task energy efficiency. A novel platform architecture permits event-resolved real-time energy measurements. EAS uses OPJ values for scheduling tasks to reduce resource contention. Compared to the Linux task scheduler (Completely Fair Scheduler), EAS improves energy efficiency by over 30% and execution time by over 24%.

Categories and Subject Descriptors

D.4.1 [**Operating Systems**]: Process Management – *scheduling, multiprocessing/multiprogramming/multitasking.*

Keywords

Energy efficiency; Resource contention; Energy aware scheduler

1. INTRODUCTION

The operating system's task scheduling policy has a well-known and significant impact on the performance and energy efficiency of computing platforms [1]. Development of task schedulers confront the challenges of ensuring low latency, meeting task deadlines, improving fairness in distribution of computing resources to tasks and load balancing among processors [2, 3]. However, the large-scale deployment of multiprocessor platforms also now requires that resource contention be minimized to ensure efficient usage of resources. This paper presents the Energy Aware Scheduler (EAS), which is a task scheduler designed for superior energy efficiency on multi-core computing platforms.

2. BACKGROUND AND RELATED WORK

2.1 Multiprocessing and Resource Contention

Multiprocessing CPU architectures are critical in the delivery of computing performance for a broad range of platforms from mobile embedded devices to server systems. Symmetric multiprocessing (SMP) CPU architectures are widely deployed to enable advances in both energy efficiency and performance

through parallel execution [3, 4]. However, the complete potential for these benefits is not realized if multiple tasks frequently contend for resources, such as CPU cache, on a multi-core CPU and lead to a loss in performance called co-run degradation [5].

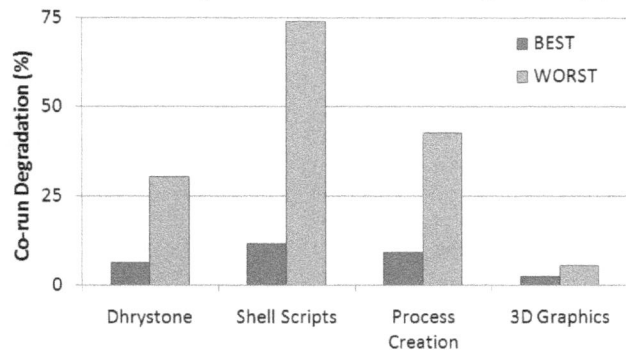

Figure 1. Co-run degradation of four benchmark applications.

The impact of co-run degradation is illustrated in Figure 1 using four benchmarks from the UnixBench suite [6] that execute in parallel on a quad-core x86 platform with the Linux 2.6.32 kernel. Execution time for parallel execution is compared with the execution time when the benchmarks are executed individually. The worst and best cases in the figure correspond to different task schedules that were observed over a thousand repetitions of the experiment. It is important to note that co-run degradation must be determined during, or after, run-time because of run-time dynamism in resource contention [5]. Thus, EAS exploits direct energy measurements along with standard CPU performance monitoring units to identify inefficient processes suffering from resource contention at run-time. The tasks corresponding to these inefficient processes have scheduling priorities adjusted to reduce co-run degradation and improve energy efficiency.

2.2 Completely Fair Scheduler

The Completely Fair Scheduler (CFS) has been adopted as the task scheduler in Linux since the 2.6.23 kernel [7]. CFS constantly attempts to maintain fairness among tasks in terms of allotted CPU time [8]. Thus, if a task has used the least amount of CPU time then CFS will assign highest scheduling priority to this task. In order to efficiently perform priority assignment and to maintain a list of executable tasks, CFS constructs a balanced binary search tree called the red-black tree [9]. Each node of the red-black tree data structure represents an executable task with the key being the CPU time used by the task. Since the tree is balanced, the scheduler can perform scheduling operations in $O(\log n)$ time complexity for a tree with n tasks. For multiprocessing platforms, CFS maintains a red-black tree structure for each CPU core. Tasks are divided among the cores via the mechanism of *load-balancing* and tasks can be moved from one core to another through the use of *task migration* [8].

2.3 Performance Monitoring Unit

Modern CPU architectures support detailed monitoring of computing platform events through the performance monitoring unit. Performance monitoring units provide access to special-purpose CPU registers called performance counters that can count important events such as cache misses. They have been recognized as an important resource for performance monitoring and improvement [10]. EAS utilizes two types of performance counters: 1) the time-stamp counter (TSC) is used as a clock for high-resolution timing of platform events, and 2) performance counters are used to measure the number of CPU operations performed during execution of a task.

2.4 DEEP Energy Measurement

Estimating the energy consumption of computing platforms has been extensively investigated in previous work. Direct energy measurements [11], platform/device energy models [12] or a combination of both [13] have all been successfully applied. In this paper, EAS utilizes energy data using a direct energy measurement platform called DEEP [11] that adds current sensing instrumentation to the computing platform. A high-frequency (10kS/s) data sampler or data acquisition unit (DAQ) is utilized to acquire energy measurements for the complete platform and important computing components such as the CPU, memory (RAM), storage systems, network and peripheral devices.

3. ENERGY AWARE SCHEDULER

3.1 Architecture

The EAS architecture is based on CFS with primary CFS features, such as load-balancing and task migration, and most of the kernel scheduler infrastructure included without significant modification.

3.1.1 OPJ

EAS uses OPJ as a run-time indicator of a task's energy efficiency. OPJ represents the number of CPU micro-operations (μops) [14] executed by the task per joule of energy consumed by the platform. A performance counter is used for each CPU core to count the number of μops executed by a task each time it is scheduled. Time-synchronized energy measurements are then used to determine energy consumption of the platform during the time quantum that the task was scheduled. The number of μops is divided by the energy consumption to obtain the latest task OPJ.

3.1.2 Priority Assignment & Efficient Co-scheduling

EAS uses red-black trees, as shown in Figure 2, to maintain its list of tasks. Each node of the red-black represents a task and uses the task's OPJ as its key. Larger OPJ values represent a higher priority as these tasks exhibited higher energy efficiency when previously co-scheduled. A red-black tree is maintained for each CPU core on the platform and the mechanisms of load-balancing along with task-migration distribute tasks among CPU cores.

3.1.3 Task Promotion

The priority assignment scheme used by EAS has the advantage of efficient task co-scheduling, but inefficient tasks with reduced OPJ values also need to be provided with opportunities for being rescheduled since task behavior varies at run-time and contention from other tasks may not be present anymore. This is accomplished through *task promotion*. For a red-black tree with n tasks, task promotion randomly selects a natural number $k \leq n$ every n scheduler time quanta so that the kth lowest priority task's

OPJ value is set to one greater than the largest OPJ value in the tree. This causes the task to be promoted to highest priority for the succeeding scheduling quantum. To preserve the algorithmic efficiency of red-black tree operations, the time complexity of performing task promotion must be limited to O(log n). Hence, EAS uses a modified red-black where each node contains an additional value, called *Size*, that represents the size of the tree if that node is the root of the tree. Such a tree is shown in Figure 2.

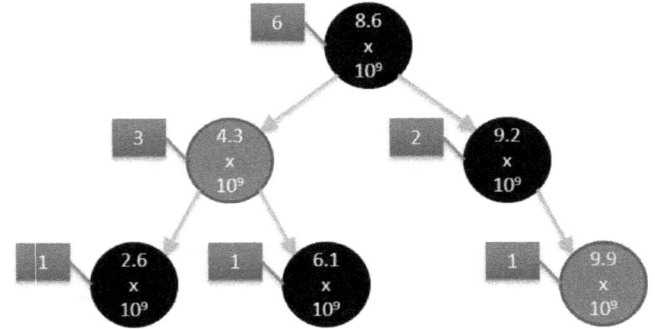

Figure 2. EAS uses modified red-black trees for its task list.

3.1.4 Scheduling Details

At the end of a scheduler time quantum due to a timer/interrupt event or yielding of control by a task, EAS performs several steps before scheduling the next task: 1) the time-stamp counter (TSC) value denoting the end of the time quantum is recorded, 2) the number of CPU μops performed during the previous time quantum is read from a performance counter and recorded, 3) the latest energy measurements are synchronized with TSC values and recorded, 4) the latest OPJ values are calculated from data obtained in previous steps, 5) the OPJ value of the previously scheduled task is updated to the latest available value, 6) the task is inserted back into the red-black tree with appropriate updates to Size values, 7) task promotion is performed if n time quanta have passed since the last task promotion, 8) the TSC value for the beginning of the next time quantum is recorded, and 9) the highest priority task is selected from tree and scheduled to execute on the CPU core. These important steps are illustrated in Figure 3.

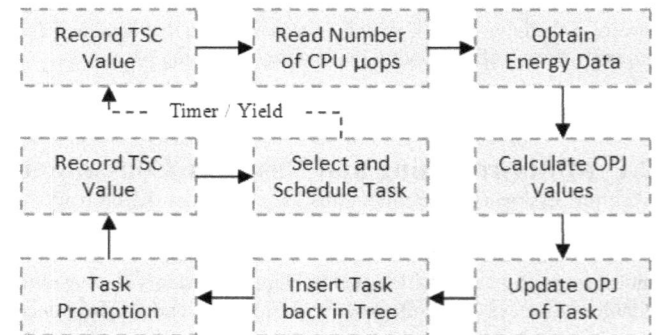

Figure 3. Vital context switching steps performed by the EAS.

3.2 Implementation

3.2.1 Modifications to CFS

EAS is implemented based on the Linux scheduler infrastructure for CFS with some modifications: 1) `vruntime` for a task, which is for recording the CPU time used, is replaced with `OPJ`, 2) each red-black tree node has an additional entry called `Size` for efficient task promotion, 3) red-black tree insertion and removal functions correctly update `Size` value at nodes, 4) a fixed scheduling quantum of 4ms is applied, and 5) scheduler functions and control-flow are modified to include steps in Figure 3.

sched_rt.c	sched_fair.c	sched_eas.c
enqueue_task_rt	enqueue_task_fair	enqueue_task_eas
dequeue_task_rt	dequeue_task_fair	dequeue_task_eas
yield_task_rt	yield_task_fair	yield_task_eas
...	...	...
SCHED_RR	**SCHED_OTHER**	**SCHED_EAS**

Figure 4. EAS creates a new scheduling class in the kernel.

3.2.2 Co-Existence with Standard Task Schedulers

The concept of modular schedulers, which is part of modern Linux kernels [15], is utilized in the implementation of EAS. Thus, EAS co-exists with other task schedulers in the Linux kernel, as shown in Figure 4, by creating its own scheduling class. This allows the abstraction of tedious EAS implementation details while exposing the required scheduler functions to the kernel.

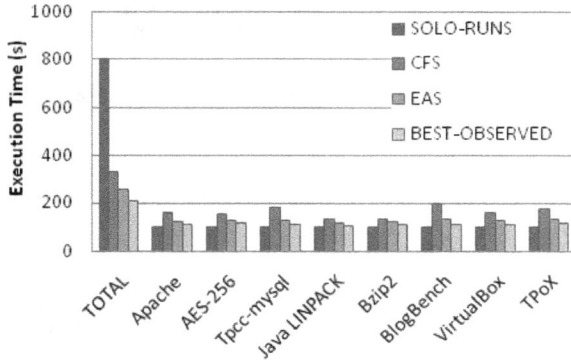

Figure 5. Benchmark execution times for the task schedulers.

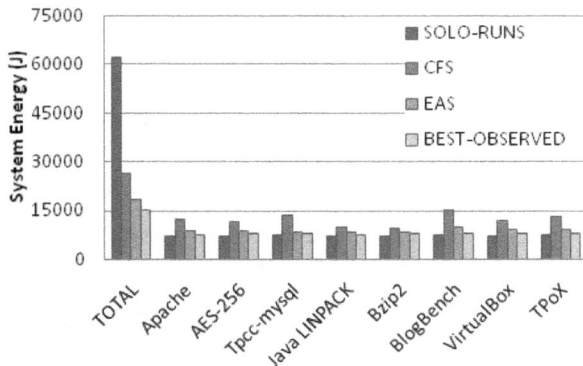

Figure 6. Platform energy usage for the task schedulers.

3.2.3 Platform Support

The implementation of EAS in this paper is based on modern x86 platforms and some of the features they provide [16]. EAS relies on standard platform features in addition to the DEEP energy monitoring infrastructure. The performance monitoring unit provides performance counters that are needed for counting the number of μops that each CPU core executes during a task's time

quantum while excluding PAUSE and NOP instructions as these don't represent work performed by a task. The TSC is required for timing of platform events and time synchronization of energy measurements.

4. RESULTS

EAS is evaluated in terms of both energy efficiency and execution time compared to CFS. The investigations reported here utilize Linux kernel 2.6.32 on an Intel x86 quad-core platform. Energy measurement infrastructure is added to the platform as described in Section 2. When measuring the energy consumption for CFS, measurements are performed by another platform with a DAQ using the instrumentation of the platform under observation so that the energy measurement overhead does not create errors in the data. For EAS this overhead is included in the data because the measurement infrastructure is an integral component of EAS.

Eight applications have been selected to create a compact, but comprehensive, suite of benchmarks: 1) Apache, 2) AES-256, 3) Tpcc-mysql, 4) Java LINPACK, 5) Bzip2, 6) BlogBench, 7) VirtualBox, and 8) TPoX. Each benchmark's input workload is normalized so that the benchmark has an average execution time of 100s using CFS when no other benchmarks execute in parallel.

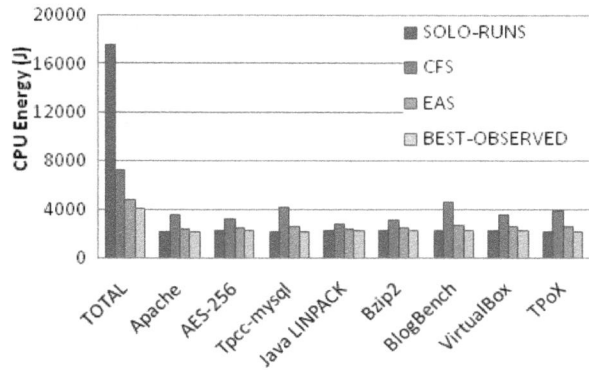

Figure 7. CPU energy consumption for the task schedulers.

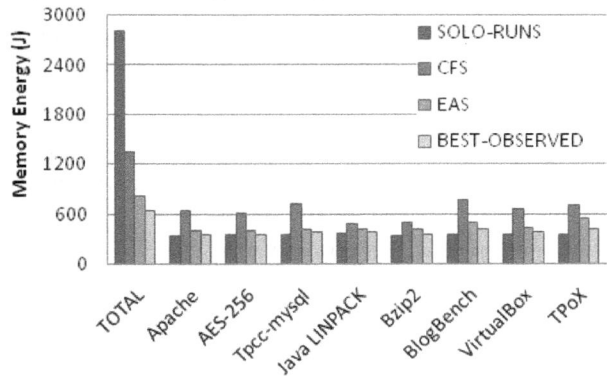

Figure 8. Memory energy usage for the task schedulers.

In Figures 5 through 12, SOLO-RUNS represent the case where each of the benchmarks is executed individually using CFS so that resource contention is absent. EAS represents the case where benchmarks begin execution in parallel and EAS is used to schedule them. CFS represents the case where CFS is used to schedule the benchmarks. Experiments for each case are repeated a thousand times and the mean values are reported in the figures. BEST-OBSERVED represents the minimum values for energy consumption and execution time observed over all thousand repetitions of the CFS and EAS experiments. This value indicates the best possible schedule that is achieved in presence of resource contention among tasks. TOTAL represents the values for execution of all benchmarks while the individual values represent the decomposition of TOTAL among each benchmark. Also, the energy data for individual benchmarks does not represent the energy consumption due to that benchmark, but the energy consumption that occurs during execution of the benchmark. This is because there can be multiple benchmarks executing in parallel.

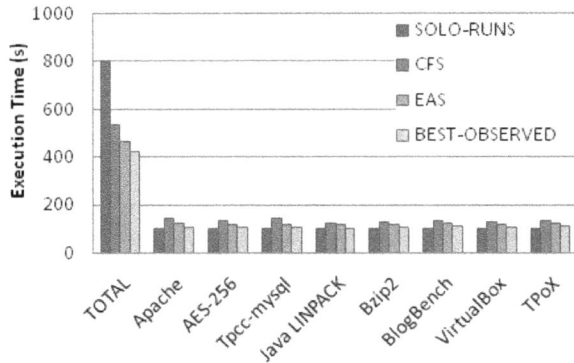

Figure 9. Execution time without L2 CPU cache contention.

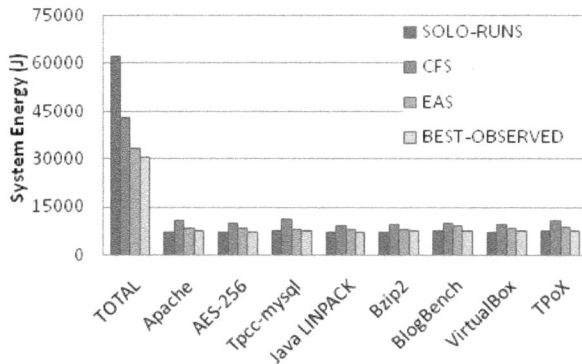

Figure 10. Platform energy usage without L2 contention.

Figures 5 through 8 illustrate the results of the comparisons between EAS and CFS. EAS demonstrates a large benefit over CFS with an average execution time improvement of 24.7% and energy efficiency improvement of 30.2% over all benchmarks. Furthermore, energy consumption and execution time with EAS are much closer to BEST-OBSERVED values.

The platform used in this evaluation has its four CPU cores arranged as two pairs with each pair sharing a level-2 (L2) cache. Therefore, if the two tasks are scheduled on cores from different pairs then L2 cache contention is absent. This enables an evaluation where the eight benchmarks are executed using only two of the four cores on the platform. In one case the benchmarks are allowed to execute on a pair of cores sharing an L2 cache and in the other case the benchmarks are executed on only one core of each pair with separate L2 cache. Both CFS and EAS are used in the experiments and the results are illustrated in Figures 9 through 12. The execution time and energy consumption are larger in the case where L2 cache is shared when using CFS, but EAS effectively reduces the impact of L2 cache contention because both the energy consumption and execution time approach values when L2 cache is not shared.

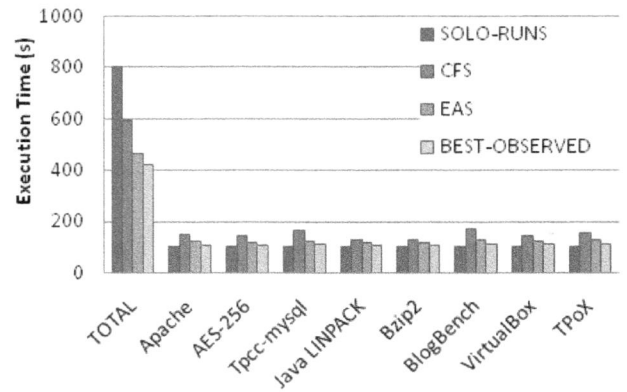

Figure 11. Execution time with L2 CPU cache contention.

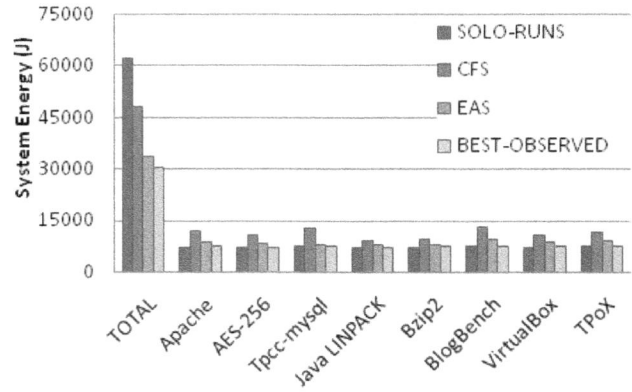

Figure 12. Platform energy consumption with L2 contention.

5. REFERENCES

[1] Zhuravlev, S., Saez, J. C., Blagodurov, S., Fedorova, A., and Prieto, M., "Survey of energy-cognizant scheduling techniques." *IEEE TPDS*, 2013.

[2] Davis, R. I., and Burns, A., "A survey of hard real-time scheduling for multiprocessor systems." *ACM CSUR*, 2011.

[3] Shiva, S. G., *Advanced Computer Architectures*. CRC Press, 2005.

[4] Woo, D. H., and Lee, H. H. S., "Extending Amdahl's law for energy-efficient computing in the many-core era." *IEEE Computer*, 2008.

[5] Blagodurov, S., Zhuravlev, S., and Fedorova, A., "Contention-aware scheduling on multicore systems." *ACM TOCS*, 2010.

[6] Smith, B., Grehan, R., Yager, T, and Niemi D. C., "Byte-unixbench: a unix benchmark suite.", 2011.

[7] Wong, C. S., Tan, I. K. T., Kumari, R. D., Lam, J. W., and Fun, W., "Fairness and interactive performance of o (1) and cfs linux kernel schedulers." *IEEE ITSim*, 2008.

[8] Wang, S., Chen, Y., Jiang, W., Li, P., Dai, T., and Cui, Y., "Fairness and interactivity of three CPU schedulers in Linux." *IEEE RTCSA*, 2009.

[9] Hinze, R., "Constructing red-black trees." *WAAAPL*, 1999.

[10] Zhang, X., Dwarkadas, S., Folkmanis, G., and Shen, K., "Processor hardware counter statistics as a first-class system resource." *HotOS*, 2007.

[11] Singh, D., and Kaiser, W. J., "Energy efficient network data transport through adaptive compression using the DEEP platforms." *IEEE WiMob*, 2012.

[12] Yoon, C., Kim, D., Jung, W., Kang, C., and Cha, H., "Appscope: application energy metering framework for android smartphone using kernel activity monitoring." *USENIX ATC*, 2012.

[13] Yan, J., Lonappan, C. K., Vajid, A., Singh, D., and Kaiser, W. J., "Accurate and low-overhead process-level energy estimation for modern hard disk drives." *IEEE GreenCom*, 2013.

[14] Slechta, B., Crowe, D., Fahs, B., Fertig, M., Muthler, G., Quek, J., Spadini, F., Patel, S. J., and Lumetta, S. S. "Dynamic optimization of micro-operations." *IEEE HPCA*, 2003.

[15] Molnar, I., "Modular scheduler core and completely fair scheduler (cfs)." *Linux Kernel Mailing List*, 2007.

[16] Bandyopadhyay, S. "A study on performance monitoring counters in x86-architecture." *Indian Statistical Institute*.

Energy-Efficient Mapping of Biomedical Applications on Domain-Specific Accelerator under Process Variation

Mohammad Khavari Tavana[†], Amey Kulkarni[‡], Abbas Rahimi[◊],
Tinoosh Mohsenin[‡] and Houman Homayoun[†]

[†]Department of Electrical and Computer Engineering, George Mason University, Fairfax County
[‡] Department of Computer Science and Electrical Engineering, University of Maryland, Baltimore County
[◊]Department of Computer Science and Engineering, UC San Diego, La Jolla
Email: [†]{mkhavari, hhomayou}@gmu.edu   [‡]{ameyk1,tinoosh}@umbc.edu   [◊]abaas@cs.ucsd.edu

ABSTRACT

The variability of deep-submicron technologies creates systems with asymmetric cores from a frequency and leakage power viewpoint, which makes an opportunity for performance-power optimization. In particular, process variation can transform a homogeneous many-core platform into a heterogeneous system where the task mapping becomes extremely difficult. In this paper, we propose a mapping algorithm that selects an appropriate task mapping along with voltage and frequency assignment for a cluster of cores. The mapping algorithm, which is based on simulated annealing, determines cluster voltages and core frequencies to minimize energy consumption and EDP under process variation. We examine the effectiveness of our proposed algorithm on a fully placed and routed 128-core biomedical accelerator in 45nm when running various applications including compressive sensing, seizure detection and ultrasound spectral Doppler and linear regression. The results indicate that exposing frequency and power variations to the mapping algorithm results in up to 22% (on average 11%) energy saving and 31% (on average19%) EDP improvement.

Categories and Subject Descriptors

C.3 [**Special-purpose and application-based systems**]: Real-time systems and embedded systems

General Terms: Algorithms, Design

Keywords: Mapping, accelerator, process variation, many-core systems, energy efficiency

1. INTRODUCTION

Unsustainable power consumption and ever-increasing computing demands have driven the computing industry to move to an era of parallelization with few to tens of computing cores integrated in a single die. Domain-specific customization such as programmable many-core accelerator has been emerged as the next disruptive technology to bring significant performance and power-efficiency improvement [1]. The International Technology Roadmap for Semiconductors (ITRS) predicts that single embedded SoCs will have tens of specialized accelerators by 2021 [2]. With embedded devices being battery powered, energy efficiency of this class of architectures becomes a major concern. In particular, as the number of cores increases in many-core accelerator the power dissipation increases and therefore limits the scalability of this class of design [3].

Among conventional low power design techniques, dynamic voltage/frequency scaling (DVFS) is one of the most effective ones. This technique has been extensively explored in managing the balance between power and performance in multi-core architectures [4]. However, in more recent technologies where the device dimensions approaching the limits of process technology capabilities, a rapid increase of manufacturing process variation is observed [6] [13]. These variations result in the spread of maximum achievable clock frequencies (*fmax*) across different cores in a chip where employing DVFS to save power and energy should be considered wisely. For example, the results acquired using *Synopsys PrimeTime-VX* for a 45nm technology shows 12% frequency variation at 1.1V. The variation further increases for lower operating voltages. As a result, the variability in the process parameters leads to a system with asymmetric cores from a frequency and leakage power viewpoint. Consequently, the process variation transforms a homogeneous many-core accelerator into a heterogeneous system. Hence, variation-aware task mapping and voltage/frequency assignment is required [14]. The energy-efficient mapping of tasks and voltage/frequency management necessitates specific strategies to exploit the diversity of the accelerator cores while meeting the energy and/or real-time constraints. In addition, in cluster-based accelerator architectures the processing cores are grouped into a set of clusters where a cluster is controlled by the same power supply voltage domain. This makes the task mapping strategy crucial and can have significant impact on the energy-efficiency of the system.

This paper highlights the challenges and investigates a solution for energy management in many-core accelerator systems in the presence of process variation and under real-time constraint. We utilize simulated annealing to find optimal task mapping, parallelization degree of tasks, and DVFS setting with few voltage domain clusters. The rest of the paper is organized as follows: Section 2 introduces models and assumptions, while Section 3 provides a motivational example about the task mapping. Section 4 introduces the mapping algorithm based. Section 5 is our evaluations and experimental results, and Section 6 concludes the paper.

2. MODELS AND ASSUMPTIONS

2.1 Architecture Model

We focus on an accelerator comprised N_{core} homogeneous cores, each of which can process its data and execute its own instruction streams through I/O ports and local memories. The cores are equipped with DVFS [4] to save power/energy consumption. Even though it is possible to assign each core a dedicated voltage DC-DC convertor, it is not efficient due to the complexity of chip design

This work was supported in part by the National Science Foundation under grant NSF CNS– 1329829.

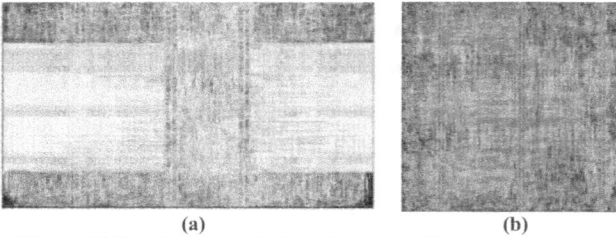

Fig. 1: (a) Core layout and (b) router layout. The core and router area footprint are 0.033 mm² and 0.035 mm² respectively in 45nm technology, where each router is shared by 4 cores.

and area overhead. This problem exacerbates when the number of cores is in the orders of hundreds each with small area footprint [5]. As a consequence, a group of cores forms a voltage domain cluster, such that the cores on the same cluster share the same power lines and supply voltage. Our accelerator platform consists of 128 processing cores divided into 8 voltage clusters where each cluster contains 16 cores.

The cores are based on a 6-stage modified RISC pipeline architecture which communicate through a simple, scalable hierarchical 4-ary tree structure that reduces the number of hops in communication. The cores are equipped with parallel loop control, parallel FFT processing and pointers to accelerate computation [11]. Note that each core is quite small and contains dedicated 128 words data and instruction memories. Hence, if there is not enough memory space to hold all the required data and instruction needed for a task execution, the data should be distributed among cores. Each core and router were synthesized, placed and routed in a 45nm CMOS process (Fig. 1). Each core operates at different clock rates through Globally Asynchronous Locally Synchronous (GALS) architecture [10] thereby eliminating global clock routing.

2.2 Application Model

We consider two cases: i) real-time applications where all tasks share a common deadline D, i.e., the application deadline. In this case, we aim at minimizing energy consumption provided that application is finished before the deadline. ii) non real-time applications where we aim at minimizing energy-delay product. Each task is either *serial* or *moldable*. In the former case a task cannot be parallelized, but in the latter the parallelization degree of a task can be determined before mapping and application execution. We assume that there is a control or data dependency among tasks in our applications which is modeled by direct acyclic graph (DAG). A sample application can be represented as $TG = (V, E, C, T)$. The first two parameters shows the topology of graph where $n_i \in V$ represents a set of nodes (i.e., tasks) and E indicates their edges (i.e., dependency among tasks). For example $(n_i, n_j) \in E$ shows there is an edge between task i and j and the latter cannot be executed before the former one due to the dependency. $c_{ij} \in C$ indicates the communication cost between node i and j in terms of number of flits, and $T_i^p \in T$ indicates execution cycles of task i with p level of parallelism. For serial tasks, p is one, but for moldable tasks p varies from one to the maximum level of parallelism which is also task dependent. Note that parallelizing tasks may impose new subtasks in the task graph, and also increases the amount of communications.

2.3 Process Variation and Power Models

Because of the imperfection during manufacturing process, the maximum frequency and the static power dissipation will be varied from one core to another. To find the effect of process variation on the frequency, the RTL description of the fabric has been

synthesized for 45nm technology, the general purpose process. The front-end flow with multi-VTH cells has been performed using *Synopsys Design Compiler* with tight timing constraint, while *Synopsys IC Compiler* has been used for the back-end. First, to observe the effect of static process variation on the fabric, we have analyzed how the critical paths of each core are affected due to within-die and die-to-die process parameters variation. Therefore, the various cores within the fabric experience different variability-induced delay and thus display various error rate. During the sign-off stage, we have injected process variation in the fabric using the variation-aware timing analysis engine of *Synopsys PrimeTime-VX*. Fig. 2 show the frequency variation of the first sixteen cores of the 128 core accelerator platform. At three higher voltage levels almost 12% variation is observed in frequency, and frequency variation exceeds 15% at the lowest voltage level. We performed the frequency binning with the step of 33 MHz for the accelerator, hence, the frequency of each core varies from 366 MHz up to 933 MHz. The dashed line in Fig. 2 indicates 633 MHz frequency. Note that only nine out of 16 cores can operate at this frequency at the voltage of 0.81V. Moreover, four cores are operational below 600 MHz at this voltage level.

Table 1: power consumption of the processing core

Operating Voltage	Freq. (MHz)	Dynamic Power(mW)	Static Power(mW)	Total Power(mW)
1.10V	900	141.39	3.90	145.29
0.99V	733	62.63	2.12	64.75
0.81V	633	34.06	1.14	35.20
0.66V	433	18.96	0.99	19.95

The energy dissipation comprises of dynamic and static energy consumption. The former is due to the activity and switching of gates in the system, and the latter is the amount of energy dissipated when the system is in the standby state. In Table 1, the power breakdown of a core at different voltage levels has been presented. The static power variation has been modeled similar to [7], moreover, for communication energy modeling we used the modeled provided by [12]. It is noteworthy that it takes 4 cycles to send a flit from router to router, or core to router in our system.

3. MOTIVATIONAL EXAMPLE

To evaluate how mapping strategy in the cluster-based accelerator and under process variation can influence energy consumption, we provide a simple example in which an application with three tasks is mapped on a system with four cores. Even though we consider dependency in our example, for simplicity, we assume there is no communication among the tasks. The system is divided into two clusters each composed of two cores and can operate at two different voltages/frequencies. The goal of mapping is to assign tasks to the cores and select the voltage and frequency to minimize the energy consumption provided that the application meets the

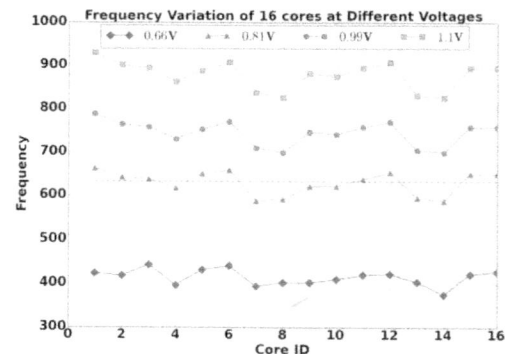

Fig. 2: Frequency variation of first sixteen cores of 128-core accelerator obtained by *Prime Time-VX* for a 45nm technology

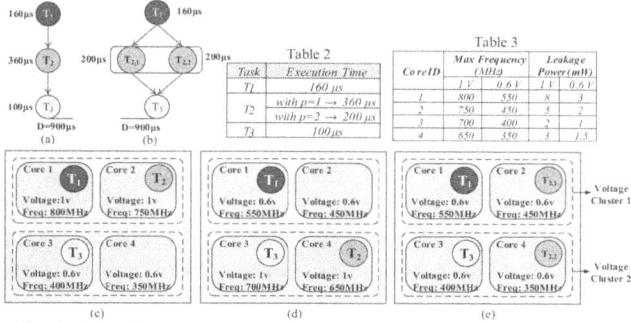

Fig. 3: Mapping an application on a 4-core system with different leakage power and frequency characteristics.

Table 2

Task	Execution Time
T_1	160 µs
T_2	with p=1 → 360 µs
	with p=2 → 200 µs
T_3	100 µs

Table 3

CoreID	Max Frequency (MHz)		Leakage Power(mW)	
	1 V	0.6 V	1 V	0.6 V
1	800	550	8	3
2	750	450	5	2
3	700	400	2	1
4	650	350	3	1.5

deadline. For each core the maximum energy saving at a given voltage is achieved by executing the task at the maximum frequency that can be supported .Therefore, whenever we determine a voltage level, we set the operating frequency at the maximum possible corresponding to that voltage. Table 2 shows tasks execution time, and Table 3 represents the maximum frequency at a given voltage and the leakage power for each core. It is important to note that T_2 can be executed either as a single task (Fig. 3 (a)) with 360 µs execution time or as two sub-tasks each with 200 µs execution time (Fig. 3 (b)). We assume that the execution time of each task is obtained through profiling on a core clocking at 800 MHz. Note that in the presence of process variation the operating frequency might be lower or higher than the profiling frequency and therefore the mapping algorithm need to be adapted accordingly, to meet the deadline. In addition, we assume 50 mW dynamic power is dissipated when each processing core operates at the maximum voltage level, and it decreases quadratically with reducing voltage level linearly [4].

Fig. 3 (c) represents a mapping where tasks T_1, T_2, T_3 are mapped on cores 1, 2 and 3 respectively. None of the tasks are mapped on core 4 because it is the weakest core among the others. Note that due to the mapping of T_2 on the core 2, the cluster 1 cannot reduce the voltage, because it leads to application deadline violation, while cores on cluster 2 can use lower voltage level to reduce energy. If we consider perfect power gating for core 4, 43.4 µj energy is consumed with this mapping. By moving task T_2 from core 2 to core 4 (i.e., the weakest core), the voltage of the first cluster can be reduced while the second cluster cannot. This case is shown in Fig. 3 (d) which results in 39.25 µj energy consumption, and consequently 10% energy saving compared to the first mapping. In Fig. 3 (e), we show how exploiting parallelism of tasks can help to increase the system utilization and further improve energy efficiency. Although breaking task T_2 into two sub-tasks lead to sub-linear speedup in our case, it allows both clusters to operate at lower voltage without violating application deadline. Mapping two sub-tasks $T_{2,1}$ and $T_{2,2}$ on cores 2 and 4 respectively lead to 29.16 µj and additional 26% energy saving compared to the mapping in Fig. 3 (d).

Mapping tasks on many-core platforms such as an accelerator where there is a variation on power and frequency is similar to mapping problem to a heterogeneous hardware platforms which is NP-hard in a strong sense [8]. The search space of the mapping problem even gets larger, assuming that tasks can be parallelized and the tasks set parameters like execution time can be changed dynamically.

4. MAPPING ALGORITHM

Simulated annealing (SA) heuristic is a popular approach for solving both discrete and continuous optimization problems and can effectively deal with nonlinear and multivariate systems [9]. Our energy-efficient mapping algorithm is based on this heuristic technique. This algorithm probabilistically allows poorer solutions to be accepted to better search the solution space and move out from local optima. A standard kind of SA-based algorithm can be found in [9], the parameters and how the new solutions are generated form the fundamental parts of this algorithm which are case dependent [9]. The algorithm begins with a random feasible mapping as the initial solution and progresses with new movements from the current state.

Determining the level of parallelism for moldable task not only has an impact on the energy consumption for a task itself, but also influences on the efficiency of mapping for the entire tasks set. Two movements have been employed in the algorithm, which allows the level of parallelism for each task to be expanded or shrunk.

- *Increasing parallelism:* randomly selects a moldable task and increases the level of parallelism for a given task. If increasing violates the upper bound of the parallelism, the action will be discarded.
- *Decreasing parallelism:* randomly selects a task and decreases the level of parallelism for a given task. If decreasing leads to elimination of the task in the mapping, the action will be discarded.

Apart from expanding or shrinking, we have also used four moves to alter mapping. It is possible that these small alternations in the mapping lead to modification of clusters voltage and as a consequence result in significant change in the energy dissipation.

- *Intra-cluster task swapping:* two random cores within a cluster are selected and their corresponding tasks are swapped together. It is possible that one of the core to be totally available (free), hence in this case we have simple task movement rather than swapping. In case where both selected cores are free, the movement is discarded.
- *Inter-cluster task swapping:* two random processing cores among the clusters are selected and their corresponding tasks are swapped together. It is possible that one of the core to be totally free. Therefore, in this case we can have simple task movement rather than swapping. In case both selected core are free, the movement is discarded.
- *Cluster swapping:* two random clusters and their tasks are swapped together. In case both selected clusters are totally free the movement is discarded. Even though this movement can be render with many inter-cluster tasks swapping, our simulations showed that adding this movement to our solution generator procedure can increase speed of the algorithm and quality of the solution.
- *Random movement:* although three former movements are systematic, adding some flavor of randomness can help the algorithm to better explore the search space and avoid from sticking at the local optima.

If any movement violate the timing constraint of the application, it will be discarded. Notice that in case of discarding any movement, the algorithm regenerates solution once again. For a given voltage, the maximum operational frequency of the processing core leads to minimum energy consumption. As the voltage is controlled at the cluster level, the minimum energy dissipation for a cluster can be found by simply checking a small set of voltage levels. The bad mapping can dramatically affect the flexibility of voltage reduction because the tightest time constraint of tasks in a cluster determines the amount of voltage/frequency reduction. We defined Δ as the

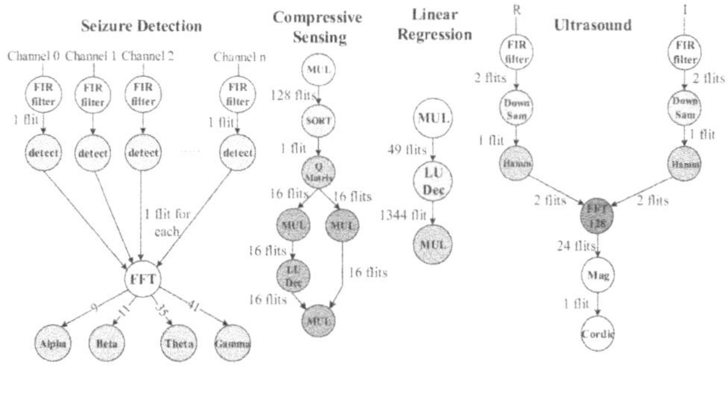

Fig. 4: task graph of our biomedical applications

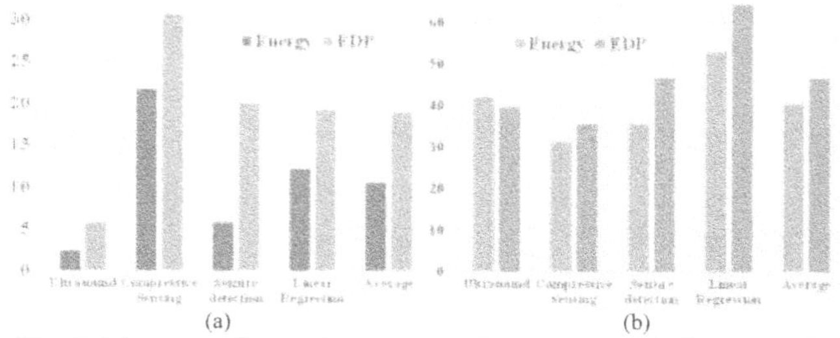

Fig. 5: (a) proposed mapping compared to process variation agnostic mapping, (b) proposed mapping compared to best random mapping

difference between energy consumption (or EDP) of new mapping and current mapping. The energy consumption includes both cores energy and communication energy.

If Δ becomes negative it means that generated solution is the better one and replaced with the current solution. Otherwise, the solution is accepted with probability of $e^{-\Delta/T}$, where T is the current temperature. When T is larger, the probability of accepting worse solution is more and by reducing T this probability reduces.

Whenever the neighbor solutions around optimal one are much closer to each other, the optimal solution hardly froze even at a very low temperature. Hence, we set a bound for minimum temperature in which crossing that will stop the algorithm. This bound is small enough (0.001) which allows the solution to be frozen most of the time.

After the predefined number of iterations, the temperature should be reducing by *cooling rate* parameter. We used exponential cooling scheme [9], which is the most common cooling decrement scheme. We set the *cooling rate* equal to 0.92, *initial temperature* equal to 60, and *initial iteration* equal to 600 in our simulations.

5. SIMULATION FRAMEWORK

For application profiling, each algorithm is partitioned into multiple tasks where each task is assigned to a single or multiple cores. Then using our many-core simulator, different application statistics are obtained. For moldable tasks, different level of parallelism is considered and investigated to analyze the execution time and communication overhead. Because the accelerator used for simulations were designed to execute biomedical domain applications effectively [11], we provide four implementation of biomedical applications for the case study (Fig. 4) including compressive sensing, seizure detection, linear regression and ultrasound. To increase the utilization of the accelerator and measure the energy and EDP, we did the mapping with four copies of each application, except the seizure detection for which we used four channels. For the energy minimization of real-time tasks we considered application deadline equal to summation of tasks execution in serial form, thus the slack time can be created by parallelizing moldable tasks and give the opportunity to reduce voltage and frequency. In Fig. 5 (a) and (b), we compared our mapping with two other mapping scenarios, the process variation agnostic scheme where the mapping scheme is not aware of the process variation, and best random scheme where 10000 feasible random mapping were generated and the best one were considered as the solution. The energy consumption reduces up to 22% and on average 11% over process variation agnostic scheme. The saving increases up to 53% and on average 40%, respectively compared to the best random mapping. The improvement of EDP is more significant. The EDP reduces up to 31% and on average 19% over the process variation agnostic mapping. The improvement

increases up to 65% and on average 47%, respectively compared to the best random mapping.

6. CONCLUSION

This paper proposes a mapping algorithm based on simulated annealing to render energy efficiency in a many-core accelerator architecture under the process variation. Leveraging the frequency and power variations in the mapping algorithm as well as the level of parallelism of the tasks, we significantly reduce the energy consumption. Energy-efficient mapping of the tasks necessitates specific strategies to exploit the diversity of the accelerator cores while meeting the application real-time constraints. The proposed mapping methodology is evaluated by biomedical applications executing on a 128-core accelerator divided into 8 voltage clusters where each cluster contains 16 cores. The results indicate that exposing frequency and power variations to the mapping algorithm results in up to 22% energy saving and 53% EDP improvement.

7. REFERENCES

[1] P. Schaumont and I. Verbauwhede, "Domain-specific codesign for embedded security." Computer, 36(4), pp. 68-74, 2003.

[2] "Semiconductor industry association, international technology roadmap for semiconductors (itrs), 2010, update 2011. [Online]. Available: http://www.itrs.net.

[3] S. Nilakantan, S. Battle and M. Hempstead, "Metrics for Early-Stage Modeling of Many-Accelerator Architectures." *Computer Architecture Letters*, 12(1), pp. 25-28, 2013.

[4] M. T. Schmitz, B. Al-Hashimi, and P. Eles. *"System-level design techniques for energy-efficient embedded systems"* (Vol. 4). Dordrecht: Kluwer Academic Publishers, 2004.

[5] S. Vangal, et al. "An 80-tile 1.28 TFLOPS network-on-chip in 65nm CMOS." *IEEE International Solid-State Circuits Conference*, Digest of Technical Papers, pp. 98-589, 2007.

[6] S. R. Sarangi, B. Greskamp, R. Teodorescu, J. Nakano, A. Tiwari, A. and J. Torrellas. "VARIUS: A model of process variation and resulting timing errors for microarchitects." *IEEE Transactions on Semiconductor Manufacturing*, 21(1), pp. 3-13, 2008.

[7] B. Raghunathan, Y. Turakhia, S. Garg and D. Marculescu. "Cherry-picking: exploiting process variations in dark-silicon homogeneous chip multi-processors." *In Proceedings of the Conference on Design, Automation and Test in Europe*, pp. 39-44, 2013.

[8] A. Schranzhofer, J. J. Chen and L. Thiele, "Dynamic power-aware mapping of applications onto heterogeneous mpsoc platforms." *IEEE Transactions on Industrial Informatics*, 6(4), pp. 692-707, 2010.

[9] J. W. Chinneck, *"Practical optimization: A gentle introduction."* 2004, Electronic document: http://www. sce. carleton. ca/faculty/chinneck/po. html.

[10] D. Chapiro, *"Globally-asynchronous locally-synchronous systems."* Ph.D. thesis, Stanford University, 1984.

[11] J. Bisasky, H. Homayoun, F. Yazdani, and T. Mohsenin, "A 64-core platform for biomedical signal processing." *In International Symposium on Quality Electronic Design (ISQED)*, pp. 368-372, 2013.

[12] J. Hu and R. Marculescu. "Energy-aware communication and task scheduling for network-on-chip architectures under real-time constraints." *In Design, Automation and Test in Europe Conference and Exhibition*, vol. 1, pp. 234-239, 2004.

[13] S. Avesta, H. Homayoun, A. Eltawil, and F. Kurdahi. "Process variation aware sram/cache for aggressive voltage-frequency scaling." *In Design, Automation & Test in Europe Conference & Exhibition*, DATE'09, pp. 911-916., 2009.

[14] A. Rahimi, A. Marongiu, P. Burgio, R. K. Gupta, L. Benini, "Variation-tolerant OpenMP Tasking on Tightly-coupled Processor Clusters" Proc. ACM/IEEE DATE, 2013, pp. 541-546.

A Memory Rename Table to Reduce Energy and Improve Performance

Joseph Pusderis, Benjamin VanderSloot, and Trevor Mudge
University of Michigan
Ann Arbor, MI
{joemp,benvds,tnm}@umich.edu

ABSTRACT

A memory rename table for improved performance, reduced complexity, and reduced energy consumption is proposed and evaluated. It gives an average 8.7% speedup and 7.9% reduction in core and cache energy. The evaluation employs a simulation model for an out-of-order core, similar to the ARM Cortex A15, and McPAT for energy measurements. The improvements are the result of filtering nearly half (45.4%) of memory accesses before they go to cache. Complexity is reduced by replacement of a load store queue with a scalable renaming system. The changes are transparent to the ISA.

Categories and Subject Descriptors

C.1.3 [**Processor Architectures**]: Other Architecture Styles—pipeline processors

Keywords

Load store unit; memory system; energy-efficiency

1. INTRODUCTION

To cope with the high cost of memory access, modern architectures provide a large number of general purpose registers. These registers offer a dense set of short term storage within the CPU to avoid accessing memory. Unfortunately, short term values cannot always take advantage of these registers. There are situations known to cause this behavior, for example:

- Register pressure cause values to be spilled and filled from memory.

- Registers must be demoted across function calls.

- Compilers are not able to disambiguate pointers and conservatively keep the values in memory to guarantee correctness.

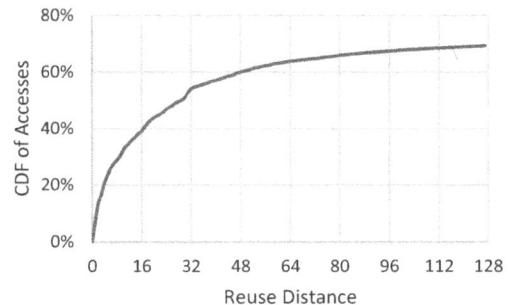

Figure 1: A CDF that depicts the locality in SPECINT when compiled for the ARM ISA. The reuse distance is measured in number of distinct addresses accessed between repeated accesses. Despite the reuse distance being low, these values are not promoted to registers by software.

While a variety of techniques to reduce these restrictions have been proposed, they have not seen widespread adoption. This is likely because of the required changes to the programming interface. The most common architectural approach used in modern out-of-order processors is not to prevent the situations listed above, but instead to speed up the short term spills via a sophisticated load-store-unit (LSU) in conjunction with a high-bandwidth, low-latency L1 cache.

To show just how prevelent these sort term spills are, we will use a metric called reuse distance. Reuse distance is the distance between accesses to the same address; the distance here is measured in number of accesses to distinct addresses. Figure 1 quantifies the reuse distance present in SPECINT. This figure shows that if we can preserve 64 of the most recently accessed values they will satisfy more than 60% of future memory accesses.

This reuse distance is so small that the L1 cache may be over equiped for the general case. Since a small reuse distance has such a high coverage, it stands to reason that a structure sized hundreds of bytes could be used instead. In traditional designs, the closest structure to that size is the store buffer within the LSU. However, since the store buffer often only holds pre-retirement stores, and does not include post-retirement stores or any loads, the values held in this structure are a small percentage of the total accesses. The low coverage of this structure is reflected by a low rate of forwarding. Infrequent forwarding motivated designers to access the data cache in parallel with the store buffer. While this is necessary to provide the lowest average latency, this

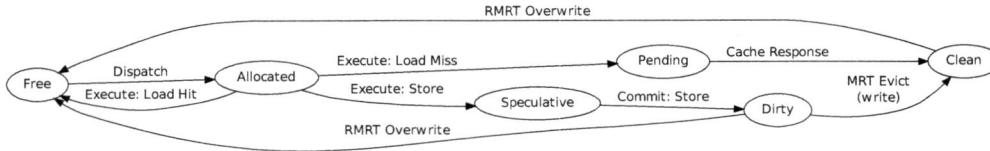

Figure 2: The FSM associated with each register in the MRF. A register is marked as allocated when a memory operation is dispatched. When the operation is executed and accesses the MRT, the register is either marked free, pending, or speculative. The registers will later be updated to Dirty and Clean, eventually being marked free when the entry is no longer referenced by the RMRT.

is unnecessarily taxing on power resources when the LSU services the request by forwarding.

There have been many LSUs implemented and proposed with differing capabilities. The baseline in this work is an LSU which restricts issue ordering such that accesses cannot pass stores to the same address. Store-to-load forwarding is also included in the baseline. These are the optimizations to be expected from an ARM Cortex A15-like core. More aggressive cores may speculatively issue with respect to memory ordering.

While effective, many LSU designs are expensive, featuring comparator matrices, storage registers, ordering logic, scheduling logic, and requiring the L1 cache to be multiported with low latency. Our design offers significant reduction in energy consumption and design complexity compared to the equivalent level of optimization in a traditional LSU. This increase in scalability will enable more aggressive optimizations which would otherwise be unattainable within the same resource budget.

An alternative to an LSU-centric approach is an L0 cache, but the L0 cache has several shortcomings. A granularity of block size instead of word size is wasteful in such a small structure. Additionally, an L0 cache does not support the storage of speculative data. Our design and traditional LSU can contain multiple uncommitted stores, unlike an L0.

2. DESIGN

Our design is intended to reduce energy consumption for out-of-order cores while requiring no modification to the ISA or programming model. With our design many memory accesses which would traditionally be L1 data cache hits no longer access the cache at all, and are instead forwarded from an earlier memory access.

Several decisions were made specifically to reduce energy consumption. One such decision is to make the design nonspeculative, requiring that correct memory ordering is enforced at execution. Many other LSU designs will issue memory operations in a speculative order and squash on detection of an incorrect prediction. By avoiding this behavior, there is no longer wasted execution that gets squashed, misspeculation detection circuity, or prediction logic. We also reduce the number of comparators to a small constant number, relative to the LSQ size. Traditional LSQ designs often need N, or even N^2 comparisons as they are fully associative, comparing every addresses to every other address either at issue or execute.

Our design is similar to a register renaming pipeline. Just as logical registers are translated to physical register indices in an out-of-order pipeline, memory addresses are translated to register file indices. These translations may index the

same register file as the register rename table, but for the remainder of this paper they will refer to a separate register file, called the *Memory Register File (MRF)*. Each entry in this MRF has associated state bits. Similar to the freelist in register renaming, this state is used to track when an entry is *Free* to be allocated, if an entry can be made *Free*, and what to do with the entry at different stages in the pipeline. The state machine for this tracking is shown in Figure 2.

The active translations of memory address to MRF entries are stored in a 4-way set associative structure called the *Memory Rename Table (MRT)*. This structure is similar to what was used for register renaming in VCA [5]. The pipeline must contain two of these MRTs. One MRT, accessed in the execute stage, contains a valid picture of memory at issue time, including the effect of the stores which have not yet been committed. The other MRT only contains committed information and it is accessed in the retire stage of the pipeline. This secondary MRT is used to recover from a branch misprediction and will be referred to as the *Retirement Memory Rename Table (RMRT)*.

The above components are placed into an out-of-order pipeline as shown in Figure 3. Unlike register renaming, the renaming done by our design happens in the execute stage, out-of-order. This is problematic as renaming in the order in which addresses are produced leads to incorrect execution. To prevent this, the address queue will restrict the order in which memory operations can issue.

2.1 Issue stage

The address queue, pictured in Figure 4, imposes the following restrictions for memory operations to issue:

- Stores cannot pass more than N other stores, where N is the associativity of the MRT.

- Accesses cannot pass stores to the same address.

- Restrictions imposed by the consistency model of the implemented ISA.

These restrictions are enforced by allowing execution of only the N oldest non-executed memory operations. The younger operations are in a FIFO buffer until space is available in the N issue slots. Note that the second restriction requires that for a load to proceed, its address must be resolved as well as any stores that precede it because of our lack of speculation.

2.2 Execution stage

Once issued, the address of a memory operation is searched in the MRT. If the instruction is a load and a hit in the MRT, the value is read from the memory register referenced by the MRT entry and releases the register which was allocated in

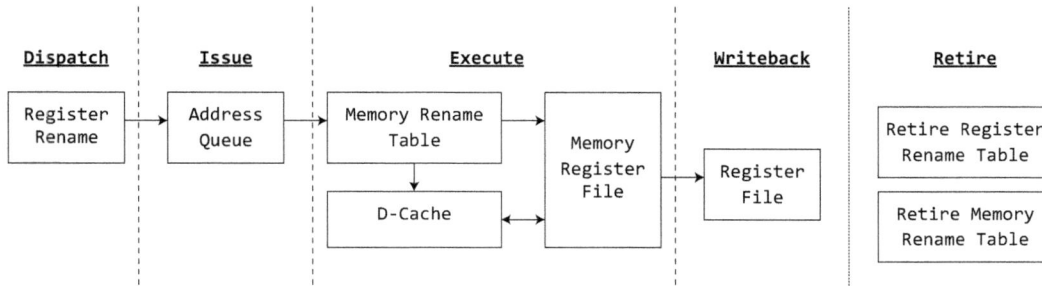

Figure 3: Our load-store unit's components placed into the proper stages of a pipeline. Only the components that are part of or interface directly with our design are depicted.

dispatch to the *Free* state. If the load's address misses in the MRT, a cache access is issued and the result is stored into the *Allocated* Memory Register. An MRT entry is also allocated, evicting the least recently used non-*Speculative* entry in that set. The address and MRF number are then written to that MRT entry and the memory register is transitioned to the *Pending* state, where it remains until it is transitioned to the *Clean* state once the cache responds. If the evicted MRT entry's register is in the *Dirty* state, indicating a store has not written back to the L1 cache, then a cache write is issued.

The net effect of the above is that the MRT filters loads before accessing the cache. This causes the cache latency to increase relative to a traditional design where the LSU and cache are accessed in parallel, but the hit rate is typically high enough that the lower latency of MRT forwarding compensates for the higher latency of the cache. The MRT is expected to have significantly higher hitrates than the store buffer in a traditional LSU since it includes values from retired instructions, is larger, includes loads, and has an even larger effective capacity since duplicates do not use additional entries.

If the issued operation is a store to an address that hit in the MRT, then the MRT entry's Memory Register is updated to the register allocated for this instruction at dispatch and marked as *Dirty*. The address component is left unchanged since it is already the address that hit, but the Memory Register Number is overwritten with the new one.

For a store, an MRT miss behaves similarly to an MRT hit, except both the address and Memory Register Number are written to an evicted MRT entry. The MRT eviction is done in the same way described for a load miss.

If all MRT entries for a set were allowed to be in the *Speculative* state a deadlock could occur. The address queue prevents this by only allowing ops to pass N stores. If this were not limited, then the N subsequent stores could execute, and therefore hold on to the entire block of entries in the MRT, potentially preventing forward progress.

2.3 Retirement stage

At retirement, memory instructions write their entry changes to the RMRT, similar to how they wrote to the MRT at execute. Since it is already known which entry number will be written, no search is needed and the RMRT can be direct mapped. The write of an RMRT entry may overwrite an older entry. In this event, the overwritten entry's register is moved to the *Free* state. In addition to this, if the instruction is a store, it must update its register's state to *Dirty*. Dirty values are not written to the cache until they

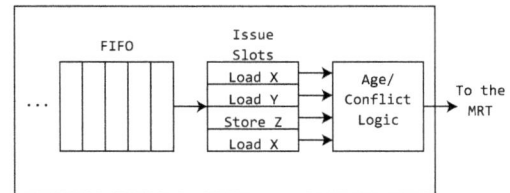

Figure 4: The address queue of our design. Instructions fill the 4 Issue Slots where they are compared to verify which are allowed to proceed. If these slots fill, then the FIFO buffer will allow the previous pipeline stages to continue execution.

are evicted from the MRT. This significantly reduces the number of stores that take place, since only the last value written to an address while it is resident in the LSU, the one evicted from the MRT, will be written. In the event of a squash, the RMRT contents are copied into the MRT, immediately returning the MRT to a valid state for continued execution.

3. METHODOLOGY

Trace-based simulation was used to evaluate the advantages of our design. This in-house simulator implements a superscalar pipeline with drop-in load-store units featuring our LSU and the LSU discussed in Section 1 as baseline.

The simulator was fed with an oracle dynamic instruction stream. This model features no instruction fetch side hazards such as branch prediction or instruction cache misses. This was considered fair since both pipelines employ near identical branch resolution mechanisms and penalty. The results should only bias in favor of the baseline because due to the RMRT, the MRT will be warm on recovery and the store buffer will not. This oracle trace was generated using gem5 [2] with the ARM instruction set.

The benchmarks used consisted of all of SPECINT 2006 [3]. Each trace includes 2 billion instructions, but no statistics are collected for the first 1 billion to allow for cache warm up. The traces were fed into each architecture model for detailed comparisons.

To monitor detailed performance and energy cost, the simulator keeps track of a variety of statistics including register file, cache, and memory read/write as well as cycle count. The simulator was configured to closely match the ARM cortex A15 [1].

We used McPat to estimate power and energy[4]. For these studies we targeted a 22nm technology node, modeling

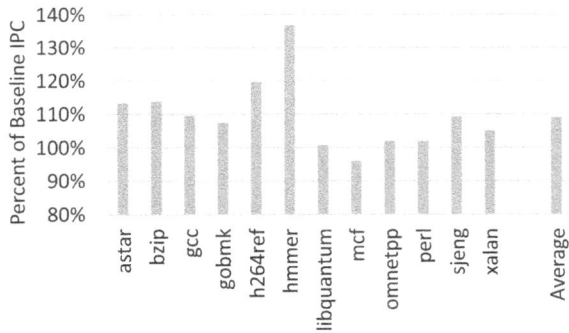

Figure 5: A detailed per-benchmark graph of the IPC reported relative to the store buffer baseline. The MRT is 4-way set associative with 64 entries.

multi-gate devices and aggressive interconnect projections on wire technologies. The nominal clock frequency was set to 1.7 GHz. This value matches the clock frequency of current industrial design, and we validated the peak power figures obtained with our model against publicly available data of comparable commercial microprocessors.

4. EVALUATION

Tests are performed across the SPECINT benchmarks using a configuration comparable to an ARM Cortex A15. The experiments performed give a sense of the energy efficiency and IPC gained by using our LSU. All values are presented relative to the baseline.

4.1 IPC

While our design increases L1 latency by deferring access until an MRT miss is confirmed, there is typically still a net performance gain. The performance of our design across SPECINT demonstrates an average increase in IPC of 8.7% over the baseline. The cause of this speedup is twofold. First, the LSU access is modeled as one cycle faster than a typical L1 access. This lets a dependent instruction proceed a cycle sooner. Second, this filtering of accesses will reduce contention on the L1 cache port(s) which would otherwise cause stalls. The per-benchmark speedup is shown in Figure 5.

4.2 Cache Bandwidth

A summary of average reduction in cache accesses is shown in Figure 6. In total, 45.4% of memory accesses are removed, from both the reads and writes relative to the baseline execution. Optimizations in the design such as post-retirement storage, store coalescing, load-to-load forwarding, and store-to-load forwarding are responsible for these results.

4.3 Power and Energy

We first evaluated the impact of our architecture on the power consumption of the data cache using McPAT. Our results report that we reduce data cache dynamic power by 42% on average. On top of this, the IPC is increased so leakage energy of the data cache per operation is reduced as a result, by 9.5%.

We then evaluated the total power and energy consumed by a core augmented with our LSU. Despite the reduction in data cache power consumption, our studies reported a slight increase in total core power consumption: 2.6%. We

Figure 6: The reduction in memory access as provided by our Load-Store Unit with a 64 entry, 4-way set associative MRT. Significant decrease is demonstrated both in the number of reads and writes performed when compared to the baseline store buffer.

justify these results with the higher IPC achieved by our design. While our design reduces the burden and the power consumed by the memory subsystem, it increases the load on the rest of the pipeline by increasing the IPC. As a result, our design improves core energy efficiency, yielding a significant reduction in the energy needed to execute a task. Our results show that a core deploying our load store unit achieves average energy savings of 7.9%.

5. CONCLUSION

As an artifact of the way software is written or generated today, the reuse distance of many values in memory is very short. Short enough to be stored in a physical register file instead of the cache. To exploit this attribute, we present a LSU that keeps most recently used memory addresses in a register file managed by a pair of set associative rename tables.

Our work supports memory optimizations at very little power cost. It has post-retirement storage, store coalescing, store-to-load, and load-to-load forwarding. With these optimizations, we can prevent 45% of cache accesses, reducing cache power. Accessing these structures sequentially increases the latency of a cache access, but this is overcome by the high hit rate in the low latency LSU and reduction in cache port contention. The net result is an 8.7% speedup and a 7.9% energy reduction.

6. REFERENCES

[1] ARM. *Cortex-A15 MPCore Technical Reference Manual, Revision: r3p3.*

[2] N. Binkert, B. Beckmann, G. Black, S. K. Reinhardt, A. Saidi, A. Basu, J. Hestness, D. R. Hower, T. Krishna, S. Sardashti, R. Sen, K. Sewell, M. Shoaib, N. Vaish, M. D. Hill, and D. A. Wood. The gem5 simulator. *SIGARCH Comput. Archit. News*, 39(2):1–7, Aug. 2011.

[3] J. L. Henning. SPEC CPU2006 Benchmark Descriptions. *SIGARCH Computer Architecture News*, 34(4):1–17, 2006.

[4] S. Li, J.-H. Ahn, R. Strong, J. Brockman, D. Tullsen, and N. Jouppi. McPAT: An integrated power, area, and timing modeling framework for multicore and manycore architectures. In *Microarchitecture, 2009. MICRO-42. 42nd Annual IEEE/ACM International Symposium on*, pages 469–480, 2009.

[5] D. W. Oehmke, N. L. Binkert, T. Mudge, and S. K. Reinhardt. How to fake 1000 registers. In *Proceedings of the 38th annual IEEE/ACM International Symposium on Microarchitecture*, pages 7–18. IEEE Computer Society, 2005.

A Deterministic-Dither-Based, All-digital System for On-chip Power Supply Noise Measurement

Kannan Sankaragomathi, William Smith, Brian Otis, Visvesh Sathe
Department of Electrical Engineering
University of Washington, Seattle
kannansa@uw.edu, wasmith2@uw.edu, botis@uw.edu, sathe@uw.edu

ABSTRACT

Supply-noise measurement techniques are becoming increasingly critical in modern digital design, driven by the trend toward smaller, lower-voltage domains. All-digital measurement modules capable of meeting bandwidth and resolution requirements would enable spatially fine supply voltage measurements across Systems-on-Chip. Existing implementations either use analog techniques, limiting their applicability, or do not meet the increasingly challenging requirements of supply noise measurement. In this paper we discuss a bandwidth-resolution-reconfigurable all-digital system that relies on a dithering technique to achieve a resolution of 2.05 mV at a bandwidth of 6.94 GHz in an industrial 65 nm CMOS process.

1. INTRODUCTION

A substantial amount of supply-voltage margin applied to modern digital designs is attributable to the inductive (L^{di}/dt) and resistive (IR) power supply droop observed on-chip. As supply voltages continue to scale driven by the need for energy efficiency, the ability to detect and measure supply noise in post-silicon testing for supply noise mitigation is becoming an increasingly important aspect of efficient, high-performance digital design, particularly in modern SoC designs.

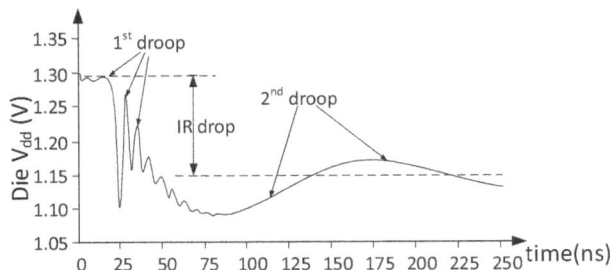

Figure 1: Typical L^{di}/dt and IR supply noise in digital integrated circuits

Figure 1 illustrates the on-die supply voltage resulting from an instantaneous load current increase in a regulated voltage domain

ISLPED'14, August 11–13, 2014, La Jolla, CA, USA.
Copyright is held by the owner/author(s). Publication rights licensed to ACM.
ACM 978-1-4503-2975-0/14/08 ...$15.00.
http://dx.doi.org/10.1145/2627369.2627656.

of a microprocessor. Inductive supply noise in the form of 1st and 2nd droop occuring at relatively lower frequencies has traditionally been dominant in digital integrated circuits. However, recent integration trends, including three-dimensional integration through chip-stacking [6] and the deployment of multiple voltage domains using integrated low drop out regulators (LDOs) [11], have resulted in increased amplitude and frequency content of supply noise. Increased per-domain package supply impedance, reduced power routing, and decap resources cause faster L^{di}/dt ringing and increased IR drop.

Integrated circuits are needed to adapt to and mitigate supply noise at design time [4,8]. Detailed post-silicon testing plays a key role in validating and optimizing these techniques and in providing sufficient learning to drive future changes. Modern digital systems require diagnostic supply noise measurement circuits which offer a small footprint, high voltage precision, and meet increasingly demanding bandwidth requirements. Implementing all-digital measurement circuits offers key additional advantages, including easy inclusion within multiple SoC sub-modules and enhanced portability from one process generation to the next.

One common digitally-compatible technique for measuring supply voltage involves using a ring oscillator (RO) as a time-to-digital converter (TDC). The temporal resolution offered by the approach for a given bandwidth is inadequate for current and future power supply noise measurement needs. A number of other supply measurement circuits have been proposed in the literature [1, 5, 9, 10]. Analog implementations tend to have large footprints, do not scale well and are not easily integrated into the design flow. Existing all-digital implementations have also been proposed, but as discussed in Section 2, these techniques place significant practical limitations on the system-under-test such as excessive test time, limited test-pattern length, or an inadequate bandwidth-resolution ratio.

In this paper we propose an all-digital power supply noise measurement circuit that has a small footprint and is capable of high-bandwidth high-resolution measurements with acceptable test time. The proposed technique achieves an elastic, user-tunable bandwidth-resolution ratio of 3.4 GHz/mV. The measurement performance in the circuit is enabled by two key techniques. The first involves periodically sampling the supply noise waveform, similar to [1,5,10]. The waveform is iteratively sampled with a small timing window to accumulate large counts. Second, we propose a novel approach involving the application of *deterministic* dither to the sampling window width to suppress quantization error over aggregate measurements, enhancing the bandwidth-resolution ratio beyond what is possible with undithered measurements.

This paper is organized as follows: Section 2 discusses the current state-of-the-art in all-digital supply noise measurement. Section 3 introduces the proposed supply noise measurement system and examines its bandwidth-resolution performance. Post-layout simulation results for the proposed measurement circuit are presented in Section 4.

2. RELATED WORK

The use of a ring oscillator (RO) to measure supply voltage is a is one of the oldest known approaches. The RO is started at a defined time and the number of oscillator transitions occurring in a sampling window are counted. Allowing τ denote the voltage-dependent delay of an inverter stage, a sampling duration of T_{samp}, the voltage resolution δ_V can be shown to be $\delta_V = \tau^2 / \left(T_{samp} \frac{\partial \tau}{\partial V_{dd}} \right)$. Improving voltage resolution (lower δ_V) requires lower τ (process limited) or increasing T_{samp} (bandwidth-limiting). Denoting f_{BW} as the 3 dB measurement bandwidth of the technique (approximated as a square-pulse sample), the bandwidth-resolution ratio of the approach is derived to be $\frac{f_{BW}}{\delta_V} = \frac{0.44}{\tau^2} \frac{\partial \tau}{\partial V_{dd}}$. This is insufficient for most SoC applications. In a technology with an inverter delay of 40 ps at 1 V, achieving 6.5 mV resolution limits the bandwidth to approximately 75MHz, inadequate even for 1st droop.

Several enhanced techniques have also been proposed, which rely on the idea of iterative sampling, illustrated in Figure 2. Sampling a narrow time-interval iteratively, and accumulating phase and quantization information enables bandwidth-resolution ratios beyond that possible with traditional RO voltage sensing [1, 9]. In [1], a uniform, randomly distributed initial phase within the RO is assumed to produce transition counts within a sampling window over multiple tests. This technique achieves an excellent bandwidth-resolution ratio, but the statistical measurement approach requires an extremely large number of iterations, making the test time impractical for supply noise measurement in several SoC and multi-core applications. For example, achieving a 3.25mV voltage resolution requires 1.6×10^5 samples. Analyzing a 200ns section of a 3ms code-trace to capture supply noise in a multi-core system [7] (assuming no I/O is required between successive tests) will require an impractical 666 hours of test time with this technique.

More recently, gated ring oscillators have been proposed to deterministically achieve bandwidth-resolution improvement over traditional RO voltage sensing [9]. Quantization error from an individual sample is accumulated between successive iterations in floating node voltages of the gated RO. However, as discussed in [9], charge leakage in scaled CMOS limits the duration of the test to approximately 100ns, making it unsuitable for most practical test vectors. A latched ring oscillator similar to Figure 2 is proposed to address the test duration limitation. However, this approach is identical to a traditional RO based measurement with stage-level counter resolution. A simulated voltage resolution of 40mV with a 1.6GHz bandwidth for the latched RO is reported in [9]. This is insufficient resolution for most measurement applications.

There are a number of analog-based measurement systems proposed [5, 10]. However, such analog techniques are not readily portable, and either area intensive or need a high frequency analog I/O, making them unsuitable for spatially-fine supply voltage measurements required by modern SOCs.

3. PROPOSED APPROACH

This section outlines the proposed all-digital power supply measurement technique. It relies on periodically sampling the supply noise with a deterministically-dithered pulse to achieve substantially finer resolution than a unit RO stage delay.

In the proposed approach, a latched RO topology similar to the one shown in Figure 2 was chosen to support an arbitrarily long test duration. For simplicity, Figure 2 illustrates the principle of operation on a single inverter. Signal in transitions, causing out to transition after $\tau(V)$. A sampling pulse asserted at the same time instant has its width deterministically-dithered from T_{min} to T_{max} over successive iterations. Only iterations where the sampling width exceeds the inverter delay will register a transition at out. Repeated measurements over a range of *uniformly* distributed pulse widths will result in an aggregated edge-count that is proportional to the ratio between the *"edge"* region in the figure and the dither range T_d. Lower voltages with higher delays ($V1 > V2$) result in narrower *"edge"* regions and lower counts. The supply noise sample is periodically generated. The applied deterministic dither exceeds the inverter delay ($T_d > \tau(V)$) and occurs over fine, discrete time intervals. To the first order, the voltage resolution achieved by this approach is determined not by the size of the RO stage delay but by the much finer dither step size.

3.1 Timing Generation

Figure 3 illustrates the system level architecture of the power supply measurement circuit. The timing generation block produces a sampling pulse, φ, that gates a ring oscillator. The width of this pulse is deterministically dithered with sub-picosecond resolution. The timing block also controls the arrival time of the sampling pulse relative to the system clock to perform a supply measurement "sweep" over the test duration.

The timing state-machine relies on its own ring oscillator for both coarse and fine delay, enabling a time offset in the sampling pulse relative to the system clock. The appropriately delayed transition is selected by a multiplexer (MUX) to generate a one-shot *edge_en* pulse. Interpolators, controlled by the state-machine, are used for generating fine-delay offsets (sub-gate delay), and for generating the deterministic dither. The fine-delay interpolator operates over a range equal to the unit delay of the timing-generator RO. Two additional interpolators provide the required deterministic dither to incrementally modulate the sampling pulse width over the dither range across successive sampling iterations. The resulting dithered pulse samples the latched RO. The pulse width is first gradually increased by delaying the falling edge of the pulse over multiple iterations and subsequently reduced by delaying the rising edge of the sampling pulse across multiple iterations. Transitions across all iterations needed to implement the uniform deterministic dither and the final state and count of the latched RO is recorded.

The phase interpolator design, shown in Figure 3, is identical across all three instantiations. The interpolator decode logic sets *clkD<63:0>* bits thermometrically to *count*, modulating nMOS current drive and causing a linear increase in edge transition delay. A fully-static interpolator design is used to generate 64 different delay values. The control logic is capable of implementing dynamic-element-matching (DEM) [3] to mitigate fabrication mismatch between the pull-down nMOS devices.

3.2 Analysis of Bandwidth-Resolution Trade-offs

The proposed approach enables runtime bandwidth configuration by controlling the sampling pulse width. Measurement resolution adjusts based on the bandwidth-resolution ratio achieved by the system. Wider pulses accumulate more phase—suppressing quantization noise more effectively—while a narrower pulse allows higher bandwidth measurement.

The rectangular sampling pulse is shaped by the applied deterministic dither. Although the dither itself is applied uniformly, all time instants are not uniformly sampled across an entire dither sequence. This results in an effective pulse shape shown in Figure 3. In the figure, T_{min} is the minimum sampling pulse width, T_d is

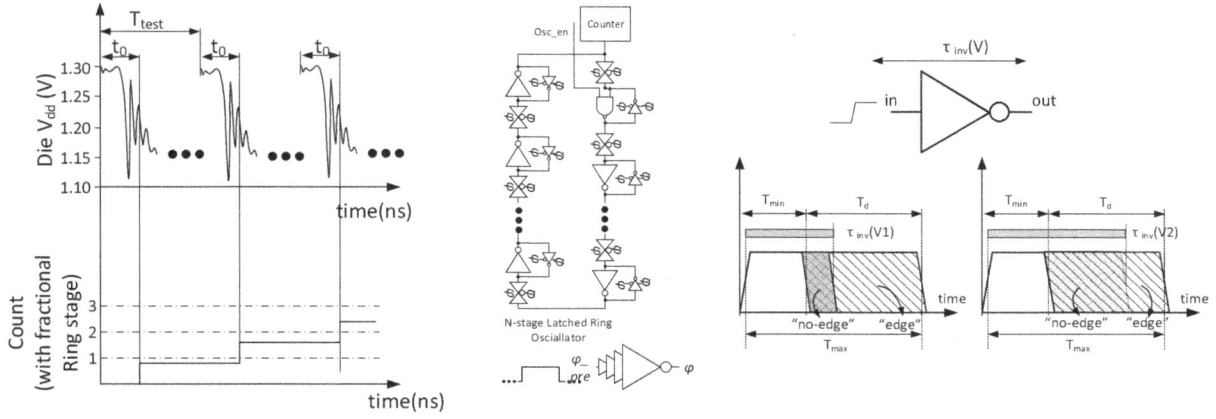

Figure 2: Proposed deterministic-dither based sampling supply noise measurement technique

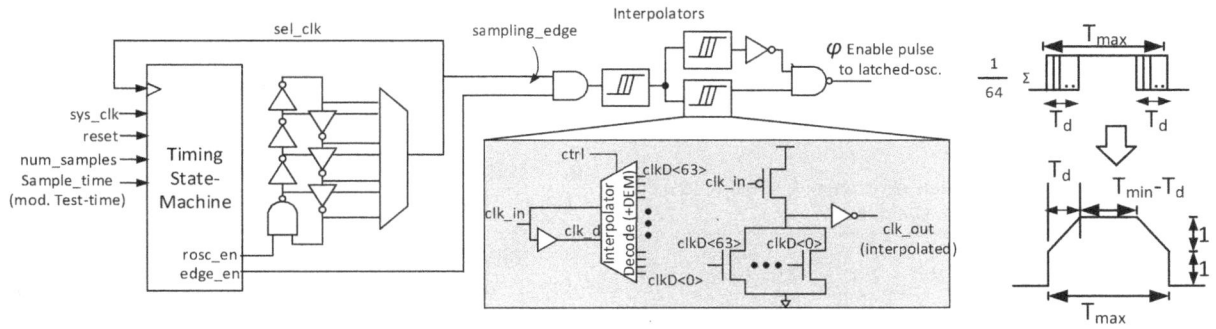

Figure 3: Proposed deterministic-dither based sampling supply noise measurement technique

the dither range, and T_{max} is the maximum sampling pulse width. Consequently, $T_{max} = T_{min} + T_d$.

The effective pulse can be viewed as a combination of three sub-waveforms, an additive square pulse and triangle pulse, and a subtractive triangle pulse. The Fourier-domain representation of the effective pulse can then be written as the sum of three Fourier representations as shown in Equation 1.

When $T_{max} \gg T_d$, the effective pulse resembles the original pulse: $f_{-3dB} = {0.44}/{T_{max}}$. When $T_{min} = T_d$, the 3dB bandwidth can be shown to be $f_{-3dB} = 0.53/T_{max}$. Voltage resolution is set by the pulse width and the dither step ΔT.

Given that the measurement circuit is capable of detecting a ΔT time difference over its longest phase-accumulation duration and that T_d exceeds τ (the unit delay within the RO), voltage resolution of the proposed circuit can be shown to be:

$$\Delta V = \frac{\Delta T}{\lfloor (\frac{T_d}{\tau}) \rfloor \lfloor (\frac{T_{max}}{\tau}) \rfloor \frac{\partial \tau}{\partial V_{dd}}}.$$

4. SIMULATION RESULTS

In this section, we present simulation results of the proposed power supply measurement circuit. The system illustrated in Figure 3 was designed using a standard industrial 65nm CMOS process. All reported results are from post-layout extracted simulations.

From Section 3.2, the importance of ΔT in setting voltage resolution places a strong emphasis on interpolator design. Interpolator simulation results are shown in Figure 4. The maximum DNL is 0.08 of a single dither step of 650 fs resulting in 52 fs worst-case pulse jitter due to the phase interpolator.

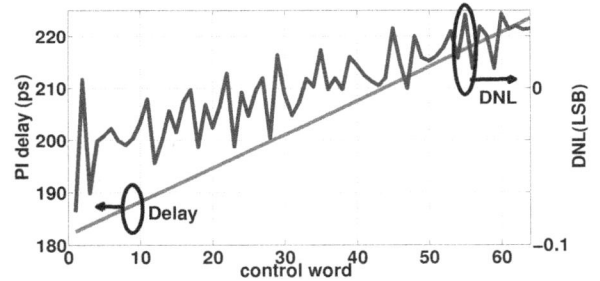

Figure 4: Phase Interpolator linearity

Figure 5a illustrates the code calibration–V_{DD} graph that is used to recover a voltage from a given code. The code displayed in the plot corresponds to 12-step dither sequence with $T_{min} = 800$ ps. Simulation was performed for fast (FF), typical (TT), and slow (SS) corners. Also shown is a finer voltage-code relationship for the TT waveform, displaying the quantization noise in the system. As expected, the simulation process corner has an impact on the V_{DD}-Code mapping. Consequently, individual calibration of each measurement system is required before post-silicon measurements.

Figures 5b and 5c illustrate the performance of the proposed supply-measurement circuit. $L^{di/dt}$ supply noise caused by 1st and 2nd droop noise is measured with the circuit, and the reconstructed waveform is overlaid over the original supply noise waveform in Figure 5b. Measurements were taken with $T_{max} = 470$ ps, corresponding to a bandwidth of 936 MHz and an effective resolution of 0.16 mV.

$$H(f) = T_{max}sinc(T_{max}f) + \frac{T_{max}^2}{4T_d}sinc^2(\frac{1}{2}T_{max}f) - \frac{(T_{min} - T_d)^2}{4T_d}sinc^2(\frac{1}{2}(T_{min} - T_d)f). \quad (1)$$

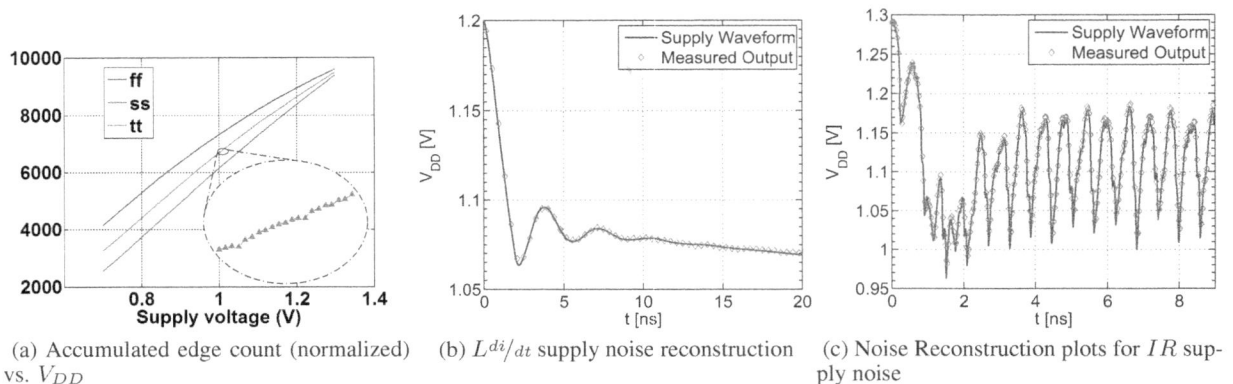

(a) Accumulated edge count (normalized) vs. V_{DD}

(b) $L^{di}/_{dt}$ supply noise reconstruction

(c) Noise Reconstruction plots for IR supply noise

Figure 5: Simulation data. In (b), the waveform was sampled at sampled at 2.56 GHz with a nominal 430ps pulse width. In (c), the waveform was sampled at 33.3 GHz with a nominal pulse width of 40 ps.

Table 1: Performance comparison of proposed work with other supply noise measurement techniques

Performance Metric	[10]	[1] [2]	[9]	[5]	This work
Bandwidth (GHz)	6.5	44	4.1	0.7[*]	6.94
Samp. rate (GHz)	100	100	8.3	200	25
Voltage Res. (mV)	—[**]	3.2	40[*,†]	0.19	2.05
Area (μm^2)	1550[*]	—	99.79	5040[*,‡]	187
Test time (min.)	0.25	39960[*]	0.25	0.25	32
Analog I/O	Yes[*]	No	No	No	No
Technology (nm)	130	90	90	65	65

[*] Drawback   [†] Latch-oscillator   [‡] From die photo   [**] Analog o/p

Figure 5c illustrates an increasingly common supply noise scenario resulting from IR drop in a micro-regulated voltage domain. Since such domains are smaller in size and limited in the amount of filter decoupling capacitance they can provide, the dominant pole frequency of the impedance of the domain as seen by the load has substantially higher frequencies. In this simulation, the dominant pole frequency is 4 GHz. As seen from both figures, the proposed circuit provides very accurate reconstruction of the original IR drop dominated supply waveform.

Table 1 summarizes the performance of the proposed system along with a comparison of previously existing supply voltage monitors. In contrast to all previous works listed in the table, the proposed circuit meets all the required criterion of sufficient signal bandwidth and resolution, all-digital construction, small footprint, and reasonable test time to measure supply noise.

5. CONCLUSION

This paper presents an all digital supply noise measurement technique using a deterministic dithering technue. The proposed technique achieves bandwidth-resolution metrics beyond possible with current approaches while using a small footprint.Post-layout simulations of an implementation in an industrial 65nm process indicate an effective resolution of 2.05 mV at 6.94 GHz measurement bandwidth.

6. REFERENCES

[1] V. Abramzon et al. Scalable circuits for supply noise measurement. In *Proc. ESSCIRC 2005*, pages 463–466, Sept 2005.

[2] E. Alon, V. Abramzon, B. Nezamfar, and M. Horowitz. On-Die Power Supply Noise Measurement Techniques. *IEEE Adv. Packag.*, 32(2):248–259, May 2009.

[3] I. Galton. Why Dynamic-Element-Matching DACs Work. *IEEE Trans. Circuits Syst. II, Exp. Briefs*, 57(2):69–74, Feb 2010.

[4] A. Grenat et al. Adaptive clocking system for improved power efficiency in a 28nm x86-64 microprocessor. In *Tech. Dig. IEEE ISSCC 2014*, pages 106–107, Feb 2014.

[5] T. Hashida and M. Nagata. An On-Chip Waveform Capturer and Application to Diagnosis of Power Delivery in SoC Integration. *IEEE J. Solid-State Circuits*, 46(4):789–796, April 2011.

[6] G. Huang, M. Bakir, A. Naeemi, H. Chen, and J. Meindl. Power Delivery for 3D Chip Stacks: Physical Modeling and Design Implication. In *Proc. IEEE Elect. Performance of Electron. Packaging 2007*, pages 205–208, Oct 2007.

[7] Y. Kim et al. AUDIT: Stress Testing the Automatic Way. In *Proc. IEEE/ACM MICRO 2012*, pages 212–223, Dec 2012.

[8] N. Kurd et al. Next Generation Intel Core Micro-Architecture (Nehalem) Clocking. *IEEE J. Solid-State Circuits*, 44(4):1121–1129, Apr. 2009.

[9] Y. Ogasahara et al. All-Digital Ring-Oscillator-Based Macro for Sensing Dynamic Supply Noise Waveform. *IEEE J. Solid-State Circuits*, 44(6):1745–1755, June 2009.

[10] M. Takamiya et al. An on-chip 100 GHz-sampling rate 8-channel sampling oscilloscope with embedded sampling clock generator. In *Tech. Dig. IEEE ISSCC 2002*, volume 1, pages 182–458 vol.1, Feb 2002.

[11] Z. Toprak-Deniz et al. Distributed system of digitally controlled microregulators enabling per-core DVFS for the POWER8 microprocessor. In *Tech. Dig. IEEE ISSCC 2014*, pages 98–99, Feb 2014.

An Open-Source Framework for Formal Specification and Simulation of Electrical Energy Systems[*]

Sara Vinco[1], Alessandro Sassone[1], Franco Fummi[2], Enrico Macii[1], Massimo Poncino[1]

[1] Department of Control and Computer Engineering, Politecnico di Torino, Italy, {name.surname@polito.it}
[2] Department of Computer Science, University of Verona, Italy, {name.surname@univr.it}

ABSTRACT

Electrical energy systems (EESs) are systems which consume, generate, distribute and store energy at various scales. This paper presents a modeling and simulation framework that uses principles borrowed from the system-level simulation of digital systems and extends them to the case of EESs. The framework relies on open-source standards such as SystemC (and its Analog and Mixed-Signal extensions) for simulation, and IP-XACT for interface definition.

The paper extends the IP-XACT standard with the formal definition of the interfaces of the typical components of an EESs. Then, it proposes a methodology to seamlessly plug such components into the simulation framework using the power configuration information contained in the IP-XACT descriptions. Simulations show that the proposed approach provides accuracy comparable to Matlab/Simulink results, with higher modularity and faster simulation times.

Categories and Subject Descriptors

J.6 [**Computer-Aided Engineering**]: Computer-aided design (CAD)

Keywords

Electrical Energy Systems; SystemC-AMS; IP-XACT; power simulation

1. INTRODUCTION

The traditional approach to Electrical Energy Systems (EES) design relies on a model-based paradigm, which uses built-in models provided by commercial simulation platforms like Matlab/Simulink. While robust and easy to use, such tools lack many important and desirable features.

First, as closed and proprietary tools, they are not easily extensible. Moreover, they are subject to changes of the underlying, proprietary simulation backbone, and across-version compatibility is not guaranteed. Furthermore, these

tools are not designed to efficiently co-simulate the physical portion and the cyber portion of the system. This feature clearly limits the possibility of designing EESs following a systematic approach guided by user-defined optimizations. To tackle these limitations, recently several approaches have appeared in the literature that aim at applying methods borrowed from the domain of electronic systems design [6, 8, 9, 14]. These solutions mainly differ in two aspects: underlying simulation engine (Matlab [6] vs. SystemC [10] vs. ad-hoc developed C/C++-based simulators [14]), and their degree of generality (specialized for some type of EES, e.g., a smart grid, [6], or general-purpose [9, 14]).

One common feature shared by these solutions is that they rely on a database of pre-characterized models of the various EES components. This does not allow to replace a model of a component with a different implementation [8].

In this work, we introduce a modeling and simulation framework that relies on open-source tools and standards such as SystemC-AMS for simulation, and IP-XACT for the definition of the models. Our solution is similar in scope to [9] because it uses standard modeling and simulation languages, and to [14] in that it targets general EES without any limitation in scope and scale. With respect to those solutions, however, we introduce two main innovative contributions. Firstly we formally define the model interfaces for EES components by extending the IP-XACT standard; this allows (1) to define abstract "meta-models" for these components with which a model must comply, and (2) using the power configuration information contained in the IP-XACT descriptions, to seamlessly plug such components into the SystemC simulation framework. Our approach allows therefore designers of EESs to implement multi-level simulations, where different components can be simulated at different levels of details, while using a single, open simulation platform.

2. BACKGROUND

2.1 The IP-XACT standard

IP-XACT is a standard XML format for describing interfaces of digital IPs [2], thus easing reuse and integration of third party IPs and assisting system level simulation.

IP-XACT supports a set of different description schemas. A *component* description describes the interface of an IP, detailed as the list of its ports. Similarly, a *bus* definition describes the interface of a bus. A *design* definition outlines the components instantiated in a system and their connections. *Ports* are characterized by a name, a direction and a type, that is assumed to be either an integer or a bit vector (analog or physical quantities are not natively supported).

[*]This work was supported by the EC co-funded CONTREX (Design of embedded mixed-criticality CONTRol systems under consideration of EXtra-functional properties) project Grant Agreement FP7-ICT- 611146

2.2 SystemC and its AMS extension

SystemC-AMS (*Analog Mixed Signal*) provides different abstraction levels to cover a wide variety of domains [1]. *Timed Data-Flow* (TDF) features the modeling of discrete time processes, that are scheduled statically by considering their producer-consumer dependencies. *Electrical Linear Network* (ELN) models electrical networks through the instantiation of predefined linear network primitives, e.g., resistors or capacitors, where each primitive is associated with an electrical equation. The SystemC-AMS AD solver analyzes the ELN system to derive the equations modeling system behavior, that will be solved to determine system state at any simulation time.

3. MODELING AND SIMULATION FRAMEWORK

3.1 Architectural Template

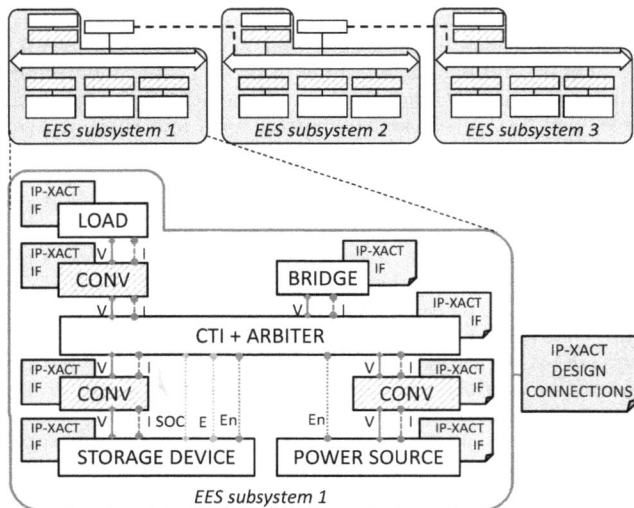

Figure 1: Template of the reference architecture, including the CTI bus and the connected components

Table 1 and Figure 1 outline the main components of a EES. In the figure, the CTI bus and the arbiter have been merged in a single component, as the goal is to provide a simple simulatable interface, rather than to reflect the physical components of the power system. This *enhanced power bus* constitutes an abstraction of the power behaviors of the overall heterogeneous system. (For the sake of clarity, it is assumed that the system contains only one component per type).

The *power interface* describes what power information is shared with the other EES components. V and I are voltage and current, respectively. SOC and E are the state of charge and the energy (i.e., capacity) of the ESD components. En is an enabling signal, used by the arbiter to activate an ESD or a power source to provide power to the system. Environmental parameters are non-power characteristics that may influence the behavior of EES components, such as temperature (T) and solar radiation (G). Parameters vary with the kind of ESD or power source.

3.2 IP-XACT Mapping of the Architecture

In the following of this Section, interfaces are formalized to define a standard interface for each EES component. This enhances composability and design space exploration, as a standard interface may correspond to different implementations. Figure 1 summarizes the ports and the connections modeled in the system.

IP-XACT power port support.

Power ports are *real values* modeling a continuous physical evolution. They are thus represented by using the IP-XACT extension for analog mixed signal modeling [3] and they are associated with a default value, annotated with the measure unit (e.g., Volt) and a prefix (e.g., kilo and milli).

Ports are annotated with a tag that qualifies the type of *carried information* (e.g., voltage, current) and with a *signal type*, that defines whether the port value is continuous or discrete, and whether energy conservation laws are satisfied. Figure 2.a shows an extract of a IP-XACT file modeling a digital input port, whose name is *data* and whose type is a vector of four bits. Similarly, Figure 2.b shows the changes necessary to model an input power port *voltg*, whose default value is 1.3 mV. The port is tagged as continuous and conservative and as carrying voltage values.

```
<port>                          <port>
  <name>data</name>               <name>voltg</name>
  <wire>                          <wire>
    <direction>in</direction>       <direction>in</direction>
    <vector>                      </wire>
      <left>3</left>              <vendorExtensions>
      <right>0</right>             <value unit="volt" prefix="milli"> 1.3
    </vector>                      </value>
    <typeName>                    <isVoltage>true</isVoltage>
      bit_vector                  <signalType>continuous-conservative
    </typeName>                   </signalType>
  </wire>                        </vendorExtensions>
</port>                         </port>
        a.                              b.
```

Figure 2: Excerpt of IP-XACT file modeling a digital port (a) and a power bort (b).

IP-XACT power component support.

IP-XACT component descriptions are provided for all components of the EES system, excluding the CTI bus. Each IP-XACT component description adopts the previously defined power ports and it is enriched with a tag conveying qualifying information about the *role of the component* in the system. Tags are: isLoad, isEsd, isSource, isController, isConverter and isArbiter. The tag evaluated to true identifies the role of the component in the system. Bus definitions are treated similarly and they are enriched by a isCti tag that, if set to true, notifies that the bus being modeled is a CTI bus, rather than a digital one.

IP-XACT power design support.

IP-XACT design descriptions model connections between EES components. Any EES system will contain a number of components, with specific connections. Thus, the IP-XACT design description must be modeled by the user. This manual step is necessary to determine the architecture of the system to be simulated and it eases its definition.

To build a power IP-XACT design description, EES components are instantiated by referencing the corresponding IP-XACT component description to determine, e.g., whether the new component is an ESD or a converter. It is then possible to configure the instantiated components by setting

Table 1: Classification and main characteristics of components of an EES system

Component	Instances (#)	Description	Power interface	Env. parameters
Load	l	Functional component that requires some power	(V, I)	-
ESD	s	Energy storage device of different natures	(V, I, SOC, E, En)	(T)
Power source	p	Almost infinite source of power (e.g., solar panel)	(V, I, En)	(T, G)
Converter	$c = s + p + l$	Component necessary to maintain compatibility of V levels between EES components	(V, I, V, I)	-
Arbiter	1	Device in charge of controlling the energy paths among ESDs and power sources at any time	$((SOC, E, En)^s, (En)^p, (V, I)^c)$	-
CTI bus	1	Ideal charge transfer interconnect used to abstract power behaviors	$((SOC, E, En)^s, (En)^p, (V, I)^c)$	-
Bridge	b	Component connecting different CTI buses	(V, I, V, I)	-

some parameters. Port bindings are modeled through ad hoc connections.

3.3 Modeling and Simulation

IP-XACT interfaces are instantiated by declaring one SystemC module per EES system element (`SC_MODULE`). Ports are declared as SystemC TDF ports (`sca_tdf::sca_in` or `sca_tdf::sca_out`) of type `double`, as adopting a TDF interface is crucial to speed up simulation (as in Figure 3). Future work will enhance the methodology with automatic generation of the SystemC interface from the IP-XACT files. Once the interface has been defined, the SystemC modules must be populated with an *implementation* of the components. The only requirement is that implemented models respect the pre-defined interface.

Models for EES components typically belong to two main categories: *functional* models and *circuit-level* models.

Functional models implement component evolution with a function (e.g., an equation or even a simple waveform over time) [11, 13]. Functional models can be reproduced by implementing the function as a digital process, activated whenever the function inputs change (left of Figure 3).

Circuit-level models emulate the behavior of a component through an equivalent electrical circuit. In literature, a variety of circuit models exists for the various elements , e.g., batteries [12], converters [5] and power sources [4]. These models can be implemented by describing the circuit as a network of SystemC-AMS ELN components, instantiated and connected in a way that reproduces the circuit specification (right of Figure 3). Wrapping the ELN subsystem through ELN-TDF converters (`sca_eln::sca_tdf` components) allows to preserve the synchronization with the rest of the system.

Figure 3 clearly shows how using a pre-defined interface allows the seamless replacement of models with different accuracy vs. complexity tradeoff levels. Moreover, this also allows simulating various parts of an EES with different degrees of accuracy, e.g., with the purpose of analyzing a particular bottleneck or the design of critical component.

4. SIMULATION RESULTS

4.1 Accuracy and Simulation Speed

The first experiment consists of an example EES made of:

- a Li-ion rechargeable battery by Qinetiq (capacity of 5.8Ah, nominal voltage of 3.69V) modeled as in [12];
- two load devices corresponding to the power state profiles of two commercial cores; loads are represented as current and voltage waveforms over time;

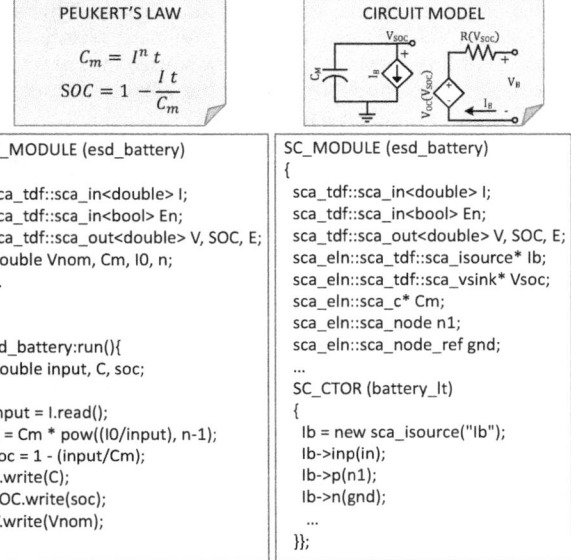

Figure 3: Example of a battery simulated with two different models.

Table 2: Accuracy and effectiveness of the proposed approach w.r.t. Matlab/Simulink.

	Time step (s)	Samples (#)	Battery LT (s)	Error (avg. %)	Time (s)
Matlab/ Simulink	Variable	9	14,101.1	7.9999	0.89
	1.0	7,505	7,501.9	0.4788	4.68
	0.1	74,973	7,497.1	-	37.59
SystemC (-AMS)	1.0	7,502	7,501.1	0.0049	0.17
	0.1	74,972	7,497.1	0.0003	1.31

- three DC-DC converters modeled as in [11];
- a CTI bus modeled as an ideal current conductor with constant reference voltage of 3.0V.

The system has first been modeled in Matlab/Simulink, in a top down approach. Then, it was described in SystemC(-AMS), by following the framework proposed in this work. Table 2 compares simulation accuracy and performance of five code versions: SystemC-AMS and Matlab/Simulink with time steps 0.1s and 1s, and the Matlab/Simulink version with variable adaptive step. The Matlab/Simulink version with time step 0.1s is used as a reference.

The SystemC versions exhibit very high accuracy, which is very little sensitive to the size of time step: the average error is 0.005% with time step 1s (max. error 0.6%) and 0.0003% with time step 0.1s (max. error 0.04%). Conversely, Matlab/Simulink accuracy decreases with larger time steps (e.g., avg. error 0.48% and max. error 3.55% with time step 1s). Concerning speed, SystemC-AMS proved to be much faster than Matlab/Simulink. The speedup w.r.t. Matlab/Simulink version is about 29x with time step 1s and 28x with time step 0.1s. The reason is that the Matlab/Simulink internal solver is far heavier than the efficient TDF and ELN SystemC implementations.

Notice that the Matlab/Simulink simulation with adaptive step, which has simulation speed comparable to ours, incurs however in a significant estimation error (average/-maximum error of 8%/15%): as shown in the table only 9 samples are recorded for the whole simulation. This shows that SystemC(-AMS) can be a very efficient alternative to Matlab/Simulink; besides being open source and extensible, it also is accurate and fast w.r.t. the corresponding Matlab/Simulink implementations.

4.2 Simulation of a Charge Allocation Policy

In the second experiment, the system described in Section 4.1 is extended by adding a power source, i.e., a photovoltaic (PV) panel composed of 5 Sunpower A300 PV cells connected to a module performing maximum power transfer tracking (MPTT) [7]. The daily solar irradiation profile is modeled as in [11]. Fig. 4 shows the resulting system.

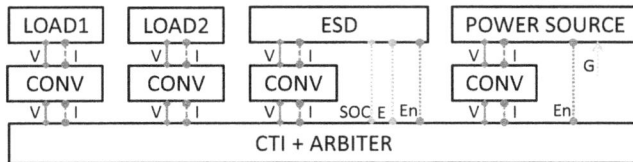

Figure 4: Charge Allocation Policy EES.

The CTI arbiter is augmented with an implementation of a "charge allocation" policy, which is as follows: As long as the power drawn from the PV panel satisfies the power demand of the loads, loads are supplied by the power source. Otherwise, the loads are supplied by the battery, until the SOC is below 10%. Finally, when the PV panel is able to provide power and the power demanded by the loads is 0, the battery is charged by the power source. Although this policy is quite simplistic, the purpose here is not to develop sophisticated policies but rather to show the efficiency and the flexibility of the system.

The system has been implemented as in the previous experiments with time step 1s. The simulated operating time is concentrated on the peak power period of the PV panel and ends when the power demand can not be satisfied.

Fig. 5(a) compares the power drawn from the PV panel P_{ps} and the power demand of the loads P_{load}. The curves are almost completely overlapped, denoting the high accuracy of the SystemC(-AMS) implementation, having an average error 0.002% w.r.t. Matlab/Simulink. Simulation time shows a speedup of 32x, consistently with the previous experiment. Fig. 5(b) shows the waveform of the activation signal En_{ps} of the PV panel during the simulation (the activation signal of the battery is the negated version of the waveform). The two waveforms coincide, as a result of correct processing of the simple charging allocation policy implemented.

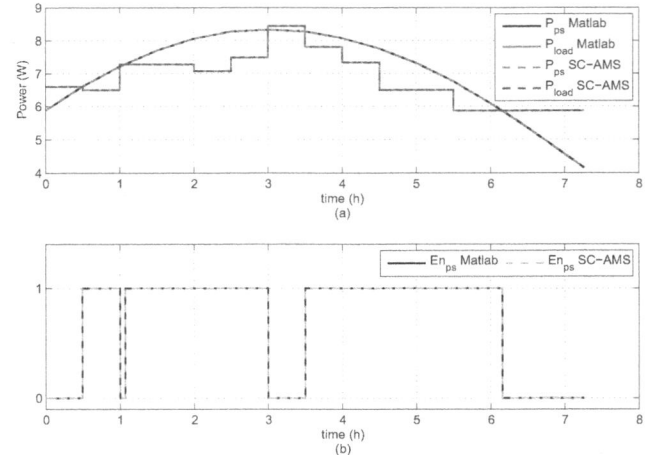

Figure 5: Comparison of Matlab/Simulink and SystemC(-AMS) simulations.

5. CONCLUSIONS

This paper proposed a framework for simulating EESs based on open source tools and standards of the digital domain. Experimental results show that the proposed approach provides a faster simulation w.r.t. Matlab/Simulink (avg. 28x), still preserving a high level of accuracy (avg. error is always lower than 0.001%). The approach proved to scale well over a set of experiments of increasing complexity and to enhance design space exploration. We envision that this solution will allow effective simulation of more complex systems, thus enhancing design of EESs. Furthermore, the adoption of a C++ based simulation environment will enable the simultaneous simulation of the power and functional domains.

6. REFERENCES

[1] Accellera. *SystemC-AMS.* www.systemc-ams.org.
[2] Accellera. *IEEE Standard 1685-2009 for IP-XACT*, 2010.
[3] Accellera. *Recommended Vendor Extensions to IEEE 1685-2009 (IP-XACT)*, 2013. www.accellera.org.
[4] A. Bauer, J. Hanisch, and E. Ahlswede. An Effective Single Solar Cell Equivalent Circuit Model for Two or More Solar Cells Connected in Series. *IEEE PHOT*, 4(1):340–347, Jan 2014.
[5] Y. Choi, N. Chang, and T. Kim. DC-DC Converter-Aware Power Management for Low-Power Embedded Systems. *IEEE TCAD*, 26(8):1367–1381, Aug 2007.
[6] M. A. Faruque and F. Ahourai. A Model-Based Design of Cyber-Physical Energy Systems. In *Proc. of IEEE ASPDAC*, pages 97–105, 2014.
[7] Y. Kim, N. Chang, et al. Maximum power transfer tracking for a photovoltaic-supercapacitor energy system. In *Proc. of ACM/IEEE ISLPED*, pages 307–312. ACM, 2010.
[8] Y. Kim, D. Shin, et al. Computer-Aided Design of Electrical Energy Systems. In *Proc. of ACM/IEEE ICCAD*, pages 194–201, 2013.
[9] J. Molina, X. Pan, et al. A Framework for Model-Based Design of Embedded Systems for Energy Management. In *Proc. of IEEE MSCPES*, pages 1–6, 2013.
[10] Open SystemC Initiative. *SystemC.* www.systemc.org.
[11] S. Park, Y. Wang, et al. Battery Management for Grid-connected PV Systems with a Battery. In *Proc. of ACM/IEEE ISLPED*, pages 115–120, 2012.
[12] M. Petricca, D. Shin, et al. An automated framework for generating variable-accuracy battery models from datasheet information. In *Proc. of ACM/IEEE ISLPED*, pages 365–370, 2013.
[13] W. Peukert. Über die Abhängigkeit der Kapazität von der Entladestromstärke bei Bleiakkumulatoren. In *Elektrotechnische Zeitschrift*, page 20, 1897.
[14] S. Yue, D. Zhu, et al. SIMES: A Simulator for Hybrid Electrical Energy Storage Systems. In *Proc. of ACM/IEEE ISLPED*, pages 33–38, 2013.

Analysis and Optimization of In-Situ Error Detection Techniques in Ultra-Low-Voltage Pipeline

Seongjong Kim, Mingoo Seok

Columbia University, New York, NY, USA, sk3667@columbia.edu

Abstract. In-situ error-detection and correction techniques have a strong potential to eliminate the worst-case margins in ultra-low-voltage (ULV) pipelines while achieving high variation tolerance. Adding the capability of error detection, however, can incur large hardware overhead, especially in ULV due to the larger variability. In this paper, we analyze the hardware overhead of error-detection techniques and propose a technique called sparse insertion of error-detecting registers. The proposed technique, applied on benchmark 3-stage pipeline operating at 0.35V, can reduce the error-detecting register count by 1.3-4.3×, total area by 15-40% and timing violation rate by 19-37×, compared to the conventional techniques.

Keywords. Ultra-low-voltage, in-situ error detection, pipeline

1. Introduction

Ultra-low-voltage (ULV) operation has gained a significant amount of attention for highly energy-efficient digital integrated circuits (ICs). Supply voltage (V_{DD}) of ICs can be scaled down to near or below transistor threshold voltage (V_{th}) for increasing energy efficiency, prolonging battery lifetime, and miniaturizing systems [14].

One of the most critical challenges in designing ULV ICs is to mitigate delay variability. In ULV regime, device current becomes exponentially sensitive to process, voltage, and temperature (PVT) variations. The large variability demands designers to add an excessive amount of margin for ensuring correct operation under the worst-case PVT conditions. Such margin, however, can severely limit the performance and energy efficiency of the ICs when they operate under nominal or best conditions. In [1] it is shown that the worst-case margin can force a chip to operate at only 10% of their potential performance although the chance to experience such worst-case condition is very low.

Error detection and correction (EDAC) techniques [2-9] coupled with dynamic voltage frequency scaling (DVFS) have been proposed to eliminate such margins while still ensuring correct operation across PVT variations. The conventional EDAC techniques use special pipeline registers having timing error detection capability. The controller for DVFS can take the error rate from error-detecting registers and modulate operating conditions, i.e., V_{DD} or cycle time (T_{CLK}), for making the circuits to operate on the edge of failure. EDAC and DVFS techniques can track and compensate static and slow-varying variations, which include systematic inter-die, intra-die, and random process variations, package and die supply voltage fluctuations, and ambient temperature variations, contributing a large portion of the entire variability of a chip. The remaining dynamic and fast-varying variations such as local V_{DD} variations, coupling noise, and cold spots need to be handled by error-detecting registers due to the limited response time of the EDAC and DVFS closed loop.

However, adding the capability of error detection to pipelined designs can incur a large amount of hardware (i.e., area) overhead, especially in ULV designs. This paper starts with analyzing the area overhead for two representative EDAC designs, one using flip-flops (or flops) [2] and the other using two-phase latches (or latches) [3], in the context of ULV designs. In order to reduce the overhead associated with in-situ error detection capability, we propose to sparsely insert error-detecting registers across pipeline stages, instead of every stage. To verify the effectiveness of the proposed technique, benchmark circuit (multiplier-based, T_{CLK}=40 Fan-Out-of-4 [FO4] delays, V_{DD}=0.35V) is designed and analyzed.

2. Overhead Analysis of the Existing Error-Detection Techniques in ULV Regime

In this section, the overhead of the two representative EDAC designs, the flop-based [2], and the latch-based [3] ones, are analyzed in near and sub-V_{th} operation. The conceptual schematics of the two designs are shown in Figs. 1(a) and 1(b) respectively.

2.1. Flop based Error Detection

Short-path padding: The existing flop based EDAC technique [2] severely suffers from the area overhead caused by short path padding. In this technique, any data arriving in error detection window is regarded as timing error. However, the signals that propagate through short paths also can arrive in this window, causing false error detection. In order to filter those correct signals arriving through short paths from actual timing errors, delay elements (e.g., buffers and inverters) are typically inserted to ensure the delay of short paths longer than that of error detection window.

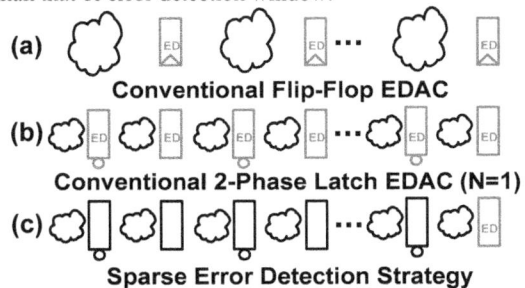

Fig. 1. (a) The conventional flop-based error detection. (b) The conventional latch-based error detection. (c) The proposed sparse error-detection. (ED – error detection pipeline registers)

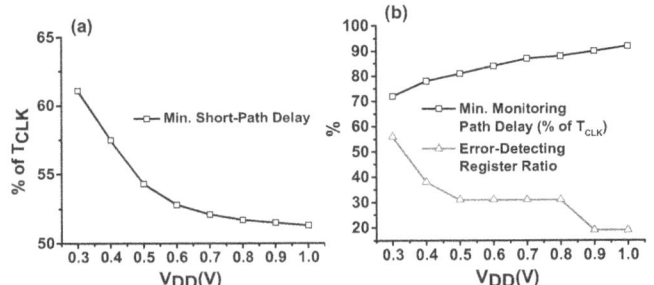

Fig. 2. At lower V_{DD}s, (a) a more number of short paths need to be delay-padded, and (b) a more number of flops needs to be replaced with error-detecting registers.

Short paths must be longer than the detection window even under the worst-case PVT condition. As shown in Fig. 2(a), this makes the overhead of short-path padding to increases at lower V_{DD} where delay variability becomes larger. In our experiment using a single-stage 16b multiplier synthesized at 40 FO4 delays in a 65nm CMOS, short paths should be longer than 62% of T_{CLK} when considering 3σ delay variation incurred by local process variations at 0.35V. As a result, a large amount of delay buffers are inserted, causing a 2.2× increase in combinational-logic area, as compared to the baseline design without error detection capability.

Error-detector insertion rate: Another major source of area overhead in the flop based technique is error-detecting registers to insert. The error-detecting registers often have 1.3-3.2× many transistors than the regular registers [2-7] and it can significantly increase sequential overhead to embed many of them on a chip. Typically, the delays of critical and near-critical paths are estimated under the worst-case dynamic variations. Those flops that receive data from the paths which can potentially violate T_{CLK} are replaced with error-detecting registers. In ULV regime, more paths are likely to violate T_{CLK} due to the higher sensitivity to the ranges of dynamic variations. We investigate the amount of critical and near-critical paths requiring error detection using the single-stage 16b multiplier across V_{DD}s from nominal down to 0.3V. As shown in Fig. 2(b), every path whose delay is longer than 76% of T_{CLK} should be monitored at 0.35V whereas only the paths longer than 92% of T_{CLK} need to be monitored at 1V. The increased amount of critical and near-critical paths require 44% of the total flops need to be replaced with error-detecting registers as compared to only 19% of the total flops at 1V.

2.2. Two-Phase Latch based Error Detection

An EDAC technique based on two-phase latch sequencing has been recently proposed [3]. One of the benefits of using the latch-based EDAC technique is to eliminate the false error detection induced by short paths since each consecutive latch stage becomes transparent at an opposite phase of clock signal.

Sequential overhead: Converting a flop based design to a latch based design can increase sequential overhead. In our experiment, such transformation performed on a 16b multiplier can increase the sequential area by 2.6× and the total area by 18%. This is because (i) a pair of latch has larger area than a single flop and (ii) the total number of latches is more than twice the number of flops in original design. i.e., 16 flops (i.e., roughly 32 latches) are transformed into 39 latches.

Error-detector insertion rate: Applying an EDAC technique to latch-based designs can significantly increase the number of error-detecting registers. This is because a latch-pipelined design has more sequential elements than a flop-based design. In addition, the delay of one latch stage is shorter (close to half of that of one flop stage), which can pronounce the impact of local variations. In our multiplier test circuits, a latch stage has 1.7× higher variability than a flop stage. As a result, 23 out of 39 latches needs to be replaced with error-detecting ones while only 7 out of 16 flops are replaced in the flop based design.

3. Sparse Error-Detecting Register Insertion

3.1. Concept

While the conventional techniques often provide error detection window of 50% of T_{CLK}, we find that more than half of the window is not utilized even under the worst-case delay variation induced by dynamic variations. To better utilize error detection window, as shown in Fig. 1(c), we propose to sparsely insert error-detecting registers in pipeline circuits. This strategy, applied onto two-phase latch based pipeline, can place error-detecting registers only every N latch stage, instead of every latch stage as in the conventional EDAC design based on latch-based sequencing as shown in Fig. 1(b) [3].

In the proposed sparse insertion of error-detecting registers, we do not intend to detect the timing violations (or delay surplus) produced in every latch stage as long as it can be passed over to the next stage via cycle-borrowing without imposing timing errors. The delay increases can then disappear while propagating through non-critical paths, or can be cycle-borrowed again to the next stage. Eventually, delay surplus can be accumulated and become larger than the size of cycle-borrowing window. Error-detecting registers are inserted before this accumulated delay is expected to exceed the size of cycle-borrowing window. This sparse insertion can significantly reduce sequential overhead associated with error-detecting registers.

Another significant benefit of sparse insertion of error-detectors is the reduced error rate. A critical path in one stage may not directly

feed another critical path in the next stage [13]. Therefore, some of the delay surplus produced in a stage can disappear in the subsequent stages via cycle-borrowing without causing errors. This self-healing effect can reduce the overhead of error detection and correction.

3.2. Inverter Chain Study - Simulation Setup

In order to evaluate the robustness and effectiveness of the proposed sparse error detection technique, we perform SPICE-level simulations using 20 latch stage circuits where each stage has a 25-FO4 long inverter chain. First, we determine the minimum T_{CLK} by measuring the delay of two latch-stages which include the delays of an inverter chain and a pair of latches. A minimal margin of 1 FO4 delay is added to T_{CLK} in order to account for input and clock uncertainties. Second, Monte-Carlo simulations with local process variations are performed. The T_{CLK} is set to the value found above. Across the simulation, the data arrival time in each latch stage is observed to determine if they are properly captured.

In this paper, the 6σ worst-case delay variability from local process variations is used to account for all the dynamic variations. The sources of dynamic variation include IR-drop (particularly across local power gating switches) [10,11], clock jitters, capacitive coupling [12], and temperature cold spots. In ULV operation, a smaller amount of driving current and relatively slow clock frequency can reduce the concern on inductive noise. In addition, device current has a positive temperature coefficient, i.e., current increases with higher temperature, in near and sub-threshold regimes, which can relieve the concern for temperature hot spots. To precisely estimate the amount of dynamic variations is a design-specific task and beyond the scope of this paper.

3.3. Inverter Chain Study - Sparseness Optimization

First, we analyze the conventional case where error-detecting registers are inserted in every stage, i.e., insertion sparseness or N is 1. The required window is defined as the minimum amount of window needed to capture 6σ worst-case delay from the Monte-Carlo simulation. As shown in Fig. 3(a), simulations show that the required amount of error-detection window increases as V_{DD} is scaled down since the variability grows. The results, however, also show that even at 0.3V, the small error-detection window of 19 % of T_{CLK} is sufficient for the worst-case dynamic variations when number of latch stages is 1(i.e. N=1), making the remaining error detection window of 31% of T_{CLK} redundant.

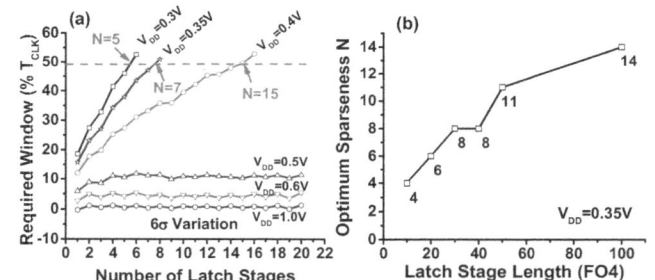

Fig. 3. (a)A significant number of latch stages can be skipped before error-detecting registers are inserted. At V_{DD}>0.4, the optimal sparseness is estimated to be larger than 20 latch stages. (b) The optimal sparseness's are estimated from 4 to 14 across the lengths of latch stages of 10-FO4 to 100-FO4 delays.

The under-utilization of error-detection window motivates us to investigate the way to sparsely insert error-detecting registers coupled with latch-based sequencing. This way we can accumulate delay surplus across stages without explicitly causing timing error, and the sparsely placed detection stage can utilize the entire error-detection window of 50% of T_{CLK}. As shown in Fig. 3(a), at 0.35V, up to 7 latch stages can be skipped without placing error-detecting registers under the 6σ worst-case dynamic variations. A notable observation is that the required error-detection window is considerably low at V_{DD}>0.4V. This is because the large cycle-borrowing window (50% of T_{CLK}) and the added 1-FO4 (2.5% of T_{CLK} in this case) margin, coupled with a smaller amount of delay variability, are sufficient to absolve all the dynamic variations at those relatively high V_{DD}s. N, therefore, can be larger than 20 latch stages (10 stages in flop based pipeline), and not found in our simulation.

We also investigate the optimal sparseness across different lengths of latch stages from 10 to 100 FO4 delays at 0.35V, particularly because the delay variability can become worse at the fine-grained pipeline stages, demanding wider error-detection window. As shown in Fig. 3(b), the optimal sparseness increases as latch stages become longer due to the larger amount of averaging effects. For the very aggressive latch stage of 10-FO4 delays, the optimal sparseness is still 4 (i.e., 2 stages in flop based pipeline). The optimal sparseness grows to 14 when latch stage is 100-FO4 long.

3.4. Optimal Sparsenes N for General Pipelines

In large-scale pipeline designs, it is not trivial to do the brute-force search for N as we did for inverter chains in Section 3.3. A strictly-non-optimal yet effort-saving approach is to find the N for the top several longest paths among all the stages. Critical paths can be found using commercial tools for static timing analysis (STA) and automatic test pattern generation (ATPG). For the found critical paths, we can run Monte-Carlo simulation with local process variations to estimate the mean (μ) and the standard deviation (σ). This μ and σ then can be used conservatively for all the other stages. Finally, based on the law of the sum of independent random variables (EQ1), we can estimate the optimal N which can fully utilize the detection window but can still cover the found worst-case dynamic variation (i.e., the 6σ value).

$$6\sqrt{N\sigma^2} < Detection\ Window \qquad (Eq.1)$$

4. Case Study with 3-Stage Pipeline

In Section 3, we propose and investigate the sparse insertion technique using FO4 inverter chains. In this section, we apply the proposed technique to more realistic benchmark circuits, a 3-stage pipeline design based on three 16b multipliers, targeting at $V_{DD}=0.35V$ and $T_{CLK}=40$-FO4 delays (Fig. 4).

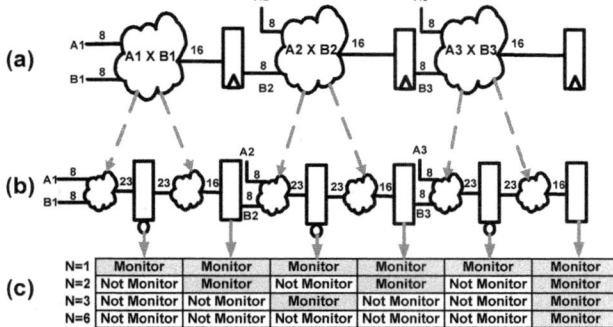

Fig. 4. Diagrams of (a) flop based, and (b) latch based 3-stage pipeline circuits using three 16b multipliers. (c) Multiple latch based pipelines are implemented for the different sparseness's.

4.1. Two-Phase Latch based Sequencing

We design the test circuits which are pipelined using two-phase latches. Using the industrial CAD tools and custom scripts, 3-stage pipeline flop based circuits are retimed into 6 latch stage ones (Fig. 4). Retiming was performed using half the T_{CLK} (20 FO4 delays) of the original flop based pipeline. We reserve cycle-borrowing window for the use when we add error-detection ability. The latches, therefore, are treated as flip-flops during retiming and the timing closure step becomes the same to that of the conventional flop based design.

Before being equipped with error-detection capability, the latch based design exhibits 18% larger area and 2.4× larger clock load than the flop based one, which translate roughly 24% energy overhead in the test circuits. This is because a pair of latches have a larger amount of clock load than a single flop and also the total number of latches is larger than twice the number of flops for the same pipeline circuits. As shown in Fig. 4, the flop based and latch based pipelines have 48 flops and 117 latches (48 transparent-high and 69 transparent-low latches),

respectively. This is inherent overhead that latch based design has. The gains from (i) cycle-borrowing and (ii) the elimination of short-path padding with the proposed technique, however, largely outweigh this intrinsic overhead as we will see in the Sections 4.2 and 4.3.

Pseudo Algorithm: Error-Detector Insertion

FIND μ and σ of the critical paths (Section 3.5)

FIND $N_{optimal}=\left(\frac{T}{12}\frac{1}{\sigma}\right)^2$ (Detection Window $=\frac{T}{2}$)

FOR N = 1 to $N_{optimal}$
    COMPUTE Required Window (RW) = $6\sqrt{N\sigma^2}$ (% of T_{CLK})
    FOR every N_{th} stages
Replace the registers that capture data from the paths having the slack that is less than the Required Window with error-detecting registers
    END FOR
END FOR

Fig. 5. Pseudo algorithm for error-detecting register insertion

4.2. Sparse Error Detection

Now we replace some of the latches and flops with the error-detecting ones based on the algorithm with several user-defined constraints (Fig. 5). The replacement process starts by finding the μ and σ of the critical path as we discussed in Section 3.4. In the latch based test circuit, the longest path appears in the first half stage (the stage having transparent-low latches at the end) which has $\mu=20$ FO4 and $\sigma=1.4$ FO4 delays (Table. 1). Next, we find the $N_{optimal}$ based on the and Eq. 1, which is found to be 6 at 0.35V. We still explore several N values from 1 to 6 for verifying the non-linearity caused by the circuit structures (Table. 1). For a given insertion sparseness of N, the algorithm finds the required window (RW) which represents the required size of error detection window for the given insertion sparseness. Then the process finds the pipeline latches which receive the data from the paths with the slack smaller than the RW. For example, for the latch based design with N=1, the RW is found to be 9.2FO4 delays (23% of T_{CLK}). The latches which receive data from the paths longer than 10.8FO4 (i.e., 20-9.2) need to be replaced with error-detecting latches. We perform the same insertion process (Fig. 5) for the flop-based design. In flop based design, however, the N is set to 1 since cycle-borrowing is not supported.

Design	T_{CLK}	μ (σ)	RW (% T_{CLK})	Error-Detector Insertion Rate
Flip-Flop N=1	40FO4	40FO4(1.6FO4)	24%	21/48(44%)
Latch N=1	40FO4	20FO4(1.36FO4)	23%	69/117(59%)
Latch N=2	40FO4	20FO4(1.36FO4)	33%	24/117(21%)
Latch N=3	40FO4	20FO4(1.36FO4)	40%	42/117(36%)
Latch N=6(opt)	40FO4	20FO4(1.36FO4)	50%	16/117(14%)

Table. 1. Required error-detector insertion rate for various N

The final and intermediate results of the insertion process are summarized in the Table. 1. At N=6, the total number of error-detecting registers is only 16 whereas at N=1 like the conventional two-phase-latch based EDAC techniques [3], the algorithm determines to replace 69 out of 117 latches with error-detecting registers. A notable observation is that the number of error-detecting registers for N=3 is larger than N=2. This is because the stage width in the middle of logic circuits is typically wider than in that in the input or output parts of logic circuits. Also, the paths ending in transparent-low latch stage were more critical than the paths ending in transparent-high latch stage. This observation implies that there is an additional overhead-reducing opportunity to place an error-detecting stage at the location of a pipeline where the width of logic is narrow.

4.3. Comparisons of Error Detection Techniques

Finally, we compare four design approaches – I. no error detection technique, II. the conventional error detection technique based on flop based sequencing [2], III. the conventional error detection technique based on two-phase latch based sequencing (N=1) [3], and IV. the proposed sparse insertion technique (N=6) – by applying them in the

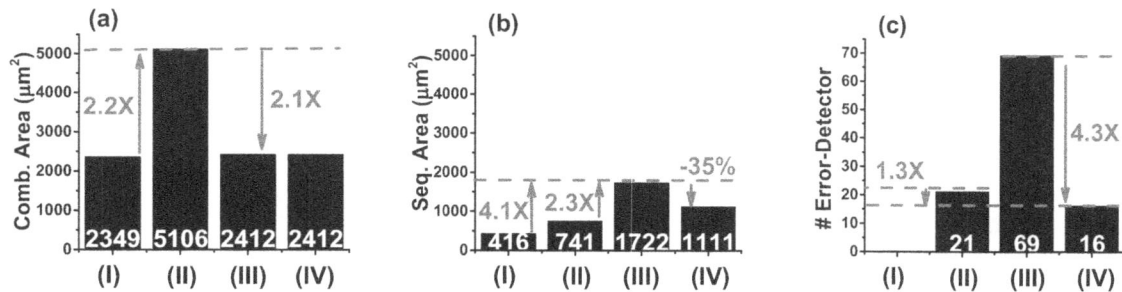

Fig. 6. Comparison of the conventional techniques and the proposed sparse insertion technique: (a) combinational area, (b) sequential area, (c) total number of error-detectors. (Abbreviation: I. baseline without error-detection capability II. conventional flop EDAC [2] III. conventional two-phase latch based EDAC with N=1 [3] IV. the proposed EDAC with sparsely inserted error-detecting registers [N=6])

same benchmark pipeline circuits. The area, error-detection register count, and timing violation rate are investigated. For the technique II, we use the well-known error-detecting register circuits having a main flip-flop, a shadow latch, an XOR gate, and a meta-stability detector [2]. For the techniques III and IV, we use the error-detecting register which has a main latch, a shadow latch with an opposite phase, and a XOR gate [3].

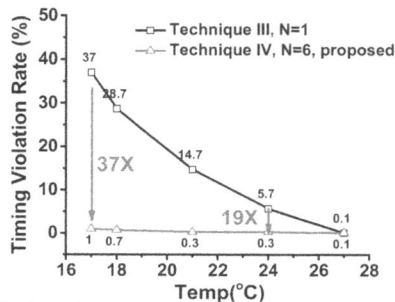

Fig. 7. Timing violation rate comparison for different N

Fig. 6(a) shows that the technique II can incur more than 2× area overhead in combinational logic due to the excessive amount of short-path padding requirement. The technique III uses two- phase latch based sequencing and incurs little increase in logic area since no short-path padding is necessary. The sequential area of technique II is increased by 1.8× (Fig. 6(b)) as 21 out of 48 flip-flops (44%) are replaced with error-detecting registers. The area for sequential circuits and the total area in technique III are increased by 4.1× and 50%, respectively as compared to the design without error detection capability, i.e., the technique I.

The proposed technique, i.e., the technique IV, significantly reduces the count of error-detecting registers by 1.3× and 4.3×, as compared to the techniques II and III, respectively (Fig. 6(c)). The total area is also reduced by 40% and 15% over the conventional techniques II and III. As compared to the baseline design having no error-detection capability, the area overhead is only 27%. Note that the error-detection technique can substantially improve performance and energy efficiency over the baseline design which is plagued by an excessive amount of margin across ranges of variations.

Fig. 7 shows the timing violation rates of the conventional error detection technique III, and the proposed technique IV. The timing violation rates are simulated by running the pipeline circuits with 300 random vectors at the fixed T_{CLK} for 10°C of temperature variations. The proposed technique can significantly reduce error rate since many of the potential timing violations (i.e., delay surpluses induced by variations) can disappear as signals propagate through non-critical paths across multiple stages. The smaller timing violation rate is critical to reduce the energy and throughput penalty associated with correction processes.

5. Conclusions

In this paper, we analyze the hardware overhead of error-detection techniques in the context of ULV design. We propose sparse error-detecting-register insertion coupled with latch-based sequencing for reducing hardware overhead and error rate. The effectiveness of proposed technique is confirmed with the experiment on the 3-stage benchmark circuits operating at 0.35V in a 65nm CMOS technology. The technique can reduce the error-detecting register count by 1.3×-4.3×, area by 15%-40% and timing violation rate by 19-37× without compromising error detection coverage.

Acknowledgement.

This work was supported by DARPA PERFECT and Catalyst Foundation.

References

[1] R. G. Dreslinski, et al., "Near-Threshold Computing: Reclaiming Moore's Law Through Energy Efficient Integrated Circuits," *Proceedings of the IEEE* , Vol.98, No. 2, pp. 253-266, 2010.

[2] S. Das, et al., "A Self-Tuning DVS Processor Using Delay-Error Detection and Correction," *Journal of Solid-State Circuits*, Vol. 41, No. 4, pp. 792-804, 2006.

[3] M. Fojtik, et al., "Bubble Razor: An Architectural-Independent Approach to Timing-Error Detection and Correction," *International Solid-State Circuits Conference*, 2012.

[4] S. Kim, et al., "Razor-Lite: A Side-Channel Error-Detection Register for Timing-Margin Recovery in 45nm SOI CMOS," *Internaltional Solid-State Circuits Conference*, 2013.

[5] K. A. Bowman, et al., "A 45nm Resilient Microprocessor Core for Dynamic Variation Tolerance," *Journal of Solid-State Circuits*, Vol. 46, No. 1, pp. 194-208, 2011.

[6] D. Bull, et al., "A Power-Efficient 32 bit ARM Processor Using Timing-Error Detection and Correction for Transient-Error Tolerance an d Adaptation to PVT Variation," *Journal of Solid-State Circuits*, Vol. 46, No. 1, pp. 18-31, 2011.

[7] R. Pawlowski, et al., "A 530mV 10-Lane SIMD Processor with Variation Resiliency in 45nm SOI," *International Solid-State Circuits Conference*, pp.492-494, 2012.

[8] S. Das, et al., "Razor II: In Situ Error Detection and Correction for PVT and SER Tolerance," *Journal of Solid-State Circuits*, Vol. 44, No. 1, pp. 32-48, 2009.

[9] I. Shin, et al., "A Pipeline Architecture with 1-cycle Timing Error Correction for Low Voltage Operations," *International Symposium on Low Power Electronics and Design*, pp. 199-204, 2013.

[10] B.H. Calhoun, et al., "Design Methodology for Fine-Grained Leakage Control in MTCMOS," *International Symposium on Low Power Electronics and Design*, pp. 104-109, 2003.

[11] M. Seok, "Decoupling Capacitor Design Strategy for Minimizing Supply Noise of Ultra Low Voltage Circuits," *ACM/DAC/IEEE Design Automation Confernece*, pp. 968-973, 2012.

[12] H. Fuketa, et al., "Increase of Crosstalk Noise Due to Imbalanced Threshold Voltage Between nMOS and pMOS in Subthreshold Logic Circuits," *Journal of Solid-State Circuits*, Vol. 48, No. 8, pp. 1986-1994, 2013.

[13] M. R. Choudhury, et al., "Masking timing errors on speed-paths in logic circuits," *Design, Automation & Test in Europe Conference & Exhibition*, pp. 87-92, 2009.

[14] M. Seok, et al., "The Phoenix Processor: A 30pW platform for sensor applications," *IEEE Symposium on VLSI Circuits*, pp. 188-189, 2008.

Quantifying the Impact of Variability on the Energy Efficiency for a Next-generation Ultra-green Supercomputer

Francesco Fraternali
University of Bologna
francesco.fraternali@unibo.it

Andrea Bartolini
University of Bologna, ETHZ
a.bartolini@unibo.it

Carlo Cavazzoni
SCAI, CINECA, Italy
c.cavazzoni@cineca.it

Giampietro Tecchiolli
Eurotech SpA, Italy
giampietro.tecchiolli@eurotech.com

Luca Benini
University of Bologna, ETHZ
luca.benini@unibo.it

ABSTRACT

Supercomputers, nowadays, aggregate a large number of nodes sharing the same nominal HW components (eg. processors and GPGPUS). In real-life machines, the chips populating each node are subject to a wide range of variability sources, related to performance and temperature operating points (i.e. ACPI p-states) as well as process variations and die binning. Eurora is a fully operational supercomputer prototype that topped July 2013 Green500 and it represents a unique 'living lab' for next-generation ultra-green supercomputers. In this paper we evaluate and quantify the impact of variability on Eurora's energy-performance tradeoffs under a wide range of workload intensity.

Categories and Subject Descriptors

B.8.0 [Performance and Reliability]

Keywords

Supercomputer, Variability, Energy Efficiency, Energy Aware.

1. INTRODUCTION AND RELATED WORK

The TOP500 organization collects and ranks worldwide the peak performance, measured in Flops (floating point operation per second), of new supercomputer installations when running Linpack Benchmarks. TOP500 rankings in the last twenty years show an exponential growth of peak performance that is predicted to enter the ExaFlops (10^{18}) range in 2018 [2]. Today's most powerful Supercomputer, Tianhe-2, reaches 33.2 PetaFlops with 17.8 MW of power dissipation that increases to 24 MW when considering also the cooling infrastructure [1]. This data shows that Exascale supercomputers cannot be built by simply expanding the number of processing nodes and leveraging technology scaling, as power demand would increase and would become unsustainable (hundreds of MW of power). According to [4], an acceptable value for an Exascale supercomputer is 20 MW. To reach this target, current supercomputer systems must achieve a goal of 50 GFlops/W. To improve the energy efficiency of supercomputers, the Green500 list ranks Top500 supercomputers by energy efficiency metric, measured as GFlops per

Watt (GOPS/W) [3]. From the Green500 perspective, the current fastest supercomputer (Tianhe-2) is only 40th delivering 1.9 GFlops/W.

Scaled process technology is increasingly affected by process variability [7, 5]. Pang et al. show that variation increase almost of 2x when moving from 90nm to 45nm [7]. Providers use speed binning [6] to reduce the impact of variability by adjusting the same nominal speed to devices that share similar performance. However, in a supercomputer that includes thousands of CPUs of the same bin the effect of process variability can become relevant. Authors in [8, 11] show that process variation can be exploited by operating systems to differentiate the peak performance of processing elements while ensuring the same target lifetime of the device. In addition, Paterna et al. propose an ILP formulation to minimize the energy consumption of a multimedia multicore platform affected by variability[12]. All these works are based on simulation results and modeling assumption without evaluating the impact of process variation in a real large-scale high-performance computing system.

In addition to process variation, the same device can operate at different frequency and voltage levels (DVFS, ACPI states) [9]. These are exploited by the operating system to adapt the power consumption to workload requirements, leading to power savings[13, 16]. The Linux operating system uses a default SW governor called "on-demand" that adapts the frequency to the CPU load [10]. Moreover today CPUs have dedicated HW capabilities to overclock (in the so-called turbo mode) dynamically when the estimated power consumption and temperature are not critical [14]. Lo et al. evaluate the impact of turbo logic on energy-delay-product squared (ED2) for different workloads running on different classes of real HW (from laptop to server node) and show that not all the benchmarks benefit from running with active turbo mode. By modulating the turbo activation accordingly to the memory access rate of the application they achieve 68% of improvements in ED2. However the ED2 metric is mainly relevant for latency critical applications, and thus the same considerations do not directly apply to purely energy and energy-per-delay (EDP) metrics[14].

More than 85% of TOP500 supercomputers are based on a scalable architecture where a "node" is replicated many times and connected to the system through a fast interconnect[2]. In almost 90% of today's supercomputers the node embeds x86 CPUs and the 96% use Linux OS. The Eurora Supercomputer prototype, developed by Eurotech and Cineca [15] has ranked first in the Green500 list in July 2013, achieving 3.2 GFlops/W on the Linpack Benchmark. Eurora has been supported by PRACE 2IP project [19] and it will serve as testbed for next generation Tier-0 system. Its outstanding performance is achieved by adopting an heterogeneous architecture and a direct liquid cooling that is suitable for

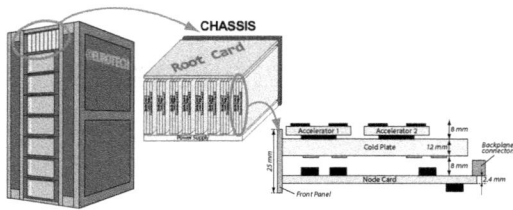

Figure 1: Eurora architecture

hot water recycling and free-cooling solutions [17]. For its characteristics Eurora is a perfect vehicle for testing and characterizing next-generation "greener" supercomputers.

In this paper we analyze the impact of different variation sources (HW and SW) on Eurora in terms of performance and energy metrics. We limit our analysis on the general purpose processors only as their impact will be visible in all the workloads. We leave the accelerator study for future works. The main contributions of the paper are: i) We classify the major sources of variability by conducting a large set of experiments on Eurora. The variation sources can be classified as desired and undesired, and software and hardware; ii) We measure the impact of process variation after speed binning in two Intel Xeon E5 processors family, which can lead up to the 15% of the energy variation; iii) We measure the impact of voltage and frequency scaling and we show that the energy figures present a minimum far from the maximum frequency and this depends on the application peculiarity;

To the authors' knowledge this is the first open study on the impact of variability on the energy efficiency of a full-scale green supercomputer. In our characterization effort we consider both well-controller "synthetic benchmarks" and a real-life workload, namely, Quantum Espresso (QE). QE is a Computational Material Science community code, publicly available and it is one of the currently "hot applications" for high-end supercomputers[1]. Furthermore, QE is included in many benchmark suites[18].

In the remainder of the paper, Section 2 presents an overview of the Eurora Platform, Section 3 provides a taxonomy of the variation sources in a supercomputer system and Section 4 shows the workloads and tests for our characterization. Finally, Section 5 shows the results obtained and the conclusions and future work are reported in Section 6.

2. EURORA

The Eurora system consists of a half-rack containing 8 stacked chassis, each of them designed to host 8 node cards and 16 expansion cards (see Fig. 1). The node card is the basic element of the system and consists of 2 Intel Xeon E5 series (SandyBridge) processors and 2 expansion cards configured to host an accelerator module. One half of the nodes use E5-2658 processors including 8 cores with 2.1 GHz clock speed (Max Turbo Frequency 2.8 GHz), 20 MB caches, and 95 W maximum TDP. The rest of the nodes use E5-2687W processors including 8 cores with 3.1 GHz clock speed (Max Turbo Frequency 3.8 GHz), 20 MB caches, and 150 W maximum TDP. The accelerator modules can be Nvidia Tesla (Kepler) or, alternatively, Intel MIC KNC.

Each node of Eurora currently executes a SMP CentOS Linux distribution version 6.3. The kernel is configured with hyper-threading HW support disabled and on-demand power governor [10]. This governor allows superusers in the system to change the CPU frequency using the */sys/dev* filesystem. Eurora features an integrated and low-overhead monitoring system made-up by a set of software daemons and parsing scripts. It allows to monitor every five second for each node and each processing element (CPUs,GPUs,Xeon

Phy) workload characteristics as well as clock frequency, power and temperature[20].

3. VARIABILITY IN SUPERCOMPUTERS

In this section we define the taxonomy of the different variability sources that are relevant in a supercomputer environment. We classify them from the user-perspective (*desired* vs. *undesired*) and from their nature (*HW* vs. *SW*).

Desired Hardware Variability: We consider in this class both the processing element heterogeneity and the ACPI performance states. Eurora nodes are build using different HW accelerators and different series of the same CPU family (speed binning). Moreover within each node, each of the above CPUs is capable of scaling its own voltage and frequency. If the fastest state is selected, then the turbo mode is enabled. In Eurora this ranges for the 32 nodes with E5-2658 from 1.2GHz to 2.1GHz with 100MHz step while for the 32 nodes with E5-2687W from 1.2GHz to 3.1GHz with 200MHz step.

Undesired Hardware Variability: This class groups all the variability sources that come from non-idealities in chip technology, fabrication and operation which can lead the same device to operate at different PVT points and ambient conditions. This can cause different power and temperature values for different CPUs of the same family while executing the same workload at the same operating point.

Desired Software Variability: This class maps the different applications which execute different type and number of operations and have a different usage of resources. This may reflect in a variable performance and energy consumption and different sensitivity to variability sources.

Undesired Software Variability: This class accounts for all the software fluctuations that introduce variations in energy and performance of the same code that runs on the same node multiple times. Those variation sources include the operating system interference, external interrupts, the effect of shared resources contention, etc.

Section 4 describes the workloads we have designed to highlight the effect of the presented variability sources. Section 5 measures their impact on the CPUs of Eurora.

4. WORKLOAD DESIGN

In this Section we present the benchmarks and tests performed. We used a combination of synthetic and real-life applications:

i) *SYNT CPU*: this synthetic parallel benchmark has one thread for core. Each thread consists of a loop where an ALU operation is executed on a circular buffer. By modulating the circular buffer size we can mimic different cache miss ratio. In this particular case, we used 2^{37} iterations and a buffer dimension of 4KB per core, that fits the L1 cache emulating a CPU bound application (the L1 size for both the Intel Xeon E5-Series is 64KB).

ii) *SYNT Mem*: this benchmark is similar to the previous one but it uses a circular buffer of 4MB per thread and 2^{33} iterations. Both the Intel Xeon E5-Series used for our tests, present a L3 shared cache of 20 MB. As each thread has its own circular buffer, the overall memory footprint (32MB) exceeds the L3 size. This is sufficient to let each memory access miss in the L1, L2, L3 cache and hit in the DRAM, emulating a strongly memory bound task execution.

iii) *QE*: Quantum ESPRESSO is a freely available integrated suite of computer codes for electronic-structure calculations and materials modeling at the nanoscale.[2] Quantum Espresso is one of the most used code in high-end supercomputers. Moreover QE main computational kernels include

---

[1]www.quantum-espresso.org

[2]Quantum ESPRESSO is an initiative of the DEMOCRITOS National Simulation Center (Trieste) and of its partners.

dense parallel linear algebra and 3D parallel FFT, which are both relevant in many HPC applications. We configure QE to calculate the electronic structure of the Al^2O^3 in 3K points and we use the thread affinity to run in parallel on all the available cores within one node.

To generate the data-set used for characterizing the variability sources in Eurora we have designed a PBS script that first scales equally the frequencies for all the cores of the node in which is running and then executes five time the same benchmark. At the beginning and at the end of each benchmark run, we save the initial time and end time. The script iterates these operations for all the available DVFS states and for the three benchmarks considered. The script is then executed in all the nodes of Eurora. Off-line the log information are used to navigate the traces generated by the Eurora monitoring framework[20] (Section 2). We do this to compute for each benchmark run: the execution time, the average node power consumption (CPUs Package Power + DRAMs Power), the average real frequency of the core, the energy and the EDP.

5. EXPERIMENTAL RESULTS

This Section quantifies the impact of all variability sources defined in Section 3 in terms of energy/performance.

Desired Hardware and Software Variability: In the first test we compare the standard operation (i.e turbo mode) of the two classes of nodes (with 2.1GHz CPUs and with 3.1GHz CPUs). Table 1 shows the energy/performance metrics for the two cases while executing the three test benchmarks. Values are averaged among all the nodes of the same class and among the repetitions of the same workload.

Nodes	Power[W]	Ex Time[s]	Energy[KJ]	EDP[MJs]
Benchmark SYNT CPU				
2.1GHz	114	459	52.4	24.0
3.1GHz	221(+94%)	283(-62%)	62.9(+20%)	17.8(-35%)
Benchmark SYNT Mem				
2.1GHz	141	440	62.4	27.4
3.1GHz	240(+70%)	435(-1.5%)	104(+67%)	45.2(+65%)
Benchmark QE				
2.1GHz	118	459	54.3	24.9
3.1GHz	223(+89%)	323(-42%)	72.4(+33%)	23.4(-7%)

Table 1: Desired Hardware Variability Results

Table 1 shows that the same application can have up to 94% of power loss, 62% of performance gain, 67% of energy loss and 65% of EDP loss when using 3.1GHz nodes w.r.t 2.1GHz nodes. These trends depends significantly on the application itself. Comparing the two synthetic benchmarks we notice that *SYNT CPU* at 3.1GHz consumes 24% more power, gains 60% speed-up, resulting in a 40% lower energy loss. In addition it saves the 35% of EDP differently from the *SYNT MEM* that loses the 65% of EDP in the same HW. The same table shows that QE benchmark is in between the two corner cases. This result is not unexpected and shows that high-speed nodes deliver significantly more performance for CPU-intensive workloads. But when the memory system effects dominate, they are extremely energy inefficient and do not provide major EDP gains even in the real-life application case. So, future green computer may decide to go for a much smaller fraction of fast nodes in case of sporadic ultra-CPU-dominated workload, and use mostly the more efficient balanced-CPU nodes.

To evaluate the impact of DVFS states on the energy/performance metrics for the different benchmarks, we report in Figure 2 the execution time, power and energy for the two classes of nodes at the different DVFS states. Looking at the graphs we can clearly notice that in all the plots the 2.1GHz nodes lay on top of the 3.1GHz for all the frequency settings. The energy is not monotonic and behaves differently for the

three cases. For the *SYNT CPU* and the *QE* the minimum energy consumption happens at around 2.0GHz, while the *SYNT MEM* has minimum energy at the lower frequency.

Benchmarks	SYNT CPU		SYNT Mem		QE	
Class Nodes [GHz]	2.1	3.1	2.1	3.1	2.1	3.1
Optimal Frequency [GHz]	1900	2000	1200	1200	1700	1800
Ex Time Overhead [%]	-11	-70	-18	-23	-20	-65
Energy Saving [%]	+2	+18	+18	+50	+3	+27

Table 2: Energy Optimization Margin

Table 2 quantifies for the three benchmarks the energy/performance improvements when the nodes operates at the optimal frequency for the energy consumption w.r.t standard operating conditions (i.e. turbo mode). Choosing the optimal frequency for minimum energy leads to energy savings up to 18% for *SYNT CPU* and savings of the 50% for the *SYNT MEM* benchmark. *QE* instead saves the 27%. From Table 2 we can see that for the majority of workloads high energy efficiency does not coincide with peak performance. Hence, for energy-constrained supercomputers new management strategy for allocating machine resources to workload can be conceived that reward energy efficiency with respect to pure performance.

Undesired Hardware Variability In this analysis we compare the energy/performance of different nodes. We focus this analysis on the synthetic benchmarks only as they highlight the corner cases and are subjected to less variability among repetitions. We consider for each benchmark the average on five run.

Figure 3a,b) quantify for the two benchmarks the effect of process variability among Eurora nodes. In addition to the previous consideration on the energy variation which differs from the performance maximum, we can notice that for both the benchmarks different nodes show a significant variability on energy consumption which is consistent at all the DVFSA point. Figure 3c) quantifies the maximum variation between all nodes of the same class at the different frequencies while executing the same benchmark. We can notice that the energy variation is entirely due to the power variation as the execution time variation is negligible. Energy variation can reach almost 9% and its average is a non-negligible 7%. For the memory-bound benchmark (Figure 4a,b)) we can see an outlier (node57). This node which has the same nominal characteristics of node33-64 has DRAM clock half of the other nodes. This explain why the same node was not an outlier for cpu-bound benchmark(Figure 3a,b)). We removed this node in the computation of the maximum variation reported in Figure 4c) between all the nodes of the same class at the different frequencies while executing the same benchmark. From the plot we can see that memory bound applications incur in higher variability w.r.t CPU bound one. With peak variation of 15% and average of 8%. This can be explained by higher sensibility to the DRAM variability. It must be noted that these values are computed on 32 nodes and thus are expected to increase in larger systems. Results suggest that, even in today's technology, node-to-node variability has significant impact and it will increase as we move to scaled-down nodes. Variability managements in software (e.g. through proper workload allocation and scheduling by a variability-aware job dispatcher) will play a key role in future Exascale systems.

Undesired Software Variability We evaluated it by laun-ching several times the same benchmark on the same hardware node. Our results show for QE a SW variability of the 5% while for the synthetic benchmarks is less than 1%.[3] This should be considered as unavoidable process noise

---

[3]Synthetic benchmarks have more simple and regular computational patterns.

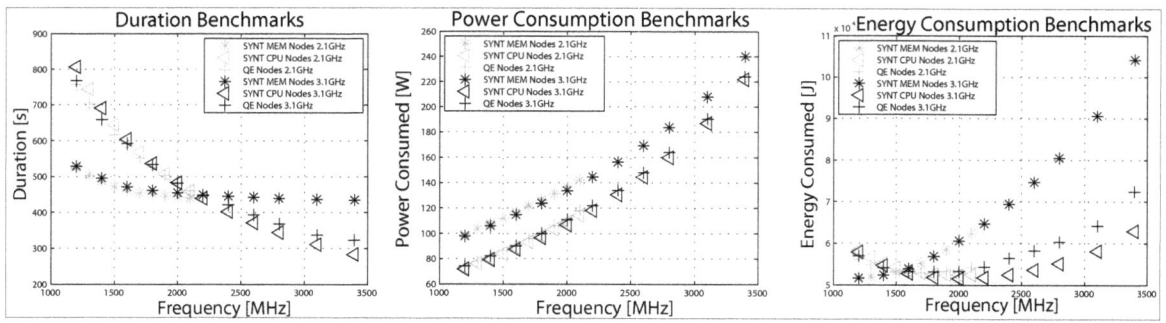

Figure 2: 3.1GHz nodes vs 2.1GHz nodes - Mean Ex Time, Power, Energy

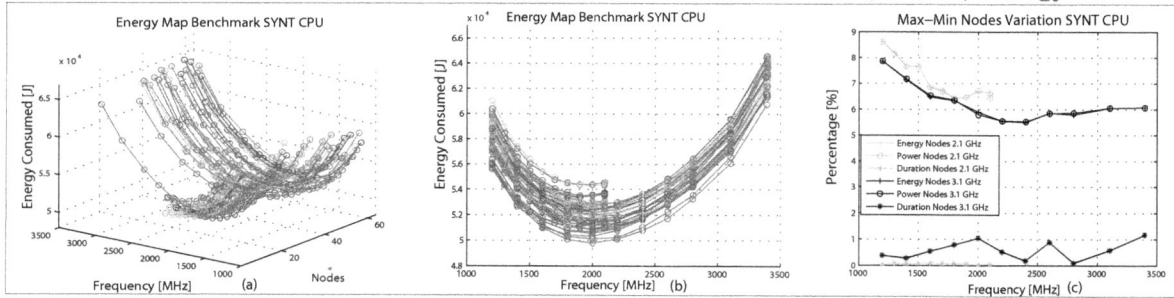

Figure 3: Energy Map SYNT CPU Results

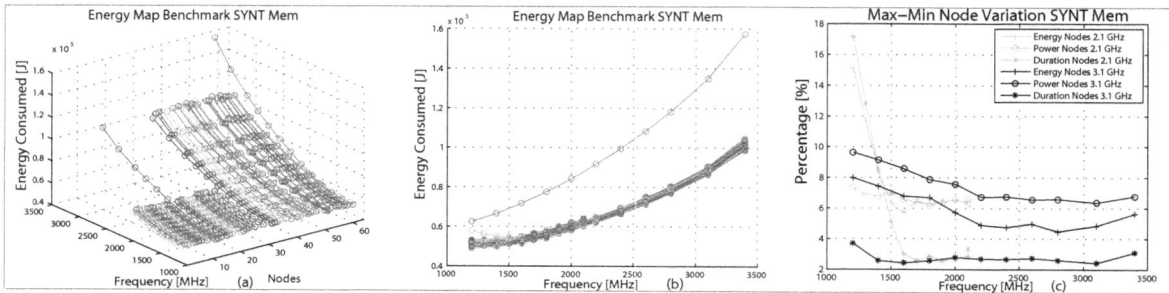

Figure 4: Energy Map SYNT MEM Results

and managed properly when designing feedback-based energy management techniques. In addition, we believe that SW variability should be analyzed deeply to derive programming guidelines and APIs for better controlling it and avoiding its blowup in future exascale systems.

6. CONCLUSION AND FUTURE WORK

In this paper we have presented the first characterization of variability effects on a real first-class "green" supercomputer. Our analysis show a clear evidence of a significant variability within the computational nodes, operation point and workload. We measured up to 15% of energy variation in between nodes at the same operating condition and under the same workload. We quantify that optimal DVFS selection can lead to an energy saving ranging between 18% and 50%: in a real supercomputer application we measure 27% energy saving w.r.t. the default turbo mode. In future work we will extend this characterization to the Eurora accelerators.

ACKNOWLEDGMENTS
This work was supported by the FP7 ERC Advance project MULTITHERMAN (g.a. 291125), by the PRACE 2IP EU project (g.a. RI-283493) and by the YINS RTD project (no. 20NA21_150939), evaluated by the Swiss NSF and funded by Nano-Tera.ch with Swiss Confederation financing.

7. REFERENCES

[1] J. Dongarra. Visit to the National University for Defense Technology Changsha, China. *Technical report*, University of Tennessee, 06 2013.

[2] J. J. Dongarra, H.W. Meuer, E. Strohmaier, et al. Top500 supercomputer sites. *Supercomputer*, 13:89-111, 1997.

[3] W. chun Feng and K. Cameron. The green500 list: Encouraging sustainable supercomputing. *Computer*, 40(12):50-55, 2007.

[4] K. Bergman, et al. Exascale computing study: Technology challenges in achieving exascale systems. Tech rep, 09 2008.

[5] K. A. Bowman, et al. Impact of die-to-die and within-die parameter fluctuations on the maximum clock frequency distribution for gigascale integration *IEEE J. Solid-StateCircuits*, vol.37, no. 2, pp. 183-190, Feb. 2002.

[6] A. Datta, et al. Speed binning aware design methodology to improve profit under parameter variations In *Proc. ASP-DAC*, 2006, pp. 712-717.

[7] L.-T. Pang, et al. Measurement and analysis of variability in 45-nm strained-Si CMOS technology *IEEE J. Solid-State Circuits*, vol. 44, no. 8, pp. 2233-2243, Aug. 2009.

[8] P. Mercati, A. Bartolini, F. Paterna, T. S. Rosing, and L. Benini. Workload and user experience-aware dynamic reliability management in multicore processors. In *Proceedings of the th Annual Design Automation Conference*, DAC '13, pages 2:1-2:6, New York, NY, USA, 2013. ACM.

[9] ACPI Advanced Configuration and Power Interface Specification http://www.Intel.com/products/processor/manuals/

[10] V. Pallipadi and A. Starikovskiy. The ondemand governor: past, present and future. In *Proceedings of Linux Symposium, vol. 2, pp. 223-258*, 2006.

[11] C. Zhuo, D. Sylvester, and D. Blaauw. Process variation and temperature-aware reliability management. In *Design, Automation Test in Europe Conference Exhibition (DATE), 2 1*, pages 580-585, march 2010.

[12] F.Paterna, et al. Variability-Aware Task Allocation for Energy-Efficient Quality of Service Provisioning in Embedded Streaming Multimedia Applications In *IEEE Transactions on Computers*. 61(7) July 2012

[13] G. Dhiman, G. Marchetti, and T. Rosing. Green: A System for Energy-Efficient Management of Virtual Machines. ACM TODAES, 16(1):6:1-6:27, 2010.

[14] D. Lo, et al. Dynamic Management of TurboMode in Modern Multi-core Chips In *Proc. HPCA*, 2014, Orlando, USA

[15] C. Cavazzoni. Eurora: a european architecture toward exascale. In Proceedings of the Future HPC Systems: the Challenges of Power-Constrained Performance, page 1. ACM, 2012.

[16] K. Flautner and T. Mudge Vertigo: Automatic performance-setting for linux. ACM SIGOPS Operating Systems Review 36 (SI), 105-116

[17] J. Kim, M. Ruggiero, and D. Atienza. Free cooling-aware dynamic power management for green datacenters. In *Proc. HPCS International Conference on*, pages 140-146, 2012.

[18] P. Giannozzi, et al J.Phys.:Condens.Matter, 21, 395502 (2009) http://dx.doi.org/10.1088/0953-8984/21/39/395502.

[19] PRACE. Partnership for Advanced Computing in Europe.

[20] A. Bartolini, et al Unveiling Eurora - Thermal and power characterization of the most energy-efficient supercomputer in the world DATE 2014, doi=10.7873/DATE2014.290

MIN: A Power Efficient Mechanism to Mitigate the Impact of Process Variations on Nanophotonic Networks

Majed Valad Beigi and Gokhan Memik

Department of EECS, Northwestern University, Evanston, IL

majed.beigi@northwestern.edu and memik@eecs.northwestern.edu

ABSTRACT

In this paper, we introduce MIN, a novel method for assigning wavelengths to nodes dynamically on a nanophotonic network to minimize the impact of process variations (PVs). Among the available wavelengths on a waveguide, a subset of them, called bubbles, are left intentionally unused. These bubbles are then borrowed by nodes dynamically to improve the channel utilization. We present an express wavelength regulation approach to manage these assignments efficiently. Evaluation results reveal that MIN can recover 80% of bandwidth loss due to PVs and achieve 41% trimming power reduction compared to state-of-the-art alternative approaches.

Categories and Subject Descriptors

C.1.2 [**Computer System Organization**]: Process Architectures – *Interconnect architectures*

General Terms

Design, Reliability, Performance

Keywords

Nanophotonic, Process variations, Networks-on-chip

1. INTRODUCTION

The advances in deep sub-micron technology have enabled the integration of a verity of components onto a single chip. Furthermore, ITRS [1] has predicted that the number of processing cores in multiprocessor systems-on-chips (MPSoCs) will reach 1,000 by 2020. Therefore, with increasing on-chip networks size, the energy efficiency, latency, and high bandwidth of on-chip networks are becoming even more important [2]. Electrical networks have several limitations in such large scales and optical interconnect networks is considered as one of the most important potential alternative for future many core microprocessors [3-5].

Optical interconnects possess many promising characteristics. However, they also face several key challenges. Arguably, the most important challenge is the reliability of nanophotonic on-chip network components. Typically, there are two crucial obstacles for reliable nanophotonic on-chip communications: Process variations (PVs) and thermal sensitivity of silicon photonic devices [6-8, 22]. PVs refer to inaccuracies in fabrication and changes in physical dimensions such as thickness of silicon or, width of waveguide caused by lithography imperfection and etch non-uniformity of devices [7]. On the other hand, thermal sensitivity relates to spatial and temporal variation in the refractive index of silicon-photonic devices [9]. Those changes will directly affect the microring resonator (μring) [10-12], which is extremely compact (3-10 μm radius). Under process and thermal variations, μrings fail to resonate at the designated wavelengths. This leads to communication errors and bandwidth loss. Several studies have reported that a 1 nm variation in the μring width can shift a μring's resonance by approximately 0.5 nm. Similarly, a single degree change in temperature can shift a μring's resonance by roughly 0.1 nm [13, 14].

ISLPED'14, August 11 – 13, 2014, La Jolla, CA, USA
Copyright is held by the owner/author(s). Publication rights licensed to ACM.
ACM 978-1-4503-2975-0/14/08...$15.00.
http://dx.doi.org/10.1145/2627369.2627660

Moreover, the spacing between two adjacent wavelengths is less than 1 nm [9] in a wavelength division multiplexing (WDM) enabled optical interconnect; this means μring diameter variation of 2 nm or thermal variation of 10°C would bring the μring to resonate at the neighboring wavelength. If a μring resonates at an unassigned wavelength, the data sent on the new wavelength is corrupted. In addition, the original wavelength is not used causing a decrease in the achievable bandwidth.

There exist two common techniques to eliminate resonance frequency shifts of μrings. The first one is post-fabrication physical trimming, where the refractive index of a μring is adjusted by employing high energy particles such as UV light or electron beam to correct the resonance [7, 8, 15]. However, since this technique requires trimming for each μring individually, it is unclear that it is practical for high volume production [7, 10]. In addition, this technique does not eliminate resonance shifts due to temperature variations. The second technique is power trimming. Specifically, to correct the resonance wavelength, μrings are either heated (for red-shifting, i.e., increase their resonance wavelength) or carrier injection is applied (for blue-shifting, i.e., to reduce the resonance wavelength). The most important problem with this approach is the high power consumption [6, 10, 13]. For example, a total of ~26W is necessary for trimming in the Corona network, which constitutes 54% of the total power dedicated to the network [5]. In this paper, we present techniques to minimize the trimming power needed for correcting resonant wavelengths.

We propose a novel methodology, called MIN, to reduce the impact of PVs in optical networks while keeping bandwidth at maximum and power consumption at minimum. The objective of this approach is to maximize the number of usable wavelengths for all nodes through properly arranging μring resonant wavelengths while considering the power consumption. To reach this goal, the first step of our approach is based on the idea that a μring should be trimmed to a nearby wavelength rather than the one statically assigned to it. Hence, we divide the wavelengths in a waveguide to a number of regions where their wavelengths are determined based on the power trimming limitation of current injection and heating. We also define a region within which the resonant wavelength can be shifted. These shifts are made possible by our initial assignment of the wavelengths. Specifically, MIN divides the wavelengths into regions and leaves a few wavelengths unused within each region. These unused wavelengths are called bubbles. Depending on the traffic rate and the conditions of the μrings, these bubbles can be allocated to different nodes. This allocation is performed at fixed intervals. At each time epoch, we perform the allocation of the bubbles to requesting nodes while minimizing the power needed for trimming. We give higher priority to nodes under heavy PVs than others. It is worthy to mention that using bubbles creates more opportunities for selecting fine-tuned μrings, which result in less trimming power to correct their resonance wavelengths. Further, the wavelength assignments are monitored periodically by an express wavelength regulation approach that is triggered to manage the wavelength assignment and also arbitrate among multiple nodes requesting access to the same bubbles efficiently.

The idea of dynamically assigning wavelengths to μrings has been explored recently: Nitta et al. and Xu et al. have shown the benefits of allowing μrings to resonate at its closest wavelength instead of the originally assigned one [6, 7]. However, these approaches rely on additional hardware cost (e.g., using additional μrings) and/or are power hungry [8]. Our results, described in Section 4, reveal that our approach achieves 41% lower consumption and 61% higher bandwidth in comparison against these state-of-art methods. We also show that this is achieved with minimal area overhead; the hardware necessary to implement MIN causes 3.5% area overhead compared to the baseline design.

The rest of this paper is organized as follows. Section 2 describes our methodology. The experimental results are presented in Section 3 and Section 4 concludes the paper with a summary.

2. MIN Methodology

In this section, we present the proposed MIN methodology. As we mentioned earlier, μrings are drifted from their resonance due to process and thermal variations. This drift can be corrected by heating or current injection. Both of these methods are power hungry. As a result, the total trimming power increases with the total number of μrings. Moreover, even using efficient μring heating approaches such as in-plane heaters and air-undercut [16, 17] does not result in significant reduction: it is estimated that μring heating power still consumes 38% of total network power with efficient trimming hardware [4]. Another important property of these techniques is that the power consumption varies with the amount of wavelength shift: on average, the power needed for blue- and red-shifting of a 3-μm μring are 130 μW/nm and 240 μW/nm, respectively [6, 10]. Hence, minimizing the amount of shift results in reduced trimming power consumption.

Our technique, described in the next section, tries to achieve that. In addition to the power limitation, another important limitation is the amount of shift possible with this technique. Specifically, current injection to shift the resonance wavelength towards the blue end of spectrum causes signal loss: 0.4nm shift results in 1 dB signal loss [7,13]. As a result, the current injection can be applied only for short shifts. By using bubbles and efficient wavelength assignment to use less trimming power under PVs, our technique can reduce the power and increase the bandwidth. Here, in order to describe the MIN approach, we first provide an overview of the proposed design. Second, the details of the MIN technique are described. Third, we explain the proposed wavelength assignment mechanism and the wavelength regulation.

2.1 Overview of MIN design

There are three alternatives to organize the optical channels to build nanophotonic crossbars, namely SWMR, MWSR, and MWMR [3-5]. In this paper we employ MWMR [4] as the baseline crossbar design. We have chosen this topology as it provides the most energy-efficient topology compared to SWMR and MWSR. We slightly modify the topology in order to support the MIN approach. The channel defined here is a set of wavelengths used to transfer packets. MWMR, which is a dynamic channel allocation scheme, can improve channel utilization and network throughput with channel sharing. Although MWMR requires additional router complexity and more μrings compared to SWMR and MWSR, the added flexibility and reduced overall power consumption makes it more attractive than other topologies. In addition, the large number of μrings in MWMR allows the design to be provisioned with any number of channels. As a result, PVs can be handled efficiently without the need of adding extra μrings. Finally, we must highlight that our approach can be easily applied to SWMR and MWSR.

In our design, a set of wavelengths is devoted for establishing bubbles to be employed in the presence of PVs. Bubbles operate similar to other wavelengths in the network but they can be borrowed by nodes for a determined period of time. However, if a node with PVs requests an idle bubble, it will have priority over other nodes. In MIN, we use a single-round data channel [4] because it reduces the waveguide length, which reduces the overall energy consumption.

2.2 MIN Mechanism

The first step in our approach is based on the idea that a μring does not have to be trimmed to a predefined wavelength that may be far from its current resonating wavelength. We first divide the waveguide into regions; each μring is shifted within its region. Specifically, for each interval, we find the region that a μring belongs to for that interval (μring resonates at a wavelength in that region). Since we focus on PVs, there is specifically one region for each μring throughout execution. If thermal variations are taken into consideration, the region should be periodically determined. The technique for computing regions is divided into two sequential phases. Figure 1 shows the different phases. Initially, the technique receives the waveguide information including the number of wavelengths and the distance between them. Besides, it also receives restrictions for trimming in both direction and the power for a given shift amount. The length of the region is denoted by d and is determined based on the number of wavelengths and the number of bubbles in the network. In the next step, one wavelength is assigned as a bubble in each region to provide a flexible wavelength assignment. The bubble is regularly put in the center of each region so that it is easily reachable from each μring that might be trimmed to it. It should be noted that, in some extreme cases regions may have an overlap; for example, if the number of wavelengths are not divisible by the number of regions, some wavelengths may fall into two regions.

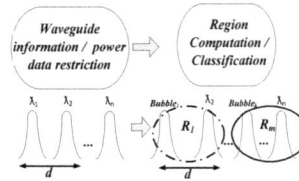

Figure 1. Region computation Technique

The Trimming policy inside the region
if $(|\lambda_{idle} - \mu_{current}| < |b_r - \mu_{current}|)$
  if $(|\lambda_{idle} - \mu_{current}| < \alpha)$ current_injection()
  else heating()
  end if
else if $(|\lambda_{idle} - \mu_{current}| > |b_r - \mu_{current}|)$
  if $(|b_r - \mu_{current}| < \alpha)$ current_injection()
  else heating()
  end if
end if

Figure 2. The pseudo-code of the proposed policy

Since MIN uses trimming algorithm only inside the region, the policy for trimming are accomplished based on the unit power for current injection and heating. In MIN, we try to trim a μring inside of the region. The reason we define (and remain within) a region is to limit the amount of shift necessary and to minimize the cost of arbitration. In other words, in each region a μring is trimmed to a nearby bubble rather than its actual wavelength, thus trimming distance is reduced and trimming power is decreased. Moreover, the mechanism of trimming in each region can reduce the number of uncorrectable μrings as their trimming distances are now smaller.

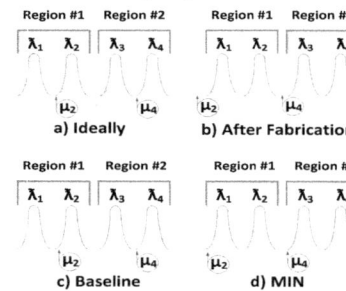

Figure 3. Trimming μrings example for both baseline design and MIN

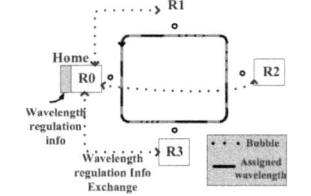

Figure 4. Wavelength regulation hardware for the data channels of R0.

The pseudo-code of the proposed policy is shown in Figure 2. In this pseudo-code λ_{idle} represents the available idle wavelength in the region, b_r shows the bubble in region r, $\mu_{current}$ illustrates the current μring location and α denotes the current injection trimming constraint and is assumed to be 0.4 [13]. Additionally, function $|a\_b|$ shows the absolute value of the difference between wavelength a and b. Current_injection() and heating() are the functions that operate for current injection and heating trimming techniques, respectively. As can be seen from pseudo-code, the policy first checks the difference between the current μring location and its nearby bubble and also the difference between the current μring location and its nearby available idle wavelength. If one of these distances is smaller than the other one the μring will be trimmed to that wavelength (actual one or bubble). In this condition if this difference is less than α, the current injection trimming technique is triggered to tune it; otherwise the heating approach is performed to shift the µring.

Figure 3 illustrates the trimming approach with a sample example. As depicted in the figure, there are four wavelengths which are distributed into two regions. Each region includes two wavelengths. λ_1 and λ_3 are bubbles while λ_2 and λ_4 are regular wavelengths. Here the assigned wavelength of µring #2 and #4 are λ_2 and λ_4, respectively. In Fig. 3-b, PVs cause µrings #2 and #4 to be closer to λ_1 and λ_3, respectively. The baseline design trims the two µrings back to their actual wavelengths as illustrated in Fig.3-c. However, with MIN, µring #2 will be trimmed to λ_1 in region #1 and µring #4 to λ_3 in region #2 which clearly consumes less trimming power than the baseline. As we mentioned before, in each region one bubble is dedicated for helping µrings with PVs. However, in high load traffic this bubble can be borrowed by any node for a period of time. So, if there are no PVs, bubbles can be used efficiently. In other words, our approach does not place a limit on the utilization of the network. In the case that PVs occur and there is no available wavelength in a region for a µring to be trimmed to, the bubble is released from its current node immediately after the time epoch and assigned to the µring affected by PVs. As we will describe in the next section, this process is completed within a few cycles, hence there is no possibility of long durations of starvation.

2.3 Wavelength Regulation

Figure 4 illustrates the wavelength regulation established by MIN which is triggered for each node. The wavelength regulator is placed at the end of the waveguide as the *home* node. Therefore, no additional physical connectivity is required. As seen in the figure, each node employs token arbitration similar to the baseline design to send its requests to use wavelengths. However, some modifications are needed to support assignement of bubbles. With no PVs, wavelengths are assigned to each node similar to the baseline design. Nevertheless, we record the region that each wavelength is located at. In some conditions, such as high traffic rate, nodes may send requests to borrow bubbles. As we mentioned previously, this happens at the boundary of time epochs of T cycles each. Each node can borrow a bubble for one epoch. After that period, if a node wants to keep the bubble it should send its request again to a wavelength regulator and the regulator decides whether to assign the bubble to the node or not.

MIN first checks the possibility that a µring can be trimmed to nearby idle wavelength in its region, if this wavelength is not a bubble, a µring will be trimmed to a wavelength in its region. However, if this wavelength is a bubble and the bubble is idle it will be shifted to it. If all the wavelengths (bubble and other wavelengths) in the region are busy, $node_i$ sends its request to the regulator to trim the µring to the bubble. Once the regulator receives the node's request, it checks the bubble in the node region and if the bubble has been borrowed by another node for bandwidth purpose ($node_j$), the regulator releases the bubble immediately after finishing its epoch time and the µring of $node_i$ is easily trimmed to the bubble. The size of the epoch should be determined efficiently to prevent increasing the time that a µring has to wait before having access to the bubble. However, during this wait time, the regulator checks the region periodically and if a nearby wavelength is released before finishing the epoch time, this wavelength is used by the µring. Hence, the number of usable wavelengths for each node is maximized and we can achieve the highest bandwidth.

2.3.1 Express wavelength regulation

With perfect fabrication process, it does not matter which wavelengths are assigned to each node. With PVs, however, determining which wavelengths are assigned to a node is crucial since a wavelength may not be usable by one node but usable by another. Therefore, in order to achieve efficient wavelength assignment, we define Associate Control Logic (ACL) that is kept at the home node. ACL manages the wavelength assignment for multiple nodes. Since a request from the nodes is sent to the ACL in the home node, it first

checks the wavelength availability and then according to the proposed approach, it assigns a suitable wavelength to the node. If multiple nodes send requests to use the wavelengths, it stores their information in its tables and assigns an appropriate wavelength dynamically to each node based on the nodes priority. ACL includes four modules: 1) wavelength control table, 2) the wavelength availability tracker, 3) node arriving/departing pointer logic, and 4) wavelength dispenser. All four modules operate independently and in parallel. The operation of each module is described as follows:

1) The wavelength control table is the core of the ACL. It is a compact table holding IDs of all nodes (Node-ID). The wavelength control table is organized by wave-ID, bubble-ID and region-ID which are established for assigning wavelengths efficiently. While the requests are sent from the nodes, their IDs are placed to the table. In each epoch, the table information is updated. If a wavelength is idle, a tag of the node relating to Node-ID is NULL. When a wavelength is allocated to the node, ACL updates the control table accordingly. In each region one wavelength is defined as a bubble and the bubble-ID of the rest of the wavelengths in each region are NULL.

2) Wavelength availability tracker keeps track of all the wavelengths in the wavelength control table that are not used. If a node makes a request, the tracker selects a wavelength based on the region-ID and the available wavelengths (which can be found by monitoring the node-ID and the wave-ID in the wavelength control table).

3) Arriving/Departing node pointer logic directly controls the node requests. It is also directly linked to wavelength control table. If multiple nodes want to access the same bubble, their requests are monitored in the node arriving/departing table and the information about them is stored in the table. For each incoming request from the node, we store the priority and the request order for the node.

The *Node-ID* is obtained according to ID of each node while the *FIFO-ID* is determined based on the time that each node has sent its request. We also rank each node considering both *FIFO-ID* and *Priority* tag. As for the regular wavelengths that are not bubbles, the values of *FIFO-ID* and *Priority* are same. However, if the wavelengths are bubbles, the *Priority* is calculated as follows:

$$Priority = FIFO\text{-}ID \times Max\,(FIFO\text{-}ID) \tag{1}$$

where max (*FIFO-ID*) is the maximum number among all the *FIFO-ID* values. By employing the priority tag, the bubbles can be assigned to the nodes affected by PVs immediately. Clearly, the nodes with higher priority values will be given priority over nodes with lower priority value.

4) The wavelength dispenser is responsible for dispensing free wavelengths to requesting nodes. The wavelength dispenser dynamically assigns wavelengths to the requesting node; they are returned to the dispenser upon release. Based on the information provided by the wavelength availability tracker, the wavelength dispenser decides whether to grant a wavelength or not.

We have implemented all the MIN structures in VHDL and compiled it using Xilinx ISE tools. Based on the results, we estimate the overall area cost of the structures to be 3.5% of the baseline interconnection network.

3. EVALUATION

In order to evaluate the proposed MIN, we first need to provide a model of the impact of PVs on the optical network. To characterize the impact of PVs on µring resonance wavelengths, we have utilized a variation model for the physical dimensions of the optical waveguide based on die-to-die (D2D), a.k.a. intra-die, and within die (WID), a.k.a. inter-die, variations [18]. We generate a set of variation parameters based on WID and D2D results [21] since both of them use small dies (2×2.2 mm^2) with 0.57nm WID variation and 1.08nm D2D variation. As for large dies, a PV modeling infrastructure for CMOS technology, called VARIUS [20] is used to model both WID and D2D variations [7]. The results from the small die in [21] are placed into VARIUS. Then VARIUS generates 100 sample dies of 400 mm^2 each. On average, these dies have 0.61nm WID variation and 1.01nm D2D variation. In the results we present in this section, we use both results from [7] and [21] for small and large dies to evaluate the effectiveness of the proposed approach. Moreover, we modify the cycle accurate network simulator booksim [19] to compare the proposed schemes with alternatives. We use a MWMR crossbar and simulate crossbar size of K=16 with single flit packets of 64 bytes. We assume Dense Wavelength Division Multiplexing where 64 wavelengths are transmitted in a single waveguide (in both directions). The power consumption of the network includes the trimming power, which is 0.13 mw/nm for current injection and 0.24 mw/nm for heating [6, 10]. We also take the distance between adjacent wavelengths, $\Delta\lambda$, into consideration. We assume that current injection can correct up to $0.5\Delta\lambda$ towards blue shift [13].

Figure 5 shows the power consumption among different schemes for the two $\Delta\lambda$ values (0.5 and 1) and with different region sizes. The epoch size is 128 cycles. The results are normalized to Closest trimming scheme. In the Closest scheme, the trimming is done based on shifting a group of μrings to their closest λs (similar to sliding window scheme by Nitta et al. [6]) while the 'Actual' trims the μrings to their originally assigned wavelength. We test two different configurations of our scheme; $d=2$ and $d=4$, where d is the region size described in the previous section. Although the Closest approach eliminates large trimming distances, MIN with $d=2$ consumes less trimming power compared to it. Specifically, 41% power reduction is observed in MIN in comparison to the Closest approach. This achievement is obtained because we provide freedom for each μring by employing a bubble and also triggering efficient wavelength regulation mechanism to manage the bubbles. However, as depicted in the figure, if the length of region increases, the trimming power in our approach rises too. The reason for such increases relies on boosting the trimming distance between the nodes in the region and the bubble.

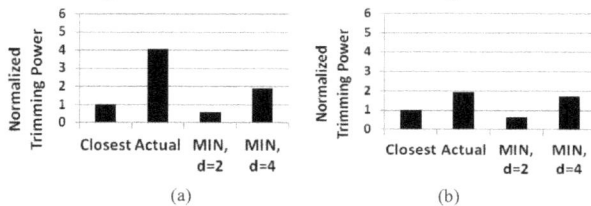

Figure 5. Normalized trimming power for two $\Delta\lambda$ values: (a) 0.5 and (b) 1.

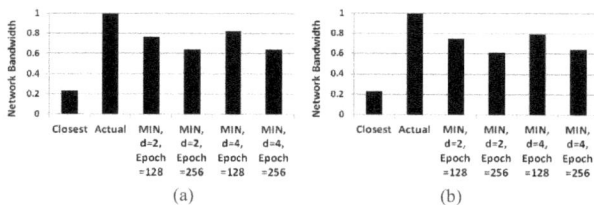

Figure 6. Normalized network bandwidth for two $\Delta\lambda$ values: (a) 0.5 and (b) 1.

Figure 6 illustrates the network bandwidth comparison between MIN and other schemes. The results are also normalized based on the 'Actual' trimming scheme. The 'Actual' scheme is assumed that it can achieve 100% bandwidth after trimming. The network bandwidth metric in our evaluation is obtained based on the number of working channels considering both tuned senders and receivers. In this figure in addition to comparing MIN with other schemes, we also contrast the proposed approach in different regions and epoch sizes to understand the effect of these parameters efficiently. As depicted in the figure, the proposed methodology achieves nearly 80 % of network bandwidth in both $\Delta\lambda$ values. The Closest approach, on the other hand, can utilize only 24% of the bandwidth. The reason of this improvement was illustrated in Figure 3: MIN can reduce the uncorrectable μring by finding a nearby wavelength without disrupting any other communication. It is worthy to note that the high network bandwidth achieved with our approach is accomplished without using spare μrings. This also helps in obtaining lower power consumption. Additionally, as illustrated in the figure, MIN acquires

higher bandwidth in epoch size of 128 compared to epoch size of 256. It is intuitive that a smaller epoch size results in higher bandwidth: if more than one μring request the same bubble and the bubble is grabbed by a node for a long period (epoch time), it will lead to underutilization of the network. On the other hand, if the epoch size is too small, it will cause frequent requests and increase the power consumption.

In summary, Figures 5 and 6 indicate that MIN provides a robust mechanism to achieve high network bandwidth and low trimming power under PVs compared to recently proposed alternatives.

4. CONCLUSION

This paper presents a novel methodology, called MIN, to alleviate the impact of PVs on optical networks. We improve the level of flexibility and accuracy of wavelength assignment by providing efficient wavelength arrangement and regulation. The proposed approach allocates bubbles and allows nodes to borrow wavelengths in order to reduce trimming power and achieve maximal bandwidth. Evaluation results show that the proposed methodology results in 41% less power consumption and over 3x improvement in bandwidth compared to state-of-the-art approaches. Hence, it provides a significant level of reliability with lower hardware overhead, latency and energy compared to alternative designs.

5. REFERENCES

[1] ITRS, International Technology Roadmap for Semiconductors, *Edition Technical Report*, 2011. http://public.itrs.net.

[2] J. Owens et al. Research challenges for on-chip interconnection networks, *IEEE Micro.*, 27(5): 96–108, 2007.

[3] N. Kirman et al. Leveraging Optical Technology in Future Bus-based Chip Multiprocessors. In *MICRO-39*, 2006.

[4] Y. Pan et al. Flexishare: Channel sharing for an energy efficient nanophotonic crossbar. In *HPCA*, pages 1–12, 2010.

[5] D. Vantrease et al. Corona: System implications of emerging nanophotonic technology. In *ISCA*, pages 153–164, 2008.

[6] C. Nitta et al. Addressing system-level trimming issues in on-chip nanophotonic networks. In *HPCA*, pages 122–131, 2011.

[7] Y. Xu et al. Tolerating process variations in nanophotonic on-chip networks. In *ISCA*, 2012.

[8] M. Mohamed et al. Reliability-aware design flow for silicon photonics on-chip interconnect. *IEEE TVLSI* (in press), 2013.

[9] C. Batten et al. Designing chip-level nanophotonic interconnection networks. *IEEE J. Emerg. Select. Topics Circuits Syst.*, 2(2):137–153, 2012.

[10] J. Ahn et al. Devices and architectures for photonic chip-scale integration, *Appl. Phy. A*, 2009.

[11] A. Kirshnamoorthy et al. Exploiting CMOS manufacturing to reduce tuning requirements for resonant optical devices, *IEEE Photonics Journal.*, 3, 2011.

[12] J. Orcutt et al. Nanophotonic integration in state-of-the-art CMOS foundries. *Optics Express.*, 19: 2335–2346, 2011.

[13] Z. Li et al. Reliability modeling and management of nanophotonic on-chip networks. In *IEEE TVLSI.*, 99, 2010.

[14] S. Manipatruni et al. Wide temperature range operation of micrometer-scale silicon electro-optic modulators, *Opt Letter.*, 33(19): 2185–2187, 2008.

[15] N. Kobayashi et al. Uv trimming of polarization-independent microring resonator by internal stress and temperature control. *Optics Express.*, 18: 906–916, 2010.

[16] C. Batten et al. Building manycore processor-to-dram networks with monolithic silicon photonics. In *Hot Interconnects*, pages 21–30, 2008.

[17] A. Joshi et al. Silicon-photonic clos networks for global on-chip communication. *In 3rd NOCS*, pages 124–133, 2009.

[18] J. Orcutt et al. Nanophotonic integration in state-of-the-art cmos foundries. *Optics Express.*, 19: 2335–2346, 2011.

[19] W. J. Dally and B. Towles. Principles and Practices of Interconnection Network, Morgan Kaufmann, 2004.

[20] S. Sarangi et al. Varius: A model of process variation and resulting timing errors for microarchitects. *IEEE Transactions on Semiconductor Manufacturing.*, 21(1):3–13, 2008.

[21] D. Xu. Polarization control in silicon photonic. *Topics in Applied Physics*, 31–70, 2011.

[22] C. Nitta et al. Resilient microring resonator based photonic networks. In *MICRO.*, 2011.

EECache: Exploiting Design Choices in Energy-Efficient Last-Level Caches for Chip Multiprocessors

Hsiang-Yun Cheng, Matt Poremba, Narges Shahidi, Ivan Stalev,
Mary Jane Irwin, Mahmut Kandemir, Jack Sampson, Yuan Xie
Department of Computer Science and Engineering, Pennsylvania State University
University Park, Pennsylvania, USA 16802
hoc5108@cse.psu.edu, mrp5060@psu.edu, nxs314@cse.psu.edu, ids103@psu.edu,
{mji, kandemir, sampson, yuanxie}@cse.psu.edu

ABSTRACT

Power management for large last-level caches (LLCs) is important in chip-multiprocessors (CMPs), as the leakage power of LLCs accounts for a significant fraction of the limited on-chip power budget. Since not all workloads need the entire cache, portions of a shared LLC can be disabled to save energy. In this paper, we explore different design choices, from circuit-level cache organization to micro-architectural management policies, to propose a low-overhead run-time mechanism for energy reduction in the shared LLC. Results show that our design (EECache) provides 14.1% energy saving at only 1.2% performance degradation on average, with negligible hardware overhead.

Categories and Subject Descriptors: B.3.2 [Memory Structures]: Design Styles - *Cache memories*

Keywords: Cache; Power management; Energy-efficiency

1. INTRODUCTION

The power consumption of modern chip-multiprocessors has become a primary design constraint. Even though Moore's law continues to provide increasing transistor counts, the limited on-chip power budget restricts the percentage of active transistors [5, 16]. In recent years, an increasing percentage of those transistors are invested on the large LLCs utilized to bridge the gap between fast CPU cores and slow off-chip memory accesses. Specifically, LLCs occupy as much as 50% of the chip area and contribute to a significant amount of the chip's leakage power [17].

The high leakage power of the LLC comes from its large size that aims to accommodate most applications' memory footprints. However, not all workloads need the entire cache. Figure 1(a) illustrates the variable sensitivity of workloads to changes in LLC capacity. On the x-axis are multi-programmed workloads with different demands on capacity (see Section 6 for workloads and simulation details). For example, workloads LL1 and LL2 do not benefit from a larger capacity, while TH1 and TH2 perform better with larger LLCs. Further, the required cache size may also vary with different program phases, as shown in Figure 1(b). When the required cache size is smaller, some parts of the LLC can be disabled to reduce leakage power. In Figure 1(a), for example, if a 5% performance degradation is acceptable, more than half of the LLC can be disabled to save power in all but two workloads.

This research was funded by NSF grants 1218867, 1213052, 1409798, and Department of Energy under Award Number DE-SC0005026.

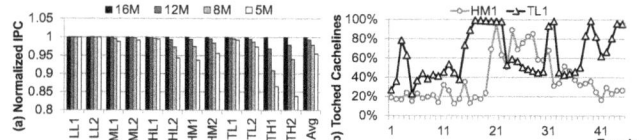

Figure 1: (a) Performance under different L3 sizes relative to 16MB L3 and (b) phase-dependent memory footprints.

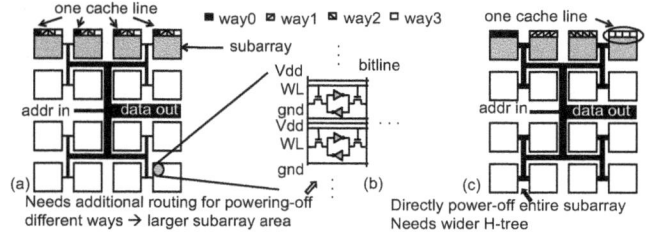

Figure 2: Physical design of (a) uniform cache architecture (b) zoomed in portion of SRAM subarray and (c) slice-based cache organization.

In this paper, we propose low-overhead run-time mechanisms to manage LLC power consumption. We first introduce a slice-based cache organization that requires only minimal circuit overhead to shut down parts of the LLC. Based on this slice-based organization, we next propose a low-overhead approach to monitor cache access behavior and determine when to power-off/on cache slices. Specifically, we consider three important and complementary metrics that guide our slice turn-on and turn-off decisions: **utilization**, **hotness**, and **the distribution of dirty cache lines**. Our evaluation reveals that considering one metric alone may not be effective across workloads. By taking advantage of the strengths of different metrics, our comprehensive approach provides 14.1% energy savings with only 1.2% performance degradation on average.

2. SLICE-BASED CACHE

We craft our design starting from the physical implementation of a uniform cache architecture. A uniform cache consists of several smaller subarrays of SRAM cells, shown as squares in Figure 2(a). An H-tree interconnect provides equal wiring distance to all subarrays in the cache. Typically, each cache set spans multiple subarrays in the horizontal direction, highlighted in grey. Further, the bits of each way can be interleaved for less wiring on each subarray output, designated by the black striped cache line. At the die layout level, the bitlines run perpendicular to the wordlines (WL), the power (Vdd), and the ground (gnd) rails, as shown in Figure 2(b).

This results in a large trade-off between area overhead and the shutdown granularity. Since the power rails are perpendicular to bitlines, they span multiple ways in the same set. This makes it difficult to turn off single ways without either adding multiple wire routes for different ways or re-routing wires parallel to the bitlines. Both of these methods would increase the area of all subarrays and incur high overheads (>10%). For example, in Figure 2(a), additional wire routing is required to power gate only 1/4 of a single subarray when turning off way0. The other option is to force a few ways, rather than all ways, to reside in a single subarray. Figure 2(c) shows an example that forces each subarray to store data from only a single way. Forcing a subset of ways into a single subarray increases the width of the H-tree. However, the size of the H-tree near the center of the cache, closest to the cache output, will be the same size. By utilizing CACTI [12] to analyze the area overhead, we found that the wider H-tree only incurs less than 0.5% additional area overhead, which is much smaller than the area overhead of larger subarrays in way-based shutdowns.

In this work, we utilize the second approach of constraining ways into subarrays, an organization which we call *slice*. A slice is a generically sized shut-down granularity which may range from one to all ways in a cache. Data ways in a slice are placed in the same subarray or group of subarrays sharing a sleep transistor. This work chooses a slice size of 1/16 of the total cache ways; 4-ways in our experimental design. Such design allows us to turn off entire subarrays. This results in lower overhead both due to (1) subarray sizes remaining static and (2) the need for fewer power gating transistors.

3. RELATED WORK

Prior studies have proposed circuit-level methods, including drowsy cache [6] and the gated-Vdd approach [13], to reduce the leakage power of on-chip caches. In this paper, we use the gated-Vdd technique to power-off slices for lower supply voltage overhead. Based on the circuit level techniques, several architectural approaches have been proposed [1, 2, 8, 9, 11, 15]. Some techniques [1, 15] attempt to partition caches by ways, and disable useless ways across the whole cache or sub-group of sets [11]. Basu et al. [2] exploited cache coherence to identify stale data and resize the cache. Kadjo et al. [8] facilitated power gating and migrated high temporal locality blocks to live partitions. Kaxiras et al. [9] disabled cache lines that are not likely to be reused. These techniques either require offline profiling, high hardware overhead to track the dead blocks, or utilize additional hardware that consumes non-negligible power to monitor cache accesses. Moreover, these prior way-based schemes do not easily generalize to the slice-based organization which incurs less power-gating circuit overhead.

4. METRICS OF INTEREST

In order to save energy by disabling cache slices, we need to exploit variability in cache size requirements. There are three main factors that can be used to make slice turn-on/turn-off decisions: utilization, hotness, and the distribution of dirty cache lines.

4.1 Utilization

Ideally, the cache capacity should be large enough to fit the active cache footprint of workloads, i.e. the unique cache lines referenced in a time epoch, and it indicates the utilization of the cache. Figure 3(a) and (b) show the utilization of two types of workloads. We define the utilization as the percentage of cache lines that are referenced in a time epoch in each slice. As shown in the figure, ML1 has low utilization, while TL1 has high utilization. Furthermore, the utilization varies across different cache slices and time epochs.

Low-utilization slices represent potential power-off opportunities, as disabling these slices would incur few additional cache misses. Figure 4 shows that if we shutdown slices with utilization less than 30%, we can turn off 68.1% of the LLC on average. Utilization alone can capture the power-off opportunity of most of the workloads. However, if the data are seldom reused, such as in TL1, TL2, TH1, and TH2, it misses some power-off opportunities. This observation motivates us to consider additional metrics.

4.2 Hotness

In addition to the active cache footprint, the access frequency of the stored data also helps to capture the power-off opportunity. Dis-

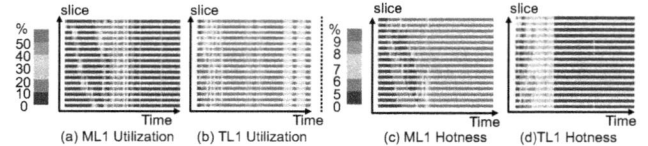

Figure 3: Utilization and hotness of ML1(with small active footprint but frequently reused data) and TL1(with large active footprint but rarely reused data).

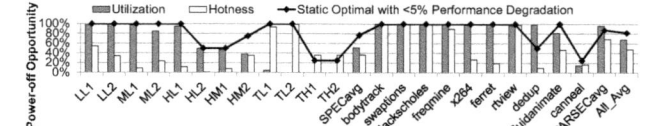

Figure 4: Power-off opportunity captured by (a) Utilization (utilization<0.3 slices) (b) Hotness (Hotness<0.075 slices) and (c) Static Optimal (statically select minimum cache size that incurs <5% performance degradation).

abling a frequently accessed slice would incur more cache misses than shutting down a seldom reused slice. In this paper, we define the hotness of a slice as the number of hits to the slice divided by the total number of LLC misses in a time epoch. Thus, the hotness implies the increase in the cache miss rate if the slice is disabled.

Disabling cold slices provides different power-off opportunities, than disabling low-utilization slices. Figure 3(c) and (d) show the hotness of two type of workloads. The active footprint of ML1 is small, but the referenced data are highly reused. Disabling only cold slices for ML1 would lose considerable power-off opportunities provided by the small active footprint. On the other hand, TL1 references a large number of cache lines in each epoch, but these referenced data are seldom reused. Therefore, disabling cold slices for TL1 may provide higher power savings than disabling low-utilization slices. Figure 4 illustrates that if we shutdown the cold slices with hotness less than 7.5%, we can disable 47.6% of the LLC on average. For workloads with large but seldom reused cache footprint, such as TL1, TL2, TH1, and TH2, the hotness of slices can better capture the power-off opportunity than utilization.

4.3 Writeback of Dirty Data

When a slice in the LLC is turned off, the dirty data need to be written back. Disabling a slice with a higher number of dirty cache lines would reduce power savings, since the slice can only be powered down once all the dirty data have been written back. Furthermore, these writes would frequently fill up the write-buffer in the memory controller and could delay critical reads. Thus, a slice with less dirty data should be chosen among the slices with the same level of utilization or hotness, when deciding which slice should be powered off.

In summary, cache utilization indicates spatial access behavior, while cache hotness indicates temporal access behavior. Low-utilization slices can be disabled to save the leakage power, while cold slices can be turned off when the stored data are seldom reused to further increase the power-off opportunity. Also, when choosing which slices to power off, the number of dirty lines should play an important role. The discussion above suggests that an ideal slice power-off/on strategy should consider all these metrics.

5. EECACHE

In this paper, we propose low-overhead methods to monitor the cache access behavior, and design the power-off, power-on, and data migration policies accordingly. Figure 5 shows the overview of the proposed scheme. In the cache controller, we add a power management unit (PMU) to determine the power state of each cache slice. At the beginning of each epoch, i.e., time t in the figure, the PMU collects the cache access status from the previous epoch. Based on the cache access behavior, the PMU first decides whether the workload will benefit from a higher capacity. It then checks whether some of the slices can be turned off to save even more

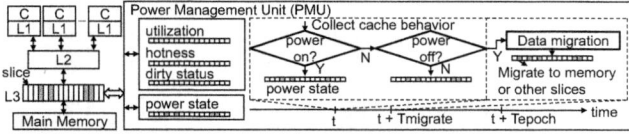

Figure 5: Overview of EECache and power management process.

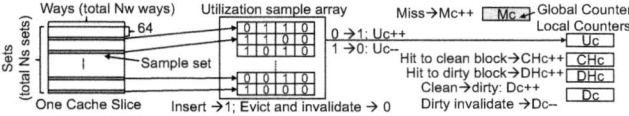

Figure 6: Profiling cache access behavior in each cache slice. Uc: Utilization counter; CHc/DHc: Clean/Dirty hit counter; Dc: Dirty counter.

power. Before turning off the victim slices selected by the power-off policy, the PMU decides whether each dirty block in the victim slices should be written back to the main memory or migrated to other slices. The clean blocks also need to be either discarded or migrated. After all the blocks in the victim slices are flushed, i.e., at time t+Tmigrate in Figure 5, the victim slices can be turned off to save leakage power. Below, we explain how to monitor the cache access behavior with low-overhead hardware, and describe our power management policies in detail.

5.1 Monitoring Cache Access Behavior

Figure 6 shows how to dynamically monitor the cache access behavior with small hardware overhead. To capture hotness, we use two counters (CHc and DHc) to count the number of hits to each clean and dirty cache line. The number of LLC misses is captured by a global counter (Mc) for all the cache slices. To monitor the distribution of dirty blocks, we utilize a counter (Dc) to count the number of dirty cache lines. For profiling the utilization, we develop a sampling-based method that is inspired by a prior set-sampling approach [14] to reduce the hardware overhead. We sample the utilization of only $1/64$ sets, which is enough to provide high accuracy ($>80\%$). When a cache line is inserted into the sample set, the corresponding utilization bit is set to one. The utilization counter (Uc) of the slice is then increased by one. When the cache line is evicted or invalidated, the mapped utilization bit is reset to zero and Uc is decreased by one. All the utilization bits are reset to zero at the beginning of each epoch to filter the stale data. Suppose that there are Nw ways and Ns sets in each slice, the utilization of a slice can be estimated by $Uc/(Nw*Ns*(1/64))$, and the hotness can be calculated by $(CHc+DHc)/Mc$.

5.2 Power-off Policy

As observed in Section 4, using the utilization alone to decide the power state would lose some power-off opportunities when the stored data are seldom reused. The hotness characteristic can help to identify these seldom reused slices. Moreover, with similar utilization and hotness, the slice with fewer dirty cache lines would incur a lower writeback penalty. Therefore, we consider all three factors when designing the power-off policy, as illustrated in Figure 7. We first select the power-off victims from the slices with less than Uth utilization. If there is no low-utilization slice, we instead select the slices with less than Hth hotness. Among the power-off candidates, at most $Noff$ slices with fewer dirty cache lines are chosen to be turned off. We analyze the impact of different threshold settings, and empirically set $Uth=30\%$, $Hth=7.5\%$, and $Noff=4$.

5.3 Power-on Policy

After some slices are powered off, the power consumption is reduced but the cache misses may increase due to the smaller LLC size. Since the cache access behavior changes in different program phases, we need to determine whether the workload would benefit from a larger LLC at each epoch. We keep the whole tag array powered-on to monitor the potential hits to the powered-off portion

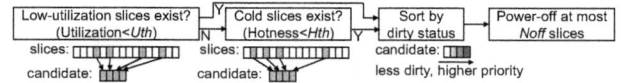

Figure 7: Flow chart of the power-off policy.

of the LLC. The tag arrays of the powered-off slices are called victim tags [4], and store the evicted cache lines from the active slices. A potential hit counter, Vhit, is increased by one when a hit occurs to the victim tags. When the hit rate to the victim tags (Vhit/Mc) is higher than a threshold, $HonTh$, $Noff$ slices are powered on to improve performance. Increasing the value of $HonTh$ provides more power saving by turning on slices less often, but the performance degradation would also increase. We analyze the impact of different $HonTh$ settings, and find that $HonTh=10\%$ is a good value.

5.4 Data Migration Policy

The goal of the data migration process is to guarantee data coherency while reducing the miss penalty due to the loss of data in the powered-off slices. One possible solution is to migrate useful data to other active slices. During each migration, a replacement victim is selected from the active slices according to the underlying replacement policy, i.e., the LRU block in active slices. The migration of a cache line may incur an additional conflict miss if the evicted replacement victim is reused later. Thus, we choose to migrate only the clean blocks in hot-clean slices ($CHc/Mc > Mth$) and dirty blocks in hot-dirty slices ($DHc/Mc > Mth$). The Mth is the migration threshold and is empirically set to 4%. Note that the data migration is performed at background and does not delay the demand requests to the cache.

Our power management mechanism requires only 0.005% storage overhead in a 16MB LLC, as shown in Table 1.

Uc	Utilization counter per slice	32bits * 16(slice) = 64B
CHc	Clean hit counter per slice	32bits * 16 = 64B
DHc	Dirty hit counter per slice	32bits * 16 = 64B
Mc	Miss counter for entire LLC	32bits = 4B
Dc	Dirty counter per slice	32bits * 16 = 64B
Vhit	hit counter for victim tags	32bits = 4B
Uarray	Utilization set-sampling array	64(way) * 64(sampled set) = 512B
All		776B/16MB $\simeq$ 0.005%

Table 1: Storage overheads.

Processor	16 cores; 2GHz; Out-of-order; issue width=4; 192 ROB; 32 LSQ
L1 cache	Private; 32KB per core; 4-way; 64B line size; 2 cycles
L2 cache	Shared; 4MB total; 16-way; 64B line size; 20 cycles
L3 cache	Shared; 16MB total(1MB per slice); 64-way(4-way per slice)
	30 cycles; MSHR=32; 5 slices are always on for inclusion property
Memory	120 cycles access latency
Epoch	10M cycles

Table 2: System Configuration

6. EXPERIMENTAL SETUP

We evaluate our designs using gem5 [3], augmented with McPAT [10]. The area overhead is evaluated using CACTI [12]. When calculating the power consumption, the leakage power saving, the increase in dynamic power due to additional cache misses, and the additional power consumption of our monitoring mechanism, are all included. The baseline system configuration is shown in Table 2. We use a set of SPEC2006 benchmarks for multi-programmed workloads and PARSEC benchmarks for multi-threaded workloads. For the SPEC benchmarks, we fast forward 500M instructions, and run in detailed mode for 1 billion instructions. The SPEC benchmarks are classfied into four categories, as shown in Table 3, according to their active cache footprint. We create the multi-programmed workloads by combining two different categories of applications to cover a broad range of cache access behavior. For the PARSEC benchmarks, we run 1 billion instructions starting from the Region of Interest (ROI) [7]. When reporting performance results, we use overall throughput ($\sum IPC_i$).

	Benchmark	Util	Benchmark	Util
LL1	GemsFDTD,tonto,tonto,povray	3.6	bodytrack	0.1
LL2	GemsFDTD,povray,povray,tonto	2.0	swaptions	0.1
ML1	dealII,xalancbmk,GemsFDTD,povray	6.8	blackscholes	0.1
ML2	gromacs,h264ref,povray,tonto	14.4	freqmine	0.7
HL1	gobmk,omnetpp,GemsFDTD,tonto	12.5	x264	4.7
HL2	hmmer,zeusmp,povray,tonto	52.9	ferret	7.5
HM1	gobmk,hmmer,dealII,gromacs	37.9	rtview	8.8
HM2	omnetpp,zeusmp,h264ref,namd	58.3	dedup	15.4
TL1	astar,mcf,GemsFDTD,povray	61.9	fluidanimate	25.9
TL2	leslie3d,libquantum,povray,tonto	98.6	canneal	72.0
TH1	astar,leslie3d,gobmk,hmmer	97.0		
TH2	libquantum,sjeng,omnetpp,zeusmp	91.6		

Table 3: Workload characteristic and classification. Util=average LLC utilization per Epoch (%). Active cache footprint: L<M<H<T.

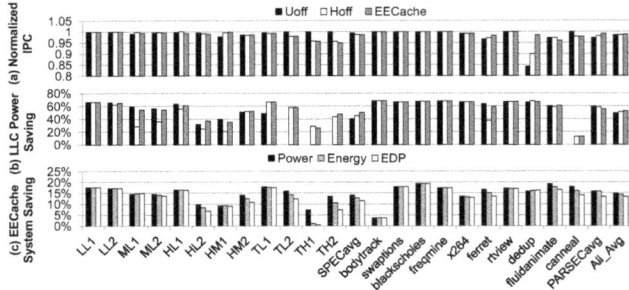

Figure 8: (a) Performance and (b) L3 power saving of differnt power-off policies, and (c) System power, energy, and EDP saving, compared to baseline 16MB LLC.

7. EXPERIMENTAL RESULTS

We first analyze the performance impact and power-saving of the proposed EECache, as shown in Figure 8(a) and (b), comparing to using only utilization (utilization $< 30\%$ slices) or hotness (hotness $< 7.5\%$ slices) alone as the power-off metric. Powering-off low-utilization slices (Uoff) can provide 48.4% power saving on average. However, when the access footprint of the workloads is large, such as in TL2, TH1, TH2, and canneal, Uoff loses the power-off opportunity when the stored data are seldom reused. Using hotness as the power-off metric (Hoff) can disable the rarely reused slices in these high-utilization workloads. However, the Hoff policy misses the power-off opportunity when the workload frequently accesses small amount of hot data, such as in ML1, ML2, HL2, HM1, and ferret. Within similar performance degradation, our EECache can better capture the power-off opportunity by taking advantage of the strengths of different metrics. On average, EECache can provide 52.5% power-saving in the LLC, while incurring only 1.2% performance degradation. EECache can also reduces the power and energy consumption of the entire system. Figure 8(c) shows that EECache provides 14.8% system power saving. The energy consumption and the energy-delay-product (EDP) of the whole system are also reduced by 14.1% and 13.4% on average.

	PGM	EECache
Storage overhead	103.25KB area=0.907mm^2 (3.3%) leakage=0.516W (2.5%)	776B area=0.100mm^2 (0.4%) leakage=0.057W (0.3%)
Gated-Vdd circuit	3.0%	1.7%
Routing overhead	larger subarrays (14.3%)	wider H-tree (0.4%)
Total area overhead	20.6%	2.5%

Table 4: Hardware overheads of PGM and EECache in a 16MB LLC.

We compare EECache against a state-of-the-art way-based power-gating approach (PGM) [8]. PGM uses a high-overhead sampling array that stores the tags of the sample sets and the instructions that recently access the blocks. They determine the required cache size by analyzing the hits to the sample tags, and rely on a high-overhead prediction scheme that hashes the instructions into a counter array to determine whether a cache line is useful and should be migrated to other active ways during the transition phase. Our EECache design consumes negligible storage overhead (0.4% extra L3 area), which is smaller than the PGM scheme, as shown in

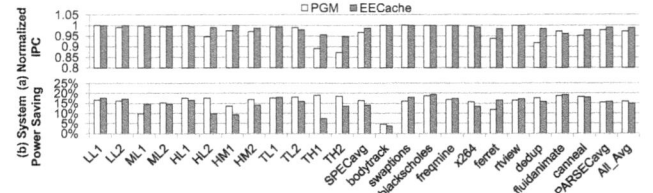

Figure 9: (a) System performance and (b) System power saving of prior way-based power-gating (PGM) [8] and our EECache.

Table 4, resulting in less leakage power consumption. Since we use slice-based shutdowns, the gated-Vdd circuit and routing overhead are smaller than the fine-grained way-based shutdowns in PGM. As a result, the overall area overhead of EECache is only 2.5%, much less than the 20.6% overhead in the PGM scheme.

Figure 9 illustrates the system performance and power saving of prior PGM and our EECache. Prior PGM approach relies on the hits to LRU ways to determine the required cache size. However, their scheme does not consider the active footprint of the LLC, thus sacrificing the performance of some high-utilization workloads, such as TH1 and TH2, to provide higher power saving. The PGM also incurs higher than 5% performance degradation for ferret and dedup, due to the failure to detect the power-on demand in these workloads. Our EECache better tradeoff performance degradation and power savings, and incurs less than 5% performance degradation in all workloads, while providing 14.8% system power saving on average. These results show that our EECache can provide similar power savings to finer grained approaches with both smaller hardware overheads and less performance degradation.

8. CONCLUSION

This paper explores low-cost LLC power management policies for multi-programmed and multi-threaded benchmarks. Based on our extensive experimental analysis, we can conclude that simultaneously exploiting three key metrics, i.e, utilization, hotness, and the distribution of dirty cache lines, is necessary to design the power management policies for an energy-efficient LLC. Our EECache achieves 14.1% energy saving with less than 2% performance degradation, and consumes negligible hardware overhead.

9. REFERENCES

[1] D. Albonesi. Selective cache ways: on-demand cache resource allocation. In *MICRO*, 1999.
[2] A. Basu et al. Freshcache: Statically and dynamically exploiting dataless ways. In *ICCD*, 2013.
[3] N. Binkert et al. The gem5 simulator. *SIGARCH Comput. Archit. News*, 2011.
[4] J. Cong et al. An energy-efficient adaptive hybrid cache. In *ISLPED*, 2011.
[5] H. Esmaeilzadeh et al. Dark silicon and the end of multicore scaling. In *ISCA*, 2011.
[6] K. Flautner et al. Drowsy caches: simple techniques for reducing leakage power. In *ISCA*, 2002.
[7] M. Gebhart et al. Running parsec 2.1 on m5. Technical report, The University of Texas at Austin, Department of Computer Science, October 2009.
[8] D. Kadjo et al. Power gating with block migration in chip-multiprocessor last-level caches. In *ICCD*, 2013.
[9] S. Kaxiras et al. Cache decay: exploiting generational behavior to reduce cache leakage power. In *ISCA*, 2001.
[10] S. Li et al. Mcpat: An integrated power, area, and timing modeling framework for multicore and manycore architectures. In *MICRO*, 2009.
[11] S. Mittal et al. Flexiway: A cache energy saving technique using fine-grained cache reconfiguration. In *ICCD*, 2013.
[12] N. Muralimanohar et al. Cacti 6.0: A tool to model large caches. Technical report, HP Lab, 2009.
[13] M. Powell et al. Gated-vdd: a circuit technique to reduce leakage in deep-submicron cache memories. In *ISLPED*, 2000.
[14] M. K. Qureshi et al. A case for mlp-aware cache replacement. In *ISCA*, 2006.
[15] K. Sundararajan et al. Cooperative partitioning: Energy-efficient cache partitioning for high-performance cmps. In *HPCA*, 2012.
[16] G. Venkatesh et al. Conservation cores: reducing the energy of mature computations. In *ASPLOS*, 2010.
[17] D. Wendel et al. The implementation of power7: A highly parallel and scalable multi-core high-end server processor. In *ISSCC*, 2010.

A Digital Dynamic Write Margin Sensor for Low Power Read/Write Operations in 28nm SRAM

Peter Beshay, Benton H. Calhoun
University of Virginia, Charlottesville, VA
{plb3qt, bcalhoun}@virginia.edu

Vikas Chandra, Rob Aitken
ARM Inc, San Jose, CA
{vikas.chandra, rob.aitken}@arm.com

ABSTRACT

The conventional guard band design approach increases the SRAM Wordline (WL) pulse duration to operate successfully in all the process, voltage and temperature (PVT) corners. This can significantly increase the dynamic energy. This work presents a digital circuit that is able to track and control the WL pulse duration of the SRAM memory across PVT variations, to minimize the dynamic energy while maintaining robust operations. The circuit is applied on a 78kbit SRAM. The results are compared to the worst case margin approach and show a maximum write energy savings of 45% and 49% relative to margining voltage/temperature (VT) and process variations, respectively.

Categories and Subject Descriptors

1. [Technology, Circuits, and Architecture]: 1.2 Circuits

Keywords

Low power SRAM; Adaptive Stability, Calibration, Dynamic Margin Sensor, Wordline Quantization, Wordline Control.

1. INTRODUCTION

The static noise margin has been traditionally used for SRAM cell stability characterization. However, recently it has been shown that the dynamic noise margin that utilizes the critical WL pulse width or TCRIT to estimate SRAM cell stability is more precise [1] because static read margin overestimates failures and static write margin underestimates failures. TCRIT is defined as the minimum WL pulse duration required to successfully write to the memory. As technology scales and the supply voltage is lowered, variability increases. This causes an SRAM cell to have a wider distribution of Wordline (WL) pulse duration required to perform successful read and write operations. The conventional worst case margin design methodology increases the WL voltage or pulse duration to operate successfully in all PVT corners. This can lead to operating the memory at much dynamic energy than what the memory requires for successful read/write operations [2]. This becomes more problematic with technology scaling due to the heightened variability effect [3] which can be a big problem in high performance System on Chips (SOCs) and multi-core processors where the SRAM memory contributes significantly to the total power consumption. Increasing the WL pulse duration increases the Read and Write energies due to the increased Precharge, WL driver, and Bit-line (BL) driver energies. Figure 1(a) shows that longer WL pulses results in larger differential voltage between BL and BLB which increases the Pre-charge energy during the Read

operation. In Figure 1(a), increasing the WL pulse from W1 to W2 results in an energy increase of $C_{BL} V_{DD} (\Delta V)$, where C_{BL} is the capacitance of the BL, V_{DD} is the supply voltage and ΔV is the difference between the developed differential voltages on BL/BLB as shown in Figure 1(a). Similarly Figure 1(b) shows that longer WL pulses results in an increased developed voltage on the WL, and hence an increased WL driver energy during both the Read and the Write operations. In Figure 1(b), increasing the WL pulse from W1 to W2 results in an energy increase of $C_{WL} V_{DD} (\Delta V)$, where C_{WL} is the capacitance of the WL.

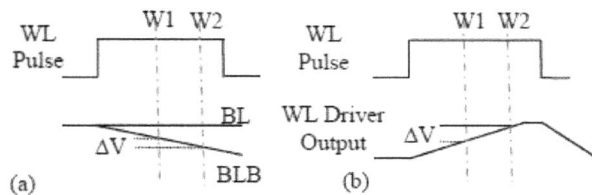

Figure 1. (a) Longer WL pulse increases the Pre-charge energy (b) Longer WL pulse increases the WL driver energy.

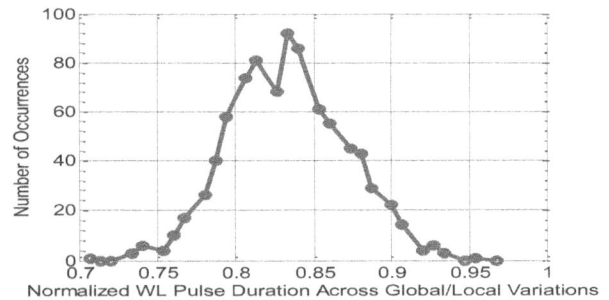

Figure 2. Distribution of the minimum WL Pulse in a 78kbit SRAM

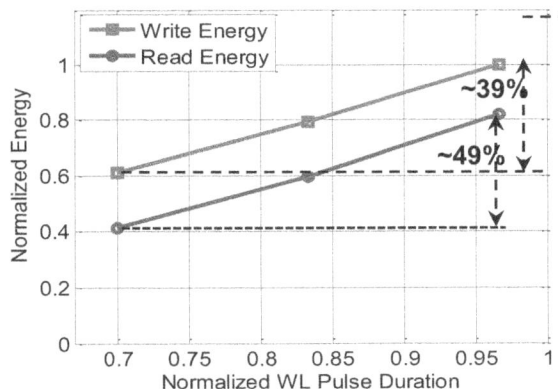

Figure 3. Total Energy versus the WL pulse

Figure 2 shows the distribution of the WL pulse duration required to successfully perform robust read/write operations to a 78kbit SRAM array across global and local process in 28nm technology node. The array has 256 rows and 312 columns. The read and write energy that corresponds to the WL pulse duration range is shown in Figure 3. The figure indicates energy savings of up to 39% and 49% can be achieved in the write and read energies, respectively by adjusting the WL pulse duration with the global and local process variations. Worst case margin design approach guards for ±10% variation in the supply voltage and a 0-100 C temperature operation range. We studied the WL pulse required to perform robust operations across the aforementioned voltage and temperature range at the typical process corner for the 78kbit SRAM array. The results indicated an energy savings of up to 34% and 45% can be achieved in the write and read energies, respectively by adjusting the WL pulse with the supply voltage and temperature variations at the typical process corner.

Hence, significant energy savings can be achieved by adjusting the WL pulse duration across PVT variations. Prior works [4][5][6] have addressed this issue. In [6], replica rows/columns were used to track the memory margins across PVT. Replica rows/columns use extra row or column of the memory to track the margins, which have high area overhead. The energy overhead is also high since the replica rows/columns are used anytime the memory is accessed. In [4], analog sensors are used to control the WL voltage across PVT. Analog sensors are less scalable than their digital counterparts, which make them less attractive for scaled technologies nodes (32nm and beyond). In [5], a Built In Self-Test (BIST) was used to tune the WL pulse duration for minimum dynamic energy after powering up the memory. However, the proposed scheme failed to track the changes in that WL pulse across voltage and temperature (VT) variations. The WL pulse duration was overdesigned to account for VT variations, which can significantly increase the dynamic energy as shown earlier in this work. The contribution of this work is the sensor and a low power WL control scheme that utilizes the sensor. The rest of this paper is organized as follows. Section 2 discuss the sensor circuit, calibration, and accuracy. Section 3 demonstrates the utilization of the sensor in a low power WL pulse control scheme and the total scheme overhead.

2. Dynamic Write Margin Sensor

In scaled technologies it has been shown that write failures are higher than the read failures [7]. In other words, TCRIT is wider than the read WL pulse duration. Therefore we can use TCRIT to successfully perform both the read and write operations. This work utilizes a sensor that generates TCRIT for different PVT conditions.

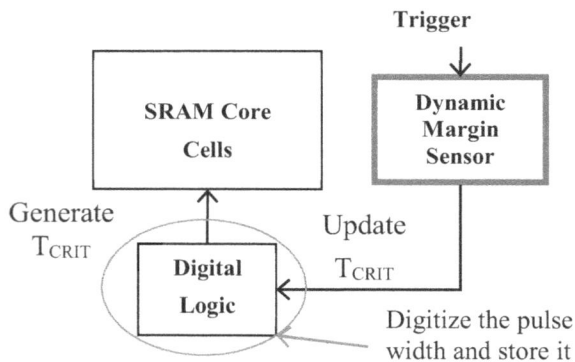

Figure 4. Dynamic Margin Sensor in a WL control scheme

Figure 4 shows a block diagram of a WL control scheme that utilizes the sensor to track and control the WL pulse duration across PVT conditions. In this work, we will refer to the bitcell with the longest TCRIT as the worst case bitcell. The sensor is calibrated to generate TCRIT of the worst case bit-cell. When a coarse change in the temperature or voltage occurs, a trigger signal is generated. The sensor then generates the new TCRIT and sends it to digital logic that digitizes and stores TCRIT and uses it to generate the WL pulse for the memory during normal operation. The sensor circuit is shown in Figure 5. The waveforms of the circuit are shown in Figure 6. The sensor consists of a 6T bitcell and circuits that measure TCRIT of this bitcell. The bitcell is initially calibrated to have the same TCRIT as the worst case bitcell of the memory as will be shown later in this section. The calibration ensures that TCRIT of the sensor's bitcell follows that of the worst case bitcell with voltage and temperature variations.

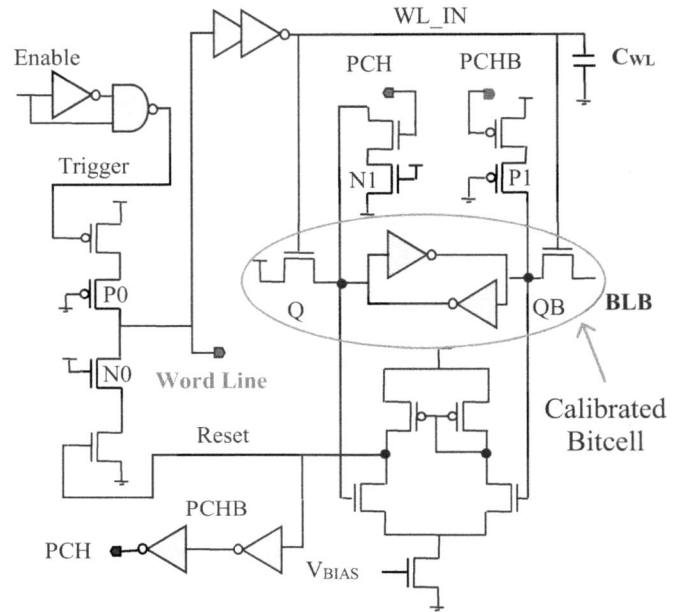

Figure 5. Dynamic Write Margin Sensor.

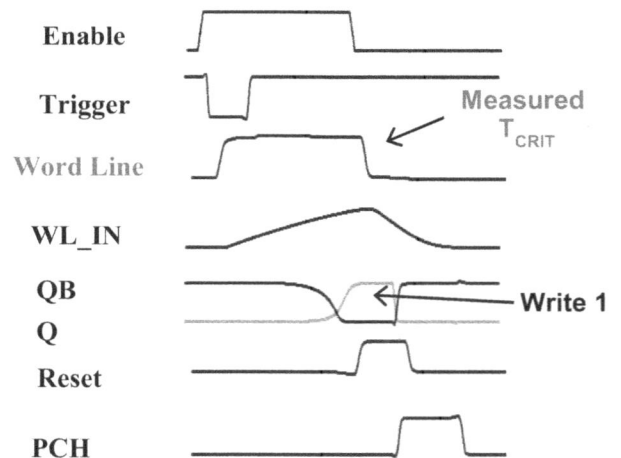

Figure 6. Write Margin Sensor Waveforms.

The sensor measures TCRIT of its bitcell as follows the bitcell initially stores 0. Once the sensor is enabled, a Trigger signal is generated that asserts the sensor's Wordline to write 1 to the bitcell. Q and QB starts charging and discharging, respectively. Once Q crosses QB, a comparator asserts a Reset signal. The Reset signal turns off the Wordline indicating the end of the write operation and asserts PCH and PCHB to 0 back again to the bitcell to be ready for the next operation. The width of the WL pulse is the measured TCRIT. Transistors P0 and N0 are used to decouple the switching effect from the Wordline signal. Similarly, transistors P1 and N1 are used to decouple the switching effect from the Q and QB nodes. The pulse generator circuit that asserts the Trigger signal is designed to ensure long output pulse enough to turn on the Wordline across process corners. The capacitor CWL is attached to the bit-cell and its value is equivalent to the WL capacitance of one row in the SRAM memory. CWL is utilized to have similar initial dynamic margin of the sensor as that of the SRAM bitcell. VBLB is the voltage set by the digital controlled voltage divider during the calibration phase.

The calibration of the sensor's bitcell to the worst case bitcell of the memory is done through digitally setting the value of BLB of the sensor's bitcell using a voltage divider circuit to adjust TCRIT of the sensor's bitcell to the same as that of the worst case bitcell. Using 3 bits resistive ladder voltage divider, the maximum error in TCRIT due to calibration is ~3.5% TCRIT.

We studied the precision of the sensor in controlling TCRIT .The sensor is calibrated to the worst case bitcell of the 78kbit memory at the typical operating point (0.9V, 25C). Figure 7 shows TCRIT generated by the sensor and TCRIT of the worst case bitcell at 0.81V, 0C and 1V, 100C. As shown, the sensor precisely adjusts the WL pulse duration needed to write to the worst case bitcell, with a slight deviation of 2% at 0.81V, 0C. We studied the process variation effects on the sensor. The analysis indicated that the sensor can be tuned to the worst case bitcell in the memory independent of process variations because of the calibration phase. The energy overhead of the margin sensor is 0.5X the energy of a single write operation to the 78kbit memory. However the sensor only operates when a coarse change in the voltage/temperature is sensed. In modern processors, where the frequency of operations is in the GHz range, the rate of coarse change of temperature or voltage is much smaller than the cycle time and hence the effective energy overhead of the sensor is amortized. For instance, if the rate of voltage/temperature coarse change is assumed to be 10X of the cycle time which is an extreme upper limit, the effective energy overhead of the sensor will be 5% the energy of the memory write operation. The area overhead is 7X the area of single bit-cell or ~0.0087% the area of the core SRAM array.

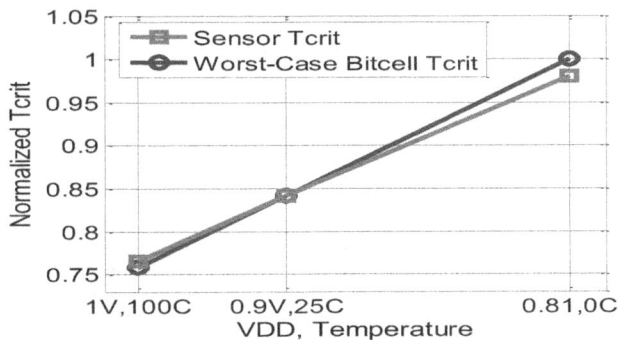

Figure 7. TCRIT measured by the sensor follows TCRIT of the worst case bitcell in the memory.

3. Wordline Control Scheme

Figure 8 shows one realization of the sensor in a Wordline (WL) pulse control scheme. The calibration flow is shown in dotted lines, while the operation flow is shown in solid lines. The control scheme uses a BIST circuit to measure the minimum WL pulse required to successfully write to the worst case bitcell in the memory. The measured pulse is then digitized and stored in the WL register. Afterwards, calibration logic uses the WL register to calibrate the sensor to enable the sensor to track TCRIT of the worst case bitcell across VT variations. This calibration step is done at powering up the memory and repeated to compensate for the aging effect. Once the temperature and/or voltage changes, the margin sensor generates the new WL pulse and sends it to a WL quantizer circuit that digitizes the pulse and stores it in the WL digital register.

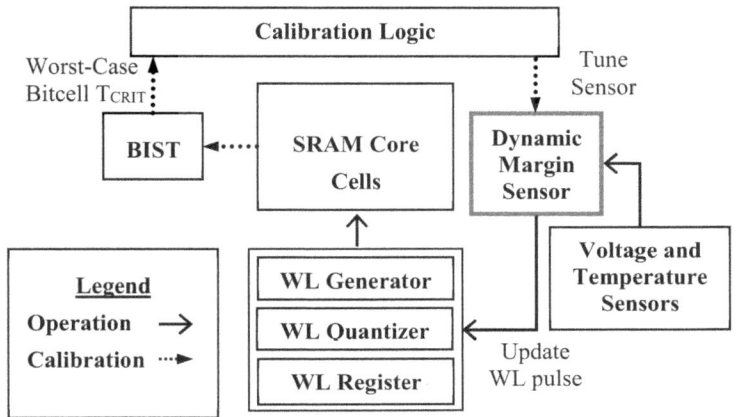

Figure 8. Wordline control scheme

The WL register is then used throughout the operation of the memory to generate the read/write WL pulses. External voltage and temperature sensors are used to sense a coarse change in voltage and temperature (VT) and trigger the margin sensor to generate TCRIT for this instantaneous VT condition. VT sensors are not discussed in this work but they are extensively used in advanced processors [8] and can be easily integrated to this work. The WL quantization circuit is shown in Figure 9. The circuit consists of 16 delay stages, a thermometer-to-binary encoder (TBE), and 4 output registers. In [9][10], the conventional delay line approach for time to digital conversion was used, which is similar to this work. In [9][10], the delay of all the delay line stages was set to the minimum sized delay in both approaches. Unlike the aforementioned approaches, we statistically designed the first stage to have a delay equal to the minimum WL pulse duration across all PVT corners through setting bias voltage VA and the rest of the delay line stages to have the minimum sized delay. This minimizes the quantization energy by ~70% through only quantizing the range of the WL pulse instead of the WL pulse itself. In addition, we sensed the delay nodes using pass transistors P0, P1, P2 as shown in Figure 15. This decreases the capacitive loading on the delay line stages, and minimizes the quantization energy by ~40% compared to the conventional TDC approach [9][10] that loads the delay line nodes with latch circuits. The error resulting from quantizing the WL pulse is ~6% of the minimum WL pulse. The WL generator circuit is shown in Figure 10. A binary to thermometer encoder converts the 4 binary registers to a thermometer code T0, T1, till T15. The delay line nodes are initially set to zero. When the clock signal (clk) changes from 0 to 1, a pulsed trigger signal is generated. The trigger signal is applied to transistor P0 to initially set the WL voltage. A pulse then propagates in the delay line and sets the delay line nodes to '1'. When the WL pulse timing is met, the pull down transistors N0, N1, N15 reset the WL pulse. The energy overhead of the WL quantizer and generator circuits is 2% and 1.2% the energy of a single write operation. The area overhead of the WL quantizer and generator circuits is 0.02% and 0.01% of the SRAM core array respectively. The BIST works as follows, the circuit first sets the WL pulse width to the min WL pulse of the design (TWL_MIN). This is the smallest WL pulse duration of the design across all PVT corners. This is also the delay of the first stage of the WL generator. The BIST then scans each row in the memory and performs a write followed by read operation to check if a successful write occurs. If the write operation didn't finish successfully the circuit increment the WL pulse duration by 1 delay unit, store the new WL pulse in the WL register and scans the next row. The min WL pulse is then stored in the WL register after scanning all the rows of the memory and used to calibrate the sensor. The total energy overhead of the control scheme is ~6.5% the energy of a single write operation to the memory including the energy of the margin sensor, WL quantization and generation circuits, calibration registers and the voltage divider circuit.

The overall area overhead of the control scheme is ~0.12% the area of the SRAM core array including the aforementioned circuits. The overhead of the BIST and the VT sensors are not included since they exist in modern processors [8] for various purposes, their output are available and can be easily integrated to this work.

4. Conclusion

We presented a dynamic margin sensor that is capable of tracking the critical WL pulse duration (TCRIT) of a memory across PVT variations. The sensor is digital and hence suitable for scaled technologies. The sensor was used in a time control scheme that utilizes WL quantization and generation circuits. The scheme was applied on a 78kbit SRAM memory with 256 rows and 312 columns in 28nm commercial technology node. The results are compared to the worst case margin approach and show a maximum write energy savings of 45% and 49% relative to margining voltage/temperature (VT) and process variations, respectively. The total energy overhead of the control scheme is ~6.5% the energy of a single write operation to the memory. The total area overhead of the scheme is ~0.12% the area of the array.

5. References

[1] Sharifkhani, Mohammad, and Manoj Sachdev. "SRAM cell stability: A dynamic perspective." *Solid-State Circuits, IEEE Journal of* 44.2 (2009): 609-619.

[2] Aitken, Robert, and Sachin Idgunji. "Worst-case design and margin for embedded SRAM." *Design, Automation & Test in Europe Conference & Exhibition, 2007. DATE'07.* IEEE, 2007.

[3] Chandra, Vikas, Cezary Pietrzyk, and Robert Aitken. "On the efficacy of write-assist techniques in low voltage nanoscale SRAMs." *Proceedings of the Conference on Design, Automation and Test in Europe*. European Design and Automation Association, 2010.

[4] Nho, Hyunwoo, et al. "A 32nm High-k metal gate SRAM with adaptive dynamic stability enhancement for low-voltage operation." Solid-State Circuits Conference Digest of Technical Papers (ISSCC), 2010 IEEE International. IEEE, 2010.

[5] Abu-Rahma, Mohamed H., Mohab Anis, and Sei Seung Yoon. "Reducing SRAM power using fine-grained wordline pulsewidth control." Very Large Scale Integration (VLSI) Systems, IEEE Transactions on 18.3 (2010): 356-364.

[6] Yamaoka, Masanao, et al. "Low-power embedded SRAM modules with expanded margins for writing." Solid-State Circuits Conference, 2005. Digest of Technical Papers. ISSCC. 2005 IEEE International. IEEE, 2005.

[7] Bhavnagarwala, Azeez, et al. "Fluctuation limits & scaling opportunities for CMOS SRAM cells." *Electron Devices Meeting, 2005. IEDM Technical Digest. IEEE International*. IEEE, 2005.

[8] Souri, Kamran, Youngcheol Chae, and Kofi Makinwa. "A CMOS temperature sensor with a voltage-calibrated inaccuracy of±0.15° C (3σ) from− 55 to 125° C." *Solid-State Circuits Conference Digest of Technical Papers (ISSCC), 2012 IEEE International*. IEEE, 2012.

[9] Joshi, R., et al. "6.6+ GHz Low Vmin, read and half select disturb-free 1.2 Mb SRAM." VLSI Circuits, 2007 IEEE Symposium on. IEEE, 2007.

[10] Helal, Belal M., et al. "A low jitter 1.6 GHz multiplying DLL utilizing a scrambling time-to-digital converter and digital correlation." VLSI Circuits, 2007 IEEE Symposium on. IEEE, 2007.

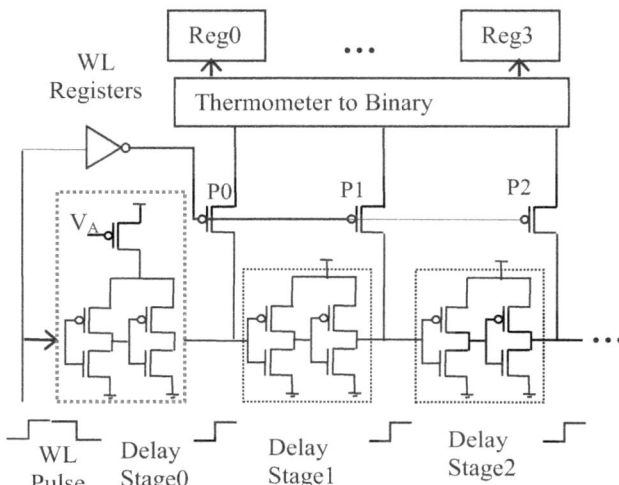

Figure 9. Wordline quantizer

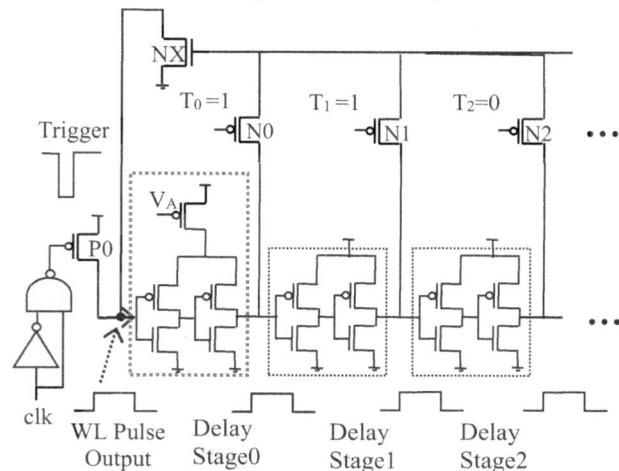

Figure 10. Wordline generator

Smart Butterfly: Reducing Static Power Dissipation of Network-on-Chip with Core-State-Awareness

Siyu Yue, Lizhong Chen, Di Zhu, Timothy M. Pinkston, and Massoud Pedram
Ming Hsieh Department of Electrical Engineering
University of Southern California
Email: {siyuyue, lizhongc, dizhu, tpink, pedram}@usc.edu

ABSTRACT

While power gating is a promising technique to reduce the static power consumption of network-on-chip (NoC), its effectiveness is often hindered by the requirement of maintaining network connectivity and the limited knowledge of traffic behaviors. In this paper, we present *Smart Butterfly*, a core-state-aware NoC power-gating scheme based on flattened butterfly that utilizes the active/sleep state information of processing cores to improve power-gating effectiveness. Smart Butterfly exploits the rich connectivity of the flattened butterfly topology to allow more on-chip routers to be power-gated when their attached cores are asleep. We present two heuristic algorithms to determine the set of routers to be turned on to maintain connectivity and allow tradeoff between power consumption and average packet latency. Simulation results show an average of 42.85% and 60.48% power reduction of Smart Butterfly over prior art on 4x4 and 8x8 networks, respectively.

Keywords

Network-on-chip, power-gating, flattened butterfly.

1. INTRODUCTION

Networks-on-chip (NoCs) have been proposed as a key component in many-core systems such as chip-multiprocessors (CMPs) and multiprocessor system-on-chips (MPSoCs). Compared with traditional bus structures, the relatively complex NoCs with routers and links can draw a substantial percentage of chip power [2][3][4][10]. This is particularly true as cores are often underutilized and therefore put into low-power sleep states (10–50% average utilization [8]).

An effective approach to reduce NoC power consumption is to apply power gating techniques. Most state-of-the-art NoC power gating schemes are traffic-oriented, in which routers are power gated when there is no traffic that needs to go through the routers [9]. However, the traffic-oriented power gating strategies use only traffic information and are unable to take full advantage of inactive cores. For example, even if a core is in sleep state and, thus, has no incoming or outgoing packets, its attached router cannot stay power-gated for long. This is because the router must be awoken intermittently to forward the passing packets to support communication of other active cores. In typical applications, the length of router idle periods is in the order of tens to hundreds of cycles – short enough to cause frequent wakeups and the associated energy overhead.

A new approach, which we refer to as core-state-aware power gating, aims to save more static power by enhancing NoCs with information of core states to make better power gating decisions. To be specific, some routers that are attached to the sleeping cores stay power-gated until the cores become active. Any traffic that

would go through the sleeping routers is detoured. As the sleep periods of cores are in the order of several milliseconds [8], this approach allows routers to be turned off for a much longer time compared to the traffic-oriented approach. Note that not all of the routers attached to sleeping cores can be turned off as the network must maintain full connectivity of the active cores. In some cases, it may even need to turn on additional routers than the minimally required in order to reduce detoured traffic, and therefore reduce packet latency.

The closest example of core-state-aware power gating to-date is the Router Parking technique, which provides core power state information in power-gating mesh networks [10]. However, conventional mesh-based NoC topologies have limited ability in utilizing core status to reduce NoC power, as many routers that are attached to the sleeping cores must be turned on to provide full connectivity and reduce packet latency to an acceptable range.

The inherent topological limitation of mesh networks prompts us to look at other topologies that have richer connectivity. One such topology is high-radix networks that have express channels added to tile-based NoCs [5][6]. In particular, the flattened butterfly topology [5], uses express channels as shortcuts to connect directly the non-neighboring tiles on the same row or column, thus bypassing intermediate routers and accelerating packet transfer. Figure 1(b) shows an example of a 4x4 flattened butterfly network, in comparison to a 4x4 mesh network in Figure 1(a). Due to its superior connectivity, flattened butterfly is very suitable for core-state-aware power gating, as the number of routers that need to be powered on to guarantee connectivity is much smaller than in meshes (more details in Section 2.2).

To this end, we propose *Smart Butterfly*, a novel NoC power gating scheme that exploits the potential of power gating in flattened butterfly NoCs, and utilizes core-state-awareness to increase power-saving effectiveness. Specifically, we first prove the minimal number of routers that need to be powered on in flattened butterflies to ensure full connectivity of a given set of active cores. We then reduce packet latency without increasing much power overhead by selectively turning on additional routers. Two heuristic algorithms are proposed to solve the problem. We show that the two algorithms are able to achieve near-optimal results. With these algorithms, Smart Butterfly is able to achieve a wide range of power-latency trade-offs by varying the number of *ON* routers.

2. PRELIMINARIES

2.1 NoC Power Gating Techniques

Power gating is an effective technique to reduce static power consumption, especially for components with sufficiently long idle periods. Recent research has started to apply power gating to on-chip routers. Matsutani, *et al.*, propose look-ahead technique to

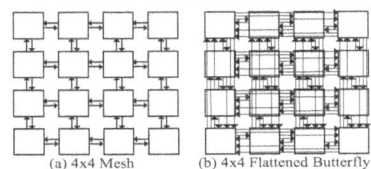

Figure 1. On-chip network topologies.

reduce run-time power consumption and wake-up latency [9]. Chen, *et al.*, present a mesh-based NoC architecture with a bypass channel which allows more sleeping routers and smaller latency penalty [2]. In addition, a Clos NoC based power-gating scheme [3] and a multiple network based scheme [4] have been proposed to increase power-gating opportunity. However, these works belong to traffic-oriented power gating approaches and cannot exploit the long idle period of sleeping cores. Samih, *et al.*, propose a novel NoC power gating technique, namely *Router Parking*, which shuts off selected routers attached to sleeping cores to achieve low NoC power consumption [10]. However, as discussed in detail later, the power efficiency of Router Parking deployment is largely restrained by the underlying mesh topology, and the adopted algorithms suffer unstable results due to randomness and lack the flexibility to trade-off between power and performance.

2.2 Connectivity Analysis
A key challenge to enable core-state-aware power gating is to ensure the connectivity of all active cores while minimizing the set of routers that needs to be powered on. Although the Router Parking work shows that the mesh is a viable candidate to allow some routers to be powered-off without disconnecting cores, flattened butterfly networks require much fewer powered-on routers due to their rich connectivity.

We first identify the minimal number of routers that need to be powered on additionally in flattened butterfly to ensure full connectivity of a given set of active cores.

Theorem: In a flattened butterfly network, in which the set of routers attached to the active cores form K connected components, full connectivity of all K components can be maintained only if a minimum of $(K - 1)$ additional routers are powered on.

Proof sketch: The proof consists of the following two parts:

1) Full connectivity => At least $(K - 1)$ additional routers.

In a flattened butterfly, all active routers in a row (or in a column) are already connected and are in the same component. For a sleeping router on the i-th row and j-th column, it can merge at most two components if turned on, one comprised of all the active routers on the i-th row and the other formed by all the active routers on the j-th column. This means that turning on one sleeping router can reduce the number of components by no more than one. Therefore, by induction, at least $(K - 1)$ additional routers exist in powered-on state to connect K components and hence maintain full connectivity of all active cores.

2) The boundary case of $(K - 1)$ additional routers is achievable.

We start from connecting two components. Assume A and B are two components. There exists at least one sleeping router which will connect A and B if turned on. We can turn on this router to merge A and B. Repeat this step $(K - 1)$ times and we can connect all K components with $(K - 1)$ additional routers. ∎

While this theorem states that a selective set of $(K - 1)$ additional routers is needed, there are different ways of choosing these routers, leading to different paths and varying packet latency among cores. Moreover, it may be beneficial to turn on extra routers besides the $(K - 1)$ routers to further reduce average packet latency. Therefore, we focus on this more complex but more important problem and present two efficient algorithms to solve it.

3. PROBLEM STATEMENT
Before presenting the problem formulation, we first describe the network topology as well as the packet latency model used.

An n by m flattened butterfly network is defined as a grid with n rows and m columns. There is a core with a router attached to it on each grid point, making $N \triangleq n \times m$ cores (and routers) in total. All the routers on the same row or column are directly connected by a physical link between them.

Each core in the network can be either active or in sleep state. Let $c_i = 1$ denote core i is active and $c_i = 0$ otherwise. The set $C \triangleq \{i | c_i = 1\}$ is the set of all active cores in the network. Similarly, let $s_i = 1$ denote router i (which is attached to core i) is active and $s_i = 0$ otherwise, and $S \triangleq \{i | s_i = 1\}$ is the set of all active routers in the network. As a router cannot be put to sleep state if the corresponding core is in the active state, the following constraint exists,

$$s_i \geq c_i, \forall i \in \{1, \ldots, N\} \quad (1)$$

For each pair of active cores (i, j), let $r_{i,j}$ denote the communication load rate, and $d_{i,j}$ denote the communication latency between them. Assuming minimal routing which forwards packets on the shortest paths, we can compute the communication latency $d_{i,j}$ by

$$d_{i,j}(S) = \big(H_{i,j}(S) + 1\big) \cdot (T_R + t_c) + L_{i,j}(S) \cdot T_L + T_S \quad (2)$$

where $H_{i,j}(S)$ and $L_{i,j}(S)$ are the number of hops and the link length (in terms of how many unit lengths), respectively, on the shortest path between router i and j with given active router set S. T_R is the router pipeline latency, typically 2-4 cycles. t_c is the per hop contention latency. T_L is the unit length link latency, typically 1 cycle. T_S is the serialization latency, which is the quotient of packet size and link bandwidth.

The goal of the proposed Smart Butterfly scheme is to determine the best active router set S based on the knowledge of current active cores C and communication rates $r_{i,j}$. The objective is to minimize the average packet latency APL, calculated by

$$APL = \frac{\sum_{i,j \in C} d_{i,j}(S) \cdot r_{i,j}}{\sum_{i,j \in C} r_{i,j}} \quad (3)$$

subject to the maximum number of active routers S_{max}, i.e.,

$$|S| \leq S_{max} \quad (4)$$

It is impractical to enumerate all the possible solutions of the above problem when N is large. Therefore we propose two efficient heuristic algorithms, both having near-optimal performance and polynomial-time complexity.

4. PROPOSED ALGORITHMS
4.1 Exact Cost-Based Approach
The first algorithm is an exact cost-based approach, which starts from the state that only the routers connected to active cores are ON, and then turns on other routers one by one as needed. At each step when we determine which router to turn on, and choose the one that minimizes APL. The pseudo code is given below:

Algorithm Input: $n, m, C, r_{i,j}, S_{max}$

Initialize $activeS = C$, $sleepS = \{1, \ldots, N\} - activeS$
For k from $|C| + 1$ to S_{max} // Turn on routers one by one
  $minAPL = \infty$
  For s in $sleepS$
    $activeS = activeS \cup \{s\}$
    Compute APL using equation (3)
    If $APL < minAPL$
      $minAPL = APL$, $mins = s$
    $activeS = activeS/\{s\}$
    $activeS = activeS \cup \{mins\}$
    $sleepS = sleepS - \{mins\}$
Return

We assume t_c is a small fixed value to compute APL in designing the heuristics. It is also worth mentioning that we define $d_{i,j}$ to be a finite large number (e.g., 10^4) instead of ∞ in the algorithm if router i and j are not connected to each other yet.

Computing APL in the algorithm involves solving an all-pairs shortest path problem. Our implementation has a runtime of

$O(N^4)$ by bookkeeping $d_{i,j}(activeS)$. When router s is added to $currentS$, we can update $d_{i,j}(activeS)$ in $O(N^2)$ time.

4.2 Merit Value-Based Approach

In case $O(N^4)$ time complexity is still not fast enough for online implementation, we propose a faster algorithm, namely the merit value-based algorithm with $O(N^2)$ time complexity. Similar to the exact cost-based approach, the merit value-based approach turns on routers one by one. At each step of deciding which router to turn on, we first consider the routers that can connect two components, with the help of a disjoint set. If there is a tie (i.e., either multiple or no routers that can connect two components), we use a pre-computed merit value associated with each router as tie-breakers. The merit value of a router serves as a rough approximation of the reward of turning on that router. The merit value of router s is computed as the sum of communication rate $r_{i,j}$ where router i and router j are not directly connected to each other but are both directly connected to router s (so that they become connected if router s is turned on). When a sleeping router is turned on, the merit values of other routers are updated accordingly.

The pseudo code is given below:

Algorithm Input: n, m, C, $r_{i,j}$, S_{max}

Initialize $activeS = C$, $sleepS = \{1, \dots, N\} - activeS$
Initialize $merit = 0$
Initialize disjoint-set $DS = \{Row_1, \dots, Row_n\} \cup \{Col_1, \dots, Col_m\}$
For c_1 in C // Compute merit values
  For c_2 in C
    If c_1 and c_2 are not on the same row or column
      s_1 =router at $c_1.row$ and $c_2.column$
      s_2 =router at $c_2.row$ and $c_1.column$
      $merit(s_1)+= r_{c1,c2}$, $merit(s_2)+= r_{c1,c2}$
For s in $activeS$ // Update disjoint-set
  $DS.union(s.row, s.column)$
For k from $|C| + 1$ to S_{max} // Turn on routers one by one
  $maxs = -1$, $maxMerit = -\infty$, $connected = true$
  For s in $sleepS$
    If $DS.find(s.row, s.column) = false$
      // Router s connects two components
      If $connected$
        $maxs = s$, $maxMerit = merit(s)$, $connected = false$
      Else If $merit(s) > maxMerit$
        $maxs = s$, $maxMerit = merit(s)$
    Else If $connected$ **And** $merit(s) > maxMerit$
      $maxs = s$, $maxMerit = merit(s)$
  $DS.union(maxs.row, maxs.col)$
  $activeS = activeS \cup \{maxs\}$
  $sleepS = sleepS - \{maxs\}$
  For s in $sleepS$ // Update merit values
    If s and $maxs$ are not on the same row or column
      c_1 =core at $s.row$ and $maxs.column$
      c_2 =core at $maxs.row$ and $s.column$
      $merit(s) -= r_{c1,c2}$

Return

We use an array-based disjoint-set implementation whose *find* operation has $O(1)$ time complexity and *union* operation has $O(n + m)$ time complexity. As computing and updating merit values take $O(N^2)$ time, the overall time complexity is $O(N^2)$, which is much smaller than that of the exact cost-based approach.

5. SIMULATION RESULTS

5.1 Simulation Setup

In the simulation, the proposed Smart Butterfly is evaluated on both 4x4 and 8x8 flattened butterfly (FB) networks with real application traces including four MPSoC traces (namely mms2, mpeg4, toybox, and vopd_t) and eight CMP traces (referred to as spec1~4 for 4x4 network and spec5~8 for 8x8 network). The

MPSoC traces are collected from 12 to 16-core real applications. For 4x4 networks, the application traces are concentrated onto 3 to 4-core traces to form the active core set. The CMP traces are synthesized based on the memory and cache access traffic from a subset of SPEC benchmarks. Cores of all the test traces are randomly mapped to the NoC tiles.

We compare the following eight schemes, including both aggressive and conservative algorithms proposed in the Router Parking work [10] (these algorithms can be applied to FB as well):

1. Mesh_BB: A branch and bound algorithm on mesh network that minimizes *APL* at given maximum number of ON routers
2. Mesh_RPA: Router Parking – Aggressive on mesh network
3. Mesh_RPC: Router Parking – Conservative on mesh network
4. FB_BB: A branch and bound algorithm on FB that minimizes *APL* at given maximum number of ON routers
5. FB_RPA: Router Parking – Aggressive on FB
6. FB_RPC: Router Parking – Conservative on FB
7. FB_EC: The proposed exact cost-based approach on FB
8. FB_MV: The proposed merit value-based approach on FB

The network configurations in the simulation are listed in Table 1. Based on a previous study [7], the on-chip traffic is composed of approximately 80% short packets and 20% long packets. For fair comparison, both mesh and flattened butterfly networks have the same total buffer size in number of bits and the same total bisection bandwidth (so the individual link width of FB is narrower than that of mesh).

The *APL*s are computed based on Equation (3). For each of the test case, the per-hop contention latency t_c is acquired by feeding the trace into Garnet, a cycle-accurate NoC simulator [1]. NoC power (comprised of router power and link power) is calculated by the NoC power model DSENT [11] with 32nm technology.

5.2 Simulation Results

5.2.1 Power-Latency Trade-offs

Figure 2 shows the simulation results of the five algorithms on flattened butterfly (aforesaid Schemes 4-8) in the form of trade-off curves between overall NoC power and average APL. Only two 4x4 and two 8x8 test cases are shown due to lack of space.

As shown in the figure, the trade-off curves of the two proposed heuristic algorithms are close to the optimal curve of branch and bound-based algorithm on 4x4 network. The branch and bound result is not shown for 8x8 network because it did not finish in a reasonable time period. Compared with Router Parking, we can see that at the same level of power consumption, FB_EC and FB_MV achieve 13% and 12% lower *APL*s on average, respectively, compared to FB_RPA. At the same level of *APL*, FB_EC and FB_MV save 28% and 27% of NoC power consumption on average, respectively, compared to FB_RPC.

It is worth mentioning that, the proposed FB_EC and FB_MV can produce a range of power-latency trade-off points that can be used by system operators under different constraints and scenarios.

5.2.2 Comparison of Eight Schemes

Figure 3 and Figure 4 compare the minimal NoC power consumption (left y-axis and the bars) that can be achieved by each of the

Table 1. Simulated network configurations.

Traffic	64-bit (80%) and 512-bit (20%) packets			
Network Size	4x4		8x8	
Network Type	Mesh	FB	Mesh	FB
Link Width (bit)	512	128	512	32
Average T_S	1	1.6	1	4.8
T_R	3	3	3	3
T_L	1	1	1	1
Router Radix	5	7	5	15

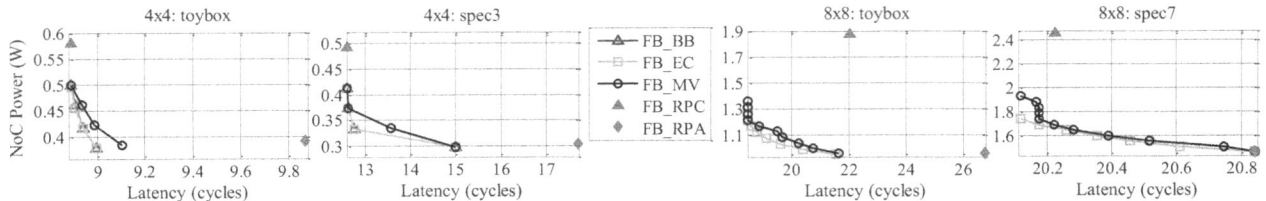

Figure 2. Tradeoff curves between overall NoC power and average packet latency.

eight schemes (x-axis), and the corresponding average packet latency (right y-axis and the curves) for different test cases. As can be seen, the power and latency results for FB_EC and FB_MV are very similar to those of FB_BB, demonstrating the effectiveness of the two proposed heuristic algorithms.

In addition, the proposed FB_EC and FB_MV schemes are considerably better than the mesh-based schemes in both power and latency. For example, FB_EC achieves on average 42.85% and 60.48% less NoC power consumption compared to the best results on 4x4 and 8x8 mesh network, respectively. This advantage mainly comes from two aspects. First, each router in the flattened butterfly (higher radix but narrower width) consumes less power compared to mesh routers (around 16% and 29% on 4x4 and 8x8 networks at the same injection rate, respectively). Second, the proposed algorithms can utilize the express channels in the flattened butterfly to maintain connectivity of active cores while allowing more routers to be powered off, thus having more power savings and less detours than the mesh. Note that although the serialization latency in flattened butterfly is slightly higher than in mesh, the reduced detours and the use of express channels in FB lead to much lower average packet latency than mesh.

5.2.3 Dynamic Power vs. Static Power

Figure 3 and Figure 4 also show the relative percentages between dynamic power and static power, which varies among different workloads. Overall, the static power percentage in flattened butterfly networks is slightly higher than that in mesh. This is because flattened butterflies have a smaller average hop count than meshes. In other words, packets in the flattened butterfly are forwarded through fewer routers, resulting in lower dynamic power and lower average injection rate per router. Table 2 shows the toybox example. As can be seen, when the same workload is executed on mesh and flattened butterfly, the static power percentage can be different due to the change in hop count and average injection rate. However, even if this relative static power percentage is higher in flattened butterfly, the absolute value of static power consumption of FB is still much lower than that of the mesh.

Table 2. Avg. hop count, inj. rate and static power percentage.

Test Case	Mesh			FB		
	Hop	Inj. Rate	Static %	Hop	Inj. Rate	Static %
toybox(4x4)	2.93	0.28	55	2.22	0.23	69
toybox(8x8)	7.73	0.24	59	3.51	0.18	76

6. CONCLUSION

In this paper, we propose *Smart Butterfly*, an effective NoC power-gating scheme that applies core-state-awareness to flattened butterfly networks. Smart Butterfly exploits the rich connectivity of flattened butterfly networks, and selectively powers off routers attached to sleeping cores to save more power. Furthermore, it achieves a wide range of power-latency trade-offs by adjusting the number of ON routers. We propose two heuristic algorithms to implement Smart Butterfly with different complexity and performance. Simulation results show that the two heuristic algorithms are able to achieve near-optimal solutions with low complexity, resulting in 42.85% and 60.48% less power consumption, on average, on 4x4 and 8x8 networks compared to a recently proposed mesh-based technique, respectively.

7. ACKNOWLEDGEMENT

This research is supported, in part, by the National Science Foundation (NSF) grant CCF-1321131 and the Software and Hardware Foundations program of the NSF.

8. REFERENCES

[1] Agarwal, N., Krishna, T., Peh, L. S., & Jha, N. K., GARNET: A detailed on-chip network model inside a full-system simulator. In *IEEE ISPASS*, pp. 33-42, 2009.

[2] Chen, L., & Pinkston, T. M., NoRD: Node-router decoupling for effective power-gating of on-chip routers. In *MICRO*, pp. 270-281, 2012.

[3] Chen, L., Zhao, L., Wang R., & Pinkston, T. M. (2014). MP3: Minimizing Performance Penalty for Power-gating of Clos Network-on-Chip", In *HPCA*, 2014.

[4] Das, R., *et al.*, Catnap: Energy Proportional Multiple Network-on-Chip," In *ISCA*, 2013.

[5] Kim, J., Balfour, J., & Dally, W., Flattened butterfly topology for on-chip networks. In *MICRO*, pp. 172-182, 2007.

[6] Kumar, A., Peh, L. S., Kundu, P., & Jha, N. K., Express virtual channels: towards the ideal interconnection fabric. In *ACM SIGARCH Comp. Architecture News*, 35(2), pp. 150-161, 2007.

[7] Ma, S., Jerger, N. E., & Wang, Z., Whole packet forwarding: Efficient design of fully adaptive routing algorithms for networks-on-chip. In *HPCA*, pp. 1-12, 2012.

[8] Madan, N., Buyuktosunoglu, A., Bose, P., & Annavaram, M., A case for guarded power gating for multi-core processors. In *HPCA*, pp. 291-300, 2011.

[9] Matsutani, H., Koibuchi, M., Amano, H., & Wang, D., Run-time power gating of on-chip routers using look-ahead routing. In *ASP-DAC*, pp. 55-60, 2008.

[10] Samih, A., *et al.*, Energy-efficient interconnect via router parking. In *HPCA*, pp. 508-519, 2013.

[11] Sun, C., *et al.*, DSENT-a tool connecting emerging photonics with electronics for opto-electronic networks-on-chip modeling. In *IEEE/ACM NOCS*, pp. 201-210, 2012.

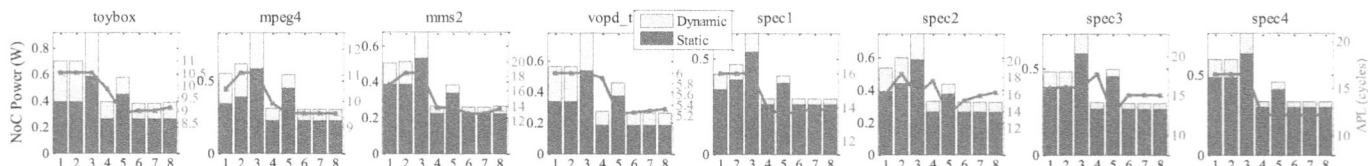

Figure 3. 4x4 results: (1-3) Mesh_BB, Mesh_RPA, Mesh_RPC, (4-5) FB_RPA, FB_RPC, (6-8) FB_BB, FB_EC, FB_MV

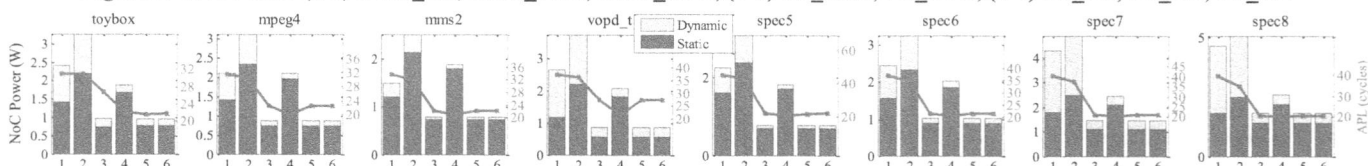

Figure 4. 8x8 results: (1-2) Mesh_RPA, Mesh_RPC, (3-4) FB_RPA, FB_RPC, (5-6) FB_EC, FB_MV

Energy-Efficient Dot Product Computation using a Switched Analog Circuit Architecture

Ihab Nahlus[†], Eric P. Kim[†], Naresh R. Shanbhag[†], and David Blaauw[*]

[†]Department of Electrical and Computer Engineering, University of Illinois, Urbana, IL 61801, USA

{nahlus2, epkim2, shanbhag}@illinois.edu

[*]Department of Electrical Engineering and Computer Science, University of Michigan, Ann Arbor, MI 48109, USA

blaauw@umich.edu

ABSTRACT

In this paper, we present switched analog circuit (SAC), a new circuit architecture, to implement an energy-efficient mixed-signal dot product (DP) kernel for machine learning and signal processing applications. SAC operates by fast switching the analog inputs to output via variable width digital pulses. The output accuracy and energy consumption of SAC is analyzed and verified for an average and Gaussian blur filter. Simulations in a commercial 130 nm process for a 120×120 image show energy savings of $19\times$-to-$32\times$ compared to a digital implementation for signal-to-noise ratios (SNRs) of 30 dB-to-24 dB, respectively.

Categories and Subject Descriptors

B.2 [**Hardware**]: Arithmetic and logic structures

Keywords

Switched analog circuit; Low-power; Dot product; Mixed-signal

1. INTRODUCTION

The demand for ubiquitous computing with learning and decision making capabilities has grown in the past several years. These applications need to process large amounts of data acquired by sensing the surrounding environment and are subject to strict energy demands. Figure 1 depicts a typical sensory data processing chain. Sensors such as CMOS image sensors acquire analog data, which is then processed by a digital processor, or an actuator. The dot product (DP) kernel within the processor implements a variety of functions including but not limited to vector inner products, correlators, filters, convolutions, multiply-accumulate, L-1 and L-2 norms, which are extensively used in classifiers such as support vector machines (SVMs), in deep learning networks, image processors, and communication receivers.

Conventionally, these kernels are designed using digital logic. This approach enables complex algorithms requiring

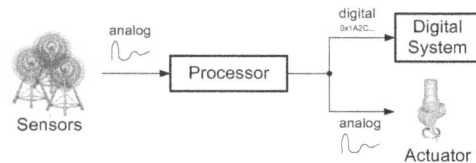

Figure 1: Block diagram of a sensory data processing chain.

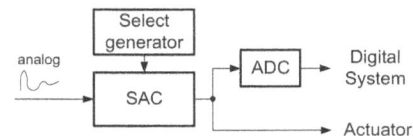

Figure 2: Switched analog circuit (SAC) implementation for processor kernel.

high precision to be implemented reliably, but at a high energy cost. Feature size scaling has reduced energy costs significantly, making digital design the favorable choice. However, as the number of sensors increase, the analog-to-digital converter (ADC) overhead can be quite large, especially if an analog output is required to drive an actuator. Analog processing has been reported to be more energy-efficient at low precision [4]. By operating in the analog domain, the overhead of ADCs and digital-to-analog converters (DACs) can be eliminated. Energy efficient designs have been proposed that use current summing, but their application has been limited to ultra high speed applications [2]. A mixed-signal approach that utilizes switched capacitors has been reported to give large energy savings [1]. However, these designs are susceptible to process, voltage and temperature (PVT) variations, and do not scale well with process technology which makes it challenging for implementing in sensory chains.

In this paper, we present switched analog circuit (SAC) (Fig. 2), which is an energy-efficient mixed-signal circuit architecture. SAC implements the DP kernel by fast switching the analog input to the output via variable width digital pulses. The input analog voltages are passed through an N input MUX with N select signals (Fig. 3(a)). By having only one select signal active at a time, and switching among the inputs at a high frequency, the output voltage is obtained as the weighted sum of the input voltages. An example operation with $N = 3$ is depicted in Fig. 3(c).

In this paper, we implement a SAC based average and

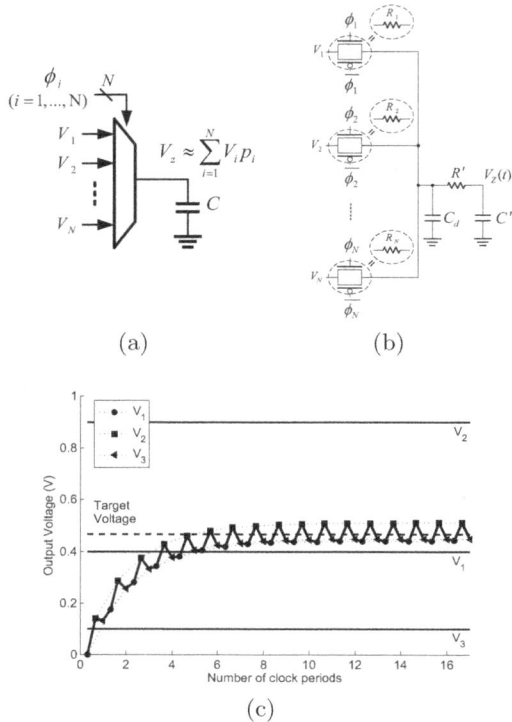

Figure 3: Switched analog circuit (SAC)-based DP kernel: (a) conceptual operation, (b) circuit implementation, and (c) output waveform for $N = 3$, $V_1 = 0.4$, $V_2 = 0.9$, $V_3 = 0.1$, and $p_1 = p_2 = p_3 = 1/3$.

Gaussian blur filter in a commercial 130 nm process. When applied to a 120×120 image, 19×-to-32× energy savings can be achieved compared to a digital implementation at a signal-to-noise ratio (SNR) of 30 dB-to-24 dB, respectively.

The remainder of the paper is organized as follows. Section 2 describes SAC in detail. Section 3 presents the behavioral model of SAC. Section 4 presents simulation results and Section 5 concludes the paper.

2. SWITCHED ANALOG CIRCUIT (SAC)

2.1 SAC-based DP kernel

A length N SAC-based DP kernel, as shown in Fig. 3(a), takes input voltages $V_1, \ldots, V_N$, and computes the output voltage $V_o = \sum_{i=1}^{N} V_i p_i$. The weights p_i are implemented by a set of non-overlapping pulses ϕ_i (i^{th} element of Φ_v) of period T and duty cycle p_i. The switch can be viewed as a switched resistor [3] network with its effective resistance divided by p_i. By designing T to be significantly smaller than the time constant of the RC network, V_z will converge to $\sum_{i=1}^{N} V_i p_i$, with accuracy increasing at an exponential rate with the number of cycles until it settles.

The circuit implementation of the SAC kernel is shown in Fig. 3(b). Transmission gates are used to implement the switches to allow full swing at the output. A detailed analysis of this kernel is given in Section 3. A series resistance R' and a capacitor C' is added to suppress the effect of variation in path resistances R_i.

2.2 Select generation

Generation of the duty-cycled clocks (select signals) with period T is needed for proper SAC operation. The select signals are generated by a *multi-phase clock generator* (MPCG) that provides clock inputs to the combinational logic. The MPCG is designed using a length M ring counter operating at a frequency $f_{CLK} \triangleq \frac{1}{T_{CLK}} = \frac{M}{T}$. The combinational logic generates pulses with variable width $\frac{x}{M}T$ with a phase offset of $\frac{y}{M}T$. For large M, the ring counter becomes expensive. An alternative would be to use a counter at the expense of complexity/energy.

2.3 Energy Consumption

For the SAC-based DP kernel, the total energy consumption per DP computation can be written as:

$$E_{tot}[n] \triangleq E_{SAC}[n] + \frac{nE_{MPCG}}{V}$$

where $E_{SAC}[n]$ is the energy consumption of the SAC DP kernel and combinational logic over n clock cycles, E_{MPCG} is the energy consumption of the MPCG per clock cycle, and V is the number of SAC DP kernels sharing the same MPCG. E_{MPCG} depends largely on the topology used and hence will be obtained through simulations. The energy dissipated in the combinational logic, gate and drain capacitors of the kernel is linear in n and dominates the energy dissipated in C', when C' and C_d are of the same order.

3. BEHAVIORAL MODEL

The transient response of the SAC computation kernel, a switched RC circuit, can be obtained using linear constant-coefficient difference equations. Let $\tau_{max} \triangleq \max_{i=1..N}(R_i)C_d$ be the largest time constant of the circuit when $R' = 0$ and $C' = 0$. Two conditions are imposed on the values of R' and C': C1) $R'C' \gg \tau_{max}$, and C2) $R' \gg \max_i(R_i)$. C1 ensures that the new time constant will be dominated by $R'C'$ while C2 will have an impact on the output accuracy as will be shown. Note: C1 is automatically satisfied if C2 is, by ensuring C' is of the same order as C_d. First, we make the following two claims:

Claim 1. If $T \ll R'C'$,

$$\tilde{V}_z \triangleq \lim_{n \to \infty} V_z[n] \approx \sum_{i=1}^{N} V_i p_i', \qquad (1)$$

where $V_z[n]$ is the DP kernel's output after n clock cycles, and $p_i' = \frac{\frac{p_i}{R'+R_i}}{\sum_{j=1}^{N} \frac{p_j}{R'+R_j}} \approx p_i$ (since $R' \gg R_j, j = 1, ..., N$).

Now, define the error at the output after n clock cycles to be $e[n] \triangleq V_0 - V_z[n]$, where $V_o = \sum_{i=1}^{N} V_i p_i$ is the ideal output.

Claim 2. The mean-square error $J[n, K]$ after n clock cycles is:

$$J[n, K] \triangleq E\{e[n]^2\} = E\{(V_0 - \tilde{V}_z)^2\} + K^n \alpha_A + K^{2n} \beta_A \quad (2)$$

where $K \triangleq e^{-\frac{T}{C'}\sum_{j=1}^{N} \frac{p_j}{R'+R_j}} \approx e^{-\frac{T}{R'C'}}$, and α_A and β_A are constants that depend largely on the input's 1st and 2nd order statistics. Note that as n increases, K^n will go to zero. Proofs for the above two claims have been omitted due to space limitations. Circuit simulation results in Section 4.3 support these claims.

Figure 5: Circuit simulation of a SAC-based Gaussian blur filter with $H = 5$ ($n = 5H$).

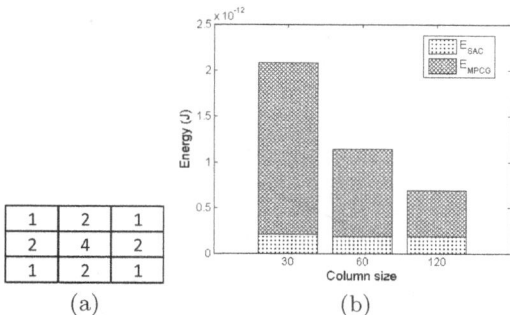

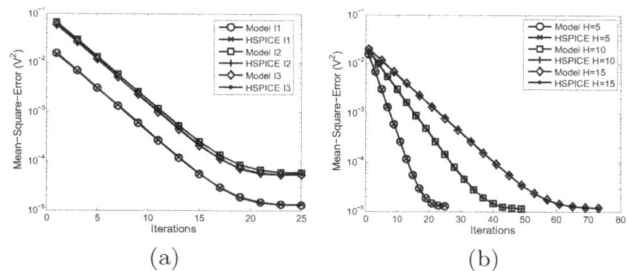

Figure 4: (a) Coefficients of a Gaussian blur filter with $\sigma^2 = 0.85$, and (b) Energy per computation breakdown of the Gaussian filter applied to 30×30, 60×60, and 120×120 images.

Let $H = \frac{R'C'}{T} = \frac{-1}{ln(K)}$. Then, decreasing H results in faster convergence but greater inaccuracy as $\tilde{V}_z$ will no longer equal V_0 since the approximation in (1) is no longer valid. As energy consumption has a strong dependence on the number of clock cycles, H and n become two important variables in the design of a SAC-based DP kernel. We finally note that the exact value of the resistor R' is unimportant as long as C2 is satisfied. A polysilicon resistor of around $1\,M\Omega$ in a commercial $130\,nm$ process with minimum width corresponds to area of 600 minimum sized transistors. This presents a large area overhead for small N ($N = 2$, e.g.) but for larger values of N ($N = 9$ in our implementation), we obtain large area savings (compared to digital implementation) since the same resistor will be shared by all N paths.

4. SIMULATIONS AND RESULTS

4.1 Simulation setup

A SAC-based DP kernel (Fig. 3(b)) is used to implement an image filter. Circuit simulations in a commercial $130\,nm$ CMOS process at the nominal corner were performed for image sizes 30×30, 60×60, and 120×120. We note that the image is processed on a per-row basis and hence $V = 30, 60$ and 120 for the different image sizes. The MPCG was designed as a ring counter that operates at $T_{CLK} = 400\,ps$ and gives $T = MT_{CLK}$, where M is the length of the ring counter. Three average filters of lengths $M = 9, 25$, and 49 were implemented which correspond to a 3×3, 5×5 and 7×7 window, respectively. These filters do not require any combinational logic at the output of the ring counter since the different phases already represent the coefficients. A 3×3 Gaussian blur filter with $\sigma^2 = 0.85$ (Fig. 4(a)) has also been implemented. For this filter, M is chosen to be 16 which is the sum of all coefficients. The D-flipflops in the ring counter are implemented using true single-phase clocking (TSPC). Select signals are generated using static-CMOS based NOR and NAND gates. Select signals corresponding to coefficient of unit value do not need a logic stage but are still passed through inverters to match the delay of other select signals. A single ring counter was shared for all parallel SAC units, while the combinational logic may be duplicated to ensure sharp rise and falls of the select signals. In our simulations, one set of logic gates for the 30×30 image, two sets for the

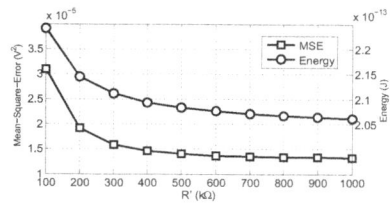

60×60 image, and four sets for the 120×120 image were used. For our design, simulations show that $E_{MPCG} \gg E_{SAC}$, and energy per single computation is dominated by $\frac{E_{MPCG}}{V}$. As more computation kernels can share the same ring counter, more energy benefits can be obtained (Fig. 4(b)).

4.2 Choice of R'

The auxiliary resistor R' and capacitor C' were designed to satisfy condition C1 and C2 (Section 3). To obtain a good value for R', the circuit was simulated at different values of R' while keeping $H = \frac{R'C'}{T}$ at a fixed value by adjusting C' accordingly. C1 was satisfied by choosing $R'C'$ large enough to dominate τ_{max}. Figure 5 shows the plot of the MSE and energy consumption of the circuit vs. R' with $H = 5$. The same trend was observed for different values of H. A total of $5H$ iterations were performed. It can be seen that MSE and energy consumption reduce as R' increases until $R' \approx 700k\Omega$ for the MSE and $R' \approx 900k\Omega$ for energy. Hence, in all simulations, R' was chosen to be $1M\Omega$, and the value of C' was set to obtain a specific value for H.

4.3 Validation of behavioral model

Comparison of circuit simulations and behavioral model for mean-square error (MSE) vs. iterations are shown in Fig. 6. Figure 6(a) shows the Gaussian filter applied to three different 30×30 images (I1,I2 and I3). I2 and I3 were chosen

Figure 6: Accuracy comparison between the behavioral model and circuit simulation for: (a) a Gaussian filter with different images and (b) Gaussian filter with varying H.

Table 1: Fitted accuracy parameter values of a Gaussian filter with $H = 5$ ($C' = 32\,fF$).

Image	α_A	β_A	$E\{(V_0 - \tilde{V}_z)^2\}$
I1	-3.07×10^{-4}	2.3×10^{-2}	1.4×10^{-5}
I2	-1.11×10^{-3}	9.83×10^{-2}	6.17×10^{-5}
I3	-1.44×10^{-3}	8.9×10^{-2}	5.96×10^{-5}

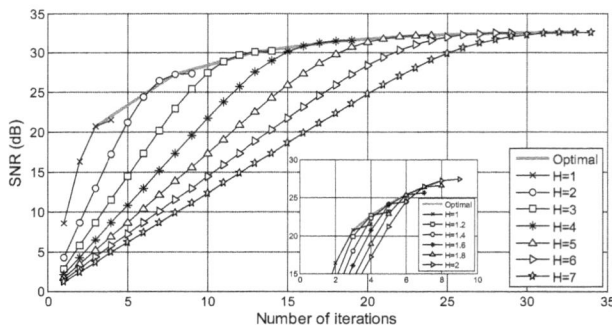

Figure 7: SNR vs. number of iterations of a Gaussian filter for a 30×30 image.

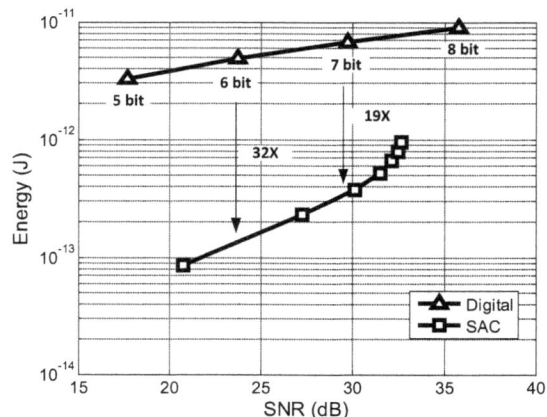

Figure 8: Comparison of SNR vs. energy per DP computation for a Gaussian filter.

to have similar statistics while being different from those of I1. Weighted least-squares fitting was applied to obtain the parameters α_A, β_A and $E\{(V_0 - \tilde{V}_z)^2\}$ in Section 3. The fitted parameters obtained for $H = 5$ ($C' = 32\,\text{fF}$) are tabulated in Table 1. It can be seen that the parameters for I2 and I3 are similar in value as expected.

In Fig. 6(b), H was varied for I1 to see its effect on MSE. As expected, the parameters α_A and β_A in this model are a weak function of H and depend largely on the input statistics. The asymptotic MSE value $E\{(V_0 - \tilde{V}_z)^2\}$ decreases as H increases as expected from Section 3. However, the decrease in MSE is minimal due to the overall accuracy being dominated by the imperfection of the select-signal generation block.

4.4 Design optimization

A large number of options exist for choosing the values of H and n to minimize the energy consumption of the SAC-based DP kernel for a given SNR. HSPICE simulations were performed on a Gaussian filter for I1, by sweeping over H at various iterations (Fig. 7). The number of iterations for a given SNR should be minimized since the linear component in E_{SAC} dominates ($\alpha_E \gg \beta_E$). From the close up view of $1 \leq H \leq 2$, it can be seen that the minimum iterations for a given SNR occur at $n = 5H - 2$. The optimal curve is obtained by joining these minimizing points. SNR improvements saturate around $H = 5$ due to the overall accuracy being dominated by the imperfection of the select-signal generation block.

4.5 Comparison to digital implementations

The SAC-based DP kernel is compared against a digital logic implementation using Baugh-Wooley multipliers (BWM) and ripple carry adders (RCA). To estimate the energy consumption of the adders and multipliers, the energy for a 1-bit full adder (E_{FA}) using a mirror-adder structure loaded with $FO4$ inverters was simulated. In a 130 nm process, $E_{FA} = 18.63\,\text{fJ}$. Energy consumption of a B_x bit RCA is then estimated to be:

$$E_{RCA}[B_x] = \alpha_{0 \to 1} B_x E_{FA} \qquad (3)$$

where $\alpha_{0 \to 1}$ is the activity factor of the RCA. We assume the inputs are uniformly distributed and hence $\alpha_{0 \to 1}$ is 0.25. The energy consumption of a B_x bit BWM is lower-bounded [5] by:

$$E_{BW}[B_x] \geq E_{FA}(B_x^2 - 2B_x + 2)$$

The SNR vs. energy per DP computation is shown in Fig. 8 for a 120×120 image. For $SNR \approx 24\,\text{dB}$, energy savings are approximately $32\times$ whereas for $SNR \approx 30\,\text{dB}$, the energy savings are approximately $19\times$. These savings are pessimistic as E_{BW} was based on a lower bound.

5. CONCLUSION

In this paper, we have presented a new energy-efficient mixed-signal DP kernel that can achieve large energy savings for the same level of accuracy. This work opens up the possibility of employing SAC to design inference kernels for various emerging applications.

6. ACKNOWLEDGEMENTS

This work was supported by Systems on Nanoscale Information fabriCs (SONIC), one of the six SRC STARnet Centers, sponsored by MARCO and DARPA.

7. REFERENCES

[1] M. Duppils and C. Svensson. Low power mixed analog-digital signal processing. In *Proc. of Int. Symp. on Low Power Elect. and Design*, pages 61–66, 2000.

[2] Y. Lu and E. Alon. Design techniques for a 66 Gb/s 46 mW 3-tap decision feedback equalizer in 65 nm CMOS. *IEEE J. Solid-State Circuits*, 48(12):3243–3257, Dec. 2013.

[3] M. H. Perrott, S. Pamarti, E. Hoffman, F. S. Lee, S. Mukherjee, C. Lee, V. Tsinker, S. Perumal, B. Soto, N. Arumugam, et al. A low-area switched-resistor loop-filter technique for fractional-N synthesizers applied to a MEMS-based programmable oscillator. In *IEEE Int. Solid-State Circuits Conf. (ISSCC)*, pages 244–245, 2010.

[4] R. Sarpeshkar. Analog versus digital: extrapolating from electronics to neurobiology. *Neural computation*, 10(7):1601–1638, 1998.

[5] J. H. Satyanarayana and K. K. Parhi. A theoretical approach to estimation of bounds on power consumption in digital multipliers. *IEEE Trans. Circuits Syst. II*, 44(6):473–481, 1997.

Gated Low-Power Clock Tree Synthesis for 3D-ICs

Tiantao Lu and Ankur Srivastava

Dept. of Electrical and Computer Engineering, University of Maryland, College Park, MD, U.S.A.

{ttlu, ankurs}@umd.edu

ABSTRACT

In this paper, we minimize 3D clock power using shutdown gates to selectively turn off unnecessary clock activities. In 3D-IC, shutdown signals require large-sized Through-Silicon-Vias(TSVs), so we propose a simulated annealing(SA) based algorithm along with a force-directed TSV placer to decide the selection of shutdown gates and the locations of TSVs under layout whitespace constraint. Furthermore, we recognize optimal power saving is achieved when the clock tree itself is designed simultaneously with the shutdown network. Experimental results show that our heuristic decreases the total clock power by more than 20% with less than 1.5% wirelength overhead while ensuring zero clock skew.

Categories and Subject Descriptors

B.7.2 [**Integrated Circuits**]: Design Aids—*Placement and routing*; J.6 [**Computer-Aided Engineering**]: Computer-aided design (CAD)

Keywords

3D-ICs; TSV; clock gating; optimization

1. INTRODUCTION

Clock gating is an effective approach to reduce the clock power in modern VLSI design, which takes up to 70% of the chip's total power[12]. The reason behind such dominant clock power dissipation is that clock network is a large netlist that spans across the whole chip, and has the fastest switching rate. Clock gating exploits the fact that instructions are not executed with even frequency, making the usage of certain sequential logics highly non-uniform temporally. This enables us to apply control signal at intermediate clock tree node to shut down all its descendants' clock signal and power supply, when clock is not needed, thereby reducing the overall power dissipated by wires, buffers, and synchronous circuits.

Clock gating for 2D clock tree has been extensively studied in the past [5, 11, 4, 8, 3, 10, 13]. Recently with the emergence of three-dimensional circuits (3D-ICs), 3D clock design has become an active research topic. Current work in 3D clock synthesis has focused on minimizing total wire length, clock skew and clock slew. For example, [7] extended the 2D deferred-merge-embedding(DME)[2] to ensure zero-skew in 3D clock tree. [15] implemented a cutting-based approach for abstract clock tree generation, and routed the 3D clock network to minimize clock slew and total wire length.

The primary concern of this paper is the design of the 3D clock shutdown network, which provides enable signals for the shutdown gates. The shutdown network in 2D clock tree is a planar *Star* network(one centralized control center delivering enable signals to each of the shutdown gates through one wire) and the wiring overhead is usually ignored, meaning that designers can always deliver the enable signals to wherever needed. Works in [5, 11, 10] insert control gate as long as the power saved by shutting down the subtree outweighs the power consumed by the gate's control network. However, the assumption that shutdown gates can be inserted at every tree node and wiring overhead of the *Star* network is negligible is no longer valid for 3D clock tree.

In 3D clock tree, *clock TSVs* deliver clock signals from clock source to each of the clock sinks while *control TSVs* provide shutdown signal from a centralized control center to shutdown gates. Since clock synthesis is usually performed after cell placement, layout whitespace for TSVs is limited. However, both TSVs occupy large placement area and reliability[6] and signal integrity[9] requirements enforce TSVs to maintain certain keep-out area, both of which constrain the usage of TSVs. In addition, although TSVs offer short and fast vertical connections, excessive usage of TSVs increases the manufacturing overhead and makes the system's reliability questionable, due to the degradation of TSVs over time. The restriction that limited number of *clock TSVs* and *control TSVs* are available to designers changes the way how 3D clock tree should be synthesized and how clock gating technique should be applied.

To summarize, given limited layout whitespace for *control TSVs* and *clock TSVs*, how to design a shutdown clock network for 3D-IC and how the design of the shutdown network affects the design of the 3D clock tree itself are new and challenging problems. An exhaustive search approach in order to determine the selection of shutdown gates will take at least $O(2^n)$, where n is the number of clock sinks. For a modern synchronizing processor, n could vary from the order of several hundred to several millions, depending on the granularity of the design. In the following sections, we are to show our methodology to smartly allocate shutdown gates such that all the TSVs can be legally placed inside layout whitespace and clock tree power is minimized. More specifically, this paper makes the following contributions:

1. We identify the problem of layout constrained shutdown network design for 3D-ICs, and discuss its significant difference from 2D clock gating techniques.

2. We develop a force-directed placer to remove the overlap between TSVs(and their KOZs) and to place the TSVs within layout whitespace.

3. We present a simulated annealing(SA) based heuristic to handle the gate insertions problem(Problem 1). Based on a given 3D clock tree, we find the optimal shutdown gates' selections and TSV locations such that the overall power consumption is minimized.

4. We solve Problem 2(Clock tree synthesis with simultaneous clock gating) by placing the *control TSVs* simultaneously with *clock TSVs*. We modified the SA approach to account for the wire length increase when *clock TSV* are moved from their optimal locations, which are determined by 3D DME algorithm[7].

5. We develop an effective linear-time heuristic to generate an initial state for SA to significantly speedup the convergence and also saves more power compared to the SA process without initial state setup.

The organization of this paper is as follows. We provide an overview of related works in 2D clock gating techniques and 3D clock tree synthesis in Section 1. Section 2 formulates the gated 3D clock tree synthesis problem. In Section 3 we present our 3D gated clock tree synthesis algorithm. Experimental results are presented in Section 4 and Section 5 concludes the paper.

2. PROBLEM FORMULATION

Let $M = \{M_1, M_2, ..., M_n\}$ denotes clock sinks(modules). Each clock sink has a fixed position(x_i, y_i, z_i). Let $V = \{v_1, v_2, ..., v_{2n-1}\}$ be the nodes of the clock tree, where $v_1, v_2, ..., v_n$ refer to leaf nodes (clock sinks) and the rest are internal nodes. We assume the clock tree is fully binary. We define an e_i to be the tree edge between v_i and its parent. We identify each edge e_i is associated with a potential gating location, G_i, where G_i offers shut-down for the subtree rooted at v_i when necessary. We assume the control center is fixed at the center of layer Z_0. All the control signal paths form a *Star* network(a routing network that each sink connects to the source through a separate wire).

We also assume that abstract clock tree topology is given. Abstract tree topology contains the ungated tree structure, with known X/Y/Z coordinates of all clock sinks. We investigate two consecutive problems, as discussed below.

2.1 Problem1: Gate insertion under constrained placement of control TSVs

Given an ungated clock tree, Problem 1 investigates where to insert shutdown gates among all 2n-1 gating candidates, (n = total number of clock sinks) such that the dynamic power of the gated clock tree is minimized while the *control TSVs* can be legally placed. Here the locations of *clock TSVs* are fixed, and *clock TSVs* are treated as placement blockages as we place the *control TSVs*.

2.2 Problem2: 3D clock tree synthesis with TSV and control TSV co-placement

Given an ungated abstract clock tree, Problem 2 aims to construct a zero-skew clock tree with simultaneous gate insertion, such that the dynamic power and total wire length of the clock tree are minimized, while the *clock TSVs* and *control TSVs* can be legally placed inside layout whitespace.

Traditionally the X/Y location of internal nodes are decided by performance metrics such as total wire length, clock skew, slew and phase delay using the deferred-merging and embedding (DME) technique[2].

In Problem 2, we propose that the X/Y location of internal nodes should be decided simultaneously with the placement of the shutdown gates and *control TSVs*. This is because when the physical routing of 3D clock tree is completely fixed and *clock TSVs* are purely treated as placement blockages, *control TSVs* may not be able to utilize all the whitespace

effectively. However, moving *clock TSVs* may increase the clock tree's overall wire length and clock skew, so there exists a trade-off between power savings, brought by clock gating, and performance-metric such as wire length and clock skew.

3. METHODOLOGY

In this section we first develop a force-directed TSV placer, and then present our algorithms to solve both Problem 1 and 2. We also discuss approaches to speed up the algorithm.

3.1 TSV placement

The number of *control TSVs*, which carry the shutdown gates' control signals, is proportional to the number of the shutdown gates used. However, since clock tree synthesis is usually performed after the placement of blocks/ standard cells/ IO pins, the layout whitespace left for TSVs is limited. Moreover, TSVs have larger dimensions than standard cells, for example, a TSV could occupy $5\mu m \times 5\mu m$ to $30\mu m \times 30\mu m$ in area, depending on different fabrication technologies, as compared to less than $1\mu m \times 1\mu m$ standard cells at sub-micro technology node. In addition, TSVs have to maintain certain distance from each other, due to mechanical[6] and signal integrity[9] considerations. The TSV placement problem is to place the *clock TSVs* and *control TSVs* such that each TSV is located inside the layout area and outside other TSVs' keep-out-zone(KOZ).

We adopt the force-directed placement idea in [14] to solve the TSV placement problem. Overlap between TSVs, and overlap between TSVs and placement boundaries produce forces to move TSVs to the overlapping-free regions during each iteration. The magnitude of the force is proportional to the area that overlaps. The direction of force is the combination of two kinds of overlap: (1) the overlap between *control TSVs* and other TSV's KOZ; (2) the overlap between *control TSVs* and the boundary region. Fig.1 illustrates these two forces. Here we assume the clock tree is given so the *clock TSVs* are fixed and treated as placement obstacles(more details in Section 3.2). We later make all *clock TSVs* and *control TSV* movable in Section 3.3.

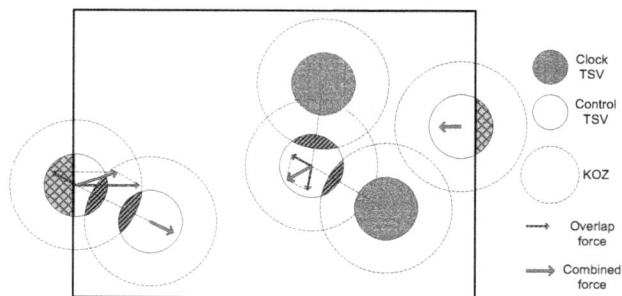

Figure 1: Force-directed placer to place *control TSVs* inside the TSV layout whitespace.

3.2 Problem 1

As mentioned in Section 2.1, Problem 1 treats *clock TSVs* as fixed placement obstacles. We use the the force-directed TSV placer to iteratively move *control TSVs* to remove overlaps. The force-directed TSV placer is integrated into a simulated annealing based (SA) framework, which aims to find the optimal selection of *control TSVs* that could fit into current chip layout, while minimizing the total clock power.

Fig.2 presents our SA based algorithm to solve Problem 1. It starts with an estimation *control TSVs* number that can fit into the whitespace. Then a set of shutdown gates are randomly selected to form the initial state. Iteration begins as we try to fit the selected *control TSVs* into the current layout whitespace, using the force-directed placer. If the placement fails, we reject the current selection immediately. Then we remove one *control TSV* in high overlapping area, hoping the remaining *control TSVs* can be legally placed in next iteration. Otherwise, if the placement is successful, simulated annealing process probabilistically accepts or rejects the current selection, based on the clock tree's total power consumption. If current selection is accepted, we add one more *control TSV*, hoping it'll bring us more power saving in the next iteration. If the selection is rejected due to an increase in clock power, we substitute one *control TSV* with one unused *control TSV*. We update the annealing temperature afterwards. When the annealing procedure converges, an optimal set of shutdown gates are chosen, which achieves maximum power saving and all the TSVs can be legally placed within the layout whitespace.

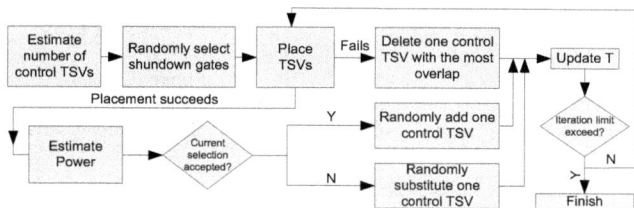

Figure 2: Flowchart of simulated annealing based approach for solving Problem 1.

3.3 Problem 2

When solving Problem 1, we notice that when the location of *clock TSVs* is fixed, layout area cannot be fully utilized. Therefore, we modified the force-directed placer to place *clock TSVs* simultaneously with *control TSVs*.

We adopt similar SA based iterative framework to solve Problem 2. The primary modification is that after each successful TSV placement, the clock tree itself needs to be resynthesized to meet the zero-skew constraint, and the clock tree's wire length might increase slightly, assuming the ungated clock tree already achieves minimum wire length. The time complexity of DME-based clock tree synthesis is bounded by O(n) where n is the number of clock sinks[7]. So this extra synthesis step won't increase the time complexity of our SA based approach asymptotically. In order to control the growth of total wire length, the objective function in simulated annealing is modified to be the weighted sum of the total clock power and total wire length.

3.4 Setting up initial state

SA's solution quality and runtime heavily rely on the initial state. In order to speed up our SA based algorithm, we develop a snippet to setup the initial state before SA begins. We start with an ungated routed zero-skew clock tree, and iteratively select the gate with maximum power saving. The procedure is summarized in Alg.1

4. EXPERIMENTAL RESULT

We evaluate the performance of our clock gating algorithm based on the benchmark circuits from ISPD clock network

---

Algorithm 1 Setting up initial state for SA

0. $S = \varnothing$; $U = \{G_1, G_2, ..., G_{2n-1}\}$;
1. m = estimation of available *control TSV* numbers;
2. Construct a zero-skew ungated clock tree using DME-3D algorithm[7];
3. **Repeat**
4.   Calculate the power saving when inserting each one of the gate in set U;
5.   Pick the gate insertion candidate G_i whose power saving is largest and add to S;
6.   Remove G_i from U;
7.   if *control TSV* is need when insert G_i, update m;
8. **Until** m = 0 or U = $\varnothing$.

---

synthesis contest[1]. Since the benchmark circuits are originally designed for 2D chip (with an area of A), we randomly partition all the clock sinks into N layers, with an area of $\sqrt{N}A$ on each layer, as in [5, 15]. We randomly generate several whitespaces for TSVs, where TSVs are to be placed.

The diameter of the TSV we use for simulation is 5 μm, and the minimum keep-out distance between centers of neighboring TSVs is 12 μm.

Table 1: Power saving(%), Wire Length Increase(%) results after solving P1 and P2

ckt	Layout whitespace constraint	Power saving(%)				WL increase(%)	
		P1	P1 (Init.)	P2	P2 (Init.)	P2	P2 (Init.)
f11	strict	6.9	7.2	13.1	15.4	0.72	0.53
	medium	18.9	22.6	25.2	25.2	0.95	0.73
	loose	27.0	27.0	28.3	28.9	1.03	0.8
f12	strict	10.5	10.8	14.7	14.9	0.74	0.69
	medium	17.3	17.3	21.2	21.3	1.14	1.14
	loose	25.8	26.0	27.3	27.4	3.1	2.09
f21	strict	7.5	8.3	17.3	20.3	1.23	1.19
	medium	15.8	16.5	23.3	24.1	1.36	1.35
	loose	27.1	27.8	30.1	30.1	1.52	1.53
f22	strict	9.2	11.9	15.1	15.1	2.23	2.15
	medium	16.5	16.5	20.6	20.6	2.92	2.58
	loose	21.6	21.6	22.5	22.9	3.03	2.32
f31	strict	14.1	19.8	21	21.4	1.49	0.93
	medium	21.4	24	26.7	27.5	1.37	1.47
	loose	27.5	28.2	29	29.4	1.92	1.88
f32	strict	11.6	12.	15.4	15.4	0.98	0.97
	medium	18.2	21.5	23.5	25.9	2.05	1.79
	loose	25.9	26.1	26.3	26.3	2.65	2.65
Average		17.9	19.2	22.3	22.9	1.69	1.49

The results for clock power saving and wire length increasement in percentage (compared to a ungated clock tree) are summarized in Tab.1. Three sets of layout whitespace constraint(for TSV placement) are imposed on six ISPD benchmarks(strict = $8100\mu m^2$, medium = $14400\mu m^2$, loose = $22500\mu m^2$). Note that the chip area is fixed for each benchmark circuit. Solving Problem 1 achieves 17.9% power reduction on average(column 3). When a loose TSV placement constraint is applied, we are able to use more *control TSVs*, which leads to more significant power saving. Initial state is set up using Alg.1, and slightly increases the power saving(compare column 4 to column 3). Since in Problem 1 we design the shutdown network after clock tree synthesis, (thus the wire length increase after solving P1 is zero and not shown) the placement of *control TSVs* is hindered by fixed locations of *clock TSVs*. However, in Problem 2 we place the *clock TSVs* simultaneously with *control TSVs*, which enables a better whitespace utility. We see a further decrease in clock power(column 5), compare to column 3, with a slight increase in total wire length(column 7). Again Alg.1 sets up the initial state for P2 and continues to reduce clock power(column 6) with less wire length overhead(column 8).

Setting up SA's initial state also improves runtime. As shown in Table.2, in both P1 and P2, SA's runtime decreases after running Alg.1 under each of the whitespace constraints. Finally, usages of *control TSVs* are reported in column 7-8 in Table.2. The co-placement of TSVs in P2 improves the whitespace utility thus more *control TSVs* are available to obtain better power savings.

Fig.3 and Fig.4 illustrate the simulated annealing process for solving Problem 1 and 2 for ISPD09f11 benchmark, respectively. Each successful move is plotted while rejected moves and failures of placement are omitted for brevity. The dash black line indicates the maximum power saving when gates are inserted at every clock tree node. Relaxing the TSV placement constraint results in better power savings since more *control TSVs* can be used. In Fig.3(b) initial state is setup using Alg.1, and SA converges faster and obtains better power results compared to Fig.3(a). Rather than treating *clock TSVs* as placement obstacles in P1(Fig.3), P2 places *control TSVs* simultaneously with *clock TSVs*, as shown in Fig.4. Compare Fig.4(a) to Fig.3(a), better power savings are achieved under every whitespace constraint. Again Fig.4(b) speeds up the convergence with initial state.

Table 2: Runtime(s) and number of *control TSV* used when solving P1 and P2

ckt	Layout whitespace constraint	Runtime(s)				# TSVs	
		P1	P1 (Init.)	P2	P2 (Init.)	P1	P2
f11	strict	9.2	6.7	55.4	28	10	21
	medium	19.4	12.5	99.2	69.3	42	72
	loose	66.7	24.9	129.9	55.3	79	116
f12	strict	9.0	6.2	15.8	10.2	9	22
	medium	30.2	23.4	43.9	32.8	20	51
	loose	32.9	26.2	62.0	43.0	44	83
f21	strict	14.3	9.5	36.5	25.9	12	24
	medium	29.8	16.7	67.0	46.4	26	53
	loose	40.2	22.5	108.3	43	45	85
f22	strict	7.3	6.9	17.9	12.4	10	18
	medium	7.7	7.0	23.6	20.7	18	39
	loose	15.1	9.8	30.5	22.6	32	57
f31	strict	29	18.3	68.7	37.7	8	17
	medium	55.2	48.2	132.9	87.8	14	38
	loose	181.1	131.1	292.9	146.3	38	75
f32	strict	21.5	11.8	69.6	45.9	9	18
	medium	58.8	23.8	137.8	59.1	17	38
	loose	99.6	65.6	253.2	111.1	37	66
Average		40.4	26.2	91.4	49.9	26.1	49.6

5. CONCLUSION

We design a shutdown network to save clock power for TSV-based 3D-ICs. We propose a simulated annealing based heuristic to select shutdown gates, while ensuring all the *clock TSVs* and *control TSVs* can be legally placed in the whitespace. We further modify the clock tree itself to enhance the usage of TSV placement area, so that more *control TSVs* can be placed and better power savings are achieved. Our experimental results show that our heuristic can effectively find the optimal selection of shutdown gates and TSV locations, with more than 20% clock power savings and less than 1.5% percent wire length overhead while ensuring zero clock skew.

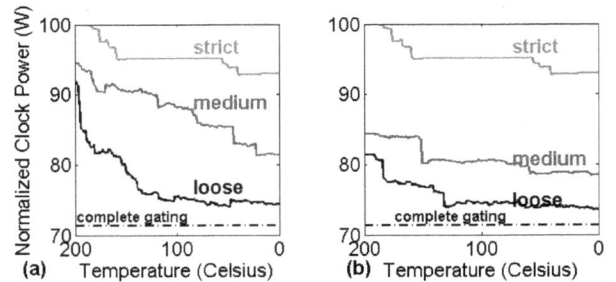

Figure 3: Simulated annealing process using ispd09f11 benchmark. Three area constraints are applied. (a) SA process when solving P1(fixed *clock TSV* position). (b) SA process when initial state is set up for P1.

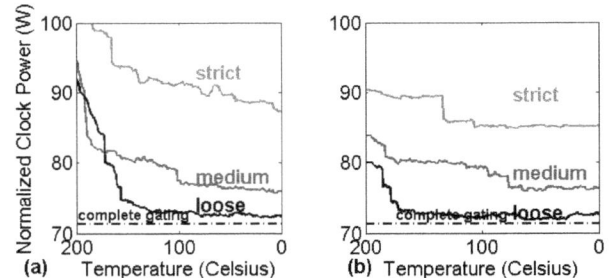

Figure 4: (a) SA process when solving P2.(co-placement of *clock TSVs* and *control TSVs*) (b) SA process with initial state for P2.

6. REFERENCES

[1] Ispd 2009 clock network synthesis contest. http://ispd.cc/contests/09/ispd09cts.html.

[2] T.-H. Chao, et al. Zero skew clock routing with minimum wirelength. *Circuits and Systems II: Analog and Digital Signal Processing, IEEE Transactions on*, 1992.

[3] W.-C. Chao and W.-K. Mak. Low-power Gated and Buffered Clock Network Construction. *ACM Trans. Des. Autom. Electron. Syst.*, 2008.

[4] M. Donno, et al. Clock-tree power optimization based on RTL clock-gating. In *DAC*, 2003.

[5] A. Farrahi, et al. Activity-driven clock design. *TCAD*, 2001.

[6] M. Jung, et al. TSV stress-aware full-chip mechanical reliability analysis and optimization for 3DIC. In *DAC*, 2011.

[7] T.-Y. Kim and T. Kim. Clock Tree Synthesis for TSV-based 3D IC Designs. *ACM Trans. Des. Autom. Electron. Syst.*, 2011.

[8] H. Li, et al. DCG: deterministic clock-gating for low-power microprocessor design. *VLSI Systems*, 2004.

[9] C. Liu, et al. Full-chip TSV-to-TSV coupling analysis and optimization in 3D IC. In *DAC*, 2011.

[10] J. Lu, et al. Fast Power- and Slew-Aware Gated Clock Tree Synthesis. *VLSI Systems, IEEE Transactions on*, 2012.

[11] J. Oh and M. Pedram. Gated clock routing for low-power microprocessor design. *Computer-Aided Des of Integrated Circ. and Sys., IEEE Transactions on*, 2001.

[12] R. S. Shelar and M. Patyra. Impact of Local Interconnects on Timing and Power in a High Performance Microprocessor. In *ISPD*, ISPD '10, 2010.

[13] W. Shen, et al. An Effective Gated Clock Tree Design Based on Activity and Register Aware Placement. *VLSI Systems, IEEE Transactions on*, 2010.

[14] N. Viswanathan and C. Chu. FastPlace: efficient analytical placement using cell shifting, iterative local refinement,and a hybrid net model. *TCAD*, 2005.

[15] X. Zhao, et al. Low-Power and Reliable Clock Network Design for Through-Silicon Via (TSV) Based 3D ICs. *Components, Packaging and Manufacturing Technology, IEEE Transactions on*, 2011.

Unlocking the True Potential of 3D CPUs with Micro-Fluidic Cooling

Caleb Serafy, Ankur Srivastava and Donald Yeung
University of Maryland, College Park, MD, USA
{cserafy1, ankurs, yeung}@umd.edu

ABSTRACT

As technology scaling is coming to an end, 3D integration is a promising technology to continue transistor density scaling in the future and facilitate new architectural designs. However heat removal is a serious challenge in 3D ICs. A promising solution is micro-fluidic (MF) cooling. In this paper we argue that aggressive cooling methods are necessary to unlock the true potential of 3D ICs. We simulate a spectrum of 3D CPU architectures which offer vast improvements to performance, but are inefficient and thermally infeasible with air cooling alone. Our results show that integrating micro-fluidic cooling can increase average performance by 2.62x and energy efficiency by 1.78x by unlocking new architectural configurations.

Categories and Subject Descriptors

B.8.2 [**Performance and Reliability**]: Performance Analysis and Design Aids

Keywords

3D-IC; liquid cooling; stacked DRAM; memory controller

1. INTRODUCTION

Vertical integration is a promising technology that allows chips to be stacked and interconnected using through silicon vias (TSVs). Such a technology can continue transistor density scaling beyond the end of technology scaling. Vertical integration can facilitate heterogeneous integration, creating new SoC architectures using disparate manufacturing processes, and reduce global wirelengths, improving critical path delays and interconnect power dissipation.

Although 3D integration has the potential to offer drastic improvements to performance, it also brings significant challenges, especially with respect to cooling. For one, 3D stacking significantly increases power density. Furthermore, there exists a layer of insulation material separating each layer in a 3D stack, creating a large thermal resistance between the heat sink and the intermediate layers of the stack. This trapped heat effect causes 3D ICs to become very hot [12, 2]. In addition to causing thermal violations, higher temperatures induce more leakage power, reducing the energy efficiency and possibly resulting in thermal runaway.

With traditional air cooling, 3D ICs must have very low power density on the intermediate layers due to the trapped heat effect. This severely limits the true potential of 3D integration. To unlock more aggressive designs, active cooling solutions must be considered. In this work we consider

micro-fluidic cooling, which removes heat from each layer by pumping liquid through micro-channels fabricated on the back side of the chip [2]. This concept is illustrated in Figure 1. Heat from each layer conducts through the substrate and into the fluid, which is then pumped out of the system. While micro-fluidic cooling does require some power overhead to pump the fluid, we show that the pumping power is quite low and micro-fluidic cooling can increase the total energy efficiency of a 3D IC (including pumping power) by reducing leakage power. With the additional cooling capacity offered by micro-fluidic cooling, new design opportunities become feasible, such as stacking cores, increasing frequency and increasing core utilization.

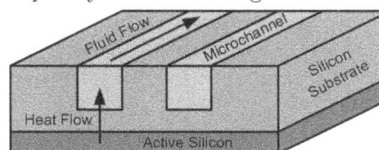

Figure 1: Micro-Fluidic Cooling

In this paper we consider 3D CPU architectures with stacked DRAM. Stacking logic layers allows core count to be increased without increasing the footprint area of the chip or reducing the complexity of each core. Heterogeneously integrating DRAM on top of logic allows the DRAM bus to be fabricated using TSVs, facilitating a faster and wider DRAM bus [9]. Because TSV counts in modern 3D processes can be on the order of 1000's of TSVs [10], parallel memory access can be achieved by implementing a separate memory controller and bus to each DRAM bank. This could significantly increase the utilization of the chip when running memory bound applications [7, 9].

Although vertical integration of CPUs potentially offers great improvements to system performance, without aggressive cooling methods many of these opportunities will be thermally infeasible. In this work we quantify the performance and energy efficiency possible in a 3D CPU architecture with traditional air cooling, and show the extent to which these metrics can be improved when micro-fluidic cooling is integrated into the system. Specifically, this work makes the following contributions:

- We propose a simulation flow for 3D CPUs with stacked DRAM and micro-fluidic cooling

- We show that many high performance architectures are thermally infeasible without aggressive localized cooling

- We quantify the improvement to performance and energy efficiency unlocked by co-design of 3D CPUs with micro-fluidic cooling

2. ANALYSIS APPROACH

In this section we detail the simulation flow used to obtain our results. The flow is illustrated in Figure 2. We simulate performance using a cycle accurate simulator, and our DRAM latency model. We use performance statistics to estimate the power of each CPU component using McPAT, and then simulate the generated power profiles using our thermal model. We account for the relationship between leakage power and temperature by iteratively solving our thermal model and scaling leakage power accordingly. Details of each simulation step are provided below.

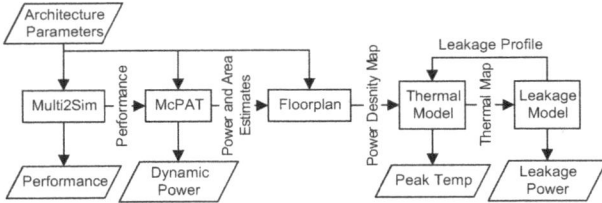

Figure 2: Flowchart of Analysis Approach

2.1 3D CPU Architecture

Cores: In this work we simulate multi-core 3D stacked DRAM processors. Architectural details are given in Table 1. The 3D CPU contains a shared L2 cache distributed in 512kB slices adjacent to each core. Each core/L2 slice has an associated router which is used to move data between any core and any L2 slice. Routers are interconnected in a 3D super-mesh configuration (see below) with a 3-cycle link latency. Each core is composed of five components: Memory management unit (MMU), load store unit (LSU), rename unit (RAT), instruction fetch unit (IFU) and execution unit (EX).

Memory Controllers: Each memory controller has a 64B bus implemented with 512 vertical interconnects (TSVs), and controls a specific region of DRAM. Each L2 slice is connected to a specific memory controller (MC), and can only contain data from that MC's region of DRAM.

Floorplan: The floor plan for each logic layer consists of a 4x4 tiling of cores and corresponding slices of the L2, with memory controllers (MCs) inserted between rows. A section of the floorplan of a single logic layer (16 cores) with 8 MCs is illustrated in Figure 4(b). Architectures containing more than 16 cores are created by stacking multiple logic layers. Figure 4(a) illustrates a 64 core 3D CPU with stacked DRAM.

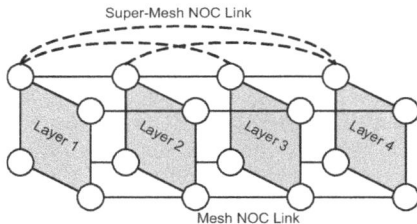

Figure 3: Example Super-Mesh NOC with four layers and four routers per layer

Cores	{**16**, 32, 64}
Technology	45 nm
Clock Rate	{**2.4**, 3.0, 3.6} GHz
Memory Controllers	{**0.125**, 0.25, 0.5} per Core
Branch Predictor	4k Entry 2-Level
Issue	Out of Order
Reorder Buffer	64 entries
Fetch/Dec/Issue Width	4
Functional Units	4 IALU, 1 IMult, 2 FPALU, 1 FPMult
BTB Size	1024 entries
Private L1 I/D Cache	256 Sets per Core, 2-Way, 64B Block (32kB per Core) @ 2 cycle
Shared L2 Cache	512 Sets per Core, 16-Way, 64B Block (512kB per Core) @ 7 cycles
NOC type	3D Super-Mesh
NOC link latency	3 cycles

Table 1: Architectural Parameters (baseline values in bold)

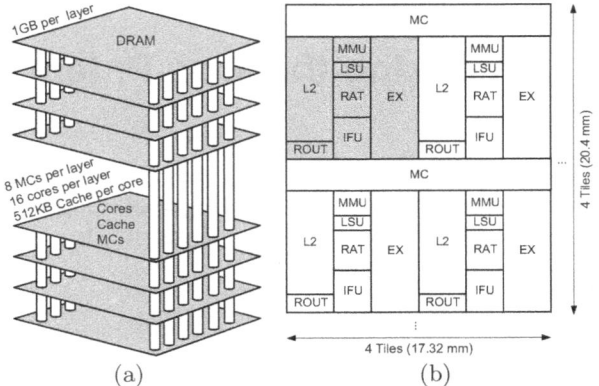

Figure 4: (a) 3D stacked DRAM architecture (b) floorplan of a logic layer (single core/L2 tile shown in gray)

3D Super-Mesh NOC: Vertical links in the 3D mesh NOC are implemented using TSVs. TSVs are very short, resulting in very low RC delays across a TSV [11]. For this reason, multiple layers can be traversed in a single NOC hop. In this work we modify a traditional 3D mesh NOC by connecting each router to *all* routers above and below, as opposed to just those that are in adjacent layers. We call this configuration a 3D super-mesh NOC, illustrated in Figure 3. Super-mesh links are shown with dashed lines for only one vertical column of routers in this figure for the purpose of readability, but in reality such links exist in each column.

2.2 Performance Estimation

In this work we use Multi2Sim (M2S) 3.4, a cycle accurate CPU simulator, to simulate performance across different benchmarks for each architectural combination. Performance simulation requires a model of DRAM latency, which we present in Section 2.2.1. Performance statistics generated from M2S are used as the inputs to the power model, which is introduced in Section 2.3.

2.2.1 DRAM Latency Model

Although in reality DRAM latency depends on many factors, many performance simulators, including the one we use in this work, simply model memory latency as a constant value. We propose a model for the average memory latency time, comprised of five different steps in the DRAM access procedure, starting at the time a last level cache (LLC) miss is detected. We estimate the average duration of each step as a function of the architectural parameters. The five steps are as follows: (1) MC Queuing Delay, (2) Memory Addr. Translation, (3) Addr. Transfer Delay, (4) DRAM Core Access (5) Data Transfer Delay. Step (1) is the only step that is a strong function of the architecture. Steps (2) through (5) are modeled as a constant delay of 5 cycles, 1 cycle, 32 ns, and 1 cycle respectively.

MC Queuing Delay: The memory controller queuing delay represents the amount of time a memory request spends waiting in the memory controller queue. This value depends on the number of memory controllers and the number of cores. The work by Awasthi et al. reports that the increase in queuing delay from a single core to a 16 core processors is about 8x [1]. Dong et al. reported that a configuration with 4 cores and one MC has a queuing latency of 116 cycles [3]. We linearly extrapolate these two observations to model queuing delay as a function of #core, and assume that memory requests are uniformly distributed across the address space [9], such that queuing delay is inversely proportional to the number of MCs. Thus we model MC queuing delay with Equation (1).

$$T_Q = \frac{388}{\#MC} \times \left[1 + \left(\#core \times \frac{1 - 1/8}{16 - 1} \right) - \left(16 \times \frac{1 - 1/8}{16 - 1} \right) \right] \quad (1)$$

2.3 Power and Area Estimation

McPAT is a power estimation tool commonly used to estimate power in computer architecture research [9, 4, 8]. Given a specific architecture and usage profile, it estimates the power and area of each component in the design. Power estimations are used as the input to our thermal model and area estimations are used to create the floorplan (see Section 2.1). All power simulations are run assuming a nominal clock frequency of $f_{nom} = 3.0\,\text{GHz}$. To simulate other frequencies, we scale dynamic power by $(\frac{f}{f_{nom}})^2$ and leakage power by $\frac{f}{f_{nom}}$. McPAT gives estimates for leakage, but these estimates assume a constant temperature across the whole chip, which is not realistic. Leakage is highly dependent on temperature [6], so we solve for the proper leakage values by using feedback from our thermal model (see Section 2.4). It has been reported in literature that an upper bound on DRAM power dissipation is 3W per GB [7]. We assume a uniform power density with a total of 3W of power dissipation on each layer of DRAM.

Pumping Power: The power required to pump fluid through a microchannel, P_{pump} is defined in Equations (2) through (6) [12], where N is the number of microchannels, f is the fluid flow rate, Δp is the pressure drop across each microchannel, γ is a function of microchannel aspect ratio ($AR = W/H$), μ is the viscosity of fluid flow, L is the length of the channel, v is the fluid velocity, D_h is the hydraulic diameter of the channel, W is the width and H is the height of the microchannel. Specific values of the parameters discussed here are given in Table 2. In the specific architectures simulated here the pumping power is $161\,\text{mW}$ per layer. The pumping power is quite low, and even though pumping power is considered in the calculation of energy efficiency, the efficiency results improve with micro-fluidic cooling (see Table 5) due to a significant reduction in leakage power.

$$P_{pump} = Nf\Delta p \quad (2) \quad f = WHv \quad (3) \quad \Delta p = 2\gamma\mu Lv D_h^{-2} \quad (4)$$

$$\gamma = 4.7 + 19.64 \times \frac{(AR^2 + 1)}{(AR + 1)^2} \quad (5) \quad D_h = \frac{2WH}{W + H} \quad (6)$$

Var	Value	Name	Var	Value	Name
W	100 m	Width	N	86 per layer	#Channels
H	200 m	Height	v	$2\,\text{m s}^{-1}$	Velocity
L	20.4 mm	Length	μ	653 Pa s	Viscosity

Table 2: Micro-Fluidic System Parameters

2.4 Temperature Estimation

We estimate temperature in the 3D stack by using our micro-fluidic cooling thermal simulator [12], which has been validated with less than 1% error against ANSYS CFX simulation. We impose a 3D grid on the stack, and calculate the power at each grid point from McPAT results. Each layer in the 3D stack is composed of the following sublayers: Si substrate, active Si, wiring layer and oxide insulation. The material properties and dimensions of each layer are given in Tabel 3. The top layer has a thick substrate that interfaces with the air-cooled heat sink, whereas the intermediate layers have thinned substrates. Microfluidic cooling adds 200 m to the substrate thickness of each logic layer to accommodate the microchannel. Heat flow is modeled using a thermal resistance network, which is an established technique that has been used in previous work [13, 5]. An example thermal resistor network is shown in Figure 5 both with and without micro-fluidic cooling. The power at each grid point is modeled as a current source, and the node voltage represents the temperature. In this work we assume a fluid flow rate of $2\,\text{m s}^{-1}$ and an ambient temperature of $40\,°\text{C}$. The air cooled heatsink is simulated as a thermal resistance between ambient temperature and the top of the stack with thermal conductance of $0.1\ \text{W}\ \text{m}^{-2}\,\text{K}^{-1}$.

Layer	Thickness	Material	Therm Cond
Top Substrate	995 m	Si	148 W/mK
Thinned Substrate	55 m	Si	148 W/mK
Active Layer	5 m	Si	148 W/mK
Wiring Layer	15 m	SiO2+Cu	2.25 W/mK
Oxide Layer	15 m	SiO2	1.4 W/mK

Table 3: Physical properties of 3D stack layers

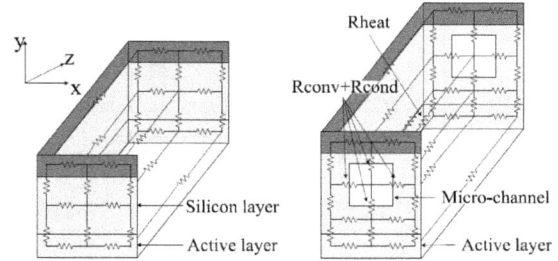

Figure 5: Thermal resistance network: without (left) and with (right) micro-fluidic cooling

Leakage Model: In order to calculate leakage power, we start with the leakage values reported from McPAT (which assume a uniform temperature T_0 across the whole chip) and solve for temperature using the thermal model. Then we use the results from the thermal model to scale the leakage power using a temperature dependent leakage model extrapolated from the McPAT source code, which is given in Equation (7). The thermal model is resolved with the scaled leakage profile, and this process repeats until it converges.

$$P_{leak}(T) = P_{leak}(T_0) \times \left(5.121\tfrac{T}{T_0}^2 - 6.013\tfrac{T}{T_0} + 1.892\right) \quad (7)$$

3. SIMULATION

In this work we simulate 3D stacked DRAM architectures with 4 GB of DRAM stacked on top of a multi-core processor. We consider three design variables: number of cores (#Cores), number of memory controllers (#MC), and core frequency (Freq). Each variable can take on three different values, (enumerated in Table 1), resulting in a total of 27 architectures considered in this work. For each architecture, we simulate 12 benchmarks from the SPLASH-2 and PARSEC benchmark suites. To simulate each benchmark, we fast-forward past the initial sequential portion of the benchmark and then simulate 1B instructions (or until the end of the benchmark, whichever comes first). Thus all simulations have 100% thread level parallelism. We use performance statistics from the simulations to estimate power and temperature, with and without the addition of micro-fluidic cooling.

To quantify the improvement due to adding micro-fluidic cooling, we use two metrics: performance and energy efficiency ("efficiency"). Performance is expressed as number of instructions per nanosecond (IPnS), and energy efficiency is the reciprocal of the energy delay product ($\frac{1}{EDP}$). When comparing two architectures running the same benchmark, raw performance and energy efficiency numbers can be used. However, in order to compare two architectures running different benchmarks, or to average the performance and efficiency of an architecture across multiple benchmarks, the metrics must be normalized to a baseline architecture. The baseline architectural parameters are shown in bold in Table 1.

3.1 Results

For each benchmark, we find the highest performing or most energy efficient architecture configuration that does not violate the peak temperature constraint of $85\,°\text{C}$. The results of these experiments are shown in Tables 4 and 5 respectively. All results are reported in units of ns, nJ, W and GHz. When optimizing for performance (efficiency),

Benchmark	Air Cooled						MF Cooled						Increase in IPnS	Increase in $\frac{1}{EDP}$
	#Cores	#MC	Freq	Power	IPnS	$\frac{1}{EDP}$	#Cores	#MC	Freq	Power	IPnS	$\frac{1}{EDP}$		
Barnes	32	16	2.4	137	43.6	13.9	64	16	3.6	357	103.1	29.8	2.37x	2.14x
Blackscholes	16	4	3.6	84	29.4	10.3	64	8	3.6	246	50.2	10.3	1.71x	0.99x
Bodytrack	16	8	3.6	110	35.9	11.7	64	32	3.6	655	57.6	5.1	1.60x	0.43x
Dedup	32	16	2.4	145	36.6	9.3	64	32	3.0	546	86.2	13.6	2.35x	1.47x
FFT	32	16	2.4	149	42.2	12.0	64	32	3.0	531	81.9	12.6	1.94x	1.06x
Fluidanimate	32	8	2.4	115	53.1	24.5	64	16	3.6	390	113.6	33.1	2.14x	1.35x
FMM	32	8	2.4	99	37.8	14.5	32	16	3.6	238	57.1	13.7	1.51x	0.94x
Ocean	32	16	2.4	123	12.3	1.2	32	16	3.6	215	17.6	1.4	1.43x	1.18x
Radix	16	8	3.6	113	38.5	13.1	64	16	3.6	337	49.4	7.3	1.28x	0.55x
Swaptions	32	16	2.4	146	51.3	18.0	64	32	3.0	534	128.0	30.7	2.50x	1.70x
Water-nsquared	32	8	2.4	125	79.0	49.8	64	16	3.6	436	180.0	74.3	2.28x	1.49x
Water-spatial	16	8	3.0	121	81.1	54.6	64	16	3.6	474	241.9	123.5	2.98x	2.26x
Average													2.01x	1.30x

Table 4: Architectures With Maximum Performance (IPnS) s.t. Thermal Constraint (85 °C) with and without Micro-Fluidic Cooling

Benchmark	Air Cooled						MF Cooled						Increase in IPnS	Increase in $\frac{1}{EDP}$
	#Cores	#MC	Freq	Power	IPnS	$\frac{1}{EDP}$	#Cores	#MC	Freq	Power	IPnS	$\frac{1}{EDP}$		
Barnes	32	8	2.4	100	42.9	18.4	64	8	3.6	282	101.6	36.6	2.37x	1.99x
Blackscholes	16	4	3.6	84	29.4	10.3	16	4	3.6	73	29.4	11.9	1.00x	1.15x
Bodytrack	16	4	3.6	89	33.8	12.9	16	4	3.6	78	33.8	14.8	1.00x	1.14x
Dedup	32	16	2.4	145	36.6	9.3	64	16	2.4	191	57.9	17.6	1.58x	1.90x
FFT	32	16	2.4	149	42.2	12.0	64	16	3.0	275	68.6	17.1	1.62x	1.43x
Fluidanimate	32	8	2.4	115	53.1	24.5	64	16	3.0	287	101.4	35.8	1.91x	1.46x
FMM	32	8	2.4	99	37.8	14.5	32	8	3.6	158	56.2	20.0	1.49x	1.38x
Ocean	16	8	3.6	94	12.0	1.5	16	8	3.6	84	12.0	1.7	1.00x	1.12x
Radix	16	8	3.6	113	38.5	13.1	16	8	3.6	102	38.5	14.6	1.00x	1.11x
Swaptions	32	16	2.4	146	51.3	18.0	64	32	3.0	534	128.0	30.7	2.50x	1.70x
Water-nsquared	32	8	2.4	125	79.0	49.8	64	16	3.6	436	180.0	74.3	2.28x	1.49x
Water-spatial	16	4	3.0	102	80.1	62.9	64	8	3.0	279	187.5	126.2	2.34x	2.00x
Average													1.67x	1.49x

Table 5: Architectures With Maximum Efficiency ($\frac{1}{EDP}$) s.t. Thermal Constraint (85 °C) with and without Micro-Fluidic Cooling

micro-fluidic cooling provides an average increase of 2.01x (1.49x). Micro-fluidic cooling can increase performance (efficiency) by thermally unlocking higher performing (more efficient) architectures. Moreover, micro-fluidic cooling can improve the efficiency of a fixed architectural configuration by decreasing the leakage power of the chip.

If we assume that the architecture must be determined at design time for all workloads, we must identify the architecture that has the best average normalized performance/efficiency across all benchmarks, and we must only consider architectures that meet the thermal constraints for all benchmarks. In our study the same architectures were found to be optimal for both performance and energy efficiency. The results of this study are shown in Table 6. For a fixed architecture design, including micro-fluidic cooling can result in an average increase to performance and energy efficiency of 2.62x and 1.78x respectively.

	#Cores	#MC	Freq	Norm Performance	Norm Efficiency
Air Cooled	16	8	3.0	3.2	7.6
MF Cooled	64	16	3.6	8.3	13.5
Increase				2.62x	1.78x

Table 6: Architectures with maximum normalized performance/efficiency averaged across all benchmarks

4. CONCLUSIONS

In this paper we have investigated how micro-fluidic cooling can unlock new architectures with higher performance and energy efficiency. When considering average performance/energy efficiency across all benchmarks micro-fluidic cooling can increase performance by 2.62x and energy efficiency by 1.78x. These results provide strong quantitative evidence that traditional air cooling limits the potential of 3D integration, and more aggressive cooling techniques are required to fully leverage this new technology.

5. ACKNOWLEDGMENTS

The authors acknowledge that this work has been funded by NSF grant CCF1302375 and the DARPA IceCool Project.

6. REFERENCES

[1] M. Awasthi, et al. Handling the problems and opportunities posed by multiple on-chip memory controllers. In *PACT'10*. ACM, 2010.

[2] M. Bakir, et al. 3D heterogeneous integrated systems: Liquid cooling, power delivery, and implementation. In *CICC'08*. IEEE, 2008.

[3] X. Dong, et al. Simple but Effective Heterogeneous Main Memory with On-Chip Memory Controller Support. In *SC'10*, 2010.

[4] M.-y. Hsieh, et al. A Framework for Architecture-level Power, Area, and Thermal Simulation and Its Application to Network-on-chip Design Exploration. *SIGMETRICS PER*, Mar. 2011.

[5] W. Huang, et al. HotSpot: a compact thermal modeling methodology for early-stage VLSI design. *TVLSI*, 2006.

[6] W. Liao, et al. Temperature and supply Voltage aware performance and power modeling at microarchitecture level. *TCAD*, 2005.

[7] G. Loh. 3D-Stacked Memory Architectures for Multi-core Processors. In *ISCA'08*, 2008.

[8] J. Meng, et al. Run-time Energy Management of Manycore Systems Through Reconfigurable Interconnects. In *GLSVLSI'11*, 2011.

[9] J. Meng, et al. Optimizing energy efficiency of 3-D multicore systems with stacked DRAM under power and thermal constraints. In *DAC'12*, 2012.

[10] M. Pathak, et al. Through-silicon-via management during 3D physical design: When to add and how many? In *ICCAD'10*, pages 387–394, 2010.

[11] I. Savidis and E. Friedman. Closed-Form Expressions of 3-D Via Resistance, Inductance, and Capacitance. *T-ED*, 2009.

[12] B. Shi, et al. Non-uniform micro-channel design for stacked 3D-ICs. In *DAC'11*, 2011.

[13] A. Sridhar, et al. 3D-ICE: Fast compact transient thermal modeling for 3D ICs with inter-tier liquid cooling. In *ICCAD'10*, 2010.

Prolonging PCM Lifetime through Energy-efficient, Segment-aware, and Wear-resistant Page Allocation

Hoda Aghaei Khouzani, Yuan Xue, Chengmo Yang, and Archana Pandurangi
Department of Electrical and Computer Engineering, University of Delaware, Newark, DE 19716 USA
{hoda,xueyuan,archicp,chengmo}@udel.edu

ABSTRACT

Improving the endurance of Phase change memory (PCM) is a fundamental issue when the technology is considered as an alternative to main memory usage. Existing wear-leveling techniques overcome this challenge through constantly remapping hot virtual pages, engendering a fair amount of extra write operations to PCM and imposing considerable energy overhead. Our observation is that it is unnecessary to fully balance the accesses to different physical pages during the execution of each process. Instead, since endurance is a lifetime factor, the hot virtual pages of different processes can be mapped to different physical pages in the PCM. Leveraging this property, we develop a wear-resistant page allocation algorithm, which exploits the diverse write characteristics of different program segments to improve PCM write endurance within almost no extra remapping cost. Experimental results show that the proposed technique can prolong PCM lifetime by hundreds of times with nearly zero searching and remapping overhead.

1. INTRODUCTION

Phase Change Memory (PCM) is regarded as a promising candidate for the next-generation main memory system. Compared to DRAM, PCM has higher storage density, lower leakage power, better scalability and non-volatility [1, 2, 3]. However, the high writing energy and short write endurance of PCM are the two limiting factors for it to completely replace DRAM. Without proper optimizations, a PCM memory system is likely to fail in a matter of days [2, 4, 5].

Existing techniques improve PCM endurance either by reducing the total number of write operations to the PCM cells [2, 4, 5, 6, 7, 8], or by evenly spreading write operations over the PCM in order to prevent some cells from being worn out quickly [4, 9, 10, 11, 12]. While techniques of the latter type are effective, they need to periodically swap the mapping of hot and cold pages, thus engendering a large number of extra write operations. The more balanced write distribution is achieved, the more extra writes needed to be performed, and hence the larger performance and energy overhead will be induced.

As each program has its own hot/cold pages, most wear-leveling techniques balance the write operations to different pages during the execution of each program. However, our observation is that this is unnecessary. Instead, since endurance is a lifetime factor, the unbalanced access characteristics of different programs can be utilized. The hot

virtual pages of different processes can be mapped to different physical page frames in the PCM, thus balancing write counts to different PCM pages without inducing extra write operations or noticeable energy overhead.

Balancing writes across different processes requires the identification of hot and cold pages by the memory management unit when it allocates a virtual page. This can be achieved by exploiting the segment information that is usually available to the OS. Different segments usually have very diverse write characteristics. The *text* segment is usually read-only, while the *data* and *stack* segments are write-entensive and their accesses display high spatial and temporal localities. Leveraging this property, we propose an energy efficient wear leveling technique. We develop a *segment-based* and *age-aware* page allocation strategy, enabling the OS to allocate page frames of different ages to different segments across PCM lifetime. This is further enhanced by a *wear out prevention* procedure, which deallocates page frames based on their age information. Both procedures are compatible with existing virtual memory management, with minimum software and hardware modifications needed. The experimental studies on SPEC benchmarks show that the proposed technique can prolong PCM lifetime by hundreds of times with nearly zero searching and remapping overhead.

In the following sections, we first provide a brief background on phase change memory and related work, and then describe the proposed segment-based wear-leveling approaches in detail. Experimental results and conclusions are presented at the end.

2. BACKGROUND AND MOTIVATION

PCM exploits chalcogenide glass, a phase-change material, to record bit information [1]. The material has large resistance contrast between the amorphous and crystalline states, which is exploited to represent one or even multiple bits per cell. Unlike DRAM that needs to periodically refresh the capacitor charge, PCM does not require standby power and consumes only a small amount of energy for read operations. However, as the phase transition of PCM is driven by a heating process, write operations are more time and energy consuming. Most importantly, with the repeated heat stress applied to the phase change material, a PCM cell can only sustain $10^6 \sim 10^9$ writes. Compared to the typical 10^{15} writes that a DRAM cell can sustain, this limited write endurance is the most critical challenge to overcome when replacing DRAM with PCM.

Researchers have proposed a number of approaches to overcome the endurance challenge mainly from two aspects. The first type of approach aims at reducing the total number of writes to PCM main memory, achieved by first comparing the value to be written [8, 13], or its negative [5], with the old value, and then writing only those different bits. The second type of approach, usually called *wear leveling* (WL), aims at evenly distributing the writes to avoid wearing out a small proportion of PCM cells at an early stage. This is achieved through remapping those *heavily written virtual pages* (referred to as

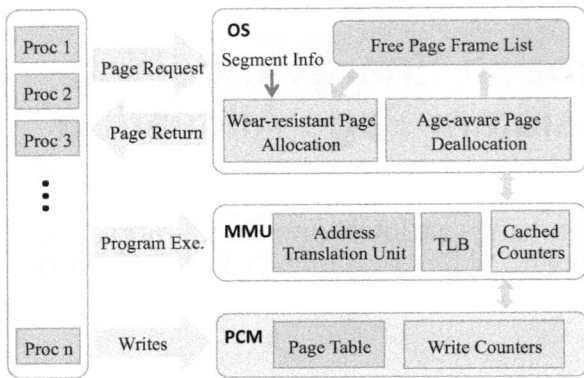

Figure 1: Functional overview of segment-aware memory management

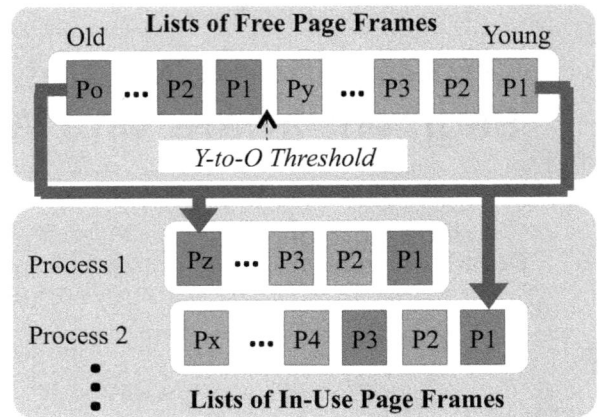

Figure 2: Data structure. Each process has its own in-use list, while a single free list is shared among all processes.

hot pages) to *physical page frames with less writes* in the past (referred to as *young* page frames).

Wear leveling techniques are either *random-based* or *age-based*. Random-based WL approaches [3, 9, 12] swap the data on PCM randomly, based on the assumption that applications display highly skewed write patterns and the hot pages/lines are less than 10% [3]. To achieve a more balanced write distribution, a high swapping rate is needed, which in turn induces a large number of extra writes to PCM and huge energy overhead. Age-based WL approaches, on the other hand, maintain precise write counts for each individual page and periodically remap hot data to young PCM pages. Techniques of this category include segment swapping [2], bucket-based [3], curling [14], and others. The remapping granularity can be a line (Row shifting [2] and Start-Gap [10]), a page (Random swapping [12], Bucket-based [3], and Curling [14]), or even a set of pages (Segment swapping [2]).

2.1 Motivation

A detailed examination reveals two types of *energy inefficiency* in traditional wear leveling techniques. First of all, most WL techniques induce a large number of extra writes in remapping hot pages during the execution of each program. Yet this is unnecessary because endurance is a lifetime factor. Our observation is that by mapping hot virtual pages of different processes to different physical page frames, the write distribution can be balanced across different processes with almost no extra writes induced.

The second type of energy inefficiency is that most WL techniques treat hot and cold pages uniformly during page allocation, and only remap a page later when it becomes hot. Our observation is that hot and cold pages can be differentiated during page allocation towards a pre-active and energy efficient wear-leveling approach. Different segments usually have very diverse write characteristics. The *text* segment is usually read-only, while the *data* and *stack* segments are write-intensive. As the segment information is available to the OS, it can use old physical page frames to hold text pages and use young page frames to hold data and stack pages. In other words, most hot pages are never remapped, while their physical page frames are reclaimed at the end of the process, and will be used to hold text pages of other processes that are guaranteed to be cold. In this way, the performance and energy overhead needed for consistently remapping those hot pages can be eliminated to a large extent.

3. SEGMENT-AWARE PAGE MANAGEMENT

The fundamental goal of the proposed work is to perform wear leveling (WL) pre-actively without energy-expensive remapping operations. This is achieved through two WL procedures that are compatible with memory management of most operation systems.

3.1 Overview

Figure 1 shows an overview of the proposed wear-leveling design. Two WL procedures as well as a set of write counters are added to the memory management system. The *Wear-Resistant Page Allocation* procedure is invoked if a memory access triggers a page fault. Based on segment information, a free page frame of appropriate age is allocated. The *Wear Out Prevention* procedure precludes an extremely hot virtual page from quickly wearing out its physical page frame. It checks the write counters cached in TLB, and remaps the currently written page to a young page frame only if its write count is tremendously high.

To provide the OS with precise age information, a *write counter* is associated with each physical page frame to precisely record its age (i.e., write counts). Moreover, the MMU (memory management unit) is augmented to cache the write counters of the pages in the TLB and absorb most counter updates, as shown in Figure 1. In this way, write counters in PCM are updated only upon TLB replacements, which will be less frequent than updating the corresponding memory page (upon replacing a dirty cache line).

3.2 Wear-resistant Page Allocation

The primary goal of page allocation is to serve page requests according to their potential writes in the future. Specifically, the allocation procedure considers both the write counts of the page frames and the writing characteristics of the corresponding segments. As mentioned before, pages of different segments display varying write intensities. Leveraging this property, the proposed page allocation algorithm serves data and stack requests with young page frames, and serves text requests with old page frames.

The latency and energy overhead of page allocation is determined by how quickly an appropriate free page frame can be identified for allocation. To achieve near-zero search cost, we organize the entire free list, shared by all processes, in two ordered queues. As shown in Figure 2, these queues respectively contain *Young* and *Old* page frames. All page frames in the same queue have similar wear level and are arranged in the decreasing order of their write count. The two queues are distinguished by the *Y-to-O threshold*, which will be adaptively adjusted throughout PCM lifetime.

When the OS receives a page request, it selects the proper queue depending on the segment information. Since pages in the same queue are already arranged in decreasing order of write count, the OS always allocates the first (i.e., the youngest) page frame in the selected queue. The search cost is therefore zero.

3.3 Age-aware Page Deallocation

As free page frames keep being allocated upon page requests, it is necessary to deallocate page frames and prevent the system from running out of free page frames.

The proposed WL framework adopts an organization that is highly compatible with existing OS memory management. As can be seen in Figure 2, each process has a dedicated *in-use list* that includes all its page frame regardless of the segment information. This allows the use of the conventional clock algorithm [15] to select a page frame for deallocation.

As the replacement procedure does not force a hot page to be deallocated, in an extreme case a hot virtual page may about to wear out its physical page frame. To prevent this undesired case, the *Wear Out Prevention* procedure will be invoked to remap an extrmely hot page, if any. Fortunately, an extremely hot virtual page is ensured to hit in the TLB, implying that its cached write counter can be monitored with no need of accessing the PCM main memory. Upon a write hit, if the write count is larger than the *Y-to-O* threshold, the physical page frame is considered "old", and will be deallocated and placed in the "old" queue of the free list.

Using the *Wear-aware Page Deallocation* and *Wear-resistant Page Allocation* procedures, wear leveling can be naturally achieved for most hot virtual pages with no need of energy-expensive remapping operations. To be more precise, assume one hot page in process A wears a page frame down to the "old" category. The page frame, once deallocated, will be placed in the "old" queue of the free list, ensuring that it will be allocated to a cold text page of another process B.

As the *Y-to-O* determines the number of old page frames that will be forced to be deallocated upon a write hit, it has a great impact on both the degree of balanced write counts and the overhead caused by extra remapping operations. In the early stage of PCM lifetime, most of pages are young and far from the worn out point. At that time a relatively high *Y-to-O* threshold is desirable, as it reduces the energy-expensive remap operations. As memory ages, more and more page frames fall into the "old" category. They will be deallocated and placed in the free list, and will not be allocated until a page request from text segment is received. At some point, a considerable number of page frames in the free list are old, and the *Y-to-O* threshold will be redefined, allowing those old pages to be used for data and stack segments.

3.4 Energy Efficiency Analysis

The proposed wear leveling scheme is highly energy efficient as it imposes negligible overhead on top of existing OS memory management. The overhead of the proposed scheme can be assessed from two perspectives, the cost for maintaining and updating write counters and the complexity of the two wear-leveling functions.

The need for write counters in PCM is undoubtedly the major hardware overhead of all the age-based wear leveling schemes, including the proposed one. Updating those write counters incurs extra energy and degrades endurance of the PCM. Yet by caching write counters in the MMU, the write counters in PCM only need to be updated upon TLB misses [3], which are quite rare compared to cache misses. In this situation, the energy and endurance impact of write counters can be largely reduced.

The two WL procedures, as they are developed to be compatible with existing memory management procedures in the OS, have very low complexity. For page allocation, the *Wear-resistant Page Allocation* procedure only needs one extra step for checking the segment information, which is already available to the OS. The complexity for selecting an appropriate page frame is $O(1)$. Likewise, the *Wear Out*

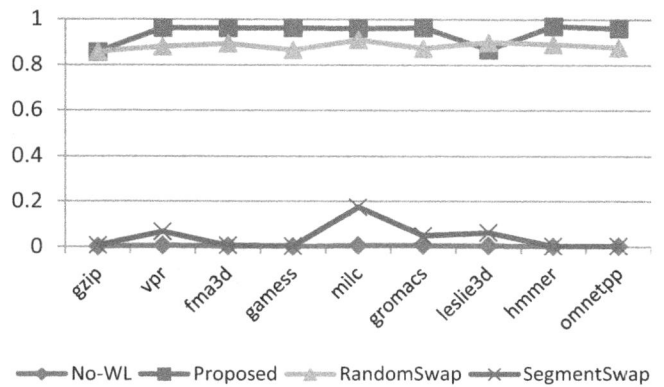

Figure 3: Normalized lifetime of different WL approaches

Prevention procedure only needs to access the write counter of the currently written page, which only involves a TLB access with a complexity of $O(1)$.

4. EXPERIMENTAL EVALUATION

To evaluate the proposed age-based and segment-aware wear leveling scheme, we developed a memory management system and incorporated the proposed wear-leveling procedures in it. The *Y-to-O* threshold is set to 2×10^5 initially, and increased linearly throughout PCM lifetime. We also implemented two representative wear leveling approaches as the comparison set. *Segment swapping* [3] swaps the hottest and coldest segments of pages periodically. The segment size is 1 MB, and the swapping interval is 2×10^5 memory writes. *Random swapping* [9] periodically swaps the page frame currently being written with a randomly selected page frame for every 512 writes to PCM pages.

Nine benchmarks that produce a high volume of memory writes are selected from the SPEC 2000 and 2006 suites. Their memory access traces are collected with Pin [16]. A 128 KB, 2-way associative instruction cache and a data cache are used, while the PCM main memory is 64 MB with 10^6 wear out limit per cell.

4.1 Lifetime Evaluation

Lifetime evaluation is conducted by repetitively executing a benchmark until one page frame wears out. The total number of write operations performed by the processor, without including the write operations caused by page fault or remap operations, is collected and considered as the lifetime metric. Figure 3 shows the normalized PCM lifetime of the baseline no-WL case, the proposed wear leveling approach and the two competitors.

It can be observed that without wear leveling, the first page frame wears out when there are still more than 99% memory writes that could be potentially performed. This clearly confirms the necessity of high-quality wear leveling techniques. The results show that *segment swapping* and *random swapping* are able to utilize 2.5% and 89% of the potential writes, which translate to 5.3 and 190 times improvement in memory lifetime over the no-WL baseline case, respectively. However, the proposed segment-aware approach still outperforms both competitors. Using the proposed page allocation and deallocation strategies, over 96% of the potential writes can be achieved, which translates to 200+ times improvement in memory lifetime over the no-WL case. Furthermore, the performance of the proposed WL scheme is very stable across the various benchmarks. This advantage is a result of the adaptation to the two thresholds throughout PCM lifetime. In comparison, the other two WL techniques, especially the *segment swap-*

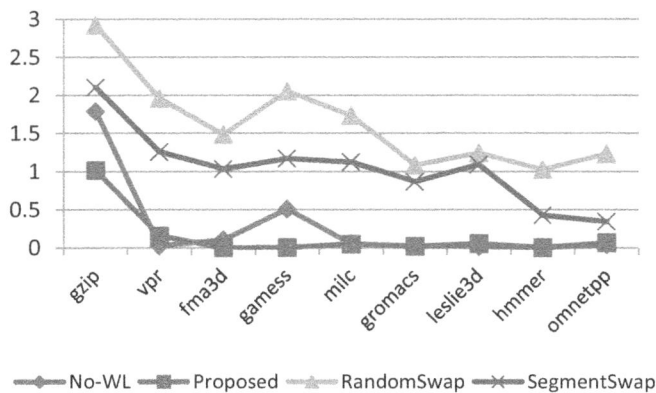

Figure 4: Normalized overhead of different WL approaches

ping approach delivers highly varying lifetime improvement across the benchmarks due to its non-adaptive, coarse granularity.

4.2 Overhead Evaluation

For wear-level techniques, the dominating overhead consists of the extra write operations caused by remapping operations or extra page faults. These extra writes not only affect endurance by reducing the potentially useful writes, but also impose sizable energy overhead. Specifically, page faults and remapping operations, as they require writing a whole page frame, consume much more energy than a write operation performed by the CPU. Assuming an average CPU write size of 8 bytes and a page size of 4 KB, writing a page frame consumes approximately 512 times the energy of a CPU write. In light of this observation, we evaluate energy overhead by computing the extra *write volume* (in terms of bytes) over the CPU write volume.

In Figure 4, the energy overhead of the no-WL case is caused by page faults. Some benchmarks, such as *gzip*, have very high energy overhead even in the no-WL case, due to a relatively high rate of page faults but small number of useful CPU writes.

For the three WL approaches, both page faults and remapping operations are considered. It can be seen that segment swapping and random swapping respectively suffer from 89% and 145% overhead. In comparison, the overhead of the proposed wear leveling scheme is just 3.1%, which is just 4% more than the no-WL baseline case but 28 times less than segment swapping and 47 times less than random swapping. Such low overhead confirms that by allocating pages in a wear-resistent manner, very few remap operations need to be performed. Among all the benchmarks, only *gzip* has an energy overhead of more than 100%. Yet by comparing all the WL cases and the no-WL case, it is clear that such high overhead is not because of remap but because of page faults.

5. CONCLUSIONS

We have proposed an energy-efficient scheme to address the endurance issue of PCM as main memory. By leveraging segment information and performing wear-leveling proactively across multiple processes, Our segment-aware and wear-resistant algorithms enhance OS page allocation and deallocation and prolongs the lifetime of PCM almost to its full potential. By leveraging segment information and performing wear-leveling proactively across multiple processes, this scheme avoids inducing too many remapping operations that may degrade memory energy and performance.

We have conducted a set of experimental studies on SPEC 2000 and 2006 benchmarks. The results show that the proposed scheme allows the CPU to exploit more than 96% of potential PCM writes. More-

over, the energy overhead caused by remapping operations or extra page faults is less than 4%, compared to a system without any wear-leveling technique. We believe that the proposed wear-level technique is appealing to various types of systems given its high effectiveness in prolonging PCM lifetime, high compatibility with OS functions, and its low energy and performance overhead.

6. REFERENCES

[1] S. Raoux, G. W. Burr, M. J. Breitwisch, C. T. Rettner, Y. C. Chen, and R. M. Shelby, "Phase-change random access memory: A scalable technology," *IBM J. Res. and Development*, vol. 52, Jul. 2008.

[2] P. Zhou, B. Zhao, J. Yang, and Y. Zhang, "A durable and energy efficient main memory using phase change memory technology," in *36th Intl. Symp. Comput. Archit. (ISCA)*, 2009, pp. 14–23.

[3] C.-H. Chen, P.-C. Hsiu, T.-W. Kuo, C.-L. Yang, and C.-Y. M. Wang, "Age-based PCM wear leveling with nearly zero search cost," in *49th Design Autom. Conf. (DAC)*, 2012, pp. 453–458.

[4] M. K. Qureshi, V. Srinivasan, and J. A. Rivers, "Scalable high performance main memory system using phase-change memory technology," in *36th Intl. Symp. Comput. Archit. (ISCA)*, 2009, pp. 24–33.

[5] S. Cho and H. Lee, "Flip-N-Write: a simple deterministic technique to improve PRAM write performance, energy and endurance," in *42nd Intl. Symp. Microarchitecture (MICRO)*, 2009, pp. 347–357.

[6] M. Zhou, Y. Du, B. Childers, R. Melhem, and D. Moose, "Writeback-aware partitioning and replacement for last-level caches in phase change main memory systems," *ACM Trans. Archit. Code Optim.*, vol. 8, Jan. 2012.

[7] J. Hu, C. Xue, W.-C. Tseng, Y. He, M. Qiu, and E. Sha, "Reducing write activities on non-volatile memories in embedded CMPs via data migration and recomputation," in *47th Design Autom. Conf. (DAC)*, Jun. 2010, pp. 350–355.

[8] B. C. Lee, E. Ipek, O. Mutlu, and D. Burger, "Architecting phase change memory as a scalable DRAM alternative," in *36th Intl. Symp. Comput. Archit. (ISCA)*, 2009, pp. 2–13.

[9] A. P. Ferreira, M. Zhou, S. Bock, B. Childers, R. Melhem, and D. Mosse, "Increasing PCM main memory lifetime," in *Design Autom. & Test in Europe (DATE)*, 2010, pp. 914–919.

[10] M. K. Qureshi, J. Karidis, M. Franceschini, V. Srinivasan, L. Lastras, and B. Abali, "Enhancing lifetime and security of PCM-based main memory with start-gap wear leveling," in *42nd Intl. Symp. Microarchitecture (MICRO)*, 2009, pp. 14–23.

[11] L. Jiang, Y. Du, Y. Zhang, B. Childers, and J. Yang, "LLS: Cooperative integration of wear-leveling and salvaging for PCM main memory," in *41st Intl. Conf. Dependable Syst. & Netw. (DSN)*, Jun. 2011, pp. 221–232.

[12] N. H. Seong, D. H. Woo, and H.-H. S. Lee, "Security refresh: prevent malicious wear-out and increase durability for phase-change memory with dynamically randomized address mapping," in *37th Intl. Symp. Comput. Archit. (ISCA)*, 2010, pp. 383–394.

[13] W. Zhang and T. Li, "Characterizing and mitigating the impact of process variations on phase change based memory systems," in *42nd Intl. Symp. Microarchitecture (MICRO)*, 2009, pp. 2–13.

[14] D. Liu, T. Wang, Y. Wang, Z. Shao, Q. Zhuge, and E. Sha, "Curling-PCM: Application-specific wear leveling for phase change memory based embedded systems," in *18th Asia & South Pacific Design Autom. Conf. (ASP-DAC)*, Jan. 2013, pp. 22–25.

[15] A. S. Tanenbaum, *Modern Operating Systems (Second Edition)*. Prentice Hall, 2001.

[16] "Pin - A Dynamic Binary Instrumentation Tool," http://software.intel.com/en-us/articles/pintool.

The New (System) Balance of Power and Opportunities for Optimizations

Parthasarathy Ranganathan
Google
Mountain View, California, USA
partha.ranganathan@google.com

Abstract

Power and energy are key design considerations across a spectrum of computing solutions, from large-scale data centers and supercomputers to mobile phones and wearable computers. Correspondingly, all these systems need to focus on *efficiency*: achieving higher performance and functionality at improved resource and energy usage. At the same time, emerging workload and technology trends provide additional unique challenges and opportunities for future efficient system designs.

In this talk, I will discuss these trends and summarize common, and not-so-common, design practices to address efficiency. I will discuss the opportunities for "balanced" system designs where all the different resources in the system are used equally efficiently, and building on the original Amdahl-Case rules for system balance from the 1960s, show how updating and rethinking the definitions for system balance can provide opportunities for significant improvements.

ACM Classification:

B. Hardware, C. Computer Systems Organizations

Author Keywords: Amdahl ratios, energy efficiency, balanced system design, warehouse-scale computing, servers and datacenters

Bio

Partha Ranganathan is currently at Google helping design their next-generation infrastructure. Before this, he was a HP Fellow and Chief Technologist at Hewlett Packard Labs where he led their research on next-generation systems, including HP's Project Moonshot and HP Labs' Data-centric Data Center program. Dr. Ranganathan has worked extensively on systems architecture and energy efficiency, and made key contributions in energy-aware user interfaces, heterogeneous multi-cores, power-capping, low-power servers, disaggregated systems, and system redesign for non-volatile memory. He holds more than 50 patents (with another 45 pending) and has published extensively including several award-winning papers. His work has been featured on numerous occasions in the popular press including in the New York Times, Wall Street Journal, Business Week, SF Chronicle, Times of India, slashdot, etc. He has been named of the world's top young innovators by MIT Technology Review and as a top 15 "tech rockstar" by Business Insider and has been recognized with several other awards including the ACM SIGARCH Maurice Wilkes award and Rice University's Outstanding Young Engineering Alumni award. Dr. Ranganathan received his B.Tech degree from the Indian Institute of Technology, Madras and his M.S. and Ph.D. from Rice University, Houston. He is also an IEEE Fellow.

ISLPED'14, August 11–13, 2014, La Jolla, CA, USA.
ACM 978-1-4503-2975-0/14/08.
http://dx.doi.org/10.1145/2627369.2631635

eDRAM-Based Tiered-Reliability Memory with Applications to Low-Power Frame Buffers

Kyungsang Cho[†‡]   Yongjun Lee[†‡]   Young H. Oh[†]   Gyoo-cheol Hwang[†]   Jae W. Lee[‡]

[†]Samsung Electronics
Hwaseong, Korea
{kyungsang.cho, yonjun80.lee, gchwang}@samsung.com

[‡]Sungkyunkwan University
Suwon, Korea
{loias, yongjunlee, garion9013, jaewlee}@skku.edu

ABSTRACT

Embedded DRAM (eDRAM) is becoming more and more popular as a low-cost alternative to on-chip SRAM. eDRAM is particularly attractive for frame buffers in video applications with ever increasing screen resolutions. However, eDRAM suffers short retention time and high refresh power, which prevents its widespread adoption. To save the refresh power of eDRAM-based frame buffers, we propose *Tiered-Reliability Memory* (TRM), where the frame buffer is divided into multiple segments with different refresh periods and hence different error rates. By allocating most-significant bits to the most reliable segment, our four-tier TRM reduces refresh power by 48% without degrading user experience.

Categories and Subject Descriptors

B.3.1 [**Hardware**]: Memory Structures—*Semiconductor Memories*

Keywords

eDRAM; Frame buffer; Refresh; Error tolerance; Low power

1. INTRODUCTION

Many complex system-on-chip's (SoCs) require large on-chip buffers, which often become a determining factor of chip area and power consumption. Recently, Embedded DRAM (eDRAM) has emerged as a low-cost replacement for conventional on-chip SRAM. For example, several multicore processors have adopted eDRAM-based last-level caches integrated with processing elements either on the same die [15] or in the same package [16]. Compared to conventional SRAM-based caches and register files, eDRAM-based caches and register files have an advantage of much higher density with lower leakage power [9, 17].

The eDRAM-based on-chip storage is attractive not only for caches but also for frame buffers in display driver and video processing SoCs. With ever increasing screen resolutions, the frame buffer organization will have an even greater impact on chip area and power. As shown in Figure 1, the

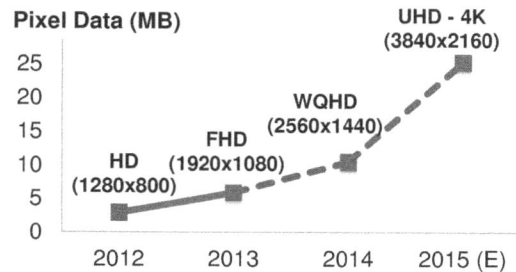

Figure 1: Trends of graphics display resolutions [3]

ultra high definition (UHD) resolution video will become commonplace in the near future for which a 24MB buffer is required to store a single video frame.

However, unlike SRAM, eDRAM cells need to be periodically refreshed to preserve stored bits, which becomes the main source of power consumption [9]. In the context of the commodity off-chip DRAM, researchers have proposed techniques to extend DRAM refresh period by using error correcting code (ECC) [11,35], retention-aware DRAM page allocation [32] and refresh [22], and memory access-aware refresh [12]. However, the cell capacitance of eDRAM is much smaller than that of the commodity DRAM, and the refresh power problem is of a greater concern for eDRAM. Even worse, with technology scaling the cell capacitance will continue to shrink only to exacerbate this problem.

One nice property of the video and display applications is that they can tolerate errors in the pixel data. Besides, the human visual system (HVS) is known to be more sensitive to a change in the higher-order bits of a pixel value than the lower-order bits. Leveraging these properties we can effectively trade the accuracy of the pixel data for power savings in frame buffers with minimal degradation of video quality.

To exploit these opportunities, there are proposals for heterogeneous SRAM-based frame buffers, which consist of multiple segments with different error rates. This heterogeneity is realized by controlling transistor sizing [20], operating voltage [10], or number of transistors per cell [8, 13]. By allocating higher-order bits to more reliable segments power consumption can be significantly reduced with an (almost) undetectable degradation of the video quality. However, they are still based on expensive SRAMs and lack flexibility since the segment configuration, specified by the number of segments and their error rates, is fixed at design time.

This paper proposes Tiered-Reliability Memory (TRM) to effectively exploit power-accuracy tradeoffs in eDRAM-based frame buffers. In TRM, the memory array is divided into multiple segments that can be independently refreshed with different periods. Unlike previous DRAM refresh control schemes targeted for general-purpose computing plat-

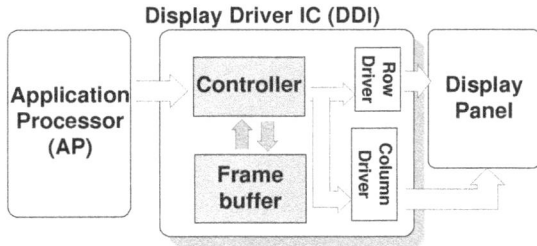

Figure 2: Mobile display sub-system

	SRAM (6T)	eDRAM	
		1T1C [6]	3T1D [24]
Cell size	1×	0.22×	0.64×
Latency	Good	Poor	Good
Process	Logic compatible	Trench capacitor	Logic compatible
Leakage	Poor	Good	Good
Retention	∞	$40\mu s$	$200\mu s$

Table 1: Comparison of SRAM and eDRAM at 65nm

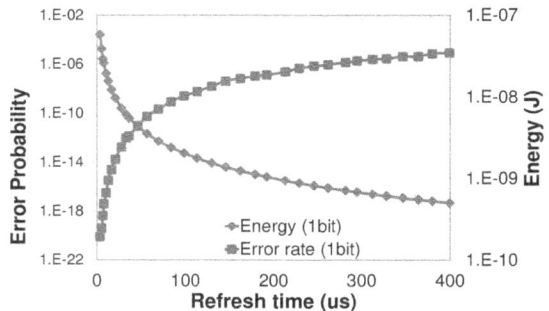

Figure 4: Tradeoff between bit error rate and refresh energy

forms [22, 23], TRM is specialized for display applications and assigns data criticality at a sub-word (i.e., sub-pixel) granularity. By allocating the highest-order bits of a pixel to the most reliable segment, TRM achieves significant savings of refresh power without compromising display quality. Moreover, unlike heterogeneous SRAM-based frame buffers [8, 10, 13, 20], the segment configuration can be adjusted in the field, depending on the application and user preference.

2. BACKGROUND

2.1 Display Sub-system

Figure 2 illustrates a mobile display sub-system, which consists of an application processor (AP), a display driver IC (DDI) and a display panel. The DDI has an on-chip frame buffer that keeps pixel data and sends them to the display panel periodically, say at 60 Hz. Each pixel consists of three color components representing red (R), green (G), and blue (B), and each component typically takes one byte. The display sub-system is the most power-consuming block in a mobile device [7, 28] whose power efficiency is highly desirable to reduce the overall system power.

In DDI, the frame buffer accounts for a dominating fraction of total chip area and power consumption [5, 19]. SRAM is a traditional choice for the frame buffer, but eDRAM is becoming more and more popular for its cost and power benefits. With ever increasing screen resolutions, the organization and power efficiency of the frame buffer will have a profound impact on the overall system cost and power.

2.2 Embedded DRAM

Recently, eDRAM has emerged as a low-cost alternative to SRAM in organizing large-capacity memories on a chip. SRAM is still the most popular technology for on-chip storage due to its low access time and compatibility with the standard CMOS logic process. However, SRAM is based on 6-transistor (6T) cells (or enhanced 8T or 10T cells [25]), which incur significant area overhead and high leakage power. Unlike SRAM, eDRAM uses much fewer transistors per cell, leading to higher density and lower leakage power.

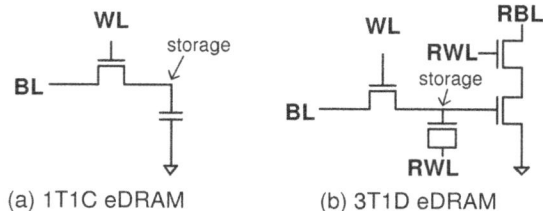

Figure 3: eDRAM cell schematics

There are two popular variants of eDRAM among others: 1T1C (trench capacitor) eDRAM and 3T1D (gain cell) eDRAM. Table 1 compares the two types of eDRAM with SRAM, and Figure 3 illustrates their cell structures. The 1T1C cell has the same structure with that of the commodity DRAM and is about 4-5× smaller than the 6T SRAM cell. However, it requires additional process masks to embed trench capacitors and has slow access time due to destructive reads [21]. In contrast, the 3T1D eDRAM uses additional transistors to overcome these limitations [24]. The 3T1D cell is based on the 3T DRAM cell in 1970s, and a gated diode is added to dynamically amplify the storage capacitance. Compared to the 1T1C eDRAM, the 3T1D eDRAM has advantages of low fabrication cost by obviating the needs for additional masks and fast access time comparable to SRAM with non-destructive reads.

Regardless of the types of eDRAM, the eDRAM cells need to be periodically refreshed to preserve stored bits, and the refresh power dominates the overall memory power consumption [35]. eDRAM has a smaller cell capacitance than the commodity DRAM. Hence, the retention time becomes shorter, and the refresh operation should be performed much more frequently. This leads to higher refresh power, which is a serious concern for eDRAM-based on-chip memories.

Both bit error rate and refresh power are functions of the refresh period, and there is a tradeoff between the two. Figure 4 illustrates this tradeoff. The refresh power, whose model is detailed in Section 4, is inversely proportional to the refresh period, whereas the eDRAM bit error rate increases exponentially as the refresh period increases [23, 35].

In video and display applications, which can tolerate bit errors (i.e., pixel inaccuracies), we can exploit power-accuracy tradeoffs by controlling refresh period. With *data criticality-aware non-uniform refreshment*, we can save a significant fraction of the refresh power with minimal degradation of the video quality.

3. TIERED-RELIABILITY MEMORY

TRM enables data criticality-aware non-uniform refreshment to save refresh power in eDRAM-based frame buffers.

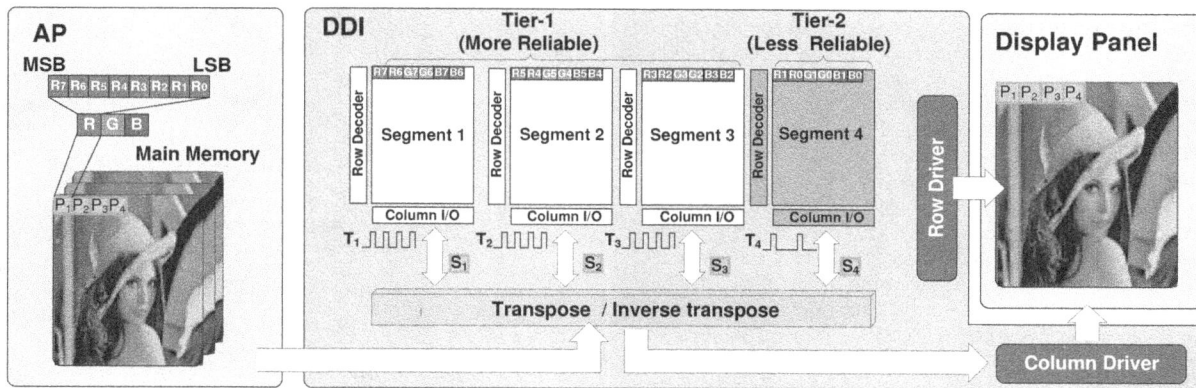

Figure 5: Mobile display sub-system augmented with eDRAM-based Tiered-Reliability Memory (TRM)

To realize this, TRM combines the following three components synergistically:

- (Multiple segments) The frame buffer is partitioned into multiple *segments* that can be refreshed independently with different periods.

- (Bit transpose) The incoming stream of pixel bits are rearranged at a sub-pixel granularity and allocated to segments according to their criticality. The MSBs of a color component are allocated to the most reliable segment, and the LSBs to the least reliable segment.

- (Optimal refresh period vector) The refresh period of each segment should be set optimally to balance refresh power savings with video quality degradation.

3.1 TRM Organization

Figure 5 illustrates a TRM-based display sub-system with a 4-segment frame buffer. The refresh period of each segment can be set independently from other segments to control its error rate. The refresh period of Segment i is denoted by T_i and represented as a multiple of the *nominal* refresh period (T_0), which is the refresh period for reliable operation. We assume that, if $T_i \leq 1$ (i.e., refresh period is equal to or shorter than the nominal refresh period), the error rate of Segment i will be zero. The nominal refresh period is determined by cell retention time.

Table 2 summarizes TRM parameters. The refresh period vector ($\mathbf{V}$) is a vector of length N containing $T_1, T_2, ..., T_N$. The number of tiers can be up to the number of segments. For example, the DDI in Figure 5 illustrates a two-tier TRM with $\mathbf{V} =< 1, 1, 1, 2 >$, where Segments 1, 2, and 3 constitute more reliable Tier 1 with a refresh period of T_0 and Segment 4 constitutes less reliable Tier 2 with a refresh period of $2T_0$.

Parameter	Descriptions
N	Number of segments
T_0	Nominal refresh period
T_i	Refresh period of Segment i
$\mathbf{V} =< T_1, T_2, ..., T_N >$	Refresh period vector

Table 2: TRM parameters

Independent refresh operation from each segment requires per-segment row and column access circuitry. However, this hardware overhead is minimal since most DDIs have already

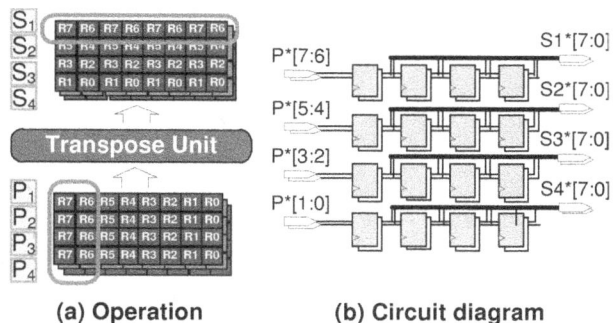

(a) Operation   (b) Circuit diagram

Figure 6: Transpose unit (* denotes either R, G, or B)

adopted multi-bank frame buffers to reduce the internal operating frequency by accessing multiple banks simultaneously. In such a case, supporting programmable refresh periods is the only required modification to the bank structure.

To make the best use of the frame buffer with multiple reliability tiers, we should sort incoming pixel data by their criticality and allocate the most critical data to the most reliable segment. By doing this refresh power is allocated to data proportionally to their criticality. In video applications, the MSBs of a pixel (or color component) are more critical for human visual perception, so they should be allocated to more reliable memory (e.g., Tier 1 in Figure 5), and LSBs to less reliable memory (e.g., Tier 2).

With the transpose unit in Figure 6, we can cluster pixel bits by their criticality, hence eliminating criticality fragmentations. In the DDI, pixel data arrive in a raster scan order and are stored across multiple banks in the frame buffer by interleaving them at a *pixel* granularity. The transpose unit in Figure 6 gathers the 7th and 6th bits (R7 and R6) of the four pixels (P1 through P4) and forwards them to Segment 1 (S1) as a group. For each set of four pixels, the three color components (R, G, and B) are processed in parallel. This circuit requires 48 flip-flops for each of transpose and inverse transpose, respectively, whose area overhead is negligible compared to the frame buffer.

3.2 TRM Parameter Selection

This section discusses various aspects to consider in selecting the following two TRM parameters: number of segments (N) and refresh period vector ($\mathbf{V}$).

Number of Segments (N): More segments enable more fine-grained control of refresh periods at the cost of additional per-segment hardware such as row decoder and refresh control logic. In the frame buffer, the maximum number of N is practically upper bounded by the number of bits for each color component, which is 8 in our setup.

Refresh Period Vector ($\mathbf{V}$): A careful selection of $\mathbf{V}$ is necessary to balance power savings and video quality degradation. $\mathbf{V}$ controls the error rate of each segment and can be adjusted/tuned in the field. Since the display panel reads (and refreshes) pixel data from the frame buffer periodically, the frame rate sets an upper bound on the refresh period. For example, for the frame rate of 60Hz, this upper bound is $1/60{=}16.7$ ms. If an image in the frame buffer does not change indefinitely, the pixel data in those segments with $T_i > 1$ will be eventually broken, hence degrading the image quality. To prevent this, we assume a fresh copy of the image is sent from the AP to the DDI every 5 minutes (300 seconds) even if the image being displayed does not change. Evaluation with varying $\mathbf{V}$ will be presented in Section 5.

4. MODELS AND METRICS

In this section we first describe the error rate model and power model that we use for evaluation, as functions of the refresh period. They are followed by the two metrics to quantify the degradation of video quality with TRM.

Error Injection Methodology

We use as baseline the eDRAM bit error model introduced by Wilkerson et al. [35], which is reproduced in Figure 4. We assume bit retention failures are distributed randomly throughout the frame buffer. By applying their methodology to a 24MB UHD frame buffer with the same target failure rate, we obtain the nominal refresh period (T_0) of $44\mu s$. Our error model assumes zero error rate for a refresh period shorter than T_0; otherwise, the bit error rate will follow the curve in Figure 4.

For evaluation the TRM simulator injects a random bit error for all bits in the frame buffer with a probability of the bit error rate corresponding to the refresh period. For each bit this injection process is repeated by the maximum number of refreshes that can happen without updating the frame buffer. Once error injection is finished for the entire frame, we compare the error-injected frame with the original frame to quantify the degradation of image quality.

Refresh Power Model

Based on the refresh power model of Tran et al. [31], the refresh power of TRM can be represented as follows:

$$P_{refresh} = \sum_{i=1}^{N} \frac{R_i \cdot E_{refresh}}{T_i} + P_C \approx \sum_{i=1}^{N} \frac{R_i \cdot E_{refresh}}{T_i}$$

where $P_{refresh}$ is a sum of the refresh power of all segments and R_i is the fraction of the size of Segment i in the frame buffer; T_i is the refresh period of Segment i; $E_{refresh}$ is per-refresh energy consumption; P_C is the constant power for refresh operation, which typically accounts for less than 10% of refresh power [18].

Video Quality Metrics

To quantify image/video quality, we use the following two metrics: Peak Signal-to-Noise Ratio (PSNR) and Structural Similarity index (SSIM). Assuming X and Y are the original

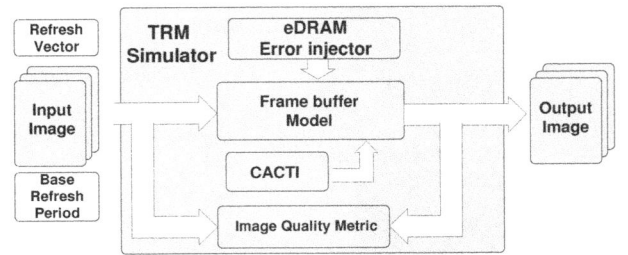

Figure 7: TRM Simulator

and error-injected images, respectively, PSNR is defined as follows:

$$PSNR(dB) = 20log(\frac{255^2}{MSE}), MSE = \sum \frac{(X_{i,j} - Y_{i,j})^2}{n}$$

where n is the total number of pixels, and mean square error (MSE) is a sum of pixel differences divided by pixel numbers. $X_{i,j}$ ($Y_{i,j}$) denotes the pixel value of X (Y) at the ith row and the jth column. If PSNR is higher than 40-45 dB, a human cannot tell the difference between the two images. Some vendors call it *visually lossless*.

SSIM is more sensitive to the structure information like the human visual perception system [33] and defined as follows:

$$SSIM = \frac{(2\mu_x\mu_y + C_1)(2\sigma_{xy} + C_2)}{(\mu_x^2 + \mu_y^2 + C_1)(\sigma_x^2 + \sigma_y^2 + C_2)}$$

where μ_x is the average pixel value of the original image and μ_y is that of the inaccurate image with TRM. σ_x, σ_y, σ_{xy} denote variance of X, variance of Y, and covariance of X and Y, respectively. C_1 and C_2 are 2.55 and 7.56 for the RGB color space. Based on the SSIM score whose range is from 0 to 1, the frame quality is classified into high (0.98-1), medium (0.96-0.98), or low (0.94-0.96).

5. EVALUATION

5.1 Methodology

To evaluate TRM, we have built a TRM simulator as shown in Figure 7. The simulator takes as input an input image, refresh period vector and nominal refresh period to output an inaccurate output image. CACTI [30] is used to model the power consumption. We assume a 4-segment TRM as shown in Figure 5 and a fresh frame sent to the frame buffer from the AP every 5 minutes (if not more frequently on the user's demand) as discussed in Section 3.2.

We choose input images from multiple sources for wide coverage of use cases, such as USC-SIPI [34], video clips [4], compress test image set [1], Kodak image set [2], and web pages (e.g., Google homepage). If an input image is not provided in the UHD resolution, we resize the image using the NumPy package [26]. To be visually loseless, PSNR should be greater than 45 dB, and SSIM greater than 0.98.

5.2 Results

An optimal refresh period vector allows us to achieve maximum power savings while staying visually lossless. To find one, we use 5 representative images taken from 5 different sources to measure PSNR, SSIM, and refresh power with varying refresh period vectors. Figure 8 shows the results,

(a) PSNR

(b) SSIM

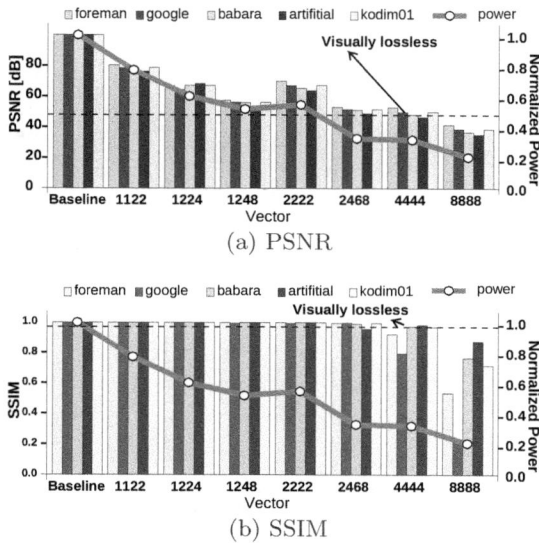

Figure 8: Video quality and refresh power with varying refresh period vectors for TRM

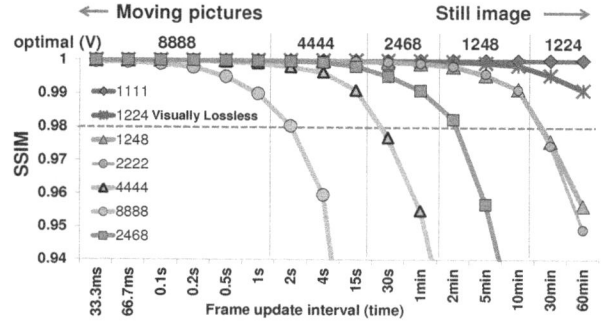

Figure 10: Frame update interval and SSIM with varying refresh vectors for TRM

where the baseline is $V=<1,1,1,1>$. All measured values are normalized to the corresponding values of the baseline. From this simulation, we obtain $<1,2,4,8>$ as an optimal vector, which has the lowest power (i.e., 48% reduction) while being visually lossless.

Figure 8 shows that most refresh period vectors are visually lossless when T_1 is 1; that is, as long as 2 MSBs are preserved, we cannot detect the degradation of image quality. This justifies criticality-aware power allocation to pixel bits. If only T_1 is one and the other T_i's are greater than one, as time goes on, all eDRAM cells except those in Segment 1 will eventually be discharged. This image represents the worst-case degradation of the image quality, and we call it *lower-bound* image.

Figure 9 shows the image quality of a wide variety of test images with $V=<1,2,4,8>$. With TRM all test images are visually loseless while consuming much less refresh power. Still, the image quality is much better than the lower bound. To bound the image quality degradation with TRM, the AP periodically resends the frame buffer with a fresh copy of the image. With this support, PSNR and SSIM stay above the cut-offs to be visually loseless while TRM achieves significant power savings.

Figure 10 shows the image quality (SSIM) with varying frame update intervals. The frame update interval is the time interval between adjacent frames sent from the AP. If the interval is shorter than 0.5 seconds (like playing video), $V=<8,8,8,8>$ is the optimal choice to minimize power consumption while remaining visually loseless. For an interval longer than 2 seconds, this vector starts to become visually lossy, and $<4,4,4,4>$ is the optimal choice, and so on. This result demonstrates that the optimal vector differs depending on the usage scenario. For a scenario displaying a still image (like reading an e-book) with a long frame update interval (say, >2 minutes), $V=<1,2,4,8>$ becomes optimal. Although $<1,2,4,8>$ and $<2,2,2,2>$ are comparable in terms of image quality, the former consumes about 7% less refresh power than the latter.

In summary, the human visual system is tolerant to errors in the low-order bits of the pixel data, but completely discarding the low-order bits would make the image visually lossy. With prolonged refreshes to those bits and periodic resubmission of the fresh frame from the AP, TRM can achieve significant power savings without degrading user experience.

6. RELATED WORK

Extending DRAM refresh period: Both Wilkerson et al. [35] and Emma el at. [11] propose to use ECC to extend refresh time. Venkatesan et al. propose retention-aware DRAM page allocation [32] to set the refresh period to be the shortest period only among the populated DRAM pages instead of all pages. Liu et al. exploit variable distribution of cell retention times to extend refresh period [22]. Ghosh et al. save refresh power and bandwidth overhead by skipping refreshes for recently accessed rows [12]. However, all of these proposals do not exploit different criticalities and error tolerance of data elements and are complementary to TRM.

Approximate computing: Approximate computing has recently drawn attention from the research community as a means to reduce power consumption by exploiting accuracy-energy tradeoffs. EnerJ [27] introduces a language extension to Java to allow the programmer to annotate which variables can be computed approximately. Also, there are several proposals to save refresh power by increasing refresh periods for non-critical data in commodity DRAM [22,23]. However, their proposals target general-purpose computing platforms with commodity DRAMs and cannot exploit bit-level criticality, hence suboptimal for video applications. In contrast, TRM is targeted for video applications to achieve much higher power efficiency than these proposals.

Hybrid on-chip memories: There are proposals for integrating multiple types of SRAM cells to handle the higher-order bits of pixel data preferentially over the lower-order bits in video applications. Kwon et al. propose Heterogeneous SRAM with varying cell sizes to trade reliability for leakage power savings [20]. Gong et al. introduce an ultra-low voltage split-data-aware 10T and 8T SRAM for the same goal [13]. Chang el al. [8] propose to mix 6T and 8T cells and save powers by aggressive voltage scaling while maintain a high signal-to-noise ratio (SNR). However, those techniques are only applicable to expensive SRAM-based frame buffers but not to eDRAM-based ones. Also, there are proposals to use non-volatile memory (NVM) for frame buffers, including DRAM-PRAM hybrid [14] and DRAM-MRAM-PRAM hybrid [29], but their main focuses are optimizing hybrid memories with different read/write characteristics and endurance.

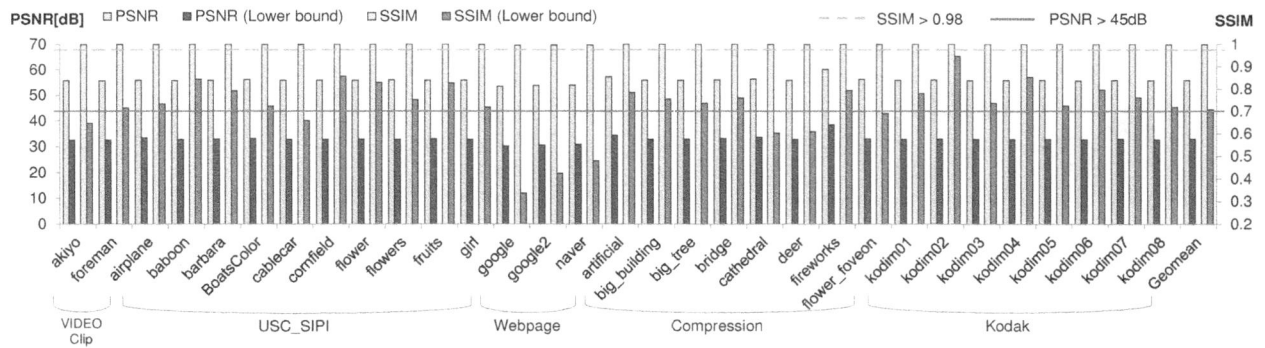

Figure 9: PSNR and SSIM for a wide variety of test images from multiple sources

7. CONCLUSION

High refresh power consumption is a serious concern for eDRAM-based on-chip memory, and the problem will get exacerbated with technology scaling, which reduces cell retention time. Furthermore, the screen resolution is expected to increase continuously in the foreseeable future, which will require even higher-capacity frame buffers, hence increasing refresh power. To save refresh power in the eDRAM-based frame buffer, we propose *Tiered-Reliability Memory* (TRM), which enables the frame buffer to allocate refresh power to pixel data non-uniformly in proportional to their criticality. By judiciously trading data accuracies for power savings, the four-tier TRM achieves 48% savings of refresh power while keeping the video frame visually lossless.

8. REFERENCES

[1] Image compression test images. http://www.imagecompression.info,.
[2] Kodak lossless true color image suite. http://r0k.us/graphics/kodak/.
[3] Samsung Analyst Day 2013: Display trends. http://www.samsung.com/.
[4] Xiph.org video test media. http://xiph.org/video/derf/.
[5] C. Argyrides, C. A. Lisboa, L. Carro, and D. K. Pradhan. A soft error robust and power aware memory design. In *Proc. 20th Annu. Symp. Integr. Circuits Syst. Des.(SBCCI)*, pages 300–305. ACM, 2007.
[6] J. Barth, W. Reohr, P. Parries, G. Fredeman, J. Golz, S. Schuster, R. Matick, H. Hunter, C. Tanner, J. Harig, et al. A 500MHz random cycle 1.5 ns-latency, soi embedded DRAM macro featuring a 3T micro sense amplifier. In *ISSCC, 2007*.
[7] A. Carroll and G. Heiser. An analysis of power consumption in a smartphone. In *Proc. of USENIX, 2010*.
[8] I. J. Chang, D. Mohapatra, and K. Roy. A priority-based 6T/8T hybrid SRAM architecture for aggressive voltage scaling in video applications. *IEEE Trans. on CSVT, 2011*.
[9] M.-T. Chang, P. Rosenfeld, S.-L. Lu, and B. Jacob. Technology comparison for large last-level caches (l3cs): Low-leakage SRAM, low write-energy STT-RAM, and refresh-optimized eDRAM. In *Proc. of HPCA, 2013*.
[10] M. Cho, J. Schlessman, W. Wolf, and S. Mukhopadhyay. Reconfigurable SRAM architecture with spatial voltage scaling for low power mobile multimedia applications. *Very Large Scale Integration (VLSI) Systems, IEEE Transactions on*, 19(1):161–165, 2011.
[11] P. G. Emma, W. R. Reohr, and M. Meterelliyoz. Rethinking refresh: Increasing availability and reducing power in DRAM for cache applications. In *Proc. of MICRO, 2008*.
[12] M. Ghosh and H.-H. S. Lee. Smart refresh: An enhanced memory controller design for reducing energy in conventional and 3D die-stacked DRAMs. In *Proc. of MICRO, 2007*.
[13] N. Gong, S. Jiang, A. Challapalli, S. Fernandes, and R. Sridhar. Ultra-low voltage split-data-aware embedded SRAM for mobile video applications. 2012.
[14] K. Han, A. W. Min, N. S. Jeganathan, and P. S. Diefenbaugh. A hybrid display frame buffer architecture for energy efficient display subsystems. In *Proc. of ISLPED, 2013*.

[15] IBM Corp. IBM Power Systems. http://www-03.ibm.com/systems/power/.
[16] Intel Corp. 72-core Knights Landing CPU. http://newsroom.intel.com/.
[17] N. Jing, H. Liu, Y. Lu, and X. Liang. Compiler assisted dynamic register file in gpgpu. In *Proc. of ISLPED, 2013*.
[18] J. Kim and M. C. Papaefthymiou. Block-based multiperiod dynamic memory design for low data-retention power. *IEEE Trans. on VLSI Systems, 2003*.
[19] K.-J. Kim, C. H. Kim, and K. Roy. TFT-LCD application specific low power SRAM using charge-recycling technique. In *Proc. of ISQED, 2005*.
[20] J. Kwon, I. J. Chang, I. Lee, H. Park, and J. Park. Heterogeneous SRAM cell sizing for low-power H.264 applications. *Circuits and Systems I: Regular Papers, IEEE Transactions on*, 59(10):2275–2284, 2012.
[21] X. Liang and et al.. Process variation tolerant 3T1D-based cache architectures. In *MICRO, 2007*.
[22] J. Liu, B. Jaiyen, R. Veras, and O. Mutlu. Raidr: Retention-aware intelligent DRAM refresh. In *ISCA, 2012*.
[23] S. Liu, K. Pattabiraman, T. Moscibroda, and B. G. Zorn. Flikker: saving DRAM refresh-power through critical data partitioning. *ACM SIGPLAN Notices*, 47(4):213–224, 2012.
[24] W. K. Luk and et al.. A 3-transistor DRAM cell with gated diode for enhanced speed and retention time. In *Symposium on VLSI Technicalogy and Circuits, June 2006*.
[25] H. Noguchi and et al.. Which is the best dual-port SRAM in 45-nm process technology?—8T, 10T single end, and 10T differential—. In *Proc. of ICICDT, 2008*.
[26] T. E. Oliphant. *A Guide to NumPy*, volume 1. Trelgol Publishing USA, 2006.
[27] A. Sampson, W. Dietl, E. Fortuna, D. Gnanapragasam, L. Ceze, and D. Grossman. Enerj: Approximate data types for safe and general low-power computation. In *ACM SIGPLAN Notices*, volume 46, pages 164–174. ACM, 2011.
[28] H. Shim, N. Chang, and M. Pedram. A compressed frame buffer to reduce display power consumption in mobile systems. In *Proc. of ASPDAC, 2004*.
[29] L. C. Stancu and et al.. Avid: Annotation driven video decoding for hybrid memories. In *Embedded Systems for Real-time Multimedia (ESTIMedia), 2012 IEEE 10th Symposium on*, pages 2–11. IEEE, 2012.
[30] S. Thoziyoor, N. Muralimanohar, J. H. Ahn, and N. P. Jouppi. Cacti 5.1. *HP Laboratories, April*, 2, 2008.
[31] L.-N. Tran and et al.. Adjustable supply voltages and refresh cycle for process variations, temperature changes, and device degradation adaptation in 1T1C embedded DRAM. In *Design and Test Workshop (IDT), 2011 IEEE 6th International*, pages 124–129. IEEE, 2011.
[32] R. K. Venkatesan, S. Herr, and E. Rotenberg. Retention-aware placement in DRAM(RAPID): software methods for quasi-non-volatile dram. In *Proc. of HPCA, 2006*.
[33] Z. Wang, A. C. Bovik, H. R. Sheikh, and E. P. Simoncelli. Image quality assessment: From error visibility to structural similarity. *Image Processing, IEEE Transactions on*, 13(4):600–612, 2004.
[34] A. G. Weber. The usc-sipi image database version 5. *USC-SIPI Report*, 315:1–24, 1997.
[35] C. Wilkerson, A. R. Alameldeen, Z. Chishti, W. Wu, D. Somasekhar, and S.-l. Lu. Reducing cache power with low-cost, multi-bit error-correcting codes. *ACM SIGARCH Computer Architecture News*, 38(3):83–93, 2010.

Enabling High-Performance LPDDRx-Compatible MRAM

Jue Wang
Pennsylvania State University
jzw175@cse.psu.edu

Xiangyu Dong
Qualcomm Technologies, Inc.
xydong@acm.org

Yuan Xie
Pennsylvania State University
yuanxie@cse.psu.edu

ABSTRACT

DRAM consumes a significant amount of energy in mobile computing devices today. Emerging non-volatile memory such as magnetoresistive memory (MRAM) offers a DRAM alternative and can potentially lead to a more energy-efficient memory system. The MRAM technology is already mature, but considering the memory industry is highly standardized, we are still unable to see any MRAM used in mainstream products. To tackle this problem, we design an LPDDRx-compatible MRAM interface by considering both MRAM pros and cons. Our design solves the pin-compatibility and the performance issues caused by MRAM small page size, and it optimizes the interface protocol by leveraging the MRAM unique feature of non-destructive reads. Combining our techniques, we boost the MRAM performance by 14% and provide a DRAM-swappable MRAM solution with 20% less energy.

Categories and Subject Descriptors

B.7.1 [**Integrated Circuits**]: Types and Design Styles—*Memory Technologies*

Keywords

MRAM, spin-transfer torque, LPDDR

1. INTRODUCTION

Battery-backed mobile devices require low energy consumption. The memory subsystem in mobile devices is unfortunately not energy-efficient, e.g. the DRAM in a smartphone today can consume 34.5% of the total energy [8]. It is because DRAM by nature is volatile: DRAM needs periodic refreshes, which can cause a 20% energy waste [17]. Ever worse, the DRAM refresh issue will soon become a system performance bottleneck [19]. Therefore, it is necessary to explore alternative memory technologies.

Magnetoresistive memory (MRAM), or known as spin-transfer torque memory (STT-RAM), is an emerging non-volatile memory (NVM), and it has potentials to provide an energy-efficient memory subsystem [15, 18]. However, enjoying the MRAM energy-saving benefit is not free. It is a consensus that MRAM

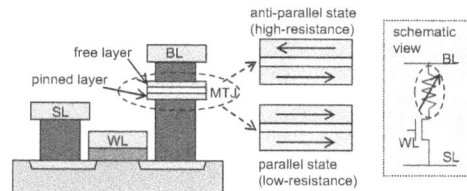

Figure 1: The conceptual view of an MRAM cell.

cannot compete with DRAM in terms of performance, and more importantly, MRAM chip internal structure is incompatible to today's memory interfaces. This compatibility is not only highly required for a successful MRAM early adoption, but also critical for enabling a tiered memory system using refresh-free MRAM and high-performance DRAM [10, 20]. Everspin's effort [22] to produce a DDR3-compatible MRAM is another example of this.

The goal of this paper is to introduce an optimized MRAM interface but totally compatible to the state-of-the-art LPDDR3 specification originally designed for DRAM. All the optimizations are done by tweaking the existing timing parameters. We start with a background introduction in Section 2, followed a discussion in Section 3 on two unique MRAM properties: MRAM small page size and MRAM non-destructive reads. These two properties bring us both challenges and opportunities to reach our goal. Then, we detail three optimization techniques in Section 4: *ComboAS* and *DynLat* to solve the compatibility and performance issues caused by MRAM small page size; *EarlyPA* to leverage the non-destructive reads. Combined all these together, we show in Section 5 that the MRAM performance is improved by 14% (up to 36%), and this DRAM-swappable MRAM solution saves 20% energy consumption.

2. BACKGROUND

We briefly explain DRAM and MRAM technology background first in this section.

2.1 MRAM Technology

Compared to DRAM, MRAM is non-volatile and consumes zero standby power [6, 13, 22, 27]. Figure 1 illustrates the basic concept of MRAM. Instead of using electrical charges, MRAM uses magnetic tunnel junctions (MTJs) to store its binary data. Each MTJ consists of two ferromagnetic layers: a pinned layer with a fixed magnetization direction and a free layer with a switchable direction. The relative direction of these two layers determines the stored data. Previous work [6] has shown that the unit cell dimension of MRAM below 30 nm can be smaller than $8\,F^2$, which is comparable to DRAM's $6\,F^2$ size.

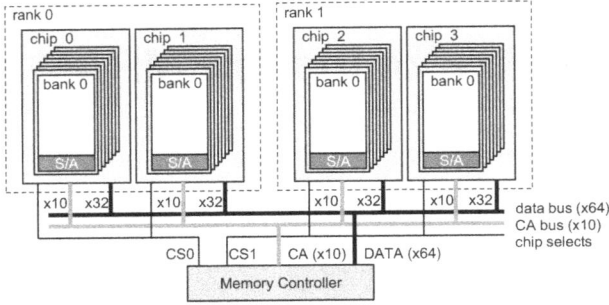

Figure 2: The memory organization for LPDDRx chips.

2.2 DRAM and LPDDRx Interface

LPDDRx memory interface is dominant in modern mobile devices. JEDEC released the first LPDDR specification in 2009. Today, almost all the mobile SoC use LPDDR2 or LPDDR3 [12]. Figure 2 shows an exemplary LPDDRx configuration, which is a 1-channel, 2-rank memory subsystem with four x32 DRAM chips.

LPDDRx uses a multiplexed command/address (CA) bus to reduce the pin count. The 10-bit CA bus contains command, address, and bank information. Each LPDDRx DRAM internally has 8 banks, and each bank can independent process a different memory request. Same as DDRx, LPDDRx accesses begin with an activation command (ACT), which includes a row access signal, a bank address, and a row address. Memory controllers send ACT commands to DRAMs, and a corresponding DRAM row is then activated (opened). After that, memory controllers issue column read or write commands with a column access signal and the starting column address for burst accesses.

2.3 MRAM Device Projection

Everspin announced the world's first MRAM (based on STT-RAM) DDR3 device in 2013 [22]. This product is DDR3-compatible, but its capacity is only 64Mb, far away from modern gigabit-scale DRAMs. Before detailing how to build DRAM-comparable gigabit-scale MRAM, we first project how the future MRAM will look like.

We use our modified CACTI [26] and NVSim [7] to simulate a 4Gb LPDDR3 DRAM and a 4Gb LPDDR3 MRAM on a 28nm process, respectively. Table 1 lists the timing and power parameters. We can verify that the estimated numbers match to the actual LPDDR3 DRAM and MRAM prototypes. The major differences between DRAM and MRAM LPDDR3 devices are:

- *Small page size*: MRAM page (row buffer) size is 16 folds smaller than DRAM. This results in an unbalanced MRAM row/column address bit ratio – 18:6 versus DRAM's 14:10. The details of this constraint is discussed later in Section 3.

- *Non-volatility*: MRAM is non-volatile and needs no refresh. Hence, MRAM has zero tREF, tRFC, auto-refresh current (IDD5[1]) and self-refresh current (IDD6).

- *Non-destructive read*: MRAM has smaller tRTP and can issue precharge command sooner because MRAM reads are non-destructive and do not need write-back.

- *Fast page close*: DRAM precharge needs to balance bitlines (BL and $\overline{BL}$) to VDD/2, but MRAM precharge can skip this step. Therefore, MRAM precharge (tRP) is faster.

- *Slow page open*: MRAM MTJ has small on/off resistance ratio (e.g. 200%), and it is hard to sense the data. Therefore, the MRAM row activation (tRCD) is slower.

[1]In auto-refresh mode, MRAM peripheral circuitry still consumes power so that IDD5 is essentially IDD2P.

Table 1: Comparison of DRAM and MRAM LPDDR3 devices

Parameters	LPDDR3 DRAM		LPDDR3 MRAM	
Clock	533 MHz		533 MHz	
Page size	4 KByte		256 Byte	
Bank bit	BA2-BA0		BA2-BA0	
Row bit	R13-R0		R17-R0	
Column bit	C9-C0		C5-C0	
tREF	3900 ns		N/A	
tRCD	10 cycle		12 cycle	
tRL	8 cycle		6 cycle	
tWL	4 cycle		4 cycle	
tRP	10 cycle		6 cycle	
tRC	32 cycle		19 cycle	
tRTP	4 cycle		2 cycle	
tRRD	6 cycle		6 cycle	
tCCD	4 cycle		4 cycle	
tWTR	4 cycle		4 cycle	
tWR	8 cycle		16 cycle	
tFAW	27 cycle		27 cycle	
tRFC	70 cycle		N/A	
Voltage	VDD1 (1.8 V)	VDD2 (1.2 V)	VDD1 (1.8 V)	VDD2 (1.2 V)
IDD0	8 mA	30 mA	5 mA	40 mA
IDD2N	2 mA	4 mA	2 mA	4 mA
IDD2P	2 mA	2 mA	2 mA	2 mA
IDD3N	3.5 mA	7 mA	3.5 mA	7 mA
IDD3P	3.5 mA	7 mA	3.5 mA	7 mA
IDD4R	3.5 mA	150 mA	0 mA	180 mA
IDD4W	3.5 mA	150 mA	0 mA	250 mA
IDD5	25 mA	80 mA	2 mA	2 mA
IDD6	1.0 mA	3.8 mA	0 mA	0 mA

- *Slow write*: MRAM has longer write latency and higher write energy. Thus, MRAM has larger tWR and IDD4W.

3. CHALLENGE AND OPPORTUNITY

The underlying technology difference poses both challenges and opportunities in designing an LPDDRx-compatible MRAM.

3.1 Challenge: Small Page Size

Although most MRAM parameters have their DRAM counterparts as we list in Table 1, a key difference is MRAM's page size.

The fundamental constraint of MRAM small page size is that MRAM reads require current sensing. Current-mode S/A is much more complicated than voltage-mode S/A used in DRAM, and it is also significantly larger. Our circuit simulation shows an MRAM S/A is 16 times larger than a DRAM S/A. To maintain chip area utilization, MRAM has to use less S/A causing a smaller page size (e.g. 16X smaller). MRAM industry also has consensus on this. For example, a 2012 EverSpin patent [2] discloses that their MRAM page is only 512-bit large, 32X smaller than a DRAM page. Unfortunately, such a small difference makes MRAM incompatible with existing memory interfaces, and worse degrades the system performance.

Unbalanced address bits: A 16x smaller page size means that a same-sized MRAM requires 4 more row address bits but 4 less column address bits[2]. However, LPDDRx uses a multiplexed CA bus for both command and address, and it can only carry 20 bits per cycle. For a row activation command, we need 2 bits for command decoding, 3 bits of bank addresses, and only have up to 15 bits for row addresses. An MRAM with 256K rows is obviously unsupported. Even though we could possibly add more CA pins to future memory interface, MRAM's unbalanced row/column address bit ratio still makes the row/column multiplexing idea highly inefficient.

[2]The "row" and "column" are both logical concept here. MRAM can still maintain a reasonable geometric aspect ratio, but partial logical row address bits are used for physical column muxing.

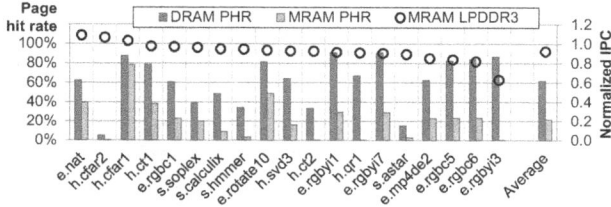

Figure 3: The IPC and page hit ratio comparison between a DRAM system and an MRAM system.

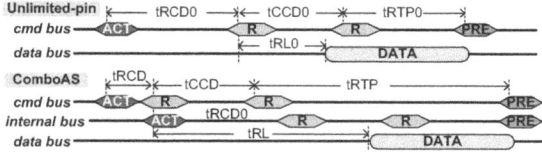

Figure 4: The timing diagrams of Unlimited-pin and ComboAS.

Table 2: Timing parameters for Unlimited-pin and ComboAS

	Unlimited-pin system	ComboAS
tRCD	$tRCD_0$	1 tCK
tCCD	$tCCD_0$	$tCCD_0$
tRL	tRL_0	$tRCD_0 + tRL_0$
tWL	tWL_0	$tRCD_0 + tWL_0$
tRTP	$tRTP_0$	$tRCD_0 + tRTP_0$

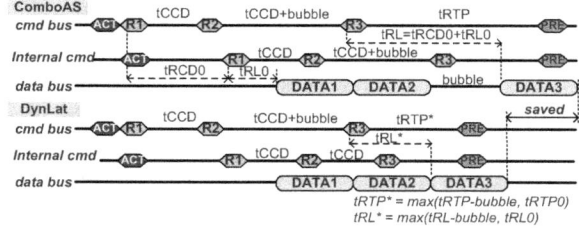

Figure 5: The timing diagrams of ComboAS and DynLat.

Performance degradation: Although a smaller page size is preferred to avoid over-activation in a memory system that uses close-page policy [28], modern mobile devices heavily adopt open-page policy, and smaller page size means high page miss rate and low performance. Figure 3 shows the page hit rate and the performance impact due to MRAM's 16x smaller page size (see Section 5 for simulation methodology details). On average, the page hit ratio is decreased by 66% and the resulting performance degradation is around 10%[3].

3.2 Opportunity: Non-destructive Read

DRAM reads are destructive and need data restoration, thus the DRAM S/A in an active bank always connect to bitlines and serves as a row buffer. On the contrary, MRAM reads are non-destructive. In another word, we can treat each row buffer as a copy of the original MRAM row data. This extra redundancy allows us to utilize the MRAM row buffer in a more aggressive way, and this is a unique opportunity for MRAM performance optimization.

4. SOLUTIONS

To overcome the drawback and leverage the advantage of MRAM, we gradually propose three optimization techniques as our solution.

4.1 ComboAS: Balance Row/Column Address

As explained in Section 3.1, the LPDDRx interface only carries 15 row address bits, but our targeted MRAM has a highly skewed row/column bit ratio (e.g 18:6). Adding two more CA pins can temporarily solve this problem, but it requires an industry-wide PHY redesign. Worse, it implies that such MRAM is not DRAM-swappable and prohibits any mixture uses of DRAM and MRAM.

Therefore, the first technique we propose is *Combinational Row/Column Address Strobe (ComboAS)*, and its goal is to re-balance the address bits carried by RAS (row access strobe, e.g. ACT command) and CAS (column access strobe, e.g. READ and WRITE commands). The basic concept is straightforward: offloading the overflowed row address from RAS to CAS.

Since we split the row address into RAS and CAS, ComboAS needs both commands before activating a new row. Consequently, instead of waiting for tRCD, we should issue a CAS command immediately after every RAS command. Figure 4 compares the

timing diagram of ComboAS against the incompatible solution of adding 2 more CA pins. In ComboAS, the actual row activation is delayed by 1 cycle to wait the remaining row address bits from CAS; read or write accesses are delayed by $tRCD_0$ (the original row activation delay). Table 2 lists the detailed adjustments.

To implement ComboAS, the modifications include:

MRAM device: We need three minor changes. (1) a new register to hold the partial row address bits carried by ACT and then later combined with the remaining row bits from READ or WRITE commands. (2) a signal generator to latch the remaining row address from the first-arrived CAS command. (3) a small register sets to temporarily hold column addresses. This is because the latency to activate a row ($tRCD_0$) is larger than the minimum delay between two column commands ($tCCD_0$), and multiple CAS commands might arrive during a new row activation. In this work, the size of this register set is 3 (i.e. $\lceil tRCD_0/tCCD_0 \rceil$).

Memory Controller: Only a small latch (4-bit in this work) after the PHY interface is needed to temporarily hold the extra row address bits from RAS command and later deposit them into the next CAS command. Second or latter CAS commands do not need to carry any row address bits. In addition, the memory timing parameters are adjusted according to Table 2.

4.2 DynLat: Remove Unnecessary Latencies

Figure 4 shows that ideally ComboAS only causes 1-cycle delay. However, that is not always true. ComboAS unconditionally adds $tRCD_0$ on top of every tRL, tWL, and tRTP to avoid internal bus conflicts, which is unnecessary for non-back-to-back accesses. For those non-ideal cases, we define a metric, **bubble**, to indicate the difference between the actual interval and the minimum interval[4]. ComboAS can be further improved if bubbles exist.

Taking a deep look into this issue, while the conventional tRL_0, tWL_0, and $tRTP_0$ are all static values and determined by the memory hardware limitation, the new tRL, tWL, and tRTP parameters in ComboAS become variable as they include the row activation latency ($tRCD_0$) which we only need to pay once for one opened row. We can deduct this $tRCD_0$ overhead from tRL/tWL/tRTP if we find bubbles on the command bus. This observation leads us to a dynamic timing parameter settings where tRL, tWL, and tRTP are adjustable on-the-fly. We call this technique *Dynamic Latency (DynLat)*.

---

[3]Note that for the workloads whose page hit ratio is less sensitive to the page size, MRAM outperforms DRAM (e.g. *e.nat*) because MRAM has faster precharge speed and needs no refresh.

[4]The minimum interval between two column accesses is max(tCCD, BL/2) where BL is the burst length. LPDDR3 has tCCD=4 and BL=8.

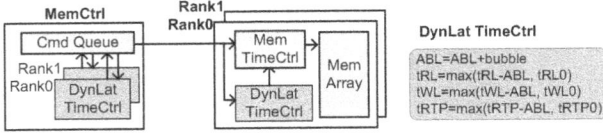

Figure 6: The DynLat implementation.

To demonstrate the idea and the benefit of DynLat, we use Figure 5 as an example. The differences between the timing diagrams without and with DynLat are:

- Accesses **R1** and **R2** are back-to-back. To avoid the memory chip internal hardware conflict, **R2** in both ComboAS and DynLat have the original tRL setting ($tRL_0 + tRCD_0$).

- Accesses **R2** and **R3** are not back-to-back. In ComboAS, the tRL of **R3** remains $tRL_0 + tRCD_0$, which causes bubbles on both the internal command bus and the data bus (the bubble between DATA2 and DATA3).

In DynLat, the bubble on the data bus is eliminated by setting the tRL for **R3** to be $max(tRL - bubbleLength, tRL_0)$. By forcing tRL larger than tRL_0, we ensure the command meets the memory chip internal hardware constraint; by subtracting bubbleLength, we guarantee the bubble is removed. We track *accumulated bubble length* (ABL) of each memory rank. We reset ABL to 0 upon every ACT command and accumulate the bubble length upon every READ or WRITE command according to Equation 1.

$$ABL' = ABL + (curCycle - lastCmdCycle) - minReqDelay \quad (1)$$

ABL keeps increasing during a page open cycle. In practice, we can limit the ABL value less than $tRCD_0$ to reduce counter overhead. Based on ABL, we then calculate the new tRL, tWL, and tRTP,

$$tRL = max(tRL_0 + tRCD_0 - ABL, tRL_0)$$
$$tWL = max(tRL_0 + tRCD_0 - ABL, tWL_0)$$
$$tRTP = max(tRTP_0 + tRCD_0 - ABL, tRTP_0) \quad (2)$$

where tRL_0, tWL_0, $tRTP_0$, and $tRCD_0$ are the original timing parameters defined by the memory device.

To implement DynLat, the hardware changes we need are:

MRAM device: Since DynLat introduces variable read and write latencies, the memory device shall track the latest tRL and tWL, so that it can return the data for read or latch the data for write at the correct cycle. For this purpose, we add a new component called *TimeCtrl* to each memory device as shown in Figure 6. TimeCtrl tracks the ABL value and updates the timing parameters to the device internal signal delaying circuitry according to Equation 2. If a memory rank contains multiple memory devices, their TimeCtrl logics behave in a lockstep mode.

Memory Controller: The same TimeCtrl logic is duplicated in the memory controller so that the optimized command intervals can be correctly generated from the controller. The number of duplications is the same as the memory subsystem rank count. For example, in Figure 6, we duplicate two TimeCtrl in the memory controller for a 2-rank configuration.

4.3 EarlyPA: Leverage Non-destructive Read

DynLat can remove the unnecessary latency and alleviate the performance drop brought by ComboAS, but it cannot mitigate the performance drop caused by reduced page hit ratio (as shown in Figure 3), which is another side effect of the MRAM small page size. As discussed in Section 3.2, the non-destructive MRAM reads give us an opportunity to improve the performance. Thus, we devise our third optimization technique: *Early*

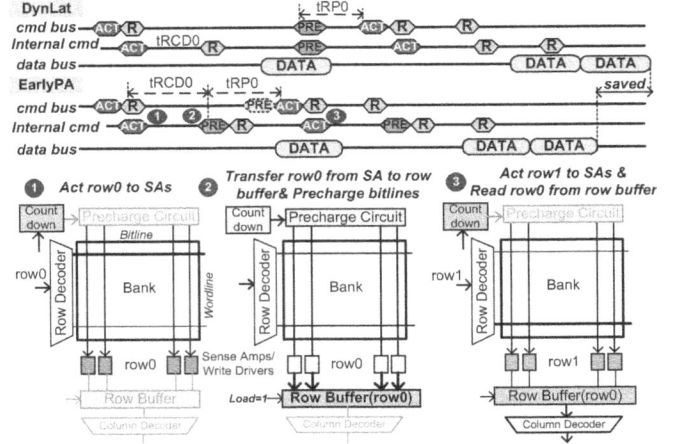

Figure 7: The timing diagrams of DynLat and EarlyPA.

Precharge/Activation (EarlyPA), in which we decouple sense amplifiers and row buffers so that bitlines can be precharged right after data sensing and the next ACT command can be issued earlier.

To implement EarlyPA, we first decouple the "data latching" out of a normal MRAM S/A by extracting the last stage amplifier and evolving it into a full SRAM cell. The decoupled row buffer allows bitlines to be early-precharged during the buffer column accesses. An example is illustrated in Figure 7:

- **Time slot 1:** Upon the first ACT, the S/A starts sensing, and a self-precharge counter starts counting down from $tRCD_0$.

- **Time slot 2:** The counter triggers a bitline self-precharge (an internal PRE command[5]) after $tRCD_0$. The S/A finishes data sensing, and the row buffer holds a copy of the data.

- **Time slot 3**: When the second ACT arrives, bitlines and S/As are ready for another row activation (row1). At the same time, all the column read accesses to row0 keep proceeding from the row buffer to I/Os.

EarlyPA improves the read performance by issuing PRE and ACT for the next row in advance. On the other hand, EarlyPA handles write accesses as follows: if it comes before the self-precharge is internally issued, we postpone the self-precharge by updating the self-precharge counter to leverage the unfinished row activation cycle; if it comes after the self-precharge, besides resetting the self-precharge counter, we need to turn on the corresponding wordline again for writing the data, which brings small latency overhead (i.e. 3 cycles in this work).

The EarlyPA implementation can be transparent to the memory controller and only requires some timing parameter manipulations. The controlling policy for column access commands (READ/WRITE) remains the same. As shown in Figure 7, we modify two precharge-related timing parameters:

- tRAS (activation-to-precharge) of EarlyPA is $tRCD_0 + tRP_0$.

- tRP (precharing time) value is set as 1 so that the next ACT command can be issued immediately when the self-precharge is finished.

To implement EarlyPA, hardware modifications are:

MRAM device: Devices ignore all the PRE commands from the memory controller as EarlyPA automatically precharges the bitlines in advance. Instead, a self-precharge counter is added to each memory device control logic. The counter is set to

---

[5]This self-precharge is different from the auto-precharge operation used in close-page policy. In EarlyPA the self-precharge only precharges the bitlines but the row buffer data remain intact.

Table 3: Simulation settings

Core	2GHz, out-of-order ARM core
SRAM I-L1/D-L1 caches	private, 32KB/32KB, 8-way, LRU, 64B cache line, write-back, write allocate
SRAM L2 cache	shared, 1MB, 16-way, LRU, 64B cache line, write-back, write allocate
Memory controller	open page policy, 32-entry read/write request queues per controller, FR-FCFS scheduler
Main Memory	1 channel, 2 ranks-per-channel, 8 banks-per-rank. Timing is configured as Table 1

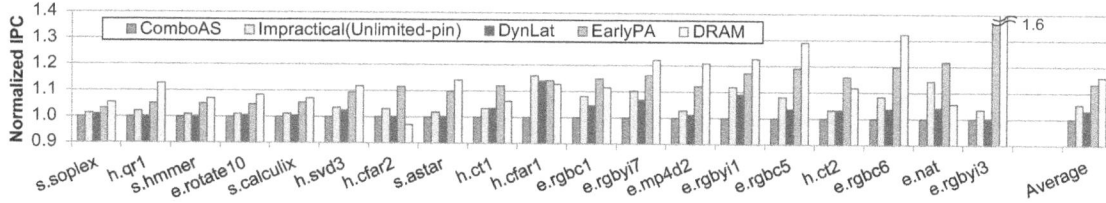

Figure 8: Normalized IPC of main memory system with each technique: ComboAS as the baseline, Unlimited-pin, DynLat, EarlyPA, and DRAM systems.

$tRCD_0$ after every ACT command and reset to $tWL+BL/2+tWR$ or $3+tWL+BL/2+tWR$ after every WRITE command depending on whether the counter reaches zero or not at the WRITE command arrival. Furthermore, the memory device skips precharge-related timing rule (e.g. tRTP checking) except the tRAS checking as S/As and row buffers are decoupled in the EarlyPA mode.

Memory controller: Symmetrically, the memory controller manipulates the timing parameters in the same way as memory devices do. An additional modification to the memory controller is the write-to-precharge latency control: after issuing a WRITE command, the minimum required delay for the next PRE command is $tWL+BL/2+tWR+tRP_0$ instead of $tWL+BL/2+tWR$.

5. EXPERIMENTS

To quantify the performance and energy improvement achieved by our techniques, we detail our simulation methodology and experiment results in this section.

5.1 Simulation Methodology

We model a 2GHz out-of-order ARMv7 microprocessor using our modified version of gem5 [3]. DRAMSim2 [23] is integrated and modified to model the main memory system. Open-page policy with FR-FCFS [21] scheduling is accurately modeled.

We use the parameters in Table 1 to simulate DRAM and MRAM and use open-page policy with row-interleaving to maximize the memory-level parallelism. More details for the simulation setting are provided in Table 3. The memory-intensive benchmarks are selected from SPEC 2006 [24], EEMBC 2.0 [9], and HPEC [11]. We fast-forward each simulation to the pre-defined breakpoint at the code region of interest, warm-up 10 million instructions, and simulate for at least 1 billion instructions.

5.2 Performance speedup

Figure 8 shows the performance speedup of the MRAM system with each proposed technique. The DRAM system performance is also provided for comparison. We use ComboAS as the baseline which has the worst performance. The second bar is the performance of an impractical implementation where 2 more pins are added (referred to as Unlimited-pin in the chart). Compared to Unlimited-pin, Figure 8 shows that the performance of ComboAS is degraded by 5% on average. However, after adopting DynLat, the sytem performance is bounced back by 3% on average (up to 14%) and is comparable to the Unlimited-pin in most cases. In addition, by leveraging the MRAM non-destructive read with EarlyPA, we improve the performance further. The total

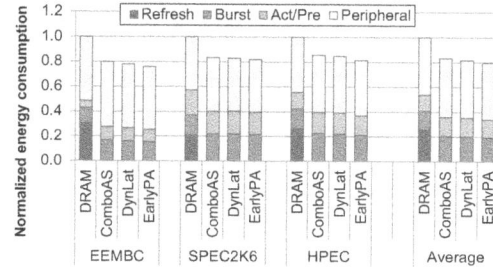

Figure 9: Normalized energy consumption of DRAM system and MRAM system adopted different techniques.

performance speedup is 14% (up to 36%). Generally, memory-intensive workloads benefit more from our proposed techniques because more efficient memory accesses provide larger system performance improvement.

After adopting all the proposed techniques, the overall MRAM performance is competitive to the DRAM counterpart (about 98%).

5.3 Energy consumption analysis

While the performance of our optimized MRAM system is similar to the conventional DRAM system, the real deal breaker is the energy consumption saving. Figure 9 shows the comparison of energy consumption between DRAM and MRAM systems, in which each value is divided to refresh energy, burst energy, activation/precharge energy and background peripheral circuit energy[6]. The energy overhead of each proposed technique is also included.

Compared to DRAM, MRAM-based system consumes zero refresh energy because of its non-volatility, and this is the major source of the MRAM energy saving. However, as shown in Table 1, the read/write energy of MRAM is larger than DRAM because MRAM has smaller sense margin and the memory cell is difficult to write. Thus, the MRAM burst energy is usually larger than the DRAM one. The energy consumed by peripheral circuits is similar between DRAM and MRAM because we do not apply any circuit optimization in this work. But we should note that the peripheral energy of MRAM can be further reduced if MRAM is allowed to go into power-collapse mode frequently during the idle state.

Figure 9 shows the ComboAS MRAM system reduces the total energy consumption by 17% on average compared to DRAM system. After adopting DynLat and EarlyPA techniques, the energy

---

[6]In this work, we do not model the self-refresh mode for DRAM systems and the power-collapse mode for MRAM systems. The realistic background energy can be smaller than our simulated numbers.

consumption of MRAM system can be further reduced by 4% on average since the performance is increased and the total execution time is reduced. Considering the comparable performance and smaller energy consumption, MRAM is an attactive candidate to build the main memory system.

6. RELATED WORK

Many previous works are focused on increasing DRAM energy efficiency by re-designing DRAM organization architecture [1, 28, 29]. Others are focused on improving DRAM performance [14,25]. The posted-RAS scheme [28] is the most similar work to our ComboAS technique as we both issue RAS and CAS commands back-to-back. However, posted-RAS only works for close-page policy where there is only one CAS command after opening one row, and it does not optimize the timing parameters to mitigate the performance overhead.

Other work aimed at NVM optimizations. PCM is studied as a main memory candidate and some techniques are proposed to reduce its energy overhead and improve its performance [4, 5, 30]. Lee *et al.* [16] proposed the technique to separate sense amplifiers and row buffers in PCM-based main memory, but unlike *EarlyPA*, their technique did not issue precharge commands in advance to hide the latency. Meza *et al.* [18] and Emre *et al.* [15] also evaluated MRAM as an main memory alternative, but they did not discuss the issue of how to build a compatible interface. Everspin [22] demonstrates a DDR3-compatible MRAM, but their MRAM capacity is so small (i.e. 64Mb) that the pin-compatibility problem is naturally hidden. Also, Everspin does not optimize for MRAM performance.

7. CONCLUSION

The shift from PCs to mobile devices is requesting low-power memory solutions, and non-volatile memories such as MRAM are promising candidates. Compared to DRAM, MRAM has many unique features such as *small page size* and *non-destructive read*. The smaller page size brings challenges in designing commodity MRAM that can be deployed on the same LPDDR interface for DRAM memory, and can cause performance degradation to mobile systems where the page hit ratio is important. In this work, we propose three techniques: *ComboAS* and *DynLat* to solve the DRAM-compatibility issue; *EarlyPA* to further improve the performance. Combined together, our solution enables a commodity MRAM on LPDDR3 interface with a much optimized performance (14% on average and up to 36%). It makes LPDDR3 MRAM have competitive performance but save 20% energy compared to LPDDR3 DRAM does. The proposed architecture is a step forward to the future energy-efficient memory design.

7.1 Acknowledgments

This research was funded by NSF grants 1218867, 1313052, 1409798, and Department of Energy under Award Number DE-SC0005026.

8. REFERENCES

[1] J. H. Ahn *et al.*, "Multicore DIMM: an energy efficient memory module with independently controlled DRAMs," *Computer Architecture Letters*, 2009.

[2] S. M. Alam *et al.*, "Memory controller and method for interleaving DRAM and MRAM accesses," US Patent 2012/0 155 160 A1, 6 21, 2012.

[3] N. Binkert *et al.*, "The gem5 simulator," *SIGARCH Computer Architecture News*, 2011.

[4] Y. Byung-Do *et al.*, "A low power phase-change random access memory using a data-comparison write scheme," in *ISCAS*, 2007.

[5] S. Cho *et al.*, "Flip-N-Write: A simple deterministic technique to improve PRAM write performance, energy and endurance," in *MICRO*, 2009.

[6] S. Chung *et al.*, "Fully integrated 54nm STT-RAM with the smallest bit cell dimension for high density memory application," in *IEDM*, 2010.

[7] X. Dong *et al.*, "NVSim: A circuit-level performance, energy, and area model for emerging non-volatile memory," *TCAD*, 2012.

[8] R. Duan *et al.*, "Exploring memory energy optimizations in smartphones," in *IGCC*, 2011.

[9] EEMBC, "EEMBC benchmark," http://www.eembc.org/.

[10] S. Hellmold, "Delivering nanosecond-class persistent memory," in *FMS*, 2013.

[11] HPEC, "HPEC benchmark," http://www.ll.mit.edu/HPECchallenge/.

[12] JEDEC Solid State Technology Association, "JESD209-3 LPDDR3 low power memory device standard."

[13] W. Kim *et al.*, "Extended scalability of perpendicular STT-MRAM towards sub-20nm MTJ node," in *IEDM*, 2011.

[14] Y. Kim *et al.*, "A case for exploiting subarray-level parallelism (SALP) in DRAM," in *ISCA*, 2012.

[15] E. Kultursay *et al.*, "Evaluating STT-RAM as an energy-efficient main memory alternative," in *ISPASS*, 2013.

[16] B. C. Lee *et al.*, "Architecting phase change memory as a scalable DRAM alternative," in *ISCA*, 2009.

[17] J. Liu *et al.*, "RAIDR: Retention-aware intelligent DRAM refresh," in *ISCA*, 2012.

[18] J. Meza, J. Li, and O. Mutlu, "A case for small row buffers in non-volatile main memories," in *ICCD*, 2012, pp. 484–485.

[19] J. Mukundan *et al.*, "Understanding and mitigating refresh overheads in high-density DDR4 DRAM systems," in *ISCA*, 2013.

[20] M. K. Qureshi *et al.*, "Scalable high performance main memory system using phase-change memory technology," in *ISCA*, 2009.

[21] S. Rixner *et al.*, "Memory access scheduling," in *ISCA*, 2000.

[22] N. Rizzo *et al.*, "A fully functional 64Mb DDR3 ST-MRAM built on 90nm CMOS technology," *Magnetics, IEEE Transactions on*, vol. 49, no. 7, 2013.

[23] P. Rosenfeld *et al.*, "DRAMSim2: A cycle accurate memory system simulator," *Computer Architecture Letters*, 2011.

[24] SPEC CPU, "SPEC CPU2006," http://www.spec.org/cpu2006/.

[25] K. Sudan *et al.*, "Micro-pages: increasing DRAM efficiency with locality-aware data placement," in *ASPLOS*, 2010.

[26] S. Thoziyoor *et al.*, "A comprehensive memory modeling tool and its application to the design and analysis of future memory hierarchies," in *ISSCC*, 2008.

[27] K. Tsuchida *et al.*, "A 64Mb MRAM with clamped-reference and adequate-reference schemes," in *ISSCC*, 2010.

[28] A. N. Udipi *et al.*, "Rethinking DRAM design and organization for energy-constrained multi-cores," in *ISCA*, 2010.

[29] H. Zheng *et al.*, "Mini-rank: Adaptive DRAM architecture for improving memory power efficiency," in *MICRO*, 2008.

[30] P. Zhou *et al.*, "A durable and energy efficient main memory using phase change memory technology," in *ISCA*, 2009.

SBAC: A Statistics based Cache Bypassing Method for Asymmetric-access Caches

Chao Zhang[†], Guangyu Sun[†], Peng Li[‡], Tao Wang[†], Dimin Niu[§] and Yiran Chen[ℒ]

[†]Center for Energy-Efficient Computing and Applications, EECS, Peking University, Beijing, 100871, China
[‡]Computer Science Department, University of California, Los Angeles, CA, 90095, USA
[§]Dept. of Computer Science and Engineering, Pennsylvania State University, University Park, PA, 16802, USA
[ℒ]Dept. of Electrical & Computer Engineering, University of Pittsburgh, Pittsburgh, PA, 15261, USA
[†]{zhang.chao, gsun, wangtao}@pku.edu.cn, [‡]pengli@cs.ucla.edu, [§]dun118@cse.psu.edu, [ℒ]yic52@pitt.edu

ABSTRACT

Asymmetric-access caches with emerging technologies, such as STT-RAM and RRAM, have become very competitive designs recently. Since the write operations consume more time and energy than read ones, data should bypass an asymmetric-access cache unless the locality can justify the data allocation. However, the asymmetric-access property is not well addressed in prior bypassing approaches, which are not energy efficient and induce non-trivial operation overhead. To overcome these problems, we propose a cache bypassing method, SBAC, based on data locality statistics of the whole cache rather than a single cache line's signature. We observe that the decision-making of SBAC is highly accurate and the optimization technique for SBAC works efficiently for multiple applications running concurrently. Experiments show that SBAC cuts down overall energy consumption by 22.3%, and reduces execution time by 8.3%. Compared to prior approaches, the design overhead of SBAC is trivial.

Categories and Subject Descriptors

B.3.2 [**Design Styles**]: Cache memories; D.4.2 [**Storage Management**]: Allocation/deallocation strategies

Keywords

Statistics; Bypass; Asymmetric-access Cache; Data Reuse Count

1. INTRODUCTION

Non-volatile memories (NVMs), such as spin-transfer torque random access memory (STT-RAM) and resistive random access memory (ReRAM), have been extensively studied to replace SRAM and embedded DRAM (eDRAM) as on-chip caches [6, 21]. Compared to traditional memory technologies, they have advantages of high storage density, low standby power consumption, good scalability, and immunity to particle based soft errors. Prior research has shown that these emerging memories can be employed as L2 and L3 caches to improve performance, reduce power consumption, and even enhance reliability against soft errors [14, 7, 17, 12].

The cache designs based on these emerging memories are normally called ***asymmetric-access caches***. It means that the read and write operations to these memories could be based on different mechanism and demonstrate different ac-cess latencies, energy consumptions, and even reliability. In most NVM techniques nowadays, the write latency and energy consumption can be several times larger than those of read. Thus, asymmetry should also be considered in architecture designs.

Prior research has demonstrated that cache bypassing is an efficient technique to mitigate cache contamination problem by selectively allocating data into a cache. There has been extensive research about bypassing techniques for traditional symmetric-access caches [8, 4, 10, 5, 20]. Prior approaches, however, cannot work efficiently with asymmetric-access cache. High overhead of the write operation is left out of consideration, leading to incorrect bypassing decisions. Moreover, in prior approaches, the bypassing decision is cache-line oriented, which means that the access history of every cache line should be tracked. It induces non-trivial design and run-time operation overhead. In addition, some bypassing techniques are designed for specific cache configurations (e.g. exclusive LLC only).

Extensive research has been proposed to mitigate write issues of asymmetric-cache. For example, write halt and P-reSET techniques are proposed to hide long write latency of these asymmetric-access caches or main memory [15, 16, 13]. The hybrid cache architecture is explored by allocating frequently updated data to the symmetric-access cache (e.g. SRAM) [15, 19]. The replacement policy can also be tailored [22] by evicting cache lines with less updated bits.

In this work, we propose a statistics based data bypassing method, SBAC, for asymmetric-access caches. The asymmetric cost of read and write operations are well addressed to achieve a proper bypassing decision. Moreover, SBAC makes bypassing decision based on statistical behavior of data in the whole cache, instead of a specific data-block. Consequently, both design and run-time overhead is significantly reduced. More importantly, the bypassing decision-making can achieve high accuracy because the statistical behavior of data is stable and predictable for many applications (details are discussed in Section 2). The results show that our method induces trivial design overhead and can achieve better performance compared to prior approaches. The contribution of this work is summarized as follows:

- We provide theoretical analysis of cost (latency or energy consumption) for allocating or bypassing data into an asymmetric-access cache.
- Based on the theoretical principle, we propose a cache bypassing method, SBAC.
- A run-time bypassing prediction technique is introduced to dynamically adjust bypassing policies.
- We further propose core-based bypassing technique to improve efficiency of SBAC in case that data with different localities are mixed together.

The rest of this paper is organized as follows. The theoretical analysis of statistics based cache bypassing is introduced in Section 2. The architecture and operation flow of SBAC and core-based bypassing techniques are proposed in Section 3.

ISLPED'14, August 11–13, 2014, La Jolla, CA, USA.
Copyright 2014 ACM 978-1-4503-2975-0/14/08$15.00.
http://dx.doi.org/10.1145/2627369.2627611.

The experimental results and discussions are presented in Section 4, followed by conclusions in the last section.

2. THEORY BASIS

In this section, we introduce terminologies and definitions used in theoretical derivation, followed by theoretically exploration of the relationship between data bypassing and data locality.

2.1 Terminologies and Definitions

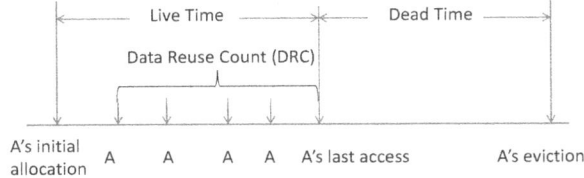

Figure 1: Illustration of data A and related terms [10, 5].

The terminologies used in this work are similar to those in prior literature [10, 5] and are illustrated in Figure 1. As shown in the figure, data A is brought into a cache line by either a read access or a prefetching operation. The life time of A in the cache is composed of live time (from allocation time to the last use) and dead time (from the last use to its eviction). The total number of accesses (hits) to data after the allocation is called **data reuse count** (DRC). The cache line A in Figure 1 has a reuse count of five. The first allocation is called **initial placement**. The data having no live time ($DRC = 0$) is normally called **instant dead block**.

$$P_i = \frac{N_{DRC=i}}{\sum_{j=0}^{\infty} N_{DRC=j}} \quad (1)$$

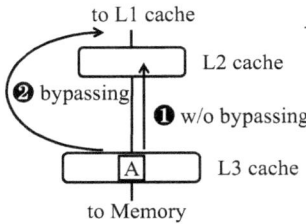

Figure 2: SBAC for loading data.

Term	Definition
DRC	Data Reuse Count
P_i	Probability of $DRC = i$
R_2	Read energy of L2 cache
$R_{2_{tag}}$	Energy of reading L2 tag
$R_{2_{data}}$	Energy of reading L2 data
W_2	Write energy of L2 cache
R_3	Read energy of L3 cache
W_3	Write energy of L3 cache
d	Bypassing depth
λ	Bypassing feature
SI	Sample Interval of DRC

Table 1: Terminologies and definitions.

With DRCs for massive data, we introduce the definition of DRC probability. Let $N_{DRC=i}$ denotes the number of data that have their DRCs equal to i. Then, a DRC probability P_i is calculated in Equation (1). Other definitions and parameters of read and write operations to L2 and L3 caches used in this case study are listed in Table 1.

2.2 Theoretical Energy for Bypassing

We first introduce a case study on data loading. Our goal in this case is **to reduce cache access energy consumption**. In order to simplify the discussion, we make some assumption. First, there are only read operations to the L2 cache. Second, L3 cache is large enough to allocate the working set. Third, the cache is non-inclusive, so the coherence of data is still kept. As shown in Figure 2, we focus on the case of loading data from L3 to L2. If data loaded from the L3 bypass the L2, they are loaded to L1 directly, as illustrated with path ❷. Otherwise, data will be loaded into L2 normally, shown with path ❶.

We derive the theoretical energy consumption as follows. Initially, the data A is allocated at the L3 only. When the processing core issues a request to access the data A, it generates cache miss at both L1 and L2 and finally receives a cache hit in the L3. If the data are loaded into the L2 without bypassing, the total access energy to L2 can be calculated in Equation (2).

$$E_{w/o\_bypass} = R_3 + W_2 + (DRC + 1) \times R_2 \quad (2)$$

From left to right, the terms on the right side of Equation (2) represent the energy of reading data from L3, writing data to L2, sending data from L2 to L1 after initial placement, and revisiting data for DRC times. If data A bypasses the L2, the total cost will be changed to that in Equation (3).

$$E_{bypass} = (DRC + 1) \times (R_{2_{tag}} + R_3) \quad (3)$$

It means that, for each data access, energy is consumed to detect a cache miss in L2 ($R_{2_{tag}}$) and load data from L3 (R_3). Obviously, we can reduce access energy with cache bypassing only when we have $E_{w/o\_bypass} > E_{bypass}$. Thus, we can obtain Equation (4) as the condition to enable cache bypassing. It means that the DRC should be large enough to ensure the benefits of data reuse, and amortize the overhead of writing data into the L2.

$$DRC < \frac{W_2 + R_2 - R_{2_{tag}}}{R_3 + R_{2_{tag}} - R_2} = \frac{W_2 + R_{2_{data}}}{R_3 - R_{2_{data}}} \quad (4)$$

To bypass or not to bypass, that is the question. For SRAM/eDRAM caches, W_2 is similar to R_2, which is several times smaller than R_3. Cache can benefit from the data allocation whenever there is at least once reuse of the data in L2. For the asymmetric-access cache, however, the W_2 can be comparable to R_3. Thus, a higher DRC is expected to justify the data allocation. In order to achieve lowest access energy, data with DRC less than $\lceil \frac{W_2 + R_{2_{data}}}{R_3 - R_{2_{data}}} \rceil$ should bypass L2.

In order to demonstrate the impact of read-write asymmetry, we compare the conditions of cache bypassing for SRAM and STT-RAM caches. Table 2 shows typical energy consumption numbers of caches based on SRAM and STT-RAM. For symmetric caches, loading data into L2 is more energy-efficient when DRC is higher than one. While in asymmetric caches, only very frequently accessed data with DRC higher than six should be loaded into L2.

2.3 Theory Basis of SBAC

In practice, it is difficult to exactly know the DRCs of all the data in cache before they all die. However, it is possible to filter out the data with specific DRC with a simple bypassing method. For example, we can assume the average DRC for unfiltered data is smaller than one, and make all initial placements bypass the L2 cache, so only the data with at least one reuse count can enter L2 cache. Thus, the key is to ensure the benefits from dead blocks bypassing can amortize the bypassing of high DRC data.

The theoretical condition of employing bypassing can be derived based on the probabilities of DRCs. Assume that the probability distribution of DRC in L2 is represented by $\{P_0, P_1, P_2, \ldots\}$ ($\sum_{i=0}^{\infty} P_i = 1$). Without bypassing technique, the average access energy of these data is noted as $\bar{E}_{w/o\_bypass}$. If initial placements of whole data bypass the L2 cache, the cache access energy consumption is noted as $\bar{E}_{bypass}$.

$$\bar{E}_{w/o\_bypass} = \sum_{i=0}^{\infty} \{P_i \times [R_3 + W_2 + (i + 1) \times R_2]\} \quad (5)$$

$$\bar{E}_{bypass} = P_0 \times (R_3 + R_{2_{tag}}) + \sum_{i=1}^{\infty} \left\{ P_i \times \left[2 \times R_3 + R_{2_{tag}} + W_2 + i \times R_2 \right] \right\} \quad (6)$$

With these two equations, it is easy to understand that such an "initial placements" bypassing can only reduce average access energy when $E_{bypass} < E_{w/o\_bypass}$. After substituting Equation (5) and (6) into it, we obtain the condition to trigger an "initial placement" bypassing, described as an Equation (7).

$$P_0 > \frac{R_3 + R_{2_{tag}} - R_2}{W_2 + R_3} \tag{7}$$

Cache Type	SRAM L2 STT-RAM L3	STT-RAM L2 STT-RAM L3
$R_{2_{data}}$ (nJ)	0.066	0.127
$W_2 (nJ)$	0.051	0.603
$R_3 (nJ)$	0.246	0.246
$\lceil \frac{W_2 + R_{2_{data}}}{R_3 - R_{2_{data}}} \rceil$	1	6

Table 2: Typical energy numbers for 2MB SRAM and STT-RAM caches, and 8MB STT-RAM cache (Technology node: 45nm).

It is interesting that the balance point where the benefits can amortize the overhead is only determined by P_0, which is the DRC probability of instant dead blocks. This is the reason why we call our technique SBAC as a statistics based cache bypassing method.

In order to have a quantitative analysis, we calculate the bypass condition for symmetric- and asymmetric-access caches, respectively. Cache bypassing can gain benefits when $P_0 > 62.8\%$ for a symmetric-access cache. For an asymmetric-access cache, however, bypassing condition is satisfied with a significant lower value of $P_0 > 15.5\%$. The parameters we used are listed in Table 2.

2.4 Bypassing Depth

After the "initial placement" bypassing is applied, the original data with once reuse count becomes instant dead block since their first loads are filtered. Thus, it is reasonable to make these new instant dead blocks bypass L2 to further reduce access energy consumption. In other words, bypass the data with $DRC < 2$. Thus, we introduce the definition of **bypassing depth**, which means that data with DRC less than bypassing depth should bypass the cache. For example, when the bypassing depth is set to "1", only initial placements are bypassed. The calculation of theoretical bypassing depth is discussed as follows.

Similar to the derivation of "initial placement" bypassing decision, we can calculate the bypassing condition with "bypassing depth = 2" as in Equation (8)

$$\frac{P_1}{1 - P_0} > \frac{R_3 + R_{2_{tag}} - R_2}{W_2 + R_3} \tag{8}$$

And we can further calculate condition for any bypassing depth d as in the following Equation:

$$\frac{P_{d-1}}{1 - \sum_{j=0}^{d-2} P_j} > \frac{R_3 + R_{2_{tag}} - R_2}{W_2 + R_3} \tag{9}$$

In this work, the $\lambda = \frac{R_3 + R_{2_{tag}} - R_2}{W_2 + R_3}$ is called **bypassing feature** of the system, which is the intrinsic cache attribute. The high write energy of asymmetric-access caches results in a small bypassing feature, making bypass more attractive to reduce energy consumption.

3. DESIGN OF SBAC

3.1 Overview

We still use the case of loading data from L3 cache to L2 cache to describe the architecture design of SBAC. As a pivot to select proper bypassing decisions, extra components

are needed to monitor and predict the distribution of DRC for data in the L2 cache. As shown in Figure 3, one extra bit is added to each cache line in L2, and two bits are added to each cache line of L3 for this purpose. In addition, they are also used to decide whether cache bypassing is needed. The extra function between L2 and L3 is called bypassing decision block (**BDB**). BDB monitors cache line transferring on the data bus. It can track information of the DRC sent with data so that probability distribution of DRC is calculated.

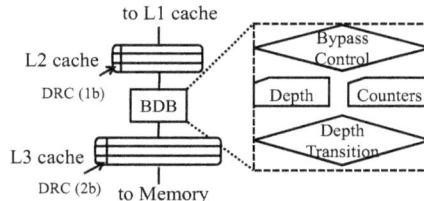

Figure 3: Architecture for cache bypassing.

A BDB includes three global DRC counters. Three DRC counters are denoted as $N_{\geq d-1}$, $N_{\geq d}$, and $N_{\geq d+1}$. They are used to count the number of DRC greater than $d-1$, d, and $d+1$, respectively. With these DRC counters, we can rewrite conditions in Equation (9) with Equation (10). Read/Write energy numbers are used to calculate the λ.

The bypassing control logic can make decision for data transferring on the bus. A cache block will bypass L2 cache if the DRC bit in the L3 cache is smaller than the bypass depth. The bypass depth transition logic is employed to calculate runtime bypassing depth. The bypass depth will be increased by one when Equation (10) is satisfied, and decreased by one when Equation (11) is satisfied.

$$\frac{N_{\geq d} - N_{\geq d+1}}{N_{\geq d}} > \lambda \tag{10}$$

$$\frac{N_{\geq d-1} - N_{\geq d}}{N_{\geq d-1}} < \lambda \tag{11}$$

3.2 Operation Flow with Cache Bypassing

Having the SBAC architecture, we describe the flow for different cache operations with an example in Figure 4. As shown in the figure, L1, L2, and L3 caches are illustrated with one, two, and four cache lines. The three DRC counters of BDB are also shown in the figure. There is one DRC bit for each cache line in L2 and two bits for each cache line in L3. The bypassing depth d is set to 2 in this example. The detailed operation flow is described as follows.

- Step (a): In the initial state, all three DRC counters are initialized as zero. The DRC bits of each line are also cleared as zero. We assume there are some initial data stored in cache lines.

- Step (b): L1 cache requests data C, since the DRC bit of data C in L3 cache is equal to zero, data C is bypassed to L1 cache directly because $DRC = 0 < d = 2$. At the same time, the DRC bit of data C in L3 cache is increased by one.

- Step (c): Similarly, when L1 cache requests data D, it is also moved from L3 to L1 directly for the same reason.

- Step (d): When L1 cache requests data C again, data C is bypassed again because we still have $DRC = 1 < d = 2$. Then, DRC of data C in L3 cache is increased to 2. At the same time, the first counter in BDB is increased by one because it counts the number of data with $DRC \geq d - 1 = 1$.

- Step (e): Similarly, when L1 cache requests data D again, it is bypassed again. And the first DRC counter of BDB is increased by one.

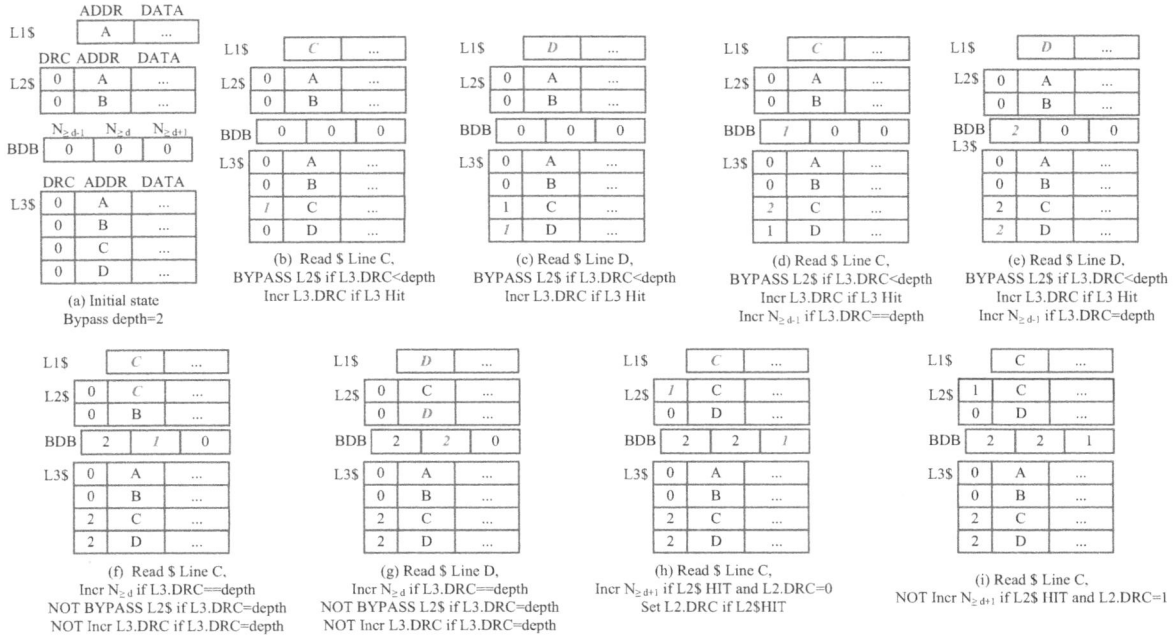

Figure 4: An example of cache bypassing flow.

- Step (f): When L1 cache requests data C for the third time, data C is finally loaded to L2 cache because we have $DRC = d$ now. At the same time, the second counter in BDB is increased by one. Note that the DRC bits of data C in L3 cache are saturated now. They are only reset to zero when data C are evicted from L3 cache.

- Step (g): Similarly, data D is also loaded to L2 cache for the third request, and the second counter in BDB is increased by one.

- Step (h): When data C is first hit in L2 cache, the third counter in BDB is increased by one because C is requested for $d + 1 = 3$ times in total. At the same time, its DRC bit in L2 is set to one.

- Step (i): When data C gets hit again with DRC bit equal to one, the third counter in BDB remains the same.

3.3 Sensitivity Control

Since the probability distribution of DRC varies during run-time execution, the bypassing depth should also be updated periodically to reflect the distribution. The length of each period, in terms of cache accesses, is called *sampling interval (SI)* in this work. At the end of a sampling interval, the BDB counters are used to calculate the current probability distribution of DRC. The distribution is used to predict the bypassing depth for the next interval.

The choice of sampling interval has an impact on the prediction accuracy of bypassing depth. Since the bypassing depth is based on DRC, we use the amount of cache access to determine a SI. If the SI is too short, the poor sampled statistics cannot represent the probability distribution of DRC. On the other hand, if the SI is too long, it may not capture the changes of DRC distribution so that the efficiency of SBAC is degraded. In addition, the size of counters in BDB is also related to SI.

Experimental results show that the optimal SI varies in the range of $10k \sim 100k$ for different workloads. Thus, we propose an algorithm to dynamically adjust SI for different data patterns. The algorithm is described as follows.

- SI is initialed as 2^{14}, which is the lower bound of SI.
- After each SI, if the bypassing depth is not changed, SI is increased by 2×.

- After each SI, if the bypassing depth is changed, SI is decreased by 2×.
- The higher bound of SI is set to 2^{20}. Thus, a 20-bit counter is needed.

3.4 SBAC Extension for Other Scenarios

Extension for Performance Optimization. To apply SBAC for cache performance optimization, we need to replace energy numbers in equation (1) - (9) with proper access latency numbers. Different from energy consumption, it is inaccurate to add the latency of a write operation directly to the total execution time. Instead, we need to estimate the time that L2 cache is blocked due to loading data from L3. The blocking time is related to cache access intensity. Previous research [15, 19, 22] pointed out that the blocking time varies from 0× to $0.6 \times write\ latency$. One solution to this problem is to calculate average run-time blocking time by monitoring the waiting time of read operations in the miss status holding registers (MSHRs).

Extension for Multi-core Optimization. For the case that there are multiple worloads running on multiple cores, more BDBs can be added to track DRC distribution of each core separately. The core ID needs to be integrated in the cache tag to identify data from each core. Thus, bypassing decisions may be different for data requested by different cores to improve efficiency of SBAC. Such an extension of SBAC is called "core-based SBAC". Extra design overhead is induced because the number of counters increase proportionally with the number of cores. Note that SBAC can be applied to both shared and private caches. For example, if L2 cache is private for each core and L3 cache is shared, each L2 needs one BDB to connect L3.

4. EXPERIMENTAL EVALUATION

In this section, we provide comprehensive evaluation to demonstrate the efficiency of SBAC for single and multiple applications under both shared and private L2 configurations.

4.1 Experiment Setup

We implement SBAC in a popular full-system simulator *gem5* [2]. It is configured to model a four-core Haswell like CMP. Each core is running at 2GHz frequency. There are three levels of caches. The IL1/DL1 caches are SRAM based and and the L2 and L3 are configured as asymmetric-access STT-RAM caches. Other details can be found in Table 3. We use cache latency and energy parameters from NVSim [3].

Component	Configuration
Processor	4 cores, 2GHz, 1-way issue
IL1/DL1 SRAM	32/32KB, 2-way, 64B, private, LRU L.P.:47.7mW, R/W Lat.: 2/2cycle, E.:6.2/2.3pJ
L2 STT-RAM	4 × 256KB, 8-way, 64B, LRU, L.P.:428mW R/W Lat.: 6/36cycle, E: 0.135/0.603nJ
L3 STT-RAM	8MB, 16-way, 64B, share, LRU, L.P.:1851mW R/W Lat.: 25/60cycle, E: 0.246/0.698nJ
Memory	8GB, DDR3, 1600MHz, 120cycle, 12.8GB/s.

Table 3: Detailed simulation setup.

Both single and multiple applications workloads are e-valuated. In order to provide a comprehensive evaluation with diversified distributions of DRC, we examine different code segments in both single and randomly mixed multi-programmed benchmarks. Both private and shared L2 configurations are used for experiments of mutli-programmed workloads. For the single application case, only the private cache with one core running is evaluated. The simulator captures all data operations such as loads, stores, and prefetching requests. The one block lookahead (OBL) approach is employed for prefetching in evaluation. All benchmarks come from SPEC CPU 2006. We fast forward one billion instructions at beginning, and execute ten billion instructions of a single benchmark. Then we construct the multi-program workloads by mixing the fast forwarded single programs. Energy consumption includes leakage and dynamic power of entire cache hierarchy, based on operation statistics.

The labels used in the rest of this section are explained: (1) Baseline: baseline case without cache bypassing; (2) S-BAC: case using SBAC; (3) SBAC-C: case using core-based SBAC; (4) Shared: case with shared L2 configuration; (5) Private: case with private L2 cache.

4.2 DRC Prediction Accuracy

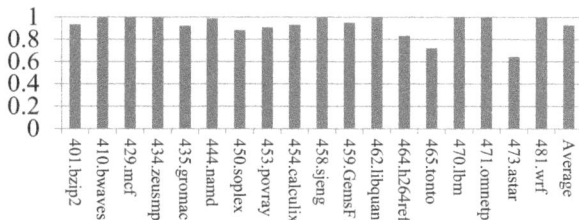

Figure 5: Prediction accuracy for various single-programmed benchmarks.

As shown in Figure 5, a high prediction accuracy of 92% on average is achieved for single program benchmarks. The prediction accuracy is about 86% on average for multiprogrammed applications (not shown due to page limit). Note that a correct bypassing decision may obtained even with a mis-prediction, as long as the bypassing depth is not affected. On the other hand, a correct prediction of DRC distribution may also lead to an incorrect decision of cache bypassing due to inaccurate estimation of read/write energy.

4.3 Evaluation for Single Application

The results of energy consumption are compared in Figure 6. We can find that the reduction of energy is related to the prediction accuracy generally. For some benchmarks,

however, the energy reduction is insignificant even with high prediction accuracy (e.g. *GemsFDTD*). The reason is that for some benchmarks the cache bypassing is not triggered for most of execution time. On average the reduction of the total cache energy consumption is about 22.3%.

The results of performance improvement is similar to energy reduction, but less significant. The reason is that the energy consumption of each load operation is reflected in total energy, but the loading time could be hidden by MSHR. On average, the total execution time is reduced by 8.3%. Detailed results are not included due to page limitation.

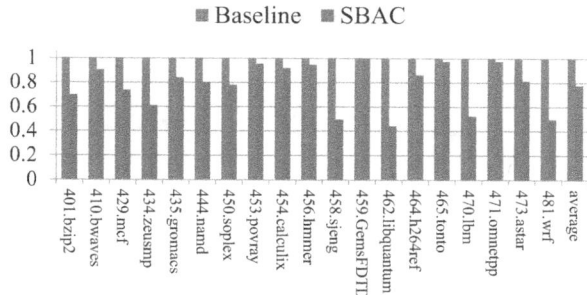

Figure 6: Normalized energy consumption for single applications.

4.4 Evaluation for Multi-programmed Applications

We evaluate energy consumption after applying SBAC to two cache configurations against corresponding baselines without cache bypassing. We show the normalized comparison in Figure 7. The results demonstrate that, for private cache configuration, the energy consumption can be reduced after using SBAC. It is because each workload is bounded to a dedicated core and the DRC distribution is estimated separately. On average, SBAC can reduce energy consumption by 7.5% for private L2 cache, but 3.8% for shared L2 cache configuration. As addressed before, mixing data with different patterns from multiple workloads makes SBAC less efficient. In order to improve SBAC for multi-programmed

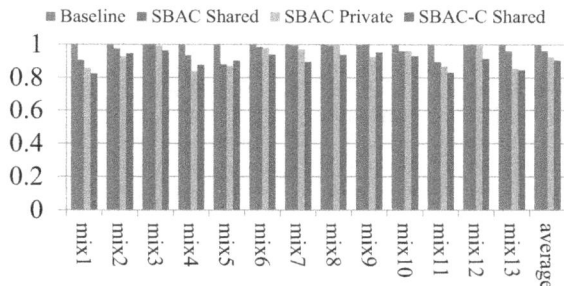

Figure 7: Normalized energy consumption after using SBAC for two cache configurations.

workloads, we propose core-based SBAC for shared L2, listed as the fourth bar in Figure 7. It is easy to find that energy consumption is further reduced after using the technique. Core-based SBAC can further reduce the energy consumption by about 9.9%, because it helps isolate the interference of data among different workloads, while shared cache supplies sufficient space. We also evaluate the results of execution time after using SBAC and compare them with the baseline. The results of applying SBAC and SBAC-C on data loaded from L3 to L2 are listed in Figure 8. We can find that the trends of these results are similar to those for energy consumption optimization. On average, the performance is improved by 2.1% and 4.3% for shared and private

Approaches	Multiprogram Support	Storage Overhead (bits)		Area Overhead (μm^2)	Operation Overhead
		per line	global		
DBP [11]	No	-	2M	102.78	2-level table lookup/update
IATAC [1]	No	31	288	293.63	6b comp + 31b update + 16-entry CAM lookup/update
IGDR [18]	No	-	42.5K	4.12×10^4	5 table lookup/update
LvP [10]	No	17	40K	62.27	5b comp + 17b update + 1 table lookup/update
AIP [10]	No	21	40K	30.34	5b comp + 21b update + 1 table lookup/update
DBRB [9]	Yes	-	13.75K	40.28	15b comp + 15b update + 3 table lookup/update
BIA [5]	Yes	3/L2+2/L3	1.8K	192.6	5b update + 16-entry CAM lookup/update
SBAC	**Yes**	**1/L2+2/L3**	**73**	**36.16**	**3b update + 2b comp + 1 counter update**
SBAC-C	Yes	1/L2+2/L3	146	144.64	3b update + 2b comp + 1 counter update

Table 4: Design overhead comparison.

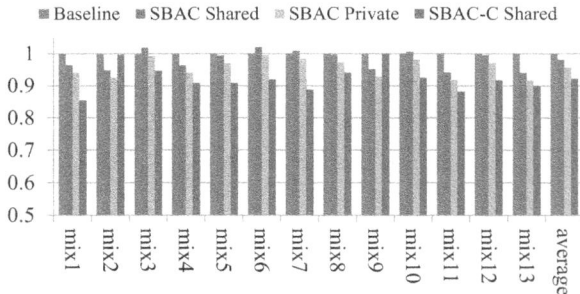

Figure 8: Normalized execution time after using S-BAC for two cache configurations.

configured L2 cache. And the core-based SBAC can improve performance by 9.4% for the shared L2 cache.

4.5 Comparison with Other Approaches

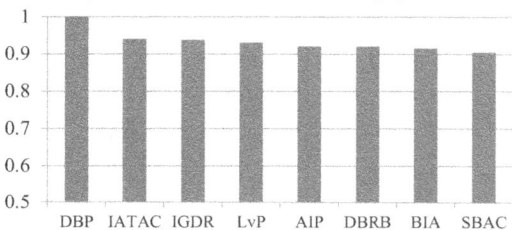

Figure 9: Comparison of performance between our bypassing scheme and other approaches.

We compare normalized average cache access latency between our bypassing scheme and prior approaches for single application, shown in Figure 9. Our bypassing scheme can outperform other approaches in respect of cache access latency. The main reason is that the asymmetry access operations are not considered in prior approaches. Note that we do not provide comparison for cases of energy optimization and multi-programmed application. It is because most prior approaches cannot work with these cases. We also compare design and operation overhead in Table 4. We estimate the design overhead by extra storage (per line and cache), area overhead of control logic, and extra cache operations. Area results are synthesized by Synopsys Design Compiler with TSMC 45nm library. It is easy to find that SBAC costs much less storage, area, and operations.

5. CONCLUSION

Emerging asymmetric-access caches are competitive for design of future cache hierarchy. Traditional cache bypassing techniques are not efficient for these asymmetric-access caches. In this work, we propose the statistics based cache bypassing method named SBAC. With the help of a theoretical model, we analyze the benefits of cache bypassing. Then, proper bypassing decisions are made based on DRC probability. In addition, we propose core-based SBAC to improve working efficiency of SBAC for multi-programmed

workloads. Compared with prior approaches, SBAC has the advantages of low design overhead and compatibility for different cache configurations. The experimental results show improvement of cache performance and energy efficiency after using SBAC.

6. ACKNOWLEDGEMENTS

This paper is supported by NSF CNS-1116171, National Natural Science Foundation of China (No.61202072 and No.61103028), and National High-tech R&D Program of China (No.2013AA013201).

7. REFERENCES

[1] J. Abella, A. González, X. Vera, and M. F. P. O'Boyle. Iatac: a smart predictor to turn-off l2 cache lines. *ACM Trans. Archit. Code Optim.*, 2(1):55–77, Mar. 2005.

[2] N. Binkert, B. Beckmann, G. Black, S. K. Reinhardt, A. Saidi, A. Basu, J. Hestness, D. R. Hower, T. Krishna, S. Sardashti, R. Sen, K. Sewell, M. Shoaib, N. Vaish, M. D. Hill, and D. A. Wood. The gem5 simulator. *SIGARCH Comput. Archit. News*, 39(2):1–7, Aug. 2011.

[3] X. Dong, C. Xu, Y. Xie, and N. Jouppi. Nvsim: A circuit-level performance, energy, and area model for emerging nonvolatile memory. *Computer-Aided Design of Integrated Circuits and Systems, IEEE Transactions on*, 31(7):994–1007, 2012.

[4] H. Dybdahl and P. Stenström. Enhancing last-level cache performance by block bypassing and early miss determination. ACSAC'06, pages 52–66. Springer-Verlag, 2006.

[5] J. Gaur, M. Chaudhuri, and S. Subramoney. Bypass and insertion algorithms for exclusive last-level caches. ISCA'11, pages 81–92. ACM, 2011.

[6] M. Hosomi, H. Yamagishi, T. Yamamoto, K. Bessho, Y. Higo, and et al. A Novel Non-Volatile Memory With Spin Torque Transfer Magnetization Switching: Spin-RAM. In *Proceedings of IEDM*, pages 459–462, 2005.

[7] A. Jadidi, M. Arjomand, and H. Sarbazi-Azad. High-endurance and performance-efficient design of hybrid cache architectures through adaptive line replacement. In *ISLPED'11*, pages 79–84, 2011.

[8] T. L. Johnson, D. A. Connors, M. C. Merten, and W.-m. W. Hwu. Run-time cache bypassing. *IEEE Trans. Comput.*, 48(12):1338–1354, Dec. 1999.

[9] S. M. Khan, Y. Tian, and D. A. Jimenez. Sampling dead block prediction for last-level caches. MICRO'10, pages 175–186, 2010.

[10] M. Kharbutli and Y. Solihin. Counter-based cache replacement and bypassing algorithms. *IEEE Trans. Comput.*, 57(4):433–447, Apr. 2008.

[11] A.-C. Lai, C. Fide, and B. Falsafi. Dead-block prediction & dead-block correlating prefetchers. ISCA'01, pages 144–154. ACM, 2001.

[12] J. Li, P. Ndai, A. Goel, H. Liu, and K. Roy. An alternate design paradigm for robust spin-torque transfer magnetic ram (stt mram) from circuit/architecture perspective. In *ASP-DAC'09*, pages 841–846, 2009.

[13] M. K. Qureshi, M. M. Franceschini, A. Jagmohan, and L. A. Lastras. Preset: improving performance of phase change memories by exploiting asymmetry in write times. ISCA '12, pages 380–391. IEEE Press, 2012.

[14] C. W. Smullen, V. Mohan, A. Nigam, S. Gurumurthi, and M. R. Stan. Relaxing non-volatility for fast and energy-efficient stt-ram caches. In *HPCA'11*, 2011.

[15] G. Sun, X. Dong, Y. Xie, J. Li, and Y. Chen. A novel architecture of the 3d stacked mram l2 cache for cmps. In *HPCA'09*, pages 239–249, feb. 2009.

[16] G. Sun, Y. Zhang, Y. Wang, and Y. Chen. Improving energy efficiency of write-asymmetric memories by log style write. ISLPED '12, pages 173–178. ACM, 2012.

[17] Z. Sun, X. Bi, and H. Li. Process variation aware data management for stt-ram cache design. ISLPED '12, pages 179–184. ACM, 2012.

[18] M. Takagi and K. Hiraki. Inter-reference gap distribution replacement: an improved replacement algorithm for set-associative caches. ICS'04, pages 20–30. ACM, 2004.

[19] X. Wu, J. Li, L. Zhang, E. Speight, R. Rajamony, and Y. Xie. Hybrid cache architecture with disparate memory technologies. ISCA'09.

[20] Y. Wu, R. Rakvic, L.-L. Chen, C.-C. Miao, G. Chrysos, and J. Fang. Compiler managed micro-cache bypassing for high performance epic processors. MICRO'02, pages 134 – 145, 2002.

[21] C. Xu, X. Dong, N. P. Jouppi, and Y. Xie. Design implications of memristor-based RRAM cross-point structures.

[22] P. Zhou, B. Zhao, J. Yang, and Y. Zhang. Energy reduction for stt-ram using early write termination. In *ICCAD'09*, pages 264–268, 2009.

Tag Check Elision

Zhong Zheng, Zhiying Wang
State Key Laboratory of High Performance
Computing & School of Computer
National University of Defense Technology
zheng_zhong@nudt.edu.cn,
zywang@nudt.edu.cn

Mikko Lipasti
Department of Electrical and Computer
Engineering
University of Wisconsin-Madison
mikko@engr.wisc.edu

ABSTRACT

For set-associative caches, accessing cache ways in parallel results in significant energy waste, as only one way contains the desired data. In this paper, we propose Tag Check Elision (TCE): a non-speculative approach for accessing set-associative caches without a tag check to save energy.

TCE can eliminate up to 86% of the tag checks (67% on average), without sacrificing any performance. These direct accesses to a 4-way set-associative data cache under TCE result in up to 56% and 85% data cache and Data Translation Look-aside Buffer (DTLB) dynamic energy saving, respectively.

Categories and Subject Descriptors

C.1.0 [**Processor Architecture**]: General; B.3.2 [**Memory Structure**]: Design Styles—*Cache memories*

1 Introduction

Caches have been playing an important role in efficiently bridging the speed gap between memory and CPU for decades. However, they consume a large fraction of the on-die area along with up to 45% of core power [19]. In addition, industrial sources and early research report that 3-17% of core power can be consumed by Translation Look-aside Buffer (TLB) [19, 9, 10]. In the many-core era, the power quota for each core is very limited, which requires simple core logic design along with more power efficient cache and TLB implementation without hurting performance.

Set-associative caches dominate the cache design in current commercial processors, as they provide higher hit rates, resulting in better performance. However, they require parallel way read and energy-hungry tag comparison. As a result, much of the energy is wasted on accessing bits that are discarded after tag check.

In this paper, we propose Tag Check Elision (TCE), a hardware approach to access set-associative caches without tag checks. TCE determines the correct cache way early in the pipeline by doing a simple bounds check that relies on the base register and offset associated with the memory

ISLPED'14, August 11–13, 2014, La Jolla, CA, USA.
Copyright 2014 ACM 978-1-4503-2975-0/14/08 ...$15.00.
http://dx.doi.org/10.1145/2627369.2627606.

instruction. In the same vein, the TLB access can also be eliminated in a physically-tagged cache. TCE memoizes the accessed cache ways and relies on a bounds check to decide if the later access is to the same line as an earlier access. The bounds check occurs as soon as the virtual address is available, and incurs no additional pipeline delay or performance degradation.

The results show that 35% to 86% (67% on average) of memory accesses in the SPEC CPU2006 benchmarks [6] can perform direct access to the cache. The cache dynamic energy saving is 15% to 56%, with 33% on average. The DTLB dynamic energy saving is 34% to 85% (66% on average). TCE outperforms two types of way prediction, including MRU and perfect prediction, in terms of Energy Delay Product (EDP).

The rest of the paper is organized as follows: The background and insight that motivate our work are presented in Section 2. The design of the TCE approach is described in Section 3. Experimental results are presented in Section 4. Related work is discussed in Section 5 and Section 6 concludes the paper.

2 Motivation

For set-associative caches, all tags in a set must be checked to decide which way contains the requested data. To provide fast access in level one caches, all tags and data ways in a set are accessed in parallel, while only one way has the requested data. This redundant tag check and data access results in much energy waste. For example, in a 4-way set-associative cache, 4 tag checks and 4 data block reads are performed. In contrast, TCE reduces the cache access to just one data block read, eliding all tag checks and 3 other data block reads.

TCE is inspired by how memory addresses are generated. The example code in Figure 1(a) adds arrays b and c to form a new array a. The addresses to the array elements are computed by adding offsets to base registers, as shown in Figure 1(b)), where the base registers are rbp, $r13$ and $r12$, respectively. The index register rsi is incremented by 4 in each loop iteration, providing the offset for the array addresses.

The addresses for these arrays comprise static base registers and an increasing index register. As the cache line size (typically 64B) is much smaller than the physical page size (typically 4KB), the same cache line access can be determined just by comparing the virtual addresses. However, this virtual address comparison cannot be performed until address generation. Fortunately, if the base address register

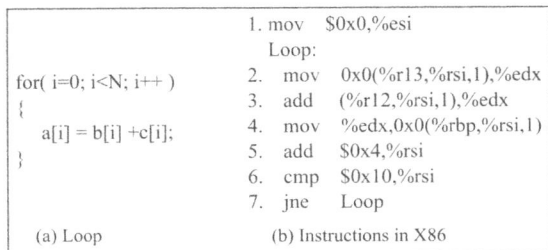

Figure 1: Loop to add two arrays and its corresponding instructions in X86 ISA.

is unchanged (e.g. base registers shown in Figure 1(b)), the same cache line determination could be simplified to just compare the offsets (e.g. register *rsi*) with a bounds check. Based on this observation, we design a mechanism to determine same cache line accesses by keeping a cache line record for the base register and comparing the offset value. Once the same cache line access is detected, the access to the cache can be performed directly without any tag check or TLB access. This type of access elides tag checks, and thus we name this approach as Tag Check Elision. The sufficient condition for the same cache line determination is:

- The same base register value,
- And the offset is within the cache line bounds.

Overall, the advantages of our TCE approach are:

(a) The stored cache line information and the offset bounds are read the same time as performing register value read, as they are indexed by base register id instead of register value or address;

(b) The offset comparison is performed in parallel with the address generation, which does not add any delays to the critical data path;

(c) TCE completely elides the tag check for the determined same cache line access;

(d) On a direct access determined by TCE, the access to the TLB is bypassed to save more energy.

3 TCE design

3.1 Cache Way Memoization

To memoize the accessed cache lines, cache way records (CWRs) are added to the processor, as shown in Figure 2. The number of CWRs matches the number of architected fixed-point registers in the ISA, as one record is kept for one register that will be used as base address register. This CWR design allows it to be indexed by the register id and be accessed early, the same time as the register read in the pipeline.

Each CWR includes three fields, namely *valid*, *bound*, and *cache pointer*. The valid field indicates if the corresponding cache block information is valid or not. The bound field gives the offset range that is located within the current cache line with the same base register value. As the range length is exactly the cache line size, we can just keep the lower bound in the record to save space. The cache pointer records the last cache line accessed based on the current base register.

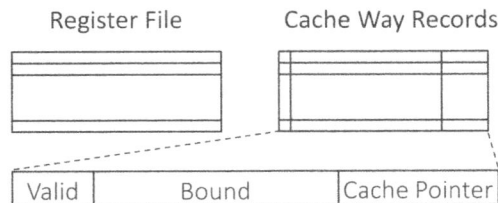

Figure 2: Example of cache way records organization.

3.2 Walkthrough Example

An example of how the TCE mechanism works is shown in Table 1. This example shows how the register *rdx* and its corresponding CWR changes.

At the beginning, we assume that the value of the register *rdx* is *0x40043c8* and the CWR for register *rdx* is invalid. The instruction in the first row accesses the memory whose address comprises the value in register *rdx* and an immediate number *4*. As the valid bit in the CWR is 0, the cache access is performed in the normal mode (probing all ways in parallel) and the cache way number (e.g. 3) of the current access is obtained to build the CWR. According to register *rdx*'s value and the current offset value, the bounds for the current accessed cache line are calculated, which are -8 and 56 (-8 + cache line size, 64). Thus, the CWR state for *rdx* becomes | 1 | -8 | 3 | after the first instruction.

When executing the second instruction, the CWR is valid and the offset 8 is within the bounds between -8 and 56. Direct access to the desired cache way is performed to fetch data. This case is what we expect, accessing cache directly and bypassing DTLB access to save dynamic energy.

On the third instruction, the offset 64 is out of bounds of the current CWR. In this situation, the cache access must be performed in normal mode, and the CWR is rebuilt after finishing cache access (assuming the accessed cache way number is 2). The CWR is invalidated after the last instruction as the value of register *rdx* is modified.

For simplicity of illustration, this example uses immediate values as offsets to describe our proposed approach. However, this approach works the same for the offsets that are stored in the register file, as shown in Figure 1.

3.3 TCE Enhancements

3.3.1 Multiple records.

Keeping one record for each register will possibly suffer from capacity misses. With multiple records, more cache line information can be kept. If we keep N records for one register, then we can track the last N cache line that have been accessed based on the same register value. However, keeping too many records will complicate the management of the CWRs.

In our design, initial experiments showed that provisioning *two* CWRs (Double Record, DR) for each register forms a reasonable compromise between complexity and performance.

3.3.2 Register value tracking.

As illustrated in Figure 3, some array accesses rely on just a single base register *rax*. The base register is incremented by 4 in each iteration, causing CWR rebuilding. To deal with the small changes to the register, another optimization is added to keep track of the register value to avoid unneces-

	Instruction	Action	Record state
1	Mov 4(%rdx), %rcx	[**Miss**]: Access the cache in normal mode, get the way pointer.	1 | -8 | 3
2	Add 8(%rdx), %rcx	[**Hit**]: The offset 8 is within the bounds between -8 and 56 (-8+64). Then access the cache block through direct access.	1 | -8 | 3
3	Mov %rcx, 64(%rdx)	[**Miss**]: The offset 64 is out of bounds between -8 and 56. Access the cache in normal mode and rebuild the record.	1 | 56 | 2
4	Mov %rax, %rdx	[**Invalidation**]: The value of the base register *rdx* has changed. The corresponding cache way record for register *rdx* must be invalidated.	0 | X | X

Table 1: An example to show how the cache way record works, using X86 ISA.

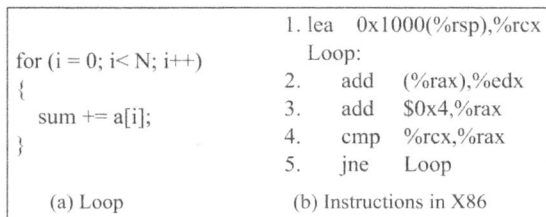

```
for (i = 0; i< N; i++)        1. lea   0x1000(%rsp),%rcx
{                             Loop:
    sum += a[i];              2.    add   (%rax),%edx
}                             3.    add   $0x4,%rax
                              4.    cmp   %rcx,%rax
                              5.    jne   Loop

      (a) Loop                    (b) Instructions in X86
```

Figure 3: Loop to sum the array *a* and its corresponding instructions in X86 ISA.

Register Value	Valid	Bound	Cache Pointer

Figure 4: Example of backup buffer design for the CWRs.

sary invalidation; this applies whenever the accesses are still located in the same cache line.

This optimization is called Register Value Tracking (RVT), which keeps the CWR valid by tracking the register value and adjusting the corresponding bound field. On the instruction *add $0x4, %rax* , we update the CWR by subtracting the bound with the same immediate 0.x4, instead of invalidating. Thus, the CWR still points to the same cache line and the next access has a chance to hit.

3.3.3 Backup buffer.

When the register value changes, the corresponding CWR entry must be invalidated. However, it is possible that this discarded CWR would be useful later. To prevent unnecessary CWR rebuilding, a backup buffer can be added to buffer the CWRs that are discarded because of the register value change.

As the CWR is strongly coupled with the register value and the offset, each item in the backup must contain the register value, as shown in Figure 4. The backup can be organized as an inexpensive direct-mapped cache. The tag is the register value, and the data is the corresponding CWR item.

3.3.4 Energy modeling.

The energy consumption of CWRs check, register value tracking, and backup buffer are carefully modeled and integrated into McPAT [12].

3.4 Coherence and Correctness

To guarantee correct access to the cache without tag check, the CWRs must be kept coherent with the cache lines. Once a cache line is evicted or invalidated, the CWR entries that point to this cache line must be invalidated. Instead of using energy-intensive associative lookups as [20], we keep backward pointers in each cache line.

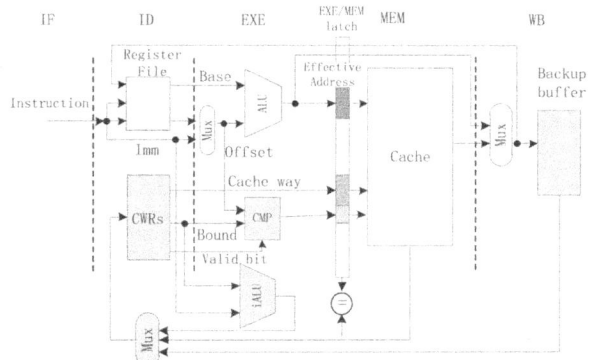

Figure 5: Pipeline integrated with TCE.

For each cache line, we add a vector to indicate which register's CWRs have pointers pointing to this cache line, one bit for each register. When the cache line is accessed in normal mode to build a CWR, the vector bit for the CWR will be set. As the number of fixed-point registers is relatively small, the cost of the vector bits will be fairly low.

For a small number of backup buffer entries, the same bit vector mechanism can be extended to cover the backup buffer. We show in the next section that a 16-entry backup buffer is a good design choice, considering the overhead and complexity of keeping it coherent.

For other events that will possibly make CWR entries go stale, for example, memory map changes, page access permission changes, and thread context switches, TCE invalidates all of the CWRs. TCE also bypasses DTLB lookups; hence, any DTLB replacement will invalidate all CWRs to guarantee correctness.

3.5 TCE Design in the Pipeline

As illustrated in Figure 5, the structures added to implement the TCE are shaded in the pipeline. For simplicity, the pipeline components that are unaffected by TCE are not shown in the figure. The register-id-indexed CWR is accessed at the same time as the register file read, and the bounds check for the offset is finished in parallel with address generation, by a dedicated comparator *CMP*. The bounds check results and the cache way information are sent to the cache to decide which mode should be adopted to finish the data access. The iALU component is dedicated for RVT, and the backup buffer is accessed in the WB stage.

The direct access information is stored in EXE/MEM latch before reaching MEM stage. The cache way information can be bypassed to the EXE/MEM latch to satisfy back-to-back access, like the first and second instruction in Table 1. When cache lines get evicted, TCE also checks the

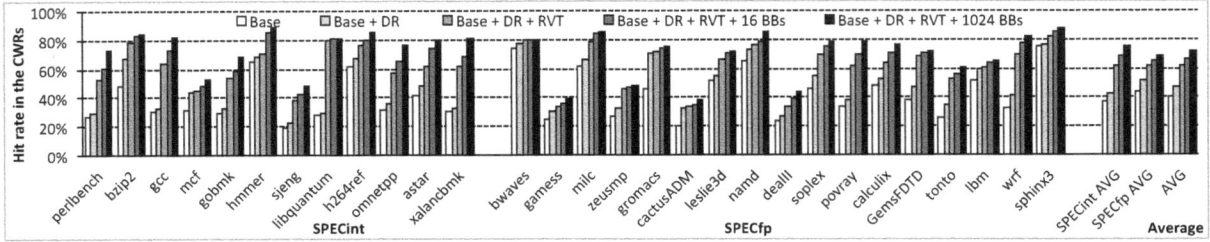

Figure 6: CWR hit rate for data cache access under different optimizations.

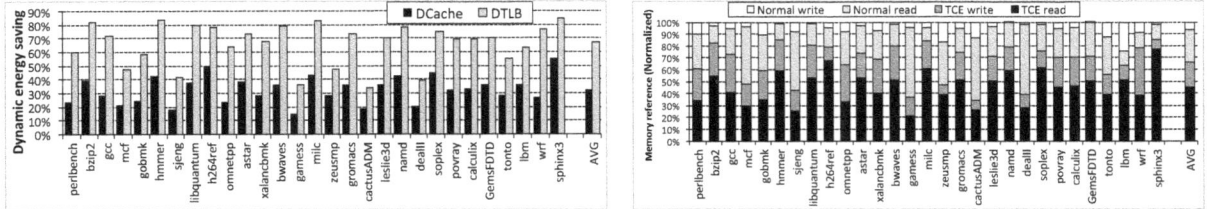

Figure 7: Data cache and DTLB dynamic energy saving (left), and TCE access breakdown (right).

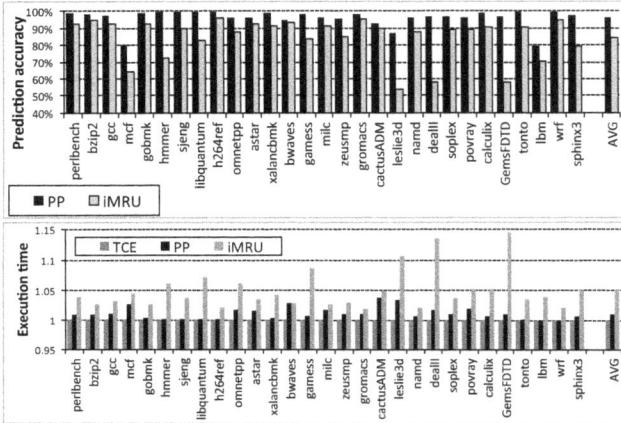

Figure 8: Prediction accuracy for PP and iMRU (top) and execution time for TCE, PP, and iMRU (bottom).

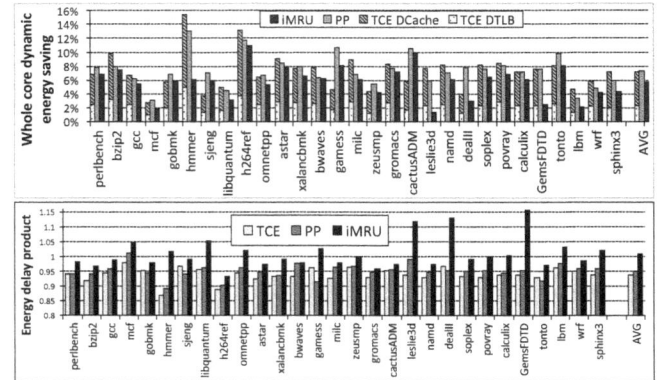

Figure 9: Whole core dynamic energy saving (top, higher is better) and energy delay product (bottom, lower is better) for TCE, PP, and iMRU.

4.4.1 Performance.

The prediction accuracy and execution time under PP and iMRU schemes are shown in Figure 8, respectively. The performance of TCE is also included, but it always the same as the baseline. As shown in the Figure 8 (top), the prediction accuracy of PP is quite high for most of the benchmarks, as it *ONLY* misses on data cache miss. The prediction accuracy for the more realistic approach, iMRU, is lower than PP, with 12% difference. Way prediction requires re-accessing the cache way on a wrong prediction, incurring performance degradation. The average performance degradations (shown in Figure 8 (bottom)) are about 1.18% and 5.02% more execution time for PP and iMRU, respectively. And the worst cases are 3.78% and 14.57% for PP and iMRU, respectively.

4.4.2 Energy delay product (EDP).

The whole core dynamic energy saving and corresponding EDP are illustrated in Figure 9. The variation of these results comes from two aspects: (a) differences in cache dynamic energy saving for TCE and way prediction on different

benchmarks; (b) cache dynamic energy accounts for different fractions of the whole core dynamic energy for different benchmarks.

TCE dynamic energy saving comes from cache dynamic energy saving and DTLB dynamic energy saving. In contrast, way prediction (PP and iMRU) only saves dynamic energy in the cache. Generally, the average whole core energy saving for TCE is almost the same as PP, better than iMRU. However, PP is not realistic, and TCE significantly outperforms iMRU across benchmarks.

On average, TCE outperforms both PP and iMRU in terms of EDP. Because of the delay caused by misprediction, TCE outperforms iMRU on *ALL* cases. TCE has significant advantages over iMRU on several benchmarks, for example, *mcf, hmmer, libquantum, leslie3d, dealII, GemsFDTD*. These big differences come from the misprediction penalty for longer execution time.

The most significant advantage of TCE is that it reduces the cache dynamic energy without hurting performance across all the benchmarks. On the contrary, EDP for way prediction can be higher than the baseline system, such as *libquantum* and *GemsFDTD*.

5   Related work

The work most similar to TCE to reduce the cache way access is way prediction. Predictive sequential associative cache [3] uses a number of prediction sources to pick the first block in a set to probe. On a miss to the predicted way, the other ways are checked. Similar way prediction techniques have been proposed in [8] and [1]. Powell et al. [16] combined way prediction and selective direct-mapping to reduce L1 dynamic cache energy. Besides performance penalty on misprediction, physical address must be obtained from TLB to check if the prediction is correct.

Instead of prediction, way caching [15] [14] records the way of recently accessed cache lines to reduce the dynamic energy of highly associative caches. A problem for this technique is that the way cache is accessed before cache access, which will add delay to the data access in the critical path. A similar approach, way memoization [13], adds the lower 14 bits of base address and displacement to index the memoized recent accessed cache ways. However, it is designed for application specific integrated processors and assumes that the 14-bit add and structure indexing can be finished in parallel with 32-bit add, which does not adapt easily to general purpose processor.

Tagless cache [17] restructures the first-level cache and TLB for more efficient storage of tags, achieving substantial energy gains, but, unlike TCE, does not elide TLB accesses, requires changes to the replacement policy, affects miss rates and performance in unpredictable ways, and complicates support for coherence and virtual address synonyms.

Before accessing the cache, techniques are proposed to filter unnecessary accesses. Sentry tag [4] determines the mismatched ways and halts them to save energy. The way halting technique [21] is an extension of the concept of sentry tags. Way decay [11] and way guard [7] adopt a bloom filter to reduce the ways that need to be checked. One problem for this type of techniques is that a new structure must be accessed serially, after address generation before accessing the cache, hence either increasing cycle time or adding a pipestage to the memory access latency.

6   Conclusion

To reduce set-associative cache access energy, we propose Tag Check Elision, which avoids tag checks and TLB access without causing performance degradation. TCE memoizes the accessed cache line and the offset of the memory address for a base address. Access to the same line elides tag checks and TLB lookups by comparing the offset of the memory address that use the same base register. To improve the base design, three optimizations are proposed, namely double records, register value tracking and a backup buffer.

We evaluated the effectiveness of the base TCE approach and further optimizations on X86 for reducing L1 data cache energy. The TCE approach avoids 35% to 86% of tag checks, which results in data cache energy savings of 15% to 56%, and DTLB dynamic energy saving of 34% to 85%. Under the TCE approach, set-associative caches achieve better energy delay product than way prediction.

7   Acknowledgments

We thank the anonymous reviewers for their insightful feedback, which has improved the content and presentation of this paper. This work is partially supported by CSC, China's 863 Program (No. 2012AA010905), NSFC (No. 61070037, 61272143, 61272144, 61103016, 61202121), NUDT's innovation fund (No. B120607), and RFDP (No.20114307120013). This work is also supported in part by NSF grant CCF-1318298.

8   References

[1] B. Batson and T. N. Vijaykumar. Reactive-associative caches. In *PACT '01*, pages 49–60, 2001.

[2] N. Binkert, B. Beckmann, G. Black, S. K. Reinhardt, A. Saidi, A. Basu, J. Hestness, D. R. Hower, T. Krishna, S. Sardashti, R. Sen, K. Sewell, M. Shoaib, N. Vaish, M. D. Hill, and D. A. Wood. The gem5 simulator. *SIGARCH CAN*, 39(2):1–7, Aug. 2011.

[3] B. Calder, D. Grunwald, and J. Emer. Predictive sequential associative cache. In *HPCA '96*, pages 244–253, 1996.

[4] Y.-J. Chang, S.-J. Ruan, and F. Lai. Sentry tag: an efficient filter scheme for low power cache. In *CRPIT '02*, pages 135–140, 2002.

[5] G. Chrysos and S. P. Engineer. Intel® xeon phi coprocessor (codename knights corner). 2012.

[6] S. P. E. Corporation. SPEC CPU2006 Site, 2013.

[7] M. Ghosh, E. Ozer, S. Ford, S. Biles, and H.-H. S. Lee. Way guard: a segmented counting bloom filter approach to reducing energy for set-associative caches. In *ISLPED '09*, pages 165–170, 2009.

[8] K. Inoue, T. Ishihara, and K. Murakami. Way-predicting set-associative cache for high performance and low energy consumption. In *ISLPED '99*, pages 273–275, 1999.

[9] T. Juan, T. Lang, and J. J. Navarro. Reducing tlb power requirements. In *ISLPED '97*, pages 196–201, 1997.

[10] I. Kadayif, A. Sivasubramaniam, M. Kandemir, G. Kandiraju, and G. Chen. Generating physical addresses directly for saving instruction tlb energy. In *MICRO-35*, pages 185–196, 2002.

[11] G. Keramidas, P. Xekalakis, and S. Kaxiras. Applying decay to reduce dynamic power in set-associative caches. In *HiPEAC'07*, pages 38–53, 2007.

[12] S. Li, J. H. Ahn, R. D. Strong, J. B. Brockman, D. M. Tullsen, and N. P. Jouppi. Mcpat: an integrated power, area, and timing modeling framework for multicore and manycore architectures. In *MICRO-42*, pages 469–480, 2009.

[13] A. Ma, M. Zhang, and K. Asanovic. Way memoization to reduce fetch energy in instruction caches. In *ISCA Workshop on Complexity Effective Design*, page 31, 2001.

[14] R. Min, W.-B. Jone, and Y. Hu. Location cache: a low-power l2 cache system. In *ISLPED '04*, pages 120–125, 2004.

[15] D. Nicolaescu, A. Veidenbaum, and A. Nicolau. Reducing power consumption for high-associativity data caches in embedded processors. In *DATE '03*, pages 1064–1068, 2003.

[16] M. D. Powell, A. Agarwal, T. N. Vijaykumar, B. Falsafi, and K. Roy. Reducing set-associative cache energy via way-prediction and selective direct-mapping. In *MICRO-34*, pages 54–65, 2001.

[17] A. Sembrant, E. Hagersten, and D. Black-Shaffer. Tlc: A tag-less cache for reducing dynamic first level cache energy. In *MICRO-46*, pages 49–61, 2013.

[18] T. Sherwood, E. Perelman, G. Hamerly, and B. Calder. Automatically characterizing large scale program behavior. In *ASPLOS X*, pages 45–57, 2002.

[19] A. Sodani. Race to exascale: Opportunities and challenges. In *MICRO 2011 Keynote talk.*, 2011.

[20] E. Witchel, S. Larsen, C. S. Ananian, and K. Asanović. Direct addressed caches for reduced power consumption. In *MICRO-34*, pages 124–133, 2001.

[21] C. Zhang, F. Vahid, J. Yang, and W. Najjar. A way-halting cache for low-energy high-performance systems. *ACM TACO*, 2(1):34–54, 2005.

Fast Photovoltaic Array Reconfiguration for Partial Solar Powered Vehicles

Jaemin Kim[1] , Yanzhi Wang[2] , Massoud Pedram[2] , and Naehyuck Chang[1]
[1]Seoul National University, Seoul, Korea
[2]University of Southern California, Los Angeles, CA, USA
[1]{jmkim,naehyuck}@elpl.snu.ac.kr, [2]{yanzhiwa,pedram}@usc.edu

ABSTRACT

This paper demonstrates that a partially solar powered EV can significantly save battery energy during cruising using innovative fast photovoltaic array (PV) reconfiguration. Use of all the vehicle surface areas, such as the hood, rooftop, door panels, quarter panels, etc., makes it possible to install more PV modules, but it also results in severe performance degradation due to inherent partial shading. This paper introduces fast online PV array reconfiguration and customization of the PV array installation according to the driving pattern and overcomes the partial shading phenomenon. We implement a high-speed, high-voltage PV reconfiguration switch network with IGBTs (insulated-gate bipolar transistors) and a controller. We derive the optimal reconfiguration period based on the solar irradiance/driving profiles using adaptive learning method, where the on/off delay of IGBT, CAN (control area network) delay, computation overhead, and energy overhead are taken into account. Experimental results show 25% more power generation from the PV array. This paper also introduces two important design-time optimization problems to achieve trade-off between performance and overhead. We derive the optimal PV reconfiguration granularity and partial PV array mounting by the car owner's driving pattern, which results in more than 20% PV cell cost reduction.

1. INTRODUCTION

Photovoltaic (PV) cells are clean, light weight, quiet, and durable, and thus may be an ideal power source for electric vehicles (EV) [1, 2, 3]. Unfortunately, PV power alone seems simply not sufficient to operate a full EV [2]. The highest solar irradiance in a day (at noon time) is at around 1000 W/m^2, and a 30% efficiency PV module with 1 m^2 area generates 300 W peak power. Typical horizontal panel areas such as the rooftop, hood and trunk of a passenger vehicle are around 4 - 5 m^2. On the other hand, modern electric vehicles (EV) aim at similar or even higher driving performance compared with conventional internal combustion engine vehicles as well as fuel economy and zero emission. Their traction motor power rating is commonly over 100 kW [4]. However, most vehicle horsepower is mainly for acceleration and uphill driving, whereas vehicles use a small fraction during cruising (e.g., less than 10 kW during city

ISLPED '14 La Jolla, CA USA
Copyright 2014 ACM 978-1-4503-2975-0/14/08 ...$15.00.
http://dx.doi.org/10.1145/2627369.2627623.

driving.) Hence, although full PV powered driving is not practical in normal passenger cars and driving conditions, partial PV power driving is certainly beneficial [2]. The PV cells can also charge the EV battery when the EV is parked, thereby mitigating the charging requirement from the grid.

PV power has lots of advantages because a large portion of electricity that charges EV is generated from fossil fuel. The current PV powered EV is equipped with PV cells on the vehicle panels that has the smallest solar incidence angle such as the hood and the rooftop. It is certainly meaningful to enlarge the onboard PV cell array using more vehicle surface area such as door panels and quarter panels.

The *string charger architecture* [5], where a single power converter is connected to both ends of the whole PV cell array (including PV modules on the hood, rooftop, door panels, quarter panels, etc.), is a practical method considering the cost. In addition, EVs are equipped with high-voltage batteries to achieve low IR loss, and thus the use of *micro-charger architecture* (i.e., multiple power converters, each connecting to a PV module mounted on the hood, the rooftop, door panels, quarter panels, etc.) is not only expensive but also inefficient to step up the PV voltage [5]. However, PV cells on the door and quarter panels may not help increase or may even decrease the PV power output because the solar irradiance on these panels may be largely different from that on the hood and the rooftop. Moreover, the solar irradiance profiles on the driver-side quarter and door panels and the passenger-side panels are virtually opposite by the driving direction and time of the day.

Combined usage of the PV modules on the rooftop, hood, trunk, quarter, and door panels are challenging in maintaining high performance in a string charger architecture. This paper introduces a fast PV cell array reconfiguration for the partial solar powered EV. We borrow the dynamic PV module reconfiguration architecture from previous work [6, 7, 8]. However, the solar irradiance levels are rapidly changing in the case of PV modules on the vehicle due to nearby shading and direction changes. We implement a high-speed, high-voltage PV reconfiguration switch network with IGBTs (insulated-gate bipolar transistors) and a controller. We derive the optimal reconfiguration period considering the on/off delay of IGBT, CAN (control-area network) delay, computation overhead, and energy overhead. We carefully decide the reconfiguration policy based on the solar irradiance/driving profiles using adaptive learning [9].

We solve a design-time optimization problem of deriving the optimal granularity of PV reconfiguration to achieve a desirable trade-off of performance and reconfiguration complexity/overhead. This paper also introduces *partial PV installation*. As PV modules are still costly, installation of a low-efficiency PV module is a waste. For example, the driver-side quarter and door panels do not have

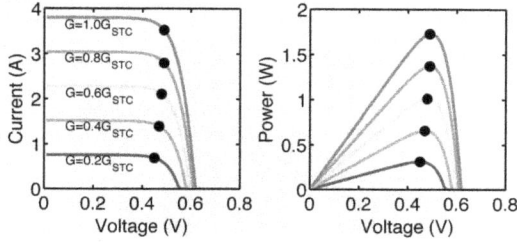

Figure 1: I-V and P-V characteristics of a PV cell.

meaningful solar irradiance when a driver commutes to the north-bound in the morning and the southbound in the afternoon. We implement an onboard PV irradiance monitoring sensor network and collect various irradiance profiles by the driving location and time, and then we customize the PV module installation according to the driving pattern.

We evaluate the proposed fast dynamic PV reconfiguration technique based on the actual implementation of reconfiguration network and controller. Experiments show that the fast dynamic PV array reconfiguration increases 423.0 W power from the baseline. The customized PV installation reduces 22.3 % PV cell cost showing only 5.6 % reduction of power generation output.

2. COMPONENT AND SYSTEM MODELS

2.1 PV Cell Modeling and Characterization

Every PV module/array is comprised of multiple PV cells. Figure 1 illustrates the PV cell I-V and P-V characteristics under different solar irradiance levels G's, where G_{STC} stands for the irradiance (1000 W/m^2) at standard test condition. One can observe that the PV cell exhibits a nonlinear output current and voltage relationship. There is an MPP under any solar irradiance level, where the output power of the PV cell is maximized. MPPs are labeled by black dots in Figure 1.

Power converters or chargers are necessary in PV systems for controlling the output voltage and current of PV modules [10]. The maximum power point tracking (MPPT) and maximum power transfer tracking (MPTT) techniques have been proposed to maximize the output power of PV systems under changing solar irradiance [10, 11, 12].

2.2 String Charger Architecture

The system diagram of the vehicular PV system is illustrated in Figure 2 based on the string charger architecture. The whole PV cell array may be comprised of multiple PV modules mounted on the hood, rooftop, door panels, quarter panels, etc., of the vehicle. Different PV modules have different areas and thus different numbers of PV cells. We use a charger between the whole PV cell array and the vehicular battery pack in order to properly regulate the operating point of the PV array. A buck-boost charger power model is proposed in [13]. In general, the charger efficiency is maximized when (i) its input and output voltages are close to each other, and (ii) the output current is within a certain range.

3. PV ARRAY RECONFIGURATION

3.1 Reconfiguration Structure

A conventional PV array consists of n series-connected PV groups, whereby each PV group has exactly m parallel-connected PV cells. Solar irradiance levels received by different PV cells in the array

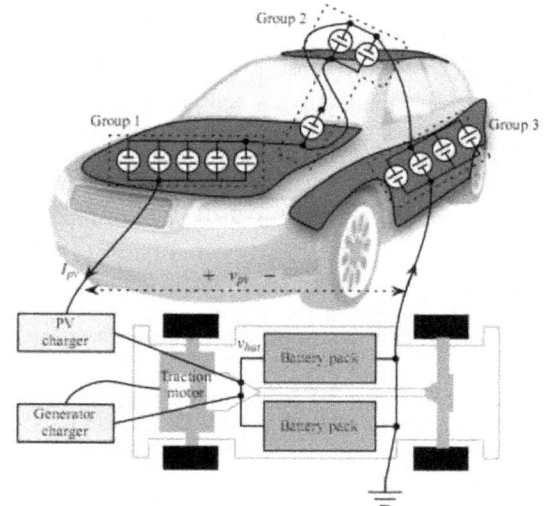

Figure 2: System diagram of a PV system on electric vehicles.

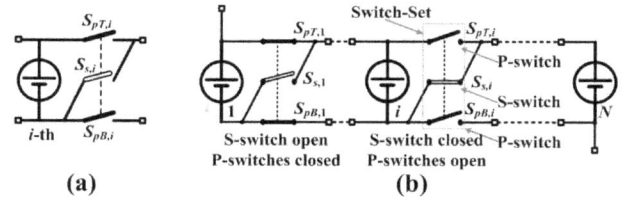

Figure 3: The structure of a reconfigurable PV array.

may be different, and such a phenomenon is known as the *partial shading effect*, which can be resulted from moving vehicles, nearby buildings and obstacles [6]. The PV array mounted on vehicles experiences more significant partial shading effect because changing directions will result in changes of solar irradiance levels at different sides of the vehicles. Partial shading not only reduces the maximum output power of the shaded PV cells, but also makes the lighted or less-shaded PV cells that are connected in series with the shaded ones deviate from their MPPs, thereby degrading the output power of the PV array.

Reference work [6, 7] suggested dynamic PV array reconfiguration to combat partial shading. The proposed reconfiguration technique can make both the shaded and lighted PV cells work at or close to their MPPs simultaneously, thereby improving the PV system output power. Figure 3 shows the structure of a reconfigurable PV array [6] with N PV cells. Please note that for the vehicular PV array, the reconfiguration structure connects all the PV cells from all PV modules mounted on the hood, rooftop, door panels, quarter panels, etc., of the vehicle[1].

As shown in Figure 3, each of the PV cells (except for the N-th PV cell) in the reconfigurable structure is integrated with three solid-state switches: a top parallel switch $S_{pT,i}$, a bottom parallel switch $S_{pB,i}$, and a series switch $S_{S,i}$. PV array reconfiguration can be conducted by controlling the ON/OFF states of the programmable switches. The two parallel switches of a PV cell are always in the same state, and the series switch of a PV cell must be in the opposite state of its parallel switches. The parallel switches connect PV cells in parallel to form a *PV group*, and the series switches connect PV groups in series. In general, a reconfigurable PV array with N PV cells can have a arbitrary number (less than or

---

[1]This requires negligible additional overhead because only two connection wires are required to connect all the PV modules as shown in Figure 3.

equal to N) of PV groups, each with arbitrary number of PV cells with consecutive IDs. Now we provide the formal definition of the configuration of a reconfigurable PV array. Consider a reconfigurable PV array comprised of N PV cells, it can have an arbitrary number (less than or equal to N) of PV groups. The number r_j (>0) of parallel-connected PV cells in the j-th PV group should satisfy:

$$\sum_{j=1}^{g} r_j = N, \tag{1}$$

where g is the number of PV groups. This configuration can be viewed as a partitioning of the PV cell index set $\mathbf{A} = \{1, 2, 3, ...N\}$, where the elements in $\mathbf{A}$ denote the indices of PV cells in the array. This partitioning is denoted by subsets $\mathbf{B}_1$, $\mathbf{B}_2$, ..., and $\mathbf{B}_g$ of $\mathbf{A}$, which correspond to the g PV groups comprised of r_1, r_2, ..., and r_g PV cells, respectively. The subsets $\mathbf{B}_1$, $\mathbf{B}_2$, ..., and $\mathbf{B}_g$ satisfy

$$\cup_{j=1}^{g} \mathbf{B}_j = \mathbf{A} \tag{2}$$

and

$$\mathbf{B}_j \cap \mathbf{B}_k = \emptyset, \quad \forall j, k \in \{1, 2, ..., g\}, \; j \neq k \tag{3}$$

The indices of PV cells in group j must be smaller than the indices of PV cells in group k for any $1 \leq j < k \leq g$ due to the structural characteristics of the reconfigurable PV array, i.e., $i_1 < i_2$ for $\forall i_1 \in \mathbf{B}_j$ and $\forall i_2 \in \mathbf{B}_k$ satisfying $1 \leq j < k \leq g$. A partitioning satisfying the above properties is called an *alphabetical partitioning*.

3.2 Reconfiguration Algorithm

Let G_{hood}, G_{roof}, G_{trunk}, G_{left} and G_{right} denote the solar irradiance levels on PV cells mounted on the hood, rooftop, trunk, left side and right side, respectively, of the vehicle. We measure these solar irradiance profiles using solar sensor network to be discussed later. Based on these irradiance levels, we derive the optimal configuration of the PV panel based on the polynomial-time reconfiguration algorithm provided in [6], which is comprised of an outer loop to find the optimal number of groups in the PV array and a kernel algorithm to determine the optimal configuration based on the number of groups. Under rapidly-changing irradiance levels on each side of the vehicle during driving, it is not possible to perform optimal reconfiguration as long as some irradiance level changes due to the timing and energy overhead associated with reconfiguration. Thus, we need to determine the optimal reconfiguration policy (and period) for the vehicular PV array based on a thorough overhead analysis.

4. SOLAR SENSOR NETWORK AND IRRADIANCE PROFILE ACQUIREMENT

We build a Zigbee-based solar sensor nodes network and a logger program to acquire real solar irradiance profile on each side of vehicles during driving. The actual implementation of a sensor node in the network is provided in Figure 4. Zigbee is a wireless network protocol to create personal area networks, which is commonly used for applications requiring low power, low data rate, and long battery life. The physical transceiving range of Zigbee protocol is up to 120 meters, however, we disable the boost mode to reduce power consumption. We use dual AAA-size batteries to supply power for each node without DC-DC converter to minimize power loss. A Zigbee transceiver module and an ambient sensor can operate by 2.4 V to 3.3 V supply voltage level, which has a enough operation margin for dual alkaline batteries. The lifetime of dual AAA batteries is more than 12 hours, which is enough for recording solar

Figure 4: Zigbee-based solar sensor node to measure the solar irradiance.

Table 1: Recorded Driving Profiles.

Location	Start time	End time	Distance
Incheon Airport	12:35	12:43	5.2km
Ontario to Riverside	08:32	08:57	27km
West LA to Indio	12:53	19:50	261.8km
West LA to Carson	14:47	16:31	44.7km
Riverside	14:15	14:36	3.1km
West LA to Riverside	09:58	11:21	112.3km

irradiance profile of one day driving. The Zigbee module automatically reads value from the ambient sensor with its internal ADC and sends it to a receiving node every 50 ms with 250 kbits/s data transmission speed. A specially designed logger program collects irradiance sensor data from the receiving node with vehicle speed and location information from GPS including latitude, longitude, altitude and time. We install magnets to each corner of a sensor node so that the sensor nodes can stick to vehicle easily and firmly. The purpose of this sensor node is to (i) easily attach to any vehicle in a very short amount of time, and (ii) so that we can test various vehicles and locations and collect benchmark solar irradiance profiles.

We attached five sensor nodes at hood, roof, trunk, left side and right side of a vehicle to measure benchmark profiles of G_{hood}, G_{roof}, G_{trunk}, G_{left} and G_{right}, respectively. Finally we drive a vehicle along six paths to collect real benchmark vehicle drive profiles: Seoul to Incheon airport, Ontario to Riverside, west Los Angeles to Indio, west Los Angeles to Carson, Riverside, and west Los Angeles to Riverside. Details are shown in Table 1.

5. RECONFIGURATION HARDWARE DESIGN AND OPTIMIZATION

5.1 PV Reconfiguration Hardware Design

In the PV reconfiguration structure proposed in [6, 8], each switch consists of one MOSFET gate driver and one pair of N-type MOSFETs. However, the reconfigurable PV module array on moving vehicles has different requirements than those in [6, 8]. First, the reconfiguration speed should be highly fast. For example, if there is a shade by an approaching four-meter-long vehicle in the opposite side and the speeds of both vehicles are 80 km/hour, the shade exists for a maximum of 180 ms. Moreover, rapid direction changes of vehicles will result in fast changing in solar irradiance levels at each side of the vehicles. Hence, fast reconfiguration within a few milliseconds reconfiguration time is required to fully exploit the potential benefits of the dynamic reconfiguration capability during vehicle driving. Second, high-voltage or high-current gate control is required for vehicular PV array reconfigurations. We implement an IGBT(insulated-gate bipolar transistor)-based reconfiguration network to meet both requirements.

We carefully select commercial IGBTs and gate drivers for switches in the reconfiguration network. The selected IGBT IXXK200N65B4 can handle voltage and current ratings of 650 V and 370 A, respectively, which is enough rating for vehicular PV arrays. We select gate driver MC33153 that has a short propagation delay of few hundreds nanoseconds to control the IGBTs. We use photo-coupler isolation between the high-voltage IGBT side and the controller logic side to prevent from damage due to power surge. We connect IGBT with 65V/5A rating power supply and apply square-wave input voltage on the gate driver to observe the step response of IGBT. The response waveform of output voltage is not distorted until the input frequency reaches tens of kHz. This shows the stability of the IGBT and gate driver selections.

Then we implement a communication system based on the controller area network, as known as CAN. The CAN standard is established specially for vehicles, which require high stability. The CAN network topology is also a bus structure so that we can easily attach sensor nodes to the communication network. We carefully select ADM3053 as an isolated CAN physical layer transceiver with LM3S2965 as the control processor, which supports hardware layers of CAN communications. 1 Mbps communication speed in transmission will make the transmission delay below 1 ms.

5.2 Overhead Analysis

In order to derive the optimal reconfiguration control policy, we need a thorough analysis of both timing overhead and energy overhead during PV array reconfiguration. During PV array reconfiguration, the following processes are required: sensing the irradiance levels, transmitting the irradiance data from sensors to the central controller, computing the optimal configuration, changing the ON/OFF states of IGBTs, and performing MPPT control after reconfiguration. Hence, the timing overhead of PV array reconfiguration is comprised of the following components:

1. *Sensing delay:* With current sensor network setup, each sensor node senses and converts the solar irradiance value in every 50 ms, which is the sensing period. The sensing delay is less than 10 μs based on the sensor ADC setup.

2. *Network delay:* The transmission delay is no more than 1 ms in the sensor network using CAN transmission protocol.

3. *Computation overhead:* The reconfiguration control algorithm is a polynomial-time optimal algorithm [6]. For a moderate-scale PV array with 60 PV cells, it takes only 3 - 4 ms to calculate the optimal configuration on a 3.0 GHz desktop computer and should take less than 10 ms on a typical ARM-based embedded processor (as the reconfiguration controller) [14].

4. *Reconfiguration delay:* Our experiments show that the gate driver and IGBT can reconfigure within 10 μs with only a little distortion of waveform. so 1 ms will be a safe (conservative) reconfiguration delay.

5. *MPPT control overhead:* The delay of a perturb & observe (P&O)-based MPPT control is typically less than 2.5 ms.

The total timing overhead is the sum of the above-mentioned delay components, and we use 15 ms in our experiments to derive the optimal reconfiguration period. The minimum reconfiguration period

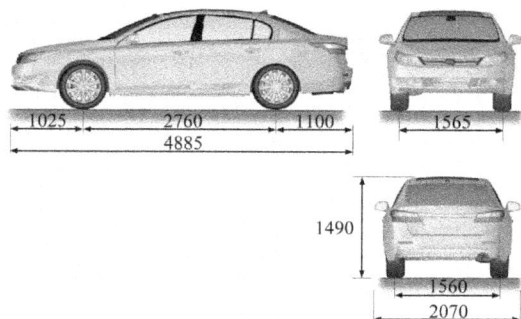

Figure 5: SM5 offical dimension from vehicle manual

is 50 ms which is limited by the sensing frequency. For the energy overhead, the vehicular PV system will have zero output power during reconfiguration (i.e., changing the ON/OFF states of IGBTs) and have sub-optimal output power during P&O-based MPPT control. We use a conservative estimate that the output power will be zero also during the MPPT control period.

5.3 Reconfiguration Period Optimization

Under rapid-changing irradiance levels on each side of the vehicle during driving, it is not possible to perform optimal reconfiguration as long as some irradiance level changes due to the timing and energy overhead associated with reconfiguration. Thus, we need to determine the optimal reconfiguration period (and policy) for the vehicular PV array based on the overhead analysis in the previous subsection. A larger reconfiguration period may not be able to capture the fast changes in solar irradiance levels. On the other hand, a smaller reconfiguration period will induce higher timing overhead and energy overhead, and may eventually degrade the PV system performance.

We use the adaptive learning method to derive the optimal reconfiguration period in an online manner [9]. We maintain multiple candidate reconfiguration period values, and choose one value with the currently highest performance at the beginning of each evaluation period (say, 10 minutes.) At the end of this evaluation period, we evaluate all the reconfiguration period values and update their performance using an exponential weighting function [15], and then choose the reconfiguration period value with the highest updated performance level.

5.4 Experimental Results

In this section, we compare the performance between the proposed reconfigurable vehicular PV system with two baseline systems. The proposed system installs reconfigurable PV array on the rooftop, hood, trunk, and left and right door panels. This should be the largest area for potential solar energy harvesting. We consider two baseline setups. Baseline B1 installs solar modules only on the rooftop, hood, and trunk panels without reconfiguration. Baseline B2 installs solar modules on the rooftop, hood, trunk, quarter, and door panels without reconfiguration. We measure a mid-size family sedan Renault-Samsung NEW-SM5 car and observe the following area parameters: hood (bonnet): 1.6 m^2 (1.024 m by 1.565 m), left door, right door: 1.7 m^2 for each (0.616 m by 2.760 m), roof: 1.99 m^2 (1.274 m by 1.565 m), trunk: 0.63 m^2 (0.400 m by 1.565 m). Note: All parameter values are measured on a real car, which are slightly smaller than official dimension in Figure 5. In this section, we assume fixed-size PV cells with 0.15 m^2 area, 20 V MPP voltage, and 2.25 A MPP current at $G = 1000$ W/m^2. We assume 200 V terminal voltage of the vehicle battery pack. We consider a realistic solar charger model with efficiency variations [13].

Table 2: Performance comparison between the proposed reconfigurable PV system with baseline PV systems on the six benchmark profiles.

Benchmark	Proposed	B1	B2
Incheon Airport	1048 W	887.8 W	730.5 W
Ontario to Riverside	518.5 W	288.4 W	343.2 W
West LA to Indio	836.2 W	715.5 W	569.7 W
West LA to Carson	785.7 W	607.2 W	514.1 W
Riverside	1028 W	706.4 W	616.1 W
West LA to Riverside	472.8 W	49.8 W	163.0 W

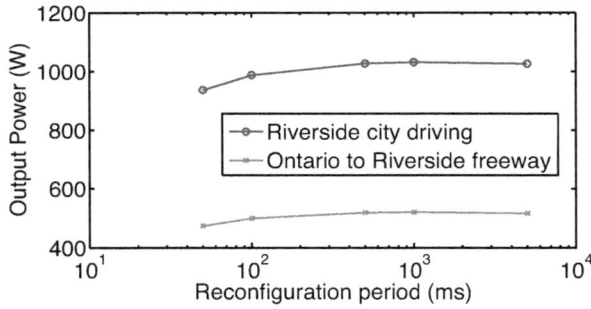

Figure 7: Performance (average output power) of the proposed reconfigurable PV system with different reconfiguration period values on two benchmark profiles.

We first consider a fixed reconfiguration period of 0.5 s, and compare the performance, i.e., the average output power, between the proposed and baseline setups on the six benchmark solar irradiance profiles. Comparison results are illustrated in Table 2. We can observe that the proposed system significantly outperforms baseline setups by a maximum of 423.0 W improvement in average output power. Comparing between two baseline systems, we observe that B1 even often outperforms B2 because the solar irradiances on the left side and right side of the vehicle are often changing and have smaller magnitude compared with the rooftop, which degrades the output power of the PV system. Moreover, we plot the PV array output power versus time of the proposed system and two baseline systems in Figure 6. We can observe that the proposed system consistently outperforms the two baseline systems over the whole time range.

Furthermore, we consider the optimization of reconfiguration period as described in Section 5.3. Figure 7 shows the average output power of the proposed reconfigurable PV system with different reconfiguration period values on two benchmark profiles "Ontario to Riverside" and "Riverside". Please note that 50 ms is the lowest possible reconfiguration period because it is the sensing period. Our experiments show that the optimal reconfiguration periods for the six benchmark profiles are around 0.5 s - 1 s in general, in order to achieve a trade-off between lower timing/energy overhead and fast reconfiguration capabilities.

6. DESIGN-TIME OPTIMIZATION OF THE VEHICULAR PV ARRAY

In this section, we discuss the design-time optimization of the vehicular PV array, including (i) deriving the optimal granularity of PV array reconfiguration, i.e., optimizing the size of a PV cell, and (ii) partial PV array installation. These optimizations are performed statically in the design time, and cannot be altered after installation.

Table 3: Performance comparison of the reconfigurable PV system with different PV cell sizes on the six benchmark profiles.

Profile	$0.1 \ m^2$	$0.15 \ m^2$	$0.25 \ m^2$	$0.5 \ m^2$
Incheon Airport	1077W	1048W	1016W	967.5W
Ontario to Riverside	537.9W	518.5W	495.3W	476.1W
West LA to Indio	865.0W	836.2W	799.3W	778.9W
West LA to Carson	809.8W	785.7W	747.5W	726.5W
Riverside	1058W	1028W	993.5W	966.1W
West LA to Riverside	495.6W	472.8W	446.9W	392.3W

6.1 Optimization of PV Cell Size

The PV cell is the basic unit in the reconfiguration technique, and its size is essentially trade-off between the lower additional capital cost and reconfiguration complexity, and performance enhancement. Basically, a larger PV cell size reduces the cost of the reconfigurable PV array architecture since fewer switches are required for reconfiguration and also reduces the computation overhead for the optimal array configuration. A smaller PV cell, on the other hand, achieves better flexibility and thus higher performance against partial shading.

The PV cell size optimization is performed at the system design stage. We aim to find the optimal PV cell size with a capital cost limit to achieve a desirable trade-off between the lower PV system capital cost and reconfiguration overhead, and enhanced performance against partial shading. In the outer loop of algorithm, we use binary search to find the most desirable PV cell size subject to the capital cost constraint. For each given PV cell size inside the loop, we evaluate the PV system performance using the six solar irradiance benchmarks using the corresponding optimal reconfiguration policy. The timing overhead and energy overhead are taken into account in this evaluation procedure.

We set the PV cell lower limit by $0.1 m^2$ and compare the performance of reconfigurable PV array with different PV cell sizes on the six solar irradiance profiles. We adopt a fixed reconfiguration period of 0.5 s. Table 3 shows the comparison results including four possible PV cell sizes: $0.1 \ m^2$, $0.15 \ m^2$, $0.25 \ m^2$, and $0.5 \ m^2$. We observe that a finer grained PV cell will result in higher average output power (at most 26.3% higher average output power when comparing between the $0.1 \ m^2$ case and $0.5 \ m^2$ case) due to the higher flexibility in reconfiguration. We would like to point out that the timing and energy overhead of all these testing cases are within the estimates provided in Section 5.2.

6.2 Partial PV Array Installation

In this section, we introduce *partial PV array installation*. As PV modules are still costly, installation of a low-efficiency PV module is a waste. For example, the driver-side quarter and door panels do not have meaningful solar irradiance when a driver commutes to the northbound in the morning and the southbound in the afternoon. Based on the PV irradiance profiles collected using the solar sensor network, we propose to customize the PV module installation according to different driving patterns.

More specifically, we consider the following partial solar array installation with reconfiguration: the rooftop, hood and trunk are equipped with PV cells, and either the left side or right side of the vehicle is equipped with PV cells. We compare the performance (output power) of these two customized PV array installation cases with the optimal reconfigurable vehicular PV system. We assume fixed-size PV cells of $0.15 \ m^2$ and adopt a fixed reconfiguration period of 0.5 s. Table 4 shows the comparison results. We can observe that for some benchmark profiles such as "Ontario to River-

(a) Riverside city driving

(b) Ontario to Riverside freeway

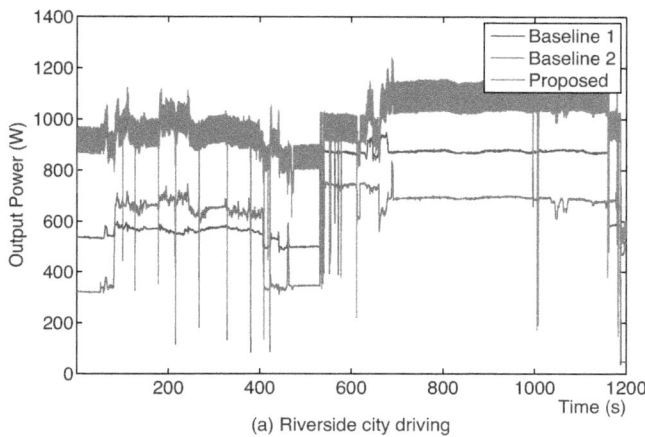

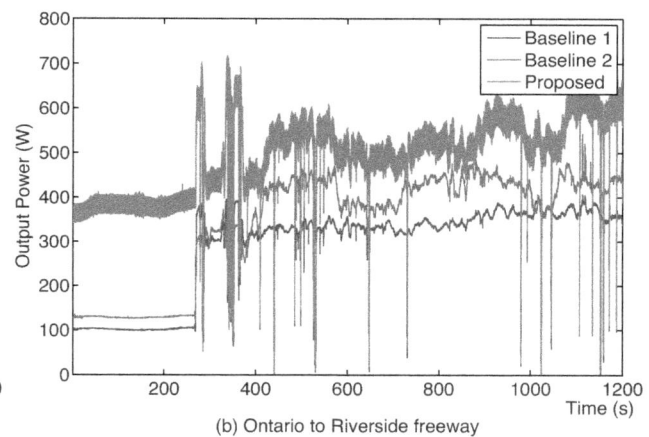

Figure 6: Performance comparison between the proposed reconfigurable PV system with baseline systems.

Table 4: Performance comparison between the optimal reconfigurable PV system with two customized PV systems on six benchmark profiles.

Benchmark	Optimal	Left Equip.	Right Equip.
Incheon Airport	1048W	945.3W	978.7W
Ontario to Riverside	518.5W	453.5W	429.9W
West LA to Indio	836.2W	770.7W	775.1W
West LA to Carson	785.7W	674.6W	715.9W
Riverside	1028W	969.9W	899.5W
West LA to Riverside	472.8W	403.3W	420.2W

side", partial PV installation will result in significant output power degradation. However, this is opposite for some other benchmark profiles such as "Riverside" or "Incheon Airport", because the solar irradiance levels on either the left side or right side (or both) of the vehicle is relatively low in the whole benchmark. In this cases, customized PV installation will be beneficial because it can significantly reduce the capital cost of the vehicular PV system. For example, if a user commutes through "Riverside" trace everyday such as a bus in a public transportation system, the customized PV installation reduces 22.3 % PV cell cost showing only 5.6 % reduction of power generation output.

7. CONCLUSIONS

In this paper, we propose fast online PV array reconfiguration and customization of the PV panel installation according to the driving pattern, in order to maximize the solar power generation for EVs. We implement a high-speed, high-voltage PV reconfiguration switch network with IGBTs and a reconfiguration controller. We derive the break-even time for reconfiguration and the corresponding adaptive reconfiguration policy based on solar irradiance/driving profiles using adaptive learning method, in which the on/off delay of IGBT, CAN delay, computation overhead, and energy overhead are taken into account. We also solve the design-time optimization problem of deriving the optimal size of each PV cell to achieve a desirable tradeoff of performance and reconfiguration complexity/overhead.

Acknowledgments

This research is supported by the Mid-Career Researcher Program and the International Research & Development Program of the NRF of Korea funded by the MSIP (NRF-2014-023320) and a grant from the Software and Hardware Foundations of the National Science Foundation.

8. REFERENCES

[1] D. Patterson and R. Spee, "The design and development of an axial flux permanent magnet brushless dc motor for wheel drive in a solar powered vehicle," IEEE Trans. Industry Applications, vol. 31, no. 5, 1995.

[2] I. Arsie, G. Rizzo, and M. Sorrentino, "Optimal design and dynamic simulation of a hybrid solar vehicle," SAE Transactions-Journal of Engines, 2007.

[3] Solar powered vehicles: http://www.designboom.com/contemporary/solarpoweredvehicles.html.

[4] A. Affanni, A. Bellini, G. Franceschini, P. Guglielmi, and C. Tassoni, "Battery choice and management for new-generation electric vehicles," IEEE Trans. Industrial Electronics, 2005.

[5] W. Xiao, N. Ozog, and W. G. Dunford, "Topology study of photovoltaic interface for maximum power point tracking," IEEE Trans. Industrial Electronics, 2007.

[6] X. Lin, Y. Wang, S. Yue, D. Shin, N. Chang, and M. Pedram, "Near-optimal dynamic module reconfiguration in a photovoltaic system to combat partial shading effects," in Proceedings of Design Automation Conference (DAC), June 2012.

[7] Y. Wang, X. Lin, N. Chang, and M. Pedram, "Dynamic reconfiguration of photovoltaic energy harvesting system in hybrid electric vehicles," in Proceedings of the International Symposium on 'Low Power Electronics and Design (ISLPED), Aug. 2012.

[8] Y. Wang, X. Lin, J. Kim, N. Chang, and M. Pedram, "Capital cost-aware design and partial shading-aware architecture optimization of a reconfigurable photovltaic system," in Proceedings of Design, Automation & Test in Europe (DATE), March 2013.

[9] C. M. Bishop, Pattern Recognition and Machine Learning. Springer, 2007.

[10] N. Femia, G. Petrone, G. Spagnuolo, and M. Vitelli, "Optimization of perturb and observe maximum power point tracking method," IEEE Trans. Power Electronics, 2005.

[11] F. Liu, S. Duan, F. Liu, B. Liu, and Y. Kang, "A variable step size inc mppt method for pv systems," IEEE Trans. Industrial Electronics, 2008.

[12] Y. Kim, N. Chang, Y. Wang, and M. Pedram, "Maximum power transfer tracking for a photovoltaic-supercapacitor energy system," in Proceedings of the International Symposium on Low Power Electronics and Design (ISLPED), Aug. 2010.

[13] Y. Wang, Y. Kim, Q. Xie, N. Chang, and M. Pedram, "Charge migration efficiency optimization in hybrid electrical energy storage (hees) systems," in Proceedings of the International Symposium on Low Power Electronics and Design (ISLPED), Aug. 2011.

[14] Samsung Exynos 4 Dual 45nm (Exynos 4210) Microprocessor, 2012.

[15] C. Hwang and C. Wu, "A predictive system shutdown method for energy saving of event-driven computation," ACM Trans. on Des. Autom. Electron. Systems, 2000.

Energy Harvesting from Anti-Corrosion Power Sources

Sehwan Kim
Dept. of Biomed. Engineering
Dankook University, S.Korea
paul.kim@dankook.ac.kr

Minseok Lee
Dept. of Medical Laser
Dankook University,S.Korea
lifeway1972@gmail.com

Pai H. Chou
University of California
Irvine, CA 92697-2625 USA
phchou@uci.edu

ABSTRACT

This work presents energy harvesting techniques from low-voltage current used to prevent galvanic corrosion between a metallic structure and a permanent copper/copper sulfate (Cu/CuSO4) reference electrode. Supercapacitors are adopted to compensate for or overcome the limitations of batteries. Then, a boost converter is used to convert the low voltage levels of galvanic corrosion to that needed by the complementary metal oxide semiconductor (CMOS) technologies used for the wireless sensor systems. Experimental results show that our proposed harvesting schemes significantly reduce the overhead of the charging circuitry, which enables nearly full charging of supercapacitors of up to 350 F under the low power conditions of 3 mW (i.e., 3 mA at 1 V). More importantly, our system enables maintenance-free operation of remote-monitoring cathodic protection (RMCP) systems in harsh environments, where sunlight or wind power may be unavailable or unpredictable.

Categories and Subject Descriptors

B.0 [**Hardware**]: General

General Terms

Design, Performance measurement

Keywords

Energy harvesting, galvanic corrosion, cathodic protection systems.

1. INTRODUCTION

Cathodic protection (CP) is the most effective electrical method of controlling and reducing corrosion on metallic structures such as water storage tanks, lock gates and dams, steel pilings, ship hulls and interiors, and water treatment equipment, located underground or underwater. In particular, the CP method has been widely used on the metal pipeline systems for the transmission and distribution of gas, petrochemical, and water [9, 10, 12]. By simply maintaining anticorrosion voltage levels, one can effectively stop corrosion of the metal pipelines.

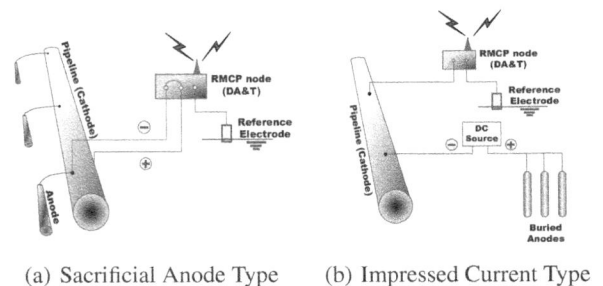

(a) Sacrificial Anode Type   (b) Impressed Current Type

Figure 1: Remote-monitoring Cathodic Protection Systems

1.1 Remote Monitoring of CP Systems

To ensure proper performance of anticorrosion, periodic monitoring of the CP system is required. To be in compliance with National Association of Corrosion Engineers (NACE) guidelines, it is necessary to take and report monthly or bimonthly measurements of the voltage potential between a reference electrode at the various test points [10]. In the conventional monitoring process for CP systems, the measurements are carried out manually using a digital multimeter on the site. These manual measurements not only incur high cost of traveling to remote sites, but they also leave the pipelines unprotected until the fault is discovered by routine measurement.

Remote-monitoring Cathodic Protection (RMCP) systems are those that combine smart corrosion sensors [3, 16] with remote monitoring functions [11, 15]. They have been receiving growing interest in recent years. They automate the data collection process and provide immediate warning of potential corrosion hazards by an RMCP node. Fig. 1 shows the representative RMCP systems with the RMCP nodes for data acquisition and transmission (DA&T): sacrificial anode and impressed current types.

1.1.1 Sacrificial Anode System

The operational principle of the first type is to connect an external anode to the metal structures to be protected, resulting in passing a positive direct current (dc) between them. The metal structure becomes a cathode that does not corrode, while the external anode is corroded. The dc current is used as a protective current by consuming iron of the anode (e.g., activated aluminum, zinc or magnesium). In other words, the anode is sacrificed by corrosion and is therefore named a *sacrificial anode system* as shown in Fig. 1(a). Due to the sacrifice of the anode, the system is required to periodically replace the sacrificed anode.

1.1.2 Impressed Current System

In Fig. 1(b), a dc source is placed between the metal structures and the anode to avoid the replacement cost of the sacrificed anode. This is called an *impressed current* system, whose anode is made durable thanks to the impressed current from the dc source. As a result, the protective current flows from the anode into the metal structures without any sacrifice of the anode.

1.1.3 Monitoring Functions

Whether sacrificial anode or impressed current is used, an RMCP node typically performs three main functions: corrosion sensing, data acquisition, and wireless data transmission [1, 7]. A reference electrode (e.g., Copper/Copper Sulfate ($Cu/CuSO_4$) or silver/silver chloride ($Ag/AgCl$)) is inevitable to determine whether it protects the metal structures against corrosion. If the potential of the metal structure against a reference cell is obtained between 850 mV and 2 V, then the corrosion is effectively protected. For CP systems to perform "on-demand" remote monitoring, the node samples the voltage level at the test points on the site and notifies the operation center if the voltage exceeds the threshold level.

1.2 Power Source for RMCP Systems

Most RMCP nodes today are powered by batteries. They are power managed by duty-cycling to extend the battery life, but the battery is still the main limiting factor associated with the RMCP nodes due to non-ideal effects such as the memory effect and the limited number of recharge cycles. As a result, batteries need to be replaced every 1-2 years and incur high replacement cost.

To address these disadvantages of batteries, researchers start proposing the use of supercapacitors, also known as ultracapacitors or electrochemical double layer capacitors (EDLCs), as the type of energy storage element (ESE) of choice. Supercapacitors have extremely long life cycles, high power density, and eco-friendly materials [2, 5, 6]. The voltage difference between an anode and a reference electrode is 0.85 to 2 V while the current varies from 2 to 4 mA depending on the soil condition surrounding a single reference electrode. This level of cumulative energy over time is nontrivial and can be sufficient for running duty-cycled remote-monitoring CP nodes. However, scavenging energy from galvanic corrosion and storing the harvested energy to supercapacitors pose new challenges on designing subwatt-scale harvesters. The voltage between the anode and the reference electrode is not directly usable unless up-converted to CMOS voltage levels, but this incurs nontrivial overhead. Also, the self-discharge (leakage) rate of supercapacitors increases rapidly near their rated voltage and can be similar to or exceed the charging current.

1.3 Contributions

The main contribution of this work is the development of an energy harvesting technique from corrosion energy: the galvanic current induced by the natural voltage difference between a cathode and a reference electrode in the remote-monitoring CP systems. We propose solutions in terms of charging and discharging phases using the supercapacitor-based energy harvester.

First, a *hysteretic charging* scheme is suggested to charge *reservoir supercapacitors* (of large capacitance) under the condition of low ambient power by offsetting the leakage of supercapacitors. The *input supercapacitor* (of small capacitance) accumulates the energy from the low-power ambient source, and then rapidly releases the accumulated energy to the reservoir supercapacitors within the hysteresis band. This charging scheme overcomes the leakage of the reservoir supercapacitors.

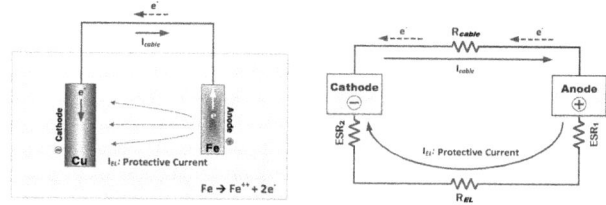

(a) Bimetallic Corrosion, (b) Equivalent Circuit

Figure 2: Corrosion Mechanism; where R_{cable} is cable path resistance, R_{EL} is electrolyte path resistance, ESR_1 is apparent or effective boundary resistance at the anode, ESR_2 is apparent or effective boundary resistance at the cathode.

Second, we propose a hybrid supply circuit for our supercapacitor-based system to efficiently power the target embedded loads in both active and low-power modes. Unlike batteries, since the voltage of a supercapacitor drops as the stored energy is released, most supercapacitors need a dc-dc converter to maintain a stable voltage level when driving target loads. However, most dc-dc converters have higher quiescent current than the sleep current of most embedded systems by 2-3 orders of magnitude. Our proposed scheme can eliminate most of the quiescent current by adding the near-constant voltage ESE for powering the load during sleep mode.

The remainder of this paper is organized as follows. Section 2 first provides theoretical background on galvanic corrosion and the characteristics of supercapacitors. We also survey current RMCP systems with energy harvesting. Section 3 describes the architecture of the harvesting system and the critical schemes. Section 4 presents the system specification and a working prototype of the proposed harvester. Section 5 presents the evaluation results of our hysteretic harvesting scheme for the RMCP system. Section 6 concludes the paper with directions for future work.

2. BACKGROUND AND RELATED WORK

Metal in the extraction from its ore has a natural tendency to revert to its original state under the action of oxygen and water. This action is called corrosion and the most common example is rusting [13]. Corrosion is an electro-chemical process related to the electrical currents on a micro or macro scale. This corrosion process is produced by the natural potential difference in galvanic couples, or the variations at different points on the surface of metallic structures such as pipeline systems. To initiate the electro-chemical process, the following four components must be included: anode, cathode, electrolyte, and connecting conductor, as shown in Fig. 2. Corrosion normally occurs at the anode but not the cathode.

2.1 Galvanic Corrosion

Galvanic corrosion (i.e., bimetallic corrosion) generates the galvanic current by connecting two dissimilar metals buried in the electrolyte such as soil. Most soils contain moisture and mineral salts and therefore make a good electrolyte. Fig. 2(a) describes the galvanic current resulting from the connection of two dissimilar metals submerged in the electrolyte. If a copper and a metal (e.g., Fe) are electrically connected in the soil, the electrolytic nature of the soil gives rise to a galvanic action in which the copper acts as a cathode and the metal as an anode. In this closed circuit, the protective current (direct current) will flow through the soil from the metal to the copper. Metal ions leave the anode by way of the electrolyte, and electrons travel from the anode to the cathode by way of the cable connection path. This galvanic corrosion occurs only at the anode (Fe) while the cathode (copper) is protected. Fig. 2(b) shows the equivalent circuit for the galvanic current loop. The current flows are a result of potential difference (i.e., $I_{cable} \cdot R_{cable}$) between the anode and the cathode. The amount of current (I_{cable} or I_{EL}) flowing in galvanic couples depends on the magnitude of the driving voltage and the total effective resistance. This electrical behavior can be equally applied to the galvanic corrosion between metallic structures and the reference electrode.

2.2 Characteristics of Supercapacitors

Supercapacitors can be an excellent ESE for the harvesters, due to their power density and durability. However, in such systems, the non-ideal behavior attributed to substantial *leakage currents* and *charge redistribution* inside the supercapacitors need to be addressed [2,17]. The charge redistribution can be reduced by repeating several charging-discharging cycles in the initial phase. However, the leakage current can still be considerable and is inevitable. According to the literature on supercapacitors modeling, their leakage power grows rapidly with the size (i.e., capacitance) and with the remaining energy. For example, at 2.5 V, the leakage power of 22 F, 100 F, and 300 F supercapacitors is 2 mW, 7 mW, and 17 mW, respectively. When the leakage power of the supercapacitor at a given voltage is higher than the ambient power of the RMCP system (at 3 mW), the RMCP system is actually at a loss. Therefore, the leakage rate should be capped by limiting the capacitance of supercapacitors, by limiting the voltage, or both. To overcome these limitations, we propose a *hysteretic charging* scheme, which is helpful to extend the upper bound on the capacitance of supercapacitors.

2.3 RMCP Systems with Energy Harvesting

Energy harvesting techniques for RMCP systems have been explored and studied extensively by researchers. The research approaches varied in their remote monitoring techniques, the types of CP systems, and data acquisition methods.

Mishra et al. [8] introduced Solar Photovoltaics (SPV) instead of a dc power source of the impressed-current CP system. Since the output of the SPV is a dc voltage, it can eliminate the rectifier that is found in conventional impressed CP systems. The SVP-based CP system simply replaces the dc power source of the conventional CP system with SVP power; it does not support DAQ and remote monitoring function, so routine manual inspection is still required.

Ghitani et al. [4] presented a prototype microprocessor-based CP system employing a photovoltaic (PV) power source. The PV array generates dc power from solar irradiation, and a microprocessor-controlled unit enables the impressed current to make automatic adjustments according to the state of corrosion of the pipeline. However, since the pipelines generally run through inaccessible remote locations, the PV power source would not be suitable for supplying stable power to the RMCP system.

Sun et al. [14] provided a corrosion-monitoring sensing framework based on the Mica mote for *reinforcing concrete* (RC) structures. The Mica mote is duty-cycled in conjunction with routing policy to extend the lifetime of the monitoring unit. However, this system uses a lithium battery, which typically requires replacement every 1-2 years.

3. HARVESTING SYSTEM DESIGN

We propose a system that harvests energy from the RMCP environments. The typical ambient power is around 3 mW, making it challenging to harvest. We define the following requirements. First, the total power budget of the harvester itself is 1 mW.

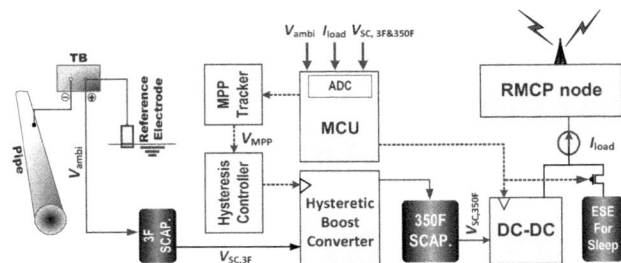

Figure 3: System block diagram for an ultra-low power consumption harvester.

max. Second, the output current of the charger should be higher than the leakage of supercapacitors. Third, the dc-dc converter on the output stage of the harvester must have very low quiescent current. To solve these problems, we propose a supercapacitor-based, hysteretic-charging energy-harvesting system named Hys-Cap, whose block diagram is shown in Fig. 3.

3.1 Hysteretic Charging Scheme

The minimum conversion voltage ($V_{conv, min}$) of most boost-up dc-dc converters to date is 0.7 V [18]. The dc-dc converters operate most efficiently when the input and output voltages are similar, but when boosting from 0.7 V to 3 V, they operate at $\leq 30\%$ efficiency. To ensure $\geq 75\%$ efficiency while considering the minimum voltage of the ambient source, the input voltage of the charger should be ≥ 0.9 V at the output voltage of 3 V. As shown in Fig. 3, given the available power of 3 mW (i.e, 3 mA at 1 V) to harvest and the charger efficiency of 75%, the output current from the charger is 0.75 mA. According to references in the literature on supercapacitors, the leakage power of supercapacitors increases exponentially with the capacitance and the (open-circuit) voltage of the supercapacitors. As their voltage approaches their rated voltage (e.g., 2.3 or 2.7 V), their leakage current can be too high such that charging will result in a net loss. For instance, the leakage current of 300 F supercapacitors is around 15 mA at 2.5 V. To charge up to 2.4 V at the charging current of 0.75 mA with a net gain, a single supercapacitor should be kept no larger than 10 F.

To overcome the high leakage issue, as well as to increase the chargeable size of supercapacitors, we propose the new scheme called *hysteretic charging*. First, the ambient source charges a smaller capacitor on the input. When it approaches the preset voltage (1 V), the charger is turned on and then starts to transfer the stored energy to the reservoir supercapacitor (350 F) until the voltage of the input supercapacitor drops by 0.1 V, which is in the hysteresis range. This technique ensures that the efficiency of the charger remains above 75% by fixing the input voltage of the charging between 0.9 V and 1 V. Furthermore, this scheme can transfer higher current than the leakage current of reservoir supercapacitors, so that it can effectively charge larger supercapacitors than those charged by the conventional continuous charging scheme.

3.2 Discharging Control

Due to the low nominal rated voltage of supercapacitors (e.g., 2.3 V or 2.7 V), most supercapacitor-based harvesters need a dc-dc converter to supply the specified voltage of the target embedded system. Buck/boost regulators are commonly used for converting a supercapacitor's lower voltage to the given target voltage. The typical target embedded system has two modes of operation: active

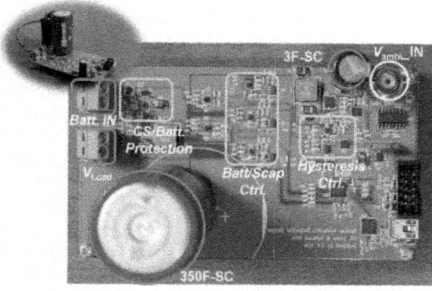

Figure 4: Prototype of HysCap harvester for an RMCP node

Table 1: Power consumption of components of HysCap

	Status	Power Consumption	Part Number
Microcontroller	Active	4 mA @ 3 V	C8051F960
	Sleep	600 nA @ 3 V	
Boost Converter	I_Q	1 μA	AS1310
Hys. & MPPT	I_Q	3.3 μA	AD8603, LT6656
	$I_{shutdown}$	< 1 μA	
DC-DC	I_Q	55 μA	TPS61200
Current Sensor	I_{supply}	0.75 μA	MAX9610

and sleep. For our application domain, the range of power consumption in active mode is from 100 to 150 mW, while in sleep mode, the power consumption ranges from 1.8 mW (3.6 V/0.5 mA) to 12.5 mW (5 V/2.5 mA), where the efficiency of a load-side dc-dc converter drops to 5%. This means 36 mW is drawn from a reservoir supercapacitor to supply 1.8 mW to the target embedded loads. In other words, the efficiency of the load-side dc-dc converter can be a crucial problem when the target load is in sleep mode.

To address the efficiency problem in sleep mode, we propose to add ESEs to power the load during sleep mode without going through the load-side dc-dc converter, which drives the load during active mode only. As shown in Fig. 3, a current sensor detects whether the target embedded load is in active or sleep mode. When in sleep mode, the current sensor outputs a low level (logic '0'), which disables the load-side dc-dc converter during sleep mode. When either the current sensor detects the high current in active mode or the voltage of the additional EHSs drops to the required minimum voltage of the target embedded loads, the load-side dc-dc converter is turned on. This discharging scheme should be able to eliminate the inefficiency of the load-side dc-dc converter during sleep mode of the target load.

4. IMPLEMENTATION

This section describes a prototype harvesting system named HysCap for an RMCP systems. The requirements for our harvester was derived from the availability of ambient power at an actual RMCP site and the power consumption of a commercial RMCP node.

4.1 System Requirements

The ambient sources are characterized as follows. The potential on the conductive wire is around 850 mV relative to a Cu/CuSO$_4$ reference electrode, and the current density from reference electrode is 2 to 4 mA depending on the soil condition surrounding a single reference electrode. Next, the power consumption of the RMCP node is measured to design the output-stage circuitry of HysCap. The power consumption of the RMCP node (DART, by Borin, USA) is 126 mW (35mA at 3.6V) in active mode and 0.65 mW (0.18mA at 3.6V) in sleep mode. In fact, the 0.18 mA

is the *root mean square* (RMS) current, since sleep mode consists of a sequence of periodical catnap signals. The duty cycle to monitor the potential between a wire connected to pipelines and the Cu/CuSO$_4$ reference electrode is 1%.

Therefore, the HysCap harvester should be designed with < 1 mW of overhead when charging the large reservoir supercapacitor under the lower ambient-power condition. It should store a sufficient amount of energy to power the RMCP node at 35 mA/3.6 V for the 1% duty cycle of continuous RF transmission for one hour, plus 0.18 mA/3.6 V during sleep mode of the RMCP node for 98% of the time (i.e., charging time = 96 hours, or 4 days).

4.2 Harvesting System

The proposed hysteretic charging and discharging system has been implemented using COTS parts. The boost converter (AS1310) has built-in hysteresis function and ultra-low quiescent current (I_Q) of 1 μA. The hysteresis band can be extended by adjusting the external resistive voltage divider, resulting in the lower-bound voltage of 0.9 V and upper-bound voltage of 1 V. As mentioned in Section 1, the voltage and the current of the ambient sources from RMCP systems can vary depending on soil conditions. Thus, the charger needs to track the maximum power point (P_{MPP}) from the RMCP environment. The microcontroller unit (MCU) detects the change of the open-circuit voltage (V_{oc}) between an anode and a reference electrode. If the voltage varies by more than 0.2 V, the MCU is waken up by the interrupt signal and moves the center voltage of the hysteresis band by adjusting the digital potentiometer on the resistive voltage divider. By setting the hysteresis band to 0.9 - 1 V, the efficiency of the buck converter can be increased.

The current sensor monitors the load current to detect whether the RMCP node is in active or sleep mode. According to Table 1, the overall power consumption of the proposed harvester is 0.46 mW at 1% duty cycle. Considering the harsh environmental conditions, both the NEMA 4+ enclosure and the conformal coating made of modified polyurethane resins (PUR) are applied to the harvester for the RMCP system. The enclosure helps protect the harvester against heavy rain, high humidity, and high temperature, while the conformal coating insulates the assembled printed circuit boards (PCBs) from the harsh environment.

5. EVALUATION

To validate the proposed charging scheme, we set up the experiment using a 3 F input supercapacitor and a 350 F reservoir supercapacitor (BCAP0350). The power of the ambient source is simulated using a regulated power supply set at 1 V/3 mA based on conditions at a representative deployment site. The hysteresis window size is 100 mV; that is, the hysteresis range is preset from 1 V to 0.9 V of the 3 F input supercapacitor.

The typical boost converter continuously transfers the charged energy of an input ceramic capacitor to either the load or ESEs. Since the value of the input capacitor is related to the efficiency and the amount of ripple of the boost converter, tens or hundreds of microfarad is usually suitable capacitance on the input. However, considering supercapacitors as a reservoir ESE, in case of low ambient power condition, it is difficult to charge supercapacitors of large capacitance due to high leakage current. To compensate for or overcome the high leakage current, we replace the input ceramic capacitor with a 3 F supercapacitor. In this experiment, we assume that the ambient source outputs power at 1 V/3 mA. Accordingly, the maximum power point (MPP) of the ambient source can be 0.95 V considering the built-in hysteresis band of 100 mV. In other words, the MPP tracker adjusts the center voltage V_{MPP} of the hysteresis comparator to 0.95 V.

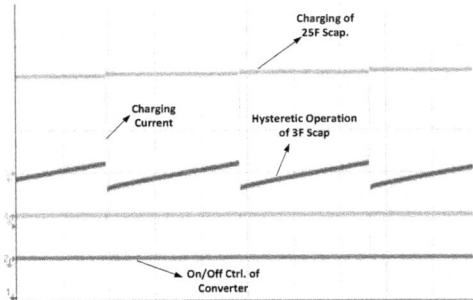

(a) Hysteretic Charging for 50 seconds.

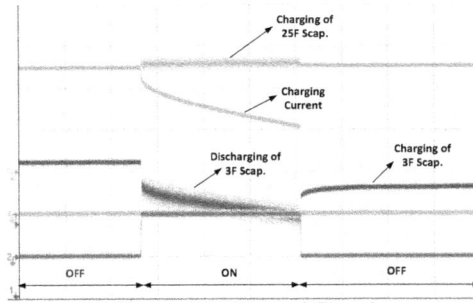

(b) Zoomed-In View of Charging.

Figure 5: Oscilloscope Snapshots showing Charging Phase of HysCap.

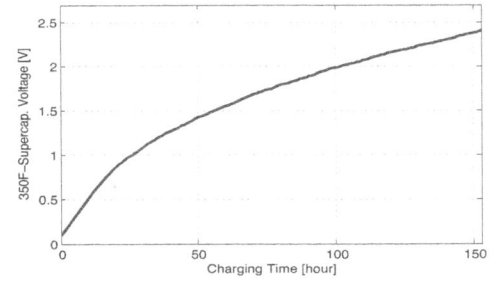

(a) Charging the reservoir supercapacitor

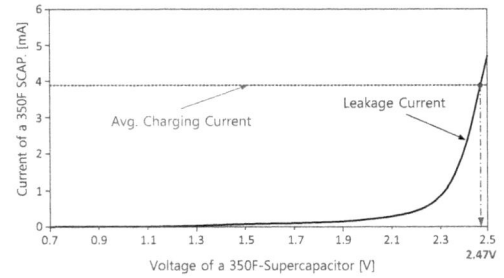

(b) Average Charging Current vs. Leakage current of the 350F Supercap.

Figure 6: Measured Charging Voltage of 350 F.

Once the voltage of the 3 F supercapacitor approaches 1 V (i.e., $V_{MPP} + V_{Hysteresis}$), the hysteresis controller turns on the boost converter and then transfers the stored energy of the 3 F input supercapacitor to the 350 F reservoir supercapacitor. After transferring the stored energy, the voltage of the 3 F supercapacitor drops to $V_{MPP} - V_{Hysteresis}$ (≈ 0.9 V). At that point, the hysteresis controller turns off the boost converter, causing the 3 F supercapacitor to start accumulating energy from the ambient source until its voltage exceeds $V_{MPP} + V_{Hysteresis}$ again.

Fig. 5 summarizes how the hysteresis operation works in the prototype energy harvester. At this moment, we use the combination of 3 F input supercapacitor and 25 F reservoir supercapacitor to show clearly the hysteretic operation based on the display range of the oscilloscope. The boost converter turns on and delivers the stored energy from the 3 F input supercapacitor to the 25 F reservoir supercapacitor at the rate of 550 mA (green solid line) for the short duration of 340 ms instantaneously. As soon as the 3 F supercapacitor's voltage (blue solid line) reaches the lower bound of the hysteretic window, the boost converter turns off (purple solid line), and the ambient source starts to charge the 3 F input supercapacitor again up to the upper bound of the hysteretic window.

5.1 Charging Phase

According to the data sheet of the BCAP0350, the leakage current of the 350 F supercapacitor is 0.30 mA, which is measured after 72 hours at 25°C and rated voltage. This means that initially, the leakage current can be much higher than that reported by the data sheet.

To accurately characterize the leakage current of the 350 F supercapacitor, we perform measurement. The average charging current during one charging cycle of 140 seconds is 3.93mA, which is higher than the leakage current of 3.5mA at 2.4V of the 350 F supercapacitor. Therefore, the 350 F reservoir supercapacitor can

also be charged under the low ambient-power source of 1 V/3 mA by the benefit of the proposed hysteretic charging scheme.

Fig. 6(b) delineates the measured leakage current of the 350 F supercapacitor and the average charging current of the hysteretic charging scheme. In this figure, the crossing point of the two lines indicates the maximum charging voltage of the 350 F supercapacitor using the proposed hysteretic charging scheme.

Fig. 6 shows the measured voltage based on the combination of a 3 F input supercapacitor and a 350 F reservoir supercapacitor by the 100 mV hysteresis window. Fig. 6(a) shows the 350 F one that has been charged to 2.0 V after about 4 days. The 350 F reservoir supercapacitor is eventually charged while alternating between a higher charging rate and a lower self-discharging rate. As the voltage of the supercapacitor approaches the maximum chargeable voltage, the leakage current increases rapidly, and therefore the charging rate decreases.

6. CONCLUSIONS AND FUTURE WORK

We have shown the feasibility of our proposed supercapacitor-charging scheme by validating its functions: hysteresis, current delivery, and charging capability. The experimental results show that the proposed scheme can charge supercapacitors of up to 350 F, larger than the upper bound of 2 F in series achieved by all previous COTS chargers at this very low power level (e.g., LTC3625, Linear Technology). As a result, this scheme makes it possible to implement the supercapacitor-based energy harvester under the low ambient power conditions. That is, the proposed scheme enables supercapacitors to be used as a reservoir energy storage element. In short, the proposed charging scheme will enhance the charging ability under the low-power ambient source and improve the charging efficiency.

Future work includes system-level optimizations. The hysteretic window size will be explored to maximize the power-conversion efficiency of the dc-dc converter. Besides, the dedicated MCU of the prototype harvester can be eliminated by either moving its functions to an existing MCU, such as the one on the RMCP node or by adding logic circuitry. Finally, we are planning to install our proposed harvesting system to validate its performance in the short term and eventually deploy an improved design for the long term.

7. REFERENCES

[1] Mohammed Zeki Al-Faiz and Liqaa Saadi Mezher. Cathodic protection remote monitoring based on wireless sensor network. *Wireless Sensor Network*, 4(7):226–233, September 2012.

[2] Davide Brunelli, Clemens Moser, Lothar Thiele, and Luca Benini. Design of a solar-harvesting circuit for batteryless embedded systems. *IEEE Transaction on Circuits and Systems I: Regular Papers*, 56(11):2519–2528, November 2009.

[3] Andy Cranny, Nick R. Harris, Mengyan Nie, Julian A. Wharton, Robert J. K. Wood, and Keith R. Stokes. Sensors for corrosion detection: Measurement of copper ions in 3.5% sodium chloride using screen-printed platinum electrodes. *IEEE Sensors Journal*, 12(6):2091–2099, June 2012.

[4] H. El Ghitani and A. H. Shousha. Design of a solar photovoltaic-powered mini cathodic protection system. *Journal of Applied Energy*, 52(2-3):299–305, September 2000.

[5] Sehwan Kim and Pai H. Chou. Energy harvesting by sweeping voltage-escalated charging of a reconfigurable supercapacitor array. In *Proceedings of International Symposium on Low Power Electronics and Design (ISLPED)*, pages 235–240, Fukuoka, Japan, August 1-3 2011.

[6] Sehwan Kim and Pai H. Chou. Size and topology considerations for supercapacitor-based micro-solar harvesters. *IEEE Transactions on Power Electronics (TPEL)*, 28(4):2068–2080, April 2013.

[7] A. Kumar and L. D. Stephenson. Comparison of wireless technologies for remote monitoring of cathodic protection systems. Technical report, U.S. Army Corps of Engineers, Engineer Research and Development Center Construction Engineering Research Laboratory, Champaign, USA, 2007.

[8] P.R. Mishra, J.C. Joshi, and B. Roy. Design of a solar photovoltaic-powered mini cathodic protection system. *Solar Energy Materials and Solar Cells*, 61(11):383–391, September 2000.

[9] M. Mohitpour, H. Golshan, and A. Murray. *Pipeline Design and Construction: A Practical Approach (3rd Edition)*. American Society of Mechanical Engineers (ASME) PRESS, 2007.

[10] A. W. Peabody. *Peabody's Control of Pipeline Corrosion (2nd Edition)*. Houston, TX, USA, January 2001.

[11] Guofu Qiao, Clemens Moser, Yi Hong, Yuelan Qiu, and Jinping Ou. Remote corrosion monitoring of the RC structures using the electrochemical wireless energy-harvesting sensors and networks. *Journal of NDT&E International*, 44(7):583–588, June 2011.

[12] Douglas P. Rieme. *Modeling cathodic protection for pipeline networks*. PhD thesis, University of Florida, 2000.

[13] Pierre R. Roberge. *Corrosion Engineering: Principles and Practice*. The McGraw-Hill companies, 2008.

[14] Guodong Sun, Guofu Qiao, and Bin Xu. Corrosion monitoring sensor networks with energy harvesting. *IEEE Sensors Journal*, 11(6):1476–1477, June 2011.

[15] Yan Yu, Guofu Qiao, and Jinping Ou. Self-powered wireless corrosion monitoring sensors and networks. *IEEE Sensors Journal*, 10(12):1901–1902, December 2010.

[16] Yan Yu, Guofu Qiao, and Jinping Ou. Optimization design of a corrosion monitoring sensor by fem for rc structures. *IEEE Sensors Journal*, 11(9):2111–2112, September 2011.

[17] Ting Zhu, Yu Gu, Tian He, and Zhi-Li Zhang. eShare: A capacitor-driven energy storage and sharing network for long-term operation. In *Proceedings of the 8th ACM Conference on Embedded Networked Sensor Systems*, pages 239–252, Zurich, Switzerland, November 3-5 2010.

[18] Ting Zhu, Ziguo Zhong, Yu Gu, Tian He, and Zhi-Li Zhang. Leakage-aware energy synchronization for wireless sensor networks. In *Proceedings of the 7th international conference on Mobile systems, applications, and services(MobiSys)*, pages 319–332, Kraków, Poland, June 22-25 2009.

Intelligent Frame Refresh for Energy-Aware Display Subsystems in Mobile Devices

Yongbing Huang[†‡§], Mingyu Chen[†], Lixin Zhang[†], Shihai Xiao[§], Junfeng Zhao[§], Zhulin Wei[§]

[†]State Key Laboratory of Computer Architecture, Institute of Computing Technology, CAS, China
[‡]University of Chinese Academy of Sciences, China
[§]Shannon Laboratory, Huawei Technologies Co., Ltd, China
Email: {huangyongbing, cmy, zhanglixin}@ict.ac.cn {xiaoshihai, junfeng.zhao, weizhulin}@huawei.com

ABSTRACT

Frame refreshes, that are used to retain frame images from frame buffers for display subsystems in mobile devices, waste energy and memory bandwidth. In this paper, we propose an intelligent frame refresh mechanism to reduce redundant frame refreshes and useless data accesses to frame buffers, which bridges the semantic gap between frame buffers and frame refreshes, and exploits the knowledge of frame buffers to guide frame refreshes. Based on this mechanism, we introduce two detailed schemes to optimize refreshes by utilizing different information. The flipping-aware frame refresh scheme uses the frame buffer switching operations to detect frame image updates and triggers useful refreshes. The row-level frame refresh scheme supports to refresh only modified rows instead of the whole frame, under the guidance of pixel status information of frame buffers. Our evaluation results show that our proposed mechanism can reduce memory requests by nearly 50% and memory power consumption up to 30%, compared to conventional fixed frame refresh mechanism.

Categories and Subject Descriptors

C.5 [**Computer System Implementation**]: Miscellaneous; B.4.2 [**Input/Output And Data Communications**]: Input/Output Devices–Image Display; I.3.1 [**Computer Graphics**]: Hardware Architecture

General Terms

Design, Experimentation

Keywords

Mobile Device; LCD; Frame Refresh; Low Power

1. INTRODUCTION

Energy consumption is regarded as a critical issue for battery-operated mobile devices, such as smartphones and

tablets. Among all components of mobile devices, display subsystems such as liquid crystal display (LCD) systems consume more than 50% of total energy [9]. LCD, especially thin-film-transistor (TFT) LCD [4] and its variants such as Super LCD and IPS, are widely used by mainstream mobile device manufacturers. While LCD panels are known to be the most power hungry portion of LCD display subsystems, frame buffers are the next in order of importance. That's because the pixel data stored in frame buffers are periodically read out in order to refresh display frames. The negative effects of frame refreshes become serious as the size of resolution of display panels increase.

Generally, frame refreshes have two purposes, that are to display new frame images and to avoid image flicker on display panels. For TFT LCD, images on the display panel do not flicker, as far as the refresh interval is lower than the discharge time of storage capacitors in TFT pixels. This requirement can be satisfied by a quite low refresh rate. Thus, the refresh rate is mainly determined by the updating frequencies of frame images. However, frame images updates are varied across different applications at different times, and consequently difficult to predict. Conventional LCD controllers periodically refresh frames at a predefined fixed rate (typically 60Hz) triggered by timing logics. Although many existing techniques have been proposed to dynamically adjust frame refresh rates [7], [10], [11], [15], they cannot accurately detect frame updates. Moreover, these techniques do not consider the data accesses to unmodified pixel data in frame buffers. Therefore, existing techniques still waste much energy incurred by useless frame refreshes and memory accesses.

Frame refreshes are mainly used to display the updated frame images contained in frame buffers, but current LCD controllers are not aware of frame buffers. Hence, there exists a semantic gap between LCD controllers and frame buffers. In this paper, we propose an intelligent frame refresh mechanism for LCD display subsystems in mobile devices, that improves energy efficiency by reducing useless frame refreshes and memory accesses, based on the knowledge of frame buffers. The key idea is that frame refresh mechanisms should combine various available information to make intelligent refresh decisions, instead of simple time-driven logics. Note that frame refreshes are demanded mainly because of the change of pixel data stored in the frame buffers, frame buffers could provide rich information to guide refreshes. Two kinds of information about frame buffers are exploited to assist frame refreshes in this paper, which are frame flipping operations and pixel status in frame buffers.

Firstly, most LCDs contain multiple frame buffers in order to improve performance, but only one frame buffer is regarded as the display buffer whose data are shown on the display panel at any time. When the newly updated frames are completely composited in other buffers, frame flipping operations are explicitly executed by runtime systems, which switch the display buffer among multiple buffers. For example, the SurfaceFlinger [3] service in the Android OS [1] is responsible for triggering frame flipping operations. Based on this observation, we introduce a flipping-aware refresh scheme to eliminate useless frame refreshes. Ideally, frame refreshes are triggered to display newly updated frame images, only when frame flipping operations are occurred. Our scheme does not need to distinguish different application types by users or OS. Moreover, to cope with the discharge of storage capacitors for TFT pixels, we enhance this scheme by adopting the timing-based refresh mechanism with a fixed low refresh rate.

Secondly, most displayed frames on the panel are changed smoothly [13], which implies that many pixel data in successive frame buffers may keep the same. But current frame refresh mechanisms read out all pixel data row by row from the display frame buffer for each refresh, and consequently result in large amount of useless data accesses. To alleviate this problem, we introduce a row-level frame refresh scheme, in which memory controllers record the status of all rows in frame buffers and only dirty rows in the display buffer are read out during frame refreshes. This scheme can be implemented with negligible hardware overhead, just by adding simple registers and signals in the row driver logic of display panels.

Our evaluation results show that flipping-aware refresh scheme can eliminate useless frame refreshes by 70% and memory requests by more than 52% for some applications in the Moby benchmark suite [14], even when we simulate a LCD with middle size and resolution. For frame flipping operations, only 50% of rows in the display buffer are modified on average. Thus, row-level refresh scheme further reduces useless memory accesses by 15%. Totally, the power consumed on memory can be reduced up to 30% by putting two proposed schemes together. As the size and resolution of mobile devices increase, our mechanism can reduce more power consumption on frame buffers.

This paper is organized as follows. Section 2 reviews some backgrounds about LCD frame refreshes, including their negative effects and frameworks. Section 3 introduces our proposed frame refresh mechanism and two detailed refresh schemes. Then, evaluation environment and results are illustrated in Section 4. Finally, we describe related work in Section 5 and conclusion in Section 6.

2. BACKGROUND

2.1 Memory Behavior of Mobile Applications

In order to study the memory behaviors presented by mobile applications, we characterize the memory access counts for the whole memory address space. Figure 1 depicts the memory access distribution of an Android web-browser benchmark BBench [12], at the granularity of 4KB page. We observe that a small portion of memory address space accounts for more than 60% of total memory read accesses. This por-

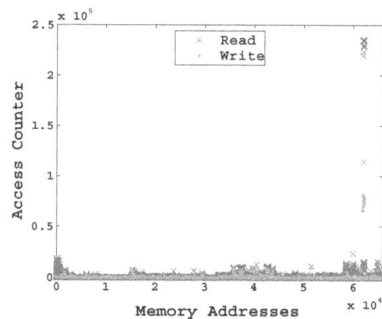

Figure 1: Memory access distribution of BBench. The small frame buffers attribute to large amounts of memory requests.

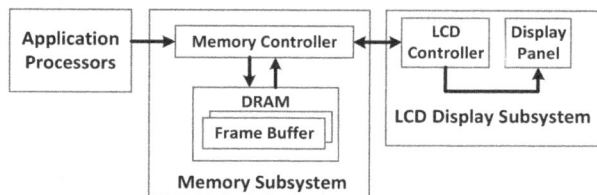

Figure 2: Conventional LCD display framework.

tion of memory address space belongs to the frame buffers used by the LCD panel. These large amounts of memory accesses will result in large power consumption, as well as interference with running applications.

Frame buffers, which store the data that drive the pixels on the panel, are read periodically by the LCD controllers. For example, for a FullHD panel ($1920 \times 1080 \times 24bpp$) with 60Hz refresh rate, more than 40 million memory requests per second [13] are issued. Therefore, there is a desire to optimize the conventional frame refresh mechanism.

2.2 LCD Frame Refresh Framework

Figure 2 illustrates the conventional LCD display framework, which consists of application processors, frame buffers in memory subsystem, LCD controller and display panel. Runtime systems in the application processors generate frame images and store them in the frame buffers. The LCD controller executes frame refresh operations triggered by refresh logics, and then issues data requests to access frame buffers, whose data will be displayed on the panel.

Frame refreshes are used to avoid frame image flicker, as well as display newly updated frame images. Conventional LCD controller utilizes simple time-driven refresh logics to generate refresh signals just according to given refresh rates. For each frame refresh operation, the LCD panel is updated row by row until all the rows are refilled, which is controlled by the row driver. The data driver of LCD panel reads the pixel data one by one for a whole row, and flushes them into their pixel circuits simultaneously [19].

2.3 Multiple Buffer Management

Multiple frame buffers are commonly supported by current LCDs in order to improve performance and prevent onscreen flickering. At any one time, only one buffer is regarded as display buffer whose data are displayed on the panel, and other buffers are draw buffers used to composite frame images.

Taking double buffers as an example, Figure 3 shows the frame buffer management in Android OS. A surface in An-

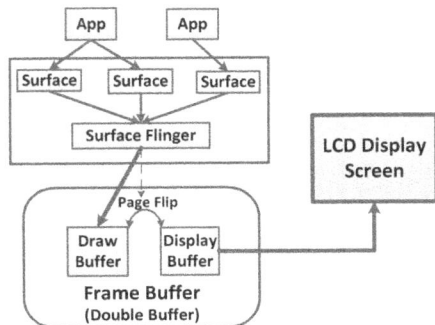

Figure 3: Double frame buffer management for Android OS.

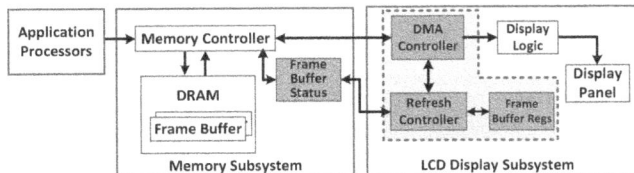

Figure 4: The framework of intelligent frame refresh mechanism.

droid, which has its position, size, content, corresponds to an off screen buffer into which application renders its content. Each application may own one or more surfaces. SurfaceFlinger is a system-wide surface composer in Android framework. It takes different surfaces from different applications and finally combine them into a main surface which will be fed to frame buffers. When the draw buffers are ready for display, SurfaceFlinger will switch buffer explicitly, which is called frame flipping operations in our paper. The frame change speed directly determines the frequency of frame flipping operations. Thus, the frame flipping operations can indicate the requirement of frame refreshes used for displaying updated frame images on the display panel.

3. INTELLIGENT FRAME REFRESH MECHANISM

Frame refreshes are mainly used to display the updated frame images contained in frame buffers, but are triggered by timing-driven refresh logics in current LCD controllers without being aware of frame buffers. Hence, there exists a semantic gap between LCD controllers and frame buffers. The main idea of our intelligent frame refresh mechanism is to bridge this semantic gap by making the LCD refresh controllers be aware of the information of frame buffers. Frame refresh decisions should be made upon as much available information as possible, instead of simple time-driven logics. In this section, we first introduce the framework of the intelligent frame refresh mechanism. Then, based on this mechanism, we illustrate two detailed refresh schemes that exploit different information to reduce useless refreshes and useless data accesses to frame buffers.

3.1 Framework

Figure 4 depicts the framework of our proposed intelligent frame refresh mechanism, mainly involving the frame buffer status module in memory subsystem, frame buffer registers, refresh and DMA controllers. Note that frame buffers are essentially a portion of main memory, their behaviors are detected by the memory controller and recorded in the frame

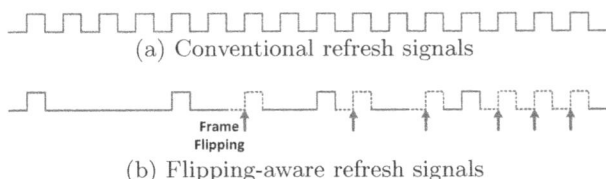

(a) Conventional refresh signals

(b) Flipping-aware refresh signals

Figure 5: Frame refresh signals. The frame flipping triggered frame refreshes can display the updated frame images on the panel in time.

buffer status module. This module can record the buffer operations at the granularity of buffer, row, or pixel. The frame buffer registers are used to indicate memory addresses of the display frame buffer. The refresh controller not only contains conventional time-driven refresh logics, but also receives information from other components such as the frame buffer status module and the frame buffer registers.

Basically, display panels are refreshed at a low fixed rate to avoid image flicker, generated by the time-driven refresh logics. When receiving the frame buffer behavior information, the refresh controller has to combine these information and decide whether frame refreshes are required or not. If so, it will notify the DMA controller to generate memory requests to access frame buffers. Moreover, unlike conventional DMA controllers which access the whole frame buffer in default, the DMA controller in Figure 4 can refer to the refresh controller to only issue necessary memory requests.

In the implementation, additional effort should be put into the information transmission from the frame buffer status module to the refresh controller. One feasible method is to allocate a small part of physical memory for the frame buffer status module, which can be accessed by the refresh controller using DMA operations. This method is efficient only when not too much information are transferred. For large amount of information, we can improve our framework by migrating some modules, such as the modules in the dashed box shown in Figure 4, from the LCD controller into the memory controller. As memory controllers and LCD controllers are integrated in the same SoC for many mobile platforms such as ARM Cortex-A9 platforms [2], above module migration is applicable with small hardware overheads.

3.2 Flipping-Aware Refresh Scheme

Note that the refresh rate is determined by the frame update speed, frame refresh mechanisms with low fixed refresh rate may not display the updated frame images in time. But high fixed refresh rate might result in useless refreshes, when frame images are not changed. Useless refreshes can be eliminated if we are able to capture the frame updates accurately. As illustrated in Section 2.3, frame updates are indicated by frame flipping operations, which can be detected by monitoring the frame buffer registers.

Based on the intelligent refresh framework, we propose a flipping-aware refresh scheme, in which frame refreshes are triggered by frame flipping operations, as well as the refresh logics with a fixed low refresh rate. By making use of frame flipping operations, frame updates can be accurately detected with little overhead. Runtime system or OS or hardware are no longer needed to study the frame behaviors of different applications, in order to predict the suitable refresh rates.

Figure 5 shows an example of the difference between conventional refresh mechanism and the flipping-aware refresh

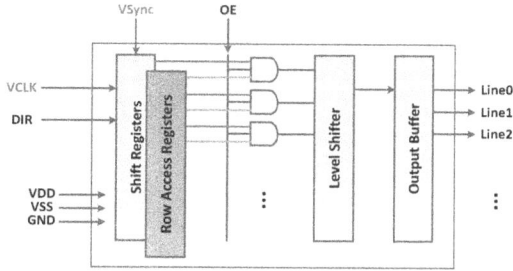

Figure 6: The block diagram of LCD's row driver architecture for row-level refresh scheme.

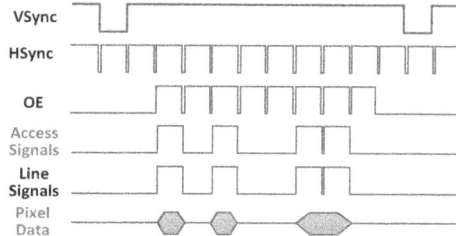

Figure 7: An example of timing diagram of row-level refresh scheme.

Table 1: Simulation Configuration

Core	2 OoO ARM cores, 1.2GHz
Cache	L1-I/D Cache: 32KB, private, 4-way
	L2 Cache: 512KB, shared, 16-way
Memory	256MB LPDDR2, 1066MHz
LCD	Resolution: 800 × 480 × 16bpp
	Frame buffer numbers: 2
	Controller: ARM PL111 [5]
OS	Android Ice Cream Sandwich 4.0.4

scheme from the point of refresh signals. For conventional refresh mechanism, signals are transmitted at high and fixed rate, such as 60Hz. For flipping-aware refresh scheme, there are two parts of refresh signals: fixed signals with low rate, and dynamical frame flipping signals. The frame flipping signals are closely related to the frame image features for different applications. Generally, the frequency of frame flipping signals is low, compared to 60Hz. For example, the frame images of a video player are updated frequently, about 30 frames per second; but only 10Hz refresh rate may be sufficient for text applications [15].

3.3 Row-Level Refresh Scheme

As illustrated in Section 2.2, TFT-LCDs refresh their frame images by scanning across the whole panel line by line, and pixel by pixel. For each frame refresh, all the pixel data are read out from the frame buffer, no matter whether the content of pixels are modified. Actually, most successive frame images are often changed smoothly, which implies that many pixel data keep the same and these pixels are not required to be refreshed. Therefore, there exist many useless data accesses even in useful frame refreshes.

In the intelligent frame refresh mechanism, the frame buffer status module shown in Figure 4 is able to monitor the status of each pixel, each row or each frame. Ideally, for each frame refresh, our mechanism supports to send only modified pixel data to LCD display panels. This method can eliminate all useless data accesses. However, there are two limits for its implementation. On one hand, the data drive logics are designed to write all pixels for each row simultaneously, in order to improve write efficiency and reduce power consumption. Writing only a specified pixel has to increase the complexity of drive logics. On the other hand, the buffer used to store the pixel data status should be quite large, as the size and resolution of display panels increase.

Considering both potential benefits and hardware overhead, we propose row-level refresh scheme, which monitors the status of frame buffers at the row granularity, and refreshes only modified rows. When frame refreshes are hap-

pened, the refresh controller obtains the information of the frame buffer status module, and guides the DMA controller to generate memory requests to access only those pixel data for the modified rows in the display buffer.

Figure 6 illustrates the block diagram of row driver logics for our row-level refresh scheme. The shift registers control the row number to be refreshed; the level shifter and output buffer generate corresponding line signals that used to drive data logics; the output enable (OE) signal can enable or disable line signals [16]. If the line signal is disabled, all the pixel circuits belonging to current row are closed and therefore no data can be written into them. Based on above row drive logics, we only add row access registers to store row status and generate access signals, and additional logic gates. Typically, row access registers contain bitmaps indicating whether the row is modified or not. These bitmaps can be read out from the frame buffer status module through DMA requests. Since the size of bitmap is small at row granularity, e.g., 100 bytes for display devices with 800 rows, filling the row access registers only result in several read requests. Hence, the hardware overhead is quite small. The access signal is quite similar with the OE signal. If current row is not modified, the access signal generated by row access registers would disable the line signal, as shown in Figure 7. For this kind of rows, pixel data are not required. Therefore, these useless memory accesses to frame buffers are avoided.

4. EVALUATION

4.1 Evaluation Setup

We use the gem5 [8] simulation infrastructure for all of our analysis. All results were obtained by simulating the RealView platform for ARM Cortex-A9 [6]. The baseline configuration of simulated platform is shown in Table 1. We run the Android Ice Cream Sandwich (ICS) operating system on the simulated ARM-based mobile platform. The resolution of the LCD display panel we choose is 800 × 480 pixels. Many high-end mobile devices may be equipped with high resolution panel 5x higher, which stands for larger frame buffers and more data accesses for frame refreshes. The memory power is calculated using the Micron Power Calculator [20].

As for experimental workloads, we use the Moby benchmark suite [14], which contains 10 different kinds of applications, such as web browser applications, document processing programs, video players and games. Each application only executes one typical operations which last for several seconds. Table 2 shows the summary of applications in Moby, including their typical operations and inputs. The diversity of these applications can present different change speed of frame images.

Table 2: Summary of Moby Benchmark Suite

Bench	Category	Typical OP	Input
BBench	Web Browser	Load web pages	Web pages
K9Mail	Email	Load/Show emails	Buffered emails
SinaWeibo	Social Network	Load information	Buffered texts
Netease	News	Check and load news	Buffered news
KingsoftOffice	Document	Open doc/xls/ppt file	A doc file
Adobe	Document	Open pdf file	A PDF file
BaiduMap	Map	Load an area's map	Buffered maps
MXPlayer	Video	Play a video	A video file
TTPod	Audio	Play a song	A music file
FrozenBubble	Game	Load game	Null

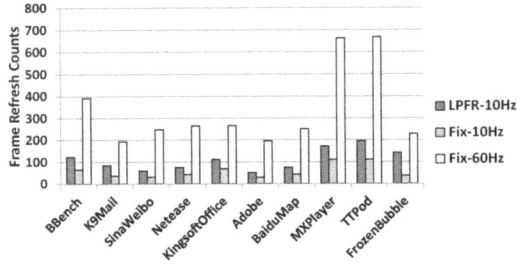

Figure 8: The reduction of frame refreshes using LPFR-10Hz scheme.

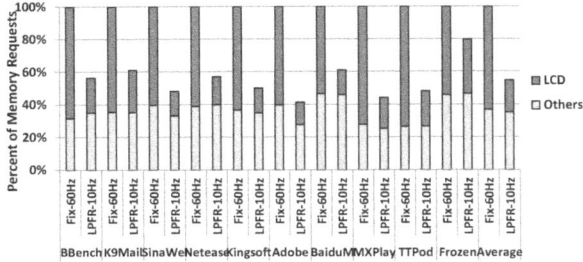

Figure 9: The reduction of memory requests using LPFR-10Hz scheme.

4.2 Experimental Results

In this subsection, we evaluate the performance of the following refresh mechanism: 1) the conventional mechanism using fixed 60Hz refresh rate (Fix-60Hz), 2) the flipping-aware refresh scheme (LPFR), and 3) both flipping-aware and row-level refresh scheme (SLFR). The fixed low refresh rate used to avoid frame image flicker is set to 10Hz for LPFR (LPFR-10Hz) and SLFR (SLFR-10Hz) scheme in our experiments. Since the discharge time of TFT LCD's storage capacitor must be longer than 0.1s, we could further decrease this fixed refresh rate.

4.2.1 Frame Refreshes

Figure 8 illustrates the number of frame refreshes executed by Moby applications using fixed refresh scheme and flipping-aware refresh scheme. When compared to Fix-60Hz, LPFR-10Hz can reduce the frame refresh by nearly 70% for applications such as Sinaweibo, Adobe, MXPlayer and TTPod. But for the game application FrozenBubble, which changes its frame images frequently, only about 28% of frame refreshes are avoided.

4.2.2 Memory Requests

Figure 9 shows the total memory requests received by the memory controller. The memory requests issued by LCD are distinguished from other requests, which mainly come

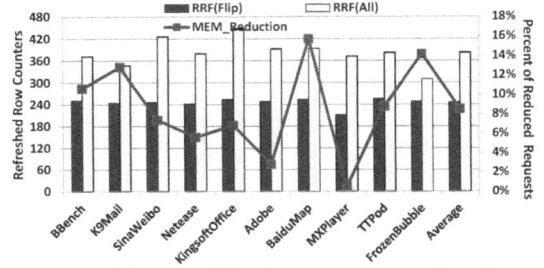

Figure 10: The modified row counts for frame refreshes, and the reduction of memory requests incurred by SLFR-10Hz compared to LPFR-10Hz.

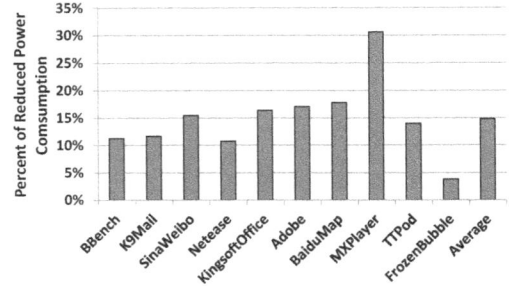

Figure 11: Memory power reduction using SLFR-10Hz scheme compared to fixed 60Hz refresh scheme.

from processors. We observe that most mobile applications are memory non-intensive. If we refresh the display panel at fixed 60Hz, more than 60% of memory requests on average access frame buffers which are issued by the LCD controller. On one hand, so many LCD requests will result in high energy consumption. On the other hand, so many regular DMA requests may compete critical memory resources with processors, and therefore degrade applications' performance. Our LPFR scheme can reduce data accesses to frame buffers by maximum 52% and average 44%.

4.2.3 SLFR vs. LPFR

Figure 10 further depicts the number of modified rows for updated frame buffers. RRF(Flip) stands for the number of modified rows per frame for frame-flipping triggered frame refreshes, and RRF(All) stands for the average number for all frame refreshes. For those frame refreshes triggered by frame-flipping, only about 240 rows are modified on average, which are half of LCD display panel's size. If we access the whole frame under this situation, at least half of memory requests can be regarded as useless. Our SLFR scheme can eliminate those memory requests belonging to useless rows, and on average another 8% of total memory requests are reduced based on the LPFR scheme.

4.2.4 Power Consumption

Figure 11 shows the reduced memory power using our proposed two refresh schemes. On average, SLFR-10Hz saves up to 30% of the energy compared to the Fix-60Hz refresh mechanism. Note that the size and resolution of LCD's display panel we choose in our experiments is small, the benefits of memory power reduction are limited. The number of useless memory requests generated in frame refreshes, which our proposed schemes can reduce, are proportional to the size and resolution of display panel. Therefore, our intelligent refresh mechanism can save more energy for larger size and resolution display panels.

5. RELATED WORK

Many researches are done to reduce LCD power consumption from the aspects of display technologies, pixel circuits, and refresh logics. As for frame buffer, previous techniques also focus on optimizing refresh rates, and data accesses.

Refresh Rate: Choi et al. [10] introduced a variable duty-ratio refresh technique, which controlled frame refreshes by setting different refresh duties. Gatti et al. [11] proposed to adjust refresh rates or even disable refreshes by applications or OS using the registers provided by LCDs. However, both of them did not give more details on how to choose suitable refresh rates. Kim et al. [15] classified applications into high-quality images or low-quality texts according to the contents in frame buffers and changed refresh rates for different types of applications.

Data Access: Patel et al. [17] exploited the spatial locality to avoid data read from frame buffer when identical adjacent pixels are detected. Shim et al. [18] adopted compression scheme to reduce the data transformation between frame buffers and LCD controllers. Han et al. [13] proposed a hybrid phase change memory and DRAM frame buffer architecture, which utilized PCM to reduce read power consumption.

6. CONCLUSION

The frame buffers of display subsystems attribute to considerable power consumption for mobile devices. In this paper, we propose an intelligent frame refresh mechanism, that aims at improving energy efficiency of display subsystems by reducing useless frame refreshes and data accesses to frame buffers. The intelligent frame refresh mechanism bridges the semantic gap between frame refresh logics and frame buffers, by utilizing the rich information of frame buffers to assist frame refreshes. By utilizing the frame buffer switching operations and pixel status for frame buffers, we introduce flipping-aware refresh scheme and row-level refresh scheme, respectively. Flipping-aware refresh scheme explores the frame flipping operations to actively trigger useful frame refreshes for frame image updates, which reduces the useless refreshes incurred by conventional refresh schemes using fixed high refresh rates. Using the row status information of frame buffers, row-level refresh scheme supports to refresh only modified rows in the display panel with negligible hardware overhead. Our evaluation results show that our proposed two schemes can save up to 30% of memory power consumption.

7. ACKNOWLEDGMENTS

We would like to thank Yungang Bao, Zehan Cui, and other teammates from ICT, and the anonymous reviewers for helpful suggestions and insightful feedback. This research is supported by the National Basic Research Program of China (973 Program) under the grant number 2011CB302502, the National Natural Science Foundation of China (NSFC) under the grant number 61272132 and 61221062, the Strategic Priority Research Program of the Chinese Academy of Sciences under the grant number XDA06010401, and the Huawei Research Program under the grant number Y-BCB2011030.

8. REFERENCES

[1] Android operating sytem for mobile devices. http://www.android.com.

[2] ARM Cortex A9. http://www.arm.com/products/processors/cortex-a/cortex-a9.php.

[3] Android graphics. https://source.android.com/devices/graphics.html, 2014.

[4] Thin-film-transistor liquid-crystal display. http://en.wikipedia.org/wiki/TFT-LCD, 2014.

[5] ARM. Primecell color LCD controller technical reference manual.

[6] ARM. Realview platform baseboard explore for Cortex-A9 user guide, 2011.

[7] A. K. Bhowmik and R. J. Brennan. System-level display power reduction technologies for portable computing and communications devices. In *Proc. IEEE Int. Conf. Portable Information Devices*, pages 1–5, 2007.

[8] N. Binkert, B. Beckmann, G. Black, S. K. Reinhardt, A. Saidi, A. Basu, J. Hestness, D. R. Hower, T. Krishna, S. Sardashti, et al. The gem5 simulator. *ACM SIGARCH Computer Architecture News*, 39(2):1–7, 2011.

[9] A. Carroll and G. Heiser. An analysis of power consumption in a smartphone. In *Proceedings of the USENIX conference on USENIX annual technical conference*, pages 21–21, 2010.

[10] I. Choi, H. Shim, and N. Chang. Low-power color TFT LCD display for hand-held embedded systems. In *Proceedings of the International Symposium on Low Power Electronics and Design*, pages 112–117. IEEE, 2002.

[11] F. Gatti, A. Acquaviva, L. Benini, and B. Ricco. Low power control techniques for TFT LCD displays. In *Proceedings of the International conference on Compilers, Architecture, and Synthesis for Embedded Systems*, pages 218–224. ACM, 2002.

[12] A. Gutierrez, R. G. Dreslinski, T. F. Wenisch, T. Mudge, A. Saidi, C. Emmons, and N. Paver. Full-system analysis and characterization of interactive smartphone applications. In *IEEE International Symposium on Workload Characterization*, pages 81–90. IEEE, 2011.

[13] K. Han, A. W. Min, N. S. Jeganathan, and P. S. Diefenbaugh. A hybrid display frame buffer architecture for energy efficient display subsystems. In *International Symposium on Low Power Electronics and Design*, pages 347–353. IEEE, 2013.

[14] Y. Huang, Z. Zha, M. Chen, and L. Zhang. Moby: A mobile benchmark suite for architectural simulators. In *IEEE International Symposium on Performance Analysis of Systems and Software*. IEEE, 2014.

[15] H. Kim, H. Cha, and R. Ha. Dynamic refresh-rate scaling via frame buffer monitoring for power-aware LCD management. *Software: Practice and Experience*, 37(2):193–206, 2007.

[16] I. Pappas, S. Siskos, and C. A. Dimitriadis. Active-matrix liquid crystal displays-operation, electronics and analog circuits design. 2009.

[17] K. Patel, E. Macii, and M. Poncino. Frame buffer energy optimization by pixel prediction. In *IEEE International Conference on Computer Design: VLSI in Computers and Processors*, pages 98–101. IEEE, 2005.

[18] H. Shim, N. Chang, and M. Pedram. A compressed frame buffer to reduce display power consumption in mobile systems. In *Proceedings of the Asia and South Pacific Design Automation Conference*, pages 818–823. IEEE Press, 2004.

[19] Y.-H. Tai. Design and operation of TFT-LCD panels. *Wu-Nan Culture Enterprise*, 3:97–100, 2006.

[20] M. Technology. Calculating memory system power for LPDDR2, 2009.

Powering the Internet of Things[*]

Hrishikesh Jayakumar, Kangwoo Lee, Woo Suk Lee, Arnab Raha,
Younghyun Kim, and Vijay Raghunathan
School of Electrical and Computer Engineering, Purdue University
{hjayakum, lee1000, lee992, araha, yhkim1, vr}@purdue.edu

ABSTRACT

Various industry forecasts project that, by 2020, there will be around 50 billion devices connected to the Internet of Things (IoT), helping to engineer new solutions to societal-scale problems such as healthcare, energy conservation, transportation, *etc.* Most of these devices will be wireless due to the expense, inconvenience, or in some cases, the sheer infeasibility of wiring them. Further, many of them will have stringent size constraints. With no cord for power and limited space for a battery, powering these devices (to achieve several months to possibly years of unattended operation) becomes a daunting challenge. This paper highlights some promising directions for addressing this challenge, focusing on three main building blocks: (a) the design of ultra-low power hardware platforms that integrate computing, sensing, storage, and wireless connectivity in a tiny form factor, (b) the development of intelligent system-level power management techniques, and (c) the use of environmental energy harvesting to make IoT devices self-powered, thus decreasing – in some cases, even eliminating – their dependence on batteries. We discuss these building blocks in detail and illustrate case-studies of systems that use them judiciously, including the QUBE wireless embedded platform, which exploits the characteristics of emerging non-volatile memory technologies to seamlessly and efficiently enable long-running computations in systems that experience frequent power loss (*i.e.*, intermittently powered systems).

Categories and Subject Descriptors

C.3 [**Computer Systems Organization**]: Special-purpose and application-based systems—*Real-time and embedded systems, Microprocessor/microcomputer applications*

Keywords

Internet of Things; Low Power; Power Management; Energy Harvesting; Perpetual Systems; Wearable Computing

[*]This research was supported in part by the National Science Foundation (NSF) through grant CCF-1018358.

1. INTRODUCTION

It is projected that, by 2020, there will be around 50 billion smart objects connected to the Internet of Things (more than six times the world's projected population at the time), making the IoT one of the fastest-growing technologies across all of computing [24]. These smart objects will pervade all aspects of our daily lives and fundamentally alter the way we interact with our physical environment, thereby revolutionizing a number of application domains such as telemetry, healthcare, home automation, energy conservation, security, wearable computing, asset tracking, maintenance of public infrastructure, *etc.*, as shown in Figure 1.

One of the biggest challenges to realizing this IoT vision is the problem of powering these tens of billions of IoT devices. Most of these devices will be battery-powered for reasons of cost, convenience, or the need for untethered operation. Despite tight constraints on size and, hence, battery capacity, many IoT devices will be required to have long operational lifetimes (from a few days to possibly several years) without the need for battery replacement, because frequent battery replacement at scale is not only expensive, but often not even feasible. The battery-powered nature of IoT devices also has significant environmental implications. For example, the Environment Protection Agency reports that more than 3 billion batteries are discarded in the USA every year and that, placed end to end, discarded AA batteries would circle the earth six times. The rapid proliferation of IoT devices will only exacerbate this problem, making the need to address it an urgent priority.

This paper highlights some promising directions for addressing this challenge and makes a case for focusing on three main building blocks: (a) the design of ultra-low power hardware platforms that integrate computing, sensing, storage, and wireless connectivity in a tiny form factor, (b) the development of intelligent system-level power management techniques that allow an IoT device to adjust its power consumption in a context-aware manner, and (c) the use of environmental energy harvesting to make IoT devices self-powered, thus decreasing - in some cases, even eliminating - their dependence on batteries. These building blocks are illustrated using examples of IoT devices, including the QUBE wireless platform, which exploits the characteristics of emerging non-volatile memory technologies to seamlessly and efficiently enable long-running computations in systems that have an intermittent and unreliable power supply.

It is important to recognize that IoT devices have very diverse power requirements and longevity requirements, which have a profound influence on how they are designed. One group of devices, henceforth referred to as *Type I* devices,

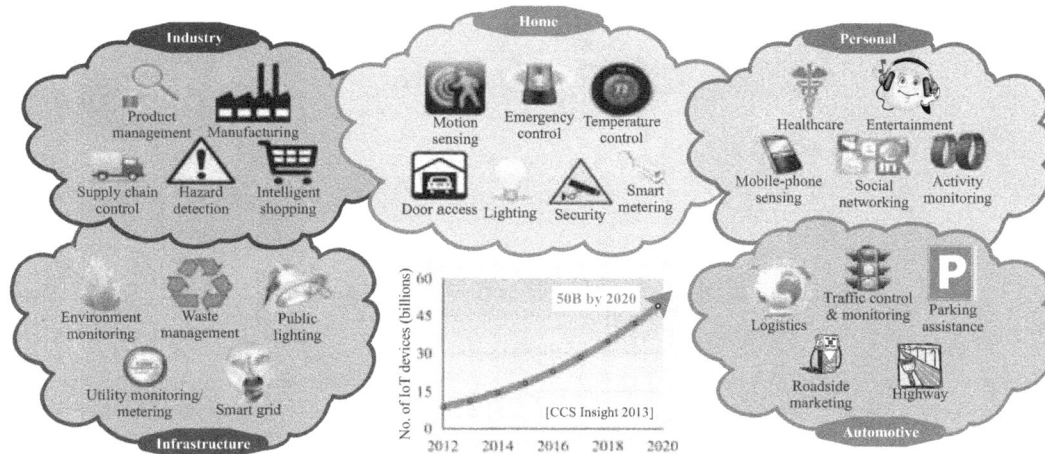

Figure 1: An overview of the envisioned applications and growth forecast for the Internet of Things.

are wearable devices (*e.g.,* smartwatches, fitness monitors, connected glasses), which have a longevity requirement of several days because a user is likely to own only a few such devices and can recharge them regularly, particularly with the advent of wireless charging technologies. A second group of devices, henceforth referred to as *Type II* devices, are set-and-forget devices (*e.g.,* home security and automation sensors, water leak sensors) that a user wants to deploy and then not tinker with for several (5 to 10) years. A user is likely to own dozens of such devices, therefore frequent battery replacement would be very inconvenient and hamper the user experience. A third group of devices, henceforth referred to as *Type III* devices, are semi-permanent devices (*e.g.,* wireless sensors that monitor public infrastructure such as bridges, highways, and parking structures), where the device is installed and needs to operate for more than a decade. The scale of these devices makes frequent battery replacement simply infeasible. A fourth group of devices, henceforth referred to as *Type IV* devices, are batteryless and passively powered (*e.g.,* RFID tags, smartcards), drawing their power from an external source such as a tag reader. Finally, a fifth group of devices, henceforth referred to as *Type V* devices, are powered appliances (*e.g.,* smart refrigerators, microwaves) that will always be plugged into a power outlet, eliminating the need for a battery.

2. LOW POWER HARDWARE FOR THE IOT

The most effective way to improve the battery life of an IoT device is to decrease the power consumed by its constituent hardware components. Even in IoT devices such as *Driblet* [3] and *SPAN* [10] that are powered through energy harvesting (discussed in Section 3), it is imperative to use low-power hardware to achieve near-perpetual operation. It is useful to note that many IoT devices are architecturally similar to wireless sensor node platforms [25, 45] and low power design techniques used for these platforms are equally applicable to the design of IoT devices [21, 49]. The following subsections discuss recent advances in low-power hardware for the computation and communication subsystems of an IoT device, respectively.

2.1 Computation Subsystem

Microcontrollers (MCUs) are at the heart of every embedded system that interfaces to (and interacts with) the real world, including IoT devices. As described in Section 1, many of these systems need to operate unattended for several years without the need for battery replacement [43, 46]. Achieving such long operational lifetime requires extreme levels of energy efficiency. Fortunately, many sensing applications operate in a heavily duty-cycled mode, wherein the system is active only for very short bursts of time (often, only milliseconds) separated by long idle intervals (often, many tens of seconds) during which the system can be placed in a low-power, sleep mode. Since the system spends greater than 90% of its time in the sleep mode, the cumulative energy spent in this mode is often the bottleneck for battery lifetime. Therefore, it is important to select an MCU that has a very low power consumption in idle state in addition to being power efficient during active computation.

To minimize idle-mode power consumption, most MCUs feature multiple low power (or sleep) modes. For example, the STM32L1 series of MCUs (based on the ARM Cortex M3 core) supports up to 7 different sleep modes. The sleep modes found in MCUs are of two types. The first is a shallow sleep mode, in which the MCU core is stopped, peripherals are disabled, and clock sources are turned off. However, the MCU stays powered up, which means that state information (consisting of the MCU registers and the contents of on-chip SRAM) is preserved during sleep. Although waking up from shallow sleep is very fast, it is (as expected) not the lowest power sleep mode possible. HYPNOS [33] addresses this problem based on the observation that the minimum voltage required for SRAM data retention is often much lower (by as much as 10x) than the minimum operating voltage of the MCU. By lowering the supply voltage when the MCU is in sleep mode to just above the SRAM data retention voltage, HYPNOS achieves dramatic reductions in sleep mode power.

The second type of sleep mode is deep sleep, in which the entire MCU, including the on-chip SRAM, is powered down. While this results in the lowest power consumption possible during sleep, it does not preserve SRAM state. Therefore, the contents of the SRAM need to be saved to non-volatile storage such as the on-chip Flash of the MCU before entering this mode. When the MCU wakes up next, the saved state is restored from the Flash to the SRAM and the MCU resumes execution. Unfortunately, due to the high erase/write time and power of Flash, the energy overhead of saving and restoring state is substantial. Recent work [32] to address this problem uses emerging non-volatile memory (NVM) technologies such as magnetoresistive RAM (MRAM) [37]

Processors and MCUs (Freq = 8 MHz)				Wireless Standards				Sensors			
Product	Architecture Family	Current Active (mA)	Sleep (μA)	Standard (Product)	Tx (mA)	Rx (mA)	Sleep (μA)	Sensor	Product	Current Active (μA)	Sleep (μA)
MSP430F5438A	MSP430	1.84	0.1	WiFi (TI CC3200)	229	59	4	Temperature	TMP102	85	0.5
STM32L051x6	ARM CM0+	1.55	0.29					Humidity	SHT21	300	0.15
STM32L100C6	ARM CM3	2.16	0.3	IEEE 802.15.4 (Atmel AT86RF231)	14	12.3	0.02	Accelerometer	ADXL362	13	0.01
SAM4S	ARM CM4	4.5	1.8					Light	ISL29033	65	0.01
PIC24FJ128GC010	PIC	1.5	0.075	Bluetooth Smart (Nordic nRF8001)	12.7	14.6	0.5	Proximity	AD7150	100	1

Table 1: Power consumption of a few representative hardware components used in IoT devices (sourced from datasheets).

or ferroelectric RAM (FRAM) [26]. These memories combine the flexibility and endurance of SRAM with the non-volatility of Flash, all at a very low power consumption. Low power MCUs with these emerging NVMs integrated are already available [48, 61]. In these MCUs, software can save the processor state and the contents of SRAM to the NVM before the MCU enters sleep mode, avoiding the need for keeping the SRAM powered during sleep. Building on this idea, recent research has led to the emergence of a new class of processors called non-volatile processors [35, 53]. In these processors, NVM memory elements are distributed throughout the MCU such that it can *automatically* save the contents of all the registers in these NVM elements before it is shutdown, resulting in a (nearly) zero-power sleep mode with state retention and rapid wakeup.

Minimizing power consumption in active mode has been extensively investigated for the past few decades and numerous techniques such as dynamic voltage and frequency scaling (DVFS), voltage islands, *etc.*, have been proposed and shown to be effective in reducing power consumption. Continued voltage scaling has led to the emergence of near-threshold and subthreshold processors [17, 58] that aim to operate at an optimal energy point. For example, the Phoenix processor [29] is an event-driven subthreshold processor that has an sleep power consumption of only 30 pW. The use of such ultra-low power MCUs, if applicable, will provide a significant boost to the battery life of IoT devices.

Table 1 shows the active-mode and sleep-mode power consumption of a few off-the-shelf hardware components (including MCUs, radios, and sensors) that are commonly used in IoT devices. As seen, most of these hardware components feature highly power-efficient sleep modes in which the power consumption is decreased by several orders of magnitude compared to the active mode.

2.2 Communication Subsystem

The IoT concept fundamentally depends on the fact that devices will communicate either directly with each other or with a cloud-based service accessible through the Internet. Hence, reliable wireless communication is an integral component of any IoT device. Typically, wireless communication is more power-hungry than other tasks such as sensing or computation. In addition, different types of IoT devices have different communication requirements depending on their deployment locations, longevity constraints, traffic patterns, *etc.* Therefore, choosing an appropriate wireless technology that is power-efficient is a vital design choice.

Despite its relatively high power consumption, WiFi is the preferred wireless standard for many IoT applications due to its near-ubiquitous nature – WiFi hotspots are present in most homes, offices, and public spaces – and the fact that it

enables convenient and straightforward access to the Internet. Advances in wireless communication have also seen the development of numerous low power wireless standards such as Bluetooth Smart, IEEE 802.15.4, *etc.* The IEEE 802.15.4 standard targets low data rate applications (*e.g.*, remote monitoring and control systems) and defines the physical and medium access control layers upon which the Zigbee and 6LoWPAN network stacks are built. The standard allows for multi-hop wireless topologies and several power-efficient IEEE 802.15.4 compliant radios are commercially available. However, one disadvantage of using IEEE 802.15.4 for IoT applications, compared to WiFi, is the need for an additional gateway device to achieve Internet access (if required). Particularly for *Type II* IoT devices, it is difficult to converge on the use of a single wireless standard due to the varying nature of applications as well as the large number of product vendors involved. Hence, it is likely that future smart homes will use IoT hubs such as *Revolv* [9] or *Ninja Spheramid* [11] that support a variety of wireless standards such as WiFi, Bluetooth Smart, Zigbee, Z-Wave, Insteon, *etc.* In addition to existing wireless standards, innovative approaches such as using the existing powerline wiring in the home as an antenna have also been proposed [12].

Bluetooth Smart is an enhanced version of the well-known Bluetooth standard that was designed for low power communication [16]. Bluetooth-based IoT devices, such as *Estimote Beacon* [23], *Lively* [41], *tado Cooling* [56], *etc.*, can directly communicate with smartphones, which are already Bluetooth-equipped. This is a key advantage that will likely cement Bluetooth Smart's position as the wireless standard of choice for IoT devices that need to frequently communicate with mobile devices such as smartphones and tablets.

Other IoT applications such as manufacturing and asset tracking could use RFID-based communication. Passive RFID technology allows devices such as batteryless smart tags to operate using power harvested from a nearby reader's RF transmissions. Recent work [40] proposed the idea of ambient backscatter, a novel technique that allows two batteryless devices to communicate with each other by backscattering existing wireless signals from TV stations and cellular transmissions. Although the technique is mainly intended for low throughput applications, it is a significant step forward because it enables tiny IoT devices to exchange small amounts of information without the need for a battery or a nearby RFID reader.

3. SELF-POWERED SYSTEMS USING ENERGY HARVESTING

Over the past decade, energy harvesting has emerged as an attractive and increasingly feasible option to address the

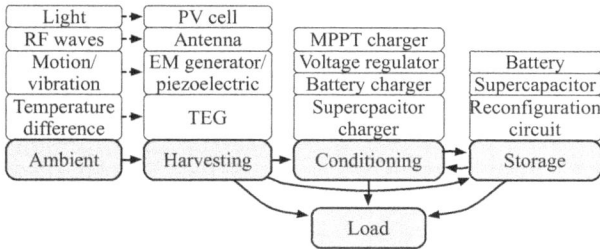

Figure 2: The power supply subsystem of an energy-harvesting IoT device.

power supply challenge in a variety of low power systems. The use of energy harvesting significantly prolongs overall system lifetime and has the potential to result in self-powered, perpetual system operation, particularly for *Type II* and *Type III* IoT devices. Figure 2 shows the power supply subsystem of an energy harvesting device. In this section, we discuss recent advances in the design of each constituent component, namely, the energy harvester (or transducer), the power conditioning unit, and the energy storage element.

3.1 Harvesting Ambient Energy

An energy harvester, in our context, is a device that converts power from ambient sources, such as electromagnetic radiation (including light and RF waves), thermal gradients, mechanical motion, *etc.*, into electrical power. Of these modalities, solar energy harvesting through photovoltaic conversion is the most mature and well-studied, in part because it has a higher power density (output power per unit area or volume) than other ambient power sources. Solar harvesting is well-suited for IoT devices that have substantial exposure to light, such as the *Flood Beacon* [5], which is an outdoor environment monitor. Flexible photovoltaic cells [34] could possibly also be integrated into clothing and used to recharge wearable IoT devices.

Kinetic energy harvesting converts the mechanical energy of motion or vibration into electrical energy through electromagnetic induction [28] or the piezoelectric effect [39]. It is particularly attractive for wearable IoT devices that are powered by human motion and for devices attached to vibrating objects such as engines or motors. For example, the *Pavegen* [6] is an energy harvesting floor tile that can be installed on a sidewalk to gather energy from footsteps, which could be used for advertising, way finding solutions, *etc.* Intelligently scavenging energy from routine human activities could play a prominent role in improving the battery lifetime of IoT devices.

RF energy harvesting uses the power received from incident RF waves for powering a device. This technique is commonly used in passive RFID systems. The source of the power can either be dedicated RF waves generated for wireless charging (*e.g.*, the Qi wireless charging standard) [31], or ambient RF signals that are transmitted for wireless data transfer (*e.g.*, WiFi or TV signals) [14]. Energy harvesting from ambient WiFi signals has been demonstrated [30], although the amount of harvested power that can be harvested is often minuscule.

Thermoelectric generators (TEGs) translate a thermal gradient between two surfaces into an electrical potential [51]. TEGs are suitable for powering IoT devices that are in contact with hot surfaces (*e.g.*, hot water pipes). Wearable IoT devices, such as smartwatches, can also use TEGs as a power

source by exploiting the difference between the body's surface temperature and the ambient temperature.

In summary, the choice of harvesting modality for a particular IoT device is dependent on its operating environment, form-factor constraints, as well as its power budget.

3.2 Power Conditioning

Electronic circuit components require a stable DC power supply to operate reliably. However, the output voltage of an energy harvester often varies significantly depending on the strength of the ambient power source (*e.g.*, the light intensity or the amplitude of vibration). Therefore, the output of the harvester needs to be converted into an appropriate (and stable) voltage level through the use of a power conditioning circuit before it can be fed to an IoT device or transferred to an energy storage element. However, power conditioning for energy harvesting is not straightforward. For example, due to the stringent form-factor constraint in most IoT devices, the output power of the harvester is very small, often only a few mW. The conditioning circuit should deliver as much of this power as possible to the IoT device with minimal loss, which requires extremely careful design. Further, some harvesters generate only tens of mV at their output, such as TEGs in body-worn devices. In such cases, a boost regulator that accepts an ultra-low input voltage is required [19].

In addition to voltage regulation, power conditioning also plays an important role in maximizing harvesting efficiency. Most energy harvesters have an optimal operating point (called the maximum power point or MPP) at which their power output is maximized. Since the MPP changes dynamically based on ambient conditions, the power conditioning unit should continuously maintain operation at the MPP, a process referred to as MPP tracking. MPP tracking is a feature available in many commercial power conditioning ICs [55, 38]. Design considerations for MPP tracking are described in [42, 36]. In [57], MPP tracking is done by modulating the average power consumption of the device, without a dedicated power conditioning unit.

3.3 Energy Storage

Since the amount of power available from an energy harvester is dynamic and unpredictable, an energy storage element is needed in IoT devices for uninterrupted operation when ambient power is not available. Often, the energy storage element is the bulkiest part of an embedded system. Therefore, energy storage elements with a high energy density are highly desirable for IoT devices to maximize lifetime and minimize device size.

Batteries are the most widely used energy storage element in untethered devices. A solid-state thin-film battery that uses solid electrolytes is a promising battery technology for IoT devices [47]. It has low power density but high energy density, making it suitable for long-lasting low-power IoT devices. Such a thin, bendable battery can also be easily integrated into small IoT devices [27]. A solid-state battery can be manufactured in conventional IC packages or even be integrated with an IC in a single package, such as Cymbet's EnerChip [22]. This enables a significant reduction in size and system integration cost. Compared to batteries, supercapacitors have a much higher cycle efficiency and extremely long cycle life. However, they require the power conditioning unit to be able to cope with their large voltage variation, in particular, the very low voltage during cold boot. Dynamic reconfiguration of multiple supercapacitors can mitigate the voltage variation issue and improve cold boot speed [20].

(a)

(b)

(c)

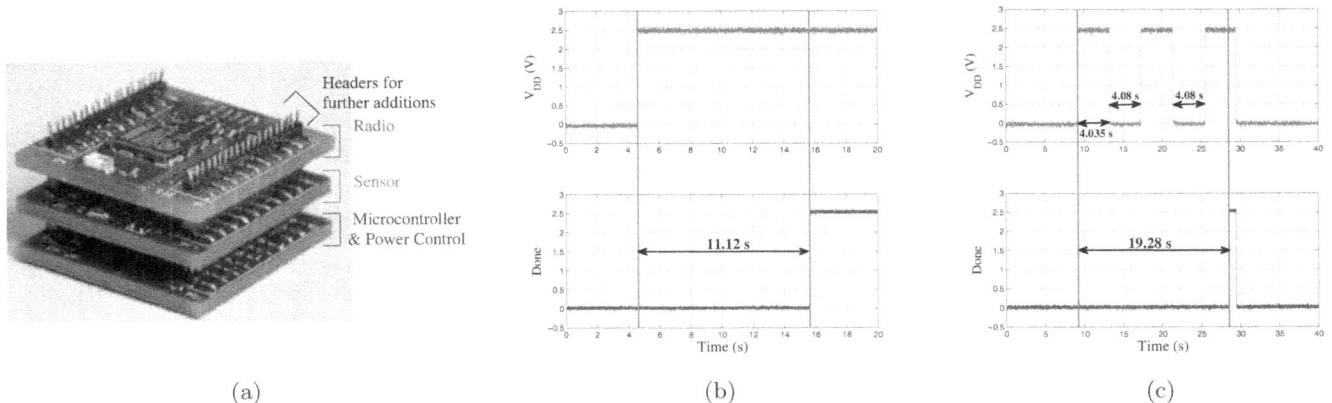

Figure 3: (a) QUBE: A modular embedded platform (1" by 1") that facilitates easy prototyping and addition/removal of features through modules, (b) Time taken (11.12s) to complete RSA encryption of 128 characters on QUBE in the presence of continuous power supply. The **Done** signal is raised at the end of the computation, and (c) QUICKRECALL implemented on QUBE. RSA encryption is successfully performed across multiple power cycles with negligible overhead (19.28s − 2 × 4.08s = 11.12s).

Recent advances in nanotechnology have also enabled flexible supercapacitors on a thin film substrate, which are well-suited for wearable applications [44].

4. HW-SW CO-DESIGN FOR LOW POWER

In addition to each hardware component being optimized for low power, system-level considerations about power consumption and management have to be carefully integrated into both the hardware and software development cycle for IoT devices.

Dynamic power management has been a well-studied technique for reducing power consumption [54]. Software controlled frequency selection of the processing unit, in conjunction with a well-designed power management unit helps in decreasing energy consumption. Modern day microcontrollers, such as TI's MSP430F5438A, have a programmable power management unit that provides software designers the option of selecting the frequency of operation according to the supply voltage used. The frequency of operation is crucial for batteryless IoT devices such as transiently powered computers (TPCs) [52] that eschew the use of voltage regulators for overhead reasons. As the power supply capacitor discharges during system operation, care must be taken to ensure that the operating frequency never exceeds the maximum frequency allowed for the current supply voltage level.

In addition to frequency scaling, another powerful technique for power management is power gating. Power gating at the system-level can be executed by careful planning of the hardware and software architecture. For IoT devices, power islands could be assigned based on functionality. For example, if the device needs to read a sensor, only the microcontroller and sensor need to be powered and other components can be power gated. As an example, QUBE (Figure 3(a)) is a wireless embedded platform that supports upto four different MCU-controlled power domains. The different functional modules make up different layers of the QUBE stack with power gating hardware residing on each module. Advances in low power circuit design have resulted in commercially available power-gating switches that consume only nanowatts of power, which is negligible compared to the active and idle mode power consumption of the modules that they power gate.

In addition to power gating, other hardware-software techniques can be used for reliable operation of IoT devices in power-constrained environments. Consider TPCs that were discussed earlier. To successfully perform computations across power cycles, TPCs resort to saving the processor and program states via checkpointing before an imminent power loss. Additional challenges are introduced by the high erase and write latency and energy overhead of Flash memory that is used in conventional microcontrollers. QUICKRECALL [32] is an *in-situ* checkpointing technique for TPCs that use an FRAM-enabled MCU. This approach is complementary to the idea of non-volatile processors discussed in Section 2. An *in-situ* checkpointing scheme decreases the checkpointing overhead by reducing the amount of data that needs to be explicitly checkpointed. However, as described in [32], a modified boot sequence is required while using such an approach. Experiments show that the latency overhead of checkpointing in QUICKRECALL is as low as 20 µs per power cycle which is over 100x lower than the corresponding overhead using Flash memory. Figures 3(b) and 3(c) show how a long-running application (in this case, RSA encryption) can be executed successfully across multiple power cycles with negligible overhead.

Communication in TPCs is a challenge as power may be lost in the midst of a transmission. As the nature of the power source is unpredictable, it is imperative to define new solutions to provide reliable communication. Bit-by-bit backscatter [60] aims to solve this problem by adaptively sizing the µframe length. Additionally, it features optimizations for decreasing the energy per backscatter operation and increasing the communication range. Another solution is to gauge the energy available and execute tasks adaptively as power requirements are satisfied [59].

For many IoT devices, maintaining a stable notion of time is critical. Conventionally, a real time clock (RTC) is used for this purpose. In addition to time keeping, the RTC is also used to perform synchronization and trigger periodic interrupts that wake the system from sleep mode. It is of utmost importance that the RTC module receives an uninterrupted power supply. Recent advances in circuit technology have seen the advent of off-the-shelf sub-threshold RTC modules that consume less than 100 nA [15]. Such low levels of current draw facilitate the use of energy harvesting to power the RTC perpetually.

Many IoT devices operate either in event-triggered mode (*e.g.,* Belkin *Wemo* [1], Quirky *Wink* [8]) or in periodic activation mode (*e.g., CubeSensors* [2], *Sensor Tags* [13]). These applications allow the user to set the trigger threshold, monitoring frequency, *etc.* The system designer's task involves considering such scenarios and architecting a power-optimized system architecture. For event-triggered systems, a hierarchical multiprocessor architecture [50] could be used, wherein a smaller MCU (which has lower power consumption than the main processor) monitors the sensor till an event is triggered, following which the main processor is woken up for further processing and communication. The smaller MCU is duty-cycled for energy efficiency according to the desired sampling frequency of the sensor and powers off when the main processor takes over. An alternative approach is to utilize MCUs whose analog components monitor the sensors without having to keep the entire MCU awake [18].

5. CONCLUSION

This paper presented some key directions to address the problem of powering the next generation of devices that form the IoT. We believe that a comprehensive solution to this problem involves three main building blocks including the design of ultra-low power embedded hardware platforms and intelligent system-level power management techniques. The third (perhaps, most promising) direction is to make IoT devices self-powered by harvesting energy from their operating environment. Doing so raises the possibility of perpetual operation of these devices, thus decreasing their dependence on batteries and the need for frequent battery replacement.

6. REFERENCES

[1] Belkin Wemo. http://www.belkin.com/us/Products/home-automation/c/wemo-home-automation/.
[2] CubeSensors. https://cubesensors.com/.
[3] Driblet. http://driblet.co/.
[4] Fitbit. http://www.fitbit.com/.
[5] Flood Beacon. http://floodbeacon.com.
[6] Pavegen. http://www.pavegen.com/.
[7] Pebble. https://getpebble.com/.
[8] Quirky Wink. https://www.quirky.com/ge.
[9] Revolv Home Automation hub. http://revolv.com/.
[10] Self-Powered Ad-Hoc Network. http://www.lockheedmartin.com/us/products/span.html.
[11] Spheramid Gateway for Ninjasphere. http://ninjablocks.com/.
[12] Wally. https://www.wallyhome.com/.
[13] Wireless Sensor Tags. https://www.mytaglist.com/.
[14] B. Allen et al. Harvesting energy from ambient radio signals: A load of hot air? In *LAPC*, pages 1–4, 2012.
[15] Ambiq Micro. AM08X5 real-time clock family. http://ambiqmicro.com/sites/default/files/AM08X5_Data_Sheet_DS0002V1p1.pdf.
[16] Bluetooth Special Interest Group.
[17] D. Bol et al. SleepWalker: A 25-MHz 0.4-V sub- mm^2 7 − μW/MHz microcontroller in 65-nm LP/GP PCMOS for low-carbon wireless sensor nodes. *IEEE J SOLID-ST CIRC*, pages 20–32, 2013.
[18] C. Brown. Low-power sampling techniques using kinetis l, 2013.
[19] E. Carlson et al. A 20 mv input boost converter with efficient digital control for thermoelectric energy harvesting. *IEEE J SOLID-ST CIRC*, pages 741–750, 2010.
[20] C.-Y. Chen and P. H. Chou. Duracap: A supercapacitor-based, power-bootstrapping, maximum power point tracking energy-harvesting system. In *ISLPED*, pages 313–318, 2010.
[21] G. Chen et al. Circuit design advances for wireless sensing applications. *Proc. IEEE*, pages 1808–1827, 2010.
[22] Cymbet. EnerChip. http://www.cymbet.com/.
[23] Estimote. Estimote beacons. http://estimote.com/.
[24] D. Evans. The internet of things: How the next evolution of the internet is changing everything. http://www.cisco.com/web/about/ac79/docs/innov/IoT_IBSG_0411FINAL.pdf, 2011.
[25] M. Fojtik et al. A millimeter-scale energy-autonomous sensor system with stacked battery and solar cells. *IEEE J SOLID-ST CIRC*, pages 801–813, 2013.

[26] G. R. Fox et al. Current and future ferroelectric nonvolatile memory technology. *J VAC SCI TECHNOL B*, pages 1967–1971, 2001.
[27] M. Gorlatova et al. Energy harvesting active networked tags (EnHANTs) for ubiquitous object networking. *IEEE WC*, pages 18–25, 2010.
[28] M. Gorlatova et al. Movers and shakers: Kinetic energy harvesting for the internet of things. In *(to appear in) ACM SIGMETRICS*, 2014.
[29] S. Hanson et al. A low-voltage processor for sensing applications with picowatt standby mode. *IEEE J SOLID-ST CIRC*, pages 1145–1155, 2009.
[30] A. M. Hawkes et al. A microwave metamaterial with integrated power harvesting functionality. *Applied Physics Letters*, 103(16), 2013.
[31] H. Jabbar et al. RF energy harvesting system and circuits for charging of mobile devices. *IEEE T CONSUM ELECTR*, pages 247–253, 2010.
[32] H. Jayakumar et al. QUICKRECALL: A low overhead HW/SW approach for enabling computations across power cycles in transiently powered computers. In *VLSID*, pages 330–335, 2014.
[33] H. Jayakumar et al. HYPNOS: An Ultra-Low Power Sleep Mode with SRAM Data Retention for Embedded Microcontrollers. CODES+ISSS '14, 2014 (to appear).
[34] C. Y. Jiang et al. High-bendability flexible dye-sensitized solar cell with a nanoparticle-modified ZnO-nanowire electrode. *APPL PHYS LETT*, 2008.
[35] S. Khanna et al. An FRAM-based nonvolatile logic MCU SoC exhibiting 100% digital state retention at vdd= 0 V achieving zero leakage with < 400-ns wakeup time for ulp applications. *IEEE J SOLID-ST CIRC*, pages 95–106, 2014.
[36] Y. Kim et al. Maximum power transfer tracking for a photovoltaic-supercapacitor energy system. In *ISLPED*, pages 307–312, 2010.
[37] H. Li and Y. Chen. *Nonvolatile Memory Design: Magnetic, Resistive, and Phase Change.* 2011.
[38] Linear Technology. LT8490-high V, high I, buck-boost battery charge controller with MPPT.
[39] J.-Q. Liu et al. A MEMS-based piezoelectric power generator array for vibration energy harvesting. *MICROELECTR J*, pages 802–806, 2008.
[40] V. Liu et al. Ambient backscatter: Wireless communication out of thin air. *COMPUT COMMUN REV*, pages 39–50, 2013.
[41] Lively. Lively. http://mylively.com/.
[42] C. Lu et al. Maximum power point considerations in micro-scale solar energy harvesting systems. In *ISCAS*, pages 273–276, 2010.
[43] S. J. A. Majerus et al. Wireless, ultra-low-power implantable sensor for chronic bladder pressure monitoring. *JETC*, pages 11:1–11:13, 2012.
[44] C. Meng et al. Ultrasmall integrated 3D micro-supercapacitors solve energy storage for miniature devices. *Advanced Energy Materials*, 2014.
[45] P. P. Mercier et al. Energy extraction from the biologic battery in the inner ear. *NAT BIOTECHNOL*, pages 1240–1243, 2012.
[46] J. Nickels et al. Find my stuff: Supporting physical objects search with relative positioning. In *UbiComp*, pages 325–334, 2013.
[47] P. H. L. Notten et al. 3-D integrated all-solid-state rechargeable batteries. *ADV MATER*, pages 4564–4567, 2007.
[48] Panasonic. MN101LR05D/04D/03D/02D datasheet. http://www.semicon.panasonic.co.jp/ds4/MN101L05_E.pdf.
[49] V. Raghunathan and P. Chou. Design and power management of energy harvesting embedded systems. In *ISLPED*, pages 369–374, 2006.
[50] V. Raghunathan et al. Emerging techniques for long lived wireless sensor networks. *IEEE COMMUN MAG*, pages 108–114, 2006.
[51] Y. Ramadass and A. Chandrakasan. A battery-less thermoelectric energy harvesting interface circuit with 35 mV startup voltage. *IEEE J SOLID-ST CIRC*, pages 333–341, 2011.
[52] B. Ransford. *Transiently Powered Computers.* PhD thesis, University of Massachusetts Amherst, Jan. 2013.
[53] N. Sakimura et al. A 90 nm 20 MHz fully nonvolatile microcontroller for standby-power-critical applications. In *ISSCC*, pages 184–185, 2014.
[54] A. Sinha and A. Chandrakasan. Dynamic power management in wireless sensor networks. *IEEE DES TEST COMPUT*, pages 62–74, 2001.
[55] STMicroelectronics. SPV1050-ULP energy harvester and battery charger with embedded MPPT and LDOs.
[56] tado. tado cooling. http://www.tado.com/.
[57] C. Wang et al. Storage-less and converter-less maximum power point tracking of photovoltaic cells for a nonvolatile microprocessor. In *ASP-DAC*, pages 379–384, 2014.
[58] B. Zhai et al. A 2.60pJ/Inst subthreshold sensor processor for optimal energy efficiency. In *Symposium on VLSI Circuits*, pages 154–155, 2006.
[59] P. Zhang et al. QuarkOs: Pushing the operating limits of micro-powered sensors. In *HotOS*, 2013.
[60] P. Zhang and D. Ganesan. Enabling bit-by-bit backscatter communication in severe energy harvesting environments. In *NSDI*, pages 345–357, 2014.
[61] M. Zwerg et al. An 82 μA/MHz microcontroller with embedded FeRAM for energy-harvesting applications. In *ISSCC*, pages 334–336, 2011.

Author Index

www.ingramcontent.com/pod-product-compliance
Lightning Source LLC
Chambersburg PA
CBHW080703220326

41598CB00033B/5295